C000061717

Frommer's®
California

My California

by Matthew Richard Poole

I'VE BEEN TRAVELING THROUGHOUT CALIFORNIA SINCE MY DAD bought a shiny new wood-paneled station wagon in 1967 and I still haven't seen every destination in this guidebook. In fact, this state is so huge and diverse that it takes a team of Frommer's travel writers to cover it from end to end. So if you're planning a vacation to California, you're going to have to make some tough decisions.

Obviously you can't see everything in a single trip, but how can you choose to visit Yosemite instead of Lake Tahoe? Or the Wine Country instead of Gold Country? San Francisco rather than San Diego? Disneyland over SeaWorld? It's the kind of conundrum that only a state as incredibly varied as California can create.

The beautiful images in the following pages will only make your decision more difficult, because it probably didn't occur to you that California's desert regions are a major international attraction (Germans love Death Valley's blistering heat), that you can hug the world's largest and tallest trees at our national parks, or that you can still find plenty of fat nuggets to pan for in the Gold Country.

My advice? Quit your job, buy a VW camper, and spend the next few years exploring California, one of the most alluring places on earth.

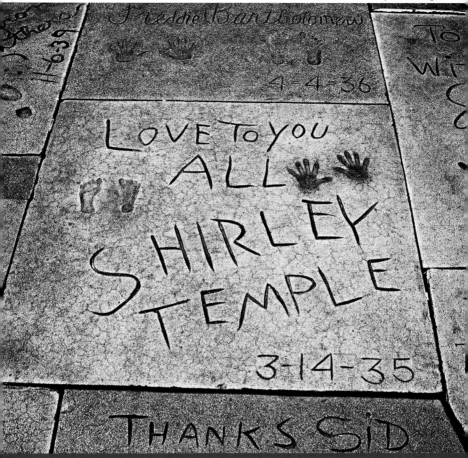

My all-time favorite LA activity is to take a leisurely ride on the 8-mile **BEACHSIDE BIKE PATH (left)** that runs along Santa Monica and Venice Beach. Here, everyone appears healthy and happy as they jog, skate, walk, and ride in the sunshine as a cool breeze blows in off the Pacific.

Some of the biggest stars in show business have their noses (Bob Hope), hair (Whoopi Goldberg), cigars (George Burns), wheels (R2-D2), hands, feet, and signatures immortalized at the famous **ENTRY COURT TO SID GRAUMAN'S CHINESE THEATER (above)**, in Los Angeles. I drop by once in a while just to admire Betty Grable's gams.

The unique warming temperatures of the desert create air currents perfect for hot-air ballooning. At each sunrise and sunset, these quiet vehicles rise into the sky, offering unparalleled views of the **COACHELLA VALLEY (left)** and the nearby Santa Rosa Mountains. Those interested in romance should choose the special champagne flight.

Along with the most famous amusement park in the world—the Disneyland Resort—the LA region hosts three other destinations for thrill-seekers: Six Flags California, Universal Studios, and **KNOTT'S BERRY FARM (below)**. That's 4 days of guaranteed fun in the sun.

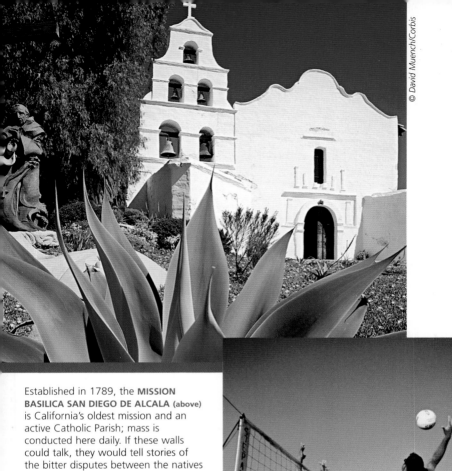

Established in 1789, the **MISSION BASILICA SAN DIEGO DE ALCALA (above)** is California's oldest mission and an active Catholic Parish; mass is conducted here daily. If these walls could talk, they would tell stories of the bitter disputes between the natives and the Spanish missionaries.

San Diego's beach scene consists of a variety of outdoor activities, like jogging, biking, and **BEACH VOLLEYBALL (right)**. On any given sunny day, dozens of volleyball games pepper San Diego's beaches. Remember, you don't have to play to enjoy this game—half the fun is in people-watching or applauding a smooth slide in the sand.

If you've seen the lines to board **SAN FRANCISCO'S CABLE CARS (above)** you can guess why most locals don't take them with regularity. But riding one is an instant reminder of why they are so fun—and romantic, thrilling, and even a bit death defying—as they slowly lunge down the city's steep hills. Seriously, this is a must-do.

Like most cities, gentrification continues to encroach on San Francisco's diversity. But the colorful **MISSION DISTRICT (right)** still celebrates its Latin community, especially through its preservation and recognition of its hundreds of murals.

Opposite page: © Chad Ehlers/Index Stock

Whether you walk it, bike it, drive it, or view it from a distance, San Francisco's most famous landmark, the **GOLDEN GATE BRIDGE,** commands attention. The bridge is a visual wonder. But its flanking backdrop of the woodsy Presidio to the south, rugged Marin Headlands to the north, and glistening waters of the Golden Gate below make it downright magical to behold.

To see the largest living thing in the world—that's one reason why you should make the drive to **SEQUOIA NATIONAL PARK (above)**. The General Sherman Tree is so massive that its branches are more than 7 feet thick. This remote region offers the most pristine wilderness in the Sierra Nevada, with 75 groves of mind-blowingly big sequoias, granite walls that rise thousands of feet, and the deepest canyon in the United States. Bring a very wide-angle lens.

When it's time to hang up my keyboard, I'm going to retire in **LAKE TAHOE (right)**. If there's a more beautiful place to live that offers as many outdoor activities, please let me know. Surrounded by the majestic peaks of the Sierra Nevada, Lake Tahoe is the largest alpine lake in North America and the best year-round playground in California. Spend a few days here and you too will consider purchasing some Sierra Nevada real estate.

The **WINE COUNTRY** (right) is all about great wine and food and leisure pursuits. Go to Napa or Sonoma to sip through a few wineries, sit down at a bucolic restaurant, and linger over a bottle of wine and a ridiculously good meal. This is about as good as life gets.

There aren't enough adjectives to describe the sensation of seeing **YOSEMITE VALLEY** (below) for the first time. Among the most beautiful and popular of America's National Parks, Yosemite is home to the highest waterfall in North America, the tallest and largest granite monolith in the world, and one of the world's largest trees.

© Charles O'Rear/Corbis

© Mike Roessler/Index Stock

If all you think of is football when some-one mentions the Forty-Niners, then spend some time touring California's rugged **GOLD COUNTRY (left)**, where many of the historic mining towns, saloons, and gold mines date back to the mid-1800s. One of the most underrated tourist desti-nations in California, the Gold Country provides the ideal vacation combination of historical interest, gorgeous scenery, cozy B&Bs, and such entertaining activi-ties as exploring active gold mines, white-water rafting, and panning for real gold (yes, you get to keep it).

One of the last great estates of America's Gilded Age, **HEARST CASTLE (below)** is among the most elaborate (and excessive) buildings on earth. This over-the-top estate of publishing magnate William Randolph Hearst is one of those you-have-to-see-it-to-believe-it kind of places, where a 100-plus-room mansion and the Greco-Roman Neptune pool (pictured here) are just part of the tour package.

California

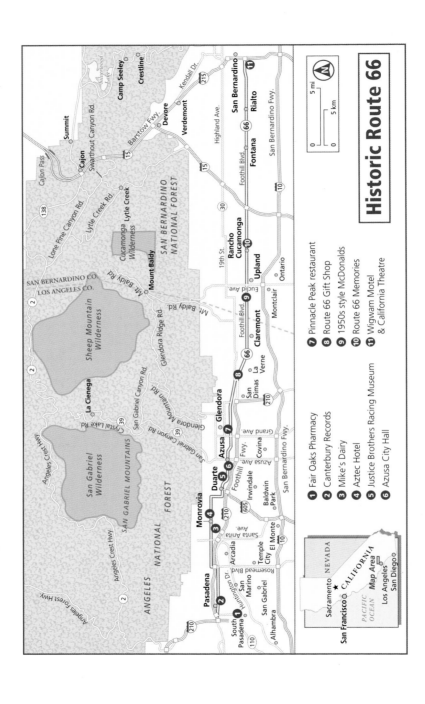

Historic Route 66

1 Fair Oaks Pharmacy
2 Canterbury Records
3 Mike's Dairy
4 Aztec Hotel
5 Justice Brothers Racing Museum
6 Azusa City Hall
7 Pinnacle Peak restaurant
8 Route 66 Gift Shop
9 1950s style McDonalds
10 Route 66 Memories
11 Wigwam Motel & California Theatre

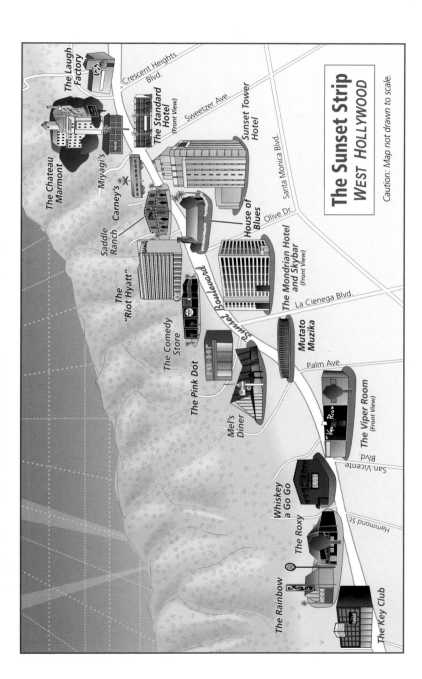

The Sunset Strip
WEST HOLLYWOOD

Caution: Map not drawn to scale.

The Wine Country

Scale: 0–1 mi / 0–1 km

Arrowood Vineyards & Winery **28**
Artesa Vineyards & Winery **22**
Beaulieu Vineyard **10**
Benziger Family Winery **29**
Beringer Vineyard **5**
Buena Vista Winery **25**
Charles Krug Winery **6**
Château St. Jean **32**
Clos Du Val **19**
Clos Pegase **1**
Domaine Chandon **18**
Frank Family Vineyards **4**
Gloria Ferrer Champagne Caves **24**

The Hess Collection **21**
Joseph Phelps Vineyards **9**
Kenwood Vineyards **30**
Kunde Estate Winery **31**
Niebaum-Coppola **11**
Opus One **15**
PlumpJack Winery **16**
Prager Winery & Port Works **8**
Ravenswood Winery **27**
Robert Mondavi Winery **14**
St. Supéry Winery **13**
Sawyer Cellars **13**
Schramsberg **3**
Sebastiani Vineyards **26**
Stag's Leap Wine Cellars **17**
Sterling Vineyards **2**
Swanson Vineyards & Winery **12**
Trefethen Vineyards **20**
V. Sattui Winery **7**
Viansa Winery **23**

Frommer's®
California 2009

by Harry Basch, Mark Hiss, Erika Lenkert & Matthew Richard Poole

Here's what the critics say about Frommer's:

"Amazingly easy to use. Very portable, very complete."
—BOOKLIST

"Detailed, accurate, and easy-to-read information for all price ranges."
—GLAMOUR MAGAZINE

"Hotel information is close to encyclopedic."
—DES MOINES SUNDAY REGISTER

"Frommer's Guides have a way of giving you a real feel for a place."
—KNIGHT RIDDER NEWSPAPERS

WILEY

Wiley Publishing, Inc.

Published by:

WILEY PUBLISHING, INC.

111 River St.
Hoboken, NJ 07030-5774

ISBN 978-0-470-28772-9

Editor: Alexia Travaglini
Production Editor: Michael Brumitt
Cartographer: Guy Ruggiero
Photo Editor: Richard Fox
Production by Wiley Indianapolis Composition Services

Front cover photo: Napa Valley: Sunset over Silverado Trail vineyard
Back cover photo: Los Angeles: Santa Monica pier entrance

For information on our other products and services or to obtain technical support, please
contact our Customer Care Department within the U.S. at 800/762-2974, outside the
U.S. at 317/572-3993 or fax 317/572-4002.

Wiley also publishes its books in a variety of electronic formats. Some content that
appears in print may not be available in electronic formats.

Manufactured in the United States of America

5   4   3   2   1

CONTENTS

4 SUGGESTED ITINERARIES 57

5 SAN FRANCISCO 65

6 THE SAN FRANCISCO BAY AREA 150

7 THE WINE COUNTRY 181

12 THE MONTEREY PENINSULA & THE BIG SUR COAST 379

13 THE CENTRAL COAST 424

14 LOS ANGELES 475

LIST OF MAPS

ABOUT THE AUTHORS

Harry Basch is the author of *Frommer's Exploring America by RV* and *RV Vacations For Dummies,* and a contributor to *Frommer's USA.* His books, articles, and photographs—many of which he produced in collaboration with his late wife, Shirley—have been published internationally for more than 25 years.

A third-generation Southern Californian, **Mark Hiss** is a writer and photographer who has spent more than 25 years in San Diego. He was founding editor of both the visitor guide *Where San Diego* and *Performances,* the playbill magazine for the city's leading performing arts venues. He is also a recovering publicist who spent many years working for several of San Diego's top theater companies.

A native San Franciscan, **Erika Lenkert** spends her time traipsing through San Francisco and across the globe in search of adventure and great food. She has written for *Travel + Leisure, Food & Wine, Bride's, Wine Country Living, San Francisco Magazine, Los Angeles Magazine,* and *Time Out.* Her latest work is an entertaining and cooking guide called *The Last-Minute Party Girl: Fashionable, Fearless, and Foolishly Simple Entertaining* (www.lastminutepartygirl.com), which mixes fun, humor, and recipes into a tasty, useful guide to living large, Bay Area–style.

Matthew Richard Poole, a native Californian, has authored more than two dozen travel guides to California, Hawaii, and abroad. A regular contributor to radio and television travel programs, he has made numerous guest appearances on the award-winning *Bay Area Backroads* television show, among other broadcast outlets. Before becoming a full-time travel writer and photographer, he worked as an English tutor in Prague, ski instructor in the Swiss Alps, and scuba instructor in Maui and Thailand. Highly allergic to office buildings and mortgage payments, he spends most of his time traveling the globe in search of new adventures. His other Frommer's titles include *California from $70 a Day, San Francisco from $70 a Day, Los Angeles, Portable Los Angeles, Irreverent Guide to San Francisco,* and *Portable Disneyland*.

AN INVITATION TO THE READER

In researching this book, we discovered many wonderful places—hotels, restaurants, shops, and more. We're sure you'll find others. Please tell us about them, so we can share the information with your fellow travelers in upcoming editions. If you were disappointed with a recommendation, we'd love to know that, too. Please write to:

Frommer's California 2009
Wiley Publishing, Inc. • 111 River St. • Hoboken, NJ 07030-5774

AN ADDITIONAL NOTE

Other Great Guides for Your Trip:

Frommer's Napa & Sonoma Day by Day

Frommer's San Francisco Day by Day

California For Dummies

Frommer's California's Best-Loved Driving Tours:
25 Unforgettable Itineraries

The Unofficial Guide to California with Kids

Frommer's San Francisco

Frommer's Los Angeles

The Unofficial Guide to Disneyland®

FROMMER'S STAR RATINGS, ICONS & ABBREVIATIONS

Every hotel, restaurant, and attraction listing in this guide has been ranked for quality, value, service, amenities, and special features using a **star-rating system.** In country, state, and regional guides, we also rate towns and regions to help you narrow down your choices and budget your time accordingly. Hotels and restaurants are rated on a scale of zero (recommended) to three stars (exceptional). Attractions, shopping, nightlife, towns, and regions are rated according to the following scale: zero stars (recommended), one star (highly recommended), two stars (very highly recommended), and three stars (must-see).

In addition to the star-rating system, we also use **seven feature icons** that point you to the great deals, in-the-know advice, and unique experiences that separate travelers from tourists. Throughout the book, look for:

(**Finds**)	Special finds—those places only insiders know about
(**Fun Facts**)	Fun facts—details that make travelers more informed and their trips more fun
(**Kids**)	Best bets for kids, and advice for the whole family
(**Moments**)	Special moments—those experiences that memories are made of
(**Overrated**)	Places or experiences not worth your time or money
(**Tips**)	Insider tips—great ways to save time and money
(**Value**)	Great values—where to get the best deals

The following **abbreviations** are used for credit cards:

AE	American Express	DISC	Discover	V	Visa
DC	Diners Club	MC	MasterCard		

FROMMERS.COM

Now that you have this guidebook to help you plan a great trip, visit our website at **www.frommers.com** for additional travel information on more than 4,000 destinations. We update features regularly to give you instant access to the most current trip-planning information available. At Frommers.com, you'll find scoops on the best airfares, lodging rates, and car rental bargains. You can even book your travel online through our reliable travel booking partners. Other popular features include:

- Online updates of our most popular guidebooks
- Vacation sweepstakes and contest giveaways
- Newsletters highlighting the hottest travel trends
- Podcasts, interactive maps, and up-to-the-minute events listings
- Opinionated blog entries by Arthur Frommer himself
- Online travel message boards with featured travel discussions

What's New in California

SAN FRANCISCO One of the greatest challenges of producing a travel guide is keeping on top of the never-ending changes that take place in San Francisco, a city that is always in flux. This section highlights the latest trends, attractions, and openings, so be sure to add them to your to-do list while exploring the city.

What's been the norm in L.A. and New York for the past half-decade has finally permeated the San Francisco hospitality industry: hip boutique hotels created by cutting-edge design companies with destination bar/lounges and restaurants run by celebrity chefs. In this edition, I've added five formerly frumpy Union Square hotels that have been transmogrified from just a place to stay to *the* place to *be*.

Take the new **Hotel Vertigo** (℅ **800/553-1900**) for instance. Playful, eclectic decor by Thomas Schoos Design, Inc., and food by celebrity chef Tyler Florence. Same with the **Hotel Frank** (℅ **800/553-1900**): A major renovation in the fall of 2008 incorporates a blend of popular design trends through the decades, from turn-of-the-20th-century Beaux Art classicism to '40s Art Deco and retro '60s chic.

Other examples include the newly renovated **Villa Florence** (℅ **866/823-4669**) and its slick new Bar Norcini wine bar; the **Hotel Metropolis** (℅ **800/553-1900**) and its yin-and-yang combo of cheeky decor and Zen ambience; and, my new favorite, the **Hotel Union Square** (℅ **800/553-1900**), built in 1913 for the 1915 Pan Pacific Exposition, yet now one of the sexiest hotels in the city. If lace curtains and

doilies just won't do, any of these five new hotels will satisfy the snob in you.

As for dining in SF, for the first time in decades someone has finally opened a true destination restaurant on the Embarcadero. Heck, they built two. The duo of **EPIC Roasthouse** (℅ **415/369-9955**) and the adjacent **Waterbar** (℅ **415/284-9922**) has managed to get even us restaurant-jaded locals excited. Design genius Pat Kuleto worked his magic yet again to create two of the sexiest restaurants in the city. Even if the prices are beyond your budget, you really need to stop by both restaurants to admire what the confluence of money, style, and setting can produce.

Two other restaurant newcomers that are getting national press are **Ducca** (℅ **415/977-0271**) and **Spruce** (℅ **415/931-5100**). The former is my new favorite Italian restaurant in the city—the things Executive Chef Richard J. Corbo can do with buffalo mozzarella are humbling—while the latter is the new darling of the Pacific Heights ladies-who-lunch crowd and worth the drive across town just for the burger and fries.

It took forever, but the city finally got around to opening the new **California Academy of Sciences** (℅ **415/379-8000**). It took 4 years and $500 million dollars, but the results are wow. It's the only institution in the world that combines an aquarium, planetarium, natural history museum, and scientific research program under one roof—and what a roof it is: a $2^{1}/_{2}$-acre undulating garden canopy carpeted with over a million plants and flowers. With so much to see and do at the Academy, you could easily spend an entire day roaming among the high-tech exhibits. Along with the brilliant de Young Museum and beautiful Conservatory of Flowers, it's yet another reason why everyone who's vacationing in San Francisco should spend at least 1 full day in Golden Gate Park.

As for nightlife in SF, the more things change . . . Your parents might remember when San Francisco's Fillmore Corridor was the swingingest jazz venue in the 1940s and 1950s. While not quite back to its halcyon days, this revitalized stretch of Fillmore Street, just south of Geary Boulevard, is once again the top West Coast destination for jazz music now that the new **Yoshi's Jazz Club** (✆ **415/655-5600**) has opened. The two-story, 28,000-square-foot jazz venue is attracting some of the finest jazz artists in the world, such as Stanton Moore, Branford Marsalis, and Diana Krall. Even if you're not a jazz fan, it's still worth the trip to revel in the coolness of it all.

On an entirely different note, I've also added some info about the best drag shows in the city. If you're out on a Friday night and looking for something that's off the straight-laced path, head to the **Cinch** (✆ **415/776-4162**) for its weekly **Charlie Horse** drag show. On weekends, check out Harry Denton's Starlight Room (✆ **415/ 395-8595**): Their **Sunday's a Drag** brunch performance is fit for a queen.

NORTHERN CALIFORNIA WINE COUNTRY While the rest of the country struggles with unstable economic times and a housing crisis, the Wine Country seems to remain unscathed, at least to the visitor. Sure, you can scoop up a house in downtown Napa at a fraction of the cost of previous years, but the multimillion-dollar homes are still as hot as ever, as are the upscale restaurants, luxury hotels, and reservations-only wineries.

Perhaps the only thing that has recently cast a cloud over the sunny skies of grape-draped wine country was the May 16, 2008, passing of Robert Mondavi, the winemaker marketing genius widely known for putting California wine on the global wine map. Still, the party goes on, just as he would have wished.

So what new finds can you expect from a visit to Napa or Sonoma? Plenty.

Downtown Napa continues to expand, with a gorgeous new riverfront walk, hotels and businesses going up faster than you can say "Pass the chardonnay," and ongoing gentrification, which shows itself in the likes of the valley's first Whole Foods Market and confirmed plans for a Ritz-Carlton to be constructed near Copia.

For the visitor, the city's most exciting addition is **Oxbow Market** (www.oxbow publicmarket.com), a co-op market hall that opened at the end of 2007. You'll find artisan and gourmet everything, from ready-made sandwiches and charcuterie to kitchen antiques and gifts.

At the other end of the valley to the north, visitors can get a taste of medieval Europe with a visit to **Castello di Amorosa** (✆ **707- 942-8200** or 707-286-7273), a 121,000-square-foot castle and winery, complete with dungeon and torture chamber.

Not new to the state but new to this book is a section dedicated to Northern Sonoma. An exceptional alternative to bustling and commercial Napa and sleepy and spread-out Sonoma Valley, this expansive region is centered on its historic town of Healdsburg, which combines exceptional accommodations, dining, shopping, world-class winery exploration, and family activities with casual country living and old-fashioned hospitality. See chapter 7 for more information.

LOS ANGELES Los Angeles and Madonna have a lot in common: They're always one step ahead of the trends. Trying to keep up with the constant changes in this amorphous metropolis is a full-time job, because what was "in" last year is probably "out" this year. Here's a short-list of what's new in L.A. that's worth checking out (or checking into).

If you haven't already made a hotel reservation, I've got some great recommendations for you. If you want to be entrenched in the Hollywood scene, you have to stay at the **Roosevelt Hotel, Hollywood** (✆ **800/950-7667;** www.hollywood roosevelt.com). The hotel just completed a $30-million renovation and is now *the* place to stay and play in the city. Hanging out by the pool while being served cocktails by model/actresses is a the classic L.A. experience. Also playing into the narcissistic Hollywood theme is the swanky new **Hotel Palomar Los Angeles** (✆ **800/472-8556;** www.hotelpalomar-lawestwood. com), where the modus operandi is to treat each guest like a celebrity V.I.P. by offering such perks as personal trainers and 24-hour in-room yoga and Pilates on your flatscreen TV.

If you'd rather stay near the beach, I have two new insider tips for you: the **Marina del Rey Marriott** (✆ **800/228-9290;** www.marriott.com) and the **Best Western Marina Pacific Hotel & Suites** (✆ **800/786-7789;** www.mphotel.com). Yes, two chain hotels, but this is L.A., where nothing is quite as it seems. At the Marriott, for example, a subtle aromatherapy mixture called Zanzibar Mist and a soundtrack of ambient world beats circulates throughout the lobby, and its outdoor lounge is ranked as one of the top hotel lounges in the country by *Playboy* magazine. The newly renovated Best Western, meanwhile, has a groovy rock-'n'-roll theme, great rates, and ocean-view rooms, and it's within easy walking distance of Venice Beach.

Then again, if all you want is a really nice room at a reasonable rate without any mist or models, the newly renovated boutique-style **Elan Hotel** (✆ **323/658-6663;** www.elanhotel.com) is my top choice. They did a fantastic job with the decor, the staff is wonderful, and the central

location makes driving around the city very convenient.

As for what's going on in L.A., the big news this year is the opening of **L.A. LIVE** (✆ **866/548-3452;** www.lalive.com) in downtown Los Angeles, a $2.5-billion mega-entertainment complex that's being optimistically hailed as Times Square West ("You, sir, are no Times Square"). Anchored by the Nokia Theatre and Staples Arena, the 6-square-block complex is crammed with restaurants, clubs, luxury condos, two hotels, a movie theater, and even a bowling alley. It's all part of the city's pricey push to revitalize the downtown area and increase convention business.

At the **Los Angeles Zoo** (✆ **323/644-4200;** www.lazoo.org), they've finally completed the new $19-million **Campo Gorilla Reserve,** a habitat for six African lowland gorillas that's designed to resemble their native West African homeland. Visitors walk along a misty, forested pathway that has glass observation areas for close-up views of the gorillas. Over at the wonderful **Natural History Museum** (✆ **213/763-DINO;** www.nhm.org), the inspiring new **Thomas the T. rex Lab** is ready for budding paleontologists. It's a specially designed workroom where visitors can watch genuine paleontologists as they prepare and assemble the fossils of a 66-million-year-old *Tyrannosaurus rex* nicknamed "Thomas." It one of many interactive exhibits that kids will find really cool.

The city has added some introspective attractions as well this year. At the **Los Angeles County Museum of Art** (✆ **323/857-6000;** www.lacma.org), the highly anticipated **Broad Contemporary Art Museum** (aka BCAM) has finally opened. The $56-million, three-story museum is one of the largest column-free art spaces in the U.S., hosting opening installations by such artists as Richard Serra, Andy Warhol, and Roy Lichtenstein. And at the **Huntington Library, Art Collections & Botanical Gardens** (✆ **626/405-2100;**

www.huntington.org), they've added a new **Chinese Garden** that is the largest classical garden outside mainland China and landscaped with 12 acres of plants native to China.

In the world of fine dining in L.A., the big news this year is the opening of **Katsuya Hollywood** (© 323/871-8777; www. sbe.com/katsuya), a collaboration between designer Philippe Starck and Master Sushi Chef Katsuya Uechi. If you want to spot celebrities on your vacation, it's a good place to start (assuming you can get a reservation). But if you're more into food than famous people, my top two picks this year are **Osteria Mozza** (© 323/297-0100; www.mozza-la.com) and **Fraîche** (© 310/839-680; www.fraicherestaurantla. com). The former is my new favorite restaurant in the city, and the latter is one of the most popular new restaurants in town (and deservedly so).

If you're more into value with a side of kitsch, I highly recommend **Luckyfish** (© 310/274-9800; www.luckyfishsushi. com), in Beverly Hills, and the **Waffle** (© 323/465-6901; www.thewaffle.us), in Hollywood. Luckyfish is a lively sushi restaurant that uses an ultramodern conveyer belt system to deliver mini-plates of fresh fish, while the Waffle is a modern take on a diner classic, serving cornmeal jalapeño waffles and maple syrup martinis to a hip crowd.

The irony of new nightclubs in L.A. is that you can't get in the ones everyone talks about. If you're under 30 and have the look, you probably won't have any problem getting into some of the newer clubs I added to this edition, such as **Green Door** (© 323/463-0008), in Hollywood, or **Winston's** (© 323/654-0105), in West Hollywood. Of course, you'll need the address because they don't have signage.

But if standing in line so a bouncer can determine your eligibility isn't your idea of a fun night out, here are a few hip alternatives that still provide that only-in-L.A.

experience: The new **Bar Nineteen12** (© 310/273-1912; www.barnineteen12. com), within the Beverly Hill Hotel, doubles as a good excuse to check out the legendary hotel and an easy way to spot celebrities; **Nic's Beverly Hills** (© 310/550-5707; www.nicsbeverlyhills.com) serves the city's best martinis in a lively, snob-free setting, despite its location; and **Glow** (© 310/578-4152; www.glow-bar. com) at the Marriott in Marina Del Rey is the sexiest hotel lounge I've ever seen. All three are good bets for a fun night in L.A.

THE CENTRAL & SOUTHERN COAST It's been a toasty summer season in Big Sur with all the wildfires burning along the Central Coast, but as far as we know, not a single tourist destination has been scorched; and by the time you read this Big Sur will be fully back in business. The blaze near Big Sur is one of more than 1,100 wildfires—most ignited by lightning—that have scorched 680 square miles and destroyed dozens of homes and buildings across Northern and Central California.

Eager for business are coastal hotels and restaurants, including newcomers to the California guidebook such as the **Monterey Bay Inn** (© 800/424-6242), where the sound of the waves lapping at your guest room is the perfect wake-up call; **Paradiso Trattoria** (© 831/375-4155), a waterfront restaurant offering spectacular sunset views; and the local favorite **Walnut Avenue Café** (© 831/457-2307), serving the best breakfasts in Santa Cruz.

A bit farther south in San Luis Obispo and Santa Barbara, we've uncovered a few more lodging and dining gems: the **Canary Hotel** (© 805/884-0300), one of the finest new hotels on the coast, with beautiful Moroccan and Spanish details; the **Tupelo Junction Café** (© 805/899-3100), beloved by locals for its pumpkin oatmeal waffles with candied walnuts and caramelized bananas; and the hugely popular **Palazzio**

(© 805/564-1985), where piled-high pasta dishes easily feed two, and garlic prevails.

The **Aqua Caliente Casino** (© **866/923-7244**; www.hotwatercasino.com) in Rancho Mirage has added a new 340-room hotel with a 10,000-square-foot spa, three restaurants, and a 2,000-seat showroom.

The newest addition to fine dining in Palm Springs is the **Purple Palm,** located in the newly refurbished **Colony Palms Hotel** on North Indian Canyon Drive (© **800/557-2187**; www.colonypalms hotel.com).

SAN DIEGO Southern California made international headlines in October 2007 when firestorms swept through the region, from Santa Barbara to the Mexican border. In San Diego, more than a half-million residents were displaced from their homes in the largest evacuation in state history; the blazes charred more than 300,000 acres and consumed some 1,700 homes and buildings. Most tragically, 10 lives were lost in San Diego. The conflagrations took place mostly in rural areas and bedroom communities, so the city's tourism infrastructure remained unaffected.

In a major governmental development, the City Council has banned drinking from all 17 miles of San Diego's beaches, as well as coastal parks and bay shores. This is a 1-year trial ban that will be in effect until January 2009. Check for posted signage after that date as to whether the prohibition is still in effect; fines run up to $250.

The newest hotel in San Diego's North County is the **Sheraton Carlsbad Resort & Spa** (© **760-827-2400**; www.sheraton carlsbad.com). Near LEGOLAND and a new golf course—the **Crossings at Carlsbad** (© **760/444-1800**; www.thecrossings atcarlsbad.com)—the Sheraton Carlsbad is designed to appeal to families and business travelers alike. Boasting ocean and fairway views, it currently has 129 rooms, but will expand to 350 by 2010.

The **Hyatt Regency Mission Bay Spa and Marina** (© **619/224-1234**; www. missionbay.hyatt.com) has unveiled its new **Blue Marble Spa,** part of the property's $65-million sprucing up. Utilizing organic products, low-flow shower heads, and other ecofriendly concepts, Blue Marble strives to be as green as possible within its 11 treatment rooms, which include five private outdoor cabanas.

You can take a culinary tour of the Caribbean at **Mangu** (© **619/269-3149**; www. mangusd.com) without leaving the Gaslamp Quarter. Serving lunch and dinner, as well as lots of rum drinks until the wee hours, Mangu takes a pan-island approach, with a menu that incorporates the tastes of Cuba, Puerto Rico, Jamaica, and the Dominican Republic—all with a helping of Miami South Beach glitz on the side.

The Gaslamp has also welcomed a "chic Greek" restaurant, **EXY** (© **619/238-0412**; www.exysandiego.com). Look for something far more creative and sophisticated than gyros—the executive chef is a veteran of several cosmopolitan eateries in San Francisco.

The Hotel del Coronado's **ENO** (© **619/ 435-6611**; www.hoteldel.com) has nothing to do with the electronic music pioneer and everything to do with wine. One of the final touches of the Del's $150-million renovation, this indoor/outdoor wine-tasting spot offers 500 wines, 35 international cheeses, and sweets created by local chocolatiers.

Burgeoning North Park adds yet another worthy entry to its growing list of high-caliber restaurants. **Urban Solace** (© **619/295-6464**; www.urbansolace.net) provides just that, serving contemporary comfort food such as lamb meatloaf (with figs, pine nuts, and feta cheese) and cider-and-molasses glazed free-range chicken. They host a live bluegrass Sunday brunch, too.

Old Town's **Jolly Boy Saloon and Restaurant** (© **619/297-3100**; www.jollyboy restaurant.com) has reemerged after an 8-month renovation. Not really such a long time to be closed, considering this historic structure dates back to 1854, when the original Jolly Boy opened. Set within Old Town State Historic Park, the Jolly Boy will feature costumed performers to go along with the meat and seafood menu.

Whether you bowl passionately or ironically, **East Village Tavern & Bowl** (© 619/ **677-2659;** www.bowlevt.com) can make room for you—especially now that it's already expanding. Featuring a logo of skull and crossbones, this hipster haven opened in late 2007 with six lanes and is now doubling that amount. Adjacent to the Gaslamp Quarter, the Tavern & Bowl also has food, good beer on tap, and ubiquitous flatscreen TVs.

San Diego's latest nightspot gem is the **Jade Theater** (© **619/814-5125;** www. jadetheater.com). This 14,000-square-foot, tri-level space not only serves imaginative Asian fare (acorn curry soup, crab *kim chi*), but is also a sexy lounge and club. Modernists will love the sleek, minimalist design.

The Best of California

by Harry Basch, Mark Hiss, Erika Lenkert & Matthew Richard Poole

In my early 20s, I took the requisite college student's pilgrimage to Europe, exploring its finer train stations and sleeping on the premier park benches from London to Istanbul. I was relatively anonymous—just another tanned and skinny, blond and blue-eyed American with a backpack. That is, until I crossed into the former Eastern Bloc.

The reaction there was dramatic, almost palpable. Like Moses parting the sea, I wandered the crowded streets of Prague and citizens would stop, stare, and step aside as if I bore a scarlet letter "A" across my chest. It wasn't until a man with faltering English approached me that I discovered the reason for my newfound celebrity status.

"Eh, you. Where you from? No, no. Let me guess." He stepped back and gave a cursory examination, followed by a pregnant pause. "Ah. I've got it! California! You're from California, no?" His eyes gleamed as I told him that, yes, he was quite correct. "Wonderful! Wonderful!" A dozen or so pilsners later with my loquacious new friend, and it all became clear to me: To him, I was a celebrity—a rich, convertible-driving surfer who spent most of his days lazing on the beach, fending off hordes of buxom blondes while arguing with his agent via cellphone. The myth is complete, I thought. I *am* the Beach Boys. I *am* *Baywatch*. Status by association. The tentacles of Hollywood have done what no NATO pact could achieve—they've leapfrogged the staid issues of capitalism versus communism by offering a far more potent narcotic: the mystique of sun-drenched California, of movie stars strolling down Sunset Boulevard, of beautiful women in tight shorts and bikini tops roller-skating along Venice Beach. In short, they've bought what the movie industry is selling.

Of course, the allure is understandable. It *is* warm and sunny most days of the year, movie stars *do* abound in Los Angeles, and you can't swing a cat by its tail without hitting an in-line skater in Venice Beach. This part of the California mystique, however exaggerated, *does* exist, and it's not hard to find.

But there's more—a lot more—to California that isn't scripted, sanitized, and broadcasted to the world's millions of mesmerized masses. Beyond the Hollywood glitter is a wondrously diverse state that, if it ever seceded from the Union, would be one of the most productive, powerful nations in the world. We've got it all: misty redwood forests, an exceptionally verdant Central Valley teeming with agriculture, the mighty Sierra Nevada Mountain Range, eerily fascinating deserts, a host of world-renowned cities, and, of course, hundreds of miles of stunning coastline.

And despite the endemic crime, pollution, traffic, and bowel-shaking earthquakes for which California is famous, we're still the golden child of the United States, America's spoiled rich kid, either loved or loathed by everyone else. (Neighboring Oregon, for example, sells lots of license-plate rims that proudly state, "I hate California.") Truth be told, however, we don't care what anyone thinks of us. Californians *know* they live in one of the most diverse and interesting places in the world, and we're proud of the state we call home.

Granted, we can't guarantee that you'll bump into Arnold Schwarzenegger or learn to surf, but if you have a little time, a little money, and an adventurous spirit, then Harry,

Mark, Erika, and I can help guide you through one of the most fulfilling vacations of your life. The four of us travel the world for a living, but we *choose* to live in California—because no other place on earth has so much to offer.

—*Matthew Richard Poole*

1 THE BEST OF NATURAL CALIFORNIA

- **Redwood National and State Parks:** Acres of inconceivably massive redwood trees, up to 350 feet tall, tower over thick, lush, oversize ferns, mosses, and wild orchids in the old-growth forests along the Northern California coast. Walking through these groves is an unforgettably humbling, serene experience. See "Redwood National & State Parks," in chapter 8.

- **Point Reyes National Seashore:** This extraordinarily scenic stretch of coast and wetlands is one of the state's best bird-watching spots for waterfowl, shorebirds, songbirds, osprey, and red-shouldered hawks. You might even catch a glimpse of a whale from the Point Reyes Lighthouse. See "Point Reyes National Seashore," in chapter 8.

- **Lake Tahoe:** One of the world's most magnificent bodies of fresh water, sparkling Lake Tahoe contains close to 40 trillion gallons—enough to cover the entire state of California to a depth of 15 inches. See "Lake Tahoe," in chapter 9.

- **Mount Shasta:** The mighty volcano Mount Shasta, a solitary tower of rock and snow, rises thousands of feet above the valley floor. If you're fit, it makes for an exhilarating climb as well. See "Mount Shasta & the Cascades," in chapter 9.

- **Yosemite National Park:** You're in for the ultimate treat at Yosemite. Nothing in the state—maybe even the world— compares to this vast wilderness and its miles of rivers, lakes, peaks, and valleys. With 3 of the 10 tallest waterfalls on earth, the largest granite monolith anywhere, and some of the world's largest trees, Yosemite is one of the most superlative natural places on the planet. See "Yosemite National Park," in chapter 10.

- **Big Sur:** Sloping redwood forests and towering cliffs pounded by the Pacific create one of the world's most dramatic coastal panoramas. See "The Big Sur Coast," in chapter 12.

- **Channel Islands National Park:** This is California in its most virginal state. Paddle a kayak into sea caves; camp among indigenous island fox and sea-birds; and swim, snorkel, or scuba dive tide pools and kelp forests teeming with wildlife. The channel waters are prime for whale-watching, and winter brings elephant-seal mating season, when you'll see them and their sea-lion cousins sunbathing on cove beaches. See "Channel Islands National Park," in chapter 13.

- **Joshua Tree National Park:** You'll find awesome rock formations; groves of flowering cacti and gnarly, eerily beautiful Joshua trees; ancient Native American petroglyphs; and shifting sand dunes in this desert wonderland. If you choose to camp here, you'll sleep under a brilliant night sky. See "Joshua Tree National Park," in chapter 16.

- **Anza-Borrego Desert State Park:** California's largest state park attracts most of its visitors during the spring wildflower season, when a kaleidoscopic carpet blankets the desert floor. Others come year-round to hike more than 100 miles of trails. See "Anza-Borrego Desert State Park," in chapter 16.

- **Torrey Pines State Reserve:** This pristine park is named for the rare, dramatic little species of pine that grows only here and on a tiny island off the coast. Eight miles of trails immerse hikers into a delicate and beautiful coastal environment featuring mesas, canyons, and marshes. One of San Diego's best

beaches awaits at the foot of the sandstone cliffs. See chapter 17.

9

2 THE BEST BEACHES

- **Sonoma Coast State Beaches:** Stretching 10 miles from Bodega Bay to Jenner, these sands draw 300 bird species. Look for osprey from December to September, seal pups from March to June, and gray whales from December to April. See "Along the Sonoma Coast," in chapter 8.

- **Santa Cruz's Beaches:** Santa Cruz has 29 miles of beaches, varied enough to please surfers, swimmers, fishers, sailboarders, the sand-pail-and-shovel set, and the bikini-and-biceps crowd. For starters, walk down the steps from the famous Santa Cruz Beach Boardwalk to the mile-long Main Beach, complete with summer lifeguards and golden-oldie tunes drifting over the sand. See "Santa Cruz," in chapter 12.

- **Pismo Beach:** Pismo's 23-mile stretch of prime beachfront has been an annual destination for generations of California families. Fishing, shopping, surfing, and renting dune buggies are just a few of the many outdoor activities here. Even dogs are welcome to play on the beach. See "Pismo Beach," in chapter 13.

- **Santa Barbara's East Beach:** This wide swath of white sand hosts beach umbrellas, sandcastle builders, and volleyball games. On Sundays, local artists display their work beneath the palm trees. See "Santa Barbara," in chapter 13.

- **Malibu's Legendary Beaches:** Zuma and Surfrider beaches inspired the 1960s surf music that embodies the Southern California coast culture. Surfrider is home to L.A.'s best waves. Zuma is loaded with snack bars, restrooms, jungle gyms, and other amenities. The beach affords some of the state's best sunbathing, in front of the Malibu Colony, a star-studded enclave of multimillion-dollar homes. See "Beaches," in chapter 14.

- **La Jolla's Beaches:** "La Jolla" may be misspelled Spanish for "the jewel," but *this* is no mistake: The bluff-lined beaches here are among the state's most beautiful. Each has a distinct personality: Surfers love Windansea's waves; harbor seals have adopted the Children's Pool; La Jolla Shores is popular for swimming, sunbathing, and kayaking; while the Cove is a top snorkeling spot—and the best place to spot the electric-orange California state fish, the garibaldi. See "Beaches," in chapter 17.

3 THE BEST GOLF COURSES

- **Pebble Beach Golf Links:** The famous 17-Mile Drive is the site of 10 national championships and the celebrity-laden AT&T Pebble Beach National Pro-Am. The nearby Pacific and a backdrop of the Del Monte Forest *almost* justify the astronomical greens fees. See "Pebble Beach & the 17-Mile Drive," in chapter 12.

- **Poppy Hills** (Pebble Beach): *Golf Digest* has called this Robert Trent Jones, Jr.–designed course one of the world's top-20. Cutting through the Del Monte Forest pines, it is kept in state-of-the-art condition. Unlike many competitors, it's rarely crowded. See "Pebble Beach & the 17-Mile Drive," in chapter 12.

- **PGA West TPC Stadium Course** (La Quinta): The par-3 17th hole has a tiny island where Lee Trevino made Skins Game history with a hole in one. The rest of Pete Dye's 7,261-yard design is flat with huge bunkers, lots of water, and severe mounding throughout. See "The Palm Springs Desert Resorts," in chapter 16.

- **Torrey Pines Golf Course** (La Jolla): Two 18-hole championship courses overlook the ocean and give players plenty of challenges—and distractions. In February, the Buick Invitational Tournament takes place here; the rest of the year, these gorgeous municipal courses are open to everyone. See "Outdoor Pursuits," in chapter 17.

4 THE BEST CALIFORNIA TRAVEL EXPERIENCES

- **Riding a Cable Car:** It's the quintessential San Francisco experience, taking the Powell–Hyde cable car down to Fisherman's Wharf. When you reach the top of Nob Hill, grab the rail with one hand and hold your camera with the other, because you're about to see a view of the bay that'll make you all weepy. See chapter 5.

- **Exploring Alcatraz Island:** Even if you loathe tourist attractions, you'll dig Alcatraz. Just looking at the Rock from across the bay is enough to give you the heebie-jeebies—and the park rangers have put together an excellent audio tour. Heck, even the boat ride across the bay is worth the price. See chapter 5.

- **Hot-Air Ballooning over Napa Valley:** Sure, you have to rise at dawn to do it, but drifting over the Napa Valley's vineyards in a balloon is the best way to view the verdant, undulating hills, meticulously striped with vines and bordered by mountains. Flights run in the morning on clear days, when the air is calm and cool. You can book a trip through your hotel or with **Bonaventura Balloon Company** (© 800/FLY-NAPA) or **Adventures Aloft** (© 800/944-4408). See "Hot-Air Ballooning over the Valley," in chapter 7.

- **Wine Tasting in Napa or Sonoma:** You don't have to be a connoisseur to appreciate the wine trail. All you need is

a decadent streak and a designated driver. Sniff and sip at a few wineries, take in the bucolic views, and see why this region is one of the hottest destinations in the country—a place to sample some of the world's best wines right at the source. See chapter 7.

- **Taking a Train Ride Through the Redwoods:** Where else on this planet would you get an opportunity to ride a historic steam train through a remote coastal redwood forest? The **Skunk Train** (© 800/866-1690), in Fort Bragg, once lugged logs and now takes tourists on an all-day outing through a redwood forest, an 80-mile journey that crosses over 31 bridges and trestles and through two deep tunnels. They even offer a Sunset Dinner BBQ excursion. See chapter 8.

- **Rafting Scenic Northern California Rivers:** You can white-water raft through cascades of raging Class IV waters or float under blue skies, through deep forests, past all sorts of wildlife. Depending on the river and the time of year, some trips are okay for children over age 6. See chapters 9, 10, and 11.

- **Spelunking a Real Gold Mine** (Sutter Creek): Don your hard hat, "tag in," board the mine shuttle, and experience what it's like to be a gold miner. The **Sutter Gold Mine** tour company (© 866/762-2837) takes you deep into a mine that's loaded with gold deposits. You'll have the chance to sluice for some real gold. See chapter 11.

- **Panning for Gold in the Gold Country:** In southern Gold Country, you can dig into living history and pan for gold. Several companies, including **Gold Prospecting Adventures** (© **800/596-0009**) in Jamestown, offer dredging lessons and gold-panning tours. You'll quickly learn that this is backbreaking labor, although an adventure. And who knows? You might get lucky and launch a new gold rush. See chapter 11.

- **Taking a Studio Tour** (Los Angeles): Studio tours are opportunities to see actual stage sets for shows such as *ER* and *The West Wing*, and you never know who you're going to spot emerging from his or her star wagon. See "Exploring the City," in chapter 14.

- **Learning How to Surf:** What could be a better experience during your California vacation than learning how to surf on the same breaks that the Beach Boys surfed? Surfing schools, such as **Learn to Surf L.A.,** in Manhattan Beach, will guarantee you'll get up on a longboard and be surfing the easy waves in one short lesson. See "Surfing," in the "Outdoor Pursuits" section, in chapter 14.

- **Cruising Sunset Boulevard:** It's a must for first-time visitors because you'll see a cross-section of everything that is L.A.: legendary clubs, studios, hotels, and zip codes that you'll instantly recognize from the silver screen and TV shows.

The journey ends with a trip to Malibu's fabled beaches, where those classy *Baywatch* episodes are filmed (how perfect). See "L.A.'s Top Attractions," in chapter 14.

- **Skating Venice Beach:** You haven't visited Southern California properly until you've rented some skates at Venice Beach and taken in the human carnival around you. Nosh on a Jody Maroni's "haute" dog; buy some cheap sunglasses, silver jewelry, or ethnic garb; and relish the wide beach, blue sea, and performers along the boardwalk. See "L.A.'s Top Attractions," in chapter 14.

- **Flying a World War II Fighter Aircraft:** Strap yourself into a vintage 600-horsepower fighter aircraft and prepare to blow your mind as you (yes, *you*) perform aerobatic maneuvers—loops, rolls, and lazy-eights—above the Carlsbad coastline, accompanied (but not flown) by a pilot from Biplane, Air Combat & Warbird Adventures (© **800/759-5667**). It's an experience you'll never forget. See p. 645.

- **Explore Wreck Alley:** Several scuttled vessels sit on the ocean floor, about 1 mile off Mission Beach, providing certified divers the chance to investigate a nautical graveyard teeming with sea life. The artificial reef includes a 366-foot Canadian destroyer, the *Yukon,* as well as the remnants of a research station toppled by a storm in 1988. See "Outdoor Pursuits," in chapter 17.

5 THE BEST OF SMALL-TOWN CALIFORNIA

- **St. Helena:** In the heart of the Napa Valley, St. Helena is known for its Main Street. In a horse and buggy, Robert Louis Stevenson and his bride once made their way down this thoroughfare lined with Victorian homes. The Victorians remain, but now they're stores for

designer clothing, hardware, bath products, you name it. Come for the old-time, tranquil mood and the food. See "Napa Valley," in chapter 7.

- **Healdsburg:** An exceptional destination within the vast wine country region of Sonoma, this charming town is centered on its historic square, which maintains old-fashion charm despite being home to world-class hotels, restaurants, and shopping. And did we mention that it's a 5-minute drive to some of the state's best wineries? See "Healdsburg," in chapter 7.

- **Mendocino:** An artists' colony with a New England flavor, Mendocino doubled as Cabot Cove, Maine, as the backdrop for *Murder, She Wrote.* On the cliffs above the Pacific Ocean, it has small art galleries, general stores, weathered wooden homes, and organic restaurants. See "Mendocino," in chapter 8.

- **Arcata:** If you're losing faith in America, restore it by spending a few days in this Northern California coastal town. Arcata has it all: its own redwood forest and bird marsh, a charming town square, great family-owned restaurants, and even its own minor-league baseball team, which draws the entire town together on many an afternoon. See "Eureka & Environs," in chapter 8.

- **Nevada City:** The entire town is a national historic landmark and the best place to understand Gold Rush fever. Settled in 1849, it offers fine dining and shopping and a stock of the multi-gabled Victorian frame houses of the Old West. Relics of the Donner Party are on display at the 1861 Firehouse No. 1. See "The Gold Country," in chapter 11.

- **Pacific Grove:** Escape beach crowds just 2 miles west of Monterey, in Pacific Grove, known for its tranquil waterfront and clean air. It draws thousands of monarch butterflies between October and March. See "Pacific Grove," in chapter 12.

- **Ojai:** When filmmakers needed a Shangri-La for the movie *Lost Horizon,* they drove to Ojai Valley, with its unspoiled eucalyptus groves and small ranches in soft, green hills. Ojai is the amiable village at the valley's heart—a mecca for artists, free spirits, and city folk in need of a restful weekend in the country. See "The Ojai Valley," in chapter 13.

- **Santa Catalina Island:** A day trip to the small town of Catalina makes for a most indulgent day: Take a scenic boat ride, shop, snorkel and dive, golf, hike, lick ice cream, get a sunburn, and barhop sans fear of a DUI. *Tip:* The helicopter taxi is cheaper than you'd expect. See "Santa Catalina Island," in chapter 15.

- **Julian:** This old mining town in the Cuyamaca Mountains near San Diego is now known for a different kind of mother lode: apples (and the ensuing apple pies). The pioneer legacy here includes a local-history museum, an Old West cemetery, and some of the town's original gold mines. See "Julian: Gold, Apple Pies & a Slice of Small-Town California," in chapter 17.

6 THE BEST FAMILY VACATION EXPERIENCES

- **San Francisco:** The City by the Bay will entertain every member of the family. If you're traveling with kids, ride the cable cars that "climb halfway to the stars," visit the Exploratorium, the Metreon, the zoo, the ships at the National Maritime Museum, Golden Gate Park, and more. See chapter 5.

- **Lake Tahoe:** Lake Tahoe has fun activities galore for families: skiing, snowboarding, hiking, tobogganing, swimming, fishing, boating, water-skiing, mountain biking, and so on. The possibilities seem endless. See "Lake Tahoe," in chapter 9.

- **Yosemite National Park:** Camping or sleeping in a cabin in Yosemite is one of California's top family attractions. Sites lie scattered over 17 campgrounds, ringed by the Sierra Nevada. By day, families can pack their schedule with hiking, bicycling, white-water rafting, scaling snowy peaks, and more. See "Yosemite National Park," in chapter 10.

- **Santa Cruz:** This funky bayside town has the stuff of an ideal family trip: surfing, sea kayaking, hiking, fishing, and shopping. And those fantastic beaches and the legendary amusement park on the boardwalk will please travelers of all ages. See "Santa Cruz," in chapter 12.
- **Monterey:** It's been called "Disneyland-by-the-Sea" because of all its tourist activities, including those on Cannery Row and Fisherman's Wharf. The state-of-the-art Monterey Bay Aquarium, however, is a class act, the best in the world. See chapter 12.
- **Disneyland Resort:** The "Happiest Place on Earth" is enhanced by its sister theme park, **Disney's California Adventure.** Whether you're wowed by the animation, thrilled by the coasters, or interested in the history and secrets of this pop-culture juggernaut, you won't leave disappointed. Get a FAST-PASS to skip those long lines! See "The Disneyland Resort," in chapter 15.
- **San Diego Zoo, Wild Animal Park, & SeaWorld:** San Diego boasts three of the world's best animal attractions. At the zoo, animals live in naturalistic habitats, and it's one of only four zoos in the U.S. with giant pandas. At the Wild Animal Park, most of the 3,500 animals roam freely over an 1,800-acre spread. And SeaWorld, with its water-themed rides, flashy animal shows, and detailed exhibits, is an aquatic wonderland of pirouetting dolphins and 4-ton killer whales with a penchant for drenching visitors. See "The Three Major Animal Parks," in chapter 17.

7 THE BEST ARCHITECTURAL LANDMARKS

- **The Golden Gate Bridge** (San Francisco): More tomato red than golden, the famous bridge remains the cheery hallmark of the San Francisco skyline. It's also an excellent expanse to walk. See "The Top Attractions," in chapter 5.
- **The Painted Ladies** (San Francisco): The so-called "Painted Ladies" are San Francisco's famous, ornately decorated Victorian homes. Check out the brilliant beauties around Alamo Square. Most of the extant 14,000 structures date from the second half of the 19th century. See chapter 5.
- **Winchester Mystery House** (San Jose): The heiress to the Winchester rifle fortune, Sarah Winchester, created one of the major "Believe It or Not?" curiosities of California, a 160-room Victorian mansion. When a fortune-teller told Sarah she wouldn't die if she'd continue to build onto her house, her mansion underwent construction day and night from 1884 to 1922. She did die eventually, and the hammers were silenced. See chapter 6.
- **The Carson Mansion** (Eureka): This ornate Victorian is one of the state's most photographed and flamboyant Queen Anne–style structures. It was built in 1885 by the Newsom brothers for William Carson, the local timber baron. Today it's the headquarters of a men's club. See chapter 8.
- **The California State Capitol Building** (Sacramento): The Golden State's dazzling white capitol was built in 1869 and renovated in 1976. Its dome—which looks like a Fabergé egg from inside—and original statuary along its eaves remain, and antiques from the original offices furnish its historic rooms. The collection of California governors' portraits is strangely compelling. See "Sacramento," in chapter 11.

- **Mission San Carlos Borromèo del Río Carmelo** (Carmel): The second mission founded in California, in 1770 by Father Junípero Serra, is perhaps the most beautiful. Its stone church and tower dome have been restored, and a garden of poppies adjoins the church. See "Carmel-by-the-Sea," in chapter 12.

- **Hearst Castle** (San Simeon): William Randolph Hearst's 165-room abode is one of the last great estates of America's Gilded Age. It's an astounding, over-the-top monument to unbridled wealth and power. See "San Simeon: Hearst Castle," in chapter 13.

- **Walt Disney Concert Hall** (Los Angeles): You would have to fly to Spain to see Frank Gehry's other architectural masterpiece, and this one is sufficiently awe inspiring. And the dramatically curvaceous stainless-steel exterior houses one of the most acoustically perfect concert halls in the world. See chapter 14.

- **The Gamble House** (Pasadena): The Smithsonian Institution calls this 1908 Arts and Crafts landmark one of the nation's most important houses. Visitors can tour the spectacular interior, designed and impeccably executed, down to the last teak armchair, by Charles and Henry Greene. See chapter 14.

- **Balboa Park** (San Diego): The Spanish Colonial Revival–style buildings along El Prado were originally built as temporary structures for the Panama-California Exposition (1915–16). The ornately decorated and imposing facades create a romantic aura amid the beautifully landscaped mesas and canyons of one of the world's finest city parks, home to many of the city's top museums. See "Exploring the Area," in chapter 17.

8 THE BEST MUSEUMS

- **de Young Museum** (San Francisco): The city's oldest museum was rebuilt from the ground up, and in late 2005 debuted as one of San Francisco's top attractions. Anchored in beautiful Golden Gate Park, surrounded by stunning flora, and shimmering in its fabulous copper exterior, it has a fantastic collection of American paintings, decorative arts and crafts, and arts from Africa, Oceania, and the Americas. Topping it off is a tower with great city views and a surprisingly good cafe with outdoor tables overlooking the sculpture garden. See p. 128.

- **The Exploratorium** (San Francisco): The hands-on, interactive Exploratorium boasts 650 exhibits that help show how things work. See p. 129.

- **California State Railroad Museum** (Sacramento): Old Sacramento's biggest attraction, the 100,000-square-foot museum was once the terminus of the transcontinental and Sacramento Valley railways. It displays dozens of locomotives and railroad cars, among other attractions. See p. 351.

- **Getty Museum at the Getty Center** (Los Angeles): Designed by Richard Meier and completed in 1997 to the tune of $1 billion, the Getty Center is a striking, starkly futuristic architectural landmark, with panoramic views of the city and ocean. The building itself is enough reason to visit, but so is the permanent collection, the crown jewel of which is Van Gogh's "Irises," which the museum paid $54 million to acquire. See p. 537.

- **Petersen Automotive Museum** (Los Angeles): This museum is a natural for Los Angeles, a city whose personality and history is so entwined with the popularity of the automobile. Impeccably restored vintage autos are displayed in life-size dioramas accurate to the last period detail (including an authentic 1930s-era service station). Upstairs galleries house celebrity vehicles, car-related artwork, and exhibits. See p. 548.

- **The Museum of Contemporary Art San Diego:** In 2007, San Diego's internationally respected contemporary art museum opened its third space, transforming a portion of the historic downtown train station into the city's newest cultural icon. Together with its other downtown annex and the flagship space that overlooks the ocean in La Jolla, MCASD stakes its claim as the boldest, most important museum in San Diego. See p. 745.

9 THE BEST LUXURY HOTELS & RESORTS

- **The Ritz-Carlton San Francisco** (Nob Hill; ✆ 800/241-3333), is the sine qua non of luxury hotels, offering near-perfect service and every possible amenity. Even if you can't afford a guest room, come for the mind-blowing Sunday brunch. See p. 88.
- **The Mandarin Oriental** (San Francisco; ✆ 800/622-0404), is perched so high above the city that the fog rolls in *below* you. It's surreal. Maybe you really did die and go to heaven? See p. 85.
- **Calistoga Ranch** (Calistoga; ✆ 707/254-2800): Napa Valley's latest upscale hotel blows away the competition, with individual luxury cabins stocked with every imaginable luxury. In a secluded canyon, it's where nature meets nurture, with a fabulous pool, spa, gym, and guest-only restaurant overlooking a lake. See p. 193.
- **Château du Sureau** (Oakhurst; ✆ 559/683-6860): Near Yosemite, the Château du Sureau and Erna's Elderberry House restaurant stand out for their European attention to quality and detail. Room furnishings are exquisite, and the cuisine is worthy of the stars. See p. 310.
- **Casa Palmero Resort** (Pebble Beach; ✆ 800/654-9300): A small, ultraluxury resort on the first tee of the Pebble Beach Golf Course, Casa Palmero has 24 intimate and private cottages and suites. Is $2,550 per night okay with you? See p. 404.

- **Post Ranch Inn** (Big Sur; ✆ 800/527-2200): Twelve hundred feet above the sea, the elevated wood-and-glass guest cottages at this romantic cliff-side retreat give guests the illusion that they're living at cloud level. See p. 418.
- **Four Seasons Resort** (Santa Barbara; ✆ 800/819-5053): Open since 1927, this Four Seasons operation, on the grounds of the historic Biltmore Hotel, has palm-studded formal gardens and prime beachfront along "America's Riviera." Wander the elegant Spanish-Moorish arcades and walkways, accented by exquisite Mexican tile, and then play croquet on manicured lawns or relax at the Coral Casino Beach and Cabana Club. The rooms are the epitome of refined luxury. See p. 460.
- **Shutters on the Beach** (Santa Monica; ✆ 800/334-9000) and **Casa del Mar** (Santa Monica; ✆ 800/898-6999): If an oceanfront room at either of these hotels doesn't put a spring in your love life, we don't know what will. Shutters is dressed up like a rich friend's contemporary-chic beach house, while glamorous Casa del Mar is an impeccably restored Art Deco–era delight. See p. 499 and 498.
- **Beverly Hills Hotel and Bungalows** (Beverly Hills; ✆ 800/283-8885): A deep dent in your credit card is a small price to pay for the chance to take afternoon tea next to Ozzy Osbourne, swim

laps in the same pool Katharine Hepburn once dove into fully clothed, and eat pancakes in the fabled Fountain Coffee Shop. See p. 503.

- **La Quinta Resort & Club** (La Quinta; ✆ **800/598-3828**): This mecca for serious golfers has morphed into an upscale family hotel without disturbing the quality of service. While Dad is putting away, Mom can luxuriate in one of more than 35 spa treatment rooms, and the kids can splash in one of the 41 outdoor pools and Jacuzzis or exercise on one of the 23 tennis courts. The property is designed to reduce the feeling of a mega resort, and the service exceeds expectations. Fido is welcome also, for a fee ($100 a night). See p. 673.

- **The Grand Del Mar** (Del Mar; ✆ **888/314-2030**): This new resort nestled in the foothills of San Diego's North County is a faux Tuscan villa padded with ornate, Vegas-style luxury. Liberally accented with fountains, courtyards, sweeping staircases, and outdoor fireplaces, it's so grandly European that you'll feel as if you are visiting the *doge* at his country estate. Its signature restaurant, Addison, is one of the city's most sumptuous dining rooms, with cuisine to match. See p. 760.

10 THE BEST AFFORDABLE SMALL HOTELS & INNS

- **Hotel Bohème** (San Francisco; ✆ **415/433-9111**): This hotel is the perfect mixture of art, style, class, romance, and location—just steps from the sidewalk cafes of North Beach. If Bette Davis were alive today, this is where she'd stay. See p. 90.

- **St. Orres** (Gualala; ✆ **707/884-3303**): Designed in a Russian style—complete with two Kremlinesque, onion-domed towers—St. Orres offers secluded accommodations constructed from century-old timbers salvaged from a nearby mill. One of the most eye-catching inns on California's North Coast. See p. 231.

- **Albion River Inn** (Albion; ✆ **800/479-7944**): One of the best rooms with a view on the coast, the Albion River Inn is on a cliff overlooking a rugged stretch of shoreline. Most of the luxuriously appointed rooms have Jacuzzi tubs for two, elevated to window level. Add champagne and you're guaranteed to have a night you won't soon forget. See p. 239.

- **River Ranch Lodge** (Lake Tahoe; ✆ **800/535-9900**): Alongside the Truckee River, the River Ranch has long been one of our favorite affordable inns around Lake Tahoe. It has everything you'd want in a mountain lodge: rustic decor, a great bar and outdoor deck overlooking the river, and a restaurant serving wood-oven-roasted Montana elk loin and other hearty dishes. See p. 282.

- **Gunn House Hotel** (Sonora; ✆ **209/532-3421**): Built in 1850 by Dr. Lewis C. Gunn, this was the first two-story adobe structure in Sonora and is now one of the best moderately priced hotels in the Gold Country. It's easy to catch the forty-niner spirit here, as the entire hotel and grounds are brimming with quality antiques and turn-of-the-20th-century artifacts. But what really makes the Gunn House one of our favorites is the hotel's beautiful pool and patio, surrounded by lush vegetation and admirable stonework. See p. 372.

- **Mount Shasta Ranch B&B** (Mount Shasta; ✆ **530/926-3870**): Built in 1923 as a private retreat and thoroughbred horse ranch for one of the country's most famous horse trainers and racing tycoons, this B&B offers one of the best deals anywhere. Rates start at $60 a night and include a full country breakfast. See p. 295.

- **Evergreen Lodge** (Yosemite; ✆ **800/935-6343**): Scattered through a grove of towering pines near the entrance to Yosemite, Evergreen's rustic cabins, with a beautiful old bar and restaurant, afford easy access to dozens of outdoor adventures. Enjoy a pitcher of beer and a game of Ping-Pong on the patio, or sit around the campfire telling stories and roasting marshmallows. See p. 307.
- **The Mosaic** (Beverly Hills; ✆ **800/463-4466**): This Beverly Hills boutique is an ideal blend of art, luxury, service, location, and value. Huge rainforest shower heads, Frette linens, Bulgari bath products, Wolfgang Puck refreshments, and piles of pillows will leave you wondering if you checked in at the pearly gates. See p. 506.
- **Huntley Santa Monica Beach** (Santa Monica; ✆ **310/394-5454**): Tucked away on the edge of a quiet Santa Monica neighborhood is my favorite Santa Monica hotel, one that combines a superb location with excellent service and strikingly stylish decor. The Huntley's 18th-floor **Penthouse** restaurant, bar, and lounge has the best nightlife scene in Santa Monica. See p. 500.
- **Casa Malibu** (Malibu; ✆ **800/831-0858**): This beachfront motel will fool you from the front; its humble entrance on Pacific Coast Highway belies the

quiet, restful haven within. Bougainvillea vines festoon the rooftops and balconies of the motel's 21 rooms around a courtyard garden. Many rooms have private decks above the sand, and one suite was reportedly Lana Turner's favorite. See p. 502.

- **Olallieberry Inn** (Cambria; ✆ **888/927-3222**): This 1873 Greek Revival house, furnished in Victorian style, is an ideal base for exploring Hearst Castle. The gracious innkeepers will provide directions to Moonstone Beach, restaurant recommendations, a scrumptious breakfast, and more. See p. 431.
- **Casa Cody** (Palm Springs; ✆ **800/231-2639**): You'll feel more like a houseguest than a client at this 1920s Spanish-style *casa,* blessed with peaceful, blossoming grounds and two pools. The southwestern-style rooms are large and equipped for extended stays, and the hotel is just a couple of easy blocks from the heart of the action. See p. 671.
- **La Pensione Hotel** (San Diego; ✆ **800/232-4683**): In Little Italy, on the fringe of downtown San Diego, this find feels like a small, modern European hotel, with tidy lodgings at bargain prices. Great dining options abound in the surrounding blocks, and you'll be perfectly situated to explore the rest of the city and region by car or trolley. The immediate neighborhood is filled with boutiques and some of the city's most dashing new architecture. See p. 709.

11 THE BEST PLACES TO STAY WITH THE KIDS

- **KOA Kamping Kabins** (Point Arena; ✆ **800/562-4188**): Once you see the adorable log cabins at this KOA campground, you'll have to admit that this is one cool way to spend the weekend on the coast. Primitive is the key word: mattresses, a heater, and a light bulb are

the standard amenities. All you need is some bedding (or sleeping bags), cooking and eating utensils, and charcoal for the barbecue. See p. 234.
- **City Hotel** and **Fallon Hotel** (Columbia; ✆ **800/532-1479**): Some parents may roll their eyes at this preserved

Gold Rush town, but it's a dream come true for rambunctious kids. Visitors can ride a 100-year-old stagecoach, visit a blacksmith shop, and view lots of mining artifacts. And the reasonably priced Victorian hotels serve a great buffet breakfast. Cars are barred from the dusty main street. See p. 371.

- **Camping at Yosemite's Tuolumne Meadows** (© **800/436-7275**): At an elevation of 8,600 feet, this is the largest alpine meadow in the High Sierra. A gateway to the "high country," it's especially memorable in late spring, when it's carpeted with wildflowers. Park authorities run the large campground and a full-scale naturalist program, but hardcore adventurers can backpack into the wilderness. See p. 322.

- **Disneyland Resort Hotels** (Anaheim; © **714/956-MICKEY**): The Holy Grail of Disney lovers has always been the "Official Hotel of the Magic Kingdom," the original **Disneyland Hotel** (p. 628). The newer **Paradise Pier Hotel** (p. 629) and **Grand Californian** (p. 628) are also an easy monorail or tram ride to Disneyland's gates (the Grand Californian opens directly into California Adventure). See p. 626.

- **Marriott's Desert Springs Spa & Resort** (Palm Desert; © **800/331-3112**): In the spirit of Disney-esque resorts, this oasis welcomes guests with a lobby featuring a 60-foot bar, tropical birds, and gondolas that tour the fairways and gardens. Once settled, kids will revel in the lagoonlike pools and play areas (with supervised children's programs). And grown-ups can luxuriate on the golf course, tennis court, or in the 30,000-square-foot day spa. See p. 672.

- **Paradise Point Resort & Spa** (San Diego; © **800/344-2626**): Right in the middle of Mission Bay, this resort is almost as much a theme park as its closest neighbor, SeaWorld. The 44-acre, tropically landscaped property can supply a seemingly endless variety of recreational toys for activities in, on, or around the bay. Adults can enjoy the fabulous spa and the excellent (kid-friendly) restaurant, Baleen. See p. 713.

12 THE BEST RESTAURANTS

- **San Francisco's Finest:** Restaurant **Michael Mina,** 335 Powell St., Union Square (© **415/397-9222**), is the place to go for Union Square fine dining. Dozens of fancifully presented small portions add up to a delightfully long, lavish meal. And then there's **Restaurant Gary Danko,** 800 North Point St., Fisherman's Wharf (© **415/749-2060**), always a sure bet for a perfect contemporary French meal complete with polished service and flambéed finales. See p. 94 and 107, respectively.

- **Chez Panisse** (Berkeley; © **510/548-5525**): This is the domain of Alice Waters, "the queen of California cuisine." Originally inspired by the Mediterranean, her kitchen has found its own style, captivating the imagination as well as the senses. Chez Panisse's delicacies include grilled fish wrapped in fig leaves with red-wine sauce, and Seckel pears poached in red wine with burnt caramel. See p. 155.

- **Bistro Don Giovanni** (Napa; © **707/224-3300**): In this large, cheery Napa Valley dining room, you can get an incredible Italian meal without a reservation. Just drop in and wait at the bar for a seat. See p. 196.

- **Restaurant 301** (Eureka; © **800/404-1390**): A recipient of *Wine Spectator*'s Grand Award, Mark Carter is passionate about food and wine, and it shows: His hotel restaurant is considered the best on the Northern Coast. Most of the herbs and many vegetables come fresh from the hotel's organic gardens. Indulge in the five-course fixed-price dinner menu; Carter pairs each course with an excellent wine, available by the glass, or as part of a wine flight. See p. 250.

- **Erna's Elderberry House** (Oakhurst; © **559/683-6800**): Erna's shines like a beacon across the culinary wasteland around Yosemite. The six-course menu, which changes nightly, is an ideal blend of Continental and Californian cuisine. Portions are bountiful, served in an elegant European setting. See p. 310.

- **bouchon** (Santa Barbara; © **805/730-1160**): With an intriguing seasonal menu derived from Santa Barbara County's wine country, this intimate restaurant (whose name means "wine cork") is hidden behind a shrubbery portal in the heart of downtown. The food and service are impeccable, and an experienced staff stands ready to help coordinate by-the-glass (or even half-glass) wines for each course. See p. 463.

- **Grace** (Los Angeles; © **323/934-4400**): The best overall dining experience in Los Angeles. Iron Chef Neal Fraser was trained by America's finest chefs, and it shows (the foie gras served two ways is worth the trip alone). Sophisticated yet unpretentious, Grace is a splurge worth making. See p. 527.

- **The Hump** (Santa Monica; © **310/313-0977**): The chefs here are deadly serious about their sushi. Flown in daily from Tokyo's Tsukijii and Fukuoka fish markets in oxygen-filled containers, it's so fresh that a sign at the entrance warns that the meat's still moving. See p. 517.

- **Koi** (West Hollywood; © **310/659-9449**): One of L.A.'s hottest restaurants has celebrities arriving nightly for addictive dishes such as baked crab rolls with edible rice paper. Koi is a killer combo of good feng shui and superb Asian fusion cuisine. See p. 525.

- **The Marine Room** (La Jolla; © **866/644-2351**): It has been around for 60-plus years, but chef Bernard Guillas keeps this senior citizen in tip-top shape. Those who come for the smashing beachside view (waves sometimes slam into the windows) may be surprised by the inventive, French-inspired food. See p. 732.

13 THE BEST CULINARY EXPERIENCES

- **Grazing at San Francisco's Farmers' Market:** In 2003, San Francisco's favorite outdoor culinary fair moved to the Ferry Building Marketplace, where some of the best artisan food producers and restaurants have storefronts. Stop by to peruse the exceptional, abundant selection of gourmet shops and restaurants, or join the locals during open-air market days to feast on the freshest vegetables, fruits, and prepared foods from beloved restaurants. See "The Top Attractions," in chapter 5.

- **Dining on Dungeness Crab at San Francisco's Fisherman's Wharf:** Eating fresh Dungeness crabmeat straight from the seafood vendors' boiling pots at the corner of Jefferson and Taylor streets is a classic San Francisco culinary experience. See p. 122.

- **A San Francisco Dim Sum Feast:** No place this side of China does dim sum as well as San Francisco. Experience a taste of Hong Kong right at your table with a myriad of mysterious and exotic little dishes—from dumplings and potstickers to salt-fried shrimp and ducks' feet. At the city's best dim sum house, **Ton Kiang** (© **415/387-8273**), you'll be wowed by the variety of mysterious dishes. For downtown dim sum, the venerable **Yank Sing** (© 415/957-9300), offers an exotic edible surprise on every cart that's wheeled to your table. See p. 114 and p. 101, respectively.

- **Point Reyes Oysters: Drake's Bay Oyster Farm** (© 415/669-1149) sells its farm-fresh oysters—by the dozen or the hundreds—for a fraction of the price you'd pay at a restaurant. See "Point Reyes National Seashore," in chapter 8.

- **Samoa Cookhouse** (Samoa; © 707/442-1659): When lumber was king in Northern California, cookhouses were the hub of Eureka. Here the mill men and longshoremen came to chow down on three hot meals before, during, and after their 12-hour workday. The Samoa is the last of the great cookhouses, and the food is still hearty, served up family style at long red-checkered tables; nobody leaves hungry. See chapter 8.

- **A Gourmet Picnic at the Hollywood Bowl:** What better way to spend a typically warm L.A. evening than under the stars with a picnic basket, bottle of wine, and some naturally amplified entertainment. Home of the Los Angeles Philharmonic, the Bowl hosts visiting performers, ranging from chamber music quartets to jazz greats to folk humorists. The imposing white Frank Lloyd Wright–designed band shell always elicits appreciative gasps from first-time Bowl-goers. See chapter 14.

- **Grand Central Market** (Los Angeles; © 213/624-2378): Fresh-produce stands, exotic-spice-and-condiment

vendors, butchers and fishmongers, and prepared-food counters create a noisy, fragrant, vaguely comforting atmosphere in this L.A. mainstay. Prepared foods of every ethnicity are served at counters throughout the market, from chili relleno burritos (around $2) to a complete Thai plate for under $5. See chapter 14.

- **A Date with the Coachella Valley:** Some 95% of the world's dates are farmed here. While the groves of date palms make evocative scenery, it's their fruit that draws visitors to the National Date Festival in Indio each February. Amid the Arabian Nights Parade and camel races, you can feast on an array of plump Medjool, amber Deglet Noor, caramel-like Halawy, and buttery Empress dates. The rest of the year, date farms and markets sell dates from the season's harvest, as well as date milkshakes, date coconut rolls, and more. See "Sweet Desert Treat: The Coachella Valley Date Gardens," in chapter 16.

- **Fish Tacos:** These tasty treats migrated north from Baja California and were popularized in San Diego some 25 years ago by **Rubio's Baja Grill.** Now a sizable chain, Rubio's is still a reliable choice, but better yet are casual fish market/eateries such as **Point Loma Seafoods** (© 619/223-1109), **Blue Water Seafood Market and Grill** (© 619/497-0914), and **Bay Park Fish Co.** (© 619/276-3474). See p. 729.

14 THE BEST OF THE PERFORMING ARTS & SPECIAL EVENTS

- **The San Francisco Opera** (© 415/864-3330): The first municipal opera in the U.S., with world-renowned productions and members, performs at the War Memorial Opera House, modeled after the Opéra Garnier in Paris. The season

opens with a gala in September and runs through December. See p. 141.

- **The San Francisco Symphony** (© 415/864-6000): The symphony is such a hot ticket, it's hard to get a seat in advance. If your concierge doesn't have any tricks up his sleeve, you can try to buy tickets at the door or from someone attempting to sell his at the last second. See p. 141.

- **The American Conservatory Theater** (San Francisco; *C* **415/749-2-ACT**): The A.C.T. is one of the nation's leading regional theaters—the American equivalent of the British National Theatre, the Berliner Ensemble, or the Comédie Française in Paris. See p. 140.
- **The Monterey Jazz Festival** (*C* **831/373-3366**): The third weekend of September, the Monterey Fairgrounds draws jazz fans from around the world. The 3-day festival, known for the sweetest jazz west of the Mississippi, usually sells out a month in advance. See "Calendar of Events," in chapter 3.
- **The Hollywood Bowl** (Los Angeles; *C* **323/850-2000**): This iconic outdoor amphitheater is the summer home of the Los Angeles Philharmonic, a stage for visiting virtuosos—including the occasional pop star—and the setting for splendid fireworks shows. See p. 590.

- **Festival of Arts/Pageant of the Masters** (Laguna Beach): These events draw crowds to the Orange County coast every July and August. Begun in 1932 by a handful of painters, the festival has grown to showcase hundreds of artists. In the evening, crowds marvel at the Pageant of the Masters' *tableaux vivants,* in which costumed townsfolk pose inside a giant frame and depict famous works of art, accompanied by music. See "The South Coast," in chapter 15.
- **The Old Globe Theatre** (San Diego; *C* **619/234-5623**): This Tony Award–winning complex of three theaters has launched Broadway hits such as *Dirty Rotten Scoundrels, The Full Monty,* and *Into the Woods,* and regularly features major film and TV actors in its casts. Since its founding more than 70 years ago, the Globe has been associated with the works of William Shakespeare; the outdoor summer Shakespeare Festival features three of the Bard's plays in nightly rotation. See p. 756.

California in Depth

by Matthew Richard Poole

The more you know about California, the more you're likely to enjoy and appreciate everything the state has to offer. In fact, it's California's incredible diversity and rough-'n'-tumble history that make it one of the most popular travel destinations in the world. With two of the nation's largest megalopolises—the San Francisco Bay Area and the greater Los Angeles basin—California has the largest, wealthiest, and most urbanized population of any state in the nation. Yet it's also an agricultural wonderland with a bounty that runs the gamut from artichokes, raisins, garlic, and asparagus to some of the finest wine-making grapes in the world. And it still manages to be home to much of the country's most striking and varied wilderness—from purple mountains' majesty to arid, marvelously barren desert to coastlines of unsurpassed beauty.

The pages that follow include a brief enlightening tale of how California came to be the most plentiful and powerful state in the nation, but the best advice we can give you about California is to just go. Bring an open mind and a sense of adventure—the rest is waiting for you.

1 CALIFORNIA TODAY

Much of California's current prosperity and popularity can be attributed to deft restructuring of the economy during the post–Cold War era. A classic example is the numerous Air Force and Naval bases that were shut down, leaving thousands of civilians unemployed. Yet thanks to an unprecedented collaboration between government and private enterprise, many of the former bases were reopened as business parks (McClellan Air Force Base in Sacramento), tourist attractions (San Francisco's Presidio is a prime example), and, in some cases, even movie studios (Treasure Island Naval Base on the San Francisco Bay). California high-tech industries, once employed to build better bombs, have also earned healthy dividends by retooling their trade toward computer and information-based enterprises. Meanwhile, the industries that have always bolstered California's economy—agriculture, tourism,

entertainment, and manufacturing—continue to thrive and profit.

So what's in store for California in the new millennium? A recent survey of the most popular name given to California's newborns says a lot about the direction in which the Golden State is headed. You probably didn't guess José, but then again, you may not have known that California is the most racially diverse state in the nation, playing host to every race, ethnic heritage, language group, and religion in the *world*. So if you're prone to xenophobia, you might want to spend your vacation elsewhere, because California will soon be the mother of all melting pots, where no single race or ethnic group will constitute a majority of the state's population.

The numbers are already bewildering: 35 million people, a whopping one-third of whom live in the Los Angeles basin. California already receives the highest

A Tale of Two States

It doesn't take a psychiatrist to figure out that California suffers from an acute case of bipolar schizophrenia. We Californians may, on the surface, appear to be one big Happy Days family, but in reality we've divided our state into separate factions worthy of Montague and Capulet. That is, you're either a northern Californian or a southern Californian, two opposing tribes that have little in common. In fact, which side you even choose to visit may reveal something about yourself.

All the California glamour, wealth, fame, fast cars, surf scenes, and buxom blondes you see on television are pure southern invention. If this is the California you're looking for, head due south, dude: Assuming you're not terribly interested in intellectual stimulation, you won't be disappointed. In fact, it's nearly impossible not to be immediately swept up by the energy and excitement that places like West Hollywood and Venice Beach exude. It's a narcotic effect, the allure of flashy wealth, gorgeous bodies, and celebrity status. Even watching it all as a bystander imparts a heady mixture of thrill and envy.

Northern California may be frightfully demure in comparison, but in the long run, its subdued charms and natural beauty prevail. Wealth is certainly in abundance, but rarely displayed. The few hard bodies that exist are usually swathed in loose jeans and shirts. The few celebrities who live here keep very low profiles and are more likely to be on their ranches than in a Rolls Royce. Ostentation in any form is looked down upon (of course, it's okay to *own* a BMW, as long as it's slightly dirty), and unlike in Los Angeles, you can actually explore smog-free San Francisco on foot.

Ironically, it's the northern Californians who think of themselves as superior for having prudently eschewed the trappings of wealth and status (L.A.–bashing is a popular pastime). Southern Californians, on the other hand, couldn't care less what the northerners think of them; it's all sour grapes as they bask poolside 300 sunny days of the year. In fact, most southern Californians would be perfectly content to form their own state. The idea has been bandied about the state capital for years, but it consistently meets its Waterloo when it comes to water rights, always a hotly contested issue in California politics. Northern California holds two-thirds of the state's watershed, and without the incredibly complex system of aqueducts, reservoirs, and dams that keep huge flows going southward, southern California's 15 million citizens would be in a world of hurt.

But regardless of our polarized views and lifestyles, most Californians do agree on one thing: We're still the best damn dysfunctional state in America.

numbers of immigrants in America each year—more than 200,000 annually. Whether this is a potential boon or time bomb for California's future is impossible to predict, but it makes for a very interesting place to live and visit. How long this social boom will last is anyone's guess, but, in the meantime, California is living up to its legacy as the land of golden promise.

EUROPEAN DISCOVERY & COLONIZATION

Although very little remains to mark the existence of West Coast Native Americans, anthropologists estimate that as many as half a million aborigines flourished on this naturally abundant land for thousands of years before the arrival of Europeans in the mid–16th century. Sailing from a small colony, established 10 years before, on the southern tip of Baja California, Portuguese explorer Juan Rodrígues Cabrillo is credited with being the first European to "discover" California, in 1542. Over the next 200 years, dozens of sailors mapped the coast, including British explorer Sir Francis Drake, who, in 1579, sailed his *Golden Hind* into what is now called Drake's Bay, and Spanish explorer Sebastian Vizcano, who, in 1602, bestowed most of the place-names that survive today, including San Diego, Santa Barbara, and Carmel.

European colonial competition and Catholic missionary zeal prompted Spain to establish settlements along the Alta (upper) California coast and claim the lands as its own. In 1769, Father Junípero Serra, accompanied by 300 soldiers and clergy, began forging a path from Mexico to Monterey. A small mission and *presidio* (fort) were established that year at San Diego, and by 1804, a chain of 21 missions, each a day's walk from the next along a dirt road called *Camino Real* (Royal Road), stretched all the way to Sonoma. Most of the solidly built missions still remain—Mission Delores, Mission San Juan Bautista, Mission San Diego de Alcala, to name just a few—and offer public tours.

During that time, thousands of Native Americans were converted to Christianity and coerced into labor. Many others died from imported diseases. Because not all the natives welcomed their conquerors with open arms, many missions and *pueblos* (small towns) suffered repeated attacks, leading to the construction of California's now ubiquitous—and fireproof—red-tile roofs.

No settlement had more than 100 inhabitants when Spain's sovereignty was compromised by an 1812 Russian outpost called Fort Ross, 60 miles north of San Francisco (which, remarkably enough, still stands and is open to the public). But the biggest threat came from the British—who had strengthened their own claims to America with the Hudson's Bay Company trading firm—and their short-lived, last-ditch effort to win back their territories in the War of 1812.

Embattled at home as well as abroad, the Spanish finally relinquished their claim to Mexico and California in 1821. Under Mexican rule, Alta California's Spanish missionaries fell out of favor and lost much of their land to the increasingly wealthy *Californios*—Mexican immigrants who had been granted vast tracts of land.

AMERICAN EXPANSION

Beginning in the late 1820s, Americans from the East began to make their way to California via a 3-month sail around Cape Horn. Most of them settled in the territorial capital of Monterey and in Northern California.

From the 1830s on, inspired by the doctrine of Manifest Destiny—an almost religious belief that the United States was destined to cover the continent from coast to coast—more and more settlers headed west. Along with them came daring explorers. In 1843, Marcus Whitman, a missionary seeking to prove that settlers could travel overland through the Oregon Territory's Blue Mountains, helped blaze the Oregon Trail; the first covered-wagon train made the 4-month crossing in 1844. Over the next few years, several hundred Americans made the trek to California over the Sierra Nevada range via Truckee Pass, just north of Lake Tahoe. A memorial to the Donner Party—the most famous tragedy in the history of westward migration—marks the site of the ill-fated travelers.

As the drive to the west increased, the U.S. government sought to extend its control over Mexican territory north of the Rio Grande, the river that now divides the United States and Mexico. In 1846, President James Polk offered Mexico $40 million for California and New Mexico. The offer might have been accepted, but America's simultaneous annexation of Texas, to which Mexico still laid claim, resulted in a war between the two countries. Within months, the United States overcame Mexico and took possession of the entire West Coast.

GOLD & STATEHOOD
In 1848, California's non–Native American population was around 7,000. That same year, flakes of gold were discovered by workers building a sawmill along the American River. Word of the find spread quickly, bringing more than 300,000 men and women into California between 1849 and 1851, one of the largest mass migrations in American history. Of course, very few prospectors unearthed a gold mine, and within 15 years the gold had dissipated, though many of the new residents remained. In fact, much of the mining equipment and Gold Rush–era buildings remain today and are on display throughout the Gold Country.

In 1850, California was admitted to the Union as the 31st state. The state constitution

on which California applied for admission included several noteworthy features. To protect the miners, slavery was prohibited. To attract women from the East Coast, legal recognition was given to the separate property of a married woman (California was the first state to offer such recognition). By 1870, almost 90% of the state's Native American population had been wiped out, and the bulk of the rest were removed to undesirable inland reservations.

Mexican and Chinese laborers were brought in to help local farmers and to work on the transcontinental railroad, which was completed in 1869. The new rail line transported Easterners to California in just 5 days, marking a turning point in the settlement of the West. Many of these original steam engines are on display at the California State Railroad Museum in Sacramento.

GROWTH & INDUSTRY
In 1875, when the Santa Fe Railroad reached Los Angeles, Southern California's population of just 10,000 was divided equally between Los Angeles and San Diego. Los Angeles, however, began to grow rapidly in 1911, when the film industry moved here from the East Coast to take advantage of cheap land and a warm climate that enabled movies to be shot outdoors year-round. The movies' glamorous, idyllic portrayal of California boosted the region's popularity and population, especially during the Great Depression of the 1930s, when thousands of families (like the Joads in John Steinbeck's *The Grapes of Wrath*) packed up their belongings and headed west in search of a better life.

World War II brought heavy industry to California, in the form of munitions

---

Fun Facts

One out of every eight Americans lives in California, the most populous state in the Union.

Impressions

California is not so much a state of the Union as it is an imagination that seceded from our reality a long time ago. . . . California became the first to discover that it was fantasy that led reality, not the other way around.

—William Irwin Thompson

factories, shipyards, and airplane manufacturing. Freeways were built, military bases were opened, and suburbs were developed. In the 1950s, California in general, and San Francisco in particular, became popular among artists and intellectuals. The so-called Beat Generation appeared, later to inspire alternative-culture groups, most notably the "flower children" of the 1960s, in San Francisco's Haight-Ashbury district. During the "Summer of Love" in 1967, as the war in Vietnam escalated, student protests increased at Berkeley and elsewhere in California, as they did across the country. A year later, amid rising racial tensions, Martin Luther King, Jr., was killed, setting off riots in the Watts section of Los Angeles and in other cities. Soon thereafter, Robert F. Kennedy was fatally shot in Los Angeles after winning the California Democratic Party presidential primary. Antiwar protests continued into the 1970s.

Perhaps in response to an increasingly violent society, the 1970s also gave rise to several exotic religions and cults, which found eager adherents in California. The spiritual "New Age" continued into the 1980s, along with a growing population, environmental pollution, and escalating social ills, especially in Los Angeles. California also became very rich. Real-estate values soared, the computer industry—centered in "Silicon Valley" south of San Francisco—boomed, and banks and businesses prospered.

RECESSION, REDEMP-TION & TERRORISM

The late 1980s and early 1990s, however, brought a devastating recession to the state. Californians, like many other Americans, became increasingly conservative. Though they remained concerned about the nation's problems—economic competition from abroad, the environment, drugs, and the blight of homelessness—their fascination with alternative lifestyles ebbed as the former campus rebels among them settled into comfortable positions in industry and politics. In short, the baby boomers were growing up and settling down.

AIDS also became a major issue of the 1990s, particularly in San Francisco, where it quickly became the number-one killer of young men. Los Angeles had its problems as well, most notably the race riots spurred by the videotaped beating of black motorist Rodney King, by four white police officers, who were subsequently acquitted. Two years later, a major earthquake caused billions of dollars in damage to L.A.'s buildings and freeways, leaving thousands injured and homeless. Oakland's hills became a raging inferno, killing 26 people and destroying 3,000 homes.

Midway through the 1990s, America's economy slowly yet surely began to improve, a welcome relief to recession-battered Californians. Crime and unemployment began to drop, while public schools received millions for much-needed improvements. Computer- and Internet-related industries flourished in the Bay Area, with entrepreneurialism fueling much of the explosive growth. As the stock market continued its record-setting pace through the end of the decade, no state reaped more benefits than California, which gained new millionaires by the day.

At the millennium, optimism in the state's strong economy and quality of life was at an all-time high. Unemployment rates were still low, and property rates still rising. Then came three out-of-the-blue sucker punches to California's rosy economy: (1) the rapid demise of many, if not most, of the dot-coms in the stock-market slump (new websites, gleefully chronicling the death throes of the fledgling enterprises, popped up to amuse the formerly envious); (2) an energy deregulation scheme gone awry, leaving irate residents with periodic rolling blackouts and escalating energy bills (never have so many taken such a sudden,

intense interest in ways to save and create energy); and (3) the September 11, 2001, terrorist attacks that left Californians, along with the rest of the country, stunned and added a near-death blow to an already reeling economy.

But even the darkest clouds had a silver lining. The dot-com bomb led to a massive rise in vacancies and declines in rent (though it's still outrageous) as the thousands of itinerant gold-diggers hitched up and moved out. We solved our energy crisis by outing those greedy Enron execs living in the empire of Texas. And since 9/11 we've even surprised ourselves at how patriotic we still are. Every Californian was knocked senseless by the shocking deeds of religious fanatics, but we quickly fought back—both literally and economically—to regain our national pride and enviable lifestyle. Oh, California— if the world hands us a lemon, we'll slice it into our imported sparkling water.

3 CALIFORNIA IN POPULAR CULTURE: BOOKS, FILM, TV & MUSIC

RECOMMENDED BOOKS

There's no shortage of reading material about the history and culture of California, one of the most romanticized places on earth. Almost from the beginning, novelists and poets were an essential part of California's cultural mosaic, and the works they've created offer a fascinating window into the lives and legends that have greatly influenced California's inception and fervid growth.

History

Readers are spoiled for choices when it comes to historical accounts of California's pioneers. Salinas native John Steinbeck, one of the state's best-known authors, paints a vivid portrayal of proletarian life in the early to mid-1900s. His *Grapes of Wrath* remains the classic account of itinerant farm laborers coming to California

in the midst of the Great Depression. *Cannery Row* has forever made the Monterey waterfront famous, and *East of Eden* brings a deep insight into the way of life in the Salinas Valley.

Famed humorist and storyteller Mark Twain penned vivid tales during California's Gold Rush era, including one of his most popular works, "The Celebrated Jumping Frog of Calaveras County" (an annual Gold Country competition that still has legs). Other good Gold Rush reads include Bret Harte's *The Luck of Roaring Camp,* a sentimental tale of hard-luck miners and their false toughness, and J. S. Holliday's *The World Rushed In,* one of the finest nonfiction accounts of the Gold Rush still in print.

San Francisco was also a popular setting for many early works, including Twain's *San Francisco,* a collection of articles that glorified "the liveliest, heartiest community on our continent." It was also the birthplace of Jack London, one of the best-known American writers, who wrote several short stories of his younger days as an oyster pirate on the San Francisco Bay, as well as *Martin Eden,* Jack London's semiautobiographical account of his life along the Oakland shores.

A work of fiction featuring San Francisco during the Gold Rush is *Daughter of Fortune* by acclaimed novelist and Marin resident Isabel Allende. The tale begins in Chile and follows the life of Eliza, an orphan adopted by a proper English spinster and her brother. In love with a boy who has sailed for the gold fields, a pregnant Eliza runs away from home to search for him and is befriended by a Chinese doctor. Allende's vivid depiction of life in California during the mid–19th century is one of the novel's strengths.

Hollywood

For what some critics consider the best novels ever written about Hollywood, turn to Nathanael West's *The Day of the Locust,* a savage and satirical look at 1930s life on the fringes of the film industry, and Bud Shulberg's *What Makes Sammy Run?,* featuring everyone's favorite amoral, desperate agent Sammy Glick. Following in these footsteps is Michael Tolkin's *The Player,* an unsentimental journey into the industry of filmmaking, and John Fante's 1939 *Ask The Dust,* wherein yet another young writer get his hopes and dreams crushed.

And while we are recommending downer (if brilliant) books, follow Los Angeles's turbulent history and speculate on its future via Mark Davis's *City of Quartz,* and equally lugubrious is Upton Sinclair's novel *Oil!,* which is representative of 1920s Southern California. You can also relive some of the state's most infamous (and brutal) moments with Vincent Bugliosi's *Helter Skelter,* the best version of the Manson murders and the book most responsible for childhood nightmares among a certain generation, or one of the many books about San Francisco's Zodiac Killer or L.A.'s Hillside Strangler.

Mystery & Mayhem

For all you mystery buffs headed to California, two must-reads include Frank Norris's *McTeague: A Story of San Francisco,* a violent tale of love and greed set in turn-of-the-20th-century San Francisco, and Dashiell Hammett's *The Maltese Falcon,* a steamy detective novel that captures the seedier side of San Francisco in the 1920s. Another favorite is Raymond Chandler's *The Big Sleep,* where private dick Philip Marlowe plies the seedier side of Los Angeles in the 1930s.

California has always been a hotbed for alternative—and, more often than not, controversial—literary styles. Joan Didion, in her novel *Slouching Toward Bethlehem,* and Hunter S. Thompson, in his columns for the *San Francisco Examiner* (brought together in the collection *Generation of Swine*), both used a "new journalistic" approach in their studies of 1960s San Francisco. Tom Wolfe's early work, *The Electric Kool-Aid Acid Test,* follows the Hell's Angels, the Grateful Dead, and Ken Kesey's Merry Pranksters as they ride through that hallucinogenic decade. Meanwhile, Jack Kerouac, Allen Ginsberg, and the rest of the "Beat" writers were penning protests against political conservatism—and promoting their bohemian lifestyle—via Ginsberg's controversial poem "Howl" (daringly published by Lawrence Ferlinghetti, poet and owner of City Lights Bookstore in San Francisco's North Beach district) and Kerouac's famous tale of American adventure, *On the Road.*

Modern Material

If you're interested in a contemporary look back at four generations in the life of an American family, you can do no better than Wallace Stegner's *Angle of Repose.* The winner of the Pulitzer Prize in 1971, this work chronicles the lives of pioneers on the western frontier. Among Stegner's many other works of fiction and nonfiction about the West is his novel *All the Little Live Things,* which explores the conflicts faced by retired literary agent Joe Allston; the book is set in the San Francisco Bay Area of the 1960s. *The Spectator Bird* (winner of the 1976 National Book Award) revisits Allston's character as he reflects on his life and his memories of a search for his roots.

Set in San Francisco, bestselling author Amy Tan's *The Joy Luck Club* is an enlightening account of bonds between Chinese-American mothers and their daughters. One of the more famous and beloved pieces of modern fiction based in San Francisco is Armistead Maupin's *Tales of the City.* Maupin is a Dickens for his time, and this is a must read for a leisurely afternoon. His 1970s soap opera covers the residents of 28 Barbary Lane (Macondry Lane on Russian Hill was the inspiration), melding sex, drugs, and growing self-awareness with enormous warmth and humor.

Special-Interest Reads

Geology buffs will want to pack a copy of *Assembling California,* John McPhee's fascinating observation of California's complex geological history. Most of this volume was previously published in *The New Yorker.*

Outdoor enthusiasts have literally dozens of sporting books to choose from, but most comprehensive is Foghorn Press's excellent outdoor series—*California Camping, California Fishing, California Golf, California Beaches,* and *California Hiking*—available at every major bookstore in the state. Another recommended choice is *Frommer's Great Outdoor Guide to Northern California* (Wiley Publishing, Inc.).

RECOMMENDED MOVIES

The beauty and metaphor that is California (Gold Rush, Land of Opportunity, Go

West Young Man, Silver Screen—the list goes on) has inspired far too many moviemakers to list in any comprehensive way, but I've compiled a short list of the California-based gems that have inspired generations of movie fans.

Vertigo (1958) is the work of possibly the greatest movie director of all time, Alfred Hitchcock, who always used locations well. Remember Mount Rushmore in *North by Northwest?* In *Vertigo,* the suspense master uses San Francisco to dizzying effect (pun intended).

Monterey Pop (1969), D.A. Pennebaker's first-rate rockumentary, chronicles the glorious 3-day music festival of the same name that was actually a better realization of the Summer of Love dream than Woodstock ever hoped to be. The film wonderfully captures '60s San Francisco's Haight–Ashbury vibe and the California sound, including groups such as the Mamas and the Papas (whose leader, the late John Phillips, was the brains behind the event), Jefferson Airplane, Janis Joplin with Big Brother and the Holding Company, Jimi Hendrix, Canned Heat, the Who, and others, including a stunning performance by Otis Redding.

Clint Eastwood made his directorial debut with *Play Misty for Me* (1971), a winningly creepy thriller costarring Jessica Walter (and Donna Mills, of quintessentially Californian *Knots Landing* fame). Young, studly Clint looks mighty fine, but the real star of the show is stunning Carmel, which Clint films with a genuine hometown love and a master's eye. (You may remember that Eastwood was elected mayor of Carmel-by-the-Sea in 1986; he still owns the Mission Ranch, an elegant country inn, and resides in town.) Watch for the great footage of Big Sur's Bixby Bridge, too.

What's Up, Doc? (1972) is a Peter Bogdanovich–directed, Buck Henry–scribed gem starring Barbra Streisand and Ryan O'Neal that shows off the hilly streets of

San Francisco—especially Chinatown—at their most colorful and romantic.

A more light-hearted view of California comes from *Gidget* (1965). Perky Sally Field is the ultimate California beach girl in the ultimate California beach movie. This innocent romp is really a joy to watch—far superior to the Frankie Avalon/Annette Funicello beach movies—with excellent footage of Malibu Beach and Pacific Coast Highway (cruisin' with the top down, of course).

Staying South, *Chinatown* (1974) is possibly the finest noir ever committed to film, using L.A. in the '70s to re-create L.A. in the '30s impeccably. Not only did director Roman Polanski (pre-exile) capture the City of Angels masterfully, but writer Robert Towne worked in an essential slice of city history: the dirty-dealing and power-grabbing of water rights that allowed—for better or worse—the infant desert city to blossom into the sprawling metropolis you see today. And, of course, this true classic features Jack Nicholson as the hard-boiled detective embroiled with femme fatale Faye Dunaway, plus legendary Hollywood heavyweight John Huston as the evil genius behind the Chandleresque web of intrigue. Its modern-day noir and crime successor is the Oscar-winning *L.A. Confidential* (1997).

Valley Girl (1983), starring a teenage Nicolas Cage, is an underdog in a teen genre that includes *Fast Times at Ridgemont High* and *Clueless,* but it comes out a winner because of its New-Wave-Boy-meets-mall-lovin'-Valley-Girl love story at the height of Valley Girl mania.

The Big Picture (1989) is director Christopher Guest's first feature, a dead-on and deadly satire of the movie industry, filmed presumably on a shoestring around Hollywood and just outside in the desert. It's hilarious, and we don't just mean the locations.

Steve Martin's *L.A. Story* (1991) is a romantic look at everything that's wonderfully silly about life in contemporary Tinseltown.

The Player (1992) all-too-realistically captures the seedy underbelly and soul-selling seductive power of Hollywood influence and celebrity. Everybody who's anybody in the movie industry knows how scarily close to home Tim Robbins's portrayal of beleaguered studio exec Griffin Mill hits.

And finally, there is the film version of *The Grapes of Wrath* (1940). The John Ford–directed, Academy Award–winning film of dispossessed "Okie" dustbowl farmers who migrate west to the promised land—California—wins a spot on this list not for its tremendous footage of the Golden State, but because it beautifully evokes California's agrarian story.

RECOMMENDED MUSIC

During its heyday in the 1950s and 1960s, San Francisco was the place to be for anyone who eschewed the conventional American lifestyle. From moody beatniks to political firebrands, the city was a vortex for poets, writers, actors, and a bewildering assortment of free thinkers and activists. Drawn by the city's already liberal views on life, liberty, and the pursuit of happiness, thousands of the country's youth—including some of America's most talented musicians—headed west to join the party. What culminated in the 1960s was San Francisco's hat trick of rock legends: It was able to lay claim to three of the rock era's most influential bands: the Grateful Dead, Big Brother and the Holding Company and Janis Joplin, and the Jefferson Airplane.

The Grateful Dead

Easily the most influential band to be spawned from the 1960s psychedelic movement was San Francisco's music guru, the Grateful Dead. Described as the "house band for the famous acid tests that transformed the City by the Bay into one endless freak-out," the Dead's music was played simultaneously on so many stereo systems (and at such high volumes) that the group almost seemed to have set the tone for one enormous, citywide jam session.

Though the group disbanded in 1995 after the death of its charismatic lead vocalist, Jerry Garcia, the band's devoted fans had already elevated the Grateful Dead to cult empire status. Tie-dyed "Deadheads" (many of whom followed the band on tour for decades) can still be found tripping within the Haight, reminiscing about the good old days when the group never traveled with a sound system weighing less than 23 tons. In fact, more than any other band produced during the 1960s, the Grateful Dead were best appreciated during live concerts, partly because of the love-in mood that frequently percolated through the acidic audiences. Many rock critics remember with nostalgia that the band's most cerebral and psychedelic music was produced in the 1960s in San Francisco, but in the 1980s and 1990s, permutations of their themes were marketed in repetitive, less threatening forms that delighted their aficionados and often baffled or bored virtually everyone else.

For better or for worse, the Grateful Dead was a musical benchmark, expressing in new ways the mood of San Francisco during one of its drug-infused and most creatively fertile periods. But the days of the Dancing Bear and peanut butter sandwiches will never be quite over: Working from a proven formula, thousands of bands around the world continue to propagate the Dead's rhythmical standards.

But reading about the Grateful Dead is like dancing to architecture: If you're looking for an album whose title best expresses the changing artistic premises of San Francisco and the ironies of the pop culture that developed here, check out its award-winning retrospective *What a Long Strange Trip It's Been.*

Janis Joplin

The wide-open moral and musical landscape of San Francisco was almost unnervingly fertile during the 1960s. Despite competition from endless numbers of less talented singers, Texas-born Janis Joplin formulated much of her vocal technique before audiences in San Francisco. Her breakthrough style was first acknowledged at the Monterey Jazz Festival in 1967. Audiences reached out to embrace a singer whose rasping, gravelly, shrieking voice expressed the generational angst of thousands of onlookers. *Billboard* magazine characterized her sound as composed of equal portions of honey, Southern Comfort, and gall. She was backed up during her earliest years by Big Brother and the Holding Company, a group she eventually outgrew.

Warned by specialists that her vocal technique would ruin her larynx before she was 30, Janis shrieked, wailed, gasped, and staggered over a blues repertoire judged as the most raw and vivid ever performed. Promoters frantically struggled to market (and protect) Janis and her voice for future artistic endeavors but, alas, her talent was simply too huge for her to handle, the time and place too destructive for her raw-edged psyche. Her style is best described as "the desperate blues," partly because it never attained the emotional nonchalance of such other blues singers as Bessie Smith or Billie Holiday.

Parts of Janis's life were the subject of such lurid books as *Going Down with Janis,* and stories of her substance abuse, sexual escapades, and general raunchiness litter the emotional landscape of modern-day San Francisco. The star died of a heroin overdose at the age of 27, a tragedy still mourned by her thousands of fans, who continue to refer to her by her nickname, "Pearl." Contemporary photographs taken shortly before her death show a ravaged body and a face partially concealed behind aviator's goggles, long hair, and a tough but brittle facade. Described as omnisexual—and completely comfortable with both male and female partners—she once (unexpectedly) announced to a group of nightclub guests her evaluation of the sexual performance of two of the era's most visible male icons: Joe Namath (not particularly memorable) and Dick Cavett (absolutely fantastic). The audience (like audiences in concert halls around California) drank in the anecdotes that followed as "Gospel According to Janis."

Jefferson Airplane

In the San Francisco suburbs of the late 1960s, hundreds of suburban bands dreamed of attaining stardom. Of the few that succeeded, none expressed the love-in ethic of that time in San Francisco better than the soaring vocals and ferocious guitar-playing of Jefferson Airplane. Singers Grace Slick and Marty Balin—as well as bass guitar player Jack Cassady—were considered at the top of their profession by their peers and highly melodic even by orchestral standards. Most importantly, all members of the band, especially Paul Kantner and Jorma Kaukonen, were songwriters. Their fertile mix of musical styles and creative energies led to songs that still reverberate in the minds of anyone who owned an AM radio during the late 1960s. The intense and lonely songs such as "Somebody to Love" and "White Rabbit" became the musical anthems of at least one summer, as American youth emerged into a highly psychedelic kind of consciousness within the creatively catalytic setting of San Francisco.

Although in 1989 the group reassembled its scattered members for a swan song as Jefferson Starship, the output was considered a banal repetition of earlier themes, and the energy of those long-faded summers of San Francisco in the late 1960s was never recovered. But despite its decline in its later years, Jefferson Airplane is still considered a band inextricably linked to the Bay Area's historic and epoch-changing Summer of Love.

4 EATING & DRINKING IN CALIFORNIA

California's agriculture industry is not only the number one producer in the nation, it's the number one in the world. No other state in the union cultivates like the Golden State: California farmers and ranchers pump more than $30 billion a year into the California economy, employ more than a million people statewide, and export billions of dollars in goods each year to markets across the globe. In fact, California's farmers produce over half the country's fruit and vegetables on just a measly 3% of its farmland. Almonds, olives, lemons, artichokes, figs, dates, and truckloads of grapes and tomatoes are just some of the commercially produced consumables that thrive in the state's mellow Mediterranean climate.

But California's cuisine is greater than the sum of its parts. Along with a rich pantry, immigration has affected what and how Californians and its visitors eat. In Northern California, the Gold Rush attracted an enormous number of Chinese from Canton Province, who stayed to work on the railroad and eventually settled into Chinatowns throughout the state. Chinese eateries opened to feed the largely male work force, but by the 1920s, adventuresome Anglos found it fashionable to give Chinese food a try, and soon you could sample Cantonese sweet and sour pork in every city, big or small.

In Southern California, Latino immigrants brought their influence to bear, introducing unfamiliar spices and changing the tastes of a population to such an extent that fast food today means tacos and burritos as much as hamburgers and fries. Los Angeles, in fact, can make its strongest claim to culinary fame (beyond the first and still champion celebrity chef, the highly influential Wolfgang Puck of Beverly Hills' iconic **Spago;** p. 524) courtesy of its many hole-in-the-wall ethnic restaurants. Reflecting the dozens (if not hundreds) of cultures that have settled in the area, the curious can nosh on Armenian, Nicaraguan, Oaxacan, Ethiopian, Issan Thai, Romanian, and Hungarian food, to name a few—a veritable United

John Thoreen, the Wine Tutor, on Tasting California Wines

Stopping at tasting rooms to sample the goods, otherwise known as wine tasting, ranks as one of the top rituals in California's Wine Country touring. It provides pleasure for everyone and the chance, if you're interested, to learn why the wines of Sonoma and Napa rank high among the wines of the world. Precautionary notes would say "taste moderately," for there are literally 200 or so tasting rooms and the virtues in wine take time to notice. Most of the attendants in tasting rooms know that, generally speaking, Americans drink very little wine (20% of the population drinks over 80% of the wine). Because we're all on a very pleasant learning curve, our goal as wine educators is to help you discover wine at many levels. If you should encounter a winery staffer with "attitude" (unfortunately, it happens), don't buy *any* of that wine and simply move on to the next stop.

The time honored techniques for tasting wine involve three steps: a good look, a good smell, and a good sip of each wine. In addition, you learn about wine most quickly if you compare them, ideally side by side. Almost any comparison will reveal features of wines you might not see by tasting one wine at a time. You might think of it as the wines talking to one another ("I'm smoother than you are." "I'm way more puckery than all of you.") By listening to these little conversations, you can discover how smooth or how puckery you want your wines to be. Tasting rooms in Napa and Sonoma have their own regimens, usually offering a series of wines. When it seems appropriate, and when the tasting room is not too busy, ask your host if you can do some comparisons.

Nations of dining experiences, and many of them within just a few blocks of each other. And that's not even discussing California rolls, which regrettably (in the minds of some purists) forever changed sushi-eating from a meditative consideration on a choice slice of fish to a circus stunt wrapped in seaweed.

Perhaps the greatest modern influence on how tuned-in Californians eat can be traced to food gurus such as Alice Waters. Her restaurant, Berkeley-based **Chez Panisse** (p. 155), began as an outgrowth of Waters's desire to feed her friends and became a philosophical training ground for many of today's important chefs. Like French cooks— and Waters was profoundly changed by a year living in Paris—she is interested not in the quantity or cost of ingredients, but strictly in quality and freshness.

In Berkeley, Waters created an infrastructure in which her restaurant is dependent on a cadre of small farmers, and vice versa. It wasn't enough, however, to provide customers with the freshest heirloom tomatoes and organic baby lettuces: The breads must be crusty and fresh; the meats must be sourced from trusted ranchers; the cheese should complement the fruits and come from local producers as well.

So along with a generation of restaurateurs, Chez Panisse inspired such robust local artisan producers as Acme Bread and Cowgirl Creamery. California cuisine—which is really about showcasing the flavors of locally grown, seasonal bounty at its peak—has spread throughout and beyond California, thanks to Waters and to the chefs who have made her vision their own.

5 THE PREMIER GRAPE VARIETIES OF THE CALIFORNIA WINE COUNTRY

Cabernet sauvignon, the transplant from Bordeaux, has become California's most well known varietal. Distinctive berry features include small size, deep color, and a thick skin. Cabernet sauvignon is regarded as a complex grape, yielding medium- to full-bodied red wines that are highly tannic when young and usually require a long aging period to achieve their greatest potential. It is often blended with other related red varieties, such as merlot and cabernet franc. Its most distinctive character is a lush blackcurrant flavor that is best matched with red meat dishes and strong cheeses. If you're looking to invest in several cases of wine, cabernet sauvignon is always a good bet.

Chardonnay is the most widely planted grape variety in the Wine Country, producing exceptional medium- to full-bodied dry white wines. In fact, it was a California chardonnay that revolutionized the world of wine when it won the legendary Paris tasting test of 1976, beating out France's top white burgundies. You'll find several types of chardonnay grown here, from delicate to rich, fruity to oaky (no other wine benefits more from the oak aging process). This highly complex and aromatic grape is one of the few grapes in the world that does not require blending and is the principle grape for making sparkling wine. It pairs well with a variety of dishes, from seafood to poultry, pork, veal, and pastas served with cream sauce and/or butter.

It has taken California vintners decades to make relatively few great wines from **pinot noir** grapes, which are difficult to grow and vinify (even in native Burgundy, the wines are excellent only a few years in a decade and are a challenge for winemakers to master). Recent attempts to grow the finicky grape in cooler climes of the Carneros District have met with promising results. When successful, however, the vine produces complex, light- to medium-bodied wines with such low tannins and silky texture that it is comparable to the finest reds in the world. It's fuller and softer than a cabernet and can be drinkable at 2 to 5 years of age, though the best will improve with additional aging. Pinot noir is versatile at the dinner table, but goes best with lamb, duck, turkey, game birds, and semi-soft cheeses.

Zinfandel is often called the "mystery" grape because its origins are uncertain. The first "Zinfandel" label appeared on California wines in the late 1800s. Hence, it has come to be known as California's grape. In fact, most of the world's zinfandel acreage is planted in the Napa Valley, though the best zinfandel grapes grow in cool coastal locations. It's by far the Wine Country's most versatile grape, popular as blush wine; as dark, spicy, and fruity red wines; and even as a port. Premium zins, such as those crafted by Ravenswood winery in Sonoma (the Wine Country's Zeus of Zins), are rich and peppery, with a lush texture and nuances of raspberries, licorice, and spice. A relatively recent addition to zinfandel winemaking is ever-quaffable white zinfandel, a lighter, more fruity-style wine, usually served chilled. Food-wise it's a free-for-all, though premium zins go well with beef, lamb, venison, hearty pastas, pizza, and stews.

Also labeled as fumé blanc, **sauvignon blanc** grapes are used to make crisp, dry white wines of medium to light body that vary in flavor from slightly grassy to tart or fruity. The grape grows very well in the Wine Country and has become increasingly popular, due to its distinctive character and pleasant acidity; indeed, it has recently become a contender to the almighty chardonnay. California's premier maker of sauvignon blanc (at least in our opinion) is Grgich Hills Cellar in Napa Valley.

Planning Your Trip to California

Whether it's your first visit or your 10th, a trip to California may require an additional degree of planning. This chapter will provide you with essential information, helpful tips, and advice for the more common problems that visitors may encounter while vacationing in the Golden State.

For additional help in planning your trip and for more on-the-ground resources, please turn to the appendix on p. 769.

1 VISITOR INFORMATION

For information on the state as a whole, log onto the **California Tourism** website at www.visitcalifornia.com. U.S. and Canadian residents can receive free travel planning information by mail by calling © **800/862-2543.** Most cities and towns also have a tourist bureau or chamber of commerce that distribute information on the area. These are listed in the following chapters, organized geographically.

PARK INFORMATION To learn more about California's national parks, contact the **Pacific West Region Information Center,** National Park Service, 1111 Jackson St., Suite 700, Oakland, CA 94607 (© **510/817-1300;** www.nps.gov). Make reservations at national park campsites—including Yosemite—via the website **www.recreation.gov,** or call © **877/444-6777** within the U.S. (for international calls dial © 001-518-885-3639).

For information on state parks, contact the **Department of Parks and Recreation,** P.O. Box 942896, Sacramento, CA

94296-0001 (© **800/777-0369;** http://cal-parks.ca.gov). Thousands of campsites are on the department's reservation system and can be booked in advance by calling **ReserveAmerica** at © **800/444-7275** or logging onto their website at **www.reserveamerica.com**.

For information on fishing and hunting licenses, contact the **California Department of Fish and Game** at © **916/445-0411,** or log onto their website at **www.dfg.ca.gov**.

To read blogs about travel within California, try **www.gocalifornia.about.com**. Numerous national travel blogs cover the state, including:

- www.gridskipper.com
- www.realtravel.com
- www.travelpost.com
- www.travelblog.com
- www.travelblog.org
- www.worldhum.com
- www.writtenroad.com

PASSPORTS

New regulations issued by the Department of Homeland Security now require virtually every air traveler entering the U.S. to show a passport. As of January 23, 2007, all persons, including U.S. citizens, traveling by air between the United States and Canada, Mexico, Central and South America, the Caribbean, and Bermuda are required to present a valid passport. As of January 31, 2008, U.S. and Canadian citizens entering the U.S. at land and sea ports of entry from within the western hemisphere will need to present government-issued proof of citizenship, such as a birth certificate, along with a government-issued photo ID, such as a driver's license. A passport is not required for U.S. or Canadian citizens entering by land or sea, but it is highly encouraged to carry one.

For information on how to obtain a passport, go to **"Fast Facts,"** in appendix A. The websites listed provide downloadable passport applications as well as the current fees for processing passport applications. For an up-to-date, country-by-country listing of passport requirements around the world, go to the "Foreign Entry Requirement" Web page of the U.S. Department of State at **http://travel.state. gov**. International visitors can obtain a visa application at the same website. *Note:* Children are required to present a passport when entering the United States at airports. More information on obtaining a passport for a minor can be found at **http:// travel.state.gov**.

VISAS

The U.S. Department of State has a **Visa Waiver Program (VWP),** allowing citizens of the following countries to enter the United States without a visa for stays of up to 90 days: Andorra, Australia, Austria, Belgium, Brunei, Denmark, Finland, France, Germany, Iceland, Ireland, Italy, Japan, Liechtenstein, Luxembourg, Monaco, the Netherlands, New Zealand, Norway, Portugal, San Marino, Singapore, Slovenia, Spain, Sweden, Switzerland, and the United Kingdom. (*Note:* This list was accurate at press time; for the most up-to-date list of countries in the VWP, consult www.travel.state.gov/ visa.) Canadian citizens may enter the United States without visas; they will need to show passports (if traveling by air) and proof of residence, however. *Note:* Any passport issued on or after October 26, 2006, by a VWP country must be an **e-Passport** for VWP travelers to be eligible to enter the U.S. without a visa. Citizens of these nations also need to present a round-trip air or cruise ticket upon arrival. E-Passports contain computer chips capable of storing biometric information, such as the required digital photograph of the holder. (You can identify an e-Passport by the symbol on the bottom center cover of your passport.) If your passport doesn't have this feature, you can still travel without a visa if it is a valid passport issued before October 26, 2005, and includes a machine-readable zone, or if it was issued between October 26, 2005, and October 25, 2006, and includes a digital photograph. For more information, go to **www.travel.state. gov/visa**.

Citizens of all other countries must have (1) a valid passport that expires at least 6 months later than the scheduled end of their visit to the U.S., and (2) a tourist visa, which may be obtained without charge from any U.S. consulate.

As of January 2004, many international visitors traveling on visas to the United States will be photographed and fingerprinted on arrival at Customs in airports and on cruise ships in a program created by the Department of Homeland Security called **US-VISIT.** Exempt from the extra scrutiny are visitors entering by land or those (mostly in Europe; see left) that don't require a visa for short-term visits.

For more information, go to the Homeland Security website at **www.dhs.gov/dhspublic**.

For specifics on getting a visa, see **"Fast Facts: California,"** in the appendix.

MEDICAL REQUIREMENTS

Unless you're arriving from an area known to be suffering from an epidemic (particularly cholera or yellow fever), inoculations or vaccinations are not required for entry into the United States. If you have a medical condition that requires **syringe-administered medications,** carry a valid signed prescription from your physician; syringes in carry-on baggage will be inspected. Insulin in any form should have the proper pharmaceutical documentation. If you have a disease that requires treatment with **narcotics,** you should also carry documented proof with you—smuggling narcotics aboard a plane carries severe penalties in the U.S.

For **HIV-positive visitors,** requirements for entering the United States are somewhat vague and change frequently. For up-to-the-minute information, contact **AIDSinfo** (© **800/448-0440,** or 301/519-6616 outside the U.S.; www.aidsinfo.nih.gov) or the **Gay Men's Health Crisis** (© **212/367-1000;** www.gmhc.org).

CUSTOMS
What You Can Bring into the U.S.

Every visitor older than 21 years of age may bring in, free of duty, the following: (1) 1 liter of wine or hard liquor; (2) 200 cigarettes, 100 cigars (but not from Cuba), or 3 pounds of smoking tobacco; and (3) $100 worth of gifts. These exemptions are offered to travelers who spend at least 72 hours in the United States and who have not claimed them within the preceding 6 months. It is forbidden to bring into the country almost any meat products (including canned, fresh, and dried meat products such as bouillon, soup mixes, and so on).

Generally, condiments including vinegars, oils, spices, coffee, tea, and some cheeses and baked goods are permitted. Avoid rice products, as rice can often harbor insects. Bringing fruits and vegetables is not advised, though not prohibited. Customs will allow produce depending on where you got it and where you're going after you arrive in the U.S. Foreign tourists may carry in or out up to $10,000 in U.S. or foreign currency with no formalities; larger sums must be declared to U.S. Customs on entering or leaving, which includes filing form CM 4790. For details regarding U.S. Customs and Border Protection, consult your nearest U.S. embassy or consulate, or **U.S. Customs** (www.customs.us treas.gov).

What You Can Take Home from the U.S.

Canadian Citizens: For a clear summary of Canadian rules, write for the booklet *I Declare,* issued by the **Canada Border Services Agency** (© **800/461-9999** in Canada, or 204/983-3500; www.cbsa-asfc. gc.ca).

U.K. Citizens: For information, contact **HM Customs & Excise** at © **0845/010-9000** (from outside the U.K., 020/8929-0152), or consult their website at **www. hmce.gov.uk.**

Australian Citizens: A helpful brochure available from Australian consulates or Customs offices is *Know Before You Go.* For more information, call the **Australian Customs Service** at © **1300/363-263,** or log on to **www.customs.gov.au.**

New Zealand Citizens: Most questions are answered in a free pamphlet available at New Zealand consulates and Customs offices: *New Zealand Customs Guide for Travellers, Notice no. 4.* For more information, contact **New Zealand Customs,** The Customhouse, 17–21 Whitmore St., Box 2218, Wellington (© **04/473-6099** or 0800/428-786; www.customs.govt.nz).

CLIMATE

California's climate is so varied that it's impossible to generalize about the state.

San Francisco's temperate marine climate means relatively mild weather year-round. In summer, temperatures rarely top 70°F (21°C; pack sweaters, even in Aug), and the city's famous fog rolls in most mornings and evenings. In winter, the mercury seldom falls below freezing, and snow is almost unheard of. Because of the fog, summer rarely sees more than a few hot days in a row. Head a few miles inland, though, and it's likely to be clear and hot.

The **Central Coast** shares San Francisco's climate, although it gets warmer as you get farther south. Seasonal changes are less pronounced south of San Luis Obispo, where temperatures remain relatively stable year-round. The Northern Coast is rainier and foggier; winters tend to be mild but wet.

Summers are cool around **Lake Tahoe** and in the **Shasta Cascades.** The climate is ideal for hiking, camping, and other outdoor activities, making these regions popular with residents of the state's sweltering deserts and valleys. From late November to early April, skiers also flock to this area, for terrific snowfall.

Southern California—including **Los Angeles** and **San Diego**—is usually much warmer than the Bay Area, and it gets significantly more sun. Even in winter, daytime temperatures regularly reach into the 60s (15°C–20°C) and warmer. Summers can be stifling inland, but Southern California's coastal communities are comfortable. The area's limited rainfall is generally seen between December and mid-April, but it's rarely intense enough to be more than a slight inconvenience. It's possible to sunbathe throughout the year, but only die-hard enthusiasts and wet-suited surfers venture into the ocean in winter. The water is warmest in summer and fall, but even then, the Pacific is too chilly for many.

The **deserts,** including **Palm Springs** and the desert national parks, are sizzling hot in summer; temperatures regularly top 100°F (38°C). Winter is the time to visit the desert resorts (and remember, it gets surprisingly cold at night in the desert).

San Francisco's Average Temperatures

	Jan	Feb	Mar	Apr	May	June	July	Aug	Sept	Oct	Nov	Dec
Avg. High (°F)	56	59	60	61	63	64	64	65	69	68	63	57
Avg. High (°C)	13	15	16	16	17	18	18	18	21	20	17	14
Avg. Low (°F)	46	48	49	49	51	53	53	54	56	55	52	47
Avg. Low (°C)	8	9	9	9	11	12	12	12	13	13	11	8

Los Angeles's Average Temperatures

	Jan	Feb	Mar	Apr	May	June	July	Aug	Sept	Oct	Nov	Dec
Avg. High (°F)	65	66	67	69	72	75	81	81	81	77	73	69
Avg. High (°C)	18	19	19	21	22	24	27	27	27	25	23	21
Avg. Low (°F)	46	48	49	52	54	57	60	60	59	55	51	49
Avg. Low (°C)	8	9	9	11	12	14	16	16	15	13	11	9

AVOIDING THE CROWDS

Given California's pleasant summer weather (with relatively low humidity), the time between Memorial Day and Labor Day is **high tourist season** virtually everywhere—except for desert areas such as Palm Springs and Death Valley, where sizzling temperatures daunt all but the hardiest bargain hunters. Naturally, prices are highest at this time, and they can drop dramatically before and after that period. (Exceptions to this rule include the aforementioned deserts

and winter ski resorts.) *Insider tip:* Many Californians think the best time to travel the state is autumn. From late September to early December, crowds drop off, shoulder-season rates kick in, and winter rains have yet to start looming.

CALENDAR OF EVENTS

For an exhaustive list of events, check **http://events.frommers.com**, where you'll find a searchable, up-to-the-minute roster of what's happening in cities all over the world.

JANUARY

Tournament of Roses, Pasadena. A spectacular parade marches down Colorado Boulevard, with lavish floats, music, and extraordinary equestrian entries, followed by the Rose Bowl football game and a nightlong party along Colorado Boulevard. Call *©* **626/449-4100** or see **www.tournamentofroses.com** for details. January 1.

Santa Barbara International Film Festival. For 10 days, Santa Barbara does its best impression of Cannes. There's a flurry of foreign and independent film premieres, appearances by actors and directors, and symposia on cinematic topics. For a rundown of events, call *©* **805/963-0023,** or see **www.sbfilmfestival.org**. Late January to early February.

FEBRUARY

Chinese New Year and Golden Dragon Parade, Los Angeles. Dragon dancers and martial arts masters parade through the streets of downtown's Chinatown. Chinese opera and other events are scheduled. For this year's schedule, contact the Chinese Chamber of Commerce at *©* **213/617-0396,** or visit **www.lachinesechamber.org**. Late January or early February.

AT&T Pebble Beach National Pro-Am, Pebble Beach. A PGA-sponsored tour where pros team up with celebrities

to compete on three famous golf courses. Call *©* **800/541-9091** or 831/649-1533, or visit **www.attpbgolf.com**. Early February.

National Date Festival, Indio. Crowds gather to celebrate the Coachella Valley desert's most beloved cash crop, with events such as camel and ostrich races, the Blessing of the Date Garden, and Arabian Nights pageants. Plenty of date-sampling booths are set up, along with rides, food vendors, and other county-fair trappings. Call *©* **800/811-3247** or 760/863-8247, or visit **www.datefest.org**. Two weeks mid-February.

Mustard Festival, Napa Valley. Celebrating the blossom of yellow-petaled mustard flowers, which coat the valley during February and March, this event was conceived to drum up visitors during this once-slow season. The festival has evolved into 6 weeks of events, from a kickoff gourmet gala to a wine auction, recipe and photography competitions, and plenty of food and wine. For a schedule, call *©* **707/944-1133,** or visit **www.mustardfestival.com**. February and March.

MARCH

Festival of Whales, Dana Point. The Dana Point community celebrates the return of the gray whales migrating off the coast with an annual street fair, food, games, entertainment, and "Majestic Migration" parade. It's great for families. Call *©* **949/496-5794,** ext. 7, or go to **www.festivalofwhales.com** for details. Early March.

Return of the Swallows, San Juan Capistrano. Each St. Joseph's Day, visitors flock to this village for the arrival of the loyal flock of swallows that nest in the mission and remain until October. The celebration includes a parade, dances, and special programs. Call © **949/234-1300,** or visit **www.missionsjc.com** for details. March 19.

Kraft Nabisco Championship, Rancho Mirage. This 33-year-old LPGA golf tournament takes place near Palm Springs. After the celebrity Pro-Am early in the week, the best female pros get down to business. For further information, call © **760/324-4546** or visit **www.nabisco championship.com.** Other special-interest events for women usually take place around the tournament, including the country's largest annual lesbian gathering. Last week of March.

Redwood Coast Dixieland Jazz Festival, Eureka. Four days of jazz featuring some of the best Dixieland, blues, and zydeco bands in the world. Call © **707/445-3378,** or see **www.redwoodcoast musicfestivals.org.** Late March.

Flower Fields in Bloom at Carlsbad Ranch. One of the most spectacular sights in San Diego's North County are the ranunculus blossoms that create a striped, floral blanket in March and April. This is a working ranch, but visitors are welcome to tour the fields. For information, call © **760/431-0352** or see **www. theflowerfields.com.** March and April.

APRIL

San Francisco International Film Festival. One of the nation's oldest film festivals, featuring more than 100 films and videos from 30-plus countries. Tickets are inexpensive, and screenings are open to the general public. Call © 925/866-9559, or visit **www.sffs.org.** Mid-April to early May.

Toyota Grand Prix, Long Beach. An exciting weekend of Indy-class auto racing and entertainment in downtown Long Beach draws world-class drivers from the United States and Europe, plus many celebrity contestants and spectators. Contact the Grand Prix Association at © **888/82-SPEED** or **www.longbeachgp.com.** Mid-April.

ArtWalk, San Diego. This free, 2-day festival in stylish Little Italy is the largest art event in the San Diego/Tijuana region, attracting some 70,000 people each year. It features visual and performing arts—painting, sculpture, photography, music, and dance—in outdoor venues, galleries, artist studios, and businesses. The event also offers hands-on art experiences for kids. Call © **619/615-1090,** or visit **www.artwalkinfo.com.** Late April.

MAY

Cinco de Mayo. A weeklong celebration of one of Mexico's most jubilant holidays takes place throughout **Los Angeles** near May 5. Large crowds, live music, dances, and food create a carnival-like atmosphere. The main festivities are held in El Pueblo de Los Angeles State Historic Park. Call © **213/628-1274** for information.

The Cinco de Mayo celebration in Old Town, **San Diego,** features folkloric music, dance, food, and historical reenactments. Call © **619/260-1700** for more information. Early May.

Calaveras County Fair and Jumping Frog Jubilee, Angels Camp. Inspired by Mark Twain's "The Celebrated Jumping Frog of Calaveras County," this race draws frog contestants and their guardians from all over. Call © **209/736-2561,** or see **www.frogtown.org.** Third weekend in May.

Paso Robles Wine Festival. What began as a small, neighborly gathering has grown into the largest outdoor wine tasting in California. The 3-day event features winery open houses and tastings, a golf tournament, 5K run and 10K bike ride, and concerts, plus a festival in downtown's City Park. For a schedule, call ✆ 805/239-8463 or visit **www. pasowine.com**. Third weekend in May.

Bay to Breakers Foot Race, San Francisco. One of the city's most popular annual events, it's more fun than run. Thousands of entrants show up dressed—or undressed—in their best costumes for the 7¹/₂-mile run. Call ✆ **415/359-2800**, or log onto **www.baytobreakers. com**. Third Sunday of May.

Carnival, San Francisco. The Mission District's largest annual event is a 2-day series of festivities culminating with a parade on Mission Street. Half a million spectators line the route, and samba musicians and dancers continue playing on 14th Street, near Harrison, after the march. Call ✆ **415/920-0125**, or visit **www.carnavalsf.com**. Memorial Day weekend.

JUNE

Ojai Music Festival. This event has been drawing world-class classical and jazz personalities to the open-air Libbey Bowl since 1947. Past events have featured Igor Stravinsky, Aaron Copland, and the Juilliard String Quartet. Seats (and local lodgings) fill up quickly; call ✆ **805/646-2094** for more information, or log onto **www.ojaifestival.org**. Early June.

San Diego County Fair. Referred to as the Del Mar Fair by locals, this is the other big happening (besides horse racing) at the Del Mar Fairgrounds. The entire county turns out for the 3-week event, with livestock competitions, rides, flower and garden shows, food and craft booths, carnival games, and home-arts exhibits. There are also grandstand concerts by big-name performers. Call ✆ **858/793-5555**, or check **www.sdfair.com**. Mid-June through early July.

Mariachi USA Festival, Los Angeles. For this 2-day, family-oriented celebration of Mexican culture at the Hollywood Bowl, festivalgoers pack their picnic baskets and enjoy music, folkloric ballet, and related performances by top groups. The all-day, all-night celebration is one of the largest mariachi festivals in the world. For tickets, call ✆ **800-MARIACHI** or 323/850-2000 (the Hollywood Bowl), or log onto **www.mariachiusa. com**. Late June.

Los Angeles Film Festival, Los Angeles. With an attendance of over 60,000, the festival showcases more than 175 American and international indies, short films, and music videos during a 10-day event. Call ✆ **866/345-6337**, or log onto **www.lafilmfest.com**. Late June.

San Francisco Lesbian, Gay, Bisexual, Transgender Pride Parade. It's celebrated over various weekends throughout the state in June and July, but San Francisco's party draws up to half a million participants. The parade heads west from Market Street and Beale to Market and Eighth Street, where hundreds of food, art, and information booths are set up around several stages. Call ✆ **415/864-3733**, or visit **www. sfpride.org** for info. Late June.

JULY

Mammoth Lakes Jazz Jubilee. This 4-day festival features 20 bands on 10 different stages, plus food, drink, and dancing—all under the pine trees and stars. Call ✆ **760/934-2478**, or see **www.mammothjazz.org**. Second weekend in July.

World Championship Over-the-Line Tournament, San Diego. This beach softball event, dating from 1953, is renowned for boisterous, beer-soaked, anything-goes behavior. More than 1,000 three-person teams compete, and upward of 50,000 people attend. It's a heap of fun for the open-minded but a bit much for small kids. It takes place on Fiesta Island in Mission Bay; admission is free. For more details, call ⓒ **619/688-0817** or visit **www.ombac.org**. Mid-July.

Gilroy Garlic Festival. A gourmet food fair with more than 85 booths serving garlicky food from almost every ethnic background, plus close to 100 arts, crafts, and entertainment booths. Call ⓒ **408/842-1625,** or visit **www.gilroy garlicfestival.com**. Last full weekend in July.

Thoroughbred Racing Season, Del Mar. The "turf meets the surf" during the thoroughbred racing season at the Del Mar Race Track. Post time is 2pm most days; the track is dark on Tuesdays. Special events are held throughout the season, including Friday afternoon concerts by top bands. For this year's schedule, call ⓒ **858/755-1141** or visit **www.dmtc.com**. Mid-July to mid-September.

Beach Festival, Huntington Beach. Two weeks of fun in the sun featuring two surfing competitions—the U.S. Open of Surfing and the world-class Pro of Surfing—plus such extreme sports as BMX biking, skateboarding, and more. The festival includes entertainment, food, product booths, and giveaways—and plenty of tanned, swimsuit-clad bodies of both sexes. For more information, call ⓒ **714/969-3492** or log onto **www. surfcityusa.com**. Late July.

Festival of Arts & Pageant of the Masters, Laguna Beach. A 60-plus-year tradition in artsy Laguna, this festival centers on a fantastic performance-art production in which actors re-create famous Old Masters paintings. Other festivities include live music, crafts sales, art demonstrations and workshops, and the grassroots Sawdust Festival across the street. Call ⓒ **800/487-FEST** or

949/494-1145; there's online info at **www.foapom.com**. July through August.

Comic-Con International, San Diego. Some 60,000 people attend America's largest comic-book convention each year when it lands at the San Diego Convention Center for a weekend of auctions, dealers, autographs, and seminars focusing on graphic novels and fantasy/sci-fi movies and television shows. Past special guests include Hugh Jackman, Matt Groening, Halle Berry, Stan Lee, Angelina Jolie, and Quentin Tarantino. For further details, call ⓒ **619/491-2475** or check **www.comic-con.org**. Late July.

U.S. Open Sandcastle Competition, Imperial Beach. The quintessential beach event: a parade and children's castle-building contest on Saturday, followed by the adult event on Sunday. Astounding creations are plundered after the awards ceremony. For details, call ⓒ **619/424-6663** or visit **www.us opensandcastle.com**. Late July.

AUGUST

Old Spanish Days Fiesta, Santa Barbara. The city's biggest annual event, this 5-day festival features a parade with horse-drawn carriages, music and dance performances, marketplaces, and a rodeo. Call ⓒ **805/962-8101,** or visit **www.old spanishdays-fiesta.org**. Early August.

La Jolla SummerFest, San Diego. This is perhaps San Diego's most prestigious annual music event. It features a range of classical and contemporary music, from tango to Tchaikovsky, with guest composers and musicians ranging from Chick Corea to Yo-Yo Ma. SummerFest also offers master classes, open rehearsals, and workshops. Contact the La Jolla Music Society at ⓒ **858/459-3728,** or visit **www.ljms.org**. Early to mid-August.

Nisei Week Japanese Festival, Los Angeles. This weeklong celebration of Japanese culture and heritage is held in the Japanese American Cultural and Community Center Plaza in Little Tokyo. Festivities include parades, food, music, arts, and crafts. Call ✆ **213/687-7193,** or see **www.niseiweek.org**. Mid-August.

SEPTEMBER

Los Angeles County Fair, Pomona. Horse racing, arts, agricultural displays, celebrity entertainment, and carnival rides are among the attractions at one of the largest county fairs in the world, at the Los Angeles County Fair and Exposition Center. Call ✆ **909/623-3111,** or visit **www.fairplex.com** for information. Throughout September.

Monterey Jazz Festival. Features top names in traditional and modern jazz. One of the oldest annual jazz festivals in the world. Call ✆ **831/373-3366,** or see **www.montereyjazzfest.com** for more info. Mid-September.

Danish Days, Solvang. Since 1936, this 3-day event has been celebrating old-world customs and pageantry with a parade, gymnastics exhibitions by local schoolchildren, demonstrations of Danish arts and crafts, and plenty of *aebleskivers* (Danish fritters) and *medisterpolse* (Danish sausage). Call ✆ **800/468-6765** for more information, or see **www.solvangusa.com**. Mid-September.

Long Beach Blues Festival, Long Beach. Great performances by blues legends such as Etta James, Dr. John, the Allman Brothers, and Ike Turner make this an event you won't want to miss. In the middle of the athletic field at Long Beach State, the event serves cold beer, wine, and food. Call ✆ **562/985-5566,** or log onto **www.kkjz.org**. Labor Day weekend.

Sausalito Art Festival, Sausalito. A juried exhibit of more than 180 artists. It's accompanied by music provided by Bay Area jazz, rock, and blues performers and international cuisine enhanced by wines from some 50 Napa and Sonoma producers. Call ✆ **415/331-3757,** or log onto **www.sausalitoart festival.org** for information. Labor Day weekend.

Simon Rodia Watts Towers Jazz Festival, Los Angeles. This event pays tribute to the roots of jazz in gospel and blues, as well as celebrating the avant-garde and Latin jazz scene. It's also a great opportunity to visit the Watts Towers. Call ✆ **213/847-4646,** or log onto **www.trywatts.com** or **www.watts towers.org**. Late September.

OCTOBER

The Half Moon Bay Art & Pumpkin Festival, Half Moon Bay. The festival features a Great Pumpkin Parade, pie-eating contests, a pumpkin-carving competition, arts and crafts, and all manner of squash cuisine. The highlight of the event is the Giant Pumpkin weigh-in. October (for exact date and details, call the Pumpkin Hot Line at ✆ **650/726-9652**).

Fleet Week, San Diego. The name is a bit of a misnomer; the nation's largest military appreciation event actually lasts a full month. It features Navy ship tours, a college football game, an auto race of classic speedsters, the renowned Miramar air-show, and more. For more info call ✆ **800/FLEET-WEEK,** or log onto **www.fleetweeksandiego.org**. Mid-September to mid-October.

Catalina Island Jazz Trax Festival, Catalina Island. Contemporary jazz artists travel to the island to play in the legendary Avalon Casino Ballroom. The festival is held over two consecutive 3-day weekends. Call ✆ **866/872-9849,** or visit **www.jazztrax.com** for advance ticket sales and a schedule of performers. Early October.

Sonoma County Harvest Fair, Sonoma County Fairgrounds. A 3-day celebration of the harvest with exhibitions, art shows, and annual judging of the local wines. Contact ℂ **707/545-4203** or **www.harvestfair.org**. Dates vary.

Hollywood Film Festival, Los Angeles. More than 50 films from the U.S. and abroad are screened, amid celebrities galore. Actors and filmmakers will find a variety of workshops and market-places. Call ℂ **310/288-1882,** or visit **www.hollywoodawards.com** for info and tickets. Mid-October.

West Hollywood Halloween Costume Carnaval, Los Angeles. This is one of the world's largest Halloween parties. More than 400,000 people, many dressed in outlandish drag couture, party all night along Santa Monica Boulevard. Call ℂ **310/289-2525,** or see **www.visitwesthollywood.com** for info. October 31.

NOVEMBER

Catalina Island Triathlon, Catalina Island. This is one of the top triathlons in the world. Participants run on unpaved roads, swim in the cleanest bay on the West Coast, and bike on chal-lenging trails. There's also a "kid's tri." Call Pacific Sports at ℂ **714/978-1528,** or visit **www.PacificSportsLLC.com**. Early November.

Doo Dah Parade, Pasadena. This outra-geous spoof of the Rose Parade features such participants as the Briefcase Preci-sion Drill Team and a kazoo-playing marching band. Call ℂ **626/440-7379,** or visit **www.pasadenadoodahparade.info**. Near Thanksgiving.

Hollywood Christmas Parade, Los Angeles. This spectacular, star-studded parade marches through the heart of Hol-lywood. For information, call ℂ **323/469-2337.** Sunday after Thanksgiving.

DECEMBER

Balboa Park December Nights, San Diego. The city's urban park is decked out in holiday splendor for a weekend of evening events, including a candle-light procession, caroling and baroque music, craft displays, ethnic food, and hot cider. The event and the park's 13 museums are free these evenings. For more information, call ℂ **619/239-0512** or visit **www.balboapark.org**. First weekend in December.

Christmas Boat Parade of Lights. Fol-lowing longstanding tradition, sailors decorate their crafts with colorful lights. Several Southern California harbors hold nighttime parades to showcase the creations, which range from tiny din-ghies draped with a single strand of lights to showy yachts with entire Nativ-ity scenes twinkling on deck. Contact the following for schedules and infor-mation: Ventura Harbor ℂ **805/382-3001;** Long Beach ℂ **562/435-4093;** Huntington Harbor ℂ **714/840-7542;** and **San Diego Bay** (www.sdparadeof lights.org). December.

Whale-Watching Season, San Diego. From mid-December to mid-March, more than 25,000 California gray whales make the trek from chilly Alaskan seas to the warm-water breeding lagoons of Baja California. Cabrillo National Monument, on the panoramic Point Loma peninsula, offers a glassed-in observatory from which to spot the whales, examine whale exhib-its, and listen to taped narration describ-ing these popular mammals. Many boating excursion companies offer whale-watching tours throughout the season. For more information, visit **www.san diego.org**. Mid-December through mid-March.

College Bowl Games, San Diego. The city hosts two college football bowl games: the **Holiday Bowl** and the **Poinsettia Bowl.** The Holiday Bowl features top teams from the Pac 10 and Big 12 Con-ferences, while the Poinsettia Bowl pits a team from the Mountain West Confer-ence against an at-large opponent. The fledgling Poinsettia Bowl (ℂ **619/285-5061;** www.poinsettiabowl.net) was inau-gurated in 2005; while the Holiday Bowl

(© **619/283-5808;** www.holidaybowl. com) has been played since 1978, augmented by several special events, including the nation's biggest balloon parade of giant inflatable characters. Late December.

New Year's Eve Torchlight Parade, Big Bear Lake. Watch dozens of nighttime skiers follow a serpentine path down Snow Summit's ski slopes bearing glowing torches—it's one of the state's loveliest traditions. Afterward, the party continues indoors with live bands, food, and drink. Call © **909/866-5766,** or log onto **www. bigbearmountainresorts.com**. December 31.

---

4 GETTING THERE & GETTING AROUND

GETTING TO CALIFORNIA
By Plane
All major U.S. carriers serve the San Francisco (SFO), Sacramento (SMF), San Jose (SJC), Los Angeles (LAX), John Wayne (Orange County; SNA), and San Diego (SAN) airports. They include **American** (© 800/433-7300; www.aa.com), **America West** (© 800/235-9292; www.americawest.com), **Continental** (© 800/525-0280; www.continental. com), **Delta** (© 800/221-1212; www.delta. com), **JetBlue** (© 800/538-2583; www.jet blue.com), **Northwest** (© 800/225-2525; www.nwa.com), **Southwest** (© 800/435-9792; www.southwest.com), **United** (© 800/241-6522; www.united.com), and **US Airways** (© 800/428-4322; www.usairways. com). The lowest round-trip fares to the West Coast from New York fluctuate between about $450 and $700; from Chicago, they range from $350 to $450. International travelers should also see "Entry Requirements" (p. 36) for information on overseas flights into California. For details on air travel within California, see "Getting Around," below.

Arriving at the Airport International visitors arriving by air, no matter what the port of entry, should cultivate patience and resignation before setting foot on U.S. soil. U.S. airports have considerably beefed up security clearances in the years since the terrorist attacks of September 11, and clearing **Customs and Immigration** can take as long as 2 hours.

By Car
If you're planning a road trip, it's a good idea to join **Automobile Association of America (AAA).** Members (who carry their cards with them) receive free roadside assistance and have access to a wealth of free travel information, including detailed maps. Also, many hotels and attractions throughout California offer discounts to AAA members—always ask. Call © **800/922-8228,** or visit **www.aaa.com** for membership details.

For listings of the major car rental agencies in California, please see "Toll-Free Numbers & Websites," in the appendix (p. 769).

By Train
Amtrak (© **800/USA-RAIL;** www. amtrak.com) connects California with about 500 American cities. The Sunset Limited is Amtrak's regularly scheduled transcontinental service, originating in Florida and making 52 stops along the way as it passes through Alabama, Mississippi, Louisiana, Texas, New Mexico, and Arizona, before arriving in Los Angeles 2 days later. The train, which runs three times weekly, features reclining seats, a sightseeing car with large windows, and a full-service dining car. Round-trip coach fares begin at around $350; several varieties of sleeping compartments are also available for an extra charge.

By Plane

In addition to the major carriers listed earlier in this section, several airlines provide service within the state, including **American Eagle** (② 800/433-7300), **Southwest** (② 800/435-9792), **United Express** (② 800/241-6522), and **US Airways Express** (② 800/428-4322). The round-trip fare between Los Angeles and San Francisco ranges from $100 to $300. See "Orientation" or "Getting There," in some of the city chapters, for more information.

Overseas visitors can take advantage of the APEX (Advance Purchase Excursion) reductions offered by all major U.S. and European carriers. In addition, some large airlines offer transatlantic or transpacific passengers special discount tickets under the name **Visit USA,** which allows mostly one-way travel from one U.S. destination to another at very low prices. Unavailable in the U.S., these discount tickets must be purchased abroad in conjunction with your international fare. This system is the easiest, fastest, cheapest way to see the country.

By Car

Unless you plan to spend the bulk of your vacation in a city where walking is the best way to get around, the most cost-effective way to travel is by car.

If you're visiting from abroad and plan to rent a car in the United States, you probably won't need the services of an additional automobile organization. If you're planning to buy or borrow a car, automobile-association membership is recommended. The **American Automobile Association,** better known as **AAA** (② 800/222-4357; http://travel.aaa. com), is the country's largest motor club and supplies its members with maps, insurance, and emergency road service. ***Note:*** Foreign driver's licenses are usually recognized in the U.S., but you should get an international one if your home license

is not in English. Check out **Breezenet. com,** which offers domestic car-rental discounts with some of the most competitive rates around. Also worth visiting are **Orbitz.com, Hotwire.com, Travelocity. com,** and **Priceline.com,** all of which offer competitive online car-rental rates from major national car rental agencies.

California's freeway signs often indicate direction by naming a town rather than a point on the compass. If you've never heard of Canoga Park, you might be in trouble—unless you have a map. The best state road guide is the comprehensive ***Thomas Guide California Road Atlas,*** a 300-plus-page book of maps with schematics of towns and cities statewide. It costs about $25, a good investment if you plan to do a lot of exploring. Smaller, accordion-style maps are handy for the entire state or for individual cities and regions; you'll find a useful one in the back of this book.

If you're heading into the Sierra or Shasta-Cascades region for a winter ski trip, top up on antifreeze and carry snow chains for your tires. (Chains are mandatory in certain areas.)

See the full-color driving distance chart inside the front cover of this book for an idea of the distance between the state's most popular destinations.

Driving Rules   California law requires both drivers and passengers to wear seat belts, and that a safety seat must be used for children under the age of 6 or less than 60 pounds. Motorcyclists must wear helmets at all times. Auto insurance is mandatory; the car's registration and proof of insurance must stay in the car.

You can turn right at a red light, unless otherwise indicated—but be sure to come to a complete stop.

Many California freeways have designated carpool lanes, also known as high-occupancy vehicle (HOV) lanes or "diamond" lanes. Some require two passengers, others three.

Most on-ramps are metered during even light congestion to regulate the flow of traffic onto the freeway; cars in HOV lanes can pass the signal without stopping. All other drivers are required to observe the stoplights—fines begin at around $271.

Demystifying Renter's Insurance Before you drive off in a rental car, be sure you're insured. Hasty assumptions about your personal auto insurance or a rental agency's additional coverage could end up costing you tens of thousands of dollars—even if you're involved in an accident that was clearly the fault of another driver.

If you already have **private auto insurance,** you are most likely covered in the U.S. for loss of or damage to a rental car, and liability in case of injury to any other party in an accident. Be sure to find out whether you're covered in the area you're visiting, whether your policy extends to all persons who will be driving the rental car, how much liability is covered in case an outside party is injured in an accident, and whether the type of vehicle you are renting is included under your contract. (Rental trucks, sport-utility vehicles, and luxury vehicles or sports cars may not be covered.)

Most **major credit cards** provide some coverage as well, if they were used to pay for the rental. Terms vary widely, however, so be sure to call your credit card company directly before you rent.

If you're **uninsured,** your credit card may provide primary coverage as long as you decline the rental agency's insurance. This means that the credit card may cover damage or theft of a rental car for the full cost of the vehicle. (In a few states, however, theft is not covered.) If you already have insurance, your credit card may provide secondary coverage—which basically covers your deductible.

Credit cards will not cover liability or the cost of injury to an outside party or damage to his or her vehicle. If you do not hold an insurance policy, you may want to consider purchasing additional liability insurance from your rental company. Be sure to check the terms, however: Some rental agencies only cover liability if the renter is not at fault.

The basic insurance coverage offered by most car-rental companies, known as the **Loss/Damage Waiver (LDW)** or **Collision Damage Waiver (CDW),** can cost as much as $20 per day. It usually covers the full value of the vehicle with no deductible if an outside party causes an accident or other damage to the rental car. Liability coverage varies according to the company policy and state law, but the minimum is usually at least $15,000. If you are at fault in an accident, however, you will be covered for the full replacement value of the car but not for liability. In California, you can buy additional liability coverage for such cases. Most rental companies will require a police report in order to process any claims you file, but your private insurer will not be notified of the accident.

By Train

Amtrak (© 800/USA-RAIL; www.amtrak. com) operates up and down the California coast, connecting San Diego, Los Angeles, San Francisco, and points in between. Multiple trains depart each day, and rates fluctuate according to season and special promotions. One-way fares for the most popular segments can range from $22 (L.A.–Santa Barbara) to $39 (L.A.–San Diego), and from $52 to $84 (San Francisco–L.A.).

International visitors can buy a **USA Rail Pass,** good for 15 or 30 days of unlimited travel on **Amtrak** (© 800/USA-RAIL; www.amtrak.com). The pass is available online or through many overseas travel agents. See Amtrak's website for the cost of travel within the western, eastern, or northwestern United States. Reservations are generally required and should be made as early as possible. Regional rail passes are also available.

By Bus

Bus travel is often the most economical form of public transit for short hops between U.S. cities, but it's certainly not an option for everyone (particularly when Amtrak, which is far more luxurious, offers similar rates). **Greyhound** (② **800/231-2222;** www.greyhound.com) is the sole nationwide bus line. International visitors can obtain information about the **Greyhound North American Discovery Pass.** The pass can be obtained from foreign travel agents or through **www.discoverypass.com** for unlimited travel and stopovers in the U.S. and Canada.

5 MONEY & COSTS

It's always advisable to bring a mix of cash, credit cards, and traveler's checks on a vacation. Before you leave home, exchange enough petty cash to cover airport incidentals, tipping, and transportation to your hotel, or withdraw money upon arrival at an airport ATM.

ATMS

Nationwide, the easiest and best way to get cash away from home is from an ATM (automated teller machine), sometimes referred to as a "cash machine" or "cashpoint." The **Cirrus** (② **800/424-7787;** www.mastercard.com) and **PLUS** (② **800/843-7587;** www.visa.com) networks span the country; you can find them even in remote regions. Be sure you know your daily withdrawal limit before you depart.

Note: Many banks impose a fee every time you use a card at another bank's ATM, and that fee is often higher for international transactions (up to $5 or more) than for domestic ones (where they're rarely more than $2). In addition, the bank from which you withdraw cash may charge its own fee. Visitors from outside the U.S. should also find out whether their bank assesses a 1% to 3% fee on charges incurred abroad.

Tip: Avoid these fees by asking for cash back at grocery, drug, and convenience stores (and most post offices) that accept ATM cards for purchases.

CREDIT CARDS & DEBIT CARDS

Credit cards are the most widely used form of payment in the United States: **Visa** (Barclaycard in Britain), **MasterCard** (Eurocard in Europe, Access in Britain, Chargex in Canada), **American Express, Diners Club,** and **Discover.** They also provide a convenient record of all your expenses and offer relatively good exchange rates. You can withdraw cash advances from your credit cards at banks or ATMs, but high fees make credit card cash advances a pricey way to get cash.

It's highly recommended that you travel with at least one major credit card. You must have a credit card to rent a car, and hotels and airlines usually require one as a deposit against expenses.

ATM cards with major credit card backing, known as **"debit cards,"** are now a commonly acceptable form of payment in most stores and restaurants.

TRAVELER'S CHECKS

Though credit cards and debit cards are more often used, traveler's checks are still widely accepted in the U.S. Foreign visitors should make sure that traveler's checks are denominated in U.S. dollars; foreign-currency checks are often difficult to exchange.

You can buy traveler's checks at most banks. Generally, you'll pay a service charge ranging from 1% to 4%.

The most popular are offered by **American Express** (© 800/807-6233; © 800/221-7282 for card holders—this number accepts collect calls, offers service in several foreign languages, and exempts Amex gold and platinum cardholders from the 1% fee); **Visa** (© 800/732-1322)—AAA members can obtain Visa checks for a $9.95 fee (for checks up to $1,500) at most AAA offices or by calling © 866/339-3378; and **MasterCard** (© 800/223-9920).

Be sure to keep a copy of the traveler's checks serial numbers separate from your checks in the event that they are stolen or lost. You'll get a refund faster if you know the numbers.

6 HEALTH & SAFETY

STAYING HEALTHY

Contact the **International Association for Medical Assistance to Travelers** (**IAMAT;** © 716/754-4883, or 416/652-0137 in Canada; **www.iamat.org**) for tips on travel and health concerns, and for lists of local doctors. The United States **Centers for Disease Control and Prevention** (© 800/311-3435; www.cdc.gov) provides up-to-date information on health hazards and offers tips on food safety. The website **www.tripprep.com** may also offer helpful advice on traveling. You can find listings of reliable clinics at the **International Society of Travel Medicine** (www.istm.org).

We list **additional emergency numbers** in "Fast Facts," in appendix A.

If you suffer from a chronic illness, consult your doctor before your departure. Pack **prescription medications** in your carry-on luggage, and carry them in their original containers, with pharmacy labels—otherwise they won't make it through airport security. Visitors from outside the U.S. should carry generic names of prescription drugs. For U.S. travelers, most reliable health-care plans provide coverage if you get sick away from home. Foreign visitors may have to pay all medical costs up front and be reimbursed later.

STAYING SAFE

An unscientific survey indicates that the biggest issue on the minds of would-be visitors to California is **earthquakes,** but the incidence of earthquakes is far surpassed by the paranoia. Major quakes are rare, and they're localized enough that it is highly unlikely you will ever feel one. Refer to "Earthquakes," in "Fast Facts: California," in the appendix, for general tips on what to do in the event of an earthquake.

Driving perils in California include winter driving on mountain roads. Chains may be required in the Sierra during icy weather at elevations above 3,000 feet. The **California Department of Transportation** provides 24-hour info at © 916/445-1534.

Conversely, driving in desert areas carries its own hazards: Always be aware of the distance to the next gas station. In some areas, they may be 50 miles apart, and summer temperatures well above 100°F (38°C) can turn a scenic drive into a disaster.

Penalties in California for drunk driving are among the nation's toughest. The legal limit is .08% blood alcohol level. In some areas, freeway speed limits are aggressively enforced after dark, as a pretext for nabbing drivers who might have imbibed.

TRAVELERS WITH DISABILITIES

California's spirit of tolerance has made it a welcoming place for travelers with disabilities. Thanks to provisions in the Americans with Disabilities Act, most public places are required to comply with disability-friendly regulations. Almost all public establishments (including hotels, restaurants, museums, and so on, but not including certain National Historic Landmarks), and at least some modes of public transportation provide accessible entrances and other facilities for those with disabilities.

The **America the Beautiful—National Park and Federal Recreational Lands Pass—Access Pass** (formerly the **Golden Access Passport**) gives visually impaired persons or those with permanent disabilities (regardless of age) free lifetime entrance to federal recreation sites administered by the National Park Service, including the Fish and Wildlife Service, the Forest Service, the Bureau of Land Management, and the Bureau of Reclamation. This may include national parks, monuments, historic sites, recreation areas, and national wildlife refuges.

The America the Beautiful Access Pass can only be obtained in person at any NPS facility that charges an entrance fee. You need to show proof of a medically determined disability. Besides free entry, the pass also offers a 50% discount on some federal-use fees charged for such facilities as camping, swimming, parking, boat launching, and tours. For more information, go to **www.nps.gov/fees_passes.htm** or call the United States Geological Survey (USGS), who issues the passes, at ℂ **888/275-8747.**

For more on organizations that offer resources to travelers with disabilities, go to **Frommers.com.**

GAY & LESBIAN TRAVELERS

California is one of the country's most progressive states when it comes to antidiscrimination legislation and workplace benefits for domestic partners. The gay and lesbian community spreads well beyond the famed enclaves of San Francisco, West Hollywood, and San Diego's Hillcrest. Gay travelers (especially men) will find a number of gay-owned inns in Palm Springs and the Russian River, north of the Bay Area.

The **International Gay and Lesbian Travel Association (IGLTA;** ℂ **800/448-8550** or 954/776-2626; www.iglta.org) is the trade association for the gay and lesbian travel industry, and offers an online directory of gay- and lesbian-friendly travel businesses and tour operators.

Many agencies offer tours and travel itineraries specifically for gay and lesbian travelers. San Francisco–based **Now, Voyager** (ℂ **800/255-6951;** www.nowvoyager. com) offers worldwide trips and cruises. **Olivia** (ℂ **800/631-6277;** www.olivia. com) offers lesbian cruises and resort vacations.

Gay.com Travel (ℂ **800/929-2268** or 415/644-8044; www.gay.com/travel or www.outandabout.com) is an excellent online successor to the popular *Out & About* print magazine. It provides regularly updated information about gay-owned, gay-oriented, and gay-friendly lodging, dining, sightseeing, nightlife, and shopping establishments in every important destination worldwide. British travelers should click on the "Travel" link at **www.uk.gay.com** for advice and gay-friendly trip ideas.

The Canadian website **GayTraveler** (gaytraveler.ca) offers ideas and advice for gay travel all over the world.

The following travel guides are available at many bookstores, or you can order them from any online bookseller: *Spartacus International Gay Guide, 35th Edition* (Bruno Gmünder Verlag; www.spartacus world.com/gayguide) and *Odysseus: The International Gay Travel Planner, 17th Edition* (Odysseus International); and the *Damron* guides (www.damron.com), with separate, annual books for gay men and lesbians.

For more gay and lesbian travel resources, visit **Frommers.com.**

SENIOR TRAVEL

Members of **AARP**, 601 E St. NW, Washington, DC 20049 (© **888/687-2277;** www.aarp.org), get discounts on hotels, airfares, and car rentals. AARP offers members a wide range of benefits, including *AARP: The Magazine* and a monthly newsletter. Anyone over 50 can join.

The U.S. National Park Service offers an **America the Beautiful—National Park and Federal Recreational Lands Pass—Senior Pass** (formerly the **Golden Age Passport**), gives seniors 62 years or older lifetime entrance to all properties administered by the National Park Service—national parks, monuments, historic sites, recreation areas, and national wildlife refuges—for a one-time processing fee of $10. The pass must be purchased in person at any NPS facility that charges an entrance fee. Besides free entry, the American the Beautiful Senior Pass also offers a 50% discount on some federal-use fees charged for such facilities as camping, swimming, parking, boat launching, and tours. For more information, go to **www.nps.gov/fees_passes.htm** or call the United States Geological Survey (USGS), who issues the passes, at © **888/275-8747.**

Frommers.com offers more information and resources on travel for seniors.

FAMILY TRAVEL

Family travel can be immensely rewarding, giving you new ways of seeing the world through smaller pairs of eyes. To make things easier for family vacationing, be sure to watch for the "Kids" icon throughout this guide.

Recommended family travel websites include **Family Travel Forum** (www.family travelforum.com), a comprehensive site that offers customized trip planning; **Family Travel Network** (www.familytravel network.com), an online magazine providing travel tips; and **TravelWithYourKids. com** (www.travelwithyourkids.com), a comprehensive site written by parents for parents, offering sound advice for long-distance and international travel with children.

Recommended family travel books include *Frommer's San Francisco with Kids, Frommer's Family Vacations in the National Parks,* and *The Unofficial Guide to California with Kids,* all published by Wiley Publishing, Inc.

For a list of more family-friendly travel resources, turn to the experts at **Frommers. com.**

STUDENT TRAVEL

A valid student ID will often qualify students for discounts on airfare, accommodations, entry to museums, cultural events, movies, and more. Check out the **International Student Travel Confederation (ISTC;** www.istc.org) website for comprehensive travel services information and details on how to get an **International Student Identity Card (ISIC),** which qualifies students for substantial savings on rail passes, plane tickets, entrance fees, and more. It also provides students with basic health and life insurance and a 24-hour helpline. The card is valid for a maximum of 18 months. You can apply for the card online or in person at **STA Travel** (© **800/ 781-4040** in North America; © 132 782 in Australia; © 0871/230-0040 in the U.K.; www.statravel.com), the biggest student travel agency in the world; check out the website to locate STA Travel offices worldwide. If you're no longer a student but are still under 26, you can get an

International Youth Travel Card (IYTC) from the same people, which entitles you to some discounts. **Travel CUTS** (© **800/ 592-2887;** www.travelcuts.com) offers similar services for both Canadians and U.S. residents. Irish students may prefer to turn to **USIT** (© **01/602-1904;** www.usit. ie), an Ireland-based specialist in student, youth, and independent travel.

TRAVELING WITH PETS

If you're thinking of taking your pet along with you to romp on a California beach, make sure you do a little research. For one thing, dogs are restricted from most public beaches in the L.A. area. To find out where you can bring man's best friend, check out the online **Pets Welcome** service (www.petswelcome.com), which lists accommodations that allow pets. The site also lists pet-related publications, medical travel tips, and links to other pet-related websites.

A good book to carry along is *The California Dog Lover's Companion: The Insider's Scoop on Where to Take Your Dog* (Avalon Travel Publishing), a source for complete statewide listings of fenced dog parks, dog-friendly beaches, and other indispensable information.

California has strict leash laws (and stiff penalties for failing to pick up waste), prompting the formation of a dog owner/ supporter group called **Freeplay** (© **310/ 301-1550;** www.freeplay.org). Contact them for the latest on dog-related issues, including information on off-leash parks around town.

---

8 SUSTAINABLE TOURISM/ECOTOURISM

California offers numerous way to be an ecofriendly visitor. The biggest favor you can do for the environment is keeping your driving to a minimum, and in California there are numerous car-free adventures to choose from. Here are a few examples:

- Instead of driving though the Wine Country, consider a self-guided but fully supported 3-day biking tour with **Wine Country Bikes** (© **866/922- 4537;** www.winecountrybikes.com).
- From San Francisco, you can take a bus to **Yosemite National Park** (p. 312) and join one of the numerous hiking, biking, and horseback riding trips that explore Yosemite Valley.
- Tour the state via **Amtrak** (www. amtrakcalifornia.com). Some of the most beautiful train routes in the U.S. wend along the California coast, stopping in such coastal cities as San Lois Obispo, Los Angeles, San Juan Capistrano, and San Diego. (At some train stops, such as Santa Barbara and Ventura, you can literally walk to your hotel from the station.)

In San Francisco there are numerous restaurants that only purchase organically grown foods (processing foods and manufacturing fertilizers and pesticides take significant amounts of energy), and the city's new $25-million **Orchard Garden Hotel** (p. 81) is the only hotel in the state that was built to the nationally accepted standards for green buildings developed by the U.S. Green Building Council. San Francisco's extensive public transportation system makes it easy to get around without a car (in fact, we recommend not driving here).

For more information on ecologically responsible travel, visit **California Vagabond** at **www.californiavagabond.com**. Here you'll find numerous tips on environmentally friendly accommodations, car rentals, and more. Other websites offering advice on ecofriendly tourism include the **International Ecotourism Society**'s website at www.ecotourism.org; **Sustainable**

It's Easy Being Green

Here are a few simple ways you can help conserve fuel and energy when you travel:

- Each time you take a flight or drive a car, greenhouse gases release into the atmosphere. You can help neutralize this danger to the planet through "carbon offsetting"—paying someone to invest your money in programs that reduce your greenhouse gas emissions by the same amount you've added. Reliable carbon offset companies include **Carbonfund** (www.carbonfund.org), **TerraPass** (www.terrapass.org), and **Carbon Neutral** (www.carbonneutral.org).

- Whenever possible, choose nonstop flights; they generally require less fuel than indirect flights that stop and take off again. Try to fly during the day—some scientists estimate that nighttime flights are twice as harmful to the environment. And pack light—each 15 pounds of luggage on a 5,000-mile flight adds up to 50 pounds of carbon dioxide emitted.

- Where you stay during your travels can have a major environmental impact. To determine the green credentials of a property, ask about trash disposal and recycling, water conservation, energy use, and if sustainable materials were used in constructing the property. The website **www.greenhotels.com** recommends green-rated member hotels around the world that fulfill stringent environmental requirements. Consult **www.environmentallyfriendlyhotels.com** for more green ratings.

- At hotels, request that your sheets and towels not be changed daily. (Many hotels already have programs like this in place.) Turn off the lights and air-conditioner (or heater) when you leave your room.

- Use public transport where possible—trains, buses, and even taxis are more energy-efficient forms of transport than driving. Even better is to walk or cycle; you'll produce zero emissions and stay fit and healthy on your travels.

- If renting a car is necessary, ask the rental agent for a hybrid, or rent the most fuel-efficient car available. You'll use less gas and save money at the tank.

- Eat at locally owned and operated restaurants that use produce grown in the area. This contributes to the local economy and cuts down on greenhouse gas emissions by supporting restaurants where the food is not flown or trucked in across long distances. Visit **Sustain Lane** (www.sustainlane.org) to find sustainable eating and drinking choices around the U.S.; also check out **www.eatwellguide.org** for tips on eating sustainably in the U.S. and Canada.

Travel International's website at www.sustainabletravel.com; and the **Conservation International**'s ecotourism website at www.ecotour.org.

In the U.K., **Tourism Concern** (www.tourismconcern.org.uk) works to reduce social and environmental problems connected to tourism and find ways of

Frommers.com: The Complete Travel Resource

Planning a trip or just returned? Head to **Frommers.com**, voted Best Travel Site by *PC Magazine*. We think you'll find our site indispensable before, during, and after your travels—with expert advice and tips; independent reviews of hotels, restaurants, attractions, and preferred shopping and nightlife venues; vacation giveaways; and an online booking tool. We publish the complete contents of over 135 travel guides in our **Destinations** section, covering over 4,000 places worldwide. Each weekday, we publish original articles that report on **Deals and News** via our free **Frommers.com Newsletters.** What's more, **Arthur Frommer** himself blogs 5 days a week, with cutting opinions about the state of travel in the modern world. We're betting you'll find our **Events** listings an invaluable resource; it's an up-to-the-minute roster of what's happening in cities everywhere—including concerts, festivals, lectures, and more. We've also added weekly **podcasts, interactive maps,** and hundreds of new images across the site. Finally, don't forget to visit our **Message Boards,** where you can join in conversations with thousands of fellow Frommer's travelers and post your trip report once you return.

improving tourism so that local benefits are increased.

The **Association of British Travel Agents** (**ABTA;** www.abtamembers.org/responsibletourism) acts as a focal point for the U.K. travel industry and is one of the leading groups spearheading responsible tourism.

The **Association of Independent Tour Operators** (**AITO;** www.aito.co.uk) is a group of interesting specialist operators leading the field in making vacations sustainable.

9 STAYING CONNECTED

TELEPHONES

Generally, hotel surcharges on long-distance and local calls are astronomical, so you're better off using your **cellphone** or a **public pay telephone.** Many convenience groceries and packaging services sell **prepaid calling cards** in denominations up to $50; for international visitors these can be the least expensive way to call home. Many public pay phones at airports now accept American Express, MasterCard, and Visa credit cards. **Local calls** made from pay phones in most locales cost either 25¢ or 35¢ (no pennies, please).

Most long-distance and international calls can be dialed directly from any phone. **For calls within the United States and to Canada,** dial 1 followed by the area code and the seven-digit number. **For other international calls,** dial 011 followed by the country code, city code, and the number you are calling.

Calls to area codes **800, 888, 877,** and **866** are toll-free. However, calls to area codes **700** and **900** (chat lines, bulletin boards, "dating" services, and so on) can be very expensive—usually a charge of 95¢ to $3 or more per minute, and they sometimes have minimum charges that can run as high as $15 or more.

For **reversed-charge or collect calls,** and for **person-to-person calls,** dial the number 0 then the area code and number; an operator will come on the line, and you should specify whether you are calling collect, person-to-person, or both. If your operator-assisted call is international, ask for the overseas operator.

For **local directory assistance** ("information"), dial 411; for long-distance information, dial 1, then the appropriate area code, and 555-1212.

CELLPHONES

Just because your cellphone works at home doesn't mean it'll work everywhere in the U.S. (thanks to our nation's fragmented cellphone system). It's a good bet that your phone will work in major cities, but take a look at your wireless company's coverage map on its website before heading out; T-Mobile, Sprint, and Nextel are particularly weak in rural areas. If you need to stay in touch at a destination where you know your phone won't work, **rent** a phone that does from **InTouch USA** (© **800/872-7626;** www.intouchglobal.com) or a rental car location, but beware that you'll pay $1 a minute or more for airtime.

If you're not from the U.S., you'll be appalled at the poor reach of the **GSM (Global System for Mobile Communications) wireless network,** which is used by much of the rest of the world. Your phone will probably work in most major U.S. cities; it definitely won't work in many rural areas. To see where GSM phones work in the U.S., check out **www.t-mobile.com/coverage**. And you may or may not be able to send SMS (text messaging) home.

For visitors arriving via LAX, a phone rental company called **Triptel** has a rental kiosk located on the arrival level of the international terminal. Triptel also has a San Francisco rental location at 1525 Van Ness Ave. The daily rental fee is $3, and nationwide coverage is $1.25 per minute. At the end of your stay, the phones can be dropped off at the airport or shipped back via Federal Express for an additional fee.

For more information, call © **877/TRIP-TEL** or log onto **www.triptel.com**.

VOICE-OVER INTERNET PROTOCOL (VOIP)

If you have Web access while traveling, you might consider a broadband-based telephone service (in technical terms, **Voice over Internet protocol,** or **VoIP**) such as Skype (www.skype.com) or Vonage (www.vonage.com), which allows you to make free international calls if you use their services from your laptop or in a cybercafe. The people you're calling must also use the service for it to work; check the sites for details.

INTERNET/E-MAIL
Without Your Own Computer

To find cybercafes in your destination check **www.cybercaptive.com** and **www.cybercafe.com**.

Most major airports have **Internet kiosks** that provide basic Web access for a per-minute fee that's usually higher than cybercafe prices. Check out copy shops like **Kinko's** (FedEx Kinko's), which offer computer stations with fully loaded software (as well as Wi-Fi).

With Your Own Computer

More and more hotels, resorts, airports, cafes, and retailers are going Wi-Fi (wireless fidelity), becoming "hot spots" that offer free high-speed Wi-Fi access or charge a small fee for usage. Wi-Fi is even found in campgrounds, RV parks, and sometimes entire towns. Most laptops sold today have built-in wireless capability. To find public Wi-Fi hot spots at your destination, go to **www.jiwire.com**; its Hotspot Finder holds the world's largest directory of public wireless hot spots.

For dial-up access, most business-class hotels in the U.S. offer dataports for laptop modems, and a few thousand hotels in the U.S. and Europe now offer free high-speed Internet access.

Wherever you go, bring a **connection kit** of the right power and phone adapters, a spare phone cord, and a spare Ethernet network cable—or find out whether your hotel supplies them to guests.

For electrical currency conversions, see "Fast Facts: California," in the appendix.

10 TIPS ON ACCOMMODATIONS

SURFING FOR HOTELS

In addition to the online travel booking sites **Travelocity, Expedia, Orbitz, Priceline,** and **Hotwire,** you can book hotels through **Hotels.com; Quikbook** (www. quikbook.com); and **Travelaxe** (www. travelaxe.net).

HotelChatter.com is a daily webzine offering smart coverage and critiques of hotels worldwide. Go to **TripAdvisor.com** or **HotelShark.com** for helpful independent consumer reviews of hotels and resort properties.

It's a good idea to **get a confirmation number** and **make a printout** of any online booking transaction.

CALIFORNIA HOUSE-SWAPPING

House-swapping is becoming a more popular and viable means of travel; you stay in their place, they stay in yours, and you both get an authentic and personal view of the area, the opposite of the escapist retreat that many hotels offer. Try **HomeLink International** (Homelink. org), the largest and oldest home-swapping organization, founded in 1952, with over 11,000 listings worldwide ($75 for a yearly membership). **HomeExchange.org** ($50 for 6,000 listings) and **InterVac.com** ($69 for over 10,000 listings) are also reliable. Many travelers find great housing swaps on Craigslist (www.craigslist.org), too, though the offerings cannot be vetted or vouched for. Swap at your own risk.

Suggested Itineraries

by Matthew Richard Poole, Erika Lenkert & Harry Basch

Because California is so vast and geographically varied—from misty redwood forests and eerily beautiful deserts to gold-sand beaches and rugged mountain ranges—it would take months to see all its major attractions. We're guessing your vacation hours are limited, so we're recommending these itineraries, to help you make the most of your time.

Essentially, we're divulging how we, the authors, would spend our own week-long dream trips. We've divided the chapter into our favorite regions and singled out the best sites, hotels, restaurants, and scenic drives. We've allowed leeway to stray from each route, but we've also mapped out enough details to guide you through an entire journey.

As you choose a route, be sure to consider the importance of timing. If you don't care to learn what it's like to drive through an Easy-Bake oven, skip the Southern California desert route in mid-July. Yosemite and Lake Tahoe are best avoided in winter, when several access roads close down due to heavy snowfall. The Wine Country is best in spring, when the Napa and Sonoma valleys are abloom and the summer crowds haven't yet arrived, or during the heady fall grape crush. Pacific Coast Highway is great year-round, as long as the sun is out and the convertible top is down.

For all of the routes in this chapter you'll need a car, so fly into the largest city near each itinerary region, and rent a vehicle for a week. See "Getting There & Getting Around," in chapter 3, for information about airports, driving rules, and rental-car companies. You'll also need a detailed map and some Dramamine if you're prone to road sickness, because most of these itineraries take you down winding roads. And since it's almost always sunny in California, splurge on a convertible Mustang—it will turn the mundane task of driving into one of the highlights of your vacation.

—*Matthew Richard Poole*

1 PACIFIC COAST HIGHWAY IN 1 WEEK (SAN FRANCISCO TO BIG SUR)

If you've ever wondered why it's outrageously expensive to buy a home in California, this seaside journey by car will resolve the mystery: Superlatives don't do justice to the views you'll see while twisting and turning, climbing and descending along Pacific Coast Highway (Hwy. 1) from San Francisco to Big Sur. It's one of the nation's most thrilling roads, gripping the mountainside while it takes you past coastal redwood forests, ocean cliffs, and secluded coves battered by the dazzling, formidable Pacific.

The trek begins with a half-day's leisurely drive from San Francisco to Santa Cruz, and then continues south past Monterey and Carmel into thickly forested Big Sur. Not a single part of this drive lacks interesting sights; even the acres of artichokes around the farming town of Castroville are pretty, and it's a wonder the ocean views around Big Sur don't cause hundreds of car wrecks a day.

Heavy traffic can afflict Carmel and Big Sur on summer weekends. If you plan your trip to avoid the congestion, you can cruise at 55 miles per hour from town to town—with the top down and your spirits up.

Day ❶: Santa Cruz & Boardwalk

From San Francisco take Highway 1 south and follow the signs to Pacifica. Continue along Highway 1 for about 60 miles to Santa Cruz. Check into the **Pleasure Point Inn** ★★ (p. 383) and make a reservation for the **Bittersweet Bistro** ★★ (p. 384). Spend some time on the **Santa Cruz Beach Boardwalk** ★★ (p. 380) and be sure to ride the wooden Giant Dipper roller coaster and the old-school carousel. The **Seymour Marine Discovery Center** (p. 381) is also worth a visit, especially for kids. Have dinner in Aptos at the **Bittersweet Bistro** and head back to the inn.

Day ❷: Monterey Bay Aquarium

Sleep in, sip coffee on the roof deck, and admire the ocean view until checkout (11am), or walk along the coastal path to **Capitola** ★ (p. 381) for a Bloody Mary. Back in the car, head south on Highway 1 to Monterey, about a 1-hour drive. Check into the **Seven Gables Inn** ★★★ (p. 399) or **Martine Inn** ★★ (p. 399) for 2 nights, and make a dinner reservation for **Montrio** restaurant ★★ (p. 395) for this evening, and **Fandango** restaurant ★★ (p. 401) and **Monterey Bay Kayaks** tour (p. 391) for tomorrow. Drive to the **Monterey Bay Aquarium** ★★★ (p. 390), the world's finest. Spend 2 to 3 hours here, and then stroll **Cannery Row** (briefly if you loathe tourist schlock; p. 387). Drive or walk to **Montrio** for dinner.

Day ❸: Kayaking & Sea Otters

Breakfast at the inn, and then drive to Del Monte Beach for a leisurely **kayak tour of Monterey Bay.** Watching sea otters and sea lions play from the water is an unforgettable experience, requiring no kayaking expertise. Afterward, stroll along **Old Fisherman's Wharf** (p. 395) and snack on all those small cups of fresh seafood sold at one of many faux fish markets. Return to the car for an afternoon/sunset drive along the **17-Mile Drive** ★★ (p. 402). Dine at **Fandango** and return to the B&B.

Day ❹: Seafood & Beer in Carmel

Eat breakfast, check out, and drive to Carmel. Check in to the **Mission Ranch** ★★ (p. 407) for 2 nights, and make a reservation for the **Flying Fish Grill** ★★ (p. 409) for tonight and the **Restaurant at Mission Ranch** ★★ (p. 410) tomorrow night. Apply sunscreen, pack a jacket, and walk along the coastal path to downtown **Carmel** for window-shopping—a beloved Carmel pastime—and a burger and beer at the **Hog's Breath Inn** (p. 410). If it's Saturday, take the 2pm **Carmel Walking Tour** (p. 406); otherwise, pick up a free map at the **Carmel Business Association** (p. 405) and check out the **San Carlos Mission** ★★ (p. 405) and **Tor House** ★ (p. 406) on your own. Have dinner at the **Flying Fish Grill,** and then stroll back to the **Mission Ranch bar** for an Irish whiskey and piano tunes.

Day ❺: Chillin' at the Beach

Take the day off. Sleep in, stock up on picnic stuff at **Neilsen Brothers Market** (p. 412), and devote the day to **Carmel Beach** ★★ (p. 405)—a welcoming stretch of pristine white sand and cypress trees. Head back to your hotel room in the late afternoon, clean up, and walk to the hotel restaurant for a fat steak dinner.

Day ❻: Big Sur

Check out, have breakfast at the **Little Swiss Cafe** (p. 411), and top off the fuel tank. Drive south on Highway 1 deep into **Big Sur** ★★★, and make various stops along the way to photograph the spectacular coastline. Have lunch at **Café Kevah**

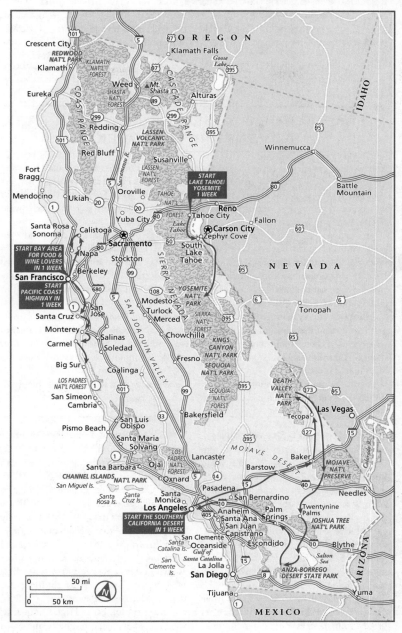

(p. 420), and then check into either **Deetjen's Big Sur Inn** ★ (p. 417) if you like extra-rustic lodgings; the **Treebones Resort** ★★ (p. 417) if you're on a budget; or the **Post Ranch Inn** ★★★ (p. 418) for a splurge.

Day ❼: Hiking & Home

Check out, then drive to **Julia Pfeiffer Burns State Park** ★★ (p. 416) and hit the trail from the parking area to **McWay Waterfall** (it's an easy trek). If you have time, return to San Francisco via Highway 1, though taking Highway 101 near Salinas is a much faster route.

2 LAKE TAHOE & YOSEMITE NATIONAL PARK ADVENTURE IN 1 WEEK

This weeklong excursion covers two of my favorite places on the planet: Lake Tahoe and Yosemite National Park. I've visited both these mountain regions countless times, yet each time I'm nonetheless awestruck by their beauty. I'd go so far as to credit them for my choice of career: The opportunity to explore natural wonders such as these is what compelled me to be a travel writer.

The trip starts in North Lake Tahoe, winds its way to South Lake Tahoe, and then veers southeast along Highway 395 to Mono Lake. From there, it cuts westward on Highway 120 and heads up, up, up to the famed Tioga Pass and into Yosemite National Park. In winter months, the scenery is even more spectacular, but Tioga Pass is usually closed due to snow. The inland route, via Highway 49, will get you there in winter, but it adds about 4 hours driving time.

The quickest way to cover this ground is to fly into Reno-Tahoe International Airport and rent a car; otherwise, take Interstate 80 east from the San Francisco or Sacramento airports to Truckee. From there, it's a short drive southward on Highway 89 to the north shore of Lake Tahoe. From Yosemite National Park, it's about a 3¹/₂-hour drive back to San Francisco.

Be sure to pack comfortable hiking shoes, a swimsuit, a small backpack, plenty of sunscreen, a wide-brimmed hat, and spare cash for the casinos.

Day ❶: Bike Ride & Slot Machines

From Tahoe City head south on West Lake Boulevard for a few miles to **Sunnyside Lodge** ★★ (p. 283). Check in for 2 nights, make dinner reservations at **Sol y Lago** ★★ (p. 286), then have lunch on the deck at Sunnyside, and soak in the view. Drive back to Tahoe City to the **Olympic Bike Shop** (p. 269). Rent a bike for a few hours and take the scenic paved bike path that follows West Lake Boulevard and the Truckee River. Return the bikes, and then drive to **Sol y Lago**. After dinner, drive to the **Cal-Neva Casino** ★ (p. 281) for some evening entertainment, and then head back to the hotel.

Day ❷: Rafting & Lakeside Dining

Eat breakfast at the **Fire Sign Café** ★ (p.287) down the street, and then drive to **Truckee River Raft Rental** (p. 272) in Tahoe City. If you're not into rafting, go on a sailboat cruise instead with **Tahoe Sailing Charters** (p. 270). After a leisurely raft trip down the mostly calm, always beautiful Truckee River, have a burger and beers on the riverside deck at the **River Ranch Lodge & Restaurant** ★★ (p. 282) while waiting for the return shuttle. Next, drive to **Squaw Valley** ★★★ (p. 266) and ride the cable car to **High Camp** ★★ (p. 267), where you can explore numerous hiking trails, ice skate, or admire the view at the **Poolside Café.** Either walk or take the cable car back to the parking lot, and then drive to **Sol y Lago** ★★ (p. 286) for dinner. (Leave time to arrive before sunset.)

Day ❸: Picnic Lunch, Beachside Mai Tais & More Gambling

Sleep in, grab breakfast at the hotel, and check out. Stock up on sandwiches and drinks at the deli, stuff them into a backpack, and head south on Highway 89 toward South Lake Tahoe. Park at **Emerald Bay** ★★ (p. 273) and walk to **Vikingsholm** ★ (p. 273) for a lakeside picnic lunch. (I recommend the hike to **Eagle Lake** as well; p. 271.) Back in the car to **South Lake Tahoe,** drive through town (heading east on Lake Tahoe Blvd./Hwy. 50) into Nevada, and check into a lakeside cabin at **Zephyr Cove** ★ (p. 279) for 2 nights. Drink a mai tai at the **beachside bar,** and then take a shuttle or taxi back toward the casinos for great sushi and *teriyaki chicken* at the **Naked Fish** ★★ (p. 285). Spend the evening at the **casinos** (p. 288).

Day ❹: Gondola Ride & Lobster

Sleep in, have breakfast at **Zephyr Cove Restaurant** (p. 279), then walk to the pier, and board the **MS *Dixie II*** (p. 272) for a 2-hour cruise to Emerald Bay. Return to the beachside bar for another mai tai, and then relax at the gold-sand beach in front of your cabin. If you can water-ski or wakeboard, consider renting a boat or jet ski. Around 4pm, hop in the car and head to the **Heavenly Resort** ★★ (p. 265) for a **gondola** ride (p. 274) to the **viewing platform** before sunset (wow!). For dinner, drive to **Fresh Ketch** ★ (p. 284) for oysters, steak, and lobster. Then win your money back at the **casinos** and/or see a **show.**

Day ❺: Mono Lake & Yosemite

Today's itinerary entails lots of driving, so rise early, eat breakfast at Zephyr Cove

Restaurant, gas up the car, and take the Kingsbury Grade to Highway 395 (it's a bit confusing to find, so bring a map). Head south to **Mono Lake** ★ (p. 331), spend an hour or so at the excellent Visitors Center, and then head east on Highway 120 into **Yosemite National Park** ★★★ (p. 312) toward **Yosemite Valley.** Be sure to stretch your legs at **Tuolumne Meadows** ★★ (p. 319) and walk around a bit, admiring the view. If you can afford it, check into the legendary **Ahwahnee Hotel** ★★★ (p. 323) for 2 nights; otherwise, stay either at the **Wawona Hotel** ★ (p. 324) or at my favorite lodging in Yosemite, the **Evergreen Lodge** ★★ (it's a bit of a drive from Yosemite Valley but worth the trip; p. 307). Dine at the hotel and call it a night.

Day ❻: Tours, Biking & Alpenglow

Sleep in, eat breakfast at the hotel, and take the 2-hour **Valley Floor Tour** (p. 316) in an open-air tram. Better yet, purchase the *Map and Guide to Yosemite Valley,* rent bikes at **Yosemite Lodge** or **Curry Village** (p. 319), and take your own tour along the paved trail that winds throughout the valley. When you return the bikes, use the *Map and Guide to Yosemite Valley*—which lists an assortment of hikes and short nature walks—to plan tomorrow's hike while you have lunch at one of the overpriced cafes in Curry Village. Save energy for the long hike on Day 7, and stroll eastward at a leisurely pace into the valley on the **John Muir Trail** ★★ (p. 317), along the Merced River toward Vernal falls—it's one of the most scenic trails in Yosemite. Make sure you have a clear view of the valley at sunset to witness the **alpenglow.** Return to the hotel for dinner. If it's a summer Saturday, mosey over to the Wawona Hotel for their old-fashioned **barbecue dinner** on the front lawn (p. 324).

Day ❼: Hiking & Drive Home

Rise early, catch a light breakfast, check out (but leave your luggage at the hotel), and unfold your *Map and Guide to Yosemite Valley* to see which hike best fits your schedule and endurance level. Some of my favorites are the **Upper Yosemite Fall Trail** ★ (a real thigh-burner but very rewarding; p. 317) or the **Mist Trail** ★ (p. 317) to Nevada Falls. Alas, after your hike, it's time to head home. If you're heading to the Bay Area or Sacramento, take Highway 120 toward Groveland and follow the signs.

3 A FOOD & WINE LOVER'S MOVABLE FEAST IN 1 WEEK

The San Francisco Bay Area is one of the nation's top destinations for world-class food and wine. The region's culinary diversity began with the California Gold Rush of 1849, when more than 300,000 people from all over the world migrated to Northern California to strike it rich. When the gold no longer panned out, many of the immigrants remained in California and used their earnings to start small farms, dairy ranches, wineries, fisheries, and restaurants that served family recipes from around the world.

Today California still harbors an impressive concentration of small, family-operated ranches, organic farms, and boutique wineries throughout Central and Northern California, providing local chefs with some of the nation's finest organic produce, artisan cheeses, hormone-free meats, and small-production wines. In fact, it was a Bay Area chef that *invented* California cuisine—the renowned Alice Waters. Even a full week of glorious gluttony won't begin to cover the range of cuisines and varietals available to serious epicureans as they indulge their inner cognoscenti, but with careful pacing and a little exercise worked into your route, you can savor the region's finest foods and still fit in your pants by the time you head home. Well, maybe.

Note: Because some of the following attractions operate only on certain days, you may need to rearrange the itinerary based on opening hours. It's also important to make restaurant reservations as far in advance as possible; the places recommended here are popular on the foodie circuit. Also, you'll need a car for the Berkeley and the Wine Country excursions.

Day ❶: Alfresco Noshing by Day & Fine Dining by Night

Start your movable feast in San Francisco at the **Ferry Building Marketplace Farmers' Market** ★★★, at the foot of Market Street in the Embarcadero (p. 121). From November through March, when produce is less abundant, the market takes place Tuesday and Saturday mornings; the rest of the year, it's open on Thursday and Sunday mornings as well. Join the throngs of locals as they browse the dozens of outdoor stalls filled with organic goods from local artisan farms, and snack on free samples of specialty foods. Inside, shop or simply gawk at delicacies from the city's finest gourmet chocolatiers, bakeries, fish and meat mongers, and tea merchants. If you haven't already filled up on free samples, have lunch at the **Slanted Door** ★★ (p. 103; reservations a must), located at the north end of the Marketplace. Afterward, burn calories with a leisurely bayside walk along the Embarcadero to Fisherman's Wharf. If your feet are up for it, continue walking to Fort Mason and the Marina (a brisk, 20- to 30-min. walk from Fisherman's Wharf) for more classic bay views (p. 133). Rest in the late afternoon to revitalize yourself for a French feast at **Restaurant Gary Danko** ★★★ (p. 107), one of the city's finest dining rooms, or for a more affordable but equally wonderful Italian meal at **A16** ★★ (p. 109). Both require advance reservations.

Day ❷: North Beach Treats & Chez Panisse

Pace yourself. Start the morning with coffee and a light breakfast at one of the sidewalk cafes in **North Beach** such as **Caffè Greco.** Wander the streets suffused with Italian heritage and the aromas of roasting garlic and pizza. Drop by **Biordi Art Imports** to pick up some **Italian pottery** (p. 139). Enjoy a leisurely lunch at **L'Osteria del Forno** ★★—classic Italian fare at reasonable prices served in a shoebox-size dining room (p. 106)—or sample authentic Hong Kong–style dining at **Great Eastern** ★, where rare delicacies are available for the adventurous palate. After lunch, it's time to find your way to Berkeley to learn how artisan chocolate is made during **Scharffen Berger Chocolate Maker's 1-hour tour** (p. 156). From the city, it's a 20-minute drive, traffic permitting (you can also take BART; call for directions, ✆ **510/465-2278**); take Columbus Avenue south and follow signs to I-80 east, which will take you across the Bay Bridge toward Oakland and Berkeley. Take the Ashby Avenue exit heading east, turn left at Seventh Street (the first signal), go to the second light, and the factory is on your right, at the corner of Seventh and Heinz streets. After the tour it's time to dine at one of the nation's most famous and influential restaurants: **Chez Panisse** ★★★. Still owned and run by Alice Waters, the godmother of contemporary California cuisine, it's a requisite pilgrimage stop for serious gourmands (p. 155). If the skies are clear on the drive back to San Francisco, revel in the **city views** from the East Bay or Treasure Island.

Day ❸: Eating Your Way Through Chinatown

Kick off another gluttonous day in San Francisco with the **"I Can't Believe I Ate**

My Way Through Chinatown" excursion—led by knowledgeable local celebrity Shirley Fong-Torres (✆ **650/355-9657; www.wokwiz.com**). Part variety show, part feast, the Chinatown food tour takes place every Saturday and some Sundays; call for details. If you're visiting on a weekday, try Fong-Torres's standard Chinatown tour, another authentic introduction to delicacies hidden throughout Chinatown. Work off lunch (included in the tour price) with a visit to **Golden Gate Park** (p. 124), where you can visit the amazing **de Young Museum** (p. 128), lounge in the grass, or ride a paddle boat. Head to the bustling Mission District for dinner at **Delfina** ★★, one of the city's best Italian restaurants, with its hip, young, fun patrons and casual setting (p. 116).

Day ❹: Union Square

Spend your last day in the city **shopping at Union Square** department stores and boutiques. Have a light lunch of antipasto and a salad at the **Emporio Armani Cafe,** and then spend the afternoon with a visit to **Alcatraz Island** ★★★ (p. 117) or the city's museums (p. 127). Or just pamper yourself with a spa treatment at the Huntington Hotel's **Nob Hill Spa** ★★ In the evening, either go for a wildly intricate and lengthy multicourse affair at **Michael Mina** ★★★ (p. 94), a more relaxed Greek-inspired feast at one of my favorite restaurants in the city, **Kokkari** ★★ (p. 102), or some of the city's finest Mediterranean-influenced cuisine at the city's beloved **Zuni Café** ★★ (p. 111). If you've still got energy after dinner, head downtown for wine tasting at **First Crush** (p. 147) or for champagne at the **Bubble Lounge** (p. 147).

Day ❺: Napa Wine Tasting

Get an early start to **Napa** on scenic Highway 101 (p. 181), which crosses the Golden Gate Bridge and is a far prettier drive than Interstate 80. Make **Artesa Vineyards & Winery** ★★ your first wine-tasting stop, as it's known for its beautiful views and contemporary architecture, as well as for its Carneros District pinot noirs (p. 200). If a cooking demo is under way, make a reservation to participate at **Copia: The American Center for Wine, Food & the Arts** ★ (p. 184). Next, stop at **Bistro Don Giovanni** ★★ for an excellent Italian lunch (don't skip the pasta); if the weather's warm, reserve a patio table overlooking the garden, whimsical fountain, and vineyards (p. 196). If you're visiting during the week, make **Shafer Vineyards'** exclusive tour and tasting (p. 186) your next stop. If it's the weekend, take the scenic drive to the **Hess Collection** winery and art gallery ★★ (p. 185) instead. Then you can satiate your appetite at the festive French brasserie **Bouchon** ★★ (p. 197). Stay the night at any of the recommended B&Bs or hotels in your price range (p. 192), but make sure you book a room as far in advance as possible.

Day ❻: Sparkling Wine, Hand-Dug Caves & Hot Springs

Take it easy on the morning meal and have just coffee and pastries (ask your concierge for the best place near you). Then head north on Highway 29 to **Schramsberg** ★★ in Calistoga (about ½ hr. from downtown Napa and 15 min. from St. Helena) for a tour of their sparkling wine–making process and hand-dug caves, followed by a tasting

(p. 191). Stop for lunch, with a huge wine selection, at **All Seasons Café** ★★ in downtown Calistoga (p. 196). Then browse the **boutiques** on the one commercial strip in town. Spend the rest of the afternoon visiting other wineries in the area, including Francis Ford Coppola's **Rubicon Estate** (p. 189) and **Swanson Vineyards** ★ (p. 188). Or relax with spa treatments at funky-cool **Dr. Wilkinson's Hot Springs** ★, one of Calistoga's numerous spas (p. 195). For an indulgent dinner, grab a bite at **Redd** ★★ (p. 196).

Day ❼: Food & Wine Gifts, Picnic & Pétanque

Reserve the day for shopping. Start with a light breakfast near your hotel. Then head to St. Helena for the Main Street boutiques. Grab mementos and gifts from **Napa Valley Olive Oil Manufacturing Company** (p. 189), follow your nose at the culinary emporium **Dean & DeLuca** (p. 198), and buy a picnic lunch from **Oakville Grocery** (p. 198). Picnic, taste wines, and play the French lawn-bowling game *pétanque* at **Clos Du Val** winery (p. 186). If you have time, you can stop in downtown **Sonoma** (p. 201) to meander around its square, or make one last stop at **Buena Vista Winery** (p. 202). Then it's back to San Francisco the same way you came, just in time to start your diet again.

San Francisco

by Matthew Richard Poole

In a city where starting off your holiday with an Irish coffee at the Buena Vista Cafe is de rigueur, it's pretty much guaranteed that you'll have a fun time. San Francisco's reputation as a rollicking city where almost anything goes dates from the boom-or-bust days of the California Gold Rush. The result is a wee bit o' heaven for everyone. In a city that is so beautiful, exciting, and cosmopolitan there's always something enjoyable to see and do no matter how long you're staying. I've lived here for 14 years, and I'm still discovering new things about this city almost every day.

But the best advice I can give you about San Francisco is to just *go*. Enjoy the cool blast of salty air as you stroll across the Golden Gate Bridge. Stuff yourself with dim sum in Chinatown. Browse the secondhand shops along Haight Street. Recite poetry in a North Beach coffeehouse. Walk along the beach, skate through Golden Gate Park, ride the cable cars, tour a Victorian mansion, explore Alcatraz Island, go to a Giants ballgame: Like an eternal world's fair, it's all happening in San Francisco, and everyone's invited. All you have to do is arrive with an open mind, this guidebook, and a sense of adventure—the rest is waiting for you.

1 ORIENTATION

GETTING THERE
By Plane

Two major airports serve the Bay Area: San Francisco International and Oakland International.

SAN FRANCISCO INTERNATIONAL AIRPORT   Almost four dozen major scheduled carriers serve **San Francisco International Airport** (© **650/821-8211;** www.flysfo.com; airport code **SFO**), 14 miles directly south of downtown on U.S. 101. Travel time to downtown during commuter rush hour is about 40 minutes; at other times, it's about 20 to 25 minutes.

The cheapest and often fastest way to get from SFO to the city is to take **BART** (Bay Area Rapid Transit; © **415/989-2278;** www.bart.gov), which offers numerous stops within downtown San Francisco. This route, which takes about 35 minutes, avoids traffic on the way and costs a lot less than taxis or shuttles (about $6 each way, depending on exactly where you're going). Just jump on the airport's free shuttle bus to the International terminal, enter the BART station there, and you're on your way. Trains leave approximately every 15 minutes.

A cab downtown from the airport is $30 to $35, plus tip. **SuperShuttle** (© **800/ BLUE-VAN** or 415/558-8500; www.supershuttle.com) will take you anywhere in town; it's $15 to a residence or business, and $8 to $15 for each additional person, depending on your destination. The shuttle requires pickup 2 hours before your flight (3 hr. during holidays).

OAKLAND INTERNATIONAL AIRPORT   About 5 miles south of downtown Oakland, at the Hegenberger Road exit off Calif. 17 (U.S. 880; if coming from the south, take 98th Ave.), Oakland International Airport (© 800/247-6255 or 510/563-3300; www.oaklandairport.com; airport code **OAK**) primarily serves passengers with East Bay destinations. Some San Franciscans prefer this less-crowded, accessible airport during busy periods—especially because by car it takes around half an hour to get there from downtown San Francisco (traffic permitting). The airport is also accessible by BART, which is not influenced by traffic because it travels on its own tracks (see below for more information).

Taxis from the Oakland airport to downtown San Francisco are expensive, costing approximately $50, plus tip.

Bayporter Express (© 877/467-1800 or 415/467-1800; www.bayporter.com) shuttle service is $26 for the first person, $12 for each additional person, to downtown San Francisco; it costs more to the city's outlying neighborhoods. Children under 12 ride for $7.

The cheapest way to reach downtown San Francisco is to take the shuttle bus from the Oakland Airport to **BART** (Bay Area Rapid Transit; © 510/464-6000; www.bart.gov). The AirBART shuttle bus runs about every 15 minutes Monday through Saturday from 5am to 12:05am and Sunday from 8am to 12:05am. It makes pickups in front of terminals 1 and 2 near the ground transportation signs. Tickets must be purchased at the Oakland Airport's vending machines prior to boarding. The cost is $2 for the 10-minute ride to BART's Coliseum station in Oakland. BART fares vary, depending on your destination; the trip to downtown San Francisco costs $3.15 and takes 15 minutes once you're on board. The entire excursion should take around 45 minutes.

By Car

San Francisco is accessible via several major highways: U.S. 101 and Highway 1 from the north and south, and I-80 and I-580 from the northeast and east, respectively. If you drive from Los Angeles, you can take either the longer coastal route along Highway 1/U.S. 101 (437 miles, 11 hr.), or the inland route along I-5 to I-580 (389 miles, 6¹/₂ hr.). From Mendocino, it's a little more than 3 hours along Highway 1, and about 3¹/₄ hours along U.S. 101; and from Sacramento, it's 88 miles, or 1¹/₂ hours, along I-80.

By Train

San Francisco–bound **Amtrak** (© 800/872-7245 or 800/USA-RAIL; www.amtrak.com) trains leave from New York and cross the country via Chicago. The journey takes about 3¹/₂ days, and seats sell quickly. At this writing, the lowest round-trip fare costs about $300 from New York and $270 from Chicago. Round-trip tickets from Los Angeles range from $120 to as much as $200. Trains arrive in Emeryville, just north of Oakland, and connect with regularly scheduled buses to San Francisco's Ferry Building and the Caltrain station in downtown San Francisco.

Caltrain (© 800/660-4287 or 415/546-4461; www.caltrain.com) operates train service between San Francisco and the towns of the peninsula. The city depot is at 700 Fourth St., at Townsend Street.

VISITOR INFORMATION

The **San Francisco Visitor Information Center,** on the lower level of Hallidie Plaza, 900 Market St., at Powell Street (© 415/391-2000; www.onlyinsanfrancisco.com), is

Money-Saving Tourist Passes

If you're the type who loves to cram as many tourist attractions as possible in one trip, then you might want to consider purchasing a **San Francisco City Pass** or **GO San Francisco Card**. The **CityPass** includes 7 days of unlimited public transportation (including cable cars, Metro streetcars, and the entire bus system), and access to some of the city's major attractions: the California Palace of the Legion of Honor and de Young museums, Aquarium of the Bay, the Asian Art Museum, the San Francisco Museum of Modern Art, the Exploratorium, and a Blue & Gold Fleet bay cruise. Discounts and coupons to other tourist-related attractions and activities are included as well. You can buy a CityPass at any of the above attractions or online at **www.citypass.net**. Current rates are $54 for adults and $44 for kids 5 to 17. For more information, visit the CityPass website at **www.citypass.net** or send an e-mail to info@citypass.com. For recorded information, call ☏ **888/330-5008.**

I think the better deal, however, is the **GO San Francisco Card** (☏ **800/887-9103;** www.gosanfranciscocard.com). It offers free or discounted admission to more than 45 of the most popular attractions, activities, and tours throughout the Bay Area and Wine Country; has far more flexibility (available in 1-, 2-, 3-, 5-, and 7-day increments over a 14-day period); and comes with a nifty little full-color guidebook that fits in your back pocket. In addition, some stores and restaurants offer discounts of up to 20% to Go San Francisco Card holders. The Go Cards are smart-technology enabled, which means they operate by calendar day and are activated the first time they are swiped, so you'll want to start your touring early in the morning to get the most value. The 2-day card costs $75 for adults ($35 for kids 3–12) and doesn't need to be used on consecutive days.

the best source of specialized information about the city. Even if you don't have a specific question, you might want to request the free *Visitors Planning Guide* and the San Francisco Visitors Kit. The kit includes a 6-month calendar of events; a city history; shopping and dining information; and several good, clear maps; plus lodging information on its members' establishments.

You can also get the latest on San Francisco at the following online addresses:

- The *Bay Guardian,* the city's free weekly paper: **www.sfbg.com**
- *SF Gate,* the city's *Chronicle* newspaper: **www.sfgate.com**
- CitySearch: **sanfrancisco.citysearch.com**

CITY LAYOUT

San Francisco occupies the tip of a 32-mile peninsula between San Francisco Bay and the Pacific Ocean. Its land area measures about 46 square miles, although the city is often referred to as being 7 square miles. At more than 900 feet high, the towering Twin Peaks (which are, in fact, two neighboring peaks), marks the geographic center of the city and is a great place to take in a vista of San Francisco.

With lots of one-way streets, San Francisco might seem confusing at first, but it will quickly become easy to negotiate. The city's downtown streets are arranged in a simple

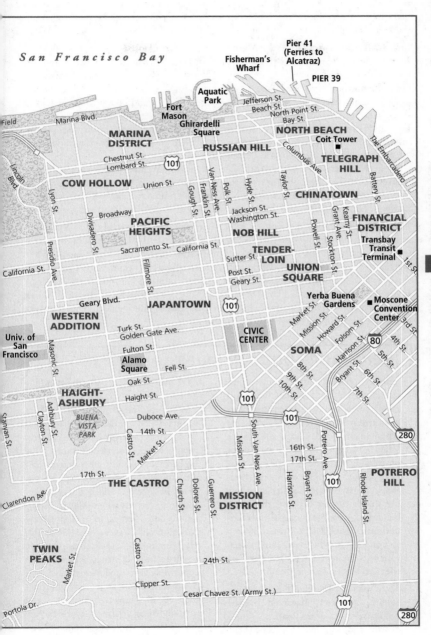

San Francisco Bay

Pier 41
(Ferries to
Alcatraz)

Fisherman's
Wharf

PIER 39

Aquatic
Park

Jefferson St.
Beach St.
North Point St.
Bay St.

Field

Marina Blvd.

Fort
Mason

Ghirardelli
Square

NORTH BEACH

Coit Tower

**MARINA
DISTRICT**

RUSSIAN HILL

Columbus Ave.

**TELEGRAPH
HILL**

The Embarcadero

Chestnut St.
Lombard St.

101

COW HOLLOW

Union St.

Van Ness Ave.

Polk St.

Hyde St.

Taylor St.

CHINATOWN

Battery St.

Lincoln
Blvd

Lyon St.

Broadway

Gough St.

Franklin St.

Jackson St.
Washington St.

Grant Ave.

Kearny St.

**FINANCIAL
DISTRICT**

**PACIFIC
HEIGHTS**

Divisadero St.

NOB HILL

Powell St.

Stockton St.

Transbay
Transit
Terminal

1st St.

California St.

Presidio Ave.

Sacramento St.

California St.

Fillmore St.

Sutter St.

**TENDER-
LOIN**

**UNION
SQUARE**

Post St.
Geary St.

Geary Blvd.

JAPANTOWN

101

Yerba Buena
Gardens

Moscone
Convention
Center

3rd St.

**WESTERN
ADDITION**

Turk St.
Golden Gate Ave.

**CIVIC
CENTER**

Market St.

Mission St.

Howard St.

Folsom St.

4th St.

80

Univ. of
San
Francisco

Masonic St.

Fulton St.

Alamo
Square

Fell St.

SOMA

Harrison St.

Bryant St.

5th St.

6th St.

Oak St.

8th St.

7th St.

**HAIGHT-
ASHBURY**

Ashbury St.

Clayton St.

Stanyan St.

Haight St.

*BUENA
VISTA
PARK*

Duboce Ave.

14th St.

Castro St.

Market St.

9th St.

10th St.

101

South Van Ness Ave.

Potrero Ave.

101

280

17th St.

16th St.
17th St.

Rhode Island St.

**POTRERO
HILL**

Clarendon Ave.

THE CASTRO

Church St.

Dolores St.

Guerrero St.

**MISSION
DISTRICT**

Harrison St.

Bryant St.

**TWIN
PEAKS**

Market St.

Castro St.

24th St.

Clipper St.

Cesar Chavez St. (Army St.)

Portola Dr.

101

280

SAN FRANCISCO

5

ORIENTATION

grid pattern, with the exceptions of Market Street and Columbus Avenue, which cut across the grid at right angles to each other. Hills appear to distort this pattern, however, and can disorient you. As you learn your way around, the hills will become your landmarks and reference points.

MAIN ARTERIES & STREETS   **Market Street** is San Francisco's main thoroughfare. Most of the city's buses travel this route on their way to the Financial District from the outer neighborhoods to the west and south. The tall office buildings clustered downtown are at the northeast end of Market; 1 block beyond lie the Embarcadero and the bay.

The Embarcadero ★ —an excellent strolling, skating, and biking route (thanks to recent renovations)—curves along San Francisco Bay from south of the Bay Bridge to the northeast perimeter of the city. It terminates at Fisherman's Wharf, the famous tourist-oriented pier. Aquatic Park, Fort Mason, and the Golden Gate National Recreation Area are on the northernmost point of the peninsula.

From the eastern perimeter of Fort Mason, **Van Ness Avenue** runs due south, back to Market Street. The area just described forms a rough triangle, with Market Street as its southeastern boundary, the waterfront as its northern boundary, and Van Ness Avenue as its western boundary. Within this triangle lie most of the city's main tourist sights.

FINDING AN ADDRESS   Because most of the city's streets are laid out in a grid pattern, finding an address is easy when you know the nearest cross street. Numbers start with 1 at the beginning of the street and proceed at the rate of 100 per block. When asking for directions, find out the nearest cross street and the neighborhood where your destination is located, but be careful not to confuse numerical avenues with numerical streets. Numerical avenues (Third Ave. and so on) are in the Richmond and Sunset Districts, in the western part of the city. Numerical streets (Third St. and so on) are south of Market Street, in the east and south parts of town.

NEIGHBORHOODS IN BRIEF

Union Square Union Square is the commercial hub of San Francisco. Most major hotels and department stores are crammed into the area surrounding the actual square, which was named for a series of violent pro-union mass demonstrations staged here on the eve of the Civil War. A plethora of upscale boutiques, restaurants, and galleries occupy the spaces tucked between the larger buildings. A few blocks west is the **Tenderloin** neighborhood, a patch of poverty and blight where you should keep your wits about you. The **Theater District** is 3 blocks west of Union Square.

The Financial District East of Union Square, this area, bordered by the Embarcadero and by Market, Third, Kearny, and Washington streets, is the city's business district and the stamping grounds for many major corporations. The pointy TransAmerica Pyramid, at Montgomery and Clay streets, is one of the district's most conspicuous architectural features. To its east sprawls the Embarcadero Center, an $8^{1}/_{2}$-acre complex housing offices, shops, and restaurants. Farther east still is the old Ferry Building, the city's prebridge transportation hub. Ferries to Sausalito and Larkspur still leave from this point. However, in 2003, the building became an attraction in itself when it was completely renovated, jam-packed with outstanding restaurants and gourmet food- and wine-related shops, and surrounded by a farmers' market a few days a week, making it one of San

Francisco residents' favorite places to stock their kitchens.

Nob Hill & Russian Hill Bounded by Bush, Larkin, Pacific, and Stockton streets, Nob Hill is a genteel, well-heeled district still occupied by the city's major power brokers and the neighborhood businesses they frequent. Russian Hill extends from Pacific to Bay and from Polk to Mason. It contains steep streets, lush gardens, and high-rises occupied by both the mon-eyed and the bohemian.

Chinatown A large red-and-green gate on Grant Avenue at Bush Street marks the official entrance to Chinatown. Beyond lies a 24-block labyrinth, bordered by Broadway, Bush, Kearny, and Stockton streets, filled with restaurants, markets, temples, shops, and, of course, a substantial percentage of San Francisco's Chinese residents. Chinatown is a great place for exploration all along Stockton and Grant streets, Portsmouth Square, and the alleys that lead off them, such as Ross and Waverly. This district has a maddening combination of incessant traffic and horrible drivers, so don't even think about driving around here.

North Beach This Italian neighborhood, which stretches from Montgomery and Jackson to Bay Street, is one of the best places in the city to grab a coffee, pull up a cafe chair, and do some serious people-watching. Nightlife is equally happening in North Beach; restaurants, bars, and clubs along Columbus and Grant avenues attract folks from all over the Bay Area, who fight for a parking place and romp through the festive neighborhood. Down Columbus, toward the Financial District, are the remains of the city's Beat Generation landmarks, including Ferlinghetti's City Lights Bookstore and Vesuvio's Bar. Broadway—a short strip of sex joints—cuts through the heart of the district. **Telegraph Hill** looms over the east side of North Beach, topped by Coit Tower, one of San Francisco's best vantage points.

Fisherman's Wharf North Beach runs into Fisherman's Wharf, which was once the busy heart of the city's great harbor and waterfront industries. Today it's a kitschy and mildly entertaining tourist area with little, if any, authentic waterfront life, except for a small fleet of fishing boats and some lethargic sea lions. What it does have going for it are activities for the entire family, with attractions, restaurants, trinket shops, and beautiful views and walkways everywhere you look.

The Marina District Created on landfill for the Pan Pacific Exposition of 1915, the Marina District boasts some of the best views of the Golden Gate, as well as plenty of grassy fields alongside San Francisco Bay. Elegant Mediterranean-style homes and apartments, inhabited by the city's well-to-do singles and wealthy families, line the streets. Here, too, are the Palace of Fine Arts, the Exploratorium, and Fort Mason Center. The main street is Chestnut, between Franklin and Lyon, which abounds with shops, cafes, and boutiques. Because of its landfill foundation, the Marina was one of the hardest-hit districts in the 1989 quake.

Cow Hollow Located west of Van Ness Avenue, between Russian Hill and the Presidio, this flat, grazeable area supported 30 dairy farms in 1861. Today Cow Hollow is largely residential and yuppie. Its two primary commercial thoroughfares are Lombard Street, known for its many relatively inexpensive motels, and Union Street, a flourishing shopping sector filled with restaurants, pubs, cafes, and shops.

Pacific Heights The ultra-elite, such as the Gettys and Danielle Steel—and those lucky enough to buy before the real-estate boom—reside in the mansions and homes in this neighborhood. When the rich meander out of their fortresses, they wander down to Union Street and join the pretty people who frequent the street's long stretch of chic boutiques and lively neighborhood restaurants, cafes, and bars.

Japantown Bounded by Octavia, Fillmore, California, and Geary, Japantown shelters only a small percentage of the city's Japanese population, but exploring these few square blocks and the shops and restaurants within them is still a cultural experience.

Civic Center Although millions of dollars have gone toward brick sidewalks, ornate lampposts, and elaborate street plantings, the southwestern section of Market Street can still feel a little sketchy due to the large number of homeless who wander the area. The Civic Center at the "bottom" of Market Street, however, is a stunning beacon of culture and refinement. This large complex of buildings includes the domed and dapper City Hall, the Opera House, Davies Symphony Hall, and the Asian Art Museum. The landscaped plaza connecting the buildings is the staging area for San Francisco's frequent demonstrations for or against just about everything.

SoMa No part of San Francisco has been more affected by recent development than the area south of Market Street (dubbed "SoMa"), the area within the triangle of the Embarcadero, Highway 101, and Market Street. Until a decade ago it was a district of old warehouses and industrial spaces, with a few scattered underground nightclubs, restaurants, and shoddy residential areas. But when it became the hub of dot-commercialization and half-million-dollar-plus lofts, its fate changed forever.

Today though, dot-coms don't occupy much of the commercial space, the area is jumping thanks to fancy loft residents, the baseball stadium, and surrounding businesses, restaurants, and nightclubs in addition to urban entertainment a la the Museum of Modern Art, Yerba Buena Gardens, Metreon, and a slew of big-bucks hotels that make tons of money from businesspeople. Though still gritty in some areas, it's growing more glittery by the year.

Mission District This is another area that was greatly affected by the city's new wealth. The Mexican and Latin American populations here, with their cuisine, traditions, and art, make the Mission District a vibrant area to visit. Some parts of the neighborhood are still poor and sprinkled with the homeless, gangs, and drug addicts, but young urbanites have also settled in the area, attracted by its "reasonably" (a relative term) priced rentals and endless oh-so-hot restaurants and bars that stretch from 16th and Valencia streets to 25th and Mission streets. Less adventurous tourists may just want to duck into Mission Dolores, cruise by a few of the 200-plus amazing murals, and head back downtown. But anyone who's interested in hanging with the hipsters and experiencing the hottest restaurant and bar nightlife should definitely beeline it here. Don't be afraid to visit this area, but do use caution at night.

The Castro One of the liveliest streets in town, the Castro is practically synonymous with San Francisco's gay community (even though it is technically a street in the Noe Valley District). Located at the very end of Market Street, between 17th and 18th streets, the Castro has dozens of shops, restaurants, and bars catering to the gay community. Open-minded straight people are welcome, too.

Haight-Ashbury Part trendy, part nostalgic, part funky, the Haight, as it's most commonly known, was the soul of the psychedelic, free-loving 1960s and the center of the counterculture movement. Today the gritty neighborhood straddling upper Haight Street, on the eastern border of Golden Gate Park, is more gentrified, but the commercial area still harbors all walks of life. Leftover aging hippies mingle with grungy, begging street kids outside Ben & Jerry's Ice Cream Store (where they might still be talking about Jerry Garcia), nondescript marijuana dealers whisper "Buds" as shoppers pass, and many people walking down the street have Day-Glo hair. But you don't need to be a freak or wear tie-dye to enjoy the Haight—the ethnic food, trendy shops, and bars cover all tastes. From Haight Street, walk south on Cole Street for a more peaceful and quaint neighborhood experience.

Richmond & Sunset Districts San Francisco's suburbs of sorts, these are the city's largest and most populous neighborhoods, consisting mainly of small (but expensive) homes, shops, and neighborhood restaurants. Although they border Golden Gate Park and Ocean Beach, few tourists venture into "The Avenues," as these areas are referred to locally, unless they're on their way to the Cliff House, zoo, or the Palace of the Legion of Honor.

2 GETTING AROUND

BY PUBLIC TRANSPORTATION

The **San Francisco Municipal Transportation Agency**, 1 S. Van Ness Ave., better known as "Muni" (© **415/673-6864;** www.sfmuni.com), operates the city's cable cars, buses, and streetcars. Together, these three services crisscross the entire city. Fares for buses and streetcars are $1.50 for adults; 50¢ for seniors over 65, children 5 to 17, and riders with disabilities. Cable cars, which run from 6:30am to 12:50am, cost a whopping $5 for all people over 5 ($1 for seniors and riders with disabilities 9pm–7am). Needless to say, they're packed primarily with tourists. Exact change is required on all vehicles except cable cars. Fares are subject to change. Muni's NextBus uses satellite technology and advanced computer modeling to track vehicles on their routes; **www.nextmuni.com** provides up-to-the-minute information about when the next bus or streetcar is coming.

For detailed route information, phone Muni or consult the Muni map at the front of the San Francisco Yellow Pages. If you plan to use public transportation extensively, you might want to invest in a comprehensive transit and city map ($2), sold at the San Francisco Visitor Information Center (p. 66), Powell/Market cable car booth, and many downtown retail outlets. Also, see the "Money-Saving Tourist Passes" box for more information.

BY CABLE CAR San Francisco's cable cars might not be the most practical means of transport, but the rolling historic landmarks are a fun ride. The three lines are concentrated in the downtown area. The most scenic, and exciting, is the Powell–Hyde line, which follows a zigzag route from the corner of Powell and Market streets, over both Nob Hill and Russian Hill, to a turntable at gaslit Victorian Square in front of Aquatic Park. The Powell–Mason line starts at the same intersection and climbs Nob Hill before descending to Bay Street, just 3 blocks from Fisherman's Wharf. The least scenic is the California Street line, which begins at the foot of Market Street and runs a straight course through Chinatown and over Nob Hill to Van Ness Avenue. All riders must exit at the last stop and wait in line for the return trip. The cable car system operates from approximately 6:30am to 12:50am, and each ride costs $5.

BY BUS   Buses reach almost every corner of San Francisco and beyond—they even travel over the bridges to Marin County and Oakland. Overhead electric cables power some buses; others use conventional gas engines. All are numbered and display their destinations on the front. Signs, curb markings, and yellow bands on adjacent utility poles designate stops, and most bus shelters exhibit Muni's transportation map and schedule. Many buses travel along Market Street or pass near Union Square and run from about 6am to midnight. After midnight, there is infrequent all-night "Owl" service. For safety, avoid taking buses late at night.

Popular tourist routes include bus nos. 5, 7, and 71, all of which run to Golden Gate Park; 41 and 45, which travel along Union Street; and 30, which runs between Union Square and Ghirardelli Square. A bus ride costs $1.50 for adults and 50¢ for seniors over 65, children 5 to 17, and riders with disabilities.

BY STREETCAR   Five of Muni's six streetcar lines, designated J, K, L, M, and N, run underground downtown and on the streets in the outer neighborhoods. The sleek rail cars make the same stops as BART (see below) along Market Street, including Embarcadero Station (in the Financial District), Montgomery and Powell streets (both near Union Sq.), and the Civic Center (near City Hall). Past the Civic Center, the routes branch off: The J line takes you to Mission Dolores; the K, L, and M lines run to Castro Street; and the N line parallels Golden Gate Park and extends all the way to the Embarcadero and AT&T Park. Streetcars run about every 15 minutes, more frequently during rush hours. They operate Monday through Friday from 5am to 12:15am, Saturday from 6am to approximately 12:15am, and Sunday from approximately 8am to 12:20am. The L and N lines operate 24 hours a day, 7 days a week, but late at night, regular buses trace the L and N routes, which are normally underground, from atop the city streets. Because the operation is part of Muni, the fares are the same as for buses, and passes are accepted.

The most recent new line to this system is not a newcomer at all, but is, in fact, an encore performance of San Francisco's beloved rejuvenated 1930s streetcar. The beautiful, retro, multicolored F-Market streetcar runs from 17th and Castro streets to Beach and Jones streets; every other streetcar continues to Jones and Beach streets in Fisherman's Wharf. This is a quick and charming way to get up- and downtown without any hassle.

BY BART   BART, an acronym for **Bay Area Rapid Transit** (✆ **415/989-2278;** www.bart.gov), is a futuristic-looking, high-speed rail network that connects San Francisco with the East Bay and the San Francisco and Oakland airports. Four stations are on Market Street. Fares range from $1.45 to $7.35, depending on how far you go. Machines in the stations dispense tickets that are magnetically encoded with a dollar amount. Computerized exits automatically deduct the correct fare. Children 4 and under ride free. Trains run every 15 to 20 minutes, Monday through Friday from 4am to midnight, Saturday from 6am to midnight, and Sunday from 8am to midnight. In keeping with its futuristic look, BART now offers online trip planners that you can download to your PDA, iPod, or phone.

BY TAXI

This isn't New York, so don't expect a taxi to appear whenever you need one—if at all. If you're downtown during rush hour or leaving a major hotel, it won't be hard to hail a cab; just look for the lighted sign on the roof that indicates the vehicle is free. Otherwise,

Curb Your Wheels!

When parking on a hill, drivers are required by law to apply the hand brake and curb their front wheels—toward the curb when facing downhill, away from it when facing uphill. Failure to curb your wheels, preventing a possible "runaway," will result in an expensive fine that is aggressively enforced.

it's a good idea to call one of the following companies to arrange a ride; **Veteran's Cab** (© **415/552-1300**), **Luxor Cabs** (© **415/282-4141**), **De Soto Cab** (© **415/970-1300**), and **Yellow Cab** (© **415/626-2345**). Rates are approximately $2.85 for the first mile and 45¢ each fifth of a mile thereafter.

BY CAR

You don't need a car to explore downtown San Francisco. In fact, with the city becoming more crowded by the minute, a car can be your worst nightmare—you're likely to end up stuck in traffic with lots of aggressive and frustrated drivers, pay upwards of $30 a day to park (plus a whopping new 14% parking lot tax), and spend a good portion of your vacation looking for a parking space. Don't bother. However, if you want to venture outside the city, driving is the best way to go.

Before heading outside the city, especially in winter, call © **800/427-7623** for California **road conditions.** You can also call © 511 for current traffic information.

CAR RENTALS　All the major rental companies operate in the city and have desks at the airports. When we last checked, you could get a compact car for a week for anywhere from $165 to $315, including all taxes and other charges, but prices change dramatically on a daily basis and depend on which company you rent from.

Some of the national car-rental companies operating in San Francisco include **Alamo** (© 800/327-9633; www.alamo.com), **Avis** (© 800/331-1212; www.avis.com), **Budget** (© 800/527-0700; www.budget.com), **Dollar** (© 800/800-4000; www.dollar.com), **Enterprise** (© 800/325-8007; www.enterprise.com), **Hertz** (© 800/654-3131; www.hertz.com), **National** (© 800/227-7368; www.nationalcar.com), and **Thrifty** (© 800/367-2277; www.thrifty.com).

PARKING　If you want a relaxing vacation, don't attempt to find street parking downtown or in Nob Hill, North Beach, Chinatown, by Fisherman's Wharf, or on Telegraph Hill. Park in a garage or take a cab or a bus. If you do find street parking, read street signs that explain when you can park and for how long. Be especially careful to avoid zones that become tow areas during rush hours.

Ⓕ *Fast Facts*　San Francisco

American Express　For travel arrangements, traveler's checks, currency exchange, and other member services, an office is at 455 Market St., at First Street (© **415/536-2600**), in the Financial District, open Monday through Friday from 9am to 5:30pm and Saturday from 10am to 2pm. To report lost or stolen traveler's checks, call © **800/221-7282.** For American Express Global Assist, call © **800/554-2639.**

Area Codes The area code for San Francisco is **415;** for Oakland, Berkeley, and much of the East Bay, **510;** for the peninsula, generally **650.** Napa and Sonoma are **707.** Most phone numbers in this chapter are in San Francisco's 415 area code, but there's no need to dial it if you're within city limits.

Earthquakes There will always be earthquakes in California, most of which you'll never notice. However, in case of a significant shaker, there are a few basic precautionary measures you should know. When you are inside a building, seek cover; do not run outside. Stand under a doorway or against a wall, and stay away from windows. If you exit a building after a substantial quake, use stairwells, not elevators. If you are in your car, pull over to the side of the road and stop—but not until you are away from bridges, overpasses, telephone poles, and power lines. Stay in your car. If you're out walking, stay outside and away from trees, power lines, and the sides of buildings. If you're in an area with tall buildings, find a doorway in which to stand.

Emergencies Call ℂ **911** to report a fire, call the police, or get an ambulance anywhere in the United States. This is a toll-free call (no coins are required at public telephones).

Hospitals **Saint Francis Memorial Hospital,** 900 Hyde St., between Bush and Pine streets on Nob Hill (ℂ **415/353-6000**), provides emergency service 24 hours a day; no appointment is necessary. The hospital also operates a **physician-referral service** (ℂ **800/333-1355** or 415/353-6566).

Safety Few locals would recommend walking alone late at night in certain areas, particularly the Tenderloin, between Union Square and the Civic Center. Compared to dodgy neighborhoods in other cities, however, even this section of San Francisco is relatively tranquil. You should also be alert in the Mission District, around 16th and Mission streets; the lower Fillmore area, around lower Haight Street; and SoMa (south of Market St.).

Taxes The United States has no value-added tax (VAT) or other indirect tax at the national level. Every state, county, and city has the right to levy its own nonrefundable local tax on all purchases, including hotel and restaurant checks, airline tickets, and so on, and is not included in the price tags you'll see on merchandise. Sales tax in San Francisco is 8.5%. Hotel tax is charged on the room tariff only (which is not subject to sales tax) and is set by the city, ranging from 12% to 17% around Northern California.

Toilets Those weird, oval-shaped, olive-green kiosks on the sidewalks throughout San Francisco are high-tech self-cleaning public toilets. It costs 25¢ to enter, with no time limit, but I don't recommend using the ones in the sketchier neighborhoods, such as the Mission, because they're mostly used by crackheads and prostitutes. Toilets can also be found in hotel lobbies, bars, restaurants, museums, department stores, railway and bus stations, gas stations, and fast-food joints; though restaurants and bars in resorts or heavily visited areas may reserve them for patrons.

San Francisco is an extensive—and expensive—hotel town, especially considering its relatively small size. I can't cover all the options in this guide; for a larger selection, check out *Frommer's San Francisco* (Wiley Publishing, Inc.), which details dozens of other lodging choices.

Most of the hotels listed below are within walking distance of Union Square and accessible via cable car. Union Square is near the city's major shops, the Financial District, and all transportation. Prices listed below do not include state and city taxes, which total 14%.

When reading over your options, keep in mind that prices listed are "rack" (published) rates. At big, upscale hotels, almost no one actually pays them, and there are always deals to be had. Therefore, you should always ask for special discounts or, even better, vacation packages. It's often possible to get the room you want for $100 less than what is quoted here, except when the hotels are packed (usually during summer and due to conventions) and bargaining is close to impossible. Use the rates listed here for the big hotels as guidelines for comparison only; prices for inexpensive choices and smaller B&Bs are closer to reality, however.

San Francisco Reservations, 360 22nd St., Suite 300, Oakland, CA 94612 (© **800/ 677-1500** or 510/628-4450; www.hotelres.com), arranges reservations for more than 150 of San Francisco's hotels and often offers discounted rates. Their nifty website allows Internet users to make reservations online. Other good online sites with discounted rates include **www.hotels.com** and **www.placestostay.com**.

UNION SQUARE
Very Expensive
Campton Place Hotel ★★   This luxury boutique hotel offers some of the best accommodations in town—not to mention the most expensive. Rooms are compact but comfy, with limestone, pear wood, and Italian-modern decor. The two executive suites and one luxury suite push the haute envelope to even more luxurious heights. Discriminating guests will find superlative service, California king-size beds, exquisite bathrooms, bathrobes, top-notch toiletries, slippers, and every other necessity and extra that's made Campton Place a favored temporary address. Alas, Campton Place Restaurant lost its award-winning chef Daniel Humm in 2005, but the restaurant still offers a respectable French/California menu. The jury's still out on whether it's a destination in its own right.

340 Stockton St. (btw. Post and Sutter sts.), San Francisco, CA 94108. © **866/332-1670** or 415/781-5555. Fax 415/955-5536. www.camptonplace.com. 110 units. $350–$485 double; $585–$2,000 suite. American breakfast $18. AE, DC, MC, V. Valet parking $38. Bus: 2, 3, 4, 30, 38, or 45. Cable car: Powell–Hyde or Powell–Mason lines (1 block west). BART: Market St. **Amenities:** Restaurant; outdoor fitness terrace; concierge; secretarial services; room service; laundry service; same-day dry cleaning. *In room:* A/C, TV w/ pay movies, minibar, hair dryer, iron, safe, T1 line.

Hotel Monaco ★★   This remodeled 1910 Beaux Arts building has plenty of atmosphere thanks to a whimsically ethereal lobby with a two-story French inglenook fireplace. The guest rooms, which were upgraded in 2006, follow suit, with canopy beds, Asian-inspired armoires, bamboo writing desks, lively stripes, and vibrant color. Everything is bold but tasteful, and rooms are as playful as they are serious, with such nifty extras as flatscreen TVs and complimentary Wi-Fi. The decor, combined with the truly

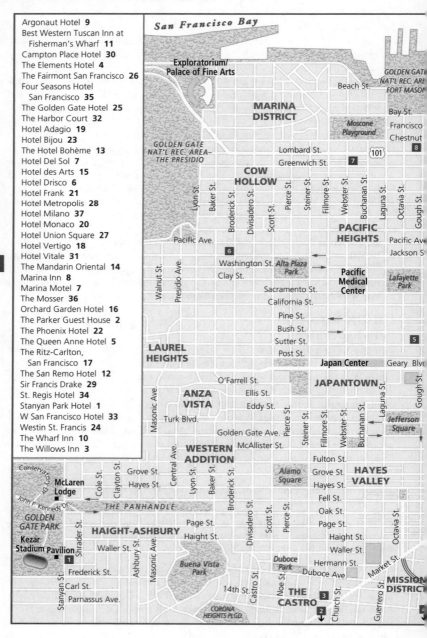

SAN FRANCISCO

5

WHERE TO STAY

Argonaut Hotel **9**
Best Western Tuscan Inn at
 Fisherman's Wharf **11**
Campton Place Hotel **30**
The Elements Hotel **4**
The Fairmont San Francisco **26**
Four Seasons Hotel
 San Francisco **35**
The Golden Gate Hotel **25**
The Harbor Court **32**
Hotel Adagio **19**
Hotel Bijou **23**
The Hotel Bohème **13**
Hotel Del Sol **7**
Hotel des Arts **15**
Hotel Drisco **6**
Hotel Frank **21**
Hotel Metropolis **28**
Hotel Milano **37**
Hotel Monaco **20**
Hotel Union Square **27**
Hotel Vertigo **18**
Hotel Vitale **31**
The Mandarin Oriental **14**
Marina Inn **8**
Marina Motel **7**
The Mosser **36**
Orchard Garden Hotel **16**
The Parker Guest House **2**
The Phoenix Hotel **22**
The Queen Anne Hotel **5**
The Ritz-Carlton,
 San Francisco **17**
The San Remo Hotel **12**
Sir Francis Drake **29**
St. Regis Hotel **34**
Stanyan Park Hotel **1**
W San Francisco Hotel **33**
Westin St. Francis **24**
The Wharf Inn **10**
The Willows Inn **3**

San Francisco Bay

Exploratorium/
Palace of Fine Arts

GOLDEN GATE
NAT'L REC. AREA
FORT MASON

Beach St.

**MARINA
DISTRICT**

Bay St.

*Moscone
Playground*

Francisco
Chestnut

8

GOLDEN GATE
NAT'L REC. AREA–
THE PRESIDIO

Lombard St.

101

7

Greenwich St.

**COW
HOLLOW**

Lyon St.
Baker St.
Broderick St.
Divisadero St.
Scott St.
Pierce St.
Steiner St.
Fillmore St.
Webster St.
Buchanan St.
Laguna St.
Octavia St.
Gough St.

**PACIFIC
HEIGHTS**

Pacific Ave.
Jackson St.

Pacific Ave.

6

Walnut St.
Presidio Ave.

Washington St.
Clay St.

*Alta Plaza
Park*

**Pacific
Medical
Center**

*Lafayette
Park*

Sacramento St.
California St.
Pine St.
Bush St.
Sutter St.
Post St.

5

**LAUREL
HEIGHTS**

Japan Center

Geary Blvd.

O'Farrell St.
Ellis St.
Eddy St.

Masonic Ave.

**ANZA
VISTA**

JAPANTOWN

Laguna St.
Gough St.

Turk Blvd.

Pierce St.
Steiner St.
Fillmore St.
Webster St.
Buchanan St.

*Jefferson
Square*

Golden Gate Ave.

McAllister St.

**WESTERN
ADDITION**

Central Ave.

Fulton St.

Conservatory Dr.

McLaren
Lodge

Grove St.
Hayes St.

Cole St.
Clayton St.

Lyon St.
Baker St.
Broderick St.

*Alamo
Square*

Grove St.
Hayes St.

**HAYES
VALLEY**

John F. Kennedy Dr.

THE PANHANDLE

Page St.

Fell St.
Oak St.
Page St.

Octavia St.

**GOLDEN
GATE PARK**

Shrader St.

HAIGHT-ASHBURY

Masonic Ave.

Haight St.

Divisadero St.
Scott St.
Pierce St.

Haight St.

Kezar
Stadium

Pavilion

1

Ashbury St.

Waller St.

Waller St.

*Buena Vista
Park*

*Duboce
Park*

Hermann St.
Duboce Ave.

Market St.

**MISSION
DISTRICT**

Stanyan St.

Frederick St.
Carl St.
Parnassus Ave.

14th St.

Noe St.
Castro St.

**THE
CASTRO**

3

2

Church St.

Guerrero St.

*CORONA
HEIGHTS PLGD.*

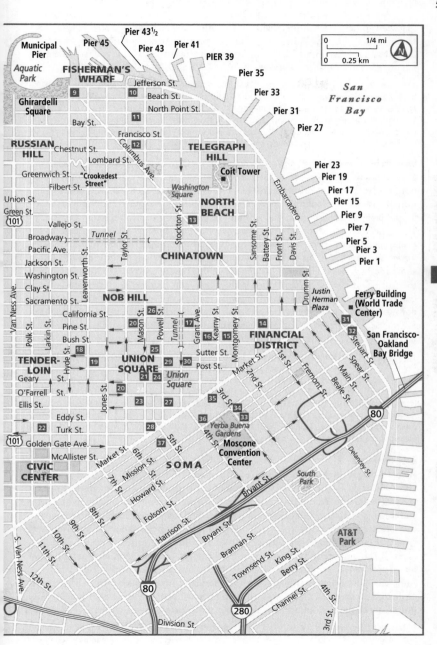

grand neighboring Grand Café restaurant that's ideal for cocktails and mingling (but also serves breakfast and lunch), would put this place on my top-10 list if it weren't for rooms that tend to be too small (especially for the price) and the lack of a sizable gym. That said, it's a fine Union Square option, which happens to include complimentary wine and cheese tasting, accompanied by shoulder and neck massages. *Tip:* If you were/are a big fan of Jefferson Airplane, inquire about their Grace Slick Shrine Suite.

501 Geary St. (at Taylor St.), San Francisco, CA 94102. (C) **866/622-5284** or 415/292-0100. Fax 415/292-0111. www.monaco-sf.com. 201 units. $229–$409 double; $279–$619 suite. Rates include evening wine and cheese tasting. Call for discounted rates. AE, DC, DISC, MC, V. Valet parking $39. Bus: 2, 3, 4, 27, or 38. Pets accepted. **Amenities:** Restaurant; exercise room; spa; Jacuzzi; sauna; steam room; concierge; courtesy car; business center; room service; in-room massage; laundry service; dry cleaning. *In room:* A/C, TV, Wi-Fi, minibar, coffeemaker w/Starbucks coffee, hair dryer, iron, safe, CD player.

Westin St. Francis ★★ (Kids) At the turn of the 20th century, Charles T. Crocker and a few of his wealthy buddies decided that San Francisco needed a world-class hotel, and up went the St. Francis. Since then, hordes of VIPs have hung their hats and hosiery here, including Emperor Hirohito of Japan, Queen Elizabeth II, Mother Teresa, King Juan Carlos of Spain, the shah of Iran, and all the U.S. presidents from Taft through Clinton. In 1972, the hotel added the 32-story Tower, doubling its capacity. The older rooms of the main building vary in size and have more old-world charm than the newer rooms, but the Tower is remarkable for its great views of the city (including from the glass elevators) from above the 18th floor. The hotel has done massive renovations, costing $185 million over the past decade, replacing the carpeting, furniture, and bedding in every main-building guest room; gussying up the lobby; restoring the facade; and adding one of the hottest downtown dining spots, the very expensive and fancy **Michael Mina** (p. 94). Although the St. Francis is too massive to offer the personal service you get at the smaller deluxe hotels on Nob Hill, few other hotels in San Francisco can match its majestic aura.

335 Powell St. (btw. Geary and Post sts.), San Francisco, CA 94102. (C) **866/500-0038** or 415/397-7000. Fax 415/774-0124. www.westinstfrancis.com. 1,195 units. Main building: $229–$529 double; Tower (Grand View): $219–$559 double; from $650 suite (in either building). Extra person $30. Continental breakfast $15–$18. AE, DC, DISC, MC, V. Valet parking $42. Bus: 2, 3, 4, 30, 38, 45, or 76. Cable car: Powell–Hyde or Powell–Mason lines (direct stop). Pets under 40 lb. accepted (dog beds available on request). **Amenities:** 2 restaurants; elaborate health club and spa; concierge; car-rental desk; business center; room service. *In room:* A/C, TV, high-speed Internet access ($15), Wi-Fi ($9.95/day), minibar, fridge available upon request, hair dryer, iron, cordless phones.

Expensive

Hotel Adagio ★★ (Value) Our local hip-hotel company, Joie de Vivre, revamped every one of this 1929 Spanish Revival hotel's 171 large, bright guest rooms in gorgeous modern style. They're real lookers, each with a walnut brown and mocha color palette and dark wood furnishings. Other pluses include firm mattresses, double-paned windows that open, quiet surroundings, voice mail, and plenty of elbowroom. Executive floors (7–16) also come with robes, upscale amenities, makeup mirrors, and stereos with iPod ports. Bathrooms are old but spotless and have resurfaced tubs. Feel like splurging? Go for one of the two penthouse-level suites; one has lovely terraces with a New York vibe. Another good reason to stay here is the restaurant/bar **Cortez,** which draws a lively crowd of locals who meet here after work to nosh on small plates in the groovy lounge. *Tip:* Rooms above the eighth floor have good, but not great, views of the city.

550 Geary St., San Francisco, CA 94102. (C) **800/228-8830** or 415/775-5000. Fax 415/775-9388. www.the hoteladagio.com. 171 units. $189–$279 double. AE, DISC, MC, V. Valet parking $35. **Amenities:** Restaurant;

bar; fitness center; concierge; business center w/free wireless Internet; room service; laundry service; dry cleaning; luggage storage room. *In room:* TV w/Nintendo and pay movies, free high-speed Internet access, minibar, fridge, hair dryer, iron, safe, CD player.

The Orchard Garden Hotel ★★   If Al Gore was a hotelier, this would be his hotel. The new $25-million Orchard Garden Hotel is California's first generation of truly "green" hotels and the only hotel in the state that was built to the nationally accepted standards for green buildings developed by the U.S. Green Building Council (USGBC). From the ecofriendly construction materials to an in-room recycling system and the use of organic cleaning products, this vanguard property is geared toward creating a healthy environment for guests and staff. It's also the first hotel in the city to use the European-style keycard system that turns power off to the entire room each time you leave. But going green doesn't mean you have to sacrifice comfort—yes, that's Egyptian cotton linen on the king-size bed, real feather down in the pillows, and plush spa-style robes in the closet. The 86 guest rooms are super-insulated and very quiet. Spacious bathrooms come with Aveda bath products (organic, of course). High-tech toys include HD LCD TVs, DVD/CD players, and iPod docking stations. The hotel also has a pleasant rooftop garden, a small fitness center (and $15 passes to Club One), and the lobby-level **Roots Restaurant**, which serves contemporary American cuisine made from locally sourced organic products. The hotel's location is ideal, with Chinatown, Union Square, and the Financial District all just a short walk away. *Note:* If the hotel is fully booked, inquire about their sister property—the Orchard Hotel—up the street.

466 Bush St. (at Grant St.), San Francisco, CA 94108. ℂ **888/717-2881** or 415/399-9807. Fax 415/393-9917. www.theorchardgardenhotel.com. 82 units. $169–$499 double. AE, DC, DISC, MC, V. Valet parking $24. Cable car: Powell–Hyde or Powell–Mason lines. **Amenities:** Restaurant; fitness center; concierge; morning car service to Financial District; business center; free DVD library; bicycle storage. *In room:* A/C, flatscreen HDTV, DVD/CD player, Wi-Fi, minibar, coffeemaker, hair dryer, iron, safe, robes, cordless phone, iPod docking station.

Sir Francis Drake ★★   This landmark hotel is one of San Francisco's grand dames, operating continuously since 1928, in the heart of Union Square. The Kimpton Hotel company has done a wonderful job renovating the hotel (which has been sorely needed since I was a kid), giving this elegant lady a much-needed makeover. I've always been a fan of the Hotel Monaco's modern, slightly offbeat interiors with bold patterns and custom furnishings, and they've incorporated a similar style at this property, though with a cream and sage color scheme. It's always a pleasure to have Tom Sweeny, the ebullient (and legendary) Beefeater doorman, handle your bags as you enter the elegant, captivating lobby, with its gilded high ceilings, glittering crystal chandeliers, and massive curved marble staircase that leads to a mezzanine overlooking bustling Powell Street.

   Scala's Bistro (p. 98), one of the most festive restaurants downtown, serves good Italian cuisine in a stylish setting on the first floor; the Italian-style Caffe Espresso does an equally commendable job serving coffees, pastries, and sandwiches daily in its spot adjacent to the hotel. **Harry Denton's Starlight Room** (p. 148), on the 21st floor, offers cocktails, entertainment, and dancing nightly, with a panoramic view of the city.

450 Powell St. (at Sutter St.), San Francisco, CA 94102. ℂ **800/795-7129** or 415/392-7755. Fax 415/391-8719. www.sirfrancisdrake.com. 417 units. $239–$289 double; from $5,200 suite. AE, DC, DISC, MC, V. Valet parking $38. Bus: 2, 3, 4, 45, or 76. Cable car: Powell–Hyde or Powell–Mason lines (direct stop). Pets welcome. **Amenities:** 2 restaurants; bar; exercise room; concierge; Wi-Fi; limited room service; same-day laundry service/dry cleaning. *In room:* A/C, TV w/movies on demand, free Wi-Fi, minibar, hair dryer, iron.

Hotel Frank ★★   Only a block from Union Square, this former Maxwell Hotel is the new darling among hip business travelers and serious shoppers. A major renovation and a clever interior makeover in the fall of 2008 brought the hotel to a far more upscale, boutique-hotel standard. The guest rooms—each with 32-inch flatscreen TVs and iPod docking stations—exude a custom designer look: houndstooth-patterned carpeting, elongated emerald green headboards in crocodile-patterned leather, sleek white leather couches, vintage 1930s artwork. Even the bathrooms are outfitted in floor-to-ceiling Carrara marble. The hotel's 28 roomy junior suites offer excellent value despite the slightly audible elevator noise, but best of all are the pair of one-bedroom penthouses on the 13th floor, both of which offer separate living rooms and exceptional views of the city.

386 Geary St. (at Mason St.), San Francisco, CA 94102. ✆ **800/553-1900** or 415/986-2000. www.personalityhotels.com. 153 units. $169–$399 double; $209–$469 junior suite; $499–$1,200 penthouse suite. AE, DC, DISC, MC, V. Valet parking $30. Bus: 2, 3, 4, 30, 38, or 45. Cable car: Powell–Hyde or Powell–Mason lines (1 block east). **Amenities:** Concierge; 24-hr. business center; meeting facilities; room service; same-day dry cleaning. *In room:* A/C, TV w/pay movies, free Wi-Fi, honor bar, hair dryer, iron, safe, bathrobes.

Hotel Metropolis ★ (Kids) (Finds)   Just off of Market Street, a few blocks from Union Square, the Hotel Metropolis is the antithesis of the corporate, frumpy McHotel. In the lobby, colorful (and curiously abstract) art created by children mixes with a cascading slate-wall waterfall for a feeling of playful serenity. As with most downtown hotels, the rooms are on the small side, but all are vibrant and cheery, with custom African Limba-wood furnishings and comfy beds with wave-shaped porthole headboards. The six Executive Rooms on the 10th floor are upgraded with feather beds and pillows, iPod alarm clocks, and robes, while the three-room Urban Explorers Kids Suite—which sleeps up to six adults and three children—is filled with pint-size furniture, bunk beds, a computer, a chalkboard wall, and bath toys. After a busy day in the city, you can relax with a bit of yoga or meditation in the hotel's "well-being room," or enjoy a cup of tea and a good read in the book-filled loft/library. Additional perks include complimentary room service via the adjacent Farmer Brown's restaurant ("farm-fresh soul food"), a 24-hour business center with complimentary computers and laser printers, free high-speed wireless Internet, and a 24-hour exercise room. All this and rates starting at $99 make the Hotel Metropolis a real find.

25 Mason St. (at Turk and Market sts.), San Francisco, CA 94102. ✆ **800/553-1900** or 415/775-4600. www.hotelmetropolis.com. 105 units. $99–$289 double; $159–$369 suite. AE, DC, DISC, MC, V. Valet parking $30. Bus: All Market St. buses. Streetcar: Powell St. station. **Amenities:** Exercise room; business center; room service; same-day laundry service/dry cleaning. *In room:* TV w/PPV, free Wi-Fi, hair dryer, iron.

Hotel Milano ★   Neoclassical Italian design patterned after Giorgio Armani's villa in Milan, elegantly streamlined rooms (with double-paned soundproof windows), moderate prices, and a central location next to the San Francisco Centre make Hotel Milano a popular choice for tourists and businesspeople alike. The hotel also has a film-production facility and private screening room to entice media types. Corporate travelers come for the spacious guest rooms, which feature everything an executive could want, from wireless Internet to video game systems and work desks. Suites have spa tubs and bidets.

55 Fifth St. (btw. Market and Mission sts.), San Francisco, CA 94103. ✆ **800/398-7555** or 415/543-8555. Fax 415/543-5885. www.hotelmilanosf.com. 108 units. $109–$199 double. Extra person $20. AE, DC, DISC, MC, V. Valet parking $33. Bus: All Market St. buses. **Amenities:** Fitness room; spa; steam room and sauna; concierge; laundry; valet. *In room:* A/C, TV w/video games, fax, Wi-Fi ($9.95/day), fridge, hair dryer, iron, safe.

Hotel Union Square ★★ Built for the 1915 Pan Pacific Exposition, San Francisco's first boutique hotel underwent a $5-million renovation in early 2008. The renovation juxtaposes contemporary and classic San Francisco, with original 1915 Egyptian-motif mosaic murals, signature staircases, completely remodeled bathrooms, and state-of-the-art technology. It's only a half-block from Union Square, in the heart of the city with cable cars passing by your window. The guest rooms feel more like urban apartments, each outfitted with platform beds with custom-made leather headboards, 600-thread-count linens, velvety chaise longues, flatscreen televisions, and custom lighting. Many have an open loftlike layout, with exposed brick walls, while the two rooftop penthouses are the ultimate in San Francisco chic, with large living rooms, wet bars, and expansive redwood decks with city views. The hotel also offers a custom Kids Suite, a Dashiell Hammett–themed suite, and "Sleep & Soak" rooms on each floor that feature spalike bathrooms outfitted with corner soaking tubs and chaise longues. Guests have complimentary use of the adjacent Hotel Diva fitness center, and Tad's Steakhouse provides complimentary delivery service.

114 Powell St. (btw. O'Farrell and Ellis sts.), San Francisco, CA 94102. ℭ **800/553-1900** or 415/397-3000. www.hotelunionsquare.com. 131 units. $149–$349 double; $199–$499 suite; $229–$799 penthouse suites. Rates include morning coffee and tea and weekday wine reception. AE, DC, DISC, MC, V. Valet parking $30. Bus: 2, 3, 4, 30, 38, 45, or 76. Cable car: Powell–Hyde or Powell–Mason lines. Streetcar: Powell St. station. **Amenities:** 24-hr. business center; room service; same-day laundry service/dry cleaning; on-site currency exchange. *In room:* TV w/PPV, free Wi-Fi, hair dryer, iron.

Hotel Vertigo ★★ I've gotten insider info that the York Hotel, currently under renovation and scheduled to reopen in fall '08 as Hotel Vertigo (the hotel occupies the former site of the Empire Hotel made famous in Alfred Hitchcock's *Vertigo*), will be *the* hot new place to stay and play in San Francisco. Locally based Personality Hotels paired cutting-edge design company Thomas Schoos Design, Inc., with celebrity chef Tyler Florence (who will open his first-ever restaurant, Bar Florence, within the hotel) to create a hotel with instant celebrity status. The restaurant's salon-style seating and Florence's shared-plates menu will bring in the locals, while Schoos's stylistic design elements will attract tourists and business travelers looking for an alternative to the W Hotel. Guest rooms will feature playful, eclectic designs such as white tufted-leather headboards, custom wingback chairs in vibrant orange, and crocodile-patterned tiles in the bathrooms. iPod docking stations and 36-inch flatscreen televisions will be standard as well. With room rates starting at $169 (half that of the W), it's a safe bet that the Vertigo will be one of the hottest new hotels in town.

940 Sutter St. (btw. Leavenworth and Hyde sts.), San Francisco, CA 94109. ℭ **800/553-1900** or 415/885-6800. www.personalityhotels.com. 97 units. $169–$399 double; $350–$495 suite. Rates include morning beverages in lobby and express breakfast. AE, DISC, MC, V. Valet parking $30. Bus: 2, 3, or 4. **Amenities:** Fitness room; concierge; business center; room service; same-day dry cleaning; overnight shoeshine. *In room:* TV w/pay movies, free Wi-Fi, hair dryer, iron, safe, robes.

Inexpensive

The Golden Gate Hotel ★ (Value) San Francisco's stock of small hotels in historic turn-of-the-20th-century buildings includes some real gems, and the Golden Gate Hotel is one of them. It's 2 blocks north of Union Square and 2 blocks down (literally) from the crest of Nob Hill, with cable car stops at the corner for easy access to Fisherman's Wharf and Chinatown. The city's theaters and best restaurants are also within walking distance. But the best thing about the 1913 Edwardian hotel—which definitely has a B&B feel—is that it's family run: John and Renate Kenaston and daughter Gabriele are hospitable innkeepers who take obvious pleasure in making their guests comfortable. Each individually decorated room has recently been repainted and carpeted and has handsome antique furnishings (plenty of wicker) from the early 1900s, quilted bedspreads, and fresh flowers. Request a room with a claw-foot tub if you enjoy a good, hot soak. Afternoon tea is served daily from 4 to 7pm, and guests are welcome to use the house fax and computer with wireless Internet free of charge.

775 Bush St. (btw. Powell and Mason sts.), San Francisco, CA 94108. © **800/835-1118** or 415/392-3702. Fax 415/392-6202. www.goldengatehotel.com. 25 units, 14 with bathroom. $85–$105 double without bathroom; $150 double with bathroom. Rates include continental breakfast and afternoon tea. AE, DC, MC, V. Self-parking $20. Bus: 2, 4, 30, 38, or 45. Cable car: Powell–Hyde or Powell–Mason lines (1 block east). BART: Powell and Market. **Amenities:** Access to health club 1 block away; activities desk; laundry service/dry cleaning next door. *In room:* TV, free Wi-Fi, hair dryer and iron upon request.

Hotel Bijou ★ (Value

Three words sum up this hotel: clean, colorful, and cheap. Although it's on the periphery of the gritty Tenderloin (just 3 blocks off Union Sq.), once inside this gussied-up 1911 hotel, all's cheery, bright, and perfect for budget travelers who want a little style with their savings. Joie de Vivre hotel group disguised the hotel's age with lively decor, a Deco theater theme, and a heck of a lot of vibrant paint. To the left of the small lobby is a "theater," where guests can watch San Francisco–based double features nightly (it has cute old-fashioned theater seating, though it's just a basic TV showing videos). Upstairs, rooms named after locally made films are small, clean, and colorful (think buttercup, burgundy, and purple), and have all the basics from clock radios, dressers, and small desks to tiny bathrooms (one of which is so small you have to close the door to access the toilet). Alas, a few mattresses could be firmer, and the lone elevator is small and slow. But considering the price—and such perks as the continental breakfast and friendly service—you can't go wrong.

111 Mason St., San Francisco, CA 94102. © **800/771-1022** or 415/771-1200. Fax 415/346-3196. www.hotelbijou.com. 65 units. $99–$159 double. Rates include continental breakfast. AE, DC, DISC, MC, V. Valet parking $27. Bus: All Market St. buses. Streetcar: Powell St. station. **Amenities:** Concierge; DSL access in lobby ($4/20 min.); limited room service; same-day laundry service/dry cleaning. *In room:* TV, high-speed Internet access, Wi-Fi ($7.95/day), hair dryer, iron.

Hotel des Arts ★★ (Value

While this bargain find has the same floor plan as San Francisco's numerous other Euro-style hotels—small lobby, narrow hallways, cramped rooms—the owners of the des Arts have made an obvious effort to distance themselves from the competition by including a visually stimulating dose of artistic license throughout the hotel. The lobby, for example, hosts a rotating art gallery featuring contemporary works by emerging local artists and is outfitted with groovy furnishings, while the guest rooms are soothingly situated with quality furnishings and tasteful accouterments. There's one suite that can sleep up to four persons at no additional charge. You'll love the lively location as well: right across the street from the entrance to Chinatown and 2 blocks from Union Square. There's even a French brasserie right downstairs. Rooms with very clean shared bathrooms start at $59, making it quite possibly the best budget hotel in the city.

447 Bush St. (at Grant St.), San Francisco, CA 94108. © **800/956-4322** or 415/956-3232. Fax 415/956-0399. www.sfhoteldesarts.com. 51 units, 26 with private bathroom. $79–$159 double with bathroom; $59–$79 double without bathroom. Rates include continental breakfast. AE, DC, MC, V. Nearby parking $18. Cable car: Powell–Hyde and Powell–Mason lines. **Amenities:** 24-hr. concierge, fax, and copy services; laundry and valet service. *In room:* TV, minifridge and microwave in many rooms, hair dryer, iron/ironing board.

Very Expensive

The Mandarin Oriental ★★★ No hotel combines better ultraluxury digs with incredible views than this gem. The only reason to pause in the lobby or mezzanine is for the traditional tea service or cocktails. Otherwise, heaven begins after a rocketing ride on the elevators to the rooms, all of which are located between the 38th and 48th floors of a high-rise. The opulent rooms also feature contemporary Asian-influenced decor, but the best details by far are the huge windows with superb city views, particularly when the fog rolls in below you. Not all rooms have tub-side views (incredible and standard with the signature rooms), but every one does have a luxurious marble bathroom stocked with terry and cotton cloth robes, a makeup mirror, and silk slippers. An added bonus: The restaurant, **Silks,** has a kitchen crew working wonders with the Asian-influenced menu. If the dining room weren't so awkwardly empty, it'd be a recommended destination. That said, even without the entire package, it's an excellent place to dine.

222 Sansome St. (btw. Pine and California sts.), San Francisco, CA 94104. © **800/622-0404** or 415/276-9888. Fax 415/433-0289. www.mandarinoriental.com. 158 units. $375–$725 double; $645–$695 signature rooms; from $1,450 suite. Continental breakfast $21; American breakfast $32. AE, DC, DISC, MC, V. Valet parking $36. Bus: All Market St. buses. Streetcar: J, K, L, or M to Montgomery. **Amenities:** Restaurant; bar; fitness center; concierge; car rental; business center; room service; in-room massage; laundry service; same-day dry cleaning. *In room:* A/C, TV w/pay movies, fax on request, Wi-Fi ($13/day), minibar, hair dryer, iron, safe, CD player.

SOMA

Very Expensive

Four Seasons Hotel San Francisco ★★★ What makes this überluxury hotel that opened in late 2001 one of my favorites in the city is its perfect combination of elegance, trendiness, and modern luxury. The entrance, either off Market or through a narrow alley off Third Street, is deceptively underwhelming, although in keeping with the hotel's overall discreetness. Take the elevators up to the lobby and you're instantly surrounded by calm, cool, and collected hotel perfection: dark mood lighting, comfy leather chairs, bottomless bowls of olives and spicy wasabi-covered peanuts, a tempting cocktail list, and a pianist playing jazz standards intermingled with No Doubt and Coldplay. Many of the oversize rooms (starting at 460 sq. ft. and including 46 suites) overlook Yerba Buena Gardens. Not too trendy, not too traditional, they're just right, with custom-made mattresses and pillows that guarantee the all-time best night's sleep, beautiful works of art, and huge luxury marble bathrooms with deep tubs and L'Occitane toiletries. Hues of taupe, beige, and green are almost as soothing as the impeccable service. Adding to the perks are free access to the building's huge Sports Club L.A. (the best hotel gym in the city), a 2-block walk to Union Square, and a vibe that combines sophistication with a hipness far more refined than the W or the Clift. Its only contender in that department is the St. Regis.

757 Market St. (btw. Third and Fourth sts.), San Francisco, CA 94103. © **800/819-5053** or 415/633-3000. Fax 415/633-3001. www.fourseasons.com/sanfrancisco. 277 units. $450–$855 double; $825 executive suite. AE, DC, DISC, MC, V. Parking $39. Bus: All Market St. buses. Streetcar: F, and all underground streetcars. BART: All trains. **Amenities:** Restaurant; bar; huge fitness center; spa; concierge; high-tech business center; secretarial services; Wi-Fi in lobby; salon; room service; in-room massage; overnight laundry service/dry cleaning. *In room:* A/C, TV w/pay movies, fax, high-speed Internet access ($13/day), minibar, hair dryer, safe.

St. Regis Hotel ★★★ The latest in full-blown high-tech luxury is yours at this überchic 40-story SoMa tower, which debuted in late 2005. Near the Museum of Modern Art and Yerba Buena Gardens, this shrine to urban luxury welcomes guests (and residents willing to pay upwards of $2 million for an apartment) with a 16-foot-long gas fireplace and streamlined lobby bar that's frequented by city socialites. A "personal butler" will take you to your room and show you how to use its coolest feature: a touchscreen control panel that works everything from the phone to the drapes to the temperature to the lights. Decor is minimalist, with such sexy touches as Barcelona benches, 42-inch plasma TVs, and leather paneling (at least in the suites). Bathrooms beckon with deep soaking tubs, 13-inch LCD TVs, rainforest shower heads, and fancy toiletries. You may want to lounge on a chaise and peek into the happenings of the downtown bustle or the Gardens, but definitely make time for an afternoon at the posh two-floor **Remède Spa,** the huge pool and fitness center, and restaurant **Ame,** where Chef Hiro Sone, who also owns Terra, in Napa Valley, presides over an Asian-influenced menu that includes delicacies, such as *hamachi* sashimi, and decadences such as foie gras and *unagi* (eel) over mushroom risotto.

125 Third St. (at Mission St.), San Francisco, CA 94103. © **877/787-3447** or 415/284-4000. Fax 415/284-4100. www.stregis.com/sanfrancisco. 260 units. From $529–$679 double; from $1,050–$8,500 suite. AE, DC, DISC, MC, V. Parking $45/day. Bus: 15, 30, or 45. Streetcar: J, K, L, or M to Montgomery. **Amenities:** 2 restaurants; bar; health club w/heated lap pool; giant spa; whirlpool; steam room; sauna; 24-hr. concierge; 24-hr. business center; Wi-Fi ($15/day); conference rooms; room service; laundry service; dry cleaning. *In room:* A/C, 2 TVs w/pay movies, fax, high-speed Internet access ($15/day), printer, scanner, copier, minibar, hair dryer, iron upon request, safe.

W San Francisco Hotel ★★ Starwood Hotels & Resorts' 31-story property is as modern and hip as its fashionable clientele. Sophisticated, slick, and stylish, it suits its neighbors, which include the Museum of Modern Art, the Moscone Center, and the Metreon entertainment center. The hip, urban guest rooms have a residential feel. Each contains a feather bed with a goose-down comforter and pillows, Waterworks linens, an oversize dark-wood desk, an upholstered chaise longue, and louvered blinds that open to (usually) great city views. Each room also contains a Sony CD/DVD player, extensive CD library, and 27-inch TV with optional high-speed Internet service. Bathrooms are super-sleek and stocked with Bliss products. Furthering the cool vibe is a bi-level **XYZ** bar and restaurant, which serves wonderful Californian cuisine within a beautiful modern interior. In 2005, the W welcomed a 5,000-square-foot outpost of NYC's **Bliss Spa** to the premises. All in all, this is one of the top places to stay in San Francisco, particularly if you enjoy nightlife.

181 Third St. (btw. Mission and Howard sts.), San Francisco, CA 94103. © **877/WHOTELS** or 415/777-5300. Fax 415/817-7823. www.whotels.com/sanfrancisco. 410 units. From $359 double; $1,800–$2,500 suite. AE, DC, DISC, MC, V. Valet parking $40. Bus: 15, 30, or 45. Streetcar: J, K, L, or M to Montgomery. **Amenities:** Restaurant; 2 bars; heated atrium pool and Jacuzzi; fitness center; spa; concierge; business center; secretarial services; Wi-Fi in public spaces; 24-hr. room service; same-day laundry service/dry cleaning. *In room:* A/C, TV w/pay movies, DVD/CD player, fax (in some rooms), high-speed Internet access ($15/day), minibar, coffeemaker, hair dryer, iron, safe.

Expensive
The Harbor Court ★★ When the Embarcadero Freeway was torn down after the Big One in 1989, one of the major benefactors was the "wellness-themed" Harbor Court hotel: The 1926 landmark building's backyard view went from a wall of cement to a dazzling vista of the Bay Bridge (request a bayview room, for an extra fee). Just off the

Embarcadero at the edge of the Financial District, this former YMCA books a lot of corporate travelers, but anyone who seeks stylish, high-quality rooms—half-canopy beds; large armoires; writing desks; soundproof windows; new beds, bedding, and carpet; and 27-inch LCD TVs in 2005—with superb views and a lively scene will be perfectly content here. A major bonus is the free use of the adjoining fitness club, a top-quality YMCA facility with a giant indoor swimming pool. There's a daily hosted evening wine reception, and the adjacent **Ozumo Sushi Bar and Robata Grill** has a hugely popular happy hour and wonderful cuisine.

165 Steuart St. (btw. Mission and Howard sts.), San Francisco, CA 94105. © **866/792-6283** or 415/882-1300. Fax 415/882-1313. www.harborcourthotel.com. 131 units. $195–$425 double. Continental breakfast $10. AE, DC, DISC, MC, V. Parking $35. Bus: 14 or 80x. Streetcar: Embarcadero. Pets accepted. **Amenities:** Access to adjoining health club and large, heated indoor pool; courtesy car weekday mornings; room service (breakfast only); same-day laundry service/dry cleaning; safe. *In room:* A/C, TV, free Wi-Fi, minibar, hair dryer, iron.

Hotel Vitale ★★　Perched at the foot of the Embarcadero with outstanding waterfront and Bay Bridge views from east-facing rooms, this 199-unit hotel opened in early 2005 to instant popularity. In addition to its prime location across from the Ferry Building Marketplace (p. 122), Hotel Vitale looks pretty darned chic, from the clean-lined lobby, lounge, and decent **Americano** restaurant (with a hopping after-work bar scene), to the modern and masculine rooms armed with such contemporary perks as flatscreen TVs, CD players with groovy compilations, gourmet minibars, for-sale bath products, and huge bathrooms with walk-in showers. Despite excellent service from the well-trained staff, a few subtleties separate Vitale from true luxury hotel status: My fancy flatscreen TV didn't face the bed or the couch and didn't swivel, and the fitness room is flat-out lame. However, they're now offering complimentary access to the nearby YMCA health club, which has all the workout essentials. But if you can live with a few quirks, it's a very attractive place to stay; especially if you book one of the suites with 270-degree San Francisco views.

8 Mission St. (at Embarcadero), San Francisco, CA 94105. © **888/890-8868** or 415/278-3700. Fax 415/278-3750. www.hotelvitale.com. 199 units. $269–$399 double; from $699 suite. Rates include morning paper, free morning yoga, and free courtesy car to downtown locations on weekdays. AE, DC, DISC, MC, V. Valet parking $42. Bus: 2, 7, 14, 21, 71, or 71L. **Amenities:** Restaurant; exercise room; spa; concierge; business center; free Internet salon; free Wi-Fi; room service; laundry service; dry cleaning. *In room:* A/C, TV w/pay movies, high-speed Internet access, Wi-Fi, minibar, hair dryer, iron, safe, CD player.

Moderate

The Mosser ★ (Value　"Hip on the Cheap" might best sum up the Mosser, a highly atypical budget hotel that incorporates Victorian architecture with modern interior design. It originally opened in 1913 as a luxury hotel only to be dwarfed by the far more modern sky-rise hotels that now surround it. But a major multimillion-dollar renovation transformed this aging charmer into a sophisticated, stylish, and surprisingly affordable SoMa lodging. Guest rooms are replete with original Victorian flourishes—bay windows and hand-carved moldings—that juxtapose well with the contemporary custom-designed furnishings, granite showers, stainless steel fixtures, Frette linens, double-paned windows, and modern electronics. The least expensive rooms are quite small and share a bathroom, but they are an incredible deal for a central location—3 blocks from Union Square, 2 blocks from the MOMA and Moscone Convention Center, and half a block from the cable car turnaround. The hotel's restaurant, **Annabelle's Bar & Bistro,** serves lunch and dinner, and the Mosser houses Studio Paradiso, a state-of-the-art recording studio.

(Finds) **Elements: A Hip Mission District Hotel**

Bad credit? No problem. There's finally a place for the perpetually young and broke to stay and play in the heart of the Mission District. The **Elements Hotel** is sort of a cross between a boutique hotel and a hostel, offering private rooms and shared dorms, all with private bathrooms. Add to that Wi-Fi access throughout the hotel, a free Internet lounge, rooftop parties, free movie nights, lockers, free continental breakfast, luggage storage and laundry facilities, free linens, TVs (in private rooms), a lively restaurant and lounge called Medjool, and a plethora of inexpensive ethnic cafes in the neighborhood, and, baby, you've got it made. The hotel is at 2524 Mission St., between 21st and 22nd streets (© **866/327-8407** or 415/647-4100; www.elementssf.com). Rates per person are between $25 and $30; expect higher rates and minimum stays during holidays.

54 Fourth St. (at Market St.), San Francisco, CA 94103. © **800/227-3804** or 415/986-4400. Fax 415/495-7653. www.themosser.com. 166 units, 112 with bathroom. $169–$259 double with bathroom; $79–$99 double without bathroom. Rates include safe-deposit boxes at front desk. AE, DC, DISC, MC, V. Parking $30, plus $10 for oversize vehicles. Streetcar: F, and all underground Muni and BART. **Amenities:** Restaurant; bar; 24-hr. concierge; same-day laundry service/dry cleaning. *In room:* Ceiling fan, TV, Wi-Fi ($9.95/day), hair dryer, iron/ironing board, AM/FM stereo w/CD player, voice mail.

NOB HILL
Very Expensive
The Fairmont San Francisco ★★★ (Kids) The granddaddy of Nob Hill's elite cadre of ritzy hotels—and the only spot in San Francisco where each of the city's cable car lines meet—the century-old Fairmont is a must-visit if only to marvel at the incredibly glamorous lobby with its vaulted ceilings, Corinthian columns, a spectacular spiral staircase, and rococo furniture (it's easy to feel underdressed in such opulent surroundings). And yes, such decadence carries to the guest rooms where luxuries abound: oversize marble bathrooms, thick down blankets, goose-down king pillows, extra-long mattresses, and large walk-in closets. Because it's perched at the top of Nob Hill, there are spectacular city views from every guest room, but nuances such as a health club and spa, a 24-hour concierge, twice-daily maid service, babysitting services, and a business center enhance every guest's stay. Within the lobby is the ornate **Laurel Court** restaurant and lounge, which serves as the hotel's centerpiece. (It's fun to indulge in afternoon tea here, served daily 2:30–4:30pm.) A local institution that's been around since I was a kid is the hotel's **Tonga Room,** a fantastically kitsch tropical bar and restaurant where happy hour hops and "rain" falls every 30 minutes.

950 Mason St. (at California St.), San Francisco, CA 94108. © **866/540-4491** or 415/772-5000. Fax 415/772-5086. www.fairmont.com. 591 units. Main building $229–$349 double; from $500 suite. Tower $289–$469 double; from $750 suite; penthouse $12,500. Extra person $30. AE, DC, DISC, MC, V. Parking $43. Cable car: California St. line (direct stop). **Amenities:** 2 restaurants/bars; health club (free for Fairmont President's Club members; $15/day or $20/2 days, nonmembers); concierge; tour desk; car-rental desk; business center; Wi-Fi in lobby; shopping arcade; salon; room service; massage; babysitting; same-day laundry service/dry cleaning. *In room:* A/C, TV w/pay movies and video games available, high-speed Internet access, kitchenette in some units, minibar, hair dryer, iron, safe.

The Ritz-Carlton, San Francisco ★★★ Ranked among the top hotels in the world, the Ritz-Carlton San Francisco has been the benchmark for the city's luxury hotels since it opened in 1991. A Nob Hill landmark, the former Metropolitan Insurance head-quarters stood vacant for years until Ritz-Carlton acquired it and embarked on a $100-million, 4-year renovation. The interior was completely gutted and restored with fine furnishings, fabrics, and artwork, including a pair of Louis XVI blue marble urns with gilt mountings, and 19th-century Waterford candelabras. Just to make sure they stay on top, the rooms were completely upgraded in 2007 to the tune of $13 million, and now include 32-inch LCD TVs, DVD/CD players, and Wi-Fi. The Italian marble bathrooms offer every possible amenity, including double sinks, name-brand toiletries, and plush terry robes. The more expensive rooms take advantage of the hotel's location to provide good views of the city. Clubrooms, on the top floors, have a dedicated con-cierge, separate elevator-key access, and complimentary small plates throughout the day. No restaurant in town has more formal service than this hotel's **Dining Room,** which serves modern French cuisine with a Japanese influence. The less formal **Terrace Restau-rant** offers contemporary Mediterranean cuisine and the city's best Sunday brunch. The Lobby lounge serves classic afternoon tea and cocktails, with low-key live entertainment daily and sushi (Wed–Sat).

600 Stockton St. (btw. Pine and California sts.), San Francisco, CA 94108. **©** **800/241-3333** or 415/296-7465. Fax 415/986-1268. www.ritzcarlton.com. 336 units. $445–$480 double; $600–$850 club-level dou-ble; from $750–$850 executive suite. Buffet breakfast $32; Sun champagne brunch $65. Weekend discounts and packages available. AE, DC, DISC, MC, V. Parking $55. Cable car: California St. cable car line (direct stop). **Amenities:** 2 restaurants; 3 bars; indoor pool; outstanding fitness center; Jacuzzi; steam room; concierge; courtesy car; business center; secretarial services; room service; in-room massage and manicure; same-day laundry service/dry cleaning. *In room:* A/C, TV w/pay movies, high-speed Internet access, Wi-Fi ($13/day), minibar, hair dryer, iron, safe.

NORTH BEACH & FISHERMAN'S WHARF
Expensive

Argonaut Hotel ★★ Ⓚⁱᵈˢ The Kimpton Hotel Group is behind Fisherman's Wharf's best hotel, a true boutique gem that's ideally located at San Francisco Maritime National Historical Park (p. 129), half a block from the bay. The four-story timber and brick landmark building was originally built in 1908 as a warehouse for the California Fruit Canners Association and was later used by William Randolph Hearst to store items that eventually ended up inside his Hearst Castle in San Simeon. Its 239 rooms and 13 suites are whimsically decorated to emulate a luxury cruise ship in cheerful nautical colors of blue, white, red, and yellow (though evidence of its modest past appears in original brick walls, large timbers, and steel warehouse doors). Along with all the stan-dard hotel amenities are special touches such as flatscreen TVs, DVD/CD players, Aveda toiletries, and leopard-spotted bathrobes. All guests are welcome at weekday evening wine receptions and can use the lobby's two popular (and free) Internet terminals. Suites have wonderful views and come fully loaded with telescopes and spa tubs. If possible, try to book a "view" room, which overlooks the wharf or bay (some rooms offer fabulous views of Alcatraz and the Golden Gate Bridge). If you're bringing the kids, know that the Argonaut's friendly staff goes out of their way to make little ones feel at home and allows each pint-size guest to pick a new plaything from the hotel's "treasure chest." *Tip:* The concierge can work wonders when you need tickets to Alcatraz—even when the trips are officially sold out.

495 Jefferson St (at Hyde St.), San Francisco, CA 94109. **©** **866/415-0704** or 415/563-0800. Fax 415/563-2800. www.argonauthotel.com. 252 units. $189–$389 double; $489–$1,089 suite. Rates include evening wine in the lobby, daily newspaper, and such kid-friendly perks as cribs and strollers. AE, DC, DISC, MC, V.

Parking $39. Bus: 10, 30, or 47. Streetcar: F. Cable car: Powell–Hyde line. **Amenities:** Restaurant; bar; fitness center; concierge; Wi-Fi in public areas; laundry service; dry cleaning; yoga video and mats. *In room:* A/C, flatscreen TV w/Nintendo and pay movies, DVD player, free high-speed Internet access, Web TV, minibar, coffeemaker, hair dryer, iron, safe, CD player.

Moderate

Best Western Tuscan Inn at Fisherman's Wharf ★★

Like an island of respectability in a sea of touristy schlock, this boutique Best Western is one of the best midrange hotels at Fisherman's Wharf. It continues to exude a level of style and comfort far beyond that of its neighboring competitors. For example, every evening in the plush lobby warmed by a grand fireplace, a wine reception is hosted by the manager, and the adjoining **Café Pescatore** serves wonderful pizzas and grilled meats from their wood-burning oven. The rooms are a definite cut above competing Fisherman's Wharf hotels: all are handsomely decorated and have writing desks and armchairs. The only caveat is the lack of scenic views—a small price to pay for a good hotel in a great location.

425 North Point St. (at Mason St.), San Francisco, CA 94133. ✆ **800/648-4626** or 415/561-1100. Fax 415/561-1199. www.tuscaninn.com. 221 units. $129–$369. Rates include coffee, tea, and evening wine reception. AE, DC, DISC, MC, V. Parking $36. Bus: 10, 15, or 47. Cable car: Powell–Mason line. Pets welcome for $50 fee. **Amenities:** Access to nearby gym; concierge; courtesy car; limited room service; same-day laundry service/dry cleaning. *In room:* A/C, TV w/video games and pay movies, free Wi-Fi, minibar, coffeemaker, hair dryer, iron.

The Hotel Bohème ★★ (Finds)

Romance awaits at the intimate Hotel Bohème. Although it's on the busiest avenue in the neighborhood, once you ascend the staircase to this narrow second-floor boutique hotel, you'll discover a style and demeanor reminiscent of a home in upscale Nob Hill. Alas, there are no common areas other than a little lobby for check-in and concierge, but rooms, though small, are truly sweet, with gauze-draped canopies, stylish decor such as ornate parasols shading ceiling lights, and walls dramatically colored with lavender, sage green, black, and pumpkin. The staff is ultrahospitable, and bonuses include sherry in the lobby each afternoon. Some fabulous cafes, restaurants, bars, and shops along Columbus Avenue are just a few steps away, and Chinatown and Union Square are within easy walking distance. *Note:* Although the bathrooms are spiffy, they're also tiny and have showers only. Also, request a room off the street side, which is quieter.

444 Columbus Ave. (btw. Vallejo and Green sts.), San Francisco, CA 94133. ✆ **415/433-9111.** Fax 415/362-6292. www.hotelboheme.com. 15 units. $164–$184 double. Rates include afternoon sherry. AE, DC, DISC, MC, V. Parking $12–$31 at nearby public garages. Bus: 12, 15, 30, 41, 45, or 83. Cable car: Powell–Mason line. **Amenities:** Concierge. *In room:* TV, free Wi-Fi, hair dryer, iron.

Inexpensive

The San Remo Hotel ★ (Value)

This small, European-style *pensione* is one of the best budget hotels in San Francisco. In a quiet North Beach neighborhood, within walking distance of Fisherman's Wharf, the Italianate Victorian structure originally served as a boardinghouse for dockworkers displaced by the great fire of 1906. As a result, the rooms are small and bathrooms are shared, but all is forgiven when it comes time to pay the bill. Rooms are decorated in cozy country style, with brass and iron beds; oak, maple, or pine armoires; and wicker furnishings. The immaculate shared bathrooms feature tubs and brass pull-chain toilets with oak tanks and brass fixtures. If the penthouse—which has its own bathroom, TV, fridge, and patio—is available, book it: You won't find a more romantic place to stay in San Francisco for so little money.

2237 Mason St. (at Chestnut St.), San Francisco, CA 94133. © **800/352-7366** or 415/776-8688. Fax 415/776-2811. www.sanremohotel.com. 62 units, 61 with shared bathroom. $65–$90 double; $175–$185 penthouse suite. AE, DC, MC, V. Self-parking $13–$14. Bus: 10, 15, 30, or 47. Streetcar: F. Cable car: Powell–Mason line. **Amenities:** Access to nearby health club; Internet kiosk in lobby; 2 massage chairs; self-service laundry; TV room. *In room:* Ceiling fan.

The Wharf Inn ★ (**Value**)   My top choice for good-value/great-location lodging at Fisherman's Wharf, the Wharf Inn offers above-average accommodations at one of the most popular tourist attractions in the world. The well-stocked rooms are done in handsome tones of earth, muted greens, and burnt orange, but more importantly, they are smack-dab in the middle of the wharf, a mere 2 blocks from Pier 39 and the cable car turnaround, and within walking distance of the Embarcadero and North Beach. The inn is ideal for car-bound families because parking is free (that saves at least $25 a day right off the bat).

2601 Mason St. (at Beach St.), San Francisco, CA 94133. © **877/275-7889** or 415/673-7411. Fax 415/776-2181. www.wharfinn.com. 51 units. $99–$209 double; $299–$439 penthouse. AE, DC, DISC, MC, V. Free parking. Bus: 10, 15, 39, or 47. Streetcar: F. Cable car: Powell–Mason or Powell–Hyde lines. **Amenities:** Access to nearby health club ($10/day); concierge; tour desk; free coffee/tea. *In room:* TV, free Wi-Fi, hair dryer on request, iron on request.

COW HOLLOW & PACIFIC HEIGHTS
Expensive

Hotel Drisco ★★ (**Finds**)   On one of the most sought-after blocks of residential property in all of San Francisco, the Drisco, built in 1903, is one of the city's best small hotels. Refinements by interior designer Glenn Texeira (who also did the Ritz-Carlton in Manila) are evident from the very small lobby and sitting areas to the calming atmosphere of the cream, yellow, and green guest rooms. As in the neighboring mansions, traditional antique furnishings and thick, luxurious fabrics abound here. The hotel's comfy beds will make you want to loll late into the morning before primping in the large marble bathrooms, complete with robes and slippers. Each suite has a couch that unfolds into a bed (although you would never guess from the looks of it), an additional phone and TV, and superior views. A 24-hour coffee and tea service is available on the ground floor, in the same comfy rooms where breakfast is served. If you're arriving by car, however, you may not want to stay here as there is no hotel parking.

2901 Pacific Ave. (at Broderick St.), San Francisco, CA 94115. © **800/634-7277** or 415/346-2880. Fax 415/567-5537. www.hoteldrisco.com. 48 units. $249 double; $369–$399 suite. Rates include buffet breakfast and evening wine hour. AE, DC, DISC, MC, V. No parking available. Bus: 3 or 24. **Amenities:** Exercise room and free pass to YMCA; concierge; business center; limited room service; same-day laundry service/dry cleaning. *In room:* TV/VCR, free high-speed Internet access, minibar, fridge, hair dryer, iron, safe, CD player.

Moderate

Hotel Del Sol ★★ (**Kids**) (**Value**)   The cheeriest motel in town is located just 2 blocks off the Marina District's bustling section of Lombard. Three-level Hotel del Sol is all about festive flair and luxury touches. The sunshine theme extends from the Miami Beach–style use of vibrant color, to the heated courtyard pool, which beckons the youngish clientele as they head for their cars parked (for free!) in cabanalike spaces. This is also one of the most family-friendly places to stay, with a "Kids are VIPs" program, including a family suite (three adjoining rooms with bunks and toys); a lending library of kids' books, toys, and videos; childproofing kits; three rooms that have been professionally baby-proofed; bonded babysitting services; evening cookies and milk; pool toys; and sunglasses and visors. The hotel boasts 57 spacious rooms (updated with all new bedding, paint, carpets, drapes, and sofas in 2006) with equally perky interior decor (read: loud and colorful) as well as unexpected extras like CD players, Aveda products, and local tips. Suites include minifridges and DVD players.

3100 Webster St. (at Greenwich St.), San Francisco, CA 94123. ℰ **877/433-5765** or 415/921-5520. Fax 415/931-4137. www.thehoteldelsol.com. 57 units. $139–$199 double; $179–$239 suite. Rates include continental breakfast and free newspapers in the lobby. AE, DC, DISC, MC, V. Free parking. Bus: 22, 28, 41, 43, 45, or 76. **Amenities:** Heated outdoor pool; same-day dry cleaning. *In room:* TV/VCR, Wi-Fi ($7.95/day), kitchenettes in 3 units, fridge and DVD player in suites only, iron, CD player.

Inexpensive

Marina Inn ★ ⓒ**Value**   Marina Inn is one of the best low-priced hotels in San Francisco. How it offers so much for so little is mystifying. Each guest room in the 1924 four-story Victorian looks like something from a country furnishings catalog, complete with rustic pinewood furniture, a four-poster bed with silky-soft comforter, pretty wallpaper, and soothing tones of rose, hunter green, and pale yellow. You also get remote-control televisions discreetly hidden in pine cabinetry—all for as little as $75 a night. Combine that with continental breakfast, friendly service, a business center in the lobby with an Internet kiosk, free Wi-Fi, and an armada of shops and restaurants within easy walking distance, and there you have it: one of my top choices for best overall value. *Note:* Traffic can be a bit noisy here, so the hotel added double panes on windows facing the street.

3110 Octavia St. (at Lombard St.), San Francisco, CA 94123. ℰ **800/274-1420** or 415/928-1000. Fax 415/928-5909. www.marinainn.com. 40 units. Nov–Feb $75–$115 double; Mar–May $85–$135 double; June–Oct $95–$145 double. Rates include continental breakfast. AE, DC, DISC, MC, V. Bus: 28, 30, 43, or 76. *In room:* TV, free Wi-Fi, hair dryer and iron on request.

Marina Motel   Established in 1939, the Marina Motel is one of San Francisco's first motels, built for the opening of the Golden Gate Bridge. The same family has owned this peach-colored, Spanish-style stucco building for three generations, and they've taken exquisite care of it. All rooms look out onto an inner courtyard, which is awash with beautiful flowering plants and wall paintings by local artists. Though the rooms show minor signs of wear and tear, they're all quite clean, bright, quiet, and pleasantly decorated with framed lithographs of old San Francisco—a thoughtful touch that adds to the motel's old-fashioned character and which makes these budget accommodations stand out from all the rest along busy Lombard Street. Two-bedroom suites with fully equipped kitchens are also available. Location-wise, the Presidio and Marina Green are mere blocks away, and you can easily catch a bus downtown. The only downside is the street noise, which is likely to burden light sleepers. *Bonus:* All rooms include a breakfast coupon valid for two entrees for the price of one at **Judy's Restaurant,** a short walk from the motel.

2576 Lombard St. (btw. Divisadero and Broderick sts.), San Francisco, CA 94123. ℰ **800/346-6118** or 415/921-9406. Fax 415/921-0364. www.marinamotel.com. 38 units. $89–$159 double; $199 suite. Lower rates in winter. Rates include 2-for-1 breakfast coupon at nearby cafe. AE, DISC, MC, V. Free covered parking. Bus: 28, 29, 30, 43, or 45. Dogs accepted with $10 nightly fee. *In room:* Fridge, coffeemaker, hair dryer, iron.

CIVIC CENTER & ENVIRONS

Moderate

The Phoenix Hotel ★★   If you'd like to tell your friends back home that you stayed in the same hotel as Linda Ronstadt, David Bowie, Keanu Reeves, Moby, Franz Ferdinand, and Interpol, this is the place to go. On the fringes of San Francisco's less-than-pleasant

Tenderloin District, which is rife with the homeless and crack addicts, this well-sheltered retro 1950s-style hotel is a gathering place for visiting rock musicians, writers, and film-makers who crave a dose of Southern California. The focal point of the Palm Springs–style hotel is a small, heated outdoor pool adorned with a mural by artist Francis Forlenza and ensconced in a modern-sculpture garden. Rooms are more pop than plush, with bright island-inspired furnishings and original local art; every room faces the pool. In addition to the usual amenities, the hotel offers movies on request and a party vibe that's not part of the package at most city hotels. Some big bonuses: free parking and the hotel's restaurant and club, the groovy and very hip **Bambuddha Lounge** (✆ **415/885-5088**), which serves Southeast Asian cuisine with cocktail-lounge flair. If you want luxury and quiet, stay else-where, but if you're looking for a great scene and fun vibe, head to the Phoenix.

601 Eddy St. (at Larkin St.), San Francisco, CA 94109. ✆ **800/248-9466** or 415/776-1380. Fax 415/885-3109. www.thephoenixhotel.com. 44 units. $149–$169 double; $219–$399 suite. Rates include continental breakfast. AE, DC, MC, V. Free parking. Bus: 19, 31, 38, or 47. **Amenities:** Bar; heated outdoor pool; concierge; tour desk; in-room massage; same-day laundry service/dry cleaning. *In room:* TV, VCR on request, high-speed Internet and Wi-Fi ($7.95/day), fridge and microwave in some rooms, hair dryer, iron.

The Queen Anne Hotel ★★ (Value) This majestic 1890 Victorian charmer was once a grooming school for upper-class young women. Restored in 1980 and renovated in early 2006, the four-story building recalls San Francisco's golden days. Walk under rich red draperies to the lavish "grand salon" lobby replete with English oak wainscoting and period antiques that evoke a different era. Guest rooms also contain a profusion of antiques—armoires, marble-top dressers, and other Victorian-era pieces. Some have corner turret bay windows that look out on tree-lined streets, as well as separate parlor areas and wet bars; others have cozy reading nooks and fireplaces. All rooms have phones and nice bath amenities in their marble-tiled bathrooms. Guests can relax in the parlor, with two fireplaces, or in the hotel library. If you don't mind staying outside the down-town area, this hotel is highly recommended and very classic San Francisco.

1590 Sutter St. (btw. Gough and Octavia sts.), San Francisco, CA 94109. ✆ **800/227-3970** or 415/441-2828. Fax 415/775-5212. www.queenanne.com. 48 units. $110–$199 double; $169–$350 suite. Extra person $10. Rates include continental breakfast on weekday mornings, local free limousine service (weekday mornings), afternoon tea and sherry, and morning newspaper. AE, DC, DISC, MC, V. Parking $14. Bus: 2, 3, or 4. **Amenities:** Access to nearby health club for $10; 24-hr. concierge; business center; same-day dry cleaning; front desk safe. *In room:* TV, free high-speed Internet access in some rooms, Wi-Fi throughout, hair dryer, iron.

HAIGHT ASHBURY & THE CASTRO

The Parker Guest House ★★ This is the best B&B option in the Castro, and one of the best in the entire city. In fact, even some of the better hotels could learn a thing or two from this fashionable, gay-friendly, 5,000-square-foot, 1909 beautifully restored Edwardian home and adjacent annex a few blocks from the heart of the Castro's action. Within the bright, cheery urban compound, period antiques abound. But thankfully, the spacious guest rooms are wonderfully updated with smart patterned furnishings, voice mail, robes, and spotless private bathrooms (plus amenities) en suite or, in two cases, across the hall. A fire burns nightly in the cozy living room, and guests are also welcome to make themselves at home in the wood-paneled common library (with fireplace and piano), sunny breakfast room overlooking the garden, and spacious garden with foun-tains and a steam room. Animal lovers will appreciate the companionship of the house pugs Porter and Patsy.

520 Church St. (btw. 17th and 18th sts.), San Francisco, CA 94114. ☎ **888/520-7275** or 415/621-3222. Fax 415/621-4139. www.parkerguesthouse.com. 21 units. $129–$199 double; $219 junior suite. Rates include extended continental breakfast and evening wine and cheese. AE, DISC, MC, V. Self-parking $17. Bus: 22 or 33. Streetcar: J Church. **Amenities:** Access to nearby health club; steam room; concierge. *In room:* TV, free Wi-Fi, hair dryer, iron.

Stanyan Park Hotel ★★ (Kids) (Value)   The only real hotel on the east end of Golden Gate Park and the west end of funky-chic Haight Street, this small inn offers classic San Francisco–style living at a very affordable price. The Victorian structure, which has operated as a hotel under a variety of names since the turn of the 20th century and is on the National Register of Historic Places, offers good-size rooms, all done in period decor. Its three stories are decorated with antique furnishings; Victorian wallpaper; and pastel quilts, curtains, and carpets. Families will appreciate the six one- and two-bedroom suites, each of which has a full kitchen and formal dining and living rooms and can sleep up to six comfortably. Tea is served each afternoon from 4 to 6pm. Continental breakfast is served in the dining room off the lobby from 6 to 10am. All rooms are nonsmoking.

750 Stanyan St. (at Waller St.), San Francisco, CA 94117. ☎ **415/751-1000.** Fax 415/668-5454. www. stanyanpark.com. 36 units. $135–$209 double; $265–$335 suite. Rates include continental breakfast and afternoon and evening tea service. Rollaway $20; cribs free. AE, DISC, MC, V. Off-site parking $14. Bus: 7, 33, 43, 66, or 71. Streetcar: N. *In room:* TV, free Wi-Fi, kitchen (in suites only), hair dryer, iron in suites or on request.

The Willows Inn ★   In the heart of the Castro, the entirely nonsmoking Willows Inn employs a staff eager to greet and attend to visitors. The country and antique willow furnishings don't strictly suit a 1903 Edwardian home, but everything's quite comfortable—especially considering the extras, which include an expanded continental breakfast (fresh fruit, yogurt, baked goods, gourmet coffee, eggs, assorted teas, and orange juice), the morning paper, nightly cocktails, a sitting room (with a DVD player), and a pantry with limited kitchen facilities. The homey rooms vary in size from large (queen-size bed) to smaller (double bed) and are priced accordingly. Each room has a vanity sink, and all the rooms share eight water closets and shower rooms.

710 14th St. (near Church and Market sts.), San Francisco, CA 94114. ☎ **800/431-0277** or 415/431-4770. Fax 415/431-5295. www.willowssf.com. 12 units, none with bathroom. $105–$135 double; $145 suite. Rates include continental breakfast. AE, DC, DISC, MC, V. Bus: 22 or 37. Streetcar: Church St. station (across the street) or F. *In room:* TV/VCR, free Wi-Fi, fridge.

---

4 WHERE TO DINE

San Francisco's dining scene is one of the best in the world. Below is a cross section of the city's best restaurants, in every price range. For a greater selection of reviews, pick up a copy of *Frommer's San Francisco* (Wiley Publishing, Inc.).

UNION SQUARE
Very Expensive
Michael Mina ★★★ AMERICAN   Chef Michael Mina takes the small-plate dining concept to extremes at this sexy, swank spot. Previously the Compass Rose tearoom in the Westin St. Francis hotel, the cream-on-cream room, with deep leather lounge chairs and tables that are too wide for romance, sets the scene for this formal prix-fixe affair. But rather than three dishes, courses arrive as a trio of different renditions of the same

theme (plus three sides to match) on custom Mina-designed modular china. That's six different preparations per dish or a total of 18 different flavors over the course of an evening. It's a bit fussy for anyone who prefers to order a few things that sound good and eat lots of bites of them, but if the idea of sampling lots of styles and flavors appeals to you, this edible food-combination case study is likely to be a culinary wonder. Take diver scallops for example. One preparation is accented with lemon Osetra caviar while the other two pair them with yellow corn and summer truffles or smoked tomato and Maine lobster—not to mention three different "chilled salads" in tiny glasses. You might also find crispy pork loin done with risotto, as pulled pork with apple ravioli, and as barbecue with a corn fritter. Some dishes hit, some miss, but in all cases this is a swank affair with an incredible wine list by Rajat Parr.

335 Powell St. (at Geary St.). (C) **415/397-9222.** www.michaelmina.net. Reservations recommended. 3-course tasting menu $98; seasonal classic tasting menu $135. AE, DC, DISC, MC, V. Mon–Sat 5:30–10pm; Sun 5:30–9:30pm. Valet parking $17. Bus: 2, 3, 4, 30, 38, 45, or 76.

Expensive

Grand Café ★ FRENCH   If you aren't interested in exploring restaurants beyond those in Union Square and want a huge dose of atmosphere with your seared salmon, Grand Café is your best bet. Its claims to fame? The most grand dining room in San Francisco, an enormous 156-seat, turn-of-the-20th-century grand-ballroom-like dining oasis that's a magnificent combination of old Europe and Art Nouveau. To match the surroundings, chef Ron Boyd, a San Francisco native and Domaine Chandon alum, serves dressed-up French-inspired California dishes such as sautéed salmon with French lentils and house-cured bacon or salade niçoise. You can also drop by for a lighter meal in the more casual front room, the Petit Café, which offers a raw bar and similar dishes for about half the price. In fact, I prefer to hang out in the cafe and nosh on pizzas from the wood-burning oven or a big bowl full of mussels swimming in broth with a side of sourdough bread—it's twice the atmosphere at half the price. There's also a wonderful selection of small-batch American whiskies and single-malt Scotches.

501 Geary St. (at Taylor St., adjacent to the Hotel Monaco). (C) **415/292-0101.** www.grandcafe-sf.com. Reservations recommended. Main courses $18–$28. AE, DC, DISC, MC, V. Mon–Fri 7–10:30am; Sat 8am–2:30pm; Sun 9am–2:30pm; Mon–Fri 11:30am–2:30pm; Sun–Thurs 5:30–10pm; Fri–Sat 5:30–11pm. Valet parking free at brunch, $15 for 3 hr. at dinner, $3 each additional half-hour. Bus: 2, 3, 4, 27, or 38.

Le Colonial ★ (Finds) VIETNAMESE   Viet-chic environs—picture slowly spinning ceiling fans, tropical plants, rattan furniture, and French Colonial decor—and quality French Vietnamese food make this an excellent choice for folks who want to nosh at one of the sexiest restaurants in town. The upstairs lounge (which opens at 4:30pm) is where romance reigns, with cozy couches, seductive surroundings, and a well-dressed cocktail crowd of post-work professionals who nosh on coconut-crusted crab cakes and Vietnamese spring rolls. In the tiled downstairs dining room and along the stunning heated front patio, guests savor the vibrant flavors of coconut curry with black tiger prawns, mangos, eggplant, and Asian basil and tender wok-seared beef tenderloin with watercress onion salad.

20 Cosmo Place (off Taylor St., btw. Post and Sutter sts.). (C) **415/931-3600.** www.lecolonialsf.com. Reservations recommended. Main courses $20–$38. AE, DC, MC, V. Sun–Wed 5:30–10pm; Thurs–Sat 5:30–11pm. Public valet parking $6 1st hr., $2 each additional half-hour. Bus: 2, 3, 4, or 27.

Moderate

Bocadillos ★★ (Finds) SPANISH/BASQUE TAPAS   The sister to Piperade (p. 105) is flat-out fabulous if you're in the mood for tapas or Spanish-influenced small plates.

A16 **3**
Ame **61**
AsiaSF **62**
Aziza **9**
B44 **49**
Beach Chalet &
   Park Chalet **11**
Belden Place **49**
Bocadillos **40**
Boudin at the Wharf **31 21, 27, 59**
Boulevard **44**
Brandy Ho's
   Hunan Food **39**
Burma Superstar **7**
Cafe Bastille **49**
Café Flore **15**
Cafe Tiramisu **49**
Capp's Corner **33**
Cha Cha Cha **13, 20**
Chez Nous **8**
Chow **16**
Cliff House **10**
Delfina **18**
Dottie's True
   Blue Café **57**
Ducca **60**
EPIC Roasthouse **46**
Fog City Diner **32**
Foreign Cinema **19**
Frjtz Fries **25**
Grand Café **58**
Greens Restaurant **1**
The Grove **2**
House of Nanking **38**
Il Pollaio **34**
Isa **4**
Jardinière **26**
Kan Zaman **14**

Kokkari **41**
Kuleto's **54**
L'Osteria del Forno **35**
Le Colonial **56**
Manora's **63**
Mario's Bohemian
   Cigar Store **36**
Mecca Café **17**
Mel's Drive-In **5, 10,**
Michael Mina **53**
Nob Hill Cafe **50**
One Market **43**
Piperade **37**
Plouf **49**
PlumpJack Café **6**
R&G Lounge **48**
Restaurant Gary
   Danko **30**
Sam's Grill & Seafood
   Restaurant **49**
Sanraku Japanese
   Restaurant **55**
Scala's Bistro **51**
Scoma's Cafe **31**
Sears Fine Foods **52**
The Slanted Door **42**
Spruce **7**
Swan Oyster Depot **28**
Tablespoon **29**
Takara **12**
Taquerias
   La Cumbre **22**
Ti Couz **23**
Ton Kiang **9**
Waterbar **47**
Yank Sing **45**
Zuni Café **24**

Executive chef Gerald Hirigoyen celebrates his Basque roots with outstanding calamari with creamy tomato-and-garlic romesco sauce, scallops "mole cortado" with sherry and orange, sautéed hot peppers, tuna carpaccio, decadent foie gras sushi rolls, and astoundingly tasty warm chocolate cake with sautéed bananas. Just watch your budget—at up to $12 per plate, the tab can creep up on you. You might also want to check out their breakfast, which includes baked eggs with chorizo and manchego cheese. But don't come anticipating a formal dining environment or a cocktail: This small Financial District space is cafe-casual and beer-and-wine only.

710 Montgomery St. (at Washington St.). ☏ **415/982-2622.** www.bocasf.com. Breakfast items $2–$6; lunch and dinner small items $3–$12. AE, DC, DISC, MC, V. Mon–Fri 7am–11pm; Sat 5–11pm. Closed Sun. Bus: 15, 30X, or 41.

Kuleto's ★ ITALIAN   Kuleto's is one of downtown's Italian darlings. Muscle your way into a seat at the antipasto bar or at the chef's counter overlooking the kitchen, and fill up on Italian specialties and selections from the wine list featuring 30 by-the-glass options. Or partake in the likes of penne pasta drenched in tangy lamb-sausage marinara sauce, clam linguine (generously overloaded with fresh clams), or any of the grilled fresh-fish specials in the casually refined dining room. If you don't arrive by 6pm, expect to wait—this place fills up fast. Not to worry though, you can always cross the hotel lobby to the wine bar, which also serves the full menu and is open from 6 to 10pm daily. Don't have time to sit down? Try Cafe Kuleto's, which is located just outside and serves panini, pastries, salads, and espresso to go, open daily from 7am to 8pm.

In the Villa Florence Hotel, 221 Powell St. (btw. Geary and O'Farrell sts.). ☏ **415/397-7720.** www.kuletos. com. Reservations recommended. Breakfast $5–$15; main courses $12–$25. AE, DC, DISC, MC, V. Mon–Fri 7–10:30am; Sat–Sun 8–10:30am; daily 11:30am–11pm. Bus: 2, 3, 4, or 38. Streetcar: All streetcars. Cable car: Powell–Mason or Powell–Hyde lines.

Scala's Bistro ★★ FRENCH/ITALIAN   Firmly entrenched at the base of the refurbished Sir Francis Drake hotel, this downtown favorite blends Italian-bistro and old-world atmosphere with jovial and bustling results. With just the right balance of elegance and informality, this is a perfect place to have some fun (and apparently most people do). Of the tempting array of Italian and French dishes, it's de rigueur to start with the "Earth and Surf" calamari appetizer or grilled portobello mushrooms. Golden beet salad and garlic cream mussels are also good bets. Generous portions of moist, rich duck-leg confit will satisfy hungry appetites, but if you can order only one thing, make it Scala's signature dish: seared salmon. Resting on a bed of creamy buttermilk mashed potatoes and accented with a tomato, chive, and white-wine sauce, it's downright delicious. Finish with Bostini cream pie, a dreamy combo of vanilla custard and orange chiffon cake with a warm chocolate glaze.

In the Sir Francis Drake hotel, 432 Powell St. (at Sutter St.). ☏ **415/395-8555.** www.scalasbistro.com. Reservations recommended. Breakfast $7–$10; main courses $12–$24 lunch and dinner. AE, DC, DISC, MC, V. Daily 8–10:30am and 11:30am–midnight. Bus: 2, 3, 4, 30, 45, or 76. Cable car: Powell–Hyde line.

Inexpensive

Dottie's True Blue Café ★ (Kids) AMERICAN/BREAKFAST   This family-owned breakfast restaurant is one of my favorite downtown diners. This is the kind of place you'd expect to see off Route 66, where most customers are on a first-name basis with the staff and everyone is welcomed with a hearty hello and steaming mug of coffee. Dottie's serves far-above-average American morning fare (big portions of French toast, pancakes, bacon and eggs, omelets, and the like), delivered to tables laminated with old movie star photos on rugged, diner-quality plates. Whatever you order arrives with delicious home-made bread, muffins, or scones, as well as house-made jelly. There are also daily specials and vegetarian dishes.

In the Pacific Bay Inn, 522 Jones St. (at O'Farrell St.). © **415/885-2767**. Reservations not accepted. Breakfast $5–$11. DISC, MC, V. Wed–Mon 7:30am–3pm (lunch 11:30am–3pm). Bus: 2, 3, 4, 27, or 38. Cable car: Powell–Mason line.

Sanraku Japanese Restaurant ★ Ⓥalue JAPANESE/SUSHI   A perfect combination of great cooked dishes and sushi at bargain prices makes this straightforward, bright, and busy restaurant the best choice in the area for Japanese food. The friendly, hardworking staff does its best to keep up with diners' demands, but the restaurant gets quite busy during lunch, when a bento-box lunch of the likes of California roll, soup, salad, deep-fried salmon roll, steamed rice, and beef with noodles comes at a very digestible $9.50. The main menu features great sesame chicken with teriyaki sauce and rice; tempura; a vast selection of *nigiri* (raw fish sushi) and rolls; and delicious combination plates of sushi, sashimi, and teriyaki. Dinner sees brisk business, too, but a table always seems to be available.

704 Sutter St. (at Taylor St.). © **415/771-0803**. www.sanraku.com. Main courses $7–$13 lunch, $10–$26 dinner; 7-course fixed-price dinner $55. AE, DC, DISC, MC, V. Mon–Sat lunch 11am–4pm and dinner 4–10pm; Sun dinner 4–10pm. Bus: 2, 3, 4, 27, or 38. Cable car: Powell–Mason line.

Sears Fine Foods ★ Ⓚids AMERICAN   Sears is not just another downtown diner—it's an old-fashioned institution, famous for its crispy, dark-brown waffles, light sourdough French toast served with house-made strawberry preserves, and silver dollar–size Swedish pancakes (18 per serving!). As the story goes, Ben Sears, a retired clown, founded the diner in 1938. His Swedish wife, Hilbur, was responsible for the legendary pancakes, which, although the restaurant is under new ownership, are still whipped up according to her family's secret recipe. Sears also offers classic lunch and dinner fare—try the Reuben for lunch and cod fish and chips for dinner, followed by a big slice of pie for dessert. Breakfast is served until 3pm every day, and plan on a brief wait to be seated on weekends.

439 Powell St. (btw. Post and Sutter sts.). © **415/986-0700**. www.searsfinefood.com. Reservations accepted for parties of 6 or more. Breakfast $3–$8; salads and soups $3–$8; main courses $6–$10. AE, DC, MC, V. Daily 6:30am–10pm (breakfast until 3pm). Cable car: Powell–Mason and Powell–Hyde lines. Bus: 2, 3, 4, or 38.

SOMA
Expensive
Ame ★★★ NEW AMERICAN   Restaurateurs Hiro Sone and Lissa Doumani, the owners of the sensational Napa Valley restaurant Terra, have blessed us foodies with an equally fantastic restaurant in the city. Located on the ground level of the new and *très* chic St. Regis Hotel, the L-shaped dining room with its mesquite flooring, red accents, and long striped curtains fits right in with the hotel's minimalist theme. Sone, a master of Japanese, French, and Italian cuisines, offers an array of exotic selections that are utterly tempting: ragout of sweetbreads with salsify and forest mushrooms; Japanese egg custard with lobster and urchin; mushroom risotto topped with foie gras; grilled Wagyu beef with fried Miyagi oysters and rémoulade sauce. If you can't figure out where to start on a menu where everything looks wonderful, opt for Sone's A Taste of Ame, an $81 five-course tasting menu that, for an additional $60, is paired with a bevy of wines by the glass. After dinner, be sure to enjoy an aperitif at the hotel's swank bar, where the city's elite congregate nightly

689 Mission St. (at Third St.). ℂ **415/284-4040.** www.amerestaurant.com. Reservations recommended. Main courses $19–$25 lunch, $22–$35 dinner. AE, DC, DISC, MC, V. Daily 5:30–10pm. Valet parking $12 for the 1st 3 hrs. Bus: 15, 30, or 45. Streetcar: J, K, L, or M to Montgomery.

Boulevard ★★ AMERICAN   Master restaurant designer Pat Kuleto and Chef Nancy Oakes are behind one of San Francisco's most beloved restaurants. Inside, the dramatically artistic Belle Epoque interior, with vaulted brick ceilings, floral banquettes, a mosaic floor, and tulip-shaped lamps, is the setting for Oakes's equally impressive sculptural and mouthwatering dishes. Starters alone could make a perfect meal, especially if you indulge in pan-seared day boat sea scallops with sautéed fresh hearts of palm, pomelo, basil, toasted shallots, and macadamia nuts, or the pan-seared foie gras with rhubarb syrup on whole grain toast. The nine or so main courses are equally creative and might include grilled Pacific sea bass with fresh gulf prawns, grilled artichoke, spring asparagus, and green garlic purée; or fire-roasted Angus filet with crispy Yukon gold potatoes, béarnaise sauce, sautéed spinach and crimini mushrooms, and red wine *jus*. Finish with warm chocolate cake with a chocolate caramel center, caramel corn, and butterscotch ice cream. Three levels of formality—bar, open kitchen, and main dining room—keep things from getting too snobby. Although steep prices prevent most from making Boulevard a regular gig, you'd be hard-pressed to find a better place for a special, fun-filled occasion.

1 Mission St. (btw. the Embarcadero and Steuart sts.). ℂ **415/543-6084.** www.boulevardrestaurant.com. Reservations recommended. Main courses $14–$22 lunch, $28–$39 dinner. AE, DC, DISC, MC, V. Mon–Fri 11:30am–2pm; Sun–Thurs 5:30–10pm; Fri–Sat 5:30–10:30pm. Valet parking $12 lunch, $10 dinner. Bus: 12, 15, 30, 32, or 41. BART: Embarcadero.

Ducca ★★★ ITALIAN   If you've never experienced what a talented chef can do with *mozzarella di bufala*, you owe it to yourself visit Ducca. Executive Chef Richard J. Corbo learned his trade at the Apicus culinary institute in Florence, and then refined it at Restaurant Gary Danko (p. 107) before being asked to run his own kitchen at Ducca. Since then he's earned nothing but kudos for his simple, seasonal Italian dishes seasoned with a hint of California influences, such as his veal chop Milanese with a fennel pollen-breadcrumb crust and preserved lemon vinaigrette, ricotta gnocchi with fava beans and fungi, and a superb yellowtail crudo with pine nuts, currants, and mint. Corbo also offers a modest selection of *cichetti*, Italian-style bar snacks such as white anchovies, salt cod crostini, and risotto fritters. You'll enjoy the ambience in either the stylish bar and lounge, alfresco terrace, or airy dining room with a bustling open kitchen. *Tip:* Arrive early to enjoy a Campari and soda in the circular lounge or outdoors by the fireplace.

50 Third St. btw. Market and Mission sts., adjacent to the Westin San Francisco Market Street hotel). ℂ **415/ 977-0271.** www.duccasf.com. Main courses $23–$51. AE, DISC, MC, V. Daily 6:30–10:30am, 11:30am–2pm, and 5:30–10:30pm. Valet parking $12. Bus: 15, 30, or 45. Streetcar: J, K, L, or M.

EPIC Roasthouse ★★ STEAKHOUSE   Why it took so long is a mystery, but for the first time in decades someone has finally created a true destination restaurant on the Embarcadero. Two, actually. The EPIC Roasthouse and its adjoining sister restaurant Waterbar (see below) were both built from the ground up on perhaps the most prime piece of real estate in the city, with spectacular views of the Bay Bridge, Treasure Island, and city skyline. They both opened on the eve of January 29, 2008, to much fanfare. At EPIC, it's all about steak. Renowned chef and co-owner Jan Birnbaum, a New Orleans man who knows his meat, runs the show in his huge exhibition kitchen, slaving over the wood-fired hearth to make sure your $76 rib-eye-for-two is cooked to your specs.

Perhaps the only thing prettier than the scenery (check out the phenomenal view of the Bay Bridge from the two-story-tall wall of windows) is Birnbaum's sizzling 26-ounce bone-in porterhouse on your plate. If you don't have a reservation, the upstairs Quiver Bar serves both bar and full menus, but the crowd usually consists of obnoxious businessmen and Gucci-toting gold-diggers from across the bridge. *Tip:* On sunny days, beg the hostess for a table on the bay-view patio.

369 Embarcadero (at Harrison St.). ℂ 415/369-9955. www.epicroasthousesf.com. Reservations recommended. Main courses $27–$54. AE, MC, V. Mon–Fri 11:30am–2pm; Sun–Thurs 5–10:30pm; Fri–Sat 5pm–midnight; brunch Sat–Sun 10:30am–3pm. Valet parking $15 lunch, $10 dinner. Bus: 1, 12, 14, or 41. Streetcar: F. BART: Embarcadero.

Waterbar ★★ SEAFOOD Built in tandem with the EPIC Roasthouse (see above), Waterbar is the surf to EPIC's turf. Whereas renowned restaurant designer Pat Kuleto went with a moderately conservative industrial look at EPIC, at Waterbar he unleashed his imagination and created the most visually playful decor since opening Farallon in 1997. The focal point of the restaurant is a pair of radiant 19-foot floor-to-ceiling circular aquariums filled with fish and marine critters from the Pacific Ocean. The aquatic theme ebbs along with a beautiful glass "caviar" chandelier and a horseshoe-shaped raw bar that has too few of the most coveted seats in town. Even the open kitchen is visually—and aromatically—pleasing. The menu offers a wide selection of market-driven, sustainable seafood such as Dover sole served whole (a whopping $80) and local halibut poached in milk with grilled asparagus; but more fun can be had at the raw bar noshing on oysters and small plates. Either way, start off with the superb sea scallop ceviche, infused with sweet potato, smoked salt, and paprika. If the weather is agreeable, request a table on the patio.

399 Embarcadero (at Harrison St.). ℂ **415/284-9922.** www.waterbarsf.com. Reservations recommended. Main courses $28–$36. AE, DISC, MC, V. Daily 11:30am–2pm and 5:30–10pm. Valet parking $15 lunch, $10 dinner. Bus: 1, 12, 14, or 41. Streetcar: F. BART: Embarcadero.

Moderate

AsiaSF ★ ASIAN/CALIFORNIA Part restaurant, part gender-illusionist musical revue, AsiaSF manages to be both entertaining and satisfying. As you're entertained by mostly Asian men dressed as women (who lip-sync show tunes when they're not waiting on tables), you can nibble on superb grilled shrimp and herb salad; baby back pork ribs with honey tamarind glaze, pickled carrots, and sweet-potato crisps; or filet mignon with Korean dipping sauce, miso eggplant, and fried potato stars. The full bar, the *Wine Spectator*-award-winning wine list, and the sake list add to the festivities. Fortunately, the food and the atmosphere are as colorful as the staff, which means a night here is more than a meal—it's a very happening event.

201 Ninth St. (at Howard St.). ℂ **415/255-2742.** www.asiasf.com. Reservations recommended. Main courses $9–$20. AE, DISC, MC, V (Mon–Wed $25 minimum). Sun–Thurs 6–10pm; Fri 6:45–10pm; Sat 5–10pm; cocktails and dancing until 2am on weekends. Bus: 9, 12, or 47. Streetcar: Civic Center on underground streetcar. BART: Civic Center.

Yank Sing ★★ CHINESE/DIM SUM Loosely translated as "a delight of the heart," Yank Sing is widely regarded as the best dim sum in the downtown area. The servers are good at guessing your gastric threshold as they wheel stainless steel carts carrying small plates of exotic dishes around the vast dining room; if they whiz right by your table there's probably a good reason. If you're new to dim sum (which, translated, means "to touch the heart"), stick with the safe, recognizable classics such as spareribs, stuffed crab claws, scallion pancakes, shrimp balls, pork buns, and steamed dumplings filled with delicious pork, beef, fish, or vegetable concoctions. A second location, open Monday through Friday from 11am to 3pm, is at 49 Stevenson St., off First Street ((C) **415/541-4949**) in SoMa, and has outdoor seating.

101 Spear St. (at Mission St. at Rincon Center). (C) **415/957-9300.** www.yanksing.com. Dim sum $3.65–$9.30 for 2–6 pieces. AE, DC, MC, V. Mon–Fri 11am–3pm; Sat–Sun and holidays 10am–4pm. Validated parking in Rincon Center Garage. Bus: 1, 12, 14, or 41. Streetcar: F. Cable car: California St. line. BART: Embarcadero.

Inexpensive
Manora's ★ THAI   Manora's cranks out some of the best Thai food in town and is well worth a jaunt to SoMa. But this is no relaxed affair: It's perpetually packed (unless you come early), and you'll be seated sardinelike at one of the cramped but well-appointed tables. During the dinner rush, the noise level can make conversation among larger parties almost impossible, but the food is so darned good, you'll probably prefer to turn toward your plate and stuff your face anyway. Start with a Thai iced tea or coffee and tangy soup or chicken satay, which comes with decadent peanut sauce. Follow these with any of the wonderful dinner dishes—which should be shared—and a side of rice. There are endless options, including a vast array of vegetarian plates. Every remarkably flavorful dish arrives seemingly seconds after you order it, which is great if you're hungry, a bummer if you were planning a long, leisurely dinner. *Tip:* Come before 7pm or after 9pm if you don't want a loud, rushed meal.

1600 Folsom St. (at 12th St.). (C) **415/861-6224.** www.manorathai.com. Reservations recommended for 4 or more. Main courses $7–$12. MC, V. Mon–Fri 11:30am–2:30pm; Mon–Sat 5:30–10:30pm; Sun 5–10pm. Bus: 9, 12, or 47.

FINANCIAL DISTRICT & EMBARCADERO
Expensive
Kokkari ★★ GREEK/MEDITERRANEAN   The funny thing is, I've been to Athens, and the food there wasn't nearly as good as the traditional Aegean dishes they're serving at Kokkari (Ko-*kar*-ee), one of my favorite restaurants in the city. My love affair starts with the setting: a beautifully rustic dining area with a commanding fireplace and oversize furnishings. Past the tiny bar, the other main room is pure rustic revelry with exposed wood beams, pretty standing lamps, and a view of the glass-enclosed private dining room. A must-order appetizer is the *Marithes Tiganites,* a beautiful platter of whole crispy smelts enhanced with garlic-potato *skordalia* (a traditional Greek dip) and lemon. Other favorites are the *pikilia* (a sampling of traditional Greek spreads served with dolmades and house-made pitas) and the fabulous mesquite-grilled octopus salad. Main courses include grilled whole petrale sole with lemon, olive oil, and braised greens; to-die-for moussaka (eggplant, lamb, potato, and béchamel); and lamb chops with oven-roasted lemon-oregano potatoes. Also consider the rotisserie specialties such as a rotisserie-roasted pork loin.

200 Jackson St. (at Front St.). (C) **415/981-0983.** www.kokkari.com. Reservations recommended. Main courses $14–$23 lunch, $19–$35 dinner. AE, DC, DISC, MC, V. Mon–Fri 11:30am–2:30pm; bar menu 2:30–5:30pm; Mon–Thurs 5:30–10pm; Fri 5:30–11pm; Sat 5–11pm. Valet parking (dinner only) $8. Bus: 12, 15, 41, or 83.

One Market ★★ CALIFORNIA   Some of the city's best food has been served at this popular Embarcadero restaurant since 1993. Amid the airy main dining room with its open exhibition kitchen, cozy banquettes, and slate flooring is a sea of diners feasting from a creative, farm-fresh menu compiled by Chef Mark Dommen, who has a passion for fresh local ingredients—they helped establish the Ferry Plaza Farmers' Market across the street. During my last visit, my table was wowed by the truly divine beet carpaccio, shellfish, and seafood sampler (*not* your everyday platter), and a superb crispy skin pork saddle with fava beans and chorizo broth. Whatever you choose, you're bound to find a perfectly accompanying wine from the "cellar," which has over 500 selections of American vintages. Arrive early to mingle with the spirited corporate crowd that convenes from 4:30 to 7pm for happy hour at the bar.

1 Market St. (at Stuart St., across from Justin Herman Plaza). ℂ **415/777-5577.** www.onemarket.com. Reservations recommended. Lunch $16–$23; dinner $20–$33. AE, DC, DISC, MC, V. Mon–Fri 11:30am–2pm and 5:30–9pm; Sat 5:30–10pm. Valet parking $10. All Market St. buses. All BART trains.

The Slanted Door ★★ VIETNAMESE   What started in 1995 as an obscure family-run restaurant in the Mission District has become one of the most popular and written-about restaurants in the city. Due to its meteoric rise—helped along by celebrity fans such as Mick Jagger, Keith Richards, and Quentin Tarantino—it's been relocated within a beautiful bay-inspired, custom-designed space at the Ferry Building Marketplace. What hasn't changed is a menu filled with incredibly fresh and flavorful Vietnamese dishes such as catfish clay-pot flavored with cilantro, ginger, and Thai chiles; an amazing green papaya salad with roasted peanuts; and fragrant peppercorn duck served with apples and watercress. If the cellophane noodles with fresh Dungeness crab meat are on the menu, *definitely* order them. Be sure to start the feast with a pot of tea from their eclectic collection.

1 Ferry Plaza (at the Embarcadero and Market). ℂ **415/861-8032.** www.slanteddoor.com. Reservations recommended. Lunch main courses $8.50–$17; most dinner dishes $15–$27; 7-item fixed-price dinner $45 (parties of 7 or more only). AE, MC, V. Daily 11am–2:30pm; Sun–Thurs 5:30–10pm; Fri–Sat 5:30–10:30pm. Bus: All Market Street buses. Streetcar: F, N-Judah line.

Ⓕinds   **Dine in the Sunshine at Belden Place**

San Francisco has always been woefully lacking in the alfresco dining department. One exception is **Belden Place,** an adorable little brick alley in the heart of the Financial District that is open only to foot traffic. When the weather is agreeable, the restaurants that line the alley break out the big umbrellas, tables, and chairs, and *voilà*—a bit of Paris just off Pine Street.

A handful of adorable cafes line Belden Place and offer a variety of cuisines all at moderate prices. There's **Cafe Bastille,** 22 Belden Place (ℂ **415/986-5673**), a classic French bistro and fun speak-easy basement serving excellent crepes, mussels, and French onion soup; it schedules live jazz on Fridays. **Cafe Tiramisu,** 28 Belden Place (ℂ **415/421-7044**), is a stylish Italian hot spot serving addictive risottos and gnocchi. **Plouf,** 40 Belden Place (ℂ **415/986-6491**), specializes in big bowls of mussels slathered in your choice of seven sauces, as well as fresh seafood. **B44,** 44 Belden Place (ℂ **415/986-6287**), serves up a side order of Spain alongside its revered paella and other seriously zesty Spanish dishes.

Sam's Grill & Seafood Restaurant ★ (Finds) SEAFOOD   Power-lunching at Sam's is a San Francisco tradition, and Sam's has done a brisk business with Financial District suits since—get this—1867. Even if you're not carrying a briefcase, this is the place to come for time-capsule dining at its most classically San Francisco. Pass the crowded entrance and small bar to get to the main dining room—packed with virtually all men—kick back, and watch yesteryear happen today. (Or conversely, slide into a curtained booth and see nothing but your dining companion.) Tuxedo-clad waiters race around, doling out big crusty cuts of sourdough bread and distributing salads overflowing with fresh crab and Roquefort vinaigrette, towering plates of seafood pasta with marinara, charbroiled fish, roasted chicken, and old-school standbys such as calves' liver with bacon and onions or Salisbury steak. Don't worry—they didn't forget classic creamed spinach. The restaurant's mildly salty service and good old-fashioned character make everything on the menu taste that much better.

374 Bush St. (btw. Montgomery and Kearny sts.). (C) **415/421-0594.** Reservations recommended for dinner and for 6 or more at lunch. Main courses $12–$24. AE, DC, DISC, MC, V. Mon–Fri 11am–9pm. Bus: 15, 45, or 76.

CHINATOWN
Inexpensive

Brandy Ho's Hunan Food ★ CHINESE   Fancy black-and-white granite tabletops and a large, open kitchen give you the first clue that the food at this casual restaurant is a cut above the usual Hunan fare. Take my advice and start immediately with fried dumplings (in sweet-and-sour sauce) or cold chicken salad and then move on to fish-ball soup with spinach, bamboo shoots, noodles, and other goodies. The best main course is Three Delicacies, a combination of scallops, shrimp, and chicken with onion, bell pepper, and bamboo shoots, seasoned with ginger, garlic, and wine, and served with black-bean sauce. Most dishes are quite hot and spicy, but the kitchen will adjust the level to meet your specifications. A full bar includes Asian-food-friendly libations like plum wine and sake from 11:30am to 11pm. *Note:* There's a second location in the Castro at 4068 18th St. (at Castro St.; (C) **415/252-8000**).

217 Columbus Ave. (at Pacific Ave.). (C) **415/788-7527.** www.brandyhos.com. Reservations recommended. Main courses $8–$13. AE, DISC, MC, V. Sun–Thurs 11:30am–11pm; Fri–Sat 11:30am–midnight. Paid parking available at 170 Columbus Ave. Bus: 15 or 41.

House of Nanking ★ CHINESE   This place would be strictly a tourist joint if it weren't for the die-hard fans who happily wait—sometimes up to an hour—for a coveted seat at this inconspicuous little restaurant serving Shanghai-style cuisine. Order the requisite potstickers, green-onion-and-shrimp pancakes with peanut sauce, or any number of pork, rice, beef, seafood, chicken, or vegetable dishes from the menu, but I suggest you trust the waiter when he recommends a special. Even with an expansion that doubled the available space, seating is tight, so prepare to be bumped around a bit and don't expect perky or attentive service—it's all part of the Nanking experience.

919 Kearny St. (at Columbus Ave.). (C) **415/421-1429.** Reservations accepted for groups of 8 or more. Main courses $6–$12. MC, V. Mon–Fri 11am–10pm; Sat–Sun noon–10pm. Bus: 9, 12, 15, or 30.

R&G Lounge ★ CHINESE   It's tempting to take your chances and duck into any of the exotic restaurants in Chinatown, but if you want a sure thing, go directly to the three-story R&G Lounge. During lunch, all three floors are packed with hungry neighborhood workers who go straight for the $5.50 rice-plate specials. Even then, you can order from the dinner menu, which features legendary deep-fried salt-and-pepper crab (a little greasy for my taste); and wonderful chicken with black-bean sauce. A personal favorite is melt-in-your-mouth R&G Special Beef, which explodes with the tangy flavor of the accompanying sauce. I was less excited by the tired chicken salad, house specialty noodles, and bland spring rolls. But that was just fine, as I saved room for generous and savory seafood in a clay pot and classic roast duck.

631 Kearny St. (at Clay St.). © **415/982-7877.** www.rnglounge.com. Reservations recommended. Main courses $9.50–$30. AE, DC, DISC, MC, V. Daily 11am–9:30pm. Parking validated across the street at Portsmouth Sq. garage 24 hr. or Holiday Inn after 5pm. Bus: 1, 9AX, 9BX, or 15. Cable Car: California.

NOB HILL & RUSSIAN HILL
Moderate

Nob Hill Cafe ★ (Finds ITALIAN/PIZZA Considering the steep cost and formality of most Nob Hill restaurants, it's no wonder that residents don't mind waiting around for a table to open up at this cozy neighborhood bistro. This is the kind of place where you can come wearing jeans and sneakers, tuck into a large plate of linguine with clams and a glass of pinot, and leave fulfilled without blowing a wad of dough (pastas are in the humble $9–$12 range). The dining room is split into two small, simple rooms, with windows looking onto Taylor Street and bright local art on the walls. Service is friendly, and one of the owners is almost always on hand to make sure everyone's content. When the kitchen is "on," expect hearty Northern Italian comfort fare worth at least twice its price; even on off days, it's still a bargain. Start with a salad or the decadent polenta with pesto and parmigiano, and then fill up on the veal piccata, any of the pastas or pizzas, or petrale sole. *Tip:* Parking can be difficult in Nob Hill; fortunately, they offer valet parking a block away at the corner of Washington and Taylor streets.

1152 Taylor St. (btw. Sacramento and Clay sts.). © **415/776-6500.** Reservations not accepted. Main courses $7–$16. DC, MC, V. Daily 11:30am–3pm and 5–10pm. Bus: 1.

Swan Oyster Depot ★★ (Finds SEAFOOD Turning 96 years old in 2008, Swan Oyster Depot is a classic San Francisco dining experience you shouldn't miss. Opened in 1912, this tiny hole in the wall, run by the city's friendliest servers, is little more than a narrow fish market that decided to slap down some bar stools. There are only 20 or so stools here, jammed cheek-by-jowl along a long marble bar. Most patrons come for a quick cup of chowder or a plate of oysters on the half shell, which arrive chilling on crushed ice. The menu is limited to fresh crab, shrimp, oyster, clam cocktails, a few types of smoked fish, Maine lobster, and Boston-style clam chowder, all of which are exceedingly fresh. *Note:* Don't let the lunchtime line dissuade you—it moves fast.

1517 Polk St. (btw. California and Sacramento sts.). © **415/673-1101.** Reservations not accepted. Seafood cocktails $7–$15; clams and oysters on the half-shell $7.95 per half-dozen. No credit cards. Mon–Sat 8am–5:30pm. Bus: 1, 19, 47, or 49.

NORTH BEACH
Moderate

Piperade ★★ BASQUE Chef Gerald Hirigoyen takes diners on a Basque adventure in this charming, small restaurant. Surrounded by a low wood-beam-lined ceiling, oak floors, and soft sconce lighting, it's a casual affair, where diners indulge in small and large plates of Hirigoyen's superbly flavorful West Coast Basque cuisine. Your edible odyssey starts with small plates—or plates to be shared—like my personal favorites: *piquillo* peppers stuffed with goat cheese; and a bright and simple salad of garbanzo beans with calamari, chorizo, and *piquillo* peppers. Share entrees, too. Indulge in New York steak with braised shallots and french fries or sop up every drop of the sweet and savory red-pepper sauce with the braised seafood and shellfish stew. Save room for orange blossom beignets: Light and airy, with a delicate and moist web of dough within and a kiss of orange essence, the beignet is dessert at its finest. There's a communal table for drop-in diners and front patio seating during warmer weather.

1015 Battery St. (at Green St.). © **415/391-2555**. www.piperade.com. Reservations recommended. Main courses $17–$24. AE, DC, DISC, MC, V. Mon–Fri 11:30am–3pm and 5:30–10:30pm; Sat 5:30–10:30pm. Bus: 10, 12, 30, or 82x.

Inexpensive

Capp's Corner ★ Value ITALIAN   Capp's is a place of givens: It's a given that high-spirited regulars are hunched over the bar and that you'll be served huge portions of straightforward Italian fare at low prices in a raucous atmosphere that prevails until closing. The waitresses are usually brusque and bossy, but always with a wink. Long tables are set up for family-style dining: bread, soup, salad, and choice of around 20 classic main dishes (herb-roasted leg of lamb, spaghetti with meatballs, *osso buco* with polenta, fettuccine with prawns and white-wine sauce)—all for $15 or $17 or so per person, around $10 for kids. You might have to wait for a table, but if you want fun old-school dining without pomp or huge prices, you'll find the wait worthwhile.

1600 Powell St. (at Green St.). © **415/989-2589**. www.cappscorner.com. Reservations accepted. Complete dinners $15–$17. AE, DC, MC, V. Daily 11:30am–2:30pm; Mon–Fri 4:30–10:30pm; Sat–Sun 4–11pm. Bus: 15, 30, or 41.

Il Pollaio ★ Value ITALIAN/ARGENTINE   Simple, affordable, and consistently good is the winning combination at Il Pollaio. When I used to live in the neighborhood I ate here at least once a week and I still can't make chicken this good. Seat yourself in the tiny, unfussy room, order, and wait expectantly for the fresh-from-the-grill lemon-infused chicken, which is so moist it practically falls off the bone. Each meal comes with a choice of salad or fries. If you're not in the mood for chicken, you can opt for rabbit, lamb, pork chop, or Italian sausage. On a sunny day, get your goods to go, and picnic across the street at Washington Square.

555 Columbus Ave. (btw. Green and Union sts.). © **415/362-7727**. Reservations not accepted. Main courses $8–$15. DISC, MC, V. Mon–Sat 11:30am–9pm. Bus: 15, 30, 39, 41, or 45. Cable car: Powell–Mason line.

L'Osteria del Forno ★★ ITALIAN   L'Osteria del Forno might be only slightly larger than a walk-in closet, but it's one of the top three authentic Italian restaurants in North Beach. Peer in the window facing Columbus Avenue, and you'll probably see two Italian women with their hair up, sweating from the heat of the oven, which cranks out the best focaccia (and focaccia sandwiches) in the city. There's no pomp or circumstance here: Locals come strictly to eat. The menu features a variety of superb pizzas, salads, soups, and fresh pastas, plus a good selection of daily specials (pray for the roast pork braised in milk), which includes a roast of the day, pasta, and ravioli. Small baskets of warm focaccia keep you going until the arrival of the entrees, which should always be accompanied by a glass of Italian red. Good news for folks on the go: You can get pizza by the slice. Note that it's cash-only here.

519 Columbus Ave. (btw. Green and Union sts.). © **415/982-1124**. www.losteriadelforno.com. Reservations not accepted. Sandwiches $6–$7; pizzas $10–$18; main courses $6–$14. No credit cards. Sun–Mon and Wed–Thurs 11:30am–10pm; Fri–Sat 11:30am–10:30pm. Bus: 15, 30, 41, or 45.

Mario's Bohemian Cigar Store ★ (Finds) ITALIAN   Across the street from Wash-

107
ington Square is one of North Beach's most venerable neighborhood hangouts. The century-old corner cafe—small, well worn, and perpetually busy—is one of the oldest and best original cappuccino cafes in United States. I stop by at least once a month for a meatball or eggplant focaccia sandwich and a slice of Mario's house-made ricotta cheese-cake, and then recharge with a cappuccino as I watch the world stroll by the picture windows. And no, they don't sell cigars.

566 Columbus Ave. (at Union St.). ℂ **415/362-0536.** www.mariosbohemiancigarstore.com. Sandwiches $7.75–$8.50. MC, V. Mon–Sat 10am–midnight; Sun 10am–11pm. Bus: 15, 30, 41, or 45.

FISHERMAN'S WHARF
Expensive
Restaurant Gary Danko ★★★ FRENCH   James Beard Award–winning chef Gary Danko presides over my top pick for fine dining. Eschewing the white-glove formality of yesteryear's fine dining, Danko offers impeccable cuisine and perfectly orchestrated service in an unstuffy environment of wooden paneling and shutters and well-spaced tables (not to mention spa-style bathrooms). The three- to five-course fixed-price seasonal menu is freestyle, so whether you want a sampling of appetizers or a flight of meat courses, you need only ask. I am a devoted fan of his trademark buttery-smooth glazed oysters with lettuce cream, salsify, and Osetra caviar; seared foie gras, which may be accompanied by peaches, caramelized onions, and *verjus* (a classic French sauce); horse-radish-crusted salmon medallions with dilled cucumbers; and adventurous Moroccan spiced squab with *chermoula* (a Moroccan sauce made with cilantro) and orange-cumin carrots. Truthfully, I've never had a dish here that wasn't wonderful. And wine? The list is stellar, albeit expensive. If, after dinner, you have the will to pass on the glorious cheese cart or flambéed dessert of the day, a plate of petit fours reminds you that Gary Danko is one sweet and memorable meal. *Tip:* If you can't get a reservation and are set on dining here, slip in and grab a seat at the 10-stool first-come, first-served bar, where you can also order a la carte.

800 North Point St. (at Hyde St.). ℂ **415/749-2060.** www.garydanko.com. Reservations required except at walk-in bar. 3- to 5-course fixed-price menu $61–$89. AE, DC, DISC, MC, V. Daily 5:30–10pm; bar open 5pm. Valet parking $10. Bus: 10. Streetcar: F. Cable car: Hyde.

Scoma's ★ SEAFOOD   A throwback to the dining of yesteryear, Scoma's eschews trendier trout preparations and fancy digs for good old-fashioned seafood served in huge portions amid a very casual windowed waterfront setting. Gourmands should skip this one. But if your idea of heaven is straightforward seafood classics—fried calamari, raw oysters, pesto pasta with rock shrimp, crab cioppino, lobster thermidor—served with a generous portion of old-time hospitality, and then Scoma's is as good as it gets. Unfortunately, a taste of tradition will cost you big time. Prices are as steep as those at some of the finest restaurants in town. Personally, I'd rather splurge at Gary Danko or A. Sabella's. But many of my out-of-town guests insist we meet at Scoma's, which is fine by me, because it's a change of pace from today's chic spots, and the parking's free.

Pier 47 and Al Scoma Way (btw. Jefferson and Jones sts.). ℂ **800/644-5852** or 415/771-4383. www.scomas.com. Reservations not accepted. Most main courses $18–$35. AE, DC, DISC, MC, V. Mon–Thurs 11:30am–10pm; Fri–Sat 11:30am–10:30pm; Sun 11:30am–10pm; bar opens 30 min. prior to lunch daily. Free valet parking. Bus: 10 or 47. Streetcar: F.

SAN FRANCISCO

5

WHERE TO DINE

Fog City Diner ★ AMERICAN   The Fog City Diner gets mixed reviews among locals, but I've always been satisfied after dining here. The restaurant looks like a genuine American metallic diner—but only from the outside. Inside, dark polished woods, inspired lighting, and a well-stocked raw bar tell you that this is no hash-slinger. Dressed-up diner dishes include juicy gourmet burgers with house-made pickles, huge salads, hot breads, soups, sandwiches, cioppino, macaroni and Gouda cheese, and pork chops. Fancier fish and meat meals include grilled catch of the day and thick-cut steaks. Light eaters can make a meal out of the long list of "small plates," which include crab cakes and quesadillas with asparagus and leek. The food is fine, but if your heart is set on coming here, do so at lunch or for early evening cocktails and appetizers—you'll be better off elsewhere if you want a special dinner. They've recently opened for weekend brunch as well.

1300 Battery St. (at the Embarcadero). © **415/982-2000.** www.fogcitydiner.com. Reservations recommended. Main courses $11–$22. DC, DISC, MC, V. Mon–Thurs 11am–10pm; Fri 11am–11pm; Sat 10:30am–11pm; Sun 10:30am–10pm. Bus: 42.

Inexpensive

Boudin at the Wharf DELI/AMERICAN   This industrial-chic Fisherman's Wharf shrine to the city's famous tangy French-style bread is impossible to miss. Even if you're not hungry, drop in to see bakers at work making 3,000 loaves daily or take the tour and learn about the city sourdough bread's history (Boudin is the city's oldest continually operating business). Good, strong coffee is served at **Peet's Coffee** (another Bay Area great), and at **Bakers Hall** you'll find picnic possibilities such as handcrafted cheeses, fruit spreads, and chocolates, as well as a wall map highlighting the town's best places to spread a blanket and feast. There's also a casual **self-serve cafe,** serving sandwiches, clam chowder bowls, salads, and pastries, and the more formal **Bistro Boudin** restaurant, which offers Alcatraz views with its Dungeness crab Louis, pizza, crab cakes, and burgers on sourdough buns.

160 Jefferson St., near Pier 43½. © **415/928-1849.** www.boudinbakery.com. Reservations recommended at bistro. Main courses cafe $6–$10, bistro $11–$33. AE, DC, DISC, MC, V. Cafe daily 8am–10pm. Bistro Mon–Fri noon–10pm; Sat 11:30am–10pm; Sun 11:30am–9pm. Bus: 10, 15, or 47. Streetcar: F.

MARINA DISTRICT & COW HOLLOW
Very Expensive

Spruce ★ CONTEMPORARY AMERICAN   In case you haven't heard of Pacific Heights, it's where most of the city's old money lives; and now the ladies-who-lunch have a new place to hang their cloches. Housed in a beautifully restored 1930s-era auto barn, Spruce consists of a restaurant, a cafe offering gourmet takeaway, an elegant bar, and a lounge, making it a destination restaurant as well as a neighborhood hangout. The 70-seat restaurant features mohair couches, faux-ostrich chairs, and a black-and-chocolate decor that's quite visually appealing, but, the cuisine isn't quite as impressive. The organic, locally sourced produce is wonderfully fresh, but many of the dishes we tried—spearmint and nettle ravioli, leek and fennel soup with salt cod dumplings, honey lacquered duck breast—were lacking in flavor, and the service suffered from mysteriously long spells of absence. Spruce is still one of the exciting new restaurants in San Francisco, but it's best enjoyed from a seat at the bar, tucked into their fantastic all-natural burger and fries, while pondering which wine to choose from their 70 by-the-glass selections.

3640 Sacramento St. (at Spruce St.). ℭ **415/931-5100.** www.sprucesf.com. Reservations recommended. **109**
Main courses $25–$40. AE, DC, DISC, MC, V. Mon–Fri 11:30am–11pm; Sat–Sun 5–11pm. Valet parking $12
dinner only. Bus: 1, 2, or 4.

Moderate

A16 ★★ ITALIAN   This sleek, casual, and wonderfully lively spot is one of San Francisco's best and busiest restaurants, featuring Neapolitan-style pizza and cuisine from the
region of Campania. Named after the motorway that traverses the region, the divided
space boasts a wine and beer bar up front, a larger dining area and open kitchen in the
back, and a wall of wines in between. But its secret weapon is the creative menu of outstanding appetizers, pizza, and entrees, which are orchestrated by chef Nate Appleman
with the same perfection as they were by opening chef Christophe Hille. Co-owner and
wine director Shelley Lindgren guides diners through one of the city's most exciting wine
lists, featuring 40 wines by the half-glass, glass, and carafe. Oddly enough, their desserts
are consistently mediocre, but perhaps that will change by the time you visit.

2355 Chestnut St. (btw. Divisadero and Scott sts.). ℭ **415/771-2216.** www.a16sf.com. Reservations
recommended. Main courses $8–$13 lunch, $14–$20 dinner. AE, DC, MC, V. Wed–Fri 11:30am–2:30pm;
Sun–Thurs 5–10pm; Fri–Sat 5–11pm. Bus: 22, 30, or 30X.

Chez Nous ★★ FRENCH   Diners get crammed into the 40-seat dining area of this
bright, cheery, small, and bustling dining room, but the eclectic tapas are so delicious and
affordable, no one seems to care. Indeed, this friendly and fast-paced neighborhood
haunt has become a blueprint for other restaurants that understand the allure of small
plates. But Chez Nous stands out as more than a petite-portion trendsetter; most of its
Mediterranean dishes taste so clean and fresh you can't wait to come back and dine here
again. Start with the soup, whatever it is; don't skip the tasty french fries with *harissa*
(Tunisian hot sauce) aioli; savor the lamb chops with lavender sea salt; and save room for
their famed mini-custard-cake-like *canneles de Bordeaux*.

1911 Fillmore St. (btw. Pine and Bush sts.). ℭ **415/441-8044.** Reservations accepted, but walk-ins welcome. Small dishes $5–$13. AE, MC, V. Daily 11:30am–3pm and 5:30–10pm (Fri–Sat until 11pm). Bus: 22,
41, or 45.

Greens Restaurant ★★ VEGETARIAN   In an old waterfront warehouse, with
enormous windows overlooking the bridge, boats, and the bay, Greens is one of the most
renowned vegetarian restaurants in the country. Executive chef Annie Somerville (author
of *Fields of Greens*) cooks with the seasons, using produce from local organic farms.
Within the quiet dining room, a weeknight dinner might feature such appetizers as
mushroom soup with Asiago cheese and tarragon; or grilled portobello and endive salad.
Entrees run the gamut from pizza with wilted escarole, red onions, lemon, Asiago, and
Parmesan, to Vietnamese yellow curry or risotto with black trumpet mushrooms, leeks,
savory spinach, white-truffle oil, Parmesan Reggiano, and thyme. Those interested in the
whole shebang should make reservations for the $48 four-course dinner served on Satur-
day only. Lunch and brunch are equally fresh and tasty. The adjacent Greens To Go sells
sandwiches, soups, salads, and pastries.

Building A, Fort Mason Center (enter Fort Mason opposite the Safeway at Buchanan and Marina sts.).
ℭ **415/771-6222.** www.greensrestaurant.com. Reservations recommended. Main courses $9.50–$14
lunch, $15–$20 dinner, fixed-price dinner $48; Sun brunch $8–$14. AE, DISC, MC, V. Tues–Sat noon–
2:30pm; Sun 10:30am–9pm; Mon–Sat 5:30–9pm. Greens To Go Mon–Thurs 8am–8pm; Fri–Sat 8am–5pm;
Sun 10:30am–4pm. Parking in hourly lot $4 for up to 2¹/₂ hrs. Bus: 28 or 30.

SAN FRANCISCO

5

WHERE TO DINE

Isa ★★ FRENCH   Luke Sung, who trained with some of the best French chefs in the city, has captured many locals' hearts by creating the kind of menu we foodies dream of: a smattering of small dishes, served a la carte family-style, that allow you to try numerous items in one sitting. It's a good thing the menu, considered "French tapas," offers small portions at reasonable prices. A party of two can choose all of these plus one or two more and not be rolled out the door afterward. Adding to the allure is the warm boutique dining environment—70 seats scattered amid a small dining room in the front, and a large tented and heated patio out back that sets the mood with a warm yellow glow. Take a peek at the "kitchen," a shoebox of a cooking space, to appreciate Sung's accomplishments that much more. Cocktailers, take note: You'll only find beer, wine, and shoju cocktails (shoju is a smooth alcohol made from sweet potato thatis used like vodka).

3324 Steiner St. (btw. Lombard and Chestnut sts.). ✆ 415/567-9588. www.isarestaurant.com. Reservations recommended. Main courses $9–$16. MC, V. Mon–Thurs 5:30–10pm; Fri–Sat 5:30–10:30pm. Bus: 22, 28, 30, 30X, 43, or 76.

PlumpJack Café ★ CALIFORNIA/FRENCH/MEDITERRANEAN   Wildly popular among San Francisco's style-setters, this small, 55-seat Cow Hollow restaurant, with a hint of whimsical Shakespearean decor, is one of the neighborhood's most "in" places to dine—partly because the place was founded and is frequented by Mayor Gavin Newsom. The extraordinarily extensive California wine list—gleaned from the Plump-Jack wine shop down the street—is sold at next-to-retail prices, with many wines available by the glass.

3127 Fillmore St. (btw. Filbert and Greenwich sts.). ✆ 415/563-4755. www.plumpjack.com. Reservations recommended. Main courses $13–$16 lunch, $20–$34 dinner. AE, DC, DISC, MC, V. Mon–Fri 11:30am–2pm; daily 5:30–10pm. Valet parking $14 for 3 hrs. after 6pm. Bus: 22, 41, or 45.

Inexpensive

The Grove ★ CAFE   The Grove is the kind of place you go just to hang out and enjoy the fact that you're in San Francisco. That the heaping salads, lasagna, pasta, sandwiches, and daily specials are predictably good is an added bonus. I like coming here on weekday mornings for the easy-going vibe, strong coffee, and friendly, fast service. Inside you can sit at one of the dark wood tables on the scuffed hardwood floor and people-watch through the large open windows, but on sunny days the most coveted seats are along the sidewalk. It's the perfect place to read the newspaper, sip an enormous mug of coffee, and be glad you're not at work right now. A second Pacific Heights location is at 2016 Fillmore St., between California and Pine Sts (✆ 415/474-1419).

2250 Chestnut St. (btw. Scott and Pierce sts.). ✆ 415/474-4843. Most main courses $6–$7. MC, V. Mon–Fri 7am–11pm; Sat–Sun 8am–11pm. Bus: 22, 28, 30, 30X, 43, 76, or 82X.

Mel's Drive-In ★ (Kids) AMERICAN   Sure, it's contrived, touristy, and nowhere near healthy, but when you get that urge for a chocolate shake and banana cream pie at the stroke of midnight—or when you want to entertain the kids—no other place in the city comes through like Mel's. Modeled after a classic 1950s diner, right down to the jukebox at each table, Mel's harkens back to the halcyon days when cholesterol and fried foods didn't jab your guilty conscience with every greasy, wonderful bite. Too bad the prices don't reflect the '50s; a burger with fries and a Coke costs about $12.

Another Mel's, at 3355 Geary St., at Stanyan Street (✆ 415/387-2244), is open from 6am to 1am Sunday through Thursday and 6am to 3am Friday and Saturday. Additional locations are: 1050 Van Ness (✆ 415/292-6357), open Sunday through Thursday 6am to 3am and Friday through Sunday 6am to 4am; and 801 Mission St. (© **415/227-4477**), open Sunday through Wednesday 6am to 1am, Thursday 6am to 2am, and Friday and Saturday 24 hours.

2165 Lombard St. (at Fillmore St.). © **415/921-3039.** www.melsdrive-in.com. Main courses $6.50–$12 breakfast, $7–$10 lunch, $8–$15 dinner. MC, V. Sun–Wed 6am–1am; Thurs 6am–2am; Fri–Sat 24 hr. Bus: 22, 30, or 43.

JAPANTOWN

Takara ★ JAPANESE/SUSHI   This unassuming restaurant tucked at the eastern end of Japantown is not only large enough that you don't have to wait in a long line (unlike other local sushi spots), but the fish is extremely fresh and affordable and the other offerings are fantastic. Their *yosenabe* is a meal for two that's under $20: a giant pot of soup is brought to the table on a burner, accompanied by a plate of fresh raw meat or seafood and vegetables. After you briefly cook the food in the liquid, you ladle it out and devour it. Even after serving two hungry people, there are always leftovers. Other favorites are anything with shrimp—pulled live from the tank—and sukiyaki, another tableside cooking experience. Bargain hunters should come for a lunch plate.

22 Peace Plaza, no. 202 (in Japan Center Miyako Mall). © **415/921-2000.** Reservations recommended. Main courses $15–$23. MC, V. Daily 11:30am–2:30pm and 5:30–10pm.

CIVIC CENTER
Expensive

Jardinière ★★ CALIFORNIA/FRENCH   Jardinière is a pre- and post-symphony favorite, and it also happens to be the perfect setting for enjoying a cocktail with your significant other. A culinary dream team created the elegant dining room and sophisticated menu: owner-designer Pat Kuleto, who created the beautiful champagne-inspired decor, and owner/chef Traci Des Jardins, one of the city's most popular chefs. On most evenings, the bi-level brick structure is abuzz with an older crowd (including ex-mayor Brown, a regular), sipping cocktails at the centerpiece mahogany bar or watching the scene discreetly from the circular balcony. The restaurant's champagne theme extends to twinkling lights and clever ice buckets built into the balcony railing, making the atmosphere conducive to splurging in the best of style—especially when live jazz is playing (at 7:30pm nightly). The daily changing menu might include seared scallops with truffled potatoes and truffle reduction; sautéed petrale sole with Alsatian cabbage and Riesling sauce; or venison with celery root, red wine, braised cabbage, and juniper sauce. The cheese selection is outstanding, and the wine list is superb— over 500 bottles, with many offered by the glass.

300 Grove St. (at Franklin St.). © **415/861-5555.** www.jardiniere.com. Reservations recommended. Main courses $26–$38; 6-course tasting menu $79. AE, DC, DISC, MC, V. Sun–Wed 5–10:30pm; Thurs–Sat 5–11:30pm. Valet parking $10. Bus: 19 or 21.

Moderate

Zuni Café ★★ (Finds) MEDITERRANEAN   Zuni Café embodies the best of San Francisco dining: Its clientele spans young hipsters to hunky gays, the cuisine is consistently terrific, and the atmosphere is electric. Its expanse of windows overlooking Market Street gives the place a sense of space, despite the fact that it's always packed. For the full effect, stand at the bustling, copper-topped bar and order a glass of wine and a few oysters from the oyster menu (a dozen or so varieties are on hand at all times). Then, because *of course* you made advance reservations, take your seat in the stylish exposed-brick two-level maze of little dining rooms or on the outdoor patio. Then do what we all do: Splurge on chef Judy Rodgers's Mediterranean-influenced menu. Although the ever-changing menu always includes meat (such as hanger steak), fish (grilled or braised on the kitchen's wood grill), and pasta (tagliatelle with nettles, applewood-smoked bacon, butter, and Parmesan), it's almost sinful not to order her brick-oven roasted chicken for two with Tuscan-style bread salad. I rarely pass up the polenta with mascarpone and a proper Caesar salad. But then again, if you're there for lunch or after 10pm, the hamburger on grilled rosemary focaccia bread is a strong contender for the city's best. Whatever you decide, be sure to order a stack of shoestring potatoes.

1658 Market St. (at Franklin St.). (✆ **415/552-2522.** www.zunicafe.com. Reservations recommended. Main courses $10–$19 lunch, $15–$29 dinner. AE, MC, V. Tues–Sat 11:30am–midnight; Sun 11am–11pm. Valet parking $10. Bus: 6, 7, or 71. Streetcar: All Market St. streetcars.

Inexpensive

Frjtz Fries ★ BELGIAN Although they serve great sandwiches and salads, Frjtz is best known for its addictively crisp french fries, piled high in a paper cone (how Euro) and served with a barrage of exotic dipping sauces such as chipotle rémoulade and balsamic mayo. I'm also a fan of their crepes—try the grilled rosemary chicken and Swiss cheese—their big, leafy salad, or the chunky focaccia sandwich packed with roasted peppers, red onions, pesto mayo, grilled eggplant, and melted Gorgonzola. Wash it down with creamy Chimay Belgian ale. *Note:* There's also a second Frjtz Fries at 590 Valencia St. (at 17th St.; (✆ **415/863-8272**) in the Mission.

581 Hayes St. (at Laguna St.). (✆ **415/864-7654.** www.frjtzfries.com. Reservations not accepted. Fries $3–$4.50; crepes $5–$8; sandwiches $7–$8.25. AE, DC, DISC, MC, V. Mon–Thurs 11am–10pm; Fri–Sat 11am–midnight; Sun 11am–9pm. Bus: 21.

HAIGHT-ASHBURY

Inexpensive

Cha Cha Cha ★★ (Value) CARIBBEAN This is one of my all-time favorite places to get festive, but it's not for everybody. Dining at Cha Cha Cha is not about a meal, it's about an experience. Put your name on the waiting list, crowd into the minuscule bar, and sip sangria while you wait. When you do get seated (it can take up to two pitchers of sangria, but by then you really don't care), you'll dine in a loud—and I mean *loud*—dining room with Santeria altars, banana trees, and plastic tropical-themed tablecloths. The best thing to do is order from the tapas menu and share the dishes family-style. Fried calamari, fried new potatoes, Cajun shrimp, and mussels in saffron broth are all bursting with flavor and accompanied by luscious sauces. This is the kind of place where you take friends in a partying mood and make an evening of it. If you want the flavor without the festivities, come during lunch. Their second, larger location, in the Mission District, at 2327 Mission St., between 19th and 20th streets ((✆ **415/648-0504**), is open for dinner only and has a full bar specializing in mojitos.

1801 Haight St. (at Shrader St.). (✆ **415/386-7670.** www.cha3.com. Reservations not accepted. Tapas $5–$9; main courses $12–$15. MC, V. Daily 11:30am–4pm; Sun–Thurs 5–11pm; Fri–Sat 5–11:30pm. Bus: 6, 7, or 71. Streetcar: N.

Kan Zaman ★ (Finds) MIDDLE EASTERN An evening dining at Kan Zaman is one of those quintessential Haight-Ashbury experiences that you can't wait to tell your friends about back in Ohio. As you pass through glass-beaded curtains, you're led by the hostess to knee-high tables under a billowed canopy tent. Shoes removed, you sit cross-legged with your friends in cushioned comfort. The most adventurous of your group requests an *argeeleh,* a large hookah pipe filled with fruity honey or apricot tobacco. Reluctantly at first, everyone simultaneously sips the sweet smoke from the cobralike tendrils emanating from the hookah; then dinner arrives—inexpensive platters offering a variety of classic Middle Eastern cuisine. The spiced wine starts to take effect, just in time for the beautiful, sensuous belly dancers who glide across the dining room, mesmerizing the rapt audience with their seemingly impossible gyrations. The evening ends, the bill arrives: $17 each. Perfect. *Note:* Belly dancing starts at 9pm Thursday though Saturday only.

1793 Haight St. (at Shrader St.). ℭ **415/751-9656.** Main courses $4–$14. MC, V. Mon–Thurs 5pm–midnight; Fri 5pm–2am; Sat noon–2am; Sun noon–midnight. Metro: N. Bus: 6, 7, 66, 71, or 73.

RICHMOND & SUNSET DISTRICTS
Moderate

Aziza ★★ MOROCCAN   If you're looking for something really different—or a festive spot for a large party—head deep into the Avenues for an exotic taste of Morocco. Chef/owner Mourad Lahlou creates an excellent dining experience through colorful and distinctly Moroccan surroundings combined with a modern yet authentic take on his native cuisine. In any of the three opulently adorned dining rooms (the front room features private booths, the middle is more formal, and the back has lower seating and a lounge feel), you can indulge in the seasonal five-course tasting menu ($49) or individual treats such as kumquat-enriched lamb shank; saffron guinea hen with preserved lemon and olives; or Paine Farm squab with wild mushrooms, bitter greens, and a *ras el hanout* reduction (a traditional Moroccan blend of 40 or so spices).

5800 Geary Blvd. (at 22nd Ave.). ℭ **415/752-2222.** www.aziza-sf.com. Reservations recommended. Main courses $10–$22; 5-course menu $39. MC, V. Wed–Mon 5:30–10:30pm. Valet parking $8 weekdays, $10 weekends. Bus: 29 or 38.

Beach Chalet Brewery & Restaurant ★ AMERICAN   While Cliff House (see below) has more historical character and better ocean views, the Beach Chalet has far better food, drinks, and atmosphere (ergo, it's where the locals go). The Chalet occupies the upper floor of a historic public lounge, adorned with WPA frescos, that originally opened in 1900 and has been fully restored. Dinner is pricey, and the ocean view disappears with the sun, so come for lunch or an early dinner when you can eat your hamburger, buttermilk fried calamari, or grilled Atlantic salmon with one of the best vistas around. In the evening, it's a more local crowd, especially on Tuesday through Sunday evenings when live bands accompany the cocktails and house-brewed ales. Breakfast is served here as well. *Note:* Be careful getting into the parking lot (accessible only from the northbound side of the highway)—it's a quick, sandy turn.

In early 2004, owners Lara and Greg Truppelli added the adjoining **Park Chalet** restaurant to the Beach Chalet. The 3,000-square-foot glass-enclosed extension behind the original landmark building offers more casual fare—with entrees ranging from $11 to $23—including rib-eye steak, fish and chips, roasted chicken, and pizza. Retractable glass walls reveal Golden Gate Park's landmark Dutch windmill, a fireplace warms the room on chillier evenings, and live music is performed Tuesday and Thursday through Sunday evenings. Weather permitting, you can eat out back on the lawn, where a weekend barbecue is held from 11am to dusk in summer. The restaurant opens at 11am daily in the summer (noon in winter) and has varying closing times, so call ahead.

1000 Great Hwy. (at west end of Golden Gate Park, near Fulton St.). ℭ **415/386-8439.** www.beachchalet. com. Main courses $8–$17 breakfast, $11–$27 lunch/dinner. AE, MC, V. Beach Chalet Mon–Fri 9am–11am;

daily 11am–5pm; Sun–Thurs 5–10pm; Fri–Sat 5–11pm; brunch Sat–Sun 9am–2pm. Park Chalet Mon–Fri noon–9pm; Sun–Thurs 5–9pm; Fri–Sat 5–11pm; brunch Sat–Sun 11am–2pm. Bus: 18, 31, or 38. Streetcar: N.

Cliff House ★ CALIFORNIA/SEAFOOD   In the old days (we're talking way back), Cliff House was *the* place to go for a romantic night on the town. Nowadays, the revamped San Francisco landmark caters mostly to tourists who arrive to gander at the Sutro Baths remains next door or dine at the two remodeled restaurants. The more formal (and pricey) **Sutro's** has contemporary decor, spectacular panoramic views, and a fancy seafood-influenced American menu that showcases local ingredients. The food, while nothing revolutionary, is well prepared and features the likes of roasted organic beet salad, or lobster and crab cakes with shaved fennel, romesco sauce, and caramelized Meyer lemon. The same spectacular views, in less dramatic but still beautiful surroundings, can be found at the **Bistro,** which offers big salads, sandwiches, burgers, and other soul-satisfiers. For the most superb ocean views, come for sunset, as long as it looks like the fog will let up. The popular Sunday champagne buffet in the **Terrace Room** features live harp music (reserve well in advance).

1090 Point Lobos (at Merrie Way). ✆ **415/386-3330.** www.cliffhouse.com. Reservations accepted for Sutro's only. Bistro main courses $9–$26 breakfast/lunch, $13–$26 dinner; Sutro main courses $18–$25 lunch, $18–$30 dinner; 3-course prix-fixe $25 lunch and $35 dinner (Mon–Fri only). AE, DC, DISC, MC, V. Bistro Mon–Sat 9am–9:30pm; Sat–Sun 9am–10pm. Sutro daily 11:30am–3:30pm and 5–9:30pm; brunch Sun 10am–2pm. Bus: 18 or 38.

Inexpensive

Burma Superstar ★★ Value BURMESE   Despite its gratuitous name, this basic dining room garners two-star status by offering exceptional Burmese food at rock-bottom prices. Unfortunately, the allure of the tea leaf salad, Burmese-style curry with potato, and sweet-tangy sesame beef is one of the city's worst-kept secrets. Add to that a no-reservations policy and you can count on waiting in line for up to an hour. (FYI, parties of two are seated more quickly than larger groups, and it's less crowded at lunch.) On the bright side, you can pencil your cellphone number onto the waiting list and browse the Clement Street shops until you receive a call.

309 Clement St. (at Fourth Ave.). ✆ **415/387-2147.** www.burmasuperstar.com. Reservations not accepted. Main courses $8–$16. MC, V. Mon–Thurs 11am–3:30pm and 5:30–9:30pm; Fri–Sat 11am–3:30pm and 5:30–10pm; Sun 11am–3:30pm and 5:30–9:30pm. Bus: 2, 4, 38, or 44.

Ton Kiang ★★ CHINESE/DIM SUM   Ton Kiang is the number one place in the city to have dim sum (served daily), only partially because they make their sauces, pickles, and other delicacies in-house. You'll have to wait in line (which is out the door 11am–1:30pm on weekends), but every tray of morsels coming from the kitchen is an absolute delight, from stuffed crab claws and roast Beijing duck, to the delicious *doa miu* (snow pea sprouts flash-sautéed with garlic and peanut oil) and a mesmerizing mango pudding. Though it's hard to get past the dim sum, which is served all day every day, the full menu of Hakka cuisine is worth investigation as well—fresh and flavorful soups; an array of seafood, beef, and chicken; and clay-pot specialties.

5821 Geary Blvd. (btw. 22nd and 23rd aves.). ✆ **415/387-8273.** www.tonkiang.net. Reservations accepted for parties of 8 or more. Dim sum $2–$5.50; main courses $9–$25. AE, DC, DISC, MC, V. Mon–Thurs 10am–10pm; Fri 10am–10:30pm; Sat 9:30am–10:30pm; Sun 9am–10pm. Bus: 38.

THE CASTRO
Expensive

Mecca ★ NEW AMERICAN   In 1996, Mecca entered the San Francisco dining scene in a decadent swirl of chocolate-brown velvet, stainless steel, cement, and brown leather. It's an industrial-chic supper club that makes you want to order a martini just so you'll match the ambience. The eclectic city clientele (with a heavy dash of same-sex couples) mingles at the oval centerpiece bar. A night here promises a live DJ spinning hot grooves, and a globally inspired meal served at tables tucked into several nooks. Chef Randy Lewis's menu items are as varied and interesting as his clientele: Moroccan-spiced lamb meatballs; "Last-Night's-Red-Wine-by-the-Glass Braised Short Ribs"; pan-seared Scottish salmon served with gnocchi, mustard seed vinaigrette, and pecan-apple relish; and a wickedly good Angus cheeseburger with tomato marmalade and garlic aioli on a brioche bun. When the place is jumping on a weekend night it's a great opportunity for tourists to experience an only-in-San-Francisco vibe.

2029 Market St. (by 14th and Church sts.). ℂ **415/621-7000.** www.sfmecca.com. Reservations recommended. Main courses $22–$34. AE, DC, MC, V. Tues–Thurs 5–10pm; Fri–Sat 5pm–midnight; Sun 4–10pm. Valet parking $10. Bus: 8, 22, 24, or 37. Streetcar: F, K, L, or M.

Inexpensive

Café Flore (Value) CALIFORNIA   Because of its large and lively patio overlooking a busy Market Street intersection, Café Flore is the top sunny-day meet-me-for-coffee spot within the Castro community. And boy is the people-watching good here—leather-wrapped bears, drag queens, trannies (Dad, is that you?), gym bunnies, and other anti-establishment types saunter down Market Street in full glory. As for dining at the cafe, here's how it works: You order drinks and desserts inside at the bar, then find a seat indoors or outside on the patio or sidewalk, and claim a spot. Next, go to the kitchen counter (there are no waiters), place your meal order and get a number, and the food will be delivered to your table. Many of the menu items are composed of mostly organic ingredients and include a succulent version of roasted chicken over rice, Niman Ranch hamburgers, soups, salads, and pastas. Breeders are always welcome as long as they behave, and breakfast is served until 3pm.

2298 Market St. (at Noe St.). ℂ **415/621-8579.** Reservations not accepted. American breakfast $5.95; main courses $4.50–$10. MC, V. Sun–Thurs 7am–11:30pm; Fri–Sat 7am–midnight. Metro: F.

Chow ★ (Value) AMERICAN   Chow claims to serve American cuisine, but the management must be thinking of today's America, because the menu is not exactly meatloaf and apple pie. And that's just fine for eclectic and cost-conscious diners. After all, what's not to like about starting with a Cobb salad before moving on to Thai-style noodles with steak, chicken, peanuts, and spicy lime-chile garlic broth, or cioppino? Better yet, everything except the fish of the day costs under $15, especially the budget-wise daily sandwich specials, which range from meatball with mozzarella (Sun) to grilled tuna with Asian-style slaw, pickled ginger, and a wasabi mayonnaise (Mon); both come with salad, soup, or fries. Although the food and prices alone would be a good argument for coming here, beer on tap, a great inexpensive wine selection, and the fun, tavernlike environment clinch the deal. A second location, **Park Chow,** is at 1240 Ninth Ave. (ℂ **415/665-9912**). You can't make reservations unless you have a party of eight or more, but if you're headed their way, you can call ahead to place your name on the wait list (recommended).

215 Church St. (near Market St.). © **415/552-2469.** Reservations not accepted. Main courses $7–$15. DISC, MC, V. Mon–Thurs 11am–11pm; Fri 11am–midnight; Sat 10am–midnight; Sun 10am–11pm; brunch served Sat–Sun 10–2:30pm. Bus: 8, 22, or 37. Streetcar: F, J, K, L, or M.

MISSION DISTRICT
Moderate

Delfina ★★ ITALIAN   Unpretentious warehouse-chic atmosphere, reasonable prices, and chef/co-owner Craig Stoll's superb seasonal Italian cuisine have made this family-owned restaurant one of the city's most cherished. Stoll, who was one of *Food & Wine*'s Best New Chefs in 2001 and a 2005 James Beard Award nominee, changes the menu daily, while his wife Annie works the front of the house (when she's not being a mom). Standards include Niman Ranch flatiron steak with french fries, and roasted chicken with Yukon Gold mashed potatoes and royal trumpet mushrooms. The winter menu might include slow-roasted pork shoulder or gnocchi with squash and chestnuts, while spring indulgences can include sand dabs with frisée, fingerling potatoes, and lemon-caper butter; or lamb with polenta and sweet peas. *A plus:* A few tables and counter seating are reserved for walk-in diners. Delfina also has a heated and covered patio that's used mid-March through November.

3621 18th St. (btw. Dolores and Guerrero sts.). © **415/552-4055.** www.delfinasf.com. Reservations recommended. Main courses $13–$22. MC, V. Mon–Thurs 5:30–10pm; Fri–Sat 5:30–11pm; Sun 5:30–10pm. Parking lot at 18th and Valencia sts., $8. Bus: 26 or 33. Streetcar: J.

Foreign Cinema ★★ MEDITERRANEAN   This place is so chic and well-hidden that it eludes me every time (*hint:* look for the valet stand). The "cinema" here is a bit of a gimmick: It's an outdoor dining area (partially covered and heated, but still chilly) where mostly foreign films are projected onto the side of an adjoining building without any audio. What's definitely not a gimmick, however, is the superb Mediterranean-inspired menu created by husband-and-wife team John Clark and Gayle Pirie. Snackers like me find solace at the oyster bar with a half-dozen locally harvested Miyagi oysters and a devilishly good *brandade* (fish purée) gratin. Heartier eaters can opt for grilled halibut with chanterelles and roasted figs in a fig vinaigrette; fried Madras curry-spiced chicken with gypsy peppers; or grilled natural rib-eye with Tuscan-style beans and rosemary-fried peppercorn sauce—all made from seasonal, sustainably farmed, organic ingredients when possible. Truth be told, even if the food weren't so good, I'd still come here—it's just that cool. If you have to wait for your table, consider stepping into their adjoining bar, Laszlo.

2534 Mission St. (btw. 21st and 22nd sts.). © **415/648-7600.** www.foreigncinema.com. Reservations recommended. Main courses $17–$26. AE, MC, V. Mon–Thurs 6–10pm; Fri–Sat 6–11pm; Sun 5–10pm; brunch Sat–Sun 11am–3pm. Valet parking $10. Bus: 14, 14L, or 49.

Inexpensive

Taquerias La Cumbre MEXICAN   If San Franciscans commissioned a flag honoring their favorite food, we'd probably all be waving a banner of the Golden Gate Bridge bolstering a giant burrito. Taquerias La Cumbre has been around forever and still retains its "Best Burrito" title, with each of the tortilla-wrapped meals deftly constructed using fresh pork, steak, chicken, or vegetables, plus cheese, beans, rice, salsa, and maybe a dash of guacamole or sour cream. The fact that it's served in a cafeterialike brick-lined room, with overly shellacked tables featuring a woman with overflowing cleavage, makes it taste even better.

515 Valencia St. (btw. 16th and 17th sts.). ℂ **415/863-8205.** Reservations not accepted. Tacos and burritos $3.50–$6.50; dinner plates $5–$7. No credit cards. Mon–Sat 11am–9pm; Sun noon–9pm. Bus: 14, 22, 33, 49, or 53. BART: Mission.

Ti Couz ★ CREPES   At Ti Couz (pronounced "Tee Cooz"), one of the most architecturally stylish and popular restaurants in the Mission, the headliner is simple: the delicate, paper-thin crepe. More than 30 choices of fillings make for infinite expertly executed combinations. The menu advises you how to enjoy these wraps: Order a light crepe as an appetizer, a heftier one as a main course, and a drippingly sweet one for dessert. Recommended combinations are listed, but you can build your own from the 15 main-course selections (such as smoked salmon, mushrooms, sausage, ham, scallops, and onions) and over 15 dessert options (caramel, fruit, chocolate, Nutella, and more). Soups and salads are equally stellar; the seafood salad, for example, is a delicious and generous compilation of shrimp, scallops, and ahi tuna with veggies and five kinds of lettuce.

3108 16th St. (at Valencia St.). ℂ **415/252-7373.** Reservations not accepted. Crepes $2–$12. MC, V. Mon and Fri 11am–11pm; Tues–Thurs 5–10pm; Sat–Sun 10am–11pm. Bus: 14, 22, 26, 33, 49, or 53. BART: 16th or Mission.

5 THE TOP ATTRACTIONS

TOP SAN FRANCISCO SIGHTS

Alcatraz Island ★★★ **(Kids)**   Visible from Fisherman's Wharf, Alcatraz Island (also known as the Rock) has seen a checkered history. Juan Manuel Ayala was the first European to discover it in 1775 and named it after the many pelicans that nested on the island. From the 1850s to 1933, when the army vacated the island, it served as a military post, protecting the bay's shoreline. In 1934, the government converted the buildings of the military outpost into a maximum-security prison. Given the sheer cliffs, treacherous tides and currents, and frigid water temperatures, it was believed to be a totally escape-proof prison. Among the famous gangsters who occupied cell blocks A through D were Al Capone, Robert Stroud, the so-called Birdman of Alcatraz (because he was an expert in ornithological diseases), Machine Gun Kelly, and Alvin Karpis. It cost a fortune to keep them imprisoned here because all supplies, including water, had to be shipped in. In 1963, after an apparent escape in which no bodies were recovered, the government closed the prison. In 1969, a group of Native Americans chartered a boat to the island to symbolically reclaim it for the Indian people. They occupied the island until 1971, the longest occupation of a federal facility by Native Americans to this day, when they were forcibly removed by the U.S. government. The next year, the island became part of the Golden Gate National Recreation Area. The wildlife that was driven away during the military and prison years has begun to return—the black-crested night heron and other seabirds are nesting here again—and a trail passes through the island's nature areas. Tours, including an audio tour of the prison block and a slide show, are given by the park's rangers, who entertain guests with interesting anecdotes.

Allow about 2¹⁄₂ hours for the round-trip boat ride and the tour. Wear comfortable shoes (the National Park Service notes that there are a lot of hills to climb on the tour) and take a heavy sweater or windbreaker, because even when the sun's out, it's cold there. You should also bring snacks and drinks with you if you think you'll want them. Although there is a beverage-and-snack bar on the ferry, the options are limited and

San Francisco Bay

expensive, and only water is available on the island. The excursion to Alcatraz is very popular and space is limited, so purchase tickets as far in advance as possible (up to 90 days) via the **Alcatraz Cruises** website at **www.alcatrazcruises.com**. You can also purchase tickets in person by visiting the Hornblower Alcatraz Landing ticket office at Pier 33. The first departure, called the "Early Bird," leaves at 9am, and ferries depart about every half-hour afterward until 2pm. Night tours (highly recommended) are also available Thursday through Monday and are a more intimate and wonderfully spooky experience.

Pier 41, near Fisherman's Wharf. © **415/981-7625.** www.alcatrazcruises.com or www.nps.gov/alcatraz. Admission (includes ferry trip and audio tour) $25 adults; $23 seniors 62 and older; $15 children 5–11. Night tours cost $32 adults; $29 seniors 62 and older; $19 children 5–11. Arrive at least 20 min. before departure time.

AT&T Park ★★ (Moments) If you're a baseball fan, you'll definitely want to schedule a visit to the magnificent AT&T Park, home of the San Francisco Giants and hailed by the media as one of the finest ballparks in America. From April through October, a sell-out crowd of 40,800 fans pack the $319-million ballpark for nearly every game—which has a smaller, more intimate feel than Monster Park (where the 49ers play) and prime views of San Francisco Bay—and root for their National League Giants.

During the Major League season, tickets to the game are usually hard to come by (and expensive when you find them), but you can try to join the Bleacher Bums by purchasing one of the 500 bleacher-seat tickets sold every day before the game. They make you work for it, however: You have to show up at the ballpark 4 hours early to get a lottery number; then come back 2 hours before the game to get your tickets (maximum four per person). The upside is that the tickets are only $8.50 to $10.

Tip: If you can't even get bleacher seats, you can always join the "knothole gang" at the Portwalk (located behind right field) to catch a free glimpse of the game through cut-out portholes into the ballpark. In the spirit of sharing, Portwalk peekers are encouraged to take in only an inning or two before giving way to fellow fans.

One guaranteed way to get into the ballpark is to take a **guided tour of AT&T Park** and go behind the scenes where you'll see the press box, the dugout, the visitor's clubhouse, a luxury suite, and more. All tours run daily at 10:30am and 12:30pm. Ticket prices are $10 for adults, $8 for seniors over 55, and $6 for kids 12 and under. There are no tours on game days, and limited tours on the day of night games. To buy tickets online log on to **www.sfgiants.com**, and then click on "AT&T Park" and "Ballpark Tours" from the drop-down list. You can also buy tour tickets at any Giants Dugout Store or Tickets.com outlet. For more tour information, call © **415/972-2400.**

At the southeast corner of SoMa at the south end of the Embarcadero (bounded by King, Second, and Thirrd sts.). © **415/972-2000.** www.sfgiants.com. Metro: N line. Bus: 10, 15, 30, 45, and 47.

Cable Cars ★★★ (Moments) (Kids) Although they may not be San Francisco's most practical means of transportation, cable cars are certainly the best loved. Designated official historic landmarks by the National Park Service in 1964, they clank up and down the city's steep hills like mobile museum pieces, tirelessly hauling thousands of tourists each day to nowhere in particular.

London-born engineer Andrew Hallidie invented San Francisco's cable cars in 1869 after watching a team of overworked horses haul a heavily laden carriage up a steep San Francisco slope. Hallidie resolved that he would invent a mechanical contraption to replace the horses, and, in 1873, the first cable car made its maiden run from the top of Clay Street. Ridiculed as "Hallidie's Folly," the cars were slow to gain acceptance. Even today, many visitors have difficulty believing that these vehicles, which have no engines, actually work. The cars, each weighing about 6 tons, run along a steel cable, enclosed under the street in a center rail. The cars move when the gripper (not the driver) pulls back a lever that closes a pincerlike "grip" on the cable. The speed of the car is determined by the speed of the cable, which is a constant $9^1/_2$ mph—never more, never less. The two types of cable cars in use hold a maximum of 90 and 100 passengers, and the limits are rigidly enforced. The best views are from the outer running boards, where you have to hold on tightly when taking curves.

Hallidie's cable cars have been imitated and used throughout the world, but all have been replaced by more efficient means of transportation. San Francisco planned to do so, too, but the proposal met with so much opposition that the cable cars' perpetuation was actually written into the city charter in 1955. The mandate cannot be revoked without the approval of a majority of the city's voters—a distant and doubtful prospect.

San Francisco's three existing cable car lines form the world's only surviving system of cable cars, which you can experience for yourself should you choose to wait in the often long boarding lines (up to a 2-hr. wait in summer).

Powell–Hyde and Powell–Mason lines begin at the base of Powell and Market sts.; California St. line begins at the foot of Market St. $5 per ride.

Coit Tower ★★ In a city known for its great views and vantage points, Coit Tower is one of the best. Atop Telegraph Hill, just east of North Beach, the round stone tower offers panoramic views of the city and the bay. Completed in 1933, the tower is the legacy of Lillie Hitchcock Coit, a wealthy eccentric who left San Francisco a $125,000 bequest "for the purpose of adding beauty to the city I have always loved" and as a memorial to its volunteer firemen (She had been saved from a fire as a child).

Inside the base of the tower are impressive murals titled *Life in California* and *1934,* which were completed under the WPA during the New Deal. They are the work of more than 25 artists, many of whom had studied under Mexican muralist Diego Rivera.

The only bummer: The narrow street leading to the tower is often clogged with tourist traffic. If you can, find a parking spot in North Beach and hoof it. It's actually a beautiful walk—especially if you take the Filbert Street Steps (p. 135).

Telegraph Hill. ⓒ **415/362-0808.** Admission is free to enter; elevator ride to the top is $4.50 adults, $3.50 seniors, $2 children 6–12. Daily 10am–6pm. Bus: 39 (Coit).

Farmers' Market ★★★ If you're heading to the Ferry Building Marketplace or just happen to be in the area at the right time (especially a sunny Sat), make a point of visiting the Farmers' Market, which is held in the outdoor areas in front of and behind the marketplace. This is where San Francisco foodies and many of the best local chefs—including the famed Alice Waters of Chez Panisse—gather, hang out, and peruse stalls hawking the finest Northern California fruits, vegetables, breads, dairy, flowers, ready-made snacks, and complete meals by local restaurants. You can also pick up locally made vinegars, preserves, olives, and oils here—they make wonderful gifts. Drop by on Saturday from 9am to noon for a serious social fest, including interviews with local farmers and culinary demos by city chefs.

The Embarcadero, at Market St. ⓒ **415/291-3276.** www.cuesa.org. Year-round Tues 10am–2pm, Sat 8am–2pm; May–Oct Tues 10am–2pm, Thurs 4–8pm, Sat 8am–2pm, Sun 10am–2pm. Bus: 2, 7, 12, 14, 21, 66, or 71. Streetcar: F. BART: Embarcadero.

San Francisco Segway Tours

Segways are those weird-looking upright scooters you've probably seen on TV. The two-wheeled "human transporter" is an ingenious electric-powered transportation device that uses gyroscopes to emulate human balance. After the free 40-minute lesson, riding a Segway becomes intuitive: lean forward, go forward; lean back, go back; stand upright, stop. Simple. The **San Francisco Electric Tour Company** offers Segway-powered narrated 2-hour tours of the San Francisco waterfront daily, starting from Fisherman's Wharf and heading out all the way to the Marina Green. For $70 it's not a bad deal, and it's the closest you'll come to being a celebrity (*everyone* checks you out). **Note:** You have to be at least 12 years old to join the tour. For more information, log on to **www.sfelectrictour.com** or call ✆ **415/474-3130.**

Ferry Building Marketplace ★★★ Finds   There's no better way to enjoy a San Francisco morning than strolling this gourmet marketplace in the Ferry Building and snacking your way through breakfast or lunch. San Franciscans can't get enough of this place; we're still amazed at what a fantastic job they did renovating the interior. The Marketplace is open daily and includes much of Northern California's best gourmet bounty: Cowgirl Creamery's Artisan Cheese Shop, Recchiuti Confections (amazing), Scharffen Berger Chocolate, Acme Breads, Wine Country's gourmet diner Taylor's Refresher, famed Vietnamese restaurant the Slanted Door, and myriad other restaurants, delis, gourmet coffee shops, specialty foods, and wine bars. Check out the Imperial Tea Court, where you'll be taught the traditional Chinese way to steep and sip your tea; nosh on premium sturgeon roe at Tsar Nicoulai Caviar, a small Parisian-style "caviar cafe"; buy cooking items at the Sur La Table shop; grab a bite and savor the bayfront views from in- and outdoor tables; or browse the Farmers' Market when it's up and running (see above). Trust me, you'll love this place.

The Embarcadero, at Market St. ✆ **415/693-0996.** www.ferrybuildingmarketplace.com. Most stores daily 10am–6pm; restaurant hours vary. Bus: 2, 7, 12, 14, 21, 66, or 71. Streetcar: F. BART: Embarcadero.

Fisherman's Wharf & PIER 39 Kids   Few cities in America are as adept at wholesaling their historical sites as San Francisco, which has converted Fisherman's Wharf into one of the most popular tourist attractions in the world. Unless you come really early in the morning to watch the few remaining fishing boats depart, you won't find many traces of traditional waterfront life—the only trolling going on here these days is for tourists' dollars. Nonetheless, everyone always seems to be enjoying themselves as they stroll down PIER 39 on a sunny day, especially the kids.

Accommodating a total of 300 boats, two marinas flank PIER 39 and house the sightseeing ferry fleets, including departures to Alcatraz. In recent years, some 900 California sea lions have taken up residence on the adjacent floating docks. Until they abandon their playground, which seems more and more unlikely, these playful, noisy (some nights you can hear them all the way from Washington Sq.) *Zalophus californianus* are one of the best free attractions on the wharf. Weather permitting, the Marine Mammal Center (✆ **415/289-SEAL**) offers an educational talk at PIER 39 on weekends from 11am to 5pm that teaches visitors about the range, habitat, and adaptability of the California sea lion.

Some people love Fisherman's Wharf; others can't get far enough away from it. Most agree that, for better or for worse, it has to be seen at least once in your lifetime. Traces of old-school San Francisco character remain, such as the convivial seafood street vendors who dish out piles of fresh Dungeness, clam chowder, and sourdough bread from their steaming stainless steel carts. Fisherman's Wharf is also one of the few places in the city where kids can be unleashed to roam through the aquarium, crawl through a real WWII submarine, play at the arcade, ride the carousel, and eat junk food galore. In short, there's something for everyone here, even us snobby locals.

At Taylor St. and the Embarcadero. (C) **415/674-7503.** www.fishermanswharf.org. Bus: 15, 30, 32, 39, 42, or 82X. Streetcar: F line. Cable car: Powell–Mason to the last stop and walk to the wharf. If you're arriving by car, park on adjacent streets or on the wharf btw. Taylor and Jones sts., for $16 per day, $8 with validation from participating restaurants.

Golden Gate Bridge ★★★ (Kids) The year 2007 marks the 70th birthday of possibly the most beautiful, and certainly the most photographed, bridge in the world. Often half-veiled by the city's trademark rolling fog, San Francisco's Golden Gate Bridge, named for the strait leading from the Pacific Ocean to the San Francisco Bay, spans tidal currents, ocean waves, and battering winds to connect The City by the Bay with the Redwood Empire to the north. With its gracefully suspended single span, spidery bracing cables, and zooming twin towers, the bridge looks more like a work of abstract art than one of the 20th century's greatest practical engineering feats. Construction was completed in May 1937 at the then-colossal cost of $35 million (plus another $39 million in interest, financed entirely by bridge tolls).

SAN FRANCISCO

5

THE TOP ATTRACTIONS

GoCar Tours of San Francisco

If the thought of walking up and down San Francisco's brutally steep streets has you sweating already, considering renting a talking GoCar instead. The tiny yellow three-wheeled convertible cars are easy and fun to drive—every time I see one of these things, the people riding in them are grinning from ear to ear—and they're cleverly guided by a talking GPS (Global Positioning System), which means that the car always knows where you are, even if you don't. The most popular computer-guided tour is a 2-hour loop around the Fisherman's Wharf area, out to the Marina District, through Golden Gate Park, and down Lombard Street, the "crookedest street in the world." As you drive, the talking car tells you where to turn and what landmarks you're passing. Even if you stop to check something out, as soon as you turn your GoCar back on, the tour picks up where it left off. Or you can just cruise around wherever you want (but not across the Golden Gate Bridge). There's a lockable trunk for your things, and the compact body makes parking a breeze. You can rent a GoCar from 1 hour (about $44) to a full day. You'll have to wear a helmet, and you must be a licensed driver of at least 18 years of age. The GoCar rental shop is at 2715 Hyde St., between Beach and North Point streets at Fisherman's Wharf. For more information, call (C) **800/91-GoCar** or (C) **415/441-5695,** or log on to their website at **www.gocarsf.com.**

The 1.7-mile bridge (including the approach), which reaches a height of 746 feet above the water, is awesome to cross. Although kept to a maximum of 45 miles an hour, traffic usually moves quickly, so crossing by car won't give you too much time to see the sights. If you drive from the city, take the last San Francisco exit, right before the toll plaza, park in the southeast parking lot, and make the crossing by foot. Back in your car, continue to Marin's Vista Point, at the bridge's northern end. Look back, and you'll be rewarded with one of the finest views of San Francisco.

Hwy. 101 N. www.goldengatebridge.org. $5 cash toll collected when driving south. Bridge-bound Golden Gate Transit buses (© 511) depart hourly during the day for Marin County, starting from Mission and First sts. (across the street from the Transbay Terminal and stopping at Market and Seventh sts., at the Civic Center, along Van Ness Ave., at Lombard and Fillmore sts., and at Francisco and Richardson sts.).

Lombard Street ★   Known (erroneously) as the "crookedest street in the world," this whimsically winding block of Lombard Street draws thousands of visitors each year (much to the chagrin of neighborhood residents, most of whom would prefer to block off the street to tourists). The angle of the street is so steep that the road has to snake back and forth to make a descent possible. The brick-lined street zigzags around the residences' bright flower gardens, which explode with color during warmer months. This short stretch of Lombard Street is one-way, downhill, and fun to drive. Take the curves slowly and in low gear, and expect a wait during the weekend. Save your film for the bottom where, if you're lucky, you can find a parking space and take a few snapshots of the silly spectacle. You can also take staircases (without curves) up or down on either side of the street. In truth, most locals don't understand what the fuss is all about. I'm guessing the draw is the combination of seeing such a famous landmark, the challenge of negotiating so many steep curves, and a classic photo op. *FYI:* Vermont Street, between 20th and 22nd streets in Potrero Hill, is even more crooked, but not nearly as picturesque.

Btw. Hyde and Leavenworth sts.

GOLDEN GATE PARK

The 1,017-acre Golden Gate Park consists of dozens of gardens and attractions connected by wooded paths and paved roads. While many worthy sites are clearly visible, there are infinite hidden treasures, so pick up information at **McLaren Lodge and Park Headquarters** (at Stanyan and Fell sts.; © **415/831-2700;** open daily; park maps $3) if you want to find the more hidden spots. Of the dozens of special gardens in the park, most recognized are **McLaren Memorial Rhododendron Dell,** the **Rose Garden, Strybing Arboretum,** and, at the western edge of the park, a springtime array of thousands of tulips and daffodils around the **Dutch windmill.**

In addition to the highlights described in this section, the park contains lots of recreational facilities: tennis courts; baseball, soccer, and polo fields; a golf course; riding stables; and fly-casting pools. The Strawberry Hill boathouse handles boat rentals. Enter the park at Kezar Drive, an extension of Fell Street; bus riders can take no. 5, 6, 7, 16AX, 16BX, 66, or 71.

BEACH CHALET   Listed on the National Register of Historic places in 1981, the Spanish-Colonial Beach Chalet, 1000 Great Hwy., at the west end of Golden Gate Park near Fulton Street (© **415/386-8439**), was designed by Willis Polk in 1925. In the 1930s, the Works Progress Administration (WPA) commissioned Lucien Labaudt (who also painted the Coit Tower frescoes) to create frescoes, mosaics, and wood carvings of San Francisco life. Today, after a renovation several years back, the chalet houses the frescoes and other historic artifacts and details downstairs, a restaurant upstairs, and a great cafe in the back. Stop upstairs for a house-made brew and a glimpse of the expansive Pacific, or head to the back dining room for glorious park views. There's even live music with some regularity.

CONSERVATORY OF FLOWERS ★★   Opened to the public in 1879, this glorious Victorian glass structure is the oldest existing public conservatory in the Western Hemisphere. A cutting-edge horticultural destination with over 1,700 species of plants, its five galleries also include the lowland tropics, aquatic plants, the largest Dracula orchid collection in the world, and special exhibits. It doesn't take long to visit, but make a point of staying awhile; outside there are good sunny spots for people-watching as well as paths leading to impressive gardens begging to be explored. The conservatory is open Tuesday through Sunday from 9am to 5pm, closed Mondays. Admission is $5 for adults; $3 for youth 12 to 17 years of age, seniors, and students with ID; $1.50 for children 5 to 11, and free for children 4 and under and for all visitors the first Tuesday of the month. For more information, visit **www.conservatoryofflowers.org** or call ✆ **415/666-7001.**

JAPANESE TEA GARDEN   John McLaren, the man who began landscaping Golden Gate Park, hired Makoto Hagiwara, a wealthy Japanese landscape designer, to further develop this garden originally created for the 1894 Midwinter Exposition. It's a quiet place with cherry trees, shrubs, and bonsai, crisscrossed by winding paths and high-arched bridges over pools of water. Focal points and places for contemplation include the massive bronze Buddha (cast in Japan in 1790 and donated by the Gump family), the Buddhist wooden pagoda, and the Drum Bridge, which, reflected in the water, looks as though it completes a circle. The garden is open daily November through February from 8:30am to 5pm (teahouse 10am–4:30pm), March through October from 8:30am to 6pm (teahouse 10am–5:30pm). For information on admission, call ✆ **415/752-4227.** For the **teahouse,** call ✆ **415/752-1171.**

STRAWBERRY HILL/STOW LAKE   Rent a paddle boat or rowboat and cruise around the circular Stow Lake as painters create still lifes, joggers pass along the grassy shoreline, ducks waddle around waiting to be fed, and turtles sunbathe on rocks and logs. Strawberry Hill, the 430-foot-high artificial island and highest point in the park that lies at the center of Stow Lake, is a perfect picnic spot; it boasts a bird's-eye view of San Francisco and the bay. It also has a waterfall and peace pagoda. For the **boathouse,** call ✆ **415/752-0347.** Boat rentals are available daily from 10am to 4pm, weather permitting; four-passenger rowboats go for $13 per hour, and four-person paddle boats run $17 per hour; fees are cash only.

STRYBING ARBORETUM & BOTANICAL GARDENS   More than 7,000 plant species grow here, among them some ancient plants in a special "primitive garden," rare species, and a grove of California redwoods. Docent tours begin at 1:30pm daily, with an additional 10:20am tour on weekends. Strybing is open Monday through Friday from 8am to 4:30pm, and Saturday, Sunday, and holidays from 10am to 5pm. Admission is free. For more information, call ✆ **415/661-1316** or visit **www.strybing.org**.

6 EXPLORING THE CITY

ARCHITECTURAL HIGHLIGHTS

The **Alamo Square Historic District** has one of the largest concentrations of the city's 14,000 **Painted Ladies,** or Victorian homes restored and ornately painted by residents.

The area is small and easy to walk—bordered by Divisadero Street on the west, Golden Gate Avenue on the north, Webster Street on the east, and Fell Street on the south, about 10 blocks west of Civic Center. From Alamo Square at Fulton and Steiner streets, you'll see one of the most famous views of San Francisco, reproduced on postcards and posters around town—sharp-edged Financial District skyscrapers towering above a row of Victorians.

City Hall and the **Civic Center** are part of a "City Beautiful" complex built in 1881, in the Beaux Arts style, designed by Brown and Bakewell. The newly renovated City Hall dome rises to 308 feet outside, ornamented with *oculi* (round windows) and topped by a lantern. The rotunda, which soars 112 feet, is finished in oak, marble, and limestone, with a marble staircase leading to the second floor.

The **Flood Mansion,** 1000 California St., at Mason Street, was built between 1885 and 1886 for James Clair Flood—who, thanks to the Comstock Lode, rose from being a bartender to one of the city's wealthiest men. The house cost $1.5 million; the fence alone was $30,000. It was designed by Augustus Laver and modified by Willis Polk to accommodate the Pacific Union Club.

The **Octagon House,** 2645 Gough St., at Union Street (© **415/441-7512**), an unusual, eight-sided, cupola-topped house, dates from 1861 and is maintained by the National Society of Colonial Dames of America. Its design was based on a past theory that people living in a space of this shape would live longer, healthier lives. Inside is a small museum where you'll find Early American furniture, portraits, silver, pewter, looking glasses, and English and Chinese ceramics. There are also some historic documents, including signatures of 54 of the 56 signers of the Declaration of Independence. Even if you're not able to visit the inside, this atypical structure is worth a look from the outside. It's open February through December on the second Sunday, and the second and fourth Thursdays of each month from noon to 3pm; it's closed January and holidays.

The **Palace of Fine Arts,** on Baker between Jefferson and Bay streets, is the only building to survive from the Pan-Pacific Exhibition of 1915. Constructed by Bernard Maybeck, it was rebuilt in concrete using molds taken from the original in the 1950s. It now houses the **Exploratorium** (p. 129).

The **TransAmerica Pyramid,** 600 Montgomery St., between Clay and Washington streets, is the tallest structure in San Francisco's skyline. It's 48 stories tall, capped by a 212-foot spire.

Although the **San Francisco–Oakland Bay Bridge** is less famous than the Golden Gate Bridge, it's more spectacular in many ways. Opened in 1936 (a year before the Golden Gate), it's one of the world's longest steel bridges, at $8^1/_4$ miles long. A dovetailed series of spans joined midbay by one of the world's widest tunnels, at Yerba Buena Island, it's not really a single bridge: West of Yerba Buena, it's two separate suspension bridges, joined at a central anchorage; east of the island, it's a 1,400-foot cantilever span, followed by a succession of truss bridges.

A ROUSING CHURCH EXPERIENCE

Glide Memorial United Methodist Church ★★ **(Moments** The best way to spend a Sunday morning in San Francisco is to visit this Tenderloin-area church to witness the exhilarating and lively sermons accompanied by an amazing gospel choir. Reverend Cecil Williams's enthusiastic and uplifting preaching and singing with the homeless and poor of the neighborhood has attracted nationwide fame over the past 40-plus years. In 1994, during the pastor's 30th-anniversary celebration, singers Angela Bofill and Bobby McFerrin joined comedian Robin Williams, author Maya Angelou, and Oprah Winfrey to honor him publicly. Even Bill Clinton has joined the crowd. Cecil Williams now shares pastor duties with Douglas Fitch and alternates presiding over the roof-raising Sunday services in front of a diverse audience that crosses all socioeconomic boundaries. Go for an uplifting experience and some hand-clapping, shoulder-swaying gospel choir music— it's an experience you'll never forget. *Tip:* Arrive about 20 minutes early to make sure you get a seat; otherwise it's SRO.

330 Ellis St. (west of Union Sq.). © **415/674-6000**. www.glide.org. Services Sun at 9 and 11am. Bus: 27. Streetcar: Powell. BART: Powell.

MUSEUMS

Asian Art Museum ★ Previously in Golden Gate Park and reopened in what was once the Civic Center's Beaux Arts–style central library, San Francisco's Asian Art Museum is one of the Western world's largest devoted to Asian art. Its collection boasts more than 15,000 art objects, such as world-class sculptures, paintings, bronzes, ceramics, and jade items, spanning 6,000 years of history and regions of south Asia, west Asia, Southeast Asia, the Himalayas, China, Korea, and Japan. Inside you'll find 40,000 square feet of gallery space showcasing 2,500 objects at any given time. Add temporary exhibitions, live demonstrations, learning activities, Cafe Asia, and a store, and you've got one very good reason to head to the Civic Center.

200 Larkin St. (btw. Fulton and McAllister sts.). © **415/581-3500**. www.asianart.org. Admission $12 adults, $8 seniors 65 and over, $7 youths 13–17 and college students with ID, free for children 12 and under, $5 flat rate for all (except children 12 and under who are free) after 5pm Thurs. Free 1st Sun of the month. Tues–Wed and Fri–Sun 10am–5pm; Thurs 10am–9pm. Bus: All Market St. buses. Streetcar: Civic Center.

Cable Car Museum ★ (**Value**) (**Kids**) If you've ever wondered how cable cars work, this nifty museum explains it all. Yes, this is a museum, but the Cable Car Museum is no stuffed shirt. It's the living powerhouse, repair shop, and storage place of the cable car system and is in full operation. Built for the Ferries and Cliff House Railway in 1887, the building underwent an $18-million reconstruction to restore its original gaslight-era look, install an amazing spectators' gallery, and add a museum of San Francisco transit history. The exposed machinery, which pulls the cables under San Francisco's streets, looks like a Rube Goldberg invention. Stand in the mezzanine gallery and become mesmerized by the massive groaning winches as they thread the cable that hauls the cars through a huge figure-eight and back into the system using slack-absorbing tension wheels. For a better view, move to the lower-level viewing room, where you can see the massive pulleys and gears operating underground. Also on display here is one of the first grip cars developed by Andrew S. Hallidie, operated for the first time on Clay Street on August 2, 1873. You can see the entire museum in about 45 minutes.

1201 Mason St. (at Washington St.). © **415/474-1887**. www.cablecarmuseum.org. Free admission. Apr– Sept daily 10am–6pm; Oct–Mar daily 10am–5pm. Closed Thanksgiving, Christmas, and New Year's Day. Cable car: Both Powell St. lines.

California Academy of Sciences ★★★ (**Kids**) San Francisco's California Academy of Sciences has been entertaining locals and tourists for more than 150 years, and with the grand opening of the all-new Academy on September 27, 2008, it's now going stronger than ever. Four years and $500 million in the making, it's the only institution in the world to combine an aquarium, planetarium, natural history museum, and scientific research program under one roof; and it's so vastly entertaining that the entire family could easily spend an entire day here. The spectacular new complex has reinvented the role of science museums, and visitors can interact with animals, educators, and biologists at hands-on exhibits such as a four-story living rainforest dome and the world's deepest living coral reef display. Even the Academy's 2¹/₂-acre undulating garden roof is an exhibit, planted with 1.7 million native California plants, including thousands of flowers.

More than 38,000 live animals fill the new Academy's aquarium and natural history exhibits, making it one of the most diverse collections of live animals at any museum or aquarium in the world. Highlights include the **Morrison Planetarium,** the world's largest all-digital planetarium that takes you on a guided tour of the solar system and beyond using current data from NASA; the **Philippine Coral Reef,** the world's deepest living coral reef tank, where 4,000 sharks, rays, sea turtles, giant clams, and other aquatic creatures live in a Technicolor forest of coral; and the **Rainforests of the World,** a living rainforest filled with croaking frogs, chirping birds, leaf cutter ants, bat caves, chameleons, and hundreds of tropical butterflies. You can climb into the tree-tops of Costa Rica, descend in a glass elevator into the Amazonian flooded forest, and walk along an acrylic tunnel beneath Amazonian river fish.

Even the dining options here are first-rate, as both the **Academy Café** and **Moss Room** restaurant are run by two of the city's top chefs, Charles Phan and Loretta Keller, and feature local, organic, sustainable foods. The only thing you won't enjoy here is the entrance fee—a whopping $25 per adult—but it includes access to all the Academy exhibits *and* the planetarium shows; if you arrive by public transportation they'll knock $3 off the fee. Combined with a visit to the spectacular de Young museum across the concourse, it makes for an entertaining and educational day.

55 Concourse Dr., Golden Gate Park. ☎ **415/379-8000.** www.calacademy.org. Admission $25 adults, $20 seniors 65 and over, $20 youths 12–17, $15 children 7–11, free for children 6 and under. Free to all 3rd Wed of each month. Mon–Sat 9:30am–5pm; Sun 11am–5pm. Closed Thanksgiving and Christmas. Bus: 5, 16AX, 16BX, 21, 44, or 71.

de Young Museum ★★★   After closing for several years, San Francisco's oldest museum (founded in 1895) reopened in late 2005 in its new state-of-the-art Golden Gate Park facility. Its vast holdings include one of the finest collections of American paintings in the United States from Colonial times through the 20th century, as well as decorative arts and crafts; Western and non-Western textiles; and arts from Africa, Oceania, and the Americas. Along with superb revolving exhibitions, the de Young has long been beloved for its educational arts programs for children and adults, and now it's equally enjoyed for its stunning architecture and sculpture-graced surroundings. The striking facade consists of 950,000 pounds of textured and perforated copper that's intended to patinate with age, while the northeast corner of the building features a 144-foot tower that slowly spirals from the ground floor and culminates with an observation floor offering panoramic views of the entire Bay Area. Surrounding sculpture gardens and lush, grassy expanses are perfect for picnicking. Adding to the allure is surprisingly good and healthy organic fare at the cafe/ restaurant. *Note:* Underground parking is accessed at 10th Avenue and Fulton Street. Also, admission tickets to the de Young may be used on the same day for free entrance to the Legion of Honor (see below).

50 Hagiwara Tea Garden Dr. (inside Golden Gate Park, 2 blocks from the park entrance at Eighth Ave. and Fulton). ☎ **415/863-3330.** www.thinker.org. Admission $10 adults, $7 seniors, $6 youths 13–17 and college students with ID, free for children 12 and under. Free 1st Tues of the month. $2 discount for Muni riders with Fast Pass or transfer receipt. AE, MC, V. Tues–Sun 9:30am–5:15pm. Closed Jan 1, Thanksgiving Day, and Dec 25. Bus: 5, 16AX, 16BX, 21, 44, or 71.

The Exploratorium ★★★ ⟨Kids⟩   *Scientific American* magazine rated the Exploratorium "the best science museum in the world"—and I couldn't agree more. With hundreds of exhibits, it's like a mad scientist's penny arcade, an educational fun house, and an experimental laboratory all rolled into one. Touch a tornado, shape a glowing electrical current, or take a sensory journey in total darkness in the **Tactile Dome** ($3 extra; call ℂ **415/561-0362** to make advance reservations); Every exhibit at the Exploratorium is designed to be interactive, educational, safe, and, most importantly, fun. Even parents inevitably end up being reluctant to leave. The museum is in the Marina District at the beautiful **Palace of Fine Arts** ★★, the only building left standing from the Panama-Pacific Exposition of 1915. The adjoining park with lagoon—good for an afternoon picnic—is home to ducks, swans, seagulls, and grouchy geese (bring bread).

3601 Lyon St., in the Palace of Fine Arts (at Marina Blvd.). ℂ **415/EXP-LORE** or 415/561-0360 (recorded information). www.exploratorium.edu. Admission $14 adults; $11 seniors, youth 13–17, visitors with disabilities, and college students with ID; $9 children 4–12; free for children 3 and under. AE, MC, V. Tues–Sun 10am–5pm. Closed Mon except MLK, Jr., Day, Presidents' Day, Memorial Day, and Labor Day. Free parking. Bus: 28, 30, or Golden Gate Transit.

The Legion of Honor ★★   Designed as a memorial to California's World War I casualties, this neoclassical structure is an exact replica of the Legion of Honor Palace in Paris, right down to the inscription HONNEUR ET PATRIE above the portal. The exterior's grassy expanses, cliffside paths, and incredible view of the Golden Gate and downtown make this an absolute must-visit attraction. The inside is equally impressive: The permanent collection covers 4,000 years of art and includes paintings, sculpture, and decorative arts from Europe, as well as international tapestries, prints, and drawings. The chronological display of 4,000 years of ancient and European art includes one of the world's finest collections of Rodin sculptures. The sunlit cafe offers indoor and outdoor seating at moderate prices. Plan to spend 2 or 3 hours here.

In Lincoln Park (34th Ave. and Clement St.). ℂ **415/750-3600** or 415/863-3330 (recorded information). www.thinker.org. Admission $10 adults, $7 seniors 65 and over, $6 youths 13–17 and college students with ID, free for children 12 and under. Fees may be higher for special exhibitions. Free 1st Tues of each month. Tues–Sun 9:30am–5:15pm. Bus: 18.

San Francisco Maritime National Historical Park ★ ⟨Kids⟩   This park includes several marine-themed sites within a few blocks of each other. Although at press time, the park's signature Maritime Museum—on Beach Street at Polk Street, shaped like an Art Deco ship, and filled with sea-faring memorabilia—is just nearing the end of its 3-year renovations, it's worth walking by just to admire the building. Head 2 blocks east to the corner of Hyde and Jefferson and you'll find SFMNHP's state-of-the-art Visitor's Center, which offers a fun, interactive look at the City's maritime heritage. Housed in the historic Haslett Warehouse building, the Center tells the stories of voyage, discovery, and cultural diversity. Across the street, at the park's Hyde Street Pier, are several historic ships, which are moored and open to the public.

Visitor's Center: Hyde and Jefferson sts. (near Fisherman's Wharf). ℂ **415/447-5000.** www.nps.gov/safr. No fee for Visitor's Center. Tickets to board ships $5, free for children 15 and under. Visitor's Center Memorial Day–Oct 15 daily 9:30am–7pm; Oct 16–May 30 daily 9:30am–5pm. Ships on Hyde St. Pier Memorial Day–Sept 30 daily 9:30am–5:30pm; Oct 16–May 27 daily 9am–5pm. Bus: 19, 30, or 47. Cable car: Powell–Hyde St. line to the last stop.

San Francisco Museum of Modern Art (SFMOMA) ★   Although it doesn't compare with similar institutions in New York City, SFMOMA is a fine museum, with more than 23,000 works to its name, though only a fraction are on display at any given time. One of the first museums to recognize photography as a major art form, SFMOMA holds more than 12,000 photographs, by notables such as Ansel Adams, Alfred Stieglitz, Edward Weston, and Henri Cartier-Bresson. Its painting and sculpture departments encompass nearly 5,000 works by Henri Matisse, Jackson Pollock, Willem de Kooning, Diego Rivera, Georgia O'Keeffe, Paul Klee, the Fauvists, Richard Diebenkorn, and others. Phone for details of special exhibitions, and whatever you do, check out the fabulous MuseumStore and cafe.

151 Third St. (2 blocks south of Market St., across from Yerba Buena Gardens). (*C*) **415/357-4000.** www. sfmoma.org. Admission $13 adults, $8 seniors, $7 students 13 and over with ID, free for children 12 and under. Half-price for all Thurs 6–9pm; free to all 1st Tues of each month. Thurs 11am–8:45pm; Fri–Tues 11am–5:45pm. Closed Wed and major holidays. Bus: 15, 30, or 45. Streetcar: J, K, L, or M to Montgomery.

NEIGHBORHOODS WORTH SEEKING OUT

For self-guided walking tours of San Francisco's neighborhoods, pick up a copy of *Frommer's Memorable Walks in San Francisco* (Wiley Publishing, Inc.).

THE CASTRO   Castro Street, between Market and 18th streets, is the center of the city's gay community as well as a lovely neighborhood teeming with shops, restaurants, bars, and other institutions that cater to the area's colorful residents. Among the landmarks are **Harvey Milk Plaza** and the **Castro Theatre** (www.castrotheatre.com), a 1930s movie palace with a Wurlitzer. The gay community began to move here in the late 1960s and early 1970s from a neighborhood called Polk Gulch, which still has a number of gay-oriented bars and stores. Castro is one of the liveliest streets in the city and the perfect place to shop for gifts and revel in free-spiritedness. Check **www.castroonline.com** for more info.

CHINATOWN   San Francisco has one of the largest communities of Chinese people in the United States. More than 80,000 people live in Chinatown, but the majority of Chinese people have moved out into newer areas like the Richmond and Sunset districts. Although frequented by tourists, the area continues to cater to Chinese shoppers, who crowd the vegetable and herb markets, restaurants, and shops. Tradition runs deep here, and if you're lucky, through an open window you might hear women mixing mah-jongg tiles as they play the centuries-old game.

THE MISSION DISTRICT   Once inhabited almost entirely by Irish immigrants, the Mission—an oblong area stretching roughly from 14th to 30th streets between Potrero Avenue in the east and Dolores on the west—is now the center of the city's Latino community. The heart of the community lies along 24th Street between Van Ness and Potrero, where dozens of ethnic restaurants, bakeries, bars, and specialty stores attract a hip crowd from all over the city. Some of San Francisco's finest Victorians still stand in the outer limits. By day the neighborhood is quite safe and highly recommended; at night, stroll through the Mission District with caution.

NOB HILL   When the cable car started operating in 1873, this hill became the city's exclusive residential area. Newly wealthy residents who had struck it rich in the Gold Rush built their mansions here, but they were almost all destroyed by the 1906 earthquake and fire. The only two surviving buildings are the Flood Mansion, which serves today as the **Pacific Union Club,** and the **Fairmont Hotel,** which was under construction when the earthquake struck and was damaged but not destroyed. Today, the burned-out sites of former mansions hold the city's luxury hotels—the InterContinental **Mark Hopkins,** the **Stanford Court,** the **Huntington Hotel,** and the spectacular **Grace Cathedral,** which stands on the Crocker mansion site. Nob Hill is worth a visit if only to stroll around **Huntington Park,** attend a Sunday service at the cathedral, or ooh and aah your way around the Fairmont's spectacular lobby.

NORTH BEACH   In the late 1800s, an enormous influx of Italian immigrants to North Beach firmly established this aromatic area as San Francisco's "Little Italy." Dozens of Italian restaurants and coffeehouses continue to flourish in what is still the center of the city's Italian community. Walk down **Columbus Avenue** on any given morning, and you'll be bombarded by the wonderful aromas of roasting coffee and savory pasta sauces. Although there are some interesting shops and bookstores in the area, it's the dozens of eclectic little cafes, delis, bakeries, and coffee shops that give North Beach its Italian-bohemian character.

FLORA & FAUNA

In addition to **Golden Gate Park** and **Golden Gate National Recreation Area** and the **Presidio,** San Francisco boasts more than 2,000 additional acres of parkland, most of which is perfect for picnicking. **Lincoln Park,** at Clement Street and 34th Avenue, on 270 acres in northwestern San Francisco, is home to both the California Palace of the Legion of Honor (see "Museums," above) and an 18-hole municipal golf course. The park's most dramatic features, however, are the 200-foot cliffs overlooking the Golden Gate Bridge and San Francisco Bay. Take bus no. 38 from Union Square to 33rd and Geary streets, and then transfer to bus no. 18 into the park.

San Francisco Zoo (& Children's Zoo) (Kids)   Founded at its present site near the ocean in 1929, the zoo is spread over 100 acres, and houses more than 930 animals including some 245 species of mammals, birds, reptiles, amphibians, and invertebrates. Exhibit highlights include the Lipman Family Lemur Forest, a forest setting for five endangered species of lemurs from Madagascar; Jones Family Gorilla World, a tranquil setting for a family of western lowland gorillas; Koala Crossing, which connects to the Australian Walkabout exhibit with its kangaroos, wallaroos, and emu; Penguin Island, home to a large breeding colony of Magellanic Penguins (join them for lunch at 2:30pm daily); and the Primate Discovery Center, home to rare and endangered monkeys. The Lion House is home to rare Sumatran and Siberian tigers and African lions. You can see the big cats fed every day at 2pm (except Mon). African Savanna is a 3-acre mixed-species habitat with giraffes, zebras, antelope, and birds. The 6-acre **Children's Zoo** offers kids and their families opportunities for close-up encounters with domestic rare breeds of goats, sheep, ponies, and horses in the Family Farm. Touch and feel small mammals, reptiles, and amphibians along the Nature Trail and gaze at eagles and hawks stationed on Hawk Hill. Don't miss the incredible Insect Zoo.

Great Highway btw. Sloat Blvd. and Skyline Blvd. (C) **415/753-7080.** www.sfzoo.org. Admission $11 adults, $8 for seniors 65 and over and youth 12–17, $5 for children 3–11, free for children 2 and under. Free to all 1st Wed of each month, except $2 fee for Children's Zoo. Carousel $2. Daily 10am–5pm, 365 days a year. Bus: 23 or 18. Streetcar: L from downtown Market St. to the end of the line.

ORIENTATION TOURS

The 49-Mile Scenic Drive ★★

The self-guided, 49-mile drive is an easy way to get oriented and to grasp the beauty of San Francisco and its extraordinary location. It's also a flat-out stunning and very worthy excursion. Beginning in the city, it follows a rough circle around the bay and passes virtually all the best-known sights, from Chinatown to the Golden Gate Bridge, Ocean Beach, Seal Rocks, Golden Gate Park, and Twin Peaks. Originally designed for the benefit of visitors to San Francisco's 1939 and 1940 Golden Gate International Exposition, the route is marked by blue-and-white seagull signs. Although it makes an excellent half-day tour, this mini-excursion can easily take longer if you decide, for example, to stop to walk across the Golden Gate Bridge or to have tea in Golden Gate Park's Japanese Tea Garden.

The **San Francisco Visitor Information Center,** at Powell and Market streets (p. 66), distributes free route maps, which are handy since a few of the Scenic Drive marker signs are missing. Try to avoid the downtown area during the weekday rush hours from 7 to 9am and 4 to 6pm.

BOAT TOURS

One of the best ways to look at San Francisco is from a boat bobbing on the bay. There are several cruises to choose from, and many of them start from Fisherman's Wharf.

Blue & Gold Fleet, Pier 39, Fisherman's Wharf (© **415/773-1188;** www.blueand goldfleet.com), tours the bay year-round in a sleek, 350-passenger sightseeing boat, complete with food and beverage facilities. The fully narrated, 1-hour cruise passes beneath the Golden Gate Bridge and comes within yards of Alcatraz Island. Don a jacket, bring the camera, and make sure it's a clear day for the best bay cruise. Frequent daily departures from Pier 39's West Marina begin at 10:45am daily during winter and 10am daily during summer. Tickets cost $21 for adults, $17 for seniors over 62 and juniors 12 to 18, and $13 for children 5 to 11; children under 5 are admitted free. There's a $2.25 charge for ordering tickets by phone; discounts are available on their website.

The **Red & White Fleet,** Pier 43¹/₂ (© **415/673-2900;** www.redandwhite.com), offers daily Golden Gate Bay Cruise tours that leave from Pier 43¹/₂. The hour-long ride cruises along the city waterfront, beneath the Golden Gate Bridge, past Angel Island, and around Alcatraz. Cruises includes a headset audio tour narrated in eight languages. Tickets are $22 for adults, $16 for youths 5 to 17, and free for kids under 5. From April to October they also offer a 2-hour California Sunset Cruise with appetizers and music, and from May to September they run a SF Explorer Cruise that sails along the city's downtown skyline while detailing history and architecture. Discounts are available through online purchase.

BUS TOURS

Gray Line (© **888/428-6937** or 415/434-8687; www.sanfranciscosightseeing.com) is San Francisco's largest bus-tour operator. It offers numerous itineraries daily (far too many to list here). Free pickup and return are available between centrally located hotels and departure locations. Advance reservations are required for all tours except motorized cable car and trolley tours. Day and evening tours depart from Pier 43¹/₂ at Fisherman's Wharf; motorized cable car tours depart from Pier 39 and Pier 41.

8 GOLDEN GATE NATIONAL RECREATION AREA & THE PRESIDIO

GOLDEN GATE NATIONAL RECREATION AREA

One could easily contend that no urban shoreline is as stunning as San Francisco's. Wrapping around the northern and western edges of the city, the Golden Gate National Recreation Area is run by the National Park Service, which lets visitors fully enjoy it as a park. Several landmarks line the shore, from which visitors have views of both the bay and the ocean. Muni runs service to most sites, including Aquatic Park, the Cliff House, and Ocean Beach. For more information, contact the National Park Service (© 415/561-4700; www.nps.gov/goga).

Here's a brief rundown of the park's major features, starting at the northern section and moving westward around the coast: **Aquatic Park,** adjacent to the Hyde Street Pier, is a small swimming beach, although it's not that appealing and the water is unbearably cold. **Fort Mason Center** runs from Bay Street to the shoreline and encompasses several buildings and piers used during World War II. Today, a variety of museums, theaters, and organizations occupies the complex. **Greens Restaurant** (p. 109) is among the best, affording views of the Golden Gate Bridge. For information on Fort Mason Center events, call © 415/441-3400 or visit **www.fortmason.org**.

Farther west along the bay, at the northern end of Fillmore, **Marina Green** is an optimum spot for flying kites or watching the sailboats on the bay. Next stop along the bay is the St. Francis Yacht Club and the start of the paved, 3.5-mile **Golden Gate Promenade,** a favorite biking-and-hiking path defining the outer limits of the Presidio. The path leads to the fantastic, recently reestablished marshland preserve **Crissy Field,** on of the city's favorite natural playgrounds. Make a point of seeing this spectacular destination with sandy beach, lots of native birds, and jogging paths.

A national historic site under the Golden Gate Bridge, **Fort Point** (© 415/556-1693; www.nps.gov/fopo) was built in 1853 to protect the entrance to the harbor. Film buffs will recognize it from Alfred Hitchcock's *Vertigo*. During the Civil War, 140 men and 90 pieces of artillery armed the brick fort to prevent a Confederate takeover of California. Rangers in Civil War regalia lead regular tours and sometimes fire the old cannons. The fort is open Friday through Sunday from 10am to 5pm, and guided tours and cannon demonstrations are given once or twice a day on open days.

Lincoln Boulevard sweeps around the western edge of the bay to two of the city's most popular beaches. **Baker Beach** is a small, beautiful strand where the waves roll ashore. A fine spot for sunbathing, walking, or fishing, it's packed on sunny days; you'll likely see some nude sunbathers here. Because of the cold water and roaring currents, swimming is risky for all but the most competent. Here you can pick up the **Coastal Trail ★**, which leads through the Presidio. A short distance from Baker, **China Beach** is a small cove where swimming is permitted. Changing rooms, showers, a sun deck, and restrooms are available. But the water is crazy-cold!

Farther around the coast, **Land's End** looks out to Pyramid Rock. A lower and upper trail provide varied hiking options amid wind-swept cypress trees and pines on the cliffs above the Pacific. **Point Lobos,** the **Sutro Baths,** and the **Cliff House** lie still farther along the coast. The latter, which underwent major renovations in 2004, has been serving refreshments to visitors since 1863. Here you can view the **Seal Rocks,** home to a colony of sea lions and marine birds. Only traces of the Sutro Baths remain today, northeast of the Cliff House. This popular swimming facility accommodated as many as 24,000 people before burning down in 1966. Farther inland (at the western end of California St.), **Lincoln Park** is home to a golf course and the Legion of Honor.

From the Cliff House, the Esplanade continues south along the 4-mile-long **Ocean Beach,** which is unsuitable for swimming, but popular with brave surfers. At the southern end of Ocean Beach, around **Fort Funston,** an easy loop trail runs across the cliffs; for information, call the ranger station (✆ **415/239-2366**). Here, too, you can watch hang gliders take advantage of the high cliffs and strong winds.

Farther south along I-280, **Sweeney Ridge** is accessible only by car but affords sweeping views of the coastline from the many trails that crisscross these 1,000 acres of land. From here, in 1769, the expedition led by Don Gaspar de Portolá first laid eyes on San Francisco Bay. In Pacifica, the ridge is accessible via Sneath Lane off Highway 35 (Skyline Blvd.) in San Bruno.

THE PRESIDIO

When the U.S. Army transferred the Presidio to the National Park Service in 1994, it became one of a handful of urban national parks that combine historical, architectural, and natural elements—not to mention a formerly private golf course and a home for filmmaker George Lucas's production companies—into one arboreal expanse.

These 1,480 acres include a variety of terrain, such as coastal scrub, dunes, and prairie grasslands that shelter many rare plants and more than 150 bird species, some of which nest here. The property also encompasses more than 350 historic buildings and a national cemetery. The National Park Service operates walking and biking tours around the Presidio, including the 2-mile **Ecology Loop Trail** through some of the Presidio's 60,000 trees, such as redwoods, spruce, cypress, and acacias; and the 2.5-mile **Coastal Trail,** from the bluff top from Baker Beach to the southern base of the Golden Gate Bridge. Reservations are required.

A former airfield, **Crissy Field** in recent years has become known as a hot arena for California's windsurfers. Between March and October, hundreds come to ply the waters, and to see and be seen. The beach affords easy water access and plenty of room to rig up, but it's not recommended for the inexperienced. Crissy Field is also a gorgeous and popular route for joggers circuiting the Marina District to Fort Point and back, with great picnic spots and a sweet cafe along the path to Fort Funston. A pier at the west end of Crissy Field is popular for fishing and crabbing.

For information, call the **Presidio Visitors Center** at ✆ **415/561-4323,** or visit **www. nps.gov/prsf** or **www.presidio.gov.** Take bus no. 28, 45, 76, or 82X to get there.

9 OUTDOOR PURSUITS

BEACHES   Most days it's too chilly to hang out at the beach, but when the fog evaporates and the wind dies down, one of the best ways to spend the day in the city is oceanside. On any truly hot day, thousands flock to the beach to worship the sun, build sandcastles, and throw the ball around. Without a wet suit, swimming is a fiercely cold endeavor. In any case, dip at your own risk—there are no lifeguards on duty and San Francisco's waters have strong undertows. On the South Bay, **Baker Beach** is ideal for picnicking, sunning, walking, or fishing against the backdrop of the Golden Gate (though pollution makes your catch not necessarily worthy of eating).

Ocean Beach, at the end of Golden Gate Park, on the westernmost side of the city, is San Francisco's largest beach—4 miles long. Just offshore, at the northern end of the beach, in front of Cliff House, are the jagged Seal Rocks, inhabited by various shorebirds and a large colony of barking sea lions (bring binoculars for a close-up view). To the left, Kelly's Cove is one of the more challenging surf spots in town. Ocean Beach is ideal for strolling or sunning, but don't swim here—tides are tricky, and each year bathers drown in the rough surf.

Stop by Ocean Beach bus terminal at the corner of Cabrillo and La Playa to learn about San Francisco's history in local artist Ray Beldner's whimsically historical sculpture garden. Then hike up the hill to explore **Cliff House** and the ruins of the **Sutro Baths,** once able to accommodate 24,000 bathers.

BIKING The San Francisco Parks and Recreation Department maintains two city-designated bike routes. One winds 7.5 miles through Golden Gate Park to Lake Merced; the other traverses the city, starting in the south, and continues over the Golden Gate Bridge. These routes are not dedicated to bicyclists, who must exercise caution to avoid pedestrians. Helmets are recommended for adults and required by law for kids under 18. A bike map is available from the San Francisco Visitor Information Center, at Powell and Mason streets, for $3, and from bicycle shops all around town.

Ocean Beach has a public walk- and bikeway that stretches along 5 waterfront blocks of the Great Highway between Noriega and Santiago streets. It's an easy ride from Cliff House or Golden Gate Park.

Avenue Cyclery, 756 Stanyan St., at Waller Street, in the Haight (© **415/387-3155**), rents bikes for $7 per hour or $28 per day. It's open daily, April through September from 10am to 7pm and October through March from 10am to 6pm. For cruising Fisherman's Wharf and the Golden Gate Bridge, your best bet is **Blazing Saddles** (© **415/202-8888; www.blazingsaddles.com**), which has five locations around Fisherman's Wharf. Bikes rent for $28 per day, including maps, locks, and helmets; tandem bikes are available as well.

CITY STAIR CLIMBING ★★ The following city stair climbs will give you not only a good workout, but seriously stunning neighborhood, city, and bay views. Check **www. sisterbetty.org/stairways** for more ideas.

Filbert Street Steps, between Sansome Street and Telegraph Hill, are a particular challenge. Scaling the sheer eastern face of Telegraph Hill, this 377-step climb winds through verdant flower gardens and charming 19th-century cottages. Napier Lane, a narrow, wooden plank walkway, leads to Montgomery Street. Turn right and follow the path to the end of the cul-de-sac, where another stairway continues to Telegraph's panoramic summit.

The **Lyon Street Steps,** between Green Street and Broadway, were built in 1916. This historic stairway street contains four steep sets of stairs totaling 288 steps. Begin at Green Street and climb all the way up, past manicured hedges and flower gardens, to an iron gate that opens into the Presidio. A block east, on Baker Street, another set of 369 steps descends to Green Street.

GOLF San Francisco has a few beautiful golf courses. One of the most lavish is the **Presidio Golf Course** (© **415/561-4661;** www.presidiogolf.com). Greens fees are $60 until 12:30pm for residents Monday through Thursday and $96 for nonresidents; rates drop to $50 until 2pm, and then to $35 for the rest of the day for residents and non-residents. Friday though Sunday, rates are $96 for residents and $108 for nonresidents from 8 to 11am; from 11am to 12:30pm, the cost is $60 for residents. After that it's $50 for everyone until 2pm and $35 for the rest of the day. Carts are included. There are also two decent municipal courses in town.

The 9-hole **Golden Gate Park Course,** 47th Avenue and Fulton Street (© **415/751-8987;** www.goldengateparkgolf.com), charges $14 per person Monday through Thursday, $18 Friday through Sunday. The 1,357-yard course is par 27. All holes are par 3, and the course is appropriate for all levels. It's a little weathered in spots, but it's casual, fun, and inexpensive. Hours are daily from sunup to sundown.

The 18-hole **Lincoln Park Golf Course,** 34th Avenue and Clement Street (© **415/221-9911;** www.parks.sfgov.org), charges greens fees of $31 per person Monday through Thursday, $36 Friday through Sunday, with rates decreasing after 4pm in summer, 2pm in winter. It's San Francisco's prettiest municipal course, with terrific views and fairways lined with Monterey cypress and pine trees. The 5,181-yard layout plays to par 68, and the 17th hole has a glistening ocean view. This is the oldest course in the city and one of the oldest in the West. It's open daily at daybreak.

SKATING Although people skate in Golden Gate Park all week, Sunday is best, when John F. Kennedy Drive, between Kezar Drive and Transverse Road, closes to cars. Disco skaters gather near the Eighth Avenue park entrance on weekends.

10 SHOPPING

Store hours vary, but most are open Monday through Saturday from 10am to 6pm, and Sunday from noon to 5pm. Most department stores stay open later, as do shops around Fisherman's Wharf. Sales tax in San Francisco is 8.5%. If you live out of state and buy an expensive item, consider asking the store to ship it home for you. You'll have to pay for transport, but you'll evade the sales tax.

UNION SQUARE & ENVIRONS San Francisco's most popular, congested shopping mecca centers on Union Square. Most of the big department stores and many high-end specialty shops are in this area. Be sure to venture to Grant Avenue, Post and Sutter streets, and Maiden Lane.

If you're into art, pick up *The San Francisco Gallery Guide,* a comprehensive, bimonthly publication listing the city's current shows (most of which are downtown). It's available free by mail; send a self-addressed stamped envelope to San Francisco Bay Area Gallery Guide, 1369 Fulton St., San Francisco, CA 94117 (© **415/921-1600**). You can also pick one up at the San Francisco Visitor Information Center at 900 Market St. (at Powell St.).

The **Catharine Clark Gallery,** on the second floor at 49 Geary St., between Kearny and Grant streets (© **415/399-1439;** www.cclarkgallery.com), exhibits the work of up-and-coming, pop culture–inspired artists (mainly from California), and nurtures novice collectors through an unusual, interest-free purchasing plan.

Century-old **Gump's,** 135 Post St., between Kearny Street and Grant Avenue (© **415/982-1616;** www.gumps.com), is a must-visit. A virtual treasure trove of household items and gifts, the shop purveys a collection of Asian antiquities, contemporary art glass, exquisite jade and pearl jewelry, and more.

Music aficionados will revel in **Virgin Megastore,** 2 Stockton St., at Market Street (© **415/397-4525**), with thousands of CDs (including an impressive collection of imports), videos, laser discs, and a multimedia department. Its literary equivalent is nearby

Amazing Grazing

There's no better way to spend a sunny Saturday morning in San Francisco than by strolling the **Ferry Building Marketplace** and **Farmers' Market,** snacking your way through some of America's finest organic produce. While foraging among the dozens of stalls crammed with Northern California fruit, vegetable, bread, shellfish, and dairy items, you're bound to bump elbows with the dozens of Bay Area chefs (such as Alice Waters) who do their shopping here. The enthusiastic vendors are always willing to educate visitors about organic produce, and often provide free samples. It's a unique opportunity for city dwellers to buy freshly picked organic produce directly from small family-operated farms.

On Saturday mornings the market is in full glory. Nearly the entire building is enrobed with local meat ranchers, artisan cheese makers, bread bakers, specialty food purveyors, and farmers. On Saturdays make sure you arrive by 10:30am to watch *Meet the Farmer,* a half-hour interview with one of the farmers, food artisans, or other purveyors who give the audience in-depth information about how and where their food is produced. Then, at 11am, Bay Area chefs give cooking demonstrations using ingredients purchased that morning from the market (you get to taste their creations then leave with the recipe). Several local restaurants also have food stalls selling their cuisine—including breakfast items. You can also pick up locally made vinegars, preserves, herbs, and oils.

The Ferry Building is located on the Embarcadero at the foot of Market Street (about a 15-min. walk from Fisherman's Wharf). Call ✆ **415/693-0996** for more information or log on to **www.ferryplazafarmersmarket.com** or **www.ferrybuildingmarketplace.com**.

Borders Books & Music, 400 Post St., at Powell (✆ **415/399-1633**), with thousands of titles and a cafe.

While the department stores have plenty of clothes, real fashion fiends will want to check out the boutiques. For men, **Cable Car Clothiers,** 200 Bush St., at Sansome Street (✆ **415/397-4740**), is popular for traditional attire, such as three-button suits with natural shoulders, Aquascutum coats, McGeorge sweaters, and Atkinson ties.

Wilkes Bashford, 375 Sutter St., at Stockton Street (✆ **415/986-4380**), is one of the most well known, expensive clothing boutiques in the city, with fashions for both sexes. It stocks only the finest garb, including men's Kiton and Brioni suits (some of the most expensive in the world, at $2,500 and up).

For fabulous, expensive women's fashions, check out **Métier,** 355 Sutter St., between Grant and Stockton streets (✆ **415/989-5395**; www.metiersf.com). Its inventory of European ready-to-wear lines is in the best taste; featured designers include Italian designer Anna Molinari Hache and Blue Marine, as well as a distinguished collection of antique-style, high-end jewelry from L.A.'s Cathy Waterman and ultrapopular custom-designed poetry jewelry by Jeanine Payer.

Although this area is too big and shops are too scattered to be suitable for strolling, you'll find good discount shopping, along with a few great regular retail shops, in warehouse spaces south of Market. Most major hotels carry discount-shopping guides. Many buses pass through this area, including nos. 9, 12, 14, 15, 19, 26, 27, 30, 42, 45, and 76.

The **SFMOMA MuseumStore,** 151 Third St., 2 blocks south of Market Street, across from Yerba Buena Gardens (© 415/357-4035; www.sfmoma.org), is a favorite among locals. The shop's art cards and books, as well as jewelry, housewares, and knickknacks are well designed. For visitors, the San Francisco mementos here are much more tasteful than those sold in Fisherman's Wharf.

Fashionable bargain hunters head to **Jeremys,** 2 S. Park, at Second Street between Bryant and Brannan streets (© 415/882-4929; www.jeremys.com), where top designer fashions, from shoes to suits, sell at rock-bottom prices. Another worthy stop is the **Wine Club San Francisco,** 953 Harrison St., between Fifth and Sixth streets (© 415/512-9086), with bargain prices on more than 1,200 domestic and foreign wines; bottles run from $4 to $1,100.

HAYES VALLEY Most neighborhoods cater to either trendy or conservative shoppers, but lower Hayes Street, between Octavia and Gough, celebrates anything vintage, artistic, and funky. The neighborhood is still in transition, but it's definitely the most interesting place to shop—with modern and retro furniture stores, trendy shoe stores, and hip clothiers. For fashionable classic clothing for men and women, check out **MAC,** 387 Grove St., at Gough Street (© 415/863-3011). Nearby, **RAG,** 541 Octavia St. at Hayes Street (© 415/621-7718; www.ragsf.com), showcases very affordable trendy fashions from upcoming local designers. **Propeller,** 555 Hayes St., between Laguna and Octavia streets (© 415/701-7767), is my favorite contemporary furniture store. Lots of great antiques shops are south on Octavia and on nearby Market Street. Bus lines include nos. 16AX, 16BX, and 21.

The Italian men's and women's shoes at **Bulo,** 437A Hayes St., at Gough Street (© 415/864-3244; www.buloshoes.com), run the gamut from casual to dressy, reserved to wildly funky. **Gimme Shoes,** 416 Hayes St. (© 415/864-0691; www.gimmeshoes.com), is ultrahip but expensive. Ferret out the sale items unless you're ready to drop around $200 per pair.

THE CASTRO You could spend a day wandering the Castro's housewares and men's clothing shops. Buses serving the area are nos. 8, 24, 33, 35, or 37.

Citizen Clothing, 536 Castro St., between 18th and 19th streets (© 415/575-3560), is a popular shop for stylish casual clothing.

Joseph Schmidt Confections, 3489 16th St., at Sanchez Street (© 415/861-8682; www.josephschmidtconfections.com), adds another dimension to designer chocolate: Sinfully luscious sweets take on sculptural shapes so exquisite you'll be reluctant to bite into them. Prices are remarkably reasonable.

CHESTNUT STREET Parallel to Union Street, a few blocks north, Chestnut likewise has endless shopping and dining choices—as well as a population of superfit, postgraduate singles who hang around cafes and bars that are good for flirting and "hooking up." The area is serviced by bus lines 22, 28, 30, 41, 42, 43, and 76.

FISHERMAN'S WHARF & ENVIRONS The tourist-oriented malls that run along Jefferson Street—Ghirardelli Square, PIER 39, the Cannery at Del Monte Square, and the Anchorage—include hundreds of shops, restaurants, and attractions. They're not particularly impressive, where merchandise is concerned.

Locals tend to avoid this part of town, but do venture to **Cost Plus World Market,** 2552 Taylor St., between North Point and Bay streets (© 415/928-6200), a vast warehouse crammed to the rafters with Chinese baskets, Indian camel bells, Malaysian batik scarves, innumerable items from Algeria to Zanzibar, and a decent wine section. Adjoining is a **Barnes & Noble** "superstore," at 2550 Taylor St., between Bay and North Point (© **415/292-6762**).

FILLMORE STREET   Some of the best women's clothes shopping in town is packed into 5 blocks of Fillmore Street in Pacific Heights, from Jackson to Sutter streets. This area is also the perfect place to grab a bite and peruse the boutiques, crafts shops, and housewares stores. It's serviced by bus lines 1, 2, 3, 4, 12, 22, and 24. One of my favorite stops is **Zinc Details,** 1905 Fillmore St., between Bush and Pine streets (© **415/ 776-2100;** www.zincdetails.com). They ply an amazing collection of modern and contemporary handcrafted glass vases, pendant lights, ceramics, and furniture.

HAIGHT STREET   Green hair, spiked hair, no hair, or mohair—even the hippies look conservative next to Haight Street's dramatic fashion freaks. The shopping in the 6 blocks of upper Haight Street, between Central Avenue and Stanyan Street, reflects its clientele and offers everything from incense to furniture, from European street styles to vintage and übertrendy—all at reasonable prices. Bus lines 7, 66, 71, or 73 run down Haight Street. The Muni Metro N line stops at Waller Street and at Cole Street.

Recycled Records, 1377 Haight St., between Central and Masonic streets (© **415/ 626-4075**), is easily one of the best used-record stores in the city. This loud shop has a good selection of promotional CDs, and cases of used classic rock LPs. You can also buy sheet music, tour programs, and old *TV Guide*s here. At the west end of Haight Street is **Amoeba Records,** 1377 Haight St., at Stanyan St. (© **415/831-1200**), a huge store that highlights, among other things, indie labels.

NORTH BEACH   Grant and Columbus avenues cater to their hip clientele with great coffee shops and a small but worthy selection of boutiques and specialty shops. You can pick up a great gift for yourself or anyone else at **Biordi Art Imports,** 412 Columbus Ave., at Vallejo Street (© **415/392-8096;** www.biordi.com). Its Italian Majolica pottery is exquisite and unique. Join the funky literary types who browse **City Lights Booksellers & Publishers,** 261 Columbus Ave., at Broadway (© **415/362-8193;** www.citylights. com), the famous bookstore owned by Beat poet Lawrence Ferlinghetti. Its shelves are stocked with a comprehensive collection of art, poetry, and political paperbacks, as well as more mainstream books.

11 SAN FRANCISCO AFTER DARK

For up-to-date nightlife information, turn to the *San Francisco Weekly* (www.sfweekly. com) and the *San Francisco Bay Guardian* (www.sfbg.com), both of which run comprehensive listings. They are available free at bars and restaurants and from street-corner boxes all around the city. *Where* (www.wheresf.com), a free tourist-oriented monthly, also lists programs and performance times; it's available in most of the city's finer hotels. The Sunday edition of the *San Francisco Chronicle* features a "Datebook" section, printed on pink paper, with information on and listings of the week's events. If you have Internet access, it's a good idea to check out **www.citysearch.com** or **www.sfstation.com** for the latest in bars, clubs, and events. And if you want to secure seats at a hot-ticket event, either buy well in advance or contact the concierge of your hotel and see if they can swing something for you.

GETTING TICKETS   **Tix Bay Area** (aka **TIX**; ✆ **415/433-7827;** www.tixbayarea.org) sells half-price tickets on the day of performance and full-price tickets in advance to select Bay Area cultural and sporting events. TIX is also a Ticketmaster outlet and sells Gray Line tours and transportation passes. Tickets are primarily sold in person with some half-price tickets available on their website. To find out which shows they are selling half-price tickets for, call their info line or check out their website. A service charge, ranging from $1.75 to $6, is levied on each ticket depending on its full price. You can pay with cash, traveler's checks, Visa, MasterCard, American Express, or Discover Card with photo ID. TIX, located on Powell Street between Geary and Post streets, is open Tuesday through Thursday from 11am to 6pm, Friday from 11am to 7pm, Saturday from 10am to 7pm, and Sunday from 10am to 3pm. *Note:* Half-price tickets go on sale at 11am.

You can also get tickets to most theater and dance events through **City Box Office,** 180 Redwood St., Suite 100, between Golden Gate and McAllister streets off Van Ness Avenue (✆ **415/392-4400;** www.cityboxoffice.com).

Tickets.com (✆ **800/225-2277;** www.tickets.com) sells computer-generated tickets (with a hefty service charge of $3–$19 per ticket!) to concerts, sporting events, plays, and special events. **Ticketmaster** (✆ **415/421-TIXS;** www.ticketmaster.com) also offers advance ticket purchases (also with a service charge).

THE PERFORMING ARTS

American Conservatory Theater (A.C.T.) (Finds)   The Tony Award–winning American Conservatory Theater made its debut in 1967 and quickly established itself as the city's premier resident theater group and one of the nation's best. The A.C.T. season runs September through July and features both classic and experimental works. Its home is the fabulous **Geary Theater,** a national historic landmark that is regarded as one of America's finest performance spaces. The 2006–07 season marked A.C.T.'s 40th anniversary. In their 4-decade history, they've reached a combined audience of seven million people. Performing at the Geary Theater, 415 Geary St. (at Mason St.). ✆ **415/749-2ACT.** www. act-sf.org. Tickets $14–$82.

The Magic Theatre   After nurturing the talents of luminary playwrights such as Sam Shepard, whose Pulitzer Prize–winning *Buried Child* premiered here, the acclaimed Magic Theatre continues its commitment to the work of new writers. The season usually runs from October through June, with performances Tuesday through Sunday. At Bldg. D, Fort Mason Center, Marina Blvd. (at Buchanan St.). ✆ **415/441-8822.** www.magictheatre.org. Tickets $20–$45; discounts for students, educators, and seniors.

Philharmonia Baroque Orchestra   This orchestra of baroque, classical, and "early Romantic" music performs in San Francisco and all around the Bay Area. The season lasts September through April. Performing in Herbst Theater, 401 Van Ness Ave. Tickets are sold through City Box Office ✆ **415/392-4400** (box office) or call 415/252-1288 (administrative offices). www.philharmonia.org. Tickets $29–$67.

San Francisco Ballet   Founded in 1933, the San Francisco Ballet is the oldest professional ballet company in the United States and is regarded as one of the country's finest. It performs an eclectic repertoire of full-length, neoclassical, and contemporary ballets. The Repertory Season generally runs February through May; the company performs the *Nutcracker* in December. The San Francisco Ballet Orchestra accompanies most performances.

San Francisco Opera   The second municipal opera in the United States, the San Francisco Opera is one of the city's cultural icons. All productions have English supertitles. The season starts in September, lasts 14 weeks, takes a break for a few months, and then picks up again in June and July. During the interim winter period, future opera stars are featured in showcases and recitals. Performances are held most evenings, except Monday, with matinees on Sundays. Tickets go on sale as early as June for subscribers, and in August for the general public. The best seats sell out quickly, but some less-coveted seats are usually available until curtain time. War Memorial Opera House, 301 Van Ness Ave. (at Grove St.). © **415/864-3330** (box office). www.sfopera.com. Tickets $24–$235; standing room $10 cash only; student rush $15 cash only.

San Francisco Symphony   Founded in 1911, the internationally respected San Francisco Symphony has long been an important part of the city's cultural life under such legendary conductors as Pierre Monteux and Seiji Ozawa. In 1995, Michael Tilson Thomas took over from Herbert Blomstedt; he has led the orchestra to new heights and crafted an exciting repertoire of classical and modern music. The season runs September through June. Summer symphony activities include a Summer Festival and a Summer in the City series. Tickets are very hard to come by, but if you're desperate, you can usually pick up a few outside the hall the night of the concert. Also, the box office occasionally has a few last-minute tickets. Performing at Davies Symphony Hall, 201 Van Ness Ave. (at Grove St.). © **415/864-6000** (box office). www.sfsymphony.org. Tickets $25–$114.

COMEDY & CABARET

Beach Blanket Babylon (Moments)   Now a San Francisco tradition, *Beach Blanket Babylon* is best known for its outrageous costumes and oversize headdresses. It's been playing almost 32 years, and nearly every performance still sells out. It's wise to write for tickets at least 3 weeks in advance, or buy them through TIX (© **415/433-7827**). At Club Fugazi, Beach Blanket Babylon Blvd., 678 Green St. (btw. Powell St. and Columbus Ave.). © **415/421-4222**. www.beachblanketbabylon.com. Tickets $25–$78.

Cobb's Comedy Club   Cobb's features such national headliners as Joe Rogan, Brian Regan, and Jake Johannsen. Comedy reigns Wednesday through Sunday, including a 15-comedian All-Pro Wednesday showcase (a 3-hr. marathon). Cobb's is open to those 18 and over, and occasionally to kids 16 and 17 when accompanied by a parent or legal guardian (call ahead). Shows are held Wednesday, Thursday, and Sunday at 8pm, Friday and Saturday at 8 and 10:15pm. 915 Columbus Ave. (at Lombard St.). © **415/928-4320**. www. cobbscomedy.com. Cover $13–$35. 2-beverage minimum.

Punch Line Comedy Club   Adjacent to the Embarcadero One office building, this is the largest comedy nightclub in the city. Three-person shows with top national and local talent are featured here Tuesday through Saturday. Showcase night is Sunday, when 15 comics take the mic. There's an all-star showcase or a special event on Monday. Doors always open at 7pm and shows are Sunday through Thursday at 8pm, Friday and Saturday at 8 and 10pm (18 and over; two-drink minimum). 444 Battery St. (btw. Washington and Clay sts.), plaza level. © **415/397-4337**, or 415/397-7573 for recorded information. www. punchlinecomedyclub.com. Cover Sun–Mon $7.50; Tues–Thurs $13–$15; Fri–Sat $18–$20.

ZinZany Dinner Party

Hungry for dinner and a damned good time? It ain't cheap, but Teatro ZinZanni is a rollicking ride of food, whimsy, drama, and song within a stunningly elegant 1926 spiegeltent on the Embarcadero. Part musical theater and part comedy show, the 3-hour dinner theater includes a surprisingly decent five-course meal served by dozens of performers who weave both the audience and astounding physical acts (think Cirque du Soleil) into their wacky and playful world. Anyone in need of a night of lighthearted laughter should definitely book a table here. Shows are held Wednesday through Sunday and tickets are $123 to $147 including dinner. The tent is located at Pier 29 on the Embarcadero at Battery Street. Call ℂ 415/438-2668, or log on to www.zinzanni.org for more details.

THE CLUB & MUSIC SCENE
Rock & Blues Clubs

Bimbo's 365 Club ★★   Originally located on Market Street when it opened in 1931, this North Beach live destination is a fabulous spot to catch outstanding live rock and jazz (think Chris Isaak and the Brian Setzer Orchestra) and dance amid glamorous surroundings. Grab tickets in advance at the box office, which is open Monday through Friday, 10am to 4pm. 1025 Columbus Ave. (at Chestnut St.). ℂ 415/474-0365. www.bimbos 365club.com.

Biscuits and Blues   With a crisp, blow-your-eardrums-out sound system, New Orleans speak-easy (albeit commercial) appeal, and a nightly lineup of live, national acts, there's no better place to muse the blues than this basement-cum-nightclub. From 7pm on, they serve drink specials, along with their signature fried chicken, namesake moist, flaky biscuits, some new small-plate entrees dubbed "Southern tapas," and a newly expanded wine list. Menu items range from $7.95 to $17. 401 Mason (at Geary St.). ℂ 415/ 292-2583. www.biscuitsandblues.com. Cover (during performances) $10–$20.

Cafe du Nord (Finds)   Although it's been around since 1907, this basement supper club is rightfully self-proclaimed as the place for a "slightly lurid indie pop scene set in a beautiful old speakeasy." It's also where you'll find an eclectic (and usually younger) crowd that flocks here to linger at the front room's 40-foot mahogany bar or dine on the likes of phyllo-wrapped prawns with romesco sauce or sip cocktails at the back room tables—while listening to such national indie rock bands as Gomez and Arab Strap, and such old school acts as Frank Black and the Pixies. 2170 Market St. (at Sanchez St.). ℂ 415/861-5016. www.cafedunord.com. Cover $5–$25. Food $5–$15.

Great American Music Hall ★★   Built in 1907 as a restaurant/bordello, the Great American Music Hall is likely one of the most gorgeous rock venues you'll encounter. With ornately carved balconies, frescoed ceilings, marble columns, and huge, hanging light fixtures, you won't know whether to marvel at the structure or watch the acts, which have ranged from Duke Ellington and Sarah Vaughan to Arctic Monkeys, The Radiators, and She Wants Revenge. 859 O'Farrell (btw. Polk and Larkin sts.). ℂ 415/885-0750. www.music hallsf.com. Ticket prices and starting times vary; call or check website for individual show information.

Lou's Pier 47 Club You won't find many locals in the place, but Lou's happens to be good, old-fashioned fun. It's a casual spot where you can relax with Cajun seafood (downstairs) and live blues bands (upstairs) nightly. A vacation attitude makes the place one of the more, um, jovial spots near the wharf. There's a $3 to $5 cover for bands that play between 4 and 8pm and a $3 to $10 cover for bands that play between 8 or 9pm and midnight or 1am. 300 Jefferson St. (at Jones St.). ✆ **415/771-5687.** www.louspier47.com.

Pier 23 If there's one good-time destination that's an anchor for San Francisco's party people, it's the Embarcadero's Pier 23. Part ramshackle patio spot and part dance floor with a heavy dash of dive bar, here it's all about fun for a startlingly diverse clientele (including a one-time visit by Bill Clinton!). The well-worn box of a restaurant with tented patio is a prime sunny-day social spot for white collars, but on weekends, it's a straight-up people zoo where every age and persuasion coexist more peacefully than the cast in a McDonald's commercial. Expect to boogie down shoulder-to-shoulder to 1980s hits and leave with a contagious feel-good vibe. Pier 23, at the Embarcadero (at Battery St.). ✆ **415/362-5125.** www.pier23cafe.com. Cover $5–$10 during performances.

The Saloon An authentic Gold Rush survivor, this North Beach dive is the oldest bar in the city. Popular with both bikers and daytime pinstripers, it schedules live blues nightly and afternoons Friday through Sunday. 1232 Grant Ave. (at Columbus St.). ✆ **415/989-7666.** Cover $5–$15 Fri–Sat.

Dance Clubs

The Endup This unique party space with a huge, heated outdoor deck (with waterfall and fountain), indoor fireplace, and eclectic clientele has always thrown some of the most kickin' parties in town. There's a different theme every night: Thursday's Wind Up offers up a variety of house DJs; Fag Friday is just what it sounds like, plus lots of throw-down dancing; and the Endup is ever-popular with the sleepless dance-all-day crowd that comes here after the other clubs close (it's open Sat morning from 6am–noon and then nonstop from Sat night around 10pm until Sun night/Mon morning at 4am). Call to confirm nights—offerings change from time to time. 401 Sixth St. (at Harrison St.). ✆ **415/357-0827.** www.theendup.com. Cover free–$15.

Ruby Skye Downtown's most glamorous and gigantic nightspot is all aglitter thanks to a dramatic renovation and the addition of killer light and sound systems within the 1890s Victorian playhouse previously known as the Stage Door. Inside, hundreds of partiers boogie on the ballroom floor to house music, mingle on the mezzanine and around the three bars, and puff freely in the smoking room while DJs or live music bring down the dancing house Thursday through Saturday. Big spenders should book the VIP

SF's Underground Entertainment

If you're really in the mood for some radical entertainment on your vacation, log on to **www.LaughingSquid.com**. Since 1995 Laughing Squid's **"Squid List"** has been the Bay Area's sine qua non online resource for underground art, culture, and technology. Along with links to local art and culture events, the Laughing Squid also hosts the Squid List, a daily event announcements list. There's some really freaky fringe stuff on this Web page, with plenty of garbage-level entertainment among several gems. Either way it makes for entertaining surfing.

lounge, which offers a glitzy place to "kick it" and bird's-eye views of the whole club scene. 420 Mason St. (btw. Geary and Post sts.). ℭ **415/693-0777.** www.rubyskye.com. Cover $10–$25.

1015 Folsom   The ginormous party warehouse at 1015 Folsom St. has three levels of dance floors that make for an extensive variety of dancing venues—complete with a 20- and 30-something gyrating mass who live for the DJs' pounding house, disco, and acid-jazz music matched to a full-color laser system. Each night is a different club that attracts its own crowd, ranging from yuppie to hip-hop. Open Thursday through Saturday 10pm to 2am. 1015 Folsom St. (at Sixth St.). ℭ **415/431-1200.** www.1015.com. Cover varies.

Supper Clubs

Jazz at Pearl's   A change of ownership in 2003 converted one of the best jazz venues in the city into one of the best supper clubs. Voted Top 30 Club Worldwide by *Condé Nast Traveler* and Best Live Jazz Venue by *San Francisco Magazine,* Jazz at Pearl's combines a 1930s vibe, Spanish tapas, and great live music. With a variety of acts throughout the week (big band on Mon to national acts Thurs–Sat), there's something for everyone at this all-ages club. Shows start at 8 and 10pm nightly; doors open at 7pm. Tickets range from $19 to $154 (for VIP seating, which includes preferred seating, champagne, and meet and greet with artist). Cash only. 256 Columbus Ave. (at Broadway). ℭ **415/291-8255.** www.jazzatpearls.com. 2-drink minimum.

Yoshi's Jazz Club ★★   What started out it 1977 as a modest sushi and jazz club in Oakland has become one of the most respected jazz venues in the world. For more than 3 decades, until the grand opening of Yoshi's in San Francisco's Fillmore District, SF locals had to cross the Bay Bridge to listen to Stanton Moore, Branford Marsalis, and Diana Krall in an intimate setting. Now, locals can take a taxi to this two-story, 28,000-square-foot, state-of-the-art jazz venue featuring the finest jazz artists, plus first-rate Japanese cuisine at the adjoining restaurant. The elegant club is awash in sculptural Japanese lanterns, and sensuously curved walls that envelop the intimate stage. It's the perfect place for a romantic date that starts with *hamachi* and ends with Harry Connick, Jr., so be sure the check Yoshi's website to see who's playing while you're in town and make reservations ASAP—you'll be glad you did. 1330 Fillmore St. (at Eddy St.). ℭ **415/655-5600.** www.yoshis.com.

Destination Bars with DJ Grooves

Bambuddha Lounge (Finds)   A hot place for the young and the trendy to feast, flirt, or just be fabulous is this restaurant/bar adjoining the funky-cool Phoenix Hotel. With a 20-foot reclining Buddha on the roof, ultramodern San Francisco–meets–Southeast Asia decor (including waterfalls in the dining room and outdoor poolside cocktail lounge and *salas,* Balinese-style lounge areas by an outdoor pool), very affordable and above-average Southeast Asian cuisine served late into the evening and topping out at $22, and a state-of-the-art sound system streaming ambient, down-tempo, soul, funk, and house music, this is the "it" joint of the moment. 601 Eddy St. (at Larkin St.). ℭ **415/885-5088.** www. bambuddhalounge.com. Cover $5–$10, $20 for special events Thurs–Sat.

The Bliss Bar   Surprisingly trendy for sleepy family-oriented Noe Valley, this small, stylish, and friendly bar is a great place to stop for a varied mix of locals, colorful cocktail concoctions, and a DJ spinning at the front window from 9pm to 2am every night except Sunday and Monday. If it's open, take your cocktail into the too-cool back Blue Room. And if you're on a budget, stop by from 4 to 7pm when martinis, lemon drops, cosmos,

watermelon cosmos, and apple martinis are $4. 4026 24th St. (btw. Noe and Castro sts.).
C **415/826-6200.** www.blissbarsf.com.

Levende Lounge A fusion of fine dining and cocktails, Levende Lounge is one of the Mission's hottest spots and has been noted as the best bar in the city for singles, romance, bar food, and a slew of other accolades. Drop in early for happy hour Monday through Friday from 5 to 7pm or sit down for a meal of "world-fusion" small plates (think French, Asian, and Nuevo Latino) in a more standard dinner setting amid exposed brick walls and cozy lighting. Later, tables are traded for lounge furnishings for some late-night noshing and grooving. *Tip:* Some nights have cover charges, but you can avoid the fee with a dinner reservation, and food is served until 11pm. 1710 Mission St. (at Duboce St.). *C* **415/864-5585.** www.levendesf.com.

Wish Bar Flirtation, fun, and a very attractive staff await at this somewhat mellow, narrow bar in the popular night crawler area around 11th and Folsom streets. Swathed in burgundy and black with exposed cinder-block walls and cement floors, all's aglow a la candlelight and red-shaded sconces. With a bar in the front, DJ spinning upbeat lounge music in the back, and seating—including cushy leather couches—in between, it's often packed with a surprisingly diverse (albeit youthful) crowd and ever filled with eye candy. Closed Sunday. 1539 Folsom St. (btw. 11th and 12th sts.). *C* **415/278-9474.** www.wishsf.com.

THE BAR SCENE

Finding your idea of a comfortable bar has a lot to do with picking a neighborhood filled with your kind of people and investigating that area further. There are hundreds of bars throughout San Francisco, and although many are obscurely located and can't be classified by their neighborhood, the following is a general description of what you'll find, and where:

- **Chestnut and Union Street** bars attract a post-collegiate-type crowd.
- Young alternatives frequent **Mission District** haunts.
- **Upper Haight** is skate- and snowboarder grungy.
- Tourists mix with theatergoers and suits in **downtown** pubs.
- **North Beach** serves all types.
- **The Castro** caters mainly to gay locals.
- **SoMa** offers an eclectic mix.

Gold Dust Lounge (Finds) If you're staying downtown and want to head to a friendly, festive bar loaded with old-fashioned style and revelry, you needn't wander far off of Union Square. This classically cheesy watering hole is all that. The red banquettes, gilded walls, dramatic chandeliers, pro bartenders, and "regulars" are the old-school real deal. Add live music and cheap drinks and you're in for a good ol' time. *Tip:* It's cash only, so come with some greenbacks. 247 Powell St. (at Geary St.). *C* **415/397-1695.**

Spec's (Finds) The location of Spec's—Saroyan Place, a tiny alley at 250 Columbus Ave.—makes it less of a walk-in bar and more of a lively local hangout. Its funky decor—maritime flags hang from the ceiling; posters, photos, and oddities line the exposed-brick walls—gives it a character that intrigues every visitor. A "museum," displayed under glass, contains memorabilia and items brought back by seamen who drop in between voyages. The clientele is funky enough to keep you preoccupied while you drink a beer. 12 Saroyan Place (at 250 Columbus Ave.). *C* **415/421-4112.**

The Tonga Room & Hurricane Bar (Finds) It's kitschy as all get-out, but there's no denying the goofy Polynesian pleasures of the Fairmont Hotel's tropical oasis. Drop in and join the crowds for an umbrella drink, a simulated thunderstorm and downpour, and a heavy dose of whimsy that escapes most San Francisco establishments. If you're on a budget, you'll definitely want to stop by for the weekday happy hour from 5 to 7pm, when you can stuff your face at the all-you-can-eat bar-grub buffet (baby back ribs, chow mein, potstickers) for $8 and the cost of one drink. Settle in and you'll catch live Top-40 music after 8pm Wednesday through Sunday, when there's a $3 to $5 cover. In the Fairmont Hotel, 950 Mason St. (at California St.). ℂ **415/772-5278.** www.tongaroom.com.

Toronado Gritty Lower Haight isn't exactly a charming street, but there's plenty of nightlife here, catering to an artistic/grungy/skateboarding 20-something crowd. While Toronado definitely draws in the young'uns, its 50-plus microbrews on tap and 100 bottled beers also entice a more eclectic clientele in search of beer heaven. The brooding atmosphere matches the surroundings: an aluminum bar, a few tall tables, minimal lighting, and a back room packed with tables and chairs. Happy hour runs 11:30am to 6pm every day for $1 off pints. 547 Haight St. (at Fillmore St.). ℂ **415/863-2276.** www.toronado.com.

Tosca Cafe (Finds) Open Tuesday through Saturday from 5pm to 2am, Sunday 7pm to 2am, Tosca is a low-key and large popular watering hole for local politicos, writers, media types, incognito celebrities such as Johnny Depp or Nicholas Cage, and similar cognoscenti of unassuming classic characters. Equipped with dim lights, red leather booths, and high ceilings, it's everything you'd expect an old North Beach legend to be. No credit cards. 242 Columbus Ave. (btw. Broadway and Pacific Ave.). ℂ **415/986-9651.**

Vesuvio Situated along Jack Kerouac Alley, across from the famed City Lights bookstore, this renowned literary beatnik hangout is packed to the second-floor rafters with neighborhood writers, artists, songsters, wannabes, and everyone else ranging from longshoremen and cabdrivers to businesspeople, all of whom come for the laid-back atmosphere. The convivial space consists of two stories of cocktail tables, complemented by changing exhibitions of local art. In addition to drinks, Vesuvio features an espresso machine. 255 Columbus Ave. (at Broadway). ℂ **415/362-3370.** www.vesuvio.com.

Zeitgeist The front door is black, the back door is adorned with a skeleton Playboy bunny, and inside is packed to the rafters with tattooed, pierced, and hard-core-looking partiers. But forge on. Zeitgeist is such a friendly and fun punk-rock-cum-biker-bar beer garden that even the occasional yuppie can be spotted mingling around the slammin' juke box featuring tons of local bands and huge back patio filled with picnic tables. Along with fantastic dive-bar environs, you'll find 30 beers on draft, a pool table, and pinball machines. The regular crowd, mostly locals and bike messengers, come here to kick back with a pitcher, and welcome anyone else interested in the same pursuit. And if your night turns out, um, better than expected, there's a hotel upstairs. Cash only. 199 Valencia St. (at Duboce). ℂ **415/255-7505.**

Brewpubs

Gordon Biersch Brewery Restaurant Gordon Biersch Brewery is San Francisco's largest brew restaurant, serving decent food and tasty beer to an attractive crowd of mingling professionals. There are always several house-made beers to choose from, ranging from light to dark. Menu items run $9.50 to $26. 2 Harrison St. (on the Embarcadero). ℂ **415/243-8246.** www.gordonbiersch.com.

San Francisco Brewing Company   The bar is one of the city's few remaining old saloons, aglow with stained-glass windows, tile floors, skylights, a mahogany bar, and, running the length of the bar, a massive overhead fan—a bizarre contraption crafted from brass and palm fronds. Menu items range from $4.15—curiously, for *edamame* (soybeans)—to $21 for a full rack of baby back ribs with all the fixings. The happy-hour special, an 8¹/₂-ounce microbrew beer for $1.50 (or a pint for $2.50), is offered daily from 4 to 6pm and midnight to 1am. 155 Columbus Ave. (at Pacific St.). ℂ 415/434-3344. www.sfbrewing.com.

ThirstyBear Brewing Company   Nine superb, handcrafted varieties of brew are always on tap at this stylish high-ceilinged brick edifice. Good Spanish food is served here, too. Pool tables and dartboards are upstairs, and live flamenco can be heard on Sunday nights. 661 Howard St. (1 block east of the Moscone Center). ℂ 415/974-0905. www. thirstybear.com.

Wine Bars
The Bubble Lounge   Toasting the town is a nightly event at this two-level champagne bar. With 300 champagnes and sparkling wines, about 30 by the glass, brick walls, couches, and velvet curtains, there's plenty of pop in this fizzy lounge. 714 Montgomery St. (btw. Washington and Jackson sts.). ℂ 415/434-4204. www.bubblelounge.com.

First Crush   If you're staying downtown and want to sip through regional specialties, stop by this wine-centric restaurant and bar. Amid a sleek and stylish interior, an eclectic clientele noshes on reasonably priced "progressive American cuisine" paired, if desired, with an outstanding selection of California wines. But plenty of people drop in simply to sample wine—especially since there are around three dozen excellent choices for filling your glass, and the joint serves until 11pm (until midnight Thurs–Sat). 101 Cyril Magnin St. (aka Fifth St., just north of Market St., at Ellis St.). ℂ 415/982-7874. www.firstcrush.com.

Nectar Wine Lounge   Catering to the Marina's young and beautiful, this ultrahip place to sip—and snack—pours an exciting and well-edited wine selection (plus 900 choices by the bottle) along with creative small plates (pairings optional). Industrial-slick decor includes cube chairs, a long bar, and lounge areas that are often packed with 20- through 40-somethings. 3330 Steiner St. (at Chestnut St.). ℂ 415/345-1377. www.nectarwine lounge.com.

Cocktails with a View
Carnelian Room   On the 52nd floor of the Bank of America Building, the Carnelian Room offers uninterrupted views of the city. From a window-front table you feel as though you can reach out, pluck up the TransAmerica Pyramid, and stir your martini with it. In addition to cocktails, the restaurant serves a four-course meal ($59 per person) as well as a la carte items ($24–$49 for main entrees). Jackets are required and ties are optional for men, but encouraged. *Note:* The restaurant has one of the most extensive wine lists in the city—1,600 selections, to be exact. 555 California St., in the Bank of America Bldg. (btw. Kearny and Montgomery sts.). ℂ 415/433-7500. www.carnelianroom.com.

Equinox   Though locals don't frequent this Fi-Di (Financial District) place, it's very popular with tourists. The hook? The 17-story Hyatt's rooftop restaurant has a revolving floor that gives each table a 360-degree panoramic view of the city every 45 minutes. Equinox serves cocktails Wednesday through Sunday from 5 to 11pm (until 1am on Fri–Sat); dinner is served from 6 to 10pm. In the Hyatt Regency Hotel, 5 Embarcadero Center. ℂ 415/788-1234.

Straight Fun at Gay Bars

You don't have to own a copy of *Brokeback Mountain* to enjoy the free-spirited atmosphere of a gay bar. San Francisco's gay and lesbian community has a long tradition of welcoming straights to their bars, and it's pretty common to see gay, straight, male, and female revelers mix it up on the dance floor. These places are not for peepers who want to see what queers look like up close; they're for nonjudgmental partiers who just want to have fun. For example, at the **Mint Karaoke Lounge** (1942 Market St., at Laguna St.; ✆ **415/626-4726;** www.themint.net), no one knows or cares what your gender or sexual preferences are, as long as you clap loudly for anyone who has the guts to get up on stage. Another good gay bar for beginners is a piano bar called **Martuni's** (4 Valencia St., at Market St.; ✆ **415/241-0205**). It has everything you want and expect in a piano bar: a neon martini glass on the sign, a huge bar in the front room, and a cozy little piano bar in the back room where you can sing along or listen in awe as I-shoulda-been-a-star types belt out classic show tunes.

Harry Denton's Starlight Room　Come dressed to the nines or in casual attire to this old-fashioned cocktail lounge turned nightclub, where tourists and locals sip drinks at sunset and boogie down to live '70s and '80s music, Motown covers, jazz, and funk Friday through Tuesday nights; "'80s vogue" on Thursday nights; and the DJs' hip-hop and Top-40 tunes after dark on Wednesdays. The room is classic 1930s San Francisco, with red-velvet banquettes, chandeliers, and fabulous views. Crowds of all ages come for a night of drinking and unrestrained dancing. Atop the Sir Francis Drake Hotel, 450 Powell St., 21st floor. ✆ 415/395-8595. www.harrydenton.com. Cover $10 Wed after 7pm; $10 Thurs–Fri after 8pm; $15 Sat after 8pm.

Top of the Mark (Moments)　This is one of the most famous cocktail lounges in the world, and for good reason—the spectacular glass-walled room features an unparalleled 19th-floor view. During World War II, Pacific-bound servicemen toasted their goodbyes to the States here. While less dramatic today than they were back then, evenings spent here are still sentimental, thanks to the romantic atmosphere. In the Mark Hopkins Inter-Continental, 1 Nob Hill (California and Mason sts.). ✆ 415/616-6916. www.topofthemark.com. Cover $5–$10.

Sports Bar

Greens Sports Bar　If you think San Francisco sports fans aren't as enthusiastic as those on the East Coast, try to get a seat at Green's during a 49ers game. It's a classic old sports bar, with lots of polished dark wood and windows that open onto Polk Street, but it's loaded with modern appliances (including two large-screen televisions and 25 smaller ones) and modern partiers (read: the mid-20s and -30s set). With 18 beers on tap, a pool table, and a happy hour Monday through Friday from 4 to 7pm, there are reasons to cheer here even when the home team's got a day off. 2239 Polk St. (at Green St.). ✆ 415/775-4287. www.greenssportsbar.citysearch.com.

The Café (Finds)   When this place first got jumping, it was the only predominantly lesbian dance club on Saturday nights in the city. Once the guys found out how much fun the girls were having, however, they joined the party. Today, it's a happening mixed gay and lesbian scene with three bars; two pool tables; a steamy, free-spirited dance floor; and a small, heated patio and balcony where smoking and schmoozing is allowed. A perk: They open at 4pm weekdays and 3pm weekends. 2369 Market St. (at Castro St.). ✆ **415/861-3846**. www.cafesf.com.

The Stud   The Stud, which has been around for almost 40 years, is one of the most successful gay establishments in town. The interior has an antiques-shop look. Music is a balanced mix of old and new, and nights vary from cabaret to oldies to disco-punk. Check their website in advance for the evening's offerings. Drink prices range from $3.25 to $8. Happy hour runs Monday through Saturday 5 to 9pm with $1 off well drinks. 399 Ninth St. (at Harrison St.). ✆ **415/863-6623** or 415/252-STUD for event info. www.studsf.com. Cover free–$10.

Twin Peaks Tavern   Right at the intersection of Castro, 17th, and Market streets is one of the Castro's most famous (at 35 years old) gay hangouts. It caters to an older crowd but often has a mixture of patrons and claims to be the first gay bar in America. Because of its relatively small size and desirable location, the place becomes fairly crowded and convivial by 8pm, earlier than many neighboring bars. 401 Castro St. (at 17th and Market sts.). ✆ **415/864-9470**.

The San Francisco Bay Area

by Matthew Richard Poole

The Bay City is captivating, but don't ignore its environs, which contain a multitude of natural spectacles such as Mount Tamalpais and Muir Woods; scenic communities such as Tiburon, Sausalito, and Half Moon Bay; and diverse, culturally rich cities such as Oakland and its youth-oriented next-door neighbor, Berkeley. Farther north stretch the valleys of Napa and Sonoma, the finest wine region in the nation (see chapter 7, "The Wine Country"). To the south lie high-tech Silicon Valley and San Jose, Northern California's largest city.

---

1 BERKELEY ★

---

10 miles NE of San Francisco

Berkeley is best known as the home of the University of California at Berkeley, which is world renowned for its academic standards, 18 Nobel Prize winners (seven are active staff), and protests that led to the most famous student riots in U.S. history. Today, there's still hippie idealism in the air, but the radicals have aged; the 1960s are present only in tie-dye and paraphernalia shops. The biggest change the town is facing is yuppification; as San Francisco's rent and property prices soar out of the range of the average person's budget, everyone with less than a small fortune is seeking shelter elsewhere, and Berkeley is one of the top picks (although Oakland is quickly becoming a favorite, too). Berkeley is a lively city, teeming with all types of people, a beautiful campus, vast parks, great shopping, and some incredible restaurants.

ESSENTIALS

The Berkeley **Bay Area Rapid Transit (BART)** station is 2 blocks from the university. The fare from San Francisco is less than $4. Call ⊘ **511** or visit **www.bart.gov** for trip info, train fares, or to download trip planners to your iPod, mobile phone, or PDA.

If you are coming **by car** from San Francisco, take the Bay Bridge (go during the evening commute, and you'll think Los Angeles traffic is a breeze). Follow I-80 east to the University Avenue exit, and follow University until you hit the campus. Parking is tight, so leave your car at the Sather Gate parking lot, at Telegraph Avenue and Durant Street, or expect to fight for a spot.

WHAT TO SEE & DO

Hanging out is the preferred Berkeley pastime, and the best place to do it is **Telegraph Avenue,** the street that leads to the campus's southern entrance. Most of the action lies between Bancroft Way and Dwight Way, where coffeehouses, restaurants, shops, great book and record stores, and crafts booths (with vendors selling everything from T-shirts

and jewelry to I Ching and tarot-card readings) swarm with life. Pretend you're a local: Plant yourself at a cafe, sip a latte, and ponder something intellectual, or survey the town's unique residents.

Bibliophiles must stop at **Cody's Books,** 1730 Fourth St. (© **510/559-9500;** www. codysbooks.com), to peruse its gargantuan selection of titles, independent-press books, and magazines. If used and antiquarian books are your thing, stop by **Moe's Books,** 2476 Telegraph Ave. (© **510/849-2087;** www.moesbooks.com). After exploring four floors of new, used, and out-of-print books, you're unlikely to leave empty-handed.

UC Berkeley Campus

The University of California at Berkeley (www.berkeley.edu) is worth a stroll. It's a beautiful campus with plenty of woodsy paths, architecturally noteworthy buildings and, of course, 33,000 students. Among the architectural highlights of the campus are a number of buildings by Bernard Maybeck, Bakewell and Brown, and John Galen Howard.

Contact the **Visitor Information Center,** 101 University Hall, 2200 University Ave., at Oxford Street (© 510/642-5215; www.berkeley.edu/visitors), to join a free 90-minute campus tour. Reservations are required; see website for details. Tours are available year-round Monday through Saturday at 10am and Sunday at 1pm. Weekday tours depart from the Visitors Center and weekend tours start from Sather Bell Tower in the middle of campus. Electric cart tours are available year-round for travelers with disabilities for $40; 2 weeks' advance reservation is required, and no tours are given the week between Christmas and New Year's Day. Or stop by the office and pick up a self-guided walking-tour brochure or a free Berkeley map. *Note:* The information center is closed on weekends, but you can find the latest information on their website.

The university's southern, main entrance is at the northern end of Telegraph Avenue, at Bancroft Way. Walk through the entrance into Sproul Plaza, and when school is in session, you'll encounter the gamut of Berkeley's inhabitants: colorful street people, rambling political zealots, and ambitious students. You might be lucky enough to stumble upon some impromptu musicians or a heated debate. There's always something going on here, so stretch out on the grass for a few minutes and take in the Berkeley vibe. You'll also find the student union, complete with a bookstore, cafes, and an information desk on the second floor, where you can pick up the student newspaper (also found in dispensers throughout campus).

For viewing more traditional art forms, there are some noteworthy museums, too. The **Lawrence Hall of Science** ★ (east of campus on Centennial Dr., just above the Botanical Gardens; © **510/642-5132;** www.lawrencehallofscience.org) offers hands-on science exploration. It's open daily from 10am to 5pm and is a wonderful place to watch the sunset. Included in the admission price is an outdoor science park called Forces That Shape the Bay, which lets visitors explore ongoing geologic forces. The site includes activity stations such as earthquake simulators, a geologic uplift bench, a water feature, telescopes, BayLab programs and demonstrations, an audio tour, and picnic sites. Admission is $9.50 for adults; $7.50 for seniors 62 and over, students, and children 5 to 18; $5.50 for children 3 or 4; and free for kids under 3. The **UC Berkeley Art Museum** ★ (2626 Bancroft Way, btw. College and Telegraph aves.; © **510/642-0808;** www.bampfa.berkeley. edu) is open Wednesday through Sunday from 11am to 5pm. Admission is $8 for adults; $5 for seniors, non-UCB students, visitors with disabilities, and children 17 and under; and $4 for UCB students. This museum contains a substantial collection of Hans Hofmann paintings, a sculpture garden, and the Pacific Film Archive.

Berkeley Convention
& Visitors Bureau **6**
College Avenue **1**
Fourth Street
Shopping District **7**
Lawrence Hall of Science **4**
Rose Garden **8**
Telegraph Avenue **2**
Tilden Park **9**
UC Berkeley Art Museum **3**
University of California
Botanical Garden **3**
Visitor Information Center **5**

Parks

Unbeknownst to many travelers, Berkeley has some of the most extensive and beautiful parks around. If you want to wear the kids out or enjoy hiking, swimming, sniffing roses, or just getting a breath of California air, jump in your car and make your way to **Tilden Park** ★. On the way, stop at the colorful terraced **Rose Garden** ★ (℃ **510/981-5151**) in north Berkeley, on Euclid Avenue between Bay View and Eunice Street. Then head high into the Berkeley hills to Tilden, where you'll find plenty of flora and fauna, hiking trails, an old steam train and merry-go-round, a farm and nature area for kids, and a chilly tree-encircled lake. The East Bay's public transit system, AC Transit (℃ **511;** www.actransit.org), runs the air-conditioned no. 67 bus line around the edge of the park on weekdays and all the way to the Tilden Visitors Center on Saturdays and Sundays. Call ℃ **510/562-PARK,** or see **www.ebparks.org** for further information.

Another worthy nature excursion is the **University of California Botanical Garden** (℃ **510/643-2755;** www.botanicalgarden.berkeley.edu), which features a vast collection of herbage ranging from cacti to redwoods. It's on campus in Strawberry Canyon on Centennial Drive. Unfortunately no public bus can take you directly there, so driving is the way to go. Call for directions. Open daily from 9am to 5pm; closed the first Tuesday of every month; docent-led tours on Thursdays, Saturdays, and Sundays at 1:30pm. Admission is $5 adults, $3 seniors 65 and over, $1 youth 3 to 17, and free for children under 3 and UC students.

Shopping

If you're itching to exercise your credit cards, head to one of two places. **College Avenue,** from Dwight Way to the Oakland border, overflows with eclectic boutiques, antiques shops, and restaurants. The other option is **Fourth Street,** in west Berkeley, 2 blocks north of the University Avenue exit. This shopping strip is the perfect place to go on a sunny morning. Grab a cup of java, read the paper at a patio table, and then hit the **Crate & Barrel Outlet,** 1785 Fourth St., between Hearst and Virginia (© **510/528-5500**). Prices are 30% to 70% off retail. It's open daily from 10am to 6pm. This area also boasts small, wonderful stores crammed with imported and locally made housewares. Nearby is **REI,** the Bay Area's favorite outdoors outfitter, 1338 San Pablo Ave., near Gilman Street (© **510/527-4140**). It's open Monday through Friday from 10am to 9pm, Saturday from 10am to 8pm, and Sunday from 10am to 7pm.

WHERE TO STAY

Unfortunately, a little research will prove that Berkeley is not even remotely close to a good hotel town. Most accommodations are extremely basic motels and funky B&Bs. The one exception (though it's overpriced) is the **Claremont Resort & Spa,** 41 Tunnel Rd., Berkeley (© **800/551-7266** or 510/843-3000; www.claremontresort.com), a grand Victorian hotel, also on the border of Oakland, with a fancy spa and gym, three restaurants, a hip bar, and grandiose surroundings. Though it's the most luxurious thing going, it's overpriced and rooms aren't nearly as charming as the exterior. Rates range from $290 to $450 for doubles and $460 to $1,050 for suites. Or you can contact the **Berkeley & Oakland Bed and Breakfast Network** (© **510/547-6380;** www.bbonline.com/ca/berkeley-oakland), which books visitors into private homes and apartments in the East Bay area.

Moderate

Rose Garden Inn   Like a Merchant-Ivory movie, the accommodations within this 40-room/five-building inn range from English Country to Victorian, making it a favorite for visiting grandparents and vacationing retirees. Despite your age or design sense, the stunning and expansive garden exploding with rose bushes, hydrangeas, and an abundance of flora and fauna is sure to delight as well as erase all memories that you're on a characterless stretch of Telegraph Avenue a few blocks south of the student action. Rooms, many of which have fireplaces, cable TVs, and all the basic amenities, show some wear and tend to be a little dark, but they are spacious, updated, and very clean, despite the obvious age of some bathroom nooks and crannies.

2740 Telegraph Ave. (at Stuart St.), Berkeley, CA 94705. © **800/992-9005** or 510/549-2145. Fax 510/549-1085. www.rosegardeninn.com. 40 units. $125–$275 double. Breakfast, coffee, and afternoon cookies included. AE, DC, DISC, MC, V. Free parking on a space-available basis. **Amenities:** Wi-Fi in lobby. *In room:* TV, high-speed Internet access in deluxe rooms, hair dryer, iron (upon request).

WHERE TO DINE

East Bay dining is a relaxed alternative to San Francisco's gourmet scene. There are plenty of ambitious Berkeley restaurants and, unlike in San Francisco, plenty of parking, provided you're not near the campus.

If you want to dine student-style, eat on campus Monday through Friday. Buy something at a sidewalk stand or in the building directly behind the Student Union. There's also the **Bear's Lair Pub and Coffee House,** the **Terrace,** and the **Golden Bear Restaurant.** All the university eateries have both indoor and outdoor seating.

Telegraph Avenue has an array of small, ethnic restaurants, cafes, and sandwich shops. Follow the students: If the place is crowded, it's good, supercheap, or both.

Expensive

Chez Panisse ★★★ CALIFORNIA   California cuisine is so much a product of Alice Waters's genius that all other restaurants following in her wake should be dated A.A.W. (After Alice Waters). Most of the produce and meat comes from local farms and is organically produced, and after all these years, Alice still tends her restaurant with great integrity and innovation. The two dining areas, the cafe and the restaurant, both serve Mediterranean-inspired cuisine. At lunch or dinner, the cafe menu might feature delicately smoked gravlax or roasted eggplant soup with pesto, followed by lamb ragout garnished with apricots, onions, and spices and served with couscous. The cozy downstairs restaurant, strewn with blossoming floral bouquets, is an appropriately warm environment in which to indulge in the $65 fixed-price four-course gourmet dinner, which is served Tuesday through Thursday. Friday and Saturday, it's $85 for four courses; and Monday is bargain night, with a three-course dinner for $50. The excellent wine list has bottles ranging from $28 to $300.

1517 Shattuck Ave. (btw. Cedar and Vine). ✆ **510/548-5525** for main restaurant reservations, 510/548-5049 for cafe reservations. Fax 510/548-0140. www.chezpanisse.com. Reservations required for the dining room and taken 1 month prior to calendar date requested. Reservations are recommended for the cafe, but walk-ins are welcomed. Restaurant fixed-price menu $50–$85; cafe main courses $15–$25. AE, DC, DISC, MC, V. Restaurant seatings Mon–Sat 6–6:30pm and 8:30–9:15pm most times of the year (in slower months, like Jan–Mar, times vary; please call to confirm). Cafe Mon–Thurs 11:30am–3pm and 5–10:30pm; Fri–Sat 11:30am–3:30pm and 5–11:30pm. BART: Downtown Berkeley. From I-80 N, take the University Ave. exit and turn left onto Shattuck Ave.

Moderate

Cafe Rouge ★ MEDITERRANEAN   After cooking at San Francisco's renowned Zuni Cafe for 10 years, chef-owner Marsha McBride launched her own restaurant, a sort of Zuni East. She brought former staff members and some of the restaurant's flavor with her, and now her sparse, loftlike dining room serves salads, rotisserie chicken with oil and thyme, grilled lamb chops, steaks, and homemade sausages. East Bay carnivores are especially happy with the burger; like Zuni's, it's top-notch. During warm days, outdoor dining overlooking the shopping square is ideal.

1782 Fourth St. (btw. Delaware and Hearst). ✆ **510/525-1440.** www.caferouge.net. Reservations recommended. Main courses $14–$32. MC, V. Mon–Fri 11:30am–3pm; Tues–Thurs 5:30–9:30pm; Fri–Sat 5:30–10pm; Sun 5–9:30pm; brunch Sun 10am–2:30pm.

Rivoli ★★ (Finds) CALIFORNIA   One of the favored dinner destinations in the East Bay, Rivoli offers top-notch food at amazingly reasonable prices. Aside from a few house favorites, the menu changes entirely every 3 weeks to feature whatever's freshest and in season; the wine list follows suit with around 10 by-the-glass options handpicked to match the food. While many love it, I'm not a fan of the portobello-mushroom fritter, a gourmet variation of the fried zucchini stick. However, plenty of dishes shine, including chicken with prosciutto di Parma, cannelloni (stuffed with wild-mushrooms, chard, and ricotta), Marsala *jus,* snap peas, and baby carrots; and braised lamb shank with green

Finds **Sweet Sensations at Berkeley's Chocolate Factory**

If you haven't had chocolate nibs, you haven't lived—at least that's what choco-holics are likely to discover upon visiting **Scharffen Berger Chocolate Maker,** California's runaway-success chocolatier that opened its factory and retail-shop doors in Berkeley in mid-2001. During regularly scheduled free tours (call or visit their website to reserve a spot as spaces are limited), visitors can not only taste the nibs (crunchy roasted and shelled cocoa beans), but also see how the famous chocolate company uses vintage European equipment. All manner of chocolate-related products are also available in the retail shop. You can have coffee, pastries, lunch, or brunch at their restaurant, Café Cacao, which is open Monday through Friday 8am to 5pm (serving lunch 11am–3pm) and Saturday and Sunday 9am to 3pm. The factory is located at 914 Heinz Ave., Berkeley (© **510/981-4066;** www.scharffenberger.com).

garlic risotto, sautéed spinach, and oven-dried tomatoes. Finish the evening with an assortment of cheeses or a warm chocolate truffle torte with hazelnut ice cream, orange crème anglaise, and chocolate sauce.

1539 Solano Ave. © **866/496-2489** or 510/526-2542. www.rivolirestaurant.com. Reservations recommended. Main courses $16–$22. AE, DC, DISC, MC, V. Mon–Thurs 5:30–9:30pm; Fri 5:30–10pm; Sat 5–10pm; Sun 5–9pm.

Inexpensive

Cafe Fanny ★★ FRENCH/ITALIAN Alice Waters's (of Chez Panisse fame) cafe is one of those local must-do East Bay breakfast traditions. Don your Birkenstocks and earth-tone apparel, grab the morning paper, and head here to wait in line for a simple yet masterfully prepared French breakfast. The menu offers such items as soft-boiled farm-fresh eggs on Levain toast, buckwheat crepes with house-made preserves, cinnamon toast, and an assortment of superb pastries. Lunch is more of an Italian experience, featuring seasonal selections. Sandwiches—such as Alice's baked ham and watercress on focaccia or grilled chicken breast wrapped in prosciutto, with sage and aioli on Acme bread—might convince you that maybe Berkeley isn't such a crazy place to live after all. There's also a selection of pizzettas, salads, and soup. Eat inside at the stand-up food bar (one bench), or outside at one of the cafe tables.

1603 San Pablo Ave. (at Cedar St.). © **510/524-5447.** Most breakfast items $5; lunch $5–$7. MC, V. Mon–Fri 7am–3pm; Sat 8am–4pm; Sun 8am–3pm. Breakfast until 11am; Sun all day. Closed major holidays.

O Chamé ★★ JAPANESE Spare and plain in its decor, this spot has a meditative air to complement the traditional, experimental, and extremely fresh Japanese-inspired cuisine. The menu, which changes daily, offers a main entree selection that always includes delicious roasted salmon, but you can also easily fill up on the meal-in-a-bowl dishes ($9–$13) that allow a choice of soba or udon noodles in a clear soup with a variety of toppings—from shrimp and *wakame* seaweed to beef with burdock root and carrot—and fresh, wholesome fixings (think roasted oysters, sea bass, and tofu skins).

1830 Fourth St. (near Hearst). © **510/841-8783.** www.themenupage.com/ochame.html. Reservations recommended Fri–Sat dinner. Main courses lunch $9–$19, dinner $18–$24. AE, MC, V. Mon–Sat 11:30am–3pm; Mon–Thurs 5:30–9pm; Fri–Sat 5:30–9:30pm.

2 OAKLAND

10 miles E of San Francisco

Although it's less than a dozen miles from San Francisco, Oakland is worlds apart from its sister city across the bay. Originally little more than a cluster of ranches and farms, Oakland exploded in size and stature practically overnight, when the last mile of transcontinental railroad track was laid down. Major shipping ports soon followed and, to this day, Oakland remains one of the busiest industrial ports on the West Coast.

The price for economic success, however, is Oakland's lowbrow reputation as a predominantly working-class city, forever in San Francisco's chic shadow. However, as The City by the Bay has become crowded and expensive in the past few years, Oakland has experienced a rush of new residents and businesses. As a result, Oak-town is in the midst of a renaissance, and its future continues to look brighter and brighter.

Rent a sailboat on Lake Merritt, stroll along the waterfront, explore the fantastic Oakland Museum—they're all great reasons to hop the bay and spend a fog-free day exploring one of California's largest and most ethnically diverse cities.

ESSENTIALS

BART connects San Francisco and Oakland through one of the longest underwater transit tunnels in the world. Fares range from $2 to $4, depending on your station of origin; children under 5 ride free. BART trains operate Monday through Friday from 4am to midnight, Saturday from 6am to midnight, and Sunday from 8am to midnight. Exit at the 12th Street station for downtown Oakland. Call ☎ **511** or visit **www.bart. gov** for more info.

By car from San Francisco, take I-80 across the San Francisco–Oakland Bay Bridge and follow signs to downtown Oakland. Exit at Grand Avenue South for the Lake Merritt area.

For a calendar of events in Oakland, contact the **Oakland Convention and Visitors Bureau,** 463 11th St., Oakland, CA 94607 (☎ 510/839-9000; www.oaklandcvb.com). The city also sponsors eight free guided tours, including African-American Heritage and downtown tours held Wednesdays and Saturdays May through October; call ☎ **510/238-3234** or visit **www.oaklandnet.com/walkingtours** for details.

Downtown Oakland lies between Grand Avenue on the north, I-980 on the west, Inner Harbor on the south, and Lake Merritt on the east. Between these landmarks are three BART stations (12th St., 19th St., and Lake Merritt), City Hall, the Oakland Museum, Jack London Square, and several other sights.

WHAT TO SEE & DO

Lake Merritt is Oakland's primary tourist attraction, along with Jack London Square (see below). Three and a half miles in circumference, the tidal lagoon was bridged and dammed in the 1860s and is now a wildlife refuge that is home to flocks of migrating ducks, herons, and geese. The 122-acre **Lakeside Park,** a popular place to picnic, feed the ducks, and escape the fog, surrounds the lake on three sides. Visit **www.oaklandnet. com/parks** for more info. At the **Municipal Boathouse** ★ (☎ 510/238-2196), in Lakeside Park along the north shore, you can rent sailboats, rowboats, pedal boats, canoes, or kayaks for $8 to $15 per hour (cash only). Or you can take an hour-long gondola ride with **Gondola Servizio** (☎ 888/737-8494; www.gondolaservizio.com). Experienced gondoliers will serenade you, June through October, as you glide across the

The USS *Potomac*: FDR's Floating White House

It took the Potomac Association's hundreds of volunteers more than 12 years—at a cost of $5 million—to restore the 165-foot presidential yacht *Potomac*, President Franklin D. Roosevelt's beloved "Floating White House." The revitalized *Potomac* is open to the public for dockside tours, as well as 2-hour History Cruises along the San Francisco waterfront and around Treasure and Alcatraz islands.

Tours are available year-round on Wednesdays and Fridays from 10am to 2:30pm, and on Sundays from noon to 3pm. Admission is $7 for ages 13 to 59, $5 for seniors over 60, and free for children age 12 and under. The History Cruise runs on Thursdays and Saturdays from early May to mid-November; the departure time is 11am. History Cruise fares are $40 for ages 13 to 59, $35 for seniors 60 and older, $20 for children 6 to 12, and free for kids 5 and under.

Tickets for the Dockside Tour can be purchased at the Visitor Center upon arrival; tickets for the History Cruise can be purchased in advance via **Ticketweb** (© **866/468-3399;** www.ticketweb.com) or by calling the **Potomac Visitor Center** (© **510/627-1215;** www.usspotomac.org). The Visitor Center is located at 540 Water St., at the corner of Clay and Water streets, adjacent to the FDR pier at the north end of Jack London Square.

lake; the cost ranges from $45 to $225 for two depending on the time and gondola style.

Another site worth visiting is Oakland's **Paramount Theatre** ★, 2025 Broadway (© **510/893-2300;** www.paramounttheatre.com), an outstanding National Historic Landmark and example of Art Deco architecture and decor. Built in 1931 and authentically restored in 1973, it's the city's main performing-arts center, hosting such big-name performers as Smokey Robinson and Alicia Keys. Guided tours of the 3,000-seat theater are given the first and third Saturday morning of each month, excluding holidays. No reservations are necessary; just show up at 10am at the box office entrance on 21st Street at Broadway. The tour lasts 2 hours, cameras are allowed, and admission is $5.

Jack London Square (© **866/295-9853;** www.jacklondonsquare.com), Oakland's only patently tourist area—which shamelessly plays up the fact that Jack London spent most of his youth along the waterfront—is a relatively low-key version of San Francisco's Fisherman's Wharf. The square fronts the harbor and houses a touristy complex of boutiques and eateries, as well as a more locals-friendly farmers' market year-round on Sundays from 10am to 2pm. Most shops are open daily from 11am to 6pm, though some restaurants stay open later. **Yoshi's World Class Jazz House & Japanese Restaurant** ★, 510 Embarcadero W. (© **510/238-9200;** www.yoshis.com), features live jazz and serves fine sushi in its adjoining restaurant. In the center of the square is a reconstruction of the Yukon cabin in which Jack London lived while prospecting in the Klondike during the gold rush of 1897.

Also in the middle of Jack London Square is a more authentic memorial: **Heinold's First and Last Chance Saloon** (© **510/839-6761;** www.heinoldsfirstandlastchance. com). This funky, friendly little bar and historic landmark is where London did some of

Legend:
- BART Station
- ⓘ Information

To 580 Bay Bridge/San Francisco

To 580 Bay Bridge/San Francisco

Grand Ave.

Children's Fairyland

LAKESIDE PARK

23rd St.

W. Grand Ave.

21st St.

22nd St.

21st St.

20th St.

Harrison St.

Municipal Boathouse (Rentals) **4**

Greyhound Bus Depot

20th St.

Williams St.

19th St.

18th St.

San Pablo Ave.

Telegraph Ave.

Broadway

19th St. BART

SNOW PARK

19th St.

Lakeside Dr.

Lake Merritt

17th St.

18th St.

17th St.

16th St.

15th St.

14th St.

The Rotunda

City Hall

Preservation Park

City Center

12th St.

11th St.

Martin Luther King Jr. Way

10th St.

Oakland Convention Center **7**

CHINATOWN

OLD OAKLAND

9th St.

8th St.

7th St.

JEFFERSON SQUARE

6th St.

Brush St.

Castro St.

Franklin St.

Webster St.

Harrison St.

Alice St.

Jackson St.

Madison St.

Oak St.

12th St./City Center BART

LINCOLN SQUARE

Asian Cultural Center

MADISON PARK

CHINESE GARDEN

15th St.

14th St.

13th St.

Post Office

12th St.

11th St.

10th St.

9th St.

8th St.

7th St.

6th St.

Camron–Stanford House **5**

Lake Merritt BART

Laney College

Fallon St.

Oakland Museum of California **6**

880

To Bay Bridge/San Francisco

5th St.

4th St.

3rd St.

2nd St.

Jefferson St.

Clay St.

Washington St.

Broadway

Franklin St.

Webster St.

Harrison St.

Alice St.

Jackson St.

Madison St.

Oak St.

5th St.

4th St.

3rd St.

2nd St.

Amtrak Terminal

ESTUARY PARK

Embarcadero

Jack London Square **9 9**

Webster St. Tube

Posey Tube

Alameda/Oakland Ferry Terminal

Ferry to Alameda & San Francisco

Water Taxi

8

0   1/4 Mi

0   0.25 Km

Berkeley

Area of Detail

San Francisco

Oakland

San Francisco Bay

101

ACCOMMODATIONS ■
Oakland Marriott City Center **7**
Waterfront Plaza Hotel **9**

DINING ◆
À Côté **1**
Citron **1**
Oliveto Cafe
  & Restaurant **2**
Yoshi's World Class Jazz House
  and Japanese Restaurant **8**

ATTRACTIONS ●
Jack London Square **9**
Lake Merritt **5**
Lakeside Park **4**
Oakland Museum of California **6**
Paramount Theatre **3**

his writing and most of his drinking; the corner table he used has remained exactly as it was nearly a century ago.

Jack London Square is at Broadway and Embarcadero. Take I-880 to Broadway, turn south, and drive to the end. Or ride BART to 12th Street station and then walk south along Broadway (about half a mile). Or take bus no. 72R or 72M to the foot of Broadway.

Oakland Museum of California ★ Two blocks south of Lake Merritt, the Oakland Museum of California incorporates just about everything you'd want to know about the state and its people, history, culture, geology, art, environment, and ecology. Inside a low, modern building set among sweeping gardens and terraces, it's actually three museums in one: exhibitions of works by California artists from Bierstadt to Diebenkorn; collections of historic artifacts, from Pomo Indian basketry to Country Joe McDonald's guitar; and re-creations of California habitats from the coast to the Sierra Mountains. The museum holds major shows of California artists as well as exhibitions dedicated to California's rich nature and history. Recent exhibits included *Aftershock: Personal Stories from the '06 Quake and Fire* and *Baseball as America*, which showcased artifacts and photos of the nation's favorite sport. The museum also frequently shows photography from its huge collections. Forty-five-minute guided tours leave from the gallery information desks on request or by appointment.

1000 Oak St. (at 10th St.). ✆ **510/238-2200.** www.museumca.org. Admission $8 adults, $5 students and seniors, free for children 5 and under. 2nd Sun of the month is free (special exhibitions excepted). Wed–Sat 10am–5pm; Sun noon–5pm; open until 9pm 1st Fri of the month. Closed Jan 1, July 4, Thanksgiving, and Dec 25. BART: Lake Merritt station; follow the signs posted in the station. From I-880 N, take the Oak St. exit; the museum is 5 blocks east. Or take I-580 to I-980 and exit at the Jackson St. ramp.

WHERE TO STAY

Two fine midrange hotel options in Oakland are the **Waterfront Plaza Hotel,** 10 Washington St., Jack London Square (✆ **800/729-3638** or 510/836-3800; www.waterfrontplaza.com), and the **Oakland Marriott City Center,** 1001 Broadway (✆ **800/228-9290** or 510/451-4000; fax 510/835-3466; www.marriott.com). Most major motel chains also have locations (and budget prices) around town and near the airport. If you want to stay near the fabulous shopping and dining neighborhood of Oakland's Rockridge and pamper yourself with a great gym, outdoor pools, and lit tennis courts, your best hotel bet (though it's undoubtedly overpriced) is the **Claremont Resort & Spa,** 41 Tunnel Rd., Berkeley (✆ **800/551-7266** or 510/843-3000; www.claremontresort.com), a grand Victorian hotel (with modern rooms) that borders both Berkeley and Oakland. It ain't downtown, but it's just a quick drive to all the action, and it is one of the area's prettiest options (see p. 154 for more information).

WHERE TO DINE

Expensive

Citron ★ FRENCH/CALIFORNIA This petite, adorable French bistro was an instant smash when it opened in 1992, and it continues to earn raves for its small yet enticingly eclectic menu. Chef and owner Chris Rossi draws the flavors of France, Italy, and Spain together with fresh California produce for results you aren't likely to have tasted elsewhere. The menu changes every few weeks; dishes range from succulent roasted Sonoma leg of lamb, served with *gigande* beans, cardoons, and fennel; to spicy bayou seafood stew brimming with fried oysters, shrimp, snapper, bell peppers, and tomato sauce; to fresh chèvre lasagna with braising greens and truffled crimini mushrooms.

A word of advice: If you're into classic foods you can identify by name, head elsewhere.
It's all about creative cooking here.

5484 College Ave. (north of Broadway, btw. Taft and Lawton sts.). (C) 510/653-5484. www.citron restaurant.com. Reservations recommended. Lunch and brunch main courses $8–$15; 3-course fixed-price menu $15; dinner main courses $20–$26; 3- to 5-course fixed-price menu $32–$48. AE, DC, DISC, MC, V. Tues–Fri 11:30am–4:30pm; Sat–Sun 10am–3pm; Mon–Tues 5:30–9pm; Wed–Thurs 5:30–9:30pm; Fri 5:30–10pm; Sat 5–10pm; Sun 5–9pm.

Oliveto Cafe & Restaurant ★★★ ITALIAN   Opened 20 years ago by Bob and Maggie Klein, and now under the helm of executive chef Paul Canales (who has been with the Kleins for 11 years, working his way up through the ranks in the kitchen), Oliveto is one of the top Italian restaurants in the Bay Area (and certainly the best in Oakland). Local workers pile in at lunchtime for wood-fired pizzas, simple salads, and sandwiches served in the lower-level cafe. The upstairs restaurant is more elegant and packed nightly with fans of the mind-blowing house-made pastas, sausages, and prosciutto. Oliveto has a wood-burning oven, flame-broiled rotisserie, and a full bar which sports a high-end liquor cabinet. An assortment of pricey grills, braises, and roasts anchor the daily changing menu, but the heavenly pastas, pizzettas, and awesome salads offer the most tang for your buck. *Tip:* Free parking is available in the lot at the rear of the Market Hall building.

Rockridge Market Hall, 5655 College Ave. (off the northeast end of Broadway at Shafter/Keith St., across from the Rockridge BART station). (C) 510/547-5356. www.oliveto.com. Reservations recommended for restaurant. Main courses cafe $2.50–$12 breakfast, $4–$8 lunch, $12–$15 dinner; restaurant $11–$15 lunch, $16–$30 dinner. AE, DC, MC, V. Cafe Mon 7am–9pm; Tues–Fri 7am–10pm; Sat 8am–10pm; Sun 8am–9pm. Restaurant Mon–Fri 11:30am–2pm; Tues–Wed 5:30–9:30pm; Thurs–Sat 5:30–10pm; Sun 5–9pm.

Moderate

À Côté ★★ FRENCH TAPAS   Jack and Daphne Knowles look to chef Matthew Colgan to serve up superb rustic Mediterranean-inspired small plates at this loud, festive, and warmly lit joint. A "limited reservations" policy means there's usually a long wait during prime dining hours, but once seated, you can join locals in a nosh fest featuring the likes of *croque-monsieur; pommes frites* with aioli; wood-oven cooked mussels in Pernod; grilled pork tenderloin with creamy polenta, and pancetta; and cheese plates—and wash it down with Belgian ales, perky cocktails, or excellent by-the-glass or -bottle selections from the great wine list. *Note:* The heated and covered outdoor seating area tends to be quieter.

5478 College Ave. (at Taft Ave.). (C) 510/655-6469. www.acoterestaurant.com. Limited reservations accepted. Small plates $5–$14. MC, V. Sun–Tues 5:30–10pm; Wed–Thurs 5:30–11pm; Fri–Sat 5:30pm–midnight.

Bay Wolf ★ CALIFORNIA   The lifespan of most Bay Area restaurants is about a year; Bay Wolf, one of Oakland's most revered restaurants, has, fittingly, been going strong for over 3 decades. The converted brown Victorian is a comfortably familiar sight for most East Bay diners, who have come here for years to let executive chef/owner Michael Wilds and his chef de cuisine Louis Le Gassic do the cooking. Bay Wolf enjoys a reputation for simple yet sagacious preparations using only fresh ingredients. Informal service means you can leave the tie at home. The front deck has heat lamps and a radiant heat floor, allowing for open-air evening dining year-round—a treat that San Franciscans rarely experience.

3853 Piedmont Ave. (off Broadway, btw. 40th St. and MacArthur Blvd.). (C) 510/655-6004. www.baywolf. com. Reservations recommended. Main courses $8.50–$18 lunch, $17–$24 dinner. AE, MC, V. Mon–Fri 11:30am–1:45pm; Mon–Thurs 5:30–9pm; Fri–Sat 5:30–10pm; Sun 5:30–9:30pm. Paid parking at Piedmont Ave. and Yosemite St.

3 SAUSALITO ★★

5 miles N of San Francisco

Just off the northeastern end of the Golden Gate Bridge is the picturesque little town of Sausalito, a slightly bohemian adjunct to San Francisco. With fewer than 8,000 residents, Sausalito feels rather like St. Tropez on the French Riviera (minus the beach). Next to the pricey bayside restaurants, antiques shops, and galleries are hamburger joints, ice cream shops, and secondhand bookstores. Sausalito's main strip is Bridgeway, which runs along the water; on a clear day the views of San Francisco far across the bay are spectacular. After admiring the view, those in the know make a quick detour to Caledonia Street, 1 block inland; not only is it less congested, but it also has a better selection of cafes and shops.

ESSENTIALS

The **Golden Gate Ferry Service** fleet, Ferry Building (© 415/923-2000; www.golden gate.org), operates between the San Francisco Ferry Building, at the foot of Market Street, and downtown Sausalito. Service is frequent, running at reasonable intervals every day of the year except January 1, Thanksgiving, and December 25. Phone for an exact schedule. The ride takes a half-hour, and one-way fares are $6.75 for adults; $3.35 for youth 6 to 18, seniors 65 plus, and passengers with disabilities (50% off full fare); children 5 and under ride free (limit two children per full-fare adult). Family rates are available on weekends.

Ferries of the **Blue & Gold Fleet** (© 415/705-5555; www.blueandgoldfleet.com) leave from Pier 41 (Fisherman's Wharf); the one-way cost is $8.50 for adults, $4.50 for kids 5 to 11. Boats run on a seasonal schedule; phone or log onto their website for departure information.

By car from San Francisco, take U.S. 101 N, and then take the first right after the Golden Gate Bridge (Alexander exit). Alexander becomes Bridgeway in Sausalito.

WHAT TO SEE & DO

Above all else, Sausalito has scenery and sunshine, for once you cross the Golden Gate Bridge, you're out of the San Francisco fog patch and under blue California sky (we hope). Houses cover the town's steep hills, overlooking a forest of masts on the waters below. Most of the tourist action, which is almost singularly limited to window-shopping and eating, takes place at sea level on Bridgeway.

Sausalito is a mecca for shoppers seeking handmade, original, and offbeat clothes and footwear, as well as arts and crafts. Many of the town's shops are in the alleys, malls, and second-floor boutiques, reached by steep, narrow staircases on and off Bridgeway. Caledonia Street, which runs parallel to Bridgeway 1 block inland, is home to more shops.

Bay Area Discovery Museum (Kids) On 7¹/₂ acres in the Golden Gate National Recreation Area at Fort Baker, this museum offers spectacular (jaw-dropping even!) views of the city and Golden Gate Bridge (you're literally at the northern base of the bridge) and is also the ultimate indoor-outdoor interactive kids' adventure. Tot Spot is tops for crawlers and toddlers; Lookout Cove is a 2¹/₂-acre outdoor area with a scaled-down model of the GGB that kids can add rivets to, a shipwreck to explore, tidal pools, and lovely site-specific art; Art Studios splits kids into groups ages 5 and under and 6 and older; and the Wave Workshop re-creates the habitat under the GGB. A small cafe serves yummy, organic food far better than typical family-friendly fare. *One thing to note:* If you're here alone with two kids of different ages, it can be difficult to navigate, as they do keep the little ones separate from the older ones in the Tot Spot. If you explain your situation, they'll give your older one (12 and up) a "Tot Spot Helper" sticker, and let them in, but they won't be allowed to play and will have to stick by you. But if it's a nice day, you can spend the entire time in Lookout Cove with both kids, have lunch outside, and still get your money's worth.

E. Fort Baker, 557 McReynolds Rd. © 415/339-3900. www.baykidsmuseum.org. Admission $8.50 adults, $7.50 children, free for children under 1 and members. Discounts available to AAA members and members of reciprocal museum organizations (see website). Tues–Fri 9am–4pm; Sat–Sun 10am–5pm. Closed Mon and all major holidays. By car: Cross the Golden Gate Bridge and take the Alexander Ave. exit. Follow signs to E. Fort Baker and the Bay Area Discovery Museum.

Bay Model Visitors Center (Kids)   The U.S. Army Corps of Engineers once used this high-tech, 1½-acre model of San Francisco's bay and delta to resolve problems and observe the impact of changes in water flow. Today the model is strictly for educational purposes and reproduces (in scale) the rise and fall of tides and the flows and currents of water. There's a 10-minute film, self-guided and audio tours ($3 donation requested), and a 1-hour tour (free; book a reservation), but the most interesting time to visit is when the model is in operation, so call ahead.

2100 Bridgeway. © **415/332-3871.** www.spn.usace.army.mil/bmvc. Free admission. Labor Day to Memorial Day (winter hours) Tues–Sat 9am–4pm; Memorial Day to Labor Day (summer hours) Tues–Fri 9am–4pm, Sat–Sun and holidays 10am–5pm.

WHERE TO STAY

Sausalito is such a desirable enclave that it offers little in the way of affordable lodging. On the bright side, it's so close to San Francisco that it takes only about 15 minutes to get here, traffic permitting.

Very Expensive

The Inn Above Tide ★★   Perched directly over the bay atop well-grounded pilings, this former luxury-apartment complex underwent a $4-million transformation in 2004 into one of Sausalito's—if not the Bay Area's—finest accommodations. The view clinches it: Every room affords an unparalleled panorama of the San Francisco Bay, including a postcard-quality vista of the city glimmering in the distance. Should you manage to tear yourself away from your private deck, you'll find that 23 of the sumptuously appointed rooms sport romantic little fireplaces. Soothing earth tones highlight the decor, which blends in well with the bayscape outside. Be sure to request that your breakfast and newspaper be delivered to your deck, and then cancel your early appointments—on sunny mornings, nobody checks out early.

30 El Portal (next to the Sausalito Ferry Landing), Sausalito, CA 94965. © **800/893-8433** or 415/332-9535. Fax 415/332-6714. www.innabovetide.com. 29 units. $295–$950 double. Rates include continental breakfast and evening wine and cheese. AE, DC, MC, V. Valet parking $12. **Amenities:** Concierge; in-room massage; same-day laundry service/dry cleaning; free shoeshine. *In room:* A/C, TV/DVD, dataport, free Wi-Fi, minibar, fridge, hair dryer, CD player.

Expensive

Casa Madrona Hotel & Spa ★★   Sooner or later most visitors to Sausalito look up and wonder at the ornate mansion on the hill. It's part of Casa Madrona, a hideaway by the bay built in 1885 by a wealthy lumber baron. The epitome of luxury in its day, the mansion had slipped into decay when John Gallagher purchased it in 1910 and converted it into a hotel. By 1976, it was damaged and facing the threat of demolition when

John Mays acquired the property and revitalized the hotel. Successive renovations and extensions added a rambling, New England–style building to the hillside below the main house. Now listed on the National Register of Historic Places, the hotel offers whimsically decorated rooms, suites, and cottages, which are accessed by steep, gorgeously landscaped pathways. The 16 free-standing units, seven cottages, and rooms in the mansion have individual themes such as Lilac and Lace, Renoir, or the Artist's Loft. Some have claw-foot tubs and others have fireplaces. Rooms in the newer adjoining building have a chic contemporary decor, four-poster beds, marble bathrooms, and great marina views from some rooms. The classy Italian **Poggio** restaurant (see below) has been a Sausalito favorite since opening, and the hotel's full-service spa offers a wide assortment of treatments and getaway packages.

801 Bridgeway, Sausalito, CA 94965. 📞 **415/332-0502.** Fax 415/332-2537. www.casamadrona.com. 63 units. $295–$450 double; $550 suite. AE, DC, DISC, MC, V. Valet parking $20. Ferry: Walk across the street from the landing. From U.S. 101 N, take the 1st right after the Golden Gate Bridge (Alexander exit); Alexander becomes Bridgeway. **Amenities:** Restaurant; spa; concierge; room service; babysitting; laundry service; dry cleaning. *In room:* TV, VCR upon availability, minibar, coffeemaker, hair dryer, robes.

WHERE TO DINE
Expensive

Horizons ★ SEAFOOD/AMERICAN   Eventually, every San Franciscan ends up at Horizons to meet a friend for Sunday Bloody Marys. It's not much to look at from the outside, but it gets better as you head past the 1960s-era dark-wood interior toward the waterside terrace. On warm days, it's worth the wait for alfresco seating if only to watch dreamy sailboats glide past San Francisco's distant skyline. The food here can't touch the view, but it's well portioned and satisfying enough. Seafood dishes are the main items, including steamed clams and mussels, freshly shucked oysters, and a variety of seafood pastas. In fine Marin tradition, Horizons has an "herb tea and espresso" bar.

558 Bridgeway. 📞 **415/331-3232.** www.horizonssausalito.com. Reservations accepted weekdays only. Main courses $9–$21; salads and sandwiches $6–$11. AE, MC, V. Mon–Fri 11:30am–9pm; Sat 10:30am–10pm; Sun 10:30am–9pm. Valet parking $4.

Poggio ★★ ITALIAN   Sausalito has historically been low on upscale dining options, but all that changed with the late-2003 opening of elegant Poggio. Adjoining the Casa Madrona hotel and across the street from the marina, its daily menu features such items as a superb salad of endive, Gorgonzola, walnuts, figs, and honey; pizzas; addictively excellent pastas (try the spinach ricotta gnocchi with beef ragout); and entrees such as whole local petrale sole deboned and served tableside, or grilled lamb chops with roasted fennel and *gremolata*. With a full bar, well-priced wine list, and great desserts, this is Sausalito's premier dining destination—excluding the more casual Sushi Ran (see below).

777 Bridgeway (at Bay St.). 📞 **415/332-7771.** www.poggiotrattoria.com. Italian-style breakfast a la carte $2.50–$5.50; main courses lunch $8–$18, dinner $13–$25. AE, DC, DISC, MC, V. Daily 6:30–11am and 11:30am–5:30pm; Sun–Thurs 5:30–10pm; Fri–Sat 5:30–11pm. Free valet parking at Casa Madrona Hotel & Spa.

Sushi Ran ★★ SUSHI/JAPANESE   San Francisco doesn't have a stellar roster of it, but right across from the Golden Gate Bridge is this compact but fashionable destination for seriously delicious Japanese cuisine. Diners cram along the counter, into the window seats, and in the more roomy dining area to sample Nori Kusakabe's nigiri sushi along with standard and specialty rolls. Executive Chef Scott Whitman turns out a slew of creative dishes, such as generously sized and unbelievably moist and buttery miso-glazed

A Picnic Lunch, Sausalito Style

If the crowds are too much or the prices too steep at Sausalito's bayside restaurants, grab a bite to go for an impromptu picnic in the park fronting the marina. It's one of the best and most romantic ways to spend a warm, sunny day in Sausalito. The best source for a la carte eats is the Mediterranean-style **Venice Gourmet Delicatessen** at 625 Bridgeway, located right on the waterfront just south of the ferry landing. Since 1964 this venerable deli has offered all the makings for a superb picnic: wines, cheeses, fruits, stuffed vine leaves, salami, lox, prosciutto, salads, quiche, made-to-order sandwiches, and fresh-baked pastries. It's open daily from 9am to 6pm (℃ **415/332-3544; www.venice gourmet.com**).

black cod (a must-have), oysters on the half-shell with *ponzu* sauce and *tobiko* (fish eggs), and a salad of Hawaiian-style ahi *poke* (Hawaiian-style minced raw tuna) that's authentic enough to make you want to hula.

107 Caledonia St. ℃ **415/332-3620.** www.sushiran.com. Reservations recommended. Sushi $5–$14; main courses $8.50–$16. AE, MC, V. Mon–Fri 11:45am–2:30pm; Mon–Sat 5:30–11pm; Sun 5–10:30pm. From U.S. 101 N, take the 1st right after the Golden Gate Bridge (Alexander exit); Alexander becomes Bridgeway in Sausalito. At Johnson St. turn left, and then right onto Caledonia.

Inexpensive

Hamburgers BURGERS   Like the name says, the specialty at this tiny, narrow cafe is juicy flame-broiled hamburgers, arguably Marin County's best. Look for the rotating grill in the window off Bridgeway, and then stand in line and salivate with everyone else. Chicken burgers are a slightly healthier option. Order a side of fries, grab a bunch of napkins, and head to the park across the street.

737 Bridgeway. ℃ **415/332-9471.** Sandwiches $5.50–$6.50. No credit cards. Daily 11am–5pm. From U.S. 101 N, take the 1st right after the Golden Gate Bridge (Alexander exit); Alexander becomes Bridgeway in Sausalito.

4 ANGEL ISLAND & TIBURON ★★

8 miles N of San Francisco

A California State Park, **Angel Island** is the largest of San Francisco Bay's three islets (the others are Alcatraz and Yerba Buena). The island has been, at various times, a prison, a quarantine station for immigrants, a missile base, and even a favorite site for duels. Nowadays, most visitors are content with picnicking on the large green lawn that fronts the docking area; loaded with the appropriate recreational supplies, they claim a barbecue pit, plop their fannies down on the lush green grass, and while away an afternoon free of phones, televisions, and traffic. Hiking, mountain biking, and guided tram tours are other popular activities here.

Tiburon, situated on a peninsula of the same name, looks like a cross between a fishing village and a Hollywood Western set—imagine San Francisco reduced to toy dimensions.

The seacoast town rambles over a series of green hills and ends up at a spindly, multicolored pier on the waterfront, like a Fisherman's Wharf in miniature. In reality, it's an extremely plush patch of yacht-club suburbia, as you'll see by the marine craft and the homes of their owners. Ramshackle, color-splashed old frame houses line Main Street, sheltering chic boutiques, souvenir stores, antiques shops, and art galleries. Other roads are narrow, winding, and hilly and lead up to dramatically situated homes. The view from here of San Francisco's skyline and the islands in the bay is a good enough reason to pay the precious price to live here.

Although there is a hotel in Tiburon, I wouldn't recommend staying there: It's a 1-block town, and the hotel is very expensive. There are no hotels on Angel Island. Both destinations are better as day trips.

ESSENTIALS

Ferries of the **Blue & Gold Fleet** (© **415/705-5555;** www.blueandgoldfleet.com) from Pier 41 (Fisherman's Wharf) travel to Angel Island and to Tiburon. Boats run on a seasonal schedule; phone or look online for departure information. The round-trip fare is $15 to Angel Island, $8.50 for kids 6 to 12, and free for kids 5 and under. The fare includes state park fees. Tickets to Tiburon are $8.50 each way for adults, $4.50 for kids 5 to 11, and free for kids 4 and under. Tickets are available at Pier 41, online, or over the phone.

By car from San Francisco, take U.S. 101 to the Tiburon/Highway 131 exit, and then follow Tiburon Boulevard all the way downtown, a 40-minute drive from San Francisco. Catch the **Tiburon–Angel Island Ferry** (© **415/435-2131;** www.angelislandferry.com) to Angel Island from the dock at Tiburon Boulevard and Main Street. The 15-minute round-trip costs $10 for adults, $8 for children 5 to 11, and $1 for bikes. One child under 5 is admitted free of charge, with each paying adult (after that it's $8 each). Boats run on a seasonal schedule, but usually depart hourly from 10am to 5pm on weekends, with a more limited schedule on weekdays. Call ahead or look online for departure information. Tickets can only be purchased when boarding and include state park fees. No credit cards.

WHAT TO SEE & DO ON ANGEL ISLAND

Passengers disembark from the ferry at **Ayala Cove,** a small marina abutting a huge lawn area equipped with tables, benches, barbecue pits, and restrooms. During the summer season, there's also a small store, a gift shop, the Cove Cafe (with surprisingly good grub), and an overpriced mountain-bike rental shop at Ayala Cove.

Angel Island's 12 miles of hiking and bike trails include the **Perimeter Road,** a paved path that circles the island. It winds past disused troop barracks, former gun emplacements, and other military buildings; several turnoffs lead to the top of Mount Livermore, 776 feet above the bay. Sometimes referred to as the "Ellis Island of the West," Angel Island was used as a holding area for detained Chinese immigrants awaiting admission papers from 1910 to 1940. You can still see faded Chinese characters on some of the walls of the barracks where the immigrants were held.

The 1-hour audio-enhanced open-air **Tram Tour** of the island costs $14 for adults, $13 for seniors, $9.50 for children 6 to 12, and is free for children 5 and under; schedules vary depending on the time of year. Your best bet is to check in at the Cove Cafe upon arrival on the island for the current day's tram schedule.

Guided **Segway tours** of the island are available as well March through November. The 2½-hour interpretive tour circles the island's paved Perimeter Trail and cost $65 (there's a shorter $35 afternoon tour as well). All riders must be 16 years and older. To make tour reservations, call © 415/435-3392 or visit www.angelisland.com.

During the warmer months you can camp at a limited number of reserved sites; call **Reserve America** at © 800/444-7275, or visit www.reserveamerica.com to find out about environmental campgrounds at Angel Island. Reservations are taken 2 days to 7 months in advance.

Guided **sea-kayak tours** ★ are also available. The 2½-hour trips combine the thrill of paddling stable, two- or three-person kayaks in an informative, naturalist-led tour around the island (conditions permitting). All equipment is provided, kids are welcome, and no experience is necessary. Rates run about $75 per person. For more information, contact the Sausalito-based **Sea Trek** (© 415/488-1000; www.seatrekkayak.com). *Note:* Tours depart from Sausalito, not Angel Island.

For more information about activities on Angel Island, call © 415/897-0715 or log onto www.angelisland.com.

WHAT TO SEE & DO IN TIBURON

The main thing to do in tiny Tiburon is stroll along the waterfront, pop into the stores, and spend an easy $50 on drinks and appetizers before heading back to the city. For a taste of the Wine Country, stop at **Windsor Vineyards,** 72 Main St. (© 415/435-3113; www.windsorvineyards.com)—its Victorian tasting room dates from 1888. Twenty or more choices are available for a free tasting. Wine accessories and gifts—glasses, cork pullers, carry packs (which hold six bottles), gourmet sauces, posters, and maps—are also available. Ask about personalized labels for your selections. The shop is open Sunday through Thursday from 10am to 6pm, Friday and Saturday from 10am to 7pm.

WHERE TO DINE IN TIBURON

Guaymas MEXICAN   Guaymas offers authentic Mexican regional cuisine and a spectacular panoramic view of San Francisco and the bay. In good weather, the two heated outdoor patios are almost always packed with diners soaking in the sun and scene. Guaymas is named after a fishing village on Mexico's Sea of Cortez, and both the town and the restaurant are famous for their *camarones* (giant shrimp). It's not fancy, nor is it gourmet, but it is a good place to come with large parties or a family. In addition to a small selection of California and Central American wines, the restaurant offers an exceptional variety of tequilas and Mexican beers.

5 Main St. © 415/435-6300. Reservations recommended. Main courses $13–$23. AE, DC, DISC, MC, V. Mon–Thurs 11:30am–10pm; Fri–Sat 11:30am–11pm; Sun 10:30am–10pm. Ferry: Walk about 10 paces from the landing. From U.S. 101, exit at Tiburon/Hwy. 131; follow Tiburon Blvd. 5 miles and turn right onto Main St. Restaurant is behind the bakery.

Sam's Anchor Café ★ (Finds) SEAFOOD   Summer Sundays are liveliest in Tiburon, when weekend boaters tie up at the docks of waterside restaurants like this one, and good-time cyclists pedal from the city to kick back here. Sam's is the kind of place where you and your cronies can take off your shoes and have a fun, relaxing time eating burgers and drinking margaritas outside on the pier. The fare is typical—sandwiches, salads, and such—but the quality and selection are inconsequential: Beers, burgers, and a designated driver are all you really need.

27 Main St. © 415/435-4527. www.samscafe.com. Main courses $9–$17 brunch, $11–$24 lunch, $15–$24 dinner. AE, DC, DISC, MC, V. Mon–Fri 11am–10pm; Sat–Sun 9:30am–10pm. Ferry: Walk from the landing. From U.S. 101, exit at Tiburon/Hwy. 131; follow Tiburon Blvd. 4 miles and turn right onto Main St.

5 MUIR WOODS & MOUNT TAMALPAIS ★★

12 miles N of the Golden Gate Bridge

While the rest of Marin County's redwood forests were being devoured to feed San Francisco's turn-of-the-20th-century building spree, Muir Woods, in a remote ravine on the flanks of Mount Tamalpais, escaped destruction in favor of easier pickings.

MUIR WOODS

Although the magnificent California redwoods have been successfully transplanted to five continents, their homeland is a 500-mile strip along the mountainous coast of southwestern Oregon and Northern California. The coast redwood, or *Sequoia sempervirens,* is one of the tallest living things known to man (!); the largest known specimen in the Redwood National Forest towers 368 feet. It has an even larger relative, the *Sequoiadendron giganteum* of the California Sierra Nevada, but the coastal variety is stunning enough. Soaring toward the sky like a wooden cathedral, Muir Woods is unlike any other forest in the world and an experience you won't soon forget.

Granted, Muir Woods is tiny compared to the Redwood National Forest farther north, but you can still get a pretty good idea of what it must have been like when these giants dominated the entire coastal region. What is truly amazing is that they exist a mere 6 miles (as the crow flies) from San Francisco—close enough, unfortunately, that tour buses arrive in droves on the weekends. You can avoid the masses by hiking up the **Ocean View Trail,** turning left on **Lost Trail,** and returning on the **Fern Creek Trail.** The moderately challenging hike shows off the woods' best sides and leaves the lazy-butts behind.

To reach Muir Woods from San Francisco, cross the Golden Gate Bridge heading north on Highway 101, take the Stinson Beach/Highway 1 exit heading west, and follow the signs (and the traffic). The park is open daily from 8am to sunset, and the admission fee is $5 per person over 16. There's also a small gift shop, educational displays, and ranger talks. For more information, call the **National Parks Service at Muir Woods** (© **415/388-2596**) or visit **www.nps.gov.**

If you don't have a car, you can book a bus trip with **San Francisco Sightseeing** (© **888/428-6937** or 415/434-8687; www.sanfranciscosightseeing.com), which takes you straight to Muir Woods and makes a short stop in Sausalito on the way back. The 3¹/₂-hour tour runs twice daily at 9:15am and 2:15pm and costs $47 for adults, $45 for seniors, $22 for children 5 through 11, and free for kids under 5. Pickup and return are offered from select San Francisco hotels. Call for information and departure times.

MOUNT TAMALPAIS

The birthplace of mountain biking, Mount Tam—as the locals call it—is the Bay Area's favorite outdoor playground and the most dominant mountain in the region. Most every local has his or her secret trail and scenic overlook, as well as an opinion on the raging debate between mountain bikers and hikers (a touchy subject). The main trails—mostly fire roads—see a lot of foot and bicycle traffic on weekends, particularly on clear, sunny days when you can see a hundred miles in all directions, from the foothills of the Sierra to the western horizon. It's a great place to escape from the city for a leisurely hike and to soak in breathtaking views of the bay.

To get to Mount Tamalpais **by car,** cross the Golden Gate Bridge heading north on Highway 101, and take the Stinson Beach/Highway 1 exit. Follow the signs up the shoreline highway for about 2¹/₂ miles, turn onto Pantoll Road, and continue for about a mile to Ridgecrest Boulevard. Ridgecrest winds to a parking lot below East Peak. From there, it's a 15-minute hike up to the top. You'll find a visitor center with a small museum, video, fun diorama, and store, as well as enthusiastic and informative "Mount Tam Hosts," who are more than happy to help you plan a hike, identify plants, and generally share their love of the mountain. Visitor center admission is free; it's open Saturday and Sunday from 11am to 4pm (standard time), and Saturday and Sunday 10am to 5:30pm (daylight saving time). Park hours are 7am to 6pm daily in winter; 7am to 9pm for about 1 month during the height of summer. Two-hour, 2-mile moonlight hikes, among many others, are offered (© 415/388-2070; www.mttam.net).

6 HALF MOON BAY ★★

28 miles SW of San Francisco

A 45-minute drive from the teeming streets of San Francisco is a heavenly little hamlet called Half Moon Bay, one of the finest—and friendliest—small towns on the California coast. While other communities like Bolinas make tourists feel unwelcome, Half Moon Bay residents are disarmingly amicable, bestowing greetings on everyone who stops for a visit.

Half Moon Bay has only recently begun to capitalize on its beaches, mild climate, and proximity to San Francisco, so it's still not tourist-tacky. Visitors will find it a peaceful slice of classic California: pristine beaches, redwood forests, nature preserves, fishing harbors, horse ranches, organic farms, and a host of superb inns and restaurants—everything for the perfect weekend getaway.

ESSENTIALS

GETTING THERE No public transportation runs from San Francisco to Half Moon Bay, but you can get there two ways by car. To save time, take Highway 92 west from I-280 or U.S. 101 out of San Francisco, which will take you over a small mountain range and drop you into Half Moon Bay. The prettier route is Highway 1, which starts at the south end of the Golden Gate Bridge and veers southwest to the shoreline a few miles south of Daly City. Both routes to Half Moon Bay are clearly marked, so don't worry about getting lost.

Downtown Half Moon Bay, however, is easy to miss since it's not on Highway 1, but a few hundred yards inland. Head 2 blocks up Highway 92 from the Highway 1 intersection, and then turn south at the Shell gas station onto Main Street until you cross a small bridge. For more information, call the **Half Moon Bay Coastside Chamber of Commerce** (© 650/726-8380; www.halfmoonbaychamber.org or www.visithalfmoonbay.org).

EXPLORING HALF MOON BAY & ENVIRONS

A wonderful **paved beach trail** winds 5 miles from Half Moon Bay to Pillar Point Harbor, where you can watch trawlers unload their catch. Be sure to keep a lookout for dolphins and whales as you walk, bike, jog, or skate along this path.

Half Moon Bay is also known for its organically grown produce, and the best place to stock up on fruits and vegetables is the **Andreotti Family Farm,** 329 Kelly Ave., off Highway 1 (© 650/726-9151), an old-fashioned outfit in business since 1926. Every Friday, Saturday, and Sunday, a member of the Andreotti family slides open the door to their old barn at 10am sharp to reveal a cornucopia of strawberries, artichokes, cucumbers, and more. Head toward the beach and you'll see the barn on your right-hand side. It's open until 6pm year-round.

BEACHES & PRESERVES   The 4-mile arc of golden sand that rings Half Moon Bay is actually three state-run beaches—Dunes, Venice, and Francis—all part of **Half Moon Bay State Beach** (© 650/726-8820). All three levy a $5-per-vehicle entrance fee. Surfing is allowed, but swimming isn't a good idea unless you happen to be cold-blooded. You can reserve campgrounds here by contacting © 800/444-PARK or visiting **www. parks.ca.gov**.

When the surf is really up, be sure to check out the banzai surfers at **Maverick Beach,** just south of the radar-tracking station past Pillar Point Harbor. To get there, take Westpoint Road to the West Shoreline Access parking lot and follow the trail to the beach. While you're there, keep a lookout for sea lions basking on the offshore rocks. Also adjacent to the parking lot is tiny **Pillar Point Marsh,** a unique fresh- and saltwater marsh that's home and way station to nearly 20% of all North American bird species—from great blue herons to snowy egrets to red-winged blackbirds.

About 7 miles farther north on Highway 1 is the **Fitzgerald Marine Reserve** (© 650/728-3584; www.fitzgeraldreserve.org), one of the most diverse tidal basins on the West Coast, as well as one of the safest, thanks to a wave-buffering rock terrace 150 feet from the beach. Call before coming to find out when it's low tide (all the sea creatures are hidden at high tide) and to get information on the docent-led tour schedules (usually offered on Sat). Rubber-soled shoes are recommended. The reserve is at the west end of California Avenue off Highway 1 in Moss Beach. Reservations are required for all groups of 10 or more; call © 650/363-4021. *Note:* Dogs, open fires, and barbecue pits are prohibited, as is collecting of any kind.

Sixteen miles south of Half Moon Bay on Highway 1 (at the turnoff to Pescadero) is the **Pescadero Marsh Natural Preserve** (see www.parks.ca.gov), one of the few remaining natural marshes on the central California coast. Part of the Pacific flyway, it's a resting stop for nearly 200 bird species, including great blue herons that nest in the northern row of eucalyptus trees. Passing through the marsh is the mile-long **Sequoia Audubon Trail,** accessible from the parking lot at Pescadero State Beach on Highway 1. (The trail starts below the Pescadero Creek Bridge.)

HMB's Best Local Lunch Spots

Very few tourists know that the tiny **Flying Fish Grill** at the corner of Main Street and Highway 92 in Half Moon Bay makes a mean fish taco, each piled with fresh cod, avocado, coleslaw, lime, and jack cheese, and then wrapped in a soft corn tortilla (don't even bother ordering just one—you'll want at least two). It's open Tuesday through Sunday from 11:30am to 8pm (99 San Mateo Rd.; © 650/712-1125). Another popular local lunch spot in town is the tiny **Garden Deli Cafe,** a hole-in-the-wall lunch counter at 356 Main St. that cranks out huge, top-notch sandwiches on thick house-made bread. It's open Monday through Friday from 11am to 3pm, and Saturday and Sunday from 11am to 3:30pm (© 650/726-3425).

| **Phipps Farm**

Because you're already in the Half Moon Bay area, you might want to stop at **Phipps Country Store and Farm,** 2700 Pescadero Rd. (© **650/879-0787;** www. phippscountry.com), located a few miles east of Duarte's Tavern on Pescadero Road. Here's you'll find a huge assortment of fresh, organically grown fruits and vegetables, homemade jams, herbs and spices, and an amazing selection of dried beans. A popular spring and early summer pastime (and a hoot for kids) is picking your own pesticide-free olallieberries, strawberries, and boysenberries in the adjacent fields for a mere $3 a pound. It's open daily from 10am to 6pm (until 5pm in the winter), and the entrance fee is $3 for ages 5 to 59.

From December through March, the **Año Nuevo State Reserve** is home to one of California's most amazing animal attractions: the breeding grounds of the northern elephant seal. Every winter, people reserve tickets for a chance to witness a fearsome clash between the 2¹⁄₂-ton bulls over mating privileges among the females. Reservations are required for the 2¹⁄₂-hour naturalist-led tours (held rain or shine Dec 15–Mar 31). For tickets, which cost $5 per person (free for children under 3), and information, call © **800/444-4445.** Even if it's not mating season, you can still see the elephant seals lolling around the shore almost year-round, particularly between April and August when they come ashore to molt.

OUTDOOR PURSUITS   For walking, biking, jogging, and skating a wonderful paved beach trail winds 3 miles from Half Moon Bay to Pillar Point Harbor (be sure to keep a lookout for dolphins and whales). Bicycles can be rented from the **Bike Works,** 20-G Stone Pine Center (© **650/726-6708**), in downtown Half Moon Bay. The rental rate for a beach cruiser is $10 per hour or $35 for all day.

Another popular tourist activity in town is horseback riding along the beach. **Sea Horse Ranch,** on **Highway 1** a mile north of Half Moon Bay (© **650/726-2362;** www. horserentals.com/seahorse.html), offers kids' pony rides and guided rides along the beach or on well-worn trails for about $60. Hours are daily from 8am to dusk.

Golfers can choose from two stellar oceanside courses at **Half Moon Bay Golf Links,** 2 Miramontes Point Rd., at the south end of Half Moon Bay (© **650/726-1800;** www. halfmoonbaygolf.com). The 18-hole "Old Course," designed by Arnold Palmer, has been rated among the top 100 courses in the country, as well as the best in the Bay Area. The newer Arthur Hills–designed Ocean Course is a true Scottish-style links layout and very challenging. Greens fees range from $90 to $185. Reserve your tee time as far in advance as possible.

If you're the adventurous type, you might want to consider a day of deep-sea fishing with **Huck Finn Sportfishing** (© **650/726-7133;** www.huckfinnsportfishing.com). They'll take you out for a full day for about $60. You don't need experience, tackle, or even a fishing license; they provide everything and will clean, fillet, and bag your catch. December through February they also offer whale-watching trips. The fishing boats depart from picturesque Pillar Point Harbor, a full-service harbor that houses over 350 commercial fishing vessels and recreational boats. Whether you plan to go fishing or not, it's worth a gander to watch the trawlers unload their daily catch.

Main Street is a browser's paradise. Dozens of small stores and boutiques line the quarter-mile strip, selling everything from feed and tack to custom furniture and camping gear. From north to south, must-see stops include **Half Moon Bay Feed & Fuel,** 331 Main St. (© **650/726-4814**), a great place to pick up a treat for your pet—and take the kids to see chicks and other cute and cuddly animals, and **Cunha's Country Store,** 448 Main St. (© **650/726-4071**), the town's beloved grocery and general store that was rebuilt in 2004 after a fire tore through the place, a mandatory stop for visitors from the Bay Area. Half Moon Bay also has a good bookstore, **Coastside Books,** 432B Main St. (© **650/726-5889**), which carries a fair selection of children's books and postcards. End your shopping spree with a stop at **Cottage Industries,** 621 Main St. (© **650/712-8078**), to marvel at the high-quality handcrafted furniture.

WHERE TO STAY

Beach House Hotel ★★   Although the facade has a rather unimaginative Cape Cod look, the rooms at this three-story hotel are surprisingly well designed and decorated with modern prints, stylish furnishings, soothing yellow and blue or red and tan tones, and spectacular views of the bay and harbor. Every room comes fully loaded with a wood-burning fireplace, king-size bed and sleeper sofa, large bathroom, and stereo with CD player. Guests also enjoy a private patio or deck access, two color TVs, *four* telephones with dataports and voice mail, and a kitchenette with microwave and fridge. Opt for one of the corner rooms, which offer a more expansive view for the same price.

4100 N. Cabrillo Hwy. (Hwy. 1), Half Moon Bay, CA 94019. © **800/315-9366** or 650/712-0220. Fax 650/712-0693. www.beach-house.com. 54 units. $195–$425 double. Rates include continental breakfast and Fri–Sat evening wine hour. AE, DC, DISC, MC, V. From Half Moon Bay, go 3 miles north on Hwy. 1. **Amenities:** Heated outdoor pool; exercise room; oceanview whirlpool; concierge; in-room massage; same-day laundry/dry cleaning. *In room:* TV, high-speed Internet (free), kitchenette, minibar, fridge, coffeemaker, hair dryer, iron, CD player.

Cypress Inn on Miramar Beach ★★   A favorite place to stay in Half Moon Bay, this three-building compound is free of Victorian charm (nary a lace curtain in *this* joint). Instead you have one modern, artistically designed and decorated building, infused with colorful folk art and rustic furniture made of pine and heavy wicker. Each room in the main building has a feather bed, private balcony, gas fireplace, private bathroom, and unobstructed ocean view. Adjacent is the Beach House building, which has rooms equipped with built-in stereo systems and hidden TVs, though they lack the Santa-Fe-meets-California effect that I like in the main house (also a few rooms don't have ocean views and one lacks a deck). This is one of the only B&Bs right on the beach.

407 Mirada Rd., Half Moon Bay, CA 94019. © **800/832-3224** or 650/726-6002. Fax 650/712-0380. www. innsbythesea.com/cypress. 18 units. $239–$380 double. Rates include breakfast; tea, wine, and hors d'oeuvres. AE, DISC, MC, V. From the junction of Hwy. 92 and 1, go 3 miles north, then turn west, and follow Medio to the end; the hotel is at Medio and Mirada. **Amenities:** Room service (breakfast only). *In room:* TV, VCR, coffeemakers in some rooms, hair dryer, iron, CD player, robes.

The Ritz-Carlton, Half Moon Bay ★★★   Set atop an ocean bluff and looking every bit like the grand seaside lodges of the 19th century is the spectacular Ritz-Carlton, Half Moon Bay. Completed in 2001, this 261-room spa and golf retreat is a popular weekend retreat for the Bay Area well-to-do. Ladies-who-lunch come for treatments at the resort's 16,000-square-foot Spa and Fitness Center, while their gents try to squeeze in 36 holes on two of the finest coastal golf courses in the state. In typical Ritz-Carlton fashion, luxuries abound throughout the contemporary guest rooms: Egyptian cotton sheets, goose-down comforters, marble bathrooms, and even personal wine cellars. Two-thirds of the rooms have ocean views, and, depending on the weather, you can opt for a fireplace or a terrace. After a day of recreating and treatments, it's de rigueur to go for a walk along the coastal path at sunset, followed by dinner at the resort's **Navio** restaurant, which serves expensive coastal cuisine prepared in a dazzling 1,000-square-foot display kitchen. Skip dessert, because the highlight of the evening is roasting s'mores at the resort's outdoor fire pit underneath a heavy wool blanket and starry skies. *Note:* It's often foggy and chilly throughout the year in this region, so pack warm clothing and don't be surprised if you see very little sunshine.

One Miramontes Point Rd., Half Moon Bay, CA 94019. © **800/241-3333** or 650/712-7000. Fax 650/712-7070. www.ritzcarlton.com. 261 units. $399–$599 double; $799–$1,699 suite. Weekend discounts and packages available. AE, DC, DISC, MC, V. Valet parking $45. **Amenities:** 3 restaurants; fitness center; full service spa; outdoor Jacuzzi; concierge; golf concierge; airport transportation; business center; secretarial services; room service; babysitting; same-day laundry service/dry cleaning. *In room:* A/C, TV w/pay movies, DVD player, high-speed Internet access, Wi-Fi ($16/day), minibar, hair dryer, iron, safe.

Seal Cove Inn ★★ This superior, sophisticated B&B blends California, New England, and European influences in a spectacular setting. All rooms have king beds, fireplaces, antiques, private bathroom with towel warmer, watercolors, and either a private balcony or a terrace with views of a colorful half-acre wildflower garden, cypress trees, and the distant ocean. You'll find coffee and a newspaper outside your door in the morning; a full breakfast waiting for you; wine, appetizers, brandy, and sherry by the living-room fireplace in the evening; and chocolates beside your turned-down bed at night. The ocean is just a short walk away.

221 Cypress Ave., Half Moon Bay, CA 94038. © **800/995-9987** or 650/728-4114. Fax 650/728-4116. www.sealcoveinn.com. 10 units. $215–$325 double. Rates include breakfast, wine and snacks, and sherry. AE, DISC, MC, V. The inn is 6 miles north of Half Moon Bay off Hwy. 1; follow signs to Moss Beach Distillery. **Amenities:** Concierge. *In room:* TV/VCR, free Wi-Fi, minibar, fridge, hair dryer, robes.

The Zaballa House ★ The oldest building in Half Moon Bay, this pretty pale-blue Victorian is refreshingly unpretentious—as soon as you walk through the door your get that *mi-casa-es-su-casa* kinda vibe from the staff. The guest rooms in the main house are pleasantly decorated with understated wallpaper and country furniture; some have fireplaces, vaulted ceilings, or Jacuzzi tubs, and all have private bathrooms. Several years ago an annex was built behind the house so the owners could add three modern suites, each equipped with a kitchenette, double Jacuzzi, fireplace, TV/VCR, fridge, and private deck (my favorite is the Casablanca room, which comes with an eponymous video). You'll like the location as well—right on Main Street next to all the shops and restaurants.

324 Main St. (at the north end of town), Half Moon Bay, CA 94019. © **650/726-9123.** Fax 650/726-3921. www.zaballahouse.net. 12 units. $109–$275 double. Rates include breakfast and afternoon tea/wine/hors d'oeuvres. AE, DISC, MC, V. *In room:* TV/VCR and kitchenette in minisuites.

WHERE TO DINE

Barbara's Fish Trap ★ Fishnets on the ceilings and a wooden fisherman guarding the entrance give you an indication of what's on the menu here. Situated on stilts above the beach with indoor and outdoor dining and panoramic bay views, this lively, popular seafood restaurant offers a wide selection of deep-fried seafood as well as healthier broiled items such as their tangy Cajun-spiced snapper. I recommend starting with the fried calamari and a cold beer, and then moving on to the excellent rock cod fish and chips with a side of house-made clam chowder. Expect to wait in line on summer weekends,

Dinner at Duarte's

Always a worthy side trip from Half Moon Bay is a jaunt down the coast to Pescadero. Nightlife in the tiny coastal community revolves around **Duarte's Tavern,** 202 Stage Rd. (*C* **650/879-0464;** www.duartestavern.com), which is owned and operated by the family that built it in 1894. The town's population literally triples on weekends as folks pile into the unassuming wood-paneled restaurant for a bowl of its legendary artichoke soup. You'll also find steak, prime rib, and plenty of fresh seafood on the menu, as well as fruits and vegetables straight from the Duartes' gardens behind the restaurant. It's open for breakfast, lunch, and dinner every day from 7am to 9pm, and reservations are recommended for dinner, when main courses cost $12 to $25. Oh, and save room for the pie.

and bring cash because they don't take credit cards. *Tip:* A free small parking lot is across from the restaurant.

281 Capistrano Rd. (4 miles north of Half Moon Bay on Hwy. 1, west on Capistrano Rd. to Pillar Point Harbor), Princeton. *C* **650/728-7049.** Main courses $11–$30. No credit cards. Sun–Thurs 11am–9pm; Fri–Sat 11am–10pm.

Café Gibraltar ★★ MEDITERRANEAN The area's most creative and highly ranked restaurant is not downtown but tucked on a nondescript side street about 5 minutes north of Half Moon Bay. This casual, romantic, and quirky spot has the kind of individual identity and personality rarely found in today's oft-too-polished restaurants. Seated at one of the well-spaced regular or low tables with seat cushions along the back wall, you'll discover that chef Jose Ugalde's menu ranges across the Mediterranean, and that each dish is made with the freshest of local coastal ingredients. The menu changes regularly. If goat cheese-stuffed zucchini blossoms with portobello mushroom sauce are available, don't pass them up. Two other recommendations are the pan-seared sashimi-grade ahi tuna with chermoula, tomato-onion confit, capers, cured olives, and house-made preserved lemons, served with a napa cabbage relish atop a savory black beluga lentil mélange; and the wood-roasted lamb sirloin marinated with basil pesto, natural *jus,* red wine–braised tarbais beans, and roasted wild mushrooms. A smart, affordable wine list and superb desserts round out what's sure to be a great meal.

425 Ave. Alhambra (at Palma St.), El Granada. *C* **650/560-9039.** www.cafegibraltar.com. Reservations recommended. Main courses $16–$24. AE, MC. V. Sun and Tues–Thurs 5–9pm; Fri–Sat 5–9:45pm.

Cetrella ★★ MEDITERRANEAN Cetrella is as close as you'll come to big-city dining in Half Moon Bay. Amidst warm, chic dining rooms—with a centerpiece fireplace—locals and visitors mingle over dishes ranging from puree of spring onion soup, steamed Washington manila clams, white-wine- and herb-braised Australian lamb shank, and mesquite-grilled Scottish salmon created by Executive Chef Robert Holt. Bonuses include an excellent cheese program and live evening jazz Friday and Saturday. If you're in the neighborhood, check it out, but make reservations first; everyone from *Gourmet* to the *San Francisco Chronicle* has trumpeted this small-town gem, so it's no secret.

845 Main St. (at Monte Vista Lane). *C* **650/726-4090.** www.cetrella.com. Reservations recommended. Most main courses bistro dinner $19–$27, main courses cafe dinner $10–$15; brunch $10–$16. Sun brunch 10:30am–2:30pm; Sun and Tues–Thurs 5:30–9:30pm; Fri–Sat 5:30–10pm.

Moss Beach Distillery ★ (Moments) CALIFORNIA/CONTINENTAL   Ever since its bootlegging days during Prohibition almost a century ago, this old stucco distillery on a cliff above Moss Beach has been a wildly popular hangout for both locals and city folk. In the 1920s, silent-film stars and San Francisco politicos frequented the distillery for drinks and the bordello next door for . . . other pastimes. Time and weather have aged it considerably, but a recent renovation spiffed things up. Although adeptly prepared, the food—blackened scallops, coastal crab cakes, panko-crusted halibut, seafood stew, seared filet mignon—has never been the main draw; rather, it's the phenomenal view of the rugged coast from the dining room windows and spacious patio. Your best bet is to come before sunset, order off the appetizer menu (the oysters are always fresh), and snuggle with your partner on the romantic patio overlooking the Pacific (they even provide blankets). Their Sunday Brunch is hugely popular as well—$29 and all the bubbly you desire.

140 Beach Way (at Ocean St.), Moss Beach (6 miles north of Half Moon Bay off Hwy. 1). (€) 650/728-5595. www.mossbeachdistillery.com. Reservations recommended. Main courses $14–$28. DC, DISC, MC, V. Mon–Thurs noon–8pm; Fri–Sat noon–9pm; Sun 11am–8pm (Sun brunch 11am–2pm).

Pasta Moon ★★ ITALIAN   I discovered Pasta Moon nearly 20 years ago and I always look forward to coming back and being greeted by the friendly, vivacious, and oh-so-Italian staff. Everything emanating from the open kitchen is made from scratch, using only fresh ingredients and always cooked perfectly. In fact, the last time I came here I had a tortellini dish—each tender piece carefully hand-cut and bursting with flavor—that was the best I have ever had on any continent (I still think about that dish with fond memories). Some of my other favorites are the house-made linguine with Manila clams, pancetta, leeks, garlic, red-pepper flakes, and clam broth; and the semolina gnocchi with sweet peppers, *pioppini* mushrooms, and pesto. The exclusively Italian wine list features nearly 50 wines by the glass. For dessert, try the wonderful tiramisu, with its layers of espresso-soaked ladyfingers and creamy mascarpone.

> (Tips)   **Half Moon Bay's Best Brunch**
>
> One of Half Moon Bay's biggest attractions is the stunning **Ritz-Carlton Half Moon Bay.** On a bluff above the Pacific, the six-story structure has the most luxurious guest rooms in the region, a fantastic spa, tennis courts, and all the usual five-star amenities—not to mention preferred access to the Half Moon Bay Golf Links. Most important for San Francisco day-trippers and those from farther afield, it's also the place to indulge in an outrageously opulent all-you-can-eat brunch. Held every Sunday in the stately open-kitchen restaurant Navio, which also has ocean views, brunch includes an endless array of gourmet edibles—including sushi, dim sum, soufflés, a raw bar, classic breakfast dishes (including great blintzes), tarts, salads, cheeses, a meat-carving station, vegetables, pastas, and desserts. The feast, which lasts from 11am to 1:30pm, will set you back $75 per adult (half price for kids 5–12 and free for those under 5). Reservations are a must. The resort is at 1 Miramontes Point Rd., Half Moon Bay ((€) **650/712-7000**). Be sure to make reservations; brunch almost always sells out.

315 Main St., Half Moon Bay. ℂ **650/726-5125.** www.pastamoon.com. Reservations recommended. Main courses $10–$21 lunch, $15–$34 dinner. AE, DC, DISC, MC, V. Mon–Fri 11:30am–2:30pm; Sat–Sun noon–3pm; Sun–Thurs 5:30–9:30pm; Fri–Sat 5:30–10pm.

Sushi Main Street ★ JAPANESE   Chef/owner Hirohito Shigeta started out his business more than a decade ago in a tiny space on Main Street and kept the old name when he moved into larger digs down the street. His wife, Karolynne, an interior designer with impeccable taste, decorated the new space with her vast collection of museum-quality Balinese artifacts (with beautiful results). But even if it looked like the inside of a trailer home, it would still be worth a visit for the tasty sushi, tempura, and soba dishes. Adventurous sushi warriors will want to try the New Zealand roll (mussels, radish, sprouts, avocado, and teriyaki), the *unagi* papaya, and the marinated salmon roll with cream cheese and spinach. For a traditional shoeless Japanese meal, request the knee-high table perched in the corner.

696 Mill St., Half Moon Bay. ℂ **650/726-6336.** www.sushimainstreethmb.com. Main courses $5–$10. MC, V. Mon–Sat 11:30am–2:30pm and 5–9pm.

7 SAN JOSE

45 miles SE of San Francisco

The San Jose of yesteryear—a sleepy town of orchards, crops, and cattle—is long gone. Founded in 1717, and hidden in the shadows of San Francisco, San Jose is now Northern California's largest city. Today the prosperity of Silicon Valley has transformed what was once an agricultural backwater into a thriving network of restaurants, shops, a state-of-the-art light-rail system, a sports arena (go Sharks!), and a reputable art scene. And despite all the growth, a number of surveys declare it one of the safest and sunniest cities in the nation.

ESSENTIALS

GETTING THERE   **BART** (ℂ **510/465-2278;** www.bart.gov) travels from San Francisco to Fremont in 1¼ hours; you can take a bus from there. **Caltrain** (ℂ **800/660-4287;** www.caltrain.com) operates frequently from San Francisco and takes about 1 hour and 25 minutes.

VISITOR INFORMATION   Free visitors guides, published by the **San Jose Convention & Visitors Bureau,** 408 Almaden Blvd. (ℂ **800/SAN-JOSE** or 408/295-9600), are available at kiosks within the **San Jose McEnery Convention Center,** 150 W. San Carlos St., San Jose, CA 95113 (ℂ **408/277-5277**). You can request information live at the visitors bureau, or log onto **www.sanjose.org** to receive a free visitors guide by mail.

GETTING AROUND   **Light Rail** (ℂ **408/321-2300**) is the best transportation option in town. A ticket is good for 2 hours, and stops include the Great America theme park, the convention center, and downtown museums. Fares are $1.75 for adults, $1.50 for children ages 5 to 17, 75¢ for seniors and travelers with disabilities, and children age 4 and under ride for free. Day passes are $5.25 for adults, $4.50 for children, $2.25 for seniors.

ATTRACTIONS

Children's Discovery Museum (Kids)   Children will find shows, workshops, and more than 150 interactive exhibitions exploring the sciences, humanities, arts, and technology.

ZOOMZone consists of science and art activities designed by kids for kids; **Bubbalogna,** an exhibit that explores the chemistry and physics of bubbles, draws rave reviews. Smaller kids will love dressing up in costumes and playing on the fire truck.

180 Woz Way. (℃ **408/298-5437.** www.cdm.org. Admission $8 children and adults, $7 seniors 60 and up, free for children under 1. Tues–Sat 10am–5pm; Sun noon–5pm.

Rosicrucian Egyptian Museum & Planetarium   The Rosicrucian is associated with an ancient Egyptian educational organization that strongly advocated belief in the afterlife and reincarnation. Permanent exhibitions display human and animal mummies, funerary boats, canopic jars, and a replica of a noble Egyptian's tomb. Less morbid artifacts include Egyptian jewelry, pottery, and bronze tool collections. The Planetarium features shows at 2pm daily. A second show on Saturday and Sunday begins at 3:30pm.

1342 Naglee Ave. (℃ **408/947-3636.** www.egyptianmuseum.org. Museum admission $9 adults, $7 seniors and students, $5 children 5–10, free for children 4 and under. Save $1 with AAA, KQED, or military ID cards. Planetarium free admission. Mon–Fri 9am–5pm; Thurs until 8pm; Sat–Sun 11am–6pm. Closed major holidays.

San Jose Historical Museum   Twenty-six restored original and replica buildings, on 25 acres in Kelley Park, recreate life in 1880s San Jose. The usual cast of 19th-century characters is here—the doctor, the printer, the postmaster—with an occasional local surprise, such as the 1888 Chinese temple and the original Stevens fruit barn. If you want to peek inside, come on the weekend or during summer months, when docents offer interior tours daily.

1650 Senter Rd. (℃ **408/287-2290.** www.historysanjose.org. Free admission. Tues–Sun noon–5pm.

San Jose Museum of Art ★   This contemporary art museum features revolving exhibitions of post-1980 works plus older 20th-century art from the permanent collection. The Historic Wing includes a cafe, bookstore, and education center. From Tuesday to Sunday, tours begin at 12:30 and 2:30pm; for group tours, call for reservations at least 1 week in advance. Docents will also sign tours for deaf and hearing-impaired visitors with 72 hours notice.

110 S. Market St. (℃ **408/294-2787** or 408/271-6840. www.sjmusart.org. Museum admission $8 adults, $5 seniors and students, free for children 5 and under. Tues–Sun 11am–5pm. Closed major holidays.

Tech Museum of Innovation ★ Kids   In a 132,000-square-foot facility, the Tech Museum allows visitors to experience a world of phenomena: Create your own virtual roller-coaster ride, survive an earthquake on a giant shake table, operate an underwater ROV (remotely operated vehicle), or ride the same virtual bobsled used to train Olympic competitors. The museum also features an IMAX dome theater.

201 S. Market St., downtown at the corner of Park and Market sts. (℃ **408/294-TECH.** www.thetech.org. Admission (IMAX and museum) $8 all ages. Daily 10am–5pm.

Winchester Mystery House   The legacy of Sarah L. Winchester, widow of the son of the famous rifle magnate, the massive Winchester house is a monument to one woman's paranoia. After the deaths of her husband and baby daughter, Mrs. Winchester consulted with a seer, who proclaimed that the family had been targeted by the evil spirits of those killed with Winchester repeaters. Convinced the spirits would only be appeased by perpetual construction on the Winchester mansion, the widow used much of her $20-million inheritance to finance the construction, which started in 1884 and went on 24 hours a day, 7 days a week, 365 days a year, for 38 years. With 160 rooms, the home sprawls across a half-dozen acres and is full of disturbing features: a staircase leading nowhere, a Tiffany window with a spider-web design, and doors that open onto blank walls. There are 13 bathrooms, 13 windows and doors in the old sewing room, 13 palms lining the main driveway, 13 hooks in the séance room, and chandeliers with 13 lights. Such schemes were designed to confound the spirits that allegedly plagued the heiress.

525 S. Winchester Blvd. (near the intersection of I-280 and I-880). (€ **408/247-2101.** www.winchester mysteryhouse.com. Admission $24 adults, $21 seniors 65 and over, $18 children 6–12, free for kids 5 and under. Tours leave every 15–30 min. Summer daily 9am–7pm; winter daily 9am–5pm.

THEME-PARK THRILLS

It's a 10-minute drive from downtown San Jose to **California's Great America,** 100 acres of family entertainment on the Great America Parkway (off U.S. 101), in Santa Clara (€ **408/988-1776;** www.pgathrills.com). A pretty cool place to lose your lunch, the park includes such favorites as the Flight Deck suspended jet coaster; the 3-acre Nickelodeon Central and KidZville for children; and their latest addition, FireFall, where riders are spun into 360-degree vertical arcs through fire and water effects. Check for concerts and special events, too. Boomerang Bay Beach Club, a 3-acre water park with 11 slides and a "lazy river," is included in the general admission; it's $45 for adults and children ages 3 to 61, $35 for seniors age 62 and anyone under 48 inches tall. Kids under 3 are free. Check the website for discounted tickets. It's open daily from Memorial Day through October but may vary according to weather, so call for details. From San Francisco, take U.S. 101 south for about 45 miles to the Great America Parkway exit.

AN EXCELLENT SHOPPING & DINING EXCURSION

Santana Row (€ **408/551-4611;** www.santanarow.com), at Winchester and Stevens Creek boulevards, is *the* hotbed for dining, shopping, and strolling in San Jose. Stores range from Urban Outfitters to Gucci. Two of the many good dining bets include supercasual, fun New England seafood house **Yankee Pier** and Asian-inspired, flavorful, and creative **Strait's Café.**

WHERE TO STAY

The Fairmont San Jose   In a landmark building near the San Jose McEnery Convention Center and the Center of Performing Arts, the Fairmont is a popular spot for afternoon tea or cocktails, and the lobby attracts many shoppers who are just passing through. For guests, the hotel places an emphasis on comfort: The guest rooms, located in two 13-story towers, feature high-tech amenities such as fax and high-speed modem lines. Other luxuries include a fourth-floor rooftop pool surrounded by tropical foliage. The most high-end restaurant of the four on the premises is the **Grill on the Alley.** The other options are an Asian fusion restaurant with a sushi lounge, an upscale seafood restaurant, and a coffee shop.

170 S. Market St., San Jose, CA 95113. (€ **866/540-4493** or 408/998-1900. Fax 408/287-1648. www. fairmont.com. 805 units. $259–$400 double; $350–$1,800 suite. AE, DC, DISC, MC, V. **Amenities:** 4 restaurants, sushi bar; bar; heated outdoor pool; health club; spa; sauna; concierge; car-rental desk; business center; secretarial services; room service; in-room massage; same-day laundry service/dry cleaning. *In room:* A/C, TV w/pay movies, high-speed Internet, minibar, hair dryer, iron, safe in tower rooms.

WHERE TO DINE

Expensive

Emile's ★★ CONTEMPORARY EUROPEAN   Since 1973, this fancy restaurant still ranks among the Bay Area's best. Mirrors, recessed lighting, and large, bold floral arrangements create an elegant atmosphere. To start, try *torchon* of foie gras with a dried fruit compote and brioche toast, or sautéed prawns Bordelaise with butter, white wine, garlic, and lemon juice over a grilled polenta crouton. Follow with beef filet in a Madagascar pepper sauce, on a bed of spinach mashed potato, served with a vegetable medley. For dessert, go with the Grand Marnier soufflé. Emile's offers "small plate" versions of entrees; a "taste" costs about two-thirds of the entree price and allows diners to snack their way through the menu.

545 S. Second St. (C) **408/289-1960.** www.emilesrestaurant.com. Reservations recommended. Main courses $26–$45. AE, DC, DISC, MC, V. Tues–Thurs 5:30–10pm; Fri–Sat 5:30–11pm.

Paolo's ★ NORTHERN ITALIAN   Paolo's attracts a business crowd at lunchtime and a cultured crowd in the evening. The cuisine is refined northern Italian, with innovative flourishes. Appetizers include tuna carpaccio or bread-crumb-crusted prawns with white wine, garlic, lemon, parsley, and butter. The main dishes range from *pappardelle* with fresh saffron egg pasta ribbons and traditional Bolognese-style meat sauce to braised chicken with artichokes, mixed herbs, and soft polenta; and grilled dry-aged angus rib-eye chop, roasted root vegetable mash, and braised winter greens. Desserts also stretch typical Italian favorites to limits: Tuscan doughnuts, filled with chocolate, in a pomegranate glaze, for example. The extensive wine list features more than 600 selections.

333 W. San Carlos St. (C) **408/294-2558.** www.paolosrestaurant.com. Reservations recommended. Main courses $15–$23 lunch, $18–$35 dinner. AE, DC, DISC, MC, V. Mon–Fri 11am–2:30pm; Mon–Sat 5:30–10pm.

Moderate

Gordon Biersch ECLECTIC   This brewpub restaurant offers a little of everything. The menu features some lighter fare, ranging from a Thai satay platter and goat cheese salads to molasses-glazed baby back ribs. Big burgers and filling pub grub are equally popular. A large outdoor patio and live music attract a youngish crowd. Four tasty home brews are always on tap.

33 E. San Fernando St. (btw. 1st and 2nd sts.). (C) **408/294-6785.** www.gordonbiersch.com. Reservations recommended. Main courses $7.50–$14. AE, DC, DISC, MC, V. Sun–Wed 11:30am–11pm; Thurs 11:30am–midnight; Fri–Sat 11:30am–2am.

Il Fornaio ★ NORTHERN ITALIAN   Il Fornaio is always a sure thing when it comes to enjoying a satisfying meal. The specialties of the house include the mesquite-grilled fresh fish and the veal chop with sage and rosemary, as well as grilled pounded chicken breast with a purée of roasted garlic and rosemary. There are about 10 pizzas to choose from; my favorite comes topped with Maui onions, Gruyère and mozzarella cheese, smoked ham, and sage. For hearty appetites, there's an excellent and tender 22-ounce steak. Salads and appetizers, including a tasty grilled polenta with wild mushrooms and provolone, round out the menu.

302 S. Market St. (on the bottom floor of the Hyatt). (C) **408/271-3366.** www.ilfornaio.com. Reservations recommended. Main courses $8–$11. AE, DC, MC, V. Mon–Thurs 7am–10:30pm; Fri 11:30am–11pm; Sat 8am–midnight; Sun 8am–11pm.

Inexpensive

Gombei Restaurant JAPANESE   On busy nights here, the ambience is barely controlled chaos, with customers diving into big bowls of *donburi* and udon (Gombei's specialty, thick wheat noodles in a chicken broth filled with dried seaweed, green onion, and tender chunks of chicken) while the sprightly staff deftly negotiates around the crowded dining room. Be sure to check the specials board, which often lists some very esoteric Japanese entrees.

193 E. Jackson St. (btw. 4th and 5th sts.). © **408/279-4311.** Main courses $6–$10. No credit cards. Mon–Sat 11:30am–2:30pm and 5–9:30pm.

Henry's World Famous Hi-Life BARBECUE   Harking back to the good ol' days—before "good" and "bad" cholesterol were invented—is Henry's World Famous Hi-Life. Formica tables lined with paper place mats and little fishnet-covered candles give you a pretty good indication that you probably won't need that dinner jacket and tie. A bib is more appropriate for tackling the huge servings of barbecued ribs, chicken, and steaks, all cooked in an oak barbecue pit that's big enough to roast a rhino, and then slathered in a sweet, tangy barbecue sauce.

301 W. St. John St. (at Almaden Blvd., near Calif. 87). © **408/295-5414.** www.henryshilife.com. Main courses $10–$25. AE, MC, V. Tues–Fri 11:30am–2pm; Mon–Thurs 5–9pm; Fri–Sat 4–9:30pm; Sun 4–9pm.

The Wine Country

by Erika Lenkert

California's Napa and Sonoma are two of the most famous wine-growing regions in the world, and two of my favorite places to visit in the state. The valleys that provide a way of life for thousands of vintners and farmers are also the ultimate retreat for wine and food lovers and romantics. Hundreds of wineries are nestled among the vines, and most are open to visitors. Even if you're a teetotaler, the country air, rolling countryside, and world-class restaurants and spas are reason enough to visit. If you can, plan to spend a couple of days just to get to know the area. No matter how long you stay, you'll probably never get enough of the romantic, indulgent way of life. It requires stamina, though; eating and drinking to excess can seriously wear you down.

While Napa Valley, Sonoma Valley, and northern Sonoma are close to each other (about 30 min. apart by car), each is attraction-packed enough that your best bet is to focus on just one of the areas, especially if your time is limited. I recommend that you read about each below and then decide which one is right for you—unless, of course, you're lucky enough to have time to explore both.

When considering the destinations, keep in mind that Napa is the most commercial, with elegant spas, a superior selection of fine restaurants and hotels, and fancy big-business wineries offering polished winery tours. Sonoma Valley is far more laid-back and small-town, with its charming town square, and a few dozen wineries—which are often family-owned—dispersed amidst winding country roads. Northern Sonoma, the most vast area to visit, combines a little of each valley, with extremely well regarded wineries, genuine country charm, the outstanding Healdsburg town square (with great shopping), and a growing number of destination-worthy hotels and restaurants.

1 NAPA VALLEY

Napa Valley is just 35 miles long, which means you can venture from one end to the other in around half an hour (traffic permitting). Most of the large wineries—as well as most of the hotels, shops, and restaurants—line a single road, Highway 29, which starts at the mouth of the Napa River, near the north end of San Francisco Bay, and continues north to Calistoga and the top of the growing region.

ESSENTIALS

GETTING THERE   From San Francisco, cross the Golden Gate Bridge and head north on U.S. 101. Turn east on Highway 37 (toward Vallejo), and then north on Highway 29, the main road through Napa Valley. Or take the scenic route: Highway 121/12, following the signs toward Napa, and turn left onto Highway 29.

VISITOR INFORMATION   Once in Napa Valley, stop first at the **Napa Valley Conference & Visitors Bureau,** 1310 Town Center Mall, Napa, CA 94559 (© **707/226-7459,**

Tips   **Shipping Wine Home**

The only thing more complex than that $800 case of cabernet you just purchased are the rules about shipping it home. Because of absurd and forever fluctuating laws—which supposedly protect the business of the country's wine distributors—wine shipping is limited by regulations that vary in each of the 50 states. Shipping rules also vary from winery to winery.

To avoid hassles, talk to the wineries and the shipping companies below before you buy. It's technically illegal to box your own wine and send it through the U.S. mail, but people do it all the time anyway (shhh). If you go that route, you might want to disguise your box and head to a post office, UPS, or other shipping company outside the Wine Country; it's far less obvious that you're shipping wine from, say, Vallejo or San Francisco than from Napa Valley.

Shipping from Napa Valley

The UPS Store, at 3212 Jefferson St. in the Grape Yard Shopping Center (© **707/ 259-1398**), claims to pack and ship anything anywhere. At press time, rates for ground shipping a case of wine were approximately $32 to Los Angeles and $65 to New York.

St. Helena Mailing Center, 1241 Adams St., at Highway 29, St. Helena (© **707/963-2686**), says they will pack and ship to certain states within the U.S. Rates for prewrapped shipments are around $30 per case for ground delivery to Los Angeles.

Shipping from Sonoma

The UPS Store, 19229 Sonoma Hwy., in Maxwell Village, Sonoma (© **707/935-3438**), has a lot of experience with shipping wine. It claims it will ship your wine to any state. Prices vary from $34 to Los Angeles to as much as $79 to the East Coast and $155 to Hawaii and Alaska.

The **Wine Exchange of Sonoma,** 452 First St. E., between East Napa and East Spain streets, Sonoma (© **707/938-1794**), will ship your wine, but there's a catch: You must buy an equal amount of any wine at the store (which they assured me would be in stock, and probably at a better rate). Shipping rates range from $20 to Los Angeles to $72 to the East Coast.

ext. 106; www.napavalley.com), and pick up the *Napa Valley Guide.* You can call or write in for the *Napa Valley Guidebook,* which includes information on lodging, restaurants, wineries, and other things to do, along with a winery map; the bureau charges a $6 postage fee. If you don't want to pay for the official publication, point your browser to **www. napavalley.org**, the NVCVB's official site, which has lots of the same information for free.

Another good source is **WineCountry.com,** where you'll find tons of information on all of California's wine-producing regions as well as a column written by *moi.*

WHEN TO GO   The beauty of the valley is striking any time of year, but it's most memorable in September and October—harvest season, when the wineries are in full production. Another great time to visit is the spring, when the mustard flowers are in full

Artesa **17**
Benziger Family **23**
Beringer Vineyard **5**
Buena Vista Winery **21**
Castello di Amorosa **3**
Château St. Jean **24**
Clos Du Val **15**
Domaine Chandon **14**
Frank Family
  Vineyards **4**
Gloria Ferrer Champagne
  Caves **19**
The Hess Collection **16**
Joseph Phelps Vineyards **6**
PlumpJack Winery **11**
Ravenswood Winery **22**

Robert Mondavi Winery **10**
Rubicon Estate **7**
St. Supéry Winery **9**
Schramsberg **2**
Sebastiani Vineyard **20**
Shafer Vineyards **12**

Stag's Leap Wine Cellars **13**
Sterling Vineyards **1**
Swanson Vineyards &
  Winery **8**
Viansa Winery and Italian
  Marketplace **18**

bloom and the tourist season is just beginning; you'll find less traffic and fewer crowds at the wineries and restaurants, and better deals on hotel rooms. Winter is still beautiful and wonderfully romantic. It promises the best budget rates, but the vines are dormant and rain is likely, so bring appropriate shoes and an umbrella. And in summer? Say hello to hot weather, traffic, crowds, and an expensive good time.

TOURING THE VALLEY & WINERIES

The Napa Valley has around 300 wineries—each with distinct wines, atmosphere, and experience—so touring the valley takes a little planning. Decide what interests you most and chart your path from there. Ask locals which vintners have the type of experience you're looking for. And don't plan to visit more than four wineries in a day. Above all, take it slowly. The Wine Country should never be rushed; like a great glass of wine, it should be savored. Besides, you're bound to get sidetracked and blow any schedule that's too tight.

Most wineries are open 10am to 5pm (some have extended hours during summer; most are closed on major holidays). Many offer tours daily from 10am to 4:30pm, which usually chart the entire winemaking process—from grafting and harvesting the vines, to pressing the grapes, to blending and aging the juice in oak casks. Tours vary in length and formality; many are free.

The towns and wineries below are organized geographically, from south to north along Highway 29, from Napa village to Calistoga. I've included a handful of my favorites below; for a complete list, be sure to pick up one of the free guides to the valley (see "Essentials," above).

Napa

55 miles N of San Francisco

Napa serves as the commercial center of the Wine Country and the gateway to Napa Valley. Most visitors whiz past it on their way to the heart of the valley, but if you veer off the highway, you'll be surprised to discover a small but burgeoning community of nearly 75,000 residents and some of the most affordable accommodations in the area. It is also in the process of gentrification, thanks to relatively affordable housing and ongoing additions of new restaurants and attractions, the latest of which is Oxbow Market, a culinary destination by the developer behind San Francisco's famed Ferry Building Marketplace. Heading north on either Highway 29 or the Silverado Trail leads you to Napa's wineries and the more quintessential Wine Country atmosphere of vineyards and wide-open country views.

A mildly interesting stop is **Copia: The American Center for Wine, Food & the Arts** ★, 500 First St. (© **707/259-1600;** www.copia.org), which explores how wine

---

 Sip Tip

You can cheaply sip your way through downtown Napa without getting behind the wheel with the new "Taste Napa Downtown" wine card. For $20, you get 10¢ tasting privileges at 10 winecentric watering holes and tasting rooms within walking distance of one other. Plus you'll get 10% discounts at tasting rooms. Available at the **Napa Valley Conference & Visitors Bureau** (1310 Napa Town Center, off First St.; © **707/226-7459,** ext. 106). Learn more at **www.napadowntown.com.**

and food influence our culture. This $50-million facility includes rotating exhibitions, organic vegetable and demonstration gardens, culinary programs, wine classes, concerts, films, and opportunities to dine and drink on the premises. Also, drop by Tuesday or Saturday morning from May through October for the outdoor farmers' market. The center's Thursday Outdoor Summer Concert Series provides great affordable alfresco entertainment.

Admission to Copia is $5 for adults, $4 for seniors and students, and free for children 12 and under. Wednesday admissions are half-price for Napa and Sonoma residents. The center is open Wednesday through Monday from 10am to 5pm. The restaurant is open Wednesday through Monday for lunch and dinner 11:30am to 9:30pm and Sundays for brunch from 11am until 3pm.

Across the street from Copia is the new **Oxbow Market** (600 First St.; www.oxbow publicmarket.com). A smaller version of San Francisco's Ferry Building Marketplace, the co-op features a cornucopia of tasty tenants, including a number of organic produce vendors, an exceptional rotisserie chicken joint called RoliRoti (try the potatoes!), a wine bar, yet another outpost of Taylor's Automatic Refresher (see "Where to Dine" for details), a food-related antiques shop, and many other reasons to loosen your belt and your grip on your wallet. Check the website to confirm opening hours, as they are subject to change.

Anyone with an appreciation for art must visit the **di Rosa Preserve ★★**, 5200 Sonoma Hwy. (Hwy. 121/12; ☎ **707/226-5991;** www.dirosapreserve.org), to explore the collection and stunning 215-acre grounds of Rene and Veronica di Rosa, who built up a world-renowned collection of 2,000-plus works by more than 900 Greater Bay Area artists. Treasures are on display in their century-old winery-turned-residence, adjoining building, two additional galleries, gardens, and along the shores of their 30-acre lake. Tours include a $10 1-hour overview at 10am and 11am (Tues–Fri), a $15 2-hour extended home tour at 1pm, and a $15 2-hour sculpture meadow tour. On Saturdays you can take a guided 2^1/2-hour tour for $15. Reservations are recommended. Drop-ins are welcome at the Gatehouse Gallery Tuesday through Friday from 9:30am to 3pm and Saturdays by appointment ($3 suggested donation).

Discount shoppers should pull off Highway 29 at Napa's First Street exit to find the **Napa Premium Outlets** (☎ **707/226-9876;** www.premiumoutlets.com), which has a Barneys New York, Tse (cashmere at low prices), Nine West, Banana Republic, BCBG, Calvin Klein, kitchenware shops, a food court, and a decent but expensive sushi restaurant. The shops are open Monday through Thursday from 10am to 8pm, Friday and Saturday 10am to 9pm, and Sunday from 10am to 6pm.

Artesa Vineyards & Winery ★★ (Finds) Views, modern architecture, seclusion, and region-specific pinot noir flights make this one of my favorite stops. On days when the wind is blowing less than 10 mph, the fountains are captivating; they automatically shut off with higher winds. Inside the winery is a very tasteful gift shop, a room outlining the history and details of the Carneros region, and a long bar with $10 to $15 flights of everything from chardonnays and pinot noirs to cabernet sauvignon and zinfandel. Sorry, but Artesa's permits don't allow for picnicking.

1345 Henry Rd., Napa. ☎ **707/224-1668.** www.artesawinery.com. Daily 10am–5pm; tours daily at 11am and 2pm. From Hwy. 121/12, turn north on old Sonoma Rd., and then turn left on Dealy Lane, which becomes Henry Rd.

The Hess Collection ★★ (Finds) Tucked into the hillside of rural Mount Veeder, this winery brings art and wine together like no other destination in the valley. Swiss art collector Donald Hess is behind the 1978 transformation of the Christian Brothers' 1903 property into a winery/art gallery exhibiting huge, colorful works by the likes of Frank Stella, Francis Bacon, and Andy Goldsworthy. A free self-guided tour leads through the collection and offers glimpses through tiny windows into the winemaking facilities. Newer guided tours and food and wine pairings, which include four to six wines and seasonal noshes, are available by appointment only Thursday through Saturday for $35 to $50 per person. But you can drop by the tasting room anytime, pay $10, and sample the current cabernet and chardonnay plus one other featured wine; $15 to $20 gets you a reserve tasting. Current-release bottles start at $22 and top off at around $120.

4411 Redwood Rd., Napa. © 707/255-1144. www.hesscollection.com. Daily 10am–5pm, except some holidays. From Hwy. 29 north, exit at Redwood Rd. west, and follow Redwood Rd. for 6¹/₂ miles.

Clos Du Val   This winery's ivy-covered building and well-manicured rose garden set the scene for a romantic wine-tasting experience. Bordeaux-born founder and winemaker Bernard Portet and his newer, younger counterpart, John Clews, are responsible for the output; Portet has garnered a reputation for his cabernet, which makes up 70% of the winery's production. Other varietals include chardonnay, pinot noir, and merlot. You can try them all in the basic tasting room. They charge a $10 tasting fee (refunded with purchase) for four wines and $20 for a reserve tasting, which includes a logo glass and a library selection or two. Grassy nooks along the grounds include facilities for picnics and the French game *pétanque.*

5330 Silverado Trail (north of Oak Knoll Ave.), Napa. © 707/259-2200. www.closduval.com. Daily 10am–5pm. Tours by appointment only.

Stag's Leap Wine Cellars   Founded in 1972, Stag's Leap shocked the oenological world 4 years later, when its 1973 cabernet won first place over French wines in a Parisian blind tasting. Visit the charmingly landscaped, unfussy winery and its very cramped "tasting room," where you can try a selection of four current release wines for $15 per person. Be prepared to pay $30 to $40 for estate wines. A 1-hour tour and tasting runs through everything from the vineyard and production facilities to the ultraswank $5-million wine caves.

5766 Silverado Trail, Napa. © 707/944-2020. www.cask23.com. Daily 10am–4:30pm. Tours by appointment only. From Hwy. 29, go east on Trancas St. or Oak Knoll Ave., and then north to the cellars.

Shafer Vineyards ★★ (Finds)   For an experience off the beaten track, reserve a tour and tasting at this Stag's Leap District destination. Unlike many Napa wineries, this one is family owned—by John Shafer, who, after 23 years in publishing, bought 209 hillside acres and planted vines on 50 of them. Today, he and his son Doug, joined by winemaker Elias Fernandez, use sustainable farming and solar energy to make exceptional chardonnay, merlot, cabernet sauvignon, and Syrah. They only produce 32,000 cases per year, but their wines are well known and extremely coveted. What's more, they share their output and winemaking philosophy during a relaxed, enjoyable $45-per-person 1¹/₂-hour tour and tasting. Most wines go for $45 to $65, but their Hillside Select cabernet is $200 (and can immediately be resold for somewhere in the $300s). *Tip:* Book your tasting tour 4 to 6 weeks in advance either online or by phone; the tours are intimate and popular.

6154 Silverado Trail, Napa. © 707/944-2877. www.shafervineyards.com. By appointment only Mon–Fri 10:30am–2pm.

(Moments) **Hot-Air Ballooning over the Valley**

Napa Valley is the busiest hot-air balloon "flight corridor" in the world. Northern California's temperate weather allows for ballooning year-round; and on summer mornings in the valley, it's a rare day when you don't see at least one of the colorful airships floating above the vineyards.

Trips depart early in the morning, when the air is cooler and the balloons have better lift. (**Note:** When weather conditions aren't optimal, balloon companies often launch flights from locations up to an hour's drive outside the valley. You won't know until the morning of the flight, but you should be able to cancel on the spot if you desire.) Flight paths vary with the direction and speed of the changing breezes, so "chase" crews on the ground must follow the balloons to their undetermined destinations. Most flights last about an hour and end with a champagne celebration and breakfast. Advance reservations are required. Prices run close to $200 per person for the basic package, which includes shuttle service from your hotel. Wedding, wine tasting, picnic, and lodging packages are also available. For more information or reservations, call Napa's **Adventures Aloft** (© 800/944-4408 or 707/944-4408; www.nvaloft.com) or **Bonaventura Balloon Company** (© 800/FLY-NAPA; www.bonaventuraballoons.com).

Yountville

70 miles N of San Francisco

The town of Yountville was founded by the first white American to settle in the valley, George Calvert Yount. While it lacks the small-town charm of neighboring St. Helena and Calistoga—primarily because its main street is rather sprawling and sprinkled with shops and restaurants rather than sites—it does serve as a good base for exploring the valley. It's also home to a handful of excellent wineries, inns, boutiques, and a small stretch of fabulous restaurants, including the world-renowned French Laundry.

Domaine Chandon ★★ (Finds)   Founded in 1973 by French champagne house Moët et Chandon, Domaine Chandon is the valley's most renowned (and hip) sparkling winery. Manicured gardens showcase locally made sculpture, and guests linger—their glasses fizzing with bubbly—by a table loaded with snacks in the festive tasting salon or under its patio's umbrella. In the valley's only fine-dining restaurant at a winery, diners indulge in formal French-inspired meals (more casual menus are available at lunchtime). If you can pull yourself away from the salon's bubbly or still wine (tastings are $7–$22), the comprehensive tours and tastings are informative and friendly. Check the website for events; Chandon often hosts live music and dancing and extends its salon hours during the summer.

1 California Dr. (at Hwy. 29), Yountville. © 707/944-2280. www.chandon.com. Daily 10am–6pm; hours vary by season, so call to confirm. Call for free tour schedules.

Oakville

68 miles N of San Francisco

Driving farther north on the St. Helena Highway (Hwy. 29) brings you to the Oakville Cross Road and the famous **Oakville Grocery Co.** (see "Gourmet Picnics, Napa Style" on p. 198), a favorite for picnic fare.

PlumpJack Winery If most wineries are like a Brooks Brothers suit, PlumpJack stands out as the Todd Oldham of wine tasting: chic, colorful, a little wild, and popular with a young, hip crowd as well as with a growing number of more mature aficionados. Like the franchise's PlumpJack restaurant and wine shop in San Francisco, as well as its resort in Lake Tahoe, this mock-medieval winery is a welcome diversion. Formerly the Villa Mt. Eden winery, it's now backed by Getty bucks, and the ample budget is in evidence beyond the atmosphere: Some serious winemaking goes down here, too. For $10 you can sample the sauvignon blanc, merlot, Syrah, and chardonnay. Alas, the winery has no tours or picnic spots.

620 Oakville Cross Rd. (just west of the Silverado Trail), Oakville. © **707/945-1220.** www.plumpjack.com. Daily 10am–4pm.

Robert Mondavi Winery ★ (Finds) The Mission-style Mondavi winery offers the most comprehensive tours in the valley. Basic jaunts—which last about an hour and 15 minutes and cost $25—lead you through the vineyards and their newest winemaking facilities. (Ask the guides anything about the process; they know a lot.) After the tour, you can taste a selection of current wines. To learn even more, ask about the in-depth tours. Mondavi offers a wide variety, including the "essence tasting" tour ($60), during which you compare wine with the scents of fruits, spices, nuts, and more. You can also sample wines without taking the tour, for $5 per 2-ounce pour or $30 per flight. Tickets to their summer series concerts are expensive, but the talent is world-class (think Buena Vista Social Club, Aimee Mann, or Chaka Kahn) and the crowd knows how to throw a picnic-party. Check the website for this season's line-up.

7801 St. Helena Hwy. (Hwy. 29), Oakville. © **888/766-6328,** ext. 2000, or 707/226-1395. www.robert mondaviwinery.com. Daily 10am–5pm. Reservations recommended for guided tour; book 1 week ahead, especially for weekend tours. Closed Easter, Thanksgiving, Christmas Day, and New Year's Day.

Rutherford

3 miles N of Oakville

If you blink after Oakville, you're likely to overlook Rutherford, the next small town that borders on St. Helena. Rutherford has its share of spectacular wineries, but you can't see most of them while driving along Highway 29.

Swanson Vineyards & Winery ★ (Finds) Swanson runs the valley's most posh and unique wine tastings, for $25 or $55, with reservations required. Here, tastings are more like a private party, known on the premises as a "SA-lon." You and up to seven other guests will sit at a round table in a coral parlor adorned with huge paintings, seashells, and a fireplace; the atmosphere is uncommonly refined yet whimsical. The table appears to be set for a dinner party rather than a tasting—with Reidel stemware, slivers of a fine cheese or two, crackers, and one superb chocolate Alexis ganache-filled bonbon (more of which are available for purchase on the premises). Over the course of the hour-plus event, a winery host will pour four to seven wines and discuss the history and fine points of each—in between casual sessions of banter among guests, of course. Expect a bright pinot grigio, rich merlot, and hearty Alexis, their signature cab-Syrah blend. If you can afford it, don't miss this place.

1271 Manley Lane, Rutherford. © **707/967-3500.** www.swansonvineyards.com. Tasting appointments available Wed–Sun 10am–5pm.

St. Supéry Winery (Kids) The outside looks like a modern corporate office building, but inside you'll find a functional, welcoming winery that encourages first-time tasters to learn more about oenology. The self-guided tour takes you through a demonstration vineyard that explains the growing techniques, and "SmellaVision" is an interactive kid-pleasing display that teaches you how to identify different wine ingredients. Adjoining it is the Atkinson House, chronicling more than 100 years of winemaking history during public tours offered at 1 and 3pm. For $20, you can sample four wines, which hopefully includes their excellent and well-priced sauvignon blanc. Even the prices make visitors feel at home: Bottles start at $19, and the tag on their high-end bordeaux red blend is $60.

8440 St. Helena Hwy. (Hwy. 29), Rutherford. © **800/942-0809** or 707/963-4507. www.stsupery.com. Daily 10am–5pm (until 5:30pm during summer). $10 tour at 1 and 3pm daily.

Rubicon Estate ★   Hollywood meets Napa Valley at Francis Ford Coppola's spectacular 1880s ivy-draped historic stone winery and grounds. Originally known as Inglenook Vineyards, then Niebaum-Coppola, it's now named after its most prestigious wine. You'll have to fork over $25 to visit the estate, but that includes valet parking, a tasting of five wines (they make dozens of different kinds under various labels), a tour of the impeccably renovated grounds, and access to the giant wine bar, retail center, and room showcasing Coppola film memorabilia, from Academy Awards to trinkets from *The Godfather* and *Bram Stoker's Dracula*. Wine, food, and gift items dominate the cavernous tasting area, where wines such as an estate-grown blend, cabernet franc, merlot, and zinfandel made from organically grown grapes are sampled. Bottles range from around $16 to more than $100. Along with the basic tour, you can pay extra for more exclusive, specialized tours as well.

1991 St. Helena Hwy. (Hwy. 29), Rutherford. © **800/RUBICON** or 707/968-1100. www.rubiconestate. com. Daily 10am–5pm. Tours daily.

St. Helena
73 miles N of San Francisco

This quiet little town, 17 miles north of Napa on Highway 29, is home to many beautiful old houses and first-rate restaurants, accommodations, and shops. The former Seventh-Day Adventist village manages to maintain a pseudo Old West feel while catering to upscale shoppers with deep pockets: It's *the* destination for retail-therapy seekers. On St. Helena's **Main Street ★**, between Pope and Pine streets, you'll find trendy fashions, chic pet gifts, estate jewelry, and European home accessories. Most stores are open 10am to 5pm Monday through Sunday.

Shopaholics should also take the sharp turn off Highway 29, 2 miles north of downtown St. Helena, to the **St. Helena Premier Outlets** (© 707/963-7282; www.sthelena marketplace.com). Featured designers include Escada, Brooks Brothers, and Tumi. The stores are open daily from 10am to 6pm.

One last favorite stop is the **Napa Valley Olive Oil Manufacturing Company,** 835 Charter Oak Ave. (© **707/963-4173**), at the end of the road behind Tra Vigne restaurant. The tiny market presses and bottles its own oils and sells them at a fraction of the price you'd pay elsewhere. It also has an extensive selection of Italian cooking ingredients, imported snacks, great deals on dried mushrooms, and a picnic table in the parking lot. You'll love the age-old method for totaling the bill—which you must discover for yourself.

If you'd like to go **bicycling,** the quieter, northern end of the valley is an ideal place to rent a set of wheels and pedal the Silverado Trail. **St. Helena Cyclery,** 1156 Main St. (© **707/963-7736;** www.sthelenacyclery.com), rents bikes for $10 per hour or $30 a day, including rear rack, helmet, and picnic bag.

Joseph Phelps Vineyards ★ Visitors interested in intimate, comprehensive tours and knockout tastings should schedule a tour at this winery. A quick turn off the Silverado Trail in Spring Valley (there's no sign—watch for Taplin Rd., or you'll blast right by), Joseph Phelps was founded in 1973 and is a major player in both the regional and the worldwide wine market. Phelps himself accomplished a long list of valley firsts, including launching the Syrah varietal in the valley and extending the 1970s Berkeley food revolution (led by Alice Waters) to the Wine Country by founding the Oakville Grocery Co. (p. 198). A visit can include an informal $20 tasting or a "seminar" ($1^1/_2$ hr. on weekdays and 1 hr. on weekends; all $30) like the Blending, Le Nez, or the Wine Appreciation seminars, which include samples of five or six wines and a short film on the history of the winery.

The three excellently located picnic tables, on the terrace overlooking the valley, are available on a first-come, first-served basis, with preference given to Phelps wine club members (join and get wine shipped a certain number of times per year, depending on level of membership), who are also able to make a reservation.

200 Taplin Rd. (off the Silverado Trail), P.O. Box 1031, St. Helena. C **800/707-5789** or 707/963-2745. www.jpvwines.com. Mon–Fri 10am–5pm; Sat–Sun 10am–4pm. $30 seminars and tastings by appointment only; Sat–Sun at 10am, 11:30am, 1pm, and 2:30pm; Mon–Fri at 11am and 2:30pm. $10 per person for 1-oz. pour of Insignia.

Beringer Vineyards ★ You won't have the most personal experience at this tourist-heavy stop, but you will find a regal 1876 estate, founded by brothers Jacob and Frederick, and hand-dug tunnels in the hillside. The oldest continually operating winery in Napa Valley, Beringer managed to stay open even during Prohibition by making "sacramental" wines. White zinfandel is the winery's most popular seller, but plenty of other varietals—including some highfalutin' options—are available. Tastings of current vintages ($5) take place in newer facilities, where a large selection of bottles sells for less than $20. Reserve wines are available for tasting in the remarkable Rhine House for $25 (applied toward purchase), and tours range from the $10 standard or $20 historical to the $35 $1^1/_2$-hour vintage legacy tour. Check the website for a complete list of tours.

2000 Main St. (Hwy. 29), St. Helena. C **707/963-7115.** www.beringer.com. Oct–May 10am–5pm (last tour 3:30pm, last tasting 4:30pm); June–Sept 10am–6pm (last tour 3:30pm, last tasting 5:30pm).

Calistoga

81 miles N of San Francisco

This last tourist town in Napa Valley was named by Sam Brannan, entrepreneur extraordinaire and California's first millionaire. After making a bundle supplying miners during the Gold Rush, he took advantage of the natural geothermal springs at the north end of Napa Valley by building a hotel and spa in 1859. Flubbing up a speech in which he compared this natural California wonder to New York State's Saratoga Springs resort, he serendipitously coined the name "Calistoga," and it stuck. With 5,190 residents and an old-time main street (no building along the 6-block stretch is more than two stories high), this small, simple resort town is popular with city folk who come here to unwind. Calistoga is a great place to relax and indulge in mineral waters, mud baths, Jacuzzis, massages and, of course, wine. The vibe is more casual—and a little groovier—than you'll find in towns to the south.

NATURAL WONDERS **Old Faithful Geyser of California,** 1299 Tubbs Lane (C **707/ 942-6463;** www.oldfaithfulgeyser.com), is one of only three "old faithful" geysers in the world. It has been blowing off steam at regular intervals for as long as anyone can remember. The 350°F (176°C) water spews at a height of about 60 feet every 40 minutes, day and night. The performance lasts about 3 minutes, and you can bring a picnic lunch to munch on between spews. An exhibit hall, gift shop, and snack bar are open every day. Admission is $8 for adults, $7 for seniors, $3 for children 6 to 12, and free for children under 6. The geyser is open daily from 9am to 6pm (to 5pm in winter). To get there, follow the signs from downtown Calistoga; it's between highways 29 and 128.

You won't see thousands of stone trees, but you'll still find many petrified specimens at the **Petrified Forest,** 4100 Petrified Forest Rd. (© **707/942-6667;** www.petrified forest.org). Volcanic ash blanketed this area after an eruption near Mount St. Helena 3 million years ago. You'll find redwoods that have turned to rock through the slow infiltration of silicas and other minerals, as well as petrified seashells, clams, and marine life indicating that water covered this area before the redwood forest appeared. Admission is $6 for adults, $5 for seniors and youths 12 to 17, $3 for children 6 to 11, and free for children under 6. The forest is open daily from 9am to 6pm (to 5pm in winter). Heading north from Calistoga on Highway 128, turn left onto Petrified Forest Road, just past Lincoln Street.

Cyclists can rent bikes from **Getaway Adventures BHK,** 1117 Lincoln Ave. (© **800/ 499-BIKE** or 707/763-3040; www.getawayadventures.com). Full-day group tours cost $125 per person, including lunch and a visit to four or five wineries, $105 per person for private groups of six or more. Bike rental without a tour costs $30 per day plus a $45 delivery fee to Napa Valley locations. You can also inquire about the company's kayaking and hiking tours.

Frank Family Vineyards ★ (Finds)   "Wine dudes" Dennis, Tim, Jeff, Rick, and Pat will do practically anything to maintain their rightfully self-proclaimed reputation as the "friendliest winery in the valley." Here it's all about down-home fun: no muss, no fuss, no intimidation. At Frank Family, you're part of their family—no joke. They'll greet you like a long-lost relative and serve you all the free bubbly tastings you want (three to four varieties: blanc de blanc, blanc de noir, and reserve rouge, for example, at $30–$55 a bottle). Still-wine lovers can sample well-received chardonnay and a cabernet sauvignon in the casual back room. Behind the tasting room, a picnic area is situated under the oaks, overlooking the vineyards.

1091 Larkmead Lane (just off the Silverado Trail), Calistoga. © **707/942-0859.** Daily 10am–5pm.

Castello di Amorosa ★ (Finds)   For a taste of medieval Europe in Napa, head to this 121,000-square-foot stone castle. The eight-level structure, with 90 feet of caves, a dungeon, and torture chamber, is surprisingly authentic (as evidenced by achy legs and feet after tromping on cobblestones). It's $10 to sample a variety of wines, including chardonnay, merlot, cabernet, and dessert wines (bottles are steeply priced btw. $30 and $75), and $25 to $30 for the 2-hour tour ($15 for children 10 or older; under 10 are not permitted). Though the castle is a far cry from quintessential Wine Country (some liken it to Disneyland), it is fun to browse this stunning architectural accomplishment.

4045 North St., Helena Hwy., Calistoga. © **707-942-8200** or 707-286-7273 (for events). www.castello diamorosa.com. Tasting daily 9:30am–6pm. Tours by reservation only: on the hour Mon–Fri 9:30am–4:30pm, and on the half-hour Sat–Sun and holidays 9:30am–5pm.

Schramsberg ★★ (Finds)   One of the valley's all-time best places to explore, this 217-acre, landmark champagne estate has a wonderful old-world feel. Schramsberg is the label that presidents serve when toasting dignitaries from around the globe—with a bevy of

> ### (Moments) Find the New You—in Mud
>
> People in Calistoga have been taking mud baths for the last 150 years. Local volcanic ash, imported peat, and naturally boiling, mineral hot springs are mulled together to produce a thick, natural mud that simmers at a temperature of about 104°F (40°C). Follow your soak with a warm mineral-water shower, a whirlpool bath, a visit to the steam room, and a relaxing blanket-wrap. Emerge rejuvenated, revitalized, and squeaky clean.
>
> Indulge yourself at any of these Calistoga spas: **Dr. Wilkinson's Hot Springs,** 1507 Lincoln Ave. (© 707/942-4102); **Golden Haven Hot Springs Spa,** 1713 Lake St. (© 707/942-6793); **Calistoga Spa Hot Springs,** 1006 Washington St. (© 707/942-6269); **Calistoga Village Inn & Spa,** 1880 Lincoln Ave. (© 707/942-0991); **Indian Springs Resort,** 1712 Lincoln Ave. (© 707/942-4913); or **Roman Spa Motel,** 1300 Washington St. (© 707/942-4441).

historic memorabilia in the front room to prove it. But the real mystique begins when you enter the champagne caves, partly hand carved by Chinese laborers in the 1800s, which wind for 2 miles—reputedly making them the longest in North America. The caves have a Tom Sawyer feel, complete with dangling cobwebs and seemingly endless passageways; you can't help but feel you're on an adventure. The comprehensive, unintimidating tour ends in the tasting room, where you'll sit around a big table and sample four surprisingly varied selections of bubbly. Tastings are $25 per person, but it's money well spent. They are offered only to those who take the free tour, and you must make reservations in advance.

1400 Schramsberg Rd. (off Hwy. 29), Calistoga. © **707/942-2414.** www.schramsberg.com. Daily 10am–4pm. Tours and tastings by appointment only at 10am, 11am, 1pm, and 2:30pm.

Sterling Vineyards ★ (Kids) (Finds)   You don't need climbing shoes to reach this dazzling white Mediterranean-style winery, 300 feet up, on a rocky knoll. Just fork over $20 ($10 for kids, which includes a goodie bag) and take the aerial tram, which yields stunning bucolic views along the way. Once you're back on land, follow the self-guided tour (one of the Wine Country's most comprehensive) of the winemaking process. The tram fare includes tastings of four varietals, in the panoramic tasting room. Limited release wines or reserve flights cost anywhere from $3 to $25, and a guided reserve tasting and tour, limited to 10 people at 11am daily, goes for $45. Expect to pay anywhere from $14 to $100 for a souvenir bottle ($20 is the average).

1111 Dunaweal Lane (off Hwy. 29, just south of downtown Calistoga), Calistoga. © **707/942-3344.** www.sterlingvineyards.com. Daily 10:30am–4:30pm. Reservations recommended for the reserve tasting and tour.

WHERE TO STAY

Accommodations here run the gamut from motels and B&Bs to world-class luxury retreats, and all are accessible from the main highway. While I recommend the more romantically pastoral areas such as St. Helena, you're definitely going to find better deals in the towns of Napa or laid-back Calistoga.

Keep in mind that during high season—between June and November—most hotels charge peak rates and sell out on weekends; many have a 2-night minimum. If you need help organizing your Wine Country vacation, contact one of the following companies: **Accommodation Bed & Breakfast Inns of Napa Valley** (© 707/944-4444; www. bbinv.com), an association of B&Bs, provides descriptions and lets you know who has vacancies. **Napa Valley Reservations Unlimited** (© 800/251-NAPA or 707/252-1985; www.napavalleyreservations.com) is also a source for booking everything from balloon rides to wine-tasting tours. Also, consider the 272-room **Napa Valley Marriott,** 3425 Solano Ave., Napa, CA 94558 (© 800/228-9290 or 707/253-8600; www.marriott. com), which has an exercise room, a heated outdoor pool and spa, and two restaurants; rates range from $129 to $329 for rooms, $350 to $500 for suites.

Very Expensive

Calistoga Ranch ★★★ Tucked into the mountainside on 157 pristine hidden-canyon acres, the 46 rural-chic free-standing luxury cottages are designed to blend into stunning natural surroundings. Guest rooms are packed with every conceivable amenity, including fireplaces, patios along a wooded area, and cushy outdoor furnishings. Reasons not to leave include a giant swimming pool, a reasonably large gym, an incredibly designed indoor-outdoor spa with a natural thermal pool, and individual pavilions with private-garden soaking tubs, as well as an open-air restaurant with stunning views of the property's Lake Lommel. Need more enticement? How about free activities such as watercolor painting, yoga, biking, and hiking. Add good food (albeit with often inexperienced service), and you've got a romantically rustic slice of Wine Country heaven.

580 Lommel Rd., Calistoga, CA 94515. © **707/254-2800.** Fax 707/254-2888. www.calistogaranch.com. 46 cottages. $600–$3,200 double. AE, DC, DISC, MC, V. **Amenities:** Restaurant; large heated outdoor pool; gym; spa; Jacuzzi; steam room; concierge; activities; Wi-Fi throughout; room service; massage; laundry service; dry cleaning (next day). *In room:* A/C, TV/DVD w/DVDs, fax upon request, free Wi-Fi, 1 lodge w/ full kitchen, minibar, fridge, coffeemaker, hair dryer, iron, safe.

Meadowood Napa Valley ★★★ (Finds) Meadowood is summer camp for wealthy grown-ups. On 250 acres of pristine mountainside amid a forest of madrona and oak trees, this resort is quiet and exclusive enough to make you forget that busy wineries are just 10 minutes away. Rooms have beamed ceilings, private patios, stone fireplaces, and wilderness views; many are individual suite-lodges so far removed from the common areas that you must drive to get to them (lazier folks can opt for more centrally located accommodations). You can spend your days playing golf, tennis, or croquet; lounging around the pools or spa; or hiking the area. Those who actually want to leave the property to do some wine tasting can check in with the hotel's wine tutor.

900 Meadowood Lane, St. Helena, CA 94574. © **800/458-8080** or 707/963-3646. Fax 707/963-3532. www.meadowood.com. 85 units. $475–$975 double; from $900–$1,700 1-bedroom suite; from $1,425–$2,675 2-bedroom; from $1,950–$3,650 3-bedroom; from $2,475–$4,625 4-bedroom. Ask about promotional offers and off-season rates. 2-night minimum stay on weekends. AE, DC, DISC, MC, V. **Amenities:** 2 restaurants; 2 large heated outdoor pools (adult and family pools); golf course; 7 tennis courts; health club and full-service spa; Jacuzzi; sauna; concierge; business center; room service; same-day laundry service/dry cleaning weekdays only; 2 croquet lawns. *In room:* A/C, TV, high-speed Internet, free Wi-Fi, kitchenette in some rooms, minibar, coffeemaker, hair dryer, iron.

Moderate

Christopher's Inn ★ (Kids) Renovations and expansions by architect-owner Christopher Layton turned these sweet old homes in downtown Calistoga into comfy hotel rooms. Options range from simple but tasteful quarters (colorful, with impressive antiques and small bathrooms) to huge, well-appointed abodes (with four-poster beds, rich fabrics, and sunken Jacuzzi tubs that face a gas fireplace). Most rooms have gas fireplaces, and some have flatscreen TVs (with cable) and DVD players. The two plain but very functional two-bedroom units are ideal for families, provided you're not expecting the Ritz. An extended continental breakfast is delivered to your room daily. *Tip:* For a quieter room, request one away from the street. Also, be warned that they have a no-refund cancellation policy and that the entire hotel is nonsmoking.

1010 Foothill Blvd., Calistoga, CA 94515. © **866/876-5755** or 707/942-5755. Fax 707/942-6895. www. christophersinn.com. 24 units. $185–$465 double; $330–$350 house sleeping 5 or 6. Rates include expanded continental breakfast. AE, MC, V. **Amenities:** 2-person massage studio. *In room:* TV, Wi-Fi.

Maison Fleurie ★★   One of the prettiest garden-set B&Bs in the Wine Country, this inn comprises a trio of beautiful 1873 brick-and-fieldstone buildings overlaid with ivy. The main house—a charming Provençal replica, with thick brick walls, terra-cotta tile, and paned windows—holds seven rooms; the rest are in the old bakery building and the carriage house. Some feature private balconies, patios, sitting areas, Jacuzzi tubs, and fireplaces. A basic breakfast is served in the little dining room; afterward, you're welcome to wander the landscaped grounds or hit the wine-tasting trail, returning in time for afternoon hors d'oeuvres and wine.

6529 Yount St. (btw. Washington St. and Yountville Cross Rd.), Yountville, CA 94599. © **800/788-0369** or 707/944-2056. Fax 707/944-9342. www.maisonfleurienapa.com. 13 units. $135–$300 double. Rates include full breakfast and afternoon hors d'oeuvres. AE, DC, DISC, MC, V. **Amenities:** Heated outdoor pool; Jacuzzi; free use of bikes. *In room:* A/C, TV, Wi-Fi, hair dryer, iron.

Rancho Caymus Inn ★   Heiress sculptor Mary Tilden Morton (of Morton Salt) was the creator of this cozy, Spanish-style hacienda. Two floors open onto wisteria-covered balconies, and guest rooms surround a garden courtyard with a huge outdoor fireplace. Morton fancied each room a work of art, so she employed the most skilled craftspeople she could find, designed adobe fireplaces in 22 of 26 rooms, and added artifacts she gathered in Mexico and South America.

The mix-and-match decor in the decent-size guest rooms is on the funky side, with braided rugs and overly varnished, imported carved-wood furnishings. It's hard to balk, though, when the rooms include wet bars, sitting areas with sofa beds, small private patios, and new beds and wall paint added in 2005. Most suites have fireplaces, one has a kitchenette, and five have whirlpools. Breakfast, served in the dining room, includes fresh fruit, granola, orange juice, and pastries.

140 Rutherford Rd., P.O. Box 78, Rutherford, CA 94573. © **800/845-1777** or 707/963-1777. Fax 707/963-5387. www.ranchocaymus.com. 26 suites. $155–$320 1-bedroom suite; $215–$410 master suite; $275–$450 2-bedroom suite. Rates include continental breakfast. AE, MC, V. From Hwy. 29 north, turn right onto Rutherford Rd./Calif. 128 east; the hotel is on your left. **Amenities:** Restaurant. *In room:* A/C, TV, Wi-Fi, kitchenette in 1 room, minibar, fridge, coffeemaker, hair dryer, iron in some rooms, microwaves in master suites.

Wine Country Inn ★★   Just off the highway, behind Freemark Abbey vineyard, this attractive, wood and stone, family-run inn, complete with a French-style mansard roof and turret, overlooks a pastoral landscape of vineyards. Inside, individually decorated rooms contain antique furnishings and handmade quilts; most have fireplaces and private terraces overlooking the valley, and others have private hot tubs. Five luxury cottages include king-size beds as well as a single bed (perfect for the tot in tow), sitting areas, fireplaces, private patios, and three-headed walk-in showers. One of the inn's best features (besides the absence of TVs) is the heated outdoor pool. Another outstanding feature is the selection of suites, which come with stereos and plenty of space and privacy. The owners make every guest feel welcome, serving wine and appetizers nightly, greeting guests hospitably in the warm living room, and offering a full buffet breakfast as well.

1152 Lodi Lane, St. Helena, CA 94574. © **888/465-4608** or 707/963-7077. Fax 707/963-9018. www.wine countryinn.com. 29 units, 12 with shower only. $215–$405 double; $535–$660 suite; $505–$590 cottages. Rates include breakfast and appetizers. MC, V. **Amenities:** Heated outdoor pool; spa services; Jacuzzi; concierge; free Wi-Fi; big-screen TV in common room. *In room:* A/C, hair dryer, iron.

Inexpensive

In addition to the listings below, **Napa Valley Railway Inn,** 6503 Washington St., Yountville, adjacent to the Vintage 1870 shopping complex (© **707/944-2000**), rents private railway cars converted into adorable hotel rooms.

Calistoga Spa Hot Springs ★ (Kids (Value

Calistoga Spa Hot Springs is one of very few hotels in the Wine Country that caters specifically to families with children. This "family resort" is a great bargain, with unpretentious yet comfortable rooms and a plethora of spa facilities. All of Calistoga's best shops and restaurants are within easy walking distance, and you can use the barbecue grills near the large pool and patio.

1006 Washington St. (at Gerard St.), Calistoga, CA 94515. © **866/822-5772** or 707/942-6269. www. calistogaspa.com. 57 units. Mar–Oct $136–$196 double. Discounted rates available Mon–Fri Nov–Feb, excluding holidays. MC, V. **Amenities:** 3 heated outdoor pools; kids' wading pool; exercise room; spa. *In room:* A/C, TV, kitchenette, fridge, coffeemaker, hair dryer, iron.

Chablis Inn ★

There's no way around it: If you want to sleep cheaply in a town where the *average* room rate tops $200 per night in high season, you're destined for a motel. Look on the bright side: Because your room is likely to be little more than a crash pad after a day of eating and drinking, a clean bed and a remote control are all you'll really need anyway. And Chablis offers much more than that. All of the motel-style rooms are super-clean, and some even boast kitchenettes or whirlpool tubs. Guests have access to a heated outdoor pool and hot tub.

3360 Solano Ave., Napa, CA 94558. © **800/443-3490** or 707/257-1944. Fax 707/226-6862. www.chablis inn.com. 34 units. May to mid-Nov $99–$250 double; mid-Nov to Apr $79–$150 double. AE, DC, DISC, MC, V. **Amenities:** Heated outdoor pool; Jacuzzi. *In room:* A/C, satellite TV, kitchenette in some rooms, fridge, coffeemaker, hair dryer.

Dr. Wilkinson's Hot Springs Resort ★

This spa/"resort," located in the heart of Calistoga, is one of the best deals in Napa Valley. The rooms range from attractive Victorian-style accommodations to modern, cozy recently renovated guest rooms in the main 1960s-style motel. All rooms are spiffier than most in the area's other hotels, with surprisingly tasteful textiles and basic motel-style accouterments. Larger rooms have refrigerators and/or kitchens. Facilities include three mineral-water pools (two outdoor and one indoor), a Jacuzzi, a steam room, and mud baths. All kinds of body treatments are available in the spa, including famed mud baths, steams, and massage—all of which I highly recommend. Be sure to inquire about their excellent packages, their new, fantastic facial held in the facial cottage, and hot stone massage therapy.

1507 Lincoln Ave. (Calif. 29, btw. Fairway and Stevenson aves.), Calistoga, CA 94515. © **707/942-4102.** www.drwilkinson.com. 42 units. $129–$239 double. Weekly discounts and packages available. AE, MC, V. **Amenities:** 3 pools; spa; Jacuzzi; steam room; mud baths; Wi-Fi in lobby. *In room:* A/C, TV, coffeemaker, hair dryer, iron, voice mail.

El Bonita Motel ★ (Kids) (Value) This 1940s Art Deco motel is a bit too close to Highway 29 for comfort, but the 2½ acres of beautifully landscaped gardens behind the building (away from the road) help even the score. The rooms, while small and nothing fancy (think motel basic), are spotlessly clean and decorated with newer furnishings and kitchenettes; some have a whirlpool bathtub. It ain't heaven, but it is cheap for St. Helena.

195 Main St. (at El Bonita Ave.), St. Helena, CA 94574. ℭ **800/541-3284** or 707/963-3216. Fax 707/963-8838. www.elbonita.com. 41 units. $89–$259 double. Rates include continental breakfast. AE, DC, DISC, MC, V. **Amenities:** Heated outdoor pool; spa; Jacuzzi; free high-speed Internet access in lobby. *In room:* A/C, TV, Wi-Fi, fridge, coffeemaker, hair dryer, iron, microwave.

WHERE TO DINE

To best enjoy Napa's restaurant scene, keep one thing in mind: You'll need reservations—especially for tables in renowned establishments.

Very Expensive

Redd ★★ CONTEMPORARY AMERICAN Chef Richard Reddington secured a spot among the valley's very best chefs when he opened this restaurant at the end of 2005. Though the modern and stark dining room is a little too white-on-white for my taste, the menu is definitely full flavored. Expect exceptional appetizers such as a delicate sashimi *hamachi* with edamame, cucumber, ginger, and sticky rice; and a cold foie gras trio with pistachios and brioche. For entrees, the Atlantic cod with chorizo, clams, and curry sauce is a dream dish that simultaneously manages to be rich *and* light. If your budget allows, definitely let the sommelier wine-pair the meal for you. Also, if you're looking for a lush brunch spot, this is it.

6480 Washington St., Yountville. ℭ **707/944-2222.** Reservations recommended. Main courses brunch and lunch $14–$25; main courses dinner $23–$29; 5-course tasting menu $70. AE, DISC, MC, V. Mon–Sat 11:30am–2:30pm; Sun 11am–2pm; daily 5:30–10pm; bar menu served 2:30pm–midnight nightly.

Moderate

All Seasons Café ★★ CALIFORNIA The best restaurant downtown balances homey charm with sophisticated, seasonally inspired dishes. Vibrant bouquets, large framed watercolors, and windows overlooking busy Lincoln Avenue soften the look of the black-and-white checkered flooring, brick red ceiling, and long, black wine bar. The laid-back service makes what arrives on the plate—such as crispy skin chicken with white truffle chicken *jus* or herb-roasted monkfish with fennel *nage*—that much more of a delicious surprise. More than 400 wines are available from their adjoining wine shop. (Buy next door, pay the $15 corkage fee, and you're still drinking for far less than at most restaurants.) Alas, the kitchen was a wee slow on my last visit, but all was forgiven when the food far surpassed my expectations.

1400 Lincoln Ave. (at Washington St.), Calistoga. ℭ **707/942-9111.** www.allseasonsnapavalley.net. Reservations recommended on weekends. Main courses $9–$11 lunch, $19–$28 dinner. DISC, MC, V. Fri–Sun noon–2:30pm; daily 6–9pm (times vary in winter, please call or go online to confirm).

Bistro Don Giovanni ★★ (Value) REGIONAL ITALIAN This bright, bustling, cheery Italian restaurant is one of my favorites in Napa Valley. The menu features pastas, risottos, pizzas (baked in a wood-burning oven), and a half-dozen other main courses. Every time I grab a menu, I can't get past the pasta with duck Bolognese and beet and green bean salad (although the latter is woefully skimpy). On the rare occasion that I venture from my favorite dishes here, I am equally smitten. The thin-crust pizzas fresh from the wood-burning oven, the seared salmon filet on buttermilk mashed potatoes, and the steak *frites* are excellent. On warm sunny days, I highly recommend dining alfresco on the patio. And no matter what, order the trifle for dessert. Seriously. *Note:* Service ranges from inattentive to great.

4110 Howard Lane (at St. Helena Hwy.), Napa. © **707/224-3300.** www.bistrodongiovanni.com. Reservations recommended. Main courses $12–$24. AE, DC, DISC, MC, V. Sun–Thurs 11:30am–10pm; Fri–Sat 11:30am–11pm.

Bistro Jeanty ★★ FRENCH BISTRO   This casual, warm bistro—with muted buttercup walls, patio seats, and two dining rooms divided by the bar—is French chef Philippe Jeanty's ode to rich French comfort food. The all-day menu includes tomato soup in puff pastry, foie gras pâté, steak tartare, and house-smoked trout with potato slices. No meal should start without a paper cone filled with fried smelt, and none should end without the crème brûlée, made with a thin layer of chocolate cream between classic vanilla custard and a caramelized sugar top. In between, prepare yourself for a rib-gripping free-for-all, including coq au vin, cassoulet, and juicy, thick-cut pork chop with *jus*, spinach, and mashed potatoes.

6510 Washington St., Yountville. © **707/944-0103.** www.bistrojeanty.com. Reservations recommended. Appetizers $8.50–$13; most main courses $15–$29. AE, MC, V. Daily 11:30am–10:30pm.

Bouchon ★★ FRENCH BISTRO   If you're looking for a delicious, moderately priced meal in city-chic, lovely environs, this is your best bet. Perhaps to appease the crowds who never get a reservation at nearby French Laundry, Thomas Keller opened this far more casual—but still delicious and very sexy—French brasserie. Along with a raw bar, expect superb renditions of steak *frites*, mussels meunière, grilled-cheese sandwiches, and other heavenly French classics (try the expensive and rich foie gras pâté, which is made at French Laundry).

6534 Washington St. (at Humboldt), Yountville. © **707/944-8037.** www.frenchlaundry.com. Reservations recommended during the week, required on weekends. Main courses $16–$30. AE, MC, V. Daily 11:30am–12:30am.

Tra Vigne Restaurant ★ Overrated ITALIAN   As much as I want to love everything about this famous, absurdly scenic restaurant, I can't—anymore. With lots of chef changes over the years and meals that range from totally rockin' to barely so-so, it's just not the sure thing it used to be. If you sit in the Tuscany-evoking courtyard, however, you'll likely enjoy yourself regardless of whether the kitchen is on the money or missing the mark. The bustling, cavernous dining room and happening bar are fine for chilly days and eves, but they're not nearly as magical. You can also count on wonderful bread (served with house-cured olives), a menu of robust California dishes cooked Italian-style, a daily oven-roasted pizza special, lots of pastas, and such tried-and-true standbys as short ribs and *fritto misto.*

1050 Charter Oak Ave., St. Helena. © **707/963-4444.** www.travigrnerestaurant.com. Reservations recommended. Main courses $15–$26. DC, DISC, MC, V. Summer daily 11:30am–10pm; winter Sun–Thurs 11:30am–9pm, Fri–Sat 11:30am–10pm.

Inexpensive
Taylor's Automatic Refresher Overrated DINER   This gourmet roadside burger shack, built in 1949, has slipped into mediocrity. Perhaps the trouble is that the owners now keep a closer watch on their San Francisco and Napa outposts. In any case, it's still the only casual burger joint in St. Helena, with ahi tuna burgers, tacos, salads, and classic

> **(Tips) Gourmet Picnics, Napa Style**
>
> You could plan your entire trip around Napa restaurants, but the valley is also an ideal place for a picnic. One of the finest gourmet food stores in the Wine Country, if not the state, the **Oakville Grocery Co.,** 7856 St. Helena Hwy., at Oakville Cross Road (© **707/944-8802;** www.oakvillegrocery.com), is the best place to fill a basket. The store is crammed with the very best breads, cheeses, pâtés, cold cuts, fresh foie gras, smoked Norwegian salmon, fresh caviar (beluga, sevruga, osetra), and prepared foods; its selection of California wines is also exceptional. Assemble your own picnic or let the staff prepare a basket for you, with 24-hours notice. The Grocery Co. is open daily from 9am to 6pm; it also has an espresso bar (Mon–Fri 7am–6pm; Sat–Sun 8am–6pm), with breakfast and lunch fare, including homemade pastries.
>
> A Manhattan import, **Dean & Deluca,** 607 S. Main St. (Hwy. 29), north of Zinfandel Lane and south of Sulphur Springs Road, in St. Helena (© **707/967-9980;** www.deananddeluca.com), is like a world's fair of beautifully displayed foods, often painfully pricey. Check out the 300 domestic and imported cheeses; tapenade, pastas, oils, hand-packed dried herbs and spices, chocolates, sauces, and cookware; an espresso bar; one heck of a bakery section; and more. The wine shop boasts a 1,200-label collection. It's open daily from 9am to 8pm (the espresso bar opens daily at 7am).

shakes. And it still draws huge lines of tourists, who love ordering at the counter or feasting alfresco at picnic tables.

933 Main St., St. Helena. © **707/963-3486.** www.taylorsrefresher.com. Main courses $4–$20. AE, MC, V. Daily 11am–8pm (9pm in summer).

ZuZu ★★ TAPAS   ZuZu lures neighborhood regulars with its no-reservation policy, its cramped but friendly wine and beer bar, and its affordable Mediterranean small plates, meant to be shared. The comfortable, warm atmosphere is anything but corporate. Equally casual and personal, the menu includes sizzling miniskillets of tangy, fantastic paella; addictive prawns with pimento dipping sauce for bread; light and delicate sea scallop ceviche salad; and Moroccan barbecued lamb chops with a sweet-and-spicy sauce. Desserts aren't as good, but with more tasty plates than you can possibly devour, who cares?

829 Main St., Napa. © **707/224-8555.** Reservations not accepted. Tapas $3–$13. MC, V. Mon–Thurs 11:30am–10pm; Fri 11:30am–11pm; Sat 4–11pm; Sun 4–9pm.

2 SONOMA VALLEY

Sonoma is often regarded as the "other" Wine Country, forever in the shadow of Napa Valley. The truth, however, is that it's a distinct experience. Sonoma still manages to feel like backcountry, thanks to its lower density of wineries, restaurants, and hotels; because it's far less traveled than Napa, it offers a more genuine escape. Small, family-owned wineries are its mainstay—as in the early days of California winemaking, when everyone

Bella Vineyards &
Wine Caves **6**
Ferrari-Carano Vineyards
& Winery **7**
J Vineyards & Winery **3**
Korbell Champagne Cellars **1**
Passalacqua **4**
Preston of Dry Creek **5**
Rochioli Vineyard & Winery **2**

THE WINE COUNTRY

7

SONOMA VALLEY

started with the intention of going broke and loving every minute of it. Unlike the rigidly structured tours at many of Napa Valley's corporate-owned wineries, tastings and tours on the Sonoma side of the Mayacamas Mountains are usually low-key, with plenty of friendly banter between staff and guests.

ESSENTIALS

GETTING THERE   From San Francisco, cross the Golden Gate Bridge and head north on U.S. 101. Exit at Highway 37; after 10 miles, turn north onto Highway 121. After another 10 miles, turn north onto Highway 12 (Broadway), which will take you directly into the town of Sonoma.

VISITOR INFORMATION   While you're in Sonoma, stop by the **Sonoma Valley Visitors Bureau,** 453 First St. E. (© **866/996-1090** or 707/996-1090; www.sonomavalley. com). It's open Monday through Saturday from 9am to 5pm (6pm in the summer) and Sunday 10am to 5pm. If you prefer advance information from the bureau, contact them to order the free *Sonoma Valley Visitors Guide,* which lists almost every lodge, winery, and restaurant in the valley. An additional **Visitors Bureau** is a few miles south of the square at Cornerstone Festival of Gardens at 23570 Arnold Dr. (Hwy. 121; © **866/996-1090**); it's open daily from 9am to 4pm, till 5pm during summer.

TOURING THE VALLEY & WINERIES

Sonoma Valley is currently home to about 40 wineries (including California's first, Buena Vista, founded in 1857) and 13,000 acres of vineyards, which produce more than five million cases a year of 25 types of wine.

The towns and wineries below are organized geographically from south to north, starting at the intersection of Highway 37 and Highway 121 in the Carneros District and ending in Kenwood. The wineries here are a little more spread out than they are in Napa, so devise a touring strategy before you set out, to avoid backtracking a lot.

I've reviewed some my favorite Sonoma Valley wineries here—more than enough to keep you busy tasting wine for a long weekend. For a complete list, pick up one of the free guides to the valley available at the Sonoma Valley Visitors Bureau (see "Visitor Information," above).

The Carneros District

As you approach the Wine Country from the south, you must pass through the Carneros District, a cool, wind-swept region that borders the San Pablo Bay and marks the entrance to both Napa and Sonoma valleys. Until the latter part of the 20th century, this mixture of marsh, sloughs, and hills was mainly used as sheep pasture (*carneros* means "sheep" in Spanish). After experimental plantings yielded slow-growing yet high-quality grapes—particularly chardonnay and pinot noir—several Napa and Sonoma wineries expanded here, eventually establishing the Carneros District as an American Viticultural Appellation.

Viansa Winery and Italian Marketplace ★ (Finds)   This sprawling Tuscan-style villa sitting atop a knoll overlooking the entire lower valley is the brainchild of Sam and Vicki Sebastiani, who left the family dynasty to create their own temple to food and wine. (*Viansa* is a contraction of "Vicki and Sam.") Here you'll find a large room crammed with a cornucopia of high-quality mustards, olive oils, pastas, salads, breads, desserts, Italian tableware, cookbooks, and wine-related gifts as well as tasting opportunities.

The winery, which does extensive mail-order business through the Tuscan Club, features Italian varietals. Tastings cost $5 per person and are offered at the east and west end of the marketplace. The self-guided tour includes a trip through the underground barrel-aging cellar, adorned with colorful hand-painted murals. Guided tours, held at 11am, 2pm, and 3pm, will set you back $10.

Viansa is also one of the few wineries in Sonoma Valley that sells deli items—the focaccia sandwiches are delicious.

25200 Arnold Dr. (Calif. 121), Sonoma. ℂ 800/995-4740 or 707/935-4700. www.viansa.com. Daily 10am–5pm. Daily self-guided tours. Guided tours daily 11am, 2pm, and 3pm, $10.

Gloria Ferrer Champagne Caves ★ (Finds) Gloria Ferrer, the grande dame of the Sonoma Valley's sparkling-wine producers, is named after José Ferrer's wife, whose family has made sparkling wine for 5 centuries. The family business, Freixenet, is the world's largest producer of sparkling wine. That legacy amounts to big bucks, and certainly a good chunk of change went into building this palatial estate. It glimmers like Oz, high atop a gently sloping hill, overlooking the verdant Carneros District. On a sunny day, enjoying a glass of dry *brut* while soaking in the magnificent views is a must.

If you're unfamiliar with the term *méthode champenoise,* take the $10 tasting and 30-minute tour of the fermenting tanks, bottling line, and caves brimming with racks of yeast-laden bottles. Afterward, retire to the elegant tasting room, order a glass of one of seven sparkling wines ($4–$10 a glass) or tastes of their eight still wines ($2–$3 per taste), find an empty chair on the veranda, and say, "Ahhh. *This* is the life." There are picnic tables, but it's usually too windy for comfort. You must buy a bottle (from around $18–$50) or glass of sparkling wine to reserve a table.

23555 Carneros Hwy. (Calif. 121), Sonoma. ℂ 707/996-7256. www.gloriaferrer.com. Daily 10am–5pm. Tours daily; call day of visit to confirm schedule.

Sonoma

Sonoma, at the northern boundary of the Carneros District along Highway 12, is the centerpiece of the valley. The midsize town owes much of its appeal to Mexican general Mariano Guadalupe Vallejo, who fashioned this pleasant, slow-paced community after a typical Mexican village—right down to its central plaza, Sonoma's geographical and commercial center. The plaza sits at the top of a T formed by Broadway (Hwy. 12) and Napa Street. Most of the surrounding streets form a grid pattern around this axis, making Sonoma easy to negotiate. The plaza's Bear Flag Monument marks the spot where the crude Bear Flag was raised in 1846, signaling the end of Mexican rule; the symbol was later adopted by the state of California and placed on its flag. The 8-acre park at the center of the plaza, complete with two ponds populated by ducks and geese, is perfect for an afternoon siesta in the cool shade.

The best way to see the town is to follow the **Sonoma Walking Tour** map, provided by the Sonoma League for Historic Preservation. Highlights include General Vallejo's 1852 Victorian-style home; the Sonoma Barracks, erected in 1836 to house Mexican army troops; and the Blue Wing Inn, an 1840 hostelry built to accommodate new settlers and travelers such as John Fremont, Kit Carson, and Ulysses S. Grant. You can purchase the $3 map at the Mission (see below).

The **Mission San Francisco Solano de Sonoma,** on Sonoma Plaza, at the corner of First Street East and Spain Street (ℂ 707/938-9560), was founded in 1823. It was the northernmost mission built in California. It was also the only one established on the Northern Coast by Mexican rulers, who wished to protect their territory from Russian fur traders. It's now part of Sonoma State Historic Park. Admission is $2 for adults, free for children ages 16 and under. It's open daily from 10am to 5pm except Thanksgiving, Christmas, and New Year's Day.

Sebastiani Vineyards & Winery   The name Sebastiani is practically synonymous with Sonoma. What started in 1904, when Samuele Sebastiani began producing his first wines, has in three generations grown into a small empire, producing some 350,000 cases a year. The original 1904 property is open to the public, with educational tours ($5–$7.50 per person), an 80-foot S-shaped tasting bar, and lots of gift-shopping opportunities. In the contemporary tasting room's minimuseum area you can see the winery's original turn-of-the-20th-century crusher and press, as well as the world's largest collection of oak-barrel carvings, crafted by bygone local artist Earle Brown. You can sample three Sonoma County wines for $5 or a flight of four for $10. Bottle prices are reasonable, ranging from $13 to $75. A picnic area adjoins the cellars; a far more scenic spot is across the parking lot in Sebastiani's Cherryblock Vineyards.

389 Fourth St. E., Sonoma. © **800/888-5532** or 707/933-3200. www.sebastiani.com. Daily 10am–5pm. Tours daily 11am, 1pm, and 3pm with an additional tour at noon Sat–Sun.

Buena Vista Winery   Count Agoston Haraszthy, the Hungarian émigré universally regarded as the father of California's wine industry, founded this historic winery in 1857. A close friend of General Vallejo, Haraszthy returned from Europe in 1861 with 100,000 of the finest vine cuttings, which he made available to all growers. Although Buena Vista's winemaking now takes place at an ultramodern facility in the Carneros District, the winery maintains a tasting room inside the restored 1862 Press House. The beautiful stone-crafted room brims with wines, wine-related gifts, and accessories.

Tastings are $5 for four wines, $10 for a flight of three library wines. You can take the free self-guided tour any time during operating hours, but their $20 "Carneros Experience" requires a reservation and pairs five wines with a small plate of food, including cheeses. A selection of cheeses, salami, bread, and spreads are all available in the tasting room.

18000 Old Winery Rd. (off E. Napa St., slightly northeast of downtown), Sonoma. © **800/926-1266** or 707/265-1472. www.buenavistawinery.com. Daily 10am–5pm

Ravenswood Winery   Ravenswood established itself as the sine qua non of zinfandel, the versatile grape that's gaining ground on cabernet sauvignon. In fact, Ravenswood was the first U.S. winery to focus primarily on zins, about three-quarters of the company's astonishing one-million-case production; it also produces merlot, cabernet sauvignon, Rhone varietals, and a small amount of chardonnay.

The winery is smartly designed—recessed into the hillside to protect its treasures from the simmering summer heat. Tours ($15 per person) follow the winemaking process from grape to glass and include a visit to the aromatic oak-barrel aging rooms. You're welcome to bring your own picnic basket to any of the tables, but if you're coming on the weekend from Memorial Day to Labor Day, consider joining one of the winery's famously fun barbecues (call for details). Tastings are $10 to $15 for four wines, and the fee is refundable with purchase.

18701 Gehricke Rd. (off Lovall Valley Rd.), Sonoma. © **888/NO-WIMPY** or 707/933-2332. www.ravenswoodwinery.com. Labor Day to Memorial Day 10am–4:30pm; Memorial Day to Labor Day 10am–5pm. Tours at 10:30am; reservations recommended.

Glen Ellen

Glen Ellen is a fraction of the size of Sonoma, 7 miles to the south, but it's home to several of the valley's finest wineries, restaurants, and inns. Aside from the addition of a few new restaurants, this charming Wine Country town hasn't changed much since the days when Jack London settled on his Beauty Ranch, a mile west. If you haven't yet decided where you want to set up camp during your visit to the Wine Country, I highly recommend this lovable little town.

Hikers, horseback riders, and picnickers will enjoy **Jack London State Historic Park,** 2400 London Ranch Rd., off Arnold Drive (© 707/938-5216; www.jacklondonpark. com). Within its 800 acres, which were once home to the renowned writer, you'll find 9 miles of trails, the remains of London's burned-down dream house, a museum, and many ideal picnic spots. The park is open daily from 9:30am to 5pm. Admission is $6 per car or $5 per seniors' car.

Benziger Family Winery ★ (Finds)   At any given time, two generations of Benzigers (*Ben*-zig-ger) may be running around tending to chores, and they instantly make you feel as if you're part of the clan. The pastoral, user-friendly property features an exceptional self-guided tour—"the most comprehensive tour in the wine industry," according to *Wine Spectator*—gardens, a spacious tasting room staffed by amiable folk, and an art gallery. The fun, informative 45-minute tram tour ($15 for adults, $5 for kids), pulled by a beefy tractor, winds through the estate vineyards and into caves, and ends with a tasting of one estate wine. *Tip:* Tram tickets—a hot item in the summer—are available on a first-come, first-served basis, so arrive early or stop by in the morning to pick up tickets for the afternoon.

Tastings for standard-release wines are $5. Tastes of limited-production, reserve, or estate wines cost $15. The winery has several picnic spots.

1883 London Ranch Rd. (off Arnold Dr., on the way to Jack London State Historic Park), Glen Ellen. © **888/ 490-2739** or 707/935-3000. www.benziger.com. Tasting room daily 10am–5pm. Tram tours daily (weather permitting) $15 adults, $5 children, every half-hour, 10:30am–3:30pm.

Kenwood

A few miles north of Glen Ellen along Highway 12 is the tiny town of Kenwood, the northernmost outpost of the Sonoma Valley. The town consists of little more than a few restaurants, wineries, and modest homes in the wooded hillsides.

Château St. Jean ★ (Finds)   Château St. Jean is notable for its exceptionally beautiful buildings, expansive landscaped grounds, gourmet market–like tasting room, and tasty wines. Among California wineries, it's a pioneer in *vineyard designation*—the procedure of making wine from, and naming it for, a single vineyard. A private drive takes you to what was once a 250-acre country retreat built in 1920; a well-manicured lawn overlooking the meticulously maintained vineyards is now a picnic area, complete with a fountain and picnic tables.

In the huge tasting room—with a charcuterie shop and housewares for sale—you can sample Château St. Jean's bounty, from chardonnays and cabernet sauvignon to fumé blanc, merlot, Johannesburg Riesling, and Gewürztraminer. Tastings are $10 per person, $15 per person for reserve wines.

8555 Sonoma Hwy. (Calif. 12), Kenwood. © **800/543-7572** or 707/833-4134. www.chateaustjean.com. Tasting daily 10am–4:30pm. Tour times vary depending on the weather, so call ahead to confirm. At the foot of Sugarloaf Ridge, just north of Kenwood and east of Hwy. 12.

WHERE TO STAY

If you are having trouble finding a room, call the **Sonoma Valley Visitors Bureau** (© **866/996-1090** or 707/996-1090; www.sonomavalley.com). The staff will try to refer you to a lodging that has a room to spare but won't make reservations for you. Another option is the **Bed and Breakfast Association of Sonoma Valley** (*©* **800/969-4667;** www.sonomabb.com), which can refer you to a B&B that belongs to the association.

Very Expensive

Fairmont Sonoma Mission Inn & Spa ★★★   As you drive through Boyes Hot Springs, you may wonder why someone decided to build a multimillion-dollar spa resort in this ordinary little town. There's no view to speak of, and it certainly isn't within walking distance of any wineries or fancy restaurants. So what's the deal? It's the naturally heated artesian mineral water, piped from directly underneath the spa into the temperature-controlled pools and whirlpools. Set on 12 meticulously groomed acres, the Sonoma Mission Inn consists of a massive, three-story replica of a Spanish mission, built in 1927; an array of satellite wings with numerous super-luxury suites; and world-class spa facilities. It's a popular retreat for the wealthy and well known, so don't be surprised if you see a famous face. The resort also has the Sonoma Golf Club, home to the PGA championship every October.

101 Boyes Blvd., corner of Boyes Blvd. and Calif. 12, P.O. Box 1447, Sonoma, CA 95476. *©* **800/441-1414** or 707/938-9000. Fax 707/938-4250. www.fairmont.com/sonoma. 226 units. $259–$1,259 double. AE, DC, MC, V. Valet parking is free for day use (spa-goers) and $14 for overnight guests. From central Sonoma, drive 3 miles north on Hwy. 12 and turn left on Boyes Blvd. **Amenities:** 2 restaurants; 3 large, heated outdoor pools; golf course; health club and spa; Jacuzzi; sauna; bike rental; concierge; business center; salon; room service; babysitting; same-day laundry service/dry cleaning; free wine tasting (4:30–5:30pm). *In room:* A/C, TV, high-speed Internet access ($13/day), minibar, hair dryer, iron, safe, free bottle of wine upon arrival.

Gaige House Inn ★★★ Finds   Recently taken over by the slick Thompson hotel group, this remains Wine Country's finest B&B. Here everything is luxurious: Silk-soft linens and premium down comforters grace firm mattresses, furniture and artwork are of museum quality, and breakfast and appetizers are prepared with herbs from the garden by an impressive in-house chef. Behind the inn is a 1½-acre oasis with perfectly manicured lawns, a 40-foot-long swimming pool, and a creekside hammock under a Heritage oak. All rooms have private bathrooms and king- or queen-size beds; two rooms have Jacuzzi tubs, and several have fireplaces. The eight spa garden suites have, among other delights, granite soaking tubs. On sunny days, breakfast is served at individual tables on the large terrace. Evenings are best spent sipping premium wines in the reading parlor.

13540 Arnold Dr., Glen Ellen, CA 95442. *©* **800/935-0237** or 707/935-0237. Fax 707/935-6411. www. thompsonhotels.com. 23 units. Summer $365–$375 double, $395–$695 suite; winter $200–$595. Rates include evening wines. AE, DC, DISC, MC, V. **Amenities:** Large heated pool; free Wi-Fi; in-room massage. *In room:* A/C, TV/DVD, high-speed Internet access, Wi-Fi, fridge, hair dryer, iron, safe.

Moderate

Beltane Ranch ★ Finds   The word *ranch* conjures up an image of a big ol' two-story house amid hundreds of rolling acres—the kind of place where you laze away the day watching the grass grow or pitching horseshoes in the garden. Well, friend, you can have all that and more at the well-located Beltane Ranch, a century-old buttercup-yellow manor that has been everything from a bunkhouse to a brothel to a turkey farm. You simply can't help but feel your tensions ease away as you prop up your feet on the shady, wraparound porch overlooking the quiet vineyards and sip a cool, fruity chardonnay while reading *Lonesome Dove* for the third time. Each room is uniquely decorated with American and European antiques; all have sitting areas and separate entrances. A big, creative country breakfast is served in the garden or on the porch overlooking the vine-yards. For exercise, you can play tennis on the private court or hike the trails meandering through the 105-acre estate. The staff here is knowledgeable and helpful. *Tip:* Request one of the upstairs rooms, which have the best views.

11775 Sonoma Hwy./Hwy. 12, P.O. Box 395, Glen Ellen, CA 95442. *(©* **707/996-6501.** www.beltaneranch. com. 5 units, 1 cottage. $150–$220 double. Rates include full breakfast. No credit cards; personal checks accepted. **Amenities:** Tennis court (unlit). *In room:* No phone.

Best Western Sonoma Valley Inn (**Kids**) Perfect for the traveling family, this simple inn with recently updated rooms offers plenty of diversions for kids on the road. There's room to run around, plus a large heated outdoor saltwater pool, gazebo-covered spa, and sauna to play in. The rooms come with a lot of perks, such as continental breakfast delivered to your room each morning, a gift bottle of white Sonoma Valley wine (chilling in the fridge), and satellite TV with HBO. Most rooms have a balcony or a deck over-looking the inner courtyard. An added bonus: If you need someone to help you get the kinks out, you can reserve one of the two spa rooms and have the staff book someone from an outside company to come in and give you a massage. The inn is also in a good location, just a block from Sonoma's plaza.

550 Second St. W. (1 block from the plaza), Sonoma, CA 95476. *(©* **800/334-5784** or 707/938-9200. Fax 707/938-0935. www.sonomavalleyinn.com. 80 units. $114–$369 double. Rates include continental breakfast. AE, DC, DISC, MC, V. **Amenities:** Heated outdoor pool; exercise room; Jacuzzi; sauna; steam room. *In room:* A/C, TV, free Wi-Fi, fridge, coffeemaker, hair dryer, iron.

The Renaissance Lodge at Sonoma ★★ Downtown Sonoma's only large-scale hotel takes into account its surroundings, offering some country charm in its 182 rooms. At the center of the resort is a U-shaped building with a classic big-hotel lobby and a large courtyard swimming pool with plenty of lounge chairs. The tasteful and spacious accommodations in the main building are decorated in earth tones and come complete with prints by local artists, artistic lighting fixtures, balconies or patios, and some fire-places and tubs with shutters that open from the bathroom to the bedroom. Surrounded by trees, flowers, and shrubs and offering a sense of seclusion, the two-story cottages along the property are especially appealing. The **Raindance Spa,** where I've consistently had exceptional massages, makes excellent use of its outdoor public space with a number of small pools surrounded by lush plants. As a bonus after your treatment, you can hang around the pool all day if you wish.

1325 Broadway, Sonoma, CA 95476. *(©* **888/710-8008** or 707/935-6600. Fax 707/935-6829. www.the lodgeatsonoma.com. 182 units. $249–$449 double. AE, MC, V. **Amenities:** Restaurant; large heated out-door pool; health club and spa; Jacuzzi; concierge; business center; room service. *In room:* A/C, TV w/pay movies, wet bar in suites and some rooms, coffeemaker, hair dryer, iron, iPod docks.

WHERE TO DINE

Though Sonoma Valley has far fewer visitors than Napa Valley, its restaurants are often equally crowded, so be sure to make reservations in advance.

Expensive

the girl & the fig ★★ COUNTRY FRENCH Chris Jones orchestrates the French-influenced nouveau country cuisine at this well-loved restaurant owned by Sondra Bern-stein. She would be the girl and, yes, figs are sure to be on the menu in one form or another. The wonderful winter fig salad contains arugula, pecans, dried figs, Laura Chenel goat cheese, and fig-and-port vinaigrette. Murray uses garden-fresh produce and

Tips **Gourmet Picnics, Sonoma Style**

Sonoma's central plaza, with its many picnic tables, is an optimal spot to set up your own lunch spread. The venerable **Sonoma Cheese Factory,** on the plaza at 2 Spain St. (*©* **707/996-1000;** daily 8:30am–5:30pm), sells award-winning house-made cheeses and imported meats and cheeses; a few are set out for tasting every day. Caviar, gourmet salads, pâté, and homemade Sonoma Jack cheese are also for sale. You can pick up some good, inexpensive sandwiches too—such as the fire-roasted pork loin or New York steak.

local meats, poultry, and fish whenever possible, in dishes such as grilled pork chops or duck confit. For dessert, try lavender crème brûlée, a glass of Jaboulet muscat, and a sliver of *raclette* from the cheese list. Sondra knows her wines, features Rhone varietals, and will be happy to choose the best accompaniment for your meal. Sunday brunch, until 3pm, is worthwhile.

110 W. Spain St., Sonoma. *©* 707/938-3634. www.thegirlandthefig.com. Reservations recommended. Main courses $13–$24. AE, DISC, MC, V. Daily 11:30am–10pm; Sun brunch 10am. Late-night brasserie menu until 11pm Fri and Sat.

Moderate

Cafe La Haye ★★ ECLECTIC   Well-prepared and wholesome food, an experienced waitstaff, friendly owners, a soothing neighborhood atmosphere, and reasonable prices— including a modestly priced wine list—make La Haye a favorite. Expect a risotto special; pasta such as fresh *tagliarini* with butternut squash, prosciutto, sage, and garlic cream; and pan-roasted chicken breast, perhaps with goat cheese–herb stuffing, caramelized shallot *jus,* and fennel mashed potatoes. The filet of beef seared with black pepper-lavender sauce, served with Gorgonzola-potato gratin, is sure to please meat lovers.

140 E. Napa St., Sonoma. *©* 707/935-5994. Reservations recommended. Main courses $14–$24. AE, MC, V. Tues–Sat 5:30–9pm.

Della Santina's ★ TUSCAN   Follow the locals to this friendly, traditional Italian restaurant. How traditional? Ask father-and-son team Dan and Robert, who will point out Signora Santina's hand-embroidered linen doilies and proudly tell you about her Tuscan recipes. (Heck, even the dining room looks like an old-fashioned Italian living room.) And their pride is merited: Dishes are authentic and well flavored, without overbearing sauces or one *hint* of California pretension. Be sure to start with traditional antipasti, especially sliced mozzarella and tomatoes, or delicious white beans. The nine pasta dishes are wonderfully authentic (gnocchi lovers, rejoice!). The spit-roasted meat dishes are a local favorite; for those who can't choose between chicken, pork, turkey, rabbit, or duck, one menu option offers a choice of three. Don't worry about breaking your bank on a bottle of wine, because many choices here go for less than $40. Portions are huge, but be sure to save room for the creamy *panna cotta.* **Tip:** The inside is small, but a huge back patio, covered in blooming trellises, is full practically every night in the summer (though the wait's never too bad). They've recently tented part of it, so you can eat back there in winter, too, weather permitting.

133 E. Napa St. (just east of the square), Sonoma. ℂ **707/935-0576.** www.dellasantinas.com. Reservations recommended. Main courses $11–$18. AE, DISC, MC, V. Daily 11:30am–3pm and 5–9:30pm.

El Dorado Kitchen ★★ CALIFORNIA Downtown Sonoma's most hip and contemporary restaurant, which has sexy seating indoors and out, entices with a seasonal menu ("Mediterranean-inspired bistro cuisine") of familiar items with unfamiliar twists— think griddled prosciutto and Vermont cheddar with San Marzano tomato soup or curry *fritto misto* (lightly battered and fried apples, cauliflower, and fall squash served with curry salt and aioli). Entrees might include Pacific salmon with white bean cassoulet, prosciutto, and sage, or lamb loin with rosemary polenta, *piquillo* peppers, Swiss chard, and Niçoise olive sauce. Don't hesitate to order the white truffle and Parmesan french fries and one of their house drinks.

405 First St. W., Sonoma. ℂ **707/996-3030.** www.eldoradosonoma.com. Reservations recommended. Lunch $8–$17, dinner $8–$26, brunch $8–$18. Daily 11:30am–2:30pm and 5:30–9pm.

Harvest Moon ★★ REGIONAL SEASONAL AMERICAN If great food is essential to your experience, don't miss this restaurant run by chef/owner Nick Demarest, whose experience at Berkeley's world famous Chez Panisse is evidenced by his use of outstanding ingredients combined into dishes of clean, pure, and glorious flavors. His chicory salad with mustard vinaigrette, house-cured bacon, and Gruyère is a case-in-point appetizer that's easily backed up by entrees such as pan-fried local rock cod with Swiss chard, fingerling potatoes, and *beurre rouge*. Sweetening the already delicious deal, his wife Jen is a pedigreed pastry chef. The interior is awkward, with the chef hard at work within the shoebox-size open kitchen and a quirky scattering of tables tucked within a cramped and warm historic adobe room. But there are great seats at the wine bar, and, weather permitting, the back garden dining is spacious and relaxed. Regardless, if it's a good meal your after, you will not find a better one this side of the Mayacamas.

487 First St. W., Sonoma. ℂ **707/933-8160.** www.harvestmoonsonoma.com. Reservations recommended. Main courses $17–$25. AE, DISC, MC, V. Sun–Thurs 5:30–9pm; Fri–Sat 5:30–9:30pm.

Shiso ★ MODERN ASIAN/SUSHI Named for a Japanese mint leaf that's referenced throughout the restaurant, this modern, airy spot is the place to come for sushi and Japanese cuisine with Americanized flair. Grab a table or sit at the sushi bar and go directly to the fresh, seasonal shared plates—miso-glazed butterfish with Chinese long beans and miso emulsion, or braised beef short ribs with glazed daikon and carrots. The specials menu changes nightly and features exotic spins on the freshest local finds (think skate with sautéed stinging nettles and *uni*—sea urchin—cream sauce). You'll find good sushi here, too, from traditional nigiri, sashimi, and rolls (tuna, *negi hama,* California) to creative combinations. Though the food is tasty, it's the little touches, such as coffee served in French press pots and luscious desserts, that makes this place a real standout.

522 Broadway (just off the plaza), Sonoma. ℂ **707/933-9331.** www.shisorestaurant.com. Reservations accepted. Entrees $9–$13 lunch; $15–$45 dinner; $3.75–$50 sushi and sashimi. AE, DISC, MC, V. Winter Wed–Sun 5:30–9:30pm; summer Wed–Sun noon–2pm and Tues–Sun 5:30–9:30pm; hours are seasonal, so please call to confirm.

Swiss Hotel ★ CONTINENTAL/NORTHERN ITALIAN With its slanting floors and beamed ceilings, the historic Swiss Hotel, in the town center, is a Sonoma landmark and the local favorite for fine, satisfying food at reasonable prices. The turn-of-the-20th-century oak bar is adorned with black-and-white photos of pioneering Sonomans. The white dining room and sidewalk patio seats are a pleasant place to enjoy lunch specials such as penne with chicken, mushrooms, and tomato cream; hot sandwiches; and California-style pizzas fired in a wood-burning oven. But the secret spot is the very atmospheric back garden patio—a secluded oasis shaded by a wisteria-covered trellis and adorned with plants, a fountain, gingham tablecloths, and a fireplace. Dinner might start with a warm winter salad of radicchio and frisée with pears, walnuts, and blue cheese. My favorite main courses include linguine and prawns with garlic, hot pepper, and tomatoes; the filet mignon wrapped in blue-cheese crust; and roasted rosemary chicken.

18 W. Spain St (at First St. W.), Sonoma. ℭ **707/938-2884.** www.swisshotelsonoma.com. Reservations recommended. Main courses lunch $8–$17, dinner $13–$28. AE, MC, V. Daily 11:30am–2:30pm; Sun–Thurs 5–9pm; Fri–Sat 5–10pm. Bar daily 11:30am–2am.

Inexpensive

Black Bear Diner ⓚⓘⓓⓢ DINER   When you're craving a classic American breakfast, with all the cholesterol and the fixings, make a beeline to this old-fashioned diner. One, it's fun, with its over-the-top bear paraphernalia, gazette-style menu listing local news from 1961 and every possible diner favorite, and absurdly friendly waitstaff. Two, it's darned cheap. Three, helpings are huge. Four, it appeals to all ages: Kids get a kick out of the coloring books, old-timers reminisce over Sinatra on the jukebox, and everyone leaves stuffed on omelets, scrambles, and pancakes. Lunch and dinner feature steak sandwiches, salads, and comfort foods such as barbecued pork ribs, roast beef, fish and chips, and spaghetti with meat sauce. You can fill up here on the cheap, especially since dinners come with salad or soup, bread, and two sides; seniors can order from a specially discounted menu.

201 West Napa St. (at Second St.), Sonoma. ℭ **707/935-6800.** www.blackbeardiner.com. Main courses breakfast $5–$8.50, lunch and dinner $5.50–$17. AE, DISC, MC, V. Daily 6am–9:30pm (closing varies on weekends, depending on business).

3 NORTHERN SONOMA

Most visitors to Northern California Wine Country relegate their vacation time to Napa Valley or Sonoma Valley. But insiders have long known that the best of both worlds can be found in Northern Sonoma. Here, amid hundreds of acres of vineyards, are family-owned wineries, adorable B&Bs, charming towns, friendly residents, classic river fun in summertime, and of course more than your share of outstanding food and wine experiences. Add to that the best shopping (in Healdsburg) and less traffic on the charming country roads and in the tasting rooms and you might begin to understand why this region has become a bona fide hot spot.

ESSENTIALS

GETTING THERE   From San Francisco, cross the Golden Gate Bridge and head north on U.S. 101. It's around 1¹⁄₂ hours to Healdsburg, the wine area's commercial and social hub.

VISITOR INFORMATION   Northern Sonoma doesn't have one major convention and visitors bureau representing the entire region. Fortunately, if you visit **www.sonoma.com**, it will direct you to the various visitors bureaus. However, there's plenty of information available should you contact the following sources. The **Santa Rosa Convention & Visitors Bureau,** 9 Fourth St., Santa Rosa, CA 95401 (ℭ **800/404-7673** or 707/577-8674), can give you the scoop on all things Santa Rosa, as well as a bit about the areas and wineries to the north. Or you can get information by visiting **www.visitsantarosa.com**.

the **Healdsburg Chamber of Commerce and Visitors Bureau** (217 Healdsburg Ave., Healdsburg; ℂ **800/648-9922** from within California or 707/433-6935; www.healdsburg. com). It's definitely worth a pit stop to get brochures and answers to any questions from their very helpful staff.

TOURING THE VALLEY & WINERIES

Touring Northern Sonoma is very different from the winery-hopping in Napa and Sonoma valleys. Sipping destinations are scattered over a vast landscape of tiny towns surrounded by open land, miles of vineyards, and great destinations for outdoor fun. And they're tucked away on one-lane roads that would be impossible to find if it weren't for the periodic white arrow signs pointing you in the right direction. They are also far more mom-and-pop, which means it's very likely you'll rub elbows with winemaker/owners as you taste at their bars. Alas, this piece of paradise has lately been touted as *the* hot vacation spot, but it's still less crowded than the alternatives. Of course, you should chart your path—or at least attempt to—before going. But keep in mind that the diversions you'll stumble upon along the way are likely to slow you down—in a good way.

Guerneville
69 miles N of San Francisco

The town closest to the Russian River may be short on wineries, but it's long on outdoor fun.

One of my all-time favorite summertime excursions—canoeing—can be embarked upon from the tiny area of Forestville, adjacent to Guerneville. At **Burke's Canoes,** 8600 River Rd., at Mirabel Rd. (ℂ **707/887-1222;** www.burkescanoetrips.com), it's an all-day adventure. You simply pack a lunch (ideally wrapped in a waterproof bag), park the car, leave all your valuables in the trunk, pay $58 (cash only) for a canoe that can comfortably fit three adults (the minimum required is two adults), throw on a bathing suit, sunscreen, and a life vest and launch yourself onto the Russian River. It's a leisurely paddle downstream, with the occasional tricky turn—especially during early summer when the water is higher. During the 10-mile journey, you'll pass beaches that beg for you to pause and bask, redwood trees, and kids jumping off rocks and rope swings, before arriving at a well-marked beach where Burke's staff will pick you up and take you back to your car. Though you can make the journey in about 3 hours, you're more likely to spend 4 or 5 with pit stops to swim, eat, and laze. Definitely reserve your canoe in advance. This is a popular activity. Also, Burke's welcomes good swimmers only—and children over 5 years of age.

Should you be more of a landlubber, you can also simply spread a towel and picnic feast at **Johnson's Beach** (near downtown Guerneville, off Church St.; ℂ **707/869-2022;** www.johnsonsbeach.com), a river resort with a big stretch of pebbly sand and snack bar that's popular with frolicking families. You can also rent a kayak, canoe, or paddleboat here from May to October. Don't come for an early morning or evening dip—the resort is only open from 10am to 6pm daily.

Another exceptional way to experience the natural beauty of this region is on **horseback.** Longtime residents Laura and Jonathan Ayers are behind the **Armstrong Woods Pack Station** (ℂ **707/887-2939;** http://redwoodhorses.com), which offers guided trail rides through old-growth redwood forests. All rides include instruction and a rest or lunch stop on top of a ridge with fabulous valley views. You can saddle up year-round, weather and trail conditions permitting. Prices start at $70 per adult and $65 per child for a 2$^{1}/_{2}$-hour ride.

To find out more about the Russian River area and its activities, contact the **Russian River Chamber of Commerce Visitors Center** (16209 First St., at the historic bridge, Guerneville; ✆ **877/644-9001** or 707/869-9000; www.russianriver.com).

Korbel Champagne Cellars   Okay, so technically they don't make—or cellar—"champagne" since they're not located in the region of the same name in France. But that doesn't stop visitors from sipping bubbly, getting a good buzz, and having a great time here. Set in a redwood grove at the eastern edge of the town of Guerneville, Korbel is a winemaking relic with more than 120 years of history under its grape-growing belt. You can peruse the ivy-draped brick winery and its stunning gardens, take an informative tour that explains their production process, and grab picnic snacks at their Delicatessen and Market. A bottle of bubbly will set you back $10 to $30, while tastes and tours are free. From mid-April through mid-October flower lovers should detour to browse the Antique Rose Gardens' 250 varieties of antique roses. To confirm tour times, call ✆ **707/824-7316.**

13250 River Rd. (at the eastern entrance of downtown), Guerneville. ✆ **707/824-7000.** www.korbel. com. Tasting room May 1–Sept 30 9am–5pm; Oct 1–Apr 30 9am–4:30pm. Tours in winter are daily, every hour on the hour 10am–3pm; in summer, Mon–Fri every 45 min. from 10am–3:45pm; weekends and holidays at 10am, 11am, and noon, and then every 45 min. until 3:45pm. Rose Garden tours are available mid-Apr through mid-Oct Tues–Sun at 11am, 1pm, and 3pm. From Hwy. 101, take the River Rd. exit, turn left (westbound) onto River Rd. and follow it for 13 miles.

Healdsburg
65 miles N of San Francisco

A mere 30- to 45-minute drive from either valley and just north of the burgeoning suburb of Santa Rosa, Healdburg's centerpiece historic square, which has been the heart of the town since its inception in 1857, captures the quaint shopping and dining experiences of downtown Sonoma—only better. Meanwhile, a few blocks away, rural roads lead to country B&Bs, homey wineries, and an abundance of Victorian architecture that gives the region an old-world charm. Adding to its intrinsic allure, the town is surrounded by all the premier viticultural areas, allowing for easy access to Russian River, Dry Creek, Alexander Valley, and Chalk Hill.

Rather than driving from winery to winery, consider maneuvering on two wheels along the quiet country roads. **Wine Country Bikes** (✆ **866/922-4537;** www.winecountrybikes.com) offers day rentals (with maps) and guided tours. A road bike goes for $55 per day and includes a helmet, lock, bag, and route suggestions. You can also rent a tandem (two-person) road bike for $95 per day. An all-day tour goes for $129 per person and includes a picnic lunch, wine tasting, and a van to lug any goodies you buy along the way.

Passalacqua ★   A romantic rural vision with a white wisteria-draped trellis, rows of old vines, umbrella-shaded tables on a patio overlooking vineyards, and a modest, welcoming tasting room pouring free samples, this family-owned winery, which was previously Pezzi King, has long been a vision of idyllic Wine Country. But since young Jason Passalacqua bought it a few years ago, a lot has changed, especially regarding winemaking, since Margaret Davenport, a veteran from Clos du Bois, was appointed winemaker. Along with overseeing the development of on-site production facilities, she garnered recognition for the winery when her 2002 Dry Creek Old Vine zinfandel made the *San Francisco Chronicle*'s top 100 wine list for 2004 and her 2001 cabernet sauvignon was awarded Double Gold and Best of Class in the *San Francisco Chronicle*'s 2005 wine-judging competition. Drop by, absorb the afternoon sun on the patio, and see for yourself why I consider this a worthy stop.

3805 Lambert Bridge Rd. (at Dry Creek Rd.), Healdsburg. ℭ **877/825-5547.** www.passalacquawinery.
com. Daily 11am–5pm. From Hwy. 101, take Dry Creek Rd. west, and turn left on Lambert Bridge Rd.

Rochioli Vineyard & Winery ★   Here it's all about the wine—no fancy logo shirts for sale, no tours, and no hard-selling or snobby staff. In fact, the only extra embellishments the simple room and its surroundings have are rotating local art and crafts and a few picnic tables on the patio. And rightly so. Rochioli (pronounced "*Ro-kee-o-lee*") makes excellent sauvignon blanc, chardonnay, and pinot noir. It's so good that at certain times of year they must limit the sales of their total annual production of 12,000 cases of wine to make sure people like you get to buy a bottle when you visit. Accordingly, the staff will sell you only a limited amount (ranging from one bottle to a case) of what's currently available; prices range from $24 to $42 per bottle.

6192 Westside Rd. (near Sweetwater Springs Rd.), Healdsburg. ℭ **707/433-2305.** www.rochioliwinery. com. Daily 11am–4pm.

Ferrari-Carano Vineyards & Winery ★   The hands-down winner for most stunning landscaping goes to this vineyard known for producing everything from fumé blanc to zinfandel. Come during spring when the air is sweet with aromas drifting from the abundant wisteria and the grounds are in bloom with literally thousands of tulips. Come any time of year to meander the formal Asian garden, abounding with rhododendron, Japanese arched bridges, boxwood, maples, magnolia, and roses—and, of course, to taste wines and enjoy quintessential wine-country views. Alas, the tasting room and gift shop is more big-business than country, with plenty of logo items and fine wines to taste and carry. If you're interested in the tour, which previews the winery and its production process and is offered Monday through Saturday at 10am only, make a reservation; it's required and can be made by calling ℭ **800/831-0381,** extension 251. Tasting prices are $5 for a selection of four current releases and are refunded with a $25 purchase.

8761 Dry Creek Rd., Healdsburg. ℭ **707/433-6700.** www.ferrari-carano.com. Daily 10am–5pm. Tours Mon–Sat 10am with a reservation. From Hwy. 101 take Dry Creek Rd. exit headed west and go 9 miles.

Bella Vineyards & Wine Caves ★★   Do yourself a favor—make a point of winding your way over to this ridiculously charming-chic winery specializing in hearty, spicy, old-vine zinfandel and red Rhone varieties. Though when you step out of the car, don't head toward the quaint barnlike building flanked by century-old olive trees. Instead, beeline through the mysterious arched doors built into the hillside to enter their too-cool cave tasting room, complete with cafe tables, chic hanging lamps, and a small casual area where staff will serve you tastes for a $5 fee. It's a very unique, scenic, and tasty experience.

9711 West Dry Creek Rd., Healdsburg. ℭ **866/572-3552** or 707/473-9171. www.bellawinery.com. Daily 11am–4:30pm. Appointment necessary for groups of 10 or more.

Preston of Dry Creek ★★   Preston's wines are fine, but what makes this one of my favorite stops in all of Northern Sonoma is everything else about the place—the winding dirt road that leads to the parking lot; the rustic grassy area outside with picnic tables, well-established wisteria, games of bocce ball; and the super-cute tasting room and store, which is located in a farmhouse and comes complete with all the charm you'd expect. Follow the neon sign's instruction and "drink zin," but also dabble in the broad selection of Rhone varietals made here—including mourvedre, viognier, roussanne, Barbera, and Syrah ($5 per tasting). By the way, you can taste more of owner Lou Preston's passions here: Organic vegetables grown on the property, and bread baked in the property's custom wood-fired brick oven are sold here daily. The bread sells out quickly, so arrive early to indulge.

9282 West Dry Creek Rd. (about 1 mile west of Yoakim Bridge Rd.), Healdsburg. ℭ **707/433-3372.** www. prestonofdrycreek.com. Daily 11am–4:30pm.

J Vineyards & Winery ★   Formerly the Piper-Sonoma winery, J is best known for its sparkling wines (hence the rabid popularity of its brand new "Bubble Room") but has also found a niche in the pinot noir and chardonnay markets. J hosts a variety of sexy winery experiences, from basic tastings to private wine and food pairings, on its 274 acres of Russian River Valley vineyards. Tastings aren't cheap, but food and bubbly lovers shouldn't balk at the expense, considering a visit here is a wine exploration and a light meal in one: It's $25 for a basic flight of four with paired hors d'oeuvres. For $55 per person, expect exquisite food pairings (which might include butternut squash soup served in a hollowed pumpkin, or foie gras), the plush couches and jacketed service of the Bubble Room, and three flights (reds, whites, or bubblies). If it's a nice day, you might also consider the $35 "al fresco" tasting that seats visitors on J's new terrace.

11447 Old Redwood Hwy., Healdsburg. ℭ **888/JWINECO** or 707/431-5310. www.jwine.com. Daily 11am–5pm. Bubble Room Fri–Mon 11am–4pm. Reservations recommended.

WHERE TO STAY

For more lodging options, check **http://Sonoma.com and http://winecountry.com**.

Very Expensive

The Farmhouse Inn & Restaurant ★★   The Farmhouse Inn, located in a speck of a town just outside of Guerneville, may be more famous for its destination restaurant than its rooms, but that doesn't mean the accommodations here aren't praiseworthy. In fact, the inn has been named one of the nation's top 30 by *Travel + Leisure* magazine. Run by the Bartolomei family, who are fourth-generation Forestvilleans, the 6-acre rural property is lined with superbly spacious and charming cottages. Each looks English-country from the outside and creatively cozy from within. Exceedingly spacious rooms are individually decorated with colorful walls adorned with whimsical sayings; surprise amenities such as saunas, whirlpool tubs, or steam showers; a fireplace; quality bath products; and a good dose of solitude. Common areas include a truly beautiful and superb European country–style restaurant complete with excellent wine list and polished service, heated outdoor pool, and a demonstration vineyard and rose garden.

7871 River Rd., Forestville, CA 95436. ℭ **800/464-6642** or 707/887-3300. www.farmhouseinn.com. 10 units. $275–$495 double. AE, MC, V. **Amenities:** Restaurant; heated outdoor pool (open May 1–Oct 31); spa; concierge; Wi-Fi; room service; massage. *In room:* Flatscreen TV w/cable, DVD player, fridge, coffee-maker (available upon request), hair dryer, iron.

Healdsburg Inn on the Plaza ★★   As the name suggests, this quaint 12-room abode run by Four Sisters boutique hotels, is smack in the middle of Healdsburg's down-town center. But what the title won't tell you is that this posh little place offers spacious, well-appointed rooms with high ceilings, contemporary-chic decor in soothing colors, fireplaces, and private baths (many with large jetted tubs). Pampering perks include complimentary afternoon wine, cheese, and fruit in the upstairs lounge and a scrumptious breakfast in bed for a mere $5 per person; and the price of a night here comes with the polished hospitality that has made Four Sisters a name in Northern California. *Tip:* Just say no to the "homey" first floor corner room. It looks onto a dark alley and doesn't have the luminous, warm quality of other rooms.

112 Matheson St. (btw. Healdsburg Ave. and Center St.), Healdsburg, CA 95448. ☏ **800/431-8663**. www. healdsburginn.com. 12 units. $275–$350 double. Rate includes full breakfast and afternoon wine and hors d'oeuvres. AE, DISC, MC, V. **Amenities:** Concierge; free Wi-Fi in the dining room; video library. *In room:* A/C, TV/VCR or DVD, hair dryer, iron.

Hotel Healdsburg ★★   The first "upscale" property to debut in Healdsburg when it opened in 2001, this home-away-from-home across the street from the plaza is a visitor favorite not only for its spacious, comfortable rooms adorned with country-chic furnishings (you'll find no doilies and lace here), but also for its amenities. Want to spend the day spa-ing it? You're golden. Lounge by a heated pool? No problem. Linger on an oversize couch over the morning paper in front of a roaring fire in the lobby? Sure thing. Dine at a refined restaurant? With **Dry Creek Kitchen** (☏ 707/431-0330; www.charlie palmer.com/dry_creek) fronting the hotel, you're already there. Rooms are minimalist-refined (think Pottery Barn) with angular, modern, dark-wood furnishings; big fluffy beds; oversize bathrooms with glass walk-in showers (some with soaking tubs); and, in many cases, balconies. Though they're comfy enough to linger in, you'll have good reason not to: The region's best shopping is outside your door around Healdsburg's historic plaza. An added bonus for the business-minded traveler (or anyone who wants to send an e-mail) is that each floor has a computer with Internet access that's free to use. Yes, it costs a pretty penny to stay here, but you might be able to find a deal on their website, where they often post promotions and packages.

25 Matheson St. (at the square), Healdsburg, CA 95448. ☏ **800/889-7199** or 707/431-2800. Fax 707/431-0414. www.hotelhealdsburg.com. 55 units. $260–$495 double; $425–$790 junior and 1-bedroom suite. Rates include a "country harvest" breakfast. AE, MC, V. **Amenities:** Restaurant; cafe; bar; heated outdoor pool; spa; Jacuzzi; concierge; free Wi-Fi; room service; laundry service; same-day dry cleaning. *In room:* A/C, TV/DVD, fridge, coffeemaker, hair dryer, iron, safe, CD player, robe.

Moderate

Best Western Dry Creek Inn   It's not exactly a romantic Wine Country getaway, but anyone looking for a wonderfully clean and affordable place to crash after a day of wining and dining will be very happy here—especially considering all the extras. The basic motel rooms were just updated and come equipped with small fridges for chilling your wine and picnic items; and the property even has a tiny fitness room for working off the pounds you're inevitably putting on. If you're willing to fork over a little extra cash, definitely opt for one of the 60 new rooms in their brand-new adjoining building. Each has a king-size bed, fireplace, Jacuzzi, and flatscreen TV. Add to that free high-speed Internet access and the great promotions featured on their website and you've found one of the Wine Country's best bargains. Yes, it's still expensive, but get used to it—that's Healdsburg for you.

198 Dry Creek Rd., Healdsburg, CA 95448. ☏ **800/222-5784** or 707/433-0300. www.drycreekinn.com. 163 units. $89–$359 double. AE, DC, DISC, MC, V. **Amenities:** Restaurant; small heated outdoor pool; exercise room; coin-op washers and dryers. *In room:* A/C, TV w/pay movies, free high-speed Internet, fridge, coffeemaker, hair dryer, iron.

Piper Street Inn   This 1882 Victorian home, located about 5 blocks from the Healdsburg Plaza, is about as homey as Wine Country digs get. With only three rental options—a one-room suite in the house, the cottage in the garden, or the entire two-bed house—the Piper Street Inn is a good place to get away from the Wine Country whirlwind. At $175 per night, the Mirror Suite, adorned with old photos and antiques, provides guests with a cozy queen-size bed, down comforter, and small sitting area and private bathroom. The cottage behind the house promises more privacy, a fireplace, and a two-person whirlpool tub. Either way, you'll enjoy a continental breakfast each morning, complimentary wine in the evening, and affordable accommodations mere blocks from the heart of Healdsburg.

402 Piper St., Healdsburg, CA 95448. ℂ **877/703-0570** or 707/433-8721. www.piperstreetinn.com. $185 1-room suite; $250 private cottage; $525 2-bed home with 1¹/₂ bathrooms, kitchen, living room, and private deck. Rate includes continental breakfast and wine evenings. No credit cards. **Amenities:** Wi-Fi, video library. *In room:* A/C, TV/VCR, robe.

Inexpensive

Sandman Motel   What sets this very clean motel apart from others in its category is an abundance of perks and thoughtful touches. Sure, you'll find the usual furnishings and expected extras such as refrigerators and coffeemakers. But you'll also get access to their large heated outdoor pool and Jacuzzi, be surrounded by well-maintained and surprisingly lush landscaping, and have the option of indulging in their free breakfast bar, which includes a make-your-own waffle station. An astoundingly cheap price makes it that much better. You'll have to drive another 15 minutes (or more with traffic) on Highway 101 to get to the heart of the region's Wine Country, but you're not likely to find a better deal in this expensive area. *Tip:* Skip dining at adjoining Carrows; it's cheap chain food.

3421 Cleveland Ave. (at Piner Rd.), Santa Rosa, CA 95403. ℂ **707/544-8570.** 136 units. $82–$92 double; $133 suite. Rates include extensive breakfast bar. AE, DC, DISC, MC, V. **Amenities:** Restaurant; heated outdoor pool; exercise room; Jacuzzi; laundry room. *In room:* A/C, TV, fridge, coffeemaker, hair dryer, iron.

WHERE TO DINE

No area in Wine Country has seen more culinary growth over the past few years than Northern Sonoma. But even before the true destination restaurants arrived, this region was still a fantastic place to dine—thanks to sweet little country restaurants and a few more contemporary staples. But now you've got even more options. Outstanding sushi, chic small plates, truly world-class experiences, excellent baked goods—they're all available, provided you make a reservation.

Very Expensive

Cyrus ★★★ (Finds   FRENCH/INTERNATIONAL   Without question, this is Sonoma County's finest dining. Run by veteran San Francisco maitre d' Nick Peyton and heralded chef Douglas Keane, it's truly a gastronome's dream destination: Romantic Burgundy, France–inspired interior, an intimate and friendly yet somewhat formal atmosphere, and to-die-for seasonal "contemporary luxury" cuisine. The intimate vaulted room is warmly lit, with colors of deep chocolate and gold brightened by ruffled white curtains. An evening appropriately starts, if your heart desires, with selections from carts showcasing caviar (measured to order on a scale against tiny gold bars) and champagne. It continues with a menu of build-your-own fixed-price three-, four-, or five-course options, which might include heavenly seared foie gras with lentil ragout, Asian pears, and vanilla bean *gastrique;* roasted quail with fennel, figs, and pine nuts; and bacon-wrapped pork loin with potato purée, "hen of the woods" (a tasty fungus), and chard. Everything is as stunning to look at as it is to taste. *FYI:* The small bar, where the specialty drinks are as creative and revered as the food, is perfect for impromptu snacking and sipping.

Moderate

Bistro Ralph ★ CALIFORNIA Located on the square, Bistro Ralph looks rather industrial-chic amid its country-town environs. The longtime standby is a prime pick for fresh, tasty, and familiar comfort foods in an upbeat and casual environment. Whether seated in the narrow dining room with high ceilings, concrete floors, and stainless-steel embellishments around the open kitchen and bar, or on the small sidewalk patio, diners who come to feast on chef/owner Ralph Tingle's Dijon chicken, Caesar salad, and sautéed mahimahi with hedgehog mushrooms will be wholly satisfied. Lunch goes lighter, with upscale salads and sandwiches.

109 Plaza St. (at Healdsburg Ave.). ℂ **707/433-1380.** Reservations recommended. Main courses $8.75–$15 lunch, $18–$36 dinner. MC, V. Mon–Sat 11:30am–2:30pm and 5:30– 9pm.

Willi's Seafood & Raw Bar ★ SEAFOOD/LATIN-INSPIRED AMERICAN Festive, modern, and city-slick with urban-Caribbean decor, this hot spot is jumping thanks to sexy environs, a tasty exotic selection of international small plates (think ceviche, skewers, and New England–style "rolls"), and 40 mostly local wines (all of which are available by the glass, carafe, and full bottle). Grab a spot at the heated sidewalk seating or at the friendly bar to try the flash-fried calamari appetizer with orange chili *gremolata* or the outstanding sliced hanger steak drizzled with *chimichurri* sauce atop a bed of cucumber salad.

403 Healdsburg Ave., (at North St.). ℂ **707/433-9191.** www.willisseafood.net. Reservations recommended for parties of 8 or more. Small plates $7–$14. DISC, MC, V. Sun–Thurs 11:30am–9pm; Fri–Sat 11:30am–10pm.

Zazu ★★ AMERICAN/ITALIAN You'll feel like you're on the road to nowhere while driving here, but chefs/owners Duskie Estes and John Stewart take roadhouse dining to gastronomic heights at this destination restaurant. The cozy, warmly lit room with comfy banquettes and a myriad of strategically placed mirrors is the perfect setting for the couple's creative and playful American and Northern Italian–inspired menu, featuring extremely generous portions of homey comfort foods such as seared duck with steamed romano beans or balsamic pork shoulder with creamy buttermilk mashed potatoes. Save room for dessert—you won't want to miss the messy and fun chocolate fondue with homemade Nutter Butter–like cookies. An added bonus is the well-priced Sonoma-centric wine list.

3535 Guerneville Rd. (about 5 miles west of Hwy. 101), Santa Rosa. ℂ **707/523-4814.** www.zazurestaurant. com. Reservations recommended. Main courses $17–$21. AE, DISC, MC, V. Wed–Sun 5:30–9:30pm.

Zin Restaurant & Wine Bar WINE BAR Locals and visitors flock to this downtown Healdsburg hot culinary outpost, where talented and innovative young chefs fuse big-city ideas with country-comfort dishes. The seasonal menu pairs a top-notch wine list with local foods and produce: I loved the sautéed shrimp with smoky tomato sauce atop crispy white corn grits followed by signature dish Coq au "Zin," chicken braised in red wine with applewood-smoked bacon, roasted mushrooms, and pearl onions, served over celery-root mashed potatoes. On my last visit, the winter menu featured few nonmeat options and only one fish entree. But vegetarians needn't fret: You can usually make a fine meal out of a few apps, and you'll have plenty of choices when you get to their exceptional wine list focusing on Dry Creek, Russian River, and Alexander Valley vintages (15 to 17 picks by the glass, around 100 by the bottle). I was lulled by the velvety '02 Stryker Sonoma old-vine zinfandel, bottled just up the road.

344 Center St., Healdsburg. (℃ **707/473-0946.** www.zinrestaurant.com. Main courses $15–$30. AE, DISC, MC, V. Mon–Fri 11:30am–2pm; daily 5:30–9pm.

Inexpensive
Jimtown Store ★★ DELI   Full of Wine Country character, this retro-hip country store promises strong coffee, a seasonal menu—focused on local farm fare—and incredible gourmet picnic grub, and charming low-key tables for on-the-spot noshing. The store, owned by cookbook author and chef Carrie Brown, sells its own brand of condiments. (Try the artichoke, caper, or fig and olive spreads.) In addition, bottles of local wine share shelf space with candy, antiques, and an assortment of wares they describe as "Gifts that are Different."

6706 State Hwy. 128, Healdsburg. (℃ **707/433-1212.** www.jimtown.com. Box lunches $9–$14. Mon–Fri 7am–5pm; Sat–Sun 7:30am–5pm.

The Northern Coast

by Matthew Richard Poole

North from San Francisco, the coast bears little resemblance to the southern part of the state. The landscape, climate, flora, and fauna are distinct, and you can forget about surfing and bikinis; instead, you'll find miles of rough shoreline with broad beaches and tiny bays harboring fantastic rock chimneystacks, blowholes, and bridges carved by the ocean waves.

You may think you've arrived in Alaska when you hit the beaches of Northern California. Take a dip and you'll agree with the locals: The Arctic waters on the Northern Coast are best left to sea lions. That doesn't mean you can't enjoy the beaches, though, whether by strolling along the water or taking in the views of towering cliffs and seascapes. And unlike their southern counterparts, the beaches here are not likely to be crowded, even during summer months.

The best season to visit is spring—when wild poppy, iris, and sea foam carpet the headlands, or fall, when the sun shines clear and bright. Summers are typically cool and windy, and the ubiquitous fog burns off by afternoon.

The most scenic way to reach Stinson Beach, Mendocino, and points north is to drive Highway 1 along the coast. U.S. 101 runs inland, much more quickly, through Healdsburg and Cloverdale, but it doesn't provide the spectacular coastal views. A good compromise if you're headed to, say, Mendocino, is to take U.S. 101 to Cloverdale and then cut over to the coast on Highway 128.

And one last thing: Dress warmly.

1 POINT REYES NATIONAL SEASHORE ★★★

35 miles NW of San Francisco

The government created the national seashore system to protect rural and undeveloped stretches of coastline from population growth and soaring real-estate values. Nowhere is the success of this system more evident than at Point Reyes. Residents of the surrounding towns—Inverness, Point Reyes Station, and Olema—have steadfastly resisted runaway development. You won't find strip malls or fast-food here—just laid-back coastal towns with cafes and country inns where gentle living prevails.

The park—a 71,000-acre hammer-shaped peninsula jutting 10 miles into the Pacific and backed by Tomales Bay—abounds with wildlife, ranging from tule elk, birds, and bobcats to gray whales, sea lions, and great white sharks. Aside from its scenery, it also boasts historical treasures that open a window into California's coastal past, including lighthouses, dairies, and ranches, the site of Sir Francis Drake's 1579 landing, plus a replica of a coastal Miwok Indian village.

Though the peninsula's people and wildlife live in harmony above the ground, the situation beneath the soil is more volatile. The San Andreas Fault separates Point Reyes—the northernmost landmass on the Pacific Plate—from the rest of California, which rests on the North American Plate. Point Reyes is making its way toward Alaska at a rate of about 2 inches per year, but it has moved faster at times. In 1906, Point Reyes jumped north almost 20 feet in an instant, leveling San Francisco and jolting the rest of the state. The half-mile **Earthquake Trail,** near the Bear Valley Visitor Center, illustrates this geological drama with a loop through an area torn by the fault. Shattered fences, rifts in the ground, and a barn knocked off its foundation illustrate how alive the earth is here. If that doesn't convince you, the seismograph in the visitor center will.

ESSENTIALS

GETTING THERE   Point Reyes is 30 miles northwest of San Francisco, but it takes at least 90 minutes to reach by car (the small towns slow you down). The easiest route is Sir Francis Drake Boulevard from U.S. 101 south of San Rafael; it takes its time to Point Reyes, but it's without detours. For a longer, more scenic route, take the Stinson Beach/Highway 1 exit, off U.S. 101 south of Sausalito, onto Highway 1 north.

VISITOR INFORMATION   As soon as you arrive at Point Reyes, stop at the **Bear Valley Visitor Center** (© 415/464-5100; www.nps.gov/pore), on Bear Valley Road (look for the small sign just north of Olema on Hwy. 1) and pick up a free Point Reyes trail map. The rangers are helpful and can answer your questions about the national seashore. Be sure to check out the great natural history and cultural displays as well. It's open Monday through Friday from 9am to 5pm, Saturday and Sunday and holidays from 8am to 5pm. Websites with information about Point Reyes include **www.pointreyes.net** and **www.pointreyes.org**.

FEES & PERMITS   Entrance to the park is free. Camping is $15 per site per night all year (up to six people), and permits are required; reservations can be made up to 3 months in advance at © **415/663-8054,** Monday through Friday from 9am to 2pm.

WHAT TO SEE & DO

When heading out to any part of the Point Reyes coast, expect to spend the day surrounded by nature. The park encompasses several surf-pounded beaches, bird estuaries, open swaths of land with roaming elk, and the Point Reyes lighthouse. As beautiful as the wilderness can be, however, it's also untamable. Waters in these areas are bone chilling, home to a vast array of sea life, including sharks, and dangerously unpredictable, with strong waves and riptides, untended by lifeguards; in other words, swimming is inadvisable. Pets are not permitted on any local trails.

The most popular attraction is the venerable **Point Reyes Lighthouse** ★, at the westernmost tip. Even if you plan to forego the 308 steps down to the lighthouse, it's worth the visit just to marvel at the scenery, which includes thousands of common murres and prides of sea lions basking on the rocks far below (binoculars come in handy). The lighthouse visitor center (© **415/669-1534**) is open Thursday through Monday from 10am to 4:30pm, weather permitting; admission is free.

The lighthouse is also the top spot on the California coast to see **gray whales** as they make their southward and northward migrations along the coast from January to April. The annual round-trip is 10,000 miles—one of the longest mammal migrations known. The whales head south in December and January and return north in March. During the southern migration (Jan), the lighthouse affords the best view. During the northern migration (Mar), you can see the whales from any of the area's beaches. *Tip:* If you plan to drive out to the lighthouse to whale-watch, arrive early as parking is limited. If possible, come on a weekday. On a weekend or holiday from December to April (weather permitting), it's wise to park at the Drake's Beach Visitor Center and take the shuttle bus

(Finds)   **Stinson Beach: The Bay Area's Best**

One of Northern California's most popular beaches, this 3-mile-wide stretch of sand, at the western foot of Mount Tamalpais, is packed with Bay Area residents (and their dogs) on those rare, fog-free summer weekends. Granted, it lacks Southern California's hard bodies and soft golden sand, but it still makes for an enjoyable day trip via the scenic drive on Highway 1. Swimming is allowed, with lifeguards on duty from May to mid-September, but notices about riptides and the cold water usually discourage beachgoers from venturing into the surf. Adjoining the beach is the small town of Stinson Beach, where you can have an enjoyable alfresco lunch at the numerous cafes along Highway 1. To reach Stinson Beach from San Francisco, cross the Golden Gate Bridge heading north on U.S. 101, take the Stinson Beach/Highway 1 exit heading west, and follow the signs (it's a winding 20 miles). The beach is free, open daily from 9am to 10pm. For more information, log onto **www.stinson beachonline.com**.

to the lighthouse, which is $5 for adults and free for kids age 12 and under. Dress warmly—it's often quite cold and windy—and bring binoculars.

Whale-watching is far from the only activity offered. Rangers conduct many different tours on weekends: You can walk along the **Bear Valley Trail** and spot the wildlife at the ocean's edge; see the waterfowl at **Fivebrooks Pond;** explore tide pools; view some of North America's most beautiful ducks in the wetlands of **Limantour;** hike to the promontory overlooking **Chimney Rock** to see sea lions, elephant seals, harbor seals, and seabirds; or take a self-guided walk along the **San Andreas Fault** to observe the epicenter of the 1906 earthquake and learn about the regional geology. Tours vary seasonally; for up-to-date details, call the **Bear Valley Visitor Center** (© **415/464-5100**) or visit the National Park Service's website (www.nps.gov/pore). Many of the tours are suitable for travelers with disabilities.

North and South **Point Reyes beaches** face the Pacific and withstand the full brunt of ocean tides and winds—so much so that the water is far too rough for even wading. Until a few years ago, entering the water was illegal, but persistent surfers went to court for their right to shred the mighty waves. Today the park service strongly advises against taking on the tides, so play it safe and content yourself to stroll the coastline. Along the southern coast, the waters of **Drake's Beach** ★ can be as tranquil and serene as Point Reyes's are turbulent. Locals come here to sun and picnic; occasionally a hearty soul ventures into the cold waters. Keep in mind, though, that storms generally come inland from the south and almost always hit Drake's before moving north or south. A powerful weather front can turn wispy waves into torrential tides.

Some of the park's best and least crowded highlights are accessible only on foot, such as **Alamere Falls** ★, a freshwater stream that cascades down a 40-foot bluff onto Wildcat Beach, or **Tomales Point Trail** ★, which passes through the Tule Elk Reserve, a protected haven for roaming herds of tule elk that once numbered in the thousands. Hiking most of the trails usually ends up being an all-day outing, however, so it's best to split a 2-day trip within Point Reyes National Seashore into a "by car" day and a "by foot" day.

(Finds) **Drake's Bay Oyster Farm**

If you want to escape the crowds and enjoy some man-made entertainment, head to **Drake's Bay Oyster Farm.** On the edge of Drakes Estero (a uniquely pristine and nutrient-rich saltwater lagoon on the Point Reyes peninsula that produces some of the finest oysters in the world), the oyster farm doesn't look like much—just a cluster of wooden shacks and oyster tanks surrounded by piles of oyster shells—but California has no better place to buy delicious fresh-out-of-the-water oysters by the sack full. The owner is very friendly and doles out all the information you'll ever want to know about the bivalves, including a lesson on how to properly shuck them. They also have picnic tables and bottled oyster sauce, so you can enjoy your recently purchased bivalves immediately (though I prefer to drive down to Point Reyes Beach), but bring your own oyster knife. Drake's Bay Oyster Farm is located at 17171 Sir Francis Drake Blvd., about 6 miles west(ish) of Inverness on the way to the Point Reyes Lighthouse. It's open daily 8am to 4:30pm (© **415/669-1149;** www.drakesbayfamilyfarms.com).

One of my favorite things to do in Point Reyes is paddle through placid Tomales Bay, a haven for migrating birds and marine mammals. **Blue Waters Kayaking** ★ (© 415/669-2600; www.bwkayak.com) organizes nature tours and hiking and kayak trips, including 3-hour morning or sunset outings, oyster tours, day trips, and longer excursions. Instruction, private groups and classes, clinics, and boat rental are available, and all ages and levels are welcome. Prices for tours start at $68. Rentals begin at $30 per person. Don't worry—the kayaks are very stable, and there aren't any waves to contend with. There are two launching points: One is on Highway 1 at the Marshall Boatworks in Marshall, 8 miles north of Point Reyes Station, and the other is on Sir Francis Drake Boulevard, in Inverness, 5 miles west of Point Reyes Station. The Marshall site is open, weather permitting, on weekends from 9am to 5pm and by appointment. Call or visit their website to confirm.

If you're into bird-watching, you'll definitely want to visit the **Point Reyes Bird Observatory** (© 415/868-0655; www.prbo.org), one of the few full-time ornithological research stations in the United States. It's at the southeast end of the park on Mesa Road. This is where ornithologists keep an eye on more than 400 feathered species. Admission to the visitor center and nature trail is free, and visitors are welcome to observe the tricky process of catching and banding the birds. The observatory is open daily from 9am to 5pm. Banding hours vary, so call the field station for exact times.

Just north of Point Reyes National Seashore, near the small coastal town of Bolinas, is the **Audubon Canyon Ranch's Bolinas Lagoon Preserve.** From March through mid-July, this 1,000-acre preserve is the annual nesting location for great egrets, snowy egrets, and great blue herons, who set up temporary shop atop 100-foot-tall redwoods, as they've been doing for the past century or so. The 2- to 4-foot birds, with wingspans of up to 6 feet, are mesmerizing to watch as they engage in their daily courtship routines, such as plume displaying, twig shaking, crooning, and bill clappering. The flailing and crash-landing of young chicks embarking on their first flights in June or July is also entertaining. The

preserve is open to the public from 10am to 4pm on weekdays and holidays from March
15 to July 13, and 2pm to 4pm Tuesday through Friday by appointment. It's free, but
donations are suggested. The address is 4900 State 1, just north of Stinson Beach; for
more information, see **www.egret.org/bolinas_lagoon.html** or call C **415/868-9244.**

WHERE TO STAY

Inns of Marin (C **800/887-2880** or 415/663-2000; www.innsofmarin.com), **Point
Reyes Lodging Association** (C **800/539-1872** or 415/663-1872; www.ptreyes.com),
and **West Marin Network** (C **415/663-9543**) are reputable services that will help you
find accommodations, from one-room cottages to inns and vacation homes. The **West
Marin Chamber of Commerce** (C **415/663-9232;** www.pointreyes.org) is also a good
source for lodging and visitor information. Keep in mind that many places here require
a 2-night minimum stay, but in slow season they may make exceptions. They'll also refer
you to restaurants, hiking trails, and other attractions in the area.

Expensive

Blackthorne Inn ★★   This redwood home with its octagonal widow's walk, spiral
staircase, turrets, and multiple decks looks more like a deluxe tree house than a B&B. My
favorite unit (also the priciest) is the Eagle's Nest, an octagonal room enclosed by glass
and topped with a sun deck, with a catwalk leading to the bathroom. The largest room
is the Forest View, a two-room suite with a deck, a private entrance, and a sitting area
facing the woods. All units have private bathrooms. The main sitting room in the house
features a stone fireplace, skylight, wet bar, and stained-glass windows, and it's surrounded by a huge deck. A country buffet breakfast, included in the room rate, is served
on the large upper deck when the sun's out.

266 Vallejo Ave. (off Sir Francis Drake Blvd., south of Inverness), Inverness Park (P.O. Box 712), Inverness,
CA 94937. C **415/663-8621.** Fax 415/663-8635. www.blackthorneinn.com. 4 units. $195–$325 double.
Rates include buffet breakfast. MC, V. **Amenities:** Nearby golf course; Jacuzzi. *In room:* Coffeemaker.

Manka's Inverness Lodge ★★★ (Finds)   If ever there was a reason to pack your
bags and leave San Francisco for a day or two, this wondrous collection of estates from
the early 1900s is it. The main property holds two redwood cabins, an annex, and an old
hunting and fishing lodge, all of which look like something out of a Hans Christian
Andersen fairy tale, right down to the tree-limb bed stands. It's all terribly romantic in a
Jack London-ish sort of way, and tastefully done. Sixteen-foot ceilings, wide plank floors,
wonderful views over Tomales Bay, and a luxurious amount of space lend rooms in the
converted 1991 boathouse a loftlike feel; all have vintage 6-foot double-ended tubs and
private outdoor showers opening up to the sky. For the ultimate romantic splurge,
inquire about the two secluded guesthouses on the ridge: Perch and Cabin 125. The
lodge's reputation was built on its rustic and romantic restaurant, where Prince Charles
and Camilla dined when they stayed for 3 nights at Manka's. While the main lodge and
restaurant were destroyed in a December 2006 fire, you can still eat like a prince: On a
nightly basis, guests are invited to indulge in either a three- or four-course fireside supper
or a private chef's meal that consists of seven or eight small courses. All ingredients are
grown, fished, gathered, or farmed within reach of the lodge. A newly refurbished din-
ning room is used during the holidays and for some special events.

30 Calendar Way (at Argyle St., off Sir Francis Drake Blvd., 1/4 mile north of downtown Inverness), P.O. Box
1110, Inverness, CA 94937. C **415/669-1034.** Fax 415/669-1598. www.mankas.com. 14 units, including
4 cabins. $215–$385 double; $365–$565 cabin and boathouse. AE, MC, V. **Amenities:** Restaurant; free

(Finds) Steep Ravine Environmental Cabins

How's this for a great deal? For $75, you and four of your best friends can stay the night in a redwood cabin on a bluff overlooking the ocean with nearby access to hiking trails and a small, secluded beach. Mount Tamalpais State Park rents 10 cabins that were once the private retreats of Bay Area politicians. All have gorgeous ocean views, available to anyone stubborn enough to get a reservation. Wood-burning stoves, platform beds, running water, and outhouses are provided, but you must bring your own sleeping bag and lantern, there's no electricity, and firewood costs extra. Each cabin sleeps five, but only one car per cabin is allowed. Off Highway 1, a mile south of Stinson Beach, look for a paved turnout and a brown metal sign. The cabins are very popular, so reserve one as far in advance as possible (you can book them up to 7 months prior). For reservations, call (C) **800/444-7275** or reserve online at **www.reserveamerica.com**. For more information, call the Mount Tamalpais State Park at (C) **415/388-2070**.

Wi-Fi; room service; in-room massage; movies on request; personal music library. *In room:* MP3 player with CD library, fireplace, redwood soaking tubs in some rooms, no phone except in guesthouses.

Moderate

Bear Valley Inn Bed & Breakfast ★ This two-story 1910 farmhouse has survived everything from a major earthquake to a recent forest fire, but you'd be hard-pressed to find a better B&B for the price in Point Reyes. Loaded with charm, down to the profusion of flowers and vines outside and comfy chairs fronting a toasty woodstove inside, it's in a great location, too, with good restaurants within walking distance and the seashore at its doorstep. One unit is a private dog-friendly cottage with a small kitchen and bunk beds that are suitable for children. The cottage comes loaded with milk and basics, but for $10 extra per person you can receive a deluxe breakfast basket (or a mere $10 gets you baked goodies and juice for your entire crew).

88 Bear Valley Rd., Olema, CA 94950. (C) **415/663-1777**. www.bearvinn.com. 3 rooms, 1 cottage. $120–$180 double; $180–$250 cottage for two ($25 per extra person up to 6 people). Rates include breakfast (house only). AE, DISC, MC, V. *In room:* A/C, TV, Wi-Fi, kitchen in cottage, some units w/coffeemaker, hair dryer, iron.

Olema Inn & Restaurant ★★ Built in 1876, the pretty Olema Inn opened on July 4, 1876, as a gathering place for farmers and ranchers, was lost in gambling debt, and survived the 1906 earthquake (Olema was the epicenter). Today it still retains much of its period charm, combining modern luxuries such as European Sleepworks mattresses, down comforters, large tub/shower combinations, and Ralph Lauren linens with antique furniture and light fixtures, Victorian-style white porcelain and chrome bathrooms, and those great high ceilings you find in old Bay Area buildings. Views are of the beautiful back garden—site of many weddings—and Olema Valley. After checking in, take a stroll on the stone pathways behind the inn to the orchard and flower gardens. The inn's romantic candle-lit restaurant features local produce and meats such as Bellwether Farms ricotta gnocchi with pine nuts and sage brown butter, duck confit and apple ravioli in a sherry reduction, and a grilled, center-cut Niman Ranch pork chop with cider glaze and a side of crispy corn cake. Much of the restaurant's produce is grown at the inn's organic garden and orchard. *Tip:* Try to reserve room no. 3—the quietest, overlooking the garden.

10000 Sir Francis Drake Blvd., Olema, CA 94950. ℂ **415/663-9559.** Fax 415/663-8783. www.theolema inn.com. 6 units. $198–$222 double. Rates include continental breakfast. AE, MC, V. Dogs are welcome at no extra charge. **Amenities:** Restaurant.

Point Reyes Country Inn & Stables ★

Are you and your horse dreaming of a country getaway? Then book a room at Point Reyes Country Inn & Stables, a ranch-style home on 4 acres with pastoral accommodations for two- and four-legged guests (horses only), plus access to plenty of hiking and riding trails. Each of the six B&B rooms has a private bathroom and either a balcony or a garden. The innkeepers have also added two studios (with kitchens) above the stables, plus they rent out two cottages on Tomales Bay, with decks, stocked kitchens, fireplaces, and a shared dock.

12050 Hwy. 1 (P.O. Box 501), Point Reyes Station, CA 94956. ℂ **415/663-9696.** Fax 415/663-8888. www. ptreyescountryinn.com. 10 units. $115–$180 double; $185–$225 cottage. $10–$15 per horse. Rates include breakfast in the B&B rooms, breakfast provisions in the cottages. MC, V. **Amenities:** Nearby golf course. *In room:* No phone.

Inexpensive

Motel Inverness (Kids) Homey, well maintained, and fronting Tomales Bay, this is the perfect pick for the spendthrift or the outdoor adventurer who plans to spend as little time indoors as possible. (Those seeking romance should dig a little deeper into their pockets and opt for Manka's; see above.) All guest rooms, except one twin-bed option, have queen-size beds and skylights. Attached to Inverness is a giant great room, complete with fireplace and pool table to distract the kids; parents can relax and children can play on the back lawn overlooking the bay, bird sanctuary, and rolling green hills. The hotel offers two, two-bedroom suites, one with wheelchair access and a deck to take in the views; the other is billed as the "luxury" suite and has a king-size bed, Jacuzzi, and a kitchenette. Both are ideal for families, as is the Dacha cottage, which is 1 mile away, on the water, and boasts three bedrooms, a living/dining room, large sitting room, and deck with bay views. *Note:* The motel is nonsmoking.

12718 Sir Francis Drake Blvd., Inverness, CA 94937. ℂ **888/669-6909** or 415/669-1081. www.motel inverness.com. 7 units, 1 cottage. $99–$140 double; $150–$200 suite; $500 Dacha Cottage. MC, V. *In room:* TV, coffeemaker.

Point Reyes Hostel (Kids)

Deep within Point Reyes National Seashore, this beautiful, old, ranchlike complex has 44 dormitory-style accommodations, including one room reserved for families (with at least one child 5 years old or younger). The two common rooms are warmed by wood-burning stoves on chilly nights, and guests can share a fully equipped kitchen, barbecue (BYO charcoal), and patio. If you don't mind sharing your sleeping quarters with strangers, this is a deal that can't be beat. Reservations (and earplugs) are strongly recommended.

Off Limantour Rd. (P.O. Box 247), Point Reyes Station, CA 94956. ℂ **888/464-4872,** ext. 191, or 415/663-8811. www.norcalhostels.org. 44 bunks, 1 private unit. $20 per adult, $10 per child under 17 with parent. 5 nights out of 30 maximum stay. MC, V. Reception hours 7:30–10am and 4:30–9:30pm daily.

WHERE TO DINE

Rosie's Cowboy Cookhouse ★ MEXICAN/AMERICAN Fresh, good, fast, cheap, and healthy: What more could you ask for in a restaurant? Taqueria La Quinta, which was a favorite lunch stop in downtown Point Reyes for years and years, is now known as Rosie's Cowboy Cookhouse. The huge selection of Mexican standards remains on the menu—try the house-made tamales—but now they've added some Tex to their

Point Reyes Mountain Biking

Mountain biking was born in Marin, so it's no surprise that miles of meandering mountain-bike trails crisscross Point Reyes National Seashore. The challenge level varies from easy to daunting, with mostly fire roads and a few single-track trails winding through densely forested knolls and sunny meadows with pretty ocean views. Because many of the hiking trails are off limits to bikes, you'll need a bike map to figure out which ones are bike-legal. They're available for free at the Bear Valley Visitor Center (p. 218). To rent a bike, call David Barnett at **Cycle Analysis** (© **415/663-9164** or 415/663-1645; www.cyclepointreyes.com).

Mex, such as rib-eye steak, pulled pork sandwiches, and excellent Niman Ranch beef chili, all prepared from scratch in their kitchen using natural, free-range, and organic ingredients. Oh, and watch out for the salsa—it's hot.

11285 Hwy. 1 (at Third and Main sts.), Point Reyes Station. © **415/663-8868.** No credit cards. Wed–Mon 11am–8pm.

Station House Café ★ AMERICAN   For more than 2 decades, the Station House Café has been a favorite pit stop for Bay Area residents headed to and from Point Reyes. It's a friendly, low-key place with a full bar, an open kitchen, an outdoor garden dining area (key on sunny days), and live music. Breakfast dishes include a Hangtown omelet with local oysters and bacon, and eggs with creamed spinach and mashed-potato pancakes. Lunch and dinner specials (such as fettuccine with fresh local mussels steamed in white wine and butter sauce, two-cheese polenta served with fresh spinach sauté and grilled garlic-buttered tomato, or a daily fresh salmon special) are all made from locally sourced produce, seasonal vegetables harvested from their kitchen garden, and organically raised Niman Ranch beef. The cafe has an extensive list of fine California wines and locally brewed beers.

11180 State Route One, at Point Reyes Station © **415/663-1515.** www.stationhousecafe.com. Reservations recommended. Breakfast $6.25–$9.25; lunch and dinner courses $7.75–$27. AE, DISC, MC, V. Fri–Mon 8am–3:30pm and 5–9pm (bar until 10pm Fri and Sat); Tues–Thurs 11am–3:30pm and 5–9:30pm.

2 ALONG THE SONOMA COAST

BODEGA BAY

Beyond the tip of the Point Reyes peninsula, the road curves around toward the coastal village of Bodega Bay, which supports a fishing fleet of around 300 boats. It's a good place to stop for lunch or a stroll. Despite the droves of tourists on summer weekends, Bodega Bay is mostly a working-class fishing town, where most locals start their day before dawn mending nets, rigging fishing poles, and talking shop. Several shops and galleries are interesting, but the best show in town—especially for kids—is at **Tides Wharf,** where the fishing boats dock, unload their catch, gut it, and pack it in ice.

Bodega Head State Park ★ is a great vantage point for whale-watching during the migration from January to April. At **Doran Beach,** a large bird sanctuary is home to willets, curlews, godwits, and more. Next door, the **UC Davis Bodega Marine Laboratory** (© 707/875-2211; www.bml.ucdavis.edu) conducts guided tours of its lab projects on Friday afternoons between 2 and 4pm. (Suggested donation is $2.)

The **Bodega Harbour Golf Links,** at 21301 Heron Dr. (© 866/905-4657 or 707/875-3538; www.bodegaharbourgolf.com), is an 18-hole, seaside Scottish-style course designed by Robert Trent Jones, Jr. A warm-up center and practice facility is free for registered golfers. Rates range from $60 with cart Monday through Thursday, $70 on Friday, and $90 on weekends. You can also ride horseback through spectacular scenery through **Chanslor Ranch** (© 707/875-3333; www.chanslor.com), which also has pony rides for kids. It's open daily from 9am to 5pm.

One of the bay's major events is the **Fisherman's Festival** in April. Local fishing boats, decked with ribbons and banners, sail out for a Blessing of the Fleet, while up to 25,000 landlubbers partake of music, a lamb-and-oyster barbecue, and an arts-and-crafts fair. For details about this festival and other events, consult the **Bodega Bay Visitors Center,** 850 Hwy. 1, Bodega Bay, CA 94923 (© 707/875-3866; www.bodegabay.com or www.visitsonomacoast.com). Open daily, it has lots of brochures, and maps of the Sonoma Coast State Beaches and the best fishing spots.

A few miles inland on Highway 1 (toward Petaluma) is the tiny town of **Bodega** (pop. 100), famous as the setting of Alfred Hitchcock's *The Birds,* filmed here in 1961. Fans will want to visit the Potter School House and St. Teresa's Church.

Where to Stay
Expensive
Bodega Bay Lodge & Spa ★★ Near Doran Beach State Park, this is Bodega Bay's best hotel. Each room has plush furnishings, a fireplace, and a private balcony with sweeping views of the bay and bird-filled marshes. If you can afford it, opt for a large luxury suite. Guests have complimentary access to a fitness center and sauna, heated pool above the bay, and a full service oceanview spa offering an array of massages and body/facial treatments. The lodge's **Duck Club Restaurant** enjoys a reputation as Bodega Bay's finest. Picture windows show off the bay view, a romantic setting for Sonoma County cuisine such as roasted Petaluma duck and fresh fish caught by the Bodega fleet.

103 Hwy. 1, Bodega Bay, CA 94923. © 888/875-3525 or 707/875-3525. Fax 707/875-2428. www.bodegabaylodge.com. 84 units. Sun–Thurs $220–$280 double, $410 suite; Fri–Sat $245–$295 double, $460 suite. 2-night minimum on weekends. Rates include a complimentary wine hour from 5–6pm. AE, DC, DISC, MC, V. **Amenities:** Restaurant; heated outdoor pool w/ocean view; nearby golf course; full-service spa and fitness center; concierge; room service; in-room massage; babysitting; coin-op laundry. *In room:* A/C, TV w/pay movies, fax, minibar, fridge, coffeemaker, hair dryer, iron, safe.

Moderate
Inn at the Tides ★ The larger of Bodega Bay's two upscale lodgings (the other being Bodega Bay Lodge), the Inn at the Tides consists of a cluster of condolike wood complexes on the side of a gently sloping hill. The selling point is the view; each unit is staggered just enough to guarantee a view of the bay across the highway. The rooms are modern and the inn's amenities are first rate, such as the attractive indoor-outdoor pool, but I would only stay here if I couldn't get a room at the Bodega Bay Lodge. The **Bay View Restaurant** is open Wednesday through Sunday for dinner only, with ocean views, a well-prepared albeit traditional choice of entrees, and a romantic, somewhat formal ambience. Be sure to check the website for special package deals.

Fun Facts   Hitchcock Haunt

Alfred Hitchcock fans will want to make the pilgrimage to Bodega, located off Highway 1 a few miles southeast of Bodega Bay. Drive past the roadside shops, turn the corner, look right, and *voilà:* a bird's-eye view of the hauntingly familiar Potter School House and St. Teresa's Church, both immortalized in Hitchcock's *The Birds,* filmed here in 1961.

800 Coast Hwy. 1 (P.O. Box 640), Bodega Bay, CA 94923. © **800/541-7788** or 707/875-2751. Fax 707/875-2669. www.innatthetides.com. 86 units. Summer Sun–Thurs $189–$259, Fri–Sat $239–$294; winter rates drop about 20%. Rates include continental breakfast. Golf packages available. AE, DC, DISC, MC, V. **Amenities:** Restaurant; indoor-outdoor heated pool; nearby golf course; exercise room; Jacuzzi; Finnish sauna; room service; in-room massage; babysitting (w/notice); self-service laundry. *In room:* TV w/pay movies, minibar, coffeemaker, hair dryer, iron.

Inexpensive

Bodega Harbor Inn ★ ⟨Value⟩   Thank Poseidon for the Bodega Harbor Inn, with some of the North Coast's best lodging bargains. On a small bluff over the bay, the inn has four single-story clapboard buildings surrounded by well-maintained lawns and gardens. The rooms are small but impeccably neat and tastefully decorated with unpretentious antiques; double beds, private bathrooms, and cable TV are standard. (The best rooms are 12 and 14, which come with small decks and partial ocean views.) The clincher is the inn's private lawn area overlooking the water. On sunny days, there's no better way to enjoy an afternoon in Bodega Bay than parking in one of the lawn chairs and watching the fishing boats bring in their daily catch. Families should inquire about the vacation homes the inn rents for as little as $135 per night.

1345 Bodega Ave., Bodega Bay, CA 94923. © **707/875-3594.** Fax 707/875-9468. www.bodegaharborinn. com. 16 units, 5 houses. $80–$155 double; $150–$350 house. Rates include continental breakfast. MC, V. *In room:* TV.

Where to Dine

In addition to the following, see the Duck Club Restaurant in the listing for Bodega Bay Lodge & Spa in "Where to Stay," above.

Dee's Bayside Deli ★ ⟨Value⟩ DELI   I always stop here when I pass through Bodega Bay. Most visitors don't even give it a glance as they head into the adjacent restaurant, but that's because they don't know about the big bowls of fresh, tangy crab cioppino doled out by the pint (in season). It's a messy affair, best devoured with a side of sourdough bread at the nearby picnic tables. Great fish and chips are available year-round as well, but the kitchen takes its sweet time getting your order to the counter.

595 Hwy. 1, Bodega Bay. © **707/875-8881.** Deli items $4–$10. MC, V. Sun–Thurs 11am–6pm; Fri–Sat 11am–7pm.

Tides Wharf Restaurant SEAFOOD/PASTA   In summer, as many as 1,000 diners a day pass through the Tides Wharf. In the early '60s, it was a set for Hitchcock's *The Birds,* but don't expect the weather-beaten, board-and-batten luncheonette you saw in the movie—a $6-million renovation gentrified, enlarged, and redecorated the place beyond recognition. The best tables have ocean views, and the fare is what you might expect: oysters on the half shell, clam chowder, and all the fish that the owners can dredge

up from the cold blue waters (they send their own boat out into the Pacific daily). Prime
rib, pasta, and poultry are available as well. A fish-processing plant, snack bar, and gift
shop are next door.

835 Hwy. 1. © **707/875-3652.** www.innatthetides.com/tideswharf.html. Main courses $15–$20. AE,
DISC, MC, V. Daily 7:30am–9:30pm.

THE SONOMA COAST STATE BEACHES, JENNER & FORT ROSS STATE HISTORIC PARK ★★

Along 13 winding and picturesque miles of Highway 1—from Bodega Bay to Goat Rock
Beach in Jenner—stretch the Sonoma Coast State Beaches. These beaches are ideal for
walking, tide pooling, abalone picking, fishing, and bird-watching for species such as
great blue heron, cormorant, osprey, and pelican. Each beach is clearly marked from the
road, and numerous pullouts are available for parking. Even if you don't stop at a beach,
the drive alone is spectacular.

At **Jenner,** the Russian River empties into the ocean. **Penny Island,** in the river's estuary, is home to otters and many species of birds; a colony of harbor seals lives out on the
ocean rocks. **Goat Rock Beach** is a popular breeding ground for the seals; pupping season begins in March and lasts until June.

From Jenner, an 11-mile, dramatic coastal drive brings you to **Fort Ross State Historic Park** (© **707/847-3286;** www.fortrossstatepark.org), a reconstruction of the fort
established in 1812 by the Russians as a base for seal and otter hunting (a post they
abandoned in 1842). At the visitor center, you can view the Russians' samovars and table
services. The compound contains several buildings, including the first Russian Orthodox
church on the North American continent outside Alaska. A short history lesson takes
place daily at various times between Memorial Day and Labor Day, and at noon and 2pm
the rest of the year. Call ahead to be sure. The park also offers beach trails and picnic
grounds on more than 1,000 acres. Admission is $6 per car per day.

North from Fort Ross, the road continues to **Salt Point State Park** (© **707/847-
3221**). This 3,500-acre expanse encompasses 30 campsites, 14 miles of trails, dozens of
tide pools, and old Pomo village sites. Your best bet is to pull off the highway any place
that catches your eye and start exploring. At the north end of the park, head inland on
Kruse Ranch Road to the **Kruse Rhododendron Reserve** (© **707/847-3221**), a forested
grove of wild pink and purple flowers, where the *Rhododendron californicum* grow up to
a height of 18 feet under the redwood-and-fir canopy.

Where to Stay

Jenner Inn & Cottages ★   The worst-kept secret on the Northern Coast is Jenner
Inn, a gallimaufry of individually designed and decorated houses and cottages along the
coast and inland along the Russian River. Couples from the Bay Area who want to stay
along the coast for a night, but dread the long drive to Mendocino, wend their way here.
Most of the houses are subdivided into suites, while second honeymooners vie for the
ultraprivate oceanfront cottages. Wicker furniture, wood paneling, and private bathrooms and entrances are standard, though each lodging has its own personality: Some
have kitchens, while others have fireplaces, hot tubs, or private decks. The private cottages overlooking the Pacific are the priciest, but for about $170, most people are content
with one of the smaller suites. A complimentary breakfast is served in the main lodge. In
addition to the B&B accommodations, the inn rents vacation homes within Jenner
Canyon or overlooking the ocean.

10400 Hwy. 1 (P.O. Box 69), Jenner, CA 95450. (℃) **800/732-2377** or 707/865-2377. Fax 707/865-0829. www.jennerinn.com. 24 units (plus several vacation homes). $108–$438 double. Rates include continental breakfast. AE, MC, V. *In room:* Kitchen in some units, coffeemaker, no phone except in cottages.

Where to Dine

River's End ★ INTERNATIONAL Established in 1927, this unpretentious yet urbane seaside restaurant offers a rugged setting, with big windows overlooking the coast (seals and sea lions might happen to be cavorting offshore). The eclectic menu offers everything from filet mignon to wild halibut, seared duck, and fresh Dungeness crab (in season). Whenever possible, the chef uses local Sonoma products—seafood, game, lamb, poultry, vegetables, microbrews, and wines. After dinner, take the remainder of your wine to the deck and watch the sun set. *Note:* The hours tend to vary as much as the menu, so call ahead if you're planning to dine here.

Hwy. 1, Jenner. (℃) **707/865-2484**, ext. 111. www.ilovesunsets.com. Reservations recommended. Main courses $13–$37. MC, V. Fri–Mon 5–9pm.

Sizzling Tandoor ⓥalue INDIAN Along a desolate stretch of Highway 1 between Bodega Bay and Jenner, the Sizzling Tandoor serves huge, inexpensive plates of Indian cuisine. The lonely location is peculiar but superb—high atop a windswept hill, with an exquisite view of the Russian River far below. An array of curries and kabobs is accompanied by soup, vegetables, *pulao* rice, and the best *naan* (Indian bread) I've ever had. Even if you're not hungry, order naan to go—it's a great road snack.

9960 Hwy. 1 (at the south end of the Russian River Bridge), Jenner. (℃) **707/865-0625**. Main courses $9–$14. AE, DISC, MC, V. Daily 11:30am–9pm.

GUALALA & POINT ARENA

Back on Highway 1 heading north, you'll pass through Sea Ranch, a series of condominium beach developments, before you reach the small coastal community of Gualala (pronounced Wah-*la*-la). In the old days, Gualala was a vivacious logging town. A few real-life, suspender-wearing lumberjacks still end their day at the Gualala Hotel's saloon, but for the most part the town's chief function is to provide gas, groceries, and hardware for area residents. Several parks, hiking trails, and about 10 ideal sunbathing beaches lie just outside town.

The **Gualala River,** adjacent to the town of the same name, is suitable for canoeing, rafting, and kayaking, because powerboats and jet skis are forbidden. Along its banks you're likely to see osprey, herons, egrets, and ducks; steelhead, salmon, and river otters make their homes in the waters. You can rent canoes and kayaks in Gualala for 2 hours, a half day, or a full day from **Adventure Rents** (℃ **888/881-4386** or 707/884-4386; www.adventurerents.com), in downtown Gualala on Highway 1 behind Century 21 Realty. Prices range from $30 for a couple of hours on a kayak to $70 for a full day on a tandem ocean kayak; canoes are available as well.

Point Arena is a few miles north of Gualala. Stop here for the view at the **Point Arena Lighthouse & Museum** ★ (℃ **877/725-4448** or 707/882-2777; www.mcn.org/1/pa light), built in 1870 after 10 ships ran aground here one night in a storm. A $5-per-person fee ($1 for children under 12) covers parking, entrance to the lighthouse museum, and an interesting tour of the six-story, 145-step lighthouse (the view through the dazzling 6-ft.-wide, lead-crystal lens is worth the hike). The lighthouse is open daily 10am to 3:30pm; half-hour tours run every 20 minutes.

Tips **Renting a Home at the Beach**

If you're taking the family for a vacation along the coast—or if you really want to impress your partner—consider renting a furnished home at the Sea Ranch, one of the most beautiful seaside communities around. All the low-swept buildings are designed to blend in with the surrounding forest, meadows, and ocean bluffs; many have outdoor hot tubs, and most have wood-burning fireplaces or stoves. About 300 homes are available as rentals with prices starting at about $140 per night. Rentals include use of the community's three outdoor heated swimming pools, tennis courts, and recreation center. The Sea Ranch also has a Scottish-style 18-hole public golf course, a fine-dining restaurant, and private access to 10 miles of coastline and several secluded beaches. For more information, log onto **www.searanchvillage.com** or call **Sea Ranch Rentals** at ✆ **888/732-7262.**

Where to Stay

St. Orres ★★ **Finds**   An extraordinary Russian-style building—complete with two onion-domed towers—St. Orres lies 1¹/₂ miles north of Gualala. The complex was built in 1972 with century-old timbers salvaged from a nearby mill. It offers cottage-style accommodations on 42 acres, as well as eight rooms in the main building (these rooms share three bathrooms decorated in brilliant colors). Other units are very private. Some have wet bars, sitting areas with Franklin stoves, and French doors leading to decks with a distant ocean view. Seven cottages border St. Orres Creek and have exclusive use of a spa facility that includes a hot tub, sauna, and sun deck. The Black Chanterelle is as exotic as it sounds, with domes, a sauna and Jacuzzi, a fireplace, and an ocean view. Full breakfast is delivered to the cottages. The hotel's restaurant (see review below), open for dinner only, is in a dramatic setting below one of the main building's domes.

36601 Hwy. 1 (P.O. Box 523), Gualala, CA 95445. ✆ 707/884-3303. Fax 707/884-1840. www.saintorres. com. 8 units (sharing 3 bathrooms), 13 cottages. Hotel $95–$130 double; cottage $155–$350 double. Rates include full breakfast. MC, V. **Amenities:** Restaurant; bar; nearby golf course; Jacuzzi; sauna; bike rental; in-room massage. *In room:* Kitchenette in some units, fridge, coffeemaker, hair dryer, iron.

Whale Watch Inn ★★   Ninety feet above the water, in five contemporary buildings on 2 cliffside acres, this inn has one of the best views of the Northern Coast. Private guest rooms all have ocean views, decks, and fireplaces. Room styles range from traditional bed-and-breakfast style to French Provençal to contemporary casual; check out the pictures on the website before you reserve one. For a closer encounter with nature, take the private stairway that leads to a half-mile-long beach with tidal pools. The Whale Watch building has a common room with a circular fireplace, floor-to-ceiling windows, and a wraparound deck for prime viewing.

35100 Hwy. 1, Gualala, CA 95445. ✆ 800/942-5342 or 707/884-3667. Fax 707/884-3667. www.whale watchinn.com. 18 units. $180–$315 double. Rates include full breakfast delivered to room at prearranged time. AE, MC, V. **Amenities:** Nearby golf course. *In room:* Kitchen, fridge, and coffeemaker in some units, phone upon request.

Pangaea ★★ (Finds) ECLECTIC Northern-coast locals have been raving about this colorful, offbeat little cafe since the day it opened in downtown Gualala. Everything that issues from Chef Rob Hunter's kitchen—from house-made charcuterie to bread baked in a wood-fired oven—is wondrously fresh, inventive, and organically grown and/or raised. Hunter created the menu after traveling the world with his wife Jill, which explains the enticingly eclectic selection. For starters, try the superb house-cured duck prosciutto appetizer, followed by the garden-fresh fava bean salad with Serrano ham, manchego cheese, hazelnuts, and sherry vinegar. Entrees range from wild Point Arena salmon with truffled golden beet relish, to wood-oven-roasted pork chop with peach-mango salsa and polenta. Desserts—strawberry tart with a topper of fresh whipped cream—are equally impressive, as is the award-winning wine list. Make a reservation well in advance, but you can leave the tie at home.

39165 S. Hwy. 1 (behind the Century 21 building), Gualala. ☎ 707/884-9669. www.pangaeacafe.com. Reservations recommended. Main courses $23–$25. MC, V. Wed–Sun 5:30pm–closing.

St. Orres Restaurant ★★ NORTH COAST CUISINE Self-taught chef Rosemary Campiformio has been wowing fans and food writers for years with her version of North Coast cuisine, which favors local organic meats and produce and wild game in dark, fruity sauces. Every day fishermen and farmers deliver their best goods to Rosemary, so you never know what will be on her prix-fixe dinner menu, but it could be stilton cheese in phyllo with smoked wild boar and tomato, followed by a garden-fresh salad and an entree of grilled veal chop with garlic mashed potatoes, foie gras, and truffle Madeira sauce. For dessert, it's a toss-up between the bread pudding with homemade nutmeg ice cream and caramel sauce, or the freshly baked individual apple pie with St. Orres cinnamon ice cream. The wine cellar stores a suitable selection of reds that pair well with the hearty entrees.

36601 Hwy. 1 (St. Orres Inn), Gualala. ☎ 707/884-3335. www.saintorres.com. Reservations recommended. Prix-fixe dinner menu $45; appetizers and desserts a la carte. Beer and wine only. MC, V. Daily 6–9:30pm (winter schedule varies).

NORTH FROM POINT ARENA

Driving north from Point Arena, you'll pass Elk (a good place to stop for lunch), Manchester, Albion, and Little River on your way to Mendocino.

Where to Stay

Elk Cove Inn & Spa ★★★ It's hard to imagine a more idyllic and romantic coastal retreat that the Elk Cove Inn. Situated on 1¹/₂ acres of quiet and secluded oceanside property about 15 miles south of Mendocino, the 15-room inn offers a variety of rooms types, ranging from modern and spacious cottages and luxury suites to cozy guest rooms within the 1883 "Victorian Mansion." The suites are heavenly—particularly the upper-level L. E. White and Sam McCanse suites, which have the best ocean views—each luxuriously appointed with a private balcony or porch, Jacuzzi tub, high ceilings, custom-made fixtures, and Arts and Crafts furniture. Most rooms have ocean views and fireplaces (perfect for those chilly North Coast nights), and all have feather beds and fluffy comforters. But you'll be spending most of your time luxuriating at the inn's European-style day spa, exploring the nearby driftwood-strewn beach (via the inn's private beach access), watching the sunset from the gazebo, or relaxing at the inn's full bar and restaurant, which serves a full buffet breakfast (you can take it back to your room if you prefer).

person $100. Rates include full breakfast and 4-course dinner. AE, MC, V. **Amenities:** Restaurant; nearby golf course; in-room massage. *In room:* Coffeemaker (in cottages), hair dryer, iron, no phone.

KOA Kamping Kabins (Kids) "What? You expect me to stay at a Kampgrounds of America?!" You bet. Once you see these neat little log "kabins," you'll admit they're a great way to spend a weekend on the coast. The cabins sleep four to six, with one or two bedrooms and log-frame double beds or bunk beds for the kids. Mattresses, a heater, and a light bulb are your standard amenities. Beyond that, you're on your own; you'll need bedding or a sleeping bag, cooking and eating utensils, and a bag of charcoal for the barbecue in front. Enjoy your meal at the picnic table or on the front porch in the log swing. If this is a little too spartan for you, opt for one of the fully furnished "kottages," both decked out with private bathrooms, fireplaces, comfy beds, and other creature comforts. Hot showers, bathrooms, laundry facilities, a small store, and a swimming pool are a short walk away, as is Manchester Beach. It's kid heaven.

On Kinney Rd. (off Hwy. 1, 5 miles north of Point Arena). ℂ **800/562-4188** or 707/882-2375. Fax 707/882-3104. www.manchesterbeachkoa.com. 24 cabins, 2 cottages. $68–$82 cabin (up to 6 people); $161–$168 cottage (up to 4 people). AE, DISC, MC, V. **Amenities:** Heated outdoor pool (seasonal); spa; children's center and playground; coin-op laundry. *In room:* TV and kitchenette in cottages, no phone.

Where to Dine

Ledford House Restaurant ★ MEDITERRANEAN If James Beard were alive, he'd feel at home at this innovative but simply decorated restaurant overlooking the pounding surf of the Pacific from a bluff above. The kitchen offers self-styled Mediterranean cuisine, experimenting with the bounty of the Golden State to fashion rich combinations and harmonious flavors using organic Northern California produce whenever possible. The bistro part of the menu is reserved primarily for the pastas and hearty stews suitable to this far-northern setting, such as their award-winning Antoine's cassoulet, a jumble of pork, lamb, garlic sausage, and duck confit slowly cooked with white beans. Although the menu changes seasonally, for a taste of California, try the salmon primavera with lemon-caper butter, or the crisp-roasted duckling with wild-huckleberry sauce. The cocktail lounge has live jazz in the evening.

3000 N. Hwy. 1, Albion. ℂ **707/937-0282.** www.ledfordhouse.com. Reservations recommended. Main courses $22–$30. AE, MC, V. Wed–Sun 5–9pm.

3 MENDOCINO ★★★

166 miles N of San Francisco

Mendocino is, to my mind, *the* premier destination on California's Northern Coast. Despite (or because of) its relative isolation, it emerged as one of Northern California's major centers for the arts in the 1950s. It's easy to see why artists were—and still are—attracted to this idyllic community, a cluster of New England–style captains' homes and stores on headlands overlooking the ocean.

At the height of the logging boom, Mendocino was an important and active port. Its population was about 3,500 residents, who constructed eight hotels, 17 saloons, and more than a dozen bordellos. Today, it has only about 1,000 residents, and most reside on the north end of town. On summer weekends, the population seems more like 10,000, as hordes of tourists drive up from the Bay Area. Despite the crowds, however, Mendocino manages to retain its charm.

GETTING THERE   The fastest route from San Francisco is via U.S. 101 north to Cloverdale. Then take Highway 128 west to Highway 1, and then go north along the coast. It's about a 4-hour drive. (You could also take U.S. 101 all the way to Ukiah or Willits and cut over to the west from there.) The most scenic route, if you have the time and your stomach doesn't mind the twists and turns, is to take Highway 1 north along the coast the entire way; it's at least a 5- to 6-hour drive.

VISITOR INFORMATION   You can stock up on lots of free brochures and maps at the **Fort Bragg/Mendocino Coast Chamber of Commerce,** 332 N. Main St. (P.O. Box 1141), Fort Bragg, CA 95437 (© 800/726-2780 or 707/961-6300; www.mendocino coast.com). Pick up a copy of the center's monthly magazine, *Arts and Entertainment,* which lists upcoming events throughout Mendocino. It's available at numerous stores and cafes, including the Mendocino Bakery, Gallery Bookshop, and Mendocino Art Center. You can also do some pretrip research on Mendocino at **MendocinoFun.com,** a nifty online events and activities website/blog to the region that's hosted by local outdoor enthusiasts, artists, and writers.

EXPLORING THE TOWN

Stroll through town, survey the architecture, and browse through the dozens of galleries and shops. My favorites include the **Highlight Gallery,** 45052 Main St. (© 707/937-3132; www.thehighlightgallery.com), for its handmade furniture, pottery, and other craft work; and the **Gallery Bookshop & Bookwinkle's Children's Books,** at Main and Kasten streets (© 707/937-2665; www.gallerybooks.com), one of the best independent bookstores in Northern California, with a wonderful selection of books for children and adults. Another popular stop is **Mendocino Jams & Preserves,** 440 Main St. (© 800/708-1196 or 707/937-1037; www.mendojams.com), which offers free tastings on little bread chips of its natural, locally made gourmet fruit spreads.

After exploring the town, walk out onto **Mendocino Headlands State Park ★**, which wraps around the town. (The visitor center is in the Ford House on Main St.; © 707/937-5397). Three miles of trails, with panoramic views of sea arches and hidden grottoes, wind through the park. At the right time of year, wildflowers blanket the area, and blackberries grow beside the trails. The headlands are home to many unique bird species, including black oystercatchers. Behind the Mendocino Presbyterian Church on Main Street, a trail leads to stairs that take you down to the beach, a small but picturesque stretch of sand where driftwood has washed ashore.

On the south side of town, **Big River Beach** is accessible from Highway 1; it's good for picnicking, walking, and sunbathing.

In town, stop by the **Mendocino Art Center,** 45200 Little Lake St. (© 707/937-5818; www.mendocinoartcenter.org), the town's unofficial cultural headquarters. It's also known for its gardens, galleries, and shops that display and sell local fine arts and crafts. Admission is free; it's open daily from 10am to 5pm.

After a day of hiking, head to **Sweetwater Spa & Inn,** 44840 Main St. (© 800/300-4140 or 707/937-4140; www.sweetwaterspa.com), which offers group and private saunas and hot-tub soaks by the hour. Additional services include Swedish or deep-tissue massages. Reservations are recommended. Private tub prices are $15 per person per half-hour, $18 per person per hour. Group tub prices are $10 per person with no time limit. Special discounts are available on Wednesdays. The spa is open daily from noon to 10pm and Saturday from noon to 11pm.

Tips **Mendocino Nightlife**

The nightlife in Mendocino is like molasses in winter. Visitors have three options: 1) Have a casual cocktail in the elegant bar and lounge at the **Mendocino Hotel** (see review below); 2) knock down a few beers with the locals at **Dick's Place** (45080 Main St.; ✆ **707/937-5643**), the town's oldest bar; or 3) get in the car and head up Highway 1 a bit to the **Caspar Inn,** the best nightclub on the North Coast. Everything from rock and jazz to reggae and blues is played live every night starting at 9:30pm. Check its website calendar for upcoming shows and bring a designated dancer and driver. It's located at 14957 Caspar Rd. (take the Caspar Rd. exit off Hwy. 1, ¼ mile north of Mendocino; ✆ **707/964-5565;** www. casparinn.com).

OUTDOOR PURSUITS

Explore the Big River by renting a canoe, kayak, or outrigger from **Catch a Canoe & Bicycles Too** (✆ **707/937-0273;** www.stanfordinn.com), open daily from 9am to sunset, on the grounds of the Stanford Inn by the Sea (see "Where to Stay," below). If you're lucky, you'll see osprey, blue herons, harbor seals, deer, and wood ducks. These same folks will also rent you a mountain bike (of higher quality than a standard rental), so you can head up Highway 1 and explore the nearby state parks on two wheels.

Visitors can ride horseback (both English and Western style) on the beach and into the woods through **Ricochet Ridge Ranch,** 24201 N. Hwy. 1, Fort Bragg (✆ **888/873-5777** or 707/964-7669; www.horse-vacation.com). Prices range from $45 for a 1½-hour beach ride to $295 for an all-day private beach-and-redwoods trail ride.

In addition to Mendocino Headlands State Park (see "Exploring the Town," above), several other state parks are within an easy drive or bike ride from Mendocino. The brochure *Mendocino Coast State Parks,* available from the visitor center in Fort Bragg, has information on all the parks, with maps of each. These areas include **Manchester State Park,** where the San Andreas Fault sweeps to the sea; **Jughandle State Reserve;** and **Van Damme State Park ★**, with a sheltered, easily accessible beach.

My favorite, on Highway 1 just north of Mendocino, is **Russian Gulch State Park ★★**. It's one of the region's most spectacular parks, where waves crash against the cliffs that protect the park's California coastal redwoods. The most popular attraction is the **Punch Bowl,** a collapsed sea cave that forms a tunnel through which waves crash, creating throaty echoes. Inland, visitors can pedal along a scenic, paved bike path, or hoof it on miles of hiking trails, including a gentle, well-marked 3-mile **Waterfall Loop** that winds past tall redwoods and damp green foliage to a 36-foot-high waterfall. Admission is $6 and camping is $25 per night. Call ✆ **800/444-7275** or log, onto **ReserveAmerica** at **www.reserveamerica.com** for camping reservations; for general state park information, call ✆ **707/937-5804** or visit **www.cal-parks.ca.gov.**

Deep-sea fishing charters are available from Fort Bragg, a short ride up the coast.

WHERE TO STAY
Expensive
Stanford Inn by the Sea ★★   Just south of Mendocino, this rustic but sumptuous lodge is on 11 acres of land abutting the Big River. The grounds are captivating, with

tiers of gardens, a pond for ducks and geese, and fenced pastures of horses, llamas, and old gnarled apple trees. The solarium-style indoor hot tub and pool surrounded by tropical plants are gorgeous. The luxurious rooms come with thick robes, down comforters, fresh flowers, and works by local artists. All units have fireplaces or stoves and private decks from which you can gaze on the Pacific. Second honeymooners should inquire about the romantic River Cottage; families will want the big renovated barn. Pets are welcome and receive the royal treatment. The inn also has a small massage studio, individual and group yoga lessons, and the **Raven's Restaurant,** the only totally vegetarian restaurant on the Mendocino coast offering a full bar and award-winning wine list.

N. Hwy. 1 and Comptche Ukiah Rd. (P.O. Box 487), Mendocino, CA 95460. ⒸⒸ **800/331-8884** or 707/937-5615. Fax 707/937-0305. www.stanfordinn.com. 33 units. $195–$305 double; $295–$785 suite. Rates include breakfast. AE, DC, DISC, MC, V. Pets accepted with $25 fee. **Amenities:** Vegetarian restaurant; solarium-style pool, spa, and sauna; nearby golf course; exercise room; kayak and canoe rental; complimentary bikes; concierge; courtesy car; business center; secretarial services; evening room service; in-room massage. In room: TV/VCR w/pay movies, kitchenette and minibar in some units, fridge, coffeemaker, hair dryer, iron.

Moderate

Agate Cove Inn ★★ Good luck trying to find an accommodation with a more beautiful coastal setting than Agate Cove Inn's. Words can barely convey the splendor of the view from the front lawn—a sweeping, unfettered vista of the sea and its surging waves crashing onto the bluffs. Situate yourself on one of the Adirondack chairs with a good book, and you'll never want to leave. The inn consists of a main house trimmed in blue and white, surrounded by a bevy of single and duplex cottages. Nine of the 10 spacious units have views of the ocean, king- or queen-size beds, down comforters, fireplaces, and private decks. In the morning, a fantastic country breakfast is served in the main house's enclosed porch (yes, with the same ocean view).

11201 N. Lansing St. (P.O. Box 1150), Mendocino, CA 95460. ⒸⒸ **800/527-3111** or 707/937-0551. Fax 707/937-0550. www.agatecove.com. 10 units. $159–$329 double. Rates include full breakfast. MC, V. **Amenities:** Nearby golf course; concierge; activities desk; laptop computer to use in main house; in-room massage. In room: TV/VCR w/complimentary videos, free Wi-Fi, coffeemaker, hair dryer, iron, CD player, complimentary sherry, robes, no phone.

Brewery Gulch Inn ★★ Built almost entirely from century-old redwood logs, the Brewery Gulch Inn is a beautiful three-story inn set high on a bluff overlooking Mendocino's Smuggler's Cove. You don't need to be a connoisseur of woodworking to marvel at the subtle red, purple, and blond tones that swirl throughout the inn's redwood beams, doors, and decks. The inn was constructed in a clean-lined Arts and Crafts style, with a massive steel-and-glass central fireplace and 10 soundproofed guest rooms, each luxuriously appointed with down comforters, gas-lit fireplaces, hardwood furnishings, leather club chairs, CD players, fresh-cut flowers, private decks, and private bathrooms with heated flooring. Most guest rooms have Jacuzzis or soaking tubs for two, as well as private decks with expansive views of the ocean and hundreds of acres of unoccupied meadow and forest. An in-house chef prepares the gourmet country breakfast with herbs and fruit from local sources, and hearty hors d'oeuvres and Mendocino County wines are offered in the evening. *Tip:* Check the website for tempting packages such as the "Romantic Escape!" and "Ocean Kayaking" deals.

9401 Coast Hwy. 1 N., Mendocino, CA 95460. ⒸⒸ **800/578-4454** or 707/937-4752. Fax 707/937-1279. www.brewerygulchinn.com. 10 units. $190–$396 double. Rates include organic gourmet country breakfast and evening wine tasting with hors d'oeuvres. AE, MC, V. **Amenities:** Concierge service; gift shop;

telescope; daily newspaper and turn-down service; common room w/fireplace; library w/wide selection of books, CDs, and videos. *In room:* TV/DVD, hair dryer, CD player, fireplace, soaking tub for 2, robes.

Joshua Grindle Inn ★★   When it was built in 1879, this stately Victorian was one of the most impressive houses in Mendocino, owned by the town's wealthiest banker. Now the oldest B&B in Mendocino, it features redwood siding, a wraparound porch, and emerald lawns. From its prettily planted gardens, the view across the village reaches all the way to the distant bay. The main house has five rooms, with two more in the cottage, and three in the water tower. All have well-lit, comfortably arranged sitting areas, some offer fireplaces, three have deep-soak tubs, and three have whirlpool tubs. Each is individually decorated: The Library Room has a New England feel, with its four-poster pine bed, floor-to-ceiling bookcase, and 19th-century tiles around the fireplace depicting Aesop's fables. Sherry, sweets, and tea are served in the parlor in front of the fireplace; breakfast is in the dining room. The proprietors also have a beautiful two-bedroom, two-bathroom oceanview rental home with floor-to-ceiling windows, a large kitchen, and a wood-burning fireplace. It's a few minutes north of Mendocino, and rates range from $245 to $375, depending on occupancy.

44800 Little Lake Rd. (P.O. Box 647), Mendocino, CA 95460. (℃) **800/GRINDLE** or 707/937-4143. www. joshgrin.com. 11 units. $189–$259 double. Rates include full breakfast, afternoon tea, and wine. MC, V. **Amenities:** Nearby golf course; concierge. *In room:* TV/DVD in some units, hair dryer, no phone.

MacCallum House Inn & Restaurant ★★ (Kids)   A historic 1882 gingerbread Victorian mansion, MacCallum House is one of Mendocino's top accommodations. Originally owned by Daisy MacCallum, the daughter of the town's richest lumber baron, the inn remained in the family until 1974, when it became a B&B. With the occasional Tiffany lamp or Persian carpet, each uniquely decorated guest room and suite is furnished with many original pieces—a Franklin stove, a handmade quilt, a cushioned rocking chair, or a child's cradle. All have private bathrooms, many with claw-foot or spa tubs for two. The luxurious barn suite with a stone fireplace can accommodate up to six. The inn also offers a variety of vacation rentals and even a separate inn, the historic 1882 Mendocino Village Inn. The popular restaurant on the premises serves sophisticated North Coast cuisine ranging from pan-seared Sonoma duck breast with huckleberry-honey-vinegar sauce, to roasted Pacific salmon with saffron-pistachio risotto and arugula pesto. Lighter fare, including a complimentary afternoon glass of wine or beer, is served at the inn's Grey Whale Bar & Cafe. Free passes to a nearby health club are available as well. And unlike most inns in the area, pets and children are both welcome.

45020 Albion St. (P.O. Box 206), Mendocino, CA 95460. (℃) **800/609-0492** or 707/937-0289. Fax 707/937-2243. www.maccallumhouse.com. 44 rooms. $175–$395 double. Extra person $25. Rates include full breakfast, afternoon wine. AE, MC, V. **Amenities:** Restaurant; cafe; bar; hot tub; bike rentals; concierge; massage and spa services; DVD library. *In room:* TV, DVD/CD player, high-speed Internet, fridge, coffeemaker, hair dryer, iron.

Mendocino Hotel & Garden Suites ★   In the heart of town, this 1878 hotel evokes California's Gold Rush era. Beveled-glass doors open into a Victorian-style lobby and parlor. Furnishings include antiques and reproductions, such as the oak reception desk from a demolished Kansas bank, Remington paintings, stained-glass lamps, and Persian carpets. Guest rooms feature hand-painted French porcelain sinks with floral designs; old-fashioned wallpaper, beds, and armoires; and memorabilia of historic Mendocino. About half the rooms are in four handsome small buildings behind the main

house. Many of the deluxe rooms have fireplaces, modern bathrooms, and good views.
Suites have an additional parlor, as well as a fireplace or balcony.

45080 Main St. (P.O. Box 587), Mendocino, CA 95460. ℂ **800/548-0513** or 707/937-0511. Fax 707/937-0513. www.mendocinohotel.com. 51 units, 37 with private bathroom. $100–$120 double with shared bathroom; $135–$295 double with private bathroom; $325–$395 suite. Extra person $20. AE, MC, V. **Amenities:** 2 restaurants; 2 bars; nearby golf course; access to nearby health club ($8); free Wi-Fi in lobby; room service. *In room:* TV, hair dryer.

In Nearby Albion & Little River

Albion River Inn and Restaurant ★★ A quarter-mile north of Albion (or 6 miles south of Mendocino), this modern, beautiful inn overlooks the mouth of the Albion River from a bluff some 90 feet above the Pacific. The view, of course, is spectacular. The rooms are decorated in a contemporary style with comfortable furnishings; all have ocean views, and most have decks. You'll find wingbacks in front of the fireplaces, down comforters on the queen- and king-size beds, well-lit desks, binoculars for wildlife viewing, and bathrobes. *Insider tip:* If you really want to impress, reserve one of the rooms with a spa tub for two, which has a picture window with dazzling views of the coast. The menu at the on-site restaurant changes daily, but the view from the tables remains the same: stellar. The award-winning wine list is also impressive. In the evening, piano music adds to the romantic atmosphere.

3790 N. Hwy. 1 (P.O. Box 100), Albion, CA 95410. ℂ **800/479-7944** or 707/937-1919. Fax 707/937-2604. www.albionriverinn.com. 22 units. $195–$275 double; $325 spa suite. Rates include full breakfast. AE, DC, DISC, MC, V. **Amenities:** Restaurant. *In room:* Fridge, coffeemaker, hair dryer, iron, CD player.

Glendeven ★★ Named one of the 12 best inns in America by *Country Inns* magazine, this 1867 farmhouse is a place of exceptional style and comfort. Accommodations spread across 2$^1/_2$ acres, encompassing the main house, the Carriage House Suite, and an addition known as Stevenscroft. Each room is individually decorated with a balanced mix of antiques, contemporary pieces, and original art. Most have ocean views, fireplaces, and porches. Etta's Suite in the Farmhouse has an antique walnut bed, while the Eastlin and Carriage House suites have king-size feather beds. The four rooms in the Stevenscroft annex are also spacious and beautifully furnished. A vacation rental house, the Barn Loft, has two bedrooms, a loft bathroom, and a kitchen. Adjacent to the inn, numerous fern-lined canyon trails lead to the ocean and beaches of Van Damme State Park.

8205 N. Hwy. 1, Little River, CA 95456. ℂ **800/822-4536** or 707/937-0083. www.glendeven.com. 11 units. $115–$325 double; $320–$410 La Bella Vista. Ask about off-season midweek specials. Rates include full breakfast. AE, DISC, MC, V. **Amenities:** Free Wi-Fi. *In room:* Hair dryer, CD player, no phone.

Heritage House Inn & Restaurant ★★ The setting of the movie *Same Time, Next Year*, this expansive (and expensive) property features guest rooms with über-romantic views of the ocean and the coastline. Thirty-seven seafront acres of lush gardens encompass a variety of accommodations, from the attractive to the outright lush. The ivy-covered, New England–style main building, built in 1877, has three guest rooms; the others are grouped, two to four, in cottages, however some of the suites are free-standing units. Rooms are individually decorated with original antiques and locally made furnishings, with every kind of amenity, including wine racks with regional wines. Most have wood-burning fireplaces or stoves, private decks, sitting areas, and ocean views. Wooded trails wind along the coastline with spectacular scenery. Heritage House Spa offers a variety of treatments in their private suites with individual decks, showers, and steam rooms. In addition to an antique rose garden and lavender fields, the inn's property features a greenhouse and Kitchen Garden with fresh herbs and produce to be used in fresh delicacies prepared in the restaurant, as well as innovative treatments at the spa. The Heritage House dining room is in a magnificent setting overlooking the ocean, with a seasonal menu and a highly touted wine cellar.

5200 N. Hwy. 1, Little River, CA 95456. (C) **800/235-5885** or 707/937-5888. Fax 707/937-0318. www. heritagehouseinn.com. 47 units. Summer $600–$1,300 double. Extra person $45. Rates include continental breakfast for 2. AE, MC, V. **Amenities:** Restaurant; spa; concierge. *In room:* TV, free Wi-Fi, complimentary minibar, coffeemaker, hair dryer, iron, iPod and Bose speakers.

WHERE TO DINE

In addition to the following, see "Where to Stay," above, for hotel restaurants.

Expensive

Café Beaujolais ★★ AMERICAN/FRENCH   This is one of Mendocino's top dining choices and one of the most celebrated restaurants on the Northern Coast. They pride themselves on using locally grown organic produce, meat from humanely raised animals, and fresh locally caught seafood. The French-style cafe is set in an early 1900s house with a modern decor featuring black-and-white photos of the local purveyors. Café Beaujolais is open for lunch and dinner with the menu changing seasonally and usually offering six to seven main courses. Their signature dish is the pan seared sturgeon filet, prepared with truffle emulsion sauce and served with house-made tagliatelle, wild mushrooms, beets, and snap peas. For dessert, try the melting chocolate lava cake served with homemade hazelnut ice cream. On a warm night request a table in the atrium overlooking the gardens.

> **Fun Facts** **Bread Winner**
>
> Few tourists know that Café Beaujolais's renowned "brickery breads" are sold daily from 11am to around 5pm at its Brickery bakery on Ukiah Street, just east of the restaurant.

961 Ukiah St. (C) **707/937-3656.** www.cafebeaujolais.com. Reservations recommended. Main courses $24–$42. DISC, MC, V. Wed–Sun 11:30am–2:30pm; daily 5:45–9pm.

The Moosse Café ★★ CALIFORNIA BISTRO   This petite cafe in a New England–style home is another one of Mendocino's most popular. The menu changes seasonally and features many items made from locally grown organic herbs and vegetables, such as the wonderful organic Rosie chicken and shiitake mushroom pot pie with a chive buttermilk biscuit crust and spring vegetables. I also enjoyed the pan-roasted natural pork chop with a sweet-onion-hazelnut crust, and the braised beef short ribs with Little River organic shiitake mushroom and yellow Finn mashed potatoes. If the cioppino is on the menu—an aromatic stew of fresh fish and shellfish simmered in a saffron-fennel-tomato broth—you're in luck. Service is friendly; my only complaint is that the tables are a bit too close together, especially if it's crowded.

390 Kasten St. (at Albion St.). (C) **707/937-4323.** www.theblueheron.com. Reservations recommended for dinner. Main courses $8–$15 lunch, $18–$29 dinner. MC, V. May–Oct daily noon–3pm and 5:30–9pm; Feb–May Thurs–Mon noon–3pm and 5:30–9pm. Closed Nov–Jan.

The 955 Ukiah Street Restaurant ★★ NORTH COAST CUISINE   Shortly after this building's construction in the 1960s, Emmy Lou Packard commandeered the premises as an art studio for the creation of a series of giant murals. Today it's a spacious yet cozy restaurant, accented with railway ties and vaulted ceilings. Ask for a window table overlooking the gardens. The cuisine is creative and reasonably priced, a worthy alternative to the perpetually booked Café Beaujolais next door. It's hard to pick a favorite dish, although the phyllo-wrapped red snapper with pesto and lime has a zesty tang, and the crispy duck with ginger, apples, and Calvados sauce would garner enthusiasm in Normandy.

955 Ukiah St. (© **707/937-1955.** www.955restaurant.com. Reservations recommended. Main courses $12–$32. MC, V. Thurs–Sun 6–10pm.

Moderate

Bay View Café ★ AMERICAN This reasonably priced cafe is one of the most popular in town. The second-floor dining area affords a sweeping view of the Pacific and faraway headlands; to reach it, climb a flight of stairs outside the town's antique water tower and then detour sideways. You'll find a menu with southwestern selections, an array of sandwiches, fish and chips, and fresh catch of the day. Breakfast ranges from the basic bacon and eggs to eggs Florentine and honey-wheat pancakes.

45040 Main St. (© **707/937-4197.** Reservations not accepted. Main courses $6–$15. No credit cards. Summer daily 8am–9pm; winter Mon–Thurs 8am–3pm, Fri–Sun 8am–9pm.

Inexpensive

Mendo Burgers (© **707/937-1111**) is arguably the best burger joint on the Northern Coast, with patties of all stripes—beef, chicken, turkey, or veggie. A side of thick, fresh-cut fries is mandatory, as is a pile of napkins. Hidden behind the Mendocino Bakery and Café at 10483 Lansing St., it's a little hard to find, but well worth searching out.

In the back of the **Little River Market** (© **707/937-5133**), directly across from the Little River Inn on Highway 1, a trio of small tables overlooks the beautiful Mendocino coastline. Order a tamale, sandwich, hamburger, or whatever else is on the menu at the tiny deli inside the market, or buy a loaf of Café Beaujolais bread, sold at the front counter, and your favorite spread.

4 FORT BRAGG

10 miles N of Mendocino; 176 miles N of San Francisco

As the Mendocino coast's commercial center—hence the site of most of the area's fast-food restaurants and supermarkets—Fort Bragg is far more down-to-earth than Mendocino. Inexpensive motels and cheap eats used to be its only attractions, but over the past few years, gentrification has spread throughout the town, as the logging and fishing industries have steadily declined. With no room left to open new shops in Mendocino, many gallery, boutique, and restaurant owners have moved up the road. The result is a huge increase in Fort Bragg's tourist trade, particularly during the Whale Festival in March and Paul Bunyan Days over Labor Day weekend.

To explore the town properly, get a free walking-tour map from the **Fort Bragg/ Mendocino Coast Chamber of Commerce,** 332 N. Main St. (P.O. Box 1141), Fort Bragg, CA 95437 (© **800/726-2780** or 707/961-6300; www.mendocinocoast.com). The friendly staff can answer most questions about Mendocino, Fort Bragg, and the surrounding region.

A Train Ride Through the Redwoods

Built as a logging railroad in 1885, the North Coast's vintage Skunk Train line was originally used for moving massive redwood logs from the rugged back country to the Mendocino Coast sawmills. Today it's one of the North Coast's largest tourist attractions, taking visitors on a scenic route through the redwood forest, crossing 31 bridges and trestles, cutting through two deep tunnels, and chugging past giant trees that are more than 1,000 years old, before reaching a secluded, forested glen accessible only by train.

The trains run daily from the Fort Bragg Depot at the foot of Laurel Avenue from March 1 to November 31, and on Saturdays December through February. Schedules vary, particularly during holidays; call for details. In the summer, it's a good idea to make reservations. Tickets cost from $47 to $75 for adults and $22 to $40 children ages 3 to 11, depending on the day, time, and train. The 4½-hour Sunset Dinner Barbecue ride includes an elaborate barbecue dinner with huge baskets and trays of homemade bread, barbecued chicken and ribs, baked beans, garden salads, and a "surprise" dessert. For more information call *©* **800/866-1690** or 707/459-1060, or see **www.skunktrain.com**.

SHOPPING & EXPLORING THE AREA

Fort Bragg doesn't have as many high-end stores and galleries as its dainty cousin to the south, but it does have some worthwhile shopping spots. **Antiques shops** line Franklin Street between Laurel and Redwood (aka Antiques Row), and several boutiques are housed within the newly refurbished **Union Lumber Company Store,** an impressive edifice built almost entirely with handcrafted redwoods (on the corner of Main and Redwood sts.).

The **Hot Pepper Jelly Company,** 330 N. Main St. (*©* **866/737-7379;** www.hotpepper jelly.com), is famous for its assortment of Mendocino food products—dozens of pepper jelly varieties, plus local mustards, syrups, and biscotti, hand-painted porcelain bowls, baskets, and more. The **Mendocino Chocolate Company,** 542 N. Main St. (*©* **800/ 722-1107** or 707/964-8800; www.mendocino-chocolate.com), makes and sells homemade chocolates and truffles, which it ships all over the world. Painters, jewelers, sculptors, weavers, potters, woodworkers, and other local artists display their works at **Northcoast Artists,** 362 N. Main St. (*©* **707/964-8266;** www.northcoastartists.org).

Fort Bragg is also the home of the **Mendocino Coast Botanical Gardens,** 18220 N. Hwy. 1 (*©* **707/964-4352;** www.gardenbythesea.org), about 7 miles north of Mendocino. This cliff-top public garden, set among the pines along the coast, nurtures rhododendrons, fuchsias, azaleas, and a multitude of flowering shrubs. The area has bridges, streams, canyons, dells, picnic areas, and trails for easy walking. Admission is $10 for adults, $7.50 for seniors ages 60 and over, $2 for children 13 to 17, $2 for children 6 to 12, and free for 5 and under. (Children under 18 must be accompanied by an adult.) The gardens are open daily March through October from 9am to 5pm, November through February from 9am to 4pm.

The **North Coast Brewing Company,** 455 N. Main St. (*©* **707/964-2739;** www. northcoastbrewing.com), is also worth investigating. Free tours are offered every Saturday at noon and reservations aren't required—just show up. Across the street, the Brewing Company's pub is open for lunch and dinner (see "Where to Dine," below).

OUTDOOR PURSUITS

Fort Bragg is the county's sport-fishing hub. South of town, **Noyo Fishing Center,** 32440 N. Harbor, Noyo (© **707/964-3000;** www.fortbraggfishing.com), is a good place to buy tackle and is the best source of information on local fishing boats. Lots of party boats leave from the town's harbor, as do whale-watching tours.

Lost Coast Kayaking, in Van Damme State Park (© **707/937-2434;** www.lostcoast kayaking.com), offers guided kayak tours of the numerous sea caves on the coast. All the necessary equipment is provided; all you need to bring is a bathing suit and $50 for the 2-hour tour (closed in winter).

Three miles north of Fort Bragg, off Highway 1, **MacKerricher State Park** (© **707/ 964-9112**), is a popular place for biking, hiking, and horseback riding. This 1,700-acre park has 142 campsites and 8 miles of shoreline. For a true biking or hiking venture, travel the 8-mile-long "Haul Road"—an old logging road (partly washed out, but safe) with fine ocean vistas all the way to Ten Mile River. Harbor seals make their home at the park's Laguna Point Seal Watching Station.

WHERE TO STAY

Beachcomber Motel (Value) If the room rates in Mendocino have you reconsidering a visit, the Beachcomber Motel may be just what you seek. Granted, the plain guest rooms are bereft of the antiques you'll find at most B&Bs (and their walls are thin), but they are spacious, comfortable, and equipped with the necessities, including private decks. Anyway, you'll be spending most of your time either on the huge back deck overlooking the Pacific, or in MacKerricher State Park's miles of beaches and dunes, across from the roadside motel. To save even more, book a room with a kitchenette, stockpile groceries, and cook your own food there or in the barbecue area. Low-end rates are for a standard room with no ocean view, and the top rate is for the deluxe suite with king bed, Jacuzzi, fireplace, and ocean view. Three units are wheelchair accessible.

1111 N. Main St., Fort Bragg, CA 95437. © **800/400-7873** or 707/964-2402. Fax 707/964-8925. www. thebeachcombermotel.com. 75 units. $69–$269 double. Rates include continental breakfast. AE, DC, DISC, MC, V. Pets accepted for $10 fee. **Amenities:** Exercise room. *In room:* TV/VCR, kitchenette in suites, fridge, coffeemaker.

Grey Whale Inn ★ (Kids) In downtown Fort Bragg, a short walk from the beach, this B&B was built as a hospital in 1915—hence the wide hallways and large guest rooms. The redwood building is now a well-run, relaxed inn, with antiques, handmade quilts, and plenty of local art. Each room is unique: Two have ocean views, four have fireplaces, one has a whirlpool tub, three have private decks, and one has a shower with wheelchair access. My favorite is the spacious, elegant Campbell Suite, with a king bed and gas-log fireplace. The buffet breakfast, served in the Craftsman-style breakfast room (with trays for carrying your food back to bed, if you prefer) includes a hot entree made from farm-fresh eggs, homemade bread or coffee cake, and fresh fruit. Kids will appreciate the game room with a pool table and foosball.

615 N. Main St., Fort Bragg, CA 95437. © **800/382-7244** or 707/964-0640. Fax 707/964-4408. www. greywhaleinn.com. 13 units. $150–$225 double. Rates include buffet breakfast. AE, MC, V. **Amenities:** Access to nearby health club; game room; in-room massage. *In room:* TV, some units w/VCR or DVD player, kitchenette, fridge, hair dryer, iron.

Thai Fix

If you're in the mood for Thai food, call **GG's Thai Café** at ℂ **707/964-7931.** Located at 500 S. Main St. (Hwy. 1) in Fort Bragg, it's the best (and only) Thai restaurant in the region.

WHERE TO DINE

North Coast Brewing Company ★ AMERICAN Since it opened in 1988, this homey brewpub has been the most happening place in town—especially during happy hour, when boisterous locals take over the bar and dark-wood tables. The building that houses the pub is a century-old redwood structure, which in previous lives functioned as a mortuary, an annex to the local Presbyterian church, an art studio, and administration offices for the College of the Redwoods. Twelve types of beer are available (to go, even) year-round, in addition to seasonal brews. Standard fare, such as fish and chips and burgers, are supplemented by more substantial dishes, ranging from pork tenderloin Dijon with garlic mashed potatoes and fresh vegetables to pasta with seafood in a light herb sauce. After your meal, browse the shop or take a free tour of the brewery (see "Shopping & Exploring the Area," above).

455 N. Main St. ℂ **707/964-3400.** www.northcoastbrewing.com. Reservations accepted for large parties only. Main courses $17–$25. DISC, MC, V. Daily noon–9pm.

The Restaurant Kids PACIFIC NORTHWEST/CALIFORNIA One of the oldest family-run restaurants on the coast, this unpretentious Fort Bragg landmark is known for its jovial atmosphere and cuisine made from scratch from local produce, seafood, meats, and wines. The menu includes dishes from just about every corner of the planet: New York strip steak, a Provençal-style seafood stew, and a few less expensive options such as the Asian noodle bowl filled with bay shrimp and fresh vegetables. My favorites are the fresh blackened rockfish and crab cakes made from local Dungeness crab. A few vegetarian specialties include grilled polenta with melted mozzarella and sautéed mushrooms, topped with tomato-herb sauce and Parmesan cheese. A nicely priced kids' menu is available as well. The booth section is the best place to sit if you want to keep an eye on the kitchen entertainment, provided by ebullient chef Jim Larsen, who has been running things here for more than 30 years.

418 N. Main St. ℂ **707/964-9800.** www.therestaurantfortbragg.com. Reservations recommended. Dinner main courses $20–$30 (includes soup or salad); $10–$15 a la carte items. AE, DISC, MC, V. Daily 5–10pm.

5 THE AVENUE OF THE GIANTS ★★

From Fort Bragg, Highway 1 continues north along the shoreline for about 30 miles before turning inland to Leggett and the Redwood Highway (U.S. 101), which runs north to Garberville. Six miles beyond Garberville, the **Avenue of the Giants** (Hwy. 254) begins around Phillipsville. The Avenue of the Giants is one of the most spectacular routes in the West, cutting along the Eel River through the 51,000-acre Humboldt Redwoods State Park. It roughly parallels U.S. 101, with about a half-dozen interchanges between the two roads, in case you don't want to drive the entire thing. The avenue ends just south of Scotia; from here, it's only about 10 miles to the turnoff to Ferndale, about 5 miles west of U.S. 101.

For more information or a detailed map of the area, go to the **Humboldt Redwoods State Park Visitor Center** in Weott (© 707/946-2263; www.humboldtredwoods.org), in the center of the Avenue of the Giants.

TOURING THE AVENUE

Thirty-three miles long, the Avenue of the Giants was left intact for sightseers when the freeway was built. The giants are the majestic coast redwoods *(Sequoia sempervirens);* more than 50,000 acres of them make up the most outstanding display in the redwood belt. Their rough-bark columns alone climb 100 feet or more and branches soar to more than 340 feet. With their fire-resistant bark and immunity to insects, they have survived for thousands of years. The oldest dated coast redwood is more than 2,200 years old.

Sadly, the route has several tacky attractions that attempt to turn the trees into some kind of freak show. My suggestion is to skip these and take advantage of the trails and campgrounds off the beaten path. As you drive along, you'll see many parking areas with short loop trails leading into the forest. From south to north, the first of these "attractions" is the **Chimney Tree,** where J. R. R. Tolkien's Hobbit is rumored to reside. This living, hollow redwood is more than 1,500 years old. A gift shop and burger place are nearby. Then there's the **One-Log House,** a small apartment-like dwelling built inside a log. You can also drive your car through a living redwood at the **Shrine Drive-Thru Tree,** at Myers Flat, midway along the avenue.

A few miles north of Weott is **Founders Grove,** named in honor of those who established the Save the Redwoods League in 1918. Farther north, close to the end of the avenue, stands the 950-year-old **Immortal Tree,** just north of Redcrest. Near Pepperwood at the end of the avenue, the **Drury Trail** and the **Percy French Trail** are two great short hikes. The park itself is also good for mountain biking. Ask the rangers for details. For more information, contact **Humboldt Redwoods State Park** (© 707/946-2409; www.humboldtredwoods.org).

The state park has three **campgrounds** with 248 campsites: Hidden Springs, half a mile south of Myers Flat; Burlington, 2 miles south of Weott, near park headquarters; and Albee Creek State Campground, 5 miles west of U.S. 101 on the Mattole Road north of Weott. Reservations are advised in summer; you can make them by calling © 800/444-7275 or online via **ReserveAmerica** at **www.reserveamerica.com**. Remaining sites are on a first-come, first-served basis. You'll also come across picnic and swimming facilities, motels, resorts, restaurants, and rest areas with parking lots.

Where to Stay & Dine Near the Southern Entrance

Benbow Inn ★ This elegant National Historic Landmark, overlooking the Eel River and surrounded by gardens, has housed notable guests such as Eleanor Roosevelt, Herbert Hoover, and Charles Laughton. Constructed in 1926 in a mock-Tudor style, it's named after the family who built it. Guests enter through a grand hall and into the lobby with its huge fireplace surrounded by cushy sofas, grandfather clocks, Oriental carpets, and cherry wood wainscoting. Rooms vary in size and amenities, though all are decorated with period antiques; the deluxe units have fireplaces, Jacuzzis, private entrances, and patios. The Honeymoon Cottage is the most popular accommodation, with vaulted ceilings, a canopy bed, wood-burning fireplace, and private patio overlooking the river. A comfortable annex with elegant woodwork was added in the 1980s. Beautiful Benbow

Lake State Park is right out the front door. Complimentary afternoon tea and scones are served in the lobby at 3pm and hors d'oeuvres in the lounge at 5pm—all very proper, of course. The dramatic, high-ceilinged dining room opens onto a spacious terrace and offers internationally inspired (and expensive) main courses. *Tip:* Ask that the house-keeping staff forego the "air freshener," which smells nothing like fresh air.

445 Lake Benbow Dr., Garberville, CA 95542. ℭ **800/355-3301** or 707/923-2124. Fax 707/923-2897. www.benbowinn.com. 55 units. $90–$330 double; $395–$425 cottage. AE, DISC, MC, V. **Amenities:** Restaurant; bar; swimming pool; nearby golf course; spa; complimentary bikes; courtesy car; babysitting (w/ advance notice). *In room:* A/C, coffeemaker, hair dryer, iron, robes, complimentary decanter of sherry.

FERNDALE ★

The village of Ferndale, beyond the Avenue of the Giants and west of U.S. 101, is a National Historic Landmark because of its Victorian homes and storefronts, including a smithy and saddlery. About 5 miles inland from the coast and close to the redwood belt, Ferndale is one of the best-preserved Victorian hamlets in Northern California. Despite its unbearably cute shops, it is nonetheless a vital part of the Northern Coastal tourist circuit.

What's less known about this small town is that it has a number of artists in residence. It's also home to one of California's oddest happenings, the **World Championship Great Arcata to Ferndale Cross-Country Kinetic Sculpture Race** (www.kineticuniverse. com), which draws more than 10,000 spectators every Memorial Day weekend. For 38 miles, over land, sand, mud, and water, participants race in whimsically designed, hand-made, people-powered vehicles that have to be seen to be believed—dragons, Christmas trees, flying saucers, and pyramids, to mention but a few. Awards range from Best Art to Best Engineering to Best Bribe. And as the grand prizes are worth about $15, inspired madness is the only incentive. Stop at the museum at 780 Main St. if you want to see a few past race entries, but bear in mind it's nothing like seeing these contrivances in glorious action.

Where to Stay

Gingerbread Mansion ★★   This peach-and-yellow structure with stained glass and other fine details is one of Ferndale's most frequently photographed Victorians. Built in 1899 for a doctor and his family, it's now run by Ken Torbert, who keeps the place furnished with beautiful antiques. Some of the large guest rooms have two old-fashioned claw-foot tubs for double bubble baths, and others have fireplaces. My favorite is the attic-level Empire Suite, with Ionic columns, a massage-jet shower, two fireplaces, and a king-size bed draped with Royal Sateen fabric. The ultraluxurious Veneto Suite is also impressive. Guests receive bathrobes and thick, extra-large towels. Staff members turn down the beds, leave hand-dipped chocolates on the nightstand, and deliver coffee or tea to your door in the morning, to sustain you until your breakfast of fruit, cheese, muffins, breads, cakes, and a baked egg dish. Afternoon tea features sandwiches, pastries, and fresh fruit.

400 Berding St. (P.O. Box 40), Ferndale, CA 95536. ℭ **800/952-4136** or 707/786-4000. Fax 707/786-4381. www.gingerbread-mansion.com. 11 units. $135–$285 double; $170–$400 suite. Extra person $40. Rates include full breakfast and afternoon tea. AE, MC, V. **Amenities:** Concierge; activities desk. *In room:* Hair dryer, no phone.

Shaw House Inn Bed and Breakfast ★★   Modeled after Hawthorne's House of the Seven Gables, this gorgeous B&B is the oldest structure in Ferndale, the oldest B&B in California, and one of the prettiest Victorian homes I've ever seen (and I've seen a *lot* of B&Bs). It was built in 1854 by Ferndale founder Seth Louis Shaw, who had a penchant for jutting gables, bay windows, balconies, and gazebos. Each of the eight individually decorated guest rooms is handsomely furnished with period antiques, plush fabrics, and private bathrooms (rare for a 19th-c. B&B). Four rooms have private entrances, and three have private balconies overlooking the 1-acre garden. My favorite is the romantic Fountain Suite, with its own fireplace, parlor, and claw-foot tub. The immaculate 1-acre park is shaded by 25 varieties of 100-plus-year-old trees and rhododendrons, and the restaurants and shops along Main Street are a short walk away.

703 Main St., Ferndale, CA 95536. (℗ **800/557-SHAW** or 707/786-9958. Fax 707/786-9758. www.shaw house.com. 8 units, all with private bathroom. $135–$275 double. Rates include breakfast and afternoon tea. DISC, MC, V. **Amenities:** Gift shop; game table. *In room:* Wi-Fi.

Where to Dine

Curley's Grill ★ CALIFORNIA GRILL   This bright, lively restaurant specializes in California-inspired grilled foods, but don't think for a moment that the menu is limited to its steaks, burgers, and baby back ribs that fall off the bone. Owner Curley Tait also grills items such as braised lamb shanks, Japanese soba noodles (with green onions, red pepper, and portobello mushroom in a tamari sauce), polenta with a sausage-tomato sauce, coconut prawns, and some of the freshest seafood and vegetables on the coast. Curley's also offers homemade breads and desserts, and an interesting selection of California wines, with a Victorian-style full bar area. On sunny afternoons, request a seat on the shaded back patio.

400 Ocean Ave., inside the Victorian Inn. (℗ **707/786-9696.** Reservations recommended. Main courses $8–$28. DISC, MC, V. Mon–Sat 11:30am–9pm; breakfast Sat 8–11am and Sun 8am–3pm.

6 EUREKA & ENVIRONS ★

296 miles N of San Francisco

EUREKA

At first glance, Eureka (pop. 27,000) looks unappealing: Fast-food restaurants, cheap motels, and shopping malls predominate on the main thoroughfare. But if you turn west off U.S. 101 anywhere between A and M streets, you'll discover **Old Town Eureka** along the waterfront, which is worth exploring. It has a large number of Victorian buildings, a museum, and some good-quality stores and restaurants.

The city's newest development is a waterfront boardwalk between C and F streets, adjacent to the Old Town historic district. This section of the waterfront, previously closed to the public, now offers sweeping views of the harbor and bay.

For more visitor information, contact or visit the **Eureka/Humboldt County Convention and Visitors Bureau,** 1034 Second St., Eureka, CA 95501 (℗ **800/346-3482** or 707/443-5097; www.redwoodvisitor.org), or the **Eureka Chamber of Commerce,** 2112 Broadway, Eureka, CA 95501 (℗ **800/356-6381;** www.eurekachamber.com).

What to See & Do

The **Clarke Historical Museum,** 240 E St. (℗ **707/443-1947;** www.clarkemuseum. org), has a fine collection of Native American baskets and other artifacts. The other popular attraction is the **Carson Mansion ★** (on the corner of Second and M sts.), built from 1884 to 1886 for lumber baron William Carson. A three-story conglomeration of ornamentation, its design is a mélange of styles—Queen Anne, Italianate, Stick, and Eastlake. It took 100 men more than 2 years to build it. Today it's a private club, so you can only marvel at the exterior of this 18-room mansion—said to be the most photographed Victorian home in the U.S. Across the street stands the **Pink Lady,** designed for William Carson as a wedding present for his son. Both buildings testify to the wealth that was once made in Eureka's lumber trade. As early as 1856, seven sawmills produced 2 million board feet of lumber per month. A restored building now houses the **Morris Graves Museum of Art,** 636 F St. (© 707/442-0278; www.humboldtarts.org), with four galleries showcasing local artists as well as traveling exhibitions.

For a good read, drop in at the **Booklegger,** 402 Second St., at E St. (© 707/445-1344), a fantastic bookstore in Old Town with thousands of used paperbacks (especially mysteries, Westerns, and science fiction), children's books, and cookbooks.

Humboldt Bay, where the town stands, was discovered by settlers in 1850. To protect the fledgling community from local Native Americans, the government established Fort Humboldt 3 years later. Ulysses S. Grant was stationed here for 5 months until he resigned after disputes with his commanding officer about his drinking. Troops abandoned the fort in 1870. Today, a self-guided trail takes visitors past a series of logging exhibits, a reconstructed surgeon's quarters, and a restored fort hospital, now a museum of Native American artifacts and military and pioneer paraphernalia. **Fort Humboldt State Historic Park** is at 3431 Fort Ave. (© 707/445-6567). Admission is free; it's open daily from 8am to 5pm.

Outdoor Pursuits

Humboldt Bay supplies a large portion of California's fish, and Eureka has a fishing fleet of about 200 boats. For an optimal view of the bay and surrounding waters, board skipper Leroy Zerlang's 1910 *Madaket*—a state historic landmark and the oldest passenger-carrying vessel in continuous service in the United States—for a 75-minute narrated **Humboldt Bay Harbor Cruise.** Tours depart from the foot of F Street in downtown Eureka Thursday through Saturday at 1, 2:30, and 4pm, and Sunday through Tuesday at 1 and 2:30pm. Tickets are $18 per person for adults, $16 for seniors, $10 for kids 5 to 12, and under 5 free. There's also a $10 cocktail cruise offered in the summer. Call © 707/445-1910 for a recorded departure schedule, or log on to **www.humboldtbay maritimemuseum.com**.

For more water recreation, you can rent kayaks, canoes, and sailboats from **Hum Boats** Friday through Monday from 9am to 5pm on Dock A, Woodley Island Marina (© 707/443-5157; www.humboats.com). Tours and lessons are also available.

Humboldt County is suitable for biking because it's relatively uncongested. You can rent bikes from **Pro Sport Center,** 1600 5th St. (© 707/443-6328; www.prosport center.com). Fishing, diving, biking, and hiking information are also available here.

Humboldt Bay, an important stopover point along the Pacific Flyway, is the winter home for thousands of migratory birds. South of town, the **Humboldt Bay National Wildlife Refuge ★**, 1020 Ranch Rd., Loleta (© 707/733-5406), provides an opportunity to see many of the 200 or so species that live in the marshes and willow groves— including Pacific black brant, western sandpiper, northern harrier, great blue heron, and green-winged teal. The egret rookery on the bay, best viewed from Woodley Island Marina across the water, is spectacular. Peak viewing for most water birds and raptors is between September and March. The entrance is off U.S. 101 north at the Hookton Road exit. Cross the overpass and turn right onto Ranch Road.

Moderate

Abigail's Elegant Victorian Mansion Bed & Breakfast ★   For owners Doug and Lily Vieyra, the restoration and upkeep of this 1888 house, a National Historic Landmark, is a labor of love. They combed the country for the fabrics and designs that provide the most authentic Victorian atmosphere I have encountered in the U.S. The wallpapers are extraordinary—brilliant blues, golds, jades, and reds in patterns that feature peacocks and mythological figures. Doug pays attention to every detail, from the butler who greets you in morning dress, to the silent movies, to period music on the phonograph. Each unit is individually furnished: The Van Gogh room contains the Belgian bedroom suite of Lily's mother. The Lillie Langtry room, named after the actress and king's mistress who stayed here when she performed locally, features a four-poster bed and Langtry memorabilia. Guests can play croquet on the beautifully manicured lawn, where the staff serves ice-cream sodas and lemonade in the afternoon.

1406 C St. (at 14th St.), Eureka, CA 95501. € 707/444-3144. www.eureka-california.com. 4 units. $165–$195 double. Additional person $50. Rates include breakfast. MC, V. **Amenities:** Sauna; complimentary bikes; massage; laundry service. *In room:* A/C.

Hotel Carter, Carter House, Bell Cottage, and Carter Cottage ★★★   At the north end of Eureka's Old Town, the Carter House launched Mark Carter's renowned hostelry empire. Mark Carter built this copy of an 1884 San Francisco Victorian as a family home in 1982. Soon afterward, he and his wife, Christi, began taking guests, and before long they also built the stately hotel across the street, the Hotel Carter. Later, they acquired the pretty Victorian Bell Cottage and the ultraluxurious Carter Cottage as well.

The 23 rooms in the large, full-service Hotel Carter have beautiful modern furnishings and pine four-posters. The suites have luxury appointments such as fireplaces and Jacuzzis with distant views of the waterfront. The original Carter House has seven rooms, furnished with antiques, Oriental rugs, and modern artwork. Rooms in the Bell Cottage are also individually decorated in grand Victorian fashion. If you want to splurge, reserve the Carter Cottage, a small home that was converted into one of the most luxurious lodgings in Northern California—a minimansion with a chef's kitchen, two fireplaces, a grand bathroom with a whirlpool tub for two, and a private deck. The Carters offer an array of luxury accommodations, ranging from classic Victorian in the house and cottage to a softer, brighter, more contemporary look in the hotel. The ground level of the Hotel Carter houses one of Eureka's finest restaurants, **Restaurant 301** (see "Where to Dine," below), where a full breakfast (included in the room rate) is served each morning.

301 L St., Eureka, CA 95501. € 800/404-1390 or 707/444-8062. Fax 707/444-8067. www.carterhouse. com. 32 units. $190–$226 double; $304–$370 suite; $612 Carter Cottage. Rates include full breakfast. Packages available. AE, DC, DISC, MC, V. From U.S. 101 north, turn left onto L St. to Third St. **Amenities:** Restaurant; nearby golf course; activities desk; in-room massage; babysitting; laundry service; wine shop. *In room:* A/C, TV/VCR w/pay movies, kitchen in some units, hair dryer, iron.

Inexpensive

Bayview Motel (Value)   Although it's not nearly so opulent as Abigail's Elegant Victorian Mansion, the modern Bayview Motel soundly takes the prize for price and privacy. In fact, it's one of the cleanest, most meticulously landscaped motels I've ever seen. Atop a small knoll on the south side of Eureka, it *does* have a bay view, but you have to peer through a seedy industrial area to see it; the gardens actually make for the better view. All rooms are minisuites with standard motel amenities, including queen-size beds. If you feel like splurging, request a Romantic Getaway room complete with a Jacuzzi and fireplace. Family units are also available, and small pets are welcome.

2844 Fairfield St. (corner of Hwy. 1 and Henderson St.), Eureka, CA 95501. © **866/725-6813** or 707/442-1673. Fax 707/268-8681. www.bayviewmotel.com. 17 units. $90–$165 double. AE, DISC, MC, V. Small pets accepted. *In room:* TV, fax, fridge, coffeemaker, hair dryer, iron.

Where to Dine

Ramone's Bakery & Cafe (Value) BAKERY   Ramone's has a bakery on one side and a small dining room on the other. The baked items are extraordinary—croissants, Danishes, cinnamon rolls, truffles, and muffins made from scratch every morning without preservatives or dough conditioners. The bakery also prepares soups, salads, and huge sandwiches, plus a few lunch specials such as lasagna and quiche. Any time of the day, it's a great place to stop for a light, inexpensive meal and cup of coffee. Ramone's has other locations, at 2223 Harrison St., in Eureka, and in Arcata at 747 13th St., at Wildberries Marketplace.

209 E St. (in Old Town). © **707/445-2923**. www.ramonesbakery.com. Main courses $4–$8. No credit cards. Mon–Sat 7am–6pm; Sun 7am–4pm.

Restaurant 301 ★★★ CALIFORNIA   This is the best restaurant in the area. The large, airy dining room adjacent to the hotel lobby has tall windows overlooking the waterfront. At dinner, patrons may order a la carte or off the highly recommended Discovery Menu—a five-course, prix-fixe feast that pairs each course with suggested wines by the glass. A typical dinner might begin with an artichoke, green lentil, and fennel salad, followed by a warm chèvre cake appetizer, followed by a grilled duck breast with a seasonal fruit and zinfandel sauce. The chef picks most of the herbs and many of the vegetables fresh from organic gardens across the street. If you love oysters, start with a few Humboldt Bays roasted with barbecue sauce. Courtesy of the hotel's 301 Wine Shop, the wine bar features an excellent, extensive list that garnered *Wine Spectator*'s Grand Award.

In the Hotel Carter, 301 L St. © **800/404-1390** or 707/444-8062. www.carterhouse.com. Reservations recommended. Main courses $22–$29. AE, DC, DISC, MC, V. Daily 6–9:30pm.

Samoa Cookhouse ★ (Finds) AMERICAN   During the lumber industry's heyday, cookhouses like this one—the last of its kind in the West, dating from 1885—were common, serving as community centers. The mill men and longshoremen chowed down on three hot meals before, during, and after their 12-hour workday. The food is still hearty (though not necessarily healthy by today's standards), served family style at long tables covered with red-checkered cloths. The price includes soup, salad, fresh-baked bread, the main course, and dessert (usually pie). And the lunch-and-dinner menu still features a daily dish—roast beef, fried or barbecued chicken, ham, or pork chops. Breakfast typically includes eggs, potatoes, sausage, bacon, pancakes, and unlimited orange juice and coffee. Adjacent to the dining room, a small museum features memorabilia from the lumbering era. Bring the kids before this place vanishes into history.

Cookhouse Rd., Samoa. © **707/442-1659**. Reservations accepted for large groups only. Main courses $7.45–$12. AE, DISC, MC, V. Mon–Sat 7am–3:30pm and 5–9pm; Sun 7am–10pm (closes 1 hr. earlier in winter). From U.S. 101, take Samoa Bridge to the end and turn left on Samoa Rd.; then take the 1st left.

ARCATA ★

From Eureka, it's 7 miles to Arcata, one of my favorite towns on the Northern Coast. Sort of a cross between Mayberry and Berkeley, it has an undeniable small-town flavor—right down to the bucolic center square—yet it possesses that intellectual and environmentally conscious esprit de corps so characteristic of university towns (Arcata is the home of Humboldt State University).

Family-type activities abound. On Wednesday, Friday, and Saturday evenings between June and July, Arcata's semipro baseball team, the **Humboldt Crabs,** plays at Arcata Ballpark (© **707/826-2333;** www.humboldtcrabs.com), at Ninth and F streets. Also check out the kid-friendly **Humboldt State University Natural History Museum,** 1315 G St. (© **707/826-4479**), open Tuesday through Saturday from 10am to 5pm; **Tin Can Mailman,** at 10th and H streets (© **707/822-6450**), a used-book store with more than 130,000 titles; and **Redwood Park** (east end of 11th St.), with an outstanding playground for kids and miles of forested hiking trails.

Home to Northern California's indigenous people, the Hoopa Indian Reservation is some 40 miles east of Eureka, and a few miles north of Willow Creek. In the Hoopa Shopping Center, the **Hoopa Tribal Museum** (© **530/625-4110**) archives Hoopa culture and history, including ceremonial regalia, basketry, canoes, and tools. By appointment, the museum organizes guided tours of Hoopa Valley historic sites, including the traditional village of Takimildiñ. Hours are Monday through Friday from 8am to noon and 1 to 5pm year-round, and in summer on Saturday from 10am to noon and from 1 to 4pm.

Outdoor Pursuits

The **Arcata Marsh and Wildlife Sanctuary** ★, at the foot of South I Street (© **707/826-2359**), is a thought-provoking excursion. The 154-acre sanctuary—which doubles as Arcata's integrated wetland wastewater treatment plant—is a stopover for marsh wrens, egrets, and other waterfowl, including the rare Arctic loon. Every Saturday at 8:30am and 2pm, free 1-hour guided tours start at the cul-de-sac at the foot of South I Street. Or just pick up a free self-guided walking tour map of the preserve, available at the **Arcata Chamber of Commerce,** 1635 Heindon Rd. (© **707/822-3619;** www.arcatachamber. com). Locals are proud of their town's wastewater solution, boasting "Arcata Residents Flush with Pride."

Where to Stay

Fairwinds Motel (Value)   Right off Highway 101, just a few blocks from Humboldt State University, the Fairwinds has simple yet spotless rooms with small balconies overlooking nothing in particular. Although the motel has been in operation since 1962 and its age-lines are showing, the rooms have been completely remodeled with new beds and modernish furnishings and prints. I recommend it only if you can't get a room at the Hotel Arcata or you're looking to save a few bucks on lodging.

1674 G St. at 17th St., Arcata, CA 95521. © **866/352-5518** or 707/822-4824. Fax 707/822-0568. www. fairwindsmotelarcata.com. 26 units. $59–$99 double. AE, DISC, MC, V. *In room:* TV, free Wi-Fi.

Hotel Arcata (Value)   This is the town's most prominent hotel, with many guests visiting their children at Humboldt State University. If you're not inclined to stay at the fancier Lady Anne B&B (see review below), this is definitely the next best choice. Located on the northeast corner of the town plaza, the Hotel Arcata has a handsome, early 1900s brick facade. The individually decorated rooms range from small, inexpensive singles to large executive suites that overlook the plaza. The minisuites are the quietest—a bargain at about $100. **Tomo,** the Japanese restaurant on the premises, is under different management.

708 Ninth St., Arcata, CA 95521. © **800/344-1221** or 707/826-0217. Fax 707/826-1737. www.hotelarcata. com. 32 units. $76–$120 double; $126–$148 executive suite. Rates include continental breakfast. AE, DC, DISC, MC, V. Pets accepted with $5-a-day fee and $50 deposit. **Amenities:** Restaurant; free passes to nearby indoor pool and health club; salon; executive suites. *In room:* TV, coffeemaker.

The Lady Anne ★   Among Arcata's finest lodgings, this beautiful Queen Anne–style inn is kept in top-notch condition by innkeepers Sharon and Sam Pennisi. The large, cozy guest rooms are individually decorated with antiques, lace curtains, Oriental rugs, and English stained glass. For second honeymooners, the Lady Sarah Angela Room is ideal, with a four-poster bed and bay view. On summer afternoons you can lounge on the veranda or play croquet on the front lawn. Several good dining options are only a few blocks away at Arcata Plaza.

902 14th St., Arcata, CA 95521. © **707/822-2797.** www.humboldt1.com/ladyanne. 5 units. $110–$140 double. MC, V. *In room:* Hair dryer, iron, no phone.

Where to Dine

Abruzzi ★ ITALIAN   The best way to review your dining options in Arcata is to stroll to Jacoby's Storehouse, a mid-19th-century brick warehouse at the southwest corner of the town plaza, and ponder the menus posted outside Abruzzi and the Plaza Grill (see below). Abruzzi is considered the best Italian restaurant in town. It's also romantic, with dark woods and dim lighting. Meals begin with a basket of warm bread sticks, focaccia, and a baguette from a local bakery. Specialties include range-fed veal piccata, well-seasoned filet steaks, and sea scallops with langoustines tossed with cheese tortellini. The standout dessert is the chocolate *paradiso*, a dense chocolate cake in a pool of champagne *mousseline*.

Jacoby's Storehouse (at the corner of Eighth and H sts.). © **707/826-2345.** Reservations recommended. Main courses $9–$26. AE, DISC, MC, V. Daily 5:30–9pm.

Folie Douce ★★ BISTRO   Humboldt hip meets cuisine chic at Folie Douce, the most energized, inventive restaurant in town. Designer wood-oven-fired pizza is its mainstay, like the grilled duck sausage fennel, chèvre, and Roquefort cheese with caramelized red onions, walnuts, and arugula, or the Mexican white shrimp with honey. Appetizers and entrees are equally intriguing; the highlight of your vacation may well be the artichoke-heart and pancetta cheesecake appetizer. Other heartier menu items range from wasabi steak with scallions and sesame, to lamb loin chops sauced with local artichokes in minted jus. Everything on the menu is 100% organic, natural, free range, and free of hormones or antibiotics. The restaurant has a serious wine list as well. This small, festive eatery is extremely popular, so make reservations.

1551 G St. (btw. 15th and 16th sts.). © **707/822-1042.** www.holyfolie.com. Reservations suggested. Main courses $13–$34. AE, DISC, MC, V. Tues–Thurs 5:30–9pm; Fri–Sat 5:30–10pm.

Plaza Grill Kids AMERICAN   If the prices at Abruzzi are a bit more than you care to spend, consider the Plaza Grill, directly upstairs. Despite efforts to make it more upscale, it can't seem to shake its image as a college-student burger joint, albeit a nice one. The menu is more substantial than you'd think, with a choice of salads, sandwiches, burgers, fish platters, chicken specialties, steaks, and all kinds of coffee drinks. The children's menu is very reasonably priced.

Jacoby's Storehouse (at the corner of Eighth and H sts.). © **707/826-0860.** Main courses $7–$17. AE, DISC, MC, V. Mon–Thurs 5–9:30pm; Fri–Sat 5–10pm

Back on U.S. 101 north of Arcata, you'll come to **Trinidad,** a tiny coastal fishing village of 400 people. One of the smallest incorporated cities in California, it's on a peninsula 25 miles north of Eureka. If you're not into fishing, there's little to do in town except poke around at the handful of shops, walk along the busy pier, and wish you owned a house here.

Five miles north of Trinidad takes you to the 640-acre **Patrick's Point State Park ★,** 4150 Patrick's Point Dr. (✆ **707/677-3570**), which has one of the finest ocean access points in the north at **Agate Beach.** It's suitable for driftwood picking, rock hounding, and camping on a sheltered bluff. The park contains a re-creation of a Sumeg village, which is used by the Yurok people and neighboring tribes. A self-guided tour takes you to replicas of family homes and sweat houses.

Where to Stay

The Lost Whale Bed & Breakfast Inn ★★ (Kids)

This modern version of a blue-and-gray Cape Cod–style house sits on 9 acres of seafront studded with firs, alders, spruces, and redwoods with a private trail leading down to Abalone Cove and a private beach. The friendly owners welcome children (there's a playground on the lawn) as much as romantically inclined couples (a very inviting Jacuzzi on the back deck offers a view of the sea). They claim their hotel is the only one in California with a private beach featuring tide pools and sea lions. The inn's five soundproof rooms have private balconies or sitting alcoves with views of the ocean or garden, two rooms have separate sleeping lofts, and all have private bathrooms and queen-size beds. In the morning, you'll marvel at the huge breakfasts, prepared by the resident cook: casseroles, quiches, home-baked muffins, fresh fruit, and locally smoked salmon.

3452 Patrick's Point Dr., Trinidad, CA 95570. ✆ **800/677-7859** or 707/677-3425. Fax 707/677-0284. www. lostwhaleinn.com. 5 units. Summer $230–$230 double, $375 suite; winter $200–$230 double, $375 suite. Rates include country breakfast and afternoon tea. AE, DISC, MC, V. **Amenities:** Oceanview Jacuzzi; children's playground; game room; free Wi-Fi. *In room:* No phone.

Trinidad Bay Bed & Breakfast ★★ (Finds)

Perched 175 feet above the ocean, this charming Cape Cod–style B&B is the best place to stay on Trinidad Bay. On a clear day, you can see up to 65 miles of rugged coastline and shimmering ocean. All the bright, colorful guest rooms are individually decorated and come with king beds, ocean views, and private bathrooms. The price is the same for all four rooms, so if it's available, opt for the Tide Pool room—it offers an amazing panoramic view from the wraparound windows, as well as a private entrance. Second choice is the Trinity Alps Room, which also has a private entrance, small kitchenette, and wonderful bay views (also, both of these rooms have a small dining area so breakfast can be delivered to your room if you prefer). The town shops and restaurants are a short walk away, as well as numerous hiking trails, beaches, and picnic spots.

560 Edwards St. (P.O. Box 849), Trinidad, CA 95570-0849. ✆ **707/677-0840.** www.trinidadbaybnb.com. 4 units. $200–$250 double. Rates include breakfast. AE, MC, V. *In room:* Free Wi-Fi, fridge, coffeemaker, hair dryer.

Trinidad Inn (Value)

You'll find a bevy of inexpensive motels in these parts, but the Trinidad Inn is the best of the lot. It's 2 miles north of Trinidad on a serene stretch of road dwarfed by redwoods. Both the motel's exterior—trimmed in shades of white and blue—and guest rooms are impeccably maintained. Each room is unique: Some are family units that hold up to four persons, while others offer a comfortable queen bed and private bathroom. A good room for couples is no. 10, an adorable little cottage complete with a full kitchen, living room, private bathroom, bedroom, and small patio. Each morning fresh coffee, tea, and homemade raspberry scones and muffins are served under the gazebo in the flower-filled garden. Guests are free to use the picnic table and barbecue, or wander through the adjacent forest to the beaches a short stroll away.

1170 Patrick's Point Dr., Trinidad, CA 95570. ℂ **707/677-3349.** www.trinidadinn.com. 10 units. $65–$175 double. Rates include continental breakfast. AE, DC, DISC, MC, V. From U.S. 101, take the Trinidad exit and head 2 miles north on Patrick's Point Dr. Pets accepted with $15 fee and $20 deposit. *In room:* TV, no phone.

Where to Dine

Larrupin Café ★★ AMERICAN   On a quiet country road 2 miles north of Trinidad, this popular, beautifully decorated restaurant sports a blend of Indonesian and African artifacts mingled with colorful urns full of exotic flowers and candlelit tables. The patio with a reflecting pool and bamboo fencing is a charmer, as is the wood-burning fireplace in winter. Dinner starts with an appetizer board stocked with gravlax, pâté, dark pumpernickel, and apple slices, followed by a red- and green-leaf salad tossed with a Gorgonzola vinaigrette; or go with the barbecued oysters. Many menu items are barbecued over mesquite fires, such as the hefty cut of halibut basted with lemon butter and served with mustard-flavored dill sauce, or pork ribs with a side of sweet-and-spicy barbecue sauce. Another recommended dish is the barbecued Cornish game hen with an orange-and-brandy glaze. *Note:* They don't take credit cards and the hours tend to vary seasonally, so be sure to call ahead and bring plenty of cash.

1658 Patrick's Point Dr. ℂ **707/677-0230.** www.larrupincafe.com. Reservations recommended. Main courses $15–$22. No credit cards. Thurs–Mon 5–9pm (hours may vary seasonally, so call ahead).

The Seascape Restaurant ★ (Finds) CALIFORNIA   Established in the 1940s, the Seascape is an unpretentious cross between a cafe and a diner, with three dining rooms, ocean views, overworked but cheerful waitresses, and a nostalgic aura. People pop in for coffee or snacks from early morning until after sundown, but by far the biggest seller here is the Trinidad Bay Platter. Heaped with halibut, scallops, and shrimp, and accompanied by salad and rice pilaf, it's even more popular than the excellent prawn brochette. How fresh is the fish? As the menu states, "Availability of seafood depends on season, weather conditions, regulations, and luck." Halibut, rock cod, sole, and other local catches come charbroiled, sautéed in garlic, onions, and mushrooms, or prepared in four other styles. For you late risers, breakfast is served until 4pm.

Beside the pier at the foot of Bay St. ℂ **707/677-3762.** Full dinners $11–$30. DISC, MC, V. Daily 7am–9pm.

7 CRESCENT CITY

79 miles N of Eureka; 375 miles N of San Francisco

Crescent City has little to offer, but it makes a good base for exploring Redwood National Park and the Smith River, one of the great recreational rivers of the West. The **Battery Point Lighthouse,** at the foot of A Street (ℂ **707/464-3089;** www.lighthouse friends.com), which is accessible on foot only at low tide, houses a museum with exhibits on the coast's history. Tours of the lighthouse ($2 for adults, 50¢ for children 12 and

Another draw is the **Smith River National Recreation Area** ★, east of Jedediah Smith State Park and part of Six Rivers National Forest. Headquarters is at 10600 U.S. 199, Gasquet (© 707/457-3131), reached via U.S. 199 from Crescent City (about a 30-min. drive). You can get maps of the forest at the Supervisor's Office in Eureka, or at either of the Redwood National Park centers in Orick and Crescent City.

The 300,000-plus acres of wilderness have five small campgrounds (with fewer than 50 sites) along the Smith River. Sixteen trails draw hikers from across the country. The easiest short trail is the **McClendon Ford,** which is 2 miles long and drops from 1,000 to 800 feet in elevation to the river. Other activities include mountain biking, white-water rafting, kayaking, and fishing for salmon and trout.

For information, contact the **Crescent City–Del Norte County Chamber of Commerce,** 1001 Front St., Crescent City, CA 95531 (© **800/343-8300** or 707/464-3174; www.northerncalifornia.net).

WHERE TO STAY

Crescent Beach Motel ⟨Value⟩   Crescent City doesn't have any fancy hotels or B&Bs, but it does have lots of modestly priced motels—the best of which is the Crescent Beach, which is also the only one on the bay. Near the highway, about a mile south of town, this single-story structure is freshly remodeled, with clean and simple refurbished rooms. Four of the units face the highway; try to get one of the others, all of which have sliding glass doors to decks and a small lawn area overlooking the water.

1455 Redwood Hwy. S. (U.S. 101), Crescent City, CA 95531. © 707/464-5436. Fax 707/464-9336. www. crescentbeachmotel.com. 27 units. Summer $77–$90 double; winter $55–$64 double. AE, DISC, MC, V. *In room:* TV, no phone.

Curly Redwood Lodge ⟨Value⟩   This is a blast from the past, the kind of place where you might have stayed as a kid during a cross-country vacation in the family station wagon. It was built in 1957 on grasslands across from the harbor, and it's trimmed with lumber from a single ancient redwood. Although they're not full of high-tech gadgets, the bedrooms are among the largest and best-soundproofed in town, and certainly the most evocative of a bygone age. In winter, about a third of the rooms are locked and sealed. I still prefer the rooms on the beach at the Crescent Beach Motel, but the Curly is a solid bet for a clean, comfortable, and inexpensive hotel room.

701 Redwood Hwy. S. (U.S. 101), Crescent City, CA 95531. © 707/464-2137. Fax 707/464-1655. www. curlyredwoodlodge.com. 36 units. Summer $64–$89 double; winter $52–$78 double. AE, DC, MC, V. *In room:* TV.

WHERE TO DINE

Beachcomber SEAFOOD   The decor is as nautical as this restaurant's name, with rough-cut planking and a scattering of driftwood, fishnets, and buoys dangling above a dimly lit space. The restaurant is beside the beach, 2 miles south of Crescent City's center. The cuisine is a joy for fish lovers who prefer not to mask the flavor of their seafood with complicated sauces. Most of the dishes are grilled over madrone-wood barbecue pits. Freshly harvested Pacific salmon, halibut, lingcod, shark, sturgeon, Pacific snapper, oysters, and steamer clams have visitors lining up. The Beachcomber also serves great flame-broiled steaks.

1400 U.S. 101. ✆ **707/464-2205.** Reservations recommended. Main courses $6–$15. MC, V. Fri–Tues 5–9pm. Closed Dec–Jan and part of Feb.

Harbor View Grotto Restaurant & Lounge SEAFOOD/STEAKS This friendly local restaurant has been specializing in fresh seafood at market prices since 1961. The food is not as good as the Beachcomber's, but it's a little less expensive, it's open for lunch, and it's far less crowded on weekend nights. The "light eaters" menu includes a cup of white chowder (made fresh daily) or a salad, a main course, and vegetables; heartier eaters can choose from among three different cuts of prime rib. Menu items include fresh, locally caught fish such as Pacific snapper and salmon. Crab or shrimp Louis, as well as crabmeat or shrimp sandwiches, are popular in season.

150 Starfish Way. ✆ **707/464-3815.** Reservations recommended. Main courses $4–$9 lunch, $6–$20 dinner. DISC, MC, V. Daily 11am–9pm (later in the summer months).

8 REDWOOD NATIONAL & STATE PARKS ★★

40 miles N of Eureka; 336 miles N of San Francisco

It's difficult to explain the feeling you get in the old-growth forests of Redwood National and State Parks without citing *Alice in Wonderland.* Like a jungle, the redwood forest is a multistoried affair, and the tall trees are just the top layer. Everything seems big and misty, from another era—flowering bushes cover the ground, 10-foot-tall ferns line the creeks, and the smells are rich and musty. It's so outsize and primeval, you half expect to turn the corner and see a dinosaur.

When Archibald Menzies first noted the botanical existence of the coast redwood in 1794, more than 2 million acres of redwood forest carpeted California and Oregon. By 1965, heavy logging had reduced that to 300,000 acres, and it was obvious something had to be done if any were to survive. The state created several parks around individual groves in the 1920s, and in 1968 the federal government created Redwood National Park. In May 1994, the National Park Service and the California Department of Parks and Recreation signed an agreement to manage these conservation areas cooperatively.

Although logging of old-growth redwoods in the region is still a major bone of contention among the government, private landowners, and environmentalists, it's auspicious that contention even exists—a sign that perhaps we have all learned to see the forest *and* the trees for what they are: the monarchs of all living things, a link to the age of the dinosaurs, and a humble reminder that mankind is but a hiccup in time compared to the venerable *Sequoia sempervirens.*

ESSENTIALS

GETTING THERE The southern gateway to the Redwood National and State Parks is the town of Orick. Even though U.S. 101 runs right through the middle of town, you can't miss it anyway: Look for the dozens of burl stands along the road. Carved with chisels and chain saws, these former redwood logs have been transformed into just about every creature you can imagine. The northern gateway to the park is Crescent City near the Oregon border. It's your best bet for a cheap motel, gas, fast food, and outdoor supplies.

VISITOR INFORMATION In Orick you'll find the **Redwood Information Center,** P.O. Box 7, Orick, CA 95555 (✆ **707/464-6101**), one of California's rare examples of well-placed tax dollars. Stop here and pick up a free map; it's open daily from 9am to

Crescent Beach
  Education Center **5**
Hiouchi Information
  Education Center **1**
Humboldt Lagoons
  Education Center **9**
Lady Bird Johnson
  Grove **7**
Prairie Creek Visitor
  Center **6**
Redwood Information
  Center **8**
Redwood National
  and State Parks
  Headquarters and
  Information Center **4**
Simpson-Reed
  Grove **2**
Stout Grove **3**
Tall Trees Grove **10**

Gasquet
199

Lake Talawa
Lake Earl
Lake Earl Dr.
North Bank Rd.
101
Walker Rd.
2
Point St. George
LAKE EARL STATE WILDLIFE AREA
Smith River
SIX RIVERS NATIONAL FOREST
SISKIYOU MOUNTAINS
JEDEDIAH SMITH REDWOODS STATE PARK
1 Hiouchi
3
Douglas Park Rd.
South Fork Rd.
Elk Valley Rd.
CRESCENT CITY
Castle Rock
4
Howland Hill Rd.
Humboldt Rd.
REDWOOD NATIONAL PARK
LITTLE MOUNTAIN
Battery Point Lighthouse
Whaler Island
Crescent Beach
5
Enderts Beach Rd.
Enderts Beach
DEL NORTE COAST REDWOODS STATE PARK
Sister Rocks
COAST RANGE
Footstep Rocks
Lagoon Creek
101
Requa Rd.
Requa
REDWOOD NATIONAL PARK
Klamath
Klamath Glen
Alder Camp Rd.
Coastal Dr.
Klamath River

PACIFIC OCEAN

PRAIRIE CREEK REDWOODS STATE PARK
Newton B. Drury Scenic Pkwy.
Fern Canyon
Gold Bluffs Beach
ELK PRAIRIE
6
Davison Rd.
101
7
HOLTER RIDGE
Orick
8
Freshwater Lagoon
Humboldt Lagoons State Park
Stone Lagoon
9
REDWOOD NATIONAL PARK
10
Bald Hills Rd.
BRIDGE CREEK RIDGE
Redwood Creek
Harry A. Merlo State Recreation Area
Big Lagoon
Patricks Point State Park
101
Patricks Point Dr.
Trinidad State Beach

0   5 mi
0   5 km

N

THE NORTHERN COAST

8

REDWOOD NATIONAL & STATE PARKS

5pm. If you missed the Orick center, don't worry: About 10 miles farther north on U.S. 101 is the **Prairie Creek Visitor Center** (✆ 707/464-6101), which carries all the same maps and information. It's open daily from 9am to 5pm in summer, daily from 10am to 4pm (sometimes later) in winter.

Before touring the park, pick up a free guide at the **Redwood National and State Parks Headquarters and Information Center,** 1111 Second St. (at K St.), Crescent City, CA 95531 (✆ 707/464-6101). It's open daily from 9am to 5pm.

If you happen to be arriving via U.S. 199 from Oregon, the rangers manning the **Hiouchi Information Station** (✆ 707/464-6101) and **Jedediah Smith Visitor Center** (✆ 707/464-6101) can also supply you with the necessary maps and advice. Both are open daily in summer from 9am to 5pm, and in winter when staffing is available. For more information about the Redwood National and State Parks, visit the website at **www.nps.gov/redw**.

FEES & PERMITS   Admission to the national park is free, but to enter any of the three state parks (which contain the best redwood groves), you'll pay a $6 day-use fee, which gains you entry into all three. The camping fee is $20 per night for drive-in sites. (Reservations are highly recommended in summer.) Walk-in sites are free, though a permit is required.

RANGER PROGRAMS   The park service runs interpretive programs—covering phenomena from trees to tide pools, legends to landforms—at the Hiouchi, Crescent Beach, and Redwood information centers in summer months, and year-round at the park headquarters in Crescent City. State rangers lead campfire programs and other activities throughout the year as well. Call the **Parks Information** service for both the national and state parks (✆ 707/464-6101) to get information on current schedules and events.

EXPLORING THE PARKS BY CAR

If you're approaching the park from the south, take the detour along U.S. 101 called the **Newton B. Drury Scenic Parkway** ★, which passes through groves of redwoods and elk-filled meadows before leading back onto the highway 8 miles later. Another spectacular route is the **Coastal Drive** ★, which winds through stands of redwoods and offers grand views of the Pacific.

The most amazing car-friendly trail in the Redwood National and State Parks is the hidden, well-maintained gravel **Howland Hill Road** ★★, which winds for 12 miles through Jedediah Smith Redwoods State Park. It's an unforgettable journey through spectacular old-growth redwoods—considered by many to be one of the most beautiful areas in the world. To get here from U.S. 101, keep an eye out for the 76 gas station at the south end of Crescent City; just before the station, turn right on Elk Valley Road, and follow it to Howland Hill Road, which will be on your right. After driving through the park, you'll end up at U.S. 199 near Hiouchi, and from here it's a short jaunt west to get back to U.S. 101. Plan at least 2 to 3 hours for the 45-mile round-trip, or all day if you want to do some hiking or mountain biking. This drive is not recommended for trailers and RVs.

SPORTS & OUTDOOR PURSUITS

BEACHES, WHALE-WATCHING & BIRD-WATCHING   The park's beaches vary from long, white-sand strands to cobblestone pocket coves. The water temperature is in the

high 40s to low 50s (low 10s Celsius) year-round; it's often rough, so swimmers and
surfers should be prepared for adverse conditions.

Crescent Beach is a long sandy beach 2 miles south of Crescent City that's popular with beachcombers, surf fishermen, and surfers. Just south of Crescent Beach is **Endert's Beach,** a protected spot with a hike-in campground and tide pools at the southern end of the beach.

High coastal overlooks (such as Klamath and Crescent Beach overlooks) make great whale-watching outposts during the southern migration in December and January and the return migration in March and April. The northern sea cliffs also provide valuable nesting sites for such marine birds as auklets, puffins, murres, and cormorants. Birders will thrill at the park's freshwater lagoons as well. These coastal lagoons are some of the most pristine shorebird and waterfowl habitats left, and they're chock-full of hundreds of different species.

HIKING   The park's official map and guide, available at any of the information centers, provides a fairly good layout of hiking trails within the park. Regardless of how short or long your hike may be, dress warmly and bring plenty of water and sunscreen. Pets are prohibited on all of the park's trails.

The most popular walk is the short, heavily traveled **Fern Canyon Trail ★**, which leads to a lush grotto of lady, deer, chain, sword, five-finger, and maidenhair ferns clinging to 50-foot-high vertical walls divided by a brook. It's only about a 1.5-mile walk from Gold Bluffs Beach, but be prepared to scramble across the creek several times on your way via small footbridges.

The **Lady Bird Johnson Grove Loop ★** is an easy, 1-hour self-guided tour that loops 1 mile around a glorious lush grove of mature redwoods. It's the site where Mrs. Johnson dedicated the national park in 1968. The **Yurok Loop Nature Trail** at Lagoon Creek is also an easy trek. The 1-mile self-guided trail gradually climbs to the top of a rugged sea bluff (with wonderful panoramic views of the Pacific) before looping back to the parking lot. If someone's willing to act as shuttle driver, have him or her meet you at the Requa Trail Head and take the 4-mile coastal trail to the mouth of the Klamath. And for the whiner in your group, there's **Big Tree Trail,** a .25-mile paved trail leading to a big tree.

Tall Trees Trail leads to one of the world's tallest trees—perhaps 365 feet tall, 14 feet in diameter, and more than 600 years old. It was once touted as the world's tallest tree, but new candidates keep getting discovered, and this proud giant has lost a couple of feet to time. Now, who knows? It's still worth it to see the contender. Go to the Redwood Information Center near Orick (see "Essentials," above) for a free map and permit to drive to the trail head. The park issues 50 permits per day, on a first-come, first-served basis. After driving to the trail head, walk a steep 1.3 miles down into the grove. The trail is 3.3 miles round-trip.

WILDLIFE VIEWING   One of the most striking aspects of Prairie Creek Redwood State Park is its 200- to 300-strong herd of **Roosevelt elk ★**, usually found in the Elk Prairie, at the southern end of the park. These beasts can weigh 1,000 pounds, and the bulls carry huge antlers from spring to fall. You can also spot elk at Gold Bluffs Beach; it's a rush to come upon them out of the fog or after a turn in the trail. Nearly 100 **black bears** also call the park home, but they're seldom seen. Unlike the bears at Yosemite and Yellowstone, these are still afraid of people. Keep them that way by giving them a wide berth, observing food-storage etiquette while camping, and disposing of garbage properly.

The national park proper has five small campgrounds. Four of the walk-in (more like backpack-in) camps are free—Little Bald Hills, Nickel Creek, Flint Ridge, and Butler Creek. Only one (the Redwood Creek Gravel Bar) requires a permit from the visitor center in advance.

Most car campsites are in the **Prairie Creek** and **Jedediah Smith state parks,** entirely inside the national park. Prairie Creek has two campgrounds, at Elk Prairie and Gold Bluffs Beach. Sites are $15 per night and can be reserved via ReserveAmerica (© **800/ 444-7275;** www.reserveamerica.com). It helps to know which campground and, if possible, which site you would like.

You'll find a number of bed-and-breakfasts and funky roadside motels in the surrounding communities of Crescent City, Orick, and Klamath. The **Crescent City/Del Norte Chamber of Commerce** (© **800/343-8300**) can probably steer you toward the proper match.

Hostelling International—Redwood National Park (Value) The only lodging in the park itself, this settler's homestead was remodeled in 1987 to accommodate 30 guests dormitory-style (in bunks with shared bathrooms), from March through December. The location is optimal—300 feet from the beach, and surrounded by hiking trails leading along the Redwood Coast (the staff lead nature walks and are well versed in local history). A private couple's room is available for an additional $31, with advance notice, and the hostel takes reservations by credit card (strongly recommended in the summer). The nightly rate includes use of the showers, common room with VCR and videos, redwood deck, help-yourself common kitchen, laundry room, dining room, pellet stove, and bicycle storage.

14480 U.S. 101 (at U.S. 101 and Wilson Creek Rd., across from False Klamath Cove), Klamath, CA 95548. © **800/295-1905,** ext. 74, or 707/482-8265. Fax 707/482-4665. www.norcalhostels.org. 30 bunks, 1 couple's room ($52). $21 adults, $11 children. Check-in daily 8–11am and 4–10pm. Closed Nov–Feb, except for groups of 10-plus. MC, V. **Amenities:** On-site parking; information desk; baggage check; groceries/snacks available.

The Far North: Lake Tahoe, Mount Shasta & Lassen Volcanic National Park

by Matthew Richard Poole

Dominated by snowcapped Mount Shasta, visible for 100 miles on a clear day, California's upper northern territory is among the least-visited parts of the state. Often called "the Far North," this region stretches from the rice fields north of Sacramento to the Oregon border. The area is so immense that the state of Ohio would fit comfortably within its borders.

For the adventurous traveler, the Far North is a superlative destination for outdoor sports such as hiking, climbing, skiing, white-water rafting, and mountain biking. Other attractions, both artificial and natural, range from the Shasta Dam, the highest overflow dam in the world; to Lava Beds National Monument, which has dozens of caves to explore; to Lassen Volcanic National Park, a towering laboratory of volcanic phenomena.

South of the Cascade Range is one of the most popular recreational regions in the Golden State: Lake Tahoe, straddling the border between California and Nevada, at 6,225 feet above sea level. Although the lake has been marred by overdevelopment—particularly along the casino-riddled southern shore—the western and eastern coastlines are still quiet havens for hiking, cycling, and watersports. The surrounding Sierra Nevada mountains offer some of the best skiing in the United States, with more than a dozen resorts.

1 LAKE TAHOE ★★★

107 miles E of Sacramento; 192 miles E of San Francisco; 45 miles SW of Reno, NV

Lake Tahoe is an American treasure. It's stunningly beautiful, the air is crisp and clear, and the sun shines 80% of the time. In summer, you can partake of boating and watersports, sandy beaches, bicycling, golf, tennis, hiking, camping, ballooning, horseback riding, rock climbing, bungee jumping, parasailing, skating, and so on, with seemingly endless possibilities. In winter, with an average snowfall of 409 inches, Lake Tahoe is one of the nation's premier ski destinations, with 15 downhill resorts, 10 cross-country ski centers, and facilities for snowboarding, ice-skating, snowshoeing, snowmobiling, sleigh riding, sledding, and snow play as well. Year-round diversions include fishing, Vegas-style gambling, and big-name entertainment in the casinos.

Then there's the lake; it's hard to imagine one as captivating. When Mark Twain first saw it, he declared it "the fairest picture the whole earth affords." It's famed for its crystal-clear

> (Tips) **A Tale of Two Shores**
>
> Before you visit Tahoe, it's important to understand the distinction between the North and the South shores. Don't let the "City" in the North Shore's "Tahoe City" fool you; you can drive through it in a couple of minutes. To the contrary, South Lake Tahoe brims with high-rise casinos, motels, and mini-malls. Where you choose to stay is important because driving from one end of the lake to the other takes an hour or more in summer and can be treacherous in winter.
>
> So which side is for you? If you're here for gambling or entertainment, go south: The selection of casinos is better, with more action and more lodgings, often at better rates. If you seek a relaxing, outdoor retreat, head to the North Shore, which has a better selection of high-quality resorts and vacation rentals. The woodsy West Shore has the most camping spots, and the East Shore, protected from development, has no commercial activity.
>
> Wherever you stay, you'll find plenty of water and mountain sports. The lake is crowded during summer and ski season, so plan far ahead. It's much easier to get reservations for the spring and fall, and rates drop significantly. Many vacation homes and condominiums are rentable; call the visitor-center bureaus or visit the websites below under "Visitor Information" for a list of rental agents.

water (a white dinner plate at the depth of 75 ft. would be visible from the surface) and its size (at 22 miles long and 12 miles wide, it's the largest alpine lake in North America). Its average depth is 989 feet, with the deepest point being 1,645 feet, containing enough water to cover the entire state of California to a depth of 15 inches. Surrounded by the imperious peaks of the Sierra Nevada, its waters soak up the colors of the sky and the mountains, creating a kaleidoscope of sparkling blues, greens, and purples—a sight that will lure you back year after year.

ESSENTIALS

GETTING THERE   It's a 4-hour drive from San Francisco; take I-80 east to Sacramento, and then U.S. 50 to the South Shore, or I-80 east to Highway 89 or Highway 267 to the North Shore. Be prepared for snow in the winter. During heavy storms, you won't be permitted to pass the CHP (California Highway Patrol) checkpoints without four-wheel-drive or chains. From Los Angeles, it's a 9-hour drive; take I-5 through the Central Valley to Sacramento, and then follow the directions above.

Reno-Tahoe International Airport (45 min. to North Shore, 90 min. to South Shore; www.renoairport.com) runs regular service by 10 major airlines, including **American** (© 800/433-7300), **Delta** (© 800/221-1212), and **United** (© 800/241-6522). Rent a car or take a shuttle up to the lake: **North Lake Tahoe Express** (© 866/216-5222; www.northlaketahoeexpress.com) serves the North and West shores; **South Tahoe Express** (© 866/898-2463; www.southtahoeexpress.com) serves the South Shore (1-day advance reservations recommended). To get to the lake, take U.S. 395 South to Route 431 for the North Shore or U.S. 50 for the South Shore. All the roads leading to

the lake are scenic, but the panorama as you descend into the Lake Tahoe Basin from Route 431 is spectacular. Pull into the overlook and enjoy the view.

Amtrak (© **800/USA-RAIL;** www.amtrak.com) stops in Truckee, 10 miles north of the lake. Public transportation (TART or Truce Trolley) is available from the train depot, or you can take a taxi to the North Shore. **Greyhound Bus Lines** (© **800/229-9424;** www.greyhound.com) serves both Truckee and South Lake Tahoe with daily arrivals from San Francisco and Sacramento.

VISITOR INFORMATION   In Tahoe City, stop by the **Tahoe City Visitor Information Center,** 380 North Lake Blvd. (© **800/824-6348;** www.PureTahoeNorth.com). In Incline Village, go to the **Incline Village/Crystal Bay Visitors Center,** 969 Tahoe Blvd. (© **800/468-2463** or 775/832-1606; www.gotahoe.com). Go to the **South Lake Tahoe Chamber of Commerce,** 3066 Lake Tahoe Blvd. (© **530/541-5255;** www.tahoeinfo. com). Many other websites offer information about Lake Tahoe, including www.virtual tahoe.com, www.skilaketahoe.com, www.laketahoeconcierge.com, www.gotahoenorth. com, and www.tahoevacationguide.com.

WHAT TO SEE & DO
Skiing & Snowboarding

With the largest concentration of ski resorts in North America, Lake Tahoe is California's best skiing destination. The ski season typically lasts from November to May and frequently extends into the summer. Lift tickets last winter ranged from $44 to $75 per day for adults, and from free to $39 for children, with special rates for seniors. Ticket prices rise every year, but bargains are available, particularly midweek. Many resorts, hotels, and motels offer ski packages. Contact the visitor centers or visit the websites listed under "Visitor Information," above, to look for these values. The resorts offer instruction for adults and children, equipment rental, special courses for snowboarding, and restaurants. Most have free shuttles.

Alpine Meadows ★★ (Kids   With more than 100 runs over 2,400 acres, Alpine has something for everyone: kids' programs, a family zone, and its "wild side" for the double black diamond crowd. In addition to its 14 lifts, this low-key resort also has a beginner surface lift designed for children, novice skiers, and snowboarders. You can get a great bargain through its Lift & Lodging packages, which provides lift tickets and lodging (© **800/949-3296**). Alpine also offers ski and snowboard instruction for all ages, excellent snowboarding-terrain parks, snowshoe rentals, and snow-play areas.

2600 Alpine Meadows Rd., Tahoe City, CA 96145. © **530/583-4232.** www.skialpine.com.

Diamond Peak ★ (Kids (Value   In the heart of quiet, upscale Incline Village, this is a great choice for a low-key, less crowded, less expensive, nonetheless beautiful skiing adventure, with spectacular lake views. Smaller than most resorts in the area, it's a premier destination for families. Skiing and snowboarding options for kids abound, with a snowboard park and sledding area, a Burton "Learn to Ride" center for snowboarders, and a snow-play program to entertain the younger ones who aren't quite ready to hit the slopes. The Diamond Peak Cross Country and Snowshoe Center (same telephone number), east of Incline Village on NV Route 431, is gorgeous and even allows dogs to share in the fun in the afternoon.

1210 Ski Way, Incline Village, NV 89451. © **775/832-1177.** www.diamondpeak.com.

Heavenly Resort ★★ (Kids)   This hugely popular resort—the only one on the South Shore—has the highest elevation (10,067 ft.) of any resort at the lake. Skiers and snowboarders of all levels will find something to challenge them, including three snowboard parks, 4,800 skiable acres, 30 lifts (including a 50-passenger aerial tram), and 86 runs. Heavenly is also the only resort with day care for infants as young as 6 weeks (up through 6 years of age), child care and ski combinations for toddlers 3 to 5, and full-day programs for older kids. With arcades, recreation centers, bowling alleys, and movie theaters nearby, it's a great choice if you have teenagers or if you want to visit the big casinos at night. The latest addition here is the $20-million **Heavenly Gondola**—cars that can transport up to eight passengers from the South Shore casino area up to an observation deck at 9,200 feet on Heavenly Mountain—a 2¹/₂-mile journey. The resort also recently invested nearly $30 million in improvements to the mountain, including two new high-speed lifts and a new 15-acre beginner's area.

P.O. Box 2180 (on Ski Run Blvd.), Stateline, NV 89449. ℭ **775/586-7000.** www.skiheavenly.com.

Homewood Mountain Resort ★ (Kids) (Value)   Homewood is one of my favorite small ski areas, a homey little resort with 1,260 acres, 56 runs, eight lifts, and spectacular lake views. It's a good family resort with child care for ages 2 to 6 and ski schools for ages 4 to 12. Lift tickets were only $39 last winter, and children under 10 skied free when accompanied by an adult.

5145 W. Lake Blvd., Homewood, CA 96141 (6 miles south of Tahoe City and 19 miles north of South Lake Tahoe on Hwy. 89). ℭ **530/525-2992.** www.skihomewood.com.

Kirkwood ★★ (Kids)   Kirkwood's only drawback is that it's 30 miles south of South Lake Tahoe; otherwise, it's one of the top ski areas in Tahoe, with lots of snow and excellent spring skiing. It has 2,300 skiable acres, 12 lifts, and 65 trails. Many programs cater to children, including child care for the younger ones (ages 2–6). The **Cross Country & Snowshoe Center** (ℭ **209/258-7248**) is one of the best around, with lessons for all ages, and spectacular scenery. Kirkwood is also ideal for summertime hiking, horseback riding, mountain biking, and rock climbing. With ample lodging (ℭ **800/967-7500**) and dining options, this is a great year-round destination. The shuttle service to South Lake Tahoe is $5.

Off Hwy. 88 at Carson Pass (P.O. Box 1), Kirkwood, CA 95646. ℭ **209/258-6000.** www.kirkwood.com.

Mt. Rose ★ (Finds)   Although Mt. Rose has been open since 1964, I've never skied it until recently. Why? Because it wasn't challenging enough. But since they opened "The Chutes," Mt. Rose has become the new darling of the Tahoe ski scene. Located 22 miles from Reno and about a 20-minute drive from the lake, Mt. Rose has always been popular with beginner and intermediate skiers, offering 1,300 acres of mostly groomed slopes with the highest base elevation (7,900 ft.) in Lake Tahoe. Now that the wickedly steep and long chutes—with names such as Chaos and Nightmare—are officially open, it's attracting skiers of all levels. The ski area has seven lifts, including two high-speed detachables, as well as three snowboard terrain parks. Money-saving specials include Two-For-One Tickets on Tuesday, and Ladies Day Thursday, when gals get a full-day ticket for only $29 (holidays excepted).

22222 Mt. Rose Hwy. (Hwy. 431), Reno, NV 89511. ℭ **800/SKI-ROSE** or 775/849-0704. www.skirose.com.

Northstar-at-Tahoe ★★ (Kids)   With 70 runs covering 2,420 acres on two mountains, Northstar is consistently rated among the top western resorts. Its sophisticated series of lifts, including an express gondola, ensure speedy access to the slopes and short lift lines. Whatever your age or experience level, you'll find what you're looking for here. Backcountry terrain on Saw Tooth Ridge will test the skills of expert skiers and snowboarders on 200 acres of ungroomed, out-of-boundary terrain. The Learning Center offers coaching in skiing, snowboarding, cross country, and the new snow toys. Child care (ages 2–6) is available, as well as instruction—including the "magic carpet" lift and special Paw Parks, Northstar's pint-size obstacle courses. Other outdoor pastimes include cross-country skiing, telemarking, snowshoeing, sleigh rides, tubing, and ice-skating in the heart of Northstar's new Village. Check out the snow toys, such as the snowscoot, the skifox, the snowbike, and the snowskate, a skateboard deck without wheels. See p. 280 for a full review of Northstar-at-Tahoe.

100 Northstar Dr., Truckee, NV 96161 (6 miles north of Kings Beach). ℂ **800/466-6784** or 530/562-1010. www.northstarattahoe.com.

Sierra-at-Tahoe ★ (Kids) Tahoe's third-largest ski area is a great all-around resort, with slightly lower rates than most comparable places in the area. With more than 2,000 acres of slopes, from bunny to expert, Sierra-at-Tahoe features four terrain parks for both boarders and skiers, and 200 acres of backcountry terrain for steeps and deeps. The runs are very wide and well groomed, giving skiers plenty of room to fly down the mountain. On a powder day, don't miss skiing the trees. If you're staying on the South Shore, it's a good alternative to Heavenly Ski Resort. Free ski shuttle service is available from about 40 locations in South Lake Tahoe.

1111 Sierra at Tahoe Rd., Twin Bridges, CA 95735 (off Hwy. 50, 12 miles west of South Lake Tahoe). ℂ **530/ 659-7453.** www.sierraattahoe.com.

Squaw Valley USA ★★★ (Kids) Site of the 1960 Olympic Winter Games, Squaw is one of the world's finest year-round resorts. Skiing is spread across six peaks with one of the most advanced lift systems on earth, providing access to more than 4,000 acres of skiable terrain—70% geared toward beginners and intermediates and 30% for the advanced, expert, and/or insane. For nonskiers and skiers alike, High Camp, at the top of the cable car, has the Olympic Ice Pavilion (year-round ice-skating), a swimming lagoon and spa (spring and summer), snow tubing, snowboarding school, restaurants, and bars. Squaw also has an arcade, climbing wall, and Central Park for snowboarders. The Nordic Center (ℂ **530/583-6300**) has 400 acres of groomed trails for cross-country skiing and snowshoeing. Squaw also offers free night skiing with the purchase of a full-day lift ticket. Children ages 12 and under ski for only $5. See p. 281 for a full review of the Resort at Squaw Creek.

Olympic Valley, CA 96146 (6 miles north of Tahoe City). ℂ **800/545-4350** or 530/583-6985. www.squaw.com.

Sugar Bowl ★★ (Kids) Sugar Bowl is excellent for skiers of all levels—especially if you are driving from the Bay Area or Sacramento on I-80 and don't want to go all the way to Tahoe. This medium-size resort (13 lifts, 1,500 skiable acres) offers child care, ski school, snowboard parks, and lodging at the foot of the mountains.

P.O. Box 5, Norden, CA 95724 (3 miles east of the Soda Springs/Norden exit of I-80). ℂ **530/426-9000.** www.sugarbowl.com.

More Winter Fun
CROSS-COUNTRY SKIING In addition to the major resorts, here are some other excellent establishments: **Royal Gorge Cross-Country Ski Resort** ★★★, Soda Springs,

Lake Tahoe's Best Cheap Thrills

Nothing beats a cheap thrill, and the Lake Tahoe region is loaded with them. Your most affordable adventures will inevitably involve getting outside and taking in the area's natural wonders. In spring, summer, and fall, take a drive around the lake, hike to a scenic spot for a picnic lunch, or soak up some rays on the beach. In winter, inexpensive outdoor fun can be had with just a sled and a slope. Here are some other offbeat things to do in and around Tahoe:

Three miles north of South Lake Tahoe off Highway 89 is the Forest Service Visitor Center's **Stream Profile Chamber** ★ (✆ 530/573-2674), a series of submerged windows that allow an up-close-and-personal study of one of nature's stranger rites: the annual spawning display of red kokanee salmon as they battle their way up Taylor Creek to lay their eggs. Although the salmon run takes place during October, the chamber and visitor center are open from Memorial Day to the end of October. When the salmon aren't stealing the show, you can watch rainbow trout, crayfish, and minnows in their natural habitat through the viewing windows.

On the north side of the lake is the popular **Fanny Bridge** (at the intersection of Calif. 28 and Calif. 89). While everybody's at the railing admiring the huge rainbow trout that congregate below the bridge, take a step back and you'll see how the bridge got its name. Rent a bike for about $7 an hour at the **Olympic Bike Shop,** 620 N. Lake Blvd., Tahoe City (✆ 530/581-2500; www.olympicbikeshop.com), and ride along the beautiful **Truckee River Bike Trail.** Helmets are included in the price, and for another small fee you can rent a trailer or a tandem-attachment to include your kids.

For the ultimate cheap sunset thrill, ride the **Squaw Valley cable car** (✆ 800/545-4350; www.squaw.com) after 5pm. From late June to the beginning of September, it's only $11 (that's $9 off the regular price). Then hang out at the High Camp, a miniresort near the top of the mountain that has an ice-skating rink, five restaurants, hiking trails, and gorgeous views of the lake basin. The 8-minute ride also offers incredible vistas as you rise 2,000 feet above the valley floor.

near Sugar Bowl (✆ **800/500-3871** or 800/666-3871; www.royalgorge.com), is one of the largest and best cross-country resorts anywhere, with 90 trails, including 28 novice trails and four ski lifts. For North Shore visitors, **Tahoe Cross Country Ski Area** ★, 925 Country Club Dr., Tahoe City (✆ **866/SKI-TXCC** or **530/583-5475;** www.tahoexc.org), is a small (14 trails), full-service ski center run by a nonprofit community group. A quiet, full-service ski center off the beaten path, **Spooner Lake Cross Country Ski Area** ★, near the intersection of Highway 28 and U.S. 50 on the East Shore (✆ **775/749-5349;** www.spoonerlake.com), offers some of the most scenic skiing at the lake.

ICE-SKATING　Accessible only by a tram ride up the mountain, **Squaw Valley's High Camp** ★★ (✆ **530/583-6985**) has an ice rink that's open year-round, with one of the world's most beautiful views for a skating rink. On the North Shore there are also ice rinks at the **Northstar-at-Tahoe** resort (✆ **530/562-0321;** p. 280), and the **Resort at**

Squaw Creek (© **800/327-3353;** p. 281). South Lake Tahoe has two rinks: the **South Tahoe Ice Arena** (1176 Rufus Allen Blvd.; © **530/542-6262**), open year-round, and the **Heavenly Village Ice Rink,** at Heavenly Village on Highway 50 (© **530/543-4230;** www.theshopsatheavenlyvillage.com).

SNOWMOBILING   Snowmobile rental and tours are available at several locations in the Lake Tahoe Area. Call ahead for reservations and directions. The **Zephyr Cove Snowmobile Center** ★, 760 U.S. 50, about 4 miles northeast of the casinos (© **800/23-TAHOE** or 775/589-4906; www.laketahoesnowmobiles.com), offers several exhilarating tours daily for all experience levels. The cost for a 2-hour tour is about $112 for a single rider, $152 for two. **Lake Tahoe Snowmobile Tours** (© **530/546-4280;** www.laketahoe snowmobiling.com) offers 90-minute to 4-hour backcountry tours from Brockway Summit, about 3 miles north of Kings Beach on Highway 267; prices start at $110 for one, $140 for two.

SNOW PLAY   For snow play beyond the resorts, try the **North Tahoe Regional Park,** at the top of National Avenue off Highway 28, Tahoe Vista (© **530/546-4212**). This ultimate snow-play hill charges a $5 fee for a choice of sled, tube, or saucer. **Taylor Creek Snow Park** off Highway 89 in South Lake Tahoe is run by the U.S. Forest Service. Bring your own equipment for sledding and tubing. For information about California Sno Park locations, call the **Sno Park Hot Line** at © **916/324-1222.**

Summer Activities

BALLOONING   See the lake and mountains from 8,000 to 10,000 feet above, with **Lake Tahoe Balloons** (© **800/872-9294** or 530/544-1221; www.laketahoeballoons.com) in South Lake Tahoe. A 4-hour tour costs about $250 per person.

BEACHES   Here are a few popular spots around the lake. All have sandy beaches, picnic areas, and restrooms; many have playgrounds. Remember that this is an alpine lake, so the water is *very* cold.

- **Baldwin Beach:** Highway 89, 4 miles north of South Lake Tahoe
- **Commons Beach Park:** Downtown Tahoe City; free movie (Fri at dusk; © **530/583-3348**)
- **Connolly Beach:** U.S. 50 at Timber Cove Lodge; boat launches
- **D. L. Bliss State Park:** South of Meeks Bay on Highway 89; camping, trails
- **El Dorado Beach:** Between Rufus Allen and Lakeview in South Lake Tahoe
- **Kings Beach State Recreation Center:** Highway 28 in Kings Beach
- **Pope Beach:** Highway 89, 2 miles north of South Lake Tahoe
- **Sand Harbor:** 4 miles south of Incline Village on Highway 28; lifeguards
- **Sugar Pine Point:** Highway 89, just south of Tahoma; camping, trails, pier
- **Zephyr Cove Beach:** U.S. 50 at Zephyr Cove

BICYCLING   Miles of paved bicycle paths surround the lake. Incline Village has a scenic, easy, 2¹/₂-mile path along Lakeshore Boulevard (a safe choice for younger children). In Tahoe City you can follow the path in three directions. The one that follows Truckee River is a relaxing, beautiful ride. On the South Shore, the Pope-Baldwin bike path runs parallel to Highway 89 through Camp Richardson and the Tallac Historic Site. Nearby, in South Lake Tahoe, a paved pathway runs from El Dorado Beach along the lake, paralleling U.S. 50. The Tahoe City trails are my favorites, especially the Truckee River section. You can rent a bicycle from any of the shops listed below.

A dizzying choice of mountain biking trails awaits mountain bikers in Lake Tahoe. For maps and information, check with one of the bicycle-rental shops. In North Lake Tahoe, try the **Olympic Bike Shop,** 620 N. Lake Blvd., Tahoe City (✆ **530/581-2500;** www.olympicbikeshop.com); **Tahoe Bike & Ski,** 8499 N. Lake Blvd., Kings Beach (✆ **530/546-7437;** www.tahoebikeski.com). In South Tahoe, try **Anderson's Bike Rental,** 645 Emerald Bay Rd. (✆ **530/541-0500),** or **Lakeview Sports,** 3131 Hwy. 50, at El Dorado Beach (✆ **530/544-0183).**

Another great choice is **Cyclepaths Mountain Bike Adventures,** 1785 W. Lake Blvd. in Tahoe Park, a few miles south of Tahoe City (✆ **800/780-BIKE** or 530/581-1171; www.cyclepaths.com), where you can arrange a guided off-road tour. Whether you're into hard-core downhill single track or easy-going scenic outings, the expert guides will provide you with the necessary gear, food, and transportation.

BOATING, KAYAKING, PARASAILING & WATERSPORTS   Nothing beats getting out on the lake and seeing the 360-degree view of Lake Tahoe—either by taking a guided tour or going off on your own to motor, sail, or paddle around. And plenty of companies around the lake would love your business. **Zephyr Cove Marina** (✆ **800/238-2463;** www.zephyrcove.com) is the lake's largest marina and home of the paddle-wheeler MS *Dixie II* (see "Lake Cruises," on p. 272). Here you can parasail, charter sport-fishing trips, or take guided tours. You can also rent motorized boats, pedal boats, kayaks, canoes, water-ski equipment, and jet skis. **Tahoe City Marina** (✆ **530/583-1039;** www.tahoe citymarina.com), at 700 N. Lake Blvd. in Tahoe City, rents motorized boats, sailboats, and fishing boats. This is also the location for **Lake Tahoe Parasailing** (✆ **530/583-7245).** **Tahoe Paddle and Oar,** North Lake Beach Center, 8299 North Lake Blvd., Kings Beach (✆ **530/581-3029;** www.tahoepaddle.com), is a good place to rent kayaks, canoes, pedal boats, and windsurfing equipment. Paddling around in the clear waters of Crystal Bay is great fun. Other companies that rent kayaks and provide a variety of guided tours—Emerald Bay tours, East Shore tours, sunset tours, moonlight/astronomy tours, to name a few—include the **Tahoe Adventure Company** (✆ **866/830-6125;** www.tahoeadventurecompany.com) and **Tahoe City Kayak** (✆ **530/581-4336;** www.tahoecitykayak.net).

Action Water Sports rents boats, kayaks, jet skis, paddleboats, and other water toys; parasailing and guided tours are also available. Action Water Sports has two locations: 3411 Lake Tahoe Blvd. at Timber Cove Marina, South Lake Tahoe (✆ **530/544-5387;** www.action-watersports.com); and across from the Hyatt in Incline Village (✆ **775/831-4386).** **Camp Richardson Marina,** 1900 Jameson Beach Rd., off Highway 89 on the South Shore (✆ **530/542-6570;** www.camprichardson.com), on a long sandy beach, rents power- and ski boats, jet skis, kayaks, and paddleboats. It also offers fishing charters, ski school, and raft and kayak tours to Emerald Bay. **SunSports,** 3564 Lake Tahoe Blvd., South Lake Tahoe (✆ **530/541-6000),** provides rentals, tours, and lessons for kayaking, rafting, sailing, and scuba diving.

CAMPING   If you have an appetite for the great outdoors, here are a few of the many good campgrounds at Tahoe:

D. L. Bliss State Park, on the western shore (✆ **530/525-7277),** has 168 campsites, fine beaches, and hiking trails.

Sugar Pine Point State Park, open year-round on the western shore (✆ **530/525-7982),** has 175 campsites, a picnic area, beach, nature center, and cross-country skiing.

Campground by the Lake, 1150 Rufus Allen Blvd., South Lake Tahoe (✆ **530/542-6096),** features 170 campsites, a boat ramp, a gym, and a history museum.

A Sailing Tour of Lake Tahoe

I can't imagine a better way to spend an afternoon in Lake Tahoe than relaxing on a beautiful sailing yacht, sipping a cold beer or chardonnay while soaking in the sunshine and incredible scenery. That's why I think you should call **Tahoe Sailing Charters** and join them on one of their scenic 2-hour afternoon or sunset cruises aboard the *Tahoe Cruz,* a sleek 50-foot Santa Cruz–class yacht with a 12-foot beam and plenty of elbowroom. Guests can take turns at the helm or relax and let captain and crew sail the deep blue. Complimentary refreshments and snacks are included. The *Tahoe Cruz* sails daily from the Tahoe City Marina on Lake Tahoe's North Shore; rates are $50 for the afternoon sail and $60 for the sunset cruise. For departure times, reservations, and information, call ✆ **530/583-6200** or log on to **www.tahoesail.com**.

Zephyr Cove RV Park and Campground, at Zephyr Cove Resort on U.S. 50 (✆ **775/589-4907;** www.zephyrcove.com), has a beach, a marina, and complete facilities.

FISHING   The cold, clear waters of Lake Tahoe are home to massive kokanee salmon and rainbow, brown, and Mackinaw trout. Fishing here is a challenge in the deep water, so most anglers opt to use a guide or charter boat. Dozens of charter companies offer daily excursions. Rates run about $65 for a half-day to $95 for a whole day (bait, tackle, fish cleaning, and food included). On the North Shore, try **Mickey's Big Mack Charters** at the Sierra Boat Company in Carnelian Bay (✆ **800/877-1462** or 530/546-4444; www.mickeysbigmack.com). On the South Shore, try **Avid Fisherman,** Zephyr Cove (✆ **775/588-7675**); **Blue Ribbon Fishing Charters,** Tahoe Keys Marina (✆ **530/544-6552;** www.blueribbonfishing.com); or **Tahoe Sportfishing,** 900 Ski Run Blvd. (✆ **800/696-7797** or 530/541-5448; www.tahoesportfishing.com). If you'd rather try your hand at fly-fishing, the **Northstar-at-Tahoe** resort (✆ **530/582-5393;** www.northstarattahoe.com) has a private 10-acre reservoir stocked with hundreds of rainbow trout, reserved for catch-and-release fly-fishing only. Equipment is available for guests at no extra cost and there's a guide on-site daily to provide helpful hints.

FITNESS CENTERS   The **Incline Recreation Center,** 980 Incline Way, Incline Village (✆ **775/832-1310;** www.inclinerecreation.com), is impressive, with a heated indoor Olympic-size swimming pool, aerobics, basketball, cardiovascular fitness room, lounge, fireplace, and on-site child care. It's $14 for adults and $8 for children.

GOLF   With its world-class golf courses, mild summer weather, and magnificent scenery, Lake Tahoe is a golfer's paradise. All of the following courses are very busy in the summer, so call *far* in advance for tee times. For more information about Tahoe-area golf courses, log on to **www.tahoesbest.com/Golf**.

The north end of the lake has four highly rated courses: **Incline Village Championship Course,** 955 Fairway Blvd., and the smaller **Incline Village Mountain (Executive) Course,** 690 Wilson Way (✆ **866/925-GOLF** for both; www.golfincline.com); **Northstar-at-Tahoe** (✆ **530/562-2490;** p. 280); and the **Resort at Squaw Creek** (✆ **800/327-3353;** p. 281).

In the south, **Edgewood,** U.S. 50 at Lake Parkway, Stateline (© **775/588-3566;** www. edgewood-tahoe.com), is home of the Celebrity Golf Championship; **Lake Tahoe Golf Course,** 2500 Emerald Bay Rd., South Lake Tahoe (© **530/577-0788;** www.laketahoe gc.com), also has some good 9-hole municipal courses. There's also **Old Brockway Golf Course,** 7900 N. Lake Blvd., Kings Beach (© **530/546-9909;** www.oldbrockway.com); **Tahoe City Golf Course,** 251 N. Lake Blvd., Tahoe City (© **530/583-1516**); and **Bijou Municipal Golf Course,** 3464 Fairway Ave., South Lake Tahoe (© **530/542-6097**).

HIKING Hiking trails for all levels of experience crisscross the mountains surrounding Lake Tahoe. Before setting out, you may wish to contact the local visitor centers or sporting-goods shops for a map and more in-depth information on particular trails, or hire a guide. Try **Tahoe Trips & Trails** (© **800/581-HIKE** or 530/583-4506; www. tahoetrips.com) for short and long guided hikes. Everything is provided: food, drinks, transportation, and information about the lake. Going on your own? Some of the most popular short hikes in the area are:

- **Eagle Falls/Eagle Lake:** This moderately easy trail is well marked and begins at Eagle Picnic Area, across Highway 89 from Emerald Bay. It's only about a third of a mile to the steel footbridge overlooking the falls and 2 miles round-trip ($1^1/_2$–2 hr.) to Eagle Lake. Be sure to sign in at the self-registration station at the trail head.
- **Emerald Bay/Vikingsholm:** The trail starts at the parking area on the north side of Emerald Bay, on Highway 89. It's a wide, well-maintained trail but fairly steep, about 2.5 miles round-trip. At the bottom of the trail is a picnic area, as well as world-famous Vikingsholm, a replica of a Scandinavian castle.
- **Nevada Shoreline:** Begin at the paved parking lot on the west side of Highway 28, 3 miles south of Sand Harbor. The trail drops to the beach and follows the shoreline, passing Chimney Beach, Secret Harbor, and Whale Beach. The trail eventually connects to a service road that can be followed back up to the parking area. It's an easy 4-mile hike, with a vertical climb of only 300 feet.
- **Shirley Lake:** This trail leads to Shirley Lake and then down to Shirley Canyon. Take the tram at Squaw Valley up to High Camp and hike down, or vice versa. The trail

THE FAR NORTH

9

LAKE TAHOE

The "Heavenly Flyer" Zip-Line Thrill Ride

If you're looking to add some high-adrenaline thrills to your Lake Tahoe vacation, head over to the Heavenly Mountain Resort on the South Shore and take a ride on their new Heavenly Flyer, the longest zip line in the lower 48 states. Located at the top of the Heavenly Gondola's Adventure Peak, the Heavenly Flyer is sort of like a flying chair attached to a thick 3,100-foot-long cable that runs from the base to way up the mountainside. You buckle in at the take-off deck, and then descend 525 feet through the pine trees at an exhilarating 50 mph. Heck, the views of Lake Tahoe alone are worth the ride. The Heavenly Flyer is open year-round from 11am to 3pm daily, and a single-ride pass costs $30. For more information log on to **www.skiheavenly.com/mountain/heavenly_flyer**, or call the resort at © **775/586-7000.**

begins at the end of Squaw Creek Road, next to the cable-car building. It's a 4-mile hike, easy to moderate in difficulty, with some steep sections.

HORSEBACK RIDING   Most stables offer a variety of guided trail rides and lessons for individuals, families, and groups. Choose the one that appeals to your sense of adventure: 1- to 2-hour trail rides; breakfast, lunch, or dinner rides; half-day, full-day, overnight, and extended pack trips. Expect to pay $20 to $25 for a 1-hour ride, $6 for a half-hour pony ride. Saddle up and savor the scenery. Try **Alpine Meadows Stables,** 355 Alpine Meadows Rd., Tahoe City (✆ **530/583-3905**); **Squaw Valley Stables,** 1525 Squaw Valley Rd., north of Tahoe City (✆ **530/583-7433**); **Camp Richardson Corral,** Highway 89, South Lake Tahoe (✆ **530/541-3113**); or **Zephyr Cove Stables,** Zephyr Cove Resort, U.S. 50 at Zephyr Cove (✆ **775/588-5664;** www.zephyrcovestables.com).

RIVER RAFTING   For a swift but gentle ride down the Truckee River (the lake's only outlet), try **Truckee River Raft Rental,** 185 River Rd., Tahoe City (✆ **530/583-0123;** www.truckeeriverraft.com). It's only available in the summer, and the rates are $35 for adults and $30 for children 6 to 12 (kids 5 and under are free). If you prefer a more exciting whitewater experience, **Tributary Whitewater Tours** (✆ **800/672-3846;** www. whitewatertours.com) offers daily excursions (in season) down the Truckee River amid Class 2 to 3-plus rapids. It's the perfect trip for neophyte rafters and families—exciting but not dangerously so. For a half-day trip, rates range from $68 to $98 for adults and $60 to $70 for kids 7 and older.

TENNIS   The mild summer weather at Lake Tahoe is perfect for great tennis. If you want to sharpen your skills, **Northstar-at-Tahoe** (✆ 530/562-0321; p. 280) offers several excellent tennis packages for its guests only. **Squaw Creek** (✆ 530/581-6694; p. 281) tennis courts are open to the public for $14 an hour. **Kirkwood** (✆ 209/258-6000;** p. 265), **MontBleu Resort Casino & Spa** (✆ 775/588-3515; p. 276), and **Harveys Casino & Resort** (✆ 775/588-2411; p. 276) all feature tennis courts for a fee.

Budget-minded players should visit Tahoe Lake School on Grove Street in Tahoe City, or Tahoe Regional Park, at the end of National Avenue in Tahoe Vista. South Tahoe Intermediate School on Lyons Avenue has eight lighted courts and charges $3 per hour. South Tahoe High School, 1735 Lake Tahoe Blvd., has free courts.

Lake Cruises

If you can fit a lake cruise into your vacation plans, you won't regret it—it's one of the best ways to see the lake. The **MS Dixie II,** located at Zephyr Cove Marina (4 miles north of the South Lake casinos on U.S. 50; ✆ 800/238-2463; www.zephyrcove.com), is a 570-passenger paddle-wheeler with bars, a dance floor, and a full dining room. Emerald Bay scenic cruises cost $41 for adults, $20 for children. They also offer champagne-brunch and breakfast cruises ($53), dinner cruises ($61), and sunset dinner-dance cruises ($71).

The **Tahoe Queen** (✆ 800/238-2463; www.zephyrcove.com), which departs from the Marina Village at Ski Run Boulevard in South Lake Tahoe, is also an authentic paddle-wheeler offering Emerald Bay sightseeing tours ($46 adults, $22 children) and dinner/dance cruises ($106 adults, $71 children). Live music, buffet breakfast, dinner, and appetizers are all available onboard.

The **Tahoe Gal** (✆ 800/218-2464 or 530/583-0141; www.tahoegal.com), departing from the Lighthouse Marina (behind Safeway) in Tahoe City, is the only cruise boat on the North Shore. Cruises include the Scenic Brunch Cruise ($34 adults, $16 children), Emerald Bay ($38 adults, $19 children), Happy Hour (4:30–6pm; $25 adults, $14 children), and Sunset Dinner ($35 adults, $16 children). *Note:* Prices are for the cruise only; food and beverages cost extra.

Woodwind Sailing Cruises (© 888/867-6394) runs daily sightseeing tours ($32 adults, $15 children 3–12), and a Sunset Champagne Cruise ($42). *Woodwind I,* a 30-passenger Searunner trimaran, sails to Emerald Bay from Camp Richardson Marina in South Lake Tahoe. The *Woodwind II,* a 50-passenger Searunner catamaran, sails from Zephyr Cove Marina.

A Drive Around the Lake

Overwhelmed by the choices? Get in your car and take a leisurely drive around the lake. It's only 72 miles, but plan on expending several hours, even in the best of weather. In the worst of weather, don't try it! Parts of the road, if not closed, can be icy and dangerous. On a mild day, it will be a memorable experience. If your car has a CD player, consider buying a self-guided CD audio tour that contains facts, legends, places of interest, and just about everything else you might want to know about the lake. You'll find them at many gift shops and bookstores around the lake.

We'll start at the California-Nevada border in South Lake Tahoe and loop around the western shore on Highway 89 to Tahoe City and beyond. U.S. 50, which runs along the South Shore, is an ugly, overdeveloped strip that obliterates any view of the lake. Keep heading west and you will be free of this boring stretch.

First stop is the **Tallac Historic Site,** site of the former Tallac Resort and a cluster of 100-year-old mansions that provide a fascinating glimpse into Tahoe's past. In its heyday, the resort included two large hotels, a casino, and numerous outbuildings. Throughout the summer, the **Valhalla Festival of Arts and Music** (© 530/541-4975; www.valhalla tahoe.com) showcases jazz, bluegrass, rock, mariachi, and classical music. Summer highlights include June's Valhalla Renaissance Festival, July's Native American Fine Arts Festival, and August's Great Gatsby Festival.

From here the highway winds north along the shore until you reach **Cascade Lake** on the left and **Emerald Bay** ★★ on the right. The Emerald Bay Lookout is a spectacular picture-taking spot. Emerald Bay's deep green water is the site of the only island in Lake Tahoe, Fannette Island. The small structure atop the island is the teahouse, built by Ms. Lora Knight, who also constructed **Vikingsholm** ★ (www.vikingsholm.com), a 38-room Scandinavian castle built in 1929, located at the head of Emerald Bay. Tours of this unique structure are available from mid-June to Labor Day every half-hour from 10am to 4pm. Even if you don't want to take the tour, it's a pleasant walk from the parking area down to the beach and the mansion's grounds. Just remember that you have to walk back up. Across the highway, there's another parking area. From here, it's a short, steep .25-mile hike to a footbridge above **Eagle Falls.** Then it's about a mile farther up to **Eagle Lake.**

It's only about 2 more miles to **D. L. Bliss State Park** (© 530/525-7277), with one of the lake's best beaches. It fills up in summer, so arrive early for a parking place. The park also has 168 campsites and several trails, including one along the shoreline.

In about 7 miles you will reach **Sugar Pine State Park** (© 530/525-7982), the largest (2,000 acres) of the lake's parks and also the only one that has year-round camping. In summer, you can visit its beaches, plus a nature center and miles of trails; in winter, you can cross-country ski on well-maintained trails.

Continuing on through the town of **Homewood** (site of the ski resort), **Sunnyside,** on the right, is a great place to stop for a lakeside lunch. Or, if you feel like taking a stroll, drive on to Tahoe City with its beautiful paved path along the Truckee River. Check out the big trout at **Fanny Bridge** ★ (p. 267) first. If you would like to see **Squaw Valley**

THE FAR NORTH

9

LAKE TAHOE

and **Alpine Meadows,** take a left at Highway 89. A ride on the Squaw Valley cable car (© 530/583-6985) will reward you with incredible vistas from 2,000 feet above the valley floor. It runs year-round and costs $22 for adults, $17 for seniors, and $6 for children under 13. Back on Highway 28, as you leave **Tahoe City,** you will pass a string of small malls at 700 through 850 North Lake Blvd. If you like to wander around, this is a good area to stop and eat, watch the activity at the **Tahoe City Marina** (parasailing, cruises on the *Tahoe Gal,* and boat rental), or visit the shops.

Continuing around the lake on Highway 28, you'll reach Carnelian Bay, Tahoe Vista, and Kings Beach before crossing the state line into Nevada. **Kings Beach State Recreation Area** ★ (© 530/546-7248), a long, wide beach and picnic area, is jammed in the summer with sunbathers and swimmers. As you approach **Crystal Bay,** you will know, from the string of small casinos, that you have crossed the state line. The **Cal-Neva Resort, Spa & Casino** (p. 281) on the right was once owned by Frank Sinatra and has a celebrity-studded history. The state line goes right through the lodge, and gambling is allowed only on the Nevada side (it's worth stopping to see).

Your journey next takes you to woodsy Incline Village, arguably the most beautiful community on the lake. Take a right on Lakeshore Boulevard to view the elegant estates. Lunch or dinner time? The **Lone Eagle Grille** (p. 279), at the Hyatt Regency Lake Tahoe, offers gorgeous panoramic lake views as well as superb food.

The east shore of the lake is largely undeveloped and very scenic. Drive about 4 miles south of Incline Village to **Sand Harbor** ★ (© 775/831-0494), one of the lake's best-loved beaches, and home to the very popular **Lake Tahoe Shakespeare Festival** (© 800/747-4697; www.tahoebard.com) every mid-July through August. In addition to turquoise blue water dotted with big boulders and a wide sandy beach, you'll find nature trails, picnic areas, and boating.

Going south you will come to an outcropping called **Cave Rock** where the highway passes through 75 feet of solid stone. Farther along is **Zephyr Cove Resort and Marina,** home to the MS *Dixie II* and a beehive of watersports activity. You'll then return to Stateline and South Lake Tahoe, your original starting point.

South Shore & South Lake Tahoe
Expensive

Black Bear Inn Bed & Breakfast ★★   Within a wooded acre near Heavenly Ski Resort, this beautiful neorustic lodge offers luxury accommodations in a tranquil setting and convenient location (though not the prettiest in town). The great room, with its beamed ceilings, grand piano, early American antiques, three-story rock fireplace, and complimentary evening hors d'oeuvres, offers a relaxing environment after a long day of outdoor activities. Or better yet, soak your tired body in the sheltered Jacuzzi. Breakfast—included in the room rate—is an event, with fresh-baked muffins, eggs Benedict, omelets, and other hearty fare. Each of the spacious guest rooms has an artful blend of modern and authentic Old West furnishings, including a king-size bed, private bathroom, and gas fireplace. For additional privacy, request one of the three cabins behind the inn, and ask for breakfast to be delivered to your door.

1202 Ski Run Blvd., South Lake Tahoe, CA 96150. (© **877/232-7466** or 530/544-4451. www.tahoeblack bear.com. 5 lodge rooms, 3 cabins. $200–$265 lodge room; $260–$470 cabin. Rates include full breakfast. AE, MC, V. **Amenities:** Nearby golf course; Jacuzzi. *In room:* A/C, TV/VCR/DVD, Wi-Fi, kitchenette, fridge, coffeemaker, hair dryer in cabins.

Embassy Suites Lake Tahoe Hotel & Ski Resort ★ (Kids)   On the edge of the state line, steps away from the Heavenly Gondola, this is the only major noncasino hotel on Tahoe's South Shore. It earns its keep by luring the upscale gambling crowd and the convention business with uncommonly large suites. The nine-story château-style hotel has a roofline pierced with a double layer of dormers; equally impressive are the three massive inner atriums featuring a collection of fine art, live plants, and a waterfall feature reminiscent of the Comstock Lode mining era. The two-room suites all have a separate living room with sofa bed, armchair, a well-lit dining/work table, a microwave, two TVs, a small refrigerator, and a wet bar. Complimentary breakfasts, cooked to order, are served in a garden atrium and a complimentary evening manager's reception is held from 4:30pm to 6:30pm daily. The resort's fine-dining restaurant, **Echo**, serves New American cuisine for lunch and dinner with large-screen TVs to view the latest sports activities. In the summer, all guests have access to a private beach and a multitude of outdoor recreational activities; and family skiers fill up the place in winter, partly because kids 18 and under stay free.

4130 Lake Tahoe Blvd., South Lake Tahoe, CA 96150. (© **877/497-8483** or 530/544-5400. Fax 530/544-4900. www.embassytahoe.com. 400 suites. $169–$399 suite. Rates include full breakfast and evening cocktail reception. Special packages available. Children 18 and under stay free in parent's room. AE, DC, DISC, MC, V. **Amenities:** Restaurant; lounge; indoor pool; health club; Jacuzzi; dry sauna; watersports equipment rental; concierge; car-rental desk; Wi-Fi in public areas; room service; in-room massage; babysitting; same-day dry cleaning; executive-level rooms. *In room:* A/C, TV, fridge, coffeemaker, hair dryer, iron.

Harrah's Lake Tahoe ★ (Kids)   Understatement is not a word that crosses your mind at Harrah's, the most luxurious and glitzy of Tahoe's casinos. Harrah's takes great pride in its special blend of luxury, beauty, unparalleled guest service, and casino entertainment. Large rooms have two bathrooms, each with a TV and telephone, with those thick, fluffy, white towels Sinatra always demanded. Most have bay windows overlooking the lake or the mountains. The casino has an enormous fun center for kids, with the latest in video and arcade games, virtual reality, and an indoor "playscape" for young children. Weddings and parties can be scheduled aboard the private yacht, the *Tahoe Star*. The newly renovated **South Shore Room** hosts showbiz stars, and last, but by no means least, the casino is a gambler's dream.

P.O. Box 8, Stateline, NV 89449. 🕽 **800/427-7247** or 775/588-6611. Fax 775/586-6601. www.harrahs. com. 525 units. $159–$349 double; $396–$596 suite. Packages available. AE, DC, DISC, MC, V. **Amenities:** 8 restaurants; cafe; deli; coffeehouse; indoor pool; full-service health club/spa; family center; game room; shopping arcade; salon; room service; in-room massage; same-day dry cleaning. *In room:* A/C, TV/VCR, coffeemaker, hair dryer, iron, safe.

Harveys Lake Tahoe Casino & Resort (Kids)

With its two massive towers and 740 rooms, Harveys is the largest (and possibly the ugliest) hotel in Tahoe. It features an 88,000-square-foot casino, eight restaurants, and a cabaret with some of the most glittering, bespangled shows in town. Harveys is like a city unto itself, with a children's day camp, beauty and barbershops, and even a wedding chapel, should you get the urge. Heck, you never have to see the real world again. *Tip:* Try to get a room between the 15th and 19th floors in the Lake Tower, where every unit has a view of Lake Tahoe and the surrounding Sierra. *Note:* The Harrah's Entertainment corporation owns Harveys, which is why they share the same toll-free number and Web address.

U.S. 50 at Stateline Ave. (P.O. Box 128), Stateline, NV 89449. 🕽 **800/427-7247** or 775/588-2411. Fax 775/588-6643. www.harrahs.com. 740 units. $129–$299 double; $299–$699 suite. AE, DC, DISC, MC, V. **Amenities:** 7 restaurants; 10 bars; outdoor heated pool; nearby golf course; health club; spa; Jacuzzi; sauna; watersports equipment rental; children's day camp; video arcade; concierge; car-rental desk; business center; shopping arcade; salon; room service; in-room massage; laundry service; same-day dry cleaning. *In room:* A/C, TV w/pay movies, minibar, coffeemaker, hair dryer, iron, safe.

MontBleu Resort Casino & Spa ★★

Et tu, MontBleu? On May 24, 2006, the iconic Caesars Tahoe changed ownership and is now run by a Kentucky-based hotel corporation that also owns the Horizon Casino across the street. Following the bandwagon of casinos offering a resort experience, the MontBleu is selling itself as "the" park-'n'-play destination in South Lake. Makeovers include a chic new lobby that makes the other hotels on the strip look frumpy, and seven stylin' new restaurants (tapas anyone?), two hip new nightclubs, the 1,500-seat MontBleu Theatre that features celebrity performers, and a new outdoor sports arena hosting pro volleyball tournaments. Changes to the 40,000-square-foot casino floor include a new race and sports book (aka "The Zone") and a new poker room offering eight tables of the popular Texas Hold 'Em at various buy-in levels. The guest rooms, many of which offer beautiful lake views, are furnished with contemporary hardwood pieces and equipped with signature Bleu Cloud Beds and extra-large tubs. Suites range from executive-style quarters to lavish suites for high rollers. Other highlights include a lagoon-style indoor pool, a Starbucks, and the new Onsen Spa.

55 U.S. 50 (P.O. Box 5800), Lake Tahoe, NV 89449. 🕽 **800/648-3353** or 775/588-3515. www.montbleu resort.com. 440 units. $99–$330 double; $390–$950 suite. Packages available. AE, DC, MC, V. **Amenities:** 7 restaurants; indoor pool; 3 outdoor tennis courts; health club; spa; Jacuzzi; sauna; video arcade; activities desk; car-rental desk; business center; shopping arcade; salon; room service; dry cleaning; executive-level rooms; 4 nightlife venues; ski rental. *In room:* A/C, TV, Wi-Fi, kitchenette and minibar in suites, fridge upon request, hair dryer, iron, safe.

Tahoe Seasons Resort

Big, modern, and loaded with luxuries, the Tahoe Seasons lies in a relatively uncongested residential neighborhood at the base of the Heavenly Valley Ski Resort, 2 miles from Tahoe's casinos. Every unit here is a spacious, attractive suite, sleeping up to four in the smaller one and six in the larger one. Most have gas fireplaces, and all have huge whirlpool spas complete with shoji screens (in case you plan to lose your shirt in more ways than one). Skiing isn't the only activity around here: Play a round of tennis on the roof or hop aboard the free casino shuttles.

Village People

That sprawling "alpine village" next to the casinos is the new 464-room Marriott's Timber Lodge & Grand Residence Club (4100 Lake Tahoe Blvd.; © **800/845-5279** or 530/542-6600; www.marriottvillarentals.com). It's the first phase of a massive redevelopment project slated for Stateline that will level most of the old, inexpensive motels with nickel-slotters and replace them with that expensive corporate faux-village thing that's taking over the world's tourist destinations. The two adjacent vacation ownership resorts also sell rooms on a per-night basis, but it's only a good deal if your family takes full advantage of the resort amenities: restaurants, bars, an ice-skating rink, two pools, a movie theater, a ski gondola, an arcade, and an alpine-style retail mini-mall. The silver lining? The new building codes are fiercely pro-environment: Holding and treatment ponds are now required to prevent polluted snowmelt and rainwater from dumping straight into the lake, and the central ski gondola and high-tech bus system are two new ecofriendly means of luring people away from their SUVs.

3901 Saddle Rd., off Ski Run Blvd. (P.O. Box 5656), South Lake Tahoe, CA 96157. © **800/540-4874** or 530/541-6700. Fax 530/541-0653. www.tahoeseasons.com. 160 suites. Summer $170–$240 double; winter $180–$250 double; spring and fall $122–$200 double. Seasonal packages available. AE, MC, V. **Amenities:** Restaurant; pub; outdoor heated pool; nearby golf course; 2 rooftop tennis courts; complimentary health club use at Harveys Resort; game room; concierge; tour and activities desk; courtesy car; room service; in-room massage; same-day dry cleaning. In room: A/C, TV/VCR, fridge, coffeemaker, hair dryer on request, iron.

Moderate

Best Western Station House Inn (Value) Ensconced amid towering pines but just 3 blocks from the casinos, the Best Western Station House Inn, built in the late 1970s, is one of the few hotels in town that still has its own private "gated" beach on the lake. The decor is corporate dull, but the location is ideal, the large swimming pool and hot tub are a huge bonus, and **LewMarNel's,** the on-site restaurant, won a *Wine Spectator* award. The complimentary breakfast, cooked to order, and free shuttle service make staying here a particularly good value.

901 Park Ave., South Lake Tahoe, CA 96150. © **800/822-5953** or 530/542-1101. Fax 530/542-1714. www. stationhouseinn.com. 100 units. $74–$138 double; $135–$165 suite; $200–$300 cabin. Rates include full breakfast. Packages available. AE, DC, DISC, MC, V. **Amenities:** Restaurant; heated outdoor pool; Jacuzzi. In room: A/C, TV, coffeemaker, hair dryer.

Camp Richardson Resort ★ (Kids) If you're planning a family vacation, a reunion, or just a weekend getaway, Camp Richardson has it all. (I *love* this place.) On a long sandy beach on the southwest shore, this woodsy retreat offers a wide array of activities and several lodging and dining options. Its two restaurants offer lakeside dining, but there are also more informal dining options, plus a general store, a candy store, and an ice-cream parlor. The sports center rents all the seasonal equipment you'll need. You can ski right along the shore, scale the rock-climbing wall, or visit the stable for horseback riding. The full-service marina rents ski boats, jet skis, kayaks, and paddleboats, and offers guided tours, cruises, and chartered fishing trips. Lodging options include a hotel, cabins, a beachside inn, a marina duplex, tent campgrounds, and an RV park. The children will fall into bed exhausted at night with all of the organized activities available.

Cabins rent only by the week in summer and fill up quickly. *Tip:* Check their website for seasonal money-saving packages.

Jameson Beach Rd. (P.O. Box 9028), South Lake Tahoe, CA 96158. © 800/544-1801 or 530/541-1801. Fax 530/541-1802. www.camprichardson.com. $95–$195 hotel; $145–$250 cabin per day winter, $745–$2,265 per week in summer. Camping or RV hookup $25–$40 per day. DISC, MC, V. **Amenities:** 2 restaurants; ice cream parlor; cafe; Jacuzzi; sports center w/bike, snowshoe, and ski rental; children's program; tour and activities desk; general store; marina. *In room:* TV in inn and duplex rooms, kitchen in cabin, coffeemaker, no phone in hotel and cabin units.

Fireside Lodge ★ (Kids) If you're more into outdoor recreation than roulette, on the opposite side of town from the big casinos is the Fireside Lodge, a small log cabin–style inn that sits on the edge of the national forest, affording easy access to a public beach and miles of hiking and biking trails. It's owned and run by the local family who also owns the Inn at Heavenly, and the location is unbeatable—close to some great restaurants and the kid-friendly facilities at Camp Richardson, but far enough from the main drag to keep your mind on the mountains. The nine country-pine rooms are well equipped with river-rock fireplaces and kitchenettes. After a hike in the woods, relax in the hot-tub room, play some pool in the rec room, and then have a barbecue outside. Dogs and kids are welcome, and the staff will even lend you bicycles, float tubes, and free videos.

515 Emerald Bay Rd., South Lake Tahoe, CA 96150-6505. © **800/692-2246** or 530/544-5515. www.tahoe firesidelodge.com. 9 rooms. $119–$199 double. Rates include continental breakfast. AE, DISC, MC, V. **Amenities:** Hot tub; rec room; Wi-Fi; barbecue facilities. *In room:* TV/VCR, fridge, coffeemaker, microwave.

Horizon Casino Resort (Value) This massive resort hotel, next to the even larger Harveys, charges less for basically the same facilities. The lobby is a cheesy sea of white marble and mirrors, and the standard rooms are bland but innocuous (although the suites are far racier). The upper floors of the two towers naturally open onto the best views of mountains and the lake. Besides the 42,000-square-foot gaming room, the resort has a multiplex movie theater, cabaret, lounge, nightclub, the largest outdoor pool in Tahoe, and restaurants ranging from buffet to gourmet.

U.S. 50 (P.O. Box C), Lake Tahoe, NV 89449. © **800/648-3322** or 775/588-6211. Fax 775/588-0349. www. horizoncasino.com. 539 units. $125–$188 double summer, $99–$169 double winter; $250–$500 suite. Children 11 and under stay free in parent's room. Packages available. AE, DC, DISC, MC, V. **Amenities:** 3 restaurants; large heated outdoor pool; nearby golf course; health club; 3 Jacuzzis; bike and ski rental; video arcade; concierge; car-rental desk; shopping arcade; salon; room service; in-room massage; laundry service; same-day dry cleaning; executive-level rooms. *In room:* A/C, TV w/pay movies, minibar, fridge, coffeemaker, hair dryer, iron in suites.

Lakeland Village Beach & Mountain Resort ★ (Kids) This 1970s condominium/hotel resort is a good choice for families. Clustered on 19 lightly forested acres of shoreline property are a labyrinth of redwood buildings that blend into the surrounding landscape. The only drawback is the proximity to traffic headed into Lake Tahoe, although some units are quieter than those in the main lodge, adjacent to the road. The units—ranging from studios and suites in the lodge to multibedroom lakeside town homes—have streamlined California architecture, and many have upstairs sleeping lofts. All accommodations come with fully equipped kitchens and fireplaces. Perks include a large private beach directly on the lake, access to a boat dock, and free private shuttle service to Heavenly and the casinos.

3535 Lake Tahoe Blvd., South Lake Tahoe, CA 96150. © **800/822-5969** or 530/544-1685. Fax 530/541-6278. www.lakeland-village.com. 209 condo units. $99–$300 double; $165–$1,500 for a 1- to 5-bedroom town house. Includes skiers free continental breakfast (winter only). Children stay free in parent's room.

AE, DISC, MC, V. **Amenities:** 2 heated outdoor pools; kids wading pool; nearby golf course; 2 outdoor tennis courts; 2 Jacuzzis; fitness room; sauna; children's play area and summer kids' activity club; same-day dry cleaning. *In room:* TV/VCR/DVD, Wi-Fi, kitchen, fridge, coffeemaker, hair dryer, iron.

Zephyr Cove ★ (Value) (Kids)   Like historic Camp Richardson Resort (see review above), this place is great for families. A lakeside bargain in a shady grove of tall pines, about 4 miles from the casinos, this Nevada-side resort has everything you need for a relaxing vacation: a beautiful gold-sand beach, volleyball courts, a beachside bar with strong mai tais, and water toys for rent: pedal boats, kayaks, canoes, and ski boats. Zephyr Cove's pier is also the launching point for cruises on the MS *Dixie II* paddle-wheeler and the *Woodwind II* catamaran. The resort's 28 cabins range in size from studios and cottages to four-bedroom cabins sleeping up to 10. The decor is low-grade Levitz, but all units are very clean with well-equipped kitchens and a front porch with patio furniture. Even in the winter, it's fun to stay here: The resort's snowmobile tours are a lot of fun, and the Heavenly ski resort is only a 10-minute drive away. The Zephyr Cove Restaurant serves hearty American fare for breakfast, lunch, and dinner daily. A free shuttle runs to the restaurants and casinos down the road.

750 Hwy. 50, at Zephyr Cove, NV 89448. © **800/23-TAHOE** or 775/589-4906. www.zephyrcove.com. 28 cabins. Summer $129–$479 cabin; off season $79–$409. AE, DISC, MC, V. Pets are allowed with $15 charge per pet, per night. **Amenities:** Restaurant; bar; gift shop; watersports; sailing; volleyball court; horseback riding; snowmobiling. *In room:* TV w/cable and HBO, Internet access, kitchen (w/fridge, oven, microwave, coffeemaker, cookware, dishes, and utensils).

Inexpensive

Big Pines Mountain House of Tahoe (Value)   It's nothing fancy, but you get a lot for your money here: agreeable accommodations, access to a private beach, and an easy walk to the casinos and the Heavenly Gondola. The rooms are clean and pleasant, with all the standard conveniences. If you're traveling with kids, you may want one of the units with a kitchen. Be sure to inquire about the ski and lake cruise packages.

4083 Cedar Ave., South Lake Tahoe, CA 96150. © **800/288-4083** or 530/541-5155. Fax 530/541-5643. www.bigpinesmountainhouse.com. 76 units. $56–$119 double. Children 11 and under stay free in parent's room. Rates include continental breakfast. Packages available. AE, DC, DISC, MC, V. **Amenities:** Outdoor heated pool; nearby golf course; Jacuzzi. *In room:* TV, kitchen in 14 units, fridge on request, coffeemaker, hair dryer, iron.

North Shore/Tahoe City
Expensive

Hyatt Regency Lake Tahoe Resort, Spa & Casino ★ (Kids)   If you like gambling but hate gauche, glitzy casinos, you'll like the Hyatt in Incline Village. Amid towering pines and mountains on the lake's pristine northeast shore, it's far classier and quieter than the casino hotels you'll find along Stateline. The private beach, loaded with water toys—catamaran cruises, boat rentals, jet skis, parasailing—is available only to guests. The adjoining Lakeside Cottages are a wee bit o' heaven for families or honeymooners who want beachfront access and large, comfortable rooms with unobstructed panoramas of the lake. Popular Camp Hyatt affords kids aged 3 to 12 a break from their parents for the day. The **Lone Eagle Grille,** one of several on-site restaurants, has one of the most beautiful dining rooms on the lake and superb cuisine. Be sure to take a walk (or a jog) down Lakeshore Boulevard to see the magnificent estates fronting the water. The latest addition is a 15,000-square-foot Stillwater Spa facility with a multitiered swimming pool and an entire 150-room wing of Spa Terrace guest rooms.

Skiing Tahoe in Squaw Valley Style

The fancy new **Village at Squaw Valley** looks expensive, but it's actually one of the best deals in Tahoe. For as little as $150 per night you can score a fully furnished condominium—fireplace, full kitchen, deck, huge TV, sofa bed, DVD player—right next to the ski lifts. And the free perks are superb: covered underground parking, eight whirlpool spas, ski and snowboard lockers, a billiards lounge, and three fitness centers with saunas. You'll never need your car because the best restaurants, bars, and shops are within walking distance. After a full day of skiing, there's no better way to finish off the day than with a Deluxe Deep Tissue massage at the Village's **Trilogy Spa** (✆ 530/584-6125; www.trilogyspa.com), followed by a drink at **Auld Dubliner** (✆ 530/584-6041; www.aulddubliner.com), an authentic Irish Pub from Ireland (literally—the pub was built in Ireland, dismantled, shipped over, and reassembled). The Dubliner has Squaw's best après-ski bar scene and serves great Irish fare. Combine all of this with Tahoe's best skiing and you have my top resort choice for a Tahoe ski vacation. For more information, log on to **www.thevillageat squaw.com** (be sure to check out the money-saving package deals) or call ✆ 866/818-6963.

Country Club at Lakeshore, 111 Country Club Dr., Incline Village, NV 89451. ✆ **888/899-5019** or 775/832-1234. Fax 775/831-2171. www.laketahoehyatt.com. 405 units, 24 cottages. $160–$330 double; $405–$1,385 cottage. Packages available. AE, DC, DISC, MC, V. **Amenities:** 4 restaurants; 4 lounges; nearby golf course; watersports equipment rental; bike rental; children's program; concierge; tour and activities desk; car-rental desk; business center; room service; laundry service; same-day dry cleaning; executive-level rooms. *In room:* A/C, TV w/pay movies, minibar, fridge, coffeemaker, hair dryer, iron, safe.

Northstar-at-Tahoe ★★ (Kids) The owners of Northstar continue to come up with more ways to have fun year-round—the list of activities here is mind-boggling. Northstar prides itself on being the ultimate self-contained family destination, and it's even better now, since completion of the new Village—seven buildings, with 213 new luxury ski-in/ski-out condominium residences, stylish boutiques, outdoor restaurants, an ice rink, and a pedestrian plaza. The Village is surrounded by a honeycomb of fully equipped redwood condos and vacation homes, all nestled among the pines. And a midmountain Ritz-Carlton resort should be complete by next year. Lodging options range from a hotel room in the lodge to a five-bedroom house, with every size in between. Summer activities include golf, swimming, tennis, mountain biking, hiking, fly-fishing, rock climbing, rope courses, and horseback riding. See "Skiing & Snowboarding," earlier in this chapter, for winter activities.

Off Hwy. 267, Box 129, Northstar-at-Tahoe, CA 96160. ✆ **800/466-6784** or 530/562-1010. Fax 530/562-2215. www.northstarattahoe.com. 250 units. $209–$349 double in lodge; $165–$989 condo, home. Packages available. AE, DISC, MC, V. **Amenities:** 2 restaurants; cafe; deli; bar; 3 pools (outdoor heated, indoor heated, children's); golf course; 10 tennis courts; health club; 3 outdoor Jacuzzis; sauna; bike rental; children and teen center; game room/video arcade; tour and activities desk; business center; babysitting; laundry facilities; ice rink. *In room:* TV/DVD and HBO in select rooms, coffeemaker w/Starbucks coffee, hair dryer, iron.

PlumpJack Squaw Valley Inn ★★ Part ski chalet, part boutique hotel, PlumpJack Squaw Valley Inn is among Tahoe's most refined, elegant lodgings. It lacks the fancy toys offered by its competitor across the valley, the Resort at Squaw Creek (see below), but the PlumpJack is unquestionably more genteel, a tribute to the melding of artistry and hostelry. The hotel is done in muted, earthy tones, with swirling sconces and sculpted metal accents. Rooms have thick hooded robes, terry-cloth slippers, down comforters on expensive mattresses, and mountain views. One unit has a kitchenette. The inn's fine restaurant, **PlumpJack Café,** is reviewed on p. 286.

1920 Squaw Valley Rd. (P.O. Box 2407), Olympic Valley, CA 96146. ✆ **800/323-7666** or 530/583-1576. Fax 530/583-1734. www.plumpjack.com. 61 units. Summer $169–$379; winter $199–$549. AE, DISC, MC, V. **Amenities:** Restaurant; bar; heated outdoor pool (seasonal); nearby golf course; 2 Jacuzzis; bike rental; concierge; room service; laundry service; same-day dry cleaning; executive-level rooms. *In room:* TV w/ pay movies, minibar, fridge, coffeemaker in suites, hair dryer.

The Resort at Squaw Creek ★★★ (**Kids**) The most deluxe resort on the lake is the Resort at Squaw Creek, a paradise for skiers, golfers, and tennis players. It's ranked among the top 50 resorts in North America by *Condé Nast Traveler.* You can't beat the resort's ski-in/ski-out access to Squaw Valley slopes; the chairlift lands just outside the door. Don't ski? Don't worry. Lots of other sports facilities will divert you, including 20 miles of groomed cross-country skiing trails (marked for hiking and biking in the summer), snowshoeing, dogsled rides, an ice-skating rink, and, in summer, a world-class golf course, on-property fly-fishing, and the newly renovated Spa at Squaw Creek, a full-service spa and salon. Trained counselors lead a Mountain Buddies program for kids ages 4 to 13, with different activities every day. The standard guest rooms are not particularly spacious, but they're well equipped with attractive furnishings, original artwork, and windows that open, with beautiful views. Suites come in all different sizes and configurations. *Tip:* Be sure to ask about the money-saving midweek package deals.

400 Squaw Creek Rd., Olympic Valley, CA 96146. ✆ **800/327-3353** or 530/583-6300. Fax 530/581-6632. www.squawcreek.com. 403 units. $309–$395 double; $450–$1,900 suite. Packages available. AE, DC, DISC, MC, V. Free valet. **Amenities:** 4 restaurants; deli; 2 bars; 3 pools (1 heated); golf course; 2 outdoor tennis courts; health club; region's largest spa; indoor and outdoor Jacuzzis; dry saunas; bike rental; children's program; video arcade; concierge; activities desk; business center; secretarial services; shopping arcade; salon; room service; in-room massage; babysitting; laundry service; same-day dry cleaning; guided hiking. *In room:* A/C, TV w/pay movies, kitchen in some units, minibar, coffeemaker, hair dryer, iron.

The Shore House at Lake Tahoe ★★ This romantic little bed-and-breakfast inn, right on the lake, is a real charmer. Each individually decorated room has its own entrance, handmade log furniture, knotty-pine walls, a gas-log fireplace, and a blissfully comfortable feather bed. Guests have access to a private beach and landscaped lawn that overlook the lake and an in-house spa. If you're planning to tie the knot, the charming hosts will provide everything you need for a beautiful ceremony, including an outdoor lakeside setting and a honeymoon cottage with a two-person spa tub.

7170 N. Lake Blvd. (P.O. Box 499), Tahoe Vista, CA 96148. ✆ **800/207-5160** or 530/546-7270. Fax 530/546-7130. www.shorehouselaketahoe.com. 8 units, 1 cottage. $190–$275 double; $275–$310 cottage. Rates include full breakfast. DISC, MC, V. **Amenities:** Jacuzzi; massage. *In room:* A/C, TV, fridge, hair dryer, no phone (phone available in dining room).

Moderate

Cal-Neva Resort, Spa & Casino ★
You might guess from the name of this place that the state line literally runs right through it, but you might never imagine its colorful, sometimes scandalous history. It's here that Marilyn Monroe allegedly had her rendezvous with

John F. Kennedy (you can even see the secret tunnel), and ownership passed around to moguls with names like Pretty Boy, Babyface, and Sinatra, who built the famed Celebrity Room. Respectability has since laid claim to the Cal-Neva, however, and it's now a popular, reputable lakeside resort. Almost all the elegantly decorated rooms have lake views. Besides the casino (on the Nevada side of the hotel, of course), the Cal-Neva offers a full array of sport and spa options, a complete wedding-planning service, and two wedding chapels. Even if you don't stay here, stop by and take a look.

2 Stateline Rd. (Box 368), Crystal Bay, NV 89402-0368. © **800/225-6382** or 775/832-4000. Fax 775/831-9007. www.calnevaresort.com. 188 units, 9 chalets, 3 bungalows. $109–$209 double; $199–$289 suite, chalet, or bungalow. Packages available. AE, DC, DISC, MC, V. **Amenities:** Lake-view restaurant; bar; heated outdoor pool; nearby golf course; 2 outdoor tennis courts; full-service European health spa; Jacuzzi; large video arcade; concierge; salon; room service. *In room:* A/C, TV, fax, coffeemaker, hair dryer, iron.

Meeks Bay Resort ★

Ten miles south of Tahoe City, rustic Meeks Bay Resort is one of the oldest hostelries on the lake and something of a historical landmark. Opened as a public campground in 1920, its sweeping lakefront location has one of the finest beaches on the lake. During the next 50 years, the resort grew to include cabins and other improvements, and attracted many celebrities from Southern California. Acquired by the U.S. Forest Service in 1974, the property is open during summers only. Most rentals are on a weekly basis and consist of motel lodging or modest wood cabins near the lake. Facilities include a full marina with boat rentals, a campground with RV access ($25 a night, 4-night minimum), a beachfront snack bar, a playground, and a visitor center with a cultural display, coffee bar, and retail store. The Kehlet Mansion, set on a rock that juts into the lake, is the resort's prime accommodation. Owned at one time by William Hewlett, cofounder of the Hewlett-Packard Corporation, and later the summer residence of billionaire Gordon Getty, it has seven bedrooms, three bathrooms, a large kitchen, a living room, and water on three sides. The entire house is rented by the week, sleeps a dozen, and costs $6,000. Make all reservations here early.

P.O. Box 787, Tahoma, CA 96142. © **877/326-3357** or 530/525-6946. Fax 530/525-4028. www.meeksbay resort.com. 21 units, 34 campsites. $90–$240 double per night, $1,350–$1,825 per week. AE, MC, V. Open May–Nov only. **Amenities:** Watersports gear rental. *In room:* Kitchen in log cabins.

River Ranch Lodge & Restaurant ★★

The River Ranch Lodge has long been one of my favorite places to stay in Lake Tahoe. Alongside the Truckee River, the lodge is minutes away from Alpine Meadows and Squaw Valley ski resorts, and a short drive (or ride along the bike path) into Tahoe City. The best rooms have balconies overlooking the river. All have a handsome mountain-home decor, lodgepole pine furniture, and down comforters. Room nos. 9 and 10, the farthest from the road, are my top choices. In summer, guests relax under umbrellas on the huge patio overlooking the river, working down burgers and beer while watching the rafters float by. During ski season, the River Ranch's spectacular circular cocktail lounge and dining area, which cantilevers over the river, is a popular après-ski hangout. Another big hit is the handsome **River Ranch Lodge Restaurant,** which serves creations by its new Executive Chef, Julia Walter. Dishes range from fresh seafood—think seared sesame-coated ahi tuna or the diver-scallop pasta—to such thick meats as a ranch rib-eye with a wild mushroom demiglacé, or the filet mignon in a California cabernet and roasted garlic sauce.

On Hwy. 89, at Alpine Meadows Rd. (P.O. Box 197), Tahoe City, CA 96145. © **800/535-9900** or 530/583-4264. Fax 530/583-7237. www.riverranchlodge.com. 19 units. $115–$200 double. Rates include continental breakfast. Packages available. AE, MC, V. **Amenities:** Restaurant; bar; golf course nearby; concierge. *In room:* TV, iron.

Sunnyside Lodge ★★ Built as a private home in 1908, this hotel and restaurant is one of the few grand old lodges left on the lake. Two miles south of Tahoe City, it looks very much like a giant, sophisticated wood cabin, complete with dormers, steep pitched roofs, and natural-wood siding. Stretching across the building, a large deck fronts a tiny marina and gravel beach. The Lakefront rooms (suites 30–31 and rooms 32–39) are the most desirable and go for about $40 more than the others—well worth the added expense. Five units have rock fireplaces. Most of the lodge's ground floor is dominated by the popular **Sunnyside Restaurant** (p. 287).

1850 W. Lake Blvd. (P.O. Box 5969), Tahoe City, CA 94145. © **800/822-2754** or 530/583-7200. Fax 530/583-2551. www.sunnysideresort.com. 23 units. $135–$295 double. Rates include continental breakfast and afternoon tea. Packages available. $10 for each additional guest. AE, MC, V. **Amenities:** Restaurant; bar; nearby golf course; watersports equipment rental; room service. *In room:* TV/VCR, fridge in some units, hair dryer, iron.

Tahoma Meadows Bed & Breakfast ★ (Kids) This historic bed-and-breakfast consists of cute red cabins nestled on a gentle forest slope surrounded by flowers and sugar pines. The units have a private bathroom, a comfy king- or queen-size bed, and are individually decorated with paintings of bucolic settings; four units have gas-log fireplaces. The largest cabins, Treehouse and Sugar Pine, sleep up to six, ideal for families. For guests staying in the B&B cottages, a family-style breakfast is served in the main lodge's common room every morning from 8 to 10am. Nearby activities include skiing at Ski Homewood (including shuttle service) and sunbathing at the lakeshore across the street. The friendly owners, Ulli and Dick White, will happily give advice on the best nearby hiking and fishing spots (Dick's an avid fly-fisherman).

6821 W. Lake Blvd. (P.O. Box 810), Homewood, CA 96141. © **866/525-1553** or 530/525-1553. www.tahomameadows.com. 14 units. $109–$375 double. Rates include full breakfast. AE, DISC, MC, V. 8¹/₂ miles from Tahoe City. Pets accepted in some units with $15 fee. **Amenities:** Nearby golf course. *In room:* TV, kitchen in some units, no phone.

Inexpensive

Ferrari's Crown Resort (Value) If you're looking for convenient lakefront accommodations at a reasonable price, this family-operated motel is a great choice. The Ferraris have proudly extended a warm welcome to guests, children included, since 1957. Family suites, completely equipped with kitchenettes and gas fireplaces, can sleep up to seven. It's nothing fancy, but it's well run, the rooms are very inviting, and you can't beat the location, which includes access to a private beach. Plan a trip during the off-season to take advantage of their great bargain rates.

8200 N. Lake Blvd. (P.O. Box 845), Kings Beach, CA 96143. © **800/645-2260** or 530/546-3388. Fax 530/546-3851. www.tahoecrown.com. 72 units. $65–$139 double; $99–$235 2-bedroom suite or lakefront room. Rates include continental breakfast. Packages available. AE, DISC, MC, V. **Amenities:** 2 heated outdoor pools (seasonal); nearby golf course; 2 Jacuzzis. *In room:* A/C, TV, high-speed Internet, stocked kitchenette, fridge, coffeemaker, hair dryer, iron in some units.

Lake of the Sky Motor Inn This remodeled 1960s-style A-frame motel in the heart of Tahoe City offers clean, quiet, inexpensive accommodations in a central location—only steps away from shops and restaurants and a main stop for the ski shuttles. You'll get just the basics here—TV, phone, bathroom—so plan on spending most of your time outdoors. Some rooms have lake views, and the landscaped picnic and barbecue area is attractive.

955 N. Lake Blvd. (P.O. Box 227), Tahoe City, CA 96145. © **530/583-3305.** Fax 530/583-7621. www.lakeoftheskyinn.com. 23 units. $89–$167 double. Children 11 and under stay free in parent's room. Rates

include continental breakfast. AE, DC, DISC, MC, V. **Amenities:** Heated outdoor pool (seasonal); nearby golf course. *In room:* TV, fridge in some units.

Pepper Tree Inn If you're the kind of person who dislikes both frills and big bills, the Pepper Tree Inn is for you. Two people can share a perfectly comfortable room for less than $50 each (considerably less in the off season). All guests have access to a redwood hot tub, heated outdoor pool with sun deck, free shuttle service to the major ski resorts, and most of the cable channels you could want, served up on 27-inch TVs. The location—right in the middle of Tahoe City with views of the lake—is great, but where the Pepper Tree Inn really shines is with its generous ski packages; so be sure to inquire when you make a reservation.

645 N. Lake Blvd. (P.O. Box 29), Tahoe City, CA 96145. ✆ **800/624-8590** or 530/583-3711. www.pepper treetahoe.com. 50 units. $99–$120 double. AE, DC, DISC, MC, V. **Amenities:** Outdoor headed pool; indoor spa. *In room:* TV, coffeemaker, hair dryer, iron.

Tamarack Lodge ★ Tamarack is one of the oldest lodges on the North Shore—so old it was a favorite haunt of Clark Gable and Gary Cooper. Now, it's one of the best bets for the frugal traveler. Hidden among a 4-acre cadre of pines just east of Tahoe City, the Tamarack Lodge consists of a few old cabins, five "poker rooms," and a modern (and far less nostalgic) motel unit. The rooms in the motel unit are the least appealing, but they're certainly clean and comfortable. The cabins all have kitchenettes and can hold up to four guests, but the most popular rooms by far are the original poker rooms (where Gable and Cooper used to play cards) lined with gleaming knotty pine. Complimentary coffee and tea are served in the lobby, Wi-Fi access is free, and rollaway beds are available for only $8 extra. The beach is within walking distance, but to get into town, you'll need to rent a car or take the Tahoe Trolley (the lodge will provide free trolley tickets).

2311 N. Lake Blvd. (P.O. Box 859), Tahoe City, CA 96145. ✆ **888/824-6323** or 530/583-3350. Fax 530/583-3531. www.tamarackattahoe.com. 17 units, 4 cabins. $52–$148 double. DISC, MC, V. *In room:* TV, Wi-Fi.

WHERE TO DINE
South Shore & South Lake Tahoe
Expensive

Evan's American Gourmet Café ★★ AMERICAN/CONTINENTAL This restaurant's impeccable service, award-winning wine list, and unyielding attention to detail serve as a perfect backdrop for the creative culinary artistry of returning chef Jimi Lasquete. Lasquete, reunited with the restaurant in 2007, bringing his accomplished techniques and creative flair that are clearly evident in the cuisine. For appetizers, typical choices are Millfeuille of goat cheese–hummus spread layered with spinach, tomato, and phyllo layers, topped with truffle honey. Entrees might include grilled filet of beef with foie-gras butter and Syrah reduction, served with white-cheddar gratin potatoes and broccoli, or prosciutto-crusted veal loin chop and wild mushroom ragout in a pearl glaze with tarragon-laced mashed potatoes. The desserts are luscious and beautiful. Seats are limited in this cozy little restaurant, so be sure to call ahead for reservations.

536 Emerald Bay Rd., South Lake Tahoe. ✆ **530/542-1990**. www.evanstahoe.com. Reservations required (must confirm by 4pm). Main courses $20–$32. AE, DISC, MC, V. Daily 5:30–9:30pm.

Fresh Ketch ★ SEAFOOD In a small marina at the foot of Tahoe Keys Boulevard, Fresh Ketch has long been regarded as South Lake's premier seafood restaurant. Try for a window table so you can watch the marina activities. For starters, I always order half a dozen oysters and the seared ahi tuna with garlic, soy, wasabi, and sesame seaweed salad.

Then it's on to the fresh catch of the day such as big Alaskan king crab, steamed in the shell and served with drawn butter. The menu also includes a modest selection of meat and poultry dishes, such as the great surf and turf of petite mignon and lobster. Prices are a bit steep, but you can also belly up with the locals and order from the extensive bar menu, with everything from blackened mahimahi to fresh-fish tacos and fish and chips for under $13. They've recently added a sushi bar as well. Live music acts perform Tuesday, Thursday, Friday, and Saturday evenings.

2433 Venice Dr. © 530/541-5683. www.thefreshketch.com. Reservations recommended. Main courses $16–$35; market price for crab and lobster. AE, DC, DISC, MC, V. Daily 11:30am–9pm (bar until 10pm).

Moderate

Cantina Bar & Grill ★ MEXICAN   The Cantina Bar & Grill is a favorite local hangout and serves the best Mexican food in South Lake. With friendly service, sports on three TVs, and 30 kinds of beer, joviality reigns. The menu is well priced and extensive, offering Cal-Mex specialties such as tacos, burritos, and enchiladas along with a half-dozen southwestern dishes such as smoked chicken polenta and blue corn salmon. The steak fajitas get a thumbs-up, as do the barbecued baby back ribs. To demonstrate their sense of whimsy and ethnic appeal, they offer an Oriental chicken salad and a southwestern Reuben sandwich, as well as a few vegetarian selections.

765 Emerald Bay Rd. © 530/544-1233. www.cantinatahoe.com. Main courses $9–$17. AE, MC, V. Daily 11:30am–10:30pm (bar until midnight).

The Naked Fish ★★ SUSHI   The Naked Fish in South Lake is the best sushi bar in Tahoe. I can never understand a word the Japanese chefs are saying to me, but I'm not paying much attention; the warm-butter-soft hamachi nigiri (yellowtail) has made my toes curl again. The colorful aquamarine theme with mermaids floating across the walls adds to the laid-back atmosphere of this locally owned Japanese restaurant. Before you open the menu, read the "specials" board above the sushi bar—this is the really fresh stuff, such as the deftly shelled live octopus sashimi. In the spirit of an authentic sushi bar, the chefs are friendly and talkative, particularly if you buy them a beer. Wimps can order cooked dinners such as sesame-crusted ahi and teriyaki chicken, but it's the flavorful rolls, tender cuts of nigiri, and festive bar that sushi hounds will appreciate.

3940 Lake Tahoe Blvd. (at the junction of Hwy. 50 and Pioneer Trail). © 530/541-3474. www.thenaked fish.com. Reservations recommended for parties of 6 or more. Main courses $14–$21; sushi $4–$12. AE, DC, DISC, MC, V. Sat–Sun 11:30am–2pm; daily 5–9pm.

Inexpensive

Ernie's Coffee Shop DINER   The undisputed king of coffee shops in South Lake Tahoe is Ernie's, which has been serving huge plates of good old American, cholesterol-laden grub to locals since the Nixon administration. The food is far from original (omelets, bacon and eggs, pancakes), so it must be the perpetually friendly service, low prices, and huge portions that attract the steady stream of customers. Another good reason to come here is that Ernie's is located next to the cheapest gas station in town, so you can top off your appetite and your tank in one stop. The milkshakes are great, too.

1207 Emerald Bay Rd./Hwy. 89. © 530/541-2161. www.erniescoffeeshop.com. Main dishes $7–$11. No credit cards. Daily 6am–2pm.

Sprouts Natural Foods Café (Value) HEALTH FOOD/JUICES   Sprouts owner Tyler Cannon has filled a much-needed niche in South Lake, serving wholesome food that looks good, tastes good, and *is* good. Most everything is made in-house, including the soups, smoothies, and fresh-squeezed juices. Menu items range from rice bowls to sandwiches (try the Real Tahoe Turkey), huge burritos, coffee drinks, muffins, fresh-fruit smoothies, and a marvelous mayo-free tuna sandwich made with yogurt and packed with fresh veggies. Order from the counter, and then scramble for a vacant seat (outdoor tables are coveted). This is also an excellent place to pack a picnic lunch.

3123 Harrison Ave. (at U.S. 50 and Alameda St., next to Lakeview Sports). (℘) **530/541-6969.** Meals $4.50–$6.75. No credit cards. Daily 8am–9pm.

Yellow Sub (Value) SANDWICHES When it comes to picnic supplies, the competition is stiff in South Lake Tahoe; this block alone has three sandwich shops. Still, my favorite is Yellow Sub, voted best deli sandwich shop by readers of the *Tahoe Daily Tribune* for 9 years straight. It sells 21 versions of overstuffed subs—made in 6-inch and 12-inch varieties—as well as several kinds of wraps. The shop is in a small shopping center across from the El Dorado Campground.

983 Tallac Ave. (at U.S. 50). (℘) **530/541-8808.** Sandwiches and wraps $3.20–$7.15. No credit cards. Daily 10:30am–8pm.

North Shore/Tahoe City
Expensive

PlumpJack Café ★★ MODERN AMERICAN Squaw Valley investors have spent oodles of money trying to turn the ski resort into a world-class destination, and one big step in the right direction is the sleek, sexy PlumpJack Café. Although dinner prices have dropped slightly (guests balked at the original rates), none of PlumpJack's standards have diminished. Expect impeccable service regardless of your attire (this is, after all, a ski resort). Menu choices range from Agave-glazed prawns, or a Sonoma duckling duo with roasted celery root in a black cherry sauce, to grilled lamb rack served in a cracked-mustard sauce with an avocado roll. There's also a more casual bar menu, and those familiar with PlumpJack in San Francisco know that the reasonably priced wine list is among the nation's best.

In the PlumpJack Squaw Valley Inn, 1920 Squaw Valley Rd., Squaw Valley. (℘) **530/583-1576.** www. plumpjack.com. Reservations recommended. Main courses $14–$45. AE, MC, V. Daily 7:30–10:30am (7am on Sat–Sun) and 11:30am–10pm.

Moderate

Gar Woods Grill & Pier ★ AMERICAN Named after the builder of those beautiful mahogany race boats that used to grace the lake in the 1930s and 1940s, Gar Woods attempts to evoke and pay homage to that era. Whether folks are watching *Monday Night Football* or drinking a famous Wet Woody, it seems as though something is always going on in the bar. On a sunny day, it's great fun to sit on the lakeside deck to enjoy the good food and good cheer. The menu is wide-ranging, covering everything from a shrimp-and-lobster bisque to beer-battered coconut prawns, blackened chicken sandwich, and grilled rib-eye—nothing out of the ordinary, but the preparation is solid and the service is friendly.

5000 N. Lake Blvd., Carnelian Bay. (℘) **800/BY-TAHOE** or 530/546-3366. www.garwoods.com. Lunch $9–$18; dinner $14–$30. AE, DISC, MC, V. Mon–Fri noon–5pm and 5:30–9:30pm; Sat–Sun 11:30am–10pm.

Sol y Lago ★★ (Finds) NUEVO LATINO It's amazing how much Tahoe's culinary scene has improved in the last 5 years. And it has only gotten better since San Francisco restaurateurs Johnny Alamilla and Brian Reccow moved to North Lake Tahoe and opened the region's only Nuevo Latino restaurant. It's right on the lake, and the gorgeous views from every window are reason enough to come here. The new decor is unique, a sort of mountain-meets-urban-chic look—rough-hewn timbers and wrought iron agreeably clash with silk shades and soft lighting. The menu will be unfamiliar territory to most diners, so it's a good idea to converse with your server before ordering; The tapas, such as the beef tenderloin served in a sizzling skillet with mild chiles, lime, onions, and cumin fries, are all very reasonably priced at $6 to $10, and ideal for family style dining. Be sure to arrive early for a pitcher of sangria with a side of yucca fries at the horseshoe-shaped bar, and beg the hostess for a table in the lower atrium, which has the best lake views.

760 North Lake Tahoe Blvd. (on the upper level of the Boatworks Mall), Tahoe City. © **530/583-0358.** www.solylago.com. Main courses $17–$29. AE, MC, V. Sun–Thurs 5:30–10pm; Fri–Sat 5:30–10:30pm (bar 4:20–11pm or later).

Sunnyside Restaurant ★ CALIFORNIA   In summer, when the sun's shining, the most highly coveted tables in Tahoe are those on Sunnyside's lakeside veranda. Guests can also dine in the lodge's more traditional Lakeside Dining Room with its 1930s aura. Nothing is extraordinary here: The lunch menu has burgers, chicken, and fish sandwiches, together with a variety of soups and salads. Dinners are fancier, with main courses such as lobster tail, lamb chops with raspberry mango sauce, and fresh salmon oven-baked on a cedar plank. In the winter, the bar has a lively après-ski scene where both tourists and locals come to watch ski flicks on the big screen and refuel on inexpensive appetizers.

At the Sunnyside Lodge, 1850 W. Lake Blvd., Tahoe City. © **800/822-2754** or 530/583-7200. www. sunnysideresort.com. Main courses $11–$36. AE, DISC, MC, V. Oct–June daily 4–9:30pm; July–Sept Sun–Thurs 11am–9:30pm, Fri–Sat 11am–10pm; year-round Sun brunch 9:30am–2pm.

Inexpensive

Bridgetender Tavern and Grill ⓥalue AMERICAN   Although it's located in one of the most popular tourist areas in North Lake, the Bridgetender has been a locals' hangout since 1977. Still, they're surprisingly tolerant of out-of-towners, who come for the cheap grub, sunny patio, and huge selection of draft beers (21). Big burly burgers, salads, hot and cold sandwiches, tacos, and hot dogs round out the menu, and the daily specials are definitely worth a taste. In summer, dine outside among the pines.

65 W. Lake Blvd. (across from Fanny Bridge), Tahoe City. © **530/583-3342.** Main courses $5–$7.25. MC, V. Daily 11am–2am.

Fire Sign Café ★ ⓥalue AMERICAN   Choosing a place to have breakfast in North Tahoe is a no-brainer. Since the late 1970s, the Fire Sign Café has been the locals' choice—which explains the lines out the door on weekends. Just about everything is made from scratch, such as the delicious coffeecake that accompanies the big plates of bacon and eggs, or blueberry pancakes. Even the salmon for chef and owner Bob Young's legendary salmon omelet is smoked in-house. Lunch—burgers, salads, sandwiches, burritos, and more—is also quite popular, particularly when the outdoor patio is open.

1785 W. Lake Blvd., Tahoe City. © **530/583-0871.** Breakfast and lunch $6–$8. MC, V. Daily 7am–3pm.

Rosie's Café ★ ⓚids AMERICAN   Two floors' worth of tables usually ensures a short wait—if one at all—at this shingled, lodge-style restaurant in the heart of downtown Tahoe City. Family owned and operated, Rosie's has been serving quality comfort food to legions of vacationers since it opened in 1980. It's noisy and casual, perfect for families (with children's menus and free balloons even), and servings are plentiful. A big menu offers breakfasts designed to carbo-load skiers, as well as hamburgers, grilled chicken sandwiches, and chef-type salads for lunch. The two-course dinners mostly star fish and meat (the Yankee pot roast with mashed potatoes and gravy is hard to resist on a cold night). You won't mistake it for gourmet, but you'll like the value and ethos.

571 North Lake Blvd., Tahoe City. © **530/583-8504.** Reservations accepted for dinner. Main courses $7–$10 lunch, $15–$20 dinner. DISC, MC, V. Daily 6:30am–10pm.

TAHOE AFTER DARK

Tahoe is not known for its nightlife, although something is always going on in the show-rooms of the major casinos on the South Shore. Call **Harrah's** (© **775/588-6611**), **Harveys** (© 775/588-2411), **MontBleu** (© 775/588-3515), and the **Horizon** (© 775/588-6211) for current show schedules and prices. Most cocktail shows cost $20 to $55. On the North Shore, **Sandy's Pub,** at the Resort at Squaw Creek (© **530/581-6617;** p. 281), hosts live music nightly. If it's just a casual cocktail you're after, my favorite spot is the cozy fireside lounge at **River Ranch Lodge,** which cantilevers over a turbulent stretch of the Truckee River, on Highway 89 at the entrance to Alpine Meadows (© **530/583-4264**).

2 MOUNT SHASTA & THE CASCADES ★★

274 miles N of San Francisco

Chances are, your first glimpse of Mount Shasta's majestic, snowcapped peak will result in a twang of awe. A dormant volcano with a 17-mile-diameter base, it stands in virtual isolation 14,162 feet above the sea. When John Muir first saw Shasta from 50 miles away in 1874, he wrote: "[I] was alone and weary. Yet my blood turned to wine, and I have not been weary since." He went on to describe it as "the pole star of the landscape," which indeed it is.

Keep in mind, however, that dining and lodging in these parts lean more toward sustenance than indulgence: It's the fresh air, not fresh fish, that lures visitors this far north. You can leave the dinner jacket home—all that's required when you visit the Far North are broken-in hiking boots, binoculars (the bald eagle is a common sight in these parts), warm clothing, and an adventurous spirit.

ESSENTIALS

GETTING THERE   From San Francisco, take I-80 to I-505 to I-5 to Redding. From the coast, pick up Highway 299 East north of Arcata, to Redding.

Redding Municipal Airport, 6751 Woodrum Circle (© **530/224-4320**), is serviced by **United Express** (© 800/241-6522) and **Horizon Air** (© 800/547-9308). **Amtrak** (© **800/USA-RAIL**) stops in Dunsmuir and Redding.

VISITOR INFORMATION   Regional information can be obtained from the following organizations: **Shasta Cascade Wonderland Association,** 1699 Hwy. 273, Anderson, CA 96007 (© **800/474-2782** or 530/365-7500; www.shastacascade.org); **Mount Shasta Visitors Bureau,** 300 Pine St., Mount Shasta, CA 96067 (© **800/926-4865** or 530/926-4865; www.mtshastachamber.com); **Redding Convention & Visitors Bureau,** 777 Auditorium Dr., Redding, CA 96001 (© **800/874-7562** or 530/225-4100; www.visitredding.org); and **Trinity County Chamber of Commerce,** 210 N. Main St., P.O. Box 517, Weaverville, CA 96093 (© **800/487-4648** or 530/623-6101; www.trinitycounty.com).

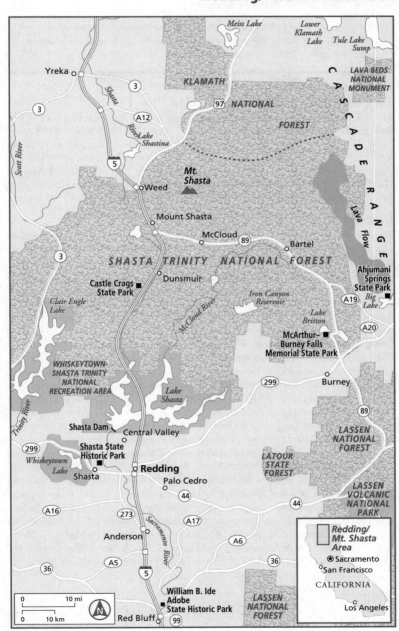

Tips **Shasta vs. Mount Shasta**

Don't confuse the old mining town, Shasta, a few miles west of Redding, with the much larger community, Mount Shasta, a major tourist destination on Interstate 5, near the base of Mount Shasta.

THE REPUBLIC OF CALIFORNIA

En route to Mount Shasta from the south, you may want to stop near Red Bluff at **William B. Ide Adobe State Historic Park,** 21659 Adobe Rd. (© **530/529-8599**), for a picnic along the Sacramento River and a visit to an adobe home dating back to 1852. The 4-acre park commemorates William B. Ide, the Republic of California's first and only president. (The Republic of California was proclaimed on June 14, 1846, following the Bear Flag Rebellion, and lasted only 3 weeks.) In summer, the park is open from 8am to sunset, and the house from noon to 4pm; call ahead in winter. Parking is $5 per vehicle.

REDDING

The major town and gateway to the area is Redding, the hub of the panoramic Shasta-Cascade region, at the top of the Sacramento Valley. From here, you can turn westward into the wilderness forest of Trinity and the Klamath Mountains, or north and east into the Cascades and Shasta Trinity National Forest.

In Redding, with its fast-food joints, gas stations, and cheap motels, summer heat generally hovers around 100°F (38°C). A city of some 80,000, Redding is the transportation hub for the upper reaches of Northern California. It has little of interest; it's mainly useful as a base for exploring the natural wonders nearby. Information is available from the **Redding Convention & Visitors Bureau,** 777 Auditorium Dr., Redding, CA 96001 (© **800/874-7562** or 530/225-4100; www.visitredding.org), west of I-5 on Highway 299. It's open Monday through Friday from 9am to 5pm. Ahead and northeast, Mount Shasta rises to a height of more than 14,000 feet. From Redding, I-5 cuts north over the Pit River Bridge, crossing Lake Shasta and leading eventually to the mount itself. Before striking north, however, you may want to explore **Lake Shasta** and see **Shasta Dam.** Another option is to take a detour west of Redding to Weaverville, Whiskeytown–Shasta Trinity National Recreation Area, and Trinity Lake (see "Whiskeytown National Recreation Area," below).

About 3 miles west, stop at the old mining town of **Shasta,** which has been converted into a state historic park (© **530/243-8194**). Founded on gold, Shasta was the "Queen City" of the northern mines in the Klamath Range. Its life was short, and it expired in 1872, when the Central Pacific Railroad bypassed it in favor of Redding. Today the business district is a ghost town, complete with a restored general store and a Masonic hall. The **1861 courthouse** is now a museum, where you can view the jail and a gallows out back, as well as a remarkable collection of California art assembled by Mae Helen Bacon Boggs. The collection includes works by Maynard Dixon, Grace Hudson, and many others. Continue along Highway 299 west to Highway 3 north, which will take you to Weaverville and then to the west side of the lake and Trinity Center.

Where to Stay

In addition to Tiffany House (see below), Redding has a **Red Lion Hotel,** 1830 Hilltop Dr., Redding (© **800/733-5466** or 530/221-8700; www.redlion.com), and a **La Quinta**

Tiffany House Bed and Breakfast Inn   On a hill above town, this beautifully refurbished Cape Cod–style inn has a sweeping view of the Lassen Mountain Range, visible from every guest room and cottage, as well as from the oversize deck above the garden in back. Common areas include the music room with a piano, and the Victorian parlor with a fireplace, games, and puzzles. Each guest room is appointed with a queen-size bed and antique furnishings, and all have private bathrooms and soft robes. Lavinia's Cottage is our top choice, with a 7-foot spa tub, sitting area, and magnificent laurel-wreath iron bed.

1510 Barbara Rd., Redding, CA 96003. © **530/244-3225.** www.tiffanyhousebb.com. 4 units. $110–$150 double. Rates include full breakfast. AE, DISC, MC, V. **Amenities:** Outdoor pool; nearby golf courses; Jacuzzi; game room. *In room:* A/C, hair dryer, no phone.

Where to Dine

Buz's Crab Seafood Restaurant, Market & Deli ★★ (Finds SEAFOOD   Don't let the Naugahyde booths and Formica tables fool you: This funky fish joint is one of the best roadside seafood stands in Northern California. What's been drawing fans here from all over the state for more than 30 years are the "seafood baskets," packed with crisp potato rounds, fresh-baked sourdough bread, and whatever's in season: prawns, oysters, scallops, clam strips, calamari, catfish, even Cajun halibut. The fish and chips are also excellent. From December to May, crab's the hot ticket, served freshly boiled from the crab pots on the patio and served with drawn butter and cocktail sauce. *Tip:* Visit Buz's website and print the fantastic cioppino recipe—I've slain 'em at dinner parties with this one.

2159 East St., at Cypress Ave. © **530/243-2120.** www.buzscrab.com. Main courses $2.50–$14. MC, V. Daily 11am–9pm.

Jack's Grill ★ STEAKHOUSE   This building was originally constructed in 1835 as a secondhand-clothing store. The second floor served as a brothel in the late 1930s, and an entrepreneur named Jack Young set up the main floor as a steakhouse (his establishment serviced all of a body's needs, you might say). Today it's a local favorite. Waiting for a table over drinks in the bar is part of the fun. Good old-fashioned red meat—thick 1-pound steaks, tender brochettes, fat steak sandwiches—is supplemented by a couple of seafood dishes, such as deep-fried jumbo prawns and ocean scallops. It's a very fetching spot, with good, honest tavern food and a jovial crowd. Be prepared to wait on weekends.

1743 California St. © **530/241-9705.** www.jacksgrillredding.com. Reservations not accepted. Main courses $12–$31. AE, DISC, MC, V. Mon–Sat 5–11pm (bar 4–11:30pm).

WEAVERVILLE

Weaverville was a gold mining town in the 1850s, and the **Jake Jackson Memorial Museum–Trinity County Historical Park,** 508 Main St. (© **530/623-5211**), captures part of its history. The collection, from firearms to household items, tells an interesting story about the residents—Native Americans, miners, pioneers, especially the Chinese. In the Gold Rush era, the town was half Chinese, with a Chinatown of about 2,500 residents. Admission is free, but a donation of $1 is suggested.

Across the parking lot, you can view the oldest continuously used Taoist temple in California at the **Joss House State Historic Park** (© **530/623-5284**). This well-preserved temple was built by immigrant Chinese miners in 1874. Admission is $1 for adults, free for children ages 16 and under.

LaGrange Café ★★ Finds CREATIVE TRADITIONAL CUISINE   Weaverville isn't exactly a star in the culinary firmament, but there is one bright spot, far and away the best food in town. Heck, it would be considered really good in Redding, Sacramento, or Tahoe. In Weaverville's historic district, two adjoining buildings were combined and stripped to the original brick walls to make a spacious, attractive dining area with a sit-down bar. Chef and owner Sharon Heryford's menu includes the local favorite—chicken enchiladas with marinated tri-tip—plus seasonal items such as the local rabbit braised with mushrooms, fresh herbs, and white wine. The tender Duane's Chicken, served with wheat pilaf, is also popular. The interesting menu includes other things such as buffalo steaks, venison bratwurst, and wild-boar sausages. Heryford's buffalo ragout won third place in a national contest. The 135-plus selections on the wine list make it one of the strongest in Northern California. Desserts, such as a sinfully rich banana cream pie and that quintessential comfort food, bread pudding, are all made on the premises.

226 Main St. ✆ **530/623-5325.** Main courses $10–$25. AE, DISC, MC, V. Mon–Thurs 11:30am–9pm; Fri–Sun 11:30am–10pm (hours vary seasonally—be sure to call ahead to confirm).

THE TRINITY ALPS

West of Weaverville stretch the Trinity Alps, with Thompson Peak rising to more than 9,000 feet. The second-largest wilderness area in the state lies between the Trinity and Salmon rivers and contains more than 55 lakes and streams. Its alpine scenery makes it popular with hikers and backpackers. You can access the **Pacific Crest Trail** west of Mount Shasta at Parks Creek, South Fork Road, or Whalen Road, and also from Castle Crags State Park. For trail and other information, contact the forest service at Weaverville (✆ **530/623-2121**).

The **Fifth Season,** 300 N. Mount Shasta Blvd. (✆ **530/926-3606;** www.thefifth season.com), offers mountaineering and backpack rentals and will provide trail maps and other information concerning Shasta's outdoor activities.

Living Waters Recreation (✆ **800/994-RAFT** or 530/926-5446; www.livingwaters rec.com) offers half-day to 4-day rafting trips on the Upper Sacramento, Klamath, Trinity, and Salmon rivers. **Trinity River Rafting Company,** on Highway 299W, in Big Flat (✆ **800/30-RIVER** or 530/623-3033; www.trinityriverrafting.com), also operates local white-water trips.

For additional outfitters and information, contact the **Trinity County Chamber of Commerce,** 210 N. Main St. (P.O. Box 517), Weaverville, CA 96093 (✆ **800/487-4648** or 530/623-6101; www.trinitycounty.com).

WHISKEYTOWN NATIONAL RECREATION AREA

In adjacent Shasta County, Whiskeytown National Recreation Area is on the eastern shore of quiet, relatively uncrowded Trinity Lake, with 157 miles of shoreline. This reservoir was originally named Clair Engle, after the politician who created it. Locals insist on calling it Trinity, however, after the river that used to rush through the region past the towns of Minersville, Stringtown, and an earlier Whiskeytown. When they dammed the river, however, they also destroyed the three towns, which now lie submerged beneath the lake's glassy surface.

Both Trinity Lake and the Whiskeytown National Recreation Area are in the Shasta Trinity National Forest, 1.3 million acres of wilderness with 1,269 miles of hiking trails. For information on trails, contact **Shasta Trinity National Forest** (✆ **530/226-2500;** www.fs.fed.us/r5/shastatrinity).

Heading north on I-5 from Redding, travel about 12 miles and take the Shasta Dam Boulevard exit to the **Shasta Dam and Power Plant** ★ (© 530/275-4463; www.shasta lake.com/shastadam/index.html), which has an overflow spillway that is three times higher than Niagara Falls. The huge dam—3,460 feet long, 602 feet high, and 883 feet thick at its base—holds back the waters of the Sacramento, Pit, and McCloud rivers. A dramatic sight indeed, it is a vital component of the Central Valley water project. At the visitor center is a series of photographs and displays covering the dam's construction. You can walk or drive over the dam, but it's far more interesting to take the **free 1-hour tours** that run on the hour daily from 9am to 5pm in summer, and at 9am, 11am, 1pm, and 3pm Labor Day to Memorial Day. The guided tour takes you deep within the dam's many chilly corridors (not a good place for claustrophobics) and below the spillway. It's an entertaining way to beat the summer heat. *Note:* Tours may be canceled due to security reasons, so call ahead first.

Lake Shasta has 370 miles of shoreline and attracts anglers (bass, trout, and king salmon), water-skiers, and other boating enthusiasts—two million, in fact, in summer. The best way to enjoy the lake is aboard a houseboat; you can rent them from several companies, including **Antlers Resort & Marina,** P.O. Box 140, Antlers Road, Lakehead, CA 96051 (© 800/238-3924; www.shastalakevacations.com); and **Packers Bay Marina,** 16814 Packers Bay Rd., Lakehead, CA 96051 (© 800/331-3137 or 530/275-5570; www. packersbay.com). There is a 1-week minimum during the summer, and a 3- to 4-day minimum during the off season.

While you're here, you can visit **Lake Shasta Caverns** (© 800/795-CAVE or 530/ 238-2341; www.lakeshastacaverns.com). These caves contain 20-foot-high stalactite and stalagmite formations—60-foot-wide curtains of them adorn the great Cathedral Room. To see the caves, drive about 15 miles north of Redding on I-5 to the O'Brien/Shasta Caverns exit. A ferry will take you across the lake and a short bus ride will follow to the cave entrance for a 2-hour-long tour. Admission is $20 for adults, $12 for children ages 3 to 15, and free for kids under 3. The caverns are open daily from 9am to 4pm in the summer, 9am to 3pm April, May, and September, and from 10am to 2pm October through March.

For information about the Lake Shasta region, contact the **Redding Convention & Visitors Bureau,** 777 Auditorium Dr., Redding, CA 96001 (© 800/874-7562 or 530/ 225-4100; www.visitredding.org), west of I-5, on Highway 299. It's open Monday through Friday from 8am to 5pm.

MOUNT SHASTA ★★★

A volcanic mountain with eight glaciers, **Mount Shasta** is a towering peak of legend and lore. It stands alone, always snowcapped, unshadowed by other mountains—visible from 125 miles away. Although it has been dormant since 1786, eruptions cannot be ruled out, and hot sulfur springs bubble at the summit. The springs saved John Muir on his third ascent of the mountain in 1875. Caught in a severe snowstorm, he and his partner took turns submersing themselves in the hot mud to survive.

Many New Agers are convinced that Mount Shasta is the center of an incredible energy vortex. These devotees flock to the foot of the mountain. In 1987, the foothills were host to the worldwide Harmonic Convergence, calling for a planetary union and a new phase of universal harmony. Yoga, massage, meditation, and metaphysics are all the rage here. These New Agers seem to coexist harmoniously with those whose metaphysical leanings begin and end with Dolly Parton song lyrics.

Those who don't want to climb can drive up to about 7,900 feet. From the town of Mount Shasta, drive 14 miles up the Everitt Memorial Highway to the end of the road near Panther Meadow. At the **Everitt Vista Turnout,** you'll be able to stop and see the Sacramento River Canyon, the Eddy Mountains to the west, and glimpses of Mount Lassen to the south. You can also take the short hike through the forests to a lava outcrop overlooking the McCloud area.

Continue on to **Bunny Flat,** a major access point for climbing in summer and also for cross-country skiing and sledding in winter. The highway ends at the Old Ski Bowl Vista, providing panoramic views of Mount Lassen, Castle Crags, and the Trinity Mountains.

While in Mount Shasta, visit the **Fish Hatchery,** at 3 N. Old Stage Rd. (© 530/926-2215), which was built in 1888. Here you can observe rainbow and brown trout being hatched to stock rivers and streams statewide—millions are born here annually. You can feed them with food purchased from the coin-operated food dispensers and observe the spawning process on certain Tuesdays during the fall and winter. Admission is free; hours are daily from 8am to sunset. Adjacent to the hatchery is the **Sisson Museum** (© 530/926-5508), which displays a smattering of local-history exhibits. It's open daily year-round, from 10am to 4pm in summer, from 1 to 4pm in winter; admission is free.

Outdoor Pursuits

GOLF & TENNIS   Golfers should head for the 27-hole Robert Trent Jones, Jr., golf course at **Lake Shastina Golf Resort,** 5925 Country Club Dr., Weed (© **800/358-4653** or 530/938-3205; www.lakeshastinagolf.com), or the 18-hole course at **Mount Shasta Resort,** 1000 Siskiyou Lake Blvd., Mount Shasta (© **800/958-3363** or 530/926-3030; www.mountshastaresort.com). The Mount Shasta resort also has tennis courts.

MOUNTAIN CLIMBING   Mount Shasta attracts thousands of hikers from around the world each year, from timid first-timers to serious mountaineers who search for the most difficult paths up. The hike isn't technically difficult, but it's a demanding ascent that takes about 8 hours of continuous exertion, particularly when the snow softens up. (*Tip:* Start early, while the snow is still firm.) Before setting out, hikers must secure a permit by signing in at the trail head or at the **Mount Shasta Ranger District** office, which also gives out plenty of good advice for amateur climbers. The office is at 204 W. Alma St., off North Mount Shasta Boulevard in Mount Shasta (© **530/926-4511**). Be sure to wear good hiking shoes and carry crampons and an ice ax, a first-aid kit, a quart of water per person, and a flashlight in case it takes longer than anticipated. Sun block is an absolute necessity. All the requisite equipment can be rented at the **Fifth Season,** 300 N. Mount Shasta Blvd. (© **530/926-3606;** www.thefifthseason.com). Mere mortals who don't feel compelled to summit can merely hike on the various low-elevation trails.

Weather can be extremely unpredictable, and every year hikers die on this dormant volcano, usually from making stupid mistakes. For **weather and climbing conditions,** call © **530/926-5555** for recorded information. Traditionally, climbers make the ascent from the Sierra Lodge at Horse Camp, accessible from the town of Mount Shasta via Alma Street and the Everitt Memorial Highway or from Bunny Flat.

For more information as well as supervised trips, contact **Shasta Mountain Guides,** 1938 Hill Rd. (© **530/926-3117;** www.shastaguides.com). This outfitter offers a 2-day climb along the traditional John Muir route for $450. It also offers a glacier climb and rock climbing in Castle Crags State Park, backpacking trips, plus cross-country and telemark skiing. The basic rock-climbing course is $150, the mountaineering course is $125, and each of the 3-day ski and snowboard descents is $550.

Also nearby is **Castle Crags State Park** (© **530/235-2684**), a 4,300-acre park with 64 campsites and 28 miles of hiking trails. Here, granite crags formed 225 million years ago tower more than 6,500 feet above the Sacramento River. The park is filled with dogwood, oak, cedar, and pine as well as tiger lilies, azaleas, and orchids in summer. You can walk the 1-mile Indian Creek nature trail or take the easy 1-mile Root Creek Trail. The entrance fee is $6 per vehicle per day. Castle Crags is off I-5, about 50 miles north of Redding.

OTHER WARM-WEATHER ACTIVITIES   Mount Shasta offers some excellent **mountain biking.** In the summer, ride the chairlifts to the top of Mount Shasta Ski Park and bike down the trails. An all-day chairlift pass is about $25 (© **530/926-8600;** www.skipark.com).

For fishing information or guided trips, call **Jack Trout Fly Fishing Guide** (© **530/926-4540;** www.jacktrout.com). Two other recommended sources are **Mount Shasta Fly Fishing** (© **530/926-6648**) and **Hart's Guide Service** (© **530/926-2431**).

SKIING   In winter, visitors can ski at **Mount Shasta Board & Ski Park,** 104 Siskiyou Ave., Mount Shasta (© **800/SKI-SHASTA** or 530/926-8610; www.skipark.com), which has 31 runs with 80% snowmaking, three triple chairlifts, and a surface lift. Lift tickets are $39. The Nordic ski center has 16 miles of groomed trails, and Terrain Park is geared toward snowboarders. The Learning Center offers instruction for adults and children. In summer you can ride the chairlifts to scenic views, mountain-bike down the trails (an all-day pass is about $15), or practice on the two-story climbing wall. Access to the park is 10 miles east of Mount Shasta (the town) on Highway 89.

WATERSPORTS   The source of the headwaters of the Sacramento River accumulates in **Lake Siskiyou,** a popular spot for boating, swimming, and fishing—and a great vantage point for photographs of Mount Shasta and its reflection. Water-skiing and jet-skiing are not allowed, but windsurfing is, and boat rentals are available at **Lake Siskiyou Camp Resort,** 4239 W. A. Barr Rd., Mount Shasta (© **888/926-2618** or 530/926-2618; www.lakesis.com).

Where to Stay

Best Western Tree House Motor Inn   Just off the main highway, this motor inn is one of the better places to stay in the town of Mount Shasta, and it keeps its prices low. The lobby and refurbished rooms, some with decks and fridges, are pleasant enough, and the huge indoor pool is usually deserted, making this a family favorite. Downhill and cross-country ski areas are 10 miles away.

111 Morgan Way (at I-5 and Lake St.), Mount Shasta, CA 96067. © **800/780-7234** or 530/926-3101. Fax 530/926-3542. www.bestwestern.com. 95 units. $97–$135 double. Rates include the breakfast buffet. AE, DC, DISC, MC, V. **Amenities:** Restaurant; bar; indoor pool; nearby golf course; exercise room; Jacuzzi; video arcade; business center; high-speed Internet; secretarial services; guest laundry. *In room:* A/C, TV w/HBO, fridge, coffeemaker, hair dryer, iron.

Mount Shasta Ranch B&B ★ Kids   One of the country's most famous horse trainers and racing tycoons, H. D. ("Curley") Brown, conceived and built the Mount Shasta Ranch as the centerpiece of a private retreat and thoroughbred-horse ranch. Despite the encroachment of nearby buildings, the main two-story house and its annex are a cozy B&B with touches of nostalgia, the occasional antique, and spectacular views of Mount Shasta. Three bedrooms with private bathrooms are in the main house; the remaining five share two bathrooms, in the carriage house. It's a 3-minute trek to the shores of nearby Lake Siskiyou (15 min. to the ski slopes), or you could stay here to enjoy the Ping-Pong tables, pool table, darts, and horseshoes. Unlike at most B&Bs, kids are welcome.

1008 W. A. Barr Rd., Mount Shasta, CA 96067. © **530/926-3870.** Fax 530/926-6882. www.stayinshasta.com. 10 units, 5 with private bathroom; 1 cottage. $60–$80 double with shared bathroom; $110 double with private bathroom; $115 cottage for 2. Rates include country breakfast (except cottage). AE, DISC, MC, V. Take Central Mount Shasta exit off I-5 to W. A. Barr Rd. Pets accepted with $10 fee. **Amenities:** Nearby golf course; game room. *In room:* A/C, TV, kitchen in 2 units, no phone.

Railroad Park Resort Ⓚⁱᵈˢ A quarter of a mile from the Sacramento River, this is an offbeat place kids will love. It's at the foot of Castle Crags with a campground and RV park, four rustic cabins, and the Caboose Motel. The guest rooms are railroad cabooses from the Southern Pacific, Santa Fe, and Great Northern Railroads, with their pipes, ladders, and lofts left in place. Surrounding the fenced-in, kidney-shaped pool, they're furnished with modern king- or queen-size brass beds, table and chairs, and dressers; most have small bay windows or rooftop cupolas. The restaurant and lounge are also in vintage railroad cars.

100 Railroad Park Rd., Dunsmuir, CA 96025. Ⓒ **800/974-RAIL** (in California only), or 530/235-4440. Fax 530/235-4470. www.rrpark.com. 27 units. $115–$120 double. Extra person $8. AE, DISC, MC, V. Take Railroad Park exit off I-5, 1 mile south of Dunsmuir. Pets accepted with $15 fee. **Amenities:** Restaurant; lounge; outdoor pool; Jacuzzi; game room; coin-op laundry. *In room:* A/C, TV, minibar (in some units), fridge, coffeemaker, microwave in some units.

Stewart Mineral Springs Resort Ⓕⁱⁿᵈˢ Stewart Mineral Springs is one of the most unusual health spas in California, rich with lore and legends. Above cold-water springs that Native Americans valued for their healing powers, the place is deliberately primitive, with as few intrusions from the urban world as possible. Don't expect anything approaching a European spa or big-city luxury here. Designed in a somewhat haphazard compound of about a dozen buildings, 4 miles west of a town called Weed, it occupies a 37-acre site of sloping, forested land accented with ponds, gazebos, and decorative bridges. The grounds are riddled with hiking and nature trails, freshwater streams, and a swimming hole.

Activities revolve around hiking, nature-watching, and the healing waters of the legendary springs. The bathhouse is the resort headquarters, with 13 private rooms where spring water is heated and run into tubs for soaking. A staff member will describe the rituals for you: A 20-minute soak is followed by a visit to a nearby wood-burning sauna and an immersion in the chilly waters of Parks Creek, just outside the bathhouse (bath price $25, sauna price $17). Other options include massages ($45 per 30-min. session, $70 for 1 hr., and $95 for 1¹/₂ hr.). On Saturdays, medicine man Walking Eagle guides guests on a spiritual journey within the Native American Purification Sweat Lodge. They even have a juice bar. If you opt for treatment and R&R here, you won't be alone. The place is popular with young Hollywood types, including soap actors, San Francisco 49ers football players, and local newscasters.

4617 Stewart Springs Rd., Weed, CA 96094. Ⓒ **530/938-2222.** Fax 530/938-4283. www.stewartmineral springs.com. 5 tepees (for up to 4 persons), 4 motel rooms, 6 apt. units, 4 cabins with kitchens, and a large A-frame house (suitable for 10 persons). $35 double tepee; $50–$110 double in motel, apts., and cabins; $360 for house. $5 for each extra person. DISC, MC, V. Leashed pets accepted with $20-per-day fee to stay in pet-designated rooms. **Amenities:** Restaurant (closed in winter); spa; sauna; massage. *In room:* Kitchen and coffeemaker in cabins and some units, no phone.

Where to Dine

Café Maddalena ★★ Ⓕⁱⁿᵈˢ WORLD CUISINE The smells wafting from this restaurant are enough to draw you into the refurbished old railroad quarter of Dunsmuir. The seasonal menu features authentic dishes from southern France, Spain, and North Africa: roasted beet and chèvre salad with hazelnut dressing; tagine of chicken in North African curry sauce with couscous; ricotta-stuffed ravioli with truffle sauce; herb-roasted lamb rack with ratatouille. Everything is fresh, including the breads and desserts. During the summer months, request a table outside under the grape arbor. *Tip:* Call to confirm the menu, which changes frequently.

5801 Sacramento Ave., Dunsmuir. (C) 530/235-2725. www.cafemaddalena.com. Reservations recommended. Main courses $17–$25. DISC, MC, V. Thurs–Sun 5–10pm. Closed Jan 1 to mid-March.

Lily's ★ WORLD CUISINE   In a white clapboard, early 1900s house, in a residential neighborhood south of the town center, this friendly little restaurant has a front porch, a picket fence, a back garden, and dining in two rooms inside and two patios out. It's popular for breakfast, with chunky breads and delicious omelets. Lunch and dinner dishes—tamale pie, Mediterranean pasta, and Kung Pao chicken salad—span the globe. Popular dishes include the chicken enchiladas, with cheese, olives, and onions; and Chicken Rosie, a tender breast of chicken simmered with raspberries, hazelnut liqueur, and cream.

1013 S. Mount Shasta Blvd., Mount Shasta. (C) 530/926-3372. www.lilysrestaurant.com. Reservations recommended. Breakfast $7–$12; lunch $8–$12; dinner $11–$23. AE, DISC, MC, V. Mon–Fri 7:30am–9:30pm.

MCARTHUR–BURNEY FALLS MEMORIAL STATE PARK ★

On its way to Lassen Volcanic National Park (see below) from Mount Shasta, Highway 89 east loops back south to the 910-acre **McArthur–Burney Falls Memorial State Park** ((C) **530/335-2777**). One of its most spectacular features is **Burney Falls ★★**, an absolutely gorgeous waterfall that cascades over a 129-foot cliff. Theodore Roosevelt once called the falls "the eighth wonder of the world." Giant springs a few hundred yards upstream feed the falls and keep them flowing—100 million gallons every day—even during California's dry spells.

The .5-mile **Headwater Trail** will take you to a good vantage point above the falls. If you're lucky, you can observe the black swifts that nest in the mossy crevices behind the cascade. Other birds to look for include barn and great horned owls, the belted kingfisher, the common flicker, and even the Oregon junco. The year-round park also has 5 miles of nature trails, 128 campsites, picnicking grounds, and good fishing for bass, crappie, and brown, rainbow, and brook trout. For **camping reservations,** call (C) **800/444-PARK** (7275).

From here, Lassen Volcanic National Park lies about 40 miles south.

3 LASSEN VOLCANIC NATIONAL PARK ★

45 miles E of Redding; 255 miles NE of San Francisco

In the far northeastern corner of California, Lassen Volcanic National Park is a remarkable reminder that North America is still forming, and that the ground below is alive with the forces of creation and, sometimes, destruction. Lassen Peak is the southernmost in a chain of volcanoes (including Mount St. Helens) that stretches all the way from British Columbia.

Although it's dormant, 10,457-foot **Lassen Peak** is still very much alive. It last awakened in May 1914, beginning a cycle of eruptions that spit lava, steam, and ash until 1921. The eruption climaxed in 1915 when Lassen blew its top, sending a cloud of ash 7 miles high, visible from hundreds of miles away. The peak has been dormant for more than three-quarters of a century now, but the area still boils with a ferocious intensity: Hot springs, fumaroles, geysers, and mud pots are all indicators that Lassen hasn't had its last word. Monitoring of geothermal features in the park shows that they are getting hotter, not cooler, and some scientists take this as a sign that the next big eruption in the Cascades is likely to happen here.

Until then, the park gives visitors an interesting chance to watch a landscape recover from the massive destruction brought on by an eruption. To the north of Lassen Peak is the aptly named **Devastated Area,** a huge swath of volcanic destruction steadily repopulating with conifer forests. Forest botanists have revised their earlier theories that forests must be preceded by herbaceous growth after watching the Devastated Area immediately revegetate with a diverse mix of eight different conifer species, four more than were present before the blast.

The 108,000-acre park is a place of great beauty. The flora and fauna are an interesting mix of species from the Cascade Range, which stretches north from Lassen, and species from the Sierra Nevada Range, which stretches south. The blend accounts for an enormous diversity of plants: 715 species have been identified in the park. Although it is snowbound in winter, Lassen is a summer feeding ground for transient herds of mule deer and numerous black bears.

In addition to the volcano and all its geothermal features, Lassen Volcanic National Park includes miles of hiking trails, 50 beautiful alpine lakes, large meadows, cinder cones, lush forests, cross-country skiing, and great backcountry camping. In fact, three-quarters of the park is designated wilderness.

And crowds? Forget it. Lassen is one of the least-visited national parks in the Lower 48, so crowd control isn't as big a consideration here as in other places. Unless you're here on the Fourth of July or Labor Day weekend, you won't encounter anything that could rightly be called a crowd. Even then, you can escape the hordes simply by skipping such popular sites as Bumpass Hell or the Sulphur Works and heading a few miles down any of the backcountry trails.

ESSENTIALS

GETTING THERE   One of the reasons Lassen Volcanic National Park is one of the least visited national parks is its remote location. The most foolproof route here is Highway 44 east from Redding, which leads directly to the northern gateway to the park. A shortcut if you're coming from the south along I-5 is Highway 36 in Red Bluff, which leads to the park's southern gateway. If you're arriving from the east via I-80, take the U.S. 395 turnoff at Reno and head to Susanville. Depending on which end of the park you're shooting for, take either Highway 44 (to the northwest entrance) or Highway 36 (to the southwest entrance) from Susanville. The $10-per-car entrance fee, valid for a week, comes with a copy of the *Lassen Park Guide,* a handy little newsletter listing activities, hikes, and points of interest. Camping fees range from $10 to $25.

Only one major road, Highway 89 (aka the Park Rd.), crosses the park, in a 39-mile half-circle with entrances and visitor centers at either end.

Most visitors enter the park at the southwest entrance station, drive through the park, and leave through the northwest entrance, or vice versa. Two other entrances lead to remote portions of the park. Warner Valley is reached from the south on the road from Chester. The Butte Lake entrance is reached by a cut-off road from Highway 44 between Highway 89 and Susanville.

VISITOR INFORMATION   **Ranger stations** are clustered near each entrance and provide the full spectrum of interpretive displays, ranger-led walks, informational leaflets, and emergency help. The largest **visitor center** is located just inside the northwest

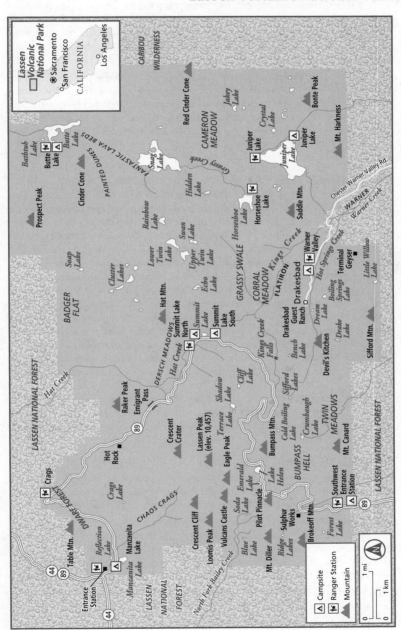

Lassen Volcanic National Park
San Francisco
Sacramento
Los Angeles
CALIFORNIA

CARIBOU WILDERNESS

Red Cinder Cone
Jakey Lake
Bonte Peak
Crystal Lake
Mt. Harkness
Bathtub Lake
Butte Lake
Cinder Cone
CAMERON MEADOW
Juniper Lake
Juniper Lake
Prospect Peak
PAINTED DUNES LAVA BEDS
FANTASTIC LAVA BEDS
Snag Lake
Hidden Lake
Grassy Creek
Horseshoe Lake
Saddle Mtn.
Chester Warner Valley Rd.
WARNER
Warner Creek
Rainbow Lake
Swan Lake
Lower Twin Lake
Upper Twin Lake
Kings Creek
Warner Valley
Hot Springs Creek
Terminal Geyser
Little Willow Lake
Soap Lake
BADGER FLAT
Cluster Lakes
Echo Lake
GRASSY SWALE
CORRAL MEADOW
FLATIRON
Boiling Springs Lake
Hat Mtn.
Summit Lake North
Summit Lake
Summit Lake South
Drakesbad
Drakesbad Guest Ranch
Dream Lake
LASSEN NATIONAL FOREST
Hat Creek
DERSCH MEADOWS
Hat Creek
Kings Creek Falls
Bench Lake
Devil's Kitchen
Drake Lake
Sifford Mtn.
Raker Peak
Emigrant Pass
Shadow Lake
Cliff Lake
Sifford Lakes
89
Crescent Crater
Lassen Peak (elev. 10,457)
Terrace Lake
Eagle Peak
Bumpass Mtn.
Cold Boiling Lake
Crumbaugh Lake
TWIN MEADOWS
Mt. Canard
LASSEN NATIONAL FOREST
Hot Rock
Crescent Cliff
Emerald Lake
Lake Helen
BUMPASS HELL
Southwest Entrance Station
89
Crags
Crags Lake
CHAOS CRAGS
Loomis Peak
Vulcans Castle
Pilot Pinnacle
Sulphur Works
Brokeoff Mtn.
Forest Lake
DIXBE FOREST
Table Mtn.
Reflection Lake
Manzanita Lake
Soda Lake
Blue Lake
Ridge Lakes
Mt. Diller
North Fork Bailey Creek
44
89
Entrance Station
Manzanita Lake
LASSEN NATIONAL FOREST
44

N

0   1 mi
0   1 km

Campsite
Ranger Station
Mountain

entrance station at the Loomis Museum. The park information number for all requests is © **530/595-4444,** or you can visit **www.nps.gov/lavo** or write Lassen Volcanic National Park, P.O. Box 100, Mineral, CA 96063-0100.

Because of the dangers posed by the park's thermal features, rangers ask that you remain on the trails at all times. Fires are allowed in campgrounds only; please make sure they're dead before leaving. Mountain bikes are prohibited on all trails.

WEATHER   Lassen Volcanic National Park is in one of the coldest places in California. Winter begins in late October and doesn't release its grip until June. Even in the summer, you should plan for possible rain and snow. Temperatures at night can drop below freezing at any time. Winter, however, shows a different and beautiful side of Lassen that more people are starting to appreciate. Since most of the park is over a mile high and the highest point is 10,457 feet, snow accumulates in incredible quantities. Don't be surprised to find snow banks lining the Park Road into July.

EXPLORING THE PARK

The highlight of Lassen is, of course, the volcano and all of its offshoots: boiling springs, fumaroles, mud pots, and more. You can see many of the most interesting sites in a day, making it possible to visit Lassen as a short detour from I-5 or U.S. 395 on the way to or from Oregon. Available at park visitor centers, the *Road Guide to Lassen Park* is a great traveling companion that will explain a lot of the features you'll see as you traverse the park.

Bumpass Hell ★, a 1.5-mile walk off the Park Road in the southern part of the park, is Lassen's largest single geothermal site—16 acres of bubbling mud pots reeking with the rotten-egg-like stench of sulfur. The hike leads you through a quiet, peaceful meadow of wildflowers and birds before it reaches the geothermal site—the name of which derives from an early Lassen hunter who lost a leg after he took a shortcut through the area and plunged into a boiling pool. Stay on the wooden catwalks that safely guide visitors past the pyrite pools, steam vents, and noisy fumaroles and you won't follow in Bumpass's footsteps.

Sulphur Works ★ is another stinky, steamy example of Lassen's residual heat. Two miles from the southwest park exit, the ground roars with seething gases escaping from the ground.

Boiling Springs Lake and **Devil's Kitchen** are two of the more remote geothermal sites; they're located in the Warner Valley section of the park, which can be reached by hiking from the main road or entering the park through Warner Valley Road from the small town of Chester.

OUTDOOR PURSUITS

In addition to the activities below, free naturalist programs are offered daily in the summer, highlighting everything from flora and fauna to geologic history and volcanic processes. For more information, call the **park headquarters** at © **530/595-4444.**

CANOEING & KAYAKING   Paddlers can take canoes, rowboats, and kayaks on any of the park lakes except Reflection, Emerald, Helen, and Boiling Springs. Motors, including electric motors, are strictly prohibited on all park waters. Park lakes are full of trout, and fishing is popular. You must have a current California fishing license, which you can obtain in Red Bluff at **Lassen Ranch and Home Store,** 22660 Antelope Rd. (© **530/527-6960**).

CROSS-COUNTRY SKIING   The park road usually closes due to snow in November, and most years it doesn't open until June, so cross-country skiers have their run of the park. Snowmobiles were once allowed but are now forbidden. Marked trails of all skill levels leave from Manzanita Lake at the north end of the park and Lassen Chalet at the south. Most visitors come to the southwest entrance, where the ski chalet offers lessons, rental gear, and a warm place to stay. Popular trips are the beginners' trails to Lake Helen or Summit Lake. More advanced skiers can make the trek into Bumpass Hell, a steaming valley of sulfuric mud pots and fumaroles.

You can also ski the popular 30-mile course of the Park Road in an overnight trek, but doing this involves a long car shuttle. For safety reasons, the park requires all skiers to register at the ranger stations before heading into the backcountry, whether for an overnight or just the day. For more information, contact the **park headquarters** at (℗ **530/595-4444.**

HIKING   Most Lassen visitors drive through in a day or two, see the geothermal hot spots, and move on. That leaves 150 miles of trails and expanses of backcountry to the few who take the time to get off-road. The *Lassen Trails* booklet at the visitor centers gives good descriptions of some of the most popular hikes and backpacking destinations. Anyone spending the night in the backcountry must have a wilderness permit, issued at the ranger stations. And don't forget to bring plenty of water, sunscreen, and warm clothing.

The most popular hike in the park is the **Lassen Peak Trail ★**, a 2.5-mile climb from the Park Road to the top of the peak. The trail may sound short, but it's steep and covered with snow until late summer. At an elevation of 10,457 feet, though, you'll get a view of the surrounding wilderness that's worth every step of the way. On clear days, you can see south all the way to Sutter Buttes near Yuba City and north into the Cascades. The round-trip takes about 4 to 5 hours.

Running a close second in popularity is **Bumpass Hell Trail.** This 1.5-mile walk off the Park Road in the southern part of the park deposits you right in the middle of the largest single geothermal site in the park. (See "Exploring the Park," above.)

The **Cinder Cone Trail,** in the northeast corner of the park, is another worthy hike, best reached from Butte Lake Campground at Lassen's far northeast corner. If 4 miles seems too short, you can extend the hike (and shorten the drive) by walking in about 8 miles from Summit Lake on the Park Road. Now dormant, Cinder Cone is generally accepted as the source of mysterious flashing lights that were seen by early settlers in the 1850s. Black and charred-looking, Cinder Cone is bereft of any life and surrounded by dunes of multihued volcanic ash.

SNOWSHOEING   From January to March, park naturalists give free 2-hour eco-adventure snowshoe hikes across Lassen's snow-packed hills. The tours take place on Saturdays at 1:30pm at the Lassen Chalet, at the park's southwestern entrance. You must be at least 8 years old, dress warmly, and wear boots. Snowshoes are free of charge on a first-come, first-served basis, although a $1 donation is requested for upkeep. For more details, call park headquarters (℗ **530/595-4444,** ext. 5133).

CAMPING

Car campers have their choice of seven park campgrounds with 375 sites, more than enough to handle the trickle of visitors who come to Lassen every summer. In fact, so few people camp in Lassen that the park is without a reservations system, except at the **Lost Creek Group Campground,** and stays there are granted a generous 14-day limit. Sites do fill up on weekends, so get to the park early on Friday to secure a place. If the park is packed, the surrounding Lassen National Forest has 43 campgrounds, so you're bound to find a site somewhere.

By far the most "civilized" campground in the park is at **Manzanita Lake,** where you can find hot showers, electrical hookups, flush toilets, and a camper store. When Manzanita fills up, rangers open the **Crags Campground** overflow camp—about 5 miles away and much more basic. Farther into the park along Highway 89 is **Summit Lake Campgrounds,** on the north and south ends of Summit Lake. It's a pretty spot, often frequented by deer, and it's a launching point for some excellent day hikes.

On the southern end of the park, you'll find **Southwest Campground,** a walk-in camp directly adjacent to the Lassen Chalet parking lot.

The two remote entrances to Lassen and Warner Valley have their own primitive campgrounds with pit toilets and no water, but the price is right—free.

Backcountry camping is allowed almost everywhere, and traffic is light. Ask about closed areas when you get your wilderness permit, which are issued at the ranger stations and required for anyone spending the night in the backcountry.

WHERE TO STAY

Inside the Park

Drakesbad Guest Ranch ★★★   Lassen Park's only lodge is Drakesbad Guest Ranch, hidden in a high mountain valley surrounded by meadows, lakes, and streams. It's famous for its rustic cabins, lodge, and steaming thermal swimming pool fed by a natural hot spring and open 24 hours a day. Drakesbad is as deluxe as a place with some electricity and no phones can be, with handmade quilts on every bed and kerosene lamps for reading. Full meal service is available, and it's very good. Because the lodge is very popular and only open from June to mid-October, reservations are booked as far as 2 years in advance (although May or June are good times to call to take advantage of cancellations).

c/o California Guest Services, 2150 N. Main St., no. 5, Red Bluff, CA 96080. ℂ **530/529-1512,** ext. 120. Fax 530/529-4511. www.drakesbad.com. 19 units. $155–$201 per person, double occupancy. Rates include meals. DISC, MC, V. **Amenities:** Restaurant; hot-spring-fed pool. *In room:* No phone.

Near the Park

The Bidwell House Bed and Breakfast Inn ★★ Kids   In 1901, General John Bidwell, a California senator who made three unsuccessful bids for the U.S. presidency, built a country retreat and summer home for his beloved young wife, Annie. After her death, when Chester had developed into a prosperous logging hamlet, the building, with its farmhouse-style design and spacious veranda, was converted into the headquarters for a local ranch. Today it's one of the most charming B&Bs in the region, with a yard of aspens and cottonwoods and sprawling views of mountain meadows and pretty Lake Almanor. The 14 individually decorated guest rooms are furnished with antiques, most have private bathrooms, a few have wood-burning stoves, and seven have Jacuzzi tubs. A cottage that sleeps up to six is ideal for families. Breakfast is presented with fanfare and many gourmet touches, including home-baked breads and delicious omelets.

1 Main St. (P.O. Box 1790), Chester, CA 96020. ℂ **530/258-3338.** www.bidwellhouse.com. 14 units, 12 with private bathroom. $85–$165 double; $175 suite or cottage (sleeps 6). Rates include full breakfast. MC, V. **Amenities:** Nearby golf course, biking, gold panning, fishing, beach, boat launch, hiking, horseback riding, snowmobile trails. *In room:* TV/DVD, free Wi-Fi.

Lassen Mineral Lodge Kids   A mere 9 miles south of Lassen Volcanic National Park's southern entrance, the Lassen Mineral Lodge offers 20 motel-style accommodations in a forested setting. In summer, the lodge is almost always bustling with guests and customers who venture into the gift shop, ski shop, general store, and full-service restaurant and bar. This is probably the best lodging option for families in the Lassen area.

On Hwy. 36E (P.O. Box 160), Mineral, CA 96063. ℂ **530/595-4422.** Fax 530/595-4452. www.minerallodge. com. 20 units. $72–$85 double. AE, DISC, MC, V. **Amenities:** Restaurant; saloon; coin-op laundry. *In room:* Kitchens in some units, no phone.

Mill Creek Resort ★   Deep in the forest next to ol' Mill Creek, the Mill Creek Resort
is that rustic mountain retreat you've always dreamed of while slaving away in the office.
A homey country general store and coffee shop serve as the resort's center, a good place
to stock up on food while exploring Lassen Volcanic National Park. Nine housekeeping
cabins, available on a daily or weekly basis, are clean, cute, and outfitted with vintage
1930s and 1940s furniture, including kitchens (a good thing, since restaurants are scarce
in this region). Pets are welcome, too. *Note:* They don't take credit cards.

1 Hwy. 172 (3 miles south of Hwy. 36), Mill Creek, CA 96061. © **888/595-4449** or 530/595-4449. www.
millcreekresort.net. 6 cabins. $70–$95 cabin. No credit cards. Pets accepted. **Amenities:** Bike rental; coin-
op laundry (May–Oct); fishing. *In room:* Kitchen, coffeemaker, no phone.

WHERE TO DINE
Near the Park
When you're this far into the wilderness, the question isn't *which* restaurant to choose,
but *whether* there is a single restaurant at all. If bacon and eggs, sandwiches, steaks,
chicken, burgers, pizza, and salads aren't part of your diet, you're in big trouble unless
you packed your own grub.

Deciding where you're going to eat near Lassen Volcanic National Park depends mostly
on which side you're on, north or south. At the south entrance to the park, the closest
restaurant is the **Lassen Mineral Lodge** (see "Where to Stay," above) in the town of Mineral, which serves the usual uninspired American fare. The best approach, however, is to
stay at a B&B or lodge that offers meals to its guests—such as the **Bidwell House** or
Drakesbad Guest Ranch—or at least provides a kitchen to cook your own meals, such as
the **Mill Creek Resort** (see above). Food and camping supplies are available at the **Lassen
Mineral Lodge,** on Highway 36 in Mineral, at the southern end of the park (© **530/595-
4422**). They also sell or rent just about every outdoor toy you'd ever want to play with in
Lassen Park, including cross-country and alpine ski equipment.

4 LAVA BEDS NATIONAL MONUMENT

324 miles NE of San Francisco; 50 miles NE of Mount Shasta

Lava Beds takes a while to grow on you. It's a seemingly desolate place with high plateaus,
cinder cones, and hills covered with lava cinders, sagebrush, and twisted junipers. Miles
of land just like it cover most of this corner of California. So why, asks the first-time
visitor, is this a national monument? The answer lies underground.

The earth here is like Swiss cheese, so porous in places that it actually makes a hollow
sound. When lava pours from a shield volcano, it doesn't cool all at once; the outer edges cool
first and the core keeps flowing, forming underground tunnels like a giant pipeline system.

More than 330 lava-tube caves lace the earth at Lava Beds—caves open to the public
to explore on their own or with park rangers. Whereas most caves fuel visitors' fear of
getting lost within their huge chambers, multiple entrances, and bizarre topography,
these tunnels are simple and relatively easy to follow. Once inside, you'll feel that this
would be a great place for a game of hide-and-seek.

ESSENTIALS
GETTING THERE   The best access to the park is from Highway 139, 4 miles south of
Tulelake.

VISITOR INFORMATION Call the **Lava Beds National Monument** (✆ **530/667-8100**; www.nps.gov/labe) for information on ranger-led hikes, cave trips, and campfire programs. The visitor center is at the southern end of the park.

ENTRY FEES The entry fee is $10 per vehicle for 7 days, $5 per bike or walk-in, and $10 a day for camping.

WHEN TO GO Park elevations range from 4,000 to 5,700 feet, and this part of California can get cold any time of year. Summer is the best time to visit, with average temperatures in the 70s Fahrenheit (20s Celsius); winter temperatures plunge down to about 40°F (4°C) in the day and as low as 20°F (–7°C) by night. Summer is also the best time to participate in ranger-led hikes, cave trips, and campfire programs.

EXPLORING THE PARK

A hike to **Schonchin Butte** (.75 mile each way) will give you a good perspective on the stark beauty of the monument and nearby Tule Lake Valley. Wildlife lovers should keep their eyes peeled for such terrestrial animals as mule deer, coyote, marmots, and squirrels, while watching overhead for bald eagles, 24 species of hawks, and enormous flocks of ducks and geese headed to the Klamath Basin, one of the largest waterfowl wintering grounds in the Lower 48. Sometimes the sky goes dark with ducks and geese during the peak migrations.

The caves at **Lava Beds** are open to the public with little restriction. All you need to see most of them are a good flashlight or headlamp, sturdy walking shoes, and a sense of adventure. Many of the caves are entered by ladders or stairs, or by holes in the side of a hill. Once inside, walk far enough to round a corner, and then shut off your light—a chilling experience, to say the least.

One-way **Cave Loop Road,** just southwest of the visitor center, is where you'll find many of the best cave hikes. About 15 lava tubes have been marked and made accessible. Two are ice caves, where the air temperature remains below freezing year-round and ice crystals form on the walls. If exploring on your own gives you the creeps, check out **Mushpot Cave.** Almost adjacent to the visitor center, this cave has been outfitted with lights and a smooth walkway; you'll have plenty of company.

Hardened spelunkers will find enough remote and relatively unexplored caves to keep themselves busy. Many caves require specialized climbing gear.

Above ground, several trails crisscross the monument. The longest of these, the **Lyons Trail** (8.25 miles one-way), spans the wildest part of the monument, where you are likely to see plenty of animals. The **Whitney Butte Trail** (3 miles one-way) leads from Merrill Cave along the shoulder of 5,000-foot Whitney Butte to the edge of the Callahan Lava Flow and monument boundary.

PICNICKING, CAMPING & ACCOMMODATIONS

The 43-unit **Indian Well Campground** near the visitor center has spaces for tents and small RVs year-round, with water available only during the summer. The rest of the year, you'll have to carry water from the nearby visitor center. Two **picnic grounds,** Fleener Chimneys and Captain Jacks Stronghold, have tables but no water; open fires are prohibited.

The monument grounds have no hotels or lodges, but many services are available in nearby Tulelake and Klamath Falls. For more information, call or write **Lava Beds National Monument,** P.O. Box 867, Tulelake, CA 96134 (✆ **530/667-2282**).

The High Sierra: Yosemite, Mammoth Lakes, Sequoia & Kings Canyon

by Matthew Richard Poole

The national parks of California's Sierra lure travelers from around the globe. The big attraction is Yosemite, of course, but the region abounds with other natural wonders as well. John Muir found in Yosemite "the most songful streams in the world . . . the noblest forests, the loftiest granite domes, the deepest ice-sculpted canyons." Few visitors would disagree with Muir's early impressions as they explore this land of towering cliffs, alpine lakes, river beaches, and dazzling fields of snow in winter.

Yosemite Valley, lush with waterfalls and regal peaks, is the most central and accessible part of the park, stretching for some 7 miles from Wawona Tunnel in the west to Curry Village in the east. If you visit during spring or early fall, you'll encounter fewer problems with crowds and have a more intimate experience of Yosemite's splendors.

Across the heart of the Sierra Nevada, in east-central California, Sequoia and Kings Canyon national parks comprise a vast, mountainous region that stretches some 1,300 square miles, taking in the giant sequoias for which they're fabled. This is a land of alpine lakes, deep canyons, and granite peaks, including Mount Whitney—at 14,495 feet, the highest point in the Lower 48 states.

Another big attraction is Mammoth Lakes, a popular playground for California residents. Glaciers carved out much of this panoramic region, where you can partake of all sorts of recreational activities against a backdrop of lakes, streams, waterfalls, and meadows.

Because of the vast popularity of the parks, facilities can be strained at peak visiting times. Always make your reservations in advance if possible (for camping as well as for hotel stays).

1 YOSEMITE'S GATEWAYS

The three most popular entrances to Yosemite (there are five total) are **Big Oak Flat** (via Hwy. 120), the west entrance, 88 miles east of Manteca and the best passage in from San Francisco; **Arch Rock** (via Hwy. 140), 75 miles northeast of Merced and the easiest route from central California; and the **South Entrance** at Wawona (via Hwy. 41), 64 miles north of Fresno and the best inroad from Southern California. Should you need to reserve accommodations outside Yosemite, it's wise to book a place near the gateway that affords you easiest access to the park.

Towns on the periphery of each gateway are built around the tourism industry, with plenty of places to stay and eat, and natural wonders of their own. The drawback is that if you stay outside Yosemite, reaching any point within the park requires at least a half-hour drive, which is especially frustrating during high season, when motor homes and congestion slow traffic to a snail's pace.

A controversial park plan would restore 180 acres to their natural state and eliminate a $3^{1}/_{4}$-mile section of road to make way for a foot-and-bike trail, but it would do so by cutting the number of day-use parking spots in Yosemite from 1,600 to 550, encouraging bus and shuttle usage, and reducing lodging rooms from 1,260 to 981.

The plan is still under debate, but various public transportation options are already in effect, allowing you to leave your car behind. You can enter Yosemite on convenient, inexpensive buses and move around the valley floor on free shuttles. The **Yosemite Area Regional Transit System (YARTS;** ✆ **877/989-2787;** www.yarts.com) runs round-trip transit from communities within Mariposa, Merced, and Mono counties to Yosemite. The Merced route along Highway 140 operates year-round, although the winter schedule is limited. Fares for riding YARTS vary, but generally range from $7 to $25 round-trip for adults, including park entrance, with discounts for children and seniors. Summer routes originate at Coulterville, Mammoth Lake and Lee Vining, and Wawona. For information on the Highway 120 east service (Mammoth Lakes to Yosemite Valley), call ✆ **877/989-2787** from May until it snows (Sept or Oct).

BIG OAK FLAT ENTRANCE

The Big Oak Flat entrance is 150 miles east of San Francisco and 130 miles southeast of Sacramento. Among the string of small communities along the way is **Groveland** (24 miles from the park's entrance)—a throwback to gold-mining days, with some semblance of a town and the oldest saloon in the state. It will take around an hour to reach the park entrance from Groveland, but at least you'll find extracurricular activity there if you're planning to stay in the area for a while. Big Oak Flat has a few hotels as well, but no town. Call the visitor information number below for details.

GETTING THERE   If you're driving from San Francisco, take I-580 (which turns into I-205) to Manteca, and then Highway 120 east.

VISITOR INFORMATION   Contact the **Yosemite Chamber of Commerce (**✆ **800/449-9120** or 209/962-0429; www.groveland.org) for an exhaustive list of hotels, motels, cabins, RV parks, and campsites in the area.

Where to Stay & Dine

Great dining options are scarce in these parts. For options beyond the places mentioned below, ask around town for further recommendations—just don't expect to discover the next Chez Panisse.

Berkshire Inn Bed & Breakfast ★   The secret to vacationing at Yosemite National Park during the crowded summer months is to stay outside the park at a quiet B&B and then make day trips into the park. Not only is it less expensive, the quality of lodgings and cuisine are usually far better as well. Ergo, consider booking a stay at the Berkshire Inn, a sprawling open-beam lodge built in 1988 on 20 wooded acres just outside Groveland. The owners expect you to treat the inn as your own house in the woods: Enjoy breakfast on the large deck overlooking the mountains, play cards in the sunny gazebo, watch TV on the couch in the family room, or warm up by the wood stove with some complimentary wine. It's so cozy here you might feel inclined to skip a day's foray into

Yosemite. The inn consists of six spacious and pleasantly decorated guest rooms and four
minisuites, all with private entrances and bathrooms. An extended continental breakfast
is included in the rate, and the innkeepers will be happy to arrange outdoor activities—
river rafting, fishing, golfing, bicycling, gold panning, hiking, snow skiing, horseback
riding, or wine tasting—for you.

19950 Hwy. 120, Groveland, CA 95321. © **888/225-2064** or 209/962-6744. www.berkshireinn.net. 10
units. $135–$180 double. Rates include continental breakfast. AE, DISC, MC, V. **Amenities:** Hiking trails;
sitting room; family room; deck.

Evergreen Lodge ★★ (Finds) (Kids)   If you're looking for *the* classic Yosemite experience at any time of the year, you'll want to book a cabin at the Evergreen Lodge. About
40 minutes east of Groveland right next to the border of Yosemite National Park, this
affordable and refreshingly crowd-free 15-acre resort has it all: cozy cabins in the woods,
a historic and lively bar, a great restaurant serving a diverse menu, and even a recreation
center and library. The 66 cabins are scattered throughout groves of towering pines and
come with private bathrooms, decks, sitting areas, Sirius Satellite Radio, and comfortable
quilted beds. In the evenings, you can enjoy a pitcher of beer or bottle of fine wine; play
a game of Ping-Pong, pool, or horseshoes; sit around the campfire roasting marshmallows; or plan your next day's outing in the recreation center. During the day, you'll have
easy access to all parts of Yosemite—particularly the beautiful and crowd-free Hetch
Hetchy area—as well as numerous hiking trails and swimming holes near the lodge. Be
sure to reserve space and join one of Evergreen's guided recreation and activities programs, which include fly-fishing trips for all levels, hikes throughout the park, bike trips
(the road biking around here is excellent), naturalist-led Yosemite tours, happy hour
sunset tours, massage therapy, and a wide variety of evening activities.

33160 Evergreen Rd. (at Hwy. 120), Groveland, CA 95321. © **800/935-6343** or 209/379-2606. Fax 209/
379-2607. www.evergreenlodge.com. 66 units. Open year-round. Rates vary with season and cabin size:
$79–$249 for 1- and 2-bedroom cabins. AE, DISC, MC, V. From San Francisco, take I-580 east (which turns
into I-205) to Manteca; take Hwy. 120 east through Groveland; turn left at Hetch Hetchy/Evergreen Rd.
Amenities: Restaurant; bar; beer garden; lake, pool, and tennis courts at neighboring Camp Mather for
day-use fee (summer only); recreation center; free Wi-Fi and long-distance phone service; general store;
massage. *In room:* TV/DVD, minifridge, hair dryer, CD player, Sirius radio, fan.

The Groveland Hotel ★   Constructed in 1849 from adobe, this California landmark is one of the oldest buildings in the region and loaded with 19th-century character.
The Victorian-style guest rooms are cozily appointed with feather beds, down comforters, private bathrooms, and attractive European antiques. The best rooms are the two-
room suites equipped with spa tubs and fireplaces. Along with an authentic Gold
Rush–era saloon, the hotel has a restaurant serving baby back ribs, rack of lamb, fresh
fish, and pasta, and a wine list that's a recipient of *Wine Spectator*'s Award of Excellence.
Be sure to visit the hotel's website for money-saving package deals.

18767 Main St. (P.O. Box 289), Groveland, CA 95321. © **800/273-3314** or 209/962-4000. Fax 209/962-
6674. www.groveland.com. 17 units. $145–$285 double. Rates include extended continental breakfast.
AE, DC, DISC, MC, V. Pets accepted with $10 fee per night. **Amenities:** Restaurant; nearby golf course;
small game room; concierge; business center; secretarial services; room service; babysitting; laundry
service. *In room:* A/C, TV/VCR in some units, free Wi-Fi, minibar, coffeemaker, hair dryer, iron, CD player.

Hotel Charlotte   Walking into the Charlotte is like stepping back in time. Built in
1918 by an Italian immigrant, and listed on the National Register of Historic Places, it's
warm, comfortable, and no-nonsense—a quintessential historic Western hotel. On the
outside, it looks like a gentrified saloon. Inside, the 10 individually decorated rooms are

Burgers & Bullets: The Iron Door Saloon

Walk through the English iron doors that were shipped around the Horn, and step into a bar that has been serving whiskey to thirsty travelers for more than 150 years. Built from solid blocks of granite, the Iron Door Saloon is a must-stop on your way to Yosemite. They say Black Bart enjoyed a tumbler or two here and put a few bullets in the walls to keep the locals jumpy (keep looking). Thousands of dollar bills are tacked to the ceiling, and a stuffed buffalo's head hangs on the wall to remind guests of the house special—a thick, juicy, char-broiled buffalo burger served with pickles, tomato, onions, and house-made coleslaw. Espressos, cappuccinos, and lattes are available as well. At 18761 Main St. in downtown Groveland, it's open daily for lunch and dinner (✆ 209/962-8904; www.iron-door-saloon.com). Live music acts (with both local and national artists) regularly play at the saloon—a remnant perk from the days when the owners used to work for concert promoter Bill Graham.

cheerily wallpapered and wainscoted. Rooms are small, quaint, and basic, with twin or queen-size beds and air-conditioning. Several units adjoin one another with connecting bathrooms (perfect for families). Two units have showers only; the rest have claw-foot tub/shower combos. The guest salons include a television, computer with Internet access (Wi-Fi also on-site), games, and a piano for impromptu sing-a-longs. The pancake buffet is great, featuring strong coffee, eggs, yogurt, cereals, fruit, breads, and juices.

18736 Main St. (Hwy. 120), Groveland, CA 95321. ✆ 800/961-7799 or 209/962-6455. Fax 209/962-6254. www.hotelcharlotte.com. 10 units. $108–$189 double. Rates include buffet breakfast. Extra person $20. AE, MC, V. 1 room accepts pets with $20 fee. **Amenities:** Restaurant; full bar; game room; Wi-Fi. In room: AC, TV.

ARCH ROCK ENTRANCE

This is the most heavily used park entrance, offering easy access to the valley.

GETTING THERE Arch Rock is 75 miles northeast of Merced. If you're driving from central California, take I-5 to Highway 99 to Merced, and then Highway 140 east through El Portal.

Greyhound (✆ 800/231-2222; www.greyhound.com) and **Amtrak** (✆ 800/USA-RAIL; www.amtrak.com) have routes to Fresno from many cities. **VIA Adventures** (✆ 800/VIA-LINE or 209/384-1315; www.via-adventures.com) offers service from Merced Amtrak Passenger Station to Yosemite Valley Visitor Center and Yosemite Lodge. Coaches, which can be wheelchair-lift equipped with advance notice, provide several round-trips daily between Merced and Yosemite.

Where to Stay

Yosemite Bug Rustic Mountain Resort (Kids) 25 miles from Yosemite Valley, this former children's camp is closer to a hostel than to a "rustic mountain resort," but if you're more interested in saving money and hiking Yosemite than in good service and fine linens, the Bug delivers (otherwise stay at the Evergreen Lodge above). Accommodations are simply furnished and come in multiple configurations: private cabins with bathrooms, B&B-style private rooms with shared bathrooms in the main lodge, Yosemite-style wood-frame tent cabins, and cottages that are best for families or small groups. The on-site **Cafe at** **the Bug** serves California-American fare—seared grilled salmon in a lemon-herb sauce with mashed potatoes, braised boneless beef short ribs with a red wine reduction sauce, vegan dishes, and box lunches to go. The cafe also doubles as the lodge's communal lounge. Other perks include a '70s vintage spa facility with an outdoor hot tub, a big sun deck, swimming hole, hammocks, and hot-rock sauna, as well as yoga classes, a game room with a pool table, a kitchen for hostel guests, and organized outings. For more reviews, check out their blog at **http://yosemitebug.blogspot.com**.

6979 Hwy. 140 (P.O. Box 81), Midpines, CA 95345. © **866/826-7108** or 209/966-6666. Fax 209/966-6667. www.yosemitebug.com. Private rooms with private bathroom $95–$125; family and private rooms with semiprivate bathroom $50–$85; dorm beds with semiprivate bathrooms $20; tent cabins $30–$55; cottages $105–$335. DISC, MC, V. **Amenities:** Restaurant; bike rentals; game room; free Wi-Fi (in lodge); coin-op laundry. *In room:* A/C, no phone.

Yosemite View Lodge (**Kids**)   It's shocking to drive onto this gargantuan compound, practically at the park gate, amid otherwise pristine natural surroundings. But the busloads of tourists need to stay somewhere, and this 335-room megamotel along the Merced River is ground zero. The motel-style units include fridges, microwaves, and HBO; some have kitchenettes, river views, balconies, and fireplaces. The indoor and outdoor pools and pizza restaurant are a big hit with the kids, though if I were a kid I'd rather stay at the Tenaya Lodge (p. 311). There's also a general store, spa, coin-op laundry, and cocktail lounge. The restaurant food is decent but pricey for a family. If this place is booked, ask about Yosemite Resort's other properties, although they're not so close to the park entrance. In the winter call ahead for information about weather and road conditions.

11156 Hwy. 140 (P.O. Box D), El Portal, CA 95318. © **888/742-4371** or 209/379-2681. Fax 209/379-2704. www.yosemiteresorts.us. 335 units. $104–$209 double. 2-night minimum on holidays. MC, V. Pets accepted with $13 fee per night. **Amenities:** Restaurant; pizza parlor; lounge; 1 indoor and 3 outdoor heated pools; 4 Jacuzzis. *In room:* A/C, TV, kitchenette in some units, fridge, hair dryer.

SOUTH ENTRANCE

The South Entrance is 332 miles north of Los Angeles, 190 miles east of San Francisco, 59 miles north of Fresno, and 33 miles south of Yosemite Valley. Fish Camp and Oakhurst are the closest towns to the South Entrance at Wawona. This entrance to the valley leads through the Wawona Tunnel to the **Tunnel View** where you *must* stop to admire the panorama; if you've never been to Yosemite before, I promise you that this is a view you'll never forget.

GETTING THERE   If you're driving from Los Angeles, take I-5 to Highway 99 north, and then Highway 41 north. **Fresno-Yosemite International Airport** (© **559/621-4500**; www.fresno.gov/flyfresno), in nearby Fresno, is 93 miles south of Yosemite Village. The airport is served by Alaska Airlines, America West, American, Continental, Delta, Horizon, United, and all the major car-rental companies. From the airport, take Highway 41 north to the South Entrance.

VISITOR INFORMATION   Ask the **Yosemite Sierra Visitors Bureau,** 40637 Hwy. 41, Oakhurst, CA 93644 (© **559/683-4636**; www.yosemitethisyear.com), for a helpful brochure on the area, and check out its excellent online guide.

Where to Stay & Dine

If you can't afford to eat at the opulent Erna's Elderberry House in Oakhurst (see below), try the pleasant **Three Sisters Café,** 40291 Junction Dr., Suite 3, off Highway 49 (© **559/642-2253**; www.threesisterscafe.com; closed Mon–Tues). For more dining and lodging options, contact the visitors bureau (see above).

Big Creek Inn ★★ Two miles from the South Entrance to Yosemite National Park, this immaculate B&B is run by owner/innkeeper Pamela Salisbury. Near the banks of Big Creek, it has everything you could want from a mountain lodging: easy access to Yosemite, great fishing outside the front door, a balcony for reading, creek sounds from every room, a telescope for stargazing, an outdoor spa tub overlooking the creek, and even in-room facials, body wraps, and foot care. The game room is filled with books, maps, and board games; Internet access is free; and more than 500 movies are available for in-room viewing. The three guest rooms have private balconies with French doors and forest views, large bathrooms with Neutrogena bath products, and cozy comforters; two come with gas fireplaces and bistro-style dining tables. A hearty, homemade buffet breakfast is served in the dining room.

1221 Hwy. 41 (P.O. Box 39), Fish Camp, CA 93623. ✆ **559/641-2828.** www.bigcreekinn.com. 3 units. $115–$239 double. Rates include buffet breakfast and self-serve hot and cold refreshments. MC, V. **Amenities:** Nearby golf course and ski areas; spa services; game room w/refreshments; Internet access; state-of-the-art robotic telescope. *In room:* Ceiling fan, TV/VCR/DVD, Wi-Fi, CD player, free local calls.

Château du Sureau ★★★ Its kudos say it all: five diamonds, five stars, hailed by *Zagat* as one of the top small hotels in the United States. The domain of Vienna-born Erna Kubin-Clanin, the Elderberries estate (*sureau* is French for elderberry) is the *sine qua non* of luxurious lodging, decadent dining, and exclusivity. The château dates from 1991 and is set back off the road on a hill. From the renowned restaurant, a pathway leads through gardens to the house, which resembles a French château, with turret and terra-cotta-tile roof. Each individually decorated room has a wood-burning fireplace and a wrought-iron balcony. Canopy beds are covered in Italian linens and goose-down comforters; several rooms have whirlpool tubs. Celebrities fleeing Los Angeles are fond of the $2,950-per-night Villa Sureau, a two-bedroom, two-bathroom luxury villa with a library, full kitchen, and 24-hour butler service (the price drops a bit without the butler). The restaurant, **Erna's Elderberry House** (✆ **559/683-6800**), is well known for its impeccable French-influenced cuisine and service—$95 six-course prix-fixe menu changes daily—and the **Spa du Sureau** pampers guests from head to toe with a wide selection of facials, body treatments, massages, dry sauna, hydrotherapy, and the latest in aroma and color therapies.

48688 Victoria Lane (P.O. Box 577), Oakhurst, CA 93644. ✆ **559/683-6860.** Fax 559/683-0800. www.chateaudusureau.com. 10 units. $445–$575 double. Rates include full breakfast. Extra person $75. AE, DISC, MC, V. **Amenities:** Restaurant; bar; outdoor pool; nearby golf course; spa services; concierge; activities desk; room service; in-room massage; laundry service; same-day dry cleaning. *In room:* A/C, TV/VCR on request, hair dryer, CD player.

The Homestead Cottages ★ Secluded on 160 acres of woodland with plenty of trails, this establishment off the beaten path is a gem. The wonderful hand-built cottages are rustic yet modern, with four-poster log beds, saltillo tile floors, vaulted ceilings, stone fireplaces, and separate sitting and dining areas, with the convenience of TV and air-conditioning. Each cabin has a unique bent, and they are all spaced far apart enough to guarantee privacy. Each cottage has a kitchen stocked with coffee, teas, fruit, muffins, and such, and a gas barbecue and picnic table is available to guests as well. Families should inquire about the Ranch House, a two-bedroom/two-bathroom accommodation that sleeps up to six guests. The top-rated River Creek Golf Club is just a mile away.

41110 Rd. 600, Ahwahnee, CA 93601. ✆ **800/483-0495** or 559/683-0495. Fax 559/683-8165. www.homesteadcottages.com. 5 cottages, 1 guest house. $145–$374 double. $25 per additional person. DISC, MC, V. 4¹⁄₂ miles north of Oakhurst on Hwy. 49, and then south on Rd. 600 for 2¹⁄₂ miles. *In room:* A/C, TV, kitchen, hair dryer, iron, no phone.

Moments   White-Water Rafting Adventures

Zephyr Whitewater Expeditions (© **800/431-3636** or 209/532-6249; www. zrafting.com) offers one of the most direct ways to interact with nature in Yosemite—especially if you're not an experienced backpacker. The half- to 3-day trips are ideal for white-water fans in the spring (when melting snow makes the ride most exciting) and for families later in the season. Although the trip doesn't go through the park, it's still an all-wilderness adventure and an experience you'll never forget. Be sure to reserve a spot well in advance, particularly in the spring.

Hound's Tooth Inn ★   This immaculate bed-and-breakfast is well located, 12 miles from Yosemite's South Entrance. It has comfortable, pretty rooms (some with spas or fireplaces), individually decorated in a Victorian style with a mix of reproductions and antiques, wallpaper, lace valances, and original art. My favorite rooms are the Hound's Tooth, with a king-size bed, fireplace, and view of the Sierra; and the Victorian Tower, with rattan chairs, and a spa. Kids are welcome by prior arrangement (rooms are set up for two people, so additional bedding must be brought in). The private garden area is the ideal spot for a relaxing read.

42071 Hwy. 41, Oakhurst, CA 93644. © **888/642-6610** or 559/642-6600. Fax 559/658-2946. www.hounds toothinn.com. 12 units, 1 cottage. $99–$199 double; $225 cottage. Extra person $20. Rates include full breakfast. AE, DC, DISC, MC, V. *In room:* A/C, TV/VCR, iron; kitchenette, minibar, fridge, and coffeemaker in some units.

The Narrow Gauge Inn & Restaurant   If you want to stay in a place that celebrates its mountainous surrounds, book a room at this friendly inn, 4 miles south of the park entrance. All of the motel-style units have a luxury cabin feel, with A-frame ceilings, little balconies or decks, antiques, quilts, and lace curtains; some have wood paneling. The higher the price of the room, the cuter it gets (nos. 40–51 are the best and most secluded; they look directly into forest). Hiking trails run through the property, and the old-fashioned, lodge-style restaurant and buffalo bar serves Angus beef, fresh seafood, chicken, and wild game; it's open Wednesday through Sunday in season from 5:30 to 9pm.

48571 Hwy. 41, Fish Camp, CA 93623. © **888/644-9050** or 559/683-7720. Fax 559/683-2139. www.narrow gaugeinn.com. 26 units. Apr–Oct $140–$195 double; Nov–Mar $79–$109 double. Extra person $10. Rates include continental breakfast. DISC, MC, V. Pets accepted with $25 fee. **Amenities:** Restaurant (seasonal); bar; outdoor heated pool (seasonal); Jacuzzi (seasonal). *In room:* TV, coffeemaker.

Tenaya Lodge ★★ **Kids**   2 miles from Yosemite National Park's southern gate, the Tenaya Lodge is a large, full-service resort that's particularly idyllic for families. The three- and four-story complex is set amid 35 acres of forest a few miles outside the park. Inside, the decor is a cross between an Adirondack hunting lodge and a Southwestern pueblo, with a lobby dominated by a three-story river-rock fireplace. The modern guest rooms have tasteful southwestern decor with quality furnishings and roomy, well-appointed bathrooms. At the Guest Experience Center on the premises, you can sign up for tours of Yosemite, white-water rafting, mountain-bike rentals, rock climbing, horseback riding, and other outdoor activities. The lodge's Adventure Club program for kids offers nature hikes, arts and crafts, games, and music for children ages 5 to 12. Baby-sitting for infants and children is also available. *Tip:* Check their website for package deals and Internet specials.

1122 Hwy. 41, Fish Camp, CA 93623. © **888/514-2167** or 559/683-6555. Fax 559/683-8684. www.tenaya lodge.com. 244 units. Winter from $129 double; summer from $255 double. Buffet breakfast $15 per person. Children 17 and under stay free in parent's room. AE, DC, DISC, MC, V. Pets accepted with a $75 fee. **Amenities:** 2 restaurants; deli; indoor and outdoor pools; 2 nearby golf courses; exercise room; full-service spa; indoor and outdoor Jacuzzis; bike rental; children's program; game room; video arcade; activities desk; business center; Wi-Fi; secretarial services; room service; massage; babysitting; laundry service; dry cleaning. *In room:* A/C, TV w/pay movies, minibar, fridge on request, coffeemaker, hair dryer, iron, safe.

2 YOSEMITE NATIONAL PARK ★★★

Yosemite is a place of record-setting statistics: the highest waterfall in North America and three of the world's 10 tallest waterfalls (Upper Yosemite Fall, Ribbon Fall, and Sentinel Falls); the tallest and largest single granite monolith in the world (El Capitan); the most recognizable mountain (Half Dome); one of the world's largest trees (the Grizzly Giant in the Mariposa Grove); and thousands of rare plant and animal species. But trying to explain its majesty is impossible; you simply must experience it firsthand.

What sets the valley apart is its geology. The Sierra Nevada formed between 10 million and 80 million years ago, when a tremendous geological uplift pushed layers of granite beneath the ocean up into a mountain range. Cracks and rifts in the rock gave erosion a start at carving canyons and valleys. During the last ice age, at least three glaciers flowed through the valley, shearing vertical faces of stone and hauling away the rubble. The last glacier retreated 10,000 to 15,000 years ago, but it left its legacy in the incredible number and size of the waterfalls pouring into the valley from hanging side canyons. From the 4,000-foot-high valley floor, the 8,000-foot tops of El Capitan, Half Dome, and Glacier Point look like the top of the world, but they're small compared to the park's highest mountains, which exceed 13,000 feet. The 7-square-mile valley acts like a huge drain for runoff from hundreds of square miles of snow-covered peaks (which explains why the valley flooded during the great storm of 1997).

High-country creeks flush with snowmelt catapult over the abyss left by the glaciers and form an outrageous variety of falls, from tiny ribbons that never reach the ground to the torrents of Nevada and Vernal falls. Combined with the shadows and lighting of the deep valley, the effect of all this falling water is mesmerizing. Hundreds of visitors flock to the park for some of the finest climbing anywhere.

The valley is also home to beautiful meadows and the Merced River. When the last glacier retreated, its debris dammed the Merced and formed a lake. Eventually, sediment from the river filled the lake and created the rich, level valley floor we see today. Tiny Mirror Lake was created later by rock fall that dammed up Tenaya Creek; the addition of a man-made dam in 1890 made it more of a lake than a pond. Rafters and inner-tubers enjoy the slow-moving Merced during the heat of summer.

Deer and **coyote** frequent the valley, often causing vehicular mayhem as one heavy-footed tourist slams on brakes to whip out the camera while another rubbernecker drives right into him. Metal crunches, tempers flare, and the deer daintily hop away.

Bears, too, are at home in the valley. Grizzlies are gone from the park now, but black bears abound, hungry for your food. Bears will rip into cars for even the smallest treats, including things you think are safe in your trunk. Each year as many as 500 bear-eats-car incidents occur, and several bears have had to be killed when they became too aggressive

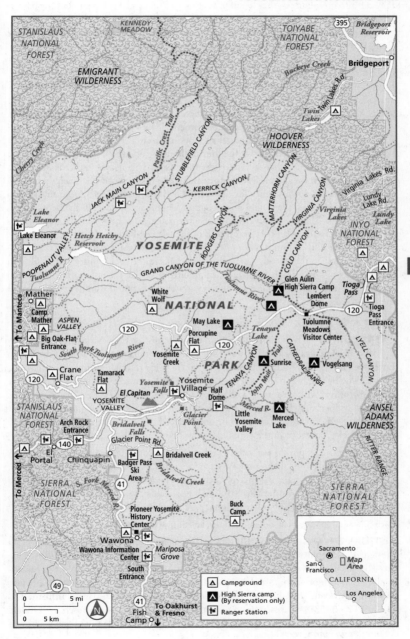

and destructive. Park officials levy a fine of up to $5,000 for feeding park animals, and they can also impound your car. Food storage lockers are available throughout the park—please use them.

In the middle of the valley's thickest urban cluster is the **Yosemite Valley Visitor Center** (*©* **209/372-0200;** www.nps.gov/yose), with exhibitions about the park's glacial geology, history, and flora and fauna. Check out the **Yosemite Museum** next door for insight into what life in the park was once like; excellent exhibits explore the Miwok and Paiute cultures that thrived here. The **Ansel Adams Gallery** (*©* **209/372-4413;** www. anseladams.com) features the famous photographer's prints as well as the work of other artists. You'll also find much history and memorabilia regarding nature writer John Muir, one of the founders of the conservation movement.

It's easy to let the beauty of the valley monopolize your attention, but remember that 95% of Yosemite is wilderness. Of the four million visitors who come to the park each year, few venture more than a mile from their cars. That leaves most of Yosemite's 750,000 acres open for anyone adventurous enough to hike a few miles. Even though the valley is the hands-down winner for drama, the high country offers a more subtle kind of beauty: glacial lakes, rivers, and miles of granite spires and domes. In the park's south-west corner, the Mariposa Grove is a forest of rare sequoias, the world's largest trees, as well as several meadows and the south fork of the Merced River.

Tenaya Lake and Tuolumne Meadows are two of the most popular high-country destinations, as well as the starting points for many trails to the backcountry. Since this area is under snow November through June, summer is more like spring. From snowmelt to the first snowfall, the high country explodes with wildflowers and wildlife trying to make the most of the short season.

ESSENTIALS

ENTRY POINTS The park has four main entrances. Most valley visitors enter through the **Arch Rock Entrance** on Highway 140. The best entrance for Wawona is the **South Entrance** on Highway 41 from Oakhurst. If you're going to the high country, you'll save a lot of time by coming in through the **Big Oak Flat Entrance,** which puts you straight onto Tioga Road without forcing you to deal with the congested valley. The **Tioga Pass Entrance** is open only in summer, and it's only relevant if you're coming from the east side of the Sierra (in which case it's your only option). A fifth, little-used entrance is the **Hetch Hetchy Entrance** in the euphonious Poopenaut Valley, on a dead-end road.

FEES It costs $20 per car per week to enter the park, or $10 per person per week (15 and younger free). Annual Yosemite Passes are a steal at $40. Wilderness permits are free, but reserving them requires a $5 fee per person. If you are 62 or older you may purchase a lifetime Golden Age Passport for $10. With reasonable proof of age, you can apply for this passport here (or at any other national park or national forest).

GAS Yosemite Valley has no gas stations, so fill up before entering.

VISITOR CENTERS & INFORMATION For general information, you can either call the central, 24-hour recorded information line for the park (*©* **209/372-0200**) or log on to the park's main website (www.nps.gov/yose). All visitor-related service lines, including hotels and information, can be accessed by phone at *©* **209/372-1000,** or at **www. yosemitepark.com.** Another good resource is **Yosemite Area Travelers Information** (*©* **209/723-3153;** www.yosemite.com). For details on lodgings within Yosemite National Park, contact **Yosemite Reservations,** P.O. Box 578, Yosemite National Park, California 95389 (*©* **801/559-5000;** www.yosemitepark.com).

The biggest visitor center is the **Valley Visitor Center** (© 209/372-0200). For trail
advice and biological and geological displays about the High Sierra, the **Tuolumne Meadows Visitor Center** (© 209/372-0263) is great (closed in winter). Each center can provide you with maps, and more newspapers, books, and photocopied leaflets than you'll ever read.

REGULATIONS   Rangers in the Yosemite Valley spend more time being cops than rangers. They even have their own jail, so don't do anything you wouldn't do in your hometown. Park regulations are pretty simple: Permits are required for overnight backpacking trips; fishing licenses are required; utilize proper food-storage methods in bear country; don't collect firewood in the valley; no off-road bicycle riding; dogs are allowed in the park but must be leashed and kept off trails; and *don't feed the animals.*

SEASONS   Winter is my favorite time to visit the valley. It isn't crowded, as it is in summer, and a dusting of snow provides a stark contrast to all that granite. To see the waterfalls at their best, come in spring when snowmelt is at its peak. Fall can be cool, but it's beautiful and much less crowded than summer. Sunshine seekers will love summer—if they can tolerate the crowds. The high country is under about 20 feet of snow November through May, so unless you're snow camping, summer is pretty much the only season to pitch a tent. Even in summer, thundershowers are a frequent occurrence, sometimes with a magnificent lightning show. Mosquitoes can be a plague during the peak of summer, but the situation improves after the first freeze.

ORGANIZED TOURS & RANGER PROGRAMS   The park offers a number of ranger-guided walks, hikes, and other programs. Check at one of the visitor centers or in the *Yosemite Guide* for current topics, start times, and locations. Walks may vary from week to week, but you can always count on nature hikes, evening discussions on park anomalies (floods, fires, or critters), and the sunrise photography program aimed at replicating some of Ansel Adams's works. The sunrise photo walk always gets rave reviews from the early risers who venture out at dawn. All photo walks require advance registration. (Get details at the visitor centers.) The living history evening program outside at Yosemite Lodge is great for young and old alike.

Several organizations host guided trips. **Yosemite Guides** ★★ (© 866/922-9111; www.yosemiteguides.com) leads tours to lesser-known areas of the park and fly-fishing trips for all levels. The **Yosemite Institute** ★ (© 209/379-9511; www.yni.org/yi) is a nonprofit group with a unique environment for learning about nature and the history of the Sierra Nevada. **Incredible Adventures** (© 800/777-8464; www.incadventures.com) runs 3-day hikes in Yosemite from San Francisco.

Yosemite Sightseeing Tours (© 559/658-TOUR; www.yosemitetours.com) conducts scheduled as well as customized trips. Tours are operated on air-conditioned buses with picture windows and cost $125. The sightseeing includes Mariposa Grove, Yosemite Valley, and Glacier Point. Guides point out geology, flora, and fauna and schedule stops for lunch, shopping, and photo opportunities. Pickup can be arranged from various motels throughout Oakhurst and Bass Lake.

A variety of **guided tram and bus tours** are also available. You can buy tickets at Yosemite Lodge, the Ahwahnee, Curry Village, or beside the Village Store in Yosemite Village. Advanced reservations are suggested for all tours; space can be reserved in person or by phone (© 209/372-1240). Always double-check for updated departure schedules and prices. Most tours depart from Yosemite Lodge, the Ahwahnee, or Curry Village, and most tours are about $75 for adults for full-day trips. Children's rates are usually 40% to 50% less, and most tours offer discounts for seniors.

The 2-hour **Valley Floor Tour** is a great way to get acclimated to the park, with a good selection of photo ops, including El Capitan, Tunnel View, and Half Dome. This ride is also available on nights when the moon is full or near full. It's an eerie but beautiful scene when moonlight illuminates the valley's granite walls. Blankets and hot cocoa are included, but dress warmly, because it can get mighty chilly after the sun goes down. Purchase tickets at valley hotels, or call ℂ **209/372-1240** for reservations.

The **Glacier Point Tour** is a 4-hour scenic bus ride through the valley to Glacier Point. Tours also depart from Yosemite Valley to **Mariposa Grove.** The Mariposa Grove trip takes 6 hours, includes the Big Trees tram tour that winds through the grove, and stops for lunch at Wawona (lunch is not provided). You can combine the trip to Glacier Point and Mariposa Grove in an 8-hour bus ride.

If you're staying in the valley, the **Park Service** and **Yosemite Concession Services** present evening programs on park history and culture. Past summer programs have included discussions on early expeditions to Yosemite, the park's flora and fauna, geology, global ecology, and the legends of the American Indians who once lived here. Other programs have focused on Mark Wellman's courageous climb of El Capitan—he made the ascent as a paraplegic—and threats to Yosemite's environment.

AVOIDING THE CROWDS   Popularity isn't always the greatest thing for wild places. Over the last 20 years, Yosemite Valley has set records for the worst crowding, noise, crime, and traffic in any California national park.

The park covers more than 1,000 square miles, but most visitors flock to the floor of Yosemite Valley, the 1-mile-wide, 7-mile-long glacial scouring that tore a deep and steep valley from the solid granite of the Sierra Nevada. It becomes a total zoo between Memorial Day and Labor Day. Cars line up bumper to bumper on almost any busy weekend, and Yosemite's superintendent has been known to close the entrances to the park occasionally between Memorial Day and mid-August, when the number of visitors reaches the park's quota.

My advice is to visit before Memorial Day or after Labor Day. If you must go in summer, do your part to help out. It's not so much the numbers of people that are ruining the valley but their insistence on driving through it. Once you're here, park your car and then bike, hike, or ride the shuttle buses. You can rent bicycles at **Curry Village** (ℂ **209/ 372-8319**) and **Yosemite Lodge** (ℂ **209/372-1208**) in summer. It may take longer to get from point A to point B, but you're in one of the most beautiful places on earth—so why hurry?

EXPLORING THE PARK
The Valley

First-time visitors are often dumbstruck as they enter the valley from the west. The first two things you'll see are the delicate and beautiful **Bridalveil Fall** ★★ and the immense face of **El Capitan** ★★, a stunning 3,593-foot-tall solid-granite rock. A short trail leads to the base of Bridalveil, which at 620 feet tall is only a medium-size fall by park standards, but one of the prettiest.

This is a perfect chance to get those knee-jerk tourist impulses under control early: Resist the temptation to rush around seeing everything. Take your time. Look around. One of the best things about the valley is that many of its most famous features are visible from all over. Instead of rushing to the base of every waterfall or famous rock face and getting a crick in your neck from staring straight up, go to the visitor center and spend a half-hour learning something. Buy the excellent *Map and Guide to Yosemite Valley* for $2.50; it describes many hikes and short nature walks. Then go take a look. Walking and biking are the best ways to get around. To cover longer distances, the park shuttles run frequently around the east end of the valley.

Three-quarters of a mile from the visitor center is the **Ahwahnee Hotel** (p. 323). Unlike other park lodgings, the Ahwahnee lives up to its surroundings. The native granite-and-timber lodge, built in 1927, reflects an era when grand hotels were, well, grand. Fireplaces bigger than most Manhattan studio apartments warm the immense common rooms. Parlors and halls are filled with antique Native American rugs. Don't worry about your attire unless you're going to dinner—this is Yosemite, after all.

The best view in the valley is from **Sentinel Bridge** ★ over the Merced River. At sunset, Half Dome's face functions as a projection screen for the many hues of the sinking sun—from yellow to pink to dark purple, and the river reflects it all. Ansel Adams took one of his most famous photographs from this very spot.

The **Nature Center at Happy Isles** ★ has great hands-on nature exhibitions for kids, plus a wheelchair-accessible path along the banks of the Merced River.

VALLEY WALKS & HIKES Yosemite Falls is within a short stroll of the visitor center. You can see it better elsewhere in the valley, but it's impressive to stand at the base of all that falling water. The wind, noise, and spray generated when millions of gallons catapult 2,425 feet through space onto the rocks below are sometimes so overwhelming you can barely stand on the bridge.

The **Upper Yosemite Fall Trail** ★ zigzags 3.5 miles from Sunnyside Campground to the top of Upper Yosemite Fall. This trail gives you an inkling of the weird, vertically oriented world that climbers enter when they scale Yosemite's sheer walls. As you climb this narrow switchback, the valley floor drops away until people below look like ants, but the top doesn't appear any closer. It's unnerving at first, but rewarding in the end. Plan on spending all day on this 7-mile round-trip trail because of the incredibly steep climb.

A mile-long trail leads from the Valley Stables (take the shuttle; no car parking) to **Mirror Lake** ★. The already tiny lake is gradually becoming a meadow as it fills with silt, but the reflections of the valley walls and sky on its surface remain one of the park's most unforgettable sights.

Also accessible from the Valley Stables or nearby Happy Isles is the best valley hike of all—the **John Muir Trail** ★★ to Vernal and Nevada falls. It follows the Sierra crest 200 miles south to Mount Whitney, but you only need go 1.5 miles round-trip to get a great view of 317-foot Vernal Fall. Add another 1.5 miles and 1,000 vertical feet for the climb to the top of Vernal Fall on the **Mist Trail** ★, where you'll get wet as you climb alongside the falls. On top of Vernal and before the base of Nevada Fall is a beautiful valley and deep pool. For an outrageous view of the valley and one heck of a workout, continue up the Mist Trail to the top of Nevada Fall. From 2,000 feet above Happy Isles, where you began, it's a dizzying view straight down the face of the fall. To the east is an interesting profile perspective of Half Dome. Return either by the Mist Trail or the slightly easier John Muir Trail for a 7-mile round-trip hike.

Half Dome ★★★ may look insurmountable to anyone but an expert rock climber, yet thousands take the strenuous yet popular cable route up the backside every year. It's almost 17 miles round-trip and a 4,900-foot elevation gain from Happy Isle on the John Muir Trail. Many do it in a day, starting at first light and rushing home to beat nightfall. A more relaxed strategy is to camp in the backpacking campground in Little Yosemite Valley just past Nevada Fall. From here, the summit is within easy striking distance of the base of Half Dome. If you plan to spend the night, you need a Wilderness Pass (see

Southern Yosemite Mountain Guides

Of the dozens of outdoor recreation companies that offer guided hiking and backpacking trips throughout the Yosemite region, the best is **Southern Yosemite Mountain Guides.** For nearly 2 decades, the professional guides from SYMG have been leading visitors to the most spectacular wilderness regions throughout Yosemite National Park and the High Sierra. SYMG founder and president Ian Elman and his staff are among the top outdoor guides in the nation and are masters at providing a fun, thrilling, and safe experience for all their clients, whether it's a casual naturalist-led day hike through the Giant Sequoias or a 7-day backpacking odyssey through Southern Yosemite's Ansel Adams Wilderness (one of the best kept secrets of the region). SYMG also offers guided fly fishing and mountaineering trips, as well as half-day and 1-day clinics on fly fishing and rock climbing. Check out the wide variety of trips they offer on their website at **www.symg.com**, and then give Ian a call at ℂ **800/231-4575.**

"Camping," below). You must climb up a very steep granite face using steel cables installed by the park service. In summer, rangers also install boards as crossbeams, but they're still far apart. Wear shoes with lots of traction and bring your own leather gloves for the cables (your hands will thank you). Given any chance of a thunderstorm, the trail closes; that cable turns into a lighting rod, so they don't take any risks. The summit yields unbeatable views of the high country, Tenaya Canyon, Glacier Point, and the awe-inspiring abyss of the valley. When you shuffle up to the overhanging lip for a look down the face, be extremely careful not to kick rocks or anything else onto the climbers below, who are earning this view the hard way.

The Southwest Corner

This corner of the park is densely forested and gently sculpted, in comparison to the stark granite that makes up so much of Yosemite. Coming from the valley, Highway 41 takes you to **Tunnel View ★★★**, site of a famous Ansel Adams photograph, and the best scenic outlook of the valley accessible by car. Virtually the entire valley is laid out below: Half Dome and Yosemite Falls straight ahead in the distance, Bridalveil to the right, and El Capitan to the left.

A few miles past the tunnel, Glacier Point Road turns off to the east. Closed in winter, this winding road leads to a picnic area at **Glacier Point ★★**, site of another fabulous view of the valley, this time 3,000 feet below. Schedule at least an hour to drive here from the valley and an hour or two to absorb the view. This is a good place to study the glacial scouring of the valley; the Glacier Point perspective makes it easy to picture the landscape below filled with sheets of ice.

Some 30 miles south of the valley on Highway 41 are the **Wawona Hotel** (p. 324) and the **Pioneer Yosemite History Center.** The Wawona, built in 1879, is the oldest hotel in the park. Its Victorian architecture evokes a time when travelers spent days in horse-drawn wagons to get here. The Pioneer Center is a collection of early homesteading log buildings across the river from the Wawona.

One of the primary reasons Yosemite was set aside as a park was the **Mariposa Grove** ★
of giant sequoias. (Many trails lead through it.) These huge trees have personalities to
match their gargantuan size. Single limbs on the biggest tree in the grove, the Grizzly
Giant, are 10 feet thick. The tree itself is 209 feet tall, 32 feet in diameter, and more than
2,700 years old. Totally out of scale with the size of the trees are the tiny sequoia cones.
Smaller than a baseball and tightly closed, the cones won't release their cargo of seeds
until opened by fire.

The High Country ★★★

Yosemite's high country is stunning. Dome after dome of crystalline granite reflects the
sunlight above deep-green meadows and icy-cold rivers.

Tioga Pass is the gateway to the high country. At times, it clings to the side of steep
rock faces; in other places, it weaves through canyon bottoms. Several good campgrounds
make it a pleasing overnight escape from summertime crowds in the valley, although use
is increasing here, too. **Tenaya Lake** ★ is popular for windsurfing, fishing, canoeing,
sailing, and swimming, but the water is chilly. Many good hikes lead into the high country from here, and the granite domes surrounding the lake are popular with climbers.
Fishing varies greatly from year to year.

Tuolumne Meadows ★★ is near the top of Tioga Pass. Covering several square miles,
this meadow is bordered by the Tuolumne River on one side and granite peaks on the
other. The meadow is cut by many trout streams, and herds of mule deer are almost
always present. The **Tuolumne Meadows Lodge** and store are a welcome counterpoint
to the overdeveloped valley. In winter, they remove the canvas roofs and the buildings fill
with snow. You can buy last-minute backpacking supplies here, or grab burgers and fries
at the on-site cafe.

TUOLUMNE MEADOWS HIKES & WALKS So many hikes lead from here into the
backcountry that it's impossible to do them justice. A good trail passes an icy-cold spring
and traverses several meadows.

On the far bank of the Tuolumne from the meadow, a trail leads downriver, eventually
passing through the grand canyon of the Tuolumne and exiting at Hetch Hetchy. Shorter
hikes will take you downriver past rapids and cascades.

An interesting geological quirk is the **Soda Springs,** on the far side of Tuolumne
Meadow from the road. This bubbling spring gushes carbonated water from a hole in the
ground; a small log cabin marks its site.

For a selection of Yosemite high-country hikes and backpacking trips, consult some of
the guidebooks to the area. Two of the best are published by Wilderness Press: *Tuolumne
Meadows,* a hiking guide by Jeffrey B. Shaffer and Thomas Winnett; and *Yosemite
National Park,* by Thomas Winnett and Jason Winnett.

SPORTS & OUTDOOR PURSUITS

BICYCLING With 10 miles of bike paths in addition to the valley roads, biking is an
ideal way to get around the park. You can rent bikes at the **Yosemite Lodge** (✆ **209/372-
1208**) or **Curry Village** (✆ **209/372-8319**) for about $7.50 per hour or $24 per day.
You can also rent bike trailers for little kids at $14 per hour or $42 per day. All hiking
trails in the park are closed to mountain bikes.

FISHING Trout season begins on the last Saturday in April and continues through
November 15. The Merced River from Happy Isles downstream to the Pohono Bridge is
catch-and-release only for native rainbow trout, and barbless hooks are required. Everyone

16 years old or more must display a California license to fish. Get licenses at the Yosemite Village Sport Shop (℃ **209/372-1286**). Guided fly-fishing trips in Yosemite for all levels are available from **Yosemite Guides** (℃ **866/922-9111** or 209/379-2231; www.yosemiteguides.com). *Note:* Yosemite Valley has special fishing regulations; get information at the visitor centers.

HORSEBACK RIDING   Three stables offer day rides and multiday excursions in the park. **Yosemite Valley Stables** (℃ **209/372-8348**) is open spring through fall. The other two—**Wawona** (℃ **209/375-6502**) and **Tuolumne Stables** (℃ **209/372-8427**)—operate only in summer. Day rides run from about $55 to $95, depending on length. Multiday backcountry trips cost roughly $100 per day and must be booked almost a year in advance. The park wranglers can also be hired to make resupply drops at any of the High Sierra Camps, if you plan an extended trip. Log on to **www.yosemiteparktours.com** (click on "Activities") for more information.

GOLF   The park has one golf course and several others nearby. **Wawona** (℃ **209/375-6572**) sports a 9-hole, par-35 course that alternates between meadows and fairways. Just outside the park is the 18-hole **Sierra Meadows Ranch Course** (℃ **559/642-1343**) in Oakhurst. Call for current fees and other information.

ICE-SKATING   The **Curry Village Ice Rink** (℃ **209/372-8319**) is fun in winter. It's outdoors, however, and melts quickly when the weather warms up. Rates are $8 for adults and $6 for children under 12. Skate rentals are $3.

RAFTING   Rafting 3 leisurely miles down the Merced River is one of the most refreshing ways to see Yosemite Valley's spectacular scenery. At the raft rental shop in Curry Village (℃ **209/372-8319**), daily fees are a mere $21 for adults and $14 for children 12 and under. Fees include a raft, paddles, mandatory life preservers, and transportation from Sentinel Beach to Curry Village. Swift currents and cold water can be deadly to young kids, so children less than 50 pounds are not permitted in rental rafts. Log on to **www.yosemiteparktours.com** (click on "Activities") for more information. Also read the "White-Water Rafting Adventures" sidebar on p. 311.

ROCK CLIMBING   Much of the most technical advancement in rock climbing grew out of the highly competitive Yosemite Valley climbing scene of the 1970s and 1980s. Other places have since stepped into the limelight, but Yosemite is still one of the most desirable climbing destinations in the world.

The **Yosemite Mountaineering School** (℃ **209/372-8344**; www.yosemite mountaineering.com) runs classes for beginning through advanced climbers. Considered one of the best climbing schools in the world, it offers private lessons that will teach you basic body moves and rappelling, and will take you on a single-pitch climb. Classes run from early spring to early October in the valley, and during summer in Tuolumne Meadows.

SKIING & SNOWSHOEING   Opened in 1935, **Badger Pass** (℃ **209/372-8430**; www.yosemitepark.com) is the oldest operating ski area in California and great for families. Four chairs and one rope tow cover a compact mountain, with beginner and intermediate runs. At $38 for adults, $32 for youths from 13 to 17, and $15 for children from 7 to 12 (kids 6 and under free with adult), it's a great place to learn how to ski or snowboard. Naturalists lead special winter children's programs, and the facility provides babysitting.

Yosemite is also popular with **cross-country skiers and snowshoers.** Both the Badger Pass ski school and the mountaineering school run trips and lessons for all abilities, ranging

Tips **Custom Camping**

If you want to experience the fun of camping without the hassle, the **Evergreen Lodge** (p. 307) might have the perfect solution for you. It's called Custom Camping, where guests sleep in spacious and fully furnished mesh-topped tents that are already set up and ready to go. Each tent includes a comfy air-bed, sleeping bags and liners, pillows, towels, quality toiletries, camping chairs, and a battery-powered lantern. Perks include a communal fire pit for roasting marshmallows, picnic tables, a spotless his-and-hers bathhouse offering private hot showers 24 hours a day, and full access to the resort's restaurant, tavern, and recreational activities. Tent rates range from $50 to $80 per night for one to four people and are available from May to October. Space is limited, so be sure to book in advance. For more information, call (*C*) **209/379-2606** or log on to **www.evergreenlodge.com**.

from basic technique to trans-Sierra crossings. Two ski huts can accommodate anyone taking guided cross-country tours, including the spiffy **Glacier Point Hut** ((*C*) 209/372-8444), with its massive stone fireplace, beamed ceilings, and bunk beds; and the **Ostrander Hut** ((*C*) 209/379-2646; www.ostranderhut.com), with 25 bunks. You have to pack in your own supplies, however. If you're on your own, Crane Flat is a good place to go, as is the groomed track up to Glacier Point, a 20-mile round-trip self-guided tour.

CAMPING

Campgrounds in Yosemite can be reserved up to 5 months in advance through the **National Park Reservation Service** ((*C*) 877/444-6777; www.recreation.gov). *Be warned:* During busy season, all valley campsites sell out within hours of becoming available on the service.

Backpacking into the wilderness and camping there is the least crowded option and takes less planning than reserving a campground. If you plan to camp in the wilderness, you must get a free **Wilderness Pass** (and pay the park entrance fee). At least 40% of each trail-head quota is allocated up to 24 hours in advance; the rest is available by mail. Write to the Yosemite Association, P.O. Box 545, Yosemite, CA 95389, specify the dates and trail heads of entry and exit, the destination, number of people, and any accompanying animals; include a $5 per person advance-registration fee. You may also call (*C*) 209/372-0740 for a pass.

Valley Campgrounds

Until January 1997, the park had five car campgrounds that were always full except in the dead of winter. Now the park has half the number of campsites, and getting a reservation on short notice takes a minor miracle. (Yosemite Valley lost almost half of its 900 camping spaces in a freak winter storm in 1997; it washed several campsites downstream and buried hundreds more beneath a foot of silt.)

The two and a half remaining campgrounds—**North Pines, Upper Pines,** and half of **Lower Pines**—charge $20 to $30 per night. All have drinking water, flush toilets, pay phones, fire pits, and heavy ranger presence. Showers are available for a small fee at Curry Village. Upper Pines, North Pines, and Lower Pines allow small RVs (less than 40 ft.

long). If you're expecting a real nature experience, skip camping in the valley unless you like doing so with 4,000 strangers.

Camp 4 (previously named Sunnyside campground) is a year-round, walk-in campground that fills quickly since it's only $5 per night. Hard-core climbers used to live here for months at a time. The park service has stopped them, but this site still has a more bohemian atmosphere than any of the other campgrounds.

Campgrounds Elsewhere in the Park

Outside the valley, things open up for campers. Two-car campgrounds near the South Entrance of the park, **Wawona** and **Bridalveil Creek,** offer a total of 210 sites with all the amenities. Wawona is open year-round, and reservations are required May through September; otherwise, it's first-come, first-served. Family sites at Wawona are $20 per night, and group sites, which hold up to 30 people, are $40 per night. Because it sits well above the snow line, at more than 7,000 feet, Bridalveil is open only in summer. Rates are $14 per night for first-come, first-served sites, and $40 for group sites.

Crane Flat, Hodgdon Meadow, and Tamarack Flat are all in the western corner of the park near the Big Oak Flat Entrance. **Crane Flat** is the nearest to the valley, about a half-hour drive away, with 166 sites, water, flush toilets, and fire pits. Its rates are $20 per night, and it's open July through September. **Hodgdon Meadow** is directly adjacent to the Big Oak Flat Entrance at 4,800 feet elevation. It's open year-round, charges $20 per night, and requires reservations May through September, through the National Park Reservation Service. Facilities include flush toilets, running water, a ranger station, and pay phones. It's one of the least crowded low-elevation car campgrounds, but you won't find lots to do here. **Tamarack Flat** is a waterless, 52-site campground with pit toilets. Open June through October, it's a bargain at $8 per night.

Tuolumne Meadows, White Wolf, Yosemite Creek, and Porcupine Flat are all above 8,000 feet, open only in summer. **Tuolumne Meadows** ★ is the park's largest campground, with more than 300 spaces. It absorbs the crowd well and has all the amenities, including campfire programs and slide shows in the outdoor amphitheater. You, however, will feel sardine-packed between hundreds of other visitors. Half of the sites are reserved in advance; the rest are set aside on a first-come, first-served basis. Rates are $18 per night.

White Wolf, west of Tuolumne Meadows, is the other full-service campground in the high country, with 74 sites available for $12 per night for family sites, $40 for group sites. It offers a drier climate than the meadow and doesn't fill up as quickly. Sites are available on a first-come, first-served basis.

(Tips) **Securing Accommodations**

All hotel reservations can be made exactly 366 days in advance. Call **Yosemite Concessions Services** at ⓒ **801/559-5000** in the morning 366 days before your intended arrival for the best chance of securing a spot. If you don't plan that far in advance, it's still worth calling, because cancellations may leave new openings. You may also book reservations online through **www.yosemitepark.com**. Reservations without a deposit must be confirmed on the scheduled day of arrival by 4pm. Otherwise, you'll lose your reservation.

(Tips)   **A Cottage in the Woods**

Yosemite West Reservations (© **559/642-2211;** www.yosemitewestreservations. com) rents a variety of privately owned accommodations, ranging from fairly simple rooms with one queen-size bed and kitchenette (suitable for one or two people) to luxurious vacation homes with full-size kitchens, two bathrooms, living rooms, and beds for as many as eight people. Kitchens and kitchenettes are fully equipped, all bedding is provided, TVs and VCRs are on hand, and outdoor decks allow you to soak up the verdant views. All units also have gas or wood-burning fireplaces. The homes are in a forested section of the park, about 10 miles from Yosemite Valley and 8 miles from Badger Pass. Most units range from $195 to $495 per night. For more information, call or see **www.yosemitewest reservations.com**.

Two primitive camps, **Porcupine Flat** and **Yosemite Creek,** are the last to fill up in the park. Both have pit toilets but no running water, and charge $10 per night on a first-come, first-served basis.

WHERE TO STAY IN THE PARK

Yosemite Concessions Services, P.O. Box 578, Yosemite National Park, California 95389 (© **801/559-5000**), operates all accommodations within the park and accepts all major credit cards. The reservations office is open Monday through Friday from 7am to 7pm, Saturday and Sunday from 8am to 5pm (PST). For more lodging options and information, or to make an online reservation request, visit **www.yosemitepark.com**.

Yosemite's five backcountry **High Sierra Camps** (© **559/253-5674**) bridge the gap between backpacking and hotel stays. The camps are good individual destinations. Or you can link several together, because they're arranged in a loose loop about a 10-mile hike from one another. Guests bunk dormitory-style in canvas tents; each camp has bathrooms and showers. Due to the huge popularity of these camps, management books reservations by lottery. They accept applications from October 15 to November 30, hold the lottery in December, and notify winners by the end of March.

The Ahwahnee Hotel ★★★   A National Historic Landmark noted for its granite-and-redwood architecture, the six-story Ahwahnee is one of the most romantic and beautiful hotels in California. With its soaring lobby, cathedral-like dining room, outstanding views, and steep prices, it's definitely worthy of the most special occasions. Try to reserve one of the more spacious cottages, which cost the same as rooms in the main hotel. For the price, the guest rooms—though pleasant—are simple to the point of austerity. On the other hand, you can look right out your window and see Half Dome, Yosemite Falls, or Glacier Point. The **Ahwahnee Restaurant** is a colossal, impressive chamber with 50-foot-tall, floor-to-ceiling leaded windows. It's more noteworthy for its ambience, however, than for its expensive cuisine.

© **209/372-1489.** www.yosemitepark.com. 99 units, 24 cottages. $408–$984 double. Children 12 and under stay free in parent's room. AE, DC, DISC, MC, V. Pets are not accepted, but they can board in the kennel at the park stables. **Amenities:** Restaurant and lounge; heated outdoor pool; nearby golf course;

2 tennis courts; Jacuzzi; concierge; room service; babysitting (need 2 weeks notice; child must be potty-trained and at least 2 years old). *In room:* A/C (ceiling fan in cottages), TV, fridge in cottages, coffeemaker, hair dryer, iron.

Curry Village (**Kids**)   Celebrating its 110th birthday in 2009, Curry Village is best known as a mass of more than 400 white canvas tents tightly packed together on the valley's south slope. It was founded in 1899 to provide inexpensive lodgings at a mere $2 a day, and it's still an economical place to crash. One downside is that these tents are basically canvas affairs, and this is bear country, so you'll need to lock up all foodstuffs and anything that bears might think is food (even toothpaste) in bear-proof lockers. They're free, but they may be a healthy walk from your tent-cabin. Curry Village also has more than 100 attractive wood cabins with private bathrooms, and about 80 wood cabins that, like the tent-cabins, share a large bathhouse. There are a number of motel rooms as well. Canvas tents have wood floors and sleep two to four people, with beds, bedding, dressers, and electrical outlets. The wood cabins and motel rooms are much more substantial and comfortable, but cost more than twice the price. *Note:* If Curry Village is full, inquire about available canvas tents-cabins at Tuolumne Meadows Lodge or White Wolf Lodge.

(*C*) **801/559-5000.** www.yosemitepark.com. 628 units. $85–$207 double. Children 12 and under stay free in parent's room. Extra person $10–$14. AE, DC, DISC, MC, V. **Amenities:** Buffet-style dining from spring to fall; fast-food court; heated outdoor pool; nearby golf course; bike rental; tour/activities desk. *In room:* No phone.

Wawona Hotel ★   Six stately white buildings, set near towering trees in a green clearing, make up this classic, Victorian-style hotel. Don't be surprised if a horse and buggy rounds the driveway by the fishpond—it's that kind of place. What makes it so wonderful? Maybe it's the wide porches, the nearby 9-hole golf course, or the vines of hops cascading from one veranda to the next. The entire place was designated a National Historic Landmark in 1987. Clark Cottage is the oldest building, dating from 1876, and the main hotel was built in 1879. Rooms are comfortable and quaint with a choice of a double and a twin bed, a king bed, or one double bed. (Most of the latter share bathrooms.) All rooms open onto wide porches and overlook green lawns. Clark Cottage is the most intimate. The main hotel has the widest porches and plenty of Adirondack chairs, and at night a pianist performs in the downstairs sunroom. *Note:* Nonguests attend the Saturday-evening summer **lawn barbecues** or Sunday brunch.

(*C*) **801/559-5000.** www.yosemitepark.com. 104 units, 52 with private bathroom. $126 double without private bathroom; $198 double with private bathroom. Children 12 and under stay free in parent's room. Extra person $16. AE, DC, DISC, MC, V. **Amenities:** Restaurant; swimming tank; golf course; tennis court. *In room:* Iron, no phone.

Yosemite Lodge at the Falls   The next step down in valley accommodations, Yosemite Lodge is not actually a lodge but a large, more modern complex with two types of accommodations: standard rooms and more spacious "Lodge" rooms with outdoor balconies have striking views of Yosemite Falls. Indeed the largest bonus—and curse—is that every Lodge room's patio or balcony has a view of the valley floor, which means you're near glorious, larger-than-life natural attractions and equally gargantuan crowds.

(*C*) **801/559-5000.** www.yosemitepark.com. 249 units. $113–$180 double. Children 12 and under stay free in parent's room. Extra person $10–$12. AE, DC, DISC, MC, V. **Amenities:** 2 restaurants; food court; bar; heated outdoor pool; nearby golf course; bike rental; tour/activities desk; Internet access.

WHERE TO DINE
In the Park

You certainly won't go hungry here; you'll find plenty of dining options in or near the park. You won't discover many bargains, however, so bring a full wallet.

In the Valley

Ahwahnee Dining Room ★★ AMERICAN/INTERNATIONAL   Even if you are a dyed-in-the-wool, sleep-under-the-stars backpacker, the Ahwahnee Dining Room will not fail to impress you. With understated elegance, the cavernous dining room, with its candelabra chandeliers hanging from the 34-foot beamed ceiling, seems intimate once you're seated. The menu changes frequently, with a good variety of creative yet recognizable dishes. The dinner menu includes suggested wines (from an extensive wine list) for each entree. An evening dress code requires men to wear a jacket and long pants (ties are optional).

Ahwahnee Hotel, Yosemite Valley. ℰ **209/372-1489.** Dinner reservations required. Breakfast $8–$20; lunch $8–$15; dinner $25–$40; Sun brunch $32 adults, $17 children. DC, DISC, MC, V. Mon–Sat 7–10am, 11:30am–3pm, and 5:30–9:15pm; Sun 7am–3pm and 5:30–9:15pm. Shuttle bus stop: 3.

Curry Dining Pavilion (Kids) AMERICAN   The Pavilion is a good spot for the very hungry. All-you-can-eat breakfast and dinner buffets offer a wide variety of well-prepared basic American selections at fairly reasonable prices.

Curry Village. Breakfast $9.25 adults, $5.50 children; dinner $12 adults, $6.25 children. DC, DISC, MC, V. Daily 7–10am and 5:30–8pm. Shuttle bus stops: 12, 13, 14, or 19.

Curry Taqueria Stand MEXICAN   A good place for a quick bite, this taco stand peddles spicy tacos, burritos, taco salads, beans, and rice.

Curry Village. $3–$6. No credit cards. Mon–Thurs 11am–5pm; Fri–Sun 8am–5pm. Closed in winter. Shuttle bus stops: 12, 13, 14, or 19.

Curry Village Ice Cream & Coffee Corner COFFEE SHOP   Specialty coffees and fresh-baked pastries are the fare here. You can also buy ice cream after 11am.

Curry Village, Yosemite Valley. Most items $1–$3. DC, DISC, MC, V. Daily 6am–10pm. Shuttle bus stops: 12, 13, 14, or 19.

Curry Village Pizza Deck ★ (Kids) PIZZA   Need to watch ESPN? This is the place, but you may have to wait in line. One of the park's few big screens awaits inside, and if you're a sports buff, this is the place to be. The scenic outdoor patio offers large umbrellas, table service, and a great view of Mother Nature, plus or minus 100 kids. The lounge also taps a few brews—nothing special, but a mix aimed to please. This is a great place to chill after a long day.

Curry Village, Yosemite Valley. Pizza $8–$16. DC, DISC, MC, V. Daily noon–9pm. Shuttle bus stop: 12, 13, 14, or 19.

Degnan's Cafe AMERICAN   Adjacent to Degnan's Deli, this cafe offers specialty coffee drinks, fresh pastries, wrap sandwiches, and ice cream. It's a good place for a quick bite when you're in a hurry.

Yosemite Village. Most items $1–$4. DC, DISC, MC, V. Daily 7am–7pm. Shuttle bus stop: D, 2, or 8.

Degnan's Deli ★★ (Value) DELI   A solid delicatessen with a large selection of generous sandwiches to order, this is our top choice for a quick, healthy lunch or supper. Sometimes the line gets long, but it moves quickly. Half market and half deli, Degnan's also sells a selection of prepared items such as soups, salads, sandwiches, desserts, and snacks. The beer and wine selection is also good.

Yosemite Village. $3–$8. DC, DISC, MC, V. Daily 7am–5pm. Shuttle bus stops: D, 2, or 8.

Degnan's Loft (Kids) ITALIAN   This cheery restaurant, with a central fireplace and high-beamed ceilings, is adjacent to Degnan's Deli and Degnan's Cafe. It's a good choice for families, with a kid-friendly atmosphere and a menu that features pizza, calzones, lasagna, salads, and desserts.

Yosemite Village. Entrees $4.25–$21. DC, DISC, MC, V. Daily noon–9pm. Shuttle bus stop: D, 2, or 8.

Mountain Room Restaurant AMERICAN   The best thing about this restaurant is the view. The food's good too, but the floor-to-ceiling windows overlooking Yosemite Falls are spectacular, and there's not a bad seat in the house. Try the chicken *champignon,* which is flavorful and moist, as is the mountain trout and the Pacific yellowfin tuna. Meals come with vegetables and bread. Soup or salad is extra. The menu includes entrees for vegetarians, and the dessert tray is amazing. The Mountain Room also has a good wine list, and the Mountain Room Bar and Lounge (open 4–10pm Mon–Fri and noon–10pm Sat–Sun) has an a la carte menu.

Yosemite Lodge. Entrees $17–$30. DC, DISC, MC, V. Daily 5:30–9pm. Shuttle bus stop: 6.

Village Grill AMERICAN   The Village Grill is a decent place to pick up fast food. It offers burgers, chicken sandwiches, and the like, and has outdoor seating.

Yosemite Village. Most items $3.75–$5.25. No credit cards. Daily 11am–5pm. Closed in winter. Shuttle bus stop: 1, 2, or 8.

Yosemite Lodge Food Court AMERICAN   You'll find breakfast, lunch, and dinner at this busy restaurant, which serves about 2,000 meals each day. A vast improvement over the traditional cafeteria, it's set up with a series of food stations, where you pick up your choices before heading to the centralized cashier. You can eat inside or in the outside seating area, which features good views of Yosemite Falls.

Yosemite Lodge. Entrees $5–$14. DC, DISC, MC, V. Daily 6:30–10am, 11:30am–2pm, and 5–8:30pm. Shuttle bus stop: 8.

Elsewhere in the Park

Tuolumne Meadows Lodge AMERICAN   One of the two restaurants in the high country, this lodge has something for everyone. The breakfast menu features the basics, including eggs, pancakes, fruit, oatmeal, and granola. Dinners always include a beef, chicken, fish, pasta, and vegetarian special, all of which change frequently. The quality can swing, but the prime rib and New York steak are consistently good.

Tuolumne Meadows, CA 120. © **209/372-8413.** Reservations required for dinner. Breakfast $3.55–$6.95; dinner $8.65–$19. DC, DISC, MC, V. Daily 7–9am and 6–8pm.

Wawona Hotel Dining Room ★★ AMERICAN   Like the hotel, the Wawona dining room is wide open, with lots of windows and sunlight, and the food is great. For breakfast, choose from a variety of items, including the Meadowloop Special, a combo of French toast, eggs, and bacon, ham or sausage—to fuel you up before you hit the golf course. Lunch features a variety of sandwiches and salads. Dinner appetizers are amazing, and a number of entrees are exceptional—such as Vietnamese shrimp lettuce wraps or a roasted eggplant lemon, herb, and garlic dip served with pita chips.

Wawona Hotel, Wawona Rd. ℂ **209/375-1425.** Breakfast $3–$13; lunch $5–$17; dinner $20–$25. Sun buffet $9.95 breakfast, $16 brunch. DC, DISC, MC, V. Mon–Sat 7:30–10am, 11:30am–1:30pm, 5:30–9pm; Sun 7:30am–10am (breakfast buffet), 10:30am–1:30pm (brunch buffet), 5:30–9pm.

White Wolf Lodge AMERICAN   This casual restaurant has a mountain lodge atmosphere and a changing menu, serving generous portions of American standards. Breakfast choices include eggs, pancakes, omelets, or biscuits and gravy; and dinner always includes beef, chicken, fish, pasta, and vegetarian dishes. Takeout lunches are also available from noon to 2pm.

White Wolf, Tioga Rd. ℂ **209/372-8416.** Reservations required for dinner. Breakfast $4–$8; dinner $7–$19. DC, DISC, MC, V. Daily 7:30–9:30am and 5–8:30pm.

3 MAMMOTH LAKES ★★

40 miles E of Yosemite; 319 miles E of San Francisco; 325 miles NE of Los Angeles

High in the Sierra, southeast of Yosemite, Mammoth Lakes is surrounded by glacier-carved, pine-covered peaks that soar up from flower-filled meadows. It's an alpine region of sweeping beauty and one of California's favorite playgrounds for hiking, biking, horseback riding, skiing, and more. It's also home to one of the world's top-rated ski resorts. At an elevation of 11,053 feet, Mammoth Mountain is higher than either Squaw or Heavenly, so the snow stays firm longer into the year for spring skiing. You won't find Tahoe's long lift lines either—just more mountain and fewer people.

ESSENTIALS

GETTING THERE   It's a 6-hour drive from San Francisco via Highway 120 over the Tioga Pass in Yosemite (closed in winter); 5 hours north of Los Angeles via Highway 14 and U.S. 395; and 3 hours south of Reno, Nevada, via U.S. 395. In winter, Mammoth is accessible via U.S. 395 from the north or the south.

   Mammoth Air Charter (ℂ **888/934-4279**) offers charter flights to the area. It servics Mammoth Lakes Airport on U.S. 395. The closest international airport is Reno-Tahoe Airport (ℂ **775/328-6400**). See "Lake Tahoe," in chapter 9, for some airlines that service the Reno-Tahoe International Airport.

VISITOR INFORMATION   Contact the **Mammoth Lakes Visitors Bureau,** Highway 203 (P.O. Box 48), Mammoth Lakes, CA 93546 (ℂ **888/466-2666** or 760/934-2712; www.visitmammoth.com).

OUTDOOR PURSUITS

At the heart of several wilderness areas, Mammoth Lakes is cut through by the San Joaquin and Owens rivers. Mammoth Mountain overlooks the Ansel Adams Wilderness Area to the west and the John Muir Wilderness Area to the southeast, and beyond to the Inyo National Forest and the Sierra National Forest.

   The **Mammoth Mountain Ski Area** ★★ (ℂ **800/626-6684** or 760/934-2571; www.mammothmountain.com) is the central focus for summer and winter activities. Visitors can ride the lifts just to see panoramic vistas, but those who want an active adventure have many options. If you do hit the slopes in winter, you can use the free **Mammoth Area Shuttle** (ℂ **760/934-2571**, ext. 9238) or **Sierra Express** taxi service (ℂ **760/934-8294**) for transportation between town and the ski area. The shuttle makes many stops and eliminates the long wait that may befall you if you drive yourself.

The state-of-the-art **Panorama Gondola** provides great viewing every day, in winter or summer, weather permitting. The gondola carries eight passengers and stops midway up the mountain and at the summit with 360-degree views. In summer, you can use it to access the hiking and biking trails on the mountain. Tickets are $18 for adults, $14 for youths 13 to 18, $9 kids 7 to 12; kids 6 and under ride free.

In addition to the most popular activities listed below, adventurers can go hot-air ballooning with **Mammoth Balloon Adventures** (© 760/937-UPUP; www.mammoth balloonadventures.com). And golfers can play at **Snowcreek Golf Course,** Old Mammoth Road (© 760/934-6633; www.snowcreekresort.com).

HIKING   Trails abound in the Mammoth Lakes Basin area. They include the half-mile **Panorama Dome Trail,** past the turnoff to Twin Lakes on Lake Mary Road, leading to the top of a plateau with a view of the Owens Valley and Lakes Basin. The 5-mile **Duck Lake Trail** starts at the end of the Coldwater Creek parking lot with switchbacks across Duck Pass past several lakes to Duck Lake. The head of the **Inyo Craters Trail** is accessible via a gravel road, off the Mammoth Scenic Loop Road. It leads you to the edge of these craters where a sign explains how they were created.

For additional trail information and maps, contact the **Mammoth Ranger Station** (© 760/924-5500). For equipment and maps, go to **Footloose Sports Center,** at the corner of Main Street and Old Mammoth Road (© 760/934-2400; www.footloose sports.com), which also rents in-line skates and mountain bikes.

HORSEBACK RIDING & PACKING TRIPS   The region is great for horseback riding, and numerous outfitters offer day rides and pack trips. Among them are **Mammoth Lakes Pack Outfit,** on Lake Mary Road past Twin Lakes (© 888/475-8747 or 760/ 934-2434; www.mammothpack.com), offering day rides, multiday riding trips, and semiannual horse drives; **Red's Meadows Pack Station** at Red's Meadows, past Minaret Vista (© 800/292-7758 or 760/934-2345; www.redsmeadow.com); and **McGee Creek Pack Station,** McGee Creek Road at Crowley Lake (© 800/854-7407 or 760/935-4324; www.mcgeecreekpackstation.com).

KAYAKING   Kayaks are available at Crowley Lake from **Caldera Kayaks** (© 760/934-1691; www.calderakayak.com), starting at $40 per day. This outfitter offers guided tours on Crowley and Mono lakes for $50, and provides instruction as well.

MOUNTAIN BIKING   In summer, the mountain becomes one huge bike park and climbing playground. The bike park is famous for its **Kamikaze Downhill Trail,** an obstacle arena and slalom course where riders can test their balance and skill. Plenty of other trails accommodate gentler folk who just want to commune with nature and get a little exercise, and one area is designed for kids. Bike shuttles will haul you and your bike to the lower mountain trails if you want to skip the uphill part, or the gondola will take you to the summit and let you find your own way down. The park operates daily from 9am to 6pm, during summer months. A 1-day pass with unlimited access to the gondola, bike shuttle, and trail system is $39 for adults, $20 for kids ages 12 and under. A variety of rent-and-ride packages is available; for more information, call © 800/MAMMOTH or log on to **www.mammothmountain.com**.

In town, the **Footloose Sports Center** rents mountain bikes, at the corner of Main Street and Old Mammoth Road (© 760/934-2400; www.footloosesports.com). The **NORBA National Mountain Bike Championships** take place here in summer.

SKIING & SNOWBOARDING   In winter, Mammoth Mountain has more than 3,500 skiable acres, a 3,100-foot vertical drop, 150 trails (32 with snowmaking), and 30 lifts,

Map legend:
- Hospital
- Post Office
- Ski Area
- Visitor Center

0 — 5 mi
0 — 5 km
N

To Bodie via 270

Conway Summit

167

Mono Lake

Lundy Lake

395

Mono Basin Visitor Center

Lee Vining
Museum

120

MONO BASIN NATIONAL FOREST SCENIC AREA

Ellery Lake

Tioga Pass

Tufa State Reserve

Tioga Lake

YOSEMITE NATIONAL PARK

Walker Lake

Mono Craters

120

June Lake Loop

Grant Lake

Devil's Punchbowl

158

June Lake

Silver Lake

Gull Lake

June Lake

Big Springs

Owens River

June Mountain

Lookout Mountain

LITTLE ANTELOPE VALLEY

Benton Crossing

Minarets

Roadside Rest

Inyo Craters

Scenic Loop

395

Hot Creek Geological Site

Fish Hatchery Road

ANSEL ADAMS WILDERNESS AREA

Minaret Vista

Mammoth Mountain

Museum

203

Fish Hatchery

Benton Crossing Road

Crowley Lake

Devils Postpile Monument

Twin Lakes

Historic Mine Sites

MAMMOTH LAKES

Owens River

Rainbow Falls

Horseshoe

Mamie

George

Mary

Convict Lake

Tom's Place

San Joaquin River

Mammoth Lakes Basin

JOHN MUIR WILDERNESS AREA

McGee Creek

Rock Creek

INYO NATIONAL FOREST

Inset — California:

Sacramento

San Francisco

Mammoth Lakes Region

CALIFORNIA

Los Angeles

Inset — Mammoth Lakes:

To Main Lodge

203

203

Main St.

Chair 7

Canyon Blvd.

Lakeview Blvd.

Visitors Bureau

203

Chair 17

Chair 16

Chair 8

Minaret Rd.

Old Mammoth Rd.

U.S. Forest Service Visitor Center

Chair 22

SKI AREA

Meridian Blvd.

Chair 15

Chair 24

Chair 25

Lake Mary Rd.

Mammoth Creek

Winter Road Closure

Mammoth Museum

Valentine Reserve (private)

Old Mammoth Rd.

Sherwin Creek Rd.

Tips **Winter Driving in the Sierra**

Winter driving in the Sierra Nevada Range can be dangerous. The most hazardous roads are often closed, but others are negotiable only by vehicles with four-wheel-drive or tire chains. Be prepared for sudden blizzards, and protect yourself by taking these important precautions:

- Check road conditions before you set out by calling ℭ **800/427-7623.**
- Let the rental-car company know you're planning to drive in snow, and ask whether the antifreeze is prepared for cold climates.
- Make sure your heater and defroster work.
- Always carry chains. In a blizzard, the police will not allow vehicles without chains on some highways. If you don't know how to put them on, you'll have to pay about $40 to have someone "chain up" your car at the side of the road.
- In your trunk, stow an ice scraper, a small shovel, sand or burlap for traction if you get stuck, warm blankets, and an extra car key (motorists often lock their keys in the car while chaining up).
- Don't think winter ends in March. Snow can pile up high as late as April on the sides of the roads leading to the valley, and cold temperatures make more snowfall more than plausible.

including seven high-speed quads. The terrain is 30% beginner, 40% intermediate, and 30% advanced. It's known for power sun, ideal spring skiing conditions, and anywhere from 8 to 12 feet of snow.

Tamarack Lodge (ℭ 760/934-2442; www.tamaracklodge.com) runs a cross-country ski center and offers snowmobiling, dog-sledding, snowshoeing, and sleigh rides for nonskiers.

If you're renting equipment, you'll save money if you do it in town instead of at the resort. We recommend **Footloose Sports Center,** at the corner of Main Street and Old Mammoth Road (ℭ 760/934-2400; www.footloosesports.com), and **Wave Rave Snowboard Shop,** on Main Street (Hwy. 203; ℭ 866/3-BOARDS or 760/934-2471; www.waveravesnowboardshop.com), for snowboards and accessories.

The **June Mountain Ski Area** ★ (ℭ 888/JUNEMTN or 760/648-7733; www.junemountain.com), 20 minutes north of Mammoth, is smaller but offers many summer activities as well as 500 skiable acres, a 2,590-foot vertical drop, 35 trails, and eight lifts, including high-speed quads. The terrain is 35% beginner, 45% intermediate, and 20% advanced. It's at the center of a chain of lakes—Grant, Silver, Gull, and June—visible from the scenic driving loop around Highway 158. It's especially beautiful in the fall, when the aspens are ablaze with gold.

TROUT FISHING Mammoth Lakes Basin sits in a canyon, a couple of miles west of town, with lakes that have made the region known for trout fishing: Mary, Mamie, Horseshoe, George, and Twin. Southeast of town, Crowley Lake is also famous for trout fishing, as are the San Joaquin and Owens rivers. For more fishing information and guides, contact **Rick's Sport Center,** at 3241 Main St. (ℭ 760/934-3416); **Trout Fitter,**

www.thetroutfitter.com); or **Kittredge Sports,** Main Street and Forest Trail (℃ **760/934-7566;** www.kittredgesports.com), which rents equipment, supplies, and guides, teaches fly-fishing, and offers backcountry trips.

EXPLORING THE SURROUNDING AREA

Bodie ★ (www.bodie.net), one of the most authentic ghost towns in the West, is about an hour's drive north of Mammoth, past the Tioga Pass entrance to Yosemite. In 1870, more than 10,000 people lived in Bodie, mining $32 million in gold; today it's an eerie shell full of ghost stories. En route to Bodie, you'll pass **Mono Lake** ★ (pronounced *Mow*-no), near Lee Vining, which has startling tufa towers arising from its surface—limestone deposits formed by underground springs. About 300 bird species nest or stop here during their migrations. Right off Highway 395 is the **Mono Basin Scenic Area Visitors Center** (℃ 760/647-3044; www.monolake.org; daily in summer, Thurs–Mon in winter), with scheduled guided tours and a terrific environmental and historical display of this hauntingly beautiful 60-square-mile desert salt lake. After touring the visitors center, head for the **South Tufa Area,** at the lake's southern end, for a closer look at the tufa formations and briny water. *FYI:* Mono means "flies" in the language of the Yokuts, the Native Americans who live south of this region; get to the lake's edge and you'll see why the nickname is suitable.

WHERE TO STAY

If you stay at the resort, you'll be steps from the lifts. If you opt for the town, you're closer to the restaurants and nightlife. Regardless, they're within a 5-minute drive of one another, so you can never be too far from the action.

More than 700 campsites service the area. They open on varying dates in June, depending on the weather. The largest are at Twin Lakes and Cold Water (both in the Mammoth Lakes Basin), Convict Lake, and Red's Meadow. For additional information, call the **Mammoth Ranger Station** (℃ 760/924-5500).

Fern Creek Lodge (Value)   The best lodging deal in the region is 25 miles north of Mammoth. Less than a mile from the June Mountain ski areas, the Fern Creek Lodge is a spread of simple, fully furnished cabins on the sunrise side of the Eastern High Sierra. Built in 1927, it has seen its ups and downs, but thanks to the latest owners—the Hart family—the year-round fishing and skiing resort is better than ever. The least expensive cabins are small, with just enough room for a bed, a table and chairs, and a bathroom. All have fully equipped kitchens, and most have fireplaces. The units are all so different, your best bet is to call and tell them what you're looking for. Rooms don't have phones, but guests may use a pay phone on the premises.

4628 Hwy. 158, June Lake, CA 93529. ℃ **800/621-9146** or 760/648-7722. www.ferncreeklodge.com. 10 cabins, 4 apts. $75–$85 cabin for 2; $145–$190 cabin for 4; $295 cabin for 8; $1,000 apt. for 4. Extra person $10. AE, DISC, MC, V. Certain pets allowed ($10 extra). **Amenities:** Common barbecue area; full kitchen; grocery and sporting-goods store. *In room:* TV w/HBO.

Holiday Inn Mammoth Lakes ★   This faux-alpine lodge is one of Mammoth's newer hotels. A woodsy exterior with a river-rock base gives the three-story hotel a rustic appeal, although the interior feels contemporary. Comfortable, generically decorated guest rooms have all the amenities you could want. A variety of configurations includes a king/kid suite with bunk beds. The suites have extra room and Jacuzzis. For romance in the great outdoors, consider a spacious honeymoon suite.

3236 Main St. (behind the Chevron station), Mammoth Lakes, CA 93546. (℃ **888/465-4329** or 760/924-1234. Fax 760/934-3626. www.holidayatmammoth.com. 72 units. $145–$359 double and suite. Packages available. AE, DC, DISC, MC, V. **Amenities:** Cafe; bar; indoor heated pool; nearby golf course; exercise room; spa; Jacuzzi; Wi-Fi; room service; coin-op laundry. *In room:* A/C, TV (VCR in some units), kitchenette in some units, fridge, coffeemaker, hair dryer, iron.

Mammoth Mountain Inn ★ (**Kids**) Opposite the ski lodge at the base of the ski resort, this inn opened in 1954 as only one building, but was expanded a decade later into a larger, glossier complex. Though it was remodeled in the early 1990s, it retains the ruggedness you'd expect from a mountain resort. Guest rooms are well equipped and pleasantly furnished. The best are the junior suites with a view of the ski area. Families love this place for its large condo units, day-care activities, cribs, playground, box lunches and picnic tables, and game room. An array of sports facilities includes bicycles, fishing or hiking guides, downhill or cross-country skiing, sleighing, horseback riding, and hay-wagon rides. Extras include free airport shuttle and occasional entertainment. The downside is the 10-minute drive into town, but skiers can't get any closer to the slopes. *Tip:* If you can get a similar or better rate at the new Westin Monache (see below), take it.

1 Minaret Rd. (P.O. Box 353), Mammoth Lakes, CA 93546. (℃ **800/626-6684** or 760/934-2581. Fax 760/934-0701. www.mammothmountain.com. 173 units, 40 condos (some suitable for up to 13 people). Winter $165–$315 double, from $325–$545 condo; summer $125–$179 double, from $170 condo. Ski and mountain-biking packages available. AE, MC, V. **Amenities:** Restaurant; bar; heated outdoor pool; nearby golf course; 2 indoor and 1 outdoor whirlpool spas; mountain-bike rental; day-care center; game room; video arcade; concierge; room service; babysitting; coin-op laundry; executive-level rooms, Wi-Fi (in bar and lobby). *In room:* TV/DVD, high-speed Internet, kitchen in some units.

Motel 6 (**Value**) The rooms may be small, but they're the nicest around in this price range. Factor in the pool, vending machines, and free coffee in the lobby, and you've got all you need to set up camp.

3372 Main St. (P.O. Box 1260), Mammoth Lakes, CA 93546. (℃ **800/4-MOTEL-6** or 760/934-6660. Fax 760/934-6989. www.motel6.com. 151 units. Winter $66–$86 double; summer from $55 double. Extra person $6. AARP discounts. AE, DC, DISC, MC, V. Pets accepted (1 pet per room). **Amenities:** Heated outdoor pool (summer only); coin-op laundry. *In room:* A/C, TV, dataport.

Sherwin Villas Outside the center of town on Old Mammoth Road, this cluster of woodsy condos is perfect for families or groups of friends traveling together. You'll find one- to four-bedroom units, each with a fully stocked kitchen, fireplace, linens, and access to a free shuttle to the slopes (a 5-min. drive away). Considering how many people you can pack into these apartments, it's a good deal—and if you stay 4 weekday nights, the fifth night is free. When making reservations, specify exactly what you're looking for: Each condo is independently owned and varies dramatically in both decor and quality; you can view a few photos of each condo on the website.

362 Old Mammoth Rd. (P.O. Box 2249), Mammoth Lakes, CA 93546. (℃ **888/626-6684.** www.sherwin villas.com. 70 condos. 1-bedroom unit for up to 4 people $100–$120 winter, from $95 summer; 2-bedroom loft for up to 6 people $140–$190 winter, from $115 summer; 3-bedroom unit for up to 8 people $155–$220 winter, from $135 summer; 4-bedroom unit for up to 10 people $195–$260 winter, from $155 summer. Extra person $10. MC, V. **Amenities:** Outdoor pool; tennis courts; 2 Jacuzzis; Finnish sauna; game room. *In room:* TV, kitchen, phone on request.

Sierra Lodge In the heart of Mammoth Lakes, this two-story inn offers contemporary lodgings without a trace of rusticity. The large guest rooms are pleasantly decorated with framed blond-wood furnishings, modern prints, track lighting, big beds, kitchenettes, and small patios or balconies with partial mountain views. The two-bedroom suite—equipped with two queen beds and a full-size pull-out sofa—is ideal for groups or families. Facilities include an outdoor Jacuzzi and a fireside room for relaxing. Other perks include ski lockers, free covered parking, continental breakfast, free shuttle service right out front, and a short walk to Mammoth's best restaurant, Nevados (see review below).

3540 Main St. (Hwy. 203; P.O. Box 9228), Mammoth Lakes, CA 93546. © **800/356-5711** or 760/934-8881. Fax 760/934-7231. www.sierralodge.com. 36 units. $79–$189 double. Rates include continental breakfast. AE, DISC, MC, V. Pets accepted for $10 per night with $100 deposit. **Amenities:** Nearby golf course. *In room:* TV, kitchenette, fridge, hair dryer, voice mail.

Tamarack Lodge & Resort ★   The lodge and cabin accommodations at this lakeside retreat aren't fancy, but that's what has kept guests coming here since the 1920s. The cabins dotted around the 6-acre property accommodate two to nine people, and they come in a variety of configurations: from rustic studios with wood-burning stoves and showers to deluxe two-bedroom/two-bathroom quarters with fireplaces. The best units are the lakefront cabins; try to request one with a lake view. The least expensive rooms, in the main lodge, come with private or shared bathrooms. **The Lakefront Restaurant** is romantic, with a seasonally changing menu. Entrees include grilled medallions of elk filet and seared sea scallops. In the winter, the lodge opens its popular cross-country ski center with more than 25 miles of trails and skating lanes, ski rentals, and a ski school. Boat and canoe rentals are also available.

Twin Lakes Rd., off Lake Mary Rd. (P.O. Box 69), Mammoth Lakes, CA 93546. © **800/MAMMOTH** or 760/ 934-2442. Fax 760/934-2281. www.tamaracklodge.com. 11 units, 6 with private bathroom; 32 cabins. $94–$300 double; $135–$485 cabin. AE, MC, V. **Amenities:** Restaurant; bar; nearby golf course; Wi-Fi. *In room:* Fax, kitchen in cabins, fridge, coffeemaker, iron.

Westin Monache Resort ★★   Don't worry, I didn't pronounce it right the first time either. It's *Mon*-ah-she, which I think is ancient Native American for condo-hotel. Located in the Village at Mammoth adjacent to a 15-passenger express gondola, this new 230-unit condo-hotel is Mono County's first upscale full-service resort hotel, featuring 24-hour room service, concierge, and bell staff; ski valet and rental shop; and a pool, hot tubs, a fitness center, and underground parking. Accommodations consist of plush one- and two-bedroom suites (most with panoramic mountain views), Westin's signature Heavenly Beds, kitchens or kitchenettes, gas fireplaces, and 32-inch flatscreen TVs. The two-bedroom suites are big enough for the entire family, with two private bedrooms, two full bathrooms, and a queen sofa bed in the living room. The hotel's **Whitebark** restaurant serves contemporary cuisine such as gilled steaks, seafood, and pizzas, or you can walk over to the numerous other restaurants in the village. *Tip:* Check the Monache website for "Hotel Offers," which can lower the rate to around $150 a night—a pretty good deal for the county's fanciest digs.

50 Hillside Dr., Mammoth Lakes, CA 93546. © **866/716-8132** or 760/934-0400. www.westin.com/ mammoth. 230 units. $199–$395 double. Ski and golf packages available. AE, DC, DISC, MC, V. **Amenities:** Restaurant; bar; heated outdoor pool; fitness center; hot tub; children's programs; concierge; room service; underground parking. *In room:* TV/DVD, Wi-Fi, kitchen or kitchenette, fireplace, bathrobe.

WHERE TO DINE

Berger's Restaurant (**Value**) (**Kids**) AMERICAN   If, after a full day of skiing, you need a hearty American meal at a fair price, head down the mountain to Berger's. Its cabinlike interior, with local photos on the wooden walls, suits the surroundings. Portions are huge and include an array of burgers, steak, ribs, chicken, sandwiches, and hefty salads. Entrees come with salad, garlic bread, and either fries or a baked potato. Sandwiches, which cost up to $8 and come with salad and fries, will also easily fill you up without emptying your wallet. The children's menu is the ultimate bargain, offering a selection of kid-friendly feasts for under $6. The daily lunch specials are most coveted by locals, but if you want to try one, come early—they almost always sell out.

6118 Minaret Rd. © **760/934-6622**. Reservations recommended. Main courses $8.25–$15. MC, V. Daily 11:30am–8:30pm. Extended summer hours.

Grumpy's Saloon and Eatery ★ (Kids) AMERICAN   For more than 2 decades, Grumpy's has been Mammoth's main "sports restaurant"—a log building with 35 TVs, pool tables, pinball machines, video games, and foosball tables. The bar has a great selection of tap beers, and the hearty, affordable grub features burgers (go for the Grumpy Burger), tasty barbecued ribs, homemade chili, a few Mexican items, and the famous quarter-pound Dogger, an unbelievably enormous hot dog. Everything on the menu comes with a choice of fries, coleslaw, or barbecued baked beans. Stop by for happy hour, which usually features a free buffet of hors d'oeuvres that may include Buffalo wings, cheese and crackers, or miniquesadillas.

361 Mammoth Rd. © **760/934-8587**. www.grumpysmammoth.com. Main courses $6.25–$16. AE, MC, V. Mon–Sun 11am–10pm; bar stays open until 2am.

The Mono Inn at Mono Lake ★★ AMERICAN   Like the Restaurant at Convict Lake (see below), the Mono Inn at Mono Lake is a special dining experience, well worth the scenic 30-mile drive from Mammoth Lakes. What started as a high-desert health resort in 1922 was eventually converted into a restaurant and art gallery in 1997 by Sarah Adams, granddaughter of photographer Ansel Adams. It's now one of the finest restaurants in the region as well, offering a combination of craftsman-style rusticity, haute-hearty cuisine, and an eerily beautiful view of Mono Lake and the White Mountains (best seen during a full moon). Dishes are satisfying and well portioned, such as the braised lamb shank with roasted garlic mashed potatoes, flat iron steak with heirloom tomatoes and *chimichurri* sauce, and crispy-skin salmon served with couscous and roasted beets. Nightly vegetarian specials are available as well. Be sure to arrive a bit early to enjoy a cocktail in the upper-level gallery and peruse the original Ansel Adams photographs and panoramic lake view from the cocktail lounge. *Tip:* When making a reservation, be sure to request a window table overlooking the lake.

Hwy. 395, Mono Lake (4 miles north of Lee Vining). © **760/647-6581**. www.monoinn.com. Reservations recommended. Main courses $14–$32. AE, DISC, MC, V. Wed–Mon 5pm–closing (closed Oct 30–May 18).

Nevados ★★ EUROPEAN/CALIFORNIA   Nevados is one of Mammoth Lakes' best restaurants and a longtime favorite with the locals and Los Angelenos on their annual ski or summer holiday. Owner/host Tim Dawson is usually on hand nightly to ensure that everyone's satisfied with the innovative cuisine and house-baked breads. Most everyone orders the prix-fixe, three-course meal, which may consist of a strudel appetizer of wild mushrooms and rabbit with roasted shallots and grilled scallions; a main course of braised Provimi veal shank with roasted tomatoes and garlic mashed potatoes; and a warm pear-and-almond tart sweetened with caramel sauce and vanilla-bean ice cream for dessert. With its casual, sweet ambience (white tablecloths, and candles) and broad choice of wines and single-malt scotches, it's no wonder this is the hangout of choice for ski instructors and race coaches.

Main St. (at Minaret Rd.). © **760/934-4466**. Reservations recommended. Main courses $21–$30; fixed-price meal $40. AE, DC, DISC, MC, V. Daily 5:30–9:30pm.

The Restaurant at Convict Lake ★★ COUNTRY FRENCH   For years, this restaurant on the edge of Convict Lake was a local secret, but the word got out when *Wine Spectator* featured it. Now you'd better make reservations if you want to enjoy a meal in this plank-sided cabin with an open-beam ceiling, wood floors, copper-hooded freestanding fireplace, and mountain views. Five miles south of Mammoth Lakes, it's well worth the drive to spend a romantic evening feasting on Long Island duckling breast with fresh blackberries, panko-crusted Hawaiian sunfish in a lime-ginger-tamari-sesame Thai chili vinaigrette, or curried lamb shank served with basmati rice. Linger a bit longer to savor the bananas Foster flambé or a cheese wedge served with dry fruit. During the summer months you can even lunch under the aspens.

Convict Lake Rd. ℂ **760/934-3803.** www.convictlake.com. Reservations recommended. Main courses $22–$40. AE, MC, V. Summer daily 11am–2pm; year-round daily 5:30–9:30pm.

Shogun ★ JAPANESE   Sushi and tempura in an alpine setting may seem out of context, but this authentic Japanese restaurant, on the second floor of a strip mall, consistently packs in both tourists and locals. Diners at the eight-seat sushi bar sup on sashimi, hand rolls, and a variety of sushi creations. Delicate tempura, sweet and tangy teriyaki dishes, and grilled *yakitori* skewers come a la carte or as combination dinners. Hearty eaters can order the Boat Dinner, which includes beef and chicken teriyaki, tempura, *tonkatsu*, sashimi or salmon, and dessert for about $24 per person (minimum two people). Sake, beer, and cocktails are also available.

Old Mammoth Rd. (in the Sierra Center Mall). ℂ **760/934-3970.** Reservations recommended. Main courses $9–$19. AE, DC, DISC, MC, V. Mon–Sun 5–9:30pm.

Skadi ★★ ECLECTIC   Suitably named after the Viking goddess of skiing and hunting, Skadi is the domain of chef/owner Ian Algerøen, a former chef at Nevados. It's the perfect place for an après-ski cocktail at the 14-seat bar, a snack from the substantial selection of appetizers and desserts, or a full dinner. Skadi's big-city, postmodern aura is a welcome change after all that local alpine simplicity. Main courses include roasted maple leaf duck with Arctic lingonberries, or braised lamb shanks with rosemary-garlic mashed potatoes and garlic comfit. Finish with lemon *panna cotta* with fresh berries or frozen caramelized macadamia nut and vanilla bean parfait topped with chocolate sauce.

587 Old Mammoth Rd. (in the Sherwin Plaza III shopping mall). ℂ **760/934-3902.** www.restaurantskadi. com. Reservations recommended. Main courses $22–$32. AE, MC, V. Daily 5:30–10pm.

Whiskey Creek Mountain Bistro ★ AMERICAN   If you favor surf-and-turf fare in an alpine atmosphere with a swinging nightlife scene, make a reservation here. Whiskey Creek's wraparound windows proffer a pretty view of the snow-clad mountains, and the menu is known for its excellent South Carolina pork chops, bacon-wrapped meatloaf, and barbecued pork spareribs, all served with a heaping side of roasted garlic mashed potatoes. The dining room may be peaceful, but the upper-level brewpub is a different world. If you're not too stuffed, head upstairs to hear live music every night from 9pm until at least 1am, making it the number-one spot in town to hear cheesy pickup lines.

24 Lake Mary Rd. (at Minaret Rd.). ℂ **760/934-2555.** Reservations recommended. Main courses $16–$28. AE, DC, DISC, MC, V. Daily 5:30–10pm; bar stays open until 2am.

4 DEVILS POSTPILE NATIONAL MONUMENT ★

10 miles W of Mammoth; 50 miles E of Yosemite's eastern boundary

Just a few miles outside Mammoth Lakes, Devils Postpile National Monument is home to one of nature's most curious geological spectacles. Formed when molten lava cracked as it cooled, the 60-foot-high, blue-gray basalt columns that form the postpile look more like an enormous, eerie pipe organ or a jumble of string cheese than anything you'd expect to see made from stone. The mostly six-sided columns formed underground and were exposed when glaciers scoured the valley during the last ice age, some 10,000 years ago. Similar columnar basalt is found in Ireland and Scotland.

Because of its high elevation (7,900 ft.) and heavy snowfall, the monument is open only from summer until early fall. Summer weather is usually clear and warm, but afternoon thundershowers are common. Nights are cold, so bring good tents and sleeping bags if you're camping. Unfortunately, all those beautiful lakes attract lots of mosquitoes. Plan for them.

GETTING THERE

From late June to early September, cars are banned in the monument between 7:30am and 5:30pm, because the roads can't handle the traffic. Visitors must take a shuttle bus to and from locations in the monument. Although it takes some planning, the resulting peace and quiet warrant the trouble and make you wonder why the park service hasn't implemented similar programs at Yosemite Valley and other traffic hot spots.

VISITOR INFORMATION   For information before you go, call ⓒ 760/934-2289 during open season, or ⓒ 760/872-4881 from November to May. You'll also find plenty of info at **www.nps.gov/depo/depomain.htm**.

HIKING

Devils Postpile is more than an impressive bunch of rocks. On the banks of the San Joaquin River, amid granite peaks and crystalline mountain lakes, the 800-acre park is a gateway to a hiker's paradise. Short paths lead from here to the top of the postpile and to **Soda Springs,** a spring of cold carbonated water.

A longer hike (about 1.3 miles) from the separate Rainbow Falls Trail head will take you to spectacular **Rainbow Falls ★**, where the middle fork of the San Joaquin plunges 101 feet from a lava cliff. From the trail, a stairway and short trail lead to the base of the falls and swimming holes below.

The **Pacific Crest Trail** and the **John Muir Trail** (which connects Yosemite National Park with Kings Canyon and Sequoia national parks) run through here. Named after the conservationist and author who is largely credited with saving Yosemite and popularizing the Sierra Nevada as a place worth preserving, the 211-mile John Muir Trail traverses some of the most difficult, remote parts of the Sierra. You can access it from two points in Devils Postpile, either near the ranger station, or from the Rainbow Falls Trail head. From here, you can hike as far as your feet will take you north or south. ***Note:*** Mountain bikes are not permitted on trails.

While most visitors stay in or around Mammoth Lakes, the monument does maintain a 21-site campground with piped water, flush toilets, fire pits, and picnic tables on a first-come, first-served basis. Rates are $8 per night. Bears are common in the park, so take proper food-storage measures. Leashed pets are permitted on trails and in camp. Call the **National Park Service** (② **760/934-2289**, or *760/872-4881 Nov–May*; www.nps.gov/depo/depomain.htm) for details. Other nearby U.S. Forest Service campgrounds include **Red's Meadow** and **Upper Soda Springs.**

5 EN ROUTE TO SEQUOIA & KINGS CANYON

Visalia is the official "gateway" and the city closest to Sequoia and Kings Canyon national parks, but it's still 40 minutes to the park entrance. Much closer is the small town of **Three Rivers,** which, until recently, had a few mediocre restaurants, coffee shops, and motels for visitors. That's changing with the opening of the **Shoshone Inn,** which has added 60 more hotel rooms in Visalia, in addition to its two restaurants.

ESSENTIALS

GETTING THERE   If you're driving from San Francisco, take I-580 east to I-5 south to Highway 198 east. The trip takes about 5 hours.

   Amtrak (② **800/USA-RAIL;** www.amtrak.com) stops at nearby Hanford, and a shuttle runs from there to Visalia.

VISITOR INFORMATION   Contact the **Visalia Chamber of Commerce,** 220 N. Santa Fe Ave., Visalia, CA 93291 (② **559/734-5876;** www.visaliachamber.org).

WHERE TO STAY

In Three Rivers, try the **Comfort Inn & Suites,** 40820 Sierra Dr. (Hwy. 198), Three Rivers, CA 93271 (② **800/331-2140** or 559/561-9000; www.sequoiahotel.com). For other options, contact the **Reservation Centre** (② **866/561-0410** or 559/561-0410; www.rescentre.com).

Ben Maddox House ★★   On a residential street of Victorian homes, 5 blocks from the town's main street, the Ben Maddox House is an impressive sight: Its triangular gable is punctuated with a round window and two tall palm trees looming over the front yard. The house, built in 1876, is built of Sequoia redwood, and its rooms retain their original dark-oak trim and white-oak floors. The six guest rooms have 18th- and 19th-century furnishings, and the two front rooms have French doors leading to two small porch/sitting areas. A full made-to-order breakfast is part of the experience.

601 N. Encina St., Visalia, CA 93291. ② **800/401-9800** or 559/739-0721. Fax 559/739-0729. www.benmaddoxhouse.com. 4 units. $130–$160 double. Rates include breakfast. AE, DISC, MC, V. **Amenities:** Outdoor pool; nearby golf course. *In room:* A/C, TV w/free movies, fridge, hair dryer, iron.

Buckeye Tree Lodge ★ (Value)   A half-mile from the entrance to Sequoia National Park, this motel is a good choice for almost anyone. Rooms are affordable and attractive, the property has rolling lawns that lead to a picturesque river, and every room has a patio or balcony with splendid views. Rooms are clean, basic, motel units, with a king bed or two queen beds. Eight rooms have showers only; the rest have tub/shower combos.

46000 Sierra Dr., Three Rivers, CA 93271. ℭ **559/561-5900.** www.buckeyetree.com. 12 units. $79–$135 double. Rates include continental breakfast. AE, DC, DISC, MC, V. Pets accepted but must be declared when making reservations. **Amenities:** Outdoor pool. *In room:* A/C, TV, VCR (video rentals available), fridge, coffeemaker, microwave (in some rooms).

Lake Elowin Resort ★★ Undoubtedly one of the best places to stay in the Sierra, this is what a mountain resort should be—a place to get away from it all, without the distraction of phones and televisions. Rustic, clean cabins under huge trees look out at Lake Elowin, a small body of water where guests can fish, above the Kaweah River. Milton Melkonian purchased the resort in the 1970s with the idea of creating a place to coexist with nature, and he is fastidious about his property, which now attracts writers, artists, and other creative types. Cabins can accommodate two to six people. I especially like cabin no. 1, close to the lake with a pretty view from the kitchen window; and Master Cabin, with a fireplace, deck, and Jacuzzi. All cabins include linens and towels, pots and pans, kitchen utensils, and barbecues. The entire property is nonsmoking; guests actually sign a contract that they won't smoke here.

43840 Dineley Dr., Three Rivers, CA 93271. ℭ **559/561-3460.** Fax 559/561-1300. www.lake-elowin.com. 10 cabins with showers only. $120–$315 double. AE, DISC, MC, V. From eastbound Sierra Dr. in Three Rivers, about 2½ miles before the park entrance, turn left on Dineley Dr. (the street sign says DINLEY) and drive across a bridge. Bear right, and it's less than ½ mile to the resort's driveway. **Amenities:** Swimming hole; free canoe use. *In room:* A/C, no phone.

Plantation Bed & Breakfast ★★★ Step into the Old South at this fun bed-and-breakfast, where the inspiration for the room names and decor comes from *Gone With the Wind.* For a quietly conservative atmosphere, request the Ashley Wilkes Room, with a king bed. Honeymooners might enjoy the luxurious Scarlett O'Hara Room, with a king bed, velvet love seat, fireplace, and marble bathroom with a Jacuzzi and separate shower. My favorite is the Belle Watling Room, done up in an elegant bordello style, with a king-size bed with an enormous mirror next to it, a red crystal chandelier, and a clawfoot bathtub with a tasteful, Renaissance-style nude painted on the side. Three rooms have showers only, while the others have showers and tubs.

33038 Hwy. 198, Lemon Cove, CA 93244 (on Hwy. 198, 16 miles west of the park entrance). ℭ **800/240-1466** or 559/597-2555. Fax 559/597-2551. www.plantationbnb.com. 8 units. $139–$229 double. Rates include full breakfast. AE, DC, DISC, MC, V. **Amenities:** Large pool; Jacuzzi; computer in common area. *In room:* A/C, TV, VCR (most rooms), no phone.

WHERE TO DINE

The Vintage Press ★★ AMERICAN/CONTINENTAL This has long been considered the best restaurant in a 100-mile radius, a bastion of culinary merit in the gastronomic wasteland between Los Angeles and San Francisco. The design is reminiscent of a *fin de siècle* gin mill in Gold Rush San Francisco, with a bar imported from that city, manufactured by the Brunswick Company (of bowling-alley fame); antiques bought at local auctions; and glittering panels of leaded glass and mirrors. The place is big enough (250 seats) to feed a boatload of Gold Rush hopefuls, and a pianist plays Thursday through Saturday, from 5:30 to 9pm, at the bustling bar and lounge.

The menu is supplemented by daily specials, such as a zesty rack of lamb roasted in a cabernet sauce with rosemary. The regular menu offers about a dozen meat and fish dishes, with steaks as well as choices such as pistachio-crusted king salmon with potato gratin; or pork tenderloin with Dijon mustard, red chile, and honey. To start, I recommend farm-raised fresh oysters on the half shell or the wild mushrooms with cognac in puff pastry. The restaurant's wine cellar, a winner of the *Wine Spectator* Award of Excellence, offers more than 1,000 selections.

216 N. Willis St., Visalia. © **559/733-3033.** www.thevintagepress.com. Reservations recommended at dinner. Main courses $12–$17 lunch, $17–$37 dinner. AE, DC, MC, V. Mon–Sat 11:30am–2pm and 5:30–10pm; Sun 10am–2pm and 5–9pm.

6 SEQUOIA & KINGS CANYON NATIONAL PARKS ★★

30 miles E of Visalia

Only 200 road miles separate Yosemite from Sequoia and Kings Canyon national parks, but they're worlds apart. While the National Park Service has taken every opportunity to modernize, accessorize, and urbanize Yosemite, resulting in a frenetic tourist scene, at Sequoia and Kings Canyon, they've treated the wilderness with respect and care. Only one road, the Generals Highway, loops through the area, and no road traverses the Sierra here. The park service recommends that vehicles over 22 feet long avoid the steep and windy stretch between Potwisha Campground and the Giant Forest in Sequoia National Park. Generally speaking, the park is much less accessible by car than most, but spectacular for those willing to head out on foot.

 Tips **Fill It Up**

Note that neither park has a gas station, so fill up your tank before you enter.

The Sierra Nevada tilts upward as it runs south. **Mount Whitney,** at 14,494 feet (the highest point in the Lower 48), is just one of many high peaks in Sequoia and Kings Canyon. The **Pacific Crest Trail** also reaches its highest point here, crossing north to south through both parks. In addition to snow-covered peaks, Sequoia and Kings Canyon are home to the largest groves of giant sequoias in the Sierra Nevada, as well as the headwaters of the Kern, Kaweah, and Kings rivers. A few high-country lakes are home to some of the only remaining pure-strain golden trout. Bears, deer, and numerous smaller animals and birds depend on the parks' miles and miles of wild habitat for year-round breeding and feeding grounds.

Technically, Sequoia and Kings Canyon are two separate but contiguous parks, managed jointly from the park headquarters at Ash Mountain, just past the entrance on Highway 198 east of Visalia.

ESSENTIALS

Most visitors make a loop through the parks by entering at Grant Grove and leaving through Ash Mountain, or vice versa.

VISITOR INFORMATION The parks have three major visitor centers open year-round, some seasonal facilities, and a museum where you can buy books and maps and discuss your plans with park rangers. In Sequoia National Park, the largest is **Foothills Visitor Center** (© **559/565-3135**), inside the Ash Mountain Entrance on Highway 198. Exhibits focus on the Sierra foothills, a biologically diverse ecosystem. The **Giant Forest Museum** (© **559/565-4480**) is housed in a historic building and offers exhibits on giant sequoias. **Lodgepole Visitor Center** (© **559/565-4436**) includes exhibits on geology, wildlife, air quality, and park history. It's 4¹/₂ miles north of Giant Forest Village,

(Tips) **Marmot Invasion**

Check under your hood before leaving a parking lot. Marmots, especially in the Mineral King area, love munching on car hoses and wiring, leaving a trail of disabled vehicles in their wake. A good number of them have stowed away in a car's engine compartment and hitched rides with unsuspecting drivers to other parts of the parks; several have ridden as far as Southern California.

and it's closed Tuesday through Thursday in winter. The visitor center in **Grant Grove,** Kings Canyon National Park (☎ **559/565-4307**), includes exhibits on logging and the role of fire in the forests. Open only in summer, a small visitor center at **Cedar Grove** in Kings Canyon and a ranger station at Sequoia's **Mineral King** dispense backcountry permits as well as information.

To research before you go, see www.nps.gov/seki, www.sequoia-kingscanyon.com, www.sequoiahistory.org, or www.visitsequoia.com, or call ☎ **559/565-3341.**

FEES & PERMITS A $20 fee per car or $10 per person on foot, bike, motorcycle or bus, is good for 7 days' entry at any park entrance. An annual pass costs $30. Wilderness permits are required for overnight backpacking in the parks. You can reserve the $15 permits in advance by downloading an application from the national park website at **www.nps.gov/seki** and mailing or faxing it to the **Wilderness Permit Office,** 47050 Generals Hwy. #60, Three Rivers, CA 93271 (☎ **559/565-3766;** fax 559/565-4239).

REGULATIONS Mountain bikes and dogs are forbidden on all park trails (dogs are permitted in developed areas but must be leashed). The park service allows firewood gathering at campgrounds, although supplies can be scarce. Removing wood from living or standing trees is forbidden.

THE SEASONS In the high altitudes, where most Sequoia and Kings Canyon visitors are headed, summers are short and winters are cold. Snow in July and August is rare but not unheard of. At mid-elevations, where the sequoias grow, spring can come as early as April or as late as June. Afternoon showers are occasional. In winter, only the main roads into the parks are usually open; the climate ranges from bitter cold to pleasant and can change by the minute. The Generals Highway, between Sequoia and Kings Canyon, closes for plowing during and after snowstorms. Be ready for anything if you head into the backcountry on skis. In summer, poison oak and rattlesnakes are common in lower elevations, and mosquitoes abound in all wet areas.

AVOIDING THE CROWDS To escape the crowds and see less-used areas of the parks, enter on one of the dead-end roads to Mineral King or Cedar Grove (both open only in summer), or South Fork. Without traffic, these parts of the parks are incredibly peaceful, even at full capacity, and gateways to some of the best hiking.

EXPLORING THE PARKS

The second-oldest national park in the U.S., Sequoia National Park was created in 1890 at the request of San Joaquin Valley residents concerned with the conservation of giant redwoods. The park has some 75 groves of giant sequoias, but the best places to see them are **Grant Grove** ★, in Kings Canyon, near the park entrance on Highway 180 from

> **(Fun Facts) A Question of Size**
>
> Until recently, the National Park Service claimed that the General Sherman Tree
> was the largest living thing on earth. Technically, though, this may not be true;
> now the claim is that it's the largest living *tree*—which is still quite a distinction.
> The reason for the change? Park officials say some underground fungi may actu-
> ally be larger, and groves of aspen trees share a common root system, making
> them one living thing, also bigger than the General.

Fresno, or **Giant Forest** ★, a huge enclave of trees with 40 miles of footpaths, 16 miles
from the entrance to Sequoia National Park on Highway 198.

The 2-mile **Congress Trail** loop in Giant Forest starts at the base of the **General Sherman Tree** ★, reputedly the largest living tree in the world. Single branches are more than
7 feet thick. Each year it grows enough wood to make a 60-foot-tall tree of normal
dimensions. Other trees in the grove are nearly as large; many of them, however peaceful-
looking they may be, bear militaristic and political monikers such as General Lee. Longer
trails lead to remote reaches of the grove and nearby meadows.

Unlike the coast redwoods, which reproduce by sprouting or by seeds, giant sequoias
only reproduce by seed. Adult sequoias rarely die of diseases and are protected from most
fire by thick bark. The huge trees have surprisingly shallow roots, and most die from
toppling when their roots are damaged and can no longer support them. These groves,
like the ones in Yosemite, were explored by conservationist and nature writer John Muir,
who named the Giant Forest.

Besides the sequoia groves, Sequoia and Kings Canyon are home to the Sierra Nevada's
most pristine wilderness. At **Road's End** on the Kings Canyon Highway (late May to
early Nov), you can stand by the Kings River and stare up at granite walls rising thousands of feet above the river, the deepest canyon in the United States.

Near Giant Forest Village, **Moro Rock** is a 6,725-foot-tall granite dome formed by
the exfoliation of rock layers. A quarter-mile trail scales the dome for a spectacular view
of the adjacent Canyon of the Middle Fork of the Kaweah. The trail gains 300 feet in
1,200 feet, so be ready for a climb.

Crystal Cave ★ is 15 miles from the Highway 198 park entrance; cave parking is
another 7 miles. Here you can take a 45-minute tour of Crystal's beautiful marble interior. The tour is $11 for adults, $10 for seniors, $6 for children ages 6 to 12, and free for
kids under 6. Tickets are not sold at the cave. Purchase them at the Lodgepole or Foothills visitor centers at least 1½ hours in advance. Wear sturdy shoes and bring a jacket.
For information, call ℭ **559/565-3759** or see **www.sequoiahistory.org**. The cave is
open mid-May to late October daily from 11am to 4pm.

Boyden Cavern, on Highway 180 in neighboring Sequoia National Forest, is a cave
where you can take an $11 45-minute tour to see stalactites and stalagmites. Call ℭ **866/
762-2837** or 209/736-2708 for details, or see **www.caverntours.com**. The cave is open
April through November daily from 10am to 5pm.

HIKING THE PARKS

Hiking and backpacking are what these parks are all about. Some 700 miles of trails
connect canyons, lakes, and high alpine meadows and snowfields.

When traveling overnight inside parks boundaries, overnight and/or day-use permits are required. If you want to do serious overnight backpacking, see "Fees & Permits" under "Essentials," above.

Some of the park's most impressive hikes start in the **Mineral King** section in the southern end of Sequoia. Beginning at 7,800 feet, trails lead onward and upward to destinations such as Sawtooth Pass, Crystal Lake, and the old White Chief Trail to the now-defunct White Chief Mine. Once an unsuccessful silver-mining town in the 1870s, Mineral King was the center of a battle in the late 1970s when developers sought to build a huge ski resort. They were defeated when Congress added Mineral King to Sequoia National Park, and the wilderness remains.

The **John Muir Trail,** which begins in Yosemite Valley, ends at Mount Whitney. For many miles it coincides with the **Pacific Crest Trail** as it skirts the highest peaks in the park. This is the most difficult part of the Pacific Crest, above 10,000 feet most of the time and crossing 12,000-foot-tall passes.

Other hikers like to explore the northern part of Kings Canyon from **Cedar Grove** and **Road's End.** The **Paradise Valley Trail,** leading to beautiful Mist Falls, is a fairly easy day trip by park standards. The **Copper Creek Trail** immediately rises into the high wilderness around Granite Pass at 10,673 feet, one of the most strenuous day hikes in the parks.

If the altitude and steepness are too much for you at these trail heads, try some of the longer hikes in **Giant Forest** or **Grant Grove.** These forests are woven with interlocking loops that allow you to take as short or as long a hike as you want. The 6-mile **Trail of the Sequoias** in Giant Forest will take you to the grove's far-eastern end, where you'll find some of the finest trees. In Grant Grove, a 100-foot walk through the hollow trunk of the **Fallen Monarch** makes a fascinating side trip. The tree has been used for shelter for more than 100 years and is tall enough inside that you can walk through without bending over.

Perhaps the most traversed trail to the park is the **Whitney Portal Trail.** It runs east of Sequoia near Lone Pine, through Inyo National Forest, to Sequoia's boundary, the summit of Mount Whitney. Though it's a straightforward walk to the summit and it's possible to do it in a long day hike, you'd better be in tip-top shape before attempting it. Almost half the people who attempt Whitney, including those who camp partway up, don't reach the summit. Weather, altitude, and fatigue can stop even the most prepared party. For more information, contact the **Mount Whitney Ranger Station** at ℭ **760/876-6200.** For wilderness permits, see "Fees & Permits" at the beginning of this section.

The official park map and guide has good road maps for the parks, but for serious hiking you'll want to check out *Sierra South: 100 Back-Country Trips,* by Thomas Winnett and Jason Winnett (Wilderness Press). Another good guide is *Kings Canyon Country,* a hiking handbook by Ginny and Lew Clark (Western Trails Publications). The Grant Grove, Lodgepole, Cedar Grove, Foothills, and Mineral King visitor centers sell a complete selection of maps and guidebooks. Books and maps are also available by mail through the **Sequoia Natural History Association** (ℭ **559/565-3759;** www.sequoia history.org).

OTHER OUTDOOR PURSUITS

FISHING The **Kaweah** drainage, the parks' lakes, and a section of the south fork of the **Kings River** are open all year for trout fishing (rainbow, brook, German brown, and golden). Most other waters are open for trout fishing from late April to mid-November, and for other species year-round. California fishing licenses (available at stores in the park) are required for anglers 16 and older, and you should also get a copy of the National Park Service's fishing regulations, available at visitor centers.

HORSEBACK RIDING   Concessionaires in both parks and the adjacent national monument during the summer run guided horseback and mule rides and overnight pack trips. In Kings Canyon, **Cedar Grove Pack Station** (© **559/565-3464** summer, 559/337-2314 winter) is a mile east of Cedar Grove Village; and **Grant Grove Stables** (© **559/335-9292** summer, 559/337-2314 winter) is near Grant Grove Village. In Giant Sequoia National Monument, **Horse Corral Pack Station** is on Big Meadows Road, 10 miles east of Generals Highway (© **559/565-3404** summer, 209/742-6400 winter; www.horsecorralpackers.com). The pack stations offer hourly rides as well as overnight treks, while the stables offer day-rides only. Rates range from $45 for a half-day ride to $75 for a full day in the saddle; call for current charges for pack trips.

RAFTING & KAYAKING   Only fairly recently have professional outfitters begun taking experienced rafters and kayakers down the Class 4 and 5 Kaweah and Upper Kings rivers outside the parks. Check the **Reservation Center** website at **www.rescentre.com** for a good list of companies running trips. Rafting and kayaking here are only for the very adventurous.

SKIING & SNOWSHOEING   **Wolverton,** 2 miles north of the General Sherman tree, has a snow-play and cross-country ski area. You can rent skis and snowshoes at the Lodgepole Market. About 50 miles of marked, cross-country trails run through the **Giant Forest** and **Grant Grove** areas. Rangers offer naturalist talks and snowshoe walks some weekends. Rental equipment (including snowshoes) and lessons are available at the Grant Grove Market. For more information on cross-country skiing, sledding, or snowshoeing at Grant Grove, call the visitor center at © **559/565-4307;** for Wolverton, call © **559/565-3435.** Kids can sled and play in the snow-play areas near Wolverton and at Big Stump, Columbine, and Azalea in Grant Grove.

The Sequoia Natural History Association operates the **Pear Lake Ski Hut** for snowshoers and cross-country skiers, which can accommodate up to 10 people. Use of the facility is by lottery. For further information, call © **559/565-3759.**

WHITE-WATER BOATING   The **Kaweah** and **Upper Kings** rivers in the parks are not open to boating (neither kayaks nor inflatable rafts), but several companies run trips just outside the parks. You're guaranteed to get wet, but this roller-coaster ride through the rapids is thrilling, and a great way to experience these scenic rivers. **Kaweah White Water Adventures** (© **800/229-8658** or 559/561-1000; www.kaweah-whitewater.com) runs Class 3, 4, and 5 trips (rated moderate to difficult) on the Kaweah River from spring to early fall. Prices range from about $95 per person for a half-day trip to $140 (with lunch) for the day. **Whitewater Voyages** (© **800/400-7238;** www.whitewatervoyages.com) runs trips on the Kaweah, Kings, Kern, and Merced rivers, with rates around $140 to $200 (including lunch) for full-day trips; multiday trips are also available (call for rates). **Kings River Expeditions** (© **800/846-3674** or 559/233-4881; www.kingsriver.com) specializes in rafting trips on the Kings. For 1-day trips, they charge $90 to $199 in spring, and $130 to $260 from mid-May until the season ends. Overnight trips are also available (call for rates).

CAMPING

Backpackers will find numerous camping opportunities in and around Sequoia and Kings Canyon national parks. It's important to remember that when camping in this

In Sequoia National Park

The only national park campgrounds that accept reservations are Dorst and Lodgepole (*C* 800/365-2267; http://reservations.nps.gov), which will do so up to 5 months in advance; the other campgrounds are first-come, first-served. Additional information on the national park campgrounds (but not reservations) can be obtained by calling the general Sequoia/Kings Canyon information line at *C* 559/565-3341.

The two biggest campgrounds in the park are in the Lodgepole area. The **Lodgepole Campground,** with flush toilets, is often crowded, but it's pretty and near some spectacular big trees. Nearby backcountry trails offer some solitude. Close to the ground are a grocery store, restaurant, visitor center, children's nature center, evening ranger programs, and gift shop. From Giant Forest, drive 5 miles northeast on the Generals Highway.

Dorst Campground, 14 miles northwest of Giant Forest via the Generals Highway, is a high-elevation campground with easy access to Muir Grove and some pleasant backcountry trails. It has flush toilets and evening ranger programs. Group campsites are also available here by reservation.

In the Foothills, **Potwisha Campground** is small, with well-spaced sites tucked beneath oak trees along the Marble Fork of the Kaweah River. The campground has flush toilets, but it gets very hot in summer. From the Ash Mountain Entrance, drive 3 miles northeast on the Generals Highway to the campground entrance. The **Buckeye Flat Campground** ★, open to tents only, is also set among oaks along the Middle Fork of the Kaweah River. It also gets hot in summer, but it's among our favorites for its scenery and flush toilets. From the Ash Mountain Entrance, drive about 6 miles northeast on the Generals Highway to the Hospital Rock Ranger Station. From there, follow signs to the campground, which is several miles down a narrow, winding road. **South Fork Campground** is the smallest and most remote campground in the park, just inside Sequoia's southwestern boundary. It is set along the South Fork of the Kaweah River and has pit toilets only. From the town of Three Rivers, go east on South Fork Road 23 miles to the campground.

The two campgrounds in the Mineral King area are open to tents only—no RVs or trailers. **Atwell Mill Campground** is a pretty, small campground, near the East Fork of the Kaweah River, at Atwell Creek, with pit toilets. From Three Rivers, take Mineral King Road east for 20 miles to the campground. **Cold Springs Campground,** which also has pit toilets, is beautiful but not very accessible. Once you get there, however, you'll be rewarded with beautiful scenery. It's also a good starting point for many backcountry hikes, given its proximity to the Mineral King Ranger Station. From Three Rivers, take Mineral King Road east for 25 miles to the campground.

In Kings Canyon National Park

All the campgrounds in Kings Canyon are first-come, first-served (no reservations), and all have flush toilets. More information can be obtained by calling the general Sequoia/Kings Canyon information line at *C* 559/565-3341.

The Grant Grove area has three attractive campgrounds near the big trees—**Azalea, Crystal Springs,** and **Sunset.** All have a nice woodsy feel, they're close to park facilities, and they offer evening ranger programs. To get to them from the Big Stump Entrance, take Highway 180 east about 1³/₄ miles.

The Cedar Grove Village area has several campgrounds, all accessed from Highway 180. All are fairly close to the facilities in Cedar Grove Village. **Sentinel,** the first to open for the season, fills up quickly. **Moraine** is the farthest from the crowds. **Sheep Creek,** along picturesque Sheep Creek, opens as needed.

WHERE TO STAY IN THE PARKS

Cedar Grove Lodge ★   This motel offers comfortable rooms on the bank of the Kings River. Getting here is half the fun—it's a 36-mile drive down a winding highway with beautiful vistas along the way. The rooms here are standard motel accommodations—clean and comfortable, but nothing special. What you're really paying for is the location, surrounded by tall trees with a pretty river running by. Most of the rooms are above the Cedar Grove Café, with communal decks with river views. I prefer the three smaller, less attractively appointed rooms on the ground level, with private patios looking onto the river.

Hwy. 180, Cedar Grove, Kings Canyon National Park (mail: Sequoia Kings Canyon Park Services Co., 5755 E. Kings Canyon Rd., Ste. 101, Fresno, CA 93727). ℂ **866/522-6966** or 559/522-6966. Fax 559/335-5507. www.sequoia-kingscanyon.com. 18 units. $119–$180 double. AE, DISC, MC, V. *In room:* A/C, fridge and microwave (ground-floor rooms only), no phone.

Grant Grove Cabins ⓥⓐⓛⓤⓔ   Although all the accommodations here are cabins, they offer a wide range of amenities and prices, from handsomely restored cabins that ooze history, with private bathrooms, to primitive tent-cabins that simply provide a comfortable bed and shelter at a very low price. Those who want to "rough it" in style should reserve one of the nine cabins, built in the 1920s, that have electricity, indoor plumbing, and full private bathrooms. A bit less modern, but still quite comfortable, the 43 basic cabins have kerosene lanterns for light and a shared bathhouse. Some are wooden; others, available in summer only, have wood floors and walls but canvas roofs. All cabins have full linen service. It's a 10-minute walk from the cabins to the Grant Grove visitor center, and the Grant Grove Restaurant is also nearby.

Hwy. 180, Grant Grove Village, Kings Canyon National Park (mail: Sequoia Kings Canyon Park Services Co., 5755 E. Kings Canyon Rd., Ste. 101, Fresno, CA 93727). ℂ **866/522-6966** or 559/522-6966. Fax 559/335-5507. www.sequoia-kingscanyon.com. 53 units, 9 with private bathroom. $62–$140 cabin. Register at Grant Grove Village Registration Center, btw. the restaurant and gift shop. AE, DISC, MC, V. *In room:* No phone.

John Muir Lodge ★★   This handsome log lodge, built in 1998, looks perfect in its beautiful national-park setting. It's an excellent choice for visitors who want quiet, comfortable, modern rooms, with full bathrooms and coffeemakers, in a forest environment. Standard rooms have two queen-size beds and wonderful views of the surrounding forest. A mountain lodge atmosphere prevails. Suites consist of two connecting standard rooms, but one of the rooms has a queen bed and a queen sofa sleeper instead of two queens.

Hwy. 180, Grant Grove Village, Kings Canyon National Park (mail: Sequoia Kings Canyon Park Services Co., 5755 E. Kings Canyon Rd., Ste. 101, Fresno, CA 93727). ℂ **866/522-6966** or 559/522-6966. Fax 559/335-5507. www.sequoia-kingscanyon.com. 36 units. $89–$180 standard room; $270 suite. Register at Grant Grove Village Registration Center, btw. the restaurant and gift shop. AE, DISC, MC, V. *In room:* Coffeemaker.

Silver City Mountain Resort ★   Three types of cabins are available here, with a variety of bed combinations (some cabins sleep up to eight) and wood stoves for heat. Wood is provided, along with blankets and pillows, but guests need to bring their own sheets, pillowcases, bath and kitchen towels, paper towels, and tall trash bags. The top- of-the-line Swiss Chalets are finished in knotty pine with completely equipped kitchens, full bathrooms, Internet access, and an outdoor barbecue. The midlevel units, dubbed Comfy Cabins, are two-bedroom units with complete kitchens, propane wall lamps and electric lights, small restrooms with toilets but no showers (you'll have to make do with the centrally located bathhouse), and decks with barbecue grills. Rustic Cabins, which were built in the 1930s, are the most basic units, with light from propane lamps, a camp kitchen with a gas stove and an oven, a cold-water sink, and an outdoor deck with barbecue.

Mineral King, Sequoia National Park (mail: PO Box 56, Three Rivers, CA 93271). © **559/561-3223,** or 805/461-3223 in winter. Fax 805/461-3116. www.silvercityresort.com. 14 cabins, 7 with shared central bathhouse. $130–$395 double (2–8 guests). Discounts June 1–15 and after Sept 18. MC, V. Closed Nov–May. Take Hwy. 198 through Three Rivers to the Mineral King turnoff. Silver City is a little more than halfway btw. Lookout Point and Mineral King. **Amenities:** Restaurant; bakery; mountain store/gift shop.

Sacramento & the Gold Country

by Matthew Richard Poole

On the morning of January 24, 1848, carpenter James Marshall was working on John Sutter's mill in Coloma when he stumbled upon a gold nugget on the south fork of the American River. Despite Sutter's wishes to keep the discovery a secret, word leaked out—a word that would change the fate of California almost overnight: *Gold!*

The news spread like wildfire, and a frenzy seized the nation: The Gold Rush was on. Within 3 years, the population of the state exploded, from 15,000 to more than 265,000. Most newcomers were single men under the age of 40, and not far behind were the merchants, bankers, and women who made their fortunes catering to the miners, most of whom went bust in their search for wealth.

Sacramento quickly grew as a supply town at the base of the goldfields. The Gold Country boom lasted less than a decade; the supply was quickly exhausted, and many towns shrank or disappeared. Sacramento, however, continued to grow as the fertile Central Valley south of it exploited another source of wealth, becoming the vegetable-and-fruit garden of the nation.

A trip along Highway 49 from the northern mines to the southern mines conveys a sense of what life was like on the mining frontier. Many of the towns along this route seem frozen in time, down to Main Street with its raised wooden sidewalks, double porches, saloons, and Victorian storefronts. Each town tells a similar story of sudden wealth and explosive growth, yet each has also left behind its own unique imprint. Any fan of movie Westerns will recognize the setting, given that hundreds, perhaps even thousands, of films have been shot in these parts.

At the base of the Gold Country's hills is the sprawling, flat Central Valley. Some 240 miles long and 50 miles wide, it's California's agricultural breadbasket, the source of bounty shipped across the nation and overseas. A lot of state history has revolved around the struggle for control of the water used to irrigate the valley and make this inland desert bloom. Yes, despite its aridity, a breathtaking panorama of orange and pistachio groves, grapevines, and strawberry fields stretches uninterrupted for miles.

1 SACRAMENTO ★

90 miles E of San Francisco; 383 miles N of Los Angeles

Sacramento, with a metro-area population of nearly 1.8 million, is one of the state's fastest-growing areas. Visitors and locals alike enjoy a day spent walking through Old Sacramento, floating down the American River, or biking the shady paths along the

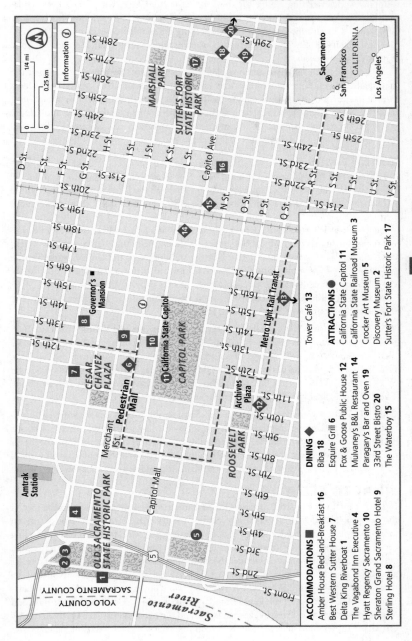

ACCOMMODATIONS ■
Amber House Bed-and-Breakfast **16**
Best Western Sutter House **7**
The Vagabond Inn Executive **4**
Hyatt Regency Sacramento **10**
Sheraton Grand Sacramento Hotel **9**
Sterling Hotel **8**

DINING ◆
Biba **18**
Esquire Grill **6**
Fox & Goose Public House **12**
Mulvaney's B&L Restaurant **14**
Paragary's Bar and Oven **19**
33rd Street Bistro **20**
The Waterboy **15**
Tower Café **13**

ATTRACTIONS ●
California State Capitol **11**
California State Railroad Museum **3**
Crocker Art Museum **5**
Discovery Museum **2**
Sutter's Fort State Historic Park **17**

Delta King Riverboat **1**

Sacramento and American rivers. In addition to being the state capital, it's a thriving shipping and processing center for the fruit, vegetables, rice, wheat, and dairy goods produced in the Central Valley. It's also become a receptacle of spillover from Silicon Valley, and a suburb for Bay Area workers seeking affordable homes. As such, the quantity and quality of downtown restaurants, such as the Esquire Grill and the Waterboy, have greatly improved.

Visitors are often surprised and how pretty the River City's downtown area is, with its tree-shaded streets lined with some impressive Victorians and well-crafted bungalows. And at its heart sits the majestic capitol building—Sacramento's most visible attraction—situated within a large park, replete with flower gardens, memorial statuary, and curious squirrels. Inside the capitol, visitors strain to get a glimpse of California's movie star governor, Arnold "The Governator" Schwarzenegger.

ESSENTIALS

GETTING THERE If you're driving from San Francisco, Sacramento is about 90 miles east on I-80. From Los Angeles, take I-5 through the Central Valley directly into Sacramento. From North Lake Tahoe, get on I-80 west, and from South Lake Tahoe take U.S. 50.

Sacramento International Airport (© **916/929-5411**), 12 miles northwest of downtown Sacramento, is served by about a dozen airlines, including Alaska Airlines, American, America West, Continental, Delta, Northwest, Southwest, and United. **SuperShuttle** (© **800/258-3826**) runs from the airport to downtown for a flat rate of $14 to the capital, a bargain compared to the $25 a conventional taxi would cost.

Amtrak (© **800/USA-RAIL;** www.amtrak.com) trains serve Sacramento daily. The Greyhound terminal is at Seventh and L streets.

VISITOR INFORMATION The **Sacramento Convention and Visitors Bureau,** 1608 I St., Sacramento, CA 95814 (© **916/808-7777;** www.discovergold.org), provides plenty of information for travelers. It's open Monday through Friday from 8am to 5pm. Once in the city, you can also stop by the **Old Sacramento Visitor Center,** 1004 Second St. (© **916/442-7644**), in Old Sacramento; it's usually open daily from 10am to 5pm. The city's major daily paper is the *Sacramento Bee* (www.sacbee.com).

ORIENTATION Suburbia sprawls around Sacramento, but its downtown area is relatively compact. Getting around the city is made easy by a gridlike pattern of streets designated by numbers or letters. The capitol, on 10th Street between N and L streets, is the key landmark. From the front of the capitol, M Street—at this point called Capitol Mall—runs 10 straight blocks to Old Sacramento, the oldest section of the city.

WHAT TO SEE & DO

In town, you'll want to stroll around **Old Sacramento** ★, 4 square blocks at the foot of the downtown area that have become a major tourist attraction. These blocks contain more than 100 restored buildings (California's largest restoration project), including restaurants and shops. Although the area has cobblestone streets, wooden sidewalks, and authentic Gold Rush–era architecture, the high concentration of T-shirt shops and other gimmicky stores has turned it into a sort of historical amusement park. Nonetheless, there are interesting things to see, such as where the Pony Express ended and the transcontinental railroad—and the Republican Party—began. The **California State Railroad Museum** (see below) is loved by railroad buffs, and the **Sacramento Jazz Festival,** mostly Dixieland, draws more than 100 bands from around the world for 4 days of madness over

Where the Wild Things Are

The best place to take little kids to let them tear around on a sunny afternoon is **Fairytale Town,** at William Land Park, Land Park Drive and Sutterville Road (© **916/264-5233;** www.fairytaletown.org). Although the slides and other climbing toys are pretty basic and show their age, kids seem to think it's the best place in the world. Across the street, at the **Sacramento Zoo** (© **916/808-5888;** www.saczoo.com), buy some cotton candy, and see the animals. Adjacent to Fairytale Town, there's also the small but pleasant **Funderland** amusement park (© **916/456-0115;** www.funderlandpark.com), with kid-size rides, open all week in summer months and on spring and fall weekends, weather permitting.

Memorial Day weekend. While you're meandering, stop at the **Discovery Museum & History Center** ★ at 101 I St. (© **916/264-7057;** www.thediscovery.org), which houses exhibits of California's history, highlighting the valley's agricultural Gold Rush and the real one in 1849. It's open Tuesday through Sunday from 10am to 5pm (daily July–Aug). Entry is $5 for adults, $4 for seniors over 60 and kids ages 13 to 17, $3 for kids 4 to 12, and free for kids 3 and under.

The Main Attractions

California State Capitol ★★★   Closely resembling a scale model of the U.S. Capitol in Washington, D.C., the beautiful, domed California state capitol was built in 1869 and renovated in 1976. Sacramento's most distinctive landmark, the capitol has been the stage of many political dramas in California history. The 1-hour guided tours provide insight into the architecture and the workings of the government it houses. *Note:* Security will ask you to put your purse or backpack through a metal detector.

10th St. (btw. N and L sts.). © **916/324-0333.** www.capitolmuseum.ca.gov. Free admission. Daily 9am–5pm. Tours offered every hour on the hour until 4pm. Closed Thanksgiving, Dec 25, and Jan 1.

California State Railroad Museum ★★★ (Kids)   With its 105 shiny antique locomotives and rail cars, this museum is the highlight of Old Sacramento. Over half a million people visit each year, and even the hordes of schoolchildren that typically mob this place shouldn't dissuade you from visiting one of the largest and best railroad museums in the country. Allow about 2 hours to see it all. From April to September, on weekends and holidays from 11am to 5pm, **steam locomotive rides** carry passengers 6 miles along the Sacramento River. Trains depart on the hour from the Central Pacific Freight Depot in Old Sacramento, at K and Front streets. Fares are $8 for adults, $3 for children 6 to 17, and free for children under 6.

125 I St. (at Second St.). © **916/445-6645.** www.californiastaterailroadmuseum.org. Admission $8 adults, $3 children 6–17, free for children 5 and under. Daily 10am–5pm. Closed Thanksgiving, Dec 25, and Jan 1.

Crocker Art Museum ★   This museum houses an outstanding collection of California art, as well as changing exhibits from around the world. It's in an imposing century-old Italianate building, with an ornate interior of carved and inlaid woods. The Crocker

Mansion Wing, the museum's most recent addition, is modeled after the Crocker family home and contains works by Northern California artists from 1945 to the present. Plan to spend about an hour here.

216 O St. (at Third St.). © **916/264-5423.** www.crockerartmuseum.org. Free on Sun 10am–1pm. Admission $6 adults, $4 seniors 65 and over, $3 students with ID, free for children 6 and under. Tues–Sun 10am–5pm; Thurs 10am–9pm. Closed major holidays.

Sutter's Fort State Historic Park ★   John Sutter established this outpost in 1839, and the park, restored to its 1846 appearance, aims to recapture the spirit of 19th-century California. Exhibits include a blacksmith's forge, cooperage, bakery, and jail—and a self-guided audio tour is available. Demonstrations and reenactments in costume are staged daily Memorial Day to Labor Day.

2701 L St. © **916/445-4422.** www.parks.ca.gov. Admission $4 adults, $2 for children 6–16, free for children 5 and under. Daily 10am–5pm.

Outdoor Pursuits

BICYCLING   One good thing about a town that's as flat as a tortilla: It's perfect for exploring on a bike. One of the best places to ride is Old Sacramento, along the paved 32-mile American River Parkway, through town. If you didn't bring your own wheels, the friendly guys at **City Bicycle Works,** 2419 K St., at 24th Street (© **916/447-2453;** www.citybicycleworks.com), will rent you one for about $15 a day.

RIVER RAFTING   Sacramento lies at the confluence of the American and Sacramento rivers, and rafting on the clear blue water of the American is popular, especially on warm weekends. Several Sacramento-area outfitters, such as **American River Raft Rentals,** 11257 S. Bridge St. (at Sunrise Ave.), Rancho Cordova (© **888/338-RAFT** or 916/635-6400; www.raftrentals.com), rent rafts for 4 to 15 persons, along with life jackets and paddles for $15 to $25 per person. Their shuttles drop you upstream and meet you 3 to 4 hours later at a predetermined point downstream.

WHERE TO STAY
Expensive

Amber House Bed-and-Breakfast ★★   Just 8 blocks from the capitol on a quiet street, Amber House offers individually decorated, antiques-filled rooms named for famous musicians and writers. The accommodations are located within historic houses: the Poet's Refuge, a 1905 Craftsman-style home with five rooms, and an 1895 Dutch colonial home called the Musician's Manor. Its Mozart Room is the B&B's best, with a four-poster queen bed, a heart-shaped Jacuzzi, a private patio, and three bay windows overlooking the tree-shaded street. A living room and library are available for guests' use. A full breakfast is served at the time and location you request—either in your room, in the large dining room, or outside on the veranda. Coffee and a newspaper are brought to your door each morning, as are freshly baked cookies every afternoon; and nonalcoholic beverages are offered all day.

1315 22nd St., Sacramento, CA 95816. © **800/755-6526** or 916/444-8085. Fax 916/552-6529. www.amberhouse.com. 10 units. $169–$279 double. Rates include breakfast. AE, DC, DISC, MC, V. **Amenities:** Concierge; laundry service; same-day dry cleaning. *In room:* A/C, TV/DVD, high-speed Internet access, hair dryer, iron.

Hyatt Regency Sacramento ★★   Sacramento's top hotel is in the heart of downtown, across from the state capitol and adjacent to the convention center. It's the high-status address for visiting politicos and is popular with conventioneers as well, as its facilities and services are unmatched in the city. While the rooms themselves are not terribly distinctive, they conform to a high standard and come with all the amenities you expect from Hyatt. The best are the corner units with views facing the state capitol.

1209 L St., Sacramento, CA 95814. (C) **800/233-1234** or 916/443-1234. Fax 916/321-3099. www.sacramento. hyatt.com. 503 units. $269–$340 double with weekend specials from $109; from $375 suite. AE, DC, DISC, MC, V. Self-parking $16; valet parking $24. **Amenities:** 2 restaurants; bar; heated outdoor pool; nearby golf course; health club; Jacuzzi; concierge; business center; full-service salon; room service; in-room massage; laundry service; same-day dry cleaning; executive-level rooms. *In room:* A/C, TV w/pay movies, Wi-Fi, minibar, fridge upon request, coffeemaker, hair dryer, iron.

Sheraton Grand Sacramento Hotel ★

This convention hotel, which opened in 2001, is praised for its high-tech amenities, a million-dollar public art collection, and the preservation of a beloved landmark. The hotel's 503 rooms are in a new 26-story building adjoining a three-story building that was originally Sacramento's public market from 1920 to the 1960s. This historic structure, designed by Julia Morgan, architect for Hearst Castle, was a favorite gathering place for three generations of Sacramentans. Now housing the lobby, bar, and two restaurants, the site is again a downtown focal point for residents and travelers alike. The accommodations are convention-type hotel rooms—a mite anonymous, but not unpleasant.

1230 J St., Sacramento, CA 95814. (C) **800/325-3535** or 916/447-1700. Fax 916/477-1701. www.sheraton. com. 503 units. $130–$289 double; from $375 suite. AE, DC, DISC, MC, V. Self-parking $13; valet parking $21. Dogs welcome. **Amenities:** 2 restaurants; bar; heated outdoor pool; health club; concierge; car-rental desk; business center; Wi-Fi in hotel only; room service; in-room massage; babysitting; laundry service; same-day dry cleaning; club-level rooms. *In room:* A/C, TV w/pay movies and video games, high-speed Internet access, minibar, coffeemaker, hair dryer, iron, dog beds available.

Sterling Hotel ★★

In the heart of Sacramento, 3 blocks from the capitol, this inn occupies a white-fronted Victorian mansion built in the 1890s and heavily renovated in 1995. The Sterling has all the charm of a small, well-managed, sophisticated inn, with a carefully tended flowering yard, tasteful decor, designer furnishings, Italian marble, and a Jacuzzi in every room. The **Chanterelle,** which serves California regional cuisine, is one of Sacramento's better restaurants.

1300 H St., Sacramento, CA 95814. (C) **800/365-7660** or 916/448-1300. Fax 916/448-8066. www.sterling hotel.com. 17 units. Sun–Thurs $176–$209 double, $335 suite; Fri–Sat $209–$257 double, $335 suite. Rates include continental breakfast. AE, DISC, MC, V. **Amenities:** Restaurant; Jacuzzi; room service. *In room:* A/C, TV w/pay movies, fridge in most units, hair dryer, iron.

Moderate

Delta King Riverboat ★

The *Delta King* carried passengers between San Francisco and Sacramento in the 1930s. Permanently moored in Sacramento since 1984, the riverboat is now a somewhat gimmicky but charming hotel. Staying here can be a novelty, but the staterooms are rather small and may bother landlubbers. All units have private bathrooms and typical low shipboard ceilings. The captain's quarters, a fancy suite, is a unique, mahogany-paneled stateroom, complete with an observation platform, private deck, and wet bar.

The riverboat's **Pilothouse Restaurant** has unparalleled river views. When the weather is nice, many patrons dine on outside decks. Live entertainment is presented below decks in two venues on Thursday through Saturday in the evening. The Mark Twain Salon hosts "Suspect's Murder Mystery Dinner Theatre," an interactive whodunit ($40 per person; drinks, tax, and gratuity extra).

1000 Front St., Old Sacramento, CA 95814. ✆ **800/825-5464** or 916/444-5464. www.deltaking.com. 44 units. Sun–Thurs $99–$139 double, $550 captain's quarters; Fri–Sat $99–$179 double, $550 captain's quarters. Riverside rooms are $15 extra. Rates include continental breakfast. AE, DC, DISC, MC, V. **Amenities:** Restaurant; lounge; laundry service; same-day dry cleaning. *In room:* A/C, TV, Wi-Fi, hair dryer, iron.

Inexpensive

Best Western Sutter House ⓥ**Value**   Its plain, motel-like exterior disguises one of the best values in Sacramento. Rooms here are as up-to-date as any offered by upscale hotels such as the Hilton or the Hyatt, including well-coordinated furnishings and lots of amenities. There's a pool in the courtyard, guest passes to a nearby fitness center, free covered parking, and complimentary coffee and pastries each morning.

1100 H St., Sacramento, CA 95814. ✆ **888/256-8040** or 916/441-1314. Fax 916/441-5961. www.thesutter house.com. 98 units. $110–$155 double. Rates include continental breakfast. AE, DC, DISC, MC, V. **Amenities:** Solar-heated outdoor pool; access to fitness center; Wi-Fi; room service; same-day dry cleaning; executive-level rooms. *In room:* A/C, TV with HBO, fax, high-speed Internet, coffeemaker, hair dryer, iron.

The Vagabond Inn Executive ⓥ**Value**   A reliable choice within walking distance of the state capitol and 1 block from historic Old Sacramento, the Vagabond Inn has many free features, including local phone calls, weekday newspapers, and continental breakfast. Bedrooms are clean and comfortable. There's an adjoining 24-hour Denny's restaurant.

909 Third St., Sacramento, CA 95814. ✆ **800/522-1555** or 916/446-1481. Fax 916/448-0364. www.vagabond inns.com. 108 units. $105–$111 double. Extra person $10. Children 18 and under stay free in parent's room. Rates include continental breakfast. AE, DC, DISC, MC, V. **Amenities:** Restaurant; heated pool; nearby golf course; exercise room; spa; free airport shuttle service; business center w/computers; laundry service; same-day dry cleaning. *In room:* A/C, TV, high-speed Internet, fridge, coffeemaker, hair dryer, iron, microwave.

WHERE TO DINE
Expensive

Biba ★★★ ITALIAN   Locals flock to this Art Deco restaurant to sample the classical Italian cuisine of Bologna-born owner Biba Caggiano, who has published nine cookbooks and also has a syndicated television show called *Biba's Italian Kitchen.* Although the menu changes seasonally, you can expect to find about 10 pastas and an equal number of main courses. There might be a delicate *pappardelle* with a fresh-seafood sauce, or linguine with clams and mussels in a butter, saffron, and white-wine sauce. For a main course, the classic *osso buco* Milanese served with a soft, creamy polenta is excellent.

2801 Capitol Ave. ✆ **916/455-2422.** www.biba-restaurant.com. Reservations recommended. Entrees $15–$30. AE, DC, MC, V. Mon–Fri 11:30am–2pm; Mon–Thurs 5:30–9:30pm; Fri–Sat 5:30–10pm.

Moderate

Esquire Grill ★ AMERICAN GRILL   Next door to Sacramento's convention center and a short walk from the capitol, Sheraton Grand, and the Hyatt Regency, the Esquire Grill was a hit as soon as it opened its handsome doors. Sacramento has been struggling for years to revive its downtown area, and this urbane place is one giant step toward creating the revitalized scene the city planners are hoping for. The bar is always lively with well-dressed folks sipping martinis and mojitos, and the restaurant's food is classic American grill. Dinner specialties might include a mixed fry of calamari, fennel, and onions; or spit-roasted pork chops with buttermilk onion rings and house-made applesauce. Though it's considered one of the city's best sites for Arnold-watching, some folks come just for the onion rings.

Mulvaney's B&L ★★ (Finds) NEW AMERICAN Sacramento's downtown restaurant scene has risen a notch with the quiet arrival of Mulvaney's B&L (the name refers to the Bailey Society Building & Loan from *It's a Wonderful Life.*) in a historic firehouse just east of the state capitol. The restaurant's classy, understated decor evokes the feel of an upscale dinner house, with original brick walls, an open kitchen, and inviting bar. Owner and executive chef Patrick Mulvaney's eclectic entrees spring from the bounteous local fare. Specialties include spinach ravioli with portobello mushroom; wild mushroom risotto cakes; and herb-crusted rack of lamb with roasted potatoes. The cuisine is complemented by a diverse wine list, and the waitstaff was hand-picked by Patrick to make sure your experience will be flawless.

1215 19th St. (off L St.). (C) **916/441-6771.** www.culinaryspecialists.com. Reservations recommended. Main courses $15–$28. AE, MC, V. Wed–Sat 5–10pm.

Paragary's Bar and Oven ★★ MEDITERRANEAN Paragary's is widely considered one of the best moderately priced restaurants in Sacramento's trendy midtown scene. In good weather, the best seats are outside amid the gorgeous fountains and plantings of the courtyard; other seating options include the formal fireplace room and the brightly lit cafe. The same menu is served no matter where you sit, with some of the best dishes coming from the kitchen's wood-burning pizza oven. But this is more than a gourmet pizza parlor, as evidenced by the grilled skirt steak with Yukon Gold mashed potatoes, grilled broccoli raab, and spicy salsa verde; or the hand-cut rosemary noodles with seared chicken, pancetta, artichokes, leeks, and garlic.

1401 28th St. (C) **916/457-5737.** www.paragarys.com. Main courses $11–$26. AE, DC, DISC, MC, V. Mon–Fri 11am–2:30pm; Mon–Thurs 5–10pm; Fri–Sat 4:30–11pm; Sun 4:30–9pm. Limited menu Mon–Fri 2:30–5pm.

33rd Street Bistro ★ BISTRO Seattle transplants Fred Haines (chef) and his brother Matt (manager) have transformed an old brick building into a hugely successful bistro. The food is good (and priced right), the staff is friendly, and the ambience is cheerful. Selections might include a variety of Italian grilled sandwiches and house favorites such as shrimp ravioli with spinach and sun-dried tomato, Uncle Bum's Jerk Ribs with Jamaican barbecue sauce and Key lime crème fraîche, and a variety of wood-fired pizzas and calzone.

3301 Folsom Blvd. (at 33rd St.). (C) **916/455-2233.** www.33rdstreetbistro.com. Main courses $9–$19. AE, MC, V. Sun–Thurs 8am–10pm; Fri–Sat 8am–11pm.

The Waterboy ★★ COUNTRY FRENCH/ITALIAN Until recently, Sacramento had a slim list of really good restaurants, but no more. At the top of everybody's list is the Waterboy. It's got everything going for it: an appealing, airy but unpretentious atmosphere; friendly and knowledgeable servers; and outstanding food cooked perfectly. Chef/owner Rick Mahan uses Niman Ranch naturally raised meats and local organic produce, and he offers a fine selection of wines. Main courses change every 4 weeks but include dishes such as saffron risotto; or boneless squab with a very crispy skin, served on sautéed greens with a squash polenta, figs, and a reduction of squab stock. Rick always has a traditional American favorite on the menu. On my last visit it was a great chili cheese dog.

2000 Capitol Ave. (C) **916/498-9891.** www.waterboyrestaurant.com. Main courses $16–$26. AE, DC, DISC, MC, V. Mon–Fri 11:30am–2:30pm; Tues–Thurs 5–9:30pm; Fri–Sat 5–10:30pm; Sun–Mon 5–9pm.

(Value) Sacramento's Best Budget Dining

I used to live in Sacramento as a starving writer, so I'm well acquainted with the city's best dining deals. Here are five of my favorites that you won't find in any other travel guide:

- **Best Burger: Willie's Burgers,** 2415 16th St., between Broadway and X Street (© **916/444-2006**), slathers food in so much chili and cheese that heavy-duty paper towel dispensers are mandatory. It's open late most nights.

- **Best Coffee Joint:** A tough one, but **Java City** (© **916/444-5282**), at the corner of Capitol Avenue and 18th Street, has been popular forever. Sure, there are a few street people around, but at least they keep the yuppies at bay.

- **Best Mexican: Taco Loco Taqueria,** 2326 J St., at 24th Street (© **916/447-0711**). Try the charbroiled black-tip shark taco, a big shrimp burrito, or snapper ceviche tostada, all so fresh the restaurant doesn't even own a freezer. Wash it all down with a Los Cabos margarita while soaking up the sun on the patio.

- **Best Breakfast:** At the **Cornerstone Restaurant,** 2330 J St., at 24th Street (© **916/441-0948**), the choices are all standard American, but the servings are huge, the service is friendly, and the price is right. A four-egg omelet with home fries, toast, and fruit costs less than $7. My dad eats here once a week.

- **Best Brewery:** The **Rubicon Brewing Company,** 2004 Capitol Ave., at 20th Street (© **916/448-7032;** www.rubiconbrewing.com), still remains my favorite hangout. A pitcher of India Pale and a side of fries is de rigueur.

Inexpensive

Fox & Goose Public House ★★ (Value) ENGLISH PUB   The Fox is your classic British pub, down to the dartboard, picture of the queen, and numerous beers from across the pond. The soups at lunch are excellent, and the specials often include bangers and mash, Welsh rarebit, and Cornish pasties. The burnt-cream dessert is famous. Arrive early for lunch or be prepared for a wait, as locals love this place (no reservations are taken and they won't seat you until all members of your party have arrived). Equally popular breakfasts include kippers, crumpets, waffles, omelets, and French toast. There's live entertainment by local bands 6 nights a week, and pub grub is served Monday through Friday from 2:30 to 9:30pm.

1001 R St. (at 10th St.). © **916/443-8825.** www.foxandgoose.com. Reservations not accepted. Main courses $5–$10. AE, MC, V. Breakfast daily 7am–2pm; lunch Mon–Fri 11am–2pm; pub grub Mon–Fri 2:30–9:30pm and Sat 5:30–9:30pm. Bar stays open until midnight Mon–Thurs, until 2am Fri–Sat.

Tower Café INTERNATIONAL   In a grand 1939 movie house with a tall Art Deco spire, the Tower Café's multicultural decor is a feast for the eyes. Dishes reflect a variety of international flavors, from the Jamaican jerk chicken to Chinese chicken salad. Usually the food is good, especially the desserts, but once in a while you get something that makes you wonder what's going on in the kitchen. On warm days it seems as if everyone in the city is lunching here on the large outdoor patio (past patrons have included Bill Clinton), so people-watching can be a real treat.

1518 Broadway. © **916/441-0222.** www.towercafe.com. Main courses $9–$18. AE, MC, V. Sun–Thurs 8am–11pm; Fri–Sat 8am–12am.

2 THE GOLD COUNTRY ★★

Cutting a serpentine swath for nearly 350 miles along Highway 49, the Gold Country's mining sites, horse ranches, ghost towns, Gold Rush architecture, and Wild West saloons stretch from Sierra City to the foothills of Yosemite. The town of Placerville, 44 miles east of Sacramento at the intersection of U.S. 50 and Highway 49, is in the approximate center of the region. To the north are the old mining towns of Grass Valley and Nevada City, while in the central and southern Gold Country are such well-preserved towns as Amador City, Sutter Creek, Columbia, and Jamestown.

The Gold Country is so immense that it would take weeks to thoroughly explore. So I have narrowed my coverage to include three of my favorite regions, each of which can be explored in just 2 or 3 days: the charismatic side-by-side towns of Nevada City and Grass Valley; the Gold Rush communities of Amador City, Sutter Creek, and Jackson; and the wonderfully authentic neighboring mining towns of Angels Camp, Murphys, Columbia, Sonora, and Jamestown.

Whether you're intent on panning for gold, exploring old mines and caverns, or rafting the area's many white-water rivers, the Gold Country is one of the most underrated and least congested tourist destinations in California, a winning combination of Old West ambience, affordable bed-and-breakfasts (many have a 2-night minimum on weekends), and outdoor adventures galore.

THE NORTHERN GOLD COUNTRY: NEVADA CITY & GRASS VALLEY

About 60 miles northeast of Sacramento, Nevada City and Grass Valley are far and away the top tourist destinations of the northern Gold Country.

These two historic towns were at the center of the hard-rock mining fields of Northern California. Grass Valley was California's richest mining town, producing more than a billion dollars' worth of gold. Both are attractive, although smaller Nevada City's wealth of Victorian homes and storefronts makes it one of the most appealing small towns in California, particularly in the fall when the maple trees are ablaze with color. (Its entire downtown has been designated a National Historic Landmark.)

From San Francisco, take I-80 to the Highway 49 turnoff in Auburn and follow the signs heading north. For information about the area, contact the **Grass Valley & Nevada County Chamber of Commerce,** 248 Mill St., Grass Valley (© **800/655-4667** in California, or 530/273-4667; www.grassvalleychamber.com), or the **Nevada City Chamber of Commerce,** 132 Main St., Nevada City (© **800/655-6569** or 530/265-2692; www. nevadacitychamber.com).

Nevada City ★★

Rumors of miners pulling a pound of gold a day out of Deer Creek brought thousands of fortune seekers to the area in 1849. Within a year, Nevada City was a boisterous town of 10,000, the third-largest city in California. In its heyday, everyone visited this rollicking Western outpost with its busy red-light district: Mark Twain lectured here in 1866, and former president Herbert Hoover lived and worked here as a gold miner.

Pick up a walking-tour map at the **Chamber of Commerce,** 132 Main St., and stroll the streets lined with impressive Victorian buildings; the **National Hotel** (built 1854–56) is here (the Gold Rush–era bar serves a spicy Bloody Mary), as is the **Nevada Theatre** (1865), one of the oldest theaters in the nation still operating as such. Today it's home to the Foothill Theatre Company.

If you want to see the source of much of the city's wealth, visit **Malakoff Diggins State Historic Park** ★, 23579 N. Bloomfield Rd. (© 530/265-2740; www.parks. ca.gov), 28 miles northeast of Nevada City. Once the world's largest hydraulic gold mine, it's an awesome (some say environmentally disturbing) spectacle of hydraulic mining: Nearly half a mountain has been washed away by powerful jets of water, leaving behind a 600-foot-deep canyon of exposed rock. In the 1870s, North Bloomfield, then located in the middle of this park, had a population of 1,500. Some of the buildings have been reconstructed and refurnished to show what life was like then. The 3,000-acre park also offers several hiking trails, swimming at Blair Lake, and 30 campsites that can be reserved through **ReserveAmerica** (© 800/444-7275; www.reserveamerica.com). The museum is open daily in summer from 11am to 4pm, on winter weekends the museum opens at 11:30am. To reach the park, take Highway 49 toward Downieville for 11 miles. Turn right onto Tyler-Foote Crossing Road for 17 miles. Turn right onto Derbec Road and then right on North Bloomfield Road, which takes you to the park entrance. The fee is $6 per car, $5 for seniors.

Another 6 miles up Highway 49 from the Malakoff Diggins turnoff brings you to Pleasant Valley Road, the exit that will take you (in about 7 miles) to one of the nation's most impressive **covered bridges.** Built in 1862, it's 225 feet long and was crossed by many a stagecoach (in fall, it makes for a spectacular photo opportunity).

Where to Stay

Deer Creek Inn Bed & Breakfast ★   An 1860 three-floor Victorian overlooking Deer Creek and within walking distance of downtown Nevada City, this inn feels like a warm home-away-from-home. Most of the individually decorated rooms, have private verandas facing the creek or town. Three bathrooms have claw-foot tubs. A stay at Deer Creek includes a three-course gourmet breakfast, served either on the deck or in the formal dining room. Guests are invited to their wine tasting, or to try a little gold panning, fishing, or simply to relax and enjoy the lawn and landscaped rose gardens along the creek.

116 Nevada St., Nevada City, CA 95959. © 800/655-0363 or 530/265-0363. Fax 530/265-0980. www. deercreekinn.com. 6 units. $160–$230 double. Rates include breakfast. MC, V. **Amenities:** Nearby golf course; bike rental. *In room:* A/C, TV/DVD, Wi-Fi.

Emma Nevada House ★★   One of the finest B&Bs in the Gold Country, this picture-perfect Victorian was the childhood home of 19th-century opera star Emma Nevada. You'll like everything about it: the quiet location, sun-drenched decks, wraparound porch, understated decor, and breakfast served in the hexagonal Sun Room. The guest rooms range from small and intimate to large and luxurious; all have private bathrooms and queen or king size beds. Top choice for honeymooners is the Empress's Chamber, with its wall of windows, ivory and burgundy tones, and—of course—the Jacuzzi tub for two. You'll also like the fact that the shops and restaurants of Nevada City's Historic District are only a short walk away.

528 E. Broad St., Nevada City, CA 95959. ℂ **800/916-EMMA** or 530/265-4415. Fax 530/265-4416. www. emmanevadahouse.com. 6 units. $169–$249 double. Rates include breakfast. AE, DISC, MC, V. **Amenities:** Concierge; creek-side or in-room massage. *In room:* A/C, Wi-Fi, hair dryer, iron, phone on request.

Nevada City Inn Ⓥ**alue**   Surely no forty-niner had it this good: his own cabinlike motel room cooled by the shade of a small tree-lined park equipped with barbecues and picnic tables. Granted, the rooms are small and simple at this restored 1940s motor lodge, but considering that you get all the standard amenities for a really low price, the cash-conscious traveler could hardly ask for more. The inn also rents seven fully fur-nished cottages with kitchens, popular with families and groups. They're a good deal for such a prime location, about a half-mile from Nevada City's historic district.

760 Zion St., Nevada City, CA 95959. ℂ **800/977-8884** or 530/265-2253. Fax 530/265-3310. www.nevada cityinn.net. 20 units, 7 cottages. $69–$139 double; $130–$189 cottage. Rates include continental break-fast. AE, DC, DISC, MC, V. *In room:* A/C, TV, Wi-Fi, in room coffee, hair dryer, iron.

Red Castle Inn Historic Lodgings ★   This elegant, comfortable hillside inn occu-pies a four-story Gothic Revival brick house built in 1860 in a secluded spot with a panoramic view of the town. The house retains its original woodwork, plaster moldings, ceiling medallions, and much of the handmade glass. It lacks modern intrusions such as TVs and phones. Guests enjoy five-course buffet breakfasts and relax on the verandas that encircle the first two floors of the house and overlook the rose gardens. My favorite rooms are the Garden Room, with a canopy bed and French doors leading into the gar-dens, and the three-room Garret Suite tucked under the eaves, with sleigh beds and Gothic arched windows.

109 Prospect St., Nevada City, CA 95959. ℂ **800/761-4766** or 530/265-5135. www.redcastleinn.com. 7 units. $120–$185 double. Rates include breakfast. MC, V. *In room:* A/C, no phone.

Where to Dine

Citronée Bistro & Wine Bar ★★ REGIONAL AMERICAN/INTERNATIONAL It took a review by the *New York Times* to get California foodies to turn their appetites from Napa and San Francisco to owner/chef Robert Perez's French country–style bistro. The menu, which focuses on locally grown organic produce, ranges from grilled filet mignon with *pommes* purée, roasted shallots, veal reduction, and black truffle oil to the "ultrarare" grilled ahi with yuzu vinaigrette, sweet peas, baby carrots, and topped with shaved fennel. My favorite dish, though, is Perez's slow-braised beef short-ribs with puréed potatoes, baby carrots, and pearl onions. You can request the casual cafe seating on the front level or the more elegant fine dining area on the brick-walled back level.

320 Broad St. ℂ **530/265-5697.** www.citroneebistro.com. Reservations recommended. Main courses $16–$34. AE, MC, V. Wed–Mon noon–2:30pm and 5pm–closing.

Country Rose Café ★ COUNTRY FRENCH The flowery country-French atmo-sphere of this popular Nevada City restaurant belies a serious (and seriously priced) menu put together by owner and chef Michael Johns. Dinner selections, written on a huge board that's lugged over to your table after you've been seated, are mostly French with a dash of Italian, Mexican, and American dishes. Skip the typical pastas and head straight for John's specialty—fresh fish prepared in a myriad of classic styles such as filet of sole *doré,* swordfish Oskar, and sea bass with garlic-basil sauce. Other regular menu items include filet mignon, lobster, rack of lamb, and roast game hen. Both lunch and dinner are served on the pretty walled-in patio in the summer, so be sure to request alfresco seating when making a reservation.

New Moon Café ★★ AMERICAN/INTERNATIONAL Nevada City's favorite chef, Peter Selaya, offers a menu of imaginatively prepared items that feature free-range and antibiotic-free meats and poultry, house-baked breads, house-made pastas using organic flours and grains, and local organic vegetables, when available—which is often, in this hotbed of natural foodstuffs. Not only is the food healthy, it tastes great. Dinner entrees include a Niman Ranch loin chop grilled with spring onion-port confit and Yukon gold mashed potatoes, or large prawns sautéed with fresh mussels, fennel, tomato, and andouille sausage. The ravioli and desserts are made fresh daily (the fresh strawberry Napoleons are beyond delicious). Nevada City's balmy climate makes the front deck a great place to dine and people-watch.

203 York St. ☎ 530/265-6399. www.thenewmooncafe.com. Reservations recommended. Main courses $15–$28. DC, MC, V. Tues–Fri 11:30am–2pm; Tues–Sun 5–8pm (or later).

Grass Valley

In contrast to Nevada City's "tourist town" image, nearby Grass Valley is the commercial and retail center of the region. Although it's lacking in high-quality restaurants and B&Bs, its wealth of historical attractions make it a worthwhile day trip. The **Empire Mine State Historic Park** ★, 10791 E. Empire St., Grass Valley (☎ **530/273-8522;** www.empiremine.org), the oldest, largest, and richest gold mine in California, is just outside of town. The mine once had 367 miles of shafts and produced an estimated 5.8 million ounces of gold between 1850 and 1956. You can look down the shaft of the mine, walk around the mine yard, and stroll through the owner's gardens. Tours are conducted and a mining technique movie is shown year-round, but check the tour and movie schedule at www.empiremine.org or call in advance. You can also enjoy picnicking, cycling, mountain biking, or hiking in the 854-acre park. It's open year-round except for Thanksgiving, Christmas, and New Year's Day. Admission to the park and museum costs $3 for adults over 16 and $1 for children over 5 (children under 5 are free). Guided tours of the mine yard and grounds are $1.50 per person.

Visitors can pick up a walking-tour map at the **Chamber of Commerce,** 248 Mill St. (☎ **530/273-4667;** www.grassvalleychamber.com), and explore the historic area along Mill and Main streets. Two museums will appeal to California-history and gold-mining buffs: the **Grass Valley Museum,** 410 S. Church St., adjacent to St. Joseph's Cultural Center (☎ **530/273-5509**), and the **North Star Mining Museum,** at the south end of Mill Street at Allison Ranch Road (☎ **530/273-4255;** May–Oct).

Grass Valley was, for a time, the home of **Lola Montez,** singer, dancer, and paramour of the rich and famous. A fully restored home that she bought and occupied in 1853 can be viewed at 248 Mill St., now the site of Grass Valley's chamber of commerce. **Lotta Crabtree,** Montez's famous protégée, lived down the street at 238 Mill St., now an apartment house. Also pop into the **Holbrooke Hotel,** 212 Main St., to see the signature of Mark Twain, who stayed here, as did four U.S. presidents. The saloon has been in continuous use since 1852, and locals still come for tall cold ones.

The surrounding region offers many recreational opportunities on its rivers and lakes and in the Tahoe National Forest. You can enjoy fishing, swimming, and boating at **Scotts Flat Lake** near Nevada City (east on Hwy. 20) and at **Rollins Lake** on Highway 174, between Grass Valley and Colfax. **Tributary Whitewater Tours,** 20480 Woodbury Dr., Grass Valley, CA 95949 (☎ **800/672-3846** or 530/346-6812; www.whitewatertours.com), offers half- to 3-day white-water rafting trips March through October. The chambers of commerce publish a trail guide for mountain biking, but you must bring your own wheels. For regional hiking information, contact **Tahoe National Forest Headquarters,** at Coyote Street and Highway 49 in Nevada City (✆ **530/265-4531;** www.r5.fs.fed.us/tahoe).

Where to Stay

Grass Valley Courtyard Suites If you like to lounge poolside with a good book, you'll appreciate the Courtyard Suites, and if you have your little dog, Toto, with you, he'll appreciate the canine cuddler (fuzzy little blanket) he's provided when you check in. In a quiet neighborhood, a block from downtown Grass Valley, this place offers enough amenities to cover your every need, including a spa, fitness facility, sauna, and seasonally heated pool. There's a generous continental breakfast in the morning, and wine and hors d'oeuvres in the evening. Some suites have fully equipped kitchens and fireplaces, and there's also a coin-operated guest laundry facility.

210 N. Auburn St., Grass Valley, CA 95945. ✆ **530/272-7696.** www.gvcourtyardsuites.com. 33 units. $150–$180 double; $195–$325 suite. Rates include continental breakfast. AE, DISC, V. Covered parking. **Amenities:** Outdoor seasonal heated pool; fitness facility; spa; sauna; coin-op laundry. *In room:* A/C, TV w/HBO, DVD player, fridge, microwave, coffeemaker, hair dryer, iron, safe, microwave, robes, voice mail.

Holbrooke Hotel ★ This Victorian-era white-clapboard building was a saloon during the Gold Rush days, and then evolved into a place for miners to "rack out." The oldest and most historic hotel in town, it's hosted a number of legendary figures: Mark Twain and presidents Ulysses Grant, Benjamin Harrison, and Grover Cleveland, among others. Seventeen of the rooms lie within the main building. The remainder are in an adjacent annex, a house occupied long ago by the hotel's owner. Each guest room is decorated with a collection of Gold Rush–era furniture and antiques. All have cable TVs in armoires, and most bathrooms have claw-foot tubs. If you can, reserve one of the larger Veranda rooms that face Main Street and have access to the balconies; it's well worth the few extra dollars. A continental breakfast is served in the library.

212 W. Main St., Grass Valley, CA 95945. ✆ **800/933-7077** or 530/273-1353. Fax 530/273-0434. www.holbrooke.com. 28 units. $109–$149 double. AE, DC, DISC, MC, V. **Amenities:** Restaurant; saloon; business center; Wi-Fi. *In room:* A/C, TV, coffeemaker, hair dryer, iron.

Where to Dine

Tofanelli's Ⓥalue INTERNATIONAL Under new ownership since May 2006, the venerable Tofanelli's restaurant continues to satisfy Grass Valley locals, as it has for decades, by serving large portions of good food at reasonable prices for lunch, dinner and Sunday brunch. You'll like the setting—a bright, cheery trio of dining areas (atrium, outdoor patio, and dining room) separated by exposed brick walls. Specials on the menu, such as Gorgonzola ravioli topped with garlic-cream sauce, or pad Thai noodles with fresh ginger and marinated beef, change quarterly. Perennial mainstays include lasagna, burgers, steaks, and chocolate cake.

302 W. Main St. (across from the Holbrooke Hotel). ✆ **530/272-1468.** www.tofanellisgoldcountrybistro.com. Main courses $12–$26. AE, DISC, MC, V. Daily 7am–9pm.

THE CENTRAL GOLD COUNTRY: AMADOR CITY, SUTTER CREEK, JACKSON & ENVIRONS

Though Placerville is technically the center of the Gold Country, it's the small trio of towns a few miles to the south—Amador City, Sutter Creek, and Jackson—that are the most appealing destination in this region of rolling hills, dotted with solitary oaks and granite outcroppings. Since the mining boom went bust, most of these restored Gold Rush towns rely solely on tourism (hence the conversion of many Victorian homes into B&Bs), though a few mines have reopened recently.

One of the advantages of staying in this area, 55 miles southeast of Sacramento, is that both the northern and the southern regions of the Gold Country are only a few hours' drive away (via very winding roads).

To reach Amador City, Sutter Creek, or Jackson from Placerville, head south along Highway 49 past Plymouth and Drytown. If you're coming straight here from Sacramento, take U.S. 50 to Placerville and head south on Highway 49; Highway 16 from Sacramento is another option, but only slightly faster. For more information about any of these towns, contact the **Amador County Chamber of Commerce,** 517 South Hwy. 49, Jackson Street (© **209/223-0350;** www.amadorcountychamber.com).

Amador City ★

Once a bustling mining town, Amador City is now devoted mostly to dredging up tourist dollars. Although Amador City sounds impressive, it's the smallest incorporated city in California. Local merchants have made the most of a refurbished block-long boardwalk, converting the historic false-fronted buildings into a gallery of sorts; the stores sell everything from early 1900s antiques and folk art to handcrafted furniture, Gold Rush memorabilia, rare books, and Native American crafts. Parking can be difficult, however, especially in summer.

Where to Stay & Dine

Imperial Hotel ★★ At the foot of Main Street overlooking Amador City, this stately 1879 brick hotel and restaurant has been beautifully restored and manages to be both elegant and whimsical. The individually decorated rooms, all with private bathrooms, are furnished with wicker, iron, or pine beds and numerous antiques. Room 6 is the quietest, but Room 1—with its high ceiling, queen-size canopy bed, comfortable seating area, and French doors that open onto the balcony overlooking Main Street—is the most requested. The smart and chic Oasis Bar is stocked with a large selection of spirits and California and imported wines and beers. Gourmet breakfast is served downstairs in the dining room with French doors opening onto the native stone patio. The **Imperial Hotel Restaurant,** serving California cuisine such as Sonoma Liberty duck breast with a port reduction and thick-cut pork chops with sautéed apples in a maple brandy sauce, has a sterling reputation.

14202 Hwy. 49, P.O. Box 212, Amador City, CA 95601. © **209/267-9172.** Fax 209/267-9249. www.imperial amador.com. 6 units. $125–$145 double. Rates include breakfast. AE, MC, V. **Amenities:** Restaurant; bar. In room: A/C, hair dryer, no phone.

Sutter Creek ★

The self-proclaimed "nicest little town in the Mother Lode," Sutter Creek was named after sawmill owner John Sutter, employer of James Marshall (whose discovery of gold triggered the 1849 Gold Rush). Railroad baron Leland Stanford made his fortune at Sutter Creek's Lincoln Mine and then invested his millions to build the transcontinental railroad and fund his successful California gubernatorial campaign.

The town is a charmer, lined with beautiful 19th-century buildings in pristine condition, including **Downs Mansion,** the former home of the foreman at Stanford's mine (now a private residence on Spanish St., across from the Immaculate Conception Church), and the landmark **Knight's Foundry,** 81 Eureka St., off Main Street, the last water-powered foundry and machine shop in the nation. There are also numerous shops and galleries along Main Street, though finding a free parking space can be a real challenge on summer weekends.

Where to Stay

The Foxes ★★ This 1857 clapboard house is Sutter Creek's most elegant hostelry. The six rooms are all unique, each with a queen-size bed, down comforters, and 1,200-count linens. Four rooms, including the Garden Room and the Fox Den, have gas-burning fireplaces. The Fox Den has a little library of its own, while the Anniversary Room features a 9-foot-tall Renaissance Revival bed and a sitting room. All have private bathrooms. Breakfast, cooked to order and delivered on silver service, can be served in your room or in the gazebo in the flower-filled garden. Located on Main Street, the inn is only steps away from Sutter Creek's shops and restaurants.

77 Main St. (P.O. Box 159), Sutter Creek, CA 95685. © **800/987-3344** or 209/267-5882. Fax 209/267-0712. www.foxesinn.com. 7 units. $160–$289 double. Rates include breakfast. AE, DISC, MC, V. **Amenities:** Concierge; business center; free phones; Wi-Fi; bell service. *In room:* A/C, TV/DVD/VCR, video library, fridge w/complimentary beverages, hair dryer, bathrobes, CD player, clock radio.

Grey Gables Inn ★ The Grey Gables Inn is a postcard-perfect replica of a Victorian manor. The two-story B&B is surrounded by terraces of gardens and embellished with fountains and vine-covered arbors. Each of the plushly carpeted guest rooms is named after a British poet; the Byron Room features hues of deep green and burgundy, dark-wood furnishings, and a four-poster king bed. All rooms have queen or king beds, gas-log fireplaces, armoires, and private bathrooms (a few with claw-foot tubs). Breakfast, delivered on English bone china, is served in the formal dining room adjacent to the Victorian parlor or in your room. The only flaw is the proximity to heavily traveled Highway 49, but once inside, you'll hardly notice. The shops and restaurants of Sutter Creek are within walking distance.

161 Hanford St., Sutter Creek, CA 95685. © **800/473-9422** or 209/267-1039. Fax 209/267-0998. www. greygables.com. 8 units. $110–$200 double. AE, DC, DISC, MC, V. *In room:* A/C, free Wi-Fi, hair dryer, no phone.

Where to Dine

Caffè Via d'Oro ★ CALIFORNIA It was a sad day in Sutter Creek when the town's most beloved restaurant, Zinfandels, closed, but with the new opening of Caffè Via d'Oro, fine dining has returned to the "nicest little town in the Mother Lode." It took owners Dennis and Julie Griffin a lot of time, work, love, and moola to renovate this 150-year-old building, with custom-made furnishings, beautiful murals of Sutter Creek scenery, and a handsome oak and copper bar (an ideal place for a Gold Country wine tasting). The upscale menu is impressive, ranging from southern-style shrimp to roasted rack of lamb and manicotti; organic, locally grown produce is used whenever possible. If you're staying at either the Foxes or Grey Gables B&Bs, feel free to sample all those superb Gold Country reds; the restaurant is only a short walk away.

36 Main St., Sutter Creek. © **209/267-0535.** www.caffeviadoro.com. Reservations recommended. Main courses $18–$32. AE, MC, V. Wed–Sun 5pm–closing (Fri–Sun bar open 2–5pm with hors d'oeuvre and dessert menu).

What to Do

Sutter Gold Mine One of the most entertaining and educational attractions in the Gold Country, the Sutter Gold Mine tours lead visitors on an hour-long excursion into the bowels of a modern hard-rock gold mine. After a ride on a mining shuttle to the mine, visitors "tag in" and go through the safety training room, as the miners once did.

Wearing your hardhat, you'll proceed deep into the mine, learning about geology and history while marveling at the gems and gold embedded in the quartz of the Comet Vein (you'll even learn to distinguish real gold from "fool's gold").

After the tour, be sure to buy a bag of mining ore—about $5 per bag—head over to the wood sluice, grab one of the gold pans or sluice boxes, and pan for real gold. Each bag is guaranteed to hold either gold or gemstones (emeralds, amethysts, topaz, and many other birthstones), and an assistant is on hand to show you how it's done. Other diversions include the Company Store gift shop filled with inexpensive semiprecious gems and minerals, and a 1-hour documentary about the Gold Rush and a half-hour movie about modern gold mining (a heavy-machinery flick that kids will love).

13660 Hwy. 49, about 1/2 mile south of Amador City, just north of Sutter Creek. (© **866/762-2837** or 209/736-2708. www.suttergold.com.)1-hr. Family Tour $18 for adults and $12 for kids 4–13; kids 3 and under are not allowed on the tour. Summer daily 9am–5pm; Oct–May daily 10am–5pm.

Coloma ★

On Highway 49 between Auburn and Placerville, the town of **Coloma** ★ is so small and unpretentious it's hard to imagine the significant role it played in the rapid development of California and the West. It was here that James Marshall first discovered that there was gold aplenty in the foothills of California. Over the next 50 years, 125 *million* ounces of gold were taken from the Sierra foothills, an amount worth a staggering $50 billion today.

Although Marshall and Sutter tried to keep the discovery secret, word soon leaked out. Sam Brannan, who ran a general store at Fort Sutter, secured some gold samples himself—as well as some choice real estate—and headed for San Francisco, where he ran through the streets shouting, "Gold! Gold! Gold! From the American River!" San Francisco rapidly emptied as men rushed off to seek their fortunes at the mines.

Coloma was quickly mined out, but its boom brought 10,000 people to the settlement and lasted long enough for residents to build a schoolhouse, a gunsmith, a general store, and a tin-roofed post office. The miners also planted oak and mimosa trees that shade the street during hot summers. About 70% of this quiet, pretty town lies in the **Marshall Gold Discovery State Historic Park** (© **530/622-3470;** www.coloma.com/gold or www.parks.ca.gov), which preserves the spot where Marshall discovered gold on the banks of the south fork of the American River.

Farther up Main Street is a replica of the mill Marshall was building when he made his discovery. The largest building in town, the mill is powered by electricity during the summer. Other attractions include the **Gold Discovery Museum,** which relates the story of the Gold Rush, and a number of Chinese stores, all that remain of the once-sizable local Chinese community. The park also has three picnic areas, four trails, recreational gold panning, and a number of buildings and exhibits relating the way of life that prevailed here in the 19th century. Admission is $5 per vehicle, $4 for seniors; hours are daily from 10am to 3pm, except on major holidays.

Folks also visit for white-water thrills on the American River. (Coloma is a popular launching point.) **White Water Connection,** in Coloma (© **800/336-7238** or 530/622-6446; www.whitewaterconnection.com), runs half- to 2-day trips down the forks of the American River. It's one of the state's most exciting outdoor adventures.

Jackson ★

Jackson, the county seat of Amador County, is far livelier than its neighboring towns to the north. (It was the last place in California to outlaw prostitution.) Be sure to stroll through the center of town, browsing in the stores and admiring the Victorian architecture.

Although the Kennedy and Argonaut mines ultimately produced more than $140 million in gold, Jackson initially earned its place in the Gold Rush as a supply center. That history is apparent in the town's wide Main Street, lined by tall buildings adorned with intricate iron railings.

Make no mistake: This is not a ghost town, but rather a modern minicity that has worked to preserve its pre-Victorian influence. At the southern end of the street, the **National Hotel,** 2 Water St., at Main Street (✆ **209/223-0500**), is one of California's oldest continuously operating hotels, since 1862. Will Rogers, John Wayne, Leland Stanford, and many other celebrities and politicos once stayed here.

The **Amador County Museum,** a huge brick building at 225 Church St. (✆ **209/ 223-6386**), is where Will Rogers filmed *Boys Will Be Boys* in 1920. Today the former home of Armistead Calvin Brown and his 11 children is filled with mining memorabilia and information on two local mines, the Kennedy and the Argonaut, that were among the deepest and richest in the nation. Within the museum is a working large-scale model of the Kennedy. The museum is open Wednesday through Sunday from 10am to 4pm; admission is pay-as-you-wish. Tours of the Kennedy Mine model cost $1 and are offered Saturday and Sunday on the hour from 11am to 3pm.

To see the real thing, head to the **Kennedy Tailing Wheels Park,** site of the Kennedy and Argonaut mines, the deepest in the Mother Lode. The mines have been closed for years, but the tailing wheels and head frames used to convey debris over the hills to a settling pond remain. To reach the park, take Main Street to Jackson Gate Road, just north of Jackson (no phone).

A few miles south of Jackson, on Highway 49, is one of the most evocative towns of the region: **Mokelumne Hill** ★. The town consists of one street overlooking a valley with a few old buildings, and somehow its sad, abandoned air has the mark of authenticity. At one time, the hill was dotted with tents and wood-and–tar paper shacks, and the town housed a population of 15,000, including an old French quarter and a Chinatown. But now many of its former residents are memorialized in the town's Protestant, Jewish, and Catholic cemeteries.

Where to Stay & Dine

Buscaglia's Ristorante   This capacious, recently renovated Italian Tuscan restaurant is situated in a building that was originally a tavern for miners and locals in 1905. The miners probably weren't eating sautéed fresh Atlantic salmon with champagne dill sauce or braised pork shank on a bed of cheese polenta, but they might have had the historically popular spaghetti and meatballs or hearty vegetable soup (aka minestrone). The menu features a wide variety of pasta, fish, meat, and pizza selections to accommodate the crankiest family member. There's patio dining in fair weather and a pianist on Friday and Saturday nights.

1218 Jackson Gate Rd. ✆ **209/223-9992.** www.villabuscaglia.net. Main courses $10–$25. MC, V. Wed–Sun 5pm–closing.

The Gate House Bed and Breakfast Inn   About a mile from downtown Jackson and a short walk to the Kennedy Tailing Wheels park, the Gate House offers an assortment of accommodations in a historic mansion surrounded by landscaped lawns, garden, and open fields. Besides the two rooms and two suites in the main house, decorated with Victorian furnishings, there's a small cottage with a gas-log stove and a Jacuzzi for two. Ping-Pong, darts, a swimming pool, and newly completed bocce ball court offer fun diversions. The three- to four-course candlelit champagne breakfast is served on fine china, and in the afternoon, wine and appetizers are served. The inn is within walking distance of two fine restaurants and close to Amador County wineries, gold mines, caverns, and Daffodil Hill.

1330 Jackson Gate Rd., Jackson, CA 95642. (*C*) **800/841-1072** or 209/223-3500. www.gatehouseinn.com. 5 units. $145–$215 double. Rates include breakfast. AE, DISC, MC, V. **Amenities:** Pool (solar heated). *In room:* A/C, hair dryer, robes, wineglasses, bottled water.

Mel and Faye's Diner (Value) AMERICAN   How can anybody not love a classic old roadside diner? In business since 1956, Mel and Faye have been cranking out the best diner food in the Gold Country for so long that it's okay not to feel guilty for salivating over the thought of a sloppy double Moo Burger smothered with onions and special sauce and washed down with a chocolate shake. And could you please add a large side of fries with that? And how much is a slice of pie? It's a time-honored Jackson tradition, so forget about your diet.

31 Hwy. 49 (at Main St.). (*C*) **209/223-0853.** www.melandfayesdiner.com. Menu items $4–$10. MC, V. Daily 5am–10pm.

Volcano

About a dozen miles east of Jackson on Highway 88 is the enchantingly decrepit town of **Volcano** ★, one of the most authentic ghost towns in the central Sierra. The town got its name in 1848, after miners mistook the origins of the craggy boulders that lie in the center of town. The dark rock and the blind window frames of a few backless, ivy-covered buildings give the town's main thoroughfare a haunted look. Sprinkled between boarded-up buildings, about 100 residents do business in the same sagging storefronts that a population of 8,000 frequented nearly 150 years ago.

The tiny, now-quiet burg has a rich history: Not only was this boomtown once home to the state's first lending library and astronomical observatory, but Volcano gold also supported the Union during the Civil War. Residents smuggled a huge cannon to the front lines in a hearse (it was never used). The story goes that had the enthusiastic blues actually fired it, it was so overcharged that "Old Abe" would have exploded. The cannon sits in the town center today, under a rusting weather vane.

Looming over the small buildings is the stately **St. George Hotel** ★ ((*C*) **209/296-4458;** www.stgeorgehotel.com), a three-story, balconied building that testifies to the $90 million in gold mined in and around the town. Its ivy-covered brick and shuttered windows will remind you of colonial New England. In 1998, new owners took over the run-down 20-room hotel and have totally turned it around. The restaurant serves brunch on Sunday, and dinner Thursday through Sunday. Even if you're not hungry, stop in for a libation at the classic old bar, the Whiskey Flat Saloon.

In summer, the **Volcano Theatre Company** performs locally written and produced comedies and mysteries at the town's outdoor amphitheater, hidden behind stone facades on Main Street, a block north of the St. George Hotel. It's a wonderful Gold Country experience. For information on performances, call (*C*) **209/274-2214** or visit **www.volcanotheatre.org**. In early spring, people come from all around to picnic amid the nearly half-million daffodils in bloom on **Daffodil Hill,** a 4-acre ranch 3 miles north of Volcano (follow the sign on Ram's Horn Grade).

Volcano is also the site of one of the National Park Service's National Natural Landmarks—the **Black Chasm** ((*C*) **866/762-2837**), a cave with stalactites, stalagmites, flowstones, and rare helictite crystals. The 50-minute Landmark Family Tour leaves every 45 minutes throughout the day, open year-round, adults $14, children $7. It follows a series of platforms, stairs, and walkways to preserve the cave environment. Aboveground, kids can mine for gemstones at a mining flume, guaranteed to find some real gemstones, $5 for a small bag. The new Visitors Center provides information on the cave's history and contents as well as on Black Chasm's connection to the Matrix trilogy. The cave site is at 15701 Pioneer-Volcano Rd.

THE SOUTHERN GOLD COUNTRY: ANGELS CAMP, MURPHYS, COLUMBIA, SONORA & JAMESTOWN

No other region in the Gold Country offers more to see and do than these towns in the south, 86 miles southeast of Sacramento. From exploring caverns to riding in the stagecoach and panning for gold, the neighboring towns of Angels Camp, Murphys, Columbia, Sonora, and Jamestown offer a cornucopia of Gold Rush–related sites, museums, and activities. It's a great place to bring the family (kids love roaming around the dusty car-free streets of Columbia), and the region offers some of the best lodgings and restaurants in the Gold Country. In short, if you're the Type A sort who needs to stay active, the southern Gold Country is for you. For information about lodging, dining, events, and the arts and entertainment in the area, contact the **Tuolumne County Visitors Bureau,** 542 W. Stockton Rd., P.O. Box 4020, Sonora, California 95370 (© **800/446-1333** or 209/533-4420; www.tcvb.com).

To reach any of these towns from Sacramento, head south on Highway 99 to Stockton, and then take Highway 4 east into Angels Camp. (From here, it's a short, scenic drive to the other towns.) For a longer but more scenic route, take U.S. 50 east to Placerville, and then head south on Highway 49, which takes you to Angels Camp.

Angels Camp ★

You've probably heard of Angels Camp, the town that inspired Mark Twain to pen "The Celebrated Jumping Frog of Calaveras County." This pretty, peaceful community is built on hills honeycombed with tunnels. In the 1880s and 1890s, five mines were located along Main Street—Sultana, Angel's, Lightner, Utica, and Stickle—and the town echoed with noise as more than 200 stamps crushed the ore. Between 1886 and 1910, the mines generated close to $20 million.

But a far-more lasting legacy than the town's gold production is the **Jumping Frog Jubilee,** started in 1928 to mark the paving of the town's streets. The ribbiting competition takes place every third weekend in May. The record, 21 feet, 5³/₄ inches, was set in 1986 by Rosie the Ribbiter, beating the old record by 4¹/₂ inches. Livestock exhibitions, pageants, cook-offs, arm-wrestling tournaments, live music, carnival rides, a rodeo, and plenty of beer and wine keep the thousands of spectators entertained between jump-offs. (You can even rent a frog if you forgot to pack one.) For more information and entry forms (around $5 per frog), call the Jumping Frog Jubilee headquarters at © **209/736-2561,** or log on to their website at **www.frogtown.org**.

Where to Stay

Best Western Cedar Inn & Suites ★ (Kids)   If you're looking for the classic, romantic B&B experience, you'll want to reserve a room at the beautiful Dunbar House in Murphys (see below), just a few miles up the road. But if all you need is a pleasant place to stay with plenty of free perks, reasonable rates, and a central location, you can't do better than the Cedar Inn. With its cheery yellow facade, river stone trim, and wraparound porch, it looks more like a sprawling two-story house than a hotel. The guest rooms are all large, comfy, and loaded with amenities such as free Internet access, four HBO channels, business desks, and double granite vanities. And on a typical sweltering summer day, that outdoor pool looks mighty inviting. Families will also appreciate the hotel's 12-and-under-stay-free policy, as well as the two-room suites with refrigerators and microwaves.

444 S. Main St., Angels Camp, CA 95222. (📞 **800/767-1127** or 209/736-4000. www.bestwesternangels camp.com. 38 units. $95–$155 double. Rate includes continental breakfast. AE, DC, DISC, MC, V. Pets allowed. **Amenities:** Outdoor heated pool; exercise room; Jacuzzi; concierge; Internet kiosk; free Wi-Fi; room service; coin-op laundry. In room: TV/DVD, high-speed Internet access, fridge, coffeemaker, hair dryer, iron, safe, microwave.

Where to Dine

Camps ★★ (Kids) CALIFORNIA   On the edge of a golf resort on the western fringes of Angels Camp is Camps, the culinary feather in the cap of Greenhorn Creek golf resort. The restaurant's architects have integrated the building into its natural surroundings by constructing the outer walls with locally mined rhyolite and painting it in natural earth tones. The interior is furnished with leather armchairs, wicker, and antique woods. The best seats in the house are on the veranda overlooking the golf course, particularly on warm summer nights. Though the menu changes seasonally, a typical dinner may start with house salad with field greens, toasted almonds, and champagne vinaigrette, followed by macadamia-crusted halibut with lemon whipped potatoes or crisp roasted duck with truffled risotto and port-braised vegetables. The lengthy wine list has been given *Wine Spectator*'s Award of Excellence for 6 years running.

676 McCauley Ranch Rd. (½ mile west of Hwy. 4/Hwy. 49 junction off Angel Oaks Dr.). (📞 **209/729-8181.** www.greenhorncreek.com. Reservations recommended. Main courses $12–$31. AE, MC, V. Wed–Sun 11:30am–5pm; Wed–Sun 5–9pm; bistro menu Wed–Fri noon–9pm; Sun brunch 10am–2pm.

Crusco's Ristorante ★ ITALIAN   The sign at the entrance says it all: RELAX AND ENJOY. THIS IS NOT FAST FOOD. The overall experience is as important as the cuisine at Crusco's, a family-run restaurant headed by Celeste Lusher, the amiable chef/owner who oversees the kitchen along with her daughter Sarah, while her husband and son-in-law cater to their customers. In the heart of old-town Angels Camp, the restaurant's decor is an attractive balance of 19th-century Gold Rush architecture—wood beams, 1½-foot-thick stone walls, dark-wood furnishings—and old-world Mediterranean objets d'art such as faux columns and bas-relief sculptures. It's an apropos setting for Lusher's classic Italian menu, made from scratch using generations of family recipes. Each meal begins with house-made focaccia, served with olive oil and balsamic vinegar; then come the tough choices: pan-seared tenderloin steak finished with a sweet brandy demiglacé, sautéed apples and prunes, the creamy polenta, or the popular penne *rigate*. For lunch, Celeste recommends the New York steak with garlic french fries. Sampling a few of the house-made desserts is highly advised as well.

1240 S. Main St. (📞 **209/736-1440.** www.goldrush.com/~ciao. Reservations recommended. Main courses $15–$23. DISC, MC, V. Thurs–Mon 11:30am–3pm and 5–9pm (closed June 3–June 19; call ahead).

Murphys ★

From Angels Camp, a 20-minute drive east along Highway 4 takes you to Murphys, one of my favorite Gold Country towns. Legend has it Murphys started as a former trading post set up by brothers Dan and John Murphy in cooperation with local Indians (John married the chief's daughter). These days, tall locust trees shade gingerbread Victorians on narrow streets. Be sure to stroll down Main Street, stopping in **Grounds** (📞 **209/ 728-8663**) for a bite, or a cool draft of Grizzly Brown Ale—direct from the **Snowshoe**

Brewing Company in nearby Arnold—at the saloon within Murphys Historic Hotel and Lodge at 457 Main St.

While you're here, you might also want to check out **Ironstone Vineyards,** 1894 Six Mile Rd., 1 mile south of downtown Murphys (*①* **209/728-1251;** www.ironstone vineyards.com), a veritable wine theme park built by the Kautz family. It's open daily from 10am to 6pm.

Also in the vicinity—just off Highway 4, 1 mile north of Murphys off Sheep Ranch Road—are the **Mercer Caverns** (*①* **209/728-2101;** www.mercercaverns.com). These caverns, discovered in 1885 by Walter Mercer, contain a variety of geological formations—stalactites and stalagmites—in a series of chambers. Tours of the well-lit caverns take nearly an hour. From Memorial Day through September, hours are Sunday through Thursday from 9am to 5pm, Friday and Saturday from 9am to 6pm; from October 1 to Memorial Day, hours are 10am to 4:30pm daily. Admission is $12 for adults, $7 for children ages 5 to 12, and free for children under 5.

Fifteen miles east of Murphys up Highway 4 is **Calaveras Big Trees State Park** ★ (*①* **209/795-2334;** www.parks.ca.gov), where you can see giant sequoias that are among the biggest and oldest living things on earth. It's a popular summer retreat that offers camping, swimming, hiking, and fishing along the Stanislaus River. It's open daily; admission is $6 per car for day use.

Where to Stay

Dunbar House, 1880 ★★   This Italianate home, built in 1880 for the bride of a local businessman, is one of the finest B&Bs in the Gold Country. The front porch, which overlooks the exquisite gardens, is decorated with wicker furniture and hanging baskets of ivy. Inside, the emphasis is on comfort and elegance. The guest rooms are furnished with quality antiques and equipped with every possible amenity. Beds have Egyptian cotton linens and down comforters, and each room has a fridge stocked with mineral water and a complimentary bottle of local wine. My favorite room, the Cedar, is a fabulous two-room suite with a private sun porch, whirlpool tub, and chilled bottle of champagne. I also like the Sugar Pine suite, with its private balcony in the trees. Lemonade and cookies are offered in the afternoon, appetizers and wine in the early evening. Breakfast is served in your room, the dining room, or the garden.

271 Jones St., Murphys, CA 95247. *①* **800/692-6006** or 209/728-2897. Fax 209/728-1451. www.dunbar house.com. 5 units. $190–$260 double. Rates include breakfast and afternoon appetizers. AE, DISC, MC, V. *In room:* A/C, flatscreen TV/DVD, Wi-Fi, hair dryer, iron.

Where to Dine

Firewood ★ Value AMERICAN   Local restaurateur River Klass opened this order-at-the-counter cafe just down the street from his Grounds restaurant (see below). The open-air establishment specializes in fast, inexpensive, and darn good dishes such as Baja-style fish tacos, drippingly juicy, "not healthy" burgers, baby back ribs with house-made barbecue sauce, and superb gourmet pizzas baked in a wood-burning oven (the prosciutto and arugula, shrimp and feta, and sausage and pepperoni versions are all big hits). Good microbrew and local wine selections are available as well.

420 Main St. *①* **209/728-3248.** Reservations not accepted. Main courses $5–$10. MC, V. Wed–Sun 11am–9pm.

Grounds ★★ ECLECTIC   When River Klass moved here from the East Coast to open his own place, Murphys's restaurant-challenged residents heaved a sigh of relief. Its nickname is the "Rude Boy Cafe," after Klass's acerbic wit, but you'll find happy smiles

and friendly service. The majority of Grounds's business is with locals addicted to the
potato pancakes that come with every made-to-order omelet. For lunch, try the killer
BLT with avocado on a house-baked French roll or the grilled eggplant sandwich stuffed
with smoked mozzarella and fresh basil. Typical dinner choices include fresh breaded
halibut with house-made lentil salsa served over garlic mashed red potatoes, or a roasted
end-bone pork chop with demiglacé, cannellini beans, and grilled vegetables. The wine
list is impressive (and reasonably priced). The long, narrow dining rooms are bright and
airy with pine-wood furnishings, wood floors, and an open kitchen. On sunny days,
request a table on the back patio.

402 Main St. (C) **209/728-8663.** Reservations recommended. Main courses $15–$26. AE, DISC, MC, V.
Daily 7am–3pm; Wed–Thurs and Sun 5:30–8pm; Fri–Sat 5:30–9pm.

Columbia

Though a little hokey, **Columbia State Historic Park ★★** ((C) **209/532-3184;** www.
columbiacalifornia.com or www.parks.ca.gov) is the best-maintained Gold Rush town in
the Mother Lode (and one of the most popular, so expect crowds in the summer). At one
point, this boisterous mining town was the state's second-largest city (and only two votes
shy of becoming the state capital). When gold mining no longer panned out in the late
1850s, most of the town's 15,000 residents departed, leaving much of the mining equipment and buildings in place. In 1945, the entire town was turned into a historic park.

As a result, Columbia has been preserved and functions much as it did in the 1850s,
with stagecoach rides, Western-style Victorian hotels and saloons, a newspaper office, a
blacksmith's forge, a Wells Fargo express office, and numerous other relics of California's
early mining days. Cars are banned from its streets, giving the shady town an authentic
feel. Merchants still do business behind some storefronts, as horse, stagecoach, and pedestrian traffic wanders by.

If Columbia's heat and dust get to you, pull up a stool at the **Jack Douglass Saloon** on
Main Street ((C) **209/533-4176**), open daily from 10am to 6pm (till 7pm on Fri). Inside
the swinging doors of the classic Western bar, you can sample homemade sarsaparilla and
wild cherry, drinks the saloon has been serving since 1857. The saloon has sandwiches and
various snacks; it serves dinners on Friday night and has live music every weekend afternoon from May to September. The storefront's large shuttered windows open onto a dusty
main street, so put up your boots, relax awhile, and watch the stagecoach go by.

Free historical tours of the park depart from the Main Museum Saturday and Sunday
at 11am. Every second Saturday the park presents Gold Rush Days from 1 to 4pm when
costumed docents take you down Main Street and into dusty old structures that are off-
limits to the general public. Special docent-led tours are available by reservation for $2
per person.

Where to Stay & Dine

City Hotel ★ (Kids)   Established in 1856, the City Hotel was restored in 1975 by the
state of California, the nonprofit City Hotel Corporation, and Columbia College. Now
the college runs it as a training center for hospitality-management students (hence the
eager-to-please staff). It's a big, beautiful building, complete with a stately parlor furnished with Victorian sofas, antiques, and Oriental rugs. The largest guest rooms have
two balconies overlooking Main Street; the units off the parlor are also spacious. The
hallway rooms are smaller but still nicely furnished with Renaissance Revival beds and
antiques. Each room has a sink and toilet, but the shower rooms are separate. A continental buffet breakfast is served in the dining room. The hotel also runs a fine-dining

restaurant serving classic Continental cuisine (roast rack of lamb, grilled salmon, and smoked duck breast) Tuesday through Sunday, as well as the What Cheer saloon. Noise from the saloon—though it's not so loud as it was when the customers packed pistols—does travel upstairs. If you're a light sleeper, bring earplugs.

Main St. (P.O. Box 1870), Columbia State Park, CA 95310. © **800/532-1479** or 209/532-1479. Fax 209/532-7027. www.cityhotel.com. 10 units, all with shared shower rooms. $125–$145 double. Rates include continental breakfast. AE, DISC, MC, V. **Amenities:** Restaurant; saloon; nearby golf courses. *In room:* A/C, no phone.

Fallon Hotel ★ ⒦ⓘⓓⓢ Opened in 1857, this hotel has been restored and decorated to evoke the 1890s. The two-story building retains many of its original antiques and furniture. The largest rooms are those along the front upper balcony. Only one unit has a full bathroom; the rest have a private sink and toilet, and showers are down the hall. Rooms are furnished with high-backed Victorian beds, marble-topped dressers, and rockers. A full breakfast is served in the downstairs parlor.

Washington St. (P.O. Box 1870), Columbia State Park, CA 95310. © **800/532-1479** or 209/532-1470. Fax 209/532-7027. www.cityhotel.com. 14 units, 13 with shared bathroom. $90–$145 double. Rates include breakfast. AE, DISC, MC, V. **Amenities:** Nearby golf course; ice-cream parlor. *In room:* A/C, no phone.

Sonora

A few miles south of Columbia, Sonora is the largest town in the southern Gold Country. (You'll know you've arrived when traffic starts to crawl.) In Gold Rush days, Sonora and Columbia were the two richest towns in the Mother Lode. Dozens of stores and cafes line the main thoroughfare. If you find parking, it's worth an hour or two to check out the sites, like the 19th-century **St. James Episcopal Church,** at the top of Washington Street, and the **Tuolumne County Museum and History Center,** 158 W. Bradford Ave. (© **209/532-1317;** www.tchistory.org), in the 1857 County Jail. Admission is free, and it's open from 10am to 4pm Sunday through Friday and 10am to 3:30pm on Sundays. It's closed on Saturdays and some holidays.

Where to Stay

Gunn House Hotel ★ ⓥⓐⓛⓤⓔ Built in 1850 by Dr. Lewis C. Gunn, the Gunn House was the first two-story adobe structure in Sonora, built to house his family, who sailed around Cape Horn from the East Coast to join him in the Gold Rush. Painstakingly restored, it's now one of the best moderately priced hotels in the Gold Country. It's easy to catch the forty-niner spirit here, as the entire hotel and grounds are brimming with quality antiques and turn-of-the-20th-century artifacts. Rare for a building this old, each guest room has a private bathroom and air-conditioning. What really makes the Gunn House one of my favorites, though, is the hotel's beautiful pool and patio, surrounded by lush vegetation and admirable stonework. It's in a convenient location as well, right in downtown Sonora.

286 S. Washington St., Sonora, CA 95370. © **209/532-3421.** www.gunnhousehotel.com. 20 units. $69–$109 double. Rates include breakfast. AE, MC, V. **Amenities:** Outdoor heated pool. *In room:* A/C, TV.

Where to Dine

Diamondback Grill ⓥⓐⓛⓤⓔ AMERICAN For more than a decade, this modest family-owned diner has whipped up the Gold Country's best burger: the Diamondback—a grilled-to-order half-pounder that comes with the works, including fries. There are about a dozen other burgers, as well as gourmet sandwiches (go for the grilled eggplant with fresh tomato and mozzarella), house-made soups and pecan pies, a zesty black-bean-and-steak

Pan for Gold

You can learn to pan for gold through Jamestown's **Gold Prospecting Adventures** (© **800/596-0009** or 209/984-4653; www.goldprospecting.com). The hour-long class is about $20, plus you get to keep any gold you might find.

chili, and great daily specials listed. There's also a good selection of beer and wine by the glass.

93 S. Washington St. © **209/532-6661.** www.thediamondbackgrill.com. Main courses $5–$10. No credit cards. Mon–Sat 11am–9:30pm; Sun 11am–8pm.

Jamestown ★

About 4 miles southwest of Sonora on Highway 49 is Jamestown, a 4-block-long town of old-fashioned storefronts and two rustic turn-of-the-20th-century hotels. There's gold in these parts, too, as the marker commemorating the discovery of a 75-pound nugget attests (panning nearby Woods Creek is a popular pastime among both locals and tourists). If Jamestown looks eerily familiar to you, that's probably because you've seen it in the movies or on television. It's one of Hollywood's favorite Western movie sets; scenes from such films as *Butch Cassidy and the Sundance Kid* were shot here.

Jamestown's most popular attraction is the **Railtown 1897 State Historic Park ★**, a train buff's paradise featuring three Sierra steam locomotives. These great machines were used in many a movie and television show, including *High Noon, Little House on the Prairie, Bonanza,* and *My Little Chickadee.* The trains at the roundhouse are on display daily year-round. Call for information on weekend rides and guided tours. The Depot Store and Museum are open daily from 9:30am to 4:30pm (10am–3pm Nov–Mar). The park is located near the center of town, on Fifth Avenue at Reservoir Road (© **209/984-3953;** www.csrmf.org/railtown or www.parks.ca.gov).

Where to Stay & Dine

Jamestown Hotel ★ The most worked-over building in town, the Jamestown was originally built in 1858; it burned down and was rebuilt twice before 1915. To achieve the old-fashioned, brick-fronted Victorian look it sports today, a lot of stucco and Spanish-revival paraphernalia had to be removed. Most of the lower floor is devoted to the front office and the bar. The second floor contains a cadre of cozy bedrooms outfitted with antiques. All of the spacious rooms are loaded with nostalgic charm; a few have sitting rooms and TVs with VCRs, and all have private bathrooms (some with claw-foot tubs, several with spa tubs). *Note:* As of press time the Jamestown was up for sale, but we don't expect much to change at this historic hotel.

18153 Main St. (P.O. Box 539), Jamestown, CA 95327. © **800/205-4901** or 209/984-3902. Fax 209/984-4149. www.jamestownhotel.com. 8 units. $90–$175 double. Rates include full breakfast. AE, MC, V. **Amenities:** Bar; activities desk; business center. *In room:* A/C, TV/VCR, hair dryer, iron.

National Hotel & Restaurant ★ In the center of town, this two-story classic Western hotel has been operating since 1859, making it one of the 10 oldest continuously operating hotels in the state. The saloon has its original 19th-century redwood bar, and you can imagine what it must have been like when miners traded gold dust for drinks.

The guest rooms blend 19th-century details (handmade quilts, oak furnishings, lace curtains, brass beds) with 20th-century comforts such as private bathrooms. All guests have access to the authentic Soaking Room, a private room equipped with a sort of 1800s claw-foot Jacuzzi for two (when cowboys longed for a good, hot soak). Brunch, lunch, and dinner are served to the public in the handsome old-fashioned dining room or pretty garden courtyard. Dishes, many with a Mediterranean flavor, range from steak, veal, and prime rib to chicken, seafood, pasta dishes, and house-made desserts.

18183 Main St. (P.O. Box 502), Jamestown, CA 95327. © **800/894-3446** or 209/984-3446. Fax 209/984-5620. www.national-hotel.com. 9 units. $100–$140 double. Rates include large buffet breakfast. AE, DC, DISC, MC, V. Pets accepted w/fee of $25 per night. **Amenities:** Restaurant; saloon; nearby golf course; concierge; tour/activities desk; business center; Wi-Fi; secretarial services; room service; in-room massage. *In room:* A/C, TV, hair dryer.

3 THE CENTRAL VALLEY & SIERRA NATIONAL FOREST

The Central Valley (also known as the San Joaquin Valley) is about as far as you can get from movie stars in stretch limos. This hot, flat strip of farms, dairies, fast-food joints, cheap motels, and truck stops stretches for 225 miles from Bakersfield to Redding. The 18,000-square-mile valley is central to the economy of the Golden State, in part because of its cultivated and irrigated fields, orchards, pastures, and vineyards.

The major traffic arteries through the valley are Highway 99 and I-5. Highway 99 links the agricultural communities, while I-5 provides access routes to the attractions in the valley. Rivers cutting through the valley offer fishing, boating, house boating on the delta, and white-water rafting on the rapids. And once you get off the freeways, the valley's spectacular landscapes provide unrivaled natural beauty. Many visitors drive through in spring just to view the orchards in bloom.

The Central Valley also stands on the doorstep of some of America's greatest attractions, the most well known being Yosemite National Park. The Central Valley town of Visalia is the gateway to Sequoia and Kings Canyon National Park, and Fresno is a popular overnight stay for travelers heading in and out of the Sierra National Forest.

FRESNO

The running joke in California is that Fresno is the "gateway to Bakersfield." For most visitors, Fresno, 185 miles southeast of San Francisco, is just a place to pass through en route to the state parks; it can, however, be a good place to stop for food and lodging, and it makes a good base for exploring the Sierra National Forest (see below).

Founded in 1874, in the geographic center of the state, Fresno is in the heart of the Central Valley and in recent years has experienced incredible growth. Like most growing cities, it has seen increases in crime, drugs, and urban sprawl.

As the seat of Fresno County, the city handles more than $3 billion annually in agricultural production. It also contains Sun Maid, the world's largest dried-fruit packing plant, and Guild, one of the country's largest wineries.

If you have any reason at all to be in Fresno, try to visit between late February and late March so you can drive the **Fresno County Blossom Trail** ★. This 62-mile, self-guided tour takes in the beauty of California's agrarian bounty at its peak. The trail courses through fruit orchards in full bloom and citrus groves with lovely orange blossoms and a

heady natural perfume. The **Fresno Convention and Visitors Bureau,** 848 M St., Third **375**
Floor, in Fresno (*€* **800/788-0836** or 559/445-8300; www.fresnocvb.org), supplies full
details, including a map.

Where to Stay

San Joaquin ★   On the northern edge of Fresno, this full-service hotel was conceived
as an apartment complex in the 1970s. Around 1985, a lobby was added, the floor plans
were adjusted, and the place was reconfigured as an all-suite hotel. A recent renovation
has added a gym, conservatory, spa, and other amenities. Suites range from junior one-
bedroom suites to three-bedroom suites with kitchens, and each is outfitted in a slightly
different style, with light, contemporary colors and furniture. Room service is available
from a restaurant down the street.

1309 W. Shaw Ave., Fresno, CA 93711. *€* **800/775-1309** or 559/225-1309. Fax 559/225-6021. www.
sjhotel.com. 68 suites. $179–$215 suite. Rates include continental breakfast. AE, DC, DISC, MC, V. **Amenities:** Outdoor pool; Jacuzzi; business center; limited room service; laundry service. *In room:* A/C, TV/VCR,
kitchen, fridge, coffeemaker, hair dryer, iron.

Where to Dine

Veni, Vidi, Vici ★ CALIFORNIA   The most innovative and creative restaurant in
Fresno occupies a prominent position about 6 miles south of the commercial center, in
a funky neighborhood known as the Tower District. The place's rustic exterior strikes an
interesting contrast to the polished and artful interior on the other side of the 15-foot
doors, where the decor is accented with exposed-brick walls, mirrors, and chandeliers
fashioned from twisted wire and metal leaves. The menu changes often but might include
grilled juniper-berry pork chops with basmati rice, toasted sesame seeds, sautéed vegetables, red Thai curry glaze, and a cilantro emulsion; or lobster ravioli with sugar snap peas,
portobello mushrooms, white cheddar, and smoked tomato sauce. There are also fresh-
fish specials nightly. This is the only restaurant in Fresno that makes its own ice cream
(the flavor of the day when I arrived was Technicolor lime sorbet). Have a scoop or two
with the restaurant's perennial dessert favorite: bittersweet chocolate cake.

1116 N. Fulton St. *€* **559/266-5510.** Reservations recommended. Main courses $20–$30. AE, DC, DISC,
MC, V. Mon–Fri 11am–2pm; Tues–Sun 5:30–10pm (late-night menu Fri–Sat 10pm–midnight).

SIERRA NATIONAL FOREST ★★

Leaving Fresno's taco joints, used-car lots, and tract houses behind, an hour's drive and
45 miles northeast gets you to the Sierra National Forest, a land of lakes and coniferous
forests between Yosemite, Sequoia, and Kings Canyon national parks. The entire eastern
portion of the park is unspoiled wilderness protected by the government. Development—some of it, unfortunately, beside the bigger lakes and reservoirs—is confined to
the western side.

The 1.3-million-acre forest encompasses 528,000 acres of wilderness. The Sierra's five
wilderness areas include Ansel Adams, Dinkey Lakes, John Muir, Kaiser, and Monarch
(see below). The forest offers lots of opportunities for fishing, swimming, sailing, boating, camping, water-skiing, white-water rafting, kayaking, and horseback riding, all
regulated by certain guidelines. Downhill and cross-country skiing, as well as hunting,
are also available, in season. Backpackers will find solace here, as some 1,100 miles of
forest hiking trails traverse the park.

GETTING THERE   After visiting the ranger station at Oakhurst, take Highway 41 to Highway 49, the major road into the northern part of the national forest. This is more convenient for visitors approaching the park from Northern California. Highway 168 via Clovis is the primary route from Fresno if you're headed for Shaver Lake. There is no approach road from the eastern Sierra, only from the west.

VISITOR INFORMATION & PERMITS   To learn about hiking, camping, or other activities, or to get the fire and wilderness permits, visit one of the ranger stations in the park's western section. These include **Bass Lake Ranger District,** 57003 North Fork (✆ 559/877-2218); and the **High Sierra Ranger District,** 29688 Auberry Rd., Prather (✆ 559/855-5355).

SUPPLIES   Shaver Lake is one place where you can stock up on goods and supplies if you're going into the wilderness, but stores in Fresno carry much of the same stuff at lower prices. Cheaper supplies are also available in Clovis, outside Fresno (which you must pass through en route to the forest), at the **Peacock Market,** at Tollhouse Road (Third St.) and Sunnyside Avenue (✆ 559/299-6627).

WEATHER   In the lower elevations, summer temperatures can frequently reach 100°F (38°C), but in the higher elevations, more comfortable temperatures in the 70s and 80s (20s Celsius) are the norm.

The Major Wilderness & Recreation Areas

ANSEL ADAMS WILDERNESS   Divided between the Sierra and Inyo national forests, this wilderness area covers 228,500 acres. Elevations range from 3,500 to 13,157 feet. The frost-free period extends from mid-July to August, the best time for a visit to the park's upper altitudes.

Ansel Adams is dotted with alpine vistas, including steep-walled gorges and granite peaks. There are several glaciers in the north and some large lakes on the eastern slope of the Ritter Range. This wilderness has excellent stream and lake fishing, especially for rainbow, golden, and brook trout, and offers challenging mountain climbing on the Minarets Range. The wilderness is accessed by the Tioga Pass Road in the north, U.S. 395 and Reds Meadow Road in the east, the Minarets Highway in the west, and Highway 168 to High Sierra in the south.

DINKEY LAKES WILDERNESS   The 30,000-acre Dinkey Lakes area, created in 1984, occupies the western slope of the Sierra Nevada, southeast of Huntington Lake and northwest of Courtright Reservoir. Most of the timbered, rolling terrain here is 8,000 feet above sea level, reaching its apex (10,619 ft.) at Three Sisters Peak. Sixteen lakes are clustered in the west-central region. You can reach the area on Kaiser Pass Road (north), Red/Coyote Jeep Road (west), Rock Creek Road (southwest), or Courtright Reservoir (southeast), generally from mid-June to late October.

JOHN MUIR WILDERNESS   Occupying 584,000 acres in the Sierra and Inyo national forests, John Muir Wilderness—named after the naturalist—extends southeast from Mammoth Lakes along the crest of the Sierra Nevada for 30 miles before forking around the boundary of Kings Canyon National Park to Crown Valley and Mount Whitney. Elevations range from 4,000 to 14,496 feet at Mount Whitney, with many of the area's peaks surpassing 12,000 feet. The wilderness can be accessed from numerous points west of U.S. 395 between Mammoth Lake and Independence.

Split by deep canyons, the wilderness is also a land of meadows (especially beautiful when wildflowers bloom), lakes, and streams. The south and middle forks of the San Joaquin River, the north fork of Kings River, and many creeks draining into Owens Valley originate in the John Muir Wilderness. Mountain hemlock, red and white fir, and white-bark and western pine dot the landscape. Temperatures vary wildly throughout the day: Summer temperatures range from 25° to 85°F (–4°–29°C), and the only frost-free period is between mid-July and August. Higher elevations are marked by expanses of granite splashed with glacially carved lakes.

KAISER WILDERNESS   North of Huntington Lake and 70 miles northeast of Fresno, Kaiser is a 22,700-acre forest tract commanding a view of the central Sierra Nevada. It was named after Kaiser Ridge, which divides the area into two regions. Four trail heads provide access to the wilderness, but the northern half is much more open than the forested southern half; the primary point of entry is the Sample Meadow Campground. All other lakes are approached cross-country. Winter storms begin to blow in late October, and the grounds are generally snow covered until early June.

MONARCH WILDERNESS   Monarch is at the southern end of the John Muir Wilderness, on the western border of Sequoia and Kings Canyon National Parks, 65 miles east of Fresno via Highway 180. The area extends across 45,000 acres in the Sierra and Sequoia national forests. The Sierra National Forest portion of the region—about 21,000 acres—is rugged and hard to traverse. Steep slopes climb from the middle and main forks of Kings River, with elevations increasing from 2,400 to more than 10,000 feet. Rock outcroppings are found throughout Monarch, and most of the lower elevations are chaparral covered with pine stands near the tops of the higher peaks. Monarch is located at the southern end of the John Muir Wilderness, on the western border of Sequoia and Kings Canyon national parks, approximately 65 miles east of Fresno via Highway 180.

HUNTINGTON LAKE RECREATION AREA   At 7,000 feet, this area is a 2-hour drive east of Fresno via Highway 168. The lake is one of the reservoirs in the Big Creek Hydroelectric System and has 14 miles of shoreline. It's a popular recreational area, offering camping, hiking, picnicking, sailing, swimming, windsurfing, fishing, and horseback riding—or you can just appreciate the beauty. The main summer season stretches from Memorial Day to Labor Day. There are seven campgrounds and four picnic areas in the Huntington Lake Basin, plus numerous hiking and riding trails.

NELDER GROVE OF GIANT SEQUOIAS ★   This 1,540-acre tract in the Sierra National Forest contains 101 mature giant sequoias in the center of the Sequoia Range, south of Yosemite National Park. A **visitor center** stands near the Nelder Grove Campground, with historical relics and displays, including two restored log cabins. The Bull Buck Tree—at one time thought to be the largest in the world—is 246 feet high and has a circumference at ground level of 99 feet. There's a mile-long, self-guided walk along the "Shadow of the Giants" National Recreational Trail in the southwest corner of the grove.

Outdoor Pursuits

CAMPING   The Sierra National Forest seems like one vast campsite. Options range from primitive wilderness camps to developed and often crowded campgrounds with snack bars, flush toilets, bathhouses, and RV hookups. For information and reservations, call the **National Recreation Reservation Service** toll-free at ℂ **877/444-6777,** or visit its website at **www.reserveusa.com.**

The major campgrounds are the Shaver Lake area; the Huntington Lake area (which has seven family campgrounds open from the end of June to Labor Day that must be reserved in advance); the Florence and Edison Lake area (first-come, first-served); the Dinkey Creek area (family and group camping); the Wishon and Courtright area (four campgrounds; first-come, first-served); the Pine Flat Reservoir (in the Sierra foothills, with two first-come, first-served campgrounds); and Upper Kings River, east of Pine Flat Reservoir (family campgrounds; first-come, first-served).

FISHING   The many streams of the Sierra are home to rainbow, golden, brown, and brook trout. The best freshwater angling is in the Pineridge and Kings River Rangers District. At the lower elevations, Shaver Lake, Bass Lake, and Pine Flat reservoirs are known for their black-bass fishing. Questions about fishing in the national forest can be directed to the **California Department of Fish and Game,** 1234 E. Shaw Ave., Fresno, CA 93710 (© **559/243-4005;** www.dfg.ca.gov).

SKIING   Sixty-five miles northeast of Fresno on Highway 168 in the Sierra National Forest, the **Sierra Summit Ski Area** offers mildly challenging alpine skiing and marked trails for cross-country skiing and snowmobiling. The resort has two triple and three double chairlifts, four surface lifts, and 30 runs (the longest is 2¼ miles). The vertical drop is 1,600 feet. Grounds include a lodge, cafeteria, restaurant, and bar, open daily from mid-November until mid-April. For resort information or a ski report, call © **559/ 893-3311** or see **www.sierrasummit.com**. The **Pineridge Ranger Station** (© **559/855-5360**) maintains several marked cross-country trails along Highway 168, from a 1-mile tour for beginners to a 6-mile trail for advanced skiers.

WHITE-WATER RAFTING   The Upper Kings River, east of Pine Flat Reservoir, offers a 10-mile rafting run through Garnet Dike to Kirch Flat Campground. Rafting season is from late April to mid-July, with the highest waters in late May and early June. To get there, take Belmont Avenue in Fresno east (toward Pine Flat Reservoir) for about 63 miles. For more information about guided rafting trips on the Kings River, call **Kings River Expeditions** (© **800/846-3674** or 559/233-4881; www.kingsriver.com).

The Monterey Peninsula & the Big Sur Coast

by Matthew Richard Poole

The Monterey Peninsula and the Big Sur coast comprise one of the world's most spectacular shorelines, skirted with cypress trees, rugged shores, and crescent-shaped bays. Monterey reels in visitors with its world-class aquarium and array of outdoor activities. Pacific Grove is so peaceful that the butterflies choose it as their yearly mating ground. Pebble Beach attracts the golfing elite. Tiny Carmel-by-the-Sea is romantic and sweet despite the throngs of tourists who come for the beaches, shops, and restaurants. Big Sur's dramatic and majestic coast, backed by pristine redwood forests and rolling hills, is one of the most breathtaking, tranquil environments on earth. If you're traveling Highway 1 (which you should be), the coastline will guide you all the way through the region.

This chapter begins with Santa Cruz, at the northwestern end of Monterey Bay—one of my favorite destinations on the coast, and home of the Santa Cruz Beach Boardwalk. Across Monterey Bay at the northern tip of the Monterey Peninsula are the seaside communities of Monterey and Pacific Grove, while Pebble Beach and Carmel-by-the-Sea hug the peninsula's south coast along Carmel Bay. Between the north and south coasts, which are only about 5 miles apart, are many golf courses, some of the state's most stunning homes and hotels, and the 17-Mile Drive, one of the most scenic coastal roads in the world.

Inland lies Carmel Valley, with its elegant inns and resorts, golf courses, and guaranteed sunshine, even when the coast is socked in with fog. Farther down the coast along Highway 1 is Big Sur, a stunning 90-mile stretch of coast south of the Monterey Peninsula and west of the Santa Lucia Mountains.

1 SANTA CRUZ ★★

77 miles SE of San Francisco

For a small bayside city, Santa Cruz has a lot to offer. The main show, of course, is the Beach Boardwalk, which attracts millions of visitors each year. But past the arcades and cotton candy is a surprisingly diverse and energetic city with a little something for everyone: Shopping, hiking, mountain biking, sailing, fishing, kayaking, surfing, wine tasting, golfing, whale-watching—the list of things to do here is almost endless, making Santa Cruz one of the premier family destinations on the California coast.

GETTING THERE Santa Cruz is 77 miles southeast of San Francisco. The most scenic route to Santa Cruz is along Highway 1 from San Francisco, which, aside from the "you fall, you die" stretch called Devil's Slide, allows you to cruise at a steady 50 mph. Faster but less romantic is Highway 17, which is accessed near San Jose from I-280, I-880, or U.S. 101, and ends at the foot of the boardwalk. The exception to this rule is on weekend mornings, when Highway 17 tends to logjam with beachgoers while Highway 1 remains relatively uncrowded.

VISITOR INFORMATION For information, contact the **Santa Cruz County Conference and Visitors Council,** 1211 Ocean St., Santa Cruz, CA 95060 (© **800/833-3494** or 831/425-1234; www.santacruzca.org), open Monday through Saturday from 9am to 5pm, Sunday from 10am to 4pm.

SPECIAL EVENTS Special events include **Shakespeare Santa Cruz** in July and August (© **831/459-2159;** http://shakespearesantacruz.org), and the **Cabrillo Music Festival** in August (© **831/426-6966;** www.cabrillomusic.org).

WHAT TO SEE & DO
Beaches, Hiking & Fishing in Santa Cruz

One of the few old-fashioned amusement parks left in the world, the **Santa Cruz Beach Boardwalk** ★★ (© **831/423-5590;** www.beachboardwalk.com) draws more than three million visitors a year to its 30 rides and arcades, shops, and restaurants. The park has two national landmarks—a 1924 wooden Giant Dipper roller coaster and a 1911 carousel with hand-carved wooden horses and a 342-pipe organ band. It's open daily in the summer (Memorial Day weekend to Labor Day) and on weekends and holidays throughout the spring and fall, from 11am (noon sometimes in winter). Admission to the boardwalk is free, but an all-day "unlimited rides" pass is $38. See **www.beachboardwalk.com** for discounts, concerts and events, and up-to-date schedules, which can often vary.

Here, too, is **Neptune's Kingdom,** 400 Beach St. (© **831/423-5590;** www.beach boardwalk.com), an enormous indoor family recreation center with a two-story miniature golf course. Also on Beach Street is the shop- and restaurant-lined **Municipal Wharf** (© **831/420-6025**), a beachfront strip serenaded by the sea lions below. You can also crab and fish from here. Most shops are open daily from 7am to 9pm; the wharf is open daily from 5am to 2am. **Stagnaro's** (© **831/427-2334;** www.stagnaros.com) runs fishing and whale-watching trips year-round, and hour-long narrated bay cruises ($12 for adults, $8 for kids under 14).

Farther down on West Cliff Drive, you'll come to a favorite surfing spot, **Steamer Lane,** where you can watch pro surfers shredding the waves. If you want to learn more about surfing, practiced here for more than 100 years, go to the **Santa Cruz Surfing Museum,** at the lighthouse (© **831/420-6289;** www.santacruzparksandrec.com), open Wednesday through Sunday from 10am to 5pm in the summer, Thursday through Monday from noon to 4pm in the winter. Antique surfboards, videos, photos, and other memorabilia depict the history and evolution of surfing worldwide.

Continue along West Cliff and you'll reach **Natural Bridges State Beach,** 2531 W. Cliff Dr. (© **831/423-4609;** www.scparkfriends.org), a large sandy beach with nearby tide pools and hiking trails. It's also home to a large colony of monarch butterflies that cluster and mate in the nearby eucalyptus grove.

Other Santa Cruz beaches worth noting are **Bonny Doon,** at Bonny Doon Road and Highway 1, an uncrowded sandy beach and a major surfing spot accessible by a steep

walkway; **Pleasure Point Beach,** East Cliff Drive at Pleasure Point Drive; and **Twin**
Lakes State Beach, which is ideal for sunning and also provides access to Schwann
Lagoon, a bird sanctuary.

In addition to cultural and sporting events, the University of California at Santa Cruz
features the **Seymour Marine Discovery Center** at the Long Marine Laboratory, 100
Shaffer Rd., at the northwest end of Delaware Avenue ((C) **831/459-3800;** www2.ucsc.
edu/seymourcenter), where you can observe marine scientists at work with aquatic species, in tide-pool touch tanks and aquariums, and learn how marine research aids ocean
conservation. Hours are Tuesday through Saturday from 10am to 5pm, and Sunday from
noon to 5pm; admission is $6 for adults, $4 for students, seniors, and children ages 4 to
16, and free for kids under 3 (free admission the first Tues of each month).

The **Santa Cruz Harbor,** 135 Fifth Ave. ((C) **831/475-6161;** www.santacruzharbor.
org), has boat rentals, open-boat fishing (cod, shark, and salmon), and whale-watching
trips. For fishing trips, contact **Santa Cruz Sportfishing Inc.** ((C) **831/426-4690;** www.
santacruzsportfishing.com) Even if you're not a fisher, it's worth browsing the shops and
restaurants in the harbor.

Bikes—mountain, kids', tandem, hybrid—are available by the hour, day, or week from
various bike-rental shops in convenient locations around town. For a list of shops, call
the **Santa Cruz Visitors Council** at (C) **800/833-3494** or see **www.santacruzca.org**.

The **Pasatiempo Golf Club,** at 18 Clubhouse Rd. ((C) **831/459-9155;** www.pasatiempo.
com), is rated among the top 100 courses in the U.S. Greens fees are $200.

Kayaking is also an option. Outfitters include **Kayak Connection,** 413 Lake Ave. No.
103 ((C) **831/479-1121;** www.kayakconnection.com), and **Venture Quest Kayaking**
((C) **831/427-2267;** www.kayaksantacruz.com), which rent single, double, and triple
kayaks at Building No. 2 on the wharf and at 125 Beach St. Classes, wildlife tours, and
moonlight paddles are also available.

You can rent surfing equipment at the **Cowell's Beach Surf Shop,** 30 Front St.
((C) **831/427-2355;** www.cowellssurfshop.com), and from the **Club Ed Surf School**
((C) **800/287-SURF** or 831/464-0177; www.club-ed.com), on Cowell Beach in front of
the West Coast Santa Cruz Hotel. Both offer lessons: Club Ed's are $85 for a 2-hour
group session and $110 per hour for private lessons (equipment included); Cowell's are
$65 for 2-hour group lessons including a board and wet suit.

In Nearby Capitola & Aptos

South along the coast, the small community of **Capitola** ★, at the mouth of the Soquel
Creek, is a spawning ground for steelhead and salmon. You can fish without a license
from the **Capitola Wharf,** 1400 Wharf Rd., or rent a boat from **Capitola Boat and Bait**
((C) **831/462-2208;** www.santacruzboatrentals.net).

Capitola Beach fronts the bustling Esplanade. Surf fishing, clamming, and camping
are popular pastimes at Capitola's **New Brighton State Beach,** 1500 State Park Dr.
((C) **831/464-6330**). Another popular activity is **antiquing** in the stores along Soquel
Drive between 41st and Capitola avenues.

Farther south around the bay is **Aptos** ★, home to the 10,000-acre **Forest of Nisene**
Marks State Park ((C) **831/763-7062**). This was the epicenter of the 1989 earthquake,
and now has hiking trails through redwoods and past abandoned mining camps. Mountain bikers and leashed dogs are welcome. It's at the end of Aptos Creek Road off Soquel
Drive, open year-round from sunrise to sunset.

In the redwood-forested mountains behind Santa Cruz, there are quite a few **wineries,**
although visitors may not be familiar with the labels because the output is small and

Seven Money-Saving Tips for Santa Cruz Tourists

- On Friday nights in summer, head to the Santa Cruz Beach Boardwalk's Beach Bandstand for **free concerts** with live music from the '60s, '70s, and '80s—Greg Kihn, Eddie Money, the Fixx, Survivor—at 6:30 and 8:30pm.

- On Mondays and Tuesdays after 5pm in summer, the Santa Cruz Beach Boardwalk holds **1907 Nights,** celebrating the year it opened by reducing prices to 65¢ a ride (that's $2.50 off). Hot dogs, sodas, and cotton candy are also just 65¢. The special typically runs from late June to the end of August.

- Great Mexican food at cheap prices is served daily from 10am to 9pm at the **Las Palmas Taco Bar** at 55 Front St. near the wharf (© **831/429-1220**). This grimy little corner cafe has been a local's favorite since 1955. You can smell the frijoles frying from the beach. Get a couple of beef tongue soft tacos brimming with *pico de gallo* and salsa verde.

- To skip the entrance fee to **Henry Cowell Redwoods State Park,** drive 1½ miles south of the main entrance on Calif. 9 to the Ox Road parking lot. Park for free and then follow the trail into the park, which takes you past a popular swimming hole called the Garden of Eden.

- A far better walk than the boardwalk is along the 2-mile ocean-side paved path on **West Cliff Drive** (west of the wharf). The scenery is spectacular, particularly at sunset, and it won't cost a cent.

- **Carmelita Cottages,** 321 Main St. (© **831/423-8304;** www.hi-santacruz. org), is a hostel in Santa Cruz that will rent you a bunk bed for $21. The gaggle of white-washed Victorian cottages is a few blocks north of the Boardwalk, in a quiet, residential neighborhood. The hostel also reserves a few rooms for couples and families. (It's not exactly Romance Central, but for $50 a night for your own room at such a prime location, it's hard to complain.)

- Don't pay to park in downtown Santa Cruz. Along Cedar and Front streets are three parking garages and 13 surface lots that offer 3 hours of **free parking.**

consumed locally. Most are clustered around Boulder Creek and Felton or around Capitola. All offer tours by appointment; some feature tastings, including the **Bargetto Winery,** 3535 N. Main, Soquel (© **800/422-7438** or 831/475-2258; www.bargetto. com), which has a courtyard wine-tasting area overlooking the creek. For information, contact the **Santa Cruz Mountains Winegrowers' Association** (© **831/685-VINE;** www.scmwa.com).

WHERE TO STAY

If you have trouble finding a vacancy, consider the **Terrace Court** (125 Beach St., © **831/ 423-3031;** www.terracecourt.com), a plain but practical motel on a hill overlooking the wharf, with ocean views and easy beach access. Santa Cruz has plenty of chain motels as well. Two **Travelodges** (© 800/578-7878; www.travelodge.com), two **Best Westerns** (© 800/780-7234; www.bestwestern.com), two **Super 8s** (© 800/800-8000; www. super8.com), and an **Econo Lodge** (© 877/424-6423; www.choicehotels.com) provide moderate- and budget-priced accommodations in addition to the nonchain recommendations below.

Expensive

Babbling Brook Bed & Breakfast Inn ★★   With charm to spare, the rooms in this popular inn are like tree houses over and around a brook running through an acre of gardens, pines, and redwoods. It's on a busy street, but what you hear from your room is running water cascading over falls and a waterwheel. Rooms are tasteful and simple, with lots of windows, skylights, open-beam ceilings, balconies, and decks; most have gas fireplaces and spa tubs. The inn is within a mile of the beach and boardwalk and a short walk from downtown Santa Cruz. Breakfast, and evening wine and snacks are served in the comfortable lobby.

1025 Laurel St., Santa Cruz, CA 95060. © 800/866-1131 or 831/427-2437. Fax 831/427-2457. www. babblingbrookinn.com. 13 units. $209–$279 double. Rates include full country-breakfast buffet. AE, DISC, MC, V. **Amenities:** Nearby golf. *In room:* TV, VCR (in some units).

The Inn at Depot Hill ★★★   A few blocks from the bay front, this converted 1910-era railroad station in nearby Capitola has been designed and decorated with such artful attention to detail that it's been ranked one of the top inns in the nation—which explains why Martha Stewart chose to stay here during her coastal tour a few years ago. All rooms and suites have fine fabrics and linens, wood-burning fireplaces, stereos, two-person showers, and full bathrooms. Most have private patios with Jacuzzis (other rooms share a common Jacuzzi). Perhaps you'll check into the Portofino Room, patterned after an Italian villa, or the Stratford-on-Avon, a replica of an English cottage. The evening wine and hors d'oeuvres and breakfast are also of prime quality, served either in your room or out back in the garden courtyard on wrought-iron tables shaded by market umbrellas.

250 Monterey Ave. (near Park Ave.), Capitola, CA 95010. © 800/572-2632 or 831/462-3376. Fax 831/462-3697. www.innatdepothill.com. 12 units. $259–$349 double. Rates include breakfast, afternoon tea or wine, hors d'oeuvres, and after-dinner dessert. AE, DC, DISC, MC, V. **Amenities:** Jacuzzi; room service. *In room:* A/C, TV/VCR, fax, dataport, hair dryer.

Pleasure Point Inn ★★ (Finds)   With the amenities of a modern hotel and the casual atmosphere of a B&B, the four-room Pleasure Point Inn has all you might want in a romantic coastal getaway: a beautiful ocean view overlooking Monterey Bay, a quiet neighborhood location, contemporary design and decor, and a rooftop deck. The Pleasure Point beach and surf break are right across the street, where local longboarders provide viewing entertainment from sunrise to sunset. Each guest room is impeccably clean, with custom furnishings, wood flooring, hand-painted tiles, private bathrooms, down comforters, a gas fireplace, and private entrances. An expanded continental breakfast is served in the oceanview dining/lounge area (I spotted a gray whale while munching on a bagel); after breakfast, guests can stroll the paved coastal path down to Capitola, walk to the beach, or relax on the sunny rooftop deck (top-side toys include an eight-person hot tub, chaise longue chairs, and surround-sound music).

2-3665 East Cliff Dr., Santa Cruz, CA 95062. © 831/475-4657. www.pleasurepointinn.com. 4 units. $225–$295 double. Rates include continental breakfast. MC, V. **Amenities:** Hot tub. *In room:* TV, Wi-Fi, fridge, coffeemaker, safe, microwave, fireplace.

Casablanca Inn   Across from the wharf in a heavily trafficked area, this aging waterfront inn and motel was once the Mediterranean-style Cerf Mansion dating from 1918. Other motel-style accommodations have grown up around the main building. Originally the home of a federal judge, it has individually decorated bedrooms, some with brass beds and velvet draperies. Some units have fireplaces and terraces, and all have microwaves. Most have ocean views. Casablanca Restaurant serves California-Continental cuisine in an oceanview setting. The Casablanca wouldn't be my first choice of lodging in Santa Cruz, but in a pinch it'll do if you can get a room well below rack rate.

101 Main St. (at the corner of Beach St.), Santa Cruz, CA 95060. ℂ **800/644-1570** or 831/423-1570. Fax 831/423-0235. www.casablanca-santacruz.com. 39 units. High season $116–$320 double. AE, DC, DISC, MC, V. **Amenities:** Restaurant; bar; nearby golf course; room service; laundry service. *In room:* TV, dataport, kitchen in some units, minibar, fridge, coffeemaker, hair dryer, iron, safe.

Edgewater Beach Motel ⟨**Value**⟩   If you're nostalgic for the good ol' days when the family took road trips to the beach in the wood-paneled station wagon, you'll find a fondness for the Edgewater Beach Motel. It looks like a time capsule from the 1960s; how they kept the furnishings in such prime condition is a mystery. The motel has a range of accommodations, from family suites with kitchens to rooms with fireplaces; most have microwaves. The Edgewater also sports a nice pool, sun deck, and barbecue area, a block from the Santa Cruz boardwalk.

525 Second St., Santa Cruz, CA 95060. ℂ **888/809-6767** or 831/423-0440. www.edgewaterbeachmotel. com. 18 units. Winter $85–$219 double; summer $139–$299 double. AE, DC, DISC, MC, V. **Amenities:** Outdoor heated pool. *In room:* TV/VCR, fully equipped kitchen in suites, fridge, coffeemaker.

Inexpensive

Fern River Resort ★ ⟨**Finds**⟩   This nifty mountain retreat is 4 miles from Santa Cruz down a curvy redwood-lined road. The "resort" consists of 13 furnished and equipped cabins on 4 forested acres with lawn, garden, or river views. Outdoor toys will keep you amused, including badminton, Ping-Pong, tetherball, horseshoes, and 20 miles of hiking and mountain-biking trails in nearby Henry Cowell Park. You'll also find an enclosed spa tub and a small beach on the San Lorenzo River for sunning, swimming, and fishing. The cabins range in size from studios to some that sleep up to six. Some have equipped kitchens, but if you plan to cook, bring some pots and pans.

5250 Hwy. 9, Felton, CA 95018. ℂ **831/335-4412.** www.fernriver.com. 16 units. High season $69–$155 double; low season $75–$130 double. AE, MC, V. **Amenities:** Jacuzzi. *In room:* TV.

WHERE TO DINE

Bittersweet Bistro ★★ CALIFORNIA   Once a tiny operation in a small strip development, this restaurant has grown into one of the most popular around Santa Cruz. Its relocation to bigger digs in Rio Del Mar hasn't tarnished chef-owner Thomas Vinolus's reputation for serving exceptional cuisine. Carefully crafted dishes range from wood-oven pizzas to grilled lamb noisettes in a rosemary cabernet demiglace. Coproprietor and wine director Elizabeth Vinolus created an exceptional wine list and often hosts winemaker dinners. Bistro Hour, from 3 to 6pm daily, features two-for-one specials on gourmet pizzas and special pricing on all by-the-glass wines, beer, and spirits.

787 Rio Del Mar Blvd., Aptos (10 miles southeast of Santa Cruz on Hwy. 1). ℂ **831/662-9799.** www. bittersweetbistro.com. Reservations recommended. Main courses $17–$30. AE, MC, V. Daily 5:30–10pm.

The Crepe Place (Value) CREPES/ECLECTIC Beloved by locals, particularly as a late-night hangout, the Crepe Place has been in business for more than 30 years. Choose from over 15 styles of crepes (Spinach Supreme, Salsa, and Jambalaya are local favorites), served in the wood-paneled dining room or outdoor garden area. Other menu items include soups (good clam chowder), salads, oven-baked whole-wheat honey bread, and a popular dessert called a Tunisian Doughnut. On weekends, egg dishes are also served, at brunch.

1134 Soquel Ave. (at Seabright Ave.). ℰ 831/429-6994. www.thecrepeplace.com. Main courses $5–$17. AE, MC, V. Mon–Thurs 11am–midnight; Fri–Sun 10am–1am.

O'mei ★ PROVINCIAL SZECHUAN Wonderfully creative dishes make up for O'mei's (pronounced Oh-*may*) mini-mall location. Named after a mountain in the Sichuan province of China, O'mei serves unusual specialties such as Chengdu–bean curd sea bass in a spicy *dou-ban* sauce (a rich, velvety wine-chile sauce), apricot-almond chicken, and litchi *pi-pa* bean-curd balls, along with familiar dishes such as chicken with cashews. The most popular dish is *gan pung chicken*—battered chicken with wood ear mushrooms, ginger, cilantro, and a sweet and spicy sauce. But I usually order the rock cod in black bean and sweet pepper sauce. Dinner starts with a dim sum-style tray of exotic vegetarian fare such as sesame-cilantro-eggplant salad or pan-roasted peppers with feta cheese. Dessert includes black-sesame ice cream.

2316 Mission St. (where Hwy. 1 turns into Mission St.). ℰ 831/425-8458. Reservations recommended. Main courses $9–$24. AE, MC, V. Tues–Sun 5–9:30pm.

Shadowbrook ★ AMERICAN/CONTINENTAL One of Capitola's most romantic restaurants has a serene setting above Soquel Creek. To reach it, diners take a cable-driven "hillavator" down, or walk the long, steep steps beside a running waterfall. At the bottom, a log cabin built in the 1920s has been enlarged to house Shadowbrook's wood-paneled Wine Cellar, airy Garden Room, Fireplace Room, and creek-side Greenhouse. The menu is unsurprising, with thick-cut prime rib and steaks, seafood such as scampi and fresh halibut, and pasta dishes such as the eggplant parmigiana. Appetizers include prawn cocktail, deep-fried artichoke hearts, and baked brie. Standout desserts are the mud pie and the Shadowbrook chocolate meltdown. If you're not ready to dine, grab a seat in the lounge and nosh on appetizers and light entrees from the wood-fired oven.

1750 Wharf Rd., Capitola. ℰ 800/975-1511 or 831/475-1511. www.shadowbrook-capitola.com. Reservations recommended. Main courses $19–$32. AE, DC, DISC, MC, V. Mon–Fri 5–8:45pm; Sat 4:30–9:45pm; Sun 10am–2:30pm and 4:30–8:30pm.

Walnut Avenue Café ★★ AMERICAN Nary a Santa Cruz resident has a bad thing to say about this downtown staple. The cafe serves breakfast and lunch only, and its creative substitutions—for example, eggs Benedict can be served with shrimp and tomato or blackened *ahi* tuna—will make you wish you could sample the entire menu at once. You won't find heavy entrees on the lunch menu, other than the daily pasta special, but the salad, soup, sandwich, and burger offerings are many. If you request to dine alfresco on a sunny day, you'll likely incur a lengthy wait (and the restaurant doesn't take reservations). So head there before the lunchtime rush, or else be prepared to settle for indoor seating.

106 Walnut Ave. ℰ 831/457-2307. www.walnutavenuecafe.com. Breakfast $5–10; lunch $8–$10. AE, MC, V. Mon–Fri 7am–3pm; Sat–Sun 8am–4pm.

On U.S. 101, **San Juan Bautista** ★ is a mission town that retains the flavor of a 19th-century village. The mission complex sits in a picturesque farming valley, surrounded by the restored buildings of the original city plaza.

From U.S. 101, take Highway 156 east (south) to the town center to the mission itself, founded in 1797. The largest church in the mission chain, San Juan Bautista is the only one in continuous service. The padres here inspired many Native Americans to convert, creating one of the largest congregations in California. The mission once boasted a formidable Native American boys' choir, and the small museum exhibits many musical instruments and transcriptions. Mission San Juan Bautista is open daily year-round from 9:30am to 4:45pm. The suggested donation is $1 per person. For more information, call © 831/623-4528 or see www.oldmissionsjb.org or www.san-juan-bautista.ca.us.

East of the church, at the edge of an abrupt drop created by the San Andreas Fault, a marker notes the path of the old **El Camino Real.** Seismographic measuring equipment and an earthquake science exhibit accompany the marker.

There's much to see on the restored city plaza as well. The **San Juan Bautista State Historic Park** comprises the old Plaza Hotel with its frontier barroom and furnished rooms; the Plaza Hall, its adjoining stables, and blacksmith shop; and the Castro House, where the Breen family lived after traveling here with the ill-fated Donner Party in 1846. Allow 1¹/₂ to 2 hours to see the entire plaza. Admission to the park buildings is $2 for adults, $1 for children ages 6 to 12 (separate from the mission admission). Hours are daily from 10am to 4:30pm. For more information, call © 831/623-4526.

2 MONTEREY ★★

45 miles S of Santa Cruz; 116 miles S of San Francisco; 335 miles N of Los Angeles

Monterey is now famous as the site of the world's longest-running jazz festival (p. 43, in the Calendar of Events), which draws nearly 50,000 visitors annually for performances by the likes of Tony Bennett, Sonny Rollins, and Branford Marsalis. The town itself, however, is much older than that—and no less significant to state history. Settled in 1770 as one of the West Coast's first European outposts, Monterey was the capital of California under Spanish, Mexican, and American rule. The state constitution was drafted here in 1849, which paved the way for admission to the Union a year later. Many early colonial buildings still stand. A major whaling center in the 1800s, Monterey eventually became the sardine capital of the Western Hemisphere when the first packing plant was built in 1900. By 1913, boats were bringing in 25 tons of sardines a night to the 18 canneries. The gritty lives of the mostly working-class residents were captured by local hero John Steinbeck in his 1945 novel *Cannery Row.*

After the sardines disappeared, Monterey was forced to fish for tourist dollars instead; hence, an array of boutiques, knickknack stores, and theme restaurants now reside in converted sardine factories along the bay. Granted, plenty of history and heritage remains along Cannery Row, but you'll have to weed through the tourist schlock to find them. Its saving grace is the world-class aquarium and beautiful Monterey Bay, where sea lions and otters still frolic in abundance.

As you distance yourself from the Row, however, you'll discover Monterey is a pleasant seaside community with magnificent vistas, historic architecture, stately Victorians, and a number of quality lodgings and restaurants. More important, Monterey is only a short

drive from Pacific Grove, Carmel, Pebble Beach, and Big Sur, and the lodgings here are
far less expensive, which makes it a great place to set up base while exploring the
Monterey coast.

ESSENTIALS

GETTING THERE The region's most convenient runway, at the **Monterey Peninsula
Airport** (© 831/648-7000; www.montereyairport.com), is 3 miles east of Monterey on
Highway 68. American Eagle, Northwest, United, and US Airways run daily flights in
and out of Monterey. Many nearby hotels offer free airport shuttle service. If you take a
taxi, it will cost about $14 to $20 to get to a peninsula hotel. Several national car-rental
companies have airport locations, including **Dollar** (© **800/800-3665;** www.dollar.
com) and **Hertz** (© **800/654-3131;** www.hertz.com).

VISITOR INFORMATION The **Monterey Peninsula Visitors and Convention
Bureau** (© 831/649-1770; www.montereyinfo.org) has two visitor centers: one in the
lobby of the Maritime Museum at Custom House Plaza near Fisherman's Wharf, the
other at Lake El Estero on Camino El Estero. Both locations, open daily, offer good maps
and free pamphlets and publications, including an excellent visitors' guide and the
magazine *Coast Weekly.* Two other good sources for Monterey information are the
Monterey Peninsula On-Line Guide at **www.monterey.com** and **Monterey-Carmel.
com** (www.monterey-carmel.com).

GETTING AROUND The free **Waterfront Area Visitor Express (WAVE)** trolley takes
passengers to and from the aquarium and other waterfront attractions from Memorial
Day to Labor Day. It departs the downtown parking garages at Tyler Street and Del
Monte Avenue every 10 to 12 minutes between 10am to 7pm Monday to Friday and
10am to 8pm Saturday to Sunday. Other WAVE stops include many hotels and motels
in Monterey and Pacific Grove. For further information, call Monterey Salinas Transit at
© **831/899-2555** (www.mst.org).

WHAT TO SEE & DO

The **National Steinbeck Center** ★ isn't in town, but fans of the author may want to
make the 20-mile drive northeast from Monterey on Highway 68 to 1 Main St. in Salinas
(© **831/796-3833;** www.steinbeck.org). The modern $11-million, 37,000-square-foot
museum features interactive exhibits, a gallery of changing exhibitions, an orientation
theater with a short video on Steinbeck's life, educational programs, a gift shop, and a
cafe. Admission is $11 for adults, $8.95 for seniors over 62, $7.95 for children ages 13
to 17, $5.95 for children 6 to 12, and free for children under 6. Hours are daily from
10am to 5pm.

If you're passing through Monterey on a Tuesday afternoon, check out the **Old
Monterey Marketplace** on Alvarado Street, from Pearl to Del Monte streets (© **831/
655-8070;** www.oldmonterey.org), from 4 to 8pm (7pm in winter), rain or shine. More
than 100 vendors contribute food, music, crafts, and entertainment.

Cannery Row (Overrated) Once the center for an industrial sardine-packing operation
immortalized by John Steinbeck as "a poem, a stink, a grating noise, a quality of light, a
tone, a habit, a nostalgia, a dream," this area today is a strip congested with tourists, tacky
gift shops, overpriced seafood restaurants, and a parking nightmare. What changed it so
dramatically? The sardines disappeared in 1948, from overfishing, changing currents,
and pollution. Fishermen left, canneries closed, and the Row fell into disrepair. Curious
tourists continued to visit the area. Steinbeck himself wrote, after visiting in the 1960s,

Cannery Row **3**

Carmel Beach City Park **15**

Carmel Mission **16**

Carmel River
State Beach **18**

Fisherman's Wharf **1**

Links at Spanish Bay **11**

Lovers Point **6**

Marine Gardens Park **7**

Monterey Bay
Aquarium **4**

Pacific Grove Municipal
Golf Course **8**

Pacific Grove Museum of
Natural History **5**

Path of History **2**

Pebble Beach
Golf Links **14**

Point Pinos Lighthouse **9**

Poppy Hills
Golf Course **12**

17-Mile Drive
Entrances **10**

Spyglass Hill
Golf Course **13**

Tor House **17**

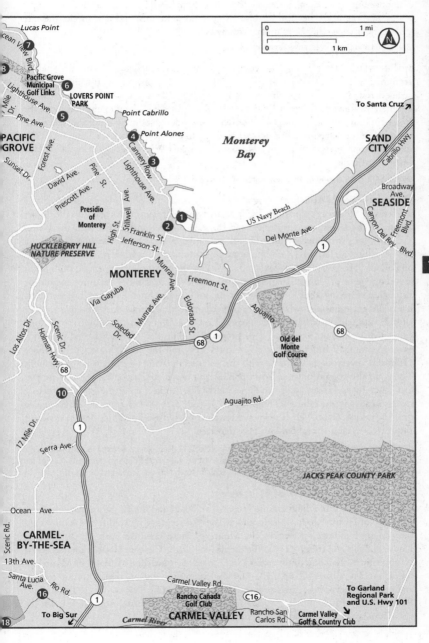

Lucas Point

7

Ocean View Blvd.

3

Pacific Grove Municipal Golf Links 6

LOVERS POINT PARK

Lighthouse Ave.

5

17 Mile Dr.

Pine Ave.

Point Cabrillo

4 Point Alones

Cannery Row

3

Lighthouse Ave.

PACIFIC GROVE

Sunset Dr.

Forest Ave.

David Ave.

Prescott Ave.

Pine St.

High St.

Stillwell Ave.

Franklin St.

Jefferson St.

Presidio of Monterey

2

1

HUCKLEBERRY HILL NATURE PRESERVE

MONTEREY

Via Gayuba

Munras Ave.

Soledad Dr.

Eldorado St.

68

1

Freemont St.

Aguajito

Old del Monte Golf Course

68

US Navy Beach

Del Monte Ave.

1

Monterey Bay

To Santa Cruz

SAND CITY

Cabrillo Hwy.

Broadway Ave.

SEASIDE

Canyon Del Rey

Freemont Blvd.

Los Altos Dr.

Scenic Dr.

Holman Hwy.

68

10

1

17 Mile Dr.

Serra Ave.

Aguajito Rd.

JACKS PEAK COUNTY PARK

Ocean Ave.

CARMEL-BY-THE-SEA

13th Ave.

Scenic Rd.

Santa Lucia Ave.

16

Rio Rd.

1

18

To Big Sur

Carmel River

Carmel Valley Rd.

Rancho Cañada Golf Club

C16

CARMEL VALLEY

Rancho San Carlos Rd.

Carmel Valley Golf & Country Club

To Garland Regional Park and U.S. Hwy 101

0   1 mi
0   1 km

N

"The beaches are clean where they once festered with fish guts and flies. The canneries that once put up a sickening stench are gone, their places filled with restaurants, antique shops, and the like. They fish for tourists now, not pilchards, and that species they are not likely to wipe out." I couldn't put it any better.

Btw. David and Drake aves. www.canneryrow.com.

Fisherman's Wharf   Like its counterpart in San Francisco, this wooden pier is crammed with crafts and gift shops, boating and fishing operations, fish markets, and seafood restaurants—all trawling for tourist dollars. But if you cast your view toward Monterey's stupendous view, with bobbing boats and sea lions, you might not notice the hordes of tourists. Grab some clam chowder in a sourdough bowl and find a seaside perch on the pier, or a bayfront seat at a seafood restaurant (see "Where to Dine," p. 395). Seafaring tour boats depart regularly from Fisherman's Wharf. See "Outdoor Pursuits," below, for details.

99 Pacific St. ✆ **831/649-6544.** www.montereywharf.com.

Monterey Bay Aquarium ★★★ (Kids)   Ranked one of the nation's top family attractions, Monterey's aquarium draws nearly two million visitors a year. On the border of one of the largest underwater canyons on earth (wider and deeper than the Grand Canyon), it's surrounded by incredibly diverse marine life. One of the world's best and largest exhibit aquariums, it's home to more than 350,000 marine animals and plants, and about 550 species. A three-story, 335,000-gallon tank with clear acrylic walls offers stunning views of leopard sharks, sardines, anchovies, and other creatures swimming through a towering kelp forest. The 1.2-million-gallon Outer Bay tank houses open-ocean life, including yellowfin tuna, large green sea turtles, barracuda, sharks, giant ocean sunfish, and schools of bonito. The Giant Octopus exhibit is also amazing. Splash Zone (designed for kids up to 9) runs daily programs and displays of black-footed penguins, invertebrates, and other inhabitants of coral reefs and the cooler waters of Northern California. Everyone falls in love with the sea otters playing in their two-story exhibit. There are also coastal streams, tidal pools, a sand beach, and a petting pool, where you can touch living bat rays and handle sea stars. *Tip:* Avoid lines at the gate by ordering tickets in advance by calling ✆ **800/756-3737** (or 831/648-4937 outside California) or online through TicketWeb at **www.ticketweb.com.** On weekdays, it's best to arrive in the afternoon after the school kids have departed.

886 Cannery Row. ✆ **831/648-4800** or 831/648-4888 for 24-hr. info line. www.mbayaq.org. Admission $25 adults, $23 students and seniors 65 and over, $16 visitors with disabilities and children 3–12, free for children 2 and under. AE, MC, V. Daily 10am–6pm (9:30am–6pm May 28–Sept 5 and holidays).

Following the Path of History

The dozen historic buildings around Fisherman's Wharf and the adjacent town constitute the "Path of History" tour, which examines the 19th-century way of life and its architecture. Many buildings are part of the **Monterey State Historic Park** ★, 20 Custom House Plaza (✆ **831/649-7118**). Highlights include the **Custom House,** the state's oldest government building (built around 1827), and the **Maritime Museum of Monterey,** 5 Custom House Plaza (✆ **831/372-2608;** www.montereyhistory.org), with ship models and other artifacts of the area's seafaring history—including a two-story, 10,000-pound Fresnel lens, used for nearly 80 years at the Point Sur lighthouse. Admission is $5; it's open Tuesday through Sunday from 10am to 5pm.

You can go the self-guided route by picking up a free tour booklet at the Monterey **391** Peninsula Visitors and Convention Bureau (see above), the Cooper Molera Adobe (at the corner of Polk St. and Munras Ave.), and various other locations. You may also opt to take the free guided tour, which departs several times daily. Call ℭ **831/649-7118** for details.

Monterey Wine Country

The congestion and price of Napa and Sonoma vineyards and the increasing popularity of winemaking have forced newcomers to plant their grapes elsewhere. Fortunately, much of the California coast offers ideal growing conditions. Any area between Monterey and Santa Barbara affords easy access to new appellations and a variety of boutique vintners making respectable wines. Stop by **A Taste of Monterey,** 700 Cannery Row (ℭ **888/ 646-5446** or 831/646-5446; www.tastemonterey.com), daily between 11am and 6pm, to learn about local wines and taste them in front of huge bayfront windows. The site also distributes maps and winery touring information.

OUTDOOR PURSUITS

Excellent for scuba diving, the waters off Monterey are also teeming with game fish. Among the public fishing boats are **Chris' Fishing Trips,** 48 Fisherman's Wharf (ℭ **831/ 375-5951;** www.chrisfishing.com). Cod and salmon are the main catches, with separate boats leaving daily. Call or log on to the website for a price list and departure schedule. Check-in is 45 minutes before departure, and equipment rental costs a bit extra.

Several outfitters rent kayaks for a spin around the bay. Contact **Monterey Bay Kayaks,** 693 Del Monte Ave. (ℭ **800/649-5357** or 831/373-5357; www.montereykayaks. com), on Del Monte Beach north of Fisherman's Wharf, which offers instruction as well as natural-history tours that introduce visitors to the Monterey Bay National Marine Sanctuary and nearby Elkhorn Slough, one of the last remaining estuaries in California (see "The Otters, Seals & Birds of the Elkhorn Slough" on p. 392). Prices start at $45 for the tours, from $30 for rentals.

For bike rentals and kayak tours and rentals, contact **Adventures by the Sea,** 299 Cannery Row (ℭ **831/372-1807;** www.adventuresbythesea.com). Bikes cost $7 per hour or $24 per day, and kayaks are $30 per person or $50 for a 2¹/₂-hour tour. Adventures by the Sea has another location at 201 Alvarado Mall (ℭ **831/648-7236**), at the Doubletree Hotel.

Experienced scuba divers can contact **Monterey Bay Dive Center,** 225 Cannery Row (ℭ **831/656-0454;** www.montereyscubadiving.com), which arranges personal dives with a dive master and has scheduled weekend dives. **Aquarius Dive Shop,** 2040 Del Monte Ave. (ℭ **831/375-1933;** www.aquariusdivers.com), also has regularly scheduled trips and dive masters. Certification cards are required.

If the kids need to let off some steam, take them to the **Dennis the Menace Playground ★** at Camino El Estero and Del Monte Avenue, near Lake Estero (ℭ **831/646-3860**), an old-fashioned playground created by Pacific Grove resident and cartoonist Hank Ketcham. It has bridges, tunnels, and an authentic Southern Pacific Railroad engine teeming with wannabe conductors. There's also a hot-dog-and-burger stand, and a big lake where you can rent paddleboats or feed the ducks. The park is open daily from 10am to sunset.

WHERE TO STAY

Monterey has three types of lodgings: lace-and-flower B&Bs, large corporate hotels, or run-of-the-mill motels. Consider where you'd like to be and how much you want to

Finds **The Otters, Seals & Birds of the Elkhorn Slough**

One of my favorite coastal stops is Moss Landing, 25 minutes north of Monterey on Highway 1, home of Captain Yohn Gideon's **Elkhorn Slough Safari** (© **831/633-5555;** www.elkhornslough.com). For $32 for adults or $24 for children 3 to 14, friendly Cap'n Gideon loads guests onto a safe, 27-foot pontoon boat and embarks on a 2-hour tour of the Elkhorn Slough Wildlife Reserve. It's not uncommon to see a "raft" of up to 50 otters, feet up and sunning themselves, harbor seals, and hundreds of species of waterfowl and migratory shorebirds. An onboard naturalist answers questions, Cap'n Gideon educates on the surroundings, and binoculars are available.

spend, and then check out the options below or contact **Resort 2 Me** (© **800/757-5646;** www.resort2me.com), a local reservations service that offers free recommendations of Monterey Bay–area hotels in all price ranges.

Expensive

In addition to the choices below, two chain hotels are popular with business travelers and conventioneers, near Fisherman's Wharf: The **Monterey Marriott,** 350 Calle Principal, at Del Monte Boulevard (© **888/236-2427** or 831/649-4234; www.marriott.com), offers some rooms with bay views, an outdoor pool, health club, Jacuzzi, and saunas. Less central but great for families and golfers, the **Hyatt Regency Monterey** resort, 1 Old Golf Course Rd. (© **800/233-1234** or 831/372-1234; www.hyatt.com), adjoins the Del Monte Golf Course, with three pools, two Jacuzzis, a gym, tennis courts, and two restaurants.

Hotel Pacific ★★ The all-suite Hotel Pacific isn't waterfront (it's near the wharf, across from the Monterey Conference Center), but it's still one of the better upscale choices in Monterey. Beyond the Spanish-Mediterranean architecture in the common areas, each unit is in one of 16 buildings clustered around courtyards and gardens with spas and fountains. All of the suites have feather beds with down comforters, stylish Spanish Colonial decor, hardwood floors, fireplaces surrounded by cushy couches and seats, separate dining areas, and French doors that open onto private patios or terraces overlooking the gardens. *Tip:* Ask for a room on the fourth level with a panoramic view of the bay.

300 Pacific St., Monterey, CA 93940. © **800/554-5542** or 831/373-5700. Fax 831/373-6921. www.hotel pacific.com. 105 suites. $179–$389 suite for 2. Rates include continental breakfast and afternoon tea. AE, DC, DISC, MC, V. Parking $16. **Amenities:** Nearby golf course; 2 Jacuzzis; room service; in-room massage; laundry service; same-day dry cleaning. *In room:* TV/DVD, dataport, coffeemaker, iron.

Monterey Bay Inn ★★ Among the tourist shuffle of Cannery Row are the quaint and quiet quarters of Monterey Bay Inn. The beds are exquisitely comfortable, and the 310-thread-count Pima cotton linens are an added bonus. Book a Bay View room for the best scenery in the house: The sound of the waves lapping against the building is the perfect wake-up call, and you can have your morning cup of joe from your private waterfront balcony. Though the hotel has no restaurant, an artfully arranged breakfast is brought to you at your request, and a handful of decent eateries are right at your doorstep. After a long day of seeing the sights, soak your weary muscles in the rooftop Jacuzzi, or book a Sanctuary Massage at the hotel spa.

Monterey Plaza Hotel & Spa ★★ One of the most formal hotels in town, the Monterey Plaza comprises three buildings—two on the water and one across the street—connected by a second-story enclosed "skywalk." The public areas are elegantly decorated with marble, Brazilian teak, and attractive artwork. The bedrooms are more upscale-corporate than most around town and have double or king beds, decor reminiscent of 19th-century Biedermeier, and Italian marble bathrooms. Many have balconies overlooking the water (sea otters included in the view). The least desirable rooms are across the street from the ocean. There's also an 11,000-square-foot European-style spa with a fitness room and ocean views, the **Duck Club Grill** serving American regional cuisine by the sea, and the adjacent **Schooner's Bistro,** which serves lighter fare.

400 Cannery Row, Monterey, CA 93940. ℂ **800/334-3999** or 831/646-1700. Fax 831/646-0285. www. montereyplazahotel.com. 290 units. $215–$760 double; $595–$3,200 suite. Children 17 and under stay free in parent's room. Packages available. AE, DC, DISC, MC, V. Parking $25 per day. From Hwy. 1, take the Soledad Dr. exit and follow the signs to Cannery Row. **Amenities:** 2 restaurants; nearby golf course; full fitness center; full-service European-style spa; Jacuzzi; dry sauna; concierge; business center; secretarial services; room service; in-room massage; laundry service; same-day dry cleaning; executive-level rooms. *In room:* TV w/pay movies, dataport, fridge, coffeemaker, hair dryer, iron.

Old Monterey Inn ★★★ This three-story, vine-covered, Tudor-style country inn is one the nation's top B&Bs and one of my favorites. It's away from the surf but a perfect choice for romantics, with rose gardens aplenty, a bubbling brook, and oak-shaded brick-and-flagstone walkways. Many rooms have private bathrooms, plush featherbeds, and down duvets, and many have wood-burning fireplaces; two open onto private patios. All guest rooms are unique and wonderful, but my two favorites are the cozy Library with its book-lined walls and stone fireplace, and the Stoneleigh for its private entrance, whirlpool for two, and fireplace facing the huge bed. The private cottage is English country, with a double Jacuzzi, magnificent king-size bed, wood-burning fireplace, sitting area, and private patio.

Breakfasts are stellar—treats may include orange-blossom French toast, or Belgian waffles, served in your room by the fire or in your bed or in the dining room. The innkeeper also provides blankets and towels for the beach. From 4:30 to 6pm, guests can retire to the living room for fireside wine and hors d'oeuvres. If you want to impress your sweetie, reserve a firelight Swedish massage for two at the inn's **SpaRetreat Salon.**

500 Martin St. (off Pacific Ave.), Monterey, CA 93940. ℂ **800/350-2344** or 831/375-8284. Fax 831/375-6730. www.oldmontereyinn.com. 9 units, 1 cottage. $250–$365 double; from $430 cottage. Rates include full breakfast, tea and cookies in the afternoon, and evening wine and hors d'oeuvres. MC, V. Free parking. From Hwy. 1, take the Soledad Dr. exit and turn right onto Pacific Ave.; then left onto Martin St. **Amenities:** Nearby golf course; passes to nearby health club; spa salon; Jacuzzi; concierge; tour desk; in-room massage. *In room:* TV/VCR, Wi-Fi, dataport, hair dryer, iron.

Spindrift Inn ★★ In the middle of honky-tonk Cannery Row, on a narrow stretch of beach, this four-story hotel is an island of Continental style in a sea of commercialism. It's elegant and well maintained, and the rooms are decorated with goose-down feather beds (a few with canopies), hardwood floors, wood-burning fireplaces, and cushioned window seats or private balconies. The bathrooms have marble and brass fixtures. Extras include terry robes and two phones. The ocean views are worth the extra cost, particularly from one of the corner rooms with cushioned window seats.

652 Cannery Row, Monterey, CA 93940. © **800/841-1879** or 831/646-8900. Fax 831/646-5342. www. spindriftinn.com. 42 units. $279–$339 double with Cannery Row view; $339–$469 double with ocean view. Rates include continental breakfast delivered to your room and afternoon wine and cheese. AE, DC, DISC, MC, V. Parking $16. **Amenities:** Nearby golf course; room service; in-room massage; same-day dry cleaning. *In room:* TV/DVD, Wi-Fi, minibar, hair dryer, CD player.

Moderate

Munras Avenue and northern Fremont Avenue are lined with moderate and inexpensive family-style motels, some independently owned and some chains. They're not as central as the downtown options, and atmosphere is seriously lacking on Fremont, but if transportation isn't an issue, you can save a bundle by staying in one of these areas. If the following places are full, try calling the Cypress Gardens Inn, 1150 Munras Ave. (© **831/ 373-2761;** www.cypressgardensinn.com), with a pool, Jacuzzi, free movie channels, and continental breakfast (dogs are welcome); the **Monterey Fireside Lodge,** 1131 10th St. (© **800/722-2624** or 831/373-4172; www.firesidemonterey.com), near Fisherman's Wharf and downtown; or the **El Adobe Inn,** 936 Munras Ave. (© **831/372-5409;** www. el-adobe-inn.com), a 26-room motor lodge close to downtown with distant bay views from several rooms.

Best Western De Anza Inn (Value) The common areas of this north Monterey motel are more modern and elaborate than most Best Westerns I've seen, but the rooms are your generic, reliable motel style. Amenities include in-room coffee, free local calls, and free wireless Internet; microwaves and refrigerators are available upon request. There's also a heated pool and Jacuzzi on the premises. The only drawback is the location, a few miles north of all of Monterey's action, but it's only a 10-minute drive and well worth the money you'll save by staying here.

2141 N. Fremont St., Monterey, CA 93940. © **800/780-7234** or 831/646-8300. Fax 831/646-8130. www. bestwestern.com. 43 units. $89–$159 double; $139–$289 suite. Extra person $8. Senior discounts available. AE, DC, DISC, MC, V. **Amenities:** Restaurant; outdoor pool; Jacuzzi. *In room:* TV, in-room movies, Wi-Fi, dataport, coffeemaker, hair dryer, iron.

Casa Munras Casa Munras was built around the original hacienda of Don Esteban Munras, the last Spanish ambassador to California. Accommodations are scattered among 11 one- and two-story buildings along the 4¹/₂-acre landscaped property. Each is decorated with pinewood furnishings and blue-and-white fabrics, and perks include Lather bath and body products and complimentary wireless Internet access. *Tip:* Spend a few extra bucks and get a deluxe room with a gas fireplace—it gets chilly at night in Monterey.

700 Munras Ave., Monterey, CA 93940. © **800/222-2558** in the U.S. except California, or 800/222-2446 in California. Fax 831/375-1365. www.hotelcasamunras.com. 171 units. $159–$229 double. AAA and Entertainment Book discounts available. AE, DC, MC, V. **Amenities:** Outdoor pool; access to nearby health club. *In room:* TV/DVD, free Wi-Fi, dataport, coffeemaker, hair dryer, iron.

The Jabberwock Bed & Breakfast ★ One of the better B&Bs in the area, the Jabberwock (from Lewis Carroll's *Through the Looking Glass & What Alice Found There*) is 4 blocks from Cannery Row. It's centrally located but tranquil; its half-acre garden with waterfalls is a respite from downtown. The seven rooms are individually furnished, some more elegantly than others; all have full bathrooms and goose-down comforters and pillows, and three have Jacuzzi tubs for two, fireplaces, and king beds. The Toves Room has a huge walnut Victorian bed and secret garden, the spacious Borogrove has a fireplace and a fine view of Monterey Bay, the Mimsy has an ocean view, and the Wabe has an Austrian carved bed. Full breakfast is served in the dining room or in guest rooms. Evening hors d'oeuvres are offered on the veranda, and a wooden Vorpal rabbit dispenses homemade **395** chocolate chip cookies, served with milk.

598 Laine St., Monterey, CA 93940. © **888/428-7253** or 831/372-4777. Fax 831/655-2946. www.jabberwock inn.com. 7 units. $179–$299 double. Rates include full breakfast, afternoon aperitifs, and bedtime cookies. MC, V. **Amenities:** Nearby golf course; Jacuzzi; concierge; activities desk; free Wi-Fi; in-room massage. *In room:* Hair dryer, robes, no phone.

Inexpensive

If you're still having trouble finding an inexpensive vacancy, try calling Monterey's chain gang: **Motel 6** (© 800/4-MOTEL-6; www.motel6.com), **Comfort Inn** (© 877/424-6423; www.choicehotels.com), **Travelodge** (© 800/578-7878; www.travelodge.com), or **Super 8** (© 800/800-8000; www.super8.com).

Cypress Tree Inn (Value) It's 2 miles from downtown, but if you're on a budget and have transportation, this inn offers a great value for such an expensive region. The staff is friendly, the large guest rooms are in decent shape, all but one have a tub/shower combination, and nine even have Jacuzzis. There are no designer soaps or other in-room treats, but the hostelry does have a handy coin-op laundry. RV spaces are also available.

2227 N. Fremont St., Monterey, CA 93940. © **800/446-8303** or 831/372-7586. Fax 831/372-2940. www. cypresstreeinn.com. 55 units. $69–$149 double. AE, DC, DISC, MC, V. **Amenities:** Jacuzzi; sauna; free Internet; coin-op laundry. *In room:* TV, kitchen or kitchenette in some units, fridge, hair dryer, iron.

WHERE TO DINE

If I had all the money in the world, I'd still have lunch the same way every day in Monterey. I'd walk down **Old Fisherman's Wharf** and snack on all those small cups of fresh seafood at the numerous faux fish markets. Priced at a couple of bucks each, fresh mussels, octopus, shrimp, crab, oysters, ceviche, and clam chowder cost a fraction of what you'd pay at a restaurant. You can either eat on foot as you head down the wharf, or cart your cups to the benches at the end of the pier (to the left of Rappa's).

Expensive

Montrio Bistro ★★ AMERICAN BISTRO Big-city sophistication meets old Monterey in this converted 1910 firehouse. The enormous dining room is the sharpest in town, a playfully chic expanse with clouds hanging from the ceiling and curvaceous walls. Order anything cooked in the open kitchen's oak-fired rotisserie grill, such as the crispy Dungeness crab cakes with spicy rémoulade or a roasted portobello mushroom with polenta and ragout of vegetables. The wine list, which received *Wine Spectator* magazine's Award of Excellence, includes numerous vintages by the glass.

414 Calle Principal (at Franklin). © **831/648-8880.** www.montrio.com. Reservations recommended. Main courses $9–$30. AE, DISC, MC, V. Sun–Thurs 5–10pm; Fri–Sat 5–11pm (open at 4:30pm for cocktails and appetizers daily).

Paradiso Trattoria ★ ITALIAN Formerly Blue Moon, this restaurant was renovated and transformed to Paradiso at the beginning of 2008. Reverting back to its original Mediterranean cuisine, the menu offers favorites such as lobster, crab risotto, eggplant parmesan, linguini and clams, and chicken scallopini. Though be warned: It's not the healthiest place to dine if you're on a diet since many of the dishes come doused in butter or cream sauce. While the food is dependably good, Paradiso's greatest offering is its waterfront seating that overlooks the bay. *Tip:* At dinnertime, request a table by the window to enjoy the sunset.

654 Cannery Row, Monterey, CA 93940. ℂ **831/375-4155.** Reservations recommended. AE, MC, V. Lunch $13–$19; dinner $16–$80. Daily 11:30am–9pm.

Stokes Restaurant and Bar ★★ CALIFORNIA/MEDITERRANEAN   This historic adobe and board-and-batten house, built in 1833 for the town doctor, has been converted into one of Monterey's finest restaurants. It's a handsome establishment, consisting of a bar and several large dining rooms, all outfitted with terra-cotta floors, bleached-wood-plank ceilings, and southwestern-style wood chairs and tables. It's the perfect rustic-yet-contemporary showcase for chef Brandon Miller's California-Mediterranean fare, such as grilled local swordfish with marinated young beets, snap peas, and salsa verde; and duck confit with warm spinach salad. Everything from Miller's wood-burning oven—chicken, fish, pizza—is recommended. Desserts are dreamy, and the wine list is excellent.

500 Hartnell St. (at Madison St.). ℂ **831/373-1110.** www.stokesrestaurant.com. Reservations recommended. Main courses $8–$24. AE, DC, DISC, MC, V. Daily 5:30pm–close.

Moderate

Bubba Gump Shrimp Co. Restaurant & Market ⓞverrated AMERICAN   Culinary cognoscenti will flee at the sight of this tourist haven, but lots of people love it. It could be the boatyard decor or location—near the aquarium, with a million-dollar, unobstructed bayfront view—that attract visitors in droves. More likely, it's the entertainment value, because Gump's (as in *Forrest Gump*) is packed with movie gimmicks and memorabilia. You're in for greasy, fried, and buttered-up seafood, suggested by the roll of paper towels at each table. The Bucket of Boat Trash, for example, is shrimp and lobster tails cooked and served in a bucket with a side of fries and coleslaw. There are also pork chops, a veggie dish, salads, and burgers. The "market" is a gift shop with T-shirts, caps, and, of course, boxes of chocolate.

720 Cannery Row (at Prescott). ℂ **831/373-1884.** Fax 831/373-0354. www.bubbagump.com. Main courses $8–$25. AE, DC, DISC, MC, V. Sun–Thurs 10am–11pm; Fri–Sat 10am–midnight.

Cafe Fina ★ ⓕinds ITALIAN/SEAFOOD   Other pier-side restaurants lure tourists with little more than a sea view, but Cafe Fina's mesquite-grilled meats, well-prepared fresh fish, brick-oven pizzas, and delicious salads and pastas give even locals a reason to head here. Betrayed by the facade of a pizza-to-go counter, the specialties are the seafood and pasta dishes, but anything that comes out of the wood broiler or wood-fired brick oven is a winner. Be sure to request a table by the back window to watch the sea otters and sea lions play in the kelp.

47 Fisherman's Wharf. ℂ **800/THE-FINA** or 831/372-5200. www.cafefina.com. Reservations recommended. Main courses $16–$30. AE, DC, DISC, MC, V. Mon–Fri 11:30am–2:30pm; Sat–Sun 11:30am–3pm; daily 5–9:30pm.

Tarpy's Roadhouse ★★ AMERICAN   A mandatory stop when I'm in Monterey, this lively southwestern-style restaurant is worth the detour a few miles east of downtown. The welcoming dining room has stylish yet rustic decor. On sunny afternoons, patrons relax under market umbrellas on the outdoor patio, sip margaritas and munch on Tarpy's locally renowned Caesar salad. Come nightfall, the place fills with tourists and locals who pile in for the hefty plate of bourbon-molasses pork chops or Dijon-crusted lamb loin. There's a modest selection of fresh fish, shellfish, and vegetable dishes, but it's the good ol' meat 'n' potato mainstays that sell the best, such as the juicy meatloaf on garlic whipped potatoes.

2999 Monterey-Salinas Hwy. (at Hwy. 68 and Canyon del Rey near the Monterey Airport). © 831/647-1444. www.tarpys.com. Reservations recommended for dinner. Most main courses $9–$45. AE, DISC, MC, V. Sun–Thurs 11:30am–9pm; Fri–Sat 11:30am–10pm.

Inexpensive

Papá Chano's Taquería MEXICAN   Don't expect cloth napkins, a formal waiter (or any server for that matter), or ambient music, but rather jumbo burritos and other Mexican specialties made from fresh ingredients. Forget about atmosphere—the cavernous ceilings, unadorned walls, and plain wooden tables and brick floors are anything but cozy. But the quesadillas, tacos, nachos, and *platillos especiales* (steak, pork, chicken, or chile relleno plates with rice, beans, cheese, lettuce, tomato, salsa, sour cream, guacamole, and tortillas) lure me back every time I'm in town.

462 Alvarado St. (at Bonifacio Place near Franklin). © 831/646-9587. Mexican plates $4–$8. No credit cards. Daily 10am–10pm.

Rosine's Value AMERICAN   Everything served at Rosine's is filling and fairly priced, which explains why this local favorite is always busy. Aside from the large, airy window seats, the place has an upscale cafeteria feel, but its menu, filled with standard entrees, aims to please all tastes. The breakfast plates are so packed they'll keep you full until dinner. Lunch features an extensive list of salads and sandwiches, and dinner offers an array of pastas, burgers, and more expensive items such as charbroiled pork chops with applesauce and mashed potatoes ($17) and prime rib ($20, Fri–Sat only). Other than steak and seafood, most entrees hover around $10 and include side salads and/or potatoes. Sugar fiends will appreciate the huge cakes behind glass as you walk in the front door (yes, you can buy them by the slice).

434 Alvarado St. (at Franklin St.). © 831/375-1400. www.rosinesmonterey.com. Breakfast $4–$10; lunch $6–$10; most dinner dishes $8–$20. AE, DC, DISC, MC, V. Sun–Thurs 8am–9pm; Fri–Sat 8am–10pm.

3 PACIFIC GROVE ★★

42 miles S of Santa Cruz; 113 miles S of San Francisco; 338 miles N of Los Angeles

Some compare 2½-square-mile Pacific Grove—the locals call it "PG"—to Carmel as it was 20 years ago. Plenty of tourists wind their way through here on oceanfront trails and dining excursions, but the town remains quaint and peaceful—amazing considering that Monterey is a stone's throw away (a quarter of the Monterey Bay Aquarium is actually in Pacific Grove). While Monterey is comparatively congested and cosmopolitan, Pacific Grove is sprinkled with historic homes, flowers, butterflies fluttering about, and deer meandering fearlessly from yard to yard.

ESSENTIALS

VISITOR INFORMATION   The **Chamber of Commerce** is on the corner of Forest and Central (© **800/656-6650** or 831/373-3304; www.pacificgrove.org).

ORIENTATION   Lighthouse Avenue is the Grove's principal thoroughfare, running from Monterey to the lighthouse at the point of the peninsula. Lighthouse Avenue is bisected by Forest Avenue, which runs from Highway 1 (where it's called Holman Hwy., or Hwy. 68) to Lover's Point, an extension of land that sticks out into the bay in the middle of Pacific Grove.

Pacific Grove is best strolled, so park the car, don walking shoes, and spend the day meandering around George Washington Park and the waterfront around the point. The **Point Pinos Lighthouse** ★, at the tip of the peninsula on Ocean View Boulevard (© 831/648-5716; www.pgmuseum.org), is the oldest working lighthouse on the West Coast. Its 50,000-candlepower beacon has illuminated the rocky shores since 1855, when Pacific Grove was little more than a pine forest. The museum and grounds are open and free to visitors, Thursday through Monday from 1 to 4pm.

Marine Gardens Park ★, a stretch of shoreline along Ocean View Boulevard on Monterey Bay and the Pacific, is renowned for ocean views, flowers, and tide-pool sea-weed beds. Walk out to **Lover's Point** (named after lovers of Jesus, not groping teenagers) and watch sea otters play and crack open an occasional abalone.

An excellent shorter alternative, or complement, to 17-Mile Drive (see "Pebble Beach & 17-Mile Drive," later) is the scenic drive or bike ride along Pacific Grove's **Ocean View Boulevard** ★. This coastal stretch starts near Monterey's Cannery Row and follows the Pacific around to the lighthouse point. Here it turns into Sunset Drive, which runs along secluded **Asilomar State Beach** ★ (© 831/648-5730). Park on Sunset and explore the trails, dunes, and tide pools of this sandy shoreline. You might find purple shore crabs, green anemone, sea bats, starfish, limpets, and all kinds of kelp and algae. The 11 build-ings of the conference center established here by the YWCA in 1913 are landmarks, designed by noted architect Julia Morgan. If you follow this route during winter, a furi-ous sea rages and crashes against the rocks.

To learn more about the region, stop in at the **Pacific Grove Museum of Natural History,** 165 Forest Ave. (© 831/648-5716; www.pgmuseum.org). It has displays on monarch butterflies and their migration, stuffed examples of the local birds and mam-mals, and temporary exhibits and special events. Admission is free; hours are Tuesday through Saturday from 10am to 5pm.

Pacific Grove is widely known as "Butterfly Town, USA," a reference to the thousands of **monarchs** that migrate here from November to February, traveling from as far away as Alaska. Many settle in the Monarch Grove sanctuary, a eucalyptus stand on Grove Acre Avenue off Lighthouse Avenue. George Washington Park, at Pine Avenue and Alder Street, is famous for its "butterfly trees." To get here, the butterflies may travel as far as 2,000 miles, covering 100 miles a day at an altitude of 10,000 feet. *Collectors beware:* The town imposes strict fines for disturbing the butterflies.

Just as Ocean View Boulevard serves as an alternative to the 17-Mile Drive, the **Pacific Grove Municipal Golf Course,** 77 Asilomar Ave. (© 831/648-5775; www.ci.pg.ca.us/golf), serves as a reasonable alternative to the high-priced courses at Pebble Beach. The back 9 of this 5,500-yard, par-70 course overlook the sea and offers the added challenge of coping with the winds. Views are panoramic, and the fairways and greens are better maintained than most semiprivate courses. There's a restaurant, pro shop, and driving range. Eighteen holes start at $40 Monday through Thursday and $45 Friday through Sunday and holidays; twilight rates are available. Optional carts cost $34.

The **American Tin Cannery Factory Premium Outlets,** 125 Ocean View Blvd., around the corner from the Monterey Bay Aquarium (© 831/372-1442), is a converted warehouse with 40 factory-outlet shops, including Bass Shoes, OshKosh B'Gosh, Sam-sonite, and Izod. It's open Monday through Saturday from 10am to 7pm, Sunday from 10am to 6pm.

If you're having trouble finding a vacancy, try calling **Resort 2 Me** (📞 **800/757-5646; www.resort2me.com**), a local reservations service that offers free recommendations of Monterey Bay area hotels in all price ranges.

Expensive

Martine Inn ★★ One glance at the lavish Victorian interior and the bay views and you'll know why this Mediterranean-style inn is one of the best B&Bs in the area. Built in 1899 for James and Laura Parke (of Parke-Davis Pharmaceuticals fame), each room has a view of the ocean or garden courtyard; most have wood-burning fireplaces. Request a room with a tub if it matters to you; some have only a shower. The inn maintains an adjacent Victorian cottage, which has been converted into a luxury suite. A full breakfast is served at lace-covered tables in the front room; hors d'oeuvres are served in the evening. Guests also have access to two additional common rooms: a room downstairs overlooking the ocean and a larger room with shelves of books.

255 Ocean View Blvd., Pacific Grove, CA 93950. 📞 **800/852-5588** or 831/373-3388. Fax 831/373-3896. www.martineinn.com. 24 units. $169–$469 double. Rates include full breakfast and evening hors d'oeuvres. AE, DISC, MC, V. **Amenities:** Nearby golf course; Jacuzzi; game room; concierge; tour desk; room service; in-room massage; babysitting; complimentary coffee, bottled water, and sodas. *In room:* Wi-Fi, fridge, hair dryer, bathrobes.

Seven Gables Inn ★★★ This is one of the most opulent B&Bs I've ever seen. Named after the seven gables that cap the inn, the compound of seven Victorian buildings was built in 1886 by the Chase family (as in Chase Manhattan Bank). Outside is the coastal road overlooking the sea; inside is a collection of mostly European antiques. Everything here is luxurious and gilded, including all of the 25 guest rooms situated among the main house, Carriage House, three cottages, Guest House, and the newly acquired Beach House (formerly the Grand View Inn). Paths through the rose gardens link the satellite accommodations to the main house. All guest rooms come with ocean views, private bathrooms, down comforters, Gilchrist & Soames bath amenities, and incredibly comfortable custom-made beds (some of which are California kings in case you like to spread out when you sleep). A full breakfast is included in all room rates.

Where the Wild Things Are

Imagine waking in a private bungalow to find a cheetah sleeping on your porch and then having an elephant deliver your breakfast basket with its trunk. That's just another morning for guests at the **Vision Quest Safari Bed & Breakfast** (📞 **800/228-7382;** www.wildthingsinc.com), one of the nation's most unique B&Bs. Amid the ranch's pride of exotic animals are deluxe Africa-style tent cabins with wild animal-theme decors, full bathrooms, sitting areas, and views that overlook a 5-acre elephant play pen and the Salinas Valley. Those are real lions and tigers roaring through your canvas walls, and guests can join trainers on their evening walks among the animals. Monterey's restaurants are a short drive away. Okay, so it's not for everyone, but at least take a look at their website and see if you might want to spend a night doing the wild thing.

555 Ocean View Blvd., Pacific Grove, CA 93950. ℰ **831/372-4341.** www.pginns.com. 25 units. $175–$405 double. Rates include breakfast and afternoon wine and cheese service. 2-night minimum on weekends. AE, MC, V. **Amenities:** Nearby golf course. *In room:* Wi-Fi, kitchenette in 1 unit, fridge in some units, hair dryer, no phone.

Moderate

The Centrella Inn ★
A couple of blocks from the waterfront and from Lover's Point Beach, the two-story Centrella is a turreted Victorian built as a boardinghouse in 1889. Today the rooms are still decorated in Victorian style with iron beds, armoires, and authentic Victorian-era antiques—even the bathrooms have claw-foot tubs. Behind the main house and connected by walkways are several cottages and suites that have fireplaces, separate bedrooms, and bathrooms. Two have private decks; the others offer decks facing the rose garden and patio, which is set with umbrella tables and chairs.

612 Central Ave., Pacific Grove, CA 93950. ℰ **800/653-5495** or 831/372-3372. Fax 831/372-2036. www.centrellainn.com. 26 units including 5 cottages. $139–$269 double; $209–$320 suite and cottage. Rates include buffet breakfast. AE, DISC, MC, V. **Amenities:** Nearby golf course. *In room:* TV in cottage, free Wi-Fi, fridge, hair dryer, iron.

Gosby House ★
Originally a boardinghouse for Methodist ministers, this Victorian was built in 1888, 3 blocks from the bay. It's one of the most charming Victorians in town, with individually decorated rooms, floral-print wallpapers, lacy pillows, and antiques. Twelve guest rooms have fireplaces, and all come with teddy bears (available for purchase if you want to keep yours). Especially noteworthy are the two Carriage House rooms, which come with a fridge and coffeemaker, fireplace, balcony, and bathroom with spa tub. The house has a separate dining room and parlor, where guests gather for breakfast and complimentary wine and hors d'oeuvres in the afternoon. Other amenities include a complimentary newspaper, twice-daily maid service, and bicycles.

643 Lighthouse Ave., Pacific Grove, CA 93950. ℰ **800/527-8828** or 831/375-1287. Fax 831/655-9621. www.gosbyhouseinn.com. 22 units. $120–$225 double. Rates include full breakfast and afternoon wine and hors d'oeuvres. AE, DC, MC, V. From Hwy. 1, take Hwy. 68 to Pacific Grove, where it turns into Forest Ave.; continue on Forest to Lighthouse Ave., turn left, and go 3 blocks. **Amenities:** Nearby golf course; complimentary bike use. *In room:* TV, hair dryer.

Green Gables Inn ★
This 1888 Queen Anne–style mansion, decorated like an English country inn, forgoes opulence (and in some cases private bathrooms) to allow for reasonable rates and less formal accommodations. The rooms are divided between the main building and the carriage houses behind it. The Carriage House rooms, which are better for families, have large private bathrooms with Jacuzzi tubs. All accommodations are individually decorated with period furnishings, including some antiques and an occasional poster bed. Most rooms in the original home have ocean views and private bathrooms. Complimentary wine, tea, and hors d'oeuvres are served each afternoon in the parlor, with an antique carousel horse.

301 Ocean View Blvd., Pacific Grove, CA 93950. ℰ **800/722-1774** or 831/375-2095. Fax 831/375-5437. www.greengablesinnpg.com. 11 units, 9 with bathroom. $135–$275 double. Rates include full breakfast and afternoon wine and hors d'oeuvres. AE, MC, V. From Hwy. 1, take the Pacific Grove exit (Hwy. 68) and continue to the Pacific Ocean; turn right on Ocean View Blvd. and drive ¹/₂ mile to Fifth St. **Amenities:** Complimentary bike use. *In room:* Iron, bathrobes.

Pacific Grove Inn ★
Five blocks from the beach, this beautifully renovated 1904 Queen Anne–style inn has a sort of Victorian-charm-meets-21st-century practicality. For example, all of the light, airy guest rooms are individually decorated with antiques and

varying color schemes, yet come with private bathrooms, queen- or king-size beds, Wi-Fi, telephones, and cable television. Several are furnished with fireplaces and have ocean views, and unique color schemes. Rates include a buffet-style breakfast along with the morning paper, and afternoon tea and refreshments served in the parlor.

581 Pine Ave., Pacific Grove, CA 93950. ✆ **800/732-2825** or 831/375-2825. Fax 831/375-0752. www.pacificgrove-inn.com. 16 units. $149–$259. Rates include buffet breakfast and afternoon tea. AE, DC, DISC, MC, V. From Calif. 1, take the Pacific Grove exit (Calif. 68) to the corner of Pine and Forest aves. *In room:* TV/VCR w/video library, Wi-Fi, fridge, hair dryer.

WHERE TO DINE
Expensive

Fandango ★★ MEDITERRANEAN   Provincial Mediterranean specialties from Spain to Greece to North Africa spice up the menu with offerings such as seafood paella with North African couscous (a 200-year-old family recipe), *cassoulet maison,* and Greek-style lamb chops. The five dining rooms are European in feel, made cozy with roaring fires, wood tables, and antiqued walls. The international wine list has won awards. In winter request the fireplace dining room, and in summer ask for the terrace. Any time of year, expect everything here, from the decor to the owner, to be lively and colorful.

223 17th St. ✆ **831/372-3456.** www.fandangorestaurant.com. Reservations recommended. Main courses $17–$34. AE, DC, DISC, MC, V. Daily 11:30am–2:30pm and 5–9:30pm. From Hwy. 1, take the Pacific Grove exit (Hwy. 68), turn left on Lighthouse Ave., and continue a block to 17th St.

Joe Rombi's ★ ITALIAN   In an area where most restaurants pack 'em in, the 11-table dining room here is refreshingly intimate with dimmed lights and antique French posters. The menu is limited to appetizers, soups, salads, pastas, and five main courses, but the food is ultra fresh. Ravioli and pastas are made fresh daily, and a basket of fresh house-made focaccia arrives upon guests' seating. Ask about the fish of the day: The last time I dined here the halibut was excellent.

208 17th St. (at Lighthouse Ave.). ✆ **831/373-2416.** www.joerombi.com. Reservations recommended. Main courses $18–$25. AE, MC, V. Wed–Sun 5–10pm.

Moderate

The Fishwife at Asilomar Beach ★★ (Kids) SEAFOOD   The restaurant dates from the 1830s, when a sailor's wife started a small food market that became famous for its Boston clam chowder. Today locals still return for the soup as well as some of the finest seafood in Pacific Grove (everyone raves about this casual, affordable place). Two bestsellers are calamari steak sautéed with shallots, garlic, tomatoes, and white wine; and Cajun catfish topped with salsa brava. All main courses come with vegetables, bread, black beans, and rice or potatoes.

1996½ Sunset Dr. (at Asilomar Beach). ✆ **831/375-7107.** www.fishwife.com. Main courses $13–$19. AE, DISC, MC, V. Mon–Sat 11am–10pm; Sun 10am–10pm. From Hwy. 1, take the Pacific Grove exit (Hwy. 68) and stay left until it becomes Sunset Dr.; the restaurant will be on your left about 1 mile ahead as you approach Asilomar Beach.

Peppers Mexicali Café ★ MEXICAN/LATIN AMERICAN   Peppers is a casual, festive place with good food at reasonable prices. The inviting dining room has wooden floors and tables, lots of pepper art, and a perpetual crowd of regulars who come to suck up beers and savor spicy but well-balanced seafood tacos and fajitas or house-made tamales and chiles rellenos. Other fire-starters include the snapper Yucatán, cooked with chiles, citrus, cilantro, and tomatoes; and grilled prawns with lime-cilantro dressing.

More than a dozen daily specials include Mexican seafood paella and grilled swordfish. The chips and salsas are addictive, and the staff is exceptionally friendly.

170 Forest Ave. (C) **831/373-6892.** www.peppersmexicalicafe.com. Reservations recommended. Main courses $7–$17. AE, DC, DISC, MC, V. Mon and Wed–Thurs 11:30am–9:30pm; Fri–Sat 11:30am–10pm; Sun 4–9:30pm.

Inexpensive

First Awakenings ★ (Value) AMERICAN This formerly dank canning factory is now a bright, huge, open restaurant with one of the cheapest and healthiest breakfasts in the area. Eye-openers include eight varieties of omelets; granola with nuts, fruit, and yogurt; walnut and wheat pancakes; and raisin French toast. At lunch there's a fine choice of salads and a slew of sandwiches ranging from albacore to zucchini. On sunny days, try snagging an outdoor patio table.

In the American Tin Cannery, 125 Ocean View Blvd. (C) **831/372-1125.** www.firstawakenings.net. Reservations not accepted. Breakfast $3–$9; lunch $5–$9. AE, DISC, MC, V. Mon–Fri 7am–2pm; Sat–Sun 7am–2:30pm. From Hwy. 1, take the Pacific Grove exit (Hwy. 68) and turn right onto Lighthouse Ave.; after a mile, turn left onto Eardley Ave., and take it to the corner of Ocean View.

Thai Bistro ★ THAI This small white house with blue trim is one of the most popular local Thai restaurants. Inside the modern, congenial dining room is usually filled with locals. The menu is a minimanifesto, with more than 60 options. Some of the most popular plates are Panang curry (with your choice of meat or seafood), *tom kha gai* soup (chicken in coconut milk), and pad Thai. There's a full vegetarian menu as well. It's all accompanied by local wines and French desserts.

159 Central Ave. (btw. David Ave. and Eardley St.). (C) **831/372-8700.** Reservations required on weekends. Most main courses $8–$12. AE, DISC, MC, V. Daily 11:30am–3pm; 5–9:30pm.

Toastie's Cafe AMERICAN Toastie's draws customers with good old-fashioned meals despite the no-frills casual dining room. Some rave about the eggs Benedict with roasted potatoes. Others swear by the hefty, sinful waffles. One thing's agreed: This place serves what everyone wants from breakfast—lots of choice, good service, endless coffee refills, and heaping plates. Weekend dinner is also a homey affair with chicken and prawn Marsala, teriyaki steak, seafood pasta, and stuffed chicken.

702 Lighthouse Dr. (C) **831/373-7543.** Breakfast and lunch dishes $5.95–$7.25; dinner main courses $9–$12. MC, V. Mon–Sat 6:30am–3pm; Sun 7am–2pm; Fri–Sat 5–8pm.

---

4 PEBBLE BEACH & 17-MILE DRIVE ★★★

Pebble Beach is a world unto itself. Polo shirts, golf shoes, and big bankrolls are standard, and if you have to ask how much accommodations and greens fees cost, you definitely can't afford them. In this elite golfers' paradise, endless grassy fairways are interrupted only by luxury resorts and cliffs where the ocean meets the land. In winter it's also the site of the AT&T Pebble Beach National Pro-Am, a celebrity tournament originally launched in 1937 by crooner Bing Crosby.

17-MILE DRIVE ★★

Set aside an afternoon, pack a picnic, fork over the $9 entrance fee, and prepare to see some of the most exclusive real estate in California. The drive is accessible from any of five gates: two from Pacific Grove to the north, one from Carmel to the south, or two from Monterey to the east. The most convenient entrance from Highway 1 is off the main road at the Holman Highway exit. You may beat traffic by entering at the Carmel Gate and doing the tour backwards. Admission to the drive includes an informative map with 26 points of interest. Other highlights include **Seal and Bird Rocks,** where you can see countless gulls and cormorants, as well as seals and sea lions; and **Cypress Point Lookout,** with a 20-mile view to the Big Sur Lighthouse. From afar, you can also admire the famous **Lone Cypress** tree that has inspired many artists and photographers (although it's no longer accessible on foot). The drive also traverses the **Del Monte Forest,** thick with tame black-tailed deer and often described as some "billionaire's private game preserve." *Note:* One of the best ways to see 17-Mile Drive is by bike. For more information on 17-Mile Drive and an interactive map, see **www.pebblebeach.com** and click on "17-Mile Drive" at the bottom of the page.

GREAT GOLF COURSES

Locals tell me it's almost impossible to get a tee time unless you're staying at the golf resort. If you're one of the lucky few, you can choose from several famous courses along the 17-Mile Drive.

PEBBLE BEACH GOLF LINKS ★★★   The most famous course is Pebble Beach Golf Links (© 800/654-9300 or 831/622-8723; www.pebblebeach.com) at the Lodge at Pebble Beach (p. 404). It's home each year to the AT&T Pebble Beach National Pro-Am, a celebrity-laden tournament televised worldwide. Jack Nicklaus has said, "If I could play only one course for the rest of my life, this would be it." He should know: He won the 1961 U.S. Amateur and the 1972 U.S. Open here. Indeed, 10 national championships have been decided here. Herbert Warren Wind, dean of 20th-century golf writers, said, "There is no finer seaside golf course in creation"—and that includes the Old Course at St. Andrews. Built in 1919, this 18-hole course is 6,799 yards and par 72. It's precariously perched over a rugged ocean. Greens fees are a staggering $475, and that doesn't include the cart fee for nonguests.

SPYGLASS HILL GOLF COURSE ★★   Also frequented by celebrities is this course at Stevenson Drive and Spyglass Hill Road (© 800/654-9300 or 831/625-8563; www. pebblebeach.com). Its slope rating of 147 means it's one of the state's toughest courses. It's justifiably famous at 6,859 yards and par 72 with five oceanfront holes. The rest reach deep into the Del Monte Forest. Greens fees are $315 plus cart. Reservations for nonguests should be made a month in advance. The excellent Grill Room restaurant is on the grounds.

POPPY HILLS ★★   This 18-hole, 6,219-yard course on 17-Mile Drive (© 831/622-8239; www.poppyhillsgolf.com) was named one of the world's top 20 by *Golf Digest*. It was designed by Robert Trent Jones, Jr., in 1986. One golf pro said the course is "long and tough on short hitters." Fees are $195, plus $34 for the cart rental. You can make reservations 30 days in advance.

THE LINKS AT SPANISH BAY ★★   On the north end of 17-Mile Drive at the Inn at Spanish Bay, Pebble Beach Resorts (© 800/654-9300 or 831/647-7495; www.pebble beach.com), this is the most easily booked course. Serious golfers say it's the most challenging of the Pebble Beach links. Robert Trent Jones, Jr., Tom Watson, and Frank Tatum (former USGA president) designed it to duplicate a Scottish links course. Its fescue grasses and natural fairways lead to rolls and unexpected bounces. Greens fees are $250 plus a cart fee. Reservations accepted 60 days in advance.

DEL MONTE GOLF COURSE ★ At 1300 Sylvan Rd. (*C* **831/373-2700;** www. pebblebeach.com) lies the oldest course west of the Mississippi, charging some of the most "reasonable" greens fees: $110 per player, plus a cart rental of $20. The course, often cited in magazines for its "grace and charm," is relatively short—only 6,339 yards. This seldom-advertised course, at the Hyatt east of Monterey, is part of the Pebble Beach complex, but is not along the 17-Mile Drive.

WHERE TO STAY & DINE

Casa Palmero Resort ★★★ The Casa Palmero is a small, ultraluxury resort on the first tee of the Pebble Beach Golf Links. The two-story villa is the newest gem in the sister properties, which include the Inn at Spanish Bay and the Lodge at Pebble Beach. The most intimate and private of the three, Casa Palmero is fashioned as a European villa with stucco walls, window boxes dripping bougainvillea, every modern comfort, and a staff to anticipate your every wish. It has 24 cottages and suites with amenities that include French doors opening onto private garden spas, oversize window-box sofas, wood-burning fireplaces, and soaking tubs that open to the main room. "Convivial" areas, where you can hang out, include a trellised patio, library, billiards parlor, living room, private dining room, executive boardroom and small conference room, intimate courtyards with fountains, and lavish outdoor pool pavilion.

1518 Cypress Dr. (on 17-Mile Dr.), Pebble Beach, CA 93953. *C* **800/654-9300** or 831/622-6650. Fax 831/622-6655. www.pebblebeach.com. 24 units. $580–$2,650 cottage or suite. Rates include continental breakfast and evening hors d'oeuvres and cocktails. AE, MC, V. From Hwy. 1 south, turn west onto Hwy. 68 and south onto 17-Mile Dr., and follow the coastal road to the hotel. **Amenities:** 3 restaurants; outdoor heated pool; golf course; tennis courts; health club; full-service spa; Jacuzzi; sauna; bike rental; concierge; room service; in-room massage; babysitting; laundry service; same-day dry cleaning; executive-level rooms. *In room:* TV/VCR w/pay movies, dataport, minibar, fridge, coffeemaker, hair dryer, iron, safe.

The Inn at Spanish Bay ★★★ Surrounded by the renowned Links at Spanish Bay golf course, the Inn at Spanish Bay is a plush three- and four-story low-rise on 236 manicured acres 4 miles north of the Lodge at Pebble Beach and Pebble Beach Golf Links. Approximately half the rooms face the ocean. Their less expensive counterparts overlook the forest. Each unit has about 600 square feet of floor space, a fireplace, and an outdoor deck or a patio. Bathrooms are finished in Italian marble. Custom-made furnishings include four-poster beds with down comforters and comfortable couches and easy chairs. My favorite time here is dusk, when a bagpiper strolls the terrace with a skirling tribute to Scotland.

2700 17-Mile Dr., Pebble Beach, CA 93953. *C* **800/654-9300** or 831/647-7500. Fax 831/644-7960. www. pebblebeach.com. 260 units. $580–$925 double; from $1,075 suite. AE, DC, MC, V. From Hwy. 1 south, turn west onto Hwy. 68 and south onto 17-Mile Dr.; the hotel is on your right, just past the gate entrance. **Amenities:** 3 restaurants; bar/lounge; heated outdoor pool; 4 world-class golf courses; 8 outdoor tennis courts (2 night lit); health club; full-service spa; Jacuzzi; sauna; bike rental; concierge; tour desk; business center; shopping arcade; room service; in-room massage; babysitting; laundry service; same-day dry cleaning; executive-level rooms; equestrian facility. *In room:* TV w/pay movies, dataport, minibar, fridge, coffeemaker, hair dryer, iron, safe.

The Lodge at Pebble Beach ★★ For the combined cost of greens fees and a room here, you could easily create a professional putting green in your own backyard—and still have money left over. But even if you're a dedicated hacker, you've got to play here at least once. Look on the bright side—at least you can expect ultraplush rooms with every amenity, including wood-burning fireplaces. Most are in two-story cottage clusters, with

1700 17-Mile Dr., Pebble Beach, CA 93953. (*€* **800/654-9300** or 831/624-3811. Fax 831/625-8598. www.
pebblebeach.com. 169 units. $665–$1,150 double; from $1,150 suite. AE, MC, V. From Hwy. 1 south, turn
west on Hwy. 68, turn south onto 17-Mile Dr., and follow the coastal road to the hotel. **Amenities:** 6
restaurants; bar/lounge; heated outdoor pool; golf course; 12 tennis courts; health club; full-service spa;
Jacuzzi; sauna; bike rental; concierge; business center; shopping arcade; room service; in-room massage;
babysitting; laundry service; same-day dry cleaning. *In room:* TV w/pay movies, dataport, minibar, fridge,
coffeemaker, hair dryer, iron, safe in most units.

5 CARMEL-BY-THE-SEA ★★

5 miles S of Monterey; 121 miles S of San Francisco; 33 miles N of Big Sur

Carmel began as a seaside artists' colony that attracted luminaries such as Sinclair Lewis, Robert Louis Stevenson, and Ansel Adams. Residents resisted assigned street numbers and lighting and carried lanterns, which they considered more romantic. The town is still intimate enough that addresses remain unnumbered—Carmel's inns, restaurants, boutiques, and galleries identify their locations by cross streets—but that ragtag bohemian village is a thing of yesteryear. Carmel is now a tourist hot spot, weekend traffic can be intolerable, and lodging rates are grossly inflated. But thousands of annual visitors are taken nonetheless with its eclectic dwellings, quaint cafes, majestic cypresses, and silky white beaches.

ESSENTIALS

The **Carmel Business Association,** P.O. Box 4444, Carmel (*€* **831/624-2522;** www.
carmelcalifornia.org), is on San Carlos Street between Fifth and Sixth streets. It distributes local maps, brochures, and publications. You'll want to pick up the *Guide to Carmel* and a schedule of events. Hours are from 10am to 5pm daily.

WHAT TO SEE & DO

A wonderful stretch of white sand backed by cypress trees, **Carmel Beach City Park** ★★ is a bit of heaven on earth (though the jammed parking lot can feel more like a car rally). There's room for families, surfers, and dogs with their owners (they can run off-leash). If the parking lot is full, try Ocean Avenue. It has some spaces, though they're mostly good for 90 minutes, and you will get a ticket if you park all day.

Farther south around the promontory, **Carmel River State Beach** ★ is less crowded, with white sand and dunes, plus a bird sanctuary with brown pelicans, black oystercatchers, cormorants, gulls, curlews, godwits, and sanderlings.

The **Mission San Carlos Borromèo del Carmelo** ★★, on Basilica Rio Road at Lasuen Drive, off Highway 1 (*€* **831/624-1271;** www.carmelmission.org), is the burial ground of Father Junípero Serra and the second-oldest of the 21 Spanish missions he established. Founded in 1771 on a site overlooking the Carmel River, it's one of the largest and most interesting of California's missions. The stone church, with its Moorish bell tower and curving walls covered with a lime plaster made of burnt seashells, was begun in 1793. The kitchen, the first library in California, the high altar, and the flower gardens are all worth visiting. More than 3,000 Native Americans are buried in the adjacent cemetery; their graves are decorated with seashells. The mission is open Monday through Saturday from 9:30am to 5pm, Sunday from 10:30am to 5pm. Admission is $5 for adults, $4 for seniors, and $1 for youth, and free for children 6 and under. Docent-led tours are $7. Call the tour office (© 831/624-1271, ext. 213) for schedules.

One of Carmel's prettiest homes and gardens is **Tor House** ★, 26304 Ocean View Ave. (© **831/624-1813;** www.torhouse.org), built by poet Robinson Jeffers. On Carmel Point, the house dates from 1918. Its 40-foot tower has stones embedded in the walls from around the world (including the Great Wall of China). Inside, an old porthole is reputed to have come from the ship on which Napoleon escaped from Elba in 1815. No photography is allowed. Admission is by guided tour only on Friday and Saturday from 10am to 3pm, and reservations are requested. It's $7 for adults, $4 for college students, and $2 for high-school students (no children under 12).

If the tourists aren't lying on the beach in Carmel, then they're probably **shopping**— the *sine qua non* of Carmel activities. This small town is home to more than 500 boutiques plying unique fashions, baskets, housewares, imported goods, and a veritable cornucopia of art galleries. Most of the commercial action is packed along the small stretch of Ocean Avenue between Junipero and San Antonio avenues.

If you want to tour the **galleries,** pick up a copy of the *Carmel Gallery Guide* from the Carmel Business Association (see "Essentials," above). Serious shoppers should also head south a few miles to the **Crossroads Shopping Center** (from Hwy. 1 south, take the Rio Rd. exit west for 1 block and turn right onto Crossroads Blvd.). As malls go, this one's a doozy, with oodles of shopping and a few good restaurants.

Carmel Walks offers 2-hour guided walks through gardens, hidden pathways, fairy-tale-like cottages and the homes of famous writers, artists, and washed-up movie stars. You'll learn about Carmel's seemingly endless spirits, strange customs, and juicy gossip. The $25 tours run Saturdays at 10am and 2pm, and Tuesday through Friday at 10am. Call © **831/642-2700** or see **www.carmelwalks.com** for reservations.

WHERE TO STAY

Most Carmel lodgings are booked solid from May to October, so make reservations as far in advance as possible. If you're traveling with pets, try the moderately priced **Cypress Inn,** Lincoln and Seventh (P.O. Box Y), Carmel-by-the-Sea, CA 93921 (© **800/443-7443** or 831/624-3871; www.cypress-inn.com), owned by actress Doris Day.

Expensive

Carriage House Inn ★★ Luxurious atmosphere and pampering make this one of my top picks downtown. Each room has a wood-burning fireplace and king-size bed with a down comforter. Most of the second-floor rooms have sunken tubs and vaulted beam ceilings; first-floor rooms have single whirlpool tubs. Staff members deliver breakfast to guests' rooms and serve wine and hors d'oeuvres in the afternoon and cappuccino, wine, and cheese in the evening. Most lodgings in this area are about frill and lace, but the Carriage House is a more mature, formal, yet cozy environment.

Junipero St., btw. Seventh and Eighth aves. (P.O. Box 1900), Carmel, CA 93921. © **800/433-4732** or 831/625-2585. Fax 831/624-0974. www.ibts-carriagehouse.com. 12 units. $299–$369 double. Rates include continental breakfast and afternoon wine and hors d'oeuvres. AE, DISC, MC, V. Free parking. From Hwy. 1, exit onto Ocean Ave. and turn left onto Junipero St. **Amenities:** Nearby golf course; concierge. *In room:* TV/VCR, minibar, fridge, coffeemaker, hair dryer, iron, safe.

Highlands Inn, Park Hyatt Carmel ★★ Four miles south of Carmel on a 12-acre cliff above Point Lobos, this inn has attracted honeymooners, business executives, and celebrities including Madonna, Walt Disney, and Marlon Brando. It's rustic yet luxurious, with wildflowers gracing its pathways, plenty of character, and an exclusive atmosphere.

The old-style main lounge, from 1916, affords panoramic coastal vistas. Guest rooms are distributed throughout a cluster of buildings terraced into the hillside; most units have decks or balconies and wood-burning fireplaces. The suites come with Jacuzzi tubs and fully equipped kitchens; four rooms have showers only.

120 Highlands Dr., Carmel, CA 93923. (C) **800/633-7313** or 831/620-1234. Fax 831/626-1574. www. highlandsinn.hyatt.com. 142 units. $220 double; $280–$735 spa suite; $510–$1,050 2-bedroom, full oceanview spa suite. AE, DC, DISC, MC, V. **Amenities:** 2 restaurants; lounge; outdoor heated pool; nearby golf course; exercise room; 3 outdoor Jacuzzis; complimentary bike use; concierge; tour/activities desk; business center; secretarial services; room service; in-room massage; babysitting; laundry service; same-day dry cleaning. *In room:* TV w/pay movies, DVD player on request, kitchen in suites, fridge, coffeemaker, hair dryer, iron, safe, CD player.

La Playa ★ The four-story La Playa is a romantic, Mediterranean-style villa 2 blocks from the beach and within walking distance of town. In 1904, Norwegian artist Christopher Jorgensen ordered its construction for his bride, an heiress of the Ghirardelli chocolate dynasty. The stylish lobby is elegant, with terra-cotta floors, Oriental rugs, and marble fireplace. In the courtyard, walkways lead through beautifully landscaped grounds surrounding a heated pool. Compared to the lobby and grounds, the standard guest rooms are disappointing, with thin walls and uninspiring furnishings. The luxury cottages—newly renovated in partnership with Restoration Hardware—are a vast (and costly) improvement—with kitchens, wet bars, garden patios, limited room service, and, in most cases, wood-burning fireplaces.

Camino Real and Eighth Ave. (P.O. Box 900), Carmel, CA 93921. (C) **800/582-8900** or 831/624-6476. Fax 831/624-7966. www.laplayahotel.com. 80 units. $190–$375 double; $425–$775 suite or cottage. Complimentary valet parking. AE, DC, MC, V. **Amenities:** Restaurant; bar; outdoor heated pool; nearby golf course; bike rental; concierge; business center; room service; babysitting; same-day dry cleaning. *In room:* TV, fridge, hair dryer, iron.

Mission Ranch ★★ If you want to stay off the beaten track, consider this converted 1850s dairy farm, restored by Clint Eastwood to preserve the vista of the nearby wetlands stretching to the bay. Accommodations are scattered amid different structures, both old and new, and surrounded by wetlands and grazing sheep. Guest rooms range from "regulars" in the main barn (less desirable) to meadow-view units with a vista across the fields to the bay. Rooms are decorated in a provincial style, with carved wooden beds bedecked in handmade quilts. Most are equipped with whirlpool baths, fireplaces, and decks or patios. The Martin Family farmhouse has six units, all arranged around a central parlor, while the Bunkhouse (the oldest structure on the property) contains separate living and dining areas, bedrooms, and a fridge. Even if you're not staying here, call for a table at the **Restaurant at Mission Ranch** (p. 410).

26270 Dolores St., Carmel, CA 93923. (C) **800/538-8221** or 831/624-6436. Fax 831/626-4163. www. missionranchcarmel.com. 31 units. $110–$275 double. Rates include continental breakfast. AE, MC, V. **Amenities:** Restaurant; 6 tennis courts; exercise room; babysitting; laundry service; dry cleaning. *In room:* TV, dataport, fridge in some units, coffeemaker, hair dryer, iron.

Moderate

Cobblestone Inn ★ The first floor of the Cobblestone Inn was built of stones from the Carmel River (hence the inn's name), and the cobblestone theme runs throughout this faux English-county charmer. The guest rooms encircle a slate courtyard and vary in size; some are small, and only the Junior Suite comes with a bathtub, but all come with a queen or king bed, fireplace, television, and refrigerator with complimentary soft drinks. The largest units have a wet bar, sofa, and separate bedroom. Guests may use the comfortable living room with a large stone fireplace (cobblestone, of course). Extras include a breakfast buffet served on the patio or sitting room, afternoon wine and hors d'oeuvres, daily maid and turndown service, and a morning newspaper.

Junipero St. (btw. Seventh and Eighth aves., 1¹/₂ blocks from Ocean Ave.; P.O. Box 3185), Carmel, CA 93921. ℂ **800/833-8836** or 831/625-5222. Fax 831/625-0478. www.cobblestoneinncarmel.com. 24 units. $155–$270 double. Rates include full breakfast and afternoon wine and hors d'oeuvres. AE, DC, MC, V. *In room:* Flatscreen TV/DVD, fridge, hair dryer, fireplace, complimentary soda and water, robes.

Normandy Inn ★   Three blocks from the beach, this French Provençal–style hotel is like something out of a storybook, with an array of colorful flowers. Some guest rooms are showing their age a little, but they're well appointed with French country decor, feather beds, and down comforters. Some have fireplaces and/or kitchenettes. The tiny heated pool is banked by a flower garden. The three large family-style units are an especially good deal and accommodate up to eight; each has three bedrooms, two bathrooms, a fully equipped kitchen, a dining room, a living room with a fireplace, and a back porch. Reserve well in advance, especially in summer.

Ocean Ave., btw. Monte Verde and Casanova sts. (P.O. Box 1706), Carmel, CA 93921. ℂ **800/343-3825** or 831/624-3825. Fax 831/624-4614. www.normandyinncarmel.com. 48 units. $98–$220 double; $165–$500 suite or cottage. Rates include continental breakfast and afternoon sherry. Extra person $10. AE, DC, MC, V. From Hwy. 1, exit onto Ocean Ave. and continue straight for 5 blocks past Junipero St. **Amenities:** Outdoor pool (seasonal); nearby golf course. *In room:* TV, kitchenette in some units, coffeemaker, hair dryer, iron.

Sandpiper Inn by the Sea ★   A flower garden welcomes visitors to this quiet, relaxing, midscale Carmel standby, in business for more than 80 years. The inn's rooms, from which you can hear the surf, offer a range of well-kept options. Corner rooms are often costliest, with four-poster beds and many windows framing the ocean view. All rooms are decorated with handsome country antiques and fresh flowers in the deluxe rooms; three have fireplaces. Carmel's white-sand beaches are 300 feet away. The complimentary buffet style breakfast is a hit with guests. While not appropriate for all families, children older than age 12 are welcome.

2408 Bay View Ave., Carmel, CA 93923. ℂ **800/590-6433** or 831/624-6433. Fax 831/624-5964. www.sandpiper-inn.com. 17 units. $140–$275 double. Rates include extended continental breakfast and afternoon sherry and tea. AE, DISC, MC, V. **Amenities:** Nearby golf course; concierge; tour desk. *In room:* No phone.

Vagabond House ★   In typical Carmel style, doting attention has been paid to every element of this English Tudor inn—from the lobby adorned with knickknack antiques and a welcoming decanter of sherry, to the wonderfully lush garden courtyard draped with greenery and dotted with blooms. Each room is warm and homey, with country decor and a private entrance; all but two have wood-burning fireplaces, which means the least-expensive rooms book quickly; call ahead if you want one. Guests are welcomed with a basket of fruit, and the extended continental breakfast is delivered to your room, though you'll most likely enjoy it best on the garden patio.

Fourth and Dolores (P.O. Box 2747), Carmel, CA 93921. ℂ **800/262-1262** or 831/624-7738. Fax 831/626-1243. www.vagabondshouseinn.com. 12 units. $145–$325 double. Rates include continental breakfast. 2-night minimum on weekends. AE, DISC, MC, V. Pets allowed for a fee. *In room:* TV, dataport, fridge, coffeemaker, hair dryer, iron.

Inexpensive

Carmel Sands Lodge ★ The Sands is a motor lodge, but it's decorated better than most, on a quiet street in Carmel. Modern rooms have pretty bedspreads and updated furnishings; some have fireplaces and wet bars. There's a small pool, but it's practically in the center courtyard parking lot. Several restaurants are nearby. I like this quiet location better than that of the comparable Carmel Village Inn (see below).

San Carlos and Fifth (P.O. Box 951), Carmel, CA 93921. © **800/252-1255** or 831/624-1255. Fax 831/624-2576. www.carmelsandslodge.com. 38 units. $85–$199 double. AE, DC, DISC, MC, V. From Ocean Ave., turn right onto San Carlos and go 2 blocks. **Amenities:** Restaurant; heated outdoor pool (seasonal); nearby golf course. In room: TV, minibar, fridge, coffeemaker, hair dryer in some units.

Carmel Village Inn (Value) Efficiently run and centrally located, the Village Inn is basically a well-kept old-school motor lodge. The rooms are always spotless, arranged around a courtyard and parking lot lined with potted geraniums, and outfitted with that ubiquitous flowery decor. The Deluxe Kings with gas fireplaces offer plenty of elbow room for the price. Continental breakfast, accompanied by the morning newspaper, is served in the downstairs lounge.

Ocean Ave. and Junipero St. (P.O. Box 5275), Carmel, CA 93921. © **800/346-3864** or 831/624-3864. Fax 831/626-6763. www.carmelvillageinn.com. 48 units. $105–$245 double. Rates include continental breakfast. AE, MC, V. From Calif. 1, exit onto Ocean Ave. and continue straight to Junipero St. **Amenities:** Babysitting. In room: TV, fax, Wi-Fi, kitchenette, fridge, coffeemaker.

WHERE TO DINE
Expensive

Anton & Michel ★ CONTINENTAL This elegant restaurant, across from Carmel Plaza, serves traditional French cuisine in one of the most formal rooms in town. By day, it's best to dine fountain-side or on the glass-encased terrace. The view is equally alluring in the evening, when the courtyard is lit and the fountain's water sparkles. Decorated with French chandelier lamps and oil paintings, the main dining room is formal, but patrons' attire need not match it. Appetizers include crab cakes with sweet corn and tomato oil or delicate ravioli filled with wild mushrooms. Specialties include rack of lamb with herb-Dijon mustard au jus and more eclectic items such as a chicken breast Jerusalem, sautéed with olive oil, white wine, cream, and artichoke hearts. The wine list is impressive.

At Court of the Fountains, Mission St. (btw. Ocean and Seventh aves.). © **831/624-2406.** www.carmels best.com. Reservations recommended. Main courses $15–$36. AE, DC, DISC, MC, V. Daily 11:30am–3pm and 5:30–9:30pm.

Flying Fish Grill ★★ PACIFIC RIM/SEAFOOD I feel more confident when a restaurant's owner runs the kitchen—and dinner here confirms that chef/proprietor Kenny Fukumoto is in the house. Dark, romantic, and Asian influenced, the 40-seat dining room has an intimate atmosphere with redwood booths (built by Kenny) and fish hanging from the ceiling. The cuisine features fresh seafood with exquisite Japanese accents. Start with *shabu-shabu*, sushi, tempura, or any of the other exotic taste teasers. Main-courses include a rare peppered ahi (tuna), blackened and served with mustard-and-sesame-soy vinaigrette and angel-hair pasta; and a pan-fried almond sea bass with whipped potatoes, Chinese cabbage, and rock shrimp stir-fry.

In Carmel Plaza, Mission St. (btw. Ocean and Seventh aves.). © **831/625-1962.** Reservations recommended. Main courses $15–$28. AE, DISC, MC, V. Wed–Mon 5–10pm.

Grasing's Coastal Cuisine ★ CALIFORNIA   Chef Kurt Grasing and renowned Bay Area restaurateur Narsai David teamed up here and opened one of Carmel's best restaurants. The bright, split-room dining area is simple yet stylish, with buttercup-yellow walls, beaded lamps, and colorful artwork. Grasing's menu reflects the decor's stylish simplicity; ultrafresh ingredients gleaned from California's coast and Central Valley are displayed modestly, belying an intense combination of textures and flavors. The warm Napa salad (with bacon, garlic, and blue cheese), for example, appears ordinary enough, but "when I took it off the menu," says Grasing, "I still made 30 a night." The Grasing's "paella" (made with prawns, clams, mussels, and sausage with saffron- and fennel-infused orzo pasta) and roast rack of pomegranate-marinated lamb with crispy polenta are also standouts. Even the bread, fresh from Gail's Bakery in Aptos, is fantastic. When the sun's out, request a table at the dog-friendly patio, and be sure to inquire about the very reasonable prix-fixe meal.

Sixth St. (at Mission St.). © 831/624-6562. www.grasings.com. Reservations recommended. Main courses $18–$36. AE, MC, V. Daily 11am–3pm and 5–9pm.

The Restaurant at Mission Ranch ★★ AMERICAN   Former Carmel Mayor Clint Eastwood bought this rustic property in 1986 and restored the ranch-style building to its original integrity. The chance of seeing him brings in some folk, but it's the views, quality food, and merry atmosphere that make the place special. The wooden building is encased with large windows that accentuate the wonderful view of the marshlands, grazing sheep, and bay. Warm days make the patio the prime spot, but the key time to come is at sunset, when the sky is transforming and happy hour is in full swing. You'll find some of the cheapest drinks around, and Clint often stops by when he's in town. As you'd expect from the ranch motif, meat is king here: New York steak, and baby back ribs. Seafood, chicken, and vegetarian options are also wonderful, and all dinners include soup or salad. Entertainment is provided at the piano bar, where locals and tourists have also been known to croon their favorites. Sunday buffet brunch, with live jazz piano, is also hugely popular; be sure to reserve a table.

At Mission Ranch, 26270 Dolores St. © 831/625-9040. www.missionranchcarmel.com. Reservations recommended. Most main courses $15–$35. DC, MC, V. Daily 5–9:30pm; Sun jazz brunch 10am–1:30pm; bar stays open until midnight.

Moderate

Club Jalapeño ★★ MEXICAN   Follow the divine aroma wafting down San Carlos Avenue and you'll end up at Club J, tearing into a plate of Oaxacan enchiladas drizzled with rich mole sauce. The fried and battered Baja fish tacos are just like the ones in Tijuana (love that salsa and lime-cilantro dressing). The coconut-encrusted fish is lightly fried then topped with spicy chipotle sauce and fruit salsa. A righteous meal for two is Club J's spicy shrimp fajitas with a side of fresh-fruit salsa. The decor is faux-hacienda-rustic with dark-wood floors, exposed beams, iron furnishings, textured walls, soft lighting, hanging chiles, and a sexy corner bar with pure agave tequila.

San Carlos (btw. Fifth and Sixth aves. in the courtyard). © 831/626-1997. www.clubjalapeno.com. Main courses $8–$25. AE, MC, V. Wed–Mon noon–close; Tues 5pm–close.

The Hog's Breath Inn AMERICAN   Clint Eastwood's involvement with this restaurant made it famous, but it's a rare day that he visits (better odds are at the Mission Ranch restaurant). No matter: The patio with tree-trunk tables and plastic chairs is ideal for taking in beer and good ol' American standbys—if you don't mind the usual wait. (Tables in the dark-wood-paneled dining room also fill up, but they're not as lively as outdoor seats.) The food—New York steak, crab cakes, chicken Marsala—is unremarkable, but the small dark sports bar is the best place to kick back on a rainy day (or a sunny one for that matter). Come for lunch, when it's more affordable.

San Carlos St. (btw. Fifth and Sixth aves.). ✆ **831/625-1044.** www.hogsbreathinn.net. Reservations not accepted. Main courses $10–$24. AE, DC, MC, V. Daily 11:30am–10pm. From Hwy. 1, take the Ocean Ave. exit and turn right onto San Carlos St.

Rio Grill ★★ AMERICAN   Serious food and a festive atmosphere (with vibrant art, including a cartoon mural of famous locals Clint Eastwood and the late Bing Crosby), have kept this place hugely popular with the locals for years. The whimsical nature of the modern Santa Fe–style dining room belies the kitchen's ambitious preparations, which include homemade soups; a rich quesadilla with almonds, cheeses, and smoked-tomato salsa; barbecued baby back ribs from a wood-burning oven; and fresh fish from an open oak grill. The good wine selection includes some rare California vintages and covers a broad price range.

Crossroads Shopping Center, 101 Crossroads Blvd. ✆ **831/625-5436.** www.riogrill.com. Reservations recommended. Main courses $8–$25. AE, DISC, MC, V. Sun–Thurs 11:30am–10pm; Fri–Sat 11:30am–11pm. From Hwy. 1, take the Rio Rd. exit west for 1 block and turn right onto Crossroads Blvd.

Tommy's Wok ★★ Ⓥalue CHINESE   Far be it for Carmel to have an ordinary Chinese restaurant. Chef/owner Tommy Mao has eschewed the typical red-and-gold color scheme for a far more austere, almost Japanese, decor. The small 12-table restaurant—with its soothing pastel hues, rice-paper posters, semi-open kitchen, and glossy wood floor—is an apt setting for Mao's stylish presentations and unique combinations of Szechuan, Hunan, and Mandarin dishes. Mao makes everything from scratch: potstickers are made with fresh Napa cabbage, moo shu vegetables with house-made pancakes, tea-smoked duck is marinated for 48 hours. The hot and spicy string beans, pine nut chicken, marinated Lover's Prawns, and Mongolian lamb are also winners. The combo lunch plates are a bargain, and a modest dim sum menu is offered for lunch as well.

Mission (btw. Ocean and Seventh, next to the Wells Fargo ATM). ✆ **831/624-8518.** Main courses $7–$16. AE, DISC, MC, V. Tues–Sun 11:30am–2:30pm and 4:30–9:30pm.

Inexpensive

Carmel Bakery BAKERY/DELI   This fancy bakery along this main street leading down to the beach serves espresso, soup, sandwiches, and pastries. It's festive and well decorated, with a few tables and chairs, and music playing from speakers overhead. Most customers grab their goods and go. For a more formal (and a mite more expensive) encounter with espresso and the like, head down the block to the Il Fornaio bakery (Ocean Ave. at Monte Verde; ✆ **831/622-5100**).

Ocean (btw. Dolores and Lincoln). ✆ **831/626-8885.** Sandwiches $4–$6. No credit cards. Daily 7am–8pm.

Little Swiss Cafe CONTINENTAL   This quirky little spot looks like a Swiss cottage. Kids may love the decor, but the grown-ups come for the best homemade blintzes and pancakes in town. Breakfast is served all day. Lunch is affordable and features sandwiches, served with potato salad, mixed green salad, or soup ($6–$9); salads; and an array of unusual entrees such as Swiss sausage with smothered onions, calves' liver sauté, and filet of red snapper with a rémoulade sauce.

Sixth Ave. (btw. Lincoln and Mission). © **831/624-5007.** Reservations not accepted. $5–$10. No credit cards. Mon–Sat 7:30am–3pm; Sun 8am–2pm.

Nielsen Brothers Market DELI   Why squander precious midday vacation minutes indoors when you can dine alfresco on Carmel Beach? A few blocks off the main drag, Nielsen Brothers market has what you need to fill a picnic basket, including sandwiches, barbecued chicken and ribs, pasta salads, and a vast selection of cheeses. You can even get french fries or veggie and meat burgers (noon–6pm), but expect a 10-minute wait—they cook to order. Call and order by phone or drop in.

San Carlos St. (at Seventh). © **831/624-6263** (deli), or 831/624-6441 (market). www.nielsenmarket.com. Picnic items $3–$5. MC, V. Daily 8am–7pm.

6 CARMEL VALLEY

3 miles SE of Carmel-by-the-Sea

Inland from Carmel stretches Carmel Valley, where the wealthy retreat beyond the reach of the coastal fog and mist. It's a scenic, perpetually sunny valley of rolling hills dotted with manicured golf courses and many a tony pony ranch.

Hike the trails in **Garland Regional Park,** 8 miles east of Carmel on Carmel Valley Road (dogs are welcome off-leash). The sun bakes you here, so bring lots of water. Several resorts and courses in the valley offer golf—notably **Quail Lodge,** 8205 Valley Green Dr. (© **888/828-8787** or 831/624-2888; www.quaillodge.com), and **Rancho Cañada Golf Club,** Carmel Valley Road (© **800/536-9459** or 831/624-0111; www.ranchocanada. com).

While you're in the area, taste the wines at the **Château Julien Winery,** 8940 Carmel Valley Rd. (© **831/624-2600;** www.chateaujulien.com), open Monday through Friday from 8am to 5pm, Saturday and Sunday from 11am to 5pm. Tours are available by reservation.

WHERE TO STAY

Bernardus Lodge ★★★   On the top-20 list of just about every luxury travel publication is this 57-room boutique "lodge" in scenic Carmel Valley. Bernardus Pon, who owns the Bernardus Winery and Vineyard, must have spent a small fortune to build his eponymous resort, which consists of a main lodge, nine adobe-style guest houses, two restaurants, a meditation garden, a croquet lawn and bocce court, two tennis courts, and a pool. The gorgeous main lodge resembles a French country home, with heavy wood beams, hand-plastered walls, copper chandeliers, antique wrought-iron, and limestone fireplaces. The guest suites are similar, with stone wood-burning fireplaces, vaulted ceilings, arched windows, feather beds with Italian linens, and French doors that open to private decks with mountain or garden views. Carmel is only a 15-minute drive, but your time is far better spent indulging in the resort's full-service spa, playing golf at nearby Carmel Valley courses or having a leisurely breakfast or lunch at the outdoor terrace, followed by an impromptu wine tasting. For dinner, chef Cal Stamenov offers exquisite California-natural cuisine and a *Wine Spectator* Award–winning wine list at the lodge's Marinus restaurant.

415 Carmel Valley Rd., Carmel Valley, CA 93924. © **888/648-9463** or 831/648-3400. Fax 831/659-3529. www.bernardus.com. 57 units. $415–$805 double; from $1,065–$1,235 suite. AE, DC, DISC, MC, V. **Amenities:** 2 restaurants; heated outdoor pool; 2 tennis courts; exercise room; full spa; sauna; concierge; room

service; bocce court; croquet lawn. *In room:* A/C, TV/DVD, minibar (w/complimentary wine and snacks), fridge, coffeemaker, hair dryer, iron, safe, CD player.

Quail Lodge Resort and Golf Club ★★ In the foothills of the Santa Lucia Range, Quail Lodge has received Mobil's five-star ratings for more than 20 years. Its pastoral setting encompasses more than 850 acres of lakes, woodlands, meadows, an 18-hole championship golf course, and a full-service spa. The guest rooms are in two-story balconied wings, with terraces overlooking the pool or one of the 10 man-made lakes, or in cottages holding five units each. Fairway villas are the most expensive, luxurious digs. Guest rooms are decorated in earthy reds, greens, yellows, and terra-cotta tones with striped and checkered patterns. Higher-priced accommodations, on the upper floors, have cathedral ceilings. Every room has a separate dressing area and French doors opening to an ample balcony, as well as spacious bathrooms with plush marble baths, deep soaking tubs, and walk-in showers; some have fireplaces and wet bars. Coffeemakers are supplied with freshly ground beans (a nice touch), and a fresh-fruit plate is delivered to each room daily as well.

8205 Valley Greens Dr., Carmel, CA 93923. © **888/828-8787** or 831/624-2888. Fax 831/624-3726. www. quaillodge.com. 97 units. $380–$465 double; $440–$575 suite. Call for winter specials. Packages available. AE, DC, DISC, MC, V. From Hwy. 1 north, past the Carmel exits (after which the highway narrows to 2 lanes), turn east on Carmel Valley Rd. and continue 3¹/₂ miles to Valley Greens Dr. Pets accepted with $25 fee per stay. Pet amenities and doggie treats included. **Amenities:** 2 restaurants; 2 bars; 2 outdoor heated pools; golf course; executive putting green; 3 tennis courts; fitness room; full spa services; Jacuzzi; concierge; room service; laundry service; same-day dry cleaning; executive-level rooms. *In room:* Big-screen plasma TV/DVD, Wi-Fi, minibar, coffeemaker, hair dryer, bathrobes.

7 THE BIG SUR COAST ★★★

3 miles S of Carmel-by-the-Sea; 123 miles S of San Francisco; 87 miles N of Hearst Castle

Big Sur is more than a drive along one of the most dramatic coastlines on earth or a peaceful repose amid a forest of California redwoods. It's a stretch of wilderness so overwhelmingly beautiful—especially when the fog glows in the moonlight—that it enchants everyone who visits. It's also home to a particular breed of nature lover who prefers a rustic lifestyle to the rest of California's offerings. When the 1997 and 1998 El Niño storms caused landslides and major road damage, cutting the area off from civilization for months, reports from Big Sur were unusual: Some residents fled, vowing never to return. The remaining residents rejoiced in the temporary solitude; Post Ranch, the area's ultimate luxury resort, shared the impromptu intimacy with deep-pocketed guests by flying them in via helicopter (for an extra fee, of course). Such is the price paid for living amid the California wilderness. The reopened roads are packed again, and driving through the region is slow; rubberneckers admiring the view and nervous Nellies fearing the cliffs drive with their foot on the brakes.

Although there is an actual Big Sur Village 25 miles south of Carmel, "Big Sur" refers to the entire 90-mile stretch of coastline between Carmel and San Simeon, blessed on one side by the majestic Santa Lucia Range and on the other by the rocky Pacific coastline. It's one of the most romantic, relaxing places in California. There's little more to do than explore the mountains and beaches, and take in the sea air—but spend a few days here and you won't need to do much else.

Visitor Information   Contact the **Big Sur Chamber of Commerce** (© 831/667-2100; www.bigsurcalifornia.org) for specialized information on places and events in Big Sur.

Orientation   Most of this stretch is state park, and Highway 1 runs its entire length, hugging the ocean the whole way. Restaurants, hotels, and sights are easy to spot—most are situated directly on the highway—but without major towns as reference points, their addresses can be obscure. For the purposes of orientation, I'll use the River Inn as a mileage guide. Located 29 miles south of Monterey on Highway 1, the inn is generally considered to mark the northern end of Big Sur.

EXPLORING THE BIG SUR COAST

Big Sur's tranquillity and natural beauty are ideal for hiking, picnicking, camping, fishing, and beachcombing. The first settlers arrived only a century ago, and the present highway, built in 1937, first made the area accessible by car. (Electricity followed in the 1950s, but it's still not available in the remote inland mountains.) Big Sur's mysterious, misty beauty has inspired several modern spiritual movements (the Esalen Institute was the birthplace of the human potential movement). Even the tourist bureau bills the area as a place in which "to catch up with your soul."

The region affords bountiful wilderness adventure opportunities. The inland **Venting Wilderness,** run by the U.S. Forest Service, has 167,323 acres straddling the Santa Lucia Mountains. Steep ridges separated by V-shaped valleys characterize it. The streams throughout the area have waterfalls, deep pools, and thermal springs. The wilderness offers 237 miles of hiking trails that lead to 55 designated trail camps—a backpacker's paradise. One of the easiest trails to access is the **Pine Ridge Trail** at Big Sur station (© 831/667-2315).

From Carmel, the first stop along Highway 1 is **Point Lobos State Reserve ★★** (© 831/624-4909; pt-lobos.parks.state.ca.us), 3 miles south of Carmel. Sea lions, harbor seals, sea otters, and thousands of seabirds reside in this 1,276-acre reserve. Between December and May you can also spot migrating California gray whales offshore, and in late April I've spotted numerous mama seals with their newly born pups. Trails follow the shoreline and lead to hidden coves. Note that parking is limited; on weekends especially, you need to arrive early to secure a place.

From here, cross the Soberanes Creek, passing **Garrapata State Park** (© 831/624-4909), a 2,879-acre preserve with 4 miles of coastline. It's unmarked and undeveloped, but the trails are maintained. To explore them, park at one of the turnouts on Highway 1 near Soberanes Point and hike in.

Ten miles south of Carmel, you'll find North Abalone Cove. From here, Palo Colorado Road leads back into the wilderness to the first of the Forest Service camping areas at **Bottchers Gap** ($12 to camp, $5 to park overnight; © 805/434-1996; www.campone.com).

Continuing south, about 13 miles from Carmel, you'll cross the **Bixby Bridge** and see the **Point Sur Lighthouse** off in the distance. The Bixby Bridge, one of the world's highest single-span concrete bridges, towers nearly 270 feet above Bixby Creek Canyon, with canyon and ocean views from observation alcoves at intervals along the bridge. The lighthouse, which sits 361 feet above the surf on a volcanic rock promontory, was built in 1889, when only a horse trail provided access to this part of the world. Tours, which take 2 to 3 hours and involve a steep half-mile hike each way, are scheduled on weekends year-round and Wednesday and Thursdays during the summer. For information, call © 831/625-4419, or visit **www.pointsur.org**. Moonlight tours are offered as well; check the website for specific dates. Admission is $8 for adults, $4 for youths ages 6 to 17, and free for kids 5 and under.

About 3 miles south of the lighthouse is **Andrew Molera State Park** (© 831/667-2315; www.bigsurcalifornia.org), the largest state park on the Big Sur coast, at 4,800 acres. It's much less crowded than Pfeiffer–Big Sur (see below). Miles of trails meander through meadows and along beaches and bluffs. Hikers and cyclists use the primitive trail camp about a third of a mile from the parking area. The 2¹/₂-mile-long beach, sheltered from the wind by a bluff, is accessible via a mile-long path flanked in spring by wildflowers and offers excellent tide pooling. You can walk the length of the beach at low tide; otherwise, take the bluff trail above the beach. Trails run through the park for horseback riders of all levels. **Molera Big Sur Trail Rides** (© 800/942-5486 or 831/625-5486; www.molerahorsebacktours.com) offers coastal trail rides daily from April to December, or until the rains come. The cost varies but starts at about $50 for a 1-hour ride along the beach. The park also has campgrounds.

Back on Highway 1, you'll reach the village of Big Sur, with commercial services. At **Big Sur Station** (© 831/667-2315), you can pick up maps and information about the region. It's located a quarter mile past the entrance to **Pfeiffer–Big Sur State Park** ★

(© 831/667-2315; www.bigsurcalifornia.org), an 810-acre park with 218 camping sites along the Big Sur River (call © 800/444-7275, for camping reservations), as well as picnicking, fishing, and hiking. It's a scenic park of redwoods, conifers, oaks, and meadows, and it gets very crowded. **The Big Sur Lodge** in the park has cabins with fireplaces and other facilities. Admission is $5 per car, and it's open daily from dawn to dusk.

Just over a mile south of the entrance to Pfeiffer–Big Sur State Park is the turnoff to Sycamore Canyon Road (unmarked), which will take you 2 winding miles down to beautiful **Pfeiffer Beach** ★, a great place to soak in the sun on the wide expanse of golden sand. It's open for day use only, there's no fee, and it's the only beach accessible by car (but not motor homes).

Back on Highway 1, the road travels 11 miles past Sea Lion Cove to Julia Pfeiffer Burns State Park. High above the ocean is the famous **Nepenthe** restaurant (p. 421), the retreat bought by Orson Welles for Rita Hayworth in 1944. A few miles farther south is the **Coast Gallery** (© 800/797-6869 or 831/667-2301; www.coastgalleries.com), the premier local art gallery which displays lithographs of works by the late writer and, yes, artist Henry Miller; it's open daily from 9am to 5pm. The gallery also has a small cafe that offers simple self-serve lunches of soup, sandwiches, baked goods, and coffee. Miller fans will also want to stop at the **Henry Miller Memorial Library** (© 831/667-2574; www.henrymiller.org) on Highway 1, 30 miles south of Carmel and a quarter mile south of Nepenthe restaurant. The library displays and sells books and artwork by Miller and houses a permanent collection of first editions. It also serves as a community art center, hosting concerts, readings, and art exhibitions (check for upcoming events on the website). The rear gallery room is a video-viewing space where films about Henry Miller can be seen. There's a sculpture garden, plus tables on the adjacent lawn where visitors can rest and enjoy the surroundings. Admission is free; hours are from 11am to 6pm daily in the summer and 11am to 6pm Thursday through Sunday winter.

Julia Pfeiffer Burns State Park ★★ (© 831/667-2315; www.bigsurcalifornia.org) encompasses some of Big Sur's most spectacular coastline. To get a closer look, take the trail from the parking area at McWay Canyon, which leads under the highway to a bluff overlooking the 80-foot-high McWay Waterfall dropping directly into the ocean. It's less crowded here than at Pfeiffer–Big Sur, and there are miles of trails to explore in the 3,580-acre park. Scuba divers can apply for permits to explore the 1,680-acre underwater reserve.

From here, the road skirts the Ventana Wilderness, passing Anderson and Marble Peaks and the Esalen Institute before crossing the Big Creek Bridge to Lucia and several campgrounds farther south. **Kirk Creek Campground** ★, about 3 miles north of Pacific Valley, offers camping with ocean views and beach access. Beyond Pacific Valley, the **Sand Dollar Beach** ★ picnic area is a good place to stop and enjoy the coastal view and take a stroll. A half-mile trail leads down to the sheltered beach, with a fine view of Cone Peak, one of the coast's highest mountains. Two miles south of Sand Dollar is **Jade Cove,** a popular spot for rock hounds. From here, it's about another 27 miles past the Piedras Blancas Light Station to San Simeon.

WHERE TO STAY

Only a handful of Big Sur's accommodations offer the kind of pampering and luxury you'd expect in a fine urban hotel; even direct-dial phones and TVs (often considered gauche in these parts) are rare. Big Sur hotels are especially busy in summer, when advance reservations are required. There are more accommodations than those listed

(**Finds**) **Big Sur Lodging at Low Rates**

If you want to stay in Big Sur but can't afford it, consider **Treebones Resort** (© **877/424-4787**; www.treebonesresort.com). This new miniresort, on a secluded bluff, shelters guests in ocean-side yurts—circular fabric structures on a wooden frame. Half-tent, half-cabin, Treebones' yurts are spacious and tastefully furnished with polished pine wood floors, queen-size beds with cozy comforters, electric lighting, gas-burning fireplaces, and French doors that open to a redwood deck with Adirondack chairs and spectacular coastal views. The yurts don't have bathrooms, but shower and restroom facilities are within a short stroll. The main lodge has a heated, oceanview pool and hot tub, and a restaurant that serves nightly dinner by a crackling fire in a casual, community setting. Private, in-yurt massage treatments are also available. Rates start at $145 for two guests with a 2-night minimum April to October, including a self-service waffle breakfast with coffee and orange juice. Treebones is at 71895 Hwy. 1, 65 miles south of Monterey.

here, so if you're having trouble securing a room or a site, contact the chamber of commerce (listed in the "Essentials" section above) for other options.

Big Sur Lodge (**Kids**)   A family-friendly place, the Big Sur Lodge is *in* the park and sheltered by towering redwoods, sycamores, and maples. The rustic motel-style cabins are spacious, with high peaked cedar- and redwood-beamed ceilings. They're clean and heated, and have private bathrooms and reserved parking spaces. Some have fireplaces and others kitchenettes. All offer porches or decks with views of the redwoods or the Santa Lucia Range. An advantage to staying here is that you're entitled to free use of all park facilities, including hiking, barbecue pits, and picnic areas. In addition, the lodge has its own grocery store. *Note:* Winter rates are significantly cheaper.

In Pfeiffer–Big Sur State Park, Hwy. 1 (P.O. Box 190), Big Sur, CA 93920. © **800/424-4787** or 831/667-3100. Fax 831/667-3110. www.bigsurlodge.com. 61 cottages. $199–$249 cottage; $259–$319 kitchen suite; $289–$359 kitchen suite with fireplace; park entrance fee included. AE, MC, V. From Carmel, take Hwy. 1 south 26 miles. **Amenities:** Restaurant; heated outdoor pool in season. *In room:* Kitchen in some units, coffeemaker, no phone.

Deetjen's Big Sur Inn ★   In the 1930s, before Highway 1 was built, this homestead in a redwood canyon was an overnight stopping place on the coastal wagon road. Norwegian homesteader Helmuth Deetjen built the original units from hand-hewn logs and lumber. Folks either love or hate them. They're cozy and adorable, with old-fashioned furnishings and a down-home feel (the hand-hewn doors don't have locks), but those who want creature comforts should go elsewhere, or at least reserve a cabin with a private bathroom. Single-wall construction rooms aren't soundproof, so children under 12 are allowed only if families reserve both rooms of a two-room building. They're not insulated, so prepare to crank up the fire or wood-burning stove. *Tip:* Cabins by the river are the most private. If you stay in one of the two-story units, request the quieter upstairs rooms. The restaurant (p. 420) is a local favorite and consists of four intimate, English country inn–style rooms lit by candlelight.

Hwy. 1, Big Sur, CA 93920. ✆ **831/667-2377.** www.deetjens.com. 20 units, 15 with bathroom. $75–$180 double with shared bathroom; $95–$200 double with private bathroom. MC, V. **Amenities:** Restaurant. *In room:* No phone.

Post Ranch Inn ★★★ (Moments) This is one of my very favorite places to stay on the planet. Perched on 98 acres of seaside ridges 1,200 feet above the Pacific, this romantic resort opened in 1992 and was instantly declared one of the world's finest retreats. Wood-and-glass guest cottages are built around existing trees—some are elevated to avoid damaging the delicate redwood root structures—and the ultraprivate Ocean and Coast cottages are so close to the edge of the earth, you get the impression that you've joined the clouds (imagine that from your private spa tub). Other cottages that face the wood-lands are as impressive in design. Each room has a king-size bed, wood-burning fireplace, private deck, digital music system with 45 channels, and wet bar with complimentary goodies. The bathrooms, fashioned out of slate and granite, have luxurious spa tubs. The best Jacuzzi I've ever encountered is here and seems to join the sky on a cliff. There is also an infinity pool and sun decks. The only drawback is that the vibe can be stuffy, which is due more to the clientele than to the staff. The **Sierra Mar** restaurant and bar is open to outside guests for lunch, afternoon appetizers, and dinner (reservations required for dinner). It, too, has floor-to-ceiling views of the ocean and offers an opportunity for people who can't afford the steep rack rates to ooh and aah at one of the most beautiful hotel settings in the world.

Hwy. 1 (P.O. Box 219), Big Sur, CA 93920. ✆ **800/527-2200** or 831/667-2200. Fax 831/667-2512. www. postranchinn.com. 30 units. $550–$1,485 double. Rates include buffet breakfast. AE, MC, V. **Amenities:** Restaurant; bar/lounge; outdoor heated pool; exercise room; spa services; cliffside Jacuzzi; game room; concierge; activities desk; room service; in-room massage. *In room:* A/C, minibar, coffeemaker, hair dryer, iron, safe, CD player.

Ventana Inn and Spa ★★★ Luxuriously rustic and utterly romantic, Ventana has been a popular wilderness outpost for more than 30 years, and with good reason. On 243 mountainous oceanfront acres, Ventana has an elegance that's atypical of the region and has attracted famous guests such as Barbra Streisand, Goldie Hawn, and Francis Ford Coppola since opening in 1975.

The accommodations, in 12 one- and two-story natural-wood buildings along wind-ing wildflower-flanked paths, blend in with the magical Big Sur countryside. The exten-sive grounds are dotted with hammocks and hand-carved benches, strategically located under shady trees and at vista points. The guest rooms are divinely decorated in warm, cozy luxury, with private terraces or balconies overlooking the ocean or forest. Most rooms offer wood-burning fireplaces, and some have Jacuzzis and cathedral ceilings. A small fitness center offers the basics—but you'll be more inspired to hike the grounds, where you'll find pastoral respite plus a pool, a rustic library, and clothing-optional tan-ning decks and spa tubs. This is one of the best retreats in the region, if not the state. I prefer the rooms at Post Ranch (see above), but the laid-back energy and the grounds at Ventana (and the spa). *Tips:* Be sure to check their website for seasonal specials. Ventana's restaurant, **Cielo** (p. 420), is a romantic and first-rate dining experience. Children are permitted in the restaurant but not encouraged.

Hwy. 1, Big Sur, CA 93920. ✆ **800/628-6500** or 831/667-2331. Fax 831/667-0537. www.ventanainn.com. 62 units. $500–$1,100 double; from $925 cottage. Rates include continental breakfast and afternoon wine and cheese. AE, DC, DISC, MC, V. **Amenities:** Restaurant; 2 heated outdoor pools; exercise room; full spa w/2 Japanese hot baths; sauna; concierge; room service; in-room massage; laundry service; execu-tive-level rooms. *In room:* A/C, TV/DVD, minibar, fridge, coffeemaker, hair dryer, iron, safe.

Camping

Big Sur is one of California's most spectacular camping destinations. One of the most glorious settings is **Pfeiffer–Big Sur State Park,** on Highway 1, 26 miles south of Carmel (© **831/667-2315**). The 810-acre state park has 218 secluded sites amid hundreds of acres of redwoods. Hiking trails, streams, and the river are steps from your sleeping bag, and the most modern amenities are the 25¢ showers (for 3 min.), and water faucets between sites. Each spot has a picnic table and fire pit but no RV hookups or electricity. Riverfront sites are most coveted, but others promise more privacy among the shaded hillsides. Campfire programs and nature walks are available. A store, gift shop, restaurant, and cafe are near the entrance. Fees are $25 per night for family sites; call © **800/444-7275** or see **www.reserveamerica.com** for reservations.

The entrance to the **Ventana Campground,** on Highway 1, 28 miles south of Carmel and 4¼ miles south of the River Inn (© **831/667-2712;** www.ventanawildernesscampground.com), is adjacent to the Ventana Resort entrance, but the comparison stops there. This is pure rusticity. The 80 campsites, on 40 acres of a redwood canyon, are spaced well apart on a hillside and shaded by towering trees. Each has a picnic table and fire ring but no electricity, RV hookups, or river access. Three conveniently located bathhouses have hot showers (25¢ fee). Reserve a space with a credit card (MasterCard or Visa) for 1 night's deposit. Or mail a deposit check, the dates you'd like to stay, and a stamped, self-addressed envelope at least 2 weeks in advance (earlier during peak months). Rates are $35 for a site for two with one vehicle. An additional person is $5 extra, and it'll cost you $5 to bring Fido. Rates include the entrance fee for your car. Open March through October.

Big Sur Campground and Cabins is on Highway 1, 26 miles south of Carmel (© **831/667-2322;** www.bigsurcalifornia.org/camping.html). Sites are cramped, so the feel is more like a camping village than an intimate retreat (romantic it ain't). However, it's very well maintained and perfect for families, who love the playground, river swimming, and inner-tube rentals. Each campsite has its own wood-burning fire pit, picnic table, and freshwater faucet within 25 feet of the pitching area. There are also RV water and electric hookups. Facilities include bathhouses with hot showers, laundry facilities, an aged volleyball/basketball court, and a grocery store. There are 81 tent sites (30 RV-ready with electricity and water hookup), plus 13 cabins (all with shower). The all-wood cabins are adorable, with stylish country furnishings, wood-burning ovens, patios, and full kitchens. Rates are $32 to $48 for a tent site for five people (plus $4 extra for electricity and water), $38 to $58 for an RV site for up to five people, $75 to $95 for a tent cabin (bed, but no heat or plumbing) for three, or $115 to $345 for a cabin for six. Rates include the entrance for your car. MasterCard and Visa are accepted. Pets cost $4 for campsites and $12 for tent cabins; pets are not allowed in the other cabins. It's open year-round.

WHERE TO DINE

In addition to the following choices, you should try the **Big Sur Bakery and Restaurant** on Highway 1, just past the post office and a mile south of Pfeiffer–Big Sur State Park (© **831/667-0520**). It offers friendly service and healthy fare, including wood-fired pizzas and portobello-mushroom burgers at lunch and salmon, tuna, and chicken selections at dinner. All the pastries are freshly baked on the premises, along with hearth-baked breads. It's open Tuesday through Sunday from 8am to 10pm; they close early on Monday.

Big Sur River Inn CALIFORNIA/AMERICAN   Popular with everyone from families to bikers, the River Inn is an unpretentious, rustic, down-home restaurant that has something for all tastes. Trying to seat a small army? No problem. Want to watch sports on TV at a local bar? Pull up a stool. Looking to snag a few rays from a deck right beside the Big Sur River? Break out the suntan lotion. In winter, the wooden dining room is the prime spot; on summer days, some folks grab their patio chairs and cocktails and hang out literally midstream. Along with the local color, attractions include a full bar and good ol' American breakfasts (steak and eggs, omelets, pancakes, and so on, plus espresso, with most dishes for around $6), lunches (an array of salads, sandwiches, and baby back ribs, or fish and chips), and dinners (fresh catch, pastas, burgers, or ribs). I usually order the Black Angus Burger with a side of beer-battered onion rings, or a big platter of the Road-house Ribs served with cowboy beans.

On Hwy. 1, 2 miles north of Pfeiffer–Big Sur State Park. ⒸＴ 831/667-2700. www.bigsurriverinn.com. Main courses $6–$13 breakfast, $8.75–$18 lunch, $8.95–$36 dinner. AE, DC, MC, V. Daily 8am–10pm; 8am–9pm in winter.

Café Kevah SOUTHWEST/CALIFORNIA   One level below Nepenthe (see below), Café Kevah offers the same celestial view at a fraction of the price, a more casual environ-ment, and—depending on your taste—better food. Seating is outdoors—a downside when the biting fog rolls in, but perfect on a clear day. You can order breakfast (served all day) or lunch from the shack of a kitchen and then grab an umbrella-shaded table. Fare here is more eclectic than Nepenthe's, with such choices as homemade granola, baby greens with broiled salmon and papaya, chicken brochettes, omelets, and new-potato hash. It ain't cheap, but innovative cuisine, the view, and a decent mocha make it worth-while. Don't forget your coat.

On Hwy. 1, 29 miles south of Carmel (5 miles south of the River Inn). ⒸＴ 831/667-2345. www.nepenthe bigsur.com. Appetizers $6.25–$12; main courses $11–$18. AE, MC, V. Daily 9am–4pm; closes when it rains.

Cielo Restaurant ★★ NEW AMERICAN   Like the resort, Ventana's "heaven" res-taurant is a woodsy but extravagant place to dine alfresco at lunch or for a romantic dinner. The airy cedar interior is divided into two spaces: the lounge, where a wooden bar and cocktail tables look onto a roaring fire and through picturesque windows; and the dining room, which overlooks the mountains and/or the ocean. But in summer it's the outdoor patio, with its views of the ocean expanse and 50 miles of Big Sur coast, that's the coveted lunch spot. Unlike some costly restaurants in the area, a meal here is as gratifying as the surroundings, and much of the organically grown produce on the menu is harvested from their own Cielo gardens. Lunch offers main courses such as grilled Atlantic salmon; dinner includes such stellar starters as a perfectly dressed Caesar salad and a well-balanced chanterelle-mushroom risotto, and main courses such as herb-mari-nated roasted *poussin* (spring chicken), rosemary scented roasted pork loin, and glazed Sonoma duck breast.

At Ventana Inn and Spa, Hwy. 1, Big Sur. ⒸＴ 831/667-4242. www.ventanainn.com. Reservations recom-mended for dinner. Main courses $11–$20 lunch, $23–$34 dinner. AE, DC, DISC, MC, V. Daily noon–3:30pm and 6–9pm.

Deetjen's Big Sur Inn Restaurant ★ AMERICAN   With the feel of an English farmhouse—white-painted wood walls, wood-burning stove, dimly lit old-fashioned lamps, country antiques—this cozy, country setting is the perfect venue for delicious comfort food and friendly service. Mornings start with a cup of strong coffee and break-fast: omelets and eggs Benedict piled high with potatoes, pancakes, and granola. Dinner might include grilled chicken with mushrooms and a garlic Marsala sauce; roasted rack

> ### (Tips) Gourmet to Go
>
> The **Big Sur Center Deli** sells fresh baked goods, salads, wine, and beer, as well as fettuccine, calzones, enchiladas, and barbecue chicken—all made on-site. Sandwiches are prepared to order, or you can grab a ready-made hoagie or vegetarian portobello mushroom on a roll. Pastries and coffee drinks are available as well. It's located on Highway 1 next to the Big Sur Post Office and is open daily from 7:30am to 8:30pm (© **831/667-2225**).

of lamb with a panko crust; prime New York steak with macadamia-nut risotto; and roast duckling with brandy, peppercorn, and molasses sauce.

On Hwy. 1. © **831/667-2377**. www.deetjens.com. Reservations recommended. Main courses $4.25–$12 breakfast, $17–$29 dinner. MC, V. Mon–Fri 9:30am–4pm; Sat noon–4pm.

Nepenthe AMERICAN   Stop by Nepenthe if only to admire the view and pay homage to Henry Miller, who wrote some of his most significant works here. At 808 feet above sea level along the cliffs overlooking the ocean, the view is celestial—especially when fog lingers above the water. On a warm day, join the crowds on the terrace. On colder days, stay indoors. The redwood and adobe structure—with a wood-burning fireplace, redwood ceilings, and bayfront windows—has been a sanctuary for writers, artists, and travelers since 1949. Unfortunately, the food is another story; elsewhere, I would scoff at a $13 burger and $19 swordfish sandwich. Here, though, I consider it a nominal admission to dine at heights only birds usually enjoy. For the most part, the food is industrial fare (big-box-store-style hamburger patties for the grown-ups and Kraft macaroni and cheese on the kids menu). Come for lunch or just a drink to see the view and save your dinner bucks for elsewhere.

Hwy. 1, 29 miles south of Carmel (5 miles south of the River Inn). © **831/667-2345**. www.nepenthe bigsur.com. Reservations accepted only for parties of 5 or more. Main courses $12–$35. AE, MC, V. Daily 11:30am–10pm.

8 PINNACLES NATIONAL MONUMENT ★

58 miles SE of Monterey

A little-known outpost 10 years ago, the 24,000-acre Pinnacles National Monument is now one of central California's most popular weekend hiking and climbing spots. In Steinbeck Country, southeast of Salinas, the mild-winter climate and plentiful routes make it an ideal off-season training ground for climbers. It's also a haven for campers, bird-watchers, and nature lovers. One of the world's most unusual chaparral ecosystems, it supports a community of plants and animals, including six endangered California condors—the largest bird in North America, with a wingspan of nearly 10 feet—and one of California's largest breeding populations of raptors. Bring binoculars!

The Pinnacles—hundreds of towering crags, spires, ramparts, and hoodoos—seem out of place amid the rolling hills of the coast range. Part of the eroded remains of a volcano formed 23 million years ago, 195 miles south in the middle of the Mojave Desert, they were brought here by the movement of the San Andreas Fault, which runs just east of the park. (The other half of the volcano remains in the Mojave.)

You could spend days here, but it's possible to cover the most interesting features in a weekend. With a single hike, you can go from the oak woodland around the Bear Gulch Visitor Center to the dry, desolate crags of the high peaks and then back down through a half-mile-long cave with underground waterfalls.

ESSENTIALS

GETTING THERE   Two entrances lead to the park: The **West Entrance** from Soledad and U.S. 101 is a dusty, winding single-lane road (not suitable for trailers) with the best drive-up view. Exit at Front Street in Soledad, turn right and then left onto Highway 46 heading east (it doesn't connect with the east side entrance). The west gate is open daily from 7:30am to 8pm (until 6pm in winter).

The alternative route is via the **East Entrance.** Unless you're coming from nearby, take the longer drive on Highway 25 through Gilroy and Hollister to enter through the east. Because most of the peaks of the Pinnacles face east and the watershed drains east, most of the interesting hikes and geologic features are on this side. The east gate is open 24 hours a day. No road crosses the park.

FEES   Park entrance fees, good for 7 days, are $2 per person or $5 per car.

VISITOR CENTER   The first place you should go when entering from the east is the **Bear Gulch Visitor Center** (🕿 831/389-4485), open daily from 9am to 5pm. This small center is rich with exhibits on the park's history, wildlife, and geology, with a great selection of nature handbooks and climbing guides for the Pinnacles. Climbers should check with rangers about closures and other information before heading out: Many routes are closed during hawk- and falcon-nesting season, and rangers like to know how many climbers are in the park.

Adjacent to the visitor center, the Bear Gulch picnic ground is a great place to fuel up before setting out on a hike. Don't leave before gazing up at the dramatic spires of the high peaks (the ultimate spot is from the west side).

For more information, log on to the park's website at **www.nps.gov/pinn**.

REGULATIONS & WARNINGS   Beware of poison oak, particularly in Bear Gulch. Rattlesnakes are common but rarely seen. Bikes and dogs are prohibited on all trails, and no backcountry camping is allowed in the park.

Hiking through this variety of landscapes demands versatility. Come prepared with a good pair of hiking shoes, snacks, lots of water, and a flashlight.

Daytime temperatures often exceed 100°F (38°C) in summer, so the best time of year to visit is spring, when the wildflowers are blooming, or in the fall. Crowds are common during spring weekends.

HIKING & EXPLORING THE PARK

To see most of the park in a single, moderately strenuous morning, take the **Condor Gulch Trail** from the visitor center. As you climb out of the parking area, the Pinnacles' wind-sculpted spires seem to grow taller. In less than 2 miles, you're among them, and Condor Gulch intersects with the **High Peaks Trail.** The view from the top spans miles: the Salinas Valley to your west, the Pinnacles below, and miles of coast to the east. And it's the most likely place to spot the elusive California condor. (Look for the white-triangle markings on the undersides of their wings.) After traversing the high peaks (including stretches of footholds carved in steep rock faces) for about a mile, the trail drops back toward the visitor center via a valley filled with eerie-looking hoodoos.

In another 1.5 miles you'll reach the reservoir marking the top of **Bear Gulch Cave,** which closes occasionally; in 1998, it closed due both to storm damage and to accommodate migrating Townsend bats, who in the past several years have come here to have their babies. It's usually open, but if you want to explore, you'll need your flashlight and you might get wet; still, this half-mile-long talus cave is a thrill. From the end of the cave, you're just a short walk (through the most popular climbing area of the park) away from the visitor center. It's also possible to hike just Bear Gulch and the cave, and then return via the **Moses Spring Trail.** It's about 2 miles round-trip, but you'll miss the view from the top.

If you're coming from the West Entrance, the **Juniper Canyon Trail** is a short (1.25 miles), but very steep, blast to the top of the high peaks. You'll definitely earn the view. Otherwise, try the short **Balconies Trail** to the monument's other talus cave, **Balconies Cave.** Flashlights are required here, too.

WHERE TO STAY

The Inn at the Pinnacles ★ (Finds)   Unless you intend to camp, the only place to stay at the Pinnacles National Monument is this sprawling hacienda-style inn a half mile from the west park entrance. Built in 2002 in the heart of a working vineyard—Brousseau Vineyards in the Chalone Appellation—the six-room inn has unblemished vistas of rolling vineyards and the Gabilan Mountain Range. Each of the individually decorated guest rooms has a private entrance, ceramic tile flooring, private patio with a gas grill and vineyard views, and a sitting area with gas fireplace; all but one have a two-person whirlpool tub (heaven after a long day of hiking). The inn's sprawling patio is a popular spot to sip wine under a shade umbrella with panoramic views of the surrounding hillsides and Pinnacles National Monument. The innkeepers serve a full breakfast each morning (in the dining room, patio, or guest rooms), and wine and cheese every evening. The nearest restaurants are 10 miles away, so you can either bring your own food to grill or ask if the innkeepers can make advance arrangements for dinner service.

32025 Stonewall Canyon Rd., Soledad, CA 93960. © **831/678-2400.** www.innatthepinnacles.com. 6 units. $200–$290 double. Rates include continental breakfast and afternoon wine and cheese. MC, V. **Amenities:** Bocce court; gas grills. *In room:* A/C, wet bar, fridge, microwave, Jacuzzi (in 5 rooms).

CAMPING

The park's campground on the west side was demolished by El Niño storms in 1997 and 1998, and it's not scheduled for repair. Now the only campground is the privately run **Pinnacles Campground, Inc.,** on the east side (© **877/444-6777;** www.nps.gov/pinn/planyourvisit/camp.htm), which charges $23 per tent and $36 per RV. It's just outside the park (off Hwy. 25, 32 miles south of Hollister), with lots of privacy and space between sites, plus showers, a store, and a large pool. It's close enough so you can hike into the park from the campground, though it will add a few miles to your outing. Surroundings here are natural, rather than overdeveloped.

The Central Coast

by Matthew Richard Poole

California's Central Coast—an amalgam of beaches, lakes, rolling hills, and mountains—is the state's most diverse region. The narrow strip that runs for more than 100 miles from San Simeon to Ventura spans several climate zones and supports an eclectic mix of college students, middle-class workers, wealthy retirees, winemakers, strawberry farmers, ranchers, immigrant laborers, and fishermen. The ride along Highway 1, which follows the ocean cliffs, is almost always packed with rental cars, RVs, and bicycles on summer weekends, but the scenery is so gorgeous nobody seems to mind a little traffic.

The Central Coast is also coming into its own as a major wine region and offers another excuse to visit some of the state's most scenic countryside. Wine snobs might tell you that Central Coast wines cannot compare to those from the northern appellations, where vintages can age to sublime flavor and astronomical price, but if you're in the market for bottles in the $20-to-$30 range that are ready to drink within a couple of years, you'll love what this up-and-coming wine destination has to offer.

Whether you're driving up from Los Angeles or down from San Francisco, Highway 1 is the most scenic and leisurely route. (U.S. 101 is faster but less picturesque.) Most bicyclists pedal from north to south, the direction of the prevailing winds. Those in cars may prefer to drive south to north so they can get a better look at the coastline as it unfolds toward the west. No matter which direction you drive, break out the camera—you're about to experience unparalleled beauty, California style.

1 SAN SIMEON: HEARST CASTLE ★★★

250 miles S of San Francisco (via Hwy. 1); 250 miles NW of Los Angeles

Few buildings on earth are as elaborate as **Hearst Castle.** The 165-room estate of publishing magnate William Randolph Hearst, high above the village of San Simeon atop a hill he called La Cuesta Encantada ("the Enchanted Hill"), is an ego trip par excellence. One of the last great estates of America's Gilded Age, it's an over-the-top monument to wealth—and to the power that money brings.

Hearst Castle is a sprawling compound, constructed over 28 years in a Mediterranean Revival style and never fully completed. The focal point of the estate is **Casa Grande,** a 100-plus-room mansion filled with art and antiques that you have to see to believe. Hearst acquired most of his collection via New York auction houses, where he bought entire rooms (including walls, ceilings, and floors) and shipped them here. The result is an old-world-style castle in a mix-and-match style. You'll see 400-year-old Spanish and Italian ceilings, 500-year-old mantels, 16th-century Florentine bedsteads, Renaissance paintings, Flemish tapestries, and innumerable other treasures.

Three opulent "guesthouses" also contain magnificent works of art. A lavish private movie theater was used to screen first-run films twice nightly—once for employees, and again for the guests and host.

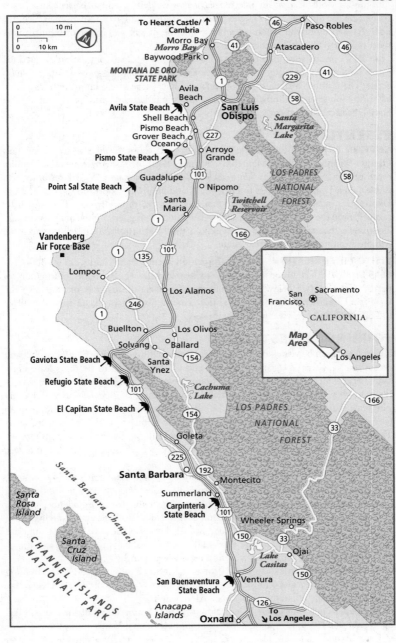

And then there are the swimming pools. The Roman-inspired indoor pool has intricate mosaic work, Carrara-marble replicas of Greek deities, and alabaster globe lamps that create the illusion of moonlight. The breathtaking outdoor Greco-Roman Neptune pool, flanked by marble colonnades that frame the distant sea, is one of the mansion's most memorable—and photographed—features.

In 1957, in exchange for a massive tax write-off, the Hearst Corporation donated the estate to the state of California (while retaining ownership of approximately 80,000 acres). The California Department of Parks and Recreation now administers it as a State Historic Monument and officially refers to it as the rather unpoetic Hearst San Simeon State Historical Monument.

ESSENTIALS

GETTING THERE   Hearst Castle is on Highway 1, about 42 miles north of San Luis Obispo, 94 miles south of Monterey, 250 miles north of Los Angeles, and 250 miles south of San Francisco. From San Francisco or Monterey, take U.S. 101 south to Paso Robles, then Highway 46 west to Highway 1, and Highway 1 north to the castle. From Los Angeles, take U.S. 101 north to San Luis Obispo, then Highway 1 north to the castle. Park in the visitor center lot; a bus takes guided tour guests up the hill to the estate. The movie theater and visitor center adjoin the parking lot and are easily accessible without heading up to the actual estate.

VISITOR INFORMATION   To get information about Hearst Castle, call © **800/444-4445** or 805/927-2020, or log on to **www.hearstcastle.org**. For more information on nearby Cambria (see below), check out **www.cambria-online.com** or stop into the **Cambria Chamber of Commerce**'s visitor center at 767 Main St., in the west village (© **805/927-3624;** www.cambriachamber.org).

TOURING THE ESTATE

Hearst Castle can be visited only by guided tours, conducted daily beginning at 8:20am, except on New Year's Day, Thanksgiving, and Christmas. Two to six tours leave every hour, depending on the season. Allow 2 hours between starting times if you plan on taking more than one tour. You can buy tickets right at the visitor center, but you have no guarantee that they'll be available—a day's slate of tours can easily sell out. You pay no fee for advance reservations, and you can make them from 1 hour to 8 weeks in advance. Tickets can be purchased by phone or online at California Reservations (© **800/444-4445;** www.hearstcastle.org). If you're ordering tickets from outside the United States, call © **916/414-8400,** ext. 4100.

Four different daytime tours run on a daily basis, each lasting 1 hour, 45 minutes, including the 15-minute bus ride to and from the castle. Docents dress in 1930s period costume and assume a variety of roles, enhancing the living history experience.

I strongly recommend setting aside 2 full days to enjoy the castle at a leisurely pace. If you're just coming to see the castle, 1 day will do, but expect it to be a longish one and sandwich it between a 2-night stay. Also, children under 6 may find walking and climbing hundreds of steps for almost 2 hours a bit overwhelming.

Tickets for the daytime tours are $24 for adults and $12 for kids 6 to 17. The Evening Tour is $30 for adults and $15 for kids. Children under 6 are free. Prices are a few bucks cheaper during the off season, September 16 to May 14.

The Experience Tour (Tour 1) is ideal for first-time visitors and is the first to get filled up. In addition to the swimming pools, this tour visits several rooms on the ground floor of Casa Grande, including Hearst's private theater, where you'll see some home movies

taken during the castle's heyday. **Tour 2** focuses on Casa Grande's upper floors, including
Hearst's opulent library, private suite of rooms, and lots of fabulous bathrooms. Tour 2
is a perfectly fine choice for first-timers if you're only planning to take one tour, particularly if your interest lies more in the home's private areas. **Tour 3,** which delves into the
construction and subsequent alterations of Hearst Castle, is fascinating for architecture
buffs and detail hounds, but it shouldn't be the first and only tour if you've never visited
the castle before. From April to October, **Tour 4** is dedicated to the estate's gardens, terraces, and walkways, the Casa del Mar guesthouse, the wine cellar of Casa Grande, and
the dressing rooms at the Neptune Pool. This tour does not visit any of the interiors of
the main house.

Evening tours are held most Friday and Saturday nights during spring and fall, and
usually nightly around Christmas (when the house, decked out for the holidays, is
magical). Thirty minutes longer than the daytime tours, they visit highlights of the main
house, the most elaborate guesthouse, and the illuminated pools and gardens.

No matter how many tours you take in a day, you must return to the visitor center
each time and ride the bus back to the top of the hill with your tour group, so allow at
least 2 hours between tours when you buy your tickets. You'll find plenty to keep you
busy at the visitor center before, after, and in between tours: an observation deck of the
Enchanted Hill, two gift shops, ball-park-quality food vendors, and a good small
museum. The permanent William Randolph Hearst Exhibit focuses on the castle's history, art, and architecture.

You can visit the giant-screen **Hearst Castle National Geographic Theater** regardless of
whether you take a tour. Larger-than-life films include the 40-minute *Hearst Castle: Building the Dream* and other films in five-story-high iWERKS format (just like IMAX) with
seven-channel surround sound. Shows begin every 45 minutes throughout the day. The
movie is included in the price of Tour 1; by itself it's $8 for adults, $6 for kids 6 to 17. For
current information, call ✆ 805/927-6811 or visit their website at www.ngtheater.com.

Wear comfortable shoes—you'll walk about a half mile per tour, each of which includes
150 to 400 steps. (Wheelchair tours are available by calling ✆ 800/444-4445 or 805/
927-2020, with 10 days notice.)

WHAT TO SEE & DO IN NEARBY CAMBRIA ★

After driving for close to an hour without passing anything but lush green hills (especially
from Hwy. 46 off U.S. 101), it's a pleasant surprise to roll into the endearing coastal town
of Cambria (pronounced *Cam*-bree-uh), 6 miles south of San Simeon. Not quite Northern
California and not quite Southern California, not quite coastal and not quite inland, this
charming artists' colony is so appealing that the town itself is reason enough to make the
drive. With little more than 4 blocks' worth of shops, restaurants, and a handful of B&Bs,
Cambria is the perfect place to escape the everyday, enjoy the endless expanses of pristine
coastal terrain, and meander through little shops selling local artwork and antiques.

Cambria has three distinct parts. Along Main Street is "the Village," which is divided into
two sections: the **West Village** and the **East Village.** The West Village is the newer, somewhat more touristy end of town where you'll find the visitor information center. The more
historic East Village is a bit quieter, more locals oriented, and a tad more sophisticated than
the West Village. If you cross Highway 1 to the coastal side at the far west end of town (or
the north end, if you're considering how the freeway runs), you'll reach Cambria's third part,
Moonstone Beach. Lined with motels, inns, and a few restaurants on the inland side of the
street, ocean-facing Moonstone Beach Drive is my favorite place to stay in Cambria.

(Fun Facts) Weekends at "the Ranch"

The lavish palace that William Randolph Hearst always referred to simply as "the ranch" took root in 1919. William Randolph ("W. R." to his friends) had inherited 275,000 acres from his father, mining baron George Hearst, and was well on his way to building a formidable media empire. He often escaped to a spot known as "Camp Hill" on his lands in the Santa Lucia Mountains above the village of San Simeon, the site of boyhood family outings. Complaining that "I get tired of going up there and camping in tents," Hearst hired architect Julia Morgan to design the retreat that would become one of the most famous private homes in the world.

An art collector with indiscriminate taste and inexhaustible funds, Hearst overwhelmed Morgan with interiors and furnishings from the ancestral collections of Europe. Each week, railroad cars carrying fragments of Roman temples, lavish doors and carved ceilings from Italian monasteries, Flemish tapestries, hastily rolled paintings by the old masters, ancient Persian rugs, and antique French furniture arrived—5 tons at a time—in San Simeon. Orson Welles's 1941 masterpiece *Citizen Kane,* which depicts a Hearst-like mogul with a similarly excessive estate called Xanadu, has a memorable scene of hoarded priceless treasures warehoused in dusty piles, stretching as far as the eye can see. Like Kane, Hearst, once described as a man with an "edifice complex," purchased so much that only a fraction of what he bought was ever installed in the estate.

In 1925, Hearst separated from his wife and began spending time in Los Angeles overseeing his movie company, Cosmopolitan Pictures. His principal actress, Marion Davies, also became his constant companion and hostess at Hearst Castle. The ranch soon became a playground for the Hollywood crowd as well as for dignitaries such as Winston Churchill and playwright George

Before you set out, pick up the Cambria Historical Society's brochure at your hotel and take a simple, fun **self-guided tour** of the historical buildings in the East Village. You'll not only get a history lesson about this picturesque village, but you'll also discover a few places you may have overlooked otherwise, such as the **blacksmith shop** at 4121 Burton Dr. or the **Santa Rosa Chapel and Cemetery** at 2352 Main St.

An overnight stay in Cambia also allows visitors to see the coastal region's "new" attraction: a spring (yes, that's the correct term—I looked it up) of elephant seals sunning themselves on the beaches year-round. Once thought to be extinct, since 1990 these 3,000-pound mammals have returned to Piedras Blancas, an **elephant seal rookery** 12 miles north of Cambria. Today more than 2,000 of these magnificent, prehistoric-looking beasts are counted here annually. Breeding takes place here December through March; molting occurs August through September. Keep your distance from the elephant seals: They're a protected species and can be dangerous if approached. Finding the beach is easy: Just stop at the packed parking lot 4¹/₂ miles north of Hearst Castle and follow the crowds along the short, sandy walk for a good vantage. Docents wearing blue jackets are usually on hand to answer questions. The beaches and coves are also great places for

Bernard Shaw, who reportedly said of the estate, "This is the way God would have done it if He had the money."

Despite its opulence, Hearst promoted "the ranch" as a casual weekend home. He regularly laid the massive refectory table in the dining room with paper napkins and bottled ketchup to evoke a camplike atmosphere. In Hearst's beautiful library, his priceless collection of ancient Greek pottery—one of the greatest collections of its kind—is arranged casually among the rare volumes, like knickknacks.

W. R. Hearst and Marion Davies hosted frequent costume parties at the ranch, which were as intricately planned as a movie production. The most legendary, the Circus Party, was held to celebrate W. R.'s 75th birthday on April 29, 1938. Much of Hollywood attended to honor the tycoon, including grande dame Bette Davis—dressed as a bearded lady. The Hollywood crowd would take Hearst's private railway car from Los Angeles to San Luis Obispo, where a fleet of limousines waited to transport them to San Simeon. Those who didn't come by train were treated to a flight on Hearst's private plane from the Burbank airport (MGM head Irving Thalberg and his wife, Norma Shearer, preferred this mode of transportation). Hearst, an avid aviator, had a landing strip built; Charles Lindbergh used it when he flew up for a visit in the summer of 1928.

Oh, if the walls could talk. Atop one of the castle towers are the hexagonal Celestial Suites. One was a favorite of Clark Gable and Carole Lombard, who would be startled out of their romantic slumber by the clamor of 18 carillon bells overhead. David Niven, a frequent guest, was one of the many who defied Hearst's edict against liquor in private rooms: Niven was called upon more than once to explain the "empties" under the bed (once owned by Cardinal Richelieu) in his customary suite.

humans to cavort as well. For more information see **www.beachcalifornia.com/piedras. html**.

Shopping

Shopping is a major pastime in the village. Boutique owners are hypersavvy about keeping their merchandise current—and priced just a hair lower than L.A. or San Francisco. This close-knit community has always attracted artists and artisans. For the finest handcrafted glass artworks, from affordable jewelry to investment-scale sculpture, head to **Seekers Collection & Gallery,** 4090 Burton Dr. (© **800/841-5250;** www.seekersglass. com). Nearby, at **Moonstones Gallery,** 4070 Burton Dr. (© **800/424-3827;** www. moonstones.com), you'll find a selection of works ranging from woven crafts to jewelry and an exceptional collection of woodcarvings and other crafts. The shopping highlight of the West Village is **Home Arts,** 727 Main St. (© **805/927-2781;** www.home-arts. com), which offers an appealingly eclectic mix of country and contemporary home fashions and gifts. If a visit to the nearby Paso Robles wine country has inspired you, **Fermentations,** 4056 Burton Dr. (© **800/446-7505;** www.fermentations.com), has wines, wine accessories, and gifts, plus Wine Country gourmet goodies open for tasting. **Heart's Ease,** 4101 Burton Dr. (© **800/266-4372** or 805/927-5224), is inside a historic cottage and is packed with an abundance of garden delights, apothecary herbs, and custom-blended potpourris.

If Cambria has aroused your artistic instincts, a few miles south is another tiny artists' colony, called **Harmony.**

WHERE TO STAY

Because of its proximity, most people use Cambria as the jumping-off point for a visit to San Simeon. Cambria's popularity in summertime and on holiday weekends makes advance planning necessary. If my favorites are full, try one of these alternatives: **Captain's Cove Inn,** 6454 Moonstone Beach Dr. (© **800/781-COVE** or 805/927-8581; www.captainscoveinn.com), is a small beachfront B&B, whose motel-style exterior belies the array of creature comforts provided by the family owners. The **Ragged Point Inn,** 19019 Hwy. 1 (© **805/927-4502;** www.raggedpointinn.com), is 21 miles north of Cambria, with ocean views from every room. It's a great choice if you're planning to explore both Hearst Castle and the Big Sur Coast from one perch.

If you want a cheaper choice, try the **Creekside Inn,** 2618 Main St., Cambria (© **800/269-5212** or 805/927-4021; www.cambriacreeksideinn.com). It's basic, but the village location is extremely convenient and the rates are considerably lower—$69 to $159 double, year-round. Still too expensive? One mile north is **San Simeon State Beach** (© **800/444-7275** or 805/927-2020), a 133-site beachfront campground.

Note: If you can't find a vacancy anywhere in Cambria, the tiny town of San Simeon, 6 miles north, has numerous run-of-the-mill motels lining both sides of Highway 1, but I only recommend staying here as a last resort.

Best Western Cavalier Oceanfront Resort ★ (Kids)
Of the dozen or so budget and midrange motels along Highway 1 near Hearst Castle, this surprisingly nice chain is the only one that's oceanfront. Sprawled across a slope, the family-owned hotel invites guests to huddle around cliffside bonfires each evening. Every room—whether you choose a basic double or opt for a fireplace, ocean view, wet bar, or oceanfront terrace—features an array of amenities. On-site extras include a whirlpool spa, an exercise room, a restaurant with room service, and a coin-op laundry. The motel welcomes pets, and it's a terrific choice for castle-bound families.

9415 Hearst Dr. (Hwy. 1), San Simeon, CA 93452. © **800/826-8168** or 805/927-4688. Fax 805/927-6472. www.cavalierresort.com. 90 units. $159–$319 double. AE, DC, DISC, MC, V. Pets accepted. **Amenities:** 2 restaurants; heated pool; exercise room; whirlpool spa; room service; coin-op laundry. *In room:* TV/DVD, free high-speed Internet access, minibar, fridge, coffeemaker, hair dryer, iron.

FogCatcher Inn ★
You'll spot the FogCatcher by its faux English Tudor architecture (though a contemporary hotel), that fits right in with the mishmash of styles on funky Moonstone Beach. The U-shaped building is situated so many rooms have unencumbered views of the crashing waves across the street; some gaze oceanward over a sea of parked cars, and others are hopelessly landlocked—be sure to inquire when reserving. Rates vary wildly according to view, but each room interior has identical amenities and comforts. Immaculately maintained and furnished in a comfy cottage style with pine furniture, each room is made cozier by a gas fireplace and also has a microwave oven. Unlike many comparably priced Moonstone Beach lodgings, the FogCatcher has a heated swimming pool and Jacuzzi. Stop by the breakfast room in the morning for basic coffee, juice, and muffins to start the day.

6400 Moonstone Beach Dr., Cambria, CA 93428. (✆ **800/425-4121** or 805/927-1400. Fax 805/927-0204. www.fogcatcherinn.com. 60 units. $169–$269 double; from $369 suite. Rates include continental breakfast. AE, DISC, MC, V. Pets accepted in select rooms with $25 fee per night. **Amenities:** Outdoor heated pool; Jacuzzi. *In room:* TV, free W-Fi, minibar, fridge, coffeemaker, hair dryer, iron, fireplace.

J. Patrick House ★ Hidden in a pine-filled neighborhood overlooking Cambria's village, this B&B is cozy, elegant, and welcoming. The main house is a two-story log cabin, where each afternoon innkeepers Ann and John host wine and hors d'oeuvres next to the living room fireplace, and each morning serve breakfast by windows overlooking a hummingbird-filled garden. Most guest rooms are in the adjacent carriage house and all feature wood-burning fireplaces, feather duvets, bedtime milk and cookies, and knotty pine, bent-twig furniture, calico prints, and hand-stitched quilts. Amenities such as a phone and guest fridge are in the common area.

2990 Burton Dr., Cambria, CA 93428. (✆ **800/341-5258** or 805/927-3812. Fax 805/927-6759. www.jpatrickhouse.com. 8 units. $165–$215 double. Rates include full breakfast, afternoon wine and hors d'oeuvres, and evening milk and cookies. Seasonal discounts and packages available. DISC, MC, V. *In room:* Hair dryer, iron, CD player/radio, no phone.

Olallieberry Inn ★★ This 1873 Greek Revival house is my favorite B&B in the area. In the afternoon the aromas of baked brie and homemade bread (served during the wine hour) waft through the main house, and the staff does everything imaginable to make your stay special. They also have a passion for cooking and gardening, but the decor doesn't fall by the wayside: A countrified berry motif reigns, and the guest rooms are lovingly and individually appointed. Each has its own fireplace and private bathroom, although some are across or down the hall. Rooms in an adjoining building overlook a creek and have a fireplace and private deck. The full breakfast—accompanied by olallieberry jam, of course—is gourmet all the way. Amenities like phone, fax, and guest fridge are available in the common area. The inn is walking distance to fine restaurants and shops.

2476 Main St., Cambria, CA 93428. (✆ **888/927-3222** or 805/927-3222. Fax 805/927-0202. www.olallieberry.com. 9 units. $130–$200 double. Rates include full breakfast and evening wine and hors d'oeuvres. AE, MC, V. **Amenities:** Massage. *In room:* Wi-Fi, hair dryer, iron, fireplace, no phone.

WHERE TO DINE

Tiny Cambria boasts an unusual concentration of superb restaurants. In addition to the restaurants listed below, consider **Moonstone Beach Bar & Grill,** 6550 Moonstone Beach Dr. (✆ **805/927-3859;** www.moonstonebeach.com), whose incredible view must be what accounts for prices on the expensive side for this tasty but casual restaurant—stick to breakfast or lunch; or local institution **Linn's Main Bin Restaurant,** 2277 Main St. (✆ **805/927-1499;** www.linnsfruitbin.com), a casual all-day farmhouse restaurant/bakery/gift shop featuring homemade potpies, fresh-from-the-farm salads, breakfast treats, and Linn's famous olallieberry fruit pies.

Mustache Pete's (Kids) ITALIAN The friendly, casual atmosphere makes this a great place for families. The main menu attraction is the gourmet pizzas, a staple that seems indigenous to California/Italian eateries. You won't be disappointed by the variety, however. Also on the menu are traditional pasta dishes that come in big portions and are served with soup or salad.

4090 Burton Dr., Cambria. (✆ **805/927-8589.** www.mustachepetes.com. Main courses $8–$30. AE, DISC, MC, V. Mon–Sat 11am–10pm; Sun 10am–10pm.

Robin's ★ INTERNATIONAL   Robin's is a restaurant with something for everyone, from exotic dishes from Mexico, Thailand, India, and beyond to more straightforward preparations such as a tasty salad, a juicy steak, and a nightly vegetarian dish, along with tofu and tempeh specials. Offerings include a salmon bisque appetizer; artichoke and Gorgonzola ravioli in a spinach-cream sauce; and other combinations such as tandoori prawns with basmati brown rice, fruit chutney, and chapati; and *rogan josh,* Indian lamb curry mixed with yogurt, almonds, and toasted coconut. Don't miss dessert—try the espresso-soaked cake with mascarpone mousse and shaved chocolate or vanilla-custard bread pudding.

4095 Burton Dr., Cambria. ℭ **805/927-5007.** www.robinsrestaurant.com. Reservations recommended. Main courses $8–$15 lunch, $17–$30 dinner. MC, V. Sun 11am–4:45pm; Sun–Thurs 5–9pm; Fri–Sat 5–9:30pm.

Sea Chest Oyster Bar ★ SEAFOOD   Feeling like a dozen other seaside old-salt hangouts, the strangely familiar Sea Chest is a must for seafood lovers. Sporting nautical kitsch and a warm, welcoming atmosphere, this gray clapboard cottage even has a game-filled lounge complete with cribbage, checkers, and chess to keep you amused during the inevitable wait for a table. Oysters are the main attraction: on the half shell, oyster stew, oysters casino, oysters Rockefeller, or "devils on horseback" (with wine, garlic, and bacon). The menu is also filled with fresh seafood from local and worldwide waters: steamed New Zealand green-lipped mussels, clams in several preparations, halibut, salmon, lobster, scampi, plus whatever looked good off the boats that morning. There's a respectable list of microbrewed and imported beers, along with a selection of Central Coast wines. *Note:* If you don't enjoy seafood, dine elsewhere—there's not even a token steak on this menu.

6216 Moonstone Beach Dr. ℭ **805/927-4514.** www.seachestrestaurant.com. Reservations not accepted. Main courses $13–$48. No credit cards. Daily 5:30–9pm (closed Tues Sept–May).

Sow's Ear Café ★★ AMERICAN/SEAFOOD   Despite the porcine moniker, this tiny old cottage at the center of the village is a rather warm and romantic hideaway. The best tables are in the fireside front room, lit just enough to highlight its rustic wood-and-brick decor. Pigs appear everywhere, in oil paintings, as ceramic or cast-iron models, and the logo is a woodcut sow. Though the menu features plenty of contemporary California cuisine, the most popular dishes are American favorites given a contemporary lift; these include a warmly satisfying chicken-fried steak with gravy, chicken and dumplings, and zesty baby pork ribs. Other standouts are parchment-wrapped salmon, and pork loin glazed with chunky olallieberry chutney. Every meal begins with the restaurant's signature marbled bread baked in terra-cotta flowerpots, and the wine list is among the area's best. *Tip:* Early birds (5–6pm nightly) choose from eight dinners priced from $13 to $20.

2248 Main St. ℭ **805/927-4865.** www.thesowsear.com. Reservations recommended. Main courses $11–$29. DISC, MC, V. Daily 5–9pm (open later in summer).

2 MORRO BAY

124 miles S of Monterey; 235 miles S of San Francisco (via Hwy. 1); 220 miles N of L.A.

Morro Bay is separated from the ocean by a long peninsula of towering sand dunes. It's best known for dramatic **Morro Rock,** an enormous egg-shaped monolith that juts 576 feet above of the water at the entrance to Morro Bay. Across from the rock, a huge oceanfront electrical plant mars the visual appeal of the otherwise pristine bay, which is filled with birds, sea mammals, and calm water offering plenty of recreational activities such as fishing, surfing, kayaking, bird-watching (Morro Rock is a protected falcon sanctuary), and beachcombing.

Other than gawking at the "Gibraltar of the Pacific," there's not all that much to see in the town itself. Tourist-trade motels, shops, and seafood restaurants line the waterfront Embarcadero and adjacent blocks, but the town's best feature is its setting: The beaches, bay, and wildlife sanctuaries are the main reason to visit.

ESSENTIALS

Morro Bay is on U.S. 101 (itself only four lanes on this stretch). The **Morro Bay Visitors Center & Chamber of Commerce,** 845 Embarcadero Rd., Morro Bay, CA 93442 (© **800/231-0592** or 805/772-4467; www.morrobay.org), offers lots of information on their website. The visitor center is open Monday through Saturday from 10am to 6pm. For additional online information, log on to **www.morrobay.com**.

EXPLORING THE AREA

Most visitors come to Morro Bay to ogle **Morro Rock,** the much-photographed Central Coast icon that anchors the mouth of the waterway. This ancient landmark, whose name comes from the Spanish word for a Moorish turban, is a volcanic remnant inhabited by the peregrine falcon and other migratory birds.

BEACHES   Popular **Atascadero State Beach,** just north of Morro Rock, has gentle waves and pretty views. Restrooms, showers, and dressing rooms are available. Just north of Atascadero is **Morro Strand State Beach,** a long, sandy stretch with normally gentle surf. Restrooms and picnic tables are available. Morro Strand has its own campgrounds; for information, call © **805/772-2560,** or reserve through **ReserveAmerica** (© **800/444-7275;** www.reserveamerica.com).

STATE PARKS   Cabrillo Peak, in the **Morro Bay State Park** (© **805/772-2560**), makes a terrific day hike and offers 360-degree views from its summit. There's a zigzagging trail, but the best way to reach the top is by bushwhacking straight up the gentle slope—a hike that takes about 2 hours round-trip. To reach the trail head, take Highway 1 south and turn left at the Morro Bay State Park/Montana de Oro State Park exit. Follow South Bay Boulevard for ³/₄ mile, and then take the left fork another half mile to the Cabrillo Peak dirt parking lot on your left. The park also offers camping and the oceanside **Morro Bay Golf Course** (aka "Poor Man's Pebble Beach"), which charges only $48 for weekend greens fees (© **805/772-8751;** www.centralcoastgolf.com).

South of Morro Bay in Los Osos is **Montana de Oro State Park** ("Mountain of Gold"), known as "petite Big Sur" because of its stony cliffs and rugged terrain. There's great swimming at Spooner's Cove and lots of easy hiking trails, including some that lead to coastal vistas or forest streams. The Hazard Reef Trail will take you up on the Morro Bay Sandspit dunes. The park's campground is in the trees, across from the beach, and is worth the detour, if you have a reservation in summer. For information or to reserve a spot, contact **ReserveAmerica** (© **800/444-7275;** www.reserveamerica.com).

ON THE WATER   You can rent sea kayaks or take a guided kayak tour around the bay with **Kayak Horizons of Morro Bay,** 551 Embarcadero (© **805/772-6444;** www.kayak horizons.com). Rentals start at $9 per hour and tours cost $55.

IN TOWN   The Embarcadero is also home to the **Giant Chessboard,** whose 3-foot-tall, 18- to 20-pound redwood pieces were inspired by open-air boards in Germany. If you're up for a game, contact the recreation and parks department for reservations at © **805/ 772-6278.** Nearby is the **Morro Bay Aquarium,** 595 Embarcadero (© **805/772-7647**), a modest operation notable for the injured or abandoned sea otters, seals, and sea lions it rescues and rehabilitates. Admission is $2 for adults, $1 for children 5 to 11.

WHERE TO STAY

Baywood Bed & Breakfast Inn (Finds)   South of Morro Bay in Baywood Park, facing out onto Morro's "back bay," this two-story gray inn is a 1970s garden-style office building that's been converted into an all-suite B&B, with each suite furnished in a distinctive (and perhaps a bit over-the-top in some cases) theme. Every room has a private outside entrance, gas fireplace, and microwave (plus a fridge stocked with complimentary sodas and snacks); all but a few have bay views. Included in your stay is a full breakfast each morning and a late-afternoon wine-and-cheese reception highlighted by a room tour. If you're looking for solitude, Baywood Park fits the bill, but I would visit their website before booking to find a room decor that suits your taste. A couple of decent restaurants are on the block, and pretty Montana de Oro is close by.

1370 Second St. (2½ blocks south of Santa Ysabel Ave.), Baywood Park, CA 93042. © **805/528-8888.** Fax 805/528-8887. www.baywoodinn.com. 18 units. $90–$200 double. Extra person $15. Rates include full breakfast and afternoon wine and cheese. MC, V. *In room:* TV/VCR, kitchenette, minibar, fridge, coffeemaker, hair dryer, fireplace.

The Inn at Morro Bay   This comfortable, moderately priced resort is smart enough to let its natural surroundings be the focus. Right on the water, the inn's two-story Cape Cod–style buildings have contemporary interiors amid a quiet garden setting. Rates vary according to view; the best rooms have unobstructed views of Morro Rock; addition upgrades include private balcony Jacuzzis and bayfront sun decks. Those in back face the swimming pool, gardens, and eucalyptus-forested golf course at Morro Bay State Park (see above). The hotel has a bayside lounge and California/Mediterranean restaurant, and a full-service spa. Beach cruiser bicycles are lent out free to guests, and even the range balls are complimentary.

60 State Park Rd., Morro Bay, CA 93442. © **800/321-9566** or 805/772-5651. Fax 805/772-4779. www.inn atmorrobay.com. 98 units. $189–$339 double; from $449 cottage. Midweek and seasonal discounts available. AE, DISC, MC, V. Take Main St. south, past park entrance. **Amenities:** 2 restaurants; lounge; outdoor heated pool; nearby golf and water recreation; full-service spa; complimentary bikes; room service; massage. *In room:* TV, fridge, hair dryer, iron, CD player.

WHERE TO DINE

Hofbrau (Value) (Kids) GERMAN/AMERICAN   *Jawohl!* When you're hungry in Morro Bay and want something other than fish and chips, Hofbrau is the place. Although they do serve the standard wharf-side fare, the star here is the roast beef French dip (their strategically placed carving station ensures its popularity). Those in the know order the minisandwich, which is a dollar less and just an inch shorter. As the name would suggest, they have a good selection of beers as well as a kids' menu.

901 Embarcadero. © **805/772-2411.** www.hofbraurestaurant.com. Reservations not accepted. Most items $5–$11. AE, DISC, MC, V. Daily 11am–9pm.

Rose's Landing CALIFORNIA/CONTINENTAL   Why eat standard seafood when you can enjoy Rose's updated takes on the classics? Situated right on the waterfront, this pretty restaurant affords a spectacular seaside view, but you'll be spending more time gazing upon your plate than at the beach. Greek scallops are big 'uns sautéed in butter and garlic, and then topped with sherry, green onion, and feta cheese; sesame teriyaki shrimp features marinated, charbroiled prawns served upon a bed of stir-fried Asian-sauced vegetables. Landlubbers won't be disappointed by Blue Beard's Steak, top sirloin stuffed with blue cheese. And all entrees are served with seafood chowder or salad, potatoes or rice, and a vegetable, so this Rose's won't land you in the poorhouse at all.

725 Embarcadero, Morro Bay. (℃) **805/772-4441.** Reservations recommended. Main courses $15–$30. AE, DC, DISC, MC, V. Mon–Thurs 4–9pm; Fri–Sun 4–10pm.

Windows on the Water ★ CALIFORNIA   If you're looking for a special meal in town, your best bet is this seaside restaurant that takes full advantage of prime waterfront views with its airy, high-ceilinged, multilevel space. The cuisine emanating from the open kitchen is a California/French/Mediterranean hybrid that incorporates local fresh seafood and produce. On a given evening the menu might include maple-leaf duck breast, shellfish braised in champagne and tossed with house-made fettuccine, or Jamaican jerk shrimp served with coconut lime rice. The first-rate wine list includes choice Central Coast vintages and select French bottles. *Tip:* Tuesday is oyster night: fresh, fried, or "shootered," they're 65¢ each all evening.

699 Embarcadero (in Marina Sq.). (℃) **805/772-0677.** www.windowsonthewater.net. Reservations recommended. Main courses $11–$35. AE, DC, DISC, MC, V. Daily 5–8:30pm.

---

3 SAN LUIS OBISPO ★

38 miles S of Cambria; 226 miles S of San Francisco; 198 miles N of L.A.

Because the town of San Luis Obispo is not visible from U.S. 101, even many Californians don't know that it's more than another fast-food-and-gasoline stopover on the highway. But its "secret" location is part of what helps this relaxed yet vital college town keep its charm and character intact—it has much of the appeal that defined Santa Barbara a few decades ago.

Sometimes referred to as "little Santa Barbara," San Luis Obispo (SLO to locals) is tucked into the mountains halfway between San Francisco and Los Angeles. It's surrounded by green, pristine mountain ranges and filled with a mix of college kids attending California Polytechnic University (Cal Poly for short), big-city transplants, and agricultural folk.

The town grew up around an 18th-century mission, and its dozens of historic landmarks, Victorian homes, shops, and restaurants are its primary attractions for visitors. Today it's still quaint, almost undiscovered, and best ventured around on foot. It also makes a good base for exploration of the region as a whole. To the west of town, a short drive away, are some of the state's prettiest swimming beaches; to the north and south you'll find the Central Coast's wine country, home to dozens of respectable wineries and bucolic scenery.

ESSENTIALS

GETTING THERE   U.S. 101, one of the state's primary north-south roadways, runs through San Luis Obispo; it's the fastest land route here from anywhere. If you're driving down along the coast, Highway 1 is the way to go for its natural beauty and oceanfront cliffs. If you're entering the city from the east, take Highway 46 or 41 to U.S. 101, and then go south. **Amtrak** (℃) **800/USA-RAIL;** www.amtrak.com) offers daily service into SLO from Oakland and Los Angeles.

VISITOR INFORMATION   At the **San Luis Obispo Visitors Center,** 1039 Chorro St. (© 805/781-2670; www.visitslo.com), downtown between Monterey and Higuera streets, you can pick up the colorful, comprehensive *Visitors Guide* and self-guided *Points of Interest Walking Tour.* It's open Sunday to Wednesday from 10am to 5pm, Thursday to Saturday from 10am to 7pm.

ORIENTATION   San Luis Obispo is about 10 miles inland, at the junction of Highway 1 and U.S. 101. The downtown is laid out in a grid, roughly centered on the historic mission and its Mission Plaza (see below). Most of the main tourist sights are around the mission, within the small triangle created by U.S. 101 and Santa Rosa and Marsh streets.

EXPLORING THE TOWN

Before heading downtown, make a pit stop at the perpetually pink **Madonna Inn,** 100 Madonna Rd., off U.S. 101 (© 805/543-3000; p. 438), if for no other reason than to use its unique public restrooms (the men's has a waterfall urinal; the women's is a barrage of crimson and pink). Every inch of this place is an exercise in excess, from the dining room, complete with pink leather booths, pink table linens, and colored sugar that's—you guessed it—piquantly pink, to the rock-walled, cavelike guest rooms. And if you think it's as gaudy as it gets, you should see it around Christmas time.

Once downtown, you can ride the free trolley that repeats a loop through downtown every 15 minutes daily from noon to 5pm. (Stops are well marked.)

Farmers Market ★   If you're in town on a Thursday, be sure to take an evening stroll down Higuera Street, when the county's largest weekly street fair fills 4 downtown city blocks. You'll find much more here than fresh-picked produce—there's an ever-changing array of street entertainment, open-pit barbecues, food stands, and market stalls selling flowers, cider, and other seasonal farm-fresh items. Surrounding stores typically stay open until 9pm.

Higuera St. (btw. Osos and Nipomo sts.). © 805/781-2777. Thurs 6–9pm (weather permitting).

Mission San Luis Obispo de Tolosa   Founded by Father Junípero Serra in 1772, California's fifth mission was built with adobe bricks by Native American Chumash people. It remains one of the prettiest, most interesting structures in the Franciscan chain. Serra chose this valley for the site of his fifth mission based on tales of friendly natives and bountiful food. Here the traditional red-tile roof was first used atop a California mission, after the original thatched tule roofs repeatedly fell to hostile Native Americans' burning arrows. The former padres' quarters are now an excellent museum chronicling both Native American and missionary life through all eras of the mission's use. Allow about 30 to 45 minutes to tour the mission and its grounds.

Mission Plaza, a garden with brick paths and park benches fronting a creek in which children love to wade, still functions as San Luis Obispo's town square. It's the focal point for local festivities and activities, from live concerts to poetry readings and dance and

---

ⓕ Fun Facts   Chew on This

Follow the alley fronting Higuera between Garden and Broad streets for a local curiosity called Gum Alley. What is it? The name says it all—it's basically an alley covered with gum.

theater productions. Check at the visitor center (see "Essentials," above) to find out what's on when you're in town.

At the south end of Mission Plaza, the **San Luis Obispo Art Center**'s (© 805/543-8562; www.sloartcenter.org) galleries display and sell an array of California-made art. Admission is free; hours are 11am to 5pm Wednesday through Monday (daily July–Aug).

751 Palm St. © 805/781-8220. www.missionsanluisobispo.org. Free admission ($2 donation requested). Daily 9am–5pm.

ATTRACTIONS OUTSIDE OF TOWN

Dozens of **wineries** offer tastings and tours daily and make for a fun diversion. See "The Central Coast Wine Country: Paso Robles & the Santa Ynez Valley," later in this chapter for further details. If you don't have time to tour the wineries or would like more information before heading out to taste, you can visit **Central Coast Wines,** 712 Higuera St. in downtown SLO (© 805/784-9463), a wine shop specializing in central coast wines, and offering daily wine tastings and weekly winemaker pourings.

WHERE TO STAY

In addition to what's listed below, there's a pristine branch of **Holiday Inn Express** (© 800/465-4329 or 805/544-8600), and a reliable **Motel 6** (© 800/4-MOTEL-6 [466-8356] or 805/541-6126).

Apple Farm Inn ★★ The popular Apple Farm Inn offers a peaceful getaway in a Disney-plantation kind of way. Every square inch of the immaculate Victorian-style farmhouse is adorable, with floral wallpaper, fresh flowers, and sugar-sweet colorful touches. No two rooms are alike, although each has a gas fireplace, large well-equipped bathroom, pine antiques, lavish country decor, and either a canopy four-poster or a brass bed. Some bedrooms open onto cozy turreted sitting areas with romantic window seats; others have bay windows and a view of San Luis Creek, where a working mill spins its huge wheel to power an apple press. The outstanding service here includes nightly turndown and a morning wake-up knock, delivered with complimentary coffee or tea and a newspaper. Other features include complimentary cribs and train and airport shuttle service, as well as a full-service spa. The hotel shares a name with their on-site restaurant, one of Highway 101's best-loved pit stops.

Budget travelers can opt for the adjoining motel-style **Apple Farm Trellis Court,** which shares the inn grounds. Rooms are smaller but well decorated, with gas fireplaces. Rates include continental breakfast and start at $79.

2015 Monterey St., San Luis Obispo, CA 93401. © 800/255-2040 or 805/544-2040. Fax 805/546-9495. www.applefarm.com. 104 units. $79–$409 double. Rates include complimentary morning coffee/tea and afternoon wine. AE, DISC, MC, V. **Amenities:** Restaurant; outdoor heated pool; spa; Jacuzzi; room service; laundry service; dry cleaning. *In room:* A/C, TV w/pay movies, free high-speed Internet access, coffeemaker, hair dryer, iron, terry robes.

Garden Street Inn ★ SLO's prettiest (and most-polished) bed-and-breakfast is this gracious Italianate/Queen Anne downtown. Built in 1887 and restored in 1990, the house is a monument to gentility and good taste. Each bedroom and suite is decorated with well-chosen antique armoires, fabric or paper wall coverings, and vintage memorabilia, and all have private bathrooms. Choose one with a claw-foot tub, fireplace, whirlpool tub, or private deck—whatever suits your fancy. Breakfast is served in the stained-glass morning room, and each evening wine and cheese are laid out for guests. The well-stocked Goldtree Library is always available.

1212 Garden St. (btw. Marsh and Pacific), San Luis Obispo, CA 93401. ✆ **800/488-2045** or 805/545-9802. Fax 805/545-9403. www.gardenstreetinn.com. 13 units. $155–$215 double. Rates include full breakfast and evening wine and cheese. AE, MC, V. *In room:* A/C.

Madonna Inn ★ (**Moments**) This one you've got to see for yourself. The creative imaginations of owners Alex (now deceased) and Phyllis Madonna gave birth to the wildest— and most superfluously showy—fantasy world this side of Graceland. For more than 50 years, the only consistency throughout the hotel has been its color scheme: perpetual pink. Beyond that, the decor is a whimsical free-for-all. For example, the lobby men's room has a cascading rock-waterfall urinal and giant clamshell sinks (I hear the women's room is a hoot as well). The "Rock Rooms" with zebra- or tiger-patterned bedspreads and cascading waterfall showers conjure up thoughts of a Flintstones's *Playboy* palace. There are also blue rooms, red rooms, and over-the-top Spanish, Italian, Irish, Alps, Currier and Ives, Native American, Swiss, and hunting rooms. One guest room even features a trapezoidal bed— it's 5 feet long on one side and 6 feet long on the other. The Silver Bar cocktail lounge and Gold Rush Steak House are also outlandishly ornate. In an effort to make the inn more a resort destination, an all-new state-of-the-art spa, pool (not just any pool, but one with a 30-foot beach-style entry and 25-foot cascading waterfall flowing into a lagoon), and fitness facility is underway on the grounds and should be completed by the time you read this. Even if you don't stay here, stop by for a liquid refresher and check it out, particularly around Christmastime.

100 Madonna Rd. (off U.S. 101), San Luis Obispo, CA 93405. ✆ **800/543-9666** or 805/543-3000. Fax 805/543-1800. www.madonnainn.com. 108 units. $179–$284 double; from $349 suite. AE, DISC, MC, V. **Amenities:** 2 restaurants; coffee shop; lounge; pool; full spa; retail shops; wine shop with daily tasting; limo service. *In room:* A/C, flatscreen TV, fridge in most rooms, coffeemaker, hair dryer, iron, safe.

Petit Soleil Bed et Breakfast ★ (**Finds**) Owners John and Dianne Conner have taken what was once an ordinary motor inn and—in the French country spirit of their other *BetB* in France—converted it into a wonderful little B&B, complete with a sunny cobblestone courtyard with cafe-style umbrellas and warm colors of Provence. Each guest room has quirky additions such as painted cupboards or a window-side reading nook; all have private bathrooms and phones for free local calls. Breakfast is served in a dining area that faces the street (coffee lovers will delight in the strong, locally roasted blend), and the hot offerings such as quiche or caramel-apple French toast are a treat. Every evening from 5 to 6:30pm there's a tasting of local and French wines paired with appetizers. You'll like the location as well—just a short walk or bike ride from downtown San Luis Obispo.

1473 Monterey St., San Luis Obispo, CA 93401. ✆ **800/676-1588** or 805/549-0321. Fax 805/549-0383. www.petitsoleilslo.com. 15 units. $159–$219 double; from $239 suite. Rates include breakfast. Extra person $10. AE, DISC, MC, V. **Amenities:** Complimentary bikes. *In room:* TV, Wi-Fi, coffeemaker, CD player.

WHERE TO DINE

Big Sky Cafe ★ AMERICAN The folk-artsy fervor of San Luis shines at this southwestern mirage, where local art and a blue, star-studded ceiling surround diners who come for fresh, healthy food. The menu is self-classified "modern food," a category that here means a dizzying international selection including Caribbean shrimp tacos with chipotle-lime yogurt, Thai shrimp salad with mint, chilled sesame-ginger noodles, and breakfast's red-flannel turkey hash—a beet-fortified ragout topped with basil-Parmesan-glazed eggs. Big Sky's owner also runs L.A.'s funky Gumbo Pot, whose Cajun-Creole influences spice up the menu at every turn. In fact, this might be the only Central Coast outlet for decent jambalaya, gumbo, or authentically airy beignets.

1121 Broad St. $\mathcal{C}$ **805/545-5401**. www.bigskycafe.com. Main courses $9–$18; lunch $8–$14; breakfast $5–$10. AE, MC, V. Mon–Fri 7am–10pm; Sat–Sun 8am–9pm.

Buona Tavola ★★ NORTHERN ITALIAN   Most choices in town are burger-and-sandwich casual, Buona Tavola offers well-prepared Italian food in a more upscale setting. You can stroll in wearing jeans, but the dining room, with checkerboard floors and original artwork, is warmer and more intimate than other spots in town. On the backyard terrace, you can enjoy your meal surrounded by magnolias, ficus, and grapevines. The menu boasts a number of salads on the antipasti list. My favorite pastas include *agnolotti de scampi allo zafferano,* house-made pockets filled with shrimp scampi and served in a cream-saffron sauce; *linguini fra diavolo* served with Manila clams, mussels, and river shrimp in a spicy tomato sauce; or the classic *timballo di Parma,* a vegetarian delight baked with two cheeses.

1037 Monterey St. $\mathcal{C}$ **805/545-8000**. www.btslo.com. Reservations recommended. Main courses $9–$32. AE, DISC, MC, V. Mon–Fri 11:30am–2:30pm; Sun–Thurs 5:30–9:30pm; Fri–Sat 5:30–10pm.

Corner View ★★ AMERICAN   It's always a memorable experience when you stumble into any old restaurant to appease your growling stomach and walk away pleasantly surprised. Perhaps that's why Corner View—in downtown San Lois Obispo at the corner of Marsh and Chorro streets—is one of the few places in the area that attracts a range of clientele, from professionals to the university students that frequent other nearby establishments. And its rather roomy interior ensures that you'll never be waiting too long. While the burger is one of the most popular items on the menu, the tomato bisque and tuna salad are a perfect lunch, and sautéed "sanddabs" are the restaurant's specialty: Corner View is one of only two places on the coast that serve this Pacific flatfish delicacy.

1141 Chorro St. $\mathcal{C}$ **805/546-8444**. www.cornerviewrestaurant.com. Lunch $9–$16; dinner $9–$27. AE, MC, V. Mon–Thurs 11am–9pm; Fri 11am–10pm; Sat 9:30am–10pm; Sun 9:30am–9pm (on weekends, the bar is open as late as 1:30am).

Mondéo Pronto (**Value** (**Kids** INTERNATIONAL   Mondéo Pronto pays particular attention to the presentation and freshness of their affordable wraps, which come with a variety of innovative international fillings. Choices range from American versions like the macadamia swordfish (grilled swordfish with macadamia butter, served with jasmine rice) to such Mediterranean selections as the Sicilian, with grilled portobello mushrooms, herb polenta, veggies, goat cheese, olives, capers, and sun-dried tomato pesto. "Fusion bowls" are satisfying, with such combinations as basil scampi, a shrimp dish over bowtie pasta with pesto, marinara, pine nuts, and herbs. Everything on the kids' menu is under $4, and as the menu states, "Substitutions and sides are no problem."

893 Higuera St. (in the plaza). $\mathcal{C}$ **805/544-2956**. Most items $5–$9. MC, V. Sun–Wed 11am–9pm; Thurs–Sat 11am–10pm.

Mo's Smokehouse BBQ ★ BARBECUE   Just about everyone in SLO is a devotee of this place, whose reputation and great barbecue belie its humble ambience. It's not fancy, but you name it, they've got it—pork or baby back ribs, barbecued beef, and chicken in either a mild or hot sauce, accompanied by baked beans, bread, potato salad, or coleslaw. Practically everything on the menu is under $10.

1005 Monterey St. $\mathcal{C}$ **805/544-6193**. www.mosbbq.com. Entrees $6–$20. AE, MC, V. Sun–Wed 11am–9pm; Thurs–Sat 11am–10pm.

4 PISMO BEACH

13 miles S of San Luis Obispo

Just outside San Luis Obispo, on Pismo's 23-mile stretch of prime beachfront, flip-flops are the shoes of choice and surf wear is the dominant fashion. It's all about beach life here, so bring your bathing suit, your board, and a good book.

If building sand castles or tanning isn't your idea of fun, you can explore isolated dunes, cliff-sheltered tide pools, and old pirate coves. Bring your dog (Fido's welcome here) and play an endless game of fetch. Or go fishing—it's permitted from Pismo Beach Pier, which also offers arcade entertainment, bowling, and billiards. Pismo is also the only beach in the area that allows all-terrain vehicles on the dunes.

Because the town itself consists of little more than tourist shops and surf-and-turf restaurants, nearby San Luis Obispo is a far more charming place to stay. But if all you want are a few lazy days on a beautiful beach at half the price of an oceanfront room in Santa Barbara, Pismo is the perfect choice.

ESSENTIALS

Pismo Beach Chamber of Commerce and Visitors Bureau, 581 Dolliver St., Pismo Beach, CA 93449 (© **800/443-7778** or 805/773-4382; www.pismochamber.com), offers free brochures and information on local attractions, lodging, and dining. The office is open Monday through Saturday from 9am to 5pm and Sunday from 10am to 4pm. You can peruse their tourist information online at **www.classiccalifornia.com**.

WHAT TO SEE & DO

Beaches in Pismo are exceptionally wide, making them some of the best in the state for sunning and playing. The beach north of Grand Avenue is popular with families and joggers. North of Wadsworth Street, the coast becomes dramatically rugged as it rambles northward to Shell Beach and Pirates Cove.

Pismo Beach was once one of the most famous places in America for **clamming,** but the famed "Pismo clam" reached near-extinction in the mid-1980s due to overharvesting. If you'd like to dig for bivalves, you'll need to obtain a license and follow strict guidelines. Or come for the annual **Clam Festival:** Held at the pier each October since 1946, the celebration features a chowder cook-off, sand-sculpture contest, and Miss Pismo Beach pageant.

If **fishing** is more your style, you'll be pleased to know that no license is required to fish from Pismo Beach Pier. Catches here are largely bottom fish such as red snapper and lingcod. There's a bait-and-tackle shop on the pier.

Pacific Dunes Riding Stables, 1205 Silver Spur Place (© **805/489-8100;** www.pacificdunesridingstables.com), in Oceano (5 min. south of Pismo Beach), runs guided hour-long horseback rides along the beach and dunes for $40.

From late November to February, thousands of migrating **monarch butterflies** take up residence in the area's eucalyptus and Monterey-pine-tree groves. The butterflies form dense clusters on the trees, each hanging with its wings over the one below it, providing warmth and shelter for the entire group. During the monarchs' stay, naturalists at Pismo State Beach conduct 45-minute narrated walks every Saturday and Sunday at 11am and 2pm (call © **805/772-2694** for tour information). The Butterfly Grove is on Highway 1, between Pismo Beach and Grover Beach, to the south.

The Rare Golden Sand Dunes of Guadalupe

The California coast was once rich in dramatic, windswept sand dunes; sheltered valleys of wildflowers and willows; and lakes full of pond turtles, red-legged frogs, muskrats, and nesting birds. San Francisco's dunes are now covered in part by Golden Gate Park, while Los Angeles's dunes were leveled to create beach towns and the airport. But travelers cruising the central coast have the chance to visit what's now a rare sight at the **Guadalupe-Nipomo Dunes Preserve** just north of the tiny agricultural hamlet of Guadalupe, about 20 minutes south of Pismo.

The preserve comprises 18 miles of the largest, most biodiverse coastal dune-lagoon ecosystem on the planet. They have been the subject of photographers such as Ansel Adams and Brett Weston; home to the Dunites, a utopian group of artists founded in 1931; and the setting for Cecil B. De Mille's spectacular 1923 film, *The Ten Commandments*. Designated by the Nature Conservancy as number one in its "Last Great Places on Earth" campaign, these dunes are now permanently protected for wildlife and passive recreation.

The **Dunes Center interpretative facility** (1055 Guadalupe St., Hwy. 1, Guadalupe; © **805/343-2455;** www.dunescenter.org), in a restored 1910 Craftsman-style home, is open Thursdays through Sundays from 10am to 4pm, and a schedule of guided walks is available on the website.

The Dunes are accessible at the southern end by driving on West Main Street (Hwy. 166) to a parking lot just below Mussel Rock Dunes, the highest coastal dunes in the world. The middle of the dunes is accessible off Highway 1, 3 miles north of Guadalupe. Turn west onto Oso Flaco Lake Road, pay a small parking fee, and walk along a rare riparian corridor to a bridge that crosses Oso Flaco Lake. A 1-mile boardwalk leads you to the ocean through one of the best examples of coastal dune scrub in the country.

WHERE TO STAY

Cottage Inn by the Sea ★   One of Pismo Beach's newer cliffside lodgings, the Cottage Inn is a good, moderately priced choice for couples and families. With its thatched roofs and Laura Ashley–style decor, the country charm is evident inside and out. Rooms, refreshingly clean and spacious, range both in price and style from traditional to ocean-view. All come with the amenities of a romantic inn (including fireplaces) as well as modern conveniences (such as complimentary Wi-Fi).

2351 Price St., Pismo Beach, CA 93449. © **888/440-8400** or 805/773-4617. Fax 805/773-8336. www. cottage-inn.com. 80 units. $199–$289 double. Rates include deluxe continental breakfast. Extra person $10. AE, DC, DISC, MC, V. Pets accepted with $20-per-night fee. **Amenities:** Oceanfront heated pool and Jacuzzi; business services. *In room:* TV w/pay movies, Wi-Fi (free), fridge, coffeemaker, hair dryer, iron, safe.

Kon Tiki Inn (Value)   The over-the-top Polynesian architecture of this three-story gem is easy to spot from the freeway and evokes memories of 1960s Waikiki hotels. Rooms are modest, small, and simply furnished with unremarkable faux bamboo furniture, yet each has an oceanfront balcony or patio. Outside, vast lawns slope gently toward the cliffs, broken only by the shielded, kidney-shaped swimming pool flanked by twin Jacuzzis. This humble hotel—which is privately owned and does no advertising—has a sandy beach with stairway access and lacks the highway noise that plagues many neighbors.

1621 Price St., Pismo Beach, CA 93449. **℡ 888/566-8454** or 805/773-4833. Fax 805/773-6541. www. kontikiinn.com. 86 units. In season $150–$180 double; off season $126–$146 double. Rates include continental breakfast. Extra person $20. AE, DISC, MC, V. **Amenities:** Restaurant; outdoor heated pool; free access to adjacent health club; 2 Jacuzzis; coin laundry. *In room:* TV w/movie channels, Wi-Fi, fridge, coffeemaker, safe, voice mail.

The Sea Venture Resort ★　If luxury accommodations overlooking the beach and an outdoor spa on your private deck sound like heaven to you, head for Sea Venture, a resort providing the most luxurious accommodations along Pismo Beach. Once in your room, you need only drag your tired feet through the thick forest-green carpeting and past the white country furnishings and feather bed, and turn on your gas fireplace to begin a relaxing stay. Rent a movie from the video library, schedule a massage, or bathe your weary bones in your own outdoor hydrotherapy spa tub. With the beach right outside your door, there's not much more you could ask for—although there is, in fact, more provided: plush robes, a wet bar, continental breakfast delivered to your room, and a restaurant on the premises with a tapas bar and Sunday brunch. Most rooms have ocean views and many have a private balcony overlooking the beach. *Tip:* Check online for specials and packages.

100 Ocean View Ave., Pismo Beach, CA 93449. **℡ 800/662-5545** or 805/773-4994. Fax 805/773-0924. www.seaventure.com. 50 units. $159–$449 double. Rates include continental breakfast. AE, DC, DISC, MC, V. Take U.S. 101 to the Price St. exit, turn west onto Ocean View (at the beach). **Amenities:** Restaurant; outdoor heated pool; complimentary bikes; room service; massage center; laundry service; dry cleaning. *In room:* TV/VCR, minibar, coffeemaker, hair dryer, iron.

WHERE TO DINE

If you like steak and ribs served in an Old West setting, you'll love Pismo's **F. McLintocks Saloon & Dining House,** on the east side of Highway 101 at 750 Mattie Rd. (**℡ 800/866-6372** or 805/773-1892; www.mclintocks.com). For diners who prefer clams over *carne,* the same outfit also runs the popular **Steamers of Pismo** restaurant, at 1601 Price St. atop the bluffs of Pismo Beach (**℡ 805/773-4711**).

Giuseppe's Cucina Italiana ★ SOUTHERN ITALIAN　This is the region's best southern Italian restaurant—would you believe owner Giuseppe Difronzo started it as his senior project at Cal Poly University? It's true, and Difronzo's love of cuisine from the Pugliese region (an Adriatic seaport) continues to bring diners a taste of the Italian countryside. Along with the homemade bread baked in a wood-burning oven imported from Italy, Giuseppe's fare uses authentic recipes, imported ingredients, and organically grown produce; the large menu of antipasti, salads, pizzas, pastas, fish, and steak makes it easy to find something you like. Highlights of the meal included linguine with shrimp, scallops, pancetta, and garlic in a vodka cream sauce; and seared ahi (tuna) with a peppercorn crust and garlic-caper aioli.

891 Price St. **℡ 805/773-2870.** http://giuseppesrestaurant.com/cm/Pismo/Home.html. Reservations not accepted. Main courses $8–$20 lunch, $11–$30 dinner. AE, DISC, MC, V. Daily 11:30am–3pm and 5pm–close.

Splash Cafe AMERICAN　This beachy burger stand, with a short menu and a few tables, gets high marks for its award-winning clam chowder in a sourdough bread bowl— more than 10,000 gallons a year are served. Fish and chips, burgers, hot dogs, and grilled ahi sandwiches are also available. Far-flung aficionados know that Splash ships its chowder frozen, overnight, anywhere in the U.S. (sourdough loaves, too). There's often a line, but it usually moves quickly.

197 Pomeroy St. (near Pismo Beach Pier). **℡ 805/773-4653.** www.splashcafe.com. Most items $3–$10. MC, V. Sun–Thurs 8am–8pm; Fri–Sat until 9pm.

5 THE CENTRAL COAST WINE COUNTRY: PASO ROBLES & THE SANTA YNEZ VALLEY

Paso Robles: 29 miles N of San Luis Obispo; Solvang: 60 miles S of San Luis Obispo

When people talk about California wines, we usually assume they mean those from the Napa and Sonoma regions north of San Francisco. But here in California—and increasingly across the country thanks to the Academy Award–winning comedy *Sideways*—wine lovers are becoming increasingly aware of quality vintages coming from the sun-drenched valleys of San Luis Obispo and Santa Barbara counties.

The truth is that the Central Coast wine country is the oldest of California's wine-growing regions. The old Franciscan missions strung along the coast, and just inland by it, attest to the area's heritage when early Spanish settlers planted grapevines and olive trees. But the area's wine production went into decline during Prohibition, and after it was repealed, Napa and Sonoma valleys shot ahead as the leading and best-known producers.

But in the last 25 years, the Central Coast has experienced a boom in grape production and winemaking, and with the new growth in winemaking has come general growth, much of it geared to visitors: hotels, spas, golf courses, restaurants, art galleries, museums, antiques stores, and even a Vegas-style casino attract a mostly well-over-40 clientele who appreciate the relaxed pace and beauty of the region (little of this area—except perhaps for the bakeries in Solvang—will thrill your kids).

The principal parts of the Central Coast Wine Country are **Paso Robles** (the town of this name and the surrounding countryside), **San Luis Obispo** (again, the town of the same name plus the nearby areas of Edna Valley and Arroyo Grande), and **northern Santa Barbara County** (the Santa Maria and Santa Ynez valleys). The great news for visitors is that these areas are distinct but sufficiently close together to make visiting all of them practical on even a short timetable. And staying in Paso Robles or San Luis Obispo is also a convenient option for visiting Hearst Castle (p. 424), offering more to do (or, at least, more to drink) than quaint Cambria.

PASO ROBLES

Paso Robles ("pass of the oaks") is suitably named for the clusters of oak trees scattered throughout the rolling hills of this inland region. The town has a faintly checkered past: It was established in 1870 by Drury James, uncle of outlaw Jesse James (who hid out in tunnels under the original Paso Robles Inn). In 1913, pianist Ignace Paderewski came to live in Paso Robles, where he brought zinfandel vines for his ranch—Paderewski played often in the Paso Robles Inn, which today maintains a small exhibit in his honor in the lobby. He really wasn't here for long, returning to Poland after World War I, but the town today treats Paderewski like a native son.

Arriving in downtown Paso Robles is like taking a step back in time and right into a movie set. The main town square is surrounded by blocks of venerable Victorian-era buildings such as the public library, a neoclassical edifice from 1907. It's worth taking a leisurely stroll around the square before heading out into the rolling vineyards for an afternoon of wine tasting.

Essentials

GETTING THERE/ORIENTATION   Paso Robles is on U.S. 101; there's an exit for the town's main thoroughfare, Spring Street. Highway 46 intersects, and briefly joins, U.S.

101. **Amtrak** (© 800/USA-RAIL; www.amtrak.com) offers daily service to Paso Robles from Oakland and Los Angeles.

Many wineries are on the winding roads off Highway 46 on either side—try to cluster your visit according to this destination, visiting one side and then the other. You'll be able to feel how the weather on the western side, which is cooler due to higher elevations and frequent coastal fog, differs from the hotter east side, on a flat plain leading inland; winemakers bicker constantly over which conditions are better for growing wine grapes.

VISITOR INFORMATION For a list of area wineries, tasting rooms, and seasonal events, contact the **Paso Robles Vintners and Growers Association,** 744 Oak St., Paso Robles, CA 93446 (© **800/549-9463** or 805/239-8463; www.pasowine.com). Additional information on the area is offered by the **Paso Robles Chamber of Commerce and Visitors & Conference Bureau,** 1225 Park St., Paso Robles, CA 93446 (© **800/ 406-4040** or 805/238-0506; fax 805/238-0527; www.pasorobleschamber.com).

Touring the Local Wineries

Growers have been tending vines in Paso Robles's fertile foothills since the turn of the century—the 20th century, that is. For decades, wine aficionados overlooked the area, even though in 1983 it was granted its own "Paso Robles" appellation (the official government designation of a recognized wine-producing region; "Napa Valley" and "Sonoma County" are probably more familiar). Around 1992, wine grapes surpassed lettuce as San Luis Obispo County's primary cash crop, and the region now has at least 75 wineries and more than 100 vineyards (which grow grapes but do not produce their own wine from them).

Paso Robles is reminiscent of Napa Valley way back in the '70s before it became a major tourist destination. Because not all wine enthusiasts are wine experts, an advantage of the area is its friendly attitude and small crowds, which make it easy to learn more about the winemaking process as you go along. Enjoy the relaxed rural atmosphere along two-lane country roads, driving leisurely from winery to winery and, more often than not, chatting with the winemaker while tasting his or her product.

Eberle Winery Owner Gary Eberle, who's been making Paso Robles wine since 1973, is sometimes called the "grandfather of Paso Robles's Wine Country," because many of the new vintners in the area honed their craft working under his tutelage. A visit to Eberle Winery includes a tour through its underground caves, where hundreds of aging barrels share space with the Wild Boar Room, site of Eberle's monthly winemaker dinners featuring guest chefs from around the country (always held on Sat nights; the prix-fixe meal is around $120, including wine). Call for current events.

3810 Hwy. 46 E. (3¹⁄₂ miles east of U.S. 101). © **805/238-9607.** www.eberlewinery.com. Complimentary tastings daily 10am–5pm (until 6pm in summer).

EOS Estate Winery at Arciero Vineyards Follow the checkered flag to the 700 acres of wine grapes owned by former race-car driver Frank Arciero, Sr. Arciero was drawn to the area by its resemblance to his native Italy; he passed through on his way to Laguna Seca, a racetrack near Salinas. (Trivia buffs know it as James Dean's intended destination in 1955, when he was killed in nearby Cholame while driving his Porsche.) The label specializes in Italian varietals (*nebbiolo, sangiovese*) and blends. The facility includes a self-guided tour, a race-car exhibit, rose gardens, a Mediterranean marketplace, and a picnic area.

5625 Hwy. 46 E. (6 miles east of U.S. 101). © **800/249-WINE.** www.eosvintage.com. Complimentary tastings daily 10am–5pm (until 6pm summer weekends).

Justin Vineyards & Winery ★★ At the end of a scenic country road lies Justin and Deborah Baldwin's boutique winery, and even a casual glance shows how much love and dedication the ex–Los Angelenos have put into their operation. The tasting room, dining room, offices, and even winemaking barns have a stylish Tuscan flair. Justin's flagship wine is Isosceles, a Bordeaux-style blend that—at about $60 a bottle—is pricier than most area wines but exudes sophistication—and earns *Wine Spectator* raves. Also worth a try is their port-style dessert wine, called Obtuse. Daily tours of the winery are $15, available by appointment only at 10:30am and 2:30pm and can be arranged by calling ✆ **805/238-6932.** The winery's tasting room is open daily from 10am to 5pm; the tasting fee is $5.

The winery also has a luxurious four-suite B&B called the **JUST Inn.** Impeccably outfitted, the romantic inn has an undeniable serenity. Room rates are $350 to $395. Nightly dinners and weekend lunches are also offered to both guests and day-trippers— call ✆ **805/238-6932** for reservations.

11680 Chimney Rock Rd. (15 miles west of U.S. 101). ✆ **805/238-6932.** www.justinwine.com.

Meridian Vineyards ★ The local vintner with the largest profile is also the Central Coast's best-known label, producing more cases each year than all the other Paso wineries combined. Veteran winemaker Chuck Ortman brought a respected Napa Valley pedigree to Meridian; as a result, here's where you'll get the most Napa-like tasting experience. In addition to the beautiful natural stone winery there's a man-made lake surrounded by rolling lawns, majestic oak trees, and landscaped herb and flower gardens. Picnicking is encouraged. There's a $5 tasting fee (refunded with wine purchase).

7000 Hwy. 46 E. (7 miles east of U.S. 101). ✆ **805/226-7133.** www.meridianvineyards.com. Tastings daily 10am–5pm.

Summerwood Winery & Inn ★★ Summerwood Winery focuses on opulent limited-edition wines—particularly cabs and Syrahs—that are only available at the West Paso Robles estate and nowhere else. With the help of award-winning winemaker Chris Cameron, Summerwood is turning out some of the best reds around, including wonderful Rhone varietals and Bordeaux-style blends. The winery also offers a gourmet deli for picnickers, plush fireside chairs for relaxed sipping, and the luxurious Summerwood Inn bed-and-breakfast set among the vines (see review below).

2175 Arbor Rd. (at Hwy. 46 W., 1 mile west of U.S. 101). ✆ **805/227-1365.** www.summerwoodwine.com. Complimentary tastings daily 10am–5:30pm (till 6pm in summer).

Tobin James Cellars ★★ Winemaker Tobin James is a walking contradiction. A lifelong wine expert who claims to wear the same pair of khaki shorts every day, Toby has patterned his winery in the spirit of local bad boys, the James Gang. The tasting room has a Wild West theme, a 100-year-old saloon bar, and plays country music, all serving to dispel the wine-snob atmosphere that prevails at so many other wineries. Tobin James's expertise lies in the production of a "user-friendly" zinfandel; the late-harvest dessert wine from zinfandel grapes is smooth and spicy.

8950 Union Rd. (at Hwy. 46 E., 8 miles east of U.S. 101). ✆ **805/239-2204.** www.tobinjames.com. Complimentary tastings daily 10am–6pm.

Where to Stay

Also see Justin Vineyards & Winery above for lodging.

Adelaide Inn Ⓥalue Tended with loving care that's rare among lower-priced accommodations, the Adelaide Inn stands out from other motels. Although it's adjacent to gas stations and coffee shops, attention has been paid to isolate this quiet, lushly landscaped property from its surroundings. The rooms are clean and comfortable with extra warmth, and the motel has a welcoming ambience. Unexpected comforts include complimentary newspaper and fruit and muffins. Facilities include a solar-heated outdoor pool and spa and even a putting green. Wine tour packages are available as well.

1215 Ysabel Ave., Paso Robles, CA 93446. ℭ **800/549-PASO** or 805/238-2770. Fax 805/238-3497. www. adelaideinn.com. 108 units. $89–$129 double. Extra person $10. Rates include continental breakfast and afternoon cookies. AE, DC, DISC, MC, V. From U.S. 101, exit Hwy. 46 E. Turn west at 24th St.; the hotel is just west of the freeway. **Amenities:** Heated outdoor pool; fitness room; Jacuzzi; sauna; coin-op laundry and laundry service; dry cleaning; complimentary newspaper. *In room:* A/C, flatscreen TV, fridge, coffeemaker, hair dryer, iron, microwave.

Paso Robles Inn ★   This Mission Revival–style inn was built to replace the 1891 Stanford White masterpiece, El Paso De Robles Hotel, that burned down in 1940. Photos of the landmark in its heyday line the Spanish-tiled lobby and adjacent dining room and cocktail lounge. Brick-lined pathways meander through the pretty oak-shaded property, and two-story motel units are scattered across the tranquil landscaped grounds. The best rooms are worth the extra bucks: the Deluxe Spa Rooms with private Jacuzzi tubs (located either on the balcony or in the spacious bathroom) that are filled from the property's mineral springs. Carports are located behind each building. The inn also has a steakhouse, retro-flavored coffee shop, and the Cattleman's Lounge, a local hot spot featuring live entertainment on weekends. *Tip:* The inn's new two-room suites with pull-out sofas are ideal for families.

1103 Spring St., Paso Robles, CA 93446. ℭ **800/676-1713** or 805/238-2660. www.pasoroblesinn.com. 100 units. $165–$185 double; $255 spa room. Extra person $15. AE, MC, V. **Amenities:** 2 restaurants; coffee shop; lounge; outdoor heated pool; Jacuzzi; business center; room service; laundry service; dry cleaning. *In room:* A/C, TV w/pay movies, high-speed Internet access, fridge, coffeemaker, hair dryer, iron, microwave.

The Summerwood Inn ★   The guest book at this elegant B&B sports more than its share of honeymooners drawn by the beautiful 46-acre vineyard estate and luxurious treatment. On the grounds of Summerwood Winery (p. 445), this three-story clapboard house looks like a cross between Queen Anne and southern-plantation styles, but it's furnished in formal English country. It's a contemporary building, though, so rooms are spacious and bathrooms ultramodern; the main floor (including two guest rooms) is wheelchair accessible. Every room has a private balcony overlooking the vineyards, a gas fireplace, fresh flowers, terry robes, satellite television, wireless Internet, and nightly turndown service. Morning brings a selection of farm-fresh breakfast entrees prepared by the inn's full-time chef.

2130 Arbor Rd. (P.O. Box 3260), Paso Robles, CA 93447. ℭ **805/227-1111.** www.summerwoodinn.com. 9 units. $239–$299 double; $469–$529 suite. Extra person $65. Rates include full breakfast, afternoon wine and hors d'oeuvres, and evening desserts. MC, V. From U.S. 101, exit Hwy. 46 W. Continue 1 mile to Arbor Rd. *In room:* A/C, TV, Wi-Fi, hair dryer.

Villa Toscana Bed & Breakfast ★★★   This new all-suites inn, in the rolling vineyards at the Martin & Weyrich winery east of downtown, is fashioned after a lavish Italian villa, with a colonnade-rimmed courtyard and fountains galore. The suites, each named after a Martin & Weyrich wine, are quite spacious and individually decorated with a profusion of elegant frills of various colors (I prefer the rich moss green, purple, and wheat tones of the Viognier suite). The beds are smartly set into recessed alcoves, and all guest rooms have Jacuzzi tubs, wood-beamed ceilings, kitchenettes, fireplaces, and expansive vineyard views. For a little extra space, reserve the winemaker's suite, a two-bedroom, two-and-a-half-bath suite with a garage, private courtyard, and a patio with Jacuzzi tub. In-room spa treatments are available. An excellent full breakfast is served either in-room, within the Bistro Kitchen, or outside in the sun-filled courtyard. *Tip:* Be sure to check out the special deals that are frequently offered on the Internet.

4230 Buena Vista Dr. (¹/₂ mile north of Circle B Rd.), Paso Robles, CA 93447. © **805/238-5600.** Fax 805/238-5605. www.myvillatoscana.com. 8 units. $425–$635 double; $2,050–$2,400 winemaker's residence. AE, DISC, MC, V. *In room:* A/C, TV/DVD/VCR w/free DVDs, high-speed Internet, kitchenette, hair dryer.

Where to Dine

You should also consider Paso's branch of the San Luis Obispo favorite, **Buona Tavola,** 943 Spring St. (© **805/237-0600;** www.btslo.com), whose house-made pastas and fresh-from-the-fields northern Italian cuisine are a welcome addition to town (see p. 439 for full review).

Bistro Laurent ★★ COUNTRY FRENCH   Executive chef/owner Laurent Grangien's sophisticated bistro caused quite a stir in this town unaccustomed to such innovations as a chef's tasting menu. But once the dust settled, everyone kept returning for the unpretentious neighborhood atmosphere, superb cuisine, and reasonable (at least by L.A. or San Francisco standards) prices. Whet your appetite with the crispy crab risotto hors d'oeuvre (the crispy tarts are addictive as well) and warm potato and goat cheese salad before plunging into main dishes such as rosemary-garlic chicken, or roasted pork chops with Dijon sauce and puréed potatoes.

1202 Pine St., Paso Robles. © **805/226-8191.** www.bistrolaurent.com. Reservations recommended. Main courses $24–$35. MC, V. Mon–Sat 10:30am–10:30pm.

McPhee's Grill ★★ (Kids) CALIFORNIA GRILL   When Ian McPhee left Ian's Restaurant in Cambria and launched this one, it didn't take long for word to get out. McPhee's is worth the short drive to the historic town of Templeton. The converted old saloon features contemporary country decor, an open kitchen, and indoor and outdoor dining. The menu offers half a dozen appetizers such as an ancho-duck quesadilla or pan-roasted black bass with artichoke pesto, roasted red pepper sauce, and fingerling potatoes. Gourmet pizza, pasta, an amazing macadamia-crusted Alaskan halibut, and four varieties of tender, juicy steaks cooked to perfection round out the Americana-with-a-twist-style menu. Especially impressive are the prices—it's rare that a restaurant "dedicated to great food and great service" offers the majority of its dishes for under $20.

416 S. Main St., Templeton. © **805/434-3204.** www.mcphees.com. Reservations recommended. Main courses $13–$16 lunch, $13–$38 dinner. MC, V. Daily 11:30am–2pm and 5pm–close.

Odyssey World Café (Value) (Kids) CONTINENTAL   Odyssey offers an eclectic range of foods reflecting world influences in a cozy, casual atmosphere at affordable prices. Lunch choices include salads, pizzas, pastas, sandwiches, wraps, gyros, Asian bowls, and rotisserie chicken, with full dinners available in the evening. The kids menu offers four choices they're sure to eat, each at $4.99. Odyssey is also the best place in Paso Robles to stock up on picnic foods.

1214 Pine St. (at 12th St.). © **805/237-7516.** www.odysseyworldcafe.com. Reservations not accepted. Main courses $7–$16. AE, MC, V. Sun–Thurs 11am–8:30pm; Fri–Sat 11am–9pm.

The Santa Ynez Valley presents a soothing and intriguing blend of Arabian horses standing beside pristine vineyards, rolling pastures dotted with spreading oaks, graceful Victorian farmhouses and barns beside cutting-edge wineries, all surrounded by imposing mountains. This is beautiful country, where the clear blue sky achieves a brilliance rarely seen in the smog-clogged cities to the south. In the Santa Ynez Valley, the pace is slower and the locals friendlier, but don't expect to find yokels gnawing on hay—this is gentleman-farmer country, where some of the nicest ranches are gated and have video surveillance, and even Disney's Davy Crockett is a respected winemaker. This balance of old-fashioned living and modern amenities is what makes the area so enjoyable: You can read in the shade of an oak tree one day and go on a wine tasting adventure the next. Just minutes away from one another, Los Olivos, Ballard, and Solvang each make an excellent base for touring the wineries of this fertile area.

Essentials

GETTING THERE   To reach the Santa Ynez Valley from the north, take Highway 101 to Highway 154 at Los Olivos. Tiny Ballard lies 3 miles south off Baseline Road. The turnoff for Solvang is just beyond, west on Highway 246, while a straight jaunt on Highway 154 will take you through the spectacular San Marcos Pass and onto Highway 101 toward Santa Barbara.

From the south, take Highway 154 off Highway 101 at Goleta (just north of Santa Barbara), up through the San Marcos Pass. A left turn heading west on Highway 246 takes you into Solvang; continuing straight along Highway 154 takes you through Los Olivos and onto Highway 101 toward San Luis Obispo.

VISITOR INFORMATION   Contact the **Santa Ynez Valley Visitors Association,** P.O. Box 1918, Santa Ynez, CA 93460 (© **800/742-2843;** www.syvva.com), for general visitors' information. The local and comprehensive website, **www.solvangca.com**, also carries information about the entire valley, as well as Santa Barbara, Lompoc, and Santa Maria. Always a definitive authority for activity in the Santa Maria and Santa Ynez valleys is the **Santa Barbara County Vintners' Association,** 3669 Sagunto St., Unit 101 (P.O. Box 1558), Santa Ynez, CA 93460 (© **800/218-0881** or 805/688-0881; www.sbcounty wines.com), which also publishes a *Winery Touring Map.* Hours are Monday through Friday from 9am to 5pm. The **Solvang Conference & Visitors Bureau,** 1511 Mission Dr., at Fifth Street (P.O. Box 70), Solvang, CA 93464 (© **800/468-6765** or 805/688-6144; www.solvangusa.com), has additional information on the Santa Ynez Valley, including maps and brochures. It's open daily from 10am to 4pm (a satellite visitor information office is at 1639 Copenhagen Dr.).

ORIENTATION   U.S. 101, Highway 246, and Highway 154 form a triangle around the six towns of the Santa Ynez Valley, all residing within a 10-mile radius. Highway 246 becomes Mission Drive within Solvang city limits and then continues east past the mission toward Santa Ynez. Alamo Pintado Road connects Solvang with Los Olivos, whose commercial stretch is along 3 blocks of Grand Avenue. This geographic arrangement may sound confusing, but in reality it all blurs together gracefully, and the friendly residents are always handy with directions.

Touring the Local Wineries

Santa Barbara County has a 200-year tradition of growing grapes and making wine—an art originally practiced by Franciscan friars at the area's missions—but only in the past

20 to 30 years have wine grape fields begun to approach the size of other crops that do so well in these fertile inland valleys.

Geography makes the area well suited for vineyards: The Santa Ynez and San Rafael mountain ranges are transverse (east-west) ranges, which allows ocean breezes to flow through, keeping the climate temperate. Variations in temperature and humidity within the valley create many microclimates, and vintners have learned how to cultivate nearly all the classic grape varietals. But it's the chardonnay, pinot noir, and Syrah that draw the most acclaim, and you'll find more than 50 wineries in the Santa Ynez Valley area, most of which have tasting rooms—a few offer tours as well. If you'd like to start with a winery tour to acquaint yourself with viticulture, Gainey Vineyard is a good bet (see below). And if you'd like to sample wines without driving around, head to **Los Olivos Tasting Room & Wine Shop,** 2905 Grand Ave. (© **805/688-7406;** www.losolivoswines.com), in the heart of town, which offers a wide selection of vintners, including those—such as Au Bon Climat and Qupé—who don't have their own tasting rooms.

Fess Parker Winery & Vineyard ★ You loved him as a child, now see what Hollywood's Davy Crockett/Daniel Boone is up to. Fess Parker has made a name for himself in Santa Barbara County, with resort hotels, cattle ranches, and now an eponymous winery that's turning out some critically acclaimed Syrahs, among other varietals. Look for the Syrah and chardonnay American Tradition Reserve vintages in the tasting room. Parker's grandiose complex, shaded by the largest oak tree I've ever seen, also features picnic tables on a terrace and an extensive gift shop where you can even buy (you guessed it) coonskin caps.

6200 Foxen Canyon Rd., Los Olivos. © **800/841-1104** or 805/688-1545. www.fessparker.com. Tastings daily 10am–5pm; tours daily at 11am, 1pm, and 3pm. Tasting fee $10, includes souvenir glass.

The Gainey Vineyard ★ This slick operation is one of the most visited wineries in the valley, thanks to its prime location on Highway 246 and its in-depth tours, offered daily. It has every hallmark of a visitor-oriented winery: a terra-cotta-tiled tasting room, plenty of logo merchandise, and a deli case for impromptu lunches at the picnic tables in a secluded vineyard garden. It bottles the most popular varietals—chardonnay, cabernet sauvignon, pinot noir, sauvignon blanc—and offers them at moderate prices.

3950 E. Hwy. 246, Santa Ynez. © **888/424-6398** or 805/688-0558. www.gaineyvineyard.com. Tastings daily 10am–5pm; tours daily 11am and 1, 2, and 3pm. Tasting fee $10, includes souvenir glass.

Sunstone Vineyards and Winery ★★★ Take a rambling drive down to this locally known winery, whose wisteria-wrapped stone tasting room belies the dirt road you take to reach it. Sunstone sits in an oak grove overlooking the river, boasting a splendid view from the lavender-fringed picnic courtyard. Inside, try its flagship merlot or treasured reserve vintages; there's also a fine selection of gourmet foods, logo ware, and cigars. The pretty setting and attractive tasting room, combined with excellent products, make this a quintessentially enjoyable wine-touring experience.

125 Refugio Rd., Santa Ynez. © **800/313-WINE** or 805/688-WINE. www.sunstonewinery.com. Tastings daily 10am–4:30pm. Tasting fee $10.

Zaca Mesa Winery ★★ One of the region's old-timers, Zaca Mesa has been in business since 1972, so one can forgive the hippie/New Age mumbo-jumbo pleasantly interwoven with the well-honed vintages. Situated on a unique plateau that the Spanish named *la zaca mesa* (the restful place), this winery's 750 acres are uniquely beautiful, with two easy nature trails for visitors. You'll also find picnic tables and a giant lawn chessboard. Inside, look for the usual Syrah and chardonnay offerings jazzed up with experimental Rhone varietals such as grenache, roussanne, and viognier.

6905 Foxen Canyon Rd., Los Olivos. (℮ **805/688-9339.** www.zacamesa.com. Daily 10am–4pm (until 5pm Fri–Sat); call for tour schedule. Tasting fee $7–$12.

Solvang: A Touristy Taste of Denmark

Immortalized in the 2004 film *Sideways,* the valley's largest community is also one of the state's most popular tourist towns, with more than a million tourists each year. Founded in 1911 by Danish immigrants longing for plenty of sunny weather, Solvang takes a lot of flack for being a Disneyfied version of its founders' vision, where everything that *can* be Danish *is* Danish ("More Danish than Denmark!" is the oft-heard local mantra). You've never seen so many windmills, cobblestone streets, flying flags, wooden shoes, and gingerbread-trimmed bakeries (even the trash cans look like little Danish farmhouses with pitched-roof lids). In fact, the whole town looks like a Thomas Kinkade painting, so it's no wonder that America's most populist painter has an outlet on the main drag, **Thomas Kinkade Places in the Heart Gallery,** 1576 Mission Dr. (℮ **805/693-8739**).

To reach Solvang from U.S. 101 south, turn east (left) onto Highway 246 at Buellton. It's a well-marked 20-minute drive along a scenic two-lane road. From Santa Barbara, take U.S. 101 north to Highway 154, a truly breathtaking 45-minute drive over San Marcos Pass. For a destination guide or hotel information, contact the **Solvang Conference & Visitors Bureau** (℮ **800/468-6765** or 805/688-6144; www.solvangusa.com).

One of the biggest attractions in Solvang is the conspicuous abundance of baked goods such as Danishes, Sarah Bernhardts, kringles, and *kransekage,* making walking-friendly Solvang a great place to stop for a leg stretch and a sugar rush between Hearst Castle and Santa Barbara. **Olsen's Danish Village Bakery,** 1529 Mission Dr. (℮ **805/688-6314;** www.olsensdanishbakery.com), is the town's best bakery.

Solvang is also full of Danish import shops stuffed with Royal Copenhagen collectibles, lace, and carvings. **Gerda's Iron Art Gift Shop,** 1676 Copenhagen Dr. (℮ **805/688-3750**), the **Royal Copenhagen Shop,** 1683 Copenhagen Dr. (℮ **805/688-6660**), all offer a large selection of china, cookware, potholders, and Danish gift items, while **Lemos Feed and Pet Supply,** 1511-C Mission Dr. (℮ **805/693-8180**), has a great selection of gifts for pets. Antiques hounds will find plenty to admire and buy at the **Solvang Antique Center,** 486 First St. (℮ **805/686-2322**), with more than 50 dealers.

Windhaven Glider Rides, Santa Ynez Airport (℮ **805/688-2517;** www.gliderrides.com), runs hang-glider rides over the gorgeous valley. For a different kind of thrill you can try your luck at the **Chumash Casino,** a huge Las Vegas–style casino on Highway 246 in Santa Ynez (℮ **800/CHUMASH;** www.chumashcasino.com).

If you want to wedge some history and culture between bites of pastries and sips of wine, the valley is the home of the historic, tragic **Mission Santa Ines,** 1760 Mission Dr. (℮ **805/688-4815;** www.missionsantaines.org; winter daily 9am–5:30; summer daily 9am–5pm), with its interpretive display of Chumash, religious, and Spanish artifacts, paintings, and documents. Built in 1804, the mission fell into disuse and disrepair after a series of natural and man-made disasters, but near-divine intervention—in the form of Capuchin monks—helped resurrect the mission, which now serves Mass and hosts an annual fiesta in midsummer.

Dedicated to documenting and preserving America's flora and fauna, the small yet wonderful **Wildling Museum,** 2329 Jonata St., Los Olivos (℮ **805/688-1082;** www.wildlingmuseum.org; Wed–Sun 11am–5pm; $2 donation requested for admission) is solely supported by donations. Its three rooms offer a changing display of photographs

Miniature Horses & More

Miniature horses supposedly make great house pets, but you may not want to mention that to your kids until you are far, far away from **Quicksilver Miniature Horse Ranch,** 1555 Alamo Pintado Rd. (✆ **800/370-4002** or 805/686-4002). No more than 34 inches high, these four-legged Lilliputians can be petted and played with during visiting hours. If you prefer full-size equines, visit **Day Dream Arabians,** 2065 Refugio Rd. (✆ **805/688-9106;** daydreamarabians.com), for a presentation, tour, and the opportunity to stroll with and feed the mares and foals. If birds are more your bag, **Ostrich Land,** 610 E. Hwy. 246, Buellton (✆ **805/686-9696**), lets you view the 8½-foot-tall, 350-pound bipeds from a safe distance, and then buy some low-fat ostrich meat (which, surprisingly, tastes like lean beef).

and paintings depicting the history of our vanishing lands and wildlife, and it's truly a labor of love.

Both the **Hans Christian Andersen Museum,** 1680 Mission Dr., upstairs (✆ **805/688-2052;** Daily 10am–5pm), and the **Elverhøj Museum,** 1624 Elverhoj Way (✆ **805/686-1211;** www.elverhoj.org; Wed–Thurs 1–4pm; Fri–Sun noon–4pm) cater to children—especially the Elverhøj, which is designed to stimulate children to celebrate the life of Denmark's most famous citizen. Downstairs is the Bookloft and Kaffe Hus, with a reading area for children.

Los Olivos: A Quiet Wine Country Town

Los Olivos is a good old-fashioned country town in the middle of the Central Coast Wine Country, complete with a flagpole at the town's main intersection. If you saw TV's *Return to Mayberry,* that was Los Olivos standing in for Andy Griffith's sentimental southern hamlet. But these days, the town's storefronts feature numerous art galleries, stylish cafes, and wine-tasting rooms. If cutesy and congested Solvang is definitely not your kind of scene, make the short, scenic drive over here along Alamo Pintado Road, spend a few hours browsing the town's 3 short blocks, and then enjoy an alfresco lunch at the Los Olivos Café or Panino gourmet sandwich shop (see "Where to Dine," below). If you're looking for a place to stay, Fess Parker runs a beautiful inn and spa here (p. 452).

Cachuma Lake: A Bald-Eagle Habitat

Created in 1953 by the damming of the Santa Ynez River, this picturesque reservoir running along Highway 154 is the primary water source for Santa Barbara County. It's also the centerpiece of a 6,600-acre county park with a flourishing wildlife population and well-developed recreational facilities. Cachuma has, through agreeable climate and diligent ranger efforts, become a notable habitat for resident and migratory birds, including rarely sighted bald eagles, which migrate south from as far as Alaska in search of food.

One of the best ways to appreciate this fine-feathered bounty is to take one of the naturalist-led **Eagle Cruises** of the lake, offered between November and February. The 48-foot *Osprey* was specially designed for wildlife observation, with unobstructed views from nearly every seat. During the rest of the year, rangers lead **Wildlife Cruises** around the lake, helping you spot resident waterfowl, deer, and the elusive bobcats and mountain lions that live here. Eagle Cruises depart Wednesday, Thursday, and Sunday between

10am and noon, with additional cruises Friday and Saturday at 2pm. Wildlife Cruises run Friday and Saturday at 3pm, and Saturday and Sunday at 10am. All cruises are 2 hours long. In addition to the park day-use fee of $5 per car, the fare is $15 for adults and $7 for children 12 and under. Reservations are recommended; call the **Santa Barbara County Parks Department** (© **805/686-5050;** www.sbparks.com).

The recreational opportunities also offer campers, boaters, and fishermen abundant facilities. Contact the **Lake Cachuma Recreation Area** (© **805/686-5054**) for recorded information.

Where to Stay

The Ballard Inn & Restaurant ★★ This two-story inn may look 100 years old, but it's actually of modern construction, offering both contemporary comforts and charming country details like wicker rockers on a wraparound porch. The entry and parlors are tastefully furnished with a comfortable mix of antiques and reproductions. Sumptuous wallpaper and fabrics lend a cozy touch, and hand-hooked rugs, bent-twig furniture, and vintage accessories lend character to the house. The guest rooms upstairs are unique—some have fireplaces and/or private balconies, and all have well-stocked bathrooms, many featuring a separate antique washbasin in the bedroom. The best (and most expensive) unit is the Mountain Room, a minisuite decorated in rich forest-green and outfitted with a fireplace and private balcony. In addition to cooked-to-order breakfast and a wine and hors d'oeuvres reception, you'll be treated to evening coffee and tea, plus addictive chocolate cookies on your nightstand at bedtime.

The inn's upscale restaurant, in a cozy room downstairs with a crackling fire, has garnered much praise since chef Budi Kazali took over a few years back. Dishes from his globally inspired menu range from herb-crusted tuna with Niçoise mashed potatoes, to roasted duck breast with sweet potato purée, and wild striped bass with potato artichoke hash.

2436 Baseline Ave., Ballard, CA 93463. © **800/638-2466** or 805/688-7770. Fax 805/688-9560. www.ballardinn.com. 15 units. $245–$315 double. Rates include full breakfast, afternoon wine and hors d'oeuvres. AE, MC, V. Take Alamo Pintado Rd. to Baseline; the inn is half a block east of the intersection. **Amenities:** Restaurant; bike rental; activities desk. *In room:* A/C, hair dryer, iron.

Fess Parker's Wine Country Inn & Spa ★★ Yes, that Fess Parker—Daniel Boone and Davy Crockett, both. But when he's not playing pioneer legends, he's a big local developer. This sprawling eponymous inn is a deep lap of luxury, with each room uniquely decorated by "Mrs. Marcy Parker" herself. The rooms are certainly pristine and comfortable, and each comes with a fireplace and cushy beds with down comforters. Other welcoming perks include a complimentary full American breakfast, a bottle of Fess Parker wine upon arrival, and a free wine tasting for two at two local tasting rooms. There is also a full spa, a pool, and Jacuzzi. And if you haven't already, buy property in these parts—this region is exploding.

2860 Grand Ave. (at Hollister St.), Los Olivos, CA 93441. © **800/446-2455** or 805/688-7788. Fax 805/688-1942. www.fessparker.com. 21 units. $380–$430 double. AE, DISC, MC, V. **Amenities:** Restaurant; pool; spa; bike rental; 24-hr. front desk. *In room:* A/C, TV, free high-speed Internet access, hair dryer, iron, fireplace.

Inn at Petersen Village ★ If you think every hotel in Solvang has a kitschy Danish theme, then step into this quiet, tasteful hotel. Rooms are decorated in a European country motif, with print wallpaper, canopy beds, and mahogany-hued furniture. But it's the little touches that impress the most, such as lighted magnifying mirrors, bathroom lights controlled by dimmers, free coffee and tea service to your room, and the complimentary food that's nearly always laid out in the hotel's friendly piano lounge. Some rooms over-look a bustling courtyard of shops, while others face Solvang's scenic hills. All are designed so everyone's happy: Smaller units have private balconies, those with noisier views are more spacious, and so on. Note that rates include a complete dinner for two and a European buffet breakfast.

1576 Mission Dr., Solvang, CA 93463. (€) **800/321-8985** or 805/688-3121. Fax 805/688-5732. www.
peterseninn.com. 42 units. $265–$380 double. Extra person $35. Rates include full dinner and breakfast buffet. AE, MC, V. **Amenities:** Restaurant; piano/wine bar; room service. In room: A/C, TV, hair dryer, iron.

Royal Scandinavian Inn   If you're looking for a traditional, full-service hotel, this attractive and comfortable mainstay in Solvang is away from the congested main drag. Popular with conventions and leisure groups, the Royal Scandinavian has an all-day restaurant and cocktail lounge and is within walking distance of downtown Solvang; the championship Alisal River Golf Course is next door. Ask for a room overlooking the courtyard—the view extends to the foothills beyond. The hotel's restaurant, **Meadows,** is one of the better options in the area, with an attractive patio for dining—equipped with heaters for cool nights and misters for hot days.

400 Alisal Rd. (P.O. Box 30), Solvang, CA 93464. (€) **800/624-5572** or 805/688-8000. Fax 805/688-0761.
www.royalscandinavianinn.com. 133 units. $141–$224 double; from $239–$299 suite. Extra person $10 in existing bedding, $15 for rollaway. AE, DC, DISC, MC, V. **Amenities:** Restaurant; lounge; outdoor pool; nearby golf; coupons for gym next door; Jacuzzi; room service; laundry service; dry cleaning. In room: A/C, TV w/pay movies, fax, coffeemaker, hair dryer, iron.

Solvang Gardens Lodge (Value)   Solvang's oldest motel is also one of the best values in the entire Santa Ynez Valley. The rooms are all nonsmoking and comfortably sized, with floral prints and marble bathrooms. The meticulously manicured grounds are replete with gardens and fruit trees, and ensconced in the backyard is a massage cottage that offers Swedish, deep tissue, aromatherapy, and hot stone massages starting at $95. Be sure to check their website for numerous money-saving package deals.

293 Alisal Rd., Solvang, CA 93463. (€) **888/688-4404** or 805/688-4404. Fax 805/688-9975. www.solvang gardens.com. 24 units. $119–$179 double; $169–$239 suite. DISC, MC, V. **Amenities:** Billiard cottage. In room: A/C, TV, Wi-Fi, wet bar, microwave.

Where to Dine

For a quick sandwich or burger on the porch—or to select prepared salads, breads, and artisan cheeses for a picnic to go—you'll be quite pleased with **Los Olivos Grocery,** 2621 W. Hwy. 154 ((€) **805/688-5115;** www.losolivosgrocery.com). This small gourmet coun-try store, open daily from 7am to 9pm, has a great selection of fine wine and foods made from scratch.

If you're looking for traditional Danish fare, head for **Bit o' Denmark,** 473 Alisal Rd. ((€) **805/688-5426**). Its smorgasbord may not be the largest in town, but it's the freshest and highest quality; you can also order from the regular menu. It's open daily from 11:30am to 9pm. **The Hitching Post,** 406 E. Hwy. 246, Buellton ((€) **805/688-0676;** www.hitchingpost2.com), is the valley's mecca for meat lovers and now famous as the restaurant featured in *Sideways.* Within these Western-themed surroundings, steaks are grilled to perfection over an oak-wood pit and, fittingly, the house label wine is better than you'd expect.

Brothers Restaurant at Mattei's Tavern ★ AMERICAN/CONTINENTAL
Mattei's is proud of its stagecoach past. Built in 1886 by Swiss-born Felix Mattei to serv-ice waiting stagecoach passengers, the tavern remained in business until 1914 when the

Tips **Picnicking in the Santa Ynez Valley**

On a sunny summer day there's no better way to enjoy lunch than having an impromptu picnic anywhere in the valley. Some of the best sandwiches in the region are made daily at **Panino,** 2900 Grand Ave., Los Olivos (© **805/688-9304**), a small gourmet sandwich shop where you can choose from about 30 varieties of sandwiches—I usually order the grilled chicken with sun-dried tomatoes, fresh basil, and provolone on fresh walnut bread—all served on Panino's fresh-baked Italian-style bread. It's open Monday through Saturday from 9am to 5pm, and Sunday from 10am to 5pm. There's even a small, grassy picnic area with tables right across the street.

Model-A Ford put the coaches out of business. Rumors abound of high-stakes poker games in Mattei's back room, where many an early rancher literally "lost the farm." As soon as you step inside this rambling white Victorian submerged in wisteria you'll be impressed by how successfully it has retained its historic charm. The restaurant is known throughout the county for its signature reduction sauces and house-made ice cream. You'll find thick steaks on the menu, along with honey-glazed Iowa pork chops, prime rib with garlic mashed potatoes, and Australian lobster tail. Bust a pant button with the sinful fudge brownie sundae with banana ice cream, and then saddle up and mosey along.

2350 Railway Ave. (just east of Grand Ave. on Hwy. 154), Los Olivos. © **805/688-4820.** www.matteis tavern.com. Reservations recommended on weekends. Dinner $18–$44. AE, MC, V. Daily 5–9pm; bar open daily from 4pm.

Los Olivos Café ★ CALIFORNIA/MEDITERRANEAN   The patio is so ensconced with wisteria that it's easy to walk right past this popular cafe and not notice it (I did it twice). The sunny patio is ideal for lunch, the inside is warm and beckoning, with its massive concrete fireplace, and the food is so consistently good that even locals eat here regularly. The menu offers mostly Mediterranean-style gourmet sandwiches, salads, and pastas—think grilled eggplant and ham on hearth bread, pesto ravioli, basil pesto pizza, and butternut-squash-and-cranberry salad. And, but of course, you can sample local wines with your meal. Don't leave without a bottle of their signature olive oil.

2879 Grand Ave., Los Olivos. © **805/688-7265.** www.losolivoscafe.com. Reservations recommended. Main courses $10–$24. AE, DISC, MC, V. Daily 11:30am–3pm and 5–9pm. Wine tasting daily 11am–9pm.

Paula's Pancake House ★ **Kids** AMERICAN/DANISH   Morning means one thing in Solvang—Paula's three-page menu of breakfast treats. Paula's is friendly and casual, in the heart of town where patio diners can watch the world go by. So, should we order the wafer-thin Danish pancakes served plain and simple or sweet and fruity? Better include some sausage and eggs with that, and a side of buttermilk pancakes. No, make that a side of whole-wheat honey pancakes, a waffle, and sourdough French toast. Hmmm, an omelet sounds pretty good too. More coffee, please.

1531 Mission Dr., Solvang. © **805/688-2867.** Most dishes under $10. AE, DISC, MC, V. Daily 6am–3pm.

6 SANTA BARBARA ★★★

45 miles S of Solvang; 105 miles S of San Luis Obispo; 92 miles NW of L.A.

Situated between palm-lined Pacific beaches and the sloping foothills of the Santa Ynez Mountains, this prosperous resort community presents a mosaic of whitewashed stucco and red-tile roofs and a gracious, relaxed attitude that has earned it the sobriquet American Riviera. It's ideal for kicking back on gold-sand beaches, prowling the shops and galleries that line the village's historic streets, and relaxing over a meal in one of many top-notch cafes and restaurants.

Downtown Santa Barbara is distinctive for its Spanish-Mediterranean architecture. But it wasn't always this way. Santa Barbara had a thriving Native American Chumash population for hundreds, if not thousands, of years. The European era began in the late 18th century around a Spanish *presidio* (fort) that's been reconstructed in its original spot. The earliest architectural hodgepodge was destroyed in 1925 by a powerful earthquake that leveled the business district. Out of the rubble rose the Spanish-Mediterranean town of today, a stylish planned community that continues to enforce strict building codes.

Visit Santa Barbara's waterfront on a Sunday, and you're sure to see the weekly **Arts and Crafts Show,** one of the city's best-loved traditions. Since 1965, artists, craftspeople, and street performers have been lining grassy Chase Palm Park, along Cabrillo Boulevard.

ESSENTIALS

GETTING THERE   By car, U.S. 101 runs right through Santa Barbara; it's the fastest and most direct route from north or south ($1^{1}/_{2}$ hr. from Los Angeles, 6 hr. from San Francisco).

By train, **Amtrak** (© **800/USA-RAIL;** www.amtrak.com) offers daily service to Santa Barbara. Trains arrive and depart from the **Santa Barbara Rail Station,** 209 State St. (© **805/963-1015**). Fares can be as low as $29 (round-trip) from Los Angeles's Union Station.

ORIENTATION   State Street, the city's primary commercial thoroughfare, is the geographic center of town. It ends at Stearns Wharf and Cabrillo Boulevard; the latter runs along the ocean and separates the city's beaches from touristy hotels and restaurants. Electric shuttles provide frequent service along these two routes if you'd rather leave the car behind.

VISITOR INFORMATION   The **Santa Barbara Conference and Visitors Bureau,** 1601 Anacapa St. (© **805/966-9222;** www.santabarbaraca.com), distributes maps, brochures, an events calendar, and information. It's open Monday through Saturday from 9am to 5pm, and Sunday from 10am to 5pm.

Be sure you pick up a copy of the *Independent,* Santa Barbara's free weekly, with articles and events listings; and *Explore Santa Barbara,* a compact visitor's guide published by the local paper, the *Santa Barbara News-Press.* Both are also available at shops and sidewalk racks throughout town.

SEEING THE SIGHTS
Historic Downtown

Following a devastating 1925 earthquake, city planners decreed that all new construction would follow codes of Spanish and Mission-style architecture. In time, the adobe-textured walls, rounded archways, glazed tile work, and terra-cotta rooftops came to symbolize the

THE CENTRAL COAST

13

SANTA BARBARA

Mediterranean ambience that still characterizes Santa Barbara. The architecture also gave a name to the **Red Tile Tour,** a self-guided walking tour of historic downtown. The visitor center (see "Visitor Information," above) has a map/guide of the tour, which can take anywhere from 1 to 3 hours, including time to visit some of the buildings, and covers about 12 blocks in total. Some of the highlights are destinations in their own right.

Santa Barbara County Courthouse ★   Built in 1929, this grand "palace" is considered the local flagship of Spanish colonial revival architecture (you've undoubtedly seen its facade on TV during the Michael Jackson trial). It's certainly the most flamboyant example, with impressive facades, beamed ceilings, striking murals, an 85-foot-high observation clock tower, and formal sunken gardens. Free guided tours are offered on Monday, Tuesday, and Friday at 10:30am.

1100 Anacapa St. ☎ **805/962-6464.** www.santabarbaracourthouse.org. Free admission. Mon–Fri 8am–5pm; Sat–Sun and holidays 10am–4:30pm.

Santa Barbara Museum of Art ★   This little jewel of a museum feels more like the private gallery of a wealthy collector. Its leaning is toward early-20th-century Western American paintings and 19th- and 20th-century Asian art, but the best displays might be the antiquities and Chinese ceramics. In addition, there are often visiting exhibits featuring small but excellent collections from other establishments.

1130 State St. ☎ **805/963-4364.** www.sbmuseart.org. Admission $9 adults, $6 seniors 65 and over, $6 students and children ages 6–17, free for children 5 and under; free for everyone every Sun. Tues–Sun 11am–5pm.

Elsewhere in the City

Stearns Wharf ★, at the end of State Street (www.stearnswharf.org), is California's oldest working wharf. It attracts visitors for strolling, shopping, dining, and exploring its exhibits, which include a Sea Center with aquariums and an outdoor touch-tank. Although the wharf no longer functions for passenger and freight shipping as it did when built in 1872 by local lumberman John C. Stearns, local fishing boats still dock to unload their daily catch. Consider taking a narrated sunset harbor cruise aboard the *Harbour Queen* at **Captain Don's** (☎ **805/969-5217;** www.captdon.com). Public parking on the wharf is free with merchant validation.

Ganna Walska Lotusland (Finds)   This secluded, lavishly landscaped 37-acre estate is renowned for exotic plants and mysterious garden paths. Named for the estate's vivacious European-born mistress and the romantic, lotus-filled ponds in her gardens, the estate reflects the late Madame Walska's eccentricity and the skill of her prestigious gardeners. She was especially fond of succulents and cacti, interspersing them artistically among native plants and decorative objects. Assembled when money was no object and import regulations were lenient (mostly in the 1940s), the garden contains priceless rare specimens—even prehistoric plants that are extinct in the wild. Advance reservations are required. Montecito is a 5-minute freeway drive south of downtown Santa Barbara. *Note:* Advance reservations are required and are available up to 6 months in advance.

695 Ashley Rd., Montecito. ☎ **805/969-9990.** www.lotusland.org. Admission $35 adults, $10 children 5–18, free for children 4 and under. 2-hr. guided tours mid-Feb to mid-Nov Wed–Sat 10am and 1:30pm.

Old Mission Santa Barbara ★   Established in 1786 by Father Junípero Serra and built by the Chumash Indians, this is a rare example in physical form of the blending of Indian and Hispanic spirituality. This hilltop structure is called the Queen of the Missions

ACCOMMODATIONS
Canary Hotel **4**
Casa del Mar Inn at
  the Beach **15**
Four Seasons Resort **19**
Franciscan Inn **15**
Hotel Oceana **14**
Simpson House Inn **10**
The Upham Victorian Hotel **9**

DINING
bouchon **1**
Brophy Bros. Clam Bar
  & Restaurant **16**
La Super-Rica Taqueria **13**
Palazzio **5**
Pan e Vino **21**
Stacky's Seaside **20**
Tupelo Junction Café **2**
Wine Cask **7**

ATTRACTIONS ●
El Paseo Mall **8**
Santa Barbara Botanic
  Garden **12**

Santa Barbara County Courthouse **6**
Santa Barbara Mission **11**
Santa Barbara Museum of Art **3**
Santa Barbara Zoo **18**
Stearns Wharf **17**

for its twin bell towers and beauty. It overlooks the town and the Channel Islands beyond. Self-guided tour booklets are available in six languages.

2201 Laguna St. (at Los Olivos St.). © **805/682-4713**. www.sbmission.org. Admission $4 adults, free for children 11 and under. Mon–Fri 9am–5pm.

Santa Barbara Botanic Garden (Finds)   The Botanic Garden is devoted to indigenous California plants. More than 5.5 miles of meandering trails on 65 acres offer glimpses of cacti, redwoods, wildflowers, and much more, many arranged in representational habitats or landscapes. The gardens were established in 1926. You'll catch the very best color and aroma just after spring showers.

1212 Mission Canyon Rd. (a short drive uphill from the mission). © **805/682-4726**. www.sbbg.org. Admission $8 adults, $6 seniors 60 and over, $6 children 13–17, $4 children 2–12, free for children 1 and under. Daily 9am–5pm (till 6pm Mar–Oct).

Santa Barbara Zoo ★ (Kids)   When you're driving around the bend on Cabrillo Boulevard, look up—you might spot the head of a giraffe poking through the palms. This zoo is an appealing, pint-size place, where all 700 animals can be seen in about 30 minutes. Most live in natural, open settings. For more stimulation, try the Discovery Area, miniature train ride, and small carousel. The picnic areas (with barbecue pits) are underused and especially recommended.

500 Niños Dr. (off Cabrillo Blvd.). © **805/962-5339** or 805/962-6310 for recorded information. www. santabarbarazoo.org. Admission $11 adults, $8 seniors and children 2–12, free for children 1 and under. Daily 10am–5pm; last admission is 1 hr. before closing. Closed Christmas. Open Thanksgiving 10am–3pm. Parking $4.

BEACHES

East Beach is Santa Barbara's favorite beach, stretching from the Santa Barbara Zoological Gardens to Chase Palm Park and the wharf. Nearer the pier you can enjoy manicured lawns, tall palms, and abundant facilities; to the east are many volleyball courts, plus the Cabrillo Pavilion, a recreational center, bathhouse, and architectural landmark dating from 1925. Picnic areas with barbecue grills, showers, and clean, well-patrolled sands make this beach a good choice for everyone.

On the other side of Santa Barbara Harbor is **Leadbetter Beach,** less sheltered than those to the south and popular with surfers. It's reached by following Cabrillo Boulevard after it turns into Shoreline Drive. This beach is also a great place to watch pleasure boats entering or leaving the harbor. Leadbetter has basic facilities, including restrooms, picnic areas, and a metered parking lot.

Two miles west of Leadbetter is secluded but popular **Arroyo Burro Beach County Park,** also known as Hendry's Beach. This gem has a grassy park beneath the cliffs and a white crescent beach with great waves for surfing and bodysurfing. There are volleyball nets, picnic areas, and restrooms.

OUTDOOR ACTIVITIES

BIKING & SURREY CYCLING   A relatively flat, palm-lined 2-mile coastal pathway, perfect for biking, runs along the beach. More adventurous riders can pedal through town (where painted bike lanes line many major routes, including one up to the mission). These routes and many more are outlined in the *Santa Barbara County Bike Map,* a free and comprehensive resource available at the visitor center or by calling **Traffic Solutions** at © **805/963-7283**.

Wheel Fun Rentals, 101 State St. (just off Cabrillo Blvd.; $\mathcal{C}$ **805/966-2282;** www. **459** wheelfunrentals.com), rents well-maintained beach cruisers, mountain bikes, tandem bikes, and an Italian four-wheel surrey that seats three adults; rates vary. It's open daily from 8am to 8pm.

BOATING The **Santa Barbara Sailing Center,** 133 Harbor Way at the Santa Barbara Harbor ($\mathcal{C}$ **800/350-9090** or 805/962-2826; www.sbsail.com), rents sailboats from 21 to 50 feet in length, as well as paddleboats, kayaks, and motorboats. Both skippered and bareboat charters are available by the day or hour. Sailing instruction for all levels of experience is also available. Coastal, island, whale-watching, dinner-cruise, and adventure tours are offered on the 50-foot sailing catamaran *Double Dolphin.* Open 9am to 6pm spring and summer; 9am to 5pm fall and winter.

GOLF At the **Santa Barbara Golf Club,** 3500 McCaw Ave., at Las Positas Road ($\mathcal{C}$ **805/687-7087**), there's a great 6,009-yard, 18-hole course and a driving range. Unlike many municipal courses, the Santa Barbara Golf Course is well maintained and presents a moderate challenge for the average golfer. Greens fees are $35 Monday through Friday and $45 on weekends. Twilight prices $22 Monday through Friday and $25 on weekends. Optional carts rent for $26.

The 18-hole, 7,000-yard **Sandpiper,** at 7925 Hollister Ave. ($\mathcal{C}$ **805/968-1541;** www. sandpipergolf.com), is a scenic ocean-side course that's rated as one of the top public courses in the U.S. It also has a driving range. Weekend greens fees are $149, and the cart fee is $16.

HIKING The foothill trails in the Santa Ynez Mountains above Santa Barbara are perfect for day hikes. In general, they aren't overly strenuous. Trail maps are available at **Pacific Travelers Supply,** 12 W. Anapamu St. (at State St.; $\mathcal{C}$ **888/PAC-TRAV** or 805/ 963-4438); at the visitor center (see "Visitor Information," above); and from **Traffic Solutions** ($\mathcal{C}$ **805/963-7283**).

One of the most popular hikes is the **Seven Falls/Inspiration Point Trail,** an easy trek that begins on Tunnel Road, past the mission, and skirts the edge of Santa Barbara's Botanic Garden (which contains some pleasant hiking trails itself).

SKATING The paved beach path that runs along Santa Barbara's waterfront is perfect for in-line skating. **Wheel Fun Rentals,** 101 State St. (just off Cabrillo Blvd.; $\mathcal{C}$ **805/ 966-2282;** www.wheelfunrentals.com), rents skates and all the requisite protective gear. It's open daily from 8am to 8pm.

WHALE-WATCHING Whale-watching cruises are offered between late December and late March, when Pacific gray whales pass by on migratory journeys from their breeding lagoons in Baja California, Mexico, to their Alaskan feeding grounds. **Shoreline Park,** west of the harbor, has high bluffs ideal for land-based whale-spotting. Sea excursions are offered by both **Captain Don's Harbor Tours** ($\mathcal{C}$ **805/969-5217;** www.captdon.com), on Stearns Wharf, and the **Condor** ($\mathcal{C}$ **888/77-WHALE** or 805/882-0088; www.condor cruises.com), located at 301 W. Cabrillo Blvd. in the Santa Barbara Harbor.

SHOPPING

State Street from the beach to Victoria Street is the city's main thoroughfare and has the largest concentration of shops. Many specialize in T-shirts and postcards, but there are a number of boutiques as well. If you get tired of strolling, hop on one of the electric shuttle buses (25¢) that run up and down State Street.

THE CENTRAL COAST

13

SANTA BARBARA

Also check out **Brinkerhoff Avenue** (off Cota St., btw. Chapala and De La Vina sts.), Santa Barbara's "antiques alley." Most shops here are open Tuesday through Sunday from 11am to 5pm. **El Paseo** (814 State St.) is a picturesque shopping arcade reminiscent of an old Spanish street. It's built around an 1827 adobe home and is lined with charming shops and art galleries. **Paseo Nuevo,** on the other side of State Street, is a modern outdoor mall, featuring familiar chain stores and cafes, and anchored by a Nordstrom department store.

WHERE TO STAY

Before you even begin calling around for reservations, keep in mind that Santa Barbara's accommodations are expensive—especially in summer. Then decide whether you'd like to stay beach side (even more expensive) or downtown. Santa Barbara is small, but not small enough to happily stroll between the two areas.

The free one-stop reservations service **Hot Spots** (© 800/793-7666 or 805/564-1637; www.hotspotsusa.com) keeps an updated list of availability for about 90% of the area's hotels, motels, inns, and B&Bs. The service will have the latest information on who might be looking to fill last-minute vacancies at reduced rates. Reservationists are available Monday through Saturday from 9am to 9pm, and Sunday from 9am to 4pm. There's no charge for using the service.

Very Expensive

Four Seasons Resort, The Biltmore Santa Barbara ★★★   This gem of the American Riviera manages to adhere to the most elegant standards of hospitality without making anyone feel unwelcome. It's easy to sense the ghosts of golden-age Hollywood celebs such as Greta Garbo, Errol Flynn, and Bing Crosby, who used to play croquet on the hotel's perfectly manicured lawns and then head over to the private Coral Casino Beach & Cabana Club—because that's exactly what today's privileged guests are *still* doing. The Four Seasons company acquired this Spanish-style hacienda (ca. 1927) in 1987 and restored the 20-acre property without spoiling a bit of its historic charm. Rooms have an airy feel, heightened by white plantation shutters, light-wood furnishings, and full marble bathrooms with all the modern amenities. Guests can amuse themselves with a putting green, shuffleboard courts, and croquet lawn. In addition to two acclaimed dining rooms, the Biltmore offers a no-holds-barred Sunday brunch that draws folks from 100 miles away. The hotel's most recent addition is the Spa, a multimillion-dollar, 10,000-square-foot Spanish-style annex that houses numerous treatment rooms, a swimming pool and two huge whirlpool baths, a state-of-the-art fitness center, and, for the big spenders, 10 oceanview deluxe suites with fireplaces, in-room bars, changing rooms, and twin massage tables (essentially, your own private treatment room).

1260 Channel Dr. (at the end of Olive Mill Rd.), Santa Barbara, CA 93108. © **800/819-5053** or 805/969-2261. Fax 805/565-8323. www.fourseasons.com/santabarbara. 207 units. $550–$8,000 double; from $1,250 suite. Extra person $55. Children age 18 and under stay free in parent's room. Special midweek and package rates available. AE, DC, MC, V. Valet parking $20; free self-parking. **Amenities:** 4 restaurants; 2 lounges; 2 outdoor heated pools; 3 lit tennis courts; health club; salon/spa services; whirlpool; complimentary bicycles; room service; laundry service; dry cleaning. *In room:* A/C, TV/VCR w/pay movies, high-speed Internet, minibar, hair dryer, iron, safe, robes.

Expensive

Canary Hotel ★★★   Formerly the Andalucia, but reopened under a new name and concept in early 2008, the Canary Hotel's combination of Moroccan flair and Spanish culture fits in perfectly with downtown Santa Barbara's casual elegance. In fact, one

The Ultimate Family Vacation, Santa Barbara Style

Now here's a family vacation idea you probably haven't thought of—a week of sun, sports, and fun at the University of California in Santa Barbara (my alma mater). During the months of July and August the **Santa Barbara Family Vacation Center** offers a recreation-oriented family vacation package using vacated university dorms as lodging. It's sort of like a mini–summer camp for the entire family. One set price includes everything for a full week's vacation: all meals, lodging (with daily housekeeping service), and daily activities such as tennis, basketball, volleyball, soccer, softball, fishing, biking, hiking, and more. Evening activities include staff shows, carnivals, casino night, dancing, talent shows, bingo, arts and crafts, and campfires. There's no rigid schedule to follow, so how you want to spend your day is entirely up to you. Children up to 18 are grouped by age and cared for by UCSB student counselors from 9am till midevening, so the parents can spend the day at the beach or touring downtown Santa Barbara. They even offer child care for infants and toddlers. Rates differ depending on age, but when you consider that you'd probably pay more just for 1 week's lodging at a Santa Barbara hotel, it's a fantastic deal. For more information, call ✆ **805/893-3123** or log on to **www.familyvacationcenter.com**.

night's visit at the centrally located establishment will make any subsequent stay in a boutique hotel pale in comparison. Every last detail has been carefully thought out and each piece of furniture finely crafted. All bedrooms boast four-poster beds, Matelasse linens, flatscreen TVs, and yoga DVDs and mats. The hotel has no spa, but offers a menu of massages, facials, and other nurturing treatments performed in-room. The rooftop's heated pool and Jacuzzi offer stunning views of the surrounding Santa Ynez mountains, nearby Channel Islands, and downtown. The hotel even caters to canines with Club Canario, a pooch program that includes a cushy bed with hotel linens, dog tags, grooming kit, treats, and a Frisbee.

31 W. Carrillo, Santa Barbara, CA 93101. ✆ **877/468-3515** or 805/884-0300. Fax 805/884-8153. www. canarysantabarbara.com. 97 units. $405–$765 double. Packages available. AE, MC, V. Dogs accepted. **Amenities:** Restaurant; bar; fitness center; concierge; room service. *In room:* TV/DVD, Wi-Fi, minibar, iron, iPod dock.

Simpson House Inn ★★★ The Simpson House is genuinely something special. Rooms within the 1874 Historic Landmark main house are decorated to Victorian perfection, with extras ranging from a claw-foot tub and antique brass shower to skylight and French doors opening to the manicured gardens; romantic cottages are nestled throughout the grounds. The rooms have everything you could possibly need, but most impressive are the extras: the gourmet Mediterranean hors d'oeuvres and Santa Barbara wines served each afternoon, the enormous video library, and the full gourmet breakfast (delivered on delicate china). Fact is, the Simpson House goes the distance—and then some—to create the perfect stay. Although this property is packed into a relatively small space, it still manages an ambience of country elegance and exclusivity—especially if you book one of the cottages.

121 E. Arrellaga St. (btw. Santa Barbara and Anacapa sts.), Santa Barbara, CA 93101. ℂ **800/676-1280** or 805/963-7067. Fax 805/564-4811. www.simpsonhouseinn.com. 15 units. $255–$615 double; $595–$605 suite and cottage. 2-night minimum on weekends. Rates include full gourmet breakfast, evening hors d'oeuvres, and wine. AE, DISC, MC, V. **Amenities:** Complimentary bicycles; concierge; in-room massage. *In room:* A/C, TV/VCR, minibar, hair dryer, iron, robes.

Moderate

Casa del Mar Inn at the Beach (Value) A half-block from the beach (sorry, no views), Casa del Mar is an excellent-value Spanish-architecture inn with one- and two-room suites in addition to standard size rooms. All the rooms were recently remodeled with fresh modern touches while still maintaining the Mediterranean feel. The flower-sprinkled grounds are well maintained, with an attractive sun deck and Jacuzzi (but no swimming pool), and the staff is eager to please. Many rooms have kitchenettes, and a variety of different room configurations guarantee something to suit your needs (especially families). Guests may order in-room spa treatments, and golf packages can be arranged. *Tip:* Despite the hotel's multitude of rates, rooms can often be an unexpected bargain. Also check the website for Internet-only specials.

18 Bath St., Santa Barbara, CA 93101. ℂ **800/433-3097** or 805/963-4418. www.casadelmar.com. 21 units. $119–$309 double. Extra person $10. AE, DC, DISC, MC, V. Free parking. From northbound U.S. 101, exit at Cabrillo, turn left onto Cabrillo, and head toward the beach; Bath is the 2nd street on the right after the wharf. From southbound U.S. 101, take the Castillo exit and turn right on Castillo, left on Cabrillo, and left on Bath. Pets accepted with $15 fee. **Amenities:** Jacuzzi; in-room massage; laundry service; dry cleaning. *In room:* TV, kitchen or kitchenette and fridge in some units, coffeemaker, hair dryer, iron.

Hotel Oceana ★ If you're going to vacation in Santa Barbara, you might as well stay in style and on the beach—ergo, at the Hotel Oceana, a "beach chic" hotel with an oceanfront setting and an L.A. makeover. The 2½-acre Spanish Mission–style property consists of four adjacent motels built in the 1940s that have been merged and renovated into one sprawling hotel. The result is a wide range of charmingly old-school accommodations—everything from apartments with real day beds (great for families) to courtyard rooms and deluxe oceanview suites—with bright modern furnishings. Each guest room, decorated by renowned interior designer Kathryn Ireland, is smartly appointed with soft Frette linens, down comforters, ceiling fans, CD players, cozy duvets, and Aveda bath products. Along with the size and location of your room, you get to choose from four color schemes—soothing blue or green, racy red, and a cheery yellow (my preferred choice). The beach and jogging path are right across the street, and the huge lawn is perfect for picnic lunches. *Note:* Yes, you will probably be paying over $250 per night for a gussied-up motel room with no A/C, but that's the going rate for oceanfront accommodations in Santa Barbara.

202 W. Cabrillo Blvd., Santa Barbara, CA 93101. ℂ **800/965-9776** or 805/965-4577. Fax 805/965-9937. www.hoteloceana.com. 122 units. $250–$360 double. 2-night minimum for weekend reservations. AE, DC, DISC, MC, V. **Amenities:** Denny's restaurant adjacent; 2 swimming pools; fitness room; spa; whirlpool; sun deck. *In room:* TV, Wi-Fi, fridge, hair dryer, iron, CD player.

The Upham Victorian Hotel and Garden Cottages This conveniently located inn combines the intimacy of a B&B with the service of a small hotel. Built in 1871, the Upham is the oldest continuously operating hostelry in Southern California. Somewhere the management made time for upgrades, though, because guest accommodations are complete with all the modern comforts. The hotel is constructed of redwood, with sweeping verandas and a Victorian cupola on top. It also has a warm lobby and a cozy restaurant.

1404 De La Vina St. (at Sola St.), Santa Barbara, CA 93101. ℂ **800/727-0876** or 805/962-0058. Fax 805/ **463**
963-2825. www.uphamhotel.com. 50 units. $195–$290 double; from $340 suite and cottage. Rates
include continental breakfast and afternoon wine and cheese. AE, DC, MC, V. **Amenities:** Restaurant;
laundry service; dry cleaning. *In room:* TV.

Inexpensive

All the best buys fill up fast in the summer months, so be sure to reserve your room—
even if you're just planning to stay at the reliable **Motel 6,** 443 Corona del Mar Dr.
(ℂ **800/466-8356** or 805/564-1392; www.motel6.com), near the beach.

Franciscan Inn The Franciscan is situated in a quiet neighborhood just a block from
the beach, near Stearns Wharf. This privately owned and meticulously maintained hotel
is an affordable retreat with enough frills that you'll still feel pampered. The small but
comfy rooms feature a country-tinged decor and finely tiled bathrooms. Services include
free local calls and afternoon cookies with spiced cider, hot cocoa, tea or coffee in the
lobby. Most second-floor rooms have unobstructed mountain views, and some suites
feature fully equipped kitchenettes. The inn stacks up as a great family choice that's classy
enough for a romantic weekend, too.

109 Bath St. (at Mason St.), Santa Barbara, CA 93101. ℂ **800/663-5288** or 805/963-8845. Fax 805/564-
3295. www.franciscaninn.com. 53 units. Summer (mid-May to mid-Sept) $165–$180 double, $195–$230
suite; winter $125–$160 double, $145–$180 suite. Extra person $10. Rates include continental breakfast
and afternoon refreshments. AE, DC, MC, V. Free parking. **Amenities:** Heated outdoor pool; whirlpool;
coin-op laundry; laundry service; dry cleaning. *In room:* A/C, TV/VCR, Wi-Fi, dataport, coffeemaker, hair
dryer, iron.

WHERE TO DINE
Expensive

bouchon ★★ CALIFORNIA You can tell that this warm and inviting restaurant is
passionate about wine just from its name—*bouchon* is French for "wine cork." And not
just any wines, but those of the surrounding Santa Barbara County. Have some fun by
enhancing each course with a glass (or half glass); knowledgeable servers help make the
perfect match from among fifty different Central Coast vintages available by the glass.
The seasonally composed, and regionally inspired, menu has included dishes such as
smoked Santa Barbara albacore "carpaccio," arranged with a tangy vinaigrette and shaved
imported Parmesan; luscious sweetbread and chanterelle ragout cradled in a potato-leek
basket; local venison sliced and laid atop cumin spaetzle in a shallow pond of green
peppercorn–Madeira demiglace; or monkfish saddle fragrant with fresh herbs and
accompanied by a creamy fennel-Gruyère gratin. Request a table on the heated front
patio, and don't miss the signature chocolate "molten lava" cake for dessert.

9 W. Victoria St. (off State St.). ℂ **805/730-1160.** www.bouchonsantabarbara.com. Reservations recommended. Main courses $25–$35. AE, DC, MC, V. Daily 5:30–10pm.

Wine Cask ★★ CALIFORNIA Take a 20-year-old wine shop, a large 1920s landmark dining room with a big stone fireplace, an outdoor dining patio, and outstanding
Italian fare, mix them with an attractive staff and clientele, and you've got the Wine
Cask—the most popular upscale dining spot in Santa Barbara. You'll be treated to comforting creations by Chef John Pettitt, such as pan-roasted arctic char in a Dijon-artichoke
emulsion. Other options include Australian lamb chops, or pasta with chanterelle mushrooms, baby artichokes, and gold beets. The wine list reads like a novel, with more than
2,000 wines ($14–$1,400), and has deservedly received the *Wine Spectator* award for
excellence. A happy hour takes place at the beautiful maple bar from 4 to 6pm daily.

In El Paseo Center, 813 Anacapa. ⓒ **800/436-9463** or 805/966-9463. www.winecask.com. Reservations recommended. Lunch $12–$17; dinner main courses $29–$36. AE, DC, MC, V. Mon–Thurs 11:30am–2pm and 5:30–10pm; Fri 11:30am–2pm and 5:30–11pm; Sat 5:30–11pm; Sun 5:30–10pm.

Moderate

Brophy Bros. Clam Bar & Restaurant ★★ SEAFOOD   This place is most known for its unbeatable view of the marina, but the dependable fresh seafood keeps tourists and locals coming back. Dress is casual, portions are huge, and favorites include New England clam chowder, cioppino, and any one of an assortment of seafood salads. The scampi and garlic-baked clams are consistently good, as is all the fresh fish, which comes with soup or salad, coleslaw, and pilaf or french fries. A great deal is the hot-and-cold shellfish combo platter for $14. Ask for a table on the narrow deck overlooking the harbor. *Be fore-warned:* The wait at this small place can be up to 2 hours on a weekend night.

119 Harbor Way (off Cabrillo Blvd. in the Waterfront Center). ⓒ **805/966-4418.** www.brophybros.com. Reservations not accepted. Main courses $9–$19. AE, MC, V. Sun–Thurs 11am–10pm; Fri–Sat 10am–11pm.

Palazzio ★ ITALIAN   I should tell you up front: This family-style restaurant is not a good place for a first date. The fresh garlic bread, which is this State Street staple's raison d'être—and the reason so many UCSB students have no problem putting on the legendary Freshman Fifteen—is potent. Offered in half-order, "normal," or family-style sizes, the main courses aren't half bad either, though normal dishes, such as their capellini with chicken meatballs and penne alla puttanesca, could easily feed two (I didn't manage to plow my way through even half of my Papa Ruby's rigatoni).

1026 State St. ⓒ **805/564-1985.** www.palazzio.com. Main courses $16–$18. AE, MC, V. Mon–Thurs 11:30am–3pm and 5:30–11pm; Fri 11:30am–3pm and 5:30–midnight; Sat 11:30am–midnight; Sun 11:30am–11pm (kitchen closes an hour before the restaurant daily).

Pan E Vino ★ ITALIAN   This popular Italian trattoria offers food as authentic as you'd find in Rome. The simplest spaghetti topped with basil-tomato sauce is so good it's hard to understand why diners would want to occupy their taste buds with more complicated concoctions. But this kitchen is capable of almost anything. Pasta puttanesca, with tomatoes, anchovies, black olives, and capers, is always tops. Pan e Vino also gets high marks for its reasonable prices, service, and casual atmosphere. Although many diners prefer to eat outside on the patio, some of the best tables are in the charming, cluttered dining room.

1482 E. Valley Rd., Montecito (a 5-min. drive south of downtown Santa Barbara). ⓒ **805/969-9274.** Reservations required. Main courses $10–$35. AE, MC, V. Mon–Sat 11:30am–9pm.

Tupelo Junction Café ★★ SOUTHERN   Most trendy restaurants have expiration dates, but the countrified Tupelo Junction has proven immune to such patterns. The unpretentious cafe, which produces Southern cuisine with a healthy California touch, is juxtaposed among the European labels and designer boutiques of State Street. Lemonade and mimosas are served up in mason jars, and Jolly Ranchers are generously doled out with the bill. If you're in Santa Barbara long enough to only dine at Tupelo once, plan your pit stop for brunch: The pumpkin oatmeal waffle with candied walnuts and caramelized bananas is divine, and the apple beignets with crème anglaise aren't to be taken lightly. On Thursday nights, the venue hosts live music, with an array of alcohol and appetizer specials on tap.

1218 State St. ⓒ **805/899-3100.** www.tupelojunction.com. Breakfast and lunch $5–$16; dinner $13–$29. AE, MC, V. Sun–Thurs 8am–2pm and 5:30–8:30pm; Fri–Sat 8am–2pm and 5:30–9pm.

La Super-Rica Taqueria ★ MEXICAN   Looking at this humble street-corner shack, you'd never guess it was blessed with an endorsement by the late Julia Child. The tacos here are authentic and no nonsense, with generous portions of filling piled onto fresh, grainy corn tortillas. My favorites are the *adobado* (marinated pork), *gorditas* (thick corn *masa* pockets filled with spicy beans), and the flank steak. A dollop of house-made salsa and green or red hot sauce is the only adornment required. Sunday's special is *pozole,* a stew of pork and hominy in red-chile sauce. On Friday and Saturday, the specialty is freshly made tamales (if the Dover sole tamales are one of the specials, order them— they're incredible). *Tip:* Always check the daily specials first, and be sure to ask for extra tortillas, no matter what you order.

622 N. Milpas St. (btw. Cota and Ortega sts.). ℂ **805/963-4940.** Most menu items $4–$10. No credit cards. Daily 11am–9pm.

Stacky's Seaside SANDWICHES   This ivy-covered shack filled with fishnets, surf-boards, and local memorabilia has been a local favorite for years. A classic seafood dive, its menu of sandwiches is enormous, as are most of their pita pockets, hoagies, and club sandwiches. A sign proudly proclaims HALF OF ANY SANDWICH, HALF PRICE—NO PROBLEM, and Stacky's has made a lot of friends because of it. Choices include the Santa Barbaran (roasted tri-tip and melted jack cheese on sourdough), the Rincon pita (jack and cheddar cheeses, green Ortega chiles, onions, and ranch dressing), and a hot pastrami hoagie with Swiss cheese, mustard, and onions. Heck, they even serve a PB&J for $4. And if you like fish and chips, they nail it here. Stacky's also serves breakfast, featuring scrambled-egg sandwiches and south-of-the-border egg dishes. An order of crispy fries is enough for two.

2315 Lillie Ave., Summerland. ℂ **805/969-9908.** Most menu items under $10. AE, DISC, MC, V. Mon–Fri 6:30am–7:30pm; Sat–Sun 7am–7:30pm. 5 min. on the freeway from Santa Barbara—take the Summerland exit, turn left under the freeway, and then take the 1st right.

7 THE OJAI VALLEY ★

35 miles E of Santa Barbara; 88 miles NW of L.A.

In a crescent-shaped valley between Santa Barbara and Ventura, surrounded by mountain peaks, lies Ojai (pronounced *Oh*-hi). It's a beautifully serene environment, selected by Frank Capra as Shangri-La, the legendary utopia of his 1936 classic *Lost Horizon.* The spectacularly tranquil setting has made Ojai a mecca for artists and a large population of New Age spiritualists, drawn by the area's mystical beauty.

Life is low key in the Ojai Valley. Perhaps the most excitement generated all year happens during the first week of June, when the **Ojai Music Festival** draws world-renowned classical artists to perform in the Libbey Bowl amphitheater (for more information, call ℂ **805/646-2094** or visit www.ojaifestival.org).

ESSENTIALS

GETTING THERE   The 45-minute drive south from Santa Barbara to Ojai is along two-lane Highway 150, a road that's as curvaceous as it is stunning. From Los Angeles, take U.S. 101 north to Highway 33, which winds through eucalyptus groves to meet Highway 150—the trip takes about 90 minutes. Highway 150 is called Ojai Avenue in the town center and is the village's primary thoroughfare.

| Fun Fact

While in Ojai, you're bound to hear folks wax poetic about the "pink moment"—a phenomenon first noticed by the earliest Native American valley dwellers, when the brilliant sunset over the nearby Pacific is reflected onto the mountainside, creating an eerily beautiful pink glow.

VISITOR INFORMATION   The **Ojai Valley Chamber of Commerce & Visitors Bureau,** 201 S. Signal St., Ojai, CA 93023 (© **805/646-8126;** www.ojaichamber.org), has free area maps, brochures, and the *Visitor's Guide to the Ojai Valley,* which lists galleries and events. It's open Monday through Friday from 9am to 4pm.

EXPLORING THE TOWN & VALLEY

Ojai is home to more than 35 artists working in a variety of media; most have home studios and are represented in one of several galleries in town. The best for jewelry and smaller pieces is **HumanArts,** 310 E. Ojai Ave. (© **805/646-1525;** www.humanarts gallery.com). It also has a home-accessories annex, **HumanArts Home,** 246 E. Ojai Ave. (© **805/646-8245**). Artisans band together each October for an organized **Artists' Studio Tour** (© **805/646-8126;** www.ojaiarttour.com). It's fun to drive from studio to studio at your own pace, meeting artists and perhaps purchasing some of their work. Ojai's most famous artist was world-renowned Beatrice Wood, who worked until her death in 1998 at 104. Her whimsical sculpture and luminous pottery are internationally acclaimed, and her spirit is still a driving force in Ojai.

Strolling the Spanish arcade shops downtown and the surrounding area will yield a treasure trove, including open-air **Bart's Books,** Matilija Street at Canada Street (© **805/ 646-3755**), an Ojai fixture for many years. Antiques hounds head for **Treasures of Ojai,** 110 N. Signal St. (© **805/646-2852**), an indoor antiques mall packed to the rafters with treasures, trash, and everything in between.

Residents of the Ojai Valley *love* their equine companions—miles of bridle paths are painstakingly maintained, and HORSE CROSSING signs are everywhere.

Ojai has long been a haven for several esoteric sects of metaphysical and philosophical beliefs. The **Krotona Institute and School of Theosophy,** 46 Krotona Hill (© **805/ 646-7679**), has been in the valley since 1926, and visitors are welcome at their library and bookstore.

In the **Lake Casitas Recreation Area** (© **805/649-2233;** www.lakecasitas.info for visitor information), the beautiful Lake Casitas boasts nearly 32 miles of shoreline and was the site of the 1984 Olympic canoeing and rowing events. You can rent rowboats and small powerboats year-round from the **boathouse** (© **805/649-2043**) or enjoy picnicking and camping by the lakeside. Because the lake serves as a domestic water supply, swimming is not allowed. From Highway 150, turn left onto Santa Ana Road, and then follow the signs to the recreation area.

When Ronald Coleman saw **Shangri-La** in *Lost Horizon,* he was really admiring the Ojai Valley. To visit the spot where he stood for his view, drive east on Ojai Avenue, up the hill, and stop at the stone bench near the top—the sight is spectacular.

Blue Iguana Inn ★ (Kids) (Value)   The Mission-style architecture, colorful Southwestern decor, and artwork by local artists (most of which are for sale) are just a few of the highlights of this small, charming hotel. The double rooms at the Blue Iguana are reasonably priced, and the fact that they are also equipped with clean, modern kitchens makes the inn an even bigger value for cook-at-home types. There's even a detached, private two-bedroom bungalow with 1¹/₂ bathrooms and a full kitchen starting at $229. Kids can play croquet on the large open lawn while parents take a breather under the shady oaks; on hot summer days it's straight to the pool for everyone. The icing on the cake is the friendly, helpful staff, which makes the Blue Iguana an excellent all-around choice. Heck, they even offer spa treatments. *Tip:* Be sure to visit their website for package deals.

11794 N. Ventura Ave., Ojai, CA 93023. ℰ **805/646-5277.** Fax 805/640-2866. www.blueiguanainn.com. 23 units. Rates $119–$155 double; $149–$268 suite; $219–$249 cottage. AE, DC, DISC, MC, V. **Amenities:** Pool; spa services; free Wi-Fi; free local calls. *In room:* A/C, TV, kitchen, coffeemaker, hair dryer.

Ojai Valley Inn & Spa ★★★   In 1923, Hollywood architect Wallace Neff designed the clubhouse that's now the focal point of this quintessentially Spanish Colonial–style resort, one of the top in the nation. The inn has a sprawling Mediterranean estate ambience and provides gracious, elegant service, and luxurious amenities. The jewel of the resort is 31,000-square-foot Spa Ojai, where stylish spa treatments—some modeled after Native American traditions—are administered inside a beautifully designed, exquisitely tiled Spanish-Moorish complex. Mind- and body-fitness classes, art classes, nifty workout machines, and a sparkling outdoor pool complete the relaxation choices. Many guest rooms have fireplaces, and most have sofas, writing desks, and secluded terraces or balconies that open onto expansive views of the valley and the mountains. Take advantage of the scenery via the resort's 220 tree-shaded acres with jogging trails and horseback riding facilities. Golfers can book a tee time at the inn's oak-studded Senior PGA Tour golf course. All guests have complimentary access to Spa Ojai with a scheduled spa treatment ($20 access fee without a scheduled spa treatment), plus free use of the fitness center, selected exercise classes, driving range, and bicycles.

905 Country Club Rd. (off Hwy. 33), Ojai, CA 93023. ℰ **800/422-6524** or 805/646-1111. Fax 805/646-7969. www.ojairesort.com. 308 units. $450–$650 double; from $600 suite. AE, DC, DISC, MC, V. Free self- and valet parking. Pets accepted with $35-per-night fee and advance notice. **Amenities:** 4 restaurants; outdoor heated 60-ft. lap pool; championship golf course; 4 tennis courts; fitness center; full-service spa; Jacuzzi; complimentary bikes; Camp Ojai for children; concierge; in-room massage; laundry service; dry cleaning. *In room:* A/C, TV w/pay movies, fax, dataport, minibar, coffeemaker, hair dryer, iron, safe, Nintendo.

WHERE TO DINE
Expensive

In addition to the choices below, check out "world famous" **Deer Lodge,** 2261 Maricopa Hwy. (ℰ **805/646-4256;** www.ojaideerlodge.net), the latest incarnation of Ojai's favorite hippie-biker hangout on Highway 33, a few minutes north of Ojai. In the valley's gorgeous foothills, the building dates back to the Depression, when it served as a country store with bait and hunting supplies for local sportsmen, but new owners have been busy sprucing the place up and expanding to include a live stage in the bar, enclosed outdoor dining, and a hearty lodge menu with enough contemporary touches to bring in an upscale, yet adventuresome, clientele.

The Ranch House ★★ CALIFORNIA   This restaurant has been placing an emphasis on the freshest vegetables, fruits, and herbs since opening its doors in 1965, long before this practice became a national craze. Freshly snipped sprigs from the restaurant's lush herb garden will aromatically transform your simple meat, fish, or game dish into a work of art. From an appetizer of cognac-laced liver pâté served with its own chewy rye bread to desserts such as fresh raspberries with sweet Chambord cream, the ingredients always shine through. And you'll love the setting, for the Ranch House offers alfresco dining year-round on the wooden porch facing the scenic valley, as well as in the romantic garden amid twinkling lights and stone fountains.

S. Lomita Ave. ℂ **805/646-2360**. www.theranchhouse.com. Reservations recommended. Main courses $21–$33; Sun brunch $22. AE, DC, DISC, MC, V. Tues–Fri 5:30–8:30pm; Sat 5:30–6:30pm or 8–8:30pm; Sun 12:30am–7:30pm. From downtown Ojai, take Hwy. 33 north to El Roblar Dr. Turn left, and then left again at Lomita Ave.

Suzanne's Cuisine ★★ CONTEMPORARY EUROPEAN   Enjoy a great meal in a comfortably sophisticated setting at this local favorite, where every little touch bespeaks a preoccupation with quality details. Ask for a table on the covered outdoor patio, where lush greenery frames a casual setting warmed by a fireplace; when it rains, a plastic curtain descends to keep water out without losing that airy garden feel. Favorites from a seasonal menu include the lunch-only Southwest salad (wild, brown, and jasmine rice tossed with smoked turkey, feta cheese, veggies, and green chiles) and pepper-and-sesame encrusted ahi, served at dinner sautéed or seared (your choice). From seafood specialties to Italian recipes from chef and owner Suzanne Roll's family, everything is fresh and natural. Veggies are crisply al dente, and even the occasional cream sauce tastes light and healthy. Don't skip dessert.

502 W. Ojai Ave. ℂ **805/640-1961**. www.suzannescuisine.com. Reservations recommended. Main courses $8–$16 lunch, $15–$34 dinner. MC, V. Wed–Mon 11:30am–2:30pm and 5:30–close.

Moderate

Boccali's ★ ITALIAN   This small, wood-frame restaurant among citrus groves is a pastoral spot where patrons eat at picnic tables under umbrellas and oak trees, or inside at tables covered with red-and-white checked oilcloths. Pizza is the main dish served, topped California-style with the likes of crab, garlic, shrimp, and chicken. I think Boccali's lasagna (served piping hot *en casserole*) would win a statewide contest hands down. Fresh lemonade, from fruit plucked from local trees, is the drink of choice. Come hungry, and plan on sharing.

3277 Ojai–Santa Paula Rd. ℂ **805/646-6116**. www.boccalis.com. Reservations recommended for dinner. Pizza $9–$23; pasta $7–$16. No credit cards. Mon–Tues 4–9pm; Wed–Sun noon–9pm.

The Oak Pit (Kids) BARBECUE   This stick-to-your-ribs joint on the road between Ojai and Ventura is worth building up an appetite for. The rust-colored shack doesn't have much going for it—just some gingham curtains, a few tables indoors and out, and stacks of wood for firing up the barbecue—but generous portions of slowly oak-smoked meats will have dedicated carnivores coming back for more. Barbecue tri-tip brisket, ham, pork, Cajun sausage, and chicken—they're all served up in sandwiches or full dinners, with available sides of coleslaw, potato salad, fries, baked beans, and corn on the cob.

820 N. Ventura Ave. (Hwy. 33), Oak View. ℂ **805/649-9903**. Reservations not accepted. Sandwiches $6; main courses $9–$13. AE, DISC, MC, V. Tues–Thurs and Sun 11am–8:30pm; Fri–Sat 11am–9pm.

8 EN ROUTE TO LOS ANGELES: VENTURA

15 miles SW of Ojai; 74 miles NW of L.A.

Snuggled between rolling foothills and the sparkling blue Pacific Ocean, Ventura may not have the cultural and gastronomic appeal of Los Angeles or even Santa Barbara, but it does boast the picturesque setting and clean sea breezes typical of California coastal towns. Southland antiques hounds have long reveled in Ventura's quirky collectible markets, but trendy home-decor shops, coffeehouses, wine bars, and fashionable restaurants are providing another lure for time-pressed vacationers who zip up from L.A. to charming bed-and-breakfasts. Ventura is also the headquarters and main point of embarkation for Channel Islands National Park (see below).

Most travelers don't bother exiting U.S. 101 for a closer look. But think about stopping to while away a few hours around lunchtime. Ventura's unforced charm might even convince you to spend a night.

ESSENTIALS

GETTING THERE   If you're traveling northbound on U.S. 101, exit at California Street; southbound, take the Main Street exit. If you're coming west on Highway 33 from Ojai, there's also a Main Street exit. By the way, don't let the directions throw you off; because of the curve of the coastline, the ocean is not always to the west, but often southward.

VISITOR INFORMATION   For a visitor's guide and genial answers to any questions you might have, stop in at the **Ventura Visitors & Convention Bureau,** 89-C S. California St., Ventura, CA 93001 (© **800/483-6214** or 805/648-2075; www.ventura-usa.com).

EXPLORING THE TOWN

Much of Ventura's recent development has taken place along the **Main Street,** the town's historic center, which grew outward from the Spanish mission of San Buenaventura (see below). The best section for strolling is between the mission (to the north) and Fir Street (to the south). While many of the antiques and thrift stores are no more, you'll find plenty of window-shopping opportunities in the revitalized downtown area.

Ventura stretches south to one of California's most picturesque harbors (the departure point for the Channel Islands; see section 9, below), but the town also has its own **pier** at the end of California Street. Well maintained and favored by area fishers, the picturesque wooden pier is the longest of its kind in the state.

Mission San Buenaventura   Founded in 1782 (current buildings date from 1815) and still in use for daily services, this whitewashed and red-tile church lent its style to the contemporary civic buildings across the street. Step back in time by touring the mission's inside garden, where you can examine the antique water pump and olive press once essential to daily life here. The mission is small and near the rest of Ventura's action. Pick up a self-guided tour brochure in the adjacent gift shop for the modest donation of $2 per adult, 50¢ per child.

211 E. Main St. © **805/643-4318.** www.sanbuenaventuramission.org. Admission donation of $2 for adults and 50¢ for children. Mon–Fri 10am–5pm; Sat 9am–5pm; Sun 10am–4pm.

San Buenaventura City Hall   This majestic neoclassical building was built in 1912 as the Ventura County Courthouse. It sits on the hillside, overlooking old downtown and the ocean. To either side on Poli Street are some of Ventura's best-preserved and most ornate late-19th- and early-20th-century houses. Notice the carved heads of Franciscan friars adorning the facade inside and out.

501 Poli St. (C) **805/654-7800**. www.ci.ventura.ca.us.

Ventura County Museum of History & Art   This museum is worth visiting for its Native American Room, filled with Chumash treasures, and its Pioneer Room, which contains a collection of artifacts from the Mexican-American War (1846–48). The art gallery features exhibits of local painters and photographers, and the museum has an enormous archive (20,000 and counting) of photos of Ventura County from its origins to the present. There is also a small archaeological museum across Main Street from the main building. Allow 1 to 2 hours for your visit.

89 S. California St. (C) **805/653-0323**. www.venturamuseum.org. Free admission. Tues–Thurs and Sat–Sun 11am–6pm; Fri 11am–8pm.

WHERE TO STAY

Crowne Plaza Ventura Beach ★ (Kids)   What this former Holiday Inn lacks in cachet it more than makes up for in location and convenience. As for location, the 12-story Crowne Plaza is Ventura's only beachfront property, is right off Highway 101, has ocean views from every guest room, is directly in front of a prime surf spot, and is a 5-minute walk from the shops and restaurants of downtown Ventura, so you don't need to use your car to get around. As for convenience, the hotel offers perks that the whole family will enjoy, including a large heated outdoor pool, a game room, a fitness center, and instant beach access. You'll also enjoy the adjacent walking/jogging/biking that winds along the coast—great for a romantic sunset stroll. The entire hotel was completely gutted and renovated in 2006 at a cost of $15 million; guest room improvements include very comfortable beds, over-size desks with handy outlets and high-speed Internet jacks, and 27-inch TVs, but it's the shimmering ocean views from the balconies that are the still the hotel's best feature. Also on the property is the **C-Street** restaurant, offering a California-inspired menu with dishes made from locally sourced organic foods, and the **AQUA Beachfront Bar** offering ocean-view outdoor seating. Pets are welcome as well, and dogs receive a special welcome package upon arrival.

450 E. Harbor Blvd., Ventura, CA 93001. (C) **800/842-0800** or 805/648-2100. Fax 805/653-6202. www. cpventura.com. 258 units. $99–$299 double. AE, DC, DISC, MC, V. Pets accepted for $30 fee. **Amenities:** Restaurant; bar and lounge; heated outdoor pool; game room; business room; laundry service; dry cleaning; covered parking. *In room:* A/C, TV, high-speed Internet access, coffeemaker, hair dryer, iron.

WHERE TO DINE

71 Palm Restaurant ★ FRENCH COUNTRY   Situated in a beautifully restored 1910 Craftsman, this country-French restaurant is a pleasant change of pace. Upstairs tables have an ocean view, while downstairs a crackling wood fire warms diners. Chef Didier Poirier hails from Le Mans, France, and takes an earnest approach to traditional specialties such as steak au poivre with french fries, New Zealand rack of lamb Provençal style, or homemade pâté served with crusty bread and tangy pickles. Poirier also dabbles with vegetarian dishes and pastas, and every night the cuisine of a different region of France is highlighted.

71 N. Palm St. (btw. Main and Poli sts.). (C) **805/653-7222**. www.71palm.com. Reservations recommended. Main courses $11–$28; lunch $5–$16. AE, DC, DISC, MC, V. Mon–Fri 11:30am–2:30pm; Mon–Sat 5–9:30pm.

Taquería Vallarta (Value) MEXICAN   There's no better place to find a snapshot of
Ventura than at the Taquería Vallarta, where young, old, rich, poor, Anglo, and Latino
come for Mexican-style comfort food. There's nothing fancy here—it's your standard
order-at-the-counter then slide-into-your-Formica-booth kind of joint, but that's no
problem. The *carnitas* are among the best you'll find anywhere, perfect in a burrito, and
the *carne asada* is best in the enchiladas. Don't forget to dress up your dishes with the
fresh salsas, limes, and chile peppers available at the condiment bar. For fans of great,
cheap Mexican food, Taquería Vallarta's a must.

278 E. Main St. *℡* **805/643-3037.** Main courses $4–$8. DC, DISC, MC, V. Mon–Fri 9:30am–9pm; Sat–Sun
7:30am–9pm.

9 CHANNEL ISLANDS NATIONAL PARK ★

Approximately 40 miles W (offshore) of Ventura

There's nothing like a visit to the Channel Islands for discovering the sense of awe explorers must have felt more than 400 years ago. It's miraculous what 25 miles of ocean can
do, for compared to the mainland, this is wild and empty land, and only 55,000 visitors
a year come to the islands. Whether you approach them by sea or air, you'll be bowled
over by how untrammeled they remain despite neighboring Southern California's teeming masses.

Channel Islands National Park encompasses the five northernmost islands of the
eight-island chain: Santa Barbara, Anacapa, Santa Cruz, Santa Rosa, and San Miguel.
The park also protects the ocean 1 nautical mile offshore from each island, thereby pro-
hibiting oil drilling, shipping, and other industrial uses.

The islands are the meeting point of two distinct marine ecosystems: The cold waters
of Northern California and the warmer currents of Southern California swirl together
here, creating an awesome array of marine life. On land, the isolation from mainland
influences has allowed distinct species—including the island fox and the night lizard—to
evolve and survive here. The islands are also the most important seabird-nesting area in
Southern California and home to one of the biggest seal- and sea-lion-breeding colonies
in the United States.

ESSENTIALS

VISITOR INFORMATION   Each of the five islands is distinct and takes some fore-
thought to reach. Odds are that you're only going to visit one island on a given trip, so
it's a good idea to study your options before going. Visit the **Channel Islands National
Park Headquarters and Visitor Center,** 1901 Spinnaker Dr., Ventura, CA 93001
(*℡* **805/658-5730;** www.nps.gov/chis), to get acquainted with the programs and individual personalities of the islands through maps and displays. Rangers run interpretive
programs both on the islands and at the center year-round.

GETTING THERE   Island Packers, near the visitor center at 1691 Spinnaker Dr.
(*℡* **805/642-7688** for recorded information, or 805/642-1393 for reservations; www.
islandpackers.com), is the park's main concessionaire for boat transportation to and from
the islands. Daylong tours are offered daily year-round to Anacapa and Santa Cruz; the
price to Anacapa is $46 for adults, $42 for seniors, and $32 for children ages 3 to 12
(Santa Cruz is slightly higher). A half-day trip is also offered to Anacapa on Saturdays.
Trips to Santa Rosa and San Miguel operate weekly May through October; boats to Santa

Barbara Island are less frequent. Boats to Anacapa leave from the Channel Islands Harbor in Oxnard, 15 minutes south of Ventura. Also see Santa Barbara–based **Truth Aquatics,** under "Diving," below.

Another option, for visiting Santa Rosa Island only, is **Channel Islands Aviation,** 305 Durley Ave., Camarillo (✆ 805/987-1301; www.flycia.com), which flies nine-passenger, fixed-wing aircraft. Flying time to Santa Rosa is 25 minutes. The fare is $160 per person for adults, $135 for children 2 to 12, which includes a guided island tour with a ranger via four-wheel-drive. Campers (that is, people camping) are flown over for about $250 round-trip (these flights scheduled on demand).

THE WEATHER   The climate is mild, with little variation in temperature year-round, but the weather is still unpredictable; 30-mph winds can blow for days, fog banks can settle in and smother the islands for weeks, and winter rains can turn trails into mud baths. In general, plan on wind, lots of sun (bring sunscreen), cool nights, and the possibility of hot days. Water temperatures are in the 50s and 60s Fahrenheit (10s–20s Celsius) year-round. If you're camping, bring a good tent. (If you don't know the difference between a good and a bad tent, the island wind will gladly demonstrate it for you.)

CAMPING   Camping is legal on all the park-owned islands but limited to a certain number of campers per night, depending on the island. Fires and pets are prohibited on all the islands. You must bring everything you'll need; there are no supplies on any of the islands. To reserve camping permits, call ✆ 800/365-CAMP or log on to **http://reservations. nps.gov**. The rate is about $20 per night, per site.

EXPLORING THE ISLANDS

ANACAPA   Most people who visit the park come to Anacapa. It's 14 nautical miles from Ventura, an easy day trip—it takes about an hour to reach by boat. At only 1¼ square miles, Anacapa—actually three small islets divided by narrow stretches of ocean—is only marginally larger than Santa Barbara and, consequently, not a place for those who need a lot of space. Only East Anacapa is open to visitors, as the other two islets are important brown pelican breeding areas. Several trails on the island will take you to beautiful overlooks of clear-watered coves and wild ocean. **Arch Rock,** a natural land bridge, is visible from the landing cove, where you'll clamber up 154 stairs to the island's flat top.

Camping is allowed on East Anacapa year-round, but don't bring more than you can carry the half mile from the landing cove. Bring earplugs and steer clear of the foghorn, which can cause permanent hearing damage. Most of the waters around the island, including the landing cove, are protected as a National Marine Preserve, where divers can look but not take anything. Pack a good wet suit, mask, fins, and snorkel; you can dive right off the landing-cove dock.

SANTA CRUZ   By far the biggest of the islands—nearly 100 square miles—Santa Cruz is also the most diverse. It has huge canyons, year-round streams, beaches, cliffs, the highest mountain in the Channel Islands (2,450 ft.), now-defunct early cattle and sheep ranches, and Native American Chumash village sites—2,000 Chumash were probably living on the island when Cabrillo first visited in 1542. The island also hosts seemingly endless displays of flora and fauna, including 680 species of plants, 45 of which are multi-island endemics and eight of which are single-island endemics; 140 land-bird species; and a small group of other land animals, including the island fox.

Most of the island is still privately owned: The Nature Conservancy holds the western three-quarters. When the park service took over the eastern end from the Gherini family, owners of a sheep ranch here, it eliminated the island's formerly exorbitant landing and camping fees, but it also eliminated the Channel Islands' only noncamping overnight options; the Gherinis currently use the ranch house and adobe bunkhouse at Scorpion Ranch under a special-use-and-occupancy permit.

Valdez Cave (aka Painted Cave, for its colorful rock types, lichens, and algae) is one of the largest and deepest known sea caves in the world. The huge cave stretches nearly ¼ mile into the island and is nearly 100 feet wide. The entrance ceiling rises 160 feet, and in the spring, a waterfall tumbles over the opening. On the northwest end of the island, the cave can only be entered via dinghy or kayak.

SANTA ROSA The second-largest of the chain, windy Santa Rosa also has a ranching past—one that ended in 1998 in a storm of controversy that pitted the National Park Service against both environmental groups and the 97-year-old Vail & Vickers cattle ranch. The cows are all gone now, taking with them a slice of California history. In the meantime, the island's native vegetation has begun to recover. Santa Rosa is home to a large concentration of endangered plant species, 34 of which occur only on the islands. And like Santa Cruz, Santa Rosa is home to the diminutive island fox, a tiny cousin of the gray fox that has become nearly fearless as it has evolved in the predator-free island environment. They'll walk right through your camp if you let them. Santa Rosa also has great beaches, a benefit somewhat outweighed by the nearly constant winds.

SAN MIGUEL People often debate what's the wildest place left in the Lower 48. They bat around such names as Montana, Colorado, and Idaho, but rarely does anyone consider San Miguel, 55 miles off Ventura. They should, for this 9,325-acre island is a wild, wild place. The wind blows constantly, and the island can be shrouded in fog for days at a time. Human presence is definitely not the status quo here.

Visitors land at Cuyler Harbor, a half-moon-shaped cove on the island's east end. Arriving here is like arriving on earth the day it was made: perfect water, perfect sand, outrageously blue water. Seals bask on the offshore rocks. The island's two most interesting features are the **Caliche Forest,** which sort of petrified when the wind exposed sandstone casts of trees that once stood on the island, and **Point Bennett,** the outrageous-sounding (and -smelling) breeding ground of four species of seals and sea lions. In winter, up to 50,000 pinnipeds carpet the beach; their barking is deafening.

The waters around San Miguel are the richest and most dangerous of all the islands. The island's 27 miles of rocky coastline is exposed to wave action from all sides—many ships have sunk here. A 3-foot-tall stone cross stands in memory of Juan Rodríguez Cabrillo, the Spanish explorer credited with being the first European to see the Channel Islands in 1542. Although his grave has never been found, Cabrillo is believed to be buried at sea, near Catalina Island.

SANTA BARBARA As you come upon Santa Barbara Island after a typical 3-hour crossing, you'll think that someone took a single, medium-size, grassy hill, ringed it with cliffs, and plunked it down in the middle of the ocean. When you drop anchor, you'll realize that your initial perception is basically on target. Landwise, there's just not a lot here. But the upside is that, of all the islands, Santa Barbara gives you the best sense of what it's like to be stranded on a desert isle. Being on Santa Barbara, far enough out to sea that the mainland is almost invisible, gives you an idea of just how immense the Pacific really is.

Other than the landing cove, there's no access to the water's edge. The snorkeling in the chilly cove is great. You can hike the entire 639-acre island in a few hours; then it's time to stare out to sea. You won't be let down. The cliffs and rocks are home to elephant seals, sea lions, and swarms of seabirds such as you'll never see on the mainland. There's also a small campground, pit toilets, and a tiny museum chronicling island history.

THE EXTRA MILE: EXPLORING THE COASTLINE & WATERS OFF THE CHANNEL ISLANDS

DIVING   A good portion of Channel Islands National Park is underwater. In fact, almost as many visitors come to dive the waters as ever set foot *on* the islands. Divers come from all over to explore stunning kelp forests, pinnacles, and underwater caves, all with the best visibility in California. Everything from sea snails and urchins to orcas and great white sharks call these waters home.

Truth Aquatics, in Santa Barbara (© **805/962-1127;** www.truthaquatics.com), is the best provider of single- and multiday dive trips to all the islands. They also offer single- and multiday hiking, kayaking, and fishing tours. **Ventura Dive & Sport** (© **805/650-6500;** www.venturadive.com) also leads trips, including a Discover Program for novice and uncertified divers accompanied by an instructor. **Channel Islands Scuba** in Thousand Oaks (© **805/230-9995;** www.cisdivers.com) and **Pacific Scuba** in Oxnard (© **805/984-2566;** www.pacificscuba.com) also lead regular trips, as do boats from San Pedro and other Southern California ports.

SEA KAYAKING   One of the best ways to explore the fascinating coastline of the islands is by sea kayak. The excursions allow you to explore sea caves and rock gardens. Fares generally run about $175 per person for full-day trips; channel crossing by charter boat, equipment, and brief lessons are included. Two- and three-day adventures to Santa Rosa—campsite, camp gear, and guide included—are offered for $275 to $340 (you'll need to bring your own food, sleeping bag, and tent). **Aquasports** (© **800/773-2309** or 805/968-7231; www.islandkayaking.com) operates most trips out of Ventura Harbor, and **Paddle Sports of Santa Barbara** (© **888/254-2094** or 805/899-4925; www.kayak sb.com) leads similar excursions.

Los Angeles

by Matthew Richard Poole

The allure of L.A.—for better or for worse—is undeniable. Los Angelenos know their city will never have the sophisticated style of Paris or the historical riches of Rome, but they cheerfully lay claim to living in the most entertaining city in the United States, if not the world. It really is warm and sunny most days of the year, movie stars actually do live and dine among the commoners, and you can't swing a cellphone without hitting an in-line skater at the beach.

L.A. can feel like an amusement park, as the line between fantasy and reality is often obscured. From the unattainable, anachronistic glamour of Beverly Hills to the vibrant street energy of the Venice Boardwalk, each of the city's diverse neighborhoods is like its own mini–theme park, offering a unique kind of adventure.

Drive down Sunset Boulevard and you'll see what I mean: The billboards are racier, the fashions trendier, the cars fancier, the bodies sexier, the sun brighter, and the energy higher than any place you've ever been.

Darlin', you ain't in Kansas anymore—you're in La-La Land. So let's go play.

1 ORIENTATION

GETTING THERE
By Plane
LAX & the Other Los Angeles–Area Airports

There are five airports in the Los Angeles area. Most visitors fly into **Los Angeles International Airport** (© **310/646-5252;** www.lawa.org/lax), better known as LAX. This behemoth—ranked fifth in the world for number of passengers handled—is situated oceanside, between Marina del Rey and Manhattan Beach. LAX is a convenient place to land; it's located within minutes of Santa Monica and the beaches, and not more than a half-hour from downtown, Hollywood, and the Westside (depending on traffic of course). Despite its huge size, the nine-terminal airport has a straightforward, easy-to-understand design. Free blue, green, and white **shuttle buses** connect the terminals and stop in front of each ticket building. Special minibuses accessible to travelers with disabilities are also available. **Travelers Aid of Los Angeles** (© **310/646-2270;** www.travelersaid.org) operates booths in each terminal.

Eight short-stay (and expensive) parking lots are within the main concourse building, and a long-stay park is on 96th Street and Sepulveda Boulevard. A free bus service runs between long-term parking and the terminals. For drivers picking up passengers, a free 24-hour **Cell Phone Waiting Lot** is at 9011 Airport Blvd. You can find extensive information about LAX—including maps, parking, and shuttle-van information, and links to weather forecasts—online at **www.lawa.org**. All car-rental agencies are in the neighborhood surrounding LAX, within a few minutes' drive; each provides a complimentary

Thousand Oaks
Canoga Park
27
405
5
210
2
SAN GABRIEL MOUNTAINS
ANGELES NATIONAL FOREST
Rancho Cucamonga
101
Burbank
Glendale
Pasadena
SANTA MONICA MTNS. NAT'L RECREATION AREA
Topanga
Sherman Oaks
North Hollywood
210
N9 N1
27
Hollywood
101
El Monte
605
39
30
66
Pomona
1
2
10
110
10
57
Ontario
Santa Monica
Inglewood
5
60
Whittier
83
71
LOS ANGELES
105
710
39
90
91
Corona
Manhattan Beach
Hermosa Beach
Redondo Beach
91
Fullerton
57
Torrance
110
605
1
405
Anaheim
55
Orange
518
Rancho Palos Verdes
San Pedro
22
Santa Ana
405
Long Beach
39
Huntington Beach
Costa Mesa
Irvine
73
5
Newport Beach
1
74
San
Pedro
Channel
San Juan Capistrano
Dana Point
San Clemente
5
Santa Catalina Island
Avalon
Outer Santa Barbara Channel
PACIFIC
OCEAN
U.S. Military Reservation
San Clemente Island
San Francisco
Sacramento
CALIFORNIA
Southern California
Los Angeles
0   20 mi
0   20 km

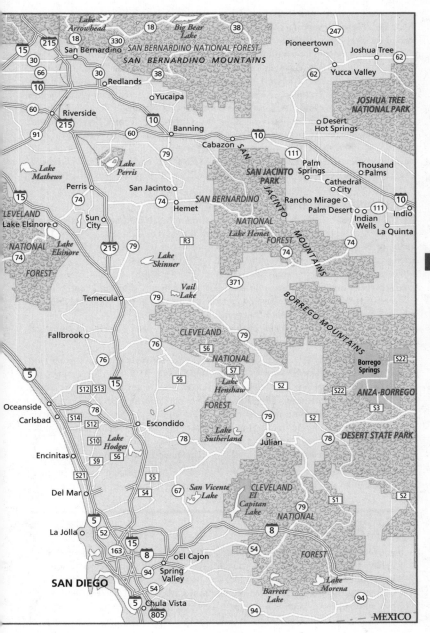

shuttle to and from the airport. For more information on car rentals, see "Getting Around," in chapter 3.

For some travelers, one of the area's smaller airports might be more convenient than LAX. **Bob Hope Airport** (2627 N. Hollywood Way, Burbank; © 818/840-8840; www.bobhopeairport.com) is the best place to land if you're headed for Hollywood or the valleys—and it's even closer to downtown L.A. than LAX. The small airport has especially good links to Las Vegas and other southwestern cities. **Long Beach Municipal Airport** (4100 Donald Douglas Dr., Long Beach; © 562/570-2600; www.lgb.org), south of LAX, is the best place to land if you're visiting Long Beach or northern Orange County and want to avoid L.A. **John Wayne Airport** (19051 Airport Way N., Anaheim; © 949/252-5200; www.ocair.com) is closest to Disneyland, Knott's Berry Farm, and other Orange County attractions. **Ontario International Airport** (Terminal Way, Ontario; © 909/937-2700; www.lawa.org/ont) is not a popular airport for tourists; businesspeople use it to head to San Bernardino, Riverside, and other inland communities. However, it's convenient if you're heading to Palm Springs and also a viable choice if you're staying in Pasadena.

Getting into Town from LAX

BY CAR To reach Santa Monica and other northern beach communities, exit the airport, take Sepulveda Boulevard north, and follow the signs to California 1 (Pacific Coast Hwy., or PCH) north. You *can* take the I-405 north, but you'll be sorry you did—that stretch of freeway is always heavily congested.

To reach Redondo, Hermosa, Newport, and the other southern beach communities, take Sepulveda Boulevard south and then follow the signs to California 1 south.

To reach Beverly Hills or Hollywood, exit the airport via Century Boulevard and then take I-405 north to Santa Monica Boulevard east.

To reach downtown or Pasadena, exit the airport, take Sepulveda Boulevard south, and then take I-105 east to I-110 north.

BY SHUTTLE Many city hotels provide free shuttles for their guests; ask when you make reservations. **SuperShuttle** (© 800/258-3826 or 310/782-6600; www.supershuttle.com) offers regularly scheduled minivans from LAX to any location in the city, as does **Prime Time Shuttle** (© 800/ RED-VANS [733-8267] or 310/536-7922; www.primetimeshuttle.com). Fares range from about $15 to $35 per person, depending on your destination. It's cheaper to cab it to most places if you're a group of three or more, but you might have to stop at other passengers' destinations before you reach your own. Reservations aren't needed for your arrival but are required for a return to the airport.

BY TAXI Taxis are located at the Arrivals level under the yellow sign outside each terminal. Be sure to ask for a list of prices to various major destinations before setting off.

(Tips) Traffic Tips

If you're renting a car at LAX, avoid arriving midweek in rush hour—particularly if you have to drive I-405. You'll save yourself several hours of stop-and-go misery. If you're driving to or from Santa Monica and Beverly Hills, West Hollywood, or Century City, try to avoid Santa Monica Boulevard. Wilshire and Pico boulevards, which run parallel to Santa Monica, are usually less congested.

The flat price between LAX and downtown Los Angeles is $42. Expect to pay at least $35 to Hollywood, $25 to Beverly Hills, $20 to Santa Monica, and $50 to $60 to the Valley and Pasadena. You'll also pay an airport surcharge of $2.50 for trips originating from LAX.

BY RAIL Budget-minded travelers heading to downtown, Universal City, or Long Beach can take L.A.'s Metro Rail service from LAX. An airport shuttle can take you to the Green Line light-rail station; from there, connections on the Blue, Gold, and Red lines can get you where you're headed. It's a good idea to contact your hotel for advice on the closest station. The service operates from 5am to midnight, and the combined fare is under $2—but you should be prepared to spend 1 to 2 hours in transit. Call the **Los Angeles County Metropolitan Transit Authority (MTA)** at ℂ **800/COMMUTE,** or see **www.mta.net** for information.

BY PUBLIC BUS The city's MTA buses also go between LAX and many parts of the city. Phone **MTA Airport Information** (ℂ **800/COMMUTE;** www.mta.net) for the schedules and fares. If you're arriving at LAX and your hotel is in Santa Monica, you can hop aboard the city's **Big Blue Bus** (ℂ **310/451-5444;** www.bigbluebus.com). It's a slow ride, but the price, 75¢, is hard to beat. Bus information is available in the baggage claim area of each LAX terminal.

By Car

Los Angeles is well connected to the rest of the United States by several major high-ways—in fact, L.A. has the highest rate of bank robberies in the U.S. because it's so easy to make a fast getaway. Among them are Interstate 5, which enters the state from the north; Interstate 10, which originates in Jacksonville, Florida, and terminates in Los Angeles; and U.S. 101, a scenic route that follows the western seaboard from Los Angeles north to the Oregon state line.

If you're driving **from the north,** you have two choices: the quick route, along I-5 through the middle of the state; or the scenic route along the coast. Heading south along I-5, you'll pass a small town called Grapevine. This marks the start of the mountain pass with the same name. Once you've reached the southern end of the pass, you'll be in the San Fernando Valley, which is the start of Los Angeles County. To reach the beach communities and L.A.'s Westside, take I-405 south (Hello traffic!); to get to Hollywood, take California 170 south to U.S. 101 south (this route is called the Hollywood Fwy. the entire way); I-5 will take you along the eastern edge of downtown and into Orange County.

If you're taking the **scenic coastal route** from the north, take U.S. 101 to I-405 or I-5, or stay on U.S. 101, following the instructions above to your destination.

If you're approaching **from the east,** you'll be coming in on I-10. For Orange County, take California 57 south. I-10 continues through downtown and terminates at the beach. If you're heading to the Westside, take I-405 north. To get to the beaches, take California 1 (PCH) north or south, depending on your destination.

From the south, head north on I-5 at the southern end of Orange County. I-405 splits off to the west; take this road to the Westside and beach communities. Stay on I-5 to reach downtown and Hollywood.

Here are some **driving times** if you're on one of those see-the-U.S.A. car trips: From Phoenix, it's about 350 miles, or 6 hours (okay, 7 if you drive the speed limit) to Los Angeles via I-10. Las Vegas is 265 miles northeast of Los Angeles (about a 4- or 5-hr. drive). San Francisco is 390 miles north of Los Angeles on I-5 (6–7 hr.), and San Diego is 115 miles south (about 2 hr.).

Amtrak (© **800/USA-RAIL;** www.amtrak.com) connects Los Angeles with about 500 American cities. As with plane travel along popular routes, fares fluctuate depending on the season and special promotions. As a general rule, heavily restricted advance tickets are competitive with similar airfares. Remember, however, that those low fares are for coach travel in reclining seats; private sleeping accommodations cost substantially more.

The L.A. train terminus is **Union Station,** 800 N. Alameda (© **213/617-0111**), on downtown's northern edge. Completed in 1939, this was the last of America's great train depots—a unique blend of Spanish Revival and Streamline Moderne architecture. From the station, you can take one of the taxis that line up outside; board the Metro Red Line to Hollywood or Universal City; or take the Metro Blue Line to Long Beach. If you're headed to the San Fernando Valley or Anaheim, Metrolink commuter trains leave from Union Station; call © **800/371-LINK** (www.metrolinktrains.com).

VISITOR INFORMATION
Information Centers

The **Los Angeles Convention and Visitors Bureau** (or **LA INC.;** © **800/228-2452** or 213/624-7300; www.discoverlosangeles.com) is the city's main source for information. In addition to maintaining an informative website, answering telephone inquiries, and sending free visitors kits, the bureau provides two **walk-in visitor centers:** downtown at 685 S. Figueroa St. at W. Seventh St. (Mon–Fri 9am–5pm), and in Hollywood at the Hollywood & Highland Center, 6801 Hollywood Blvd. at Highland Avenue (daily 10am–11pm).

Many Los Angeles–area communities also have their own information centers and often maintain detailed and colorful websites that are loaded with timely information. These include the following:

- The **Beverly Hills Visitors Bureau,** 239 S. Beverly Dr. (© **800/345-2210** or 310/248-1015; www.beverlyhillscvb.com), is open Monday through Friday from 8:30am to 5pm.
- The **Hollywood Arts Council,** P.O. Box 931056, Dept. 1995, Hollywood, CA 90093 (© **323/462-2355;** www.discoverhollywood.com), publishes the magazine *Discover Hollywood,* a biannual publication that contains listings and schedules for the area's many theaters, galleries, music venues, and comedy clubs; the current issue is always available online. You can also load up on visitor information at the **Hollywood Visitor Center,** 6801 Hollywood Blvd., Suite 237 (© **323/467-6412**), on the second level of the Hollywood & Highland mall (btw. Babylon Court and Awards Walk).
- The **West Hollywood Convention and Visitors Bureau,** 8687 Melrose Ave., M-26, West Hollywood, CA 90096 (© **800/368-6020** or 310/289-2525; www.visitwest hollywood.com), is located in the Pacific Design Center and is open Monday through Friday from 9am to 6pm.
- The **Santa Monica Convention and Visitors Bureau** (© **800/544-5319** or 310/393-7593; www.santamonica.com) is the best source for information about Santa Monica. The Palisades Park walk-up center is located near the Santa Monica Pier, at 1400 Ocean Ave. (btw. Santa Monica Blvd. and Broadway), and is open daily from 10am to 4pm. Also check out **www.malibu.org** for information about Malibu, to the northwest.
- The **Pasadena Convention and Visitors Bureau,** 171 S. Los Robles Ave. (© **626/795-9311;** www.pasadenacal.com), is open Monday through Friday from 8am to 5pm and Saturday from 10am to 4pm.

(Value) **Money-Saving Tourist Passes**

If you're the type who loves to cram as many tourist attractions as possible in one trip, then you might want to consider purchasing a **Hollywood CityPass** or **GO Los Angeles Card.** The CityPass ((*C*) **888/330-5008;** www.citypass.com) booklet includes tickets to four attractions, all within 2 blocks of each other: the **Hollywood Wax Museum, Star Line Tour of Hollywood, Redline Tours,** and the **Kodak Theatre Guided Tour** *or* **The Hollywood Museum.** Purchase the pass at any of the above attractions, or visit the CityPass website to buy advance passes online. The pass costs $50 for adults ($39 for kids 4–11) and will expire 9 days from the first use. Is it a good deal? If you use all the tickets, you end up saving about 45% over individual, full-price admission.

A better deal is the **GO Los Angeles Card** ((*C*) **800/887-9103;** www.golos angelescard.com). It offers free or discounted admission to more than 45 of L.A.'s most popular attractions, activities, and tours; has more flexibility (available in 1-, 2-, 3-, 5-, and 7-day increments over a 14-day period); and comes with a full-color guidebook that fits in your pocket. The 2-day card costs $89 for adults ($69 for kids 3–13) and doesn't need to be used on consecutive days. The 3-, 5-, and 7-day cards include admission to Universal Studios Hollywood (a great bargain). You can purchase the GO Cards via their website or at the Hollywood Visitor Information Center (6801 Hollywood Blvd. at Highland Ave.; (*C*) **323/467-6412**).

LOS ANGELES

14

ORIENTATION

OTHER INFORMATION SOURCES

L.A. Weekly (www.laweekly.com), a free listings magazine, is packed with information on current events around town. It's available from sidewalk news racks and in many stores and restaurants around the city; it also has a lively website.

The *Los Angeles Times* "**Calendar**" section of the Sunday paper, an excellent guide to the world of entertainment in and around L.A., includes listings of what's doing and where to do it. The *Times* also maintains a comprehensive website at **www.calendarlive. com**; once there, you can find departments with names such as "Southland Scenes," "Tourist Tips," "Family & Kids," and "Recreation & Fitness." Information is culled from the newspaper's many departments and is always up-to-date. If you want to check out L.A.'s most immediate news, the *Times's* main website is **www.latimes.com**.

Los Angeles magazine (**www.lamag.com**) is a glossy city-based monthly full of real news and pure gossip, plus guides to L.A.'s art, music, and food scenes. Its calendar of events gives an excellent overview of goings-on at museums, art galleries, musical venues, and other places. The magazine is available at newsstands around town and in other major U.S. cities; you can also access stories and listings from the current issue on the Internet. Web-surfers should visit @ L.A.'s website, **www.at-la.com**; its exceptional search engine provides links to more than 23,000 sites in the greater L.A. region, including destinations covered in chapter 15, "Side Trips from Los Angeles."

CITY LAYOUT

Los Angeles isn't a compact, cohesive city like San Francisco, but a sprawling suburbia comprising dozens of disparate communities on either the ocean or the flatlands of a huge desert basin. Ocean breezes push the city's infamous smog inland, through mountain passes, into the sprawl of the San Fernando and San Gabriel valleys. Downtown Los Angeles is in the center of the basin, about 12 miles east of the Pacific Ocean. Most visitors spend the bulk of their time along the coast or on the ever-trendy Westside (see "Neighborhoods in Brief," below, for details on all the city's sectors).

Main Arteries & Streets

An extensive system of toll-free, high-speed freeways connects the city's patchwork of communities. The system works well to get you where you need to be, although rush-hour (roughly 6–9am and 3–7pm) traffic is often bumper-to-bumper, particularly on the dreaded I-405. Here's an overview of the city's main freeways (best read with an L.A. map in hand):

U.S. 101, called the Ventura Freeway in the San Fernando Valley and the Hollywood Freeway in the city, runs across L.A. in a roughly northwest-southeast direction, from the San Fernando Valley to the center of downtown. You'll encounter heavy rush-hour traffic.

California 134 continues as the Ventura Freeway after U.S. 101 turns into the city and becomes the Hollywood Freeway. This branch of the Ventura Freeway continues directly east, through the valley towns of Burbank and Glendale, to I-210 (the Foothill Fwy.), which takes you through Pasadena and out toward the eastern edge of Los Angeles County.

I-5, otherwise known as the Golden State Freeway north of I-10 and the Santa Ana Freeway south of I-10, bisects downtown on its way from Sacramento to San Diego.

I-10, labeled the Santa Monica Freeway west of I-5 and the San Bernardino Freeway east of I-5, is the city's major east-west freeway, connecting the San Gabriel Valley with downtown and Santa Monica.

I-405, known as the San Diego Freeway, runs north-south through L.A.'s Westside, connecting the San Fernando Valley with LAX and southern beach areas. *Tip:* This is one of the area's busiest freeways; avoid it as much as possible (and like the plague during rush hour).

I-105, Los Angeles's newest freeway—called the Century Freeway—extends from LAX east to I-605.

I-110, commonly known as the Harbor Freeway, starts in Pasadena as California 110 (the Pasadena Fwy.); it becomes an interstate in downtown Los Angeles and runs directly south, where it dead-ends in San Pedro. The section that is now the Pasadena Freeway was Los Angeles's first freeway, known as the Arroyo Seco when it opened in 1940.

I-710, aka the Long Beach Freeway, runs in a north-south direction through East Los Angeles and dead-ends at Long Beach. Crammed with big rigs leaving the port in San Pedro in a rush, this is the ugliest and most dangerous freeway in California.

I-605, the San Gabriel River Freeway, runs from the I-405 near Seal Beach to the I-210 interchange at Duarte. It follows the San Gabriel River (hence the moniker), roughly paralleling the I-710 to the east. Most important, it gets you through the San Gabriel Valley up to the edge of the San Gabriel Mountains.

California 1—called Highway 1, Pacific Coast Highway, or simply PCH—is more of a scenic parkway than a freeway. It skirts the ocean, linking all of L.A.'s beach communities, from Malibu to the Orange Coast. It's often slow going due to all the stoplights but is far more scenic than the freeways.

A complex web of surface streets complements the freeways. From north to south, the major east-west thoroughfares connecting downtown to the beaches are **Sunset, Santa Monica, Wilshire, Olympic, Pico,** and **Venice boulevards.**

NEIGHBORHOODS IN BRIEF

Los Angeles can confuse newcomers in that downtown isn't the city center. The city itself is more of a juxtaposition of disparate communities that loosely form a metropolis (67 suburbs searching for a city, so they say). The best way to grasp the geography is to break it into six regions: Santa Monica and the beaches, L.A.'s Westside and Beverly Hills, Hollywood and West Hollywood, downtown, Pasadena, and—beyond the Hollywood Hills—the San Fernando Valley ("The Valley" to locals). Each encompasses a more-or-less distinctive patchwork of city neighborhoods and independently incorporated communities.

SANTA MONICA & THE BEACHES

These are nearly everyone's favorite L.A. communities and get my highest recommendation as the premier place to book a hotel during your vacation. The 60-mile beachfront stretching from Malibu to the Palos Verdes peninsula has milder weather and less smog than the inland communities, and traffic is nominally lighter, except on summer weekends. The towns along the coast all have a distinct mood and charm, and most are connected via a walk/bike path. They're listed below from north to south.

Malibu, at the northern border of Los Angeles County, 25 miles from downtown, was once a privately owned ranch—purchased in 1857 for 10¢ an acre and now the most expensive real estate in L.A. Today its 27 miles of wide beaches, beachfront cliffs, sparsely populated hills, and relative remoteness from the inner city make it popular with rich recluses such as Cher and Mel Gibson. Indeed, the resident lists of Malibu Colony and nearby Broad Beach—oceanfront strips of closely packed mansions—read like a who's who in Hollywood. With plenty of green space and dramatic rocky outcroppings, Malibu's rural beauty is unsurpassed in L.A., and surfers flock to "the 'Bu" for great, if crowded, waves.

Santa Monica, Los Angeles's premier beach community, is known for its festive ocean pier, stylish oceanfront hotels, artsy atmosphere, and large population of homeless residents (I know, that's an oxymoron, but it fits). Shopping is king here, especially along the Third Street Promenade, a pedestrian-only outdoor mall lined with dozens of shops and restaurants.

Venice Beach was created by tobacco mogul Abbot Kinney, who set out in 1904 to transform a worthless marsh into a resort town modeled after Venice, Italy—hence, the series of narrow canals connected by one-lane bridges that you'll see as you explore this refreshingly eclectic community. It was once infested with grime and crime, but gentrification has brought scores of great restaurants, boutiques, and rising property values for the canal-side homes and apartment duplexes. Even the movie stars are moving in: Dennis Hopper, Anjelica Huston, Nicolas Cage, and Julia Roberts reside in this pseudo-bohemian community. Some of L.A.'s most innovative and interesting architecture lines funky Main Street. But without question, Venice Beach is best known for its Ocean Front Walk, a nonstop Mardi Gras of thong-wearing skaters, vendors, fortunetellers, street musicians, and poseurs of all ages, colors, types, and sizes.

Marina del Rey, just south of Venice, is a somewhat quieter, more upscale waterside community best known for its manmade small-craft harbor, the largest of its kind in the world. Fittingly, it offers a wide variety of public boating opportunities, including fishing trips, harbor tours, dinner cruises, boat rentals, and private sailing charters.

ACCOMMODATIONS ■
The Ambrose **6**
Best Western Marina Pacific
   Hotel & Suites **26**
Cal Mar Hotel Suites **12**
Casa del Mar **17**
Casa Malibu **2**
Fairmont Miramar
   Hotel Santa Monica **8**
The Hotel California **15**
Huntley Santa Monica Beach **10**
Le Merigot **16**
Marina del Rey Marriott **27**
Marriott Los Angeles Airport **30**
Sea Shore Motel **20**
Sheraton Gateway Hotel **28**
Shutters on the Beach **18**
Travelodge at LAX **29**
Venice Beach House **23**
Westin Los Angeles Airport **31**

DINING ◆
Beau Rivage **1**
Boa Steakhouse **13**
Border Grill **11**
Bread & Porridge **5**
Duke's Malibu **3**
Gladstone's 4 Fish **4**
The Hump/Typhoon **19**
Jody Maroni's
   Sausage Kingdom **25**
Joe's Restaurant **22**
The Lobster **14**
Locanda del Lago **9**
Michael's **7**
Restaurant Hama
   (Hama Sushi) **24**
Sidewalk Café **21**

Manhattan, Hermosa, and **Redondo beaches** are laid-back, mainly residential neighborhoods with modest homes (except for oceanfront real estate), mild weather, and residents happy to have fled the L.A. hubbub. There are excellent beaches for volleyball, surfing, and tanning here, but when it comes to cultural activities, pickings can be slim. The restaurant scene, while limited, has been improving steadily, and some great new bars and clubs have opened near their respective piers.

L.A.'s Westside & Beverly Hills

The **Westside,** sandwiched between Hollywood and the city's coastal communities, includes some of Los Angeles's most prestigious neighborhoods, virtually all with names you're sure to recognize:

Beverly Hills is politically distinct from the rest of Los Angeles—a famous enclave best known for its palm tree–lined streets of palatial homes, famous residents (Jack Nicholson, Warren Beatty, and Annette Bening), and high-priced shops. But it's not all glitz and glamour; the healthy mix of filthy rich, wannabes, and tourists that peoples downtown Beverly Hills creates a unique—and often snobby-surreal—atmosphere.

West Hollywood is a key-shaped community whose epicenter is the intersection of Santa Monica and La Cienega boulevards. Nestled between Beverly Hills and Hollywood, this politically independent—and blissfully fast-food–free—town is home to some of the area's best restaurants, clubs, shops, and art galleries. WeHo, as it's come to be known, is also the center of L.A.'s gay community—you'll know you've arrived when you see the risqué billboards. Encompassing about 2 square miles, it's a pedestrian-friendly place with plenty of metered parking. Highlights include

the 1½ miles of Sunset Boulevard known as Sunset Strip, the chic Sunset Plaza retail strip, and the liveliest stretch of Santa Monica Boulevard.

Bel Air and **Holmby Hills,** located in the hills north of Westwood and west of Beverly Hills, are old-money residential areas featured prominently on most maps to the stars' homes.

Brentwood is best known as the famous backdrop to the O. J. Simpson melodrama. If Starbucks ever designed a neighborhood, this is what it would look like—a generic, relatively upscale mix of tract homes, restaurants, and strip malls. The Getty Center looms over Brentwood from its hilltop perch next to I-405.

Westwood, an urban village founded in 1929 and home to the University of California at Los Angeles (UCLA), used to be a hot destination for a night on the town, but it lost much of its appeal in the past decade due to overcrowding and even some minor street violence. Although Westwood is unlikely to regain its old charm, the vibrant culinary scene has brought new life to the village. Combined with the high concentration of movie theaters, it's now the premier L.A. destination for dinner and a flick.

Century City is a compact and rather bland high-rise area sandwiched between West Los Angeles and Beverly Hills. The primary draws here are the 20th Century Fox studios, Shubert Theatre, and the Westside Pavilion, a huge open-air shopping mall. Century City's three main thoroughfares are Century Park East, Avenue of the Stars, and Century Park West.

West Los Angeles is a label that generally applies to everything that isn't one of the other Westside neighborhoods. It's basically the area south of Santa Monica Boulevard, north of Venice

ACCOMMODATIONS ■
Avalon Hotel 9
Beverly Hills Hotel & Bungalows 7
Beverly Laurel Motor Hotel 33
Chamberlain West Hollywood 21
Chateau Marmont 22
Elan Hotel 32
Farmer's Daughter 35
Four Seasons Hotel Los Angeles at Beverly Hills 15
Hotel Angeleno Los Angeles 3
Hotel Palomar Los Angeles 4
Le Parc Suite Hotel 25
Mondrian 23
The Mosaic 8
The Orlando 37
The Standard 24
Sunset Tower 19

DINING ◆
The Apple Pan 5
Beacon 43
Fogo de Chão 34
Fraîche 42
Il Pastaio 12
The Ivy 16
Jar 31
Koi 27
La Cachette 6
Luckyfish 11
Lucques 29
Mastro's Steakhouse 13
Matsuhisa 40
Ortolan 36
The Palm 18
Providence 28
Republic 30
Spago Beverly Hills 14
Versailles 41

ATTRACTIONS ●
The Getty Center 2
Los Angeles County Museum of Art 38
Museum of Tolerance 10
Pacific Design Center 17
Peterson Automotive Museum 39
Schindler House 26
Skirball Cultural Center 1
Sunset Strip 20

Boulevard, east of Santa Monica and Venice, and west and south of Century City.

HOLLYWOOD

Yes, they still come to the mecca of the film industry—young hopefuls with stars in their eyes gravitate to this historic heart of L.A.'s movie production like moths fluttering to the glare of neon lights. But today's Hollywood is more illusion than industry. Many of the neighborhood's former movie studios have moved to more spacious venues in Burbank, the Westside, and other parts of the city.

Despite the downturn, visitors continue to flock to Hollywood's landmark attractions, such as the star-studded Walk of Fame and Grauman's Chinese Theatre. And now that the city's $1-billion, 30-year revitalization project is in full swing, Hollywood Boulevard is, for the first time in decades, showing signs of rising out of a seedy slump, with refurbished movie houses and stylish restaurants and clubs making a fierce comeback. The centerpiece Hollywood & Highland complex anchors the neighborhood, with shopping, entertainment, and a luxury hotel built around the beautiful Kodak Theatre designed specifically to host the Academy Awards (really, you'll want to poke your head into this gorgeous theater).

Melrose Avenue, scruffy but fun, is the city's funkiest shopping district, catering to often-raucous youth with second-hand and avant-garde clothing shops. There are also several good restaurants.

The stretch of Wilshire Boulevard running through the southern part of Hollywood is known as the **Mid-Wilshire** district, or the Miracle Mile. It's lined with tall, contemporary apartment houses and office buildings. The section just east of Fairfax Avenue, known as Museum Row, is home to almost a dozen museums, including the Los Angeles County Museum of Art, the La Brea Tar Pits, and that shrine to L.A. car culture, the Petersen Automotive Museum.

Griffith Park, up Western Avenue in the northernmost part of Hollywood, is one of the country's largest urban parks, home to the Los Angeles Zoo, the famous Griffith Observatory, and the outdoor Greek Theater.

DOWNTOWN

Despite the relatively recent construction of several major cultural and entertainment centers (such as the Walt Disney Concert Hall, L.A. LIVE, and Cathedral of Our Lady of the Angels) and a handful of trendy restaurants, L.A.'s downtown isn't the tourist hub that it would be in most cities. When it comes to entertaining visitors, the Westside, Hollywood, and beach communities are all far more popular.

Easily recognized by the tight cluster of high-rise offices—skyscrapers bolstered by earthquake-proof technology—the business center of the city is eerily vacant on weekends and evenings, but the outlying residential communities, such as Koreatown, Little Tokyo, Chinatown, and Los Feliz, are enticingly ethnic and vibrant. If you want a tan, head to Santa Monica, but if you want a refreshing dose of non-90210 culture, come here.

El Pueblo de Los Angeles Historic District, a 44-acre ode to the city's early years, is worth a visit. **Chinatown** is small and touristy, but can be plenty of fun for souvenir hunting or traditional dim sum. **Little Tokyo,** on the other hand, is a genuine gathering place for the Southland's Japanese population, with a wide array of shops and restaurants with an authentic flair.

Silver Lake, a residential neighborhood just north of downtown and adjacent to **Los Feliz** (home to the Los Angeles

ACCOMMODATIONS ■
Best Western Hollywood
Hills Hotel **4**
Days Inn Hollywood **14**
Magic Castle Hotel **13**
Roosevelt Hotel,
Hollywood **11**

DINING ◆
Campanile **30**
El Cholo **31**
Grace **22**
Katana Robata & Sushi Bar **17**
Katsuya Hollywood **7**
Kings Road Cafe **25**
The Little Door **24**
Musso & Frank Grill **15**
Osteria Mozza **21**
Pink's Hot Dogs **20**
Pizzeria Mozza **19**

Roscoe's House of
Chicken 'n' Waffles **8**
The Waffle **6**

ATTRACTIONS ●
Capital Records Building **5**
Craft & Folk Art Museum **28**
The Egyptian Theatre **16**
Farmers market &
The Grove **23**
Freeman House **10**
Griffith Observatory **1**
The HOLLYWOOD Sign **3**
Hollywood Walk of Fame **9**

Los Angeles County
Museum of Art **27**
Los Angeles Zoo **2**
Grauman's Chinese
Theatre **12**
Museum of the
American West **1**
Paramount Pictures **18**
Petersen Automotive
Museum **26**
Rancho La Brea Tar Pits **29**
Sunset Ranch
Hollywood Stables **3**

ACCOMMODATIONS ■
Hotel Figueroa **25**
Hotel Stillwell **23**
Millennium Biltmore Hotel Los Angeles **21**
Westin Bonaventure Hotel & Suites **19**

DINING ◆
Ciudad **18**
The Original Pantry Cafe **24**
Patina **12**
Philippe the Original **5**
R23 **10**
Tantra **2**
Water Grill **22**

ATTRACTIONS ●
Angelino Heights **3**
The Bradbury Building **16**
California Science Center **25**
Cathedral of Our Lady of the Angels **11**
Central Library **20**
Chinatown **4**
City Hall **13**
Dodger Stadium **1**
El Pueblo de Los Angeles Historic District
(Olvera Street) **6**
Grand Central Market **17**
Japanese American National Museum **9**
Museum of Contemporary Art/
Geffen Contemporary at MOCA **8**
Main Building **15**
Natural History Museum
of Los Angeles County **27**
Performing Arts Center of L.A. County **14**
L.A. Live/Staples Center **26**
Union Station **7**
University of Southern California (USC) **27**
Walt Disney Concert Hall **12**

LOS ANGELES

14

NEIGHBORHOODS IN BRIEF

Information ⓘ
Parking Ⓟ

W. Temple St.
S. Virgil Ave.
Commonwealth Ave.
Hoover St.
Benton Way
Rampart Blvd.
LAFAYETTE PARK
Westmoreland Ave.
S. Hoover St.
MacARTHUR PARK
W. 8th St.
W. 9th St.
San Marino St.
Westlake Ave.
S. Burlington Ave.
Bonnie Brae St.
S. Union Ave.
W. 11th St.
W. 12th St.
Magnolia Ave.
W. Pico Blvd.
W. Venice Blvd.
W. Washington Blvd.
W. 20th St.
Santa Monica Freeway
W. 23rd St.

101
101
5
101
10
1
10
405
110
710
LAX
105
405
PACIFIC OCEAN
Map area
0   15mi
0   15 km

0   1/2 mi
0   1/2 km

Zoo and Griffith Park), just to the west, has arty areas with unique cafes, theaters, graffiti, and art galleries—all in equally plentiful proportions. The local music scene has been burgeoning of late.

Exposition Park, south and west of downtown, is home to the Los Angeles Memorial Coliseum and the L.A. Sports Arena, as well as the Natural History Museum, the African-American Museum, and the California Science Center. The University of Southern California (USC) is next door.

The San Fernando Valley

The San Fernando Valley, known locally as "The Valley," was nationally popularized in the 1980s by the notorious mall-loving "Valley Girl" stereotype. Sandwiched between the Santa Monica and the San Gabriel mountain ranges, most of The Valley is residential and commercial and off the beaten track for tourists. But some of its attractions are bound to draw you over the hill. **Universal City,** located west of Griffith Park between U.S. 101 and California 134, is home to Universal Studios Hollywood and the supersize shopping and entertainment complex CityWalk. About the only reason to go to **Burbank,** west of these other suburbs and north of Universal City, is to see one of your favorite TV shows being filmed at NBC or Warner Brothers Studios. There are also a few good restaurants and shops along Ventura Boulevard, in and around Studio City.

Glendale is a largely residential community north of downtown between the Valley and Pasadena. Here you'll find Forest Lawn, the city's best cemetery for very retired movie stars.

LOS ANGELES

14

NEIGHBORHOODS IN BRIEF

Pasadena & Environs

Best known as the site of the Tournament of Roses Parade each New Year's Day, **Pasadena** was spared from the tear-down epidemic that swept L.A., so it has a refreshing old-time feel. Once upon a time, Pasadena was every Angeleno's best-kept secret: a quiet community whose slow and careful gentrification meant nonchain restaurants and boutique shopping without the crowds, in a revitalized downtown respectful of its old brick and stone commercial buildings. Although the area's natural and architectural beauty still shines through—so much so that Pasadena remains Hollywood's favorite backyard location for countless movies and TV shows—Old Town has become a pedestrian mall similar to Santa Monica's Third Street Promenade, complete with huge crowds, midrange chain eateries, and standard-issue mall stores. It still gets our vote as a scenic alternative to the congestion of central L.A., but it has lost much of its small-town charm.

Pasadena is also home to the famous California Institute of Technology (CalTech), which boasts 22 Nobel Prize winners among its alumni. The CalTech-operated Jet Propulsion Laboratory was the birthplace of America's space program, and CalTech scientists were the first to report earthquake activity worldwide in the 1930s.

The residential neighborhoods in Pasadena and its adjacent communities—**Arcadia, La Cañada–Flintridge, San Marino,** and **South Pasadena**—are renowned for well-preserved historic homes, from humble bungalows to lavish mansions. These areas feature public gardens, historic neighborhoods, house museums, and quiet bed-and-breakfast inns.

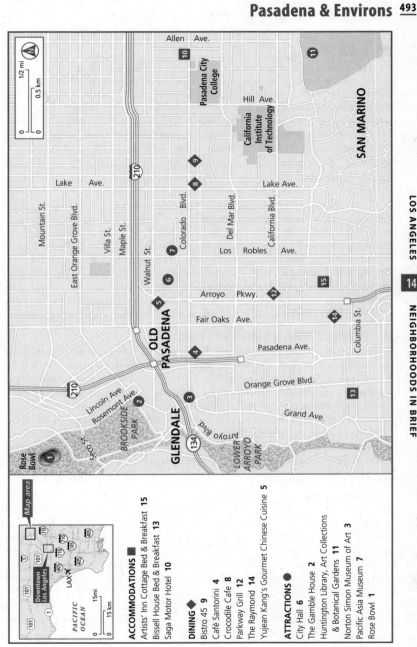

ACCOMMODATIONS ■
Artists' Inn Cottage Bed & Breakfast **15**
Bissell House Bed & Breakfast **13**
Saga Motor Hotel **10**

DINING ◆
Bistro 45 **9**
Café Santorini **4**
Crocodile Cafe **8**
Parkway Grill **12**
The Raymond **14**
Yujean Kang's Gourmet Chinese Cuisine **5**

ATTRACTIONS ●
City Hall **6**
The Gamble House **2**
Huntington Library, Art Collections
& Botanical Gardens **11**
Norton Simon Museum of Art **3**
Pacific Asia Museum **7**
Rose Bowl **1**

2 GETTING AROUND

BY CAR

Need I tell you that Los Angeles is a car-crazed city? Los Angeles is a sprawling metropolis; ergo, you're really going to need some wheels to get around easily (there *is* public transportation in L.A., but you really don't want to rely on it). An elaborate network of well-maintained freeways connects this urban sprawl, but you have to learn how to make sense of the system and cultivate some patience for dealing with the traffic—purchasing one of those plastic-covered fold-out maps is a smart investment. For a detailed view of L.A.'s freeway system, see the tear-out map tucked inside the back cover of this guide.

RENTALS   Los Angeles is one of the cheapest places in America to rent a car. Major national car-rental companies usually rent economy- and compact-class cars for about $40 per day and $130 per week, with unlimited mileage.

All the major car-rental agencies have offices at the airport and in the larger hotels; I highly recommend booking a car online before you arrive. If you're thinking of splurging on a dig-me road machine such as a Maserati, Ferrari, Rolls-Royce, Lamborghini, or Hummer, the places to call are either **Budget Beverly Hills Car Collection,** 9815 Wilshire Blvd. (© **800/227-7117** or 310/881-2335; www.budgetbeverlyhills.com); or **Beverly Hills Rent-A-Car,** 9732 Little Santa Monica Blvd., Beverly Hills (© **800/479-5996** or 310/337-1400; www.bhrentacar.com). Both car-rental companies have additional locations in Santa Monica, LAX, Orange County, and Newport Beach, and both offer complimentary delivery to local hotels or pickup service at LAX.

BY PUBLIC TRANSPORTATION

There are visitors who successfully tour Los Angeles entirely by public transportation (I've met them both), but we can't honestly recommend that plan for most readers. L.A. is a metropolis that's grown up around—and is best traversed by—the automobile, and many areas are inaccessible without one. As a result, an overwhelming number of visitors rent a car for their stay. Still, if you're in the city for only a short time, are on a very tight budget, or don't expect to be moving around a lot, public transport might be for you.

The city's trains and buses are operated by the **Los Angeles County Metropolitan Transit Authority (MTA;** © **213/922-2000;** www.mta.net), and MTA brochures and schedules are available at every area visitor center.

By Bus or Shuttle

Spread-out stops, sluggish service, and frequent transfers make extensive touring by bus impractical. For short hops and occasional jaunts, however, buses are economical and environmentally correct. However, I don't recommend riding buses late at night.

The basic bus fare is $1.25 for all local lines, with transfers costing 25¢. A Metro Day Pass is $55 and gives you unlimited bus and rail rides all day long; these can be purchased while boarding any Metro Bus (exact change is needed) or at the self-service vending machines at the Metro Rail stations. *Note:* Two kids under age 5 may travel free with each fare-paying adult.

The **Downtown Area Short Hop (DASH)** shuttle system operates buses throughout downtown, Hollywood, and the west side of L.A. Service runs every 5 to 20 minutes, depending on the time of day, and costs just 25¢. Contact the Department of Transportation (© **213/808-2273;** www.ladottransit.com) for schedules and route information (it's pretty confusing—you'll definitely need a weekday *and* weekend map).

The **Cityline** shuttle is a great way to get around West Hollywood on weekdays (9am–4pm) and Saturday (10am–7:30pm). For 50¢, it'll take you to most of the major shops and restaurants throughout WeHo (very handy if you park your car in a flat-fee lot). For more information, call © **800/447-2189.**

By Rail & Subway

The **MetroRail** system is a sore subject around town. For years, the MTA has been digging up the city's streets, sucking in huge amounts of tax money, and pushing exhaust vents up through peaceful parkland—and for what? Let's face it, L.A. will never have New York's subway or San Francisco's BART. Today the system is still in its infancy, mainly popular with commuters from outlying suburbs. Here's an overview of what's currently in place:

The **Metro Blue Line,** an aboveground rail line, connects downtown Los Angeles with Long Beach. Trains operate daily from 6am to 9pm.

The **Metro Red Line,** L.A.'s first subway, has been growing since 1993 and opened a highly publicized Hollywood–Universal City extension in 2000. The line begins at Union Station, the city's main train depot, and travels west underneath Wilshire Boulevard, looping north into Hollywood and the San Fernando Valley. Discount tokens are available at Metro service centers and many area convenience stores.

The **Metro Purple Line** subway starts at Union Station, shares six stations with the Red Line downtown, and continues to the Mid-Wilshire area.

The **Metro Green Line** runs for 20 miles along the center of I-105, the Glenn Anderson (Century) Freeway, and connects Norwalk in eastern Los Angeles County to LAX and Redondo Beach. A connection with the Blue Line offers visitors access from LAX to downtown L.A. or Long Beach.

The **Metro Gold Line** is a 14-mile link between Pasadena and Union Station, in downtown L.A. Stops include Old Pasadena, the Southwest Museum, and Chinatown.

The base Metro fare is $1.25 for all lines. A Metro Day Pass is $5 and weekly passes are $17. Passes are available at Metro Customer Centers and local convenience and grocery stores. For more information on public transportation, including construction updates, timetables, and details on purchasing tokens or passes, call **MTA** at © **213/922-2000** or, better yet, log on to their handy website at **www.mta.net.**

BY TAXI

Distances are long in Los Angeles, and cab fares are high; even a short trip can cost $20 or more. Taxis currently charge $2.65 at the flag drop, plus $2.45 per mile. A service charge of $2.50 is added to fares originating from LAX.

Except in the heart of downtown, cabs will usually not pull over when hailed. Cabstands are located at airports, at downtown's Union Station, and at major hotels. To ensure a ride, order a taxi in advance from **Checker Cab** (© **323/654-8400**), **L.A. Taxi** (© **213/627-7000**), or **United Taxi** (© **213/483-7604**).

⌒Fast Facts   Los Angeles

American Express In addition to those at 327 N. Beverly Dr., Beverly Hills (© **310/274-8277**), and at the Beverly Connection, 8493 W. Third St., Los Angeles (© **310/659-1682**), offices are located throughout the city. To locate the one nearest you, call © **800/221-7282.**

Area Codes Within the past 20 years, L.A. has gone from having a single area code (213) to a whopping seven. Even residents can't keep up. As of press time, here's the basic layout: Those areas west of La Cienega Boulevard, including Beverly Hills and the city's beach communities, use the **310** area code. Portions of Los Angeles County east and south of the city, including Long Beach, are in the **562** area. The San Fernando Valley has the **818** area code, while points east, including parts of Burbank, Glendale, and Pasadena, use the newly created **626** code. What happened to 213, you ask? The downtown business area still uses **213.** All other numbers, including Griffith Park, Hollywood, and parts of West Hollywood (east of La Cienega Blvd.) now use the area code **323.** If it's all too much to remember, just call directory assistance at © **411.**

Babysitters If you're staying at one of the larger hotels, the concierge can usually recommend a reliable babysitter. If not, contact the **Baby-Sitters Guild** in Glendale (© **310/837-1800** or 818/552-2229), L.A.'s oldest and largest babysitting service.

Business Hours Offices are usually open weekdays from 9am to 5pm. Banks are open weekdays from 9am to 3pm or later and sometimes Saturday mornings. Stores typically open between 9 and 10am and close between 5 and 6pm from Monday through Saturday. Stores in shopping complexes or malls tend to stay open late: until about 9pm on weekdays and weekends, and many malls and larger department stores are open on Sundays.

Dentists For a recommendation in the area, call the **Dental Referral Service** (© **800/422-8338**).

Emergencies Call © **911** to report a fire, call the police, or get an ambulance anywhere in the United States. This is a toll-free call (no coins are required at public telephones).

If you encounter traveler's problems, call the Los Angeles chapter of the **Traveler's Aid Society** (© **310/646-2270;** www.travelersaid.org), a nationwide, nonprofit, social service organization that helps travelers in need.

Hospital The centrally located (and world-famous) **Cedars-Sinai Medical Center,** 8700 Beverly Blvd., Los Angeles (© **310/423-3277**), has a 24-hour emergency room staffed by some of the country's finest MDs.

Newspapers & Magazines The ***Los Angeles Times*** (www.latimes.com) is a high-quality daily with strong local and national coverage. Its Sunday "Calendar" section (www.calendarlive.com) is an excellent guide to entertainment in and around L.A., and includes listings of what's doing and where to do it. The ***L.A. Weekly*** (www.laweekly.com), a free weekly listings magazine, is packed with information on current events around town. ***Los Angeles*** magazine (www.lamag.com) is a city-based monthly full of news, information, and previews of L.A.'s art, music, and food scenes. **World Book & News Co.,** at 1652 N. Cahuenga Blvd. (☎ **323/465-4352**), near Hollywood and Vine and Grauman's Chinese Theatre, stocks lots of out-of-town and foreign papers and magazines. No one minds if you browse through the magazines, but you'll be reprimanded for thumbing through the newspapers. It's open 24 hours.

Police In an emergency, dial ☎ **911.** For nonemergency police matters, call ☎ **213/485-2121;** in Beverly Hills, dial ☎ **310/550-4951.**

Post Office Call ☎ **800/ASK-USPS** to find the one closest to you.

Weather Call **Los Angeles Weather Information** (☎ **213/554-1212**) for the daily forecast. For beach conditions, call the **Zuma Beach Lifeguard** recorded information (☎ **310/457-9701**).

3 WHERE TO STAY

Due to space constraints, I've had to limit the number of hotels included here. For dozens of additional options, check out *Frommer's Los Angeles 2009* (Wiley Publishing, Inc.).

CHOOSING A LOCATION In sprawling Los Angeles, location is everything. The neighborhood you choose as a base can make or break your vacation. If you plan to spend your days at the beach but stay downtown, for example, you're going to lose a lot of valuable relaxation time on the freeway. For business travelers, choosing a location is easy: Pick a hotel near your work event—don't get on the freeways if you don't have to. For vacationers, though, the decision about where to stay is more difficult. Consider where you want to spend most of your time before you commit yourself to a base. But wherever you stay, count on doing a good deal of driving—no hotel in Los Angeles is convenient to everything.

The relatively smog-free beach communities such as **Santa Monica** and **Venice** are understandably popular with visitors—just about everybody loves to stay at the beach. Book ahead because hotels fill up quickly, especially in summer.

If they're not at one of the beach communities, most visitors stay on the city's **Westside,** a short drive from the beach and close to most of L.A.'s colorful sights. The city's most elegant and expensive accommodations are in **Beverly Hills** and **Bel Air;** a few of the hotels in these neighborhoods, such as the Beverly Hills Hotel, have become visitor attractions unto themselves. As well as one of the focal points of L.A. nightlife, **West Hollywood** is also home to the greatest range and breadth of hotels, from $300-plus-per-night boutiques to affordably priced motels.

There are fewer hotels in **Hollywood** than you might expect. Accommodations are generally moderately priced and well maintained but unspectacular. Centrally located between downtown and Beverly Hills, just a stone's throw from Universal Studios, Hollywood makes a convenient base if you're planning to do a lot of exploring, but it has more tourists and is less visually appealing than some other neighborhoods.

Downtown hotels are generally business-oriented, but thanks to direct Metro (L.A.'s subway) connections to Hollywood and Universal Studios, the demographic has begun to shift. The top hotels offer excellent deals on weekend packages. But chances are good that downtown doesn't embody the picture of L.A. you've been dreaming of; you need a coastal or Westside base for that.

Families might want to head to **Universal City** to be near Universal Studios, or straight to **Anaheim and Disneyland** (see chapter 15). **Pasadena** offers historic charm, small-town ambience, easy access to downtown L.A., and Stepford-wives beauty, but driving to the beach can take forever.

To locate the hotels reviewed below, see the individual neighborhood maps in section 1, "Orientation."

RATES The **rates** quoted in the listings that follow are the rack rates—the maximum rates that a hotel charges for rooms. But rack rates are only guidelines, and there are often many ways around them. *Always* **check each hotel's website for package deals and special Internet rates.** The hotels listed in this section have provided their best estimates for 2009. **Be aware that rates can change at any time** and are subject to availability, seasonal fluctuations, and plain ol' increases.

SANTA MONICA & THE BEACHES
Very Expensive

Casa del Mar ★★★ In a former 1920s Renaissance Revival beach club, this Art Deco stunner is a real resort hotel, equal in every respect to its sister resort, Shutters, located across the street (see below). While Shutters is outfitted like a chic East Coast beach house, this impeccable, U-shape villalike structure radiates period glamour. The building's shape awards ocean views to most of the guest rooms. You're unlikely to be too disappointed, thanks to the gorgeous, summery, European-inspired decor, plus abundant luxuries such as big Italian marble bathrooms with extra-large whirlpool tubs and separate showers.

Downstairs is a big, elegant living room with ocean views, a stylish veranda lounge, and the **Catch Restaurant,** which has earned justifiable kudos (and more than a few celebrity fans) for its beautiful setting, great service, and finest seasonal seafood. The hotel's spa features the exclusive product line of Dr. Howard Murad, one of the country's foremost authorities on skin care.

1910 Ocean Way (next to the Santa Monica Pier), Santa Monica, CA 90405. © **800/898-6999** or 310/581-5533. Fax 310/581-5503. www.hotelcasadelmar.com. 129 units. $460–$735 double; from $1,085 suite. AE, DC, DISC, MC, V. Valet parking $26. **Amenities:** Oceanfront restaurant; lobby lounge for cocktails and light fare; cafe for daytime dining; heated outdoor Roman-style pool; plunge pool; state-of-the-art health club w/spa services; Jacuzzi overlooking Santa Monica Beach; 24-hr. concierge; virtual business center; 24-hr. room service; laundry service; dry cleaning. *In room:* A/C, TV/DVD, high-speed Internet, minibar, hair dryer, iron, laptop-size safe, iPod stations.

Fairmont Miramar Hotel & Bungalows ★★ The Fairmont Miramar is for people who prefer their luxury hotels low-key and unobtrusive, yet within walking distance of the beach and Santa Monica's perpetually crowded Third Street Shopping Promenade. The hotel consists of two towers and a bevy of bungalows on 5 acres of grounds. The older, larger rooms in the Palisades Building are ideal for families, but I prefer the newer, more modern rooms in the taller Ocean Tower—particularly the corner rooms on the 8th through 10th floors overlooking the Santa Monica Pier or Malibu coastline. All rooms are well-appointed with such luxuries as goose-down duvets and soundproof windows; rooms in the Ocean Tower have balconies. The über-romantic garden bungalows are outfitted with hardwood floors, deep soaking tubs, and original artwork (they're almost as nice as the Beverly Hills Hotel bungalows and far less expensive). Other amenities include an outdoor pool and whirlpool, a pretty outdoor lounge serving drinks and food, and a fitness center and day spa.

101 Wilshire Blvd. (at Ocean Ave.), Santa Monica, CA 90401. © **800/257-7544** or 310/576-7777. Fax 310/
458-7912. www.fairmont.com/santamonica. 270 rooms, 32 bungalows. $319–$769 double; $579–$1,429
bungalow. AE, DC, DISC, MC, V. Valet parking $30. **Amenities:** Restaurant; outdoor lounge; lobby lounge;
heated outdoor pool and whirlpool; 24-hr. health and fitness center; Exhale Spa; 24-hr. concierge; business center; Wi-Fi access in lobby; 24-hr. room service; laundry service; dry cleaning. *In room:* A/C, TV/
DVD, high-speed Internet, minibar, hair dryer, iron, safe.

Le Merigot ★★   If you prefer hotels that are roomier and more contemporary than
the historic Georgian, yet not as pricey and prestigious as the Shutters or Casa del Mar
properties, this low-key luxury hotel is a comfortable setting for your seaside vacation.
On the sandy side of Ocean Avenue in the heart of Santa Monica's beach scene, the 175-
room property houses a well-regarded French-California restaurant, **Cézanne,** and the
5,500-square-foot SPA Le Merigot, which offers a full range of services along with an
outdoor pool and a state-of-the-art fitness center. Some guest rooms offer partial ocean
views, and all are plushly furnished with thick carpeting, marble-tiled bathrooms, and
pillow-top beds with Italian cotton linens, down comforters, and feather pillows. What
I really like about this hotel, however, are the clever package deals, such as the "California
Dreamin'," which includes your choice of a convertible Porsche Boxster or a BMW Z4
Roadster rental car; and the "California Surfin' Safari," a deluxe package, a 2-hour surf
lesson, a rejuvenating full-session Swedish massage, and celebratory Blue Crush gradua-
tion martinis (how very L.A.).

1740 Ocean Ave., Santa Monica, CA 90401. © **877/MERIGOT** or 310/395-9700. Fax 310/395-9200. www.
lemerigothotel.com. 175 units. $340–$635 double; from $800 suite. AE, DISC, MC, V. Valet parking $28.
Amenities: Full-service restaurant; lobby bar; outdoor pool; fitness facilities and spa; concierge; business
services; 24-hr. room service; gift shop. *In room:* A/C, TV, fax machine on request, high-speed Internet
access, minibar, iron/ironing board, laptop-size safe, 3 dual-line phones w/voice mail.

Shutters on the Beach ★★★   This Cape Cod–style luxury hotel enjoys one of the
city's most prized locations: directly on the beach, a block from Santa Monica Pier. Only
the Shutters' sister property—Casa del Mar (see above) can compete, but Shutters bests
the Casa with alfresco balconies on every guest room and a boutique hotel–like ambience. Views of the ocean are the most outstanding qualities of the spacious, luxuriously
outfitted, Cape Cod–inspired rooms, some of which have fireplaces and/or whirlpool
tubs; all have floor-to-ceiling windows that open up and elegant marble bathrooms. The
small swimming pool and the sunny lobby lounge overlooking the sand are great perches
for spotting celebrities. **One Pico,** the hotel's premier restaurant, serves modern American cuisine in a seaside setting; the best meals at the more casual **Coast Beach Café &
Bar** come from the wood-burning grill. *Tip:* The beach-cottage rooms overlooking the
sand are more desirable and no more expensive than those in the towers.

1 Pico Blvd., Santa Monica, CA 90405. © **800/334-9000** or 310/458-0030. Fax 310/458-4589. www.
shuttersonthebeach.com. 198 units. $490–$785 double; from $1,175 suite. AE, DC, DISC, MC, V. Valet
parking $26. **Amenities:** Restaurant; cafe; lobby lounge; outdoor heated pool and Jacuzzi; health club w/
spa services; sauna; extensive beach equipment rentals; concierge; activities desk; courtesy car; Wi-Fi
throughout property; business center w/secretarial services; 24-hr. room service; babysitting; laundry service; dry cleaning; video library. *In room:* TV/DVD, minibar, hair dryer, iron, laptop-size safe, iPod station.

Expensive
The Ambrose ★★   If being near the ocean isn't crucial, but a soothing, peaceful
environment is, this "green" hotel in a residential neighborhood fits the bill. The eco-
minded Ambrose is quickly becoming a favorite boutique hideaway for CEOs who enjoy
its soothing Asian influences. Guest rooms are on the small side but are luxuriously

appointed with Italian Matteo bedding, Frette kimonos and bath linens, goose-down pillows, and surround-sound CD/DVD music systems. Studio rooms are the most luxurious and come with terraces or balconies, but it was the complimentary amenities that really sold me: underground parking with direct elevator access, Wi-Fi, breakfast from a gourmet restaurant, modern 24-hour fitness room, Aveda bath products, and even shuttle service around Santa Monica via the hotel's London taxi.

1255 20th St. (at Arizona Ave.), Santa Monica, CA 90404. © **877-AMBROSE** or 310/315-1555. Fax 310/315-1556. www.ambrosehotel.com. 77 units. From $229 double. Rates include continental breakfast. AE, DC, DISC, MC, V. Valet parking free. **Amenities:** Fitness center; complimentary local taxi; 24-hr. room service. *In room:* TV/VCR, CD/DVD surround sound, Wi-Fi, minibar, hair dryer, safe.

Huntley Santa Monica Beach ★★ (**Finds**) If you're looking for a hotel that's on the beach and you can afford it, stay at Shutters; otherwise, the Huntley is my top choice for vacationing in style in Santa Monica. Even though it's housed in one of Santa Monica's tallest buildings (18 floors), the Huntley is a hidden gem—tucked away behind the Fairmont on the edge of a quiet neighborhood, yet close to Third Street Promenade dining and shopping and just a short walk from the beach. I love everything about this hotel, from its non-snobbish staff and lively bar scene to the incredible views of the Santa Monica skyline; but the coup de grâce is the new 18th-floor **Penthouse** restaurant, bar, and lounge. The Huntley's modern, earth-toned guest rooms offer ocean or mountain views, good work desks, 42-inch flatscreen TVs, pillow-top beds with Egyptian cotton linens, and bathrooms with Italian marble tile. If you want an ocean view, book a room on floors 9 to 17.

1111 Second St. (north of Wilshire Blvd.), Santa Monica, CA 90403. © **310/394-5454.** Fax 310/458-9776. www.thehuntleyhotel.com. 209 units. $289–$335 double. AE, DC, DISC, MC, V. Valet parking $18. **Amenities:** Restaurant and bar; lobby cafe; fitness center; concierge; business center; Wi-Fi; 24-hr. room service; laundry; dry-cleaning. *In room:* A/C, flatscreen TV/DVD, coffeemaker, hair dryer, iron, CD player.

Marina del Rey Marriott ★★ (**Finds**) In order to attract a more hip clientele, this Marriott that is popular among the business crowd has made some rather unorthodox modifications. Each guest room is spacious and comfortably appointed with down comforters and pillows, 32-inch HDTVs, bathrobes, Jacuzzi-style tubs, and small balconies with views of the marina or ocean. The 10-story hotel's location is excellent as well—across the street from the glimmering harbor and footpath, within walking distance of several Marina del Rey restaurants and Venice Beach, a short drive to Santa Monica, and easy freeway access to Hollywood, downtown, and the airport. The hotel has a steakhouse, but you're better off noshing on small plates and swilling martinis at **Glow,** their outdoor lounge that's ranked as one of the top in the country (p. 593). Check their website for heavily discounted weekend rates.

4100 Admiralty Way (at the north end of the marina), Marina del Rey, CA 90292. © **800/228-9290** or 310/301-3000. Fax 310/448-4870. www.marriott.com. 370 rooms. AE, DC, DISC, MC, V. Valet parking $26. **Amenities:** Restaurant; lobby bar; outdoor lounge; pool; fitness center; whirlpool; business center; barber/salon; room service; laundry service; dry cleaning. *In room:* A/C, HDTV, high-speed Internet, coffeemaker, hair dryer, iron, safe.

Moderate
The Hotel California ★ (**Finds**) Situated on enviable real estate along Ocean Avenue—right next door to the behemoth Loews—this welcoming hacienda-style beachfront motel embodies the surfer/sun-worshiper ambience you'd expect from a Santa Monica lodging. The well-tended complex sits above and across an alley from the beach

but offers excellent views and direct access to the sand via a private path. The inn offers cheery rooms with beds with down comforters, Egyptian-cotton sheets, and surfboard headboards; hardwood floors; and Spanish-tiled bathrooms. Five one-bedroom suites also have kitchenettes and trundle beds that make them great for families or longer stays; all rooms have minifridges, 27-inch TVs, and ceiling fans, as well as free wireless Internet. A handful of rooms have showers only in the bathrooms. (And no, it's not the hotel from the Eagles' hit—that hotel is rumored to be in Mexico and the album's cover photo is of the Beverly Hills Hotel.) *Tip:* Pay a few bucks extra for a courtyard view, as the cheapest rooms face the parking lot and noisy Ocean Avenue. Be sure to check their website for specials.

501

1670 Ocean Ave. (south of Colorado Ave.), Santa Monica, CA 90401. ☏ **866/571-0000** or 310/393-2363. Fax 310/393-1063. www.hotelca.com. 26 units. $179–$279 double or suite. AE, DISC, MC, V. Self-parking $20. **Amenities:** Jacuzzi; activities desk; discount car-rental desk; high-speed Internet access, fax/copier, and coffeemaker in front office. *In room:* TV/VCR, Wi-Fi, fridge, hair dryer, iron.

Venice Beach House ★ (Finds)   Listed on the National Register of Historic Places, this two-story, ivy-covered 1911 Craftsman bungalow is now a homey bed-and-breakfast on one of funky Venice's unique sidewalk streets, just a block from the beach. The interior has a lived-in look that adds charm for romantics but won't live up to the expectations of travelers who like designer appointments and private bathrooms. What's more, the inn hums noisily with activity when there's a full house. Still, the huge repeat clientele base doesn't seem to mind these minor caveats. My favorite room is the upstairs Venice Pier Suite—light and airy, with a wood-burning fireplace, king-size bed, private bathroom, and sunny sitting room. An expanded continental breakfast with homemade baked goods is served in the sunroom overlooking a splendid garden.

15 30th Ave. (at Speedway, 1 block west of Pacific Ave.), Venice, CA 90291. ☏ **310/823-1966.** Fax 310/823-1842. www.venicebeachhouse.com. 9 units, 5 w/private bathroom. $145 double w/shared bathroom; $170–$235 double w/private bathroom. Extra person after 2 people $20. Rates include expanded continental breakfast. AE, MC, V. On-site parking $12 a day. **Amenities:** Jacuzzi (some rooms). *In room:* TV, high-speed Internet, fireplace (some rooms).

Inexpensive

Best Western Marina Pacific Hotel & Suites ★ (Value) (Kids)   This recently renovated coastal hotel is a haven of smart value just off the Venice boardwalk. The hotel's spacious rooms are brightened with beachy colors, and many rooms have at least partial ocean views (and top-floor rooms have full ocean views). Terrific for families, the one-bedroom suites offer master bedrooms with king-size beds, fully outfitted kitchens with microwave and dishwasher, dining areas, queen-size sofa sleepers, balconies, and fireplaces. Photos of local scenes and rock-'n'-roll legends along with works by local artists lend public spaces a cool L.A. vibe. Stay elsewhere if you need a lot in the way of service or if you don't relish the human carnival of Venice Beach.

1697 Pacific Ave. (at 17th Ave.), Venice, CA 90291. ☏ **800/786-7789** or 310/452-1111. Fax 310/452-5479. www.mphotel.com. 88 units. $189–$309 double; $209–$429 suite. Rates include continental breakfast. Extra person $10. Children 12 and under stay free in parent's room. Ask about AAA, senior, and other discounts; weekly and monthly rates also available. AE, DC, DISC, MC, V. Self-parking $9. **Amenities:** Free shuttle to Santa Monica and Marina del Rey; coin-op laundry; laundry service; dry cleaning; secured covered parking. *In room:* A/C, cable TV w/HBO, high-speed Internet, fridge, coffeemaker, hair dryer, iron.

Cal Mar Hotel Suites ★ (Value)   In a residential neighborhood 2 blocks from the ocean, this 1950s garden apartment complex delivers a lot of bang for your vacation buck. Each unit is an apartment-style suite with a living room and pullout sofa, a full-size kitchen with utensils, and a separate bedroom; most are spacious enough to accommodate four in comfort. While the furnishings aren't luxurious, they're all quite modern and very clean, and everything is well kept. It's easy to be comfortable here for stays of a week or more, especially since it's so well located, a mere block from the Third Street Promenade and a short walk to the beach. The staff is attentive and courteous, and the garden courtyard has an inviting swimming pool and chaises for lounging. *Tip:* Request a room on the second floor to avoid the sound of stomping feet.

220 California Ave., Santa Monica, CA 90403. (C) **800/776-6007** or 310/395-5555. Fax 310/451-1111. www.calmarhotel.com. 36 units. $129–$229 suite. Extra person $10. Children under 10 stay free in parent's room. AE, DC, DISC, MC, V. Free parking. **Amenities:** Heated outdoor pool; coin-op laundry. *In room:* TV, full kitchen w/fridge and coffeemaker, hair dryer, iron, CD player.

Casa Malibu ★★ (Finds) Right on its very own beach, this leftover jewel from Malibu's golden age doesn't try to play the sleek resort game. Instead, the modest, low-rise inn has a traditional California-beach-cottage look that's cozy and timeless. Wrapped around a palm-studded inner courtyard, the 21 rooms are comfortable and thoughtfully outfitted. Many have been upgraded, but even the older ones are in great shape and boast top-quality bedding and bathrobes. You might also find a fireplace, a kitchenette (in a half-dozen or so), a CD player (in suites), a tub (instead of shower only), and/or a private deck over the sand. The upstairs Catalina Suite (Lana Turner's old hideout) has the best view, while the gorgeous Malibu Suite is the best room in the house and, like the beachfront rooms, right on the beach. More than half have ocean views, but even those facing the courtyard offer easy beach access to the private beach. The handsome, wind-shielded sun deck extends directly over the sand, allowing everyone to enjoy the blue Pacific even in cool months. Book well ahead for summer.

22752 Pacific Coast Hwy. (about ¹/₄ mile south of Malibu Pier), Malibu, CA 90265. (C) **800/831-0858** or 310/456-2219. Fax 310/456-5418. 21 units. $129–$229 garden or oceanview double; $289–$299 beachfront double; $269–$429 suite. Rates include continental breakfast. Extra person $15. AE, MC, V. Free parking. **Amenities:** Access to nearby private health club; room service for lunch and dinner; in-room massage; laundry service; dry cleaning. *In room:* TV/DVD, Wi-Fi, fridge, coffeemaker, hair dryer, iron, 2-line telephone.

Sea Shore Motel (Value) In the heart of Santa Monica's Main Street dining and shopping sector, this small, friendly, family-run motel is one of the best bargains near the beach. The Sea Shore is such a well-kept secret that most denizens of stylish Main Street are unaware of the incredible value in their midst. Arranged around a parking courtyard, rooms are small and unremarkable from the outside, but the conscientious management has done a nice job with the interiors, installing attractive terra-cotta floor tiles, granite countertops, and conveniences such as voice mail and Internet access. Complete with a living room and full kitchen, the 800-square-foot suites that sleep up to six are a phenomenal deal; book them as far in advance as possible. With a full slate of restaurants out the front door and the Santa Monica Pier and beach just a couple of blocks away, it's a terrific bargain base for exploring the sandy side of the city.

2637 Main St. (south of Ocean Park Blvd.), Santa Monica, CA 90405. (C) **310/392-2787.** Fax 310/392-5167. www.seashoremotel.com. 24 units. $110–$145 double; $160–$260 suite. Extra person $5. Children under 12 stay free in parent's room. Midweek discounts available. AE, DISC, MC, V. Free parking. Pets accepted for $10-per-night fee. **Amenities:** Deli; complimentary Wi-Fi; coin-op laundry; sun deck. *In room:* TV, 27-inch flatscreen HDTV, fridge, coffeemaker, iron.

If you have an early morning flight and need an airport hotel, the **Westin Los Angeles Airport,** 5400 W. Century Blvd. (© **800/937-8461** or 310/216-5858; www.westin.com/losangelesairport), is a cut above the rest, with its patented Westin Heavenly Beds. Two other good, moderately priced choices are the **Sheraton Gateway Hotel,** 6101 W. Century Blvd., near Sepulveda Boulevard (© **800/325-3535** or 310/642-1111; www.sheratonlosangeles.com), a comfortable, California-style hotel that overlooks the runway; and the **Marriott Los Angeles Airport,** 5855 Century Blvd. (© **800/228-9290** or 310/641-5700; www.marriott.com), a reliable choice for travelers on the fly.

An inexpensive option is the **Travelodge at LAX,** 5547 W. Century Blvd. (© **800/421-3939** or 310/649-4000; www.travelodgelax.com), an otherwise standard member of the reliable chain with a beautiful tropical garden around the pool area.

L.A.'S WESTSIDE & BEVERLY HILLS
Very Expensive

Beverly Hills Hotel and Bungalows ★★★ Behind the famous facade (remember the Eagles' *Hotel California* album?) lies this world-class haven where legends were, and still are, made: The "Pink Palace" was center stage for both deal- and star-making in Hollywood's golden days. Stars and industry hotshots can still be found lounging around the Olympic-size pool or digging into Dutch apple pancakes in the iconic **Polo Lounge,** where Hunter S. Thompson kicked off his adventure to Las Vegas, and where Ozzy Osbourne has been known to sip his afternoon tea. Following a $100-million restoration, the lavish guest rooms boast every state-of-the-art luxury, including extra-large bathrooms with double Grecian marble sinks. The management has assembled an unpretentious, service-oriented staff, and the best original touches have been retained, such as butler service at the touch of a button. Many rooms feature private patios, Jacuzzi tubs, kitchens, fireplaces, and/or dining rooms. The 21 bungalows are more luxurious than ever, and the lush, tropical-like grounds are brimming with exotic trees and flowers. The **Beverly Hills Hotel Spa by La Prairie** offers European and Asian-influenced massage and expert facials.

Named in honor of the year the hotel first opened, **Bar NINETEEN12** has an inside area with a living-room feel and a lighted terrace. Tableside bottle service can cost anywhere from $475 to $23,000, but you never know who might be next to you doing business over drinks. *Tip:* For a more affordable time, try the inexpensive, informal, and groovily retro-chic **Fountain Coffee Shop,** open daily 7am to 7pm.

9641 Sunset Blvd. (at Rodeo Dr.), Beverly Hills, CA 90210. © **800/283-8885** or 310/276-2251. Fax 310/887-2887. www.beverlyhillshotel.com. 204 units. $485–$665 double; from $1,025 suite or bungalow. AE, DC, MC, V. Parking $23. Pets accepted in bungalows only. **Amenities:** 3 restaurants; 2 bars; 2 lounges; Olympic-size outdoor heated pool; 2 outdoor tennis courts (lit for night play); fitness center; full spa services; whirlpool; concierge; car-rental desk; courtesy limo; business center w/computers; 24-hr. room service; in-room or poolside massage; babysitting; laundry service; dry cleaning; video rentals. *In room:* A/C, TV/VCR, fax/copier/scanner, high-speed Internet, minibar, hair dryer, safe, CD player.

Four Seasons Hotel Los Angeles at Beverly Hills ★★ This intimate-feeling 16-story hotel attracts a mix of A-list jet-setters and an L.A. showbiz crowd who cherish the hotel as an après-event gathering place. Lush gardens will help you forget you're in the heart of the city; the concierge is famously well connected; and service goes the distance. Guest rooms are sumptuously furnished, with luxuries including custom Sealy mattresses with heavenly linens and pillows, marble bathrooms, and French doors leading to private balconies. Room rates rise with the elevator, so bargain hunters need to sacrifice the view. Along with a full-service spa, try the California Sunset Massage at one of the private candlelit poolside cabanas, the view-endowed fourth-floor deck has a lap pool, poolside grill, and glass-walled fitness center. **Gardens** is a refined, excellent California-French eatery often overlooked by locals.

300 S. Doheny Dr. (at Burton Way), Los Angeles, CA 90048. (C) **800/819-5053,** 800/332-3442, or 310/273-2222. Fax 310/859-3824. www.fourseasons.com/losangeles. 285 units. $395–$475 double; from $595 suite. AE, DC, DISC, MC, V. Valet parking $21. Pets under 15 lb. welcomed (no charge). **Amenities:** Restaurant; lounge; poolside grill; rooftop heated pool; exercise room; full-service spa; Jacuzzi; children's program; concierge; courtesy limo within 2-mile radius; business center; 24-hr. room service; in-room massage; laundry service; dry cleaning. In room: A/C, TV w/pay movies (suites have DVD), free Wi-Fi, minibar, hair dryer, iron, safe, CD player.

Hotel Palomar Los Angeles ★★

Where else but L.A. would you find a hotel that combines dramatic movie-themed design elements with four-star service and an environmentally friendly focus? If you're looking for the kind of hotel experience that enhances your Hollywood vacation by treating you like a VIP, the new Hotel Palomar in Westwood is now playing. The 19-story Palomar oozes with elements of opulence and exoticism, from the grand rouge marble fireplace in the shimmering lobby to velvet shams and faux snakeskin chests in each guest room. Other high-end perks include L'Occitane bath products, 42-inch LCD flatscreen TVs, plush terry bathrobes, lighted make-up and full-length mirrors, and Fuji spa tubs in the suites. Sure, it's all a bit over the top, but it's fun: So go ahead and book the hotels' personal trainer. Or watch 24-hour in-room yoga and Pilates on the LCD flatscreen TV. Or have James drive you to Spago in the hotel's Lexus Hybrid town car. Or sip Manhattans while sunbathing at the pool with your cockapoo (it's a pet-friendly place). It's your turn to play diva, though I doubt Mariah is sorting her trash at the in-room recycling bins.

10740 Wilshire Blvd., Los Angeles, CA 90024. (C) **800/472-8556** or 310/475-8711. Fax 310/475-5220. www.hotelpalomar-lawestwood.com. 238 rooms, 30 suites. $269–$459 double; $369–559 suite. Includes evening wine reception. AE, DC, DISC, MC, V. Valet parking $30. **Amenities:** Blvd 16 Restaurant and lounge; heated pool; 24-hr. fitness center; in-room spa treatments; concierge; car service; business center; 24-hr. room service; laundry service; dry cleaning; complimentary overnight shoe shine. In room: A/C, TV, free high-speed Internet, minibar, hair dryer, iron, safe, iPod station.

Mondrian ★★

Theatrical, coveted, sophisticated—this is the kind of place superhotelier Ian Schrager has created from a once-drab apartment building. Working with *enfant terrible* French designer Philippe Starck, Schrager used the Mondrian's breathtaking views (from every room) as the starting point for his vision of a "hotel in the clouds." Purposely underlit hallways lead to bright, clean rooms outfitted with simple furniture casually slipcovered in white; about three-quarters of the rooms and suites have fully outfitted kitchenettes. The accommodations themselves are only secondary to the super-hip, star-studded scene. Booking a room guarantees admission to **Skybar,** one of L.A.'s hottest watering holes. (Soundproof windows on the south side of the building have eliminated a troublesome noise problem in rooms overlooking the raucous late-night scene.) In addition to its terrific and ultrahip Asian-Latin fusion restaurant **Asia de Cuba,** light meals and sushi are served at a quirky communal table in the lobby. The elegant **Agua Spa** offers a full range of spa treatments in a Zen-like atmosphere. The beautiful-people staff isn't strong on service, but they look great.

www.mondrianhotel.com. 237 units. $330–$580 double; from $405 suite. Weekend rates available. AE, DC, DISC, MC, V. Valet parking $23. **Amenities:** 2 restaurants; bar; outdoor pool; fitness room; Agua Spa; concierge; business center; 24-hr. room service; in-room massage; laundry service; dry cleaning; video, DVD, and CD libraries. *In room:* A/C, TV (DVD player available upon request), Wi-Fi, minibar, coffeemaker, hair dryer, iron, safe, CD player.

Expensive

Avalon Hotel ★★ (Finds)   The first style-conscious boutique hotel on the L.A. scene, this mid-20th-century–inspired gem in the heart of Beverly Hills still leads the pack. With classic atomic-age furnishings—Eames cabinets, Heywood-Wakefield chairs, Nelson bubble lamps—and smart custom designs, every room looks as if it could star in a *Metropolitan Home* photo spread. The property is comprised of the former Beverly Carlton, as well as two neighboring 1950s-era apartment houses. The main building is the hub of a chic but low-key scene, but I prefer the quieter Canon building, where many of the units have kitchenettes and/or furnished terraces. All rooms are stocked with terry bathrobes and Miscioni linens, and you'll have easy access to the sunny courtyard with its retro-hip amoeba-shape pool, the fitness room, and **blue on blue,** the groovy blue-hued restaurant and bar that mixes a terrific pomegranate mojito. Service is friendlier than you'll find in other style-minded hotels. *Note:* Light sleepers should request a room away from the noisy party-prone pool area.

9400 W. Olympic Blvd. (at Beverly Dr.), Beverly Hills, CA 90212. ℂ **800/670-6183** or 310/277-5221. Fax 310/277-4928. www.avalonbeverlyhills.com. 86 units. $289–$319 double; from $369–$419 junior or 1-bedroom suite. Extra person $25. AE, DC, MC, V. Valet parking $22. **Amenities:** Restaurant and lounge; courtyard pool; concierge; 24-hr. room service; in-room spa and massage; laundry service; dry cleaning. *In room:* A/C, TV/VCR w/pay movies and video games, fax, minibar, coffeemaker, hair dryer, iron, safe, CD player.

Chateau Marmont ★★   Perched secretively in a curve above the Sunset Strip, the château modeled after an elegant Loire Valley castle is a landmark from 1920s-era Hollywood. Greta Garbo regularly checked in as Harriet Brown, and Jim Morrison was one of many celebrities to call this home in later years. This historic landmark built its reputation on exclusivity and privacy, which was shattered when John Belushi overdosed in Bungalow No. 2. Now under the guiding hand of boutique hotelier Andre Balazs, the funky luxury oasis is hipper and more exclusive than ever. No two of the antiques-filled standard rooms, suites, cottages, or bungalows are alike. Many units have fireplaces and CD stereos, and all but 11 have kitchenettes or full kitchens.

The Chateau Marmont is beautifully kept, eternally chic, faultlessly service oriented, and overflowing with Hollywood and rock-'n'-roll lore (not to mention a look-at-me/don't-look-at-me clientele), but it's not for everybody. Quirkiness rules, so don't expect traditional luxuries.

8221 Sunset Blvd. (btw. La Cienega and Crescent Heights boulevards), West Hollywood, CA 90046. ℂ **800/242-8328** or 323/656-1010. Fax 323/655-5311. www.chateaumarmont.com. 63 units. $370 double; $480 suite; $520 cottage; $1,800 bungalow. AE, DC, MC, V. Valet parking $21. Pets accepted with $100-per-pet fee. **Amenities:** Restaurant (serves in lobby, garden, and dining room); bar; outdoor heated pool w/ brick sun deck; exercise room; access to nearby health club; 24-hr. concierge; business center; secretarial services; 24-hr. room service; in-room massage; babysitting; same-day laundry and dry cleaning; CD library. *In room:* A/C, TV/VCR, free Wi-Fi, minibar, fridge, coffeemaker, hair dryer, iron, laptop-size safe, CD player.

Le Parc Suite Hotel ★★   On a quiet residential street, this sophisticated and stylish all-suite hotel attracts an interesting mix of clientele: Designers stay here because it's a few minutes' walk to the Pacific Design Center; music-industry celebs stay for its low-key neighborhood location; patients and medical consultants check in because it's close to

LOS ANGELES

14

WHERE TO STAY

Cedars-Sinai; and tourists enjoy being near the Farmers Market, the Beverly Center, and Museum Row. The renovated apartment-like units are extra large—studios are 650 square feet, one-bedrooms 875 to 1,000 square feet—and each has a well-outfitted kitchenette, a dining area, a living room with a fireplace, and a balcony. What the hotel lacks in views it makes up for in value and elbowroom, and the rooftop night-lit tennis court is a rare perk in this area. The hotel's intimate bistro-style restaurant, **Knoll,** is a hidden gem, offering very good contemporary American cuisine and romantic alfresco seating at the rooftop dining area.

733 N. West Knoll Dr., West Hollywood, CA 90069. © **800/578-4837** or 310/855-8888. Fax 310/659-7812. www.leparcsuites.com. 154 units. $215–$500 junior or 1-bedroom suite. Check for theater and bed-and-breakfast packages. AE, DC, DISC, MC, V. Parking $18. Pets accepted for $75 fee. **Amenities:** Restaurant w/full bar; outdoor heated pool and Jacuzzi; rooftop night-lit tennis court; well-equipped exercise room w/sauna; access to nearby health club; concierge; courtesy car; business center; 24-hr. room service; massage; babysitting; coin-op laundry; laundry service; dry cleaning. *In room:* A/C, TV/VCR (w/pay movies, video games, and on-screen Internet access), high-speed Internet, kitchenette, minibar, coffeemaker, hair dryer, iron, CD player, microwave.

The Mosaic Hotel Beverly Hills ★★★ (Finds)

The owners pumped $3 million into completely renovating this boutique hotel (formerly the Beverly Hills Inn), and the result is spectacular. The lobby is a showcase of functional art, with gleaming tile mosaics; fabrics in deep, rich tones; and a profusion of artfully arranged orchids. Continuing a recent trend that I'm all for, a wall has been removed to allow direct access from the check-in desk to the bar and lounge, where guests are encouraged to sample the house special—a Mosaic sake martini. The guest rooms are equally impressive, with 300-count linens, goose-down comforters and piles of pillows, windows that open onto the quiet street or garden courtyard, stocked minibars, and sparkling bathrooms with Bulgari bath products and huge rain shower heads. Other perks include free high-speed Internet access, poolside cabanas, CD players, and DVD players in the suites. *Tip:* The corner deluxe rooms are worth the extra $15.

125 S. Spalding Dr., Beverly Hills, CA 90212. © **800/463-4466** or 310/278-0303. Fax 310/278-1728. www. mosaichotel.com. 49 units. $285–$520 double; from $600 2-bedroom suite. AE, DC, MC, V. Parking $15. Small pets accepted. **Amenities:** Restaurant; full bar; heated outdoor pool; exercise room w/sauna; tour desk; business services; full room-service menu until 10pm; laundry service; dry cleaning. *In room:* A/C, TV, high-speed Internet, fridge, hair dryer, iron, CD player.

Sunset Tower Hotel ★★★

The Sunset Tower has everything you could hope for in a Los Angeles hotel: a storied history, glamour, elegance, impeccable service, beautiful views, Deco-era decor, Sunset Strip location, full-service spa, romantic restaurant, celebrity clientele, and nary a smidgeon of snobbery from the staff. The 15-story Sunset Tower was built in 1921 as a luxury apartment for Hollywood's top movie stars, but the building lost its luster and was nearly demolished in the '80s. When hotelier Jeff Klein bought and renovated the hotel in 2005 it became the darling of the Hollywood hotel scene. It's been meticulously restored with fine woods, muted colors of natural brown and beige, and brass fittings. Guest rooms have floor-to-ceiling windows with wonderful city views, as well as oversize tubs, Frette sheets, and a soothing aura of old-Hollywood elegance. What better way to spend a day in L.A. than to have a massage and spa treatments at the hotel's **Argyle Spa,** spend the afternoon sunbathing at the pool while noshing on blinis and rosé from the **Terrace** poolside grill, settle into a Plymouth martini and lobster Cobb at the beautiful **Tower Bar,** then step out the front door, and stroll along the famous Sunset Strip?

8358 Sunset Blvd. (on the Sunset Strip), West Hollywood, CA 90069. ℰ **800/225-2637** or 323/654-7100.
Fax 323/654-9287. www.sunsettowerhotel.com. 74 units. $345–$445 double; from $495 suite; from $2,500 penthouse. AE, DC, DISC, MC, V. Valet parking $28. **Amenities:** Restaurant; poolside grill; bar and lounge; heated outdoor pool; full-service spa; in-room spa treatments; 24-hr. fitness center; concierge; 24-hr. room service; laundry service; dry cleaning; pet amenities. *In room:* A/C, TV/DVD, high-speed Internet, minibar, hair dryer, iPod stations.

Moderate

Chamberlain West Hollywood ★   This four-story boutique hotel in a tree-lined residential West Hollywood neighborhood looks and feels much like a high-quality Manhattan apartment building (probably because it used to be an apartment building). The location alone is reason enough to stay here, as it's only 2 blocks from the Sunset Strip and Santa Monica Boulevard. If you're young and hip and have plenty of room on your credit card, you won't need your car once it's parked in the underground garage (hell, you won't even need comfortable shoes). Each guest room is a suite with a separate living and sleeping area, and comes pleasantly equipped with a plush king-size bed with Mascioni 250-count sheets, gas-log fireplace, small balcony, flatscreen TV, DVD/VCR combo, CD player, and large desk with Internet access. The rooftop pool and cabana are ideal for sunbathing, and the roof has a great view of the city. The small restaurant and bar are good for meeting friends for a drink and appetizers before you hit the town (though I suggest you have dinner elsewhere).

1000 Westmount Dr. (1 block west of La Cienega Blvd.), West Hollywood, CA 90069. ℰ **800/201-9652** or 310/657-7400. Fax 310/854-6744. www.chamberlainwesthollywood.com. 112 units. $289–$389 studio to 1-bedroom suites. AE, DC, DISC, MC, V. Valet parking $24 with in/out privileges. **Amenities:** Heated rooftop pool; fitness center; 24-hr. concierge service; room service; coin-op laundry; laundry service; dry cleaning; grocery shopping service. *In room:* A/C, TV/DVD, high-speed Internet, coffeemaker, hair dryer, iron, CD player.

Elan Hotel ★★ (Finds)   The Elan is not only one of L.A.'s best boutique-style hotels, it's one of its best values as well. Rebuilt and freshly renovated from the bones of a 1969 retirement home, the modern structure blends elements from the original 1969 facade with a modern, sophisticated decor. A mod, loungey lobby leads to handsomely appointed guest rooms that are amenity-laden and surprisingly luxurious for the price. Standard rooms aren't huge but have high ceilings; thoughtfully designed custom furnishings; beautifully made beds—with cushioned headboards, goose-down comforters, and 350-thread-count Egyptian cotton linens; bathrooms with cotton robes; and the thickest, plushest bath sheets in town. On the downside, there's no view, no pool, no fitness center (although you can purchase an $8 pass to the nearby health club), and this stretch of Beverly Boulevard isn't exactly the hippest. But double-paned glass ensures that rooms are quiet, and the location in central L.A. is ideal (shoppers will love the walking-distance proximity to the Beverly Center).

8435 Beverly Blvd. (btw. La Cienega Blvd. and Fairfax Ave.), Los Angeles, CA 90048. ℰ **888/611-0398** or 323/658-6663. Fax 323/658-6640. www.elanhotel.com. 49 units. Rooms start at $195. Rates include continental breakfast and managers' wine and cheese reception. Extra person $15. AE, DC, DISC, MC, V. Valet parking $19. **Amenities:** Exercise room; business center; room service from coffee shop across street (5am–2am); laundry service; dry cleaning. *In room:* A/C, HDTV, free Wi-Fi and high-speed Internet, minibar, coffeemaker, hair dryer, iron, safe.

Hotel Angeleno Los Angeles ★★   This L.A. landmark building is the last of a breed of circular hotels from the 1960s and 1970s. Formerly a Holiday Inn, it was bought by the Joie de Vivre hotel group that made its name in San Francisco by revamping tired hotels into hip, modern destinations, and this is the company's first L.A. venture. The location alone is a good reason to stay here: It's perched beside the city's busiest freeway, a short hop from the popular Getty Center and centrally located between the beaches, Beverly Hills, and the San Fernando Valley. Each pie-shaped room comes with a private balcony and double-paned glass to keep most of the freeway din at bay, while comfort comes in the form of 300-count Italian linens, feather duvets, and pillow-top mattresses. Little extras such as 30-inch plasma TVs, wireless Internet access, and great views add to the panache. Also a hot spot is the 17-story hotel's penthouse-level **West** supper club and cocktail lounge, the city's first Italian steakhouse. Additional perks include an outdoor pool with cabanas and a fire pit, a lobby-level cafe, and complimentary pickup and drop-off service to the Getty Center, UCLA, and Westwood. *Tip:* Check the hotel's website to see what package deals are being offered.

170 N. Church Lane (at intersection of Sunset Blvd. and I-405), Los Angeles, CA 90049. (C) **866/ANGELENO** or 310/476-6411. Fax 310/472-1157. www.hotelangeleno.com. 209 units. $189–$239 double; from $295 suite. Includes evening wine reception. AE, DC, DISC, MC, V. Valet parking $18. **Amenities:** Rooftop restaurant and lounge; lobby cafe; heated outdoor pool and fireplace; fitness center; business center; 24-hr. concierge; free shuttle to Getty Center and within a 3-mile radius; room service; laundry service; dry cleaning. *In room:* A/C, TV w/pay movies and free HBO, Wi-Fi and high-speed Internet, minibar, coffeemaker, hair dryer, safe, CD player.

The Orlando ★★   If you came to L.A. to shop, you'll definitely want to stay at the Orlando. Not only is it situated between Beverly Hills and West Hollywood in the heart of the Third Street Shopping District, it's also within walking distance of the Grove, the Farmers Market, the Beverly Center, and Restaurant Row. The large guest rooms are comfortably equipped with custom furnishings, 2-inch plasma TVs, iPod docking stations, minibars, and beds with Egyptian cotton sheets, but you'll probably spend most of your time at the rooftop deck, floating in the saltwater pool. If you're in a splurging mood, request a spacious Executive Garden room with a big ol' king-size bed and private patio. Other hotel perks include a complimentary European breakfast buffet, $10 taxi vouchers per day (smart), and a wonderful Italian restaurant called **La Terza.** Numerous other amenities are available at the Orlando that you would typically only find at a much larger luxury hotel, including in-room spa treatments. *Tip:* Celebrities like to stay here because of the hotel's low-key location and privacy.

8384 W. Third St. (at Orlando St.), Los Angeles, CA 90048. (C) **800/62-HOTEL** or 323/658-6600. Fax 323/653-4737. www.theorlando.com. 98 units. From $279 standard rooms; from $410 Executive rooms. AE, DC, DISC, MC, V. Valet parking $26. Pets welcome. **Amenities:** Restaurant; bar; outdoor heated pool; 24-hr. fitness center; 2 dry saunas; 24-hr. concierge; business center; free Wi-Fi; room service; in-room massage. *In room:* A/C, TV w/movies on demand, minibar, coffeemaker, hair dryer, iron, laptop-size safe, CD player.

The Standard ★★   Designed to appeal to the under-35 "it" crowd, André Balazs's swank West Hollywood neo-motel is sometimes absurd, sometimes brilliant, and always provocative (not to mention crowded!). It's a scene worthy of its Sunset Strip location: shag carpeting on the lobby ceiling, blue Astroturf around the swimming pool, a DJ spinning ambient sounds while a performance artist showing more skin than talent poses in a display case behind the check-in desk. Look past the retro clutter and often-raucous party scene, and you'll find a level of service more often associated with pricier hotels. A revamped 1962 motel, it boasts comfortably sized rooms outfitted with cobalt blue indoor-outdoor carpeting, silver beanbag chairs, safety-orange tiles in the bathrooms, and Warhol's poppy-print curtains, plus private balconies, and minibars whose contents include goodies such as sake, condoms, and animal crackers. On the downside, the cheapest rooms face noisy Sunset Boulevard, and the relentless scene can get tiring if you're not into it.

Note: The 12-story **Downtown Standard,** 550 S. Flower St. (© **213/892-8080**), brings a similar dose of retro-future style and cool attitude to downtown. It's worth visiting just to check out the retro-glam rooftop bar with its vibrating waterbed pleasure pods, movies projected onto neighboring buildings, and hot waitresses.

8300 Sunset Blvd. (at Sweetzer Ave.), West Hollywood, CA 90069. © **323/650-9090.** Fax 323/650-2820. www.standardhotel.com. 139 units. $160–$295 double; from $500 suite. AE, DC, DISC, MC, V. Valet parking $22. Pets under 20 lb. accepted for $100-per-pet fee. **Amenities:** 24-hr. coffee shop; poolside cafe; bar/lounge; outdoor heated pool; access to nearby health club; concierge; business center; barbershop; 24-hr. room service; in-room massage; babysitting; laundry service; dry cleaning. *In room:* A/C, big-screen TV/DVD, complimentary Wi-Fi, minibar, iPod docking stations.

Inexpensive

Beverly Laurel Motor Hotel ⓥalue Touted by the *New York Times* for its Gen-X appeal and value, the Beverly Laurel is a great choice for wallet-watching travelers who want a central location and a room with more style than your average motel. Overlooking the parking lot, the budget-basic but well-kept rooms are smartened up with diamond-print spreads and eye-catching artwork; other features include a minifridge, microwave, and ample closet space, and a large kitchenette for an extra 10-spot. The postage-stamp-size outdoor pool is a little public for carefree sunbathing, but it does the job on hot summer days. Best of all is the motel's own excellent coffee shop, **Swingers**—nobody serves better burgers and malts, and you may even spot your favorite alt-rocker tucking into a 3pm breakfast in the vinyl booth next to yours.

8018 Beverly Blvd. (btw. La Cienega Blvd. and Fairfax Ave.), Los Angeles, CA 90048. © **800/962-3824** or 323/651-2441. Fax 323/651-5225. 52 units. $107–$150 double. AAA and senior discounts may be available. AE, DC, MC, V. Free parking. **Amenities:** Heated outdoor pool; laundry service. *In room:* A/C, TV, minifridge, hair dryer, microwave.

Farmer's Daughter ⓥalue Most people end up at the Farmer's Daughter hotel fortuitously because they're waiting to be the next contestants on *The Price Is Right.* The CBS Studios across the street recommend the budget motel to its game show fans, but I recommend it just because I dig this chic little lodge. It's cheery from the moment you walk in the lobby. Bright yellows and cool blues mix well with the country-kitsch theme: rooster wallpaper, faded barn-wood paneling, denim bedspreads, cow-skin rugs, and a parade of inflatable animals that float around the pool. It's obvious that someone with smart fashion sense and a little money turned a dumpy motel into an oasis of stylish affordability for people like me who drive Jettas and wear flip-flops in the winter. Money-saving perks include free Internet hookup, free parking, a free DVD library, and across-the-street access to an entire Farmers Market of inexpensive foodstuffs (p. 537). But now that the hotel opened its own French-country restaurant, **TART,** there's little reason to leave. *Tip:* Request a room facing the alley—the view is terrible, but you don't get the 24-hour road noise off Fairfax Avenue.

115 S. Fairfax Ave. (btw. Beverly Dr. and Third St.), Los Angeles, CA 90036. © **800/334-1658** or 323/937-3930. Fax 323/932-1608. www.farmersdaughterhotel.com. 66 units. $215 double; from $275 suite. Includes morning coffee and tea service. AE, DISC, MC, V. Valet parking $12. **Amenities:** Restaurant; bar; swimming pool; concierge services; daily laundry and dry cleaning. *In room:* A/C, TV/DVD, complimentary DVD library, high-speed Internet, minifridge, coffeemaker, personal safe, CD player, voice mail.

Expensive

Roosevelt Hotel, Hollywood ★★   After finally completing a $30-million renovation, this venerable 12-story landmark smack dab in the touristy section of Hollywood Boulevard, across from Grauman's Chinese Theatre and along the Walk of Fame, is now *the* place to stay in Hollywood. It's got everything you'd want in a Hollywood Boulevard hotel: history, exclusivity, models-slash-actresses serving cocktails at the poolside bar, a raucous nightlife scene, and just the right amount of L.A. attitude. Host to the first Academy Awards in 1929—not to mention a few famous-name ghosts—this national treasure is Hollywood's only historic hotel still operating today. The renovation harmoniously melds the Roosevelt's historical highlights (such as the 1927 Spanish-influenced sunken lobby) with modern hotel luxuries. The guest rooms have been tastefully upgraded with extra-large bathrooms, dark-wood platform beds with luxurious Frette linens, and all the latest high-tech accessories. Rooms on the upper floors have skyline views, while the individually decorated cabana rooms have a balcony or terrace overlooking the Olympic-size pool (whose mural was originally painted by David Hockney). The über-hip **Dakota** steakhouse serves a superb porterhouse, and **25 Degrees** is a popular late-night 1950s-style burger bar. Long story short, the Roosevelt Hotel has once again become the playground for the young, hot Hollywood set, with antics from the poolside **Tropicana** bar and exclusive **Teddy's** lounge getting as much press as Lindsay Lohan on a bender.

7000 Hollywood Blvd., Hollywood, CA 90028. (ℭ **800/950-7667** or 323/466-7000. Fax 323/462-8056. www.hollywoodroosevelt.com. 300 units. $285–$360 double; from $425 suite; poolside cabana rooms from $300. AE, DC, DISC, MC, V. Valet parking $18. **Amenities:** 2 restaurants; 3 bars; outdoor pool; spa and fitness center; Jacuzzi; concierge; activities desk; 24-hr. room service; poolside massage service; babysitting; laundry service; dry cleaning; executive-level rooms; complimentary shoe shine. *In room:* A/C, TV w/ pay movies, high-speed Internet, minibar, coffeemaker, hair dryer, safe, CD player, video games.

Inexpensive

Best Western Hollywood Hills Hotel ★   Location is a big selling point for this family-owned (since 1948) member of the reliable Best Western chain: It's just off U.S. 101 (the Hollywood Fwy.); a Metro Line stop just 3 blocks away means easy, car-free access to Universal Studios; and the famed Hollywood and Vine intersection is just a 5-minute walk away. The entire hotel has been recently renovated in a contemporary style, and all the spiffy guest rooms come with a refrigerator, coffeemaker, microwave, and wireless Internet. The rooms in the back building are my favorites, as they sit well back from busy Franklin Avenue, face the gleaming blue-tiled, heated outdoor pool, and have an attractive view of the neighboring hillside. A major convenience is the **101 Hills Coffee Shop** located off the lower lobby.

6141 Franklin Ave. (btw. Vine and Gower sts.), Hollywood, CA 90028. (ℭ **800/287-1700** or 323/464-5181. Fax 323/962-0536. www.bestwestern.com/hollywoodhillshotel. 86 units. $129–$169 double. AAA and AARP discounts available. AE, DISC, MC, V. Free covered parking. Small pets accepted with $25-per-night fee. **Amenities:** Coffee shop; heated outdoor pool; access to nearby health club; tour desk; coin-op laundry. *In room:* A/C, TV, Wi-Fi, fridge, coffeemaker, hair dryer, iron, microwave.

Days Inn Hollywood   While it's east of the prime Sunset Strip action, this freshly renovated motel is safe and convenient, and extras such as free underground parking and continental breakfast make it an especially good value. Doubles are large enough for families. Some rooms have microwaves, fridges, and coffeemakers; if yours doesn't have a hair dryer or an iron, they're available at the front desk. For maximum bang for your **511** buck, ask for a room overlooking the pool.

7023 Sunset Blvd. (btw. Highland and La Brea aves.), Hollywood, CA 90028. ✆ **800/329-7466** or 323/ 464-8344. Fax 323/962-9748. www.daysinn.com. 72 units. $130–$180 double; $145–$220 Jacuzzi suite. Rates include continental breakfast. Ask about AAA, AARP, and other discounted rates (as low as $95 at press time). AE, DC, DISC, MC, V. Free secured parking. **Amenities:** Heated outdoor pool; laundry service. *In room:* A/C, TV.

Magic Castle Hotel ★ (Kids) (Value)   Located a stone's throw from Hollywood Boulevard's attractions, this garden-style hotel/motel at the base of the Hollywood Hills offers L.A.'s best cheap sleeps and is ideal for wallet-watching families or long-term stays. You won't see the Magic Castle Hotel in *Travel + Leisure* anytime soon—the rooms are done in high Levitz style—but the units are spacious, comfortable, and well kept. Named for the Magic Castle, the illusionist club just uphill, the hotel was once an apartment building; it still feels private and insulated from Franklin Avenue's constant stream of traffic. The units are situated around a central swimming pool. Most are large apartments with fully equipped kitchens complete with a microwave and coffeemaker (grocery shopping service is available as well).

7025 Franklin Ave. (btw. La Brea and Highland aves.), Hollywood, CA 90028. ✆ **800/741-4915** or 323/ 851-0800. Fax 323/851-4926. www.magiccastlehotel.com. 40 units. $129 double; $149–$239 suite. Extra person $10. Off-season and other discounts available. Free continental breakfast. AE, DC, DISC, MC, V. Parking $8. **Amenities:** Outdoor heated pool; full-service or coin-op laundry. *In room:* A/C, TV, free Wi-Fi, coffeemaker, hair dryer, iron, safe.

DOWNTOWN
Expensive/Moderate
Traditionally the domain of business folk and convention attendees, downtown L.A. is becoming increasingly attractive to leisure travelers for several reasons: a Rudy Giuliani–style cleanup in the late 1990s; a growing number of cultural attractions and destination dining; excellent-value weekend packages at luxury hotels that empty out once the work-week ends; and easy, car-free access via the Metro Line to Hollywood and Universal Studios. Every freeway passes through downtown, so it's a breeze to hop in the car and head to other neighborhoods, except during rush hour. Consider yourself forewarned, however: Despite low weekend rates, downtown L.A. can feel like a ghost town, particularly after dusk. And all the hoopla about urban revival? Let's just say downtown has had more comebacks than Madonna.

Figueroa Hotel ★ (Finds)   With an artistic eye and a heartfelt commitment to creating exotic, whimsical, and oh-so-anti-corporate accommodations, charming owner Uno Thimansson has transformed a 1925-vintage former YWCA residence into my top pick for affordable downtown lodging. This venerable 12-story property sits in an increasingly gentrified corner of downtown, within shouting distance of the ever-growing L.A. LIVE entertainment complex. The big, airy lobby exudes a romantic Spanish Colonial–Gothic vibe, and elevators lead to equally artistic guest rooms that, although poorly lit, are very comfortable. Each comes with a firm, well-made bed with a wrought-iron headboard or canopy, a Mexican-tiled bathroom, and East Asian fabrics that double as blackout drapes. My favorite room is no. 1130, a large double-queen with a Spanish terra-cotta print chaise, but you can't go wrong with any room. The Casablanca Suite is a Moroccan pleasure den, ideal for romance. Out back you'll find a desert-garden deck with a mosaic-tiled pool and Jacuzzi, and the Verandah Bar, the poolside place to go on warm Southern California nights for a minty mojito.

939 S. Figueroa St. (at Olympic Blvd.), Los Angeles, CA 90015. ℂ **800/421-9092** or 213/627-8971. Fax 213/689-0305. 285 units. $144 double; $245 Casablanca suite; $195–$205 other suites. www.figueroa hotel.com. AE, DC, MC, V. Parking $8. **Amenities:** Restaurant; bar; outdoor pool area; Jacuzzi; laundry service; dry cleaning. *In room:* A/C, TV, Wi-Fi, minifridge.

Millennium Biltmore Hotel Los Angeles ★★

The Biltmore is one of those hotels that's worth a visit even if you're not staying here. Built in 1923 and encompassing almost an entire square block, this Italian-Spanish Renaissance landmark is the grande dame of L.A.'s hotels. Chances are you've seen it in many movies, including the *Wedding Crashers, Chinatown, Ghostbusters, Bugsy,* and *Beverly Hills Cop.* The hotel lobby—JFK's campaign headquarters during the 1960 Democratic National Convention—appeared upside-down in *The Poseidon Adventure.* Always in fine shape and host to world leaders and luminaries, the sense of refinement and graciousness endures. Spend the few bucks to appreciate the Art Deco health club, with its gorgeous Roman-style pool. The "wow" factor ends at guest rooms, however, which are a little on the small side (common for older hotels) and aren't quite as eye-popping as the public spaces. Bathrooms are on the small side as well, but peach-toned marble adds a luxurious edge.

A range of dining and cocktail outlets includes **Sai Sai** for modern Asian cuisine and sushi. Pretty, casual **Smeraldi's** serves homemade pastas and lighter Mediterranean fare. Off the lobby is the stunning **Gallery Bar,** named by *Los Angeles* magazine as one of the sexiest cocktail lounges in L.A. Afternoon tea and cocktails are served in the **Rendezvous Court,** which used to be the hotel's original lobby and resembles the interior of a Spanish cathedral.

506 S. Grand Ave. (btw. Fifth and Sixth sts.), Los Angeles, CA 90071. ℂ **800/245-8673** or 213/624-1011. Fax 213/612-1545. www.thebiltmore.com. 683 units. $159–$375 double; from $450 suite. Leisure discount packages available. AE, DC, DISC, MC, V. Parking $40. **Amenities:** 3 restaurants; bar; health club w/ original 1923 inlaid pool, Jacuzzi, steam, and sauna; concierge; courtesy car; business center; gift shop; salon; room service; in-room massage; babysitting; laundry service; dry cleaning; executive-level rooms. *In room:* A/C, TV w/pay movies, minibar, coffeemaker, hair dryer.

Westin Bonaventure Hotel & Suites ★

This 35-story, 1,354-room monolith is the hotel that locals love to hate. The truth is that the Bonaventure is a terrific hotel. It's certainly not for travelers who want intimacy or personality in their accommodations—but with numerous restaurants and bars, a full-service spa, a monster health club, and much more on hand, you'll be hard-pressed to want for anything here (except maybe some individualized attention). The hotel's five gleaming glass silos encompass an entire square block and form one of downtown's most distinctive landmarks. The pie-shaped guest rooms are on the small side, but a wall of windows offering great views, and Westin's unparalleled Heavenly Bed—the ultimate in hotel-bed comfort—make for a very comfortable cocoon. With executive workstation, fax, and wet bar, guest office suites are great for business travelers, while tower suites—with living room, extra half-bathroom, minifridge, microwave, and two TVs—are ideal for families.

404 S. Figueroa St. (btw. Fourth and Fifth sts.), Los Angeles, CA 90071. ℂ **866/716-8132** or 213/624-1000. Fax 213/612-4800. www.westin.com/bonaventure. 1,354 units. $237–$289 double; from $297 suite. Ask about specials and packages. AE, DC, DISC, MC, V. Valet parking $40. **Amenities:** 17 restaurants and fast-food outlets; 5 bars and lounges; outdoor heated lap pool; 15,000-sq.-ft. full-service spa, running track, and access to 4,500-sq.-ft. health club; Westin Kids Club; concierge; car-rental desk; full-service business center; shops; salon; 24-hr. room service; babysitting; valet; laundry service; dry cleaning. *In room:* A/C, TV, high-speed Internet, coffeemaker, hair dryer, iron, laptop-size safe.

Inexpensive

Hotel Stillwell   The Stillwell is far from fancy, but its modestly priced rooms are a good option in a generally pricey neighborhood. Built in 1906, this once-elegant 250-room hotel is conveniently located near the STAPLES Center, the Civic Center, and the Museum of Contemporary Art. Rooms are clean, basic, and simply decorated with decent furnishings. The hotel is quiet, though, and hallways feature East Indian artwork. That said, I much prefer the Hotel Figueroa, but this is a less eccentric and perfectly reasonable choice. The lobby-level Indian restaurant is a popular lunch spot for downtown office workers; other options include a casual Mexican restaurant and the so-old-it's-retro **Hanks Cocktail Lounge.**

838 S. Grand Ave. (btw. Eighth and Ninth sts.), Los Angeles, CA 90017. © **800/553-4774** or 213/627-1151. Fax 213/622-8940. www.hotelstillwell.com. 250 units. $79 double; $85–$115 suite. AE, DC, DISC, MC, V. Parking $4.50. **Amenities:** 2 restaurants; lounge; activities desk; business center; coin-op laundry; laundry service; dry cleaning. *In room:* A/C, TV, fax, fridge, iron.

SAN FERNANDO VALLEY & UNIVERSAL CITY
Moderate

Beverly Garland's Holiday Inn (Kids)   The "Beverly Garland" in this 258-room hotel's name is the actress who played Fred MacMurray's wife on *My Three Sons*. Grassy areas and greenery abound at this North Hollywood Holiday Inn, a virtual oasis in the concrete jungle. The Mission-influenced buildings are a bit dated, but if you grew up with *Brady Bunch* reruns, this only adds to the charm. Southwestern-themed fabrics complement the natural-pine furnishings in the spacious (and soundproof) guest rooms, attracting your attention away from the somewhat unfortunate painted cinder-block walls. On the plus side, all of the well-outfitted rooms have balconies overlooking the pleasant grounds, which include a pool and two lighted tennis courts. With Universal Studios just down the street and a free shuttle to the park, the location can't be beat for families. Since proximity to the 101 and 134 freeways also means the constant buzz of traffic, ask for a room facing Vineland Avenue for maximum quiet. *Tip:* If you're bringing the kids along, be sure to inquire about the KidSuites.

4222 Vineland Ave., North Hollywood, CA 91602. © **800/238-3759** or 818/980-8000. Fax 818/766-0112. www.beverlygarland.com. 255 units. $139–$189 double; from $220 suite. Ask about AAA, AARP, corporate, military, Great Rates, weekend, and other discounted rates. Kids 12 and under stay free in parent's room and eat free. AE, DC, DISC, MC, V. Free parking. **Amenities:** Restaurant; bar; heated outdoor pool; lighted tennis courts; sauna; car-rental desk; complimentary shuttle to Universal Studios. *In room:* A/C, TV, coffeemaker, hair dryer, iron.

Sheraton Universal Hotel ★ (Kids)   Despite the addition of the sleekly modern Hilton just uphill, the 21-story Sheraton is still considered *the* Universal City hotel of choice for tourists, businesspeople, and industry folks visiting the studios' production offices. On the back lot of Universal Studios, it has a spacious 1960s feel, with updated styling and amenities. Although the Sheraton does its share of convention/event business, the hotel feels more leisure-oriented than the Hilton next door (an outdoor elevator connects the two properties). Choose a Lanai room for balconies that overlook the lushly planted pool area, or a Tower room for stunning views and solitude. The hotel is very close to the Hollywood Bowl, and you can practically roll out of bed and into the theme park (via a continuous complimentary shuttle). An extra $35 per night buys a Club Level room—worth the money for the extra in-room amenities and free continental breakfast and afternoon hors d'oeuvres.

333 Universal Hollywood Dr., Universal City, CA 91608. ✆ **800/325-3535** or 818/980-1212. Fax 818/985-4980. www.sheraton.com/universal. 436 units. $209–$239 double; from $420 suite. Children stay free in parent's room. Ask about AAA, AARP, and corporate discounts; also inquire about packages that include theme-park admission. AE, DC, DISC, MC, V. Valet parking $21; self-parking $16. **Amenities:** Casual indoor/outdoor restaurant; outdoor pool; health club; whirlpool; game room; concierge; free shuttle to Universal Studios every 15 min.; business center; room service; babysitting; laundry service; dry cleaning; executive Club Level rooms. *In room:* A/C, TV w/pay movies, high-speed Internet connection, minibar, safe (hair dryer and iron in Club Level rooms).

Inexpensive

Best Western Mikado Hotel   This Asian-flavored garden hotel has been a Valley fixture for 40-plus years. The kitsch value extends from the pagoda-style exterior to the sushi bar (the Valley's oldest) across the driveway. Two-story motel buildings face two well-maintained courtyards, one with a koi pond and wooden footbridge, the other with a shimmering blue-tiled pool and hot tub. Guest rooms are suitably comfortable and well outfitted. Furnished in 1970s-era chic (leather sofas, earth tones), the one-bedroom apartment is a steal, with enormous rooms and a full-size kitchen.

12600 Riverside Dr. (btw. Whitsett and Coldwater Canyon), North Hollywood, CA 91607. ✆ **800/780-7234** or 818/763-9141. Fax 818/752-1045. www.bestwestern.com/mikadohotel. 58 units. $129–$159 double; $250 1-bedroom apt. Ask about AAA, senior, and other discounted rates (as low as $98 at press time). Extra person $10. Children under 12 stay free in parent's room. Rates include full American breakfast. AE, DC, DISC, MC, V. Free parking. **Amenities:** Japanese restaurant and sushi bar; cocktail lounge; outdoor pool; Jacuzzi; fax and copying services at front desk. *In room:* A/C, TV, complimentary high-speed Internet, coffeemaker, hair dryer, iron.

PASADENA & ENVIRONS
Moderate

Artists' Inn & Cottage Bed & Breakfast   Pleasantly unpretentious and furnished with wicker throughout, this yellow-shingled Victorian-style inn was built in 1895 as a farmhouse and expanded to include a neighboring 1909 home. Each of the 10 rooms is decorated to reflect the style of a particular artist or period. Among the inspired choices are the country-cozy New England–style Grandma Moses room; the soft, pastel-hued Degas suite; and the bold-lined, primary-hued Expressionist suite, a nod to such artists as Picasso and Dufy. Every room is thoughtfully arranged and features a private bathroom (many with period fixtures, three with Jacuzzi tubs), fresh roses from the front garden, port wine, and chocolates. The quiet residential location is just 5 minutes from the heart of Old Town Pasadena, just a few stops on the Metro Gold Line.

1038 Magnolia St., South Pasadena, CA 91030. ✆ **888/799-5668** or 626/799-5668. Fax 626/799-3678. www.artistsinns.com. 10 units. $135–$225 double. Rates include full breakfast and afternoon tea. Check for midweek specials. Extra person $20. AE, MC, V. Free parking. *In room:* A/C, TV (upon request), hair dryer.

Bissell House Bed & Breakfast ★   If you enjoy the true B&B experience, you'll love the Bissell House. Hidden behind hedges that carefully isolate it from busy Orange Grove Avenue, this antiques-filled 1887 gingerbread Victorian—the former home of the vacuum heiress and now owned by the Hoyman family—offers a taste of life on what was once Pasadena's "Millionaire's Row." Outfitted in a traditional chintz-and-cabbage-roses style, all individually decorated rooms have private bathrooms (two with an antique claw-foot tub, one with a whirlpool tub, four with showers only), Internet access, and comfortable beds. If you don't mind stairs, request one of the more spacious top-floor rooms. The modern world doesn't interfere with the mood in these romantic sanctuaries, but the downstairs library features a TV with VCR and a telephone. The landscaped grounds boast an inviting pool, Jacuzzi, and deck with lounge chairs. Included in the room rate is an elaborately prepared breakfast served in the large dining room, as well as an afternoon tea, cookie, and wine service. A self-serve continental breakfast is also available weekdays for business guests.

201 Orange Grove Ave. (at Columbia St.), South Pasadena, CA 91030. © **800/441-3530** or 626/441-3535. Fax 626/441-3671. www.bissellhouse.com. 5 units. $150–$350 double. Rates include full breakfast. AE, MC, V. Free parking. **Amenities:** Outdoor pool; Jacuzzi; CD and video libraries. *In room:* A/C, hair dryer, iron, robes, no phone.

INEXPENSIVE

Saga Motor Hotel (Value)   This 1950s relic of old Route 66 has far more character than most other motels in its price range. The rooms are small, clean, and simply furnished with the basics. The double/doubles are spacious enough for shares, but budget-minded families will prefer the extra-large configuration dedicated to them, which has a king-size bed and two doubles. The best rooms are in the front building surrounding the gated swimming pool, shielded from the street and inviting in warm weather. The grounds are attractive and well kept, if you don't count the Astroturf "lawn" on the pool deck. The location is relatively quiet (considering it's on a busy strip of Colorado Blvd. directly across from the Pasadena Community College) and very convenient, just off the Foothill (210) Freeway about a mile from the Huntington Library and within 10 minutes of both the Rose Bowl and Old Pasadena.

1633 E. Colorado Blvd. (btw. Allen and Sierra Bonita aves.), Pasadena, CA 91106. © **800/793-7242** or 626/795-0431. Fax 626/792-0559. www.thesagamotorhotel.com. 70 units. $76–$92 double; $110–$135 family suite. Rates include continental breakfast. AE, DC, DISC, MC, V. Free parking. **Amenities:** Outdoor heated pool; free self-serve laundromat; laundry service; dry cleaning. *In room:* A/C, TV.

4 WHERE TO DINE

As one of the world's cultural crossroads, Los Angeles is an international atlas of exotic cuisines: Afghan, Argentinean, Armenian, Burmese, Cajun, Cambodian, Cuban, Ethiopian, Jewish, Korean, Lebanese, Moroccan, Oaxacan, Peruvian, Persian, Spanish, Vietnamese, and so on. Whatever you're in the mood for, this town has got it. All you need to join the dinner party is an adventurous palate, because half the fun of visiting Los Angeles is experiencing worldly dishes.

The famous celebrity chefs and celebrity-owned restaurants attract most of the limelight, but most of L.A.'s best dining experiences are in the kind of restaurants you'd never find unless someone let you in on the secret. For a greater selection, pick up *Frommer's Los Angeles 2009* (Wiley Publishing, Inc.). For additional late-night dining options, see "Late-Night Bites" under "Los Angeles After Dark," later in this chapter. To locate the restaurants reviewed below, see the individual neighborhood maps in section 1, "Orientation."

SANTA MONICA & THE BEACHES
Expensive

Boa Steakhouse ★★ STEAKHOUSE   It's a no-brainer: Combine the best quality steaks with a sexy decor, lively bar, and a key corner location at the foot of Santa Monica Boulevard, and you'll do well. The sophisticated decor eschews the traditional dim steakhouse ambience in favor of a warm, sleek interior highlighted with floor-to-ceiling windows that allow natural light to filter in. Tough decisions await you: Should you order the bone-in filet mignon, Kobe filet mignon, 35-day dry-aged New York strip, bone-in rib-eye, flatiron steak, or porterhouse? Non-meat-eaters may prefer the lump crab cake appetizer with heart of palm salad and Cajun rémoulade, or sides such as the homemade crispy fries, macaroni and cheese, and roasted garlic whipped potatoes. For a pick-me-up dessert, try the refreshing blackberry crush cocktail, a mojito-like mixture made with fresh fruit and top-shelf vodka. *Note:* A second Boa steakhouse is located along the Sunset Strip in West Hollywood (8462 W. Sunset Blvd; ℂ 323/650-8383).

101 Santa Monica Blvd. (at Ocean Ave.), Santa Monica. ℂ 310/899-4466. www.boasteak.com. Reservations recommended. Main courses $25–$39. AE, DC, DISC, MC, V. Mon–Sat 11:30am–11:30pm; Sun 11am–11pm. Valet parking $5.

The Lobster ★★ SEAFOOD   A seafood shack called the Lobster has stood on the Santa Monica Pier since 1923—almost as long as the pier's been standing—but a new sophistication presides at this perpetually crowded and lively local favorite. The interior is completely rebuilt but still accentuates a seaside ambience and a million-dollar ocean view with its floor-to-ceiling windows. Allyson Thurber's menu consistently presents a multitude of ultrafresh fish with thoughtful and creative preparation. Specialties range from sautéed tiger prawns "scampi" style to jumbo lump crab cakes and lobster grilled, steamed, or pan-roasted. Creative appetizers include ahi carpaccio with tangy *tobiko* wasabi, steamed mussels and Manila clams with apple-wood bacon, and oysters plain or fancy. For something truly decadent, try the sake-*kasu*-marinated sea bass accompanied by a bottle of dry chardonnay from the well-stocked cellar. The menu offers a couple of fine steaks for landlubbers, and the practiced bar serves lots of Bloody Marys garnished with jumbo shrimp to dedicated locals. For dessert, chocolate bread pudding is terrific. *Tip:* Request a table on the deck and enjoy the 180-degree panoramic view of the Pacific.

1602 Ocean Ave. (at Colorado), Santa Monica. ℂ 310/458-9294. www.thelobster.com. Reservations recommended. Main courses $19–$41. AE, DC, DISC, MC, V. Mon–Thurs 11:30am–10pm; Fri–Sat 11:30am–11pm. Valet parking $4.50.

Michael's ★★ CALIFORNIA   Owner Michael McCarty, L.A.'s answer to Alice Waters, is considered by many to be the father of California cuisine. Since Michael's opened in 1979 (when McCarty was only 25), several top L.A. restaurants have caught up to it, but this fetching Santa Monica venue remains one of the city's best. The dining room is filled with contemporary art by Michael's wife, Kim, and the restaurant's garden is Santa Monica's most romantic setting for always-inventive menu choices such as grilled Mediterranean *loup de mer* with chorizo and mussels, oven-roasted Channel spiny lobster with garlic-fennel potato purée, or grilled pork chop with Calvados apple pan sauce. Don't miss Michael's famous warm mushroom salad, tossed with crumbled goat cheese, watercress, caramelized onion, and mustard-sage vinaigrette. The dry-aged New York strip is also fantastic, as are the steak *frites*.

1147 Third St. (north of Wilshire Blvd.), Santa Monica. ℂ 310/451-0843. www.michaelssantamonica. com. Reservations recommended. Main courses dinner $23–$45, lunch $16–$23. AE, DC, DISC, MC, V. Mon–Fri noon–2:30pm and 6–10:30pm; Sat 6–10:30pm. Valet parking $5.50.

Moderate

Border Grill ★★ MEXICAN   Before Mary Sue Milliken and Susan Feniger spiced up cable TV with *Too Hot Tamales*, they started this hugely popular haute Mexican restaurant in West Hollywood. Since then the Border Grill has moved to a vibrantly painted, cavernous, and *muy* loud space in Santa Monica that's packed every night with

---

(Finds) **L.A.'s Best Sushi & Stir-Fried Crickets**

If you want to start a heated argument with L.A.'s foodies, just claim that you know where the best sushi in the city is served. Well, let the tongue-fu begin, because I'm claiming that the **Hump** ★★★ (① **310/313-0977; www.the hump.biz**) serves L.A.'s best. Much of the seafood here is flown in daily from Tokyo's Tsukijii and Fukuoka fish markets in oxygen-filled containers and is so fresh that the management had to put a sign at the entrance to warn the faint-of-heart from sitting at the sushi bar.

Directly below the Hump is the much larger **Typhoon** ★★ (① **310/390-6565;** www.typhoon-restaurant.com), a very popular and high-energy Pan-Asian restaurant where stir-fried Taiwanese spicy crickets, dried Manchurian ants, and Thai-style crispy white sea worms punctuate a family-style menu filled with less exotic fare from throughout Southeast Asia, most in the $7 to $12 range.

Both restaurants are located on the second and third floors of the airport's administration building at 3221 Donald Douglas Loop Rd., in Santa Monica.

---

locals and tourists. The duck tamale appetizer I ordered the last time I was here was *the* most flavorful and unique Mexican dish I've ever had: freshly made corn masa filled with tender roast duck, *guajillo* chile sauce, roasted sweet peppers, and then topped with an exquisite cranberry salsa. Another favorite are the plantain empanadas with *chipotle* salsa and Mexican *crema*, and the über-tender roasted lamb tacos with strips of poblano chiles and manchego cheese. If it's on the specials menu, you must order the grilled chicken enchiladas verdes simmered in green mole sauce with Oaxacan cheese and hand-rolled corn tortillas. The best meatless dish is the *mulitas*, a layering of portobello mushrooms, roasted peppers, and pickled onions. *Tip:* The happy-hour menu (Mon–Fri 4–7pm, Fri–Sat after 10pm) has tasty $3 treats such as tacos, empanadas, and tostadas; and margaritas are only $3.50.

1445 Fourth St. (btw. Broadway and Santa Monica Blvd.), Santa Monica. ① **310/451-1655.** www.border grill.com. Reservations recommended. Main courses $12–$29. AE, DC, DISC, MC, V. Sun–Thurs 11:30am–10pm; Fri–Sat 11:30am–11pm. Metered parking lots; valet parking $4.

Joe's Restaurant ★★ (Value) AMERICAN ECLECTIC   This is one of L.A.'s best dining bargains. Chef/owner Joseph Miller excels in simple New American cuisine, particularly grilled fish and roasted meats accented with piquant herbs. Formerly a tiny, quirky storefront, the entire restaurant was gutted and completely remodeled, with a more spacious dining room and display wine room (though the best tables are still tucked away on the trellised outdoor patio complete with a gurgling waterfall). Don't let the upscale additions dissuade your budgeted appetite: For lunch, California sand dabs with cherry tomato, arugula, and Maine sweet shrimp goes for a mere $13. And this *includes* a fresh mixed green salad or one of Miller's exquisite soups. Dinner entrees are equally sophisticated: beet risotto with grilled asparagus, fallow deer wrapped in bacon (served in a black currant sauce with a side of roasted root vegetables), monkfish in a saffron broth, wild striped bass with curried cauliflower coulis. A double whammy is Joe's grilled ahi tuna *and* Hudson Valley foie gras appetizer served with *rösti* potatoes and a red-wine herb sauce.

Sea Breezes & Sunsets: Ocean-View Dining in Malibu

Beau Rivage, 26025 Pacific Coast Hwy. (at Corral Canyon; ✆ **310/456-5733;** www.beaurivagerestaurant.com) is my only pick located on the *other* side of PCH from the beach, but this romantic Mediterranean restaurant (whose name means "beautiful shore") has nearly unobstructed ocean views. The baby-pink villa and its flagstone dining patio are overgrown with flowering vines. The place is prettiest at sunset; romantic lighting takes over after dark. The menu is composed of country French and Italian dishes with plenty of moderately priced pastas, many with seafood. Other main courses are more expensive; they include chicken, duck, rabbit, and lamb, all traditionally prepared. An older, nicely dressed crowd tends to dine at this special-occasion place. It's open Monday through Saturday from 5 to 10pm, and Sunday from 11am to 10pm. Valet parking is $4 (Fri–Sat only; otherwise, free self-parking). **Tip:** Sunday's brunch menu, which isn't limited to breakfast dishes, is a less pricey alternative to dinner.

Duke's Malibu ★, 21150 Pacific Coast Hwy. (at Las Flores Canyon; ✆ **310/317-0777;** www.dukesmalibu.com) allows lovers of Hawaii and all things Polynesian to thrive in this outpost of the Hawaiian chain. Imagine a South Pacific T.G.I. Fridays where the food is secondary to the decor, then add a rocky perch atop breaking waves, and you have this surfing-themed crowd-pleaser. It's worth a visit for the memorabilia alone—the place is named for Hawaiian surf legend "Duke" Kahanamoku. Duke's offers up pretty good food at inflated, but not outrageous, prices. You'll find plenty of fresh fish prepared in the Hawaiian regional style, hearty surf and turf, a smattering of chicken and pasta dishes, and plenty of pupus to accompany Duke's Day-Glo tropical cocktails. The Sunday brunch buffet (10am–3pm) is a tasty deal at $22 for adults and $12 for kids. It's open Monday through Friday from 11:30am to 9pm, Saturday from 11:30am to 9:30pm, and Sunday from 11:30am to 10pm. Valet parking is $2 (dinner and weekends only; otherwise, free self-parking).

Gladstone's 4 Fish, 17300 Pacific Coast Hwy. (at Sunset Blvd.; ✆ **310/454-3474;** www.gladstones.com), a local tradition, is totally immersed in the Malibu scene. It shares a parking lot with a public beach, so the restaurant's wooden deck has a constant view of surfers, bikini-clad sunbathers, and other beachgoers. At busy times, Gladstone's even sets up picnic-style tables on the sand. Prices are moderate, and the atmosphere is casual. The menu offers several pages of fresh fish and seafood, augmented by a few salads and other meals for landlubbers—it's mostly fried tourist food, but the large portions get the job done. Gladstone's is popular for afternoon/evening drinking and offers nearly 20 seafood appetizer platters; it's also known for its decadent chocolate dessert, the Mile High Chocolate Cake, large enough for the whole table. It's open Sunday through Thursday from 8am to 10pm, Friday and Saturday from 8am to 11pm. Parking is $4.50.

Main courses dinner $18–$28, lunch 14–$18. AE, MC, V. Tues–Thurs noon–2:30pm and 6–10pm; Fri noon–2:30pm and 6–11pm; Sat 11am–2:30pm and 6–11pm; Sun 11:30am–2:30pm and 6–10pm. Free street parking or valet parking in rear of building.

Locanda del Lago ★★ NORTHERN ITALIAN In a sea of mediocre restaurants along Santa Monica's Third Street Shopping Promenade is Locanda del Lago (Trattoria of the Lake). This corner trattoria is the only restaurant in Los Angeles that specializes in cuisine from Northern Italy's Lombardy region. Both the co-owner and executive chef were born in Milan, worked in Bellagio, and share a passion for food that hasn't waned since this warm, friendly restaurant opened more than 14 years ago. On sunny days there's no better place in L.A. to people-watch than at the trattoria's outdoor patio, savoring a glass of chianti while tucking into the house specialty—*osso buco alla Milanese*, a veal shank slow-cooked in white wine and vegetables, topped with traditional *gremolata* (a parsley, garlic, and lemon zest mixture) and served with saffron risotto. Other outstanding dishes include the butternut squash risotto with seared scallops, and *tagliatelle Lago*, house-made tagliolini tossed with pink trout and escarole in a thyme-infused white-wine sauce. After a hard day's shopping there's no better place on the Promenade to relax than Lago.

231 Arizona Ave. (at Third St.), Santa Monica. 𝄪 310/451-3525. www.lagosantamonica.com. Reservations recommended. Main courses $14–$30. AE, DC, DISC, MC, V. Mon–Thurs and Sun 11:30am–10pm; Fri–Sat 11am–11pm. Valet parking $5.

Restaurant Hama (Hama Sushi) ★★ (Finds) It's called a sushi "bar" for a reason—a place where people gather to socialize, drink, and have a good time. Most California sushi bars focus more on presentation than salutation, so imagine my surprise when I walked into Hama Sushi for the first time and was greeted with a chorus of "Heeeyyy!!!" from the six jolly chefs behind the bar. In Venice, at the town's only roundabout, the restaurant is usually packed each night with regulars, so expect to wait a bit before diving into Hama's melt-in-your-mouth yellowtail, albacore, *unagi*, and specialty rolls. Standard Japanese hot plates such as chicken teriyaki and grilled Chilean sea bass are available along with a wide selection of premium, chilled sake. *Tip:* Stay long enough to close the place down, and you'll be in for a singing surprise.

213 Windward Ave. (at Main St.), Venice. 𝄪 310/396-8783. www.hamasushi.com. Main courses $6–$25. AE, DC, DISC, MC, V. Mon–Thurs 6–11pm; Fri–Sat 6–11:30pm; Sun 5:30–10:30pm. Valet parking $4.

Inexpensive

Bread & Porridge ★ (Value) AMERICAN/BREAKFAST A dozen tables are all that comprise this neighborhood cafe, but steady streams of locals mill outside, reading their newspapers and waiting for a vacant seat. Once inside, surrounded by the vintage fruit-crate labels adorning the walls and tabletops, you can sample the delicious breakfasts, fresh salads and sandwiches, and super-affordable entrees. There's a vaguely international twist to the menu, which leaps from breakfast quesadillas and omelets—all served with black beans and salsa—to the Southern comfort of Cajun crab cakes and coleslaw and typical Italian pastas adorned with Roma tomatoes and plenty of garlic. All menu items are cheap—truck-stop cheap—but with an inventive elegance that truly makes this a best-kept secret. This place thoughtfully serves breakfast all day; get a short stack of one of five varieties of pancakes with any meal.

2315 Wilshire Blvd. (3 blocks west of 26th St.), Santa Monica. 𝄪 310/453-4941. Main courses $6–$9. AE, MC, V. Daily 7am–9pm. Metered street parking.

Jody Maroni's Sausage Kingdom ★ (Finds) SANDWICHES   Your cardiologist might not approve, but Jody Maroni's all-natural, preservative-free "haute dogs" are some of the best wieners served anywhere. The grungy walk-up (or in-line-skate-up) counter looks fairly foreboding—you wouldn't know there was gourmet fare behind that aging hot dog stand facade, from which at least 14 different grilled-sausage sandwiches are served up. Bypass the traditional hot Italian and try the Toulouse garlic, Bombay curried lamb, all-chicken apple, or orange-garlic-cumin. Each is served on a freshly baked onion roll and smothered with onions and peppers. Burgers, BLTs, and rotisserie chicken are also served, but why bother?

Other locations include the Valley's Universal CityWalk ((C) **818/622-5639**), and inside LAX Terminals 3, 4, and 6, where you can pick up some last-minute vacuum-packed sausages for home. Having elevated sausage worship to an art form, Jody's now boasts a helpful and humorous cookbook, plus its own website offering franchising opportunities.

2011 Ocean Front Walk (north of Venice Blvd.), Venice. (C) **310/822-5639**. www.jodymaroni.com. Sandwiches $4–$8. No credit cards. Daily 10am–sunset.

Sidewalk Cafe AMERICAN/BREAKFAST   Nowhere in L.A. is the people-watching better than along Ocean Front Walk. The constantly bustling Sidewalk Cafe is ensconced in one of Venice's few remaining early-20th-century buildings. The best seats, of course, are out front, around overcrowded open-air tables, all with perfect views of the crowd, which provides nonstop entertainment. The menu is extensive, and the food is a whole lot better than it has to be at a location like this. Choose from the seriously overstuffed sandwiches or other oversize American favorites: omelets, salads, and burgers.

1401 Ocean Front Walk (btw. Horizon Ave. and Market St.), Venice. (C) **310/399-5547**. www.thesidewalk cafe.com. Main courses $8–$13. MC, V. Daily 8am–11pm. Free parking w/validation.

L.A.'S WESTSIDE & BEVERLY HILLS
Expensive

Fogo de Chão ★★ BRAZILIAN STEAKHOUSE   What was started long ago by four brothers in São Paulo, Brazil, has finally made its way to Beverly Hills, and is now one of the most popular restaurants in the city. Pronounced fogo-dee-*shown,* this enormous Southern Brazilian–style steakhouse is packed nightly with fans of the *churrasco* style of cooking carne—large cuts of meat slow-roasted over an open wood flame, then deftly sliced, and continuously served onto your plate until you give in and flip your disk to red (you'll see). Truly, it's bacchanalia revisited as you wander wide-eyed around what must be the most dazzling salad bar ever conceived. The gluttony continues with mountains of freshly roasted meats and endless side dishes, all washed down with rich red wines from among the 10,000 bottles that surround you in two-story temperature-controlled towers of glass and steel.

133 N. La Cienega Blvd. (btw. W. Third St. and Beverly Blvd.), Los Angeles. (C) **310/289-7755**. www.fogo dechao.com. Reservations recommended. Fixed-price menu $53. AE, DC, DISC, MC, V. Mon–Thurs 5–10pm; Fri 5–10:30pm; Sat 4:30–10:30pm; Sun 4–9:30pm. Valet parking $5.50.

The Ivy ★★ NEW AMERICAN   If you're willing to endure the cold shoulder to ogle L.A.'s celebrities and pay lots for a perfect meal, the Ivy can be enjoyable. This snobby place attracts one of the most industry-heavy crowds in the city and treats celebrities and nobodies as differently as Brahmins and untouchables. Just past the cool reception lie two disarmingly countrified dining rooms, filled with rustic antiques, comfortably worn chintz, and hanging baskets of fragrant flowers. Huge roses bloom everywhere, including out on the charming brick patio, where the highest-profile patrons are seated. The Ivy's Caesar salad is perfect, as are the plump and crispy crab cakes. Recommended dishes include spinach linguine with a peppery tomato-basil sauce, prime rib dusted with Cajun spices, and tender lime-marinated grilled chicken. There's even a great burger and kick-ass fried chicken, and the wine list is notable.

113 N. Robertson Blvd. (btw. Third St. and Beverly Blvd.), West Hollywood. ✆ **310/274-8303.** Reservations recommended on weekends. Main courses dinner $22–$38, lunch $10–$25. AE, DC, DISC, MC, V. Mon–Sat 11:30am–10:30pm; Sun 10:30am–10:30pm. Valet parking $4.

Jar ★★★ MODERN CHOP HOUSE   Jar offers everything you could hope for in a restaurant: a warm and relaxed setting, excellent service, and generous servings of reliably fantastic food. During my last visit I devoured not one but two of the most flavorful meat dishes I've ever tasted: the braised Kurobuta pork shank and a Kobe-style filet of beef—both perfectly cooked, simply seasoned, and divinely flavorful. It was always Chef Suzanne Tracht's dream to open a contemporary version of a 1940s-era chop house, and you can tell that she's putting her best into every plate that leaves the kitchen. Everything she makes is a lesson in quality and simplicity. Among her most popular dishes are the Niman Ranch *char sui* pork chops and her coup de grâce—a sensational pot roast with caramelized onions and carrots (if you've had a better one let me know). An extensive wine list and martini menu are two good reasons to arrive early and stay for a nightcap at the beautiful Parisian-style bar. *Tip:* Suzanne's Sunday brunch is one of the best in the city.

8225 Beverly Blvd. (at Harper Ave.), Los Angeles. ✆ **323/655-6566.** www.thejar.com. Reservations recommended. Main courses $21–$48. AE, DC, DISC, MC, V. Mon–Thurs 5:30–10pm; Fri–Sat 5:30–11pm; Sun 10am–2pm and 5:30–9:30pm. Valet parking $6.

La Cachette ★★★ FRENCH   Widely considered one of the most influential French chefs in America, Jean François Meteigner literally wrote the book on this cuisine—*Cuisine Naturelle*—a revolutionary approach to fine French cuisine that favors dishes that are simple, light, full of flavor, and 90% free of cream and butter. Meteigner began his career as a chef in France, moved to Los Angeles in 1980 to serve as executive chef at L'Orangerie, and then opened La Cachette ("The Hideaway") in 1994. On the edge of a residential neighborhood in Century City, the elegant, romantic dining room is a bit hard to find—you have to access it from an alley off Little Santa Monica Boulevard—but it only adds to the restaurant's charm. I found Meteigner's dairy-free crab and lobster bisque to be intensely flavorful if lacking in richness (cream is an option, however), but all was forgiven as I devoured my braised Kurobuta black pork shank with braised baby back ribs and Banyul vinegar sauce, with roasted apples and Yukon mashed potatoes. The wine list has earned the *Wine Spectator* Award of Excellence, and the warm fruit tart is a fitting finale—light and flavorful.

10506 Santa Monica Blvd. (btw. Beverly Glen Blvd. and Overland Ave.), Century City. ✆ **310/470-4992.** www.lacachetterestaurant.com. Reservations recommended. Dinner main courses $26–$35; lunch $15–$32. AE, DC, MC, V. Mon–Fri noon–2pm; Mon–Thurs 6–9:30pm; Fri–Sat 5:30–10:30pm; Sun 6–9pm. Valet parking $3.50.

Lucques ★★ FRANCO-MEDITERRANEAN   Once Los Angeles became accustomed to this restaurant's unusual name—"Lucques" is a variety of French olive, pronounced "Luke"—local foodies fell hard for this quietly and comfortably sophisticated home of former Campanile chef Suzanne Goin. Goin cooks with bold flavors, fresh-from-the-farm produce, and an instinctive feel for Mediterranean flavors. The short and oft-changed menu makes the most of unusual ingredients such as salt cod and oxtails. Standout dishes include Tuscan bean soup with tangy greens and pistou, grilled duck breast served alongside braised red cabbage with chanterelle mushrooms and chestnuts, braised beef short ribs with potato purée and horseradish cream, and a perfect vanilla *pòt de crème* for dessert. Lucques's bar menu, featuring steak *frites* béarnaise, omelets, and tantalizing hors d'oeuvres (olives, warm almonds, sea salt, chewy bread), is a godsend for late-night diners, and the bartenders make a mean vodka Collins. *Tip:* On Sundays, Lucques offers a bargain $40 prix-fixe three-course dinner from a weekly changing menu.

8474 Melrose Ave. (east of La Cienega), West Hollywood. ✆ 323/655-6277. www.lucques.com. Reservations recommended. Main courses $18–$30. AE, DC, MC, V. Mon 6–10pm; Tues–Sat noon–2:30pm and 6–11pm; Sun 5–10pm. Metered street parking or valet ($5.50).

Mastro's Steakhouse ★★★ STEAKS/SEAFOOD   Down the street from Spago— so you know it's expensive—is one of the best steakhouses in Southern California: Mastro's. Typical of an upscale steakhouse, the dimly lit dining room on the first floor has a dark, leathery, serious men's club feel to it, so be sure to request a table on the second floor, where the bar, live music, and cool vibe are located. Slide into a plush black leather booth, order a Mastro Dry Ice Martini, and start off the feast with an Iced Seafood Tower—a massive pyramid of crab legs, lobster, shrimp, clams, and oysters the size of your palm. Fred Flintstone–size slabs of hand-cut USDA beef served on sizzling plates heated to 400°F (204°C) so your steak stays warm and juicy throughout the meal. The bad news is that a bone-in rib-eye runs about $50, but it will feed three people.

246 N. Canon Dr. (btw. Dayton Way and Wilshire Blvd.), Beverly Hills. ✆ 310/888-8782. www.mastrossteakhouse.com. Reservations recommended. Dinner main courses $26–$84. AE, DC, MC, V. Mon–Sun 5pm–2am. Valet parking $7.

Matsuhisa ★★ JAPANESE/PERUVIAN   Japanese chef/owner Nobuyuki Matsuhisa arrived in Los Angeles via Peru in 1987 and opened what may be the most creative restaurant in the city. A true master of fish cookery, Matsuhisa creates unusual dishes by combining Japanese flavors with South American spices and salsas (he was the first to introduce Americans to yellowtail sashimi with sliced jalapeños). Broiled sea bass with black truffles, miso-flavored black cod, sautéed squid with garlic and soy, tempura sea urchin in a *shiso* leaf, and Dungeness crab tossed with chiles and cream are just a few examples of the masterfully prepared dishes available, in addition to thickly sliced nigiri and creative sushi rolls. Matsuhisa is perennially popular with celebrities and hard-core foodies, so reserve well in advance for those hard-to-get tables. The small, crowded main dining room suffers from poor lighting and precious lack of privacy; many big names are ushered through to private dining rooms. Expect a bit of attitude from the staff as well. *Tip:* If you're feeling adventurous, ask for *omakase,* and the chef will personally compose a selection of eccentric dishes.

129 N. La Cienega Blvd. (north of Wilshire Blvd.), Beverly Hills. ✆ 310/659-9639. www.nobumatsuhisa.com. Reservations recommended. Main courses $15–$50; sushi $4–$13 per order; full *omakase* dinner from $75. AE, DC, MC, V. Mon–Fri 11:45am–2:15pm; daily 5:45–10:15pm. Valet parking $5.

Ortolan ★★ FRENCH   Named after a small bird that's been savored to near extinction by French gourmands (and now an outlawed delicacy), this wonderful restaurant is a partnership between former L'Orangerie chef Christophe Emé and Jeri Ryan, the stunning *Boston Public* actress. The restaurant is cleverly designed into four separate sections to match your mood: a glamorous main dining room with creamy leather booths and crystal chandeliers; a more rustic dining room with Pennsylvania barn-plank flooring and a long communal family style table; a small, dimly lit bar replete with dark woods, potted **523** herbs, and a zinc top; and a cozy fireplace lounge for small dinner parties or romancing couples. Emé's sophisticated French cuisine is cleverly arranged as well: bread dippings arrive in a trio of test tubes; John Dory is served on a hot river stone; dessert arrives in baby ice-cream cones. His most popular dishes include crispy langoustines with a shot of minestrone, a superb lamb *pastilla* wrapped in phyllo and served in thick slices, and the most tender squab I've ever tasted. *Tip:* If you don't have a reservation, join the dinner party at the enormous communal table or find a spot in the fireside lounge.

8338 W. Third St. (at N. Kings Rd.), Los Angeles. ☏ **323/653-3300.** www.ortolanrestaurant.com. Reservations recommended. Main courses $19–$43. AE, DISC, MC, V. Tues–Thurs 6–10pm; Fri–Sat 6–10:30pm (bar until midnight). Valet parking $4.

The Palm ★★ STEAKS/LOBSTER   The child of the famous New York restaurant of the same name, the Palm is widely regarded by local foodies as one of the best traditional American steakhouses in the city. The glitterati seem to agree, as stars and their handlers are regularly in attendance. The restaurant is brightly lit, bustling with energy, and playfully decorated with dozens of celebrity caricatures on the walls. Live Nova Scotia lobsters are flown in almost daily and then broiled over charcoal and served with big bowls of melted butter. Most are enormous (3–7 lb.), and, although they're obscenely expensive, can be shared. The steaks and swordfish are similarly sized, perfectly grilled to order, and served a la carte by cheeky white-jacketed waiters who have been around since the Nixon administration. Diners also swear by the creamed spinach and celebrated Gigi Salad—a mixture of lettuce, shrimp, bacon, green beans, pimento, and avocado. For dessert, stick with the Palm's perfect New York cheesecake, flown in straight from the Bronx.

9001 Santa Monica Blvd. (btw. Doheny Dr. and Robertson Blvd.), West Hollywood. ☏ **310/550-8811.** www.thepalm.com. Reservations recommended. Main courses dinner $17–$41, lobsters $18 per pound; lunch $10–$19. AE, DC, MC, V. Mon–Fri noon–10:30pm; Sat 5–10:30pm; Sun 5–9:30pm. Valet parking $5.

Providence ★★★ MODERN AMERICAN SEAFOOD   The city's best seafood chef and the city's best maitre d' have combined their talents to create the city's preeminent seafood experience. After 6 years at Water Grill—one of L.A.'s finest seafood restaurants—Chef Michael Cimarusti and his quadrilingual Italian compatriot, Donato Poto, opened Providence. It's a pleasure to just relax at this sleek, modern space and converse with Donato at the bar. Because Cimarusti visits the fish market daily for the choicest seafood available, I recommend asking the waiter which are the evening's best dishes or, better yet, inquire if Michael has time to make a brief visit to your table and offer his advice. Because his philosophy is to let the divine flavors of wild fish prevail, sauces are never overpowering—striped sea bass in a pea tendril broth, wild king salmon with truffle vinaigrette, kelp-marinated fluke. If you're in a mood to splurge, go with the $140 Market Menu: nine memorable courses paired with superb wines (the young sommelier here is a wizard). Lastly, be sure to order anything Cimarusti makes with sea urchin, especially if you don't like sea urchin. Trust me, he'll convert you.

5855 Melrose Ave. (at N. Cahuenga Blvd.), Los Angeles. ☏ **323/460-4170.** www.providencela.com. Reservations recommended. Main courses $32–$49. AE, MC, V. Fri noon–2:30pm; Mon–Fri 6–10pm; Sat 5:30–10pm; Sun 5:30–9pm. Valet parking $6.

Republic ★ CONTEMPORARY AMERICAN   If you like a lot of pomp with your pulled pork, you'll want to make a reservation at Republic, where the scene is as important as the cuisine (if not more). Artistic elements prevail throughout the multilevel restaurant—giant parchment paper light fixtures, glass-beaded wall finishes, python upholstery, Brazilian walnut trim, chain mail draping—but the coup de grâce is certainly the 20-foot-tall "Tower of Wine" featuring "wine fairies" that float trapeze-style to retrieve the bottles. Following the trend toward hefty servings of meaty comfort food, the Southern-enhanced menu offers dishes ranging from a mesquite-grilled veal porterhouse to a venison chop. Naturally there's a mac and cheese on the sides menu, though I prefer the sweet potato gratin and truffle grits. After dinner you'll want to waddle over to the lounge's leather sofa for a *digestif* and watch L.A.'s pretty people in their element.

650 N. La Cienega Blvd. (just N. of Melrose Place), Los Angeles. ✆ 310/360-7070. www.therepublicla. com. Reservations recommended. Main courses $23–$44. AE, DC, DISC, MC, V. Daily 6–11pm (bar until 2am). Valet parking $7.

Spago Beverly Hills ★★★ CALIFORNIA Wolfgang Puck is more than a great chef; he's also a masterful businessman and publicist who has made Spago one of the best-known restaurants in the United States. Despite years of stiff competition, Spago remains one of L.A.'s top-rated restaurants and continues to live up to the hype. Talented Puck henchman Lee Hefter presides over the kitchen, delivering the culinary sophistication demanded by an upscale Beverly Hills crowd. Spago is also one of the last places in L.A. where men will feel most comfortable in jacket and tie (suggested, but not required). All eyes may be on the romantically twinkle-lit outdoor patio (the most coveted tables), but the food takes center stage. You simply can't choose wrong—highlights include the appetizer of foie gras "three ways"; crawfish salad; savory duck either honey-lacquered and topped with foie gras or Cantonese-style with a citrus tang; slow-roasted Sonoma lamb with braised greens; and rich Austrian dishes from "Wolfie's" childhood, such as spicy beef goulash or perfect veal schnitzel.

176 N. Canon Dr. (north of Wilshire). ✆ 310/385-0880. www.wolfgangpuck.com. Reservations required. Jacket and tie advised for men. Main courses $17–$42; tasting menu $125. AE, DC, DISC, MC, V. Mon–Fri 11:30am–2:15pm; Sat noon–2:30pm; Sun–Thurs 5:30–10:30pm; Fri–Sat 5:30–11pm. Valet parking $4.50.

Moderate

Beacon ★★ Value ASIAN FUSION Ranked number one in a "Top 25 Restaurants" article in *Los Angeles Magazine*, Beacon is the best thing to happen to the Culver City dining scene in years. For more than a decade, Chef Kazuto Matsusaka has worked in the kitchen of some of L.A.'s top restaurants (Spago, Chinois on Main), mastering the art of fusion cooking. Along with his wife Vicki Fan (she's the GM), the duo opened this small, minimally decorated cafe within the Helms Bakery complex. On most nights, you'll see a stern-faced Kazuto in the open kitchen (he's actually a hilarious guy), while Vicki oversees the L-shaped dining room. The reasonably priced cuisine is simple yet superb, combining fresh California ingredients with traditional Asian cooking styles and a dash of Vicki's family recipes. If available, you must start with the outstanding Kaki Fry appetizer—warm crispy oysters set in cool lettuce cups and topped with *yuzu* tartar sauce (a steal at $6.25)— and the stir-fried mushroom salad, a heavenly mix of organic mushrooms, mixed greens, manchego cheese, and tangy *yuzu* dressing. Other fantastic dishes I devoured were the miso-marinated black cod with sesame-tossed green beans, the ever-so-tender grilled hangar steak spiced with wasabi relish, and a savory bowl of *kakuni udon*—thick wheat-flour noodles flavored with a generous cut of braised pork belly, bamboo shoots, baby bok choy, and warm broth. *Tip:* On sunny days request a table at the back patio.

3280 Helms Ave. (at Washington Blvd.), Culver City. ✆ 310/838-7500. www.beacon-la.com. Reservations recommended. Main courses $13–$20. AE, DISC, MC, V. Mon–Sat 11:30am–2pm; Sun and Tues–Wed 5:30–9pm; Thurs–Sat 5:30–10pm. Free lot parking.

Fraîche ★★★ FRENCH/ITALIAN   Like many of L.A.'s rising-star chefs, Jason Travi cut his chops as a sous chef at Spago, cranking out 400 plates a night. Dues paid, he's now at the helm of one on the most talked-about new restaurants in Southern California, a tribute to the ingredient-driven dishes that make eating your way through the Mediterranean such a joy. Mornings are spent at the farmers market, while evenings find him in his impressive open kitchen whipping up plates of rustic dishes such as tortelli with braised rabbit or lamb *spezzatino* atop celery root gnocchi. His standout dish, however, is the *branzino* (European sea bass) served *en papillote* (cooked in parchment) with fennel, roasted peppers, and fingerling potatoes. The decor is reminiscent of a country estate with earthy Tuscan colors and textures, walls clad in weather-worn farmhouse stone, distressed walnut flooring, and a lively indoor-outdoor terrace overlooking Culver and Main streets. *Tip:* The bar menu is served every night until 1am.

9411 Culver Blvd. (at Main St.), Culver City. © **310/839-6800.** www.fraicherestaurantla.com. Reservations recommended. Main courses dinner $16–$26, lunch $10–$22. AE, DC, DISC, MC, V. Mon–Fri 11:30am–2:30pm and 5:30–10:30pm; Sat–Sun 5:30–10:30pm.

Il Pastaio ★★ NORTHERN REGIONAL ITALIAN   Sicilian-born chef/owner Giacomino Drago (scion of L.A.'s well-known Drago restaurateur family) hit the jackpot with this hugely successful, value-priced trattoria, located on a busy corner in the shopping district of Beverly Hills. All day long, Giacomino's fans take a break from work or shopping and converse over glasses of chianti and plates of authentic pasta. With 57 menu items to choose from, I haven't come close to trying everything, but I can tell you with certainty that you will swoon over the *arancini*, breaded rice cones that are filled with mozzarella cheese and peas, and then fried crispy brown (highly addictive); the pumpkin tortelloni in a light sage-and-cream sauce; the *arrabbiata*, a simple penne pasta dish in a fantastic spicy tomato-and-garlic sauce; and for dessert, the *panna cotta* (the silkiest in Southern California). There's almost always a wait—and not much room to wait in—but by meal's end it always seems worth it.

400 N. Canon Dr. (at Brighton Way), Beverly Hills. © **310/205-5444.** www.giacominodrago.com. Main courses dinner $16–$30, lunch $10–$27. AE, DC, MC, V. Mon–Sat 11:30am–11pm; Sun 11:30am–10pm.

Koi ★★ ASIAN-FUSION   If your goal is to spot Hollywood's A-list of celebrities, make a reservation at Koi, the current fave of L.A.'s glam scene. Or just make a reservation because the food is so wonderful (overpriced, but wonderful). Either way, you won't be disappointed. Incorporating feng shui elements of trickling water, votive candles, open-air patios, and soft lighting, the minimalist earthen-hued interior has a calming ambience that is a welcome relief from the hectic Melrose scene just outside the ornately carved gates. The chef's brilliant fusions of Japanese and Californian cuisine accounts for the repeat clientele. Start with the refreshing cucumber *sunomono* tower flavored with sweet vinegar and edible flowers, followed by a baked crab roll with edible rice paper (fantastic), the tuna tartare and avocado on crispy wontons, the yellowtail carpaccio delicately flavored with grapeseed oil, and the house specialty of black cod bronzed with miso that's warm-butter soft and exploding with sweet flavor. *Tip:* Request one of the horseshoe booths on the back patio amid Buddha statues and candlelight.

730 N. La Cienega Blvd. (btw. Melrose Ave. and Santa Monica Blvd.), West Hollywood. © **310/659-9449.** www.koirestaurant.com. Reservations recommended. Main courses $13–$27. AE, DC, DISC, MC, V. Sun–Thurs 6–10pm; Fri–Sat 6pm–midnight. Valet parking $5.

Luckyfish ★   Yes, another sushi restaurant in L.A., but this time with a clever twist. It's called *kaiten-zushi* style of dining, where sushi and sashimi wind through the restaurant on little covered plates via a conveyor belt (the term *kaiten* literally means "going in circles"). Everything about Luckyfish exudes modernity, from the gleaming white leather booths and nickel-plated chairs, to the ultramodern 38-foot conveyer belt lined with little high-tech sushi plates—each with a radio frequency chips embedded in it so that, after 45 minutes, an unloved dish is automatically whisked off the belt and replaced with a fresh item. The chefs prepare about 100 different types of Japanese dishes—including entree items from the menu such as miso-marinated cod—and a little cheat-sheet on each table helps you identify the wide variety of nigiri sushi and rolls. While it's not the best sushi in L.A., it's relatively inexpensive, you get to eye before you try, and it's fun. You'll like the location in the heart of Beverly Hills amid all those ritzy boutiques. *Tip:* When you're sated on sushi, walk across the street to Nic's Martini Lounge (p. 593) and order their superb pear martini (yum).

338 N. Cañon Dr. (btw. Brighton and Dayton ways), Beverly Hills. ℭ 310/274-9800. www.luckyfishsushi. com. Reservations not accepted. Main courses $9–$14. AE, DC, DISC, MC, V. Daily 11:30am–10:30pm. Valet parking $7.

Inexpensive

The Apple Pan ★ SANDWICHES/AMERICAN There are no tables, just a U-shape counter, at this classic American burger shack and hugely popular L.A. landmark. Open since 1947, the Apple Pan is a diner that looks—and acts—the part. It's famous for juicy burgers, grumpy service, and an authentic frills-free atmosphere. The hickory burger is best, though the tuna sandwich also has its share of fans. Ham, egg-salad, and Swiss-cheese sandwiches round out the menu. Definitely order fries and, if you're in the mood, the house-baked apple pie. Expect to wait a bit during the lunch rush (don't worry, the line moves pretty fast).

10801 Pico Blvd. (east of Westwood Blvd.). ℭ 310/475-3585. Most menu items under $6. No credit cards. Tues–Thurs and Sun 11am–midnight; Fri–Sat 11am–1am. Free parking.

Versailles ★ ⓥⓐⓛⓤⓔ CARIBBEAN/CUBAN Outfitted with Formica tabletops and looking something like an ethnic IHOP, Versailles feels much like any number of restaurants in Miami that cater to the Cuban community. The menu reads like a veritable survey of Havana-style cookery and includes specialties such as "Moors and Christians" (flavorful black beans with white rice), *ropa vieja* (a stringy beef stew), and fried whole fish (usually sea bass). Anybody who's eaten here will tell you the same thing: "Order the shredded roast pork." Tossed with the restaurant's trademark garlic-citrus sauce, it's highly addictive. Equally fetching is the garlic chicken—succulent, slow roasted, and smothered in onions and garlic-citrus sauce. Almost everything is served with black beans and rice; wine and beer are available. Because meals are good, bountiful, and cheap, there's often a wait.

1415 S. La Cienega Blvd. (south of Pico Blvd.). ℭ 310/289-0392. Main courses $5–$13. AE, MC, V. Daily 11am–10pm. Free parking.

HOLLYWOOD
Expensive

Campanile ★★★ BRUNCH/CALIFORNIA-MEDITERRANEAN Built as Charlie Chaplin's private offices in 1928, this Tuscan-style building has a multilevel layout with flower-bedecked interior balconies, a bubbling fountain, and a skylight through which diners can see the campanile (bell tower). Consistently ranked as one of L.A.'s finest restaurants, a meal here might begin with fried zucchini flowers drizzled with melted mozzarella or lamb carpaccio surrounded by artichoke leaves—a dish that arrives looking like one of van Gogh's sunflowers. Spago alumnus chef/owner Mark Peel heads up the kitchen and is particularly known for his grills and roasts. Try the wood-grilled prime rib smeared with black-olive tapenade; pappardelle with braised rabbit, roasted tomato, and collard greens; or the rosemary-charred lamb with artichokes and fava beans. The weekend brunch is a surprising crowd-pleaser and a terrific way to appreciate this beautiful space on a budget. One of the most popular nights is still Grilled Cheese night on Thursdays, when the menu offers 12 different gourmet sandwiches along with appetizers. *Tip:* On Monday nights, chef Peel offers a $40 three-course family-style themed menu that's been voted Best Monday Night Dinner by *Los Angeles Magazine.*

624 S. La Brea Ave. (north of Wilshire Blvd.). (C) **323/938-1447.** www.campanilerestaurant.com. Reservations required. Main courses $26–$38. AE, DC, DISC, MC, V. Mon–Wed 11:30am–2:30pm and 6–10pm; Thurs–Fri 11:30am–2:30pm and 5:30–11pm; Sat 9:30am–1:30pm and 5:30–11pm; Sun 9:30am–1:30pm. Valet parking $5.50.

Grace ★★★ NEW AMERICAN   I'm going to start an argument here by stating that Grace is the best restaurant in Los Angeles. I dined here with two friends, and everything was flawless: the service, the cuisine, the wine, the decor—even the patrons were well dressed, well behaved, and unpretentious (a rarity in this town). High ceilings, well-spaced tables, and soothing earth tones of orange, green, brown, and rose evoke a relaxed atmosphere at Grace, which is fortuitous because you'll want to slowly savor each dish created by executive chef and co-owner Neal Fraser, a culinary scion of Wolfgang Puck, Thomas Keller, and Joachim Splichal, an Iron Chef veteran. Our memorable dinner started with plump Kumamoto oysters with a trio of superb dipping sauces, a roast beet salad with grilled radicchio and onion marmalade, pumpkin risotto with sea urchin and sweet Maine shrimp, a carpaccio of tuna with fried green olives and pepper vinaigrette, and the most beautiful plate of foie gras I've ever seen (and I live for foie gras), served both as a pâté and sautéed with pistachio-cocoa nib crust and a dab of huckleberry compote. Entrees included generous servings of wild-boar tenderloin with violet mustard sauce, and slow-braised pork shank with smoked shallots and cider-sage sauce—both paired with an excellent pinot noir by the glass. The coup de grâce of our unrivaled meal was a sublime warm Cajeta bread pudding topped with pumpkin-seed ice cream. Yes, it's expensive, but if you're going to splurge on a meal in L.A., Grace is where I'd go.

7360 Beverly Blvd. (at N. Fuller Ave.), Los Angeles. (C) **323/934-4400.** www.gracerestaurant.com. Reservations recommended. Main courses $26–$38. AE, DC, DISC, MC, V. Tues–Thurs 6–10:30pm; Fri–Sat 6–11pm; Sun 6–10pm. Valet parking $5.50.

Katana Robata & Sushi Bar ★★ JAPANESE ROBATA   In the City of Sushi, you need to stand out from the crowd if you want to run a successful Japanese restaurant. And that's just what they did at Katana. Location being everything, first they perched above the perpetually busy Sunset Strip. Then they hired red-hot designer Dodd Mitchell to give the restaurant sex appeal by using aesthetically pleasing accents such as steel beams, perforated metallic screens, exotic woods, and worn brick. Next they introduced *robata-yaki* to mainstream L.A.—a traditional Japanese style of cooking where meats, fish, and vegetables are cooked on small bamboo skewers over imported *bincho tan* coal that imparts a unique smoky essence to the food. Lastly, they trained their waitstaff well (a rarity in L.A.), hired a sake sommelier to create the city's best sake list, and converted the patio above Sunset Boulevard into a coveted alfresco dining area. The result? Well, you'd better make a reservation at least a week in advance, because the only walk-in seating you'll find is at the sushi and *robata* bars. Yes, the sushi is very good, but it's the incredibly flavorful skewers that you'll want to sample: foie gras and asparagus wrapped with filet mignon, fresh lobster with a peppercorn-miso glaze, giant seared scallops with shiitake mushrooms, Kurobuta pork and pineapple drizzled with plum sauce (okay, now I'm hungry). Each comes with a trio of dipping sauces, adding yet more complexity to the mingling of flavors. Sushi, tempura, steak, and noodles are available as well. Be sure to start the adventure with a $15 Sake Sampler and a glass of their house-special Red Sun beer, brewed exclusively for the restaurant.

8439 W. Sunset Blvd. (near La Cienega Blvd.), West Hollywood. ✆ 323/650-8585. www.katanarobata. com. Reservations recommended. Main courses $11–$44. AE, DC, DISC, MC, V. Mon 6–11pm; Tues–Wed 6–11:30pm; Thurs–Sat 6pm–12:30am; Sun 6–11pm. Valet parking $7.

Katsuya Hollywood ★★★   Every year somebody opens an über-hip new restaurant that has all the L.A. foodies and snooties agog, and this time it's the opening of Katsuya Hollywood. Capitalizing on their raging success of the original Katsuya in Brentwood, the SBE Restaurant & Nightlife Group spent a small fortune hiring celebrated designer Philippe Starck to collaborate with Master Sushi Chef Katsuya Uechi and create a shrine to sushi and design (at Hollywood and Vine!). Looking more like a scene from a David Lynch movie than a restaurant, the decor is an intriguing mix of gleaming white leather and chrome furniture, overblown images of a geisha's facial parts, and a sinister black banner bearing the *kanji* symbol for Katsuya, who is one of only four Master Sushi Chefs in Los Angeles. Before you order, loosen up with their signature cocktail, the Burning Mandarin: Absolute Mandarin vodka with crushed Serrano chili and a dash of freshly squeezed juices. Katsuya's must-try signature dishes include the crispy rice with spicy tuna, the Kobe filet with foie gras and plum soy sauce, and the baked white fish with truffle in a shell of salt. But if you really want the true Katsuya experience, throw down a Franklin and order *omakase*—a chef's choice selection of the freshest fish available. Reservations may be difficult to get, particularly on a weekend night, so be sure to call as far in advance as possible.

6300 Hollywood Blvd. (at Vine St.), Hollywood. ✆ 323/871-8777. www.sbe.com/katsuya. Reservations recommended. Main courses $12–$28. AE, DC, DISC, MC, V. Mon–Fri 11am–3pm and 5pm–midnight; Sat–Sun 11am–1am. Valet parking $6.

The Little Door ★★ FRENCH MEDITERRANEAN   For more than a decade this provincial hideaway off Third Street has been voted one of L.A.'s most romantic restaurants. From the street all you see is a high fence and two carved little wooden doors, but pass through them and voila!—a bastion of quaint French countryside in the midst of the bustling city. The Little Door consists of four dining areas situated throughout a converted cottage-style house, the most popular being the "Patio" with its tile fountain, koi pond, wrought-iron candelabras, and lush greenery. If you can't get a table here, ask for one in the back room by the fireplace, which is both quieter and roomier. Fittingly, the cuisine is French/Mediterranean, ranging from a terrine of duck foie gras with strawberries to pistachio-encrusted scallops with Moroccan greens to rosemary-encrusted rack of lamb in a parsnip purée. Because the chef shops at the local farmers' market daily, the menu changes often—ergo, be sure to ask your waiter for recommendations. All wines on the list are also served by the glass, which makes for some fun wine paring with the medley of menu choices. Caveats? It's pricey ($30 for fettuccine?), the tables are a tad too close together, and the attitude from the servers can be a bit . . . er . . . French as well. But when it all comes together perfectly—the candlelit table you requested, an attentive waiter, a warm summer night, you looking marvelous in the candlelight, a nice glass of wine, a soupçon of foie gras melting on your tongue—it's easy to see why the Little Door **529** is where the locals go when they're in the mood for romance.

8164 W. Third St. (btw. Crescent Heights and La Jolla sts.), Los Angeles. © **323/951-1210.** www.thelittle door.com. Reservations recommended. Main courses $30–$48. AE, MC, V. Mon–Thurs 6–10:30pm; Fri–Sat 6–11:30pm. Valet parking $5.50.

MODERATE

Kings Road Cafe ★★ AMERICAN   This is the cafe you wish was down the street from your place instead of that Starbucks. The Kings Road Cafe has the perfect combo of everything you'd want in a neighborhood cafe—sunny sidewalk seating along bustling Beverly Boulevard, excellent coffee served in big bowl-like cups, great people-watching, attitude-free service, the occasional celebrity sighting, a huge magazine stand right next door, and fresh, healthy, inexpensive food served in large portions. It's open from morning until night, so you can drop by anytime for such local favorites as their banana-pecan buttermilk pancakes, fluffy French toast, spinach and shiitake mushroom omelet, chipotle chicken salad, Baja fish tacos, blackened ahi with sweet mashed potatoes, and their signature panini-style sandwiches (the chicken breast with garlic aioli is my favorite). You can pretty much count on waiting for an outside table on weekends, but it gives you time to do a bit of inconspicuous star searching, pick up a few magazines, and check out the Kings Road Cafe Bakery next door (the blackcurrant scones are wonderful).

8361 Beverly Blvd. (at Kings Rd.), Los Angeles. © **323/655-9044.** www.kingsroadcafe.com. Reservations not accepted. Main courses breakfast $6–$11, lunch/dinner $8–$14. MC, V. Mon–Sat 7:30am–10pm; Sun 7:30am–7pm. Metered street parking.

Musso & Frank Grill ★ AMERICAN/CONTINENTAL   A survey of Hollywood restaurants that leaves out Musso & Frank is like a study of Las Vegas singers that fails to mention Wayne Newton. As Hollywood's oldest eatery (since 1919), Musso & Frank is the paragon of Old Hollywood grillrooms. This is where Faulkner and Hemingway drank during their screenwriting days and where Orson Welles used to hold court. The restaurant is still known for its bone-dry martinis and perfectly seasoned Bloody Marys. The setting is what you'd expect: oak-beamed ceilings, gruff red-coated waiters, red-leather booths and banquettes, mahogany room dividers, and chandeliers with tiny shades. The extensive old-school menu is a veritable survey of American/Continental cookery. Hearty dinners include veal scaloppini Marsala, roast spring lamb with mint jelly, and broiled lobster. Grilled meats (particularly the Welsh rarebit) are a specialty, as is the Thursday-only chicken potpie. Regulars also flock in for Musso's trademark flannel cakes, crepe-thin pancakes flipped to order. *Tip:* Sit at either the counter for the full M&F effect, or request table no. 1 in the west room, which was Charlie Chaplin's regular table.

6667 Hollywood Blvd. (at Cherokee Ave.). © **323/467-7788.** Reservations recommended. Main courses $13–$32. AE, DC, MC, V. Tues–Sat 11am–11pm. Self-parking $2.25 w/validation.

Osteria Mozza ★★★   When's the last time you had a dining experience that was so wonderful you kept thinking about for days afterward? If it's been too long, come here. If you've read my review of Pizzeria Mozza (see below), then you already know what a fan I am of Nancy Silverton and Mario Batali. Well, nothing succeeds like success, and they've open yet another restaurant together, right next to their original—an airy, lively, Italianesque space with a central free-standing mozzarella bar of dark wood and marble (Nancy's helm), a full bar along the south wall with beautiful millwork, and an indoor/outdoor dining area that opens onto Melrose Avenue. Osteria Mozza continues the

> **(Tips)** **Hallelujah! A Brunch Worth Singing About**
>
> Have mercy and say "Hallelujah!" for the Gospel Brunch at the **House of Blues** (8430 Sunset Blvd., West Hollywood; www.hob.com). For more than a decade, it's been a Sunday tradition at the HOB to feed both the body and soul with inspiring gospel performances and heaping plates of all-you-can-eat Southern home cookin'. Every week different gospel groups from around the region perform uplifting and energetic music that invariably gets the crowd on its feet and raising the roof. Seatings are every Sunday at 10am and 1pm. Tickets are $40, including tax and gratuity, and are available only through the HOB Sunset Strip box office; call ⓒ **323/848-5100.**

Silverton-Batali formula of using only the finest and freshest ingredients to create dishes gleaned from their culinary adventures in New York and Bologna. The result is small-dish heaven for the adventurous epicurean, and of the dozen or so dishes we ordered—all praiseworthy—these were the standouts: the fresh ricotta and egg ravioli with browned butter, the monkfish *alla diavolo*, the *bufala* mozzarella with caperberry relish (sigh), and for dessert the *bombolini*, a huckleberry compote with vanilla gelato. Reservations can be tough, so make them as far in advance as possible, and take me with you.

6602 Melrose Ave. (at N. Highland Ave.), Los Angeles. ⓒ **323/297-0100.** Reservations recommended. Main courses $17–$29. AE, MC, V. Mon–Fri 5:30–11pm; Sat 5–11pm; Sun 5–10pm. Valet parking $6.

Pizzeria Mozza ★★ ITALIAN   One of the hardest reservations to get in town is at this little pizza place on the corner of Melrose and Highland. Locals are calling up to a month in advance for an opportunity to experience celeb-chef Nancy Silverton's artisanal pies. Nancy's passion for all things Italian and bread-related—she founded the famed La Brea Bakery—has culminated in her quest for baking the perfect Italian-style pizza (which, according to her, is all in the crust). So when she and Mario Batali partnered in an attempt to create the best pizza outside of Italy, L.A.'s foodies swooned. I had to call a friend of Nancy's just to reserve a table, and I still had to wait 20 minutes (then again, so did Scarlet Johansson and Paul Reiser, which made me feel a little better). In contrast to the restaurant's celebrity status, the ambience and decor are entirely unpretentious. The interior consists of a boxlike space with a high ceiling, a small wine bar, about a dozen tables, some counter seating, and an open kitchen where Nancy can usually be spotted most evenings ensuring quality control. The menu is modest as well—about 15 styles of pizza, a special entree each day of the week, and several small plates of antipasti, panini, *bruschette, insalate,* and salami. The pizzas are small and inexpensive enough for everyone to order their own. Favorites are the house-made fennel sausage with *panna* and red onion; the Gorgonzola dolce with fingerling potatoes, radicchio, and rosemary; and the *rapini* with black olives, cherry tomatoes, and anchovy. But the toppings are secondary to Nancy's complex crust—in true Italian style each is wafer thin in the middle, yet impossibly puffy, crunchy, and flavorful on the edges (I dare you to replicate it in your kitchen). Fittingly, the wines are all Italian, and moderately priced between $25 and $50. The only common complaint I've heard so far is the noise level—with so many people packed into such a small space, you'll need to speak up to be heard. Oh, and make that reservation now.

LOS ANGELES

14

WHERE TO DINE

Inexpensive

El Cholo ★ MEXICAN L.A.'s oldest Mexican restaurant (Gary Cooper and Bing Crosby were regulars, and Jack Nicholson and Warren Beatty still are), El Cholo has been serving up authentic Mexican cuisine in this pink adobe hacienda since 1925, even though the once-outlying mid-Wilshire neighborhood around it has since turned into Koreatown. El Cholo's *muy* strong margaritas, invitingly messy nachos—the first served in the U.S.—and classic combination dinners don't break new culinary ground, but the kitchen has perfected these standards over 80 years (I wish they bottled their rich enchilada sauce). Other specialties include seasonally available green-corn tamales and creative sizzling vegetarian fajitas that go way beyond just eliminating the meat. The atmosphere is festive, as people from all parts of town dine happily in the many rambling rooms that compose the restaurant. There's valet parking as well as a free self-parking lot directly across the street. Westsiders head to El Cholo's Santa Monica branch at 1025 Wilshire Blvd. (at 11th St.; © **310/899-1106**). *Note:* Be prepared for a long wait on weekends.

1121 S. Western Ave. (south of Olympic Blvd.). © 323/734-2773. www.elcholo.com. Reservations suggested. Main courses $8–$15. AE, DC, DISC, MC, V. Mon–Sat 11am–10pm; Sun 11am–9pm. Free self-parking or valet parking $5.

Pink's Hot Dogs Kids SANDWICHES/BURGERS/HOT DOGS Pink's isn't your usual guidebook recommendation, but then again, this crusty corner stand isn't your typical hot dog shack. Name another hot dog stand that has its own valet who deftly parks the stream of Rolls-Royces and Mercedes that pull up regularly. This L.A. icon grew around the late Paul and Betty Pink, who opened for business in 1939 selling 10¢ wieners from a used hot dog cart. Now 2,000 of them are served every day on Pink's soft steamed rolls. There are 24 varieties of dogs available, many of them coined by the celebrities who order them. Martha Stewart once stopped her caravan to order a 10-incher with mustard, relish, onions, chopped tomatoes, sauerkraut, bacon, and sour cream, and now you too can order a "Martha Stewart" dog. The heartburn-inducing chili dogs (made from Betty's chili formula that's still a secret) are craved by even the most upstanding, health-conscious Angelenos. There's lots of folklore emanating from this wiener shack as well: Bruce Willis reportedly proposed to Demi Moore in the parking lot, and Orson Welles holds the record for the most hot dogs consumed in one sitting (18). Even though the dogs are churned out every 30 seconds, expect to wait in line even at midnight—you'll invariably meet a true crossroads of Los Angeles cultures. Pray that greedy developers spare this little nugget of Americana.

709 N. La Brea Ave. (at Melrose Ave.). © 323/931-4223. www.pinkshollywood.com. Chili dog $2.85. No credit cards. Sun–Thurs 9:30am–2am; Fri–Sat 9:30am–3am.

Roscoe's House of Chicken 'n' Waffles BREAKFAST/SOUTHERN It sounds like a bad joke—fried chicken and waffles on the same plate. But Roscoe's is one of those places that you have to visit at least once to see how it works (and judging by the wait, it definitely works). This Hollywood institution's proximity to CBS Television City has turned this Harlem-inspired restaurant into a kind of de facto commissary for the network. A chicken-and-cheese omelet isn't everyone's ideal way to begin the day, but it's de rigueur at Roscoe's. At lunch, few calorie-unconscious diners can resist the juicy fried chicken smothered in gravy and onions, a house specialty that's served with waffles or grits and biscuits. Large chicken-salad bowls and chicken sandwiches also provide plenty of cluck for the buck. Homemade corn bread, sweet-potato pie, homemade potato salad, and corn on the cob are available as side orders. Granted, the waffles are of Eggo quality and come with enough whipped butter to stop your heart, but the Southern-fried chicken is addictive. *Tip:* The waffles tend to come a bit undercooked, so ask for them crispy.

1514 N. Gower St. (at Sunset Blvd.). ℂ **323/466-7453.** www.roscoeschickenandwaffles.com. Main courses $4–$15. No credit cards. Sun–Thurs 9am–midnight; Fri–Sat 8:30am–4am. Metered street parking.

The Waffle ★★ This is another one of those restaurants that you wish was right down the street from where you lived. It's got everything on the menu a country girl needs to survive, and then some. The Waffle is the brainchild of Chef Scooter Kanfer-Cartmill, a protégé of Wolfgang Puck and one of the most respected chefs in L.A. Her philosophy is that "you can have plenty of fun, even with serious food," and that's exactly what she serves up at her neo-classic American coffee shop. Plop your bum in a booth, rest your elbows on the Formica table, and ponder her enticingly eclectic menu while sipping good coffee from a plain ol' white mug: cornmeal jalepeno waffles, French toast soaked in vanilla bean custard, chicken pot pie with flakey buttermilk biscuit crust. Oy vey! This being no ordinary diner, the Waffle also has a full bar and even a signature cocktail—the Maple Syrup Martini. And this being L.A., there's also a fair selection of vegan and vegetarian items, such as Scooter's vegan Ruben with tofurkey and soy cheese. Friendly service, too. Trust me, you'll wish the Waffle was near your home too.

6255 W. Sunset Blvd. (at Vine St.), Los Angeles. ℂ **323/465-6901.** www.thewaffle.us. Reservations not accepted. Main courses $8–$12. AE, DC, DISC, MC, V. Sun–Thurs 6:30am–2:30am; Fri–Sat 6:30am–4:30am.

DOWNTOWN

Expensive

Patina ★★ FRENCH When celebrity L.A. restaurateur Joachim Splichal moved his flagship Patina restaurant from Melrose Avenue to the new Walt Disney Concert Hall, it raised one pertinent question: "Is it as good as the old Patina?" If you arrived after a performance ended, you wouldn't hear the answer anyway. Billowing walls of laser-cut walnut and floor-to-ceiling glass panels only augment the hubbub as droves of smartly clad fans of the performing arts dine on Splichal's signature dishes of wild game and the de rigueur ahi tuna appetizer. The après-show performances continue with a trio of carts—mounds of caviar, giant rib-eye steaks for two, and expensive cheeses—crisscross the dining room. My dinner started with soft, thin slices of *hamachi* matched with green-apple granite and mango, met its match with the seared foie gras atop caramel-poached apples, and segued into an entree of crispy skinned yellowtail snapper served on a bed of fava bean purée. Dishes I reluctantly passed on included a puff pastry–encrusted grouse with caramelized endive-and-black-olive reduction sauce, sautéed black-truffled Brussels sprouts with a sweet-potato purée, and roasted venison loin with porcini-foie gras polenta. Vegetarian dishes and wine pairings are also available, as are prix-fixe theater menus. Jackets are suggested but not required for dinner, and valet service is recommended as it's a bit of a hike from the nearest pay lot. *Tip:* If you want a quiet, romantic dinner, ask the hostess to schedule it at the *start* of a performance.

141 S. Grand Ave. (near First St.), Los Angeles. ℂ **213/972-3331.** www.patinagroup.com. Reservations recommended. Main courses dinner $31–$45, lunch $15–$30. AE, DC, MC, V. Tues–Fri 11:30am–1:30pm; Tues–Sat 5–9:30pm; Sun 4–9:30pm (on LA Philharmonic evenings, Tues–Sat 5–11pm; Sun 4–10:30pm). Closed on Mon. Valet parking $8.

Water Grill ★★ SEAFOOD Widely considered by L.A. foodies to be the best seafood house in the city, Water Grill is popular with the suit-and-tie crowd at lunch and with concertgoers en route to the Music Center at night. The dining room is a stylish and sophisticated fusion of wood, leather, and brass, but it gets a lighthearted lift from cavorting papier-mâché fish that play against an aquamarine ceiling painted with bubbles. The restaurant is known for its shellfish; among the appetizers are a dozen different oysters, Nantucket Bay scallops with Queensland blue pumpkin, and crispy sweetbreads with crayfish, chanterelles, and roasted asparagus. Main courses are imaginative dishes influenced by the cuisines of Hawaii, the Pacific Northwest, New Orleans, and New England. A good start to the feast is the appetizer seafood platter, a mouthwatering assortment served with well-made aioli. Other selections from the menu may range from Santa Barbara spot prawns paired with fingerling potato salad to line-caught pan-roasted Alaskan halibut with Niman Ranch bacon and sweet pea tendril juice. For dessert, try the mascarpone with figs and cherries, or the chocolate bread pudding. Better yet, splurge on the $95 seven-course tasting menu.

544 S. Grand Ave. (btw. 5th and 6th sts.). ✆ **213/891-0900**. www.watergrill.com. Reservations recommended. Main courses $19–$49. AE, DC, DISC, MC, V. Mon–Fri 11:30am–9:30pm; Sat 5–9:30; Sun 4:30–8:30pm. Valet parking $5.

Moderate

Ciudad ★★ LATIN The latest L.A. venture of celebrity chefs Susan Feniger and Mary Sue Milliken is this intriguing restaurant in the heart of downtown. *Ciudad* means "city" in Spanish and is a nod to the partners' long-ago venture City Restaurant. Here, amid juicy sherbet pastel walls and Miró-esque abstract designs, exuberant crowds gather to revel in a menu that brings together cuisines from the world's great Latin urban centers: Havana, Rio de Janeiro, Barcelona, and so on. Standout dishes include the tortilla soup, Argentine empanadas, Swiss chard with tomatillo sauce, citrus-roasted Cuban-style chicken (served with Puerto Rican rice and fried plantains), and a Brazilian *moqueca*—shrimp, mussels, and other seafood in a coconut-lime broth over coconut rice. Between 4 and 9pm on Sundays, Ciudad presents happy-hour tapas served at the bar; it's easy to make a meal of several, choosing from *carnitas* tacos, goat cheese fritters with sherry-soaked cherries, lamb meatballs with *chimichurri*, and more. As with the pair's superb Border Grill (p. 516), desserts are worth saving room for and are large enough to share. *Tip:* From Tuesday through Saturday Ciudad provides free shuttle service to the Music Center, the Walt Disney Concert Hall, and select STAPLES Center events.

445 S. Figueroa St., at Fifth St. ✆ **213/486-5171**. www.ciudad-la.com. Reservations recommended. Main courses $16–$29; tapas $4–$6. AE, MC, V. Mon–Tues 11:30am–9pm; Wed–Thurs 11:30am–10pm; Fri 11:30am–11pm; Sat 5–11pm; Sun 5–9pm. Day parking $3 w/validation; valet parking (after 5pm) $5.

R23 ★★ (Finds) JAPANESE/SUSHI This gallery-like space in downtown's out-of-the-way warehouse/artist loft district has been the secret of sushi connoisseurs since 1991 and has consistently ranked as one of the city's top sushi restaurants. At the back of R23's single, large exposed-brick dining room, the 12-seat sushi bar shines like a beacon; what appear at first to be ceramic wall ornaments are really stylish sushi platters hanging in wait for large orders. More functional art reveals itself in the corrugated cardboard chairs designed by renowned architect Frank Gehry—they're funky yet far more comfortable than wood. Genial sushi wizards stand in wait, cases of the finest fish before them. Salmon, yellowtail, shrimp, tuna, and scallops are among the always-fresh selections; an excellent and unusual offering is seared *toro,* in which the rich belly tuna absorbs a faint and delectable smoky flavor from the grill. Though R23's sublimely perfect sushi is the star, the short but inventive menu includes pungent miso-based soup with mixed seafood, sautéed scallops with shiitake mushrooms, deep-fried *sawa* crab, and several other choices. Browse a wide selection of premium wines and sakes (try the addictively sweet *nigori*).

923 E. Second St. (btw. Alameda St. and Santa Fe Ave.). © **213/687-7178.** www.r23.com. Reservations recommended. Main courses $12–$20; sushi $4–$12. AE, DC, DISC, MC, V. Mon–Fri 11:30am–2pm and 5:30–10pm; Sat 5:30–10pm. Free parking.

Tantra ★ INDIAN   In typical L.A. over-the-top fashion, Tantra owner Navraj Singh hired a studio design company to create an Indian restaurant unlike any you've ever seen. Hammered copper doors, iron-and-silk light fixtures, curtains of oxidized metals, murals of gender-fused beings, and black-and-white Bollywood movies shown on a giant plasma screen are just a few of the unorthodox props that vie for your attention. Part restaurant and part nightclub, Tantra is one of L.A.'s current "in" destinations, both for its scene and the cuisine. The gym-size building is equally divided: Veer right at the foyer and join the eclectic Silver Lake hipsters sipping too-cool cocktails such as Tears of Ganesha and Shiva's Revenge while the DJ spins vinyl; veer left and behold Lord Ganesha, god of prosperity, perched high above the temple-style dining room. Just about all of the curries, stir-fries, masalas, and kabobs are expertly prepared, but two are standout dishes: Coconut curry shrimp flavored with *ajwain* (caraway seeds) and stir-fried with palm vinegar, red onions, and peppers, and then finished with tomato coconut broth; and the *Mumbai* crepes—chickpea-and-corn crepes with a tangy cream-cheese filling and topped with mango sauce.

3705 W. Sunset Blvd., Silver Lake. © **323/663-8268.** www.tantrasunset.com. Reservations for parties of 6 or more. Main courses $11–$16. AE, MC, V. Tues–Wed and Sun 5–11pm; Thurs 5pm–midnight; Fri–Sat 5pm–1am. Valet parking $3.50.

Inexpensive

The Original Pantry AMERICAN/BREAKFAST   An L.A. institution in a city that thrives on change, this bastion of blue-collar cooking has been serving huge portions of comfort food round-the-clock since 1924. In fact, there isn't even a key to the front door. Owned by former L.A. mayor and botched governor contender Richard Riordan, the cash-only Pantry is popular with politicos, who come here for weekday lunches, and with conference-goers en route to the nearby L.A. Convention Center. The well-worn restaurant is also a welcoming beacon to clubbers after-hours, when downtown becomes a virtual ghost town. A bowl of celery stalks, carrot sticks, and whole radishes greets you at your Formica table, and creamy coleslaw and sourdough bread come free with every meal. The menu? It's a chalkboard hanging on the wall. Famous for quantity rather than quality, the Pantry serves huge T-bone steaks, densely packed hamburger loaf, macaroni and cheese, and other American favorites to an already overfed crowd. A typical breakfast—served all day—consists of a huge stack of hotcakes, a big slab of sweet cured ham, home fries, and coffee.

877 S. Figueroa St. (at Ninth St.). © **213/972-9279.** www.pantrycafe.com. Main courses $6–$14. No credit cards. Daily 24 hr. Free parking across the street w/validation.

Philippe The Original Ⓥalue BREAKFAST/SANDWICHES   Good old-fashioned value is what this legendary landmark cafeteria is all about. Popular with both South Central project residents and Beverly Hills elite, Philippe's unspectacular dining room with sawdust floors is one of the few places in L.A. where everyone can get along. Philippe's claims to have invented the French-dipped sandwich at this location in 1908; it remains the most popular menu item. Patrons push trays along the counter and watch while their choice of beef, pork, ham, turkey, or lamb is sliced and layered onto crusty

French bread that's been dipped in meat juices. Other menu items include house-made beef stew, navy bean soup, chili, and pickled pigs' feet. A hearty breakfast, served daily from 6 to 10:30am, is worthwhile if only for Philippe's uncommonly good cinnamon-dipped French toast. Beer and wine are available. For added entertainment, request a booth in the Train Room, which houses the nifty Model Train Museum.

Tip: A regular coffee at Philippe The Original is the same price it was when the diner opened in 1924: 9¢. That explains why they serve more than 20,000 cups per week.

1001 N. Alameda St. (at Ord St.). ℭ 213/628-3781. www.philippes.com. Most menu items under $7. No credit cards. Daily 6am–10pm. Free parking.

PASADENA & ENVIRONS
Expensive
Bistro 45 ★★ CALIFORNIA-FRENCH   All class, yet never stuffy, Bistro 45 is a favorite among Pasadena's old guard and nouvelle riche. The restaurant's warm, light ambience and gallery-like decor are an unexpected surprise after the ornately historic Art Deco exterior (the building is a former bank) and provide a romantic backdrop for owner Robert Simon's award-winning cuisine. The seasonally inspired menu changes frequently; dishes might include braised veal short ribs with Asian five spice, rock shrimp risotto with saffron, pan-roasted monkfish with garlic polenta, roasted veal loin filled with Roquefort, Fanny Bay oyster salad, and Nebraska pork with figs. For dessert, try the "chocolate soup," a creamy soufflé served with chocolate-kirsch sauce and vanilla ice cream. The knowledgeable waitstaff can answer questions about the excellent wine list; Bistro 45 appears regularly on *Wine Spectator*'s Best Of lists and hosts special-event wine dinners.

45 S. Mentor Ave. (btw. Colorado and Green), Pasadena. ℭ 626/795-2478. www.bistro45.com. Reservations recommended. Main courses dinner $17–$36, lunch $13–$33. AE, DC, MC, V. Tues–Thurs 11:30am–2pm and 6–9pm; Fri 11:30am–2pm and 6–9:30pm; Sat 6–9:30pm; Sun 5–9pm. Valet parking $4.50.

Parkway Grill ★★ CALIFORNIA   This vibrant, quintessentially Southern California restaurant has been one of the L.A. area's top-rated spots since 1985, quickly gaining a reputation for avant-garde flavor combinations and gourmet signature pizzas to rival Spago's. Although some critics find many dishes too fussy, others thrill to appetizer innovations such as lobster-stuffed cocoa crepes or Dungeness crab cakes with ginger cream and two salsas. Take my advice and start with the hot cheese-pear-walnut flatbread and the roasted beet salad, followed by any main dish from the iron mesquite grill. The richly sweet and substantial desserts can easily satiate two appetites. Located where the old Arroyo Seco Parkway glides into an ordinary city street, the Parkway Grill is within a couple of minutes' drive from Old Pasadena and thoughtfully offers free valet parking.

510 S. Arroyo Pkwy. (at California Blvd.), Pasadena. ℭ 626/795-1001. www.theparkwaygrill.com. Reservations recommended. Main courses $8–$27. AE, DC, MC, V. Mon–Fri 11:30am–2:30pm and 5–10pm; Sat 5:30–11pm; Sun 5:30–10pm. Free valet parking.

The Raymond ★★ NEW AMERICAN/CONTINENTAL   With its easy-to-miss setting in a sleepy part of Pasadena, the Raymond is a jewel even few locals know about. This Craftsman cottage was once the caretaker's house for a grand Victorian hotel called The Raymond. Though the city has grown to surround it, the place maintains an enchanting air of seclusion, romance, and serenity. In 2005, the classic restaurant got a face-lift, as did the haute American and European-inspired menu, which changes seasonally. A typical dinner may start with a pancetta-wrapped shrimp appetizer tossed in an orange reduction sauce, followed by roast Long Island duckling with raspberry port sauce and the coup de grâce—chocolate Moelleux soufflé cake with a melted chocolate center served with vanilla ice cream. Tables are scattered throughout the house and in the lush English garden, and there's plenty of free, non–valet parking (you won't find *that* on the Westside). *Note:* If you're a fan of finger sandwiches, afternoon tea (a great excuse to drink champagne under the sun) is offered Friday through Sunday from 1:30 to 3pm.

1250 S. Fair Oaks Ave. (at Columbia St.), Pasadena. ✆ **626/441-3136.** www.theraymond.com. Reservations required. Main courses dinner $16–$36, lunch $9–$24. AE, DC, DISC, MC, V. Tues–Fri 11:30am–2:30pm and 5:30–10pm; Sat 10am–2:30pm and 5:30–10pm; Sun 10am–2:30pm and 5–9pm. Free parking.

MODERATE

Café Santorini ★ GREEK
Located at ground zero of Pasadena's crowded Old Town shopping mecca, this second-story gem has a secluded Mediterranean ambience, due in part to its historic brick building with patio tables overlooking, but insulated from, the plaza below. In the evening, lighting is subdued and romantic, but ambience is casual; many diners are coming from or going to an adjacent movie-theater complex. The food is terrific and affordable, featuring grilled meats and kabobs, pizzas, fresh and tangy hummus, plenty of warm pita, and other staples of Greek cuisine. The menu includes regional flavors such as lamb, feta cheese, spinach, or Armenian sausage; the vegetarian baked butternut squash is filled with fluffy rice and smoky roasted vegetables.

64 W. Union St. (main entrance at the shopping plaza at the corner of Fair Oaks and Colorado), Pasadena. ✆ **626/564-4201.** www.cafesantorini.com. Reservations recommended on weekends. Main courses $9–$29. AE, DC, DISC, MC, V. Mon–Thurs 11:30am–10pm; Fri–Sat 11:30am–midnight; Sun 11am–10pm. Valet or self-parking $7.

Yujean Kang's Gourmet Chinese Cuisine ★★ CHINESE
Many Chinese restaurants put the word *gourmet* in their name, but few really mean it—or deserve it. Not so at Yujean Kang's, where Chinese cuisine is taken to an entirely new level. A master of fusion cuisine, the eponymous chef/owner snatches bits of techniques and flavors from both China and the West, commingling them in an entirely fresh way. Can you resist such provocative dishes as "Ants on Tree" (beef sautéed with glass noodles in chile and black sesame seeds), lobster with caviar and fava beans, or Chilean sea bass in passion-fruit sauce? Kang is also a wine aficionado and has assembled a magnificent cellar of California, French, and particularly German wines. Try pairing a German Spätlese with tea-smoked duck salad. The red-wrapped dining room is less subtle than the food, but just as elegant.

67 N. Raymond Ave. (btw. Walnut St. and Colorado Blvd.), Pasadena. ✆ **626/585-0855.** Reservations recommended. Main courses $8–$19. AE, MC, V. Sun–Thurs 11:30am–2:30pm and 5–9:30pm; Fri–Sat 11:30am–2:30pm and 5–10pm. Street parking.

INEXPENSIVE

Crocodile Cafe AMERICAN/TRADITIONAL/INTERNATIONAL
Casual and colorful, this offshoot of Pasadena's groundbreaking Parkway Grill builds a menu around simple crowd-pleasers (pizza, pasta, burgers, salads) prepared with fresh ingredients and jazzed up with creative marinades, vinaigrettes, and salsas. It's a formula that works; this Lake Avenue branch is the original location, but siblings have sprung up throughout the San Fernando and San Gabriel Valleys—even as far away as San Diego. Popular selections include the oakwood-grilled burger with curly french fries, the Croc's signature blue-corn chicken tostada with warm black beans and fresh guacamole, wood-grilled gourmet pizzas in the California Pizza Kitchen style, excellent chili, zesty tortilla soup, and ooey-gooey desserts.

140 S. Lake Ave., Pasadena. ✆ **626/449-9900.** www.crocodilecafe.com. Main courses $8–$18. AE, MC, V. Sun–Thurs 11am–10pm; Fri–Sat 11am–midnight. Free self-parking.

Farmers Market and The Grove ★ (Kids)   Now entering its 8th decade, the original market was little more than an empty lot with wooden stands set up by farmers during the Depression so they could sell directly to city dwellers. Eventually, permanent buildings grew up, including the trademark shingled 10-story clock tower. Today the place has evolved into a sprawling marketplace with a carnival atmosphere, a kind of "turf" version of San Francisco's Fisherman's Wharf. About 70 restaurants, shops, and grocers cater to a mix of workers from the CBS Television City complex, locals, and tourists brought here by the busload. Retailers sell greeting cards, kitchen implements, candles, and souvenirs, but everyone comes for the food stands, which offer oysters, hot donuts, Cajun gumbo, fresh-squeezed orange juice, corned beef sandwiches, fresh-pressed peanut butter, and all kinds of international fast foods. You can still buy produce here—it's no longer a farm-fresh bargain, but the selection's better than at the grocery store. Don't miss **Kokomo** (© 323/933-0773), a "gourmet" outdoor coffee shop that has become a power breakfast spot for showbiz types. Red turkey hash and sweet-potato fries are the dishes that keep them coming back. The seafood gumbo and gumbo ya ya at the **Gumbo Pot** (© 323/ 933-0358) are also very popular.

At the eastern end of the Farmers Market is the **Grove,** a massive 575,000-square-foot Vegas-style retail complex composed of various architectural styles ranging from Art Deco to Italian Renaissance. Miniature streets link the Grove to the Market via a double-deck electric trolley. Granted, it's all a bit Disney-gaudy, but the locals love it. Where else can you power-shop until noon, check all your bags at a drop-off station, get a spa treatment at **Amadeus Aveda Spa** (© 323/297-0311; www.amadeusspa.com), see a movie at the 14-screen **Grove Theatre** (© 323/692-0829; www.thegrovela.com), have an early dinner at **Maggiano's Little Italy** (© 323/965-9665; www.maggianos.com), and be home by 7pm?

6333 W. Third St. (at Fairfax Ave.), Hollywood. © 888/315-8883 or 323/900-8080. www.thegrovela.com. Mon–Thurs 10am–9pm; Fri–Sat 10am–10pm; Sun 11am–8pm.

The Getty Center Los Angeles ★★ (Kids)   Since opening in 1997, the Richard Meier–designed Getty Center has quickly assumed its place in the L.A. landscape (literally and figuratively) as the city's cultural acropolis and international mecca. Headquarters for the Getty Trust's research, education, philanthropic, and conservation concerns, the postmodernist complex—perched on a hillside in the Santa Monica mountains and swathed in Italian travertine marble—is most frequently visited for the museum galleries displaying the Getty's enormous collection of Impressionist paintings, truckloads of glimmering French furniture and decorative arts, fine illuminated manuscripts, contemporary photography, and European drawings. The area that's open to the public consists of five two-story pavilions set around an open courtyard, and each gallery within is specially designed to complement the works on display. A sophisticated system of programmable window louvers allows many works (particularly paintings) to be displayed in the natural light in which they were created for the first time in the modern era. One of these is van Gogh's *Irises,* one of the museum's finest and most popular holdings. Trivia buffs will enjoy knowing that the museum spent $53.9 million to acquire this painting; it's displayed in a complex that cost roughly $1 *billion* to construct.

A new addition to the Getty Center is the Fran and Ray Stark Sculpture Collection. This collection of 28 modern and contemporary outdoor sculptures from the collection of the late legendary film producer Ray Stark and his wife Fran was donated to the Getty Museum by the Ray Stark Revocable Trust and features many of the 20th century's greatest sculptors, including works by Roy Lichtenstein, Joan Miró, and Isamu Noguchi.

Visitors to the center park at the base of the hill and ascend via a cable-driven electric tram. On clear days, the sensation is of being in the clouds, gazing across Los Angeles and the Pacific Ocean (and into a few chic Brentwood backyards). If you're like me and don't remember a thing from your college art appreciation class (like I even went), get one of the new GettyGuide Audio Guides at the information desk. The nifty device allows visitors to take their own guided tour through the Getty Museum. The 45-minute human-led architectural tours, offered throughout the day, are also worth looking into. Dining options include several espresso/snack carts, a cafeteria, a self-service cafe, and the elegant (though informal) "Restaurant" offering table service for lunch (Tues–Sun) and dinner (Fri–Sat), with breathtaking views overlooking the ocean and mountains (restaurant reservations are recommended, though walk-ins are accepted; call *C* **310/440-6810,** or make reservations online at www.getty.edu).

Realizing that fine-art museums can be boring for kids, the center provides several clever programs for kids, including a family room filled with hands-on activities for families; weekend family workshops; Art Detective cards to help parents and kids explore the grounds and galleries, and self-guided audio tours made specifically for families.

Entrance to the Getty Center is free and no reservations are required. Cameras and video cams are permitted, but only if you use existing light (flash units are *verboten*).

1200 Getty Center Dr., Los Angeles. *C* **310/440-7300.** www.getty.edu. Free admission. Tues–Thurs and Sun 10am–6pm; Fri–Sat 10am–9pm. Closed major holidays. Parking $8.

The Getty Villa Malibu ★★ (Kids)

After 8 years and $275 million, the magnificent Getty Villa is receiving guests again. As the Getty Center was the cultural coup of 1997, a ticket to the newly renovated Villa is still one of the most sought-after items in the city. This former residence of oil tycoon J. Paul Getty, built in 1974 on the edge of a Malibu bluff with dazzling views of the ocean, was modeled after a first-century Roman country house buried by the eruption of Mount Vesuvius in A.D. 79—the Villa dei Papiri in Herculaneum, Italy. In fact, as you enter the sun-filled inner courtyard, it's not hard to imagine toga-clad senators wandering the gardens where fountains and bronze busts occupy the same spots as the original villa.

The museum's permanent collection of Greek, Roman, and Etruscan artifacts—dating from 6,500 B.C. to A.D. 400—consists of more than 1,200 works in 23 galleries arranged by theme, and five additional galleries for changing exhibitions. Exhibits on display range from everyday items such as coins, jewelry, and sculpture to modern interactive exhibits that illustrate key moments in the history of the ancient Mediterranean. Highlights include *Statue of a Victorious Youth,* a large-scale bronze discovered in an Adriatic shipwreck that is kept in a special climate-controlled room to preserve the metal (it's one of the few life-size Greek bronzes to have survived to modern times), as well as a beautiful 450-seat open-air theater where visitors are encouraged to take a break. And for keeping the kids entertained, the Villa's education team created a hands-on space called the Family Forum where children can partake in art-related activities.

For a more enlightening museum experience, I strongly suggest you rent a $3 GettyGuide Audio Player, which features commentary from curators and conservators on over 150 works (it's available at the Pick-Up Desk on Floor 1). Admission to the Getty Villa is free but, unlike the Getty Center, advance tickets are required and can be obtained online or by phone.

17985 Pacific Coast Hwy. (1 mile N. of Sunset Blvd.), Malibu. ℂ **310/440-7300.** www.getty.edu. Free **539** admission, but tickets required. Thurs–Mon 10am–5pm. Closed major holidays. Parking $8.

Grauman's Chinese Theatre ★   This is one of the world's great movie palaces and one of Hollywood's finest landmarks. The theater was opened in 1927 by impresario Sid Grauman, a brilliant promoter who's credited with originating the idea of the paparazzi-packed movie "premiere." Outrageously conceived, with both authentic and simulated Chinese embellishments, Grauman's theater was designed to impress. Original Chinese heavenly doves top the facade, and two of the theater's columns once propped up a Ming dynasty temple.

Visitors by the millions flock to the theater for its famous entry court, where stars such as Elizabeth Taylor, Paul Newman, Ginger Rogers, Humphrey Bogart, Frank Sinatra, Marilyn Monroe, and about 160 others set their signatures and hand-/footprints in concrete (a tradition started when actress Norma Talmadge "accidentally" stepped in wet cement during the premiere of Cecil B. De Mille's *King of Kings*). It's not always hands and feet: Betty Grable's shapely leg; the hoofprints of Gene Autry's horse, Champion; Jimmy Durante's and Bob Hope's trademark noses; Whoopi Goldberg's dreadlocks; George Burns's cigar; and even R2D2's wheels.

6925 Hollywood Blvd. (btw. Highland and La Brea Ave.). ℂ **323/464-8111.** www.manntheaters.com/chinese. Movie tickets $11. Call for showtimes.

Griffith Observatory ★★   Made world-famous in the film *Rebel Without a Cause*, Griffith Observatory's bronze domes have been Hollywood Hills landmarks since 1935. Closed for renovation for what seemed like forever, it finally reopened in November of '06 after a $93-million renovation. The central dome houses the 300-seat **Samuel Oschin Planetarium,** where hourly screenings of a narrated half-hour projection show called "Centered in the Universe" reveal the stars and planets that are hidden from the naked eye by the city's ubiquitous lights and smog.

The Observatory also features 60 space-related exhibits designed to "sparkle your imagination," the highlight being the largest astronomically accurate image ever produced—a 20×152-foot porcelain enamel dazzler that's cleverly called "The Big Picture." It supposedly encompasses a million galaxies, but I lost count after 11. There's also a new 200-seat Leonard Nimoy Event Horizon Theater (go Spock!), a Wolfgang Puck "Café at the End of the Universe," and several Zeiss and solar telescopes for public use both day and night.

Truth be told, most locals never actually go inside the observatory; they come to this spot on the south slope of Mount Hollywood for unparalleled city views. On warm nights, with the lights twinkling below, this is one of the most romantic places in L.A.

2800 E. Observatory Rd. (in Griffith Park, at the end of Vermont Ave.). ℂ **213/473-0800.** www.griffithobservatory.org. Planetarium tickets $7 adults, $5 seniors 60 or older and students with ID, $3 children ages 5–12. Tues–Fri noon–10pm; Sat–Sun 10am–10pm. Call or check website for planetarium showtimes.

The HOLLYWOOD Sign ★   These famous 50-foot-high white sheet-metal letters have come to symbolize the movie industry and the city itself. The sign was erected on Mount Lee in 1923 as an advertisement for a real-estate development. The full text originally read HOLLYWOODLAND and was lined with thousands of 20-watt bulbs around the letters (changed periodically by a caretaker who lived in a small house behind the sign). The sign gained dubious notoriety when actress Peg Entwistle leapt to her death from the "H" in 1932. The LAND section was damaged by a landslide, and the entire sign fell into major disrepair until the Hollywood Chamber of Commerce spearheaded a campaign to repair it (Hugh Hefner, Alice Cooper, Gene Autry, and Andy Williams were all major contributors). Officially completed in 1978, the 450-foot-long installation is now protected by a fence and motion detectors. The best view is from down below, at the corner of Sunset Boulevard and Bronson Avenue. *Tip:* It may look like it on a map, but Beachwood Drive does not lead to the sign. If you want to reach the sign on foot, it requires a rather arduous 5-mile round-trip hike on the Brush Canyon Trail in Griffith Park—the trail head is at the end of Canyon Drive. For more information, call the Griffith Park headquarters at ✆ **323/913-4688.**

Hollywood Walk of Fame ★ Kids When the Hollywood honchos realized how limited the footprint space was at Grauman's Chinese Theatre, they came up with another way to pay tribute to the stars. Since 1960, more than 2,200 celebrities have been honored along the world's most famous sidewalk. Each bronze medallion, set into the center of a terrazzo star, pays homage to a famous television, film, radio, theater, or recording personality. Although about a third of them are just about as obscure as Michael Jackson's sexual preference—their fame simply hasn't withstood the test of time—millions of visitors are thrilled by the sight of famous names such as **James Dean** (1719 Vine St.), **John Lennon** (1750 Vine St.), **Marlon Brando** (1765 Vine St.), **Rudolph Valentino** (6164 Hollywood Blvd.), **Marilyn Monroe** (6744 Hollywood Blvd.), **Elvis Presley** (6777 Hollywood Blvd.), **Greta Garbo** (6901 Hollywood Blvd.), **Louis Armstrong** (7000 Hollywood Blvd.), **Barbra Streisand** (6925 Hollywood Blvd.), and **Eddie Murphy** (7000 Hollywood Blvd.). **Gene Autry** is all over the place: The singing cowboy earned five different stars (a sidewalk record), one in each category.

The sight of bikers, metalheads, homeless wanderers, and hordes of disoriented tourists all treading on memorials to Hollywood's greats makes for a bizarre and somewhat tacky tribute. But the Hollywood Chamber of Commerce has been doing a terrific job sprucing up the pedestrian experience with filmstrip crosswalks, swaying palms, and more. And at least 1 weekend a month, a group of fans calling themselves Star Polishers busy themselves scrubbing tarnished medallions.

The legendary sidewalk is continually adding new names, such as Muhammad Ali in front of the Kodak Theatre. The public is invited to attend dedication ceremonies; the honoree—who pays a whopping $15,000 for the eternal upkeep—is usually in attendance. Contact the **Hollywood Chamber of Commerce,** 6255 Sunset Blvd., Suite 911, Hollywood, CA 90028 (✆ **323/469-8311**), for information.

Hollywood Blvd., btw. Gower St. and La Brea Ave.; and Vine St., btw. Yucca St. and Sunset Blvd. ✆ **323/ 469-8311.** www.hollywoodchamber.net.

La Brea Tar Pits & Page Museum ★ Kids An odorous swamp of gooey asphalt oozes to the earth's surface in the middle of Los Angeles. No, it's not a low-budget horror-movie set—it's La Brea Tar Pits, a truly bizarre primal pool on Museum Row where hot tar has been bubbling from the Earth for more than 40,000 years. The bubbling pools may look like a fake Disney set, but they're the real thing and have enticed thirsty animals throughout history. Nearly 400 species of mammals, birds, amphibians, and fish—many of which are now extinct—walked, crawled, landed, swam, or slithered into the sticky sludge, got stuck in the worst way, and stayed forever. In 1906, scientists began a systematic removal and classification of entombed specimens, including ground sloths, giant vultures, mastodons, camels, bears, lizards, and even prehistoric relatives of today's super-rats. Today it's one of the world's richest excavation sites for Ice Age fossils. The best finds are on display in the adjacent **Page Museum at the La Brea Tar Pits,** which houses the largest and most diverse collection of Ice Age plants and tar-stained skeletons in the world. Archaeological work is ongoing; you can watch as scientists clean, identify, and catalog new finds in the Paleontology Laboratory. An entertaining 15-minute film documenting the recoveries is also shown.

5801 Wilshire Blvd. (east of Fairfax Ave.), Los Angeles. © 323/934-7243. www.tarpits.org. Museum admission $7 adults, $4.50 seniors 62 and older and students with ID, $2 children ages 5–12, free for kids 4 and under; free for everyone the 1st Tues of every month. Mon–Fri 9:30am–5pm; Sat–Sun 10am–5pm (museum). Parking $6 with validation.

L.A. LIVE If you watched the Grammys last year you probably already know about the new L.A. LIVE "entertainment campus" that is the keystone of L.A.'s downtown gentrification project. This being Los Angeles, L.A. LIVE will eventually become one of the largest and flashiest mixed-used entertainment complexes in the world, costing $2.5 billion to build and covering more than 6 city blocks (hence its nickname—Times Square West). It's anchored by the **NOKIA Theatre,** the **STAPLES Center** (where the Lakers and Clippers play their home games), and the **Los Angeles Convention Center,** and is crammed with a dozen trendy restaurants and cafes, two huge nightclubs, the **GRAMMY Museum,** a bowling center, and **ESPN's West Coast broadcast headquarters.** Future plans include JW Marriott and Ritz-Carlton hotels (both within a 54-story tower), luxury condominiums, a 40,000-square-foot outdoor plaza, and a 14-screen movie complex. Log on to the L.A. LIVE website to see who's playing or performing while you're in town.

Figueroa St. btw. Venice and Olympic boulevards, Los Angeles. © 866/548-3452 or 213/763-5483. www.lalive.com.

Santa Monica Pier ★★ (Moments (Kids) Piers have been a tradition in Southern California since the area's 19th-century seaside resort days. Many have long since disappeared (such as Pacific Ocean Park, an entire amusement park perched on offshore pilings), and others have been shortened by battering storms and are now mere shadows (or stumps) of their former selves, but you can still experience those halcyon days of yesteryear at world-famous Santa Monica Pier.

Built in 1908 for passenger and cargo ships, the Santa Monica Pier does a pretty good job of recapturing the glory days of Southern California. The wooden wharf is now home to seafood restaurants and snack shacks, a touristy Mexican cantina, a gaily colored turn-of-the-20th-century indoor wooden **carousel** (which Paul Newman operated in *The Sting*), and an **aquarium** filled with sharks, rays, octopus, eels, and other local sea life. Summer evening concerts, which are free and range from big band to Miami-style Latin, draw crowds, as does the small amusement area perched halfway down. Its name, **Pacific Park** (© 310/260-8744; www.pacpark.com), hearkens back to the granddaddy pier amusement park in California, Pacific Ocean Park; this updated version has a **solar-powered Ferris wheel,** a mild-mannered **roller coaster,** and 10 other rides, plus a high-tech **arcade** shootout. But anglers still head to the end to fish, and nostalgia buffs to view the photographic display of the pier's history. This is the last of the great pleasure piers, offering rides, romance, and perfect panoramic views of the bay and mountains.

The pier is about a mile up Ocean Front Walk from Venice; it's a great round-trip stroll. Parking is available for $6 to $8 on both the pier deck and the beachfront nearby. Limited short-term parking is also available. For information on twilight concerts (generally held Thurs btw. mid-June and the end of Aug), call © 310/458-8900 or visit **www. santamonicapier.org.**

Ocean Ave. at the end of Colorado Blvd., Santa Monica.

14

L.A.'S TOP ATTRACTIONS

Six Flags California (Magic Mountain and Hurricane Harbor) ★★ **(Kids)** What started as a countrified little amusement park with a couple of relatively tame roller coasters in 1971 has been transformed by Six Flags into a thrill-a-minute daredevil's paradise called the Xtreme Park. Located about 20 to 30 minutes north of Universal Studios, Six Flags Magic Mountain is one of the only ones out of the 38 Six Flags parks that is open year-round. The 17 world-class roller coasters (more than any other place in the world) make it enormously popular with teenagers and young adults, and the children's playland—Bugs Bunny World—creates excitement for the pint-size set (kids under 48 in. tall). Bring an iron constitution; rides with names such as Goliath, Déjà Vu, Ninja, Viper, Colossus, and Psyclone will have your cheeks flapping with the G-force, and queasy expressions are common at the exit. Some rides are themed to action-film characters (such as Superman The Escape and The Riddler's Revenge); others are loosely tied to their themed surroundings, such as a Far East pagoda or gold rush mining town. The newest thrill rides are TATSU, a "flying beast" that's the tallest, fastest, and longest flying coaster in the world; Scream!, where riders are strapped into a "flying chair" and raced upside down seven times at 65 mph; and X, the world's first and only roller coaster where riders rotate 360 degrees forward and backward. Arcade games and summer-only entertainment (stunt shows, animal shows, and parades) round out the park's attractions.

Hurricane Harbor is Six Flags's tropical paradise. It's located right next door to Magic Mountain and is open May through September. You really can't see both in 1 day—combo tickets allow you to return sometime before the end of the season. Bring your own swimsuit; the park has changing rooms with showers and lockers. Like Magic Mountain, areas have themes like a tropical lagoon or an African river (complete with ancient temple ruins). The primary activities are swimming, going down the 23 water slides, rafting, playing volleyball, and lounging; many areas are designed especially for the little "buccaneer."

Note: Be sure to check their website for money-saving discounts on admission tickets—you could save up to $25 per ticket by buying online.

Magic Mountain Pkwy. (off Golden State Fwy. [I-5 N]), Valencia. ℂ **661/255-4100** or 818/367-5965. www. sixflags.com. Magic Mountain $60 adults, $30 children under 48 in. high, free for kids 2 and under; Hurricane Harbor $30 adults, $21 children under 48 in. high, free for kids 2 and under; 2-park combo ticket $70. Magic Mountain daily Apr to Labor Day, and weekends and holidays the rest of the year; Hurricane Harbor daily Memorial Day to Labor Day, weekends May and Sept, closed Oct–Apr. Both parks open at 10:30am, and closing hours vary btw. 6pm and midnight. Parking $15. All prices and hours are subject to change without notice, so please call before you arrive.

Sunset Boulevard & The Sunset Strip ★★

Unless you were raised in a cave, you've undoubtedly heard of L.A.'s Sunset Boulevard. The most famous of the city's many legendary boulevards, it winds dozens of miles over prime real estate as it travels from downtown to the beach, taking its travelers on both a historical and microcosmic journey that defines Los Angeles as a whole—from tacky strip malls and historic movie studios to infamous strip clubs and some of the most coveted zip codes on earth. In fact, driving the stretch from Hollywood to the Pacific should be required for all first-time visitors because it is such a good example of what L.A. is all about: instant gratification.

Bam! From the start, you'll see the **Saharan Motor Hotel,** of many a movie shoot; the Guitar Center's **Hollywood RockWalk,** where superstars such as Chuck Berry, Little Richard, Santana, and the Van Halen brothers left handprints or signatures; the **"Riot Hyatt,"** where The Doors, Led Zeppelin, and Guns N' Roses crashed and smashed from the '60s through the '80s; and **Chateau Marmont,** where Greta Garbo lived and John Belushi died.

Phew! And you've barely even started. Once you pass the Chateau Marmont, you're officially cruising the **Sunset Strip**—a 1³/₄-mile stretch of Sunset Boulevard from Crescent Heights Boulevard to Doheny Drive. The tour continues with the **Comedy Store,** where Roseanne, Robin Williams, and David Letterman rose to stardom; Dan Aykroyd's ramshackle **House of Blues,** where the rock stars still show up for an impromptu show; the **Sunset Tower Hotel,** where Clark Gable, Marilyn Monroe, and John Wayne once lived; the ultra-exclusive **Skybar** within the Mondrian hotel; Johnny Depp's **Viper Room,** where River Phoenix overdosed in 1993; **Whisky A Go-Go,** where The Doors were once a house band; and the **Rainbow Bar & Grill,** where Jimi Hendrix, Bruce Springsteen, and Bob Marley became legends.

Once you emerge from the strip, things calm down considerably as you drive through the tony neighborhoods of **Beverly Hills, Bel Air, Brentwood,** and **Pacific Palisades.** By the time you've reached **Malibu** and the beach where *Baywatch* was filmed, you'll have seen a vivid cross section of the city and have a pretty good idea of what L.A. is all about.

Universal Studios Hollywood & CityWalk ★★ (Kids Believing that filmmaking itself is a bona fide attraction, Universal Studios began offering tours to the public in 1964. The concept worked: Today Universal is more than just one of the largest movie studios in the world—it's one of the largest theme parks as well. By integrating shows and rides with behind-the-scenes presentations on moviemaking, Universal created a new genre of theme park, stimulating a number of clone and competitor parks.

The main attraction continues to be the **Studio Tour,** a nearly 1-hour guided tram ride around the company's 420 acres that's "hosted" (via video screen) by Whoopi Goldberg. En route you pass stars' dressing rooms and production offices before visiting famous back-lot sets that include a clean New York City street, the famous town square from the *Back to the Future* films, and newer sets such as *Curse of the Mummy's Tomb, Jurassic Park III, The Grinch,* and the airplane crash site from *War of the Worlds.* Along the way, the tram encounters several staged "disasters," which I won't divulge here lest I ruin the surprise (they're all very tame), and a staged street race "accident" echoing the action in Universal's "Fast and Furious" movie series. Though the wait to board might appear long, don't be discouraged—each tram carries several hundred people and departures are frequent, so the line moves quickly.

Other attractions are more typical of high-tech theme-park fare, but all have a film or TV-oriented slant. **The Simpsons Ride** allows guests to join Homer, Marge, Bart, Lisa, and Maggie as they soar high above the fictional "Krustyland" theme park in a "virtual roller coaster," creating the sensation of thrilling drops and turns and a full 360-degree loop. **Revenge of the Mummy** is a high-tech indoor roller coaster that whips you backward and forward through a dark Egyptian tomb filled with creepy Warrior Mummies (and ends a bit too soon). **Jurassic Park—The Ride** is short in duration as well but long on dinosaur animatronics; riders in jungle boats float through a world of five-story-tall T-rexes and airborne raptors that culminates in a pitch-dark vertical drop with a splash

LOS ANGELES

14

L.A.'S TOP ATTRACTIONS

ending. **Terminator 2: 3D** is a high-tech cyberwar show that combines live action along with triple-screen 3-D technology, explosions, spraying mists, and laser fire (Arnold prevails, of course). **Shrek 4D** is one of the park's best attractions, a multisensory animated show that combines 3-D effects, a humorous storyline, and "surprise" special effects—the flying dragon chase is wild.

There are also several live shows performing daily. At the **Fear Factor Live** show—based upon the NBC hit—park guests compete against each other in a progression of extreme stunts. **Waterworld** is a fast-paced outdoor theater presentation (and far better than the film that inspired it) featuring stunts and special effects performed on and around a small man-made lagoon (most performances are sold out, so arrive at the theater at least 15 min. before the show time listed in the handout park map). In **Backdraft,** guests move from theater to theater amid realistic ruptured fuel lines, melting metal, and scorching warehouse scenes. On the **Animal Actors Stage** trained monkeys, pigs, hawks, and other animals perform various entertaining tricks (well, most of the time). Also be sure to check out the **Wardrobe Dept.,** a retail store offering an eclectic array of men's and women's clothing from popular television and movie productions all accompanied by a certificate of authenticity, documenting the television or movie production on which the item was originally worn.

Straight ahead of the park's main entrance on Main Street is the **Hollywood Ticket Office,** where you can obtain free tickets (subject to availability) for any TV shows that are taping during your visit—including *The Tonight Show with Jay Leno*—as well as tickets and passes to other local museums, sporting events, and entertainment attractions.

Universal Studios is an exciting place for kids and teens, but just as in any theme park, lines can be brutally long; the wait for a 5-minute ride can sometimes last more than an hour. In summer, the stifling Valley heat can dog you all day. To avoid the crowds, try not to visit on weekends, school vacations, and Japanese holidays. If you're willing to pay extra money to skip the hassle of standing in line, the park offers a **"Front of Line" pass** with—obviously—front-of-the-line privileges, as well as VIP passes (essentially private tours). You can also save time standing in line by purchasing and printing your tickets online. Log on to **www.universalstudioshollywood.com** for more information. Another ticket option is the **"All You Can Eat"** pass, which allows guests to dine all day at selected in-park restaurants for one price.

For the freeway phobic or those visiting car-less at Disneyland, Universal offers an **Anaheim Shuttle Service** available to guests who purchase a full-price admission ticket to Universal Studios online via Print@Home ticketing at **www.universalstudios hollywood.com**. The shuttle bus departs from various Anaheim-area hotels twice daily. Additionally, the **Southern California CityPass** (*C* 888/330-5008; www.citypass.com) offers admission to five So Cal attractions including Universal Studios Hollywood and the Disneyland Resort.

Located just outside the gate of Universal Studios Hollywood is **Universal CityWalk** (*C* 818/622-4455; www.citywalkhollywood.com). If you have any money left from the amusement park, you can spend it at this 3-block-long pedestrian promenade crammed thick with flashy name-brand stores (Billabong, Fossil, Skechers, Abercrombie and Fitch), nightclubs (Blues at B. B. King's, Howl at the Moon dueling piano bar, Rumba Room Latin dance club), restaurants (Hard Rock Cafe, Daily Grill, Bubba Gumps, Saddle Ranch), a six-story 3-D IMAX theater, the 18-screen **CityWalk Cinemas,** a 6,200-seat amphitheater, an indoor skydiving wind tunnel, NASCAR virtual racing, and even a bowling alley (Take *that*, Disney!). Be sure to stop into the **Zen Zone** (*C* 818/ 487-7889) where you can get an inexpensive 20-minute "aqua massage." You lay down fully clothed in what looks like a tanning bed, and strong rotating jets of water massage **545** your backside from neck-to-toe (a blue rubber sheet keeps you dry). Entrance to City-Walk is free; it's open until 9pm on weekdays and until midnight Friday and Saturday. *Tip:* The sushi at the Wasabi at CityWalk restaurant (© **818/622-7224**) was surprisingly good and very reasonably priced.

Hollywood Fwy. (Universal Center Dr. or Lankershim Blvd. exits), Universal City. © **800-UNIVERSAL** or 818/622-3801. www.universalstudioshollywood.com. Admission $65 adults, $55 children under 48 in. tall, free for kids 2 and under. Parking $10. Winter hours 10am–6pm; summer hours 9am–7pm. Hours are subject to change.

Venice Beach's Ocean Front Walk ★★★ (Kids)   This has long been one of L.A.'s most colorful areas and a must-visit for any first-time tourist. Founded at the turn of the last century, Venice was a development inspired by its Italian namesake. Authentic gondolas plied miles of inland waterways lined with rococo palaces. In the 1950s, Venice became the stomping grounds of Jack Kerouac, Allen Ginsberg, William S. Burroughs, and other Beats. In the 1960s, this was the epicenter of L.A.'s hippie scene.

Today, Venice is still one of the world's most engaging bohemian locales. It's not an exaggeration to say that no visit to L.A. would be complete without a stroll along the famous paved beach path, an almost surreal assemblage of every L.A. stereotype—and then some. Among stalls and stands selling cheap sunglasses, Mexican blankets, and "herbal ecstasy" pills swirls a carnival of humanity that includes bikini-clad in-line skaters, tattooed bikers, tan hunks pumping iron at Muscle Beach, panhandling vets, beautiful wannabes, and plenty of tourists and gawkers. On any given day, you're bound to come across all kinds of performers: mimes, break-dancers, stoned drummers, chain-saw jugglers, talking parrots, and the occasional apocalyptic evangelist.

On the beach, btw. Venice Blvd. and Rose Ave., Venice. www.venicebeach.com.

Walt Disney Concert Hall ★★★   The strikingly beautiful Walt Disney Concert Hall isn't just the new home of the Los Angeles Philharmonic; it's a key element in an urban revitalization effort now underway downtown. The Walt Disney family insisted on the best and, with an initial gift of $50 million to build a world-class performance venue, that's what they got: A masterpiece of design by world-renowned architect Frank Gehry, and an acoustical quality that equals or surpasses those of the best concert halls in the world. Similar to Gehry's most famous architectural masterpiece, the Guggenheim Museum in Bilbao, the concert hall's dramatic stainless-steel exterior consists of a series of undulating curved surfaces that partially envelop the entire building, presenting multiple glimmering facades to the surrounding neighborhood. Within is a dazzling 2,273-seat auditorium replete with curved woods and a dazzling array of organ pipes (also designed by Gehry), as well as Joachim Splichal's Patina restaurant, the hip Concert Hall Cafe, a bookstore, and a gift shop.

The 3¹/₂-acre Concert Hall is open to the public for viewing, but to witness it in its full glory, do whatever it takes to attend a concert by the world-class Los Angeles Philharmonic. Also highly recommended are the $12 audio tours, which lead visitors through the Concert Hall's history from conception to creation. The 45-minute self-guided tour is narrated by actor John Lithgow and includes interviews with Frank Gehry, Los Angeles Philharmonic music director Esa-Pekka Salonen, and acoustician Yasuhisa Toyota, among others. One big caveat is that you see just about everything except the auditorium: There's almost always a rehearsal in progress, and the acoustics are so good that there's no discreet way to sneak a peek. The audio tours are available on most non-matinee days from 10am to 2pm (be sure to check their website for the monthly tour schedule).

111 S. Grand Ave. (at First St.). 𝄐 **323/850-2000** or 213/972-4399. www.disneyhall.com or www.music center.org.

---

6 EXPLORING THE CITY

To locate the attractions discussed below, see the individual neighborhood maps in section 1, "Orientation."

MUSEUMS & GALLERIES
L.A.'s Westside & Beverly Hills

Hammer Museum ★ Created by the former chairman and CEO of Occidental Petroleum, the Hammer Museum is ensconced in a two-story Carrara marble building attached to the oil company's offices. It's better known for its high-profile and often provocative visiting exhibits. With a reputation for championing contemporary political and experimental art, the Hammer continues to present often daring and usually popular special exhibits, and it's definitely worth calling ahead to find out what will be there during your visit to L.A. The permanent collection (Armand Hammer's personal collection) consists mostly of traditional western European and Anglo-American art, and contains noteworthy paintings by Toulouse-Lautrec, Rembrandt, Degas, and van Gogh.

10899 Wilshire Blvd. (at Westwood Blvd.). 𝄐 310/443-7000. www.hammer.ucla.edu. Admission $5 adults, $3 seniors 65 and over, free for kids ages 17 and under; free for everyone Thurs. Tues–Wed and Fri–Sat 11am–7pm; Thurs 11am–9pm; Sun 11am–5pm. Parking $3 for first 3 hr. with validation.

Museum of Tolerance ★ The Museum of Tolerance is designed to expose prejudices, bigotry, and inhumanity while teaching racial and cultural tolerance. Since its opening in 1993, it's hosted four million visitors from around the world, including King Hussein of Jordan and the Dalai Lama. It's located in the Simon Wiesenthal Center, an institute founded by the legendary Nazi hunter. While the Holocaust figures prominently here, this is not a Jewish museum—it's an academy that broadly campaigns for a live-and-let-live world. Tolerance is an abstract idea that's hard to display, so most of this $50-million museum's exhibits are high-tech and conceptual in nature. Fast-paced interactive displays are designed to touch the heart as well as the mind, and engage everyone from heads of state to the MTV generation.

9786 W. Pico Blvd. (at Roxbury Dr.). 𝄐 310/553-8403. www.museumoftolerance.com. Admission $13 adults, $11 seniors 62 and above, and $10 students with ID and youth 5–18, free for children ages 4 and under. Advance purchase recommended; photo ID required for admission. Mon–Fri 10am–5:00pm; Sun 11am–5:00pm. Closed Sat and many Jewish and secular holidays; call for schedule.

Hollywood

Craft & Folk Art Museum This gallery, housed in a prominent Museum Row building, has grown into one of the city's largest. "Craft and folk art" encompasses everything from clothing, tools, religious artifacts, and other everyday objects to woodcarvings, papier-mâché, weaving, and metalwork. The museum displays folk objects from around the world, but its strongest collection is masks from India, America, Mexico, Japan, and China. The museum is also known for its annual International Festival of Masks, held each October in Hancock Park, across the street. Be sure to stop in the funky, eclectic Museum Shop to peruse the wearable art, folk-art books, and various handmade crafts.

5814 Wilshire Blvd. (btw. Fairfax and La Brea aves.). (℃ 323/937-4230. www.cafam.org. Admission $5 adults, $3 seniors and students, free for children 11 and under; free to all 1st Wed each month. Tues–Wed and Fri 11am–5pm; Thurs 11am–7pm; Sat–Sun noon–6pm.

The Hollywood Museum   The historic Max Factor Building—Max Factor was the patriarch of the Hollywood makeup industry—has finally been restored to its original 1935 Art Deco splendor and is now the home of the Hollywood Museum, which features four floors of famous and rare props (including Hannibal Lecter's cell), costumes (Nicole Kidman's from *Moulin Rouge*), scripts, cameras, awards, and numerous vintage photos and posters from the television, stage, and recording industries. It's arranged for the visitor to experience Hollywood chronologically—from the Silent Era and Golden Era to current production technology and a glimpse into the future of the industry. The museum, located across from the Hollywood & Highland entertainment complex, also houses a library, a screening room, an education center, and a museum-studio gift shop. Private guided tours are available upon request.

1660 N. Highland Ave. (at Hollywood Blvd.), Hollywood. (℃ 323/464-7776. www.thehollywoodmuseum. com. Admission and tour $15 adults, $12 seniors and children 11 and under. Thurs–Sun 10am–5pm. Parking $2 with validation.

Los Angeles County Museum of Art (LACMA) ★★   For more than 50 years the LACMA has been one of the finest art museums in the nation, housing a 110,000-piece collection that includes works by Degas, Rembrandt, Hockney, and Monet. The huge 20-acre complex—it's the largest visual arts museum west of Chicago—has been expanded even more with the recent opening of the $56-million, three-story **Broad Contemporary Art Museum** (aka BCAM). Boasting 60,000 square feet of exhibition space, it's the first new art museum built in L.A. since the Getty Center opened in 1997. BCAM is one of the largest column-free art spaces in the U.S., and opening installations include works by contemporary artists such as Richard Serra, Jeff Koons, Jasper Johns, Andy Warhol, and Roy Lichtenstein.

Other highlights include LACMA's **Pavilion for Japanese Art,** which has exterior walls made of Kalwall, a translucent material that, like shoji screens, permits the entry of soft natural light. Inside is a collection of Japanese Edo paintings that's rivaled only by the holdings of the emperor of Japan. The **Ahmanson Building** houses the majority of the museum's permanent collections—everything from 2,000-year-old pre-Columbian Mexican ceramics to 19th-century portraiture, to a unique glass collection spanning the centuries. Other displays include one of the nation's largest holdings of costumes and textiles, and an important Indian and Southeast Asian art collection. Free 50-minute guided tours of many of LACMA's special exhibitions are offered weekly—check the museum's online calendar for times and locations.

5905 Wilshire Blvd. (℃ **323/857-6000.** www.lacma.org. Admission $12 adults, $8 students and seniors ages 62 and over, free for children 17 and under; regular exhibitions free for everyone after 5pm and all day the 2nd Tues of each month. Mon–Tues and Thurs noon–8pm; Fri noon–9pm; Sat–Sun 11am–8pm. Parking $5.

Museum of the American West ★★   Located north of downtown in Griffith Park, this is one of the country's finest and most comprehensive museums of the American West. More than 78,000 artifacts showcasing the history of the region west of the Mississippi River are intelligently displayed. Evocative exhibits illustrate the everyday lives of early pioneers, not only with antique firearms, tools, saddles, and the like, but with many hands-on displays that successfully stir the imagination and the heart. You'll find footage from Buffalo Bill's Wild West Show, movie clips from the silent days, contemporary films, the works of Wild West artists, and plenty of memorabilia from Gene "The Singing Cowboy" Autry's film and TV projects. The Hall of Merchandising displays Roy Rogers bedspreads, Hopalong Cassidy radios, and other items from the collective consciousness—and material collections—of baby boomers. Provocative visiting exhibits usually focus on cultural or domestic regional history. Docent-led tours are generally scheduled on Saturdays at 11am and noon. Admission is free every second Tuesday of the month.

4700 Western Heritage Way (in Griffith Park). ℂ **323/667-2000.** www.autrynationalcenter.org. Admission $9 adults, $5 seniors 60 and over and students ages 13–18, $3 children ages 2–12, free for children 1 and under; free to all Thurs after 4pm. Tues–Sun 10am–5pm (Thurs until 8pm). Parking free.

Petersen Automotive Museum ★ (Kids) When the Petersen opened in 1994, many locals were surprised that it had taken this long for the city of freeways to salute its most important shaper. Indeed, this museum says more about the city than probably any other in L.A. Named for Robert Petersen, the publisher responsible for *Hot Rod* and *Motor Trend* magazines, the four-story, 300,000-square-foot museum displays more than 200 cars and motorcycles, from the historic to the futuristic. Cars on the first floor are exhibited chronologically in period settings. Other floors are devoted to frequently changing shows of race cars, early motorcycles, famous movie vehicles, and celebrity wheels such as Jack Benny's old Chrysler Imperial. On the third floor is the Discovery Center, a 6,500-square-foot interactive "hands-on" learning center that teaches adults and kids the basic scientific principles of how a car works. Past shows have included a comprehensive exhibit of "woodies" and surf culture, Hollywood "star cars," and the world's fastest and most valuable cars.

6060 Wilshire Blvd. (at Fairfax Ave.). ℂ **323/930-CARS.** www.petersen.org. Admission $10 adults, $5 seniors and students, $3 children ages 5–12, free for kids ages 4 and under. Tues–Sun 10am–6pm. Parking $6.

Downtown

California Science Center ★★ (Kids) A $130-million renovation—reinvention, actually—has turned the former Museum of Science and Industry into Exposition Park's most popular attraction. Using high-tech sleight of hand, the center stimulates kids of all ages with questions, answers, and lessons about the world. The museum is organized into themed worlds, and one of the museum's highlights is Tess, a 50-foot animatronic woman whose muscles, bones, organs, and blood vessels are revealed, demonstrating how the body reacts to a variety of external conditions and activities. (Appropriate for children of all ages, Tess doesn't possess reproductive organs.) Another highlight is the **Air and Space Gallery,** a seven-story space where real air- and spacecraft are suspended overhead.

There are nominal fees, ranging from $2 to $5, to enjoy the science center's more thrilling attractions. You can pedal a bicycle across a high-wire suspended 43 feet above the ground (demonstrating the principle of gravity and counterweights) or get strapped into the Space Docking Simulator for a virtual-reality taste of zero gravity. There's plenty more, and plans for expansion are always in the works. The IMAX theater screen is seven stories high and 90 feet wide, with state-of-the-art surround-sound and 3-D technology. Films are screened throughout the day until 9pm and are nearly always breathtaking, even the two-dimensional ones.

700 State Dr., Exposition Park. ℂ **323/724-3623**; IMAX theater ℂ **213/744-7400**. www.casciencectr. **549**
org. Free admission to the museum; IMAX theater $8 adults, $5.75 seniors 61 and over and children ages
13–17, $4.75 ages 4–12. Multishow discounts available. Daily 10am–5pm. Closed Thanksgiving, Christmas, and New Year's Day. Parking $6.

The Museum of Contemporary Art, Los Angeles (MOCA)   MOCA is Los
Angeles's only institution devoted to art from 1940 to the present. Displaying one of the
country's finest collections of American and European art, the MOCA holds roughly
5,000 objects of various visual media—ranging from masterpieces of abstract expressionism and pop art to recent works by young and emerging artists—housed in three distant
buildings. The Grand Avenue main building (250 S. Grand Ave.), which has received
numerous design accolades, is a contemporary red sandstone structure by renowned
Japanese architect Arata Isozaki. Also at the Grand Avenue location is the museum's
popular restaurant, **Patinette** (Mon and Fri 11am–5pm; Wed 11am–2pm; Thurs 11am–
8pm; Sat–Sun 11am–6pm; ℂ **213/626-1178**), the casual-dining creation of celebrity
chef Joachim Splichal (Patina, p. 532).

The museum's second space, on Central Avenue in Little Tokyo (152 N. Central Ave.),
was the "temporary" Contemporary while the Grand structure was being built and now
presents rotating exhibits in a warehouse-type space that's been renamed the **Geffen
Contemporary at MOCA** for entertainment mogul and art collector David Geffen.
Unless there's a visiting exhibit of great interest at the main museum, I recommend that
you start at the Geffen building, where it's also easier to park.

The third gallery is the **MOCA Pacific Design Center** (8687 Melrose Ave., West
Hollywood)—it's the compact building next to the Pacific Design Center. Unlike the
other two, admission to this gallery is free, and emphasis is on contemporary architecture
and design, as well as new work by emerging and established artists.

Main MOCA information line: ℂ **213/626-6222**. www.moca.org. Admission (to all 3 galleries) $8 adults,
$5 seniors 65 and over and students, free for children ages 11 and under. Free admission to all MOCA
galleries every Thurs 5–8pm. Mon and Fri 11am–5pm; Thurs 11am–8pm; Sat–Sun 11am–6pm.

Natural History Museum of Los Angeles County ★ (Kids)   The "Fighting Dinosaurs" are not a high school football team, but the trademark symbol of this massive
museum: *Tyrannosaurus rex* and triceratops skeletons poised in a stance so realistic that
every kid feels inspired to imitate their *Jurassic Park* bellows (think *Calvin & Hobbes*).
Opened in 1913 in a beautiful domed Spanish Renaissance building, this massive
museum—it's the largest natural and historical museum in the western United States—is
a 35-hall warehouse of Earth's history, chronicling the planet and its inhabitants from
600 million years ago to the present day, and housing more than 33 million specimens
and artifacts. There's a mind-numbing array of exhibits of prehistoric fossils, bird and
marine life, gems and minerals, and North American mammals. The kid-friendly **Discovery Center** entertains children via hands-on, interactive exhibits: Kids can make
fossil rubbings, dig for fossils, and view live animals such as snakes and lizards. **Thomas
the T. rex Lab** is a specially designed workroom where visitors can watch the actual work
of paleontologists as they prepare and assemble the fossils of a 66-million-year-old *Tyrannosaurus rex*. The best permanent displays include the world's rarest shark, a walk-
through vault of priceless gems (including the largest collection of gold in the United
States), and an Insect Zoo.

The **Dinosaur Shop** sells ant farms and exploding volcano and model kits, the **Ethnic
Arts Shop** has one-of-a-kind folk art and jewelry from around the world, and the bookstore has an extensive selection of scientific titles and hobbyists' field guides.

900 Exposition Blvd., Exposition Park. (℅ **213/763-DINO.** www.nhm.org. Admission $9 adults; $6.50 children ages 13–17, seniors, and students with ID; $2 children ages 5–12; free for kids 4 and under; free for everyone 1st Tues of month. Mon–Fri 9:30am–5pm; Sat–Sun 10am–5pm.

SANTA MONICA

Santa Monica Museum of Art at Bergamot Station ★★

One of Santa Monica's primary cultural destinations is this campuslike art complex located just off the I-10 freeway. The location dates from 1875 when it was a stop for the Red Line trolley, and it retains a quasi-industrial look. Filled with more than 20 galleries, the unique installations on display here range from photography and sculpture to interactive pieces that are both eclectic and cutting edge. Its central location allows visitors to park in the free lot and spend the day seeing art rather than drive from one gallery to the next. Most pieces are available for purchase.

2525 Michigan Ave. (off Cloverfield Blvd.), Santa Monica. (℅ **310/586-6488.** www.smmoa.org. Free admission. Tues–Fri 11am–6pm; Sat 11am–8pm. Closed Sun–Mon and all legal holidays.

PASADENA

Norton Simon Museum of Art ★★★ (Finds)

Named for a food-packing king and financier who reorganized the failing Pasadena Museum of Modern Art, the Norton Simon displays one of the finest private collections of European, American, and Asian art in the world (and yet another feather in the cap of architect Frank Gehry, who redesigned the interior space). Comprehensive collections of masterpieces by Degas, Picasso, Rembrandt, and Goya are augmented by sculptures by Henry Moore and Auguste Rodin, including *The Burghers of Calais,* which greets you at the gates. The "Blue Four" collection of works by Kandinsky, Jawlensky, Klee, and Feininger is impressive, as is a superb collection of Southeast Asian sculpture. *Still Life with Lemons, Oranges, and a Rose* (1633), an oil by Francisco de Zurbarán, is one of the museum's most important holdings. Perhaps the most popular piece is *The Flower Vendor/Girl with Lilies,* by Diego Rivera, followed by Goya's *Disasters of War.* The collection of paintings, sculptures, pastels, and prints by French Impressionist Edgar Degas is among the best in the world. *Tip:* Unless you're an art expert, you'll probably want to take the "Acoustiguide" audio tour—it's $3 well spent.

411 W. Colorado Blvd., Pasadena. (℅ **626/449-6840.** www.nortonsimon.org. Admission $8 adults, $4 seniors, free for students and kids 17 and under; free for everyone the 1st Fri of each month 6–9pm. Wed–Mon noon–6pm (Fri until 9pm). Free parking.

Pacific Asia Museum

The most striking aspect of this museum is the building itself. Designed in the 1920s in Chinese Imperial Palace style, it's rivaled in flamboyance only by Grauman's Chinese Theatre in Hollywood (see "L.A.'s Top Attractions," earlier in this chapter). Rotating exhibits of 14,000 rare Asian and Pacific Islands art and artifacts span the centuries, from 100 B.C. to the current day. This manageable-size museum is worth a visit, particularly if you're an adherent of Buddhism.

46 N. Los Robles Ave., Pasadena. (℅ **626/449-2742,** ext. 10. www.pacificasiamuseum.org. Admission $7 adults, $5 students and seniors, free for children 11 and under; free for everyone the 4th Fri of each month. Wed–Sun 10am–6pm. Free parking.

ARCHITECTURAL HIGHLIGHTS

Los Angeles is a veritable Disneyland of architecture—home to an amalgam of styles, from Art Deco to Spanish Revival to coffee-shop kitsch to suburban ranch to postmodern, and more. Over-the-top styles that would be out of place in other cities are perfectly at home here. The newest gem on the scene is the Frank Gehry–designed **Walt Disney**

Santa Monica & the Beaches

When you're strolling the historic canals and streets of Venice, be sure to check out the **Chiat/Day** offices at 340 Main St. What would otherwise be an unspectacular contemporary office building is made fantastic by a **three-story pair of binoculars** that frames the entrance. The sculpture is modeled after a design created by Claes Oldenburg and Coosje van Bruggen.

When you're on your way in or out of LAX, be sure to stop for a moment to admire the **Control Tower** and **Theme Building.** The spacey *Jetsons*-style Theme Building, which has always loomed over LAX, has been joined by a more recent silhouette. The main control tower, designed by local architect Kate Diamond to evoke a stylized palm tree, is tailored to present Southern California in its best light. You can go inside to enjoy the view from the Theme Building's observation deck, or have a space-age cocktail at the Technicolor bachelor pad that is the **Encounter at LAX** restaurant.

L.A.'s Westside & Beverly Hills

In addition to the sights below, don't miss the **Beverly Hills Hotel and Bungalows** (p. 503), and be sure to wind your way through the streets of Beverly Hills off Sunset Boulevard.

Pacific Design Center   The bold architecture and overwhelming scale of the Pacific Design Center, designed by Argentine architect Cesar Pelli, aroused controversy when it was erected in 1975. Sheathed in gently curving cobalt-blue glass, the seven-story building houses more than 750,000 square feet of wholesale interior-design showrooms and is known to locals as "the Blue Whale." When the property for the design center was acquired in the 1970s, almost all of the small businesses that lined this stretch of Melrose Avenue were demolished. Only Hugo's Plating, which still stands in front of the center, successfully resisted the wrecking ball. In 1988, a second boxlike structure, dressed in equally dramatic Kelly green, was added to the design center and surrounded by a protected outdoor plaza.

8687 Melrose Ave., West Hollywood. © **310/657-0800.** www.pacificdesigncenter.com.

Schindler House ★   A protégé of Frank Lloyd Wright and contemporary of Richard Neutra, Austrian architect Rudolph Schindler designed this innovative modern house for himself in 1921 and 1922. It's now home to the Los Angeles arm of Austria's Museum of Applied Arts (MAK). The house is noted for its complicated interlocking spaces; the interpenetration of indoors and out; simple, unadorned materials; and technological innovations. Docent-guided tours are conducted at no additional charge on weekends only.

The MAK Center offers guides to L.A.-area buildings by Schindler and other Austrian architects, and presents visiting related exhibitions and creative arts programming. Call for schedules.

835 N. Kings Rd. (north of Melrose Ave.), West Hollywood. © **323/651-1510.** www.makcenter.com. Admission $7 adults, $6 students and seniors, free to children ages 12 and under; free to all every Fri after 4pm, Sept 10 (Schindler's birthday), May 24 (International Museum Day), and Dec 1. Wed–Sun 11am–6pm.

Hollywood

In addition to the buildings listed below, don't miss the **Griffith Observatory** (p. 539), **Grauman's Chinese Theatre** (p. 539), and the **Roosevelt Hotel, Hollywood** (p. 510).

> **(Fun Facts)   Not Quite S.O.S., but . . .**
>
> The light on the rooftop spire of the Capitol Records building flashes "H-O-L-L-Y-
> W-O-O-D" in Morse code. Really, it does.

Capitol Records Building   Opened in 1956, this 13-story tower, just north of the legendary intersection of Hollywood and Vine, is one of the city's most recognizable buildings. The world's first circular office building is often, but incorrectly, said to have been made to resemble a stack of 45s under a turntable stylus (it kinda does, though). Nat "King" Cole, songwriter Johnny Mercer, and other 1950s Capitol artists populate a giant exterior mural. Look down and you'll see the sidewalk stars of Capitol's recording artists (including John Lennon). In the lobby, numerous gold albums are on display.

1750 Vine St. ℂ **323/462-6252.**

The Egyptian Theatre   Conceived by grandiose impresario Sid Grauman, the Egyptian Theatre is just down the street from his better-known Chinese Theatre, but it remains less altered from its original design, which was based on the then-headline-news discovery of hidden treasures in pharaohs' tombs—hence the hieroglyphic murals and enormous scarab decoration above the stage. Hollywood's first movie premiere, *Robin Hood,* starring Douglas Fairbanks, was shown here in 1922, followed by the premiere of *The Ten Commandments* in 1923. The building recently underwent a sensitive restoration by American Cinematheque, which now screens rare, classic, and independent films. *Tip:* Check the website schedule for screenings hosted by celebrity guest speakers and directors such as Ron Howard and George Clooney.

6712 Hollywood Blvd. ℂ **323/466-FILM.** www.egyptiantheatre.com.

Freeman House   Frank Lloyd Wright's Freeman House, built in 1924, was designed as an experimental prototype of mass-produced affordable housing. The home's richly patterned "textile-block" exterior was Wright's invention and is the most famous aspect of the home's design. Situated on a dramatic site overlooking Hollywood, Freeman House is built with the world's first glass-to-glass corner windows. Dancer Martha Graham, bandleader Xavier Cugat, art collector Galka Sheye, photographer Edward Weston, and architects Philip Johnson and Richard Neutra all lived or spent significant time at this house, which became known as an avant-garde salon. The house is currently closed for restoration; call ahead to see if it's open.

1962 Glencoe Way (off Hillcrest, near Highland and Franklin aves.). ℂ **323/851-0671.**

Downtown

For a taste of what downtown's Bunker Hill was like before the bulldozers, visit the residential neighborhood of **Angelino Heights,** near Echo Park. Entire streets are still filled with stately gingerbread Victorian homes; most still enjoy the beautiful views that led early L.A.'s elite to build here. The 1300 block of Carroll Avenue is the best preserved. Don't be surprised if a film crew is scouting locations while you're there; these blocks appear often on the silver screen.

The Bradbury Building   This National Historic Landmark, built in 1893 and designed by George Wyman, is Los Angeles's oldest commercial building and one of the city's most revered architectural achievements. Legend has it that an inexperienced drafts-man named George Wyman accepted the $125,000 commission after communicating with his dead brother through a Ouija board. Capped by a magical five-story skylight, Bradbury's courtyard combines glazed brick, ornate Mexican tile floors, rich Belgian marble, Art Nouveau grillwork, handsome oak paneling, and lacelike wrought-iron railings—it's one of the great interior spaces of the 19th century. The glass-topped atrium is often used as a movie and TV set; you've probably seen it before in *Chinatown* and *Blade Runner.*

304 S. Broadway (at Third St.). (*C*) 213/626-1893. Mon–Fri 9am–6pm; Sat–Sun 9am–5pm.

Cathedral of Our Lady of the Angels ★   Completed in September 2002 at a cost of $163 million and built to last 500 years, this ultracontemporary cathedral is one of L.A.'s newest architectural treasures and the third-largest cathedral in the world. It was designed by award-winning Spanish architect Jose Rafael Moneo and features a 20,000-square-foot plaza with a meditation garden, more than 6,000 crypts and niches (making it the largest crypt mausoleum in the U.S.), Mission-style colonnades, biblically inspired gardens, and numerous artworks created by world-acclaimed artists. While most Angelinos admit that the exterior of this austere, sand-colored structure is rather unin-spiring and uninviting (the church doors don't face the street, but rather a private plaza in back surrounded by fortresslike walls), the view from the inside is breathtaking: Soar-ing heights, 12,000 panes of translucent alabaster, and larger-than-life tapestries lining the walls create an awe-inspiring sense of magnificence and serenity. The 25,000-pound bronze doors, created by sculptor Robert Graham, pay homage to Ghiberti's bronze baptistery door in Florence. Free self-guided tours are available, and there's a small cafe and gift shop as well.

555 W. Temple St. (at Grand Ave.), Los Angeles. (*C*) 213/680-5200. www.olacathedral.org. Mon–Fri 6:30am–6pm; Sat 9am–6pm; Sun 7am–6pm.

City Hall   Built in 1928, the 27-story Los Angeles City Hall was the tallest building in the city for more than 30 years. The structure's distinctive ziggurat tower was designed to resemble the Mausoleum at Halicarnassus, one of the seven wonders of the ancient world. The building has been featured in numerous films and television shows, but it is probably best known as the headquarters of the *Daily Planet* in the *Superman* TV series (or *Beverly Hills Cop,* depending on your birth date). When it was built, City Hall was the sole exception to an ordinance outlawing buildings taller than 150 feet. While you're here, be sure to take the elevator to the rarely used 27th-floor Observation Deck—on a clear day (yeah, right), you can see to Mount Wilson 15 miles away. Free docent-led tours are available at 10 and 11am Monday through Friday, and self-guided tours are available at other times. Call (*C*) 213/978-1995 for tour information.

200 N. Spring St. (*C*) 213/485-2121. www.lacityhall.org. Mon–Fri 8am–5pm.

L.A. Central Library ★★   This is one of L.A.'s early architectural achievements and the third-largest library in the United States. The city rallied to save the library when arson nearly destroyed it in 1986; the triumphant restoration has returned much of its original splendor. Working in the early 1920s, architect Bertram G. Goodhue employed the Egyptian motifs and materials popularized by the discovery of King Tut's tomb, and combined them with a more modern use of concrete block to great effect. Walking tours are the best way to explore this old beauty; they're led Monday through Friday at 12:30pm, Saturday at 11am and 2pm, and Sunday at 2pm. *Warning:* Parking in this

Stargazing in L.A., Part 2: The Less-Than-Lively Set

Almost everybody who visits L.A. hopes to see a celebrity—they are, after all, our most common export. But celebrities usually don't cooperate, failing to gather in readily viewable herds. There is, however, an absolutely guaranteed method to approach within 6 feet of many famous stars. Cemeteries are *the* place for star (or at least headstone) gazing: The star is always available, and you're going to get a lot more up close and personal than you probably would to anyone who's actually alive. Here is a guide to the most fruitful cemeteries, listed in order of their friendliness to stargazers. If you're looking for someone in particular, log on to **www.findagrave.com** (there's a website for *everything*).

Weathered Victorian and Art Deco memorials add to the decaying charm of **Hollywood Forever** ★ (formerly Hollywood Memorial Park), 6000 Santa Monica Blvd., Hollywood (© **323/469-1181;** www.hollywoodforever.com). Fittingly, there's a terrific view of the HOLLYWOOD sign over the graves, as many of the founders of the community rest here. The most notable tenant is Rudolph Valentino, who rests in an interior crypt. Outside are Tyrone Power, Jr.; Douglas Fairbanks, Sr.; Cecil B. De Mille (facing Paramount, his old studio); Carl "Alfalfa" Spitzer from the *Little Rascals* (the dog on his grave is not Petey); Hearst mistress Marion Davies; John Huston; and a headstone for Jayne Mansfield (she's really buried in Pennsylvania with her family). In 2000, Douglas Fairbanks, Jr., joined his dad at Hollywood Forever. The best epitaph is Mel Blanc's "That's all, Folks." Grab a map at the entrance for a self-guided tour.

The Catholic **Holy Cross Cemetery,** 5835 W. Slauson Ave., Culver City (© **310/836-5500**), founded in 1939, hands out maps to the stars' graves. In one area, within mere feet of each other, lie Bing Crosby, Bela Lugosi (buried in his Dracula cape), and Sharon Tate; not far away are Rita Hayworth and Jimmy Durante. Also here are "Tin Man" Jack Haley and "Scarecrow" Ray Bolger, Mary Astor, John Ford, and Gloria Morgan Vanderbilt. More recent arrivals include John Candy and Audrey Meadows.

The front office at **Hillside Memorial Park,** 6001 Centinela Ave., Baldwin Hills (© **800/576-1994;** www.hillsidememorial.com), can provide a guide to this Jewish cemetery, which has an L.A. landmark: the behemoth tomb of Al Jolson. His rotunda, complete with a bronze reproduction of Jolson and cascading fountain, is visible from I-405. Also on hand are Jack Benny, Eddie Cantor, Vic Morrow, and Michael Landon.

area can involve a heroic effort. Try visiting on the weekend and using the Flower Street parking entrance; the library will validate your ticket, and you can escape for only $2.

630 W. Fifth St. (btw. Flower St. and Grand Ave.). © **213/228-7168.** www.lapl.org/central.

Union Station ★   Union Station, completed in 1939, is one of the finest examples of California Mission-style architecture and one of the last of America's great rail stations.

You just know developers get stomachaches looking at **Westwood Village Memorial Park,** 1218 Glendon Ave., Westwood ((C) **310/474-1579;** the staff can direct you around), smack-dab in the middle of some of L.A.'s priciest real estate (behind the AVCO office building south of Wilshire Blvd.). But it's not going anywhere, especially when you consider its most famous resident: Marilyn Monroe (entombed in a simple wall crypt, number 24). It's also got Truman Capote, Roy Orbison, John Cassavetes, Armand Hammer, Donna Reed, and Natalie Wood. Walter Matthau and Jack Lemmon are buried here as well, a fitting ending for the Odd Couple.

Forest Lawn Glendale, 1712 S. Glendale Ave. ((C) **800/204-3131;** www.forestlawn.com), likes to pretend it has no celebrities. The most prominent of L.A. cemeteries, it's also the most humorless. The place is full of bad art, all part of the continuing vision of founder Huburt Eaton, who thought cemeteries should be happy places. So he banished those gloomy upright tombstones and monuments in favor of flat, pleasant, character-free, flush-to-the-ground slabs. Contrary to urban legend, Walt Disney was *not* frozen and placed under Cinderella's castle at Disneyland. His cremated remains are in a little garden to the left of the Freedom Mausoleum. Turn around, and just behind you are Errol Flynn and Spencer Tracy. In the Freedom Mausoleum itself are Nat "King" Cole, Chico Marx, and Gracie Allen—finally joined by George Burns. In a columbarium near the Mystery of Life is Humphrey Bogart. Unfortunately, some of the best celebs—such as Clark Gable, Carole Lombard, and Jean Harlow—are in the Great Mausoleum, which you often can't get into unless you're visiting a relative.

You'd think a place that encourages people to visit for fun would understand what the attraction is. But no—Forest Lawn Glendale won't tell you where any of their illustrious guests are, so don't ask. This place is immense—and, frankly, dull in comparison to the previously listed cemeteries, unless you appreciate the kitsch value of the Forest Lawn approach to art.

Forest Lawn Hollywood Hills, 6300 Forest Lawn Dr. ((C) **800/204-3131;** www.forestlawn.com), is slightly less anal than the Glendale branch, but the same basic attitude prevails. On the right lawn, near the statue of George Washington, is Buster Keaton. In the Courts of Remembrance are Lucille Ball, Charles Laughton, and the not-quite-gaudy-enough tomb of Liberace. Outside, in a vault on the Ascension Road side, is Andy Gibb. Bette Davis's sarcophagus is in front of the wall, to the left of the entrance to the Courts. Gene Autry is also buried here, almost within earshot of the museum that bears his name.

LOS ANGELES

14

EXPLORING THE CITY

It was built with the opulence and attention to detail that characterize 1930s WPA projects, such as its cathedral-like size and richly paneled ticket lobby and waiting area. When you're strolling through these grand historic halls, it's easy to imagine the glamorous movie stars who once boarded *The City of Los Angeles* and *The Super Chief* to journey back East during the glory days of rail travel; it's also easy to picture the many heartfelt reunions between returning soldiers and loved ones following the victorious end to

World War II, in the station's heyday. Movies shot here include *Bugsy, The Way We Were,* and *Blade Runner.*

800 N. Alameda St. (at Cesar E. Chavez Ave.).

US Bank Tower (aka Library Tower)   Designed by renowned architect I. M. Pei, L.A.'s most distinctive skyscraper (it's the round one) is the tallest building between Chicago and Singapore. Built in 1989 at a cost of $450 million, the 76-story monolith is both square and rectangular, rising from its Fifth Street base in a series of overlapping spirals and cubes. The Bunker Hill Steps wrapping around the west side of the building were inspired by Rome's Spanish Steps. *Gee whiz fact:* The glass crown at the top—illuminated at night—is the highest building helipad in the world.

633 W. Fifth St. (at S. Grand Ave.).

Watts Towers & Art Center   Watts became notorious as the site of riots in the summer of 1965, during which 34 people were killed and more than 1,000 were injured. Today, a visit to Watts is a lesson in inner-city life. It's a high-density land of gray strip malls, well-guarded check-cashing shops, and fast-food restaurants; but it's also a neighborhood of hardworking families struggling to survive in the midst of gangland. Although there's not much for the casual tourist here, the Watts Towers are truly a unique attraction, and the adjoining art gallery illustrates the fierce determination of area residents to maintain cultural integrity.

The Towers—the largest piece of folk art created by a single person—are colorful, 99-foot-tall cement and steel sculptures ornamented with mosaics of bottles, seashells, cups, plates, pottery, and ceramic tiles. They were completed in 1955 by folk artist Simon Rodia, an immigrant Italian tile-setter who worked on them for 33 years in his spare time. True fans of decorative ceramics will enjoy the fact that Rodia's day job was at the legendary Malibu Potteries (are those fragments of valuable Malibu tile encrusting the Towers?). Closed in 1994 due to earthquake damage, the towers were triumphantly reopened in 2001 and now attract more than 20,000 visitors annually. Tours are by request.

Note: Next to these designated Cultural Landmarks is the Art Center, which has an interesting collection of ethnic musical instruments as well as several visiting art exhibits throughout the year.

1727 E. 107th St., Los Angeles. ℂ 213/847-4646. www.trywatts.com. Art Center: Free admission. Tues–Sat 10am–4pm; Sun noon–4pm. Towers: Admission $7 adults, $3 seniors 55 and over and teens 13–17, free for children 12 and under. Fri–Sat 11am–3pm; Sun 12:30–3pm.

Pasadena & Environs

For a quick but profound architectural fix, stroll past Pasadena's grandiose and baroque **City Hall,** 100 N. Garfield Ave., 2 blocks north of Colorado Boulevard; closer inspection will reveal its classical colonnaded courtyard, formal gardens, and spectacular tiled dome.

The Gamble House ★★   The huge two-story Gamble House, built in 1908 as a California vacation home for the wealthy family of Procter and Gamble fame, is a sublime example of Arts and Crafts architecture. The interior, designed by the famous Pasadena-based Greene & Greene architectural team, abounds with handcraftsmanship, including intricately carved teak cornices, custom-designed furnishings, elaborate carpets, and a fantastic Tiffany glass door. No detail was overlooked. Every oak wedge, downspout, air vent, and switch plate contributes to the unified design. Admission is by 1-hour guided tour only, which departs every 15 minutes. Tickets go on sale on tour days in the bookstore at 10am Thursday through Saturday, and at 11:30am on Sunday. No

(Fun Facts   House Hygiene

The restoration of the Gamble House was so meticulous that workers used dental picks to scrape gunk from the home's 262 rafters.

reservations are necessary, but tours are often sold out, especially on weekends by 2pm. And don't wear high heels or they'll make you put on slippers.

If you can't fit the tour into your schedule but have an affection for Craftsman design, visit the well-stocked bookstore and museum shop located in the former garage (you can also see the exterior and grounds of the house this way). The bookstore is open Tuesday through Saturday 10am to 5pm, and Sunday 11:30am to 5pm.

Additional elegant Greene & Greene creations (still privately owned) abound 2 blocks away along **Arroyo Terrace,** including nos. **368, 370, 400, 408, 424,** and **440.** The Gamble House bookstore can give you a walking-tour map and also conducts guided neighborhood tours by appointment.

4 Westmoreland Place (in the 300 block of N. Orange Grove Blvd.), Pasadena. ℂ **626/793-3334.** www. gamblehouse.org. Tours $10 adults, $7 students and seniors 65 and over, free for children 11 and under. Tours Thurs–Sun noon–3pm. Closed holidays.

PARKS & GARDENS

In addition to the two examples of urban parkland below, check out **Pan Pacific Park,** a hilly retreat near the Farmers Market and CBS Studios, named for the Art Deco auditorium that unfortunately no longer stands at its edge.

Griffith Park ★★ (Kids   Mining tycoon Col. Griffith J. Griffith donated these 4,107 acres to the city in 1896 as a Christmas gift. Today Griffith Park is the largest urban park in America. There's a lot to do here, including 53 miles of hiking trails (the prettiest is the Fern Dell trail near the Western Ave. entrance, a shady hideaway cooled by waterfalls and ferns), horseback riding, golfing, swimming, biking, and picnicking. For a general overview of the park, drive the mountainous loop road that winds from the top of Western Avenue, past Griffith Observatory, and down to Vermont Avenue. For a more extensive foray, turn north at the loop road's midsection, onto Mount Hollywood Drive. To reach the golf courses, the **Museum of the American West** (p. 547), or **Los Angeles Zoo** (p. 560), take Los Feliz Boulevard to Riverside Drive, which runs along the park's western edge.

Near the zoo, in a particularly dusty corner of the park, you can find the **Travel Town Transportation Museum,** 5200 Zoo Dr. (ℂ **323/662-5874**), a little-known outdoor museum with a small collection of vintage locomotives and old airplanes. Kids love the miniature train ride that circles the perimeter of the museum. The museum is open Monday through Friday from 10am to 4pm, and Saturday and Sunday from 10am to 5pm; admission is free.

Hollywood; entrances are along Los Feliz Blvd., at Riverside Dr., Vermont Ave., and Western Ave. ℂ **323/ 913-4688.** Free admission.

Huntington Library, Art Collections & Botanical Gardens ★★ (Kids   The Huntington Library is the jewel in Pasadena's crown. The 207-acre hilltop estate was once home to industrialist and railroad magnate Henry E. Huntington (1850–1927), who bought books on the same massive scale on which he acquired businesses. The continually expanding collection includes dozens of Shakespeare's first editions, Benjamin Franklin's handwritten autobiography, a Gutenberg Bible from the 1450s, and the earliest known manuscript of Chaucer's *Canterbury Tales.* Although some rare works are available only to visiting scholars, the library has a regularly changing (and always excellent) exhibit showcasing different items in the collection.

If you prefer canvas to parchment, Huntington also put together a terrific 18th-century British and French art collection. The most celebrated paintings are Gainsborough's *The Blue Boy* and *Pinkie,* a companion piece by Sir Thomas Lawrence depicting the youthful aunt of Elizabeth Barrett Browning. These and other works are displayed in the stately Italianate mansion on the crest of this hillside estate, so you can also get a glimpse of its splendid furnishings. American art and Renaissance paintings are exhibited in two additional galleries.

But it's the vast **botanical gardens** featuring more than 14,000 different species of plants that draw most locals to the Huntington. The Japanese Garden comes complete with a traditional open-air Japanese house, koi-filled stream, and serene Zen garden. There's also an exotic **Desert Garden,** intriguing **Jungle Garden, Bing Children's Garden** (designed specifically for kids ages 2 to 7), and the glass-and-steel **Conservatory for Botanical Science** where visitors learn some of the fundamentals of botany via state-of-the-art science stations. The latest addition is a new 12-acre **Chinese Garden,** the largest classical garden outside mainland China and one of the largest of the Huntington's 14 specialized gardens. Highlights include a lake, tea house, pavilions, and bridges within a landscape of plants native to China.

Because the Huntington surprises many with its size and wealth of activities to choose from, first-timers might want to start with a tour. One-hour garden tours are offered daily; no reservations or additional fees are required. Times vary, so check at the information desk upon arrival. I also recommend that you tailor your visit to include the popular **English high tea** served Tuesday through Friday from noon to 4:30pm, and Saturday and Sunday from 10:45am to 4:30pm (last seating at 3:30pm). The tearoom overlooks the Rose Garden (home to 1,000 varieties displayed in chronological order of their breeding), and since the finger sandwiches and desserts are served buffet style, it's a genteel bargain even for hearty appetites at $20 per person (please note that museum admission is a separate required cost). Phone © **626/683-8131** for tearoom reservations, which are required and should be made at least 2 weeks in advance.

1151 Oxford Rd., San Marino. © **626/405-2100.** www.huntington.org. Admission $15 adults, $12 seniors 65 and over, $10 students and children ages 12–18, $6 children ages 5–11, free to children 4 and under; free to all the 1st Thurs of each month. Sept–May Mon and Wed–Fri noon–4:30pm, Sat–Sun 10:30am–4:30pm; June–Aug daily 10:30am–4:30pm, excluding Tues. Closed major holidays. Free parking.

Will Rogers State Historic Park Will Rogers State Historic Park was once Will Rogers's private ranch and grounds. Willed to the state of California in 1944, the 168-acre estate is now both a park and a historic site, supervised by the Department of Parks and Recreation. Visitors may explore the grounds, the former stables, and the 31-room house filled with the original furnishings, including a porch swing in the living room and many Native American rugs and baskets. Charles Lindbergh and his wife, Anne Morrow Lindbergh, hid out here in the 1930s during part of the craze that followed the kidnap and murder of their first son. There are picnic tables, but no food is sold. Guided Ranch House tours are available as well.

Who's Will Rogers, you ask? He was born in Oklahoma in 1879 and became a cowboy in the Texas Panhandle before drifting into a Wild West show as a folksy, speechifying

(Value) **Free Culture**

To beef up attendance and give indigent folk like us travel writers a break, almost all of L.A.'s art galleries and museums are open free to the public 1 day of the week or month (or both), and several charge no admission. Use the following list to plan your week around the museums' free-day schedules; refer to the individual attractions listings in this chapter for more information on each museum.

Free Every Day
- J. Paul Getty Museum at the Getty Center
- The Getty Villa Malibu
- Museum of Television and Radio (donation suggested)
- Los Angeles County Museum of Art, *after* 5pm
- California African American Museum
- California Science Center
- Bergamot Arts Station & Santa Monica Museum of Art

Free Every Thursday
- Museum of Contemporary Art (MOCA), from 5 to 8pm
- Museum of the American West, from 4 to 8pm
- UCLA Hammer Museum, from 11am to 9pm
- Japanese American National Museum, from 5 to 8pm
- Skirball Cultural Center, from noon to 9pm
- Geffen Contemporary at MOCA, from 5 to 8pm

Free Every Friday
- Schindler House, from 4 to 6pm

Free Every First Tuesday
- Natural History Museum of Los Angeles County, from 9:30am to 5pm
- Page Museum at La Brea Tar Pits, from 9:30am to 5pm

Free Every First Wednesday
- Craft & Folk Art Museum, from 11am to 5pm

Free Every First Thursday
- Huntington Library, Art Collections & Botanical Gardens, from noon to 4:30pm

Free Every First Friday
- Norton Simon Museum of Art, from 6 to 9pm

Free Every Second Tuesday
- Museum of the American West, from 10am to 5pm
- Los Angeles County Museum of Art, from noon to 8pm

Free Every Third Tuesday
- Los Angeles County Arboretum and Botanic Garden, from 9am to 4:30pm
- Japanese American National Museum, from 10am to 8pm

Free Every Fourth Friday
- Pacific Asia Museum, from 10am to 8pm

roper. The "cracker-barrel philosopher" performed lariat tricks while carrying on a humorous deadpan monologue on current events. The showman moved to Los Angeles in 1919, where he become a movie actor as well as the author of numerous books detailing his down-home "cowboy philosophy."

1501 Will Rogers State Park Rd., Pacific Palisades (btw. Santa Monica and Malibu). ✆ **310/454-8212.** Park entrance $7 per vehicle. Daily 8am–sunset. House opens daily 10am–5pm; guided Ranch House tours offered Tues–Sun at 11am, 1pm, and 2pm. From Santa Monica, take the Pacific Coast Hwy. (Calif. 1) north, turn right onto Sunset Blvd., and continue to the park entrance.

THE ZOO

Los Angeles Zoo ★ (Kids) The L.A. Zoo has been welcoming visitors and busloads of school kids since 1966. In 1982, the zoo inaugurated a display of cuddly koalas, still one of its biggest attractions among 1,200 animals from around the world. Although it's smaller than the world-famous San Diego Zoo, the L.A. Zoo is far easier to explore. As much an arboretum as a zoo, the grounds are thick with mature shade trees from around the world that help cool the once-barren grounds, and new habitats are light-years ahead of the cruel concrete roundhouses originally used to exhibit animals (though you can't help feeling that, despite the fancy digs, all the creatures would rather be in their natural habitat).

The zoo's latest attraction is new $19-million **Campo Gorilla Reserve,** a habitat for six African lowland gorillas that closely resembles their native West African homeland. Visitors partake in a pseudo-African-jungle experience as they journey along a misty, forested pathway with glassed viewing areas for close-up views of the gorillas living in two separate habitats: one for a family troop of gorillas, led by a silverback male; and a separate habitat for two bachelors.

Other highlights include the **Sea Lion Cliffs** habitat, home to the zoo's five sea lions where visitors can view the saltwater habitat from an underwater glass viewing area; the **Chimpanzees of the Mahale Mountains** habitat, where visitors can see plenty of primate activity; the **Red Ape Rainforest,** a natural orangutan habitat; the entertaining **World of Birds** show; the **Pachyderm Forest** (climate-controlled digs for the elephants and hippos, complete with an underwater viewing area); and the **Mandrills Exhibit** (the world's largest and most colorful baboons). The gargantuan Andean condor had me enthralled as well (the facility is renowned in zoological circles for the successful breeding and releasing of California condors, and occasionally some of these majestic and endangered birds are on exhibit). Kids will also enjoy the **Winnick Family Children's Zoo,** which contains a petting area, exhibition animal care center, Adventure Theater storytelling and puppet show, and other kid-hip exhibits and activities. *Tip:* To avoid the busloads of rambunctious school kids, arrive after noon.

5333 Zoo Dr., Griffith Park. ✆ **323/644-4200.** www.lazoo.org. Admission $10 adults, $7 seniors 62 and over, $5 kids ages 2–12, free to children 1 and under. Daily 10am–5pm (until 6pm July 1 to Labor Day). Closed Christmas Day. Free parking.

ORGANIZED TOURS
Studio Tours

NBC Studios (Kids) According to a security guard, John Wayne and Redd Foxx once got into a fight here after Wayne refused to ride in the same limo as Foxx, who called the movie star a "redneck." Well, your NBC tour will probably be a bit more docile than that. The guided indoor walking tour includes a behind-the-scenes unstaged look at *The Tonight Show with Jay Leno* set (p. 544 on how to get free Jay Leno tickets); wardrobe, makeup, and set-building departments; and several sound studios. In fact, NBC is the only TV studio that offers the public a behind-the-scenes look at the inner workings of its television operation, and it's a lot less expensive than the competition's studio tours. Granted, it doesn't have the cachet of a major motion picture studio tour, but it's entertaining nonetheless.

Tours depart at the top of the hour Monday through Friday from 9am to 3pm, and tickets are sold at the Guest Relations Department (bring cash—they don't take credit cards). Also, this is one of the few studio tours that doesn't have a minimum age requirement. *Note:* Before you make the drive to Burbank, be sure to call the studio and make sure tours are being offered that day and aren't already sold out.

3000 W. Alameda Ave. (off California St.), Burbank. © **818/840-3537.** Tours $8.50 adults, $7.50 seniors 60 and over, $5 children ages 5–12, free for children 4 and under. Mon–Fri 9am–3pm.

Paramount Pictures ★★ Paramount is the only major studio still located in Hollywood, which makes the 2-hour "cart tour" around its Hollywood headquarters far more historically enriching than the modern studios in Burbank (even the wrought-iron gates Gloria Swanson motored through in Sunset Boulevard are still there). The tour is both a historical ode to filmmaking and a real-life, behind-the-scenes look at a working movie and television facilities in day-to-day operation; ergo, no two tours are alike, and chances of spotting a celebrity are pretty good. Visits typically include a walk-through of the soundstages of TV shows or feature films, though you can't enter while taping is taking place. The $35 tours depart Monday through Friday by advance reservations only. You need to be 12 or older to take the tour, and cameras and recording equipment are verboten. *Tip:* After the tour, have lunch at the Paramount Studio's world-famous commissary; you never know who might drop in for a bite, and the food's pretty darn good.

5555 Melrose Ave. ✆ **323/956-1777.** www.paramount.com. Tours $35 per person by advance reservation only. Mon–Fri 10am–2pm.

Sony Pictures Studio Tour   Although it doesn't have quite the historical cachet as Warner Brothers or Paramount, a lot of movie history was made at this Culver City lot. The 2-hour walking tour includes stops at classic stage scenes such as the Yellow Brick Road winding through Munchkinland, sets from modern thrillers such as *Spiderman,* and an opportunity to drop in on the *Jeopardy!* or *Wheel of Fortune* sets. But the main reason for the tour is the chance to catch a glimpse at the stars who work here (it's one of the busiest studio lots in the world). Tours depart from the Sony Pictures Plaza near the parking lot; be sure to call ahead and make a reservation.

Sony Picture Studios, 10202 W. Washington Blvd., Culver City. ✆ **323/520-8687.** www.sonypictures studios.com. Reservations highly recommended; children under 12 not admitted. Tours $28 per person. Tours depart Mon–Fri at 9:30am, 10:30am, 1:30pm, and 2:30pm. Photo ID required. Free parking.

Universal Studios ★   Universal offers daily 1-hour tram tours of its studio lot as part of the general admission price to the amusement park, which is open from 9am to 7pm in the summer and from 10am to 6pm in the winter. See p. 543 for more information.

Warner Bros. Studios ★   The Warner Brothers' "VIP Tour" takes visitors on a 2¼-hour jaunt around the world's busiest movie and TV studio. After a brief introductory film about the history of WB, groups of 12 pile into stretch golf carts for an intimate view of the inner workings of a motion picture and television studio: back-lot streets, sound stages, sets, and craft shops. Because nothing is staged there's no telling what or who you might encounter, and no two tours are the same. The tour ends with a visit to the Warner Bros. Museum, which contains original costumes, props, sets, scripts, and correspondence from classic WB films and television shows. Advance tickets are recommended and available online via their website, or by calling ✆ **866/777-8932;** otherwise, tickets are sold the day of the tour on a first-come, first-served basis, but they recommended arriving at the ticket office early to make sure they don't sell out. Children under 8 are not admitted, you must bring valid photo ID, and they recommended you show up about 30 minutes before the tour starts.

3400 Riverside Dr., Burbank. ✆ **818/972-8687.** www.wbstudiotour.com. Advance reservations recommended. Tours $45 per person. Tours depart Mon–Fri every half hour btw. 8:20am–3:20pm (extended hours during spring and summer).

Bus/Van Tours

L.A. Tours (✆ **323/460-6490;** www.latours.net) operates regularly scheduled tours of the city. Plush shuttle buses pick up riders from major hotels for morning or afternoon tours of Sunset Strip, the movie studios, the Farmers Market, Hollywood, homes of the stars, and other attractions. Different itineraries are available, from downtown and the Music Center to Disneyland, Universal Studios, or Six Flags Magic Mountain. Tours vary in length from a half-day Beaches & Shopping tour to a full-day Grand City tour. Advance reservations are required.

The other major tour company in L.A. is **Starline Tours** ★ (© 800/959-3131; www.starlinetours.com)—you'll see their air-conditioned minibuses, double-decker Big Red buses, and open-air trolleys all over the city. Since 1935, Starline has been offering a wide selection of L.A. tours, including the first-ever Movie Stars' Homes tour. Its most popular tour, the 2-hour neighborhood jaunt, departs every half-hour from the front of Grauman's Chinese Theatre between 9:30am and 4pm (you'll see the Starline kiosk to the right of the theater entrance at 6925 Hollywood Blvd.). If you really like driving tours, sign up for the piece d' resistance: the 5¹/₂-hour Grand Tour of L.A. Check out their website for more tour information.

Walking Tours

If you want the classic Hollywood walking tour, **Red Line Tours** (© 323/402-1074; www.redlinetours.com) offers daily sightseeing expeditions to all the famous (and infamous) landmarks in Hollywood. Its unique "live-audio" system allows customers to hear the tour guide even over the city noise. Customers wear an audio headset receiver while the tour guide wears a headset microphone transmitter (pretty clever, actually). Trips depart from the Stella Adler Academy & Theatres (6773 Hollywood Blvd.) at 10am, noon, 2pm, and 4pm, 7 days a week. Rates are $20 for adults, $18 for students and seniors, and $15 for children ages 9 to 15. Tours of downtown L.A. are offered as. Log on to the Red Line Tour website for more information.

The **L.A. Conservancy** (© 213/623-2489; www.laconservancy.org) conducts about a dozen entertaining walking tours of historic downtown L.A. In Pasadena, **Pasadena Heritage** (© 626/441-6333; www.pasadenaheritage.org) offers a walking tour of Old Pasadena.

Bicycle Tours

Perry's Beach Café & Rentals in Santa Monica offers 1¹/₂-hour bicycle tours of the Santa Monica and Venice beach communities. It's a great way to explore the area while learning about its history and landmark architecture. The package costs $30 per person and includes a tour guide, a 3-hour bike rental with protective gear, water, a bike lock, and goody bag. *Note:* A minimum of three people are required for the tour. For more information or to make a reservation, call © **310/372-3138.**

Helicopter Tours

Touring L.A. from above is certainly a unique perspective. Just the thrill of riding in a helicopter is worth the price. **Celebrity Helicopters** (© 877/999-2099; www.celebheli.com) offers a wide array of themed trips, ranging from a 35-minute Celebrity Home Tour ($169) to a 25-minute fly-by of the L.A. coastline ($99). Other tour packages are available as well: Check their website for more information.

Jogging Tour

Off 'N Running Tours (© 310/246-1418; www.offnrunningtours.com) combines sporting with sightseeing, taking joggers on guided runs through Los Angeles. The themed tours such as "Running from the Paparazzi" are customized to take in the most entertaining areas around the city and can accommodate any skill level for 4 to 12 miles. One of the most popular routes is up to Holmby Hills, past the Playboy Mansion and other massive estates. It's a fun way to get the most out of your morning jog. Tours cost about $60 and include a T-shirt, a light breakfast, snacks, and plenty of water.

The city of Beverly Hills offers inexpensive trolley tours that detail the city's history as well as little-known facts and celebrity tidbits. The tour takes visitors on a 40-minute docent-led tour through the tony avenues of Beverly Hills, including Rodeo Avenue and the Golden Triangle. It runs every Saturday on the hour from 11am to 4pm. The fare is a mere $5 for adults and $1 for kids 12 and under. The trolley departs at the "Trolley Stop" at the intersection of Rodeo Drive and Dayton Way. For more information, call ✆ 310/285-2438 or log on to **www.beverlyhills.org**.

---

7 TV TAPINGS

Being part of the audience for the taping of a television show might be the quintessential L.A. experience. This is a great way to see Hollywood at work, to find out how your favorite sitcom or talk show is made, and to catch a glimpse of your favorite TV personalities. Timing is important—remember that most series go on hiatus between March and July. And tickets to the top shows are in greater demand than others, so getting your hands on them takes advance planning—and possibly some waiting in line.

Request tickets as far in advance as possible. Several episodes may be shot on a single day, so you may be required to remain in the theater for up to 4 hours (in addition to the recommended 1-hr. early check-in). If you phone at the last moment, you may luck into tickets for your top choice. More likely, however, you'll be given a list of shows that are currently filming, and you won't recognize many of the titles; studios are always taping pilots, few of which end up on the air. But you never know who may be starring in them—look at all the famous faces that have launched new sitcoms in the past couple of years. Tickets are always free, are usually limited to two per person, and are distributed on a first-come, first-served basis. Many shows don't admit children under the age of 10; in some cases, no one under the age of 18 is admitted.

Tickets are sometimes given away to the public outside popular tourist sites such as Grauman's Chinese Theatre in Hollywood and Universal Studios in the Valley; L.A.'s visitor information centers in downtown and Hollywood often have tickets as well. But if you're determined to see a particular show, contact the following suppliers:

Audiences Unlimited, Inc. (✆ 818/753-3470; www.tvtickets.com) is a good place to start. It distributes tickets for most of the top sitcoms, including *Two and a Half Men, Wizards of Waverly Place,* and more. This service is organized and informative (as is its website), and fully sanctioned by production companies and networks. ABC, for example, no longer handles ticket distribution directly, but refers all inquiries to Audiences Unlimited, Inc. **TVTIX.COM** (✆ 323/653-4105; www.tvtix.com) also distributes

---

Tips **The Cold Truth About Talk Shows**

The sets of most talk shows are kept at a cool temperature (the hot lights raise the temperature on stage), so be sure to bring a sweater or jacket. And if you dress well—no T-shirts or shorts—your chances of getting a front-row seat increase dramatically.

You also may want to contact the networks for information on a specific show, including some whose tickets are not available at the above agencies. At **ABC,** all ticket inquiries are referred to Audiences Unlimited (see above), but you may want to check out ABC's website at **www.abc.com** for a colorful look at their lineup and links to specific show sites.

For **CBS Television City,** 7800 Beverly Blvd., Los Angeles, CA 90036, call ℂ **323/ 575-2458** between Monday and Friday from 9am to 5pm to see what's being filmed while you're in town. Tickets for CBS tapings are distributed on a first-come, first-served basis; you can write in advance to reserve them or pick them up at the studio up to an hour before taping. Tickets for many CBS sitcoms are also available from Audiences Unlimited (see above). For tickets to *The Price Is Right,* call the 24-hour ticket hot line at ℂ **323/575-2449** or log on to **www.cbs.com/daytime/price/tickets**.

For **NBC,** 3000 W. Alameda Ave., Burbank, CA 91523 (ℂ **818/840-3537**), call to see what's on while you're in L.A. Tickets for NBC tapings, including *The Tonight Show with Jay Leno* (minimum age to attend this show is 16), can be obtained three ways: 1) Pick them up at the NBC ticket counter on the day of the show—two tickets per person are distributed on a first-come, first-served basis at the ticket counter off California Avenue starting at 8am (be sure to get there early); 2) at least 6 weeks before your visit, send a self-addressed, stamped envelope with your ticket request to the address above; 3) go to the Audiences Unlimited ticket booth at Universal Studios Hollywood (p. 543). Be sure to include show name, number of tickets (four per request), and dates desired. All the NBC shows are represented online at either **www.nbc.com** or **www.tvtickets.com**.

Paramount Studios also offers free tickets to their live audience shows. All you need to do is call one of the friendly employees at Paramount Guest Relations (ℂ **323/956-1777**) between 9am and 6pm on weekdays and make a reservation. For seating reservations for *Dr. Phil,* call ℂ **323/461-7445. Universal Studios** (ℂ **800/UNIVERSAL;** www.universal studios.com) also offers free tickets to their live audience shows. At the amusement park's **Audiences Unlimited ticket booth,** you can obtain free tickets to join the audience for any TV shows that are taping during your visit (subject to availability).

8 BEACHES

Los Angeles County's 72-mile coastline sports more than 30 miles of beaches, most of which are operated by the **Department of Beaches & Harbors,** 13837 Fiji Way, Marina del Rey (ℂ **310/305-9503**). County-run beaches usually charge for parking ($4–$8). Alcohol, bonfires, and pets are prohibited. For recorded **surf conditions** (and coastal weather forecast), call ℂ **310/457-9701.** The following are the county's best beaches, listed from north to south.

EL PESCADOR, L.A. PIEDRA & EL MATADOR BEACHES   These rugged and isolated beaches (real finds) front a 2-mile stretch of Pacific Coast Highway (Calif. 1) between Broad Beach and Decker Canyon roads, a 10-minute drive from the Malibu Pier. Picturesque coves with unusual rock formations are great for sunbathing and picnicking, but swim with caution, as there are no lifeguards. The beaches can be difficult to find; only small signs on the highway mark them. There are a limited number of parking spots atop the bluffs. Descend to the beach via stairs that cling to the cliffs.

SIGHTS & ATTRACTIONS

Aquarium of the Pacific **22**
Chiat/Day Headquarters **16**
Getty Center **12**
Getty Villa Malibu **13**
Pepperdine University **8**
Queen Mary **23**
Venice Beach
  Ocean Front Walk **18**
Will Rogers
  State Historic Park **11**
Santa Monica Pier **15**

BEACHES

El Pescador, La Piedra,
  & El Matador Beaches **3**
Hermosa City Beach **20**
Leo Carrillo Beach **2**
Malibu Lagoon
  State Beach **7**
Manhattan State Beach **19**
North County Line Beach **1**
Paradise Cove **6**
Point Dume Beach **5**
Redondo State Beach **21**
Santa Monica
  State Beach **14**
Surfrider Beach **9**
Topanga State Beach **10**
Venice Beach **17**
Will Rogers State Beach **13**
Zuma Beach County Park **4**

ZUMA BEACH COUNTY PARK ★   Jampacked on warm weekends, L.A. County's largest beach park is located off Pacific Coast Highway (Calif. 1), a mile past Kanan Dume Road. While it can't claim to be the most scenic beach in the Southland, Zuma has the most comprehensive facilities: plenty of restrooms, lifeguards, playgrounds, volleyball courts, and snack bars. The southern stretch, toward Point Dume, is Westward Beach, separated from the noisy highway by sandstone cliffs. A trail leads over the point's headlands to Pirate's Cove, once a popular nude beach.

PARADISE COVE   This private beach in the 28000 block of Pacific Coast Highway (Calif. 1) charges $25 to park and $5 per person if you walk in. Changing rooms and showers are included in the price. The beach is often full by noon on weekends.

MALIBU LAGOON STATE BEACH ★★   Not just a pretty white-sand beach, but an estuary and wetlands area as well, Malibu Lagoon is the historic home of the Chumash Indians. The entrance is on Pacific Coast Highway (Calif. 1) south of Cross Creek Road, and there's a small admission charge. Marine life and shorebirds teem where the creek empties into the sea, and the waves are always mild. The historic **Adamson House** is here, a showplace of Malibu tile now operating as a museum.

SURFRIDER BEACH   Without a doubt, L.A.'s best waves roll ashore here. One of the city's most popular surfing spots, this beach is located between the Malibu Pier and the lagoon. In surf lingo, few "locals-only" wave wars are ever fought here—surfing is not as territorial here as it can be in other areas, where out-of-towners can be made to feel unwelcome. Surfrider is surrounded by all of Malibu's hustle and bustle; don't come here for peace and quiet as the surf is always crowded.

TOPANGA STATE BEACH   Highway noise prevents solitude at this short, narrow strip of sand located where Topanga Canyon Boulevard emerges from the mountains. Why go? Ask the surfers who wait in line to catch Topanga's excellent right point breaks. There are restrooms and lifeguard services here, and across the street you'll find one of the best fresh fish restaurants around, the **Reel Inn,** 18661 Pacific Coast Hwy., Malibu (② **310/ 456-8221**).

WILL ROGERS STATE BEACH   Three miles along Pacific Coast Highway (Calif. 1), between Sunset Boulevard and the Santa Monica border, are named for the American humorist whose ranch-turned-state-historic-park is nestled above the palisades that provide the backdrop for this popular beach. A pay parking lot extends the entire length of Will Rogers, and facilities include restrooms, lifeguards, and a snack hut in season. While the surfing is not the best, the waves are friendly for swimmers, and there are always competitive volleyball games to be found.

SANTA MONICA STATE BEACH   The family-friendly beaches on either side of the Santa Monica Pier are popular for their white sands and accessibility. There are big parking lots, cafes, and well-maintained restrooms. A paved beach path runs along here, allowing you to walk, bike, or skate to Venice and points south. Colorado Boulevard leads to the pier; turn north on Pacific Coast Highway (Calif. 1) below the coastline's bluffs, or south along Ocean Avenue; you can find parking in both directions.

VENICE BEACH ★★   Moving south from the city of Santa Monica, the paved pedestrian Promenade becomes Ocean Front Walk and gets progressively weirder until it reaches an apex at Washington Boulevard and the Venice fishing pier. Although there are people who swim and sunbathe, Venice Beach's character is defined by the sea of humanity on the Ocean Front Walk, plus the bevy of boardwalk vendors and old-fashioned

MANHATTAN STATE BEACH   The Beach Boys used to hang out at this wide, friendly beach backed by beautiful oceanview homes. Plenty of parking on 36 blocks of side streets (btw. Rosecrans Ave. and the Hermosa Beach border) draws weekend crowds from the L.A. area. Manhattan has some of the best surfing around, restrooms, lifeguards, and volleyball courts. Manhattan Beach Boulevard leads west to the fishing pier and adjacent seafood restaurants.

HERMOSA CITY BEACH ★★   This very wide white-sand beach is one of the best in Southern California and my favorite. Hermosa extends to either side of the pier and includes the Strand, a wide, smooth pedestrian lane that runs its entire length. Main access is at the foot of Pier Avenue, which is lined with interesting shops and cafes with outdoor seating. There's plenty of street parking, as well as restrooms, lifeguards, volleyball courts, a fishing pier, playgrounds, and good surfing.

REDONDO STATE BEACH   Popular with surfers, bicyclists, and joggers, Redondo's white sand and ice-plant-carpeted dunes are just south of tiny King Harbor, along the Esplanade (South Esplanade Dr.). Get there via Pacific Coast Highway (Calif. 1) or Torrance Boulevard. Facilities include restrooms, lifeguards, and volleyball courts.

9 OUTDOOR PURSUITS

Bisected by the Santa Monica Mountains and fronted by long stretches of beach, L.A. is one of the world's best cities for nature and sports lovers. Where else can you hike in the mountains, skate on the beach, swim in the ocean, eat a gourmet meal, and take in a basketball, ice-hockey, or baseball game—all in the same day?

BICYCLING   Los Angeles, being mostly flat, is great for biking. If you're into distance pedaling, you can do no better than the flat, paved bicycle trail that follows about 22 miles of state beaches, harbors, LAX, and laid-back beach towns such as Venice, Manhattan Beach, Hermosa Beach, and Redondo Beach. The first stretch starts at Will Rogers State Beach in Pacific Palisades and runs south through Santa Monica and Venice to Marina del Rey—about 8 miles. The second stretch—called the South Bay Bike Trail—starts at the south end of Marina del Rey and takes you all the way to Torrence Beach. If you want to ride the entire path you'll have to detour around Marina del Rey, which only takes about 15 minutes. The bike path attracts all levels of riders and gets pretty busy on weekends, so ixnay the time trials. Don't worry about packing food and water—plenty of fountains, snack stands, and public restrooms are along the trail. For information on this and other city bike routes, log on to **www.labikepaths.com**. For **guided bicycle tours** of the Santa Monica and Venice beach communities, see "Bicycle Tours" on p. 563.

The best place to mountain bike in the L.A. region is along the trails of **Malibu Creek State Park** (© **818/880-0367**), in the Santa Monica Mountains between Malibu and the San Fernando Valley in Calabasas. Fifteen miles of trails rise to a maximum of 3,000 feet and are appropriate for intermediate to advanced bikers. Pick up a trail map at the park entrance, 4 miles south of U.S. 101 off Las Virgenes Road, just north of Mulholland Highway. Park admission is $5 per car. For more information on mountain bike trails in the L.A. region, log on to **www.latrails.com**.

Topanga Canyon: Nature's Solution to L.A.'s Noise Pollution

When you've had enough of cellphones, cement, and Mercedes, then it's time to take the short drive from L.A. to Topanga Canyon to bargain shop, drink margaritas, and play cowgirl for a day. Here's the game plan: Call **Los Angeles Horseback Riding** (© **818/591-2032;** www.losangeleshorsebackriding.com) and make a reservation for a guided horseback ride in the late afternoon. Next, take the winding drive up Topanga Canyon Boulevard to tiny **Topanga,** one of the last art communities left in Southern California—it was the former haunt of Fleetwood Mac, Neil Young, and other music legends of the '60s and '70s—and the perfect antidote to the dig-me L.A. scene. Spend an hour or so picking though the treasure-trove of vintage clothes, accessories, and antiques at **Hidden Treasures** (154 S. Topanga Canyon Blvd.; © **310/455-2998**), one of the funkiest little shops I've ever seen (the custom-made sea-theme toilet seat lids are mesmerizing). After the scenic horseback ride through the boulder-strewn Topanga canyons, lined with oaks, sycamores, chaparral, and sage, finish off your relaxing day with a leisurely dinner in Topanga at **Abuelitas** (137 S. Topanga Canyon Rd.; © **310/455-8688;** www. abuelitastopanga.com), a popular Mexican restaurant.

Spokes 'N Stuff Bike Rental has four locations, one of which is located 4175 Admiralty Way, Marina del Rey (© 310/306-3332), which is only open on weekends, and another at 1715 Ocean Front Walk, behind Loews Hotel, Santa Monica (© 310/395-4748), which is open every day. They rent 10-speed cruisers for about $7 per hour and $16 per day; 15-speed mountain bikes rent for about $8 per hour and $20 per day. Another good Santa Monica rental shop is **Blazing Saddles Bike Rentals** (Santa Monica Pier; © 310/393-9778). The rates are about the same as those at Spokes 'N Stuff. Be sure to ask for a free **self-guided tour map** (it's really handy).

In Hollywood, **Hollywood Pro Bicycles** (6731 Hollywood Blvd., Hollywood; © 323/466-5890; www.hollywoodprobicycles.com) rents mountain bikes at $30 for a 24-hour period and $20 for each additional day. Every rental comes with a free tour map, a safety helmet, a bike lock, and a handlebar bag for storage.

In the South Bay, bike rentals—including tandem bikes—are available 1 block from the Strand at **Hermosa Cyclery,** 20 13th St. (© 310/374-7816; www.hermosacyclery. com). Cruisers are $7 per hour; tandems are $13 per hour. FYI, the Strand is an excellent car-free path that's tailor-made for a leisurely bike ride.

FISHING   **Del Rey Sport Fishing,** 13759 Fiji Way, Marina del Rey (© 800/822-3625; www.marinadelreysportfishing.com), has three deep-sea boats departing daily on half- and full-day ocean fishing trips. Of course, it depends on what's running when you're out, but bass, barracuda, halibut, and yellowtail are the most common catches on these party boats. Excursions start at $35 for half-day trips; tackle rental is available as well. Phone for reservations.

No permit is required to cast from shore or drop a line from a pier. Local anglers will hate me for giving away their secret spot, but the **best saltwater fishing spot** in all of L.A. is at the foot of Torrance Boulevard in Redondo Beach.

GOLF The greater Los Angeles area has more than 100 golf courses, which vary in quality from abysmal to superb. Most of the city's public courses are administered by the Department of Recreation and Parks, which follows a complicated registration/reservation system for tee times. While visitors cannot reserve start times in advance, you're welcome to play any of the courses by showing up and getting on the call sheet. Expect to wait for the most popular tee times, but try to use your flexible vacationer status to your advantage by avoiding the early morning rush.

Of the city's seven 18-hole and three 9-hole courses, you can't get more central than the **Rancho Park Golf Course,** 10460 W. Pico Blvd. (© 310/838-7373; www.rpgc. org), located smack-dab in the middle of L.A.'s Westside. The par-71 course has lots of tall trees, but not enough to blot out the towering Century City buildings next door. For the money, it's a real bargain (heck, even Bill Clinton golfed here). Rancho also has a 9-hole, par-3 course, as well as a driving range.

For a genuinely woodsy experience, try one of the three courses inside Griffith Park, northeast of Hollywood. The courses are extremely well maintained, challenging without being frustrating, and (despite some holes alongside I-5) a great way to leave the city behind. Bucolic pleasures abound, particularly on the 9-hole **Roosevelt,** on Vermont Avenue across from the Greek Theatre; early morning wildlife often includes deer, rabbits, raccoons, and skunks (fore!). **Wilson** and **Harding** are each 18 holes and start from the main clubhouse off Riverside Drive, the park's main entrance.

Greens fees on all city courses are $24 Monday through Friday, and $31 on weekends and holidays; 9-hole courses cost $15 on weekdays and $19 on weekends and holidays. For details on other city courses, or to contact the starter directly by phone, call the Department of Recreation and Parks at © 888/527-2757, or log on to the city's parks website at **www.laparks.org**.

If you're not a fan of crowded city courses, it's well worth the 20-minute drive north to play **Robinson Ranch,** 27734 Sand Canyon Rd., Santa Clarita (© 661/252-8484; www.robinsonranchgolf.com), one of the best and least-crowded public courses in the L.A. region (my golfing buddy loves this place). Golfers can choose between two Troon-managed courses, Mountain or Valley, both of which offer challenging, hilly terrain—bring extra balls—and great views of the Santa Clarita Valley. The striking 25,000-square-foot clubhouse makes a nice view as well, and houses a well-stocked pro shop and full-service restaurant. Greens fees for both courses are $87 Monday through Thursday, $117 Friday through Sunday. Carts and practice balls are included.

The **Trump National Golf Club,** 1 Ocean Trails Dr. (© 310/265-5000; www.trump golf.com/trumplosangeles), recently opened in Rancho Palos Verdes. Perched on a bluff overlooking the Pacific Ocean, the course provides a spectacular view from every hole. Originally designed by Pete Dye as the Ocean Trails Golf Course, the property was purchased by developer Donald Trump, who spent more than $250 million to redesign it with elements such as lakes and waterfalls. Located on the Palos Verdes Peninsula, 30 minutes south of downtown Los Angeles, the course also offers a 45,000-square-foot clubhouse with locker rooms, a pro shop, three dining options, conference rooms, and a grand ballroom. Greens fees at the public course are $275 Monday through Thursday, $375 Friday through Sunday.

(Fun Facts)   **The Big Sprawl**

How crowded is L.A.? If the five-county area was a state, it would surpass all states in total population size, with the exception of California, New York, and Texas.

Industry Hills Golf Club, 1 Industry Hills Pkwy., City of Industry (© **626/810-4653;** www.ihgolfclub.com), has two 18-hole courses designed by William Bell. Together they encompass eight lakes, 160 bunkers, and many long fairways. The Eisenhower Course, consistently ranked among *Golf Digest*'s top 25 public courses, has extra-large undulating greens and the challenge of thick *Kikuyu* grass. (*Kikuyu,* even coarser than Bermuda's broad-leaf terrain, is often called Bermuda on steroids.) An adjacent driving range is lit for night use. Greens fees are $85 Monday through Friday and $120 Saturday and Sunday, including a cart; call in advance for tee times.

For more information on regional golf courses, log on to **www.golfcalifornia.com.**

HANG GLIDING   Up and down the California coast, it's not uncommon to see people poised on the crests of hills, hanging from enormous colorful kites. **Windsports Soaring Center,** 12623 Gridley St., Sylmar (© **818/367-2430;** www.windsports.com), offers instruction and rentals for both novices and experts. A 1-day lesson in a solo hang glider on a bunny hill costs $120. If it's more of a thrill you're looking for, choose the 3,000-foot-high tandem flight for $199. Beginner lessons are waterside at Dockweiler State Beach Training Flight Park (near LAX), while tandem flights take off from a San Fernando Valley hilltop. Phone for reservations.

HIKING   The **Santa Monica Mountains,** a small range that runs only 50 miles from Griffith Park to Point Mugu, on the coast north of Malibu, makes Los Angeles a great place for hiking. The mountains, which peak at 3,111 feet, are part of the Santa Monica Mountains National Recreation Area, a contiguous conglomeration of 350 public parks and 65,000 acres. Many animals live in this area, including deer, coyote, rabbit, skunk, rattlesnake, fox, hawk, and quail. The hills are also home to almost 1,000 drought-resistant plant species, including live oak and coastal sage.

Hiking is best after spring rains, when the hills are green, flowers are in bloom, and the air is clear. Summers can be very hot; hikers should always carry fresh water. Beware of poison oak, a hearty shrub that's common on the West Coast. Usually found among oak trees, poison oak has leaves in groups of three, with waxy surfaces and prominent veins. If you come into contact with this itch-producing plant, you'll end up with a California souvenir that you'll soon regret.

Santa Ynez Canyon, in Pacific Palisades, is a long and difficult climb that rises steadily for about 3 miles. At the top, hikers are rewarded with fantastic views over the Pacific. At the top is **Trippet Ranch,** a public facility providing water, restrooms, and picnic tables. From Santa Monica, take Pacific Coast Highway (Calif. 1) north. Turn right onto Sunset Boulevard and then left onto Palisades Drive. Then continue for 2¹/₂ miles, turn left onto Verenda de la Montura, and park at the cul-de-sac at the end of the street, where you can find the trail head.

Temescal Canyon, in Pacific Palisades, is far easier than the Santa Ynez trail and far more popular, especially among locals. This is one of the quickest routes into the wilderness. Hikes here are anywhere from 1 to 5 miles. From Santa Monica, take Pacific Coast

(Tips) Segway Rentals in Santa Monica

Those weird-looking upright electronic scooters zipping around the Santa Monica beach scene are coming from the **Segway Los Angeles** rental shop near the Santa Monica Pier. Riding these human transporters is a hoot: lean forward, go forward; lean back, go back; stand straight up, stop. Simple. After the free 25-minute lesson it becomes intuitive, and then you're on your own to scoot around the paved shoreline path around Venice Beach and the Santa Monica Pier (*everyone* checks you out). It's the closest you'll come to being a celebrity. A 2-hour rental with lesson is $75. Guided tours are available as well. **Note:** You have be at least 21 to rent one. 1660 Ocean Ave., 1 block south of the pier, Santa Monica; (C) **310/395-1395;** www.segway.la.

Highway (Calif. 1) north; turn right onto Temescal Canyon Road, and follow it to the end. Sign in with the gatekeeper, who can also answer your questions.

Will Rogers State Historic Park, Pacific Palisades, is also a terrific place for hiking. An intermediate-level hike from the park's entrance ends at Inspiration Point, a plateau from which you can see a good portion of L.A.'s Westside.

For more information on hiking in the L.A. region, log on to **www.latrails.com.**

HORSEBACK RIDING **Griffith Park Horse Rental,** 480 Riverside Dr. (in the Los Angeles Equestrian Center), Burbank ((C) **818/840-8401**), rents horses by the hour for guided rides through Griffith Park's hills; no experience is necessary. Horse rental costs $25 for 1 hour, cash only. The stables are open daily from 8am to 5pm (till 6pm in the summer), and you must be at least 6 years old to ride. If you have a rider younger than 6, you can either opt for the pony rides in Griffith Park (p. 557), or arrange for a private 1-hour lesson by calling (C) **818/569-3666.**

Another popular horseback-riding outfit is **Sunset Ranch,** located at 3400 Beachwood Dr. off of Franklin Avenue, just under the HOLLYWOOD sign. Horse rentals are offered daily from 9am to 5pm for all levels of riders. The ranch is on the edge of Griffith Park with access to 52 miles of trails. Also available are private night rides (very romantic), dinner rides, and riding lessons. Rates are $25 for a 1-hour ride, $40 for 2 hours, not including tip. No reservations are required. For more information, call (C) **323/469-5450** or log on to **www.sunsetranchhollywood.com.**

Closer to the ocean in Topanga Canyon is **Los Angeles Horseback Riding** (2623 Old Topanga Canyon Rd., Topanga; (C) **818/591-2032;** www.lahorsebackriding.com), a small, friendly outfit that offers guided Western-style trail rides for beginners to advanced riders. It's situated at the top of a 1,800-foot ridgeline—about a 25-minute drive from Santa Monica—with panoramic views of the ocean and San Fernando Valley (best seen on one of the sunset or full-moon rides). What I like about this outfit is that, if the guide feels that the group is experienced enough, she'll pick up the pace to a canter. Although same-day reservations are sometimes possible, try to book at least 3 days in advance. Kids 6 and older are welcome, and kids 17 and under must wear helmets (bring a bike helmet, if possible). Prices start at about $60 for a guided 70-minute ride, plus tip; 2-hour canyon rides and full-moon trips are available as well.

SAILING Marina del Rey, the largest man-made marina in the world, is the launching point for L.A.'s sailboat charters such as **Free Spirit Sailing Adventures,** which offers

LOS ANGELES

14

OUTDOOR PURSUITS

> ### (Fun Facts) The Surfing Rabbi
>
> This is *so* only-in-L.A.: Surfing instructor and orthodox rabbi Nachum Shifren hosts "Surf and Soul" sermons on the sand in Santa Monica. Not only will the rabbi teach you how to surf, his wise words will empower you to succeed in this competitive world we live in. Yes, even gentiles are welcome (© **310/877-1482; www.surfingrabbi.com**).

trips ranging from a 2-hour harbor tour ($96 per person) to full-day outings along the coast and even 4-day voyages to the Channel Islands. Your host is Captain Larry, and the boat is the *Carmina Mare,* a 46-foot cutter-rigged motorsailer. You can either bring your own food and drinks or have Captain Larry prepare lunch and dinner for you. Bring your own rods and tackle and you can even go fishing. For more information, call Captain Larry's cellphone number, © **310/780-3432,** or log on to **www.captlarry.com**.

SEA KAYAKING A simple and serene way to explore the southern coastline, sea kayaking is all the rage in Southern California. **Southwind Kayak Center** (17855 Skypark Circle, Irvine; © **800/768-8494** or 949/261-0200; www.southwindkayaks.com) rents sit-on-top sea kayaks for use in the bay or open ocean at their Newport Beach and Dana Point rental bases. Rates are $50 per day; instructional classes are available on weekends only. The center also conducts several easygoing guided outings, including a $55 Back to Nature trip that highlights the marine life around Dana Point. Visit their website for more details.

SKATING The 22-mile-long South Beach Trail that runs from Pacific Palisades to Torrance is one of the premier skating spots in the country. In-line skating is especially popular, but conventional skates are often seen here, too. Skating is allowed just about everywhere bicycling is, but be advised that cyclists have the right of way. **Spokes 'N Stuff,** 4175 Admiralty Way, Marina del Rey (© **310/306-3332;** weekends only), is just one of many places to rent wheels near the Venice portion of Ocean Front Walk. In the South Bay, in-line skate rentals are available 1 block from the Strand at **Hermosa Cyclery,** 20 13th St. (© **310/374-7816;** www.hermosacyclery.com). Skates cost $6 per hour ($18 for the day); kneepads and wrist guards come with every rental.

SURFING George Freeth (1883–1918), who first surfed Redondo Beach in 1907, is widely credited with introducing the sport to California. But surfing didn't catch on until the 1950s, when CalTech graduate Bob Simmons invented a more maneuverable lightweight fiberglass board. The Beach Boys and other surf-music groups popularized Southern California in the minds of beach-babes and -dudes everywhere, and the rest, as they say, is history.

If you're a first-timer eager to learn the sport, contact **Learn to Surf L.A.** (© **310/663-2479;** www.learntosurfla.com). This highly respected school features a team of experienced instructors that will supply all necessary equipment and get you up and riding a foam board on your first day (trust me, it's a blast). Private lessons are $120, and group lesson are $75. Another great source for learning to surf is **Malibu Longboards** (© **310/467-6898** or 818/990-7633; www.malibulongboards.com), the official surf instruction for Santa Monica College (don't you wish you'd spent a semester here?). The company offers private lessons for $60 per hour, as well as group lessons and 5-day surf camps.

If you want to try it on your own, surfboards are available for rent at shops near all top surfing beaches in the L.A. area. **Zuma Jay Surfboards,** 22775 Pacific Coast Hwy., Malibu (© **310/456-8044;** www.zumajays.com), Malibu's oldest surf shop, is about a quarter-mile south of Malibu Pier. Rentals are about $20 per day, plus $10 for wet suits in winter. For more information about surfing in Southern California, log on to **www. surfline.com.**

TENNIS While soft-surface courts are more popular on the East Coast, hard surfaces are most common in California. If your hotel doesn't have a court and can't suggest any courts nearby, try the well-maintained, well-lit **Griffith Park Tennis Courts,** on Commonwealth Road, just east of Vermont Avenue (© **323/662-7772**). Call or log on to the website of the **City of Los Angeles Department of Recreation and Parks** (© **888/527-2757;** www.laparks.org) to see a long list of free tennis courts or make a reservation at a municipal court near you. *Tip:* Spectators can watch free collegiate matches at the UCLA campus's L.A. Tennis Center from October through May. For a schedule of tournaments, call © **310/206-6831.**

10 SPECTATOR SPORTS

BASEBALL The **Los Angeles Dodgers** (© **866/Dodgers** [363-4377]; www.dodgers. com), winner of eight National League championships and five World Series titles, play at Dodger Stadium, located at 1000 Elysian Park near Sunset Boulevard. Watching a game at this old-school ballpark is a great way to spend the day, chomping on Dodger Dogs and basking in the sunshine. Tickets are reasonably priced, too. And even if you can't score tickets, you can still take a 90-minute **"Championship Tour" of Dodger Stadium,** including access to the field, the Dodger Dugout, the Dugout Club, the press box, and the Tommy Lasorda Training Center. Tours are offered Tuesdays, Thursdays, Saturdays, and Sundays at 10 and 11:30am through October. The cost is $15 for adults, $10 for seniors (55 and up), and children 14 and under. You can reserve and purchase tour tickets online at **www.dodgers.com** (click on "Dodger Stadium," then scroll down to "Stadium Tours").

The 2002 World Series champion **Los Angeles Angels of Anaheim** (© **888/796-HALO;** http://losangeles.angels.mlb.com) play American League ball at Anaheim Stadium, at 2000 Gene Autry Way, in Anaheim, about 30 minutes from downtown L.A. The regular Major League baseball season runs from April to October. Log on to either team's website for ticket information.

BASKETBALL Los Angeles has two NBA franchises: the **L.A. Lakers** (www.lakers. com), who have won 14 NBA titles, and the **L.A. Clippers** (www.clippers.com), who haven't. Both teams play in the **STAPLES Center** in downtown L.A., 1111 S. Figueroa St. Celebrity fans such as Jack Nicholson, Leonardo DiCaprio, Heather Locklear, and Dyan Cannon have the best tickets, but this 20,000-seater should have room for you— that is, if you have the big bucks for a Lakers ticket or the interest in watching a Clippers game. The season runs from October to April, with 2 months of playoffs following. For tickets to see either team, call © **213/742-7340** or log on to **www.staplescenter.com.**

FOOTBALL Los Angeles suffers from an absence of major-league football, but it gets by just fine with two popular college teams and an Arena League team. The college season runs September through November; if you're interested in checking out a game, contact **UCLA Bruins Football** (© **310/825-2101;** www.uclabruins.com) or **USC**

Polo, Anyone?

Way back in 1930 cowboy humorist Will Rogers got a hankerin' to play some polo, so he cleared the field in front of his Pacific Palisades home for a friendly match with his ponies and celebrity pals. Shortly after, he started his famed **Will Rogers Polo Club,** and of the 25 polo organizations that existed at the time, his polo field is the only one that remains. Matches are still held on weekends from mid-April through early October, and the bucolic setting of wide green fields, whitewashed fences, and majestic oaks is ideal for a leisurely picnic lunch and a bit of respite from the city. The polo field is located at 1501 Will Rogers State Park Rd. in Pacific Palisades, off West Sunset Boulevard. For more information, call the club at (℃ **310/573-5000,** or log on to its website at **www. willrogerspolo.org** (there's a great feature on "How to Watch a Polo Game").

Trojan Football ((℃ **213/740-2311;** www.usctrojans.com). Described as "fun, fast, and furious," Arena League football tends to be action-packed and exciting, and it sure costs a lot less than its NFL counterpart. The local team is the **L.A. Avengers** ((℃ **888/ AVENGER** [283-6437]; www.laavengers.com); games run April through July and are played downtown at the STAPLES Center (see "Basketball," above).

HORSE RACING   One of the most beautiful tracks in the country, **Santa Anita Racetrack,** 285 W. Huntington Dr., Arcadia ((℃ **626/574-7223;** www.santaanita.com), offers racing from late December through late April (a separate racing event called the Oak Tree Meeting runs early Oct through early Nov). Set against the majestic San Gabriel Mountains, the track was featured in the Marx Brothers' film *A Day at the Races* and in the 1954 version of *A Star Is Born.* On weekdays during the season, the public is invited to watch morning workouts from 5:00am to 9:30am at Clockers' Corner. Admission is free; be sure to call or check the website for exact post times. *Tip:* The infield is ideal for picnics, as well as getting an up-close look at the horses and jockeys in action—it even has a children's playground.

Located just down the road from LAX, the scenic **Hollywood Park Racetrack,** 1050 S. Prairie Ave., in Inglewood ((℃ **310/419-1500;** www.hollywoodpark.com), with its lakes and flowers, features thoroughbred racing from mid-April to July, as well as from mid-November through mid-December. Opened in 1938, it had shareholders that included movie mogul Harry Warner, Walt Disney, and Bing Crosby. Well-placed monitors project views of the backstretch as well as stop-action replays of photo finishes. Races are usually held Thursday through Monday. Post times are 1pm in summer (7pm on Fri) and 12:30pm on weekends and holidays. General admission is $7; admission to the clubhouse is $10.

ICE HOCKEY   The **L.A. Kings** ((℃ **888/546-4752;** www.lakings.com) hold court at the STAPLES Center home (see above); and down the road in Orange County, the **Mighty Ducks** ((℃ **714/940-2900;** www.mightyducks.com) play at the Arrowhead Pond in Anaheim. The hockey season typically runs from October through mid-April, with playoffs following. Tickets are available at either arena or through Ticketmaster.

SOCCER   Since its inaugural season in 1996, the **Los Angeles Galaxy** (© 877-3GAL-AXY;** www.lagalaxy.com) has already won the Major League Soccer Cup and earned a reputation as a major force in MLS. But the big news in the last couple of years is all about soccer superstar David Beckham joining the roster. He and his pop star wife, Victoria Beckham, have made international headlines by making Los Angeles their new home. In fact, within the first hour following the announcement, the LA Galaxy sold more than 500 home game tickets. Visitors can catch a game at the Home Depot Center stadium at 18400 Avalon Blvd. in Carson. Tickets for individual games are available through the Galaxy box office and Ticketmaster.

11   SHOPS & SPAS

Whether you're looking for trendsetting fashions or just some tourist schlock mementos, Los Angeles has your shopping needs covered like no other place in the world. Heck, Los Angeles practically *invented* the shopping mall.

But to really shop L.A.-style, you need to combine your outing with a trip to a day spa and make it an all-day event. For example, if you're planning an outing to the Grove outdoor mall (highly recommended), first you make an appointment at the **Amadeus Aveda** spa (© **323/297-0311;** www.amadeusspa.com); make a lunch reservation at **Maggiano's Little Italy** (© **323/965-9665;** www.maggianos.com); then go online to buy movie tickets to the **Grove Theatres** (© **323/692-0829;** www.thegrovela.com). When the big day arrives, you meet your friends for coffee in the morning, hit the shops, check your packages with the Grove concierge, have lunch, enjoy your spa treatments, see a matinee, pick up your purchases, and call it a day. Nicely done.

Here's a rundown of the primary shopping areas, with descriptions of their best stores. The sales tax in Los Angeles is 8.25%, but out-of-state shoppers know to have more expensive items shipped home, thereby avoiding the tax.

L.A.'S WESTSIDE & BEVERLY HILLS

BEVERLY BOULEVARD (from Robertson Blvd. to La Brea Ave.) ★   Beverly is L.A.'s premier boulevard for mid-20th-century furnishings. Expensive showrooms line the street, but the shop that started it all is **Modernica,** 7366 Beverly Blvd. (© **323/933-0383;** www.modernica.net). You can still find vintage Stickley and Noguchi pieces, but Modernica has become best known for the authentic—and more affordable—replicas they offer (Eames storage units are one popular item). **Scent Bar,** 8327 Beverly Blvd. (© **323/782-8300),** the sleek retail shop from the wildly popular fragrance website **www.luckyscent.com,** is the place to go for exclusive fragrances from Monyette Paris and Parfums de Nicolai.

British designer and rock royalty **Stella McCartney** (8823 Beverly Blvd.; © **310/273-7051;** www.stellamccartney.com) opened her eponymous digs in an ivy-covered 1920s cottage. Here you'll find the entire collection, from ready-to-wear and fragrance to footwear and handbags. If you complain that they just don't make 'em like they used to . . . well, they do at **Re-Mix,** 7605½ Beverly Blvd. (btw. Fairfax and La Brea aves.; © **323/936-6210;** www.remixvintageshoes.com). This shop sells only vintage (1940s–1970s)—but brand-new (as in unworn)—shoes for men and women, such as wingtips, Hush Puppies, Joan Crawford pumps, and 1970s platforms. It's more like a shoe-store museum. A rack of unworn vintage socks all display their original tags and stickers, and

Urban Shopping Adventures

Shopping may be a casual pastime in other cities, but in the urban jungle of Los Angeles it's a competitive sport. If you're a shopping rookie at best, you might consider an outing with **Urban Shopping Adventures,** which offers custom guided shopping tours to the L.A. Fashion District—90 sprawling blocks loaded with wholesale and retail venues—and the trendy Melrose Heights Shopping District, L.A.'s Westside destination for celebrity-frequented boutiques. Hosted by shopping expert Christine Silvestri, the 3-hour walking tours start at just $36 per person, and merchants are often willing to provide deep discounts to her tour guests. All shopping excursions include an ample-size shopping bag, district map, bottled water, snack, and plenty of time to browse at your own pace. She also offers round-trip transportation options such as shuttle, bus, or limousine service from your hotel to either district for an additional cost. Advance reservations are required for all tours, and additional shopping districts are also available upon request. Call *C* **213/683-9715** or log on to **www.urbanshoppingadventures.com.**

the prices are downright reasonable. Celebrity hipsters and hepcats from Madonna to Roseanne are often spotted here.

Other vintage wares are found at **Second Time Around Watch Co.,** 8840 Beverly Blvd. (west of Robertson Blvd.; *C* **310/271-6615;** www.secondtimearoundwatchco. com). The city's best selection of collectible timepieces includes dozens of classic Tiffanys, Cartiers, and Rolexes, plus rare pocket watches. Priced for collectors, but a fascinating browse for the Swatch crowd, too.

When it's time to unwind and beautify, hit **Ona Spa** for a tension-relieving massage. The attached **Privé Salon** is one of the city's trendiest salons where celebrity-sighting is common. One of the best-kept secret spas in the neighborhood is **Skin Haven Spa Studio,** 300 N. Crescent Heights Blvd. (at Beverly Blvd.; *C* **323/658-7546**), where owner Sharon Ronen's customized facials will leave you glowing for weeks.

LA BREA AVENUE (north of Wilshire Blvd.) ★ This is L.A.'s artiest shopping strip. La Brea is anchored by the giant **American Rag, Cie** alterna-complex, and is also home to lots of great urban antiques stores dealing in Art Deco, Arts and Crafts, 1950s modern, and the like. You'll also find vintage clothiers, furniture galleries, and other warehouse-size stores, as well as some of the city's hippest restaurants, such as Campanile (p. 526).

Bargain hunters find flea-market furnishings at **Nick Metropolis,** 100 S. La Brea Ave. (*C* **323/934-3700**), while more upscale seekers of home decor head to **Mortise & Tenon,** 446 S. La Brea Ave. (*C* **323/937-7654**), where handcrafted heavy wood pieces sit next to overstuffed velvet-upholstered sofas and even vintage steel desks. The best place for a snack is Nancy Silverton's **La Brea Bakery,** 624 S. La Brea Ave. (*C* **323/939-6813;** www.labreabakery.com), which foodies know from gourmet markets and the attached Campanile restaurant.

Stuffed to the rafters with hardware and fixtures of the past 100 years, **Liz's Antique Hardware,** 453 S. La Brea Ave. (*C* **323/939-4403;** www.lahardware.com), thoughtfully keeps a canister of wet wipes at the register—believe us, you'll need one after sifting

through bags and crates of doorknobs, latches, finials, and any other home hardware you
can imagine. Perfect sets of Bakelite drawer pulls and antique ceramic bathroom fixtures
are some of the more intriguing items. Be prepared to browse for hours, whether you're
redecorating or not. There's a respectable collection of coordinating trendy clothing for
men and women, too.

ROBERTSON BOULEVARD (btw. Wilshire and Beverly boulevards) ★ If you're a fan
of celeb magazines such as *US Weekly*, you simply must pay a visit to one of L.A.'s most
popular shopping streets. It's common to see the likes of Jessica Simpson, Lindsey Lohan,
and Paris Hilton shopping at trend-obsessed boutiques such as **Kitson,** 115 S. Robertson
Blvd. (✆ **310/859-2652**); and **Lisa Kline,** 136 S. Robertson Blvd. (✆ **310/246-0907**).
At nearby **Erica Courtney,** 117 N. Robertson Blvd. (✆ **310/858-6700**), guys can watch
ESPN on the flatscreen while gals browse drop-dead gorgeous diamonds. Julia Roberts,
Sandra Bullock, and Eva Longoria Parker are all fans of Courtney's creations. After shop-
ping like a celebrity, dine among them at the **Ivy** (p. 520).

Just up the street, two of L.A.'s most unique day spas beckon the tired, the stressed,
and the famous. **L.A. Vie L'Orange,** 638½ N. Robertson Blvd. (✆ **310/289-2501;** www.
lavielorange.com), specializes in manicures and pedicures that use yummy ingredients
such as milk, honey, oatmeal, and orange-scented oils. Two doors away, you can spend an
entire afternoon at the **Kinara Spa & Café,** 656 North Robertson Blvd. (✆ **310/657-9188;**
www.kinaraspa.com), just like faithful fans Halle Berry, Naomi Watts, and Jennifer Garner.

RODEO DRIVE & BEVERLY HILLS' GOLDEN TRIANGLE (btw. Santa Monica Blvd.,
Wilshire Blvd., and Crescent Dr., Beverly Hills) ★★ Everyone knows about Rodeo
Drive, the city's most famous shopping street. Couture shops from high fashion's Old
Guard are located along these 3 hallowed blocks, along with plenty of newer high-end
labels. And there are two examples of the Beverly Hills version of mini-malls, albeit more
insular and attractive: the **Rodeo Collection,** 421 N. Rodeo Dr., a contemporary center
with towering palms; and **2 Rodeo,** a cobblestoned Italianate piazza at Wilshire Boulevard.
The 16-square-block area surrounding Rodeo Drive is known as the Golden Triangle.
Shops off Rodeo are generally not as name-conscious as those on the strip (and you might
actually be able to afford something), but they're nevertheless plenty upscale. Little Santa
Monica Boulevard has a particularly colorful line of specialty stores, and Brighton Way is
as young and hip as relatively staid Beverly Hills gets. Parking is a bargain, with nine city-
run lots offering 2 hours of free parking and a flat fee of $2 after 2pm.

The big names to look for here are **Prada,** 343 N. Rodeo Dr. (✆ 310/278-8661);
Chanel, 400 N. Rodeo Dr. (✆ 310/278-5500); **Bulgari,** 201 N. Rodeo Dr. (✆ 310/
858-9216); **Gucci,** 347 N. Rodeo Dr. (✆ 310/278-3451); **Hermès,** 434 N. Rodeo Dr.
(✆ 310/278-6440); **Louis Vuitton,** 295 N. Rodeo Dr. (✆ 310/859-0457); **Polo/Ralph
Lauren,** 444 N. Rodeo Dr. (✆ 310/281-1500); and a three-story **Tiffany & Co.,** 210 N.
Rodeo Dr. (✆ 310/273-8880). Other ultrachic clothiers include **Dolce & Gabbana,** 312
N. Rodeo Dr. (✆ 310/888-8701); British plaid palace **Burberry Limited,** 9560 Wilshire
Blvd. (✆ 310/550-4500); and **NikeTown,** on the corner of Wilshire Boulevard and Rodeo
Drive (✆ 310/275-9998), a behemoth shrine to the reigning athletic-gear king.

Wilshire Boulevard is also home to New York–style department stores (each in spectacular landmark buildings) such as **Saks Fifth Avenue,** 9600 Wilshire Blvd. (✆ **310/
275-4211**); **Barneys New York,** 9570 Wilshire Blvd. (✆ 310/276-4400); and **Neiman
Marcus,** 9700 Wilshire Blvd. (✆ **310/550-5900**).

When all that walking and gawking tires you out, do what all the Beverly Hills beauties do: Hit a spa. Aida Thibiant has been offering classic treatments at **Thibiant Beverly**

Hills Day Spa, 449 N. Canon Dr. (© **310/278-7565;** www.thibiantspa.com), since the 1970s. Guys have a place of their own at the new high-end barbershop, the **Shave,** 230 S. Beverly Dr. (© **310/888-2898;** www.theshavebeverlyhills.com). You don't need to stay in one of the fabulously luxurious Beverly Hills hotels to get all the pampering services. At the **Spa at the Four Seasons** (p. 503), California-flavored treatments use everything from tequila to caviar in decadent massages and facials. At the **Beverly Hills Hotel Spa by La Prairie** (p. 503), the facials and massages are some of the most expensive in town, but it's a great reason to spend a decadent day at the "Pink Palace" without having to drop $1,000 a night on a room.

THE SUNSET STRIP (btw. La Cienega Blvd. and Doheny Dr., West Hollywood) The monster-size billboards advertising the latest rock god make it clear this is rock-'n'-roll territory. The Strip is lined with trendy restaurants, industry-oriented hotels, and dozens of shops offering outrageous fashions and stage accessories. One anomaly is Sunset Plaza, an upscale cluster of Georgian-style shops resembling Beverly Hills at its snootiest. You'll find **Billy Martin's,** 8605 Sunset Blvd. (© **310/289-5000**), founded by the legendary Yankees manager in 1978. This chic men's Western shop—complete with fireplace and leather sofa—stocks hand-forged silver and gold belt buckles, Lucchese and Liberty boots, and stable staples such as flannel shirts. **Book Soup,** 8818 Sunset Blvd. (© **310/659-3110;** www.booksoup.com), has long been one of L.A.'s most celebrated bookshops, selling mainstream and small-press books and hosting book signings and readings.

The Sunset Strip's trendiest hotels have in-house spas and spa services—such as **Agua at the Mondrian,** 8440 Sunset Blvd. (© **323/848-6070;** www.mondrianhotel.com)— which offer great added amenities for hotel guests. But to feel like a real super star on the Strip, go to the "facialist of the stars": **Ole Henriksen Face/Body,** 8622 W. Sunset Blvd. (© **310/854-7700;** www.olehenriksen.com/spa), is where stunners such as Ashley Judd and Charlize Theron get glowing skin.

WEST THIRD STREET (btw. Fairfax and Robertson blvds.) ★ You can shop until you drop on this trendy strip, anchored on the east end by the **Farmers Market and The Grove** (p. 537). Many of Melrose Avenue's shops have relocated here, along with terrific up-and-comers, several cafes, and the much-lauded restaurant **Locanda Veneta.** *Fun* is more the catchword here than *funky,* and the shops (including the vintage clothing stores) are a bit more refined than those along Melrose. The **Cook's Library,** 8373 W. Third St. (© **323/655-3141;** www.cookslibrary.com), is where the city's top chefs find classic and offbeat cookbooks, wine guides, and other food-oriented tomes. Browsing is welcomed, even encouraged, with tea, tasty treats, and rocking chairs. **Traveler's Bookcase,** 8375 W. Third St. (© **323/655-0575;** www.travelbooks.com), is one of the best travel bookshops in the West, stocking a huge selection of guidebooks and travel literature, as well as maps and travel accessories.

There's lots more to see along this always-growing street. Refuel at **Chado Tea Room,** 8422 W. Third St. (© **323/655-2056**), a temple for tea lovers. Chado is designed with a nod to Paris's renowned Mariage Frères tea purveyor; one wall is lined with nooks whose recognizable brown tins are filled with more than 250 different varieties of tea from around the world. Among the choices are 15 kinds of Darjeeling, Indian teas blended with rose petals, and ceremonial Chinese and Japanese blends. You can also get tea meals here, featuring delightful sandwiches and individual pots of any loose tea in the store.

Tips   **Celebrity Cloned Clothing**

If your dream is to dress like your favorite celebrity who may have stepped right off the red carpet at one of Hollywood's numerous award shows, then a visit to **A.B.S. by Allen Schwartz** should be on your to-do list. As soon as one of these high-profile events is over (think Golden Globes, SAG Awards, Oscars), A.B.S. has already produced a knockoff version that is every bit as lovely, but also much more affordable. 1533 Montana Ave. (at 15th St.); © **310/393-8770.**

HOLLYWOOD

HOLLYWOOD BOULEVARD (btw. Gower St. and La Brea Ave.)   One of Los Angeles's most famous streets is, for the most part, a cheesy tourist strip. But along the Walk of Fame, between the T-shirt shops and greasy pizza parlors, you'll find some excellent poster shops, souvenir stores, and Hollywood-memorabilia dealers worth getting out of your car for—especially if there's a chance of getting your hands on that long-sought-after Ethel Merman autograph or *200 Motels* poster.

Some long-standing purveyors of memorabilia include **Hollywood Book and Poster Company,** 6562 Hollywood Blvd. (© **323/465-8764;** www.hollywoodbookandposter. com), which has an excellent collection of posters (from about $15 each), strong in horror and exploitation flicks. Photocopies of about 5,000 movie and television scripts are sold for $10 to $15 each—*Pulp Fiction* is just as good in print, by the way—and the store carries music posters and photos.

The legendary **Fredericks of Hollywood,** 6751 Hollywood Blvd. (© **323/957-5953;** www.fredericks.com), located just a block east of Hollywood & Highland, is worth a stop if you're looking for devilish dainties. The flagship store features lingerie once worn by celebrities such as Sharon Stone, Julianne Moore, and Halle Berry.

LARCHMONT BOULEVARD (btw. Beverly Blvd. and Second St.)   Neighbors congregate on this old-fashioned street just east of busy Vine Avenue. As the surrounding Hancock Park homes become increasingly popular with artists and young industry types, the shops and cafes lining Larchmont get more stylish. Sure, chains such as Jamba Juice and the Coffee Bean are infiltrating this formerly mom-and-pop terrain, but plenty of unique shopping awaits amid charming elements such as diagonal parking, shady trees, and sidewalk bistro tables.

One of L.A.'s landmark independent bookstores is **Chevalier's Books,** 126 N. Larchmont Blvd. (© **323/465-1334**), a 60-year Larchmont tradition. If your walking shoes are letting you down, stop into **Village Footwear,** 248 N. Larchmont Blvd. (© **323/ 461-3619**), which specializes in comfort lines such as Josef Siebel. Or even better, stop in for a foot—or full body—massage at **Healing Hands Wellness Center,** 414 N. Larchmont Blvd. (© **323/461-7876;** www.healinghandswc.com), which has affordable 1-hour massages starting at $55. An entire afternoon of pampering can be had at **Le Petite Retreat Day Spa,** 331 N. Larchmont Blvd. (© **323/466-1028;** www.lprdayspa. com), which offers great packages for couples or a girls' day out.

MELROSE AVENUE (btw. Fairfax and La Brea aves.) ★★   It's showing some wear—some stretches have become downright ugly—but this is still one of the most exciting shopping streets in the country for cutting-edge fashions (and some eye-popping

GR8 Finds in West L.A.'s J-Town

What started off as a magazine has spawned two of L.A.'s most talked-about stores—**GR2,** 2062 Sawtelle Blvd. (✆ 310/445-9276); and **Giant Robot,** 2015 Sawtelle Blvd. (✆ 310/478-1819)—and **gr/eats** restaurant, 2050 Sawtelle Blvd. (✆ 310/478-3242; www.gr-eats.com). Located across the street from each other in West L.A.'s Japantown (at Sawtelle and Olympic blvds.), both shops specialize in a wide range of Asian-American pop-culture items, including T-shirts, books, music, stationery, toys, art, and accessories. There are several other cool shops and restaurants along this 1½-block stretch as well. One of my favorite stores is **Happy Six,** 2115 Sawtelle Blvd. (✆ 310/479-5363), which looks like Hello Kitty on acid and sells playful apparel and accessories for men and women. If you're hungry, my favorites along Sawtelle are **Manpuku,** 2125 Sawtelle Blvd. (✆ 310/473-0580); **Sawtelle Kitchen,** 2024 Sawtelle Blvd. (✆ 310/445-9288); and **Hurry Curry,** 2131 Sawtelle Blvd. (✆ 310/473-1640). Or you can pop into **Nijiya Market,** 2130 Sawtelle Blvd. (✆ 310/575-3300), and grab a *bento* (Japanese boxed lunch) to go.

people-watching, to boot). Melrose is always an entertaining stroll, dotted with plenty of hip restaurants and funky shops selling the latest in clothes, gifts, jewelry, and accessories that are sure to shock. Where else could you find green patent-leather cowboy boots, a working 19th-century pocket watch, an inflatable girlfriend, and glow-in-the-dark condoms on the same block? From east to west, here are some highlights.

l.a. Eyeworks, 7407 Melrose Ave. (✆ 323/653-8255), revolutionized eyeglass designs from medical supply to stylish accessory, and now their brand is nationwide. **Off the Wall** is filled with neon-flashing, bells-and-whistles kitsch collectibles, from vintage Wurlitzer jukeboxes to life-size fiberglass cows. The L.A. branch of a Bay Area hipster hangout, **Wasteland** has an enormous steel-sculpted facade. There's a lot of leather and denim, and some classic vintage—but mostly funky 1970s-style garb, both vintage and contemporary. More racks of vintage treasures (and trash) are found at **Aardvark's Odd Ark,** which stocks everything from suits and dresses to neckties, hats, handbags, and jewelry. This place also manages to anticipate some of the hottest new street fashions. An outpost of the edgy **Floyd's Barbershops,** 7300 Melrose Ave. (✆ 323/965-7600), keeps the street's style-for-less theme by charging around $24 for men's and women's cuts. It's like a salon, funky music store, and Internet cafe all rolled into one.

MELROSE HEIGHTS (btw. La Cienega Blvd. and Fairfax Ave.) ★★ This posh section of Melrose, anchored by the venerable favorite **Fred Segal,** 8100 Melrose Ave. (✆ 323/655-3734), houses designer boutiques such as **Diane Von Furstenberg,** 8407 Melrose Ave. (✆ 323/951-1947); and **Paul Smith,** 8221 Melrose Ave. (✆ 323/951-4800). L.A. jewelry designer **Suzanne Felsen,** 8332 Melrose Ave. (✆ 323/653-5400), is a celebrity favorite—she transformed a 1920s Spanish home to house her gold and platinum baubles lined with Peruvian opals and Mandarin garnets. Perennial fashion favorite **Marc Jacobs** has three stores at 8400, 8409, and 8410 Melrose Ave., featuring ready-to-wear, accessories, menswear, and the less expensive Marc by Marc Jacobs collection.

MAIN STREET (btw. Pacific St. and Rose Ave., and Santa Monica and Venice blvds.) ★ An excellent street for strolling, Main Street is crammed with a combination of mall standards as well as upscale, left-of-center individual boutiques. You can also find plenty of casually hip cafes and restaurants. The primary strip connecting Santa Monica and Venice, Main Street has a relaxed, beach-community vibe that sets it apart from similar strips. The stores here straddle the fashion fence between upscale trendy and beach-bum edgy. Highlights include **Obsolete,** 222 Main St. (near Rose Ave; © 310/399-0024), the hippest antiques store I've ever seen. Collectibles range from antique carnival curios to 19th-century anatomical charts from Belgium (you'd be amazed at how much some of that junk in your attic is worth). **CP Shades,** 2937 Main St. (btw. Ashland and Pier sts.; © 310/392-0949), is a San Francisco ladies' clothier whose loose and comfy cotton and linen line is carried by many department stores and boutiques. **Horizons West,** 2011 Main St. (south of Pico Blvd.; © 310/392-1122), sells brand-name surfboards, wet suits, leashes, magazines, waxes, lotions, and everything else you need to catch the perfect wave. If you're looking for some truly sophisticated, finely crafted eyewear, the friendly **Optical Shop of Aspen,** 2904 Main St. (btw. Ashland and Pier sts.; © 310/392-0633), is for you. Ask for frames by cutting-edge L.A. designers Bada and Koh Sakai. For aromatherapy nirvana, it's **Cloud's,** 2719 Main St. (© 310/399-2059), where Jill Cloud (happily assisted by her lovely mom) carries the most heavenly scented candles. Then there's **Arts & Letters,** 2665 Main St. (© 310/314-7345), a stationery haven that includes invitations by the owner herself, Marilyn Golin. Outdoors types will get lost in 5,600-square-foot **Patagonia,** 2936 Main St. (© 310/314-1776; www.patagonia.com), where climbers, surfers, skiers, and hikers can gear up in the functional, colorful duds that put this environmentally friendly firm on the map. For a dose of beachy pampering, check out the **Bey's Garden,** 2919 Main St. (© 310/399-5420; www.beysgarden.com). Part aromatherapy apothecary, part gift shop, part day spa, you'll find everything from waxing to "energy work" available.

MONTANA AVENUE (btw. 17th and 7th sts., Santa Monica; www.montanaave.com) This breezy stretch of slow-traffic Montana has gotten a lot more pricey than in the late 1970s, when tailors and laundromats ruled the roost, but the specialty shops still

A Mecca for High-End Vintage

If your style is more Hepburn than Hilton, you won't want to miss the motherlode of high-end vintage shopping L.A. has to offer. Doris Raymond's **The Way We Wore,** 334 S. La Brea Ave. (© 323/937-0878), is a favorite among celebs and stylists for vintage Chanel, Balenciaga, and Fortuny. Cameron Silver's **Decades,** 8214½ Melrose Ave. (© 323/655-0223), is an L.A. institution, where you'll find frocks from Halston, Gucci, Lilly Pulitzer, and Missoni. **Lily et Cie,** 9044 Burton Way (© 310/724-5757), supplies many of the glamour gowns you see on the red carpet. Owner and vintage maven Rita Watnick has an impeccable collection of pieces from important designers such as Yves Saint Laurent, Givenchy, and Trigere.

Abbot Kinney Boulevard: L.A.'s Antithesis to Rodeo Drive

When you're finally fed up with the Rodeo Drive attitude and megamall conformity, it's time to drive to Venice and stroll the eclectic shops along **Abbot Kinney Boulevard.** This refreshingly anti-establishment stretch of street has the most diverse array of shops, galleries, and restaurants in Los Angeles. (Locals still cheer that there are no franchises in the neighborhood.) You can easily spend the entire afternoon here poring over vintage clothing, antique furniture, vintage Vespas, local art, and amusing gifts. For one-of-a-kind designed jewelry, check out **Nagual,** 1142 Abbott Kinney Blvd. (© **310/396-8500**), whose "metals with an edge" designs have caught the eye of many celebrities. Or if you're looking for a unique gift, you'll want to walk into the shop of **Strange Invisible Perfumes,** 1138 Abbot Kinney Blvd. (© **310/314-1505**), where they can custom-make a scent to match your musk. Then there's **Firefly,** 1413 Abbot Kinney Blvd. (© **310/450-6288**), a local favorite. It's that one store you can go into and find great baby gifts, stationery, books, quirky handbags, and cool clothing. **DNA Clothing Co.,** 411 Rose Ave. (© **310/399-0341**), is the mother lode for those in search of the coolest, most current styles for men and women at great prices. You'll find all your major brands as well as their own private label wear, and fresh stock arrives weekly. When you're ready to sit down and look over your loot, take a break to eat at one of the boulevard's many restaurants, including **Joe's** (the best California cuisine in L.A.; p. 517), **Primitivo, Axe, Lilly's, Massimo's, Jin's Patisserie, French Market Café,** and, of course, **Hal's Bar & Grill,** with its live jazz music. Heck, there are even 2 hours of free street parking.

outnumber the chains. Look around and you can see upscale moms with strollers and cellphones shopping for designer fashions, country home decor, and gourmet takeout.

Montana is still original enough for residents from across town to make a special trip here, seeking out distinctive shops such as **Shabby Chic,** 1013 Montana Ave. (© 310/394-1975), a much-copied purveyor of slipcovered sofas and flea-market furnishings, while clotheshorses shop for designer wear at minimalist **Savannah,** 706 Montana Ave. (© 310/458-2095); ultrahip **Jill Roberts,** 920 Montana Ave. (© 310/260-1966); and sleekly professional **Weathervane,** 1209 Montana Ave. (© 310/393-5344). **Leona Edmiston,** 1007 Montana Ave. (© 310/587-1100), houses the Aussie designer's famed frocks. For more grown-up style, head to **Ponte Vecchio,** 702 Montana Ave. (© 310/394-0989), which sells Italian hand-painted dishes and urns; If Valentine's Day is approaching, duck into **Only Hearts,** 1407 Montana Ave. (© 310/393-3088), for heart-themed gifts and seductively comfortable intimate apparel. And don't forget the one-of-a-kind shops such as **Sun Precautions,** 1600 Montana Ave. (© 310/451-5858), specializing in 100% UV protection apparel, and the second-largest **Kiehl's** store outside of NYC, 1516 Montana Ave. (© 310/255-0055). Skin is taken incredibly seriously at the flagship store and spa, **Dermalogica on Montana,** 1022 Montana Ave. (© 310/260-8682), where "touch therapies" and "skin mapping" are just the beginning of the dynamite facials.

Enjoy a meal at the local favorite, **Café Montana,** 1534 Montana Ave. (© 310/829-
3990), for great people-watching through its floor-to-ceiling glass windows.

THIRD STREET PROMENADE (Third St. btw. Wilshire Blvd. and Broadway; www.
downtownsm.com) ★   Packed with those ubiquitous corporate chain stores, restaurants,
and cafes (gee, another Starbucks), Santa Monica's pedestrians-only section of Third Street
is one of the most popular shopping areas in the city. The Promenade bustles all day and
well into the evening with a seemingly endless assortment of street performers among the
shoppers, bored teens, and home-challenged. There are, however, a few shopping gems
squeezed between Gap, Abercrombie & Fitch, and Old Navy. You can easily browse for
hours at **Hennessey & Ingalls,** 214 Wilshire Blvd. (© **310/458-9074**), a bookstore
devoted to art and architecture. **Restoration Hardware,** 1221 Third Street Promenade
(© **310/458-7992**), is still the retro-current leader for reproduction home furnishings and
accessories. **Puzzle Zoo,** 1413 Third Street Promenade (© **310/393-9201**), voted "Best in
L.A." by *Los Angeles* magazine, is where you'll find the double-sided World's Most Difficult
Puzzle, the Puzzle in a Bottle, and many other brain-teasing challenges.

Music lovers can get CDs and vinyl at **Hear Music** while sipping a latte from the
Starbucks inside the record store. **Exhale** is perfect for those seeking quiet time and relief
from the crowds. There's yoga and Core Fusion classes, the Healing Waters sanctuary
with eucalyptus steam rooms, relaxing spa services, and the simply titled "Quiet Room"
for rejuvenation. Stores stay open late (often until 1 or 2am on the weekends) for the
movie-going crowds, and there's plenty of public parking in six structures along Second
and Fourth streets between Broadway and Wilshire Boulevard.

DOWNTOWN

Since the late lamented Bullock's department store closed in 1993 (its Art Deco masterpiece salons were rescued to house the Southwestern Law School's library), downtown
has become less of a shopping destination than ever. Although many of the once-splendid
streets are lined with cut-rate luggage and electronics stores, shopping here can be a
rewarding—albeit gritty—experience for the adventuresome.

Savvy Angelenos still go for bargains in the garment and fabric districts; florists and
bargain hunters arrive at the vast **Los Angeles Flower District,** 766 Wall St. (btw. E.
Eighth St. and E. Seventh sts.; © **213/622-1966**; www.laflowerdistrict.com), before
dawn for the city's best selection of fresh blooms; and families of all ethnicities stroll the
Grand Central Market ★★, 317 S. Broadway (btw. Third and Fourth sts.; © **213/624-
2378**; www.grandcentralsquare.com). Opened in 1917, this bustling market has watched
the face of downtown L.A. change while changing little. On weekends, you'll be greeted by
a mariachi band at the Hill Street entrance, near my favorite market feature, the fruit-juice
counter, which dispenses 20 fresh varieties from wall spigots and blends the tastiest,
healthiest "shakes" in town. Farther into the market you'll find produce sellers and prepared-food counters, spice vendors who seem straight out of a Turkish bazaar, and a grain-
and-bean seller who'll scoop out dozens of exotic rices and dried legumes. It's open 9am to
6pm daily.

Another of my favorite downtown shopping zones is **Olvera Street** ★ (© **213/628-
1274**; www.olvera-street.com), a lively brick pedestrian lane near Union Station that's
been lined with stalls selling Mexican wares since the 1930s. Everything that's sold south
of the border is available here, including custom leather accessories, huarache sandals,
maracas, and—but of course—freshly baked *churros.* On weekends, you're bound to see
strolling bolero musicians, mariachis, folk dancers, and performances by Aztec Indians.
It's open daily from 10am to about 8pm.

At the base of The Fashion Institute of Design & Merchandising's downtown campus you'll find the **FIDM Scholarship Store,** where donated new merchandise is sold at bargain prices. All sales go toward scholarships for FIDM students, so you can shop with the karmic awareness that you're helping the fashion industry's next generation of designers with their tuition. It's located at 919 S. Grand Ave. at West Ninth Street (© **213/624-1200**).

If you're looking to find *the* best shopping deals in handbags, luggage, shoes, costume jewelry, and trendy fashions, then try your best to find a parking meter or park in one of the parking structures from Olympic Boulevard to 12th Street and explore **Santee Alley,** located in the alley between Santee Street and Maple Avenue. Often referred to as the heart of the fashion district, you'll find everything you've ever wanted at bargain prices. Go early on Saturday mornings if you want to blend in with the locals.

Okay, so you have to wake up a little early to experience the **Southern California Flower Mart,** 742 Maple Ave. between Seventh and Eighth streets (© 213/627-2482), but if you do it right—wear comfortable shoes, bring cash, and pick up a cup o' joe—you'll find walking through the myriad of flower stalls a very tranquil experience. Besides the usual buds and stems that you see in *Sunset Magazine,* you'll be surprised to find tropicals such as torch ginger, protea, and bird of paradise. You can purchase flowers by the bundles at amazingly low prices.

12 LOS ANGELES AFTER DARK

The City of Angels has some of the most cutting-edge clubs and bars in the world and is the polestar for the best and brightest in the music scene. Entertainment of all stripes—from Hollywood Bowl picnic performances to cool jazz venues, retro chic bars, and rock-'n'-roll clubs—can be found in the following pages.

Your best bet for current entertainment info is the *L.A. Weekly* (www.laweekly.com), a free weekly paper available at sidewalk stands, shops, and restaurants. It has all the most up-to-date news on what's happening in Los Angeles's playhouses, cinemas, museums, and live-music venues. The Sunday **"Calendar"** and Thursday **"Weekend"** sections of the *Los Angeles Times* (www.calendarlive.com) are also a good source of information for what's going on throughout the city.

To purchase tickets in advance, try buying them directly from the venue to avoid paying a surcharge. If that doesn't work, log on to **Good Time Tickets** at www.goodtime-tickets.com or call © 800/464-7383. The privately owned company specializes in selling tickets to sporting, theater, concerts, and other entertainment events throughout Los Angeles—at a markup, of course. If all else fails, take out a loan and call **Ticketmaster** (© 213/480-3232; www.ticketmaster.com), but beware of their absurdly high processing fees.

THEATER

Tickets for most plays usually cost $10 to $35, although big-name shows at the major theaters can fetch up to $75 for the best seats. **LA Stage Alliance** (© 213/614-0556), a

Half-Priced Theater Tickets

The new **Hollywood Visitor Information Center,** located at the Hollywood & Highland Center at 6801 Hollywood Blvd., has three staffers on duty from 10am to 11pm daily who will sell you half-price theater tickets for up to 100 venues throughout the city. Tickets are released on Tuesdays for shows that week, so visitors can select not only the production but the specific day they would like to attend (you'll get a printout of your reservation, and the tickets are held at the theater until the night of the performance).

nonprofit association of live theaters and producers in Los Angeles, offers full- and half-price tickets to more than 100 venues via their Internet-only service at **www.LAStage TIX.com**. This handy site features a frequently updated list of shows and availability. Tickets can be purchased online with a credit card and they'll be waiting for you at the box office; a service fee is applied depending on the cost of the ticket. *Note:* One caveat of the half-price bargain is that the seating assignments are solely at the discretion of the theater—there's no guarantee you'll be sitting next to your partner—and you must bring a printed or faxed copy of your e-mail confirmation to the box office.

The all-purpose **Music Center of Los Angeles County,** 135 N. Grand Ave., downtown, houses the city's top two playhouses: the **Ahmanson Theatre** and **Mark Taper Forum.** They're both home to the Center Theater Group (www.taperahmanson.com), as well as traveling productions (often Broadway or London bred). Each season, the Ahmanson Theatre (© 213/628-2772) hosts a handful of high-profile shows, such as the Tony Award–winning *Jersey Boys,* Andrew Lloyd Webber's *Phantom of the Opera,* and Oprah Winfrey's musical *The Color Purple. Tip:* The best seats in the theater are in the mezzanine section.

The **Mark Taper Forum** (© 213/628-2772; www.marktaperforum.com) is a more intimate theater with a thrust stage—where the audience is seated on three sides of the acting area—that performs contemporary works by international and local playwrights.

One of L.A.'s most venerable landmarks, the **Orpheum Theatre,** 842 S. Broadway (at Ninth St.; © 213/749-5171; www.laorpheum.com), recently reopened after a 75-year hiatus. Built in 1926, this renowned venue has hosted an array of theatrical productions, concerts, film festivals, and movie shoots—from Judy Garland's 1933 vaudeville performance to *Ally McBeal.* The 2,000-seat theater is home to the Mighty Wurlitzer, one of three original theater organs still existing in Southern California theaters.

Across town, the moderate-size **Geffen Playhouse,** 10886 Le Conte Ave., Westwood (© 310/208-5454; www.geffenplayhouse.com), presents dramatic and comedic work by prominent and emerging writers. UCLA purchased the theater—which was originally built as a Masonic temple in 1929, and later served as the Westwood Playhouse—back in 1995 with a little help from philanthropic entertainment mogul David Geffen. This striking venue is often the West Coast choice of many acclaimed off-Broadway shows, and also attracts locally based TV and movie actors eager for the immediacy of stage work. One recent production featured the world premiere of *Wishful Drinking,* a poignant comedy written and performed by Carrie Fisher. Always audience-friendly, the Playhouse prices tickets in the $28 to $43 range.

You've probably already heard of the **Kodak Theatre,** 6834 Hollywood Blvd. (© 323/308-6300; www.kodaktheatre.com), home of the Academy Awards. The crown jewel of the Hollywood & Highland entertainment complex, this modern beauty hosts a wide range of international performances, musicals, and concerts ranging from Alicia Keys and David Gilmour to the Moscow Stanislavsky Ballet and Sesame Street Live. Guided tours are given 7 days a week from 10:30am to 2:30pm.

The recently restored **Pantages Theatre,** 6233 Hollywood Blvd. between Vine and Argyle (© 323/468-1770; www.pantages-theater.com), reflects the full Art Deco glory of L.A.'s theater scene. Opened in 1930, this historical and cultural landmark was the first Art Deco movie palace in the U.S. and site of the Academy Awards from 1949 to 1959. The theater recently presented *Cats, Les Miserables,* and *Wicked.*

At the foot of the Hollywood Hills, the 1,245-seat outdoor **John Anson Ford Amphitheatre** (© 323/461-3673; www.fordamphitheatre.org) is located in a county regional park and is set against a backdrop of cypress trees and chaparral. It is an intimate setting, with no patron more than 96 feet away from the stage. Music, dance, film, theater, and family events run May through September. The indoor theater space, a cozy 87-seat space that was extensively renovated in 1998 and renamed **[Inside] The Ford,** features live music and theater year-round.

One of the most highly acclaimed professional theaters in L.A., the **Pasadena Playhouse,** 39 S. El Molino Ave., near Colorado Boulevard, Pasadena (© **626/356-7529;** www.pasadenaplayhouse.org), is a registered historic landmark that has served as the training ground for many theatrical, film, and TV stars, including William Holden and Gene Hackman. Productions are staged on the main theater's elaborate Spanish colonial revival.

For a schedule at any of the above theaters, check the listings in *Los Angeles* magazine (www.lamag.com), available at most area newsstands, or the "Calendar" section of the Sunday *Los Angeles Times* (www.calendarlive.com); or call the box offices at the numbers listed above.

Smaller Playhouses & Companies

On any given night, there's more live theater to choose from in Los Angeles than in New York City, due in part to the surfeit of ready actors and writers chomping at the bit to make it in Tinseltown. Many of today's familiar faces from film and TV spent plenty of time cutting their teeth on L.A.'s busy theater circuit, which is home to nearly 200 small and medium-size theaters and theater companies, ranging from the 'round-the-corner, neighborhood variety to high-profile, polished troupes of veteran actors. With so many options, navigating the scene to find the best work can be a monumental task. A good bet is to choose one of the theaters listed below, which have established excellent reputations for their consistently high-quality productions; otherwise, consult the *L.A. Weekly* (www.laweekly.com), which advertises most current productions, or call **Theatre L.A.** (© **213/614-0556;** www.theatrela.org) for up-to-date performance listings.

In the same complex as Walt Disney Concert Hall, **REDCAT** (an acronym for the Roy and Edna Disney/CalArts Theater) is a relatively new multiuse forum for cutting-edge performance and media arts. Befitting its ultramodern location, the REDCAT is one of the most versatile and technologically advanced presentation spaces in the world. Be sure to arrive a bit early so you can visit the REDCAT lounge and bookstore for a pre-performance espresso or cocktail—wrapped in signature Frank Gehry plywood, it's one of the best-kept secret bars in the city. The REDCAT is located at 631 W. Second St. at the southwest corner of the Walt Disney Concert Hall (© **213/237-2800;** www.redcat.org).

The **Colony Studio Theatre,** 555 N. Third St., Burbank (© **818/558-7000;** www.colonytheatre.org), was formed in 1975 and has developed from a part-time ensemble of

TV actors longing for their theatrical roots into a nationally recognized company. The
company produces plays in all genres at the 276-seat Burbank Center Stage, which is shared with other performing arts groups.

Actors Circle Theater, 7313 Santa Monica Blvd., West Hollywood (© **323/882-6805;** www.actorscircle.net), is a 47-seater that's as acclaimed as it's tiny. Look for original contemporary works throughout the year.

Founded in 1965, **East West Players,** 120 N. Judge John Aiso St., Los Angeles (© **213/625-7000;** www.eastwestplayers.org), is the oldest Asian-American theater company in the United States. It's been so successful that the company moved from a 99-seat venue to the 200-seat David Henry Hwang Theater in downtown L.A.'s Little Tokyo.

The **L.A. Theatre Works** (© **310/827-0808**) is renowned for its marriage of media and theater and has performed more than 200 plays and logged more than 350 hours of on-air programming. Performances are held at the Skirball Cultural Center, nestled in the Sepulveda Pass near the Getty Center. In the past, personalities such as Richard Dreyfuss, Julia Louis-Dreyfus, Jason Robards, Annette Bening, and John Lithgow have given award-winning performances of plays by Arthur Miller, Neil Simon, Joyce Carol Oates, and more. For nearly a decade, the group has performed simultaneously for viewing and listening audiences in its radio theater series. Tickets are usually around $35; a full performance schedule can be found online at **www.latw.org**.

CLASSICAL MUSIC & OPERA

While L.A. is best known for its pop realms, other types of music here consist of top-flight orchestras and companies—both local and visiting—to fulfill the most demanding classical music appetites; scan the papers to find out who's performing while you're in the city.

The world-class **Los Angeles Philharmonic** (© **323/850-2000;** www.laphil.org) the only major classical music company in Los Angeles, just got a whole lot more popular with the completion of its incredible home: the **Walt Disney Concert Hall** (p. 545), at the intersection of First Street and Grand Avenue in historic Bunker Hill. Designed by world-renowned architect Frank O. Gehry, this addition to the Music Center of L.A. includes a breathtaking concert hall, outdoor park, restaurant, cafe, bookstore, and gift shop.

The Philharmonic's Finnish-born music director, Esa-Pekka Salonen, concentrates on contemporary compositions; despite complaints from traditionalists, he does an excellent job attracting younger audiences. In addition to performances at the Walt Disney Concert Hall, the Philharmonic plays a summer season at the **Hollywood Bowl** (see "Concerts Under the Stars" below) and a chamber music series at the **Skirball Cultural Center,** 2701 N. Sepulveda Boulevard, at Mulholland Drive (© **310/440-4500.** www.skirball.org).

Slowly but surely, the **Los Angeles Opera** (© **213/972-8001;** www.losangelesopera.com), which performs at the **Dorothy Chandler Pavilion,** is gaining respect and popularity with inventive stagings of classic pieces, modern operas, visiting divas, and the contributions from high-profile artistic director Plácido Domingo. The 120-voice **Los Angeles Master Chorale** sings a varied repertoire that includes classical and pop compositions. Concerts are held at the **Walt Disney Concert Hall** (© **213/972-7200**) October through June.

The **UCLA Center for the Performing Arts** (© **310/825-2101;** www.uclalive.org) has presented music, dance, and theatrical performances of unparalleled quality for more than 60 years and continues to be a major presence in the local and national cultural landscape. Presentations occur at several different theaters around Los Angeles, both on and off campus. UCLA's **Royce Hall** is the Center's pride; it has even been compared to

New York's Carnegie Hall. Recent standouts from the Center's busy calendar included the famous Gyuto Monks Tibetan Tantric Choir and the Cinderella story *Cendrillon*, with an original score by Sergei Prokofiev.

CONCERTS UNDER THE STARS

Hollywood Bowl ★★★ (Moments)   Built in the early 1920s, the Hollywood Bowl has just undergone a major overhaul. The elegant Greek-style natural outdoor amphitheater, cradled in a small mountain canyon, is the summer home of the Los Angeles Philharmonic and Hollywood Bowl orchestras, and often hosts internationally known conductors and soloists on Tuesday and Thursday nights. Friday and Saturday concerts typically feature orchestral swing or pops concerts. The summer season also includes a jazz series; past performers have included Natalie Cole, Dionne Warwick, and Chick Corea. Other events, from standard rock-'n'-roll acts such as Radiohead to Garrison Keillor programs, summer fireworks galas, and the annual Mariachi Festival, are often on the season's schedule.

To round out an evening at the Bowl, many concertgoers use the occasion to enjoy a picnic dinner and a bottle of wine—it's one of L.A.'s grandest traditions. Call ℂ 323/850-1885 by 4pm the day before you go to place your food order. Arrive a couple of hours before the show starts, in order to dine while listening to the orchestra or band tune up. 2301 N. Highland Ave. (at Pat Moore Way), Hollywood. ℂ 323/850-2000. www.hollywoodbowl.org.

THE CLUB & MUSIC SCENE

The Avalon Hollywood   Formerly known as the Palace, this 1,200-capacity theater and nightclub—just across Vine from the famed Capitol Records tower—was the site of numerous significant alternative-rock shows throughout the late '90s and has been given a much-needed makeover. Club nights feature famous DJs such as Moby and Paul Oakenfeld. 1735 N. Vine St., Hollywood. ℂ 323/462-8900. www.avalonhollywood.com.

Babe's & Ricky's Inn ★ (Finds)   Located in South Central L.A.'s up-and-coming Leimert Park, this blues club stands out as an original, a place where you can imagine B. B. King himself would have played before he became famous. Mama Laura Gross is the cultivator of the fabulous, endangered sound and the house goddess of this intimate bar. Great guitarists are the rule, not the exception here. 4339 Leimert Blvd., Leimert Park. ℂ 323/295-9112. www.bluesbar.com.

B. B. King's Blues Club   Nestled away in Universal CityWalk's commercial plaza, this three-level club/restaurant—the ribs alone are worth the trip—hosts plenty of great local and touring national blues acts and is a testament to the establishment's venerable namesake. There's no shortage of good seating, but if you find yourself on the top two levels, it's best to grab a table adjacent to the railing to get an ideal view of the stage. CityWalk, Universal City. ℂ 818/622-5464. www.bbkingclubs.com.

Ivan Kane's Forty Deuce   Owner Ivan Kane reopened this suave nightclub, formerly known as Kane. Designed as a "back-alley, striptease lounge," the low bar, lounge chair seating, vintage brass registers, and cocktail tables with chic lamps all chip in to create a sexy, burlesque vibe. Models use the bar as a runway, so watch your cocktail. 5574 Melrose Ave., Hollywood. ℂ 323/465-4242. www.fortydeuce.com.

House of Blues ★   With three great bars, cutting-edge Southern art, and a key Sunset Strip location, there are plenty of reasons music fans and industry types keep coming back to House of Blues. Night after night, audiences are dazzled by performances from nationally and internationally acclaimed acts as diverse as Jeff Beck, the Black Eyed Peas, and Motorhead. The food in the upstairs restaurant can be great (reservations are a must), and the Sunday Gospel Brunch, though a bit pricey, puts a mean raise on the roof. 8430 Sunset Blvd., West Hollywood. © **323/848-5100. www.hob.com.**

The Knitting Factory   Straight from the New York City legend, a West Coast branch of the famous Knitting Factory has arrived in the redeveloping Hollywood Boulevard nightlife district. The Main Stage was inaugurated by a Posies performance and sees such diverse bookings as Kristin Hersh, Pere Ubu, and Jonathan Richman; a secondary Alter-Knit stage has sporadic shows. The Factory is totally wired for digital, including interactive online computer stations throughout the club. 7021 Hollywood Blvd., Hollywood. © **323/463-0204. www.knittingfactory.com.**

The Roxy Theatre   Veteran record producer/executive Lou Adler opened this Sunset Strip club in the mid-1970s with concerts by Neil Young and a lengthy run of the pre-movie *Rocky Horror Show*. Since then, it's remained among the top showcase venues in Hollywood. Although the revitalized Troubadour and such new entries as the House of Blues challenge its preeminence among cozy clubs, you can still find national acts such as the Black Crowes, who will pop in, and great local bands. 9009 W. Sunset Blvd. © **310/ 278-9457. www.theroxyonsunset.com.**

Spaceland ★   The wall-to-wall mirrors and shiny brass posts decorating the interior create the feeling that, in a past life, Spaceland must've been a seedy strip joint, but the club's current personality offers something entirely different. Having hosted countless performances by artists such as Pavement, Mary Lou Lord, Elliot Smith, and Beck, this hot spot on the fringe of east Hollywood has become one of the most important clubs on the L.A. circuit. 1717 Silver Lake Blvd., Silver Lake. © **323/661-4380. www.clubspaceland.com.**

The Troubadour   This West Hollywood mainstay radiates rock history—from the 1960s to the 1990s, the Troub really has seen 'em all. Audiences are consistently treated to memorable shows from the already-established or young-and-promising acts that take the Troubadour's stage. But bring your earplugs—this beer- and sweat-soaked club likes it loud. All ages are accepted. 9081 Santa Monica Blvd., West Hollywood. © **310/276-6168. www.troubadour.com.**

Viper Room   This world-famous club on the Strip has been king of the hill since it was first opened by actor Johnny Depp and co-owner Sal Jenco back in 1993. With an intensely electric and often star-filled scene, the intimate club is also known for unforgettable late-night surprise performances from such powerhouses as the late Johnny Cash, Iggy Pop, Tom Petty, Slash, and Trapt (to name but a few) after headline gigs elsewhere in town. 8852 Sunset Blvd., West Hollywood. © **310/358-1880. www.viperroom.com.**

Whisky A Go-Go ★   This legendary bi-level venue personifies L.A. rock 'n' roll, from Jim Morrison and X to Guns N' Roses and Beck. Every trend has passed through this club, and it continues to be the most vital venue of its kind. With the hiring of an in-house booker a few years ago, the Whisky began showcasing local talent on free-admission Monday nights. All ages are welcome. 8901 Sunset Blvd., West Hollywood. © **310/ 652-4202, ext. 15. www.whiskyagogo.com.**

Winston's   The lack of a sign gives you a pretty good indication of the type of hip in-the-know crowd you'll encounter at this tiny West Hollywood bar opened by über-hip owners Andy Fiscella (of "Dime" fame) and *GQ* editor Chris Huvane. The decor is pure 1920s tinseltown with DJs spinning vintage '80s and '90s for young starlets such as

Dinner-&-a-Movie-&-DJs-&-Dancing

If your big night on the town involves dinner, a movie, DJs, and dancing, **Cine-Space** has got it all covered. Every Thursday through Saturday this stylish, intimate Hollywood supper club serves contemporary American cuisine—and stiff cocktails—while screening recent hits, indies, classics, and shorts. When the (free) film's over, the DJ party starts at around 10pm and goes until 2am. It's located in the heart of Hollywood at 6356 Hollywood Blvd. at Ivar Street on the second level (℃ **323/817-3456**; www.cine-space.com).

Lindsay Lohan, Mary Kate Olsen, and Jessica Alba. Plan on snotty service, strong drinks, and attitude in abundance. Oh, and good luck getting in on a weekend night if you don't have the right look. 7746 Santa Monica Blvd., West Hollywood. ℃ **323/654-0105.**

Dance Clubs

The Derby   This class-A east-of-Hollywood club has been at ground zero of the swing revival since the very beginning. Located at a former Brown Derby site, the club was restored to its original luster and detailed with a heavy 1940s edge. With Big Bad Voodoo Daddy as the one-time house band and regular visits from Royal Crown Revue, hep guys and dolls knew that the Derby was money even before *Swingers* transformed it into one of the city's most happenin' hangs. But if you come on the weekends, expect a wait to get in, and once you're inside, dance space is at a premium. 4500 Los Feliz Blvd., Los Feliz. ℃ **323/663-8979.** www.clubderby.com. Cover $7–$10.

El Floridita ⓕFindsⓑThis tiny Cuban restaurant-and-salsa club is hot, hot, hot. Despite its modest strip-lot locale, it draws the likes of Jennifer Lopez, Sandra Bullock, Jimmy Smits, and Jack Nicholson, in addition to a festive crowd of Latin-dance devotees who groove well into the night. The hippest nights continue to be Mondays, when Johnny Polanco and his swinging New York–flavored salsa band get the dance floor jumpin'. 1253 N. Vine St., Hollywood. ℃ **323/871-8612.** www.elfloridita.com. Cover $10.

Nacional ★   At what is quickly becoming Hollywood's most desirable dance floor, you'll find a hip and gorgeous crowd engaging in an orgiastic celebration of youth. It also has a well-designed balcony where you can watch all the flirting in a lively outdoor smoking area. So grab a mojito and mingle among the young, beautiful, and unshakably self-assured, and remember, even the rest of us can have fun here. 1645 Wilcox Ave., Hollywood. ℃ **323/962-7712.** www.nacional.cc.

Viper Room ★   Every Tuesday night, this live-music hot spot (see "The Club & Music Scene," above) hosts Atmosphere, featuring the sounds of trance, drum and bass, garage, techno, and hip-hop spun by an eclectic assemblage of DJs, MCs, and mix masters. On Mondays, a head-banging tribute to '80s metal/hard rock shakes the walls. 8852 Sunset Blvd., West Hollywood. ℃ **310/358-1880.** www.viperroom.com. Cover $10.

BARS & COCKTAIL LOUNGES

Bar Nineteen12   I'll take any excuse to walk through the front doors of the luscious Beverly Hills Hotel and rub shoulders with the celebs who love to hang out here. Suck on an apple martini popsicle while striking a pose on the golden-toned velvet sofas and high-backed leather chairs. Me, I'm out on the veranda nursing a $14 Manhattan while pretending not to notice Pamela's cleavage. **Tip:** Thursdays are the hot night, but arrive before 9pm or you might not make it in. 9641 Sunset Blvd., Beverly Hills. © 310/273-1912. www.barnineteen12.com.

Beauty Bar   It's a proven concept in New York, Las Vegas, and San Francisco: a cocktail lounge/beauty salon. Decorated with vintage salon gear and sporting a hip-retro vibe, the Beauty Bar is both campy and trendy. Where else can you actually get a manicure while sipping cocktails with such names as Blue Rinse (made with blue Curaçao) or Prell (their version of a grasshopper)? 1638 N Cahuenga Blvd., Hollywood. © 323/464-7676. www.beautybar.com.

The Dresden Room ★   Hugely popular with L.A. hipsters because of its longevity, location, often-overlooked cuisine, and elegant ambience, "The Den" was pushed into the mainstream of L.A. nightlife thanks to its inclusion in the movie *Swingers*. But it's the timeless lounge act of Marty and Elayne (the couple has been performing there up to 5 nights a week since 1982) that has proven that, fad or no fad, this place is always cool. Sidle up to the bar for a blue glass of the house classic, Blood and Sand—a space-age margarita of sorts. 1760 N. Vermont Ave., Hollywood. © 323/665-4294.

Glow ★ (Finds)   Yes, it's at the Marriot Hotel in Marina del Rey, but I know what you're thinking and you're wrong—this place is swank. How swank you ask? Playboy.com recently ranked it as one of the top 10 lounges in the U.S., joining the ranks of notable nightlife hot spots such as the Tropicana Bar at the Roosevelt Hotel in Hollywood, and the Palms Pool and Bungalows in Las Vegas. It's an outdoor venue that literally glows in shades of deep amber as young L.A. hipsters and surprised hotel guests lounge in semi-private booths and order bottle service from the lithe staff. 4100 Admiralty Way, Marina del Rey. © 310/578-4152. www.glow-bar.com.

Good Luck Bar   Until they installed a flashing neon sign outside, only locals and hipsters knew about this kung fu–themed room in the Los Feliz/Silver Lake area. The dark red windowless interior boasts Asian ceiling tiles, fringed Chinese paper lanterns, sweet-but-deadly drinks such as the Yee Mee Loo (translated as "blue drink"), and a jukebox with selections ranging from Thelonious Monk to Cher's "Half Breed." The spacious sitting room, furnished with mismatched sofas, armchairs, and banquettes, provides a great atmosphere for conversation or romance. Arrive early to avoid the throngs of L.A. scenesters. 1514 Hillhurst Ave. (btw. Hollywood and Sunset boulevards), Los Angeles. © 323/666-3524.

Green Door   Unless you're in your 20s, live in L.A., and go clubbing a lot, you've probably heard of Johnny Zander and Chris Breed, two key players in the resurgence of Hollywood's nightlife scene. The Green Door is their latest creation²a quasi nightclub, lounge, and salon that's been elaborately made over to resemble an old-world French Saloon complete with regal couches, antique mirrors, and a massive chandelier hanging from the high ceiling. It's divided into three areas depending on your mood: smoke, drink, or dance. I suggest arriving early (around 9pm) or you might get turned away at the door for reasons only the egomaniacal bouncers can fathom. 1439 Ivar Ave., Hollywood. © 323l/463-0008.

Nic's Beverly Hills ★★   There's nothing like a really good martini to take the edge off, and some of the best I've ever had are poured at Nic's (the pear martini with Grey Goose La Poire vodka and Parmesan cheese garnish is sublime). Unlike the surrounding Beverly Hills establishments, there's no attitude here, just lots of retro-groovy slippery white leather, bold colorful stripes, and laid-back locals noshing on cocktail cuisine while listening to good jazz bands and big-band trios. Owner Larry Nicola takes pride in his self-anointed title as "Vodkateur™," which means he's an expert regarding all things vodka. In fact, he built a walk-in freezer called a VODBOX just so he could have a proper tasting room so his guests can sample the best vodkas from around the world. 453 N. Canon Dr., Beverly Hills. ℭ **310/550-5707.** www.nicsbeverlyhills.com.

Skybar ⓪verrated Since its opening in hotelier Ian Schraeger's refurbished Sunset Strip hotel, Skybar has been a favorite among L.A.'s most fashionable of the fashionable set. This place was at one time so hot that even the agents to the stars needed agents to get in. Nevertheless, a little image consulting—affect the right look, strike the right pose, and look properly disinterested—might get you in to rub elbows with some of the faces that regularly appear on the cover of *People* (but please don't stare). 8440 W. Sunset Blvd., West Hollywood. ℭ **323/848-6025.**

The Standard Downtown ★★ This rooftop bar, located atop the Standard Hotel in downtown L.A. (formerly Superior Oil headquarters), is surrounded by high office towers and helipads, and the view is magnificent. The skyscrapers act like strangely glowing lava lamps in the night sky as exotic ladies sip exotic cocktails amid waterbeds and bent-plastic loungers. 550 S. Flower St. ℭ **213/892-8080.** www.standardhotel.com.

Star Shoes ★ From the same club gurus who run Beauty Bar around the corner, Star Shoes is a combo shoe store and dance club. It's usually packed with a trendy young crowd who bump around the narrow dance floor while a projectionist plasters the walls with vintage celluloid (a stony effect). The scene here is far more energetic than that at the Beauty Bar, and the DJs are among the best in town. 6364 Hollywood Blvd., Hollywood. ℭ **323/462-7827.**

Whiskey Blue When ascending the dramatic backlit staircase and entering the dimly lit, seductive interior, it's hard to believe Whiskey Blue in the W Hotel is situated on UCLA's Sorority Row. The atmosphere is as chic as the decor, which features high screen partitions, low cushioned couches, sleek private rooms, and a row of carved stumps of wood where manicured martinis may be set. Patrons are encouraged to dress their best, especially on the weekends when the Westside's glitterati come out to this scene to be seen. Hotel guests are given priority entrance. 930 Hilgard Ave., Westwood. ℭ **310/443-8232.**

COMEDY CLUBS

Acme Comedy Theater The Acme players provide a barrage of laughs with their improv and sketch comedy acts—a veritable grab bag of funnies. 135 N. La Brea Ave., Hollywood. ℭ **323/525-0202.** www.acmecomedy.com. Cover $8–$15.

Comedy Store ★ You can't go wrong here: New comics develop their material, and established ones work out their kinks at this landmark owned by Mitzi Shore (Pauly's mom). The **Best of the Comedy Store Room,** which seats 400, features professional stand-ups continuously on Friday and Saturday nights. Several comedians are always featured, each doing about a 15-minute stint. The talent is always first-rate and includes comics who regularly appear on *The Tonight Show* and other shows. The **Original Room** features a dozen or so comedians back-to-back nightly. Sunday night is amateur night: Anyone with enough guts can take the stage for 3 minutes—Lord only knows what you'll get. 8433 Sunset Blvd., West Hollywood. ℭ **323/650-6268.** www.comedystore.com. Cover $10–$20, plus 2-drink minimum.

Groundling Theater ★ L.A.'s answer to Chicago's Second City has been around for more than 25 years, yet it remains the most innovative and funny group in town. The skits change every year or so, but they take new improvisational twists every night and the satire is often savage. The Groundlings were the springboard to fame for Pee-Wee Herman, Elvira, and former *Saturday Night Live* stars Jon Lovitz, Phil Hartman, and Julia "It's Pat" Sweeney. Phone for showtimes and reservations. 7307 Melrose Ave., Los Angeles. ⓒ 323/934-4747. www.groundlings.com. Tickets $11–$21.

The Improv   A showcase for top stand-ups since 1975, the Improv offers something different each night. Although it used to have a fairly active music schedule, the place is now mostly doing what it does best—showcasing comedy. Owner Budd Freedman's buddies—such as Jay Leno, Billy Crystal, and Robin Williams—hone their skills here more often than you would expect. But even if the comedians on the bill are all unknowns, they won't be for long. Shows are at 8pm Sunday and Thursday, and at 8:30 and 10:30pm Friday and Saturday. 8162 Melrose Ave., West Hollywood. ⓒ 323/651-2583. www.improvclubs.com. Tickets $5–$12, plus 2-drink minimum.

Laugh Factory ★   Yes, this is where Michael Richards made his infamous racist comments toward two black men who were heckling him (and where Mr. Richards is no longer welcome). In fact, just about every comedian you've seen on TV—living or dead—has been a regular at the Laugh Factory: Rodney Dangerfield, Dave Chappelle, Robin Williams, Richard Pryor, Jim Carrey, Jerry Seinfeld, and others. The best night to attend is the Friday All Star Comedy show, because you never know when a celebrity guest is going to sneak onstage and try out a new routine. 8001 Sunset Blvd., Hollywood. ⓒ 323/656-1336. www.laughfactory.com. Tickets $18–$30, plus 2-drink minimum.

LATE-NIGHT BITES

Finding places to dine in the wee hours is getting easier in L.A., as each year sees the opening of more 24-hour and after-midnight restaurants and diners.

The Apple Pan ★★   This classic American burger shack, an L.A. landmark, hasn't changed much since 1947—and its burgers and pies continue to hit the spot. Open until 1am Friday and Saturday, and until midnight other nights; closed Monday. See p. 526 for a full review. 10801 W. Pico Blvd., West L.A. ⓒ 310/475-3585.

Canter's Fairfax Restaurant, Delicatessen & Bakery   This 24-hour Jewish deli has been a winner with late-nighters since it opened more than 66 years ago. If you show up after the clubs close, you're sure to spot a bleary-eyed celebrity or two alongside the rest of the after-hours crowd, chowing down on a giant pastrami sandwich, matzo-ball soup, potato pancakes, or other deli favorites. Try a potato knish with a side of brown gravy—trust me, you'll love it. 419 N. Fairfax Ave., West Hollywood. ⓒ 323/651-2030.

Dolores's   One of L.A.'s oldest surviving coffee shops, Dolores's offers just what you might expect: Naugahyde, laminated counters, lots of linoleum, and comforting predictability. Expect the usual coffee-shop fare of pancakes, burgers, and eggs at this 24-hour joint. 11407 Santa Monica Blvd., Los Angeles. ⓒ 310/477-1061.

Du-par's Restaurant & Bakery ★   During the week, this popular Valley coffee shop serves up blue-plate specials until 1am; come the weekend, they're slingin' hash until 5:30am. 12036 Ventura Blvd. (1 block east of Laurel Canyon), Studio City. ⓒ 818/766-4437.

Jerry's Famous Deli ★   Valley hipsters head to 24-hour Jerry's to satiate the late-night munchies. 12655 Ventura Blvd. (east of Coldwater Canyon Ave.), Studio City. ⓒ 818/980-4245.

Cinema at the Cemetery

If you prefer your movie settings to be slightly macabre, boy are you in luck. Every other Saturday in the summer, the **Hollywood Forever Cemetery** (**www.cinespia.org**) hosts civilized screenings of rarely seen movie classics, which are projected against the cemetery's massive mausoleum wall. Guests are encouraged to arrive early for a picnic on the lush lawn while listening to DJs spin records (Grateful Dead, mostly). A $10 donation admission is suggested, and parking is free within the cemetery. Bring a sweater, a flashlight, and—if you're having a picnic—a trash bag as well. Hollywood Forever Cemetery is located at 6000 Santa Monica Blvd., between Gower Street and Van Ness Avenue.

Kate Mantilini ★   Kate's serves stylish nouveau comfort food in a striking setting. It's open until midnight Sunday and Monday, Tuesday through Thursday until 1am, and Friday and Saturday until 2am. 9101 Wilshire Blvd. (at Doheny Dr.), Beverly Hills. ✆ **310/278-3699.**

Mel's Drive-In   Straight from an episode of *Happy Days,* this 24-hour 1950s diner on the Sunset Strip attracts customers ranging from chic shoppers during the day to rock-'n'-rollers at night. The fries and shakes here are among the best in town. 8585 Sunset Blvd. (west of La Cienega), West Hollywood. ✆ **310/854-7200.**

101 Coffee Shop   A retro coffee shop right out of the early '60s with rock walls, funky colored tiles, comfy booths, and cool light fixtures, all pulled together nicely in a hip yet subdued fashion. Count on tasty grinds until 3am (try the breakfast burritos). 6145 Franklin Ave., Hollywood. ✆ **323/467-1175.**

The Original Pantry   Owned by former Los Angeles mayor Richard Riordan, this downtown diner has been serving huge portions of comfort food round-the-clock for more than 60 years; in fact, they don't even have a key to the front door. See p. 534 for a full review. 877 S. Figueroa St. (at Ninth St.), downtown. ✆ **213/972-9279.**

Pink's Hot Dogs   Many a woozy hipster has awakened with the telltale signs of a post-cocktailing trip to this greasy street-side hot-dog stand—the oniony morning-after breath and chili stains on your shirt are dead giveaways. Open Friday and Saturday until 3am, and all other nights until 2am. See p. 531 for a full review. 709 N. La Brea Ave., Los Angeles. ✆ **323/931-4223.**

Swingers ★   This hip coffee shop keeps L.A. scene-stealers happy with its retro comfort food. Open daily until 4am. A second location is at 802 Broadway (at Lincoln Ave.; ✆ **310/393-9793**) in Santa Monica. 8020 Beverly Blvd. (west of Fairfax Ave.), Hollywood. ✆ **323/653-5858.**

Toi on Sunset ★   Those requiring a little more *oomph* from their late-night snack should come here. At this colorful and *loud* hangout, garbled pop-culture metaphors mingle with the tastes and aromas of "rockin' Thai" cuisine in delicious ways until 4am nightly. 7505½ Sunset Blvd. (at Gardner), Hollywood. ✆ **323/874-8062.**

MOVIES

This being L.A., it's saturated with megaplexes catering to high-budget, high-profile flicks featuring the usual big-ticket lures such as Hanks, Willis, and DiCaprio. But there are times when those polished Hollywood-studio stories just won't do. Below are some

The World's Most Private Public Theater

Part of the culture of L.A. is to always avoid standing in line because you're far too important and busy. So it was only a matter of time before someone came up with the idea of treating everyone like a VIP at the movie theater. **ArcLight Cinemas** (© **323/464-4226;** www.arclightcinemas.com) is specifically designed for anyone who abhors rude patrons (ushers keep it quiet), late arrivals (forbidden), searching for seats (reserved in advance by customer preference), uncomfortable chairs (think La-Z-Boy), neck strain (the first rows start 25 ft. from the screen), pimply teenage employees (most of the staff are struggling actors or film students), crappy popcorn (real butter and freshly made caramel popcorn), and paying for parking (4 free hr. are included in the ticket price). And there's a full bar and groovy lounge where themed cocktails are served with appetizers.

The ArcLight shows a mix of indie and Hollywood films, and ticket prices—as you would expect—are higher than the industry average: $11 for an afternoon show and $14 on weekend nights. But the sound and picture quality are so good that filmmakers come here to host Q&A sessions, and celebrities such as Brad Pitt and Leonardo DiCaprio prefer the ArcLight's reserved seating system. It's located at 6360 W. Sunset Blvd., between Vine and Ivar streets.

non-mainstream options that play movies from bygone eras or those with an indie bent. Consult the *L.A. Weekly* (www.laweekly.com) to see what's playing.

Film festivals are another great way to explore the other side of contemporary movies. Aside from the American Film Institute's yearly October fete, the **Film Independent's Los Angeles Film Festival** (© **866/345-6337** or 310/432-1240; www.lafilmfest.com) looks at what's new in American indies, short films, and music videos during a weeklong event in late June. Each July since 1982, the **Gay and Lesbian Film Festival** (© **213/ 480-7088;** www.outfest.org), also known as Outfest, has aimed to bring high-quality gay, lesbian, bi, and transgender films to a wider public awareness. In 1998, the festival became Los Angeles's largest, with more than 32,000 audience members.

Promoting moving pictures as this country's great art form, the **American Cinematheque** in Hollywood (© **323/466-3456;** www.egyptiantheatre.com) presents not-readily-seen videos and films, ranging from the wildly arty to the old classics. Since relocating to the historic and beautifully refurbished 1923 **Egyptian Theatre,** 6712 Hollywood Blvd. in Hollywood, American Cinematheque has hosted several film events, including a celebration of contemporary flicks from Spain, a tribute to the femme fatales of film noir, and a retrospective of the films of William Friedkin. Events highlighting a specific individual are usually accompanied by at least one in-theater audience Q&A session with the honoree.

The **Leo S. Bing Theater** at the **L.A. County Museum of Art,** 5905 Wilshire Blvd., Los Angeles (© **323/857-6010;** www.lacma.org), presents a themed film series each month. Past subjects have ranged from 1930s blond bombshell films to Cold War propaganda flicks to contemporary British satire (complete with a 3-day *Monty Python's Flying Circus* marathon).

Despite being a multiplex in a bright outdoor mall, **Laemmle's Sunset 5,** 8000 Sunset Blvd., West Hollywood (℃ **323/848-3500;** www.laemmle.com), features films that most theaters of its ilk won't even touch. This is the place to come to see interesting independent art films. There's often a selection of gay-themed movies.

The Nuart Theater, 11272 Santa Monica Blvd., Los Angeles (℃ **310/281-8223**), digs deep into its archives for real classics, ranging from campy to cool. They also feature frequent in-person appearances and Q&A sessions from stars and filmmakers, and screen *The Rocky Horror Picture Show* (yes, still!) every Saturday at midnight.

Although it's only open for social events and once-a-month movies when the new owner fancies, fans of silent-movie classics will enjoy the **Silent Movie Theatre,** 611 N. Fairfax Ave. ($^1/_2$ block south of Melrose), near the Miracle Mile (℃ **323/655-2520** for recorded program information, or 323/655-2510 for main office; www.silentmovie theatre.com). Tickets are $10.

If TV's more your thing, the **Museum of Television and Radio,** 465 N. Beverly Dr., Beverly Hills (℃ **310/786-1025;** www.mtr.org), celebrates this country's long relationship with the tube. The museum often features a movie of the month, and it also shows free selections from past television programs.

Side Trips from Los Angeles

by Matthew Richard Poole

The area within a 100-mile radius of Los Angeles is one of the world's most diverse regions. You can find arid deserts, rugged mountains, historic towns, alpine lakes, and even an island paradise. In the following pages, I've covered a variety of the best attractions beyond Los Angeles County, such as the smog-free mountain communities of Big Bear and Lake Arrowhead, Disneyland and Knott's Berry Farm amusement parks, SoCal beach towns such as Newport and Huntington Beach, and the ultimate L.A. weekend getaway, Catalina Island. From L.A., you can reach most of these scenic side trips in less than an hour by car or by boat—for an easy, refreshing diversion from the big-city scene.

---

1 LONG BEACH & THE QUEEN MARY

21 miles S of downtown L.A.

The fifth-largest city in California, Long Beach is best known as the permanent home of the former cruise liner *Queen Mary* and the Long Beach Grand Prix, whose star-studded warm-up race has included hipster Jason Priestly and formerly perennial racer Paul Newman burning rubber through the streets of the city in mid-April.

ESSENTIALS

GETTING THERE   See chapter 3 for airport and airline information. Driving from Los Angeles, take either I-5 or I-405 to I-710 south, which leads directly to both downtown Long Beach and the *Queen Mary* Seaport.

ORIENTATION   Downtown Long Beach is at the eastern end of the vast Port of Los Angeles; Pine Avenue is the central restaurant and shopping street, which extends south to Shoreline Park and the Aquarium. The *Queen Mary* is docked just across the waterway, gazing south toward tiny Long Beach marina and Naples Island. See the beginning of this guide for a color map of the Long Beach area.

VISITOR INFORMATION   Contact the **Long Beach Area Convention & Visitors Bureau,** One World Trade Center, Suite 300 (© **800/452-7829** or 562/436-3645; www.visitlongbeach.com). For information on the **Long Beach Grand Prix,** call © **562/981-2600** or check out **www.longbeachgp.com**.

THE MAJOR ATTRACTIONS

Aquarium of the Pacific ★ (Kids)   This enormous aquarium—one of the largest in the U.S.—is the cornerstone of Long Beach's ever-changing waterfront. Figuring that what stimulated flagging economies in Monterey and Baltimore would work in Long Beach, planners gave their all to this project, creating a crowd-pleasing attraction just

(Tips) **Save Some Cash**

If you plan on visiting the *Queen Mary* and the Aquarium the same day, you can purchase a combined ticket package at either venue for $34 ($19 for kids 3–11). You'll save about $10 (hey, that's a free lunch).

across the harbor from Long Beach's other mainstay, the Queen Mary. The vast facility—it has enough exhibit space to fill three football fields—re-creates three areas of the Pacific: the warm Baja and Southern California regions, the Bering Sea and chilly northern Pacific, and faraway tropical climes, including impressive re-creations of a lagoon and barrier reef. There are more than 12,500 creatures in all, from 150 sharks (some you can touch, some you can't) prowling a 90,000-gallon habitat to delicate sea horses, moon jellies, and gaggles of tropical birds within the Lorikeet Forest. Learn little-known aquatic facts at the many educational exhibits, or come nose-to-nose with sea lions, moray eels, and other inhabitants of giant, three-story-high tanks.

100 Aquarium Way, off Shoreline Dr., Long Beach. ℂ 562/590-3100. www.aquariumofpacific.org. Admission $21 adults, $18 seniors ages 62 and over, $12 ages 3–11, free for kids under 3. Daily 9am–6pm. Closed Christmas Day and Toyota Grand Prix weekend (mid-Apr). Parking $6.

The Queen Mary ★ It's easy to dismiss this old cruise ship/museum as a barnacle-laden tourist trap, but it's the only surviving example of this particular kind of 20th-century elegance and excess. From the staterooms paneled lavishly in now-extinct tropical hardwoods to the perfectly preserved crew quarters and the miles of hallway handrails made of once-pedestrian Bakelite, wonders never cease aboard this 81,237-ton Art Deco luxury liner. Stroll the teakwood decks with just a bit of imagination and you're back in 1936 on the maiden voyage from Southampton, England. Don't miss the stream-lined modern observation lounge, featured often in period motion pictures; have drinks and listen to some live jazz. Kiosk displays of photographs and memorabilia are every-where—following the success of the movie *Titanic*, the *Queen Mary* even hosted an exhibit of artifacts from its less fortunate cousin. The Cold War–era Soviet submarine *Scorpion* resides alongside; separate admission is required to tour the sub. *Tip:* Buy a First Class Passage ticket to both the sub and the ship and you'll also get a behind-the-scenes guided tour, peppered with worthwhile anecdotes and details—well worth the extra $7.

1126 Queen's Hwy. (end of I-710), Long Beach. ℂ 562/435-3511. www.queenmary.com. Admission $23 adults, $20 seniors ages 55 and over and military, $12 children ages 5–11, free for kids under 5. First Class Passage admission $30 adults, $27 seniors ages 55 and over and military, $19 children ages 5–11, free for kids under 5. 10am–6pm daily. Parking $10.

WHERE TO STAY

Hotel Queen Mary ★ (Finds) The *Queen Mary* isn't only a piece of maritime history; it's also a hotel. But although the historic ocean liner is considered the most luxurious vessel ever to sail the Atlantic, with some of the largest rooms built aboard a ship, the quarters aren't exceptional when compared to those on terra firma today, nor are the amenities. The idea is to enjoy the novelty and charm of features such as the original bathtub water faucets ("cold salt," "cold fresh," "hot salt," "hot fresh"). The beautifully carved interior is a feast for the eye and fun to explore, and the weekday rates are hard to beat. Three onboard restaurants are overpriced but convenient, and the shopping arcade has a decidedly British feel (one shop sells great *Queen Mary* souvenirs). An elegant Sunday champagne brunch—complete with ice sculpture and harpist—is served in the ship's Grand Salon, and it's always worthwhile to have a cocktail in the Art Deco Observation Bar. If you're too young to have traveled on the old luxury liners, this is the perfect opportunity to experience the romance of an Atlantic crossing—with no seasickness or cabin fever.

1126 Queen's Hwy. (end of I-710), Long Beach, CA 90802-6390. (C) 562/437-3511. www.queenmary. com. 365 units. Inside cabin from $119; deluxe cabin from $179; suite from $360. Many packages available. AE, DC, MC, V. Valet parking $20; self-parking $12. **Amenities:** 3 restaurants; spa; shopping arcade. *In room:* A/C, TV.

WHERE TO DINE

The Sky Room ★★ CALIFORNIAN/FRENCH   It takes a 40-minute drive from Los Angeles to Long Beach to get a sense of what fine dining must have been like during Hollywood's Golden Age. Built in 1926 and meticulously restored by proprietor Bernard Rosenson, the restaurant's Art Deco–period design inspires oohs and aahs among first-time guests. Awash in brilliant white, the interior's massive pillars, curvaceous ramps, glimmering brass, elevated maple-and-ebony dance floor, and classic jazz band playing enticing dance tunes all combine to create the illusion of dining on a luxury ocean liner (the beautiful view of the stately *Queen Mary* certainly enhances the effect). Opulence continues with white Frette linens, custom black-rimmed china, Villeroy & Boch tableware, and a *Wine Spectator*–award-winning wine list. The Californian/French menu offers a pleasing presentation of the classics: grilled chicken breast in a chanterelle au jus, line-caught salmon with goat cheese pesto, New York steak on a grilled onion brioche. Nothing groundbreaking here, but that's not what the Sky Room is about. I highly recommend that you take the advice of the experienced waitstaff and sommelier; our duo handled the task flawlessly. A night of dinner, drinking, dancing, and romance—what's not to like?

40 S. Locust Ave. (at Ocean Blvd.), Long Beach, CA 90802. (C) 562/983-2703. www.theskyroom.com. Reservations recommended. Dinner main courses $24–$41. AE, DC, DISC, MC, V. Mon–Thurs 5:30–10:30pm; Fri–Sat 5:30pm–midnight. Valet parking $6.

Yard House ★ AMERICAN ECLECTIC   Not only does it have one of the best outdoor dining venues in Long Beach, the Yard House also features one of the *world's* largest selection of draft beers. The keg room houses more than 1,000 gallons of beer, all visible through a glass door where you can see the golden liquids transported to a signature oval bar via miles of nylon tubing to the dozens of taps. The restaurant takes its name from the early Colonial tradition of serving beer in 36-inch-tall glasses—or yards—to weary stagecoach drivers. Customers are encouraged to partake in this tradition and can drink from the glass yards, as well as half-yards and traditional pint glasses. Signature dishes range from the tortelike California roll to the crab cake hoagie and an impressive selection of steaks and chops. There's also an extensive list of appetizers—perfect for a tapas-style meal—salads, pasta, and rice dishes, as well as sandwiches and individual pizzas (the Thai chicken pizza is excellent, as are the crab cakes and coconut-encrusted shrimp). On sunny days, be sure to request a table on the deck overlooking the picturesque harbor.

401 Shoreline Village Dr., Long Beach. (C) 562/628-0455. www.yardhouse.com. Reservations not accepted. Main courses $10–$30. AE, DC, MC, V. Sun–Thurs 11am–11pm; Fri–Sat 11am–1am.

2 SANTA CATALINA ISLAND

22 miles W of mainland Los Angeles

After an unhealthy dose of the mainland's soupy smog and freeway gridlock, you'll appreciate an excursion to Santa Catalina Island, with its clean air, crystal-clear water, and the blissful absence of traffic. In fact, there isn't a single traffic light on "The Island of Romance." Conditions like these can fool you into thinking that you're miles away from the hustle and bustle of the city, but the reality is that you're only 22 miles off the Southern California coast and *still* in L.A. County.

Because of its relative isolation, out-of-state tourists tend to ignore Santa Catalina—which Californians call simply Catalina—but those who do make the crossing have plenty of elbow room to boat, fish, swim, scuba, and snorkel. Despite the miles of hiking and biking trails, plus golf, tennis, and horseback riding, the main sport here seems to be barhopping.

Catalina is so different from the mainland that it almost seems like a different country, remote and unspoiled. In 1919, the island was purchased by William Wrigley, Jr., the chewing-gum magnate, who had plans to develop it into a fashionable pleasure resort. To publicize the new vacationland, Wrigley brought big-name bands to the Avalon Ballroom and moved the Chicago Cubs, which he owned, to the island for spring training. His marketing efforts succeeded and Catalina soon became a world-renowned playground, luring such celebrities as Laurel and Hardy, Cecil B. De Mille, John Wayne, and even Winston Churchill.

In 1975, the Santa Catalina Island Conservancy—a nonprofit operating foundation organized to preserve and protect the island's nature habitat—acquired about 88% of Catalina Island, protecting virtually all of the hilly acreage and rugged coastline that make up what is known as the interior. In fact, some of the most spectacular outlying areas can only be reached by arranged tour (see "Exploring the Island," below).

ESSENTIALS

GETTING THERE   The most common way to get to and from the island is on the **Catalina Express** ferryboat (© **800/481-3470;** www.catalinaexpress.com), which operates up to 30 daily departures year-round from Long Beach, San Pedro, and Dana Point. High-speed catamarans make the trip in about an hour. Captain's and Commodore Lunge upgrades are available. Round-trip fares are $60 for adults, $54 for seniors 55 and over, $47 for children ages 2 to 11, and $4 for infants. Fares for Dana Point are $2 more, except for infants. In San Pedro, the Catalina Express departs from the **Sea/Air Terminal,**

(Fun Facts)   Cart Culture

One of the first things you'll notice when you arrive in Avalon is the abundance of golf carts in a comical array of styles and colors. Since Avalon is the only city in California authorized by the state legislature to regulate the number of vehicles allowed to drive on city streets, there are no rental cars and only a handful of privately owned vehicles.

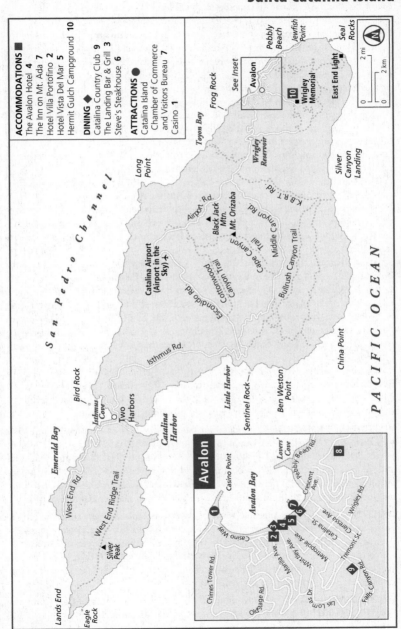

ACCOMMODATIONS ■
The Avalon Hotel **4**
The Inn on Mt. Ada **7**
Hotel Villa Portofino **2**
Hotel Vista Del Mar **5**
Hermit Gulch Campground **10**

DINING ◆
Catalina Country Club **9**
The Landing Bar & Grill **3**
Steve's Steakhouse **6**

ATTRACTIONS ●
Catalina Island
Chamber of Commerce
and Visitors Bureau **7**
Casino **1**

Berth 95; take the Harbor Freeway (I-110) south to the Harbor Boulevard exit, and then follow signs to the terminal. In Long Beach, boats leave from the **Catalina Landing;** take the 710 Freeway south into Long Beach. Stay to the left, follow signs to downtown, and exit Golden Shore. Turn right at the stop sign and follow around to the terminal on the right. Parking is in the parking structure on the left. In Dana Point; boats depart from Dana Wharf Sportfishing. From San Diego, take I-5 North and exit at Beach Cities Hwy 1, left at Dana Point Harbor Drive, and then left at Golden Lantern. Call ahead for reservations. *Note:* Check-in at the ticket window is required and begins 1 hour prior to each departure. Passengers must be checked in, holding tickets, and ready to board 15 minutes prior to departure, or the reservation will be canceled and the credit card will be charged for the full amount of the round-trip fare. Luggage is limited to 70 pounds per person; reservations are necessary for bicycles, surfboards, and dive tanks; and there are restrictions on transporting pets. You can leave your car at designated lots at each departure terminal; the parking fee is around $10 per 24-hour period.

The **Catalina Flyer,** 400 Main St., Balboa (© 949/673-5245; www.catalinainfo. com), the largest passenger-carrying catamaran on the West Coast, departs daily from Newport Beach's historic Balboa Pavilion. The boat leaves once a day at 9am and returns to Newport at 4:30pm daily. Travel time is about 75 minutes each way. Round-trip fares are $61 for adults, $46 for children 3 to 12, $56 for seniors, and $4 for infants. Pets are not allowed.

Island Express Helicopter Service, 1175 Queens Way Dr., Long Beach (© 800/ 2-AVALON or 310/510-2525; www.islandexpress.com), flies from Long Beach or San Pedro to Avalon in about 15 minutes. The expense is definitely worth the thrill and convenience, particularly if you're prone to seasickness. It flies on demand between 8am and sunset year-round, charging $84 plus tax each way, or $162 round-trip. The weight limit for luggage, however, is a mere 25 pounds. It also offers brief air tours over the island; prices vary. In Long Beach, the heliport is located a few hundred yards southwest of the *Queen Mary.*

Catalina Marina del Rey Flyer, 13737 Fiji Way, Suite C, Marina del Rey (© 310/ 305-7250; www.catalinaferries.com), departs from Fisherman's Village at Marina del Rey. Schedule varies. Travel time to Avalon is $1^3/_4$ hours. Round-trip fare is $62 for adults, $53 for children 2 to 11 years old, $64 for seniors, $6 for infants.

VISITOR INFORMATION The **Catalina Island Chamber of Commerce and Visitors Bureau,** P.O. Box 217, Avalon, CA 90704 (© 310/510-1520; fax 310/510-7606; www.CatalinaChamber.com), located on the Green Pleasure Pier, distributes brochures and information on island activities, hotels, and transportation. Call for a free 75-page visitors' guide. Its colorful website, **www.CatalinaChamber.com**, offers hotel availability and local weather, in addition to updated activities, events, and general information.

ORIENTATION The picturesque town of **Avalon** is both the port of entry for the island and the island's only city. From the ferry dock, you can wander along Crescent Avenue, the main road along the beachfront, and easily explore adjacent side streets.

Northwest of Avalon is the village of **Two Harbors,** accessible by boat or shuttle bus. Its twin bays are favored by pleasure yachts from L.A.'s various marinas, so there's more camaraderie and a less touristy ambience overall.

GETTING AROUND Once in Avalon, take a taxi from the **Catalina Cab Company** (© 310/510-0025) from the heliport or dock to your hotel, and enjoy the quick and colorful trip through town (don't blink or you'll miss it). Only a limited number of cars is permitted on the island; visitors are not allowed to drive cars on the island, and most

Catalina's Grand Casino

No trip to Catalina is complete without taking the **Casino Tour** (see "Organized Tours," above). The Casino Building, Avalon's world-famous Art Deco landmark, is not—and never was—a place to gamble your vacation money away (*casino* is an Italian word for a place of entertainment or gathering). Rather, the incredibly ornate structure (the craftsmanship inside and out is spectacular) is home to the island's only movie theater and the world's largest circular ballroom. Virtually every big band in the '30s and '40s played in the 158-foot-diameter ballroom, carried over CBS radio since its grand opening in May 1929. Today it's a coveted venue for elaborate weddings, dances, gala dinners, and the Catalina Jazz Festival. The 3-week **JazzTrax Festival** (*©* **866/872-9849;** www. jazztrax.com) takes place every October. To experience the festival, be sure to book your tickets and accommodations as far in advance as possible.

residents motor around in golf carts (many of the homes only have golf cart–size driveways). Don't worry, though—you'll be able to get everywhere you want to go by renting a cart yourself or just hoofing it, which is what most visitors do.

If you want to explore the area around Avalon beyond where your feet can comfortably carry you, rent a mountain bike or tandem from **Brown's Bikes,** 107 Pebbly Beach Rd. (*©* **310/510-0986**). If you'll be exploring, you'll want to rent a gas-powered golf cart from **Cartopia Golf Cart Rentals** on Crescent Avenue at Pebbly Beach Road (*©* **310/510-2493**), or **Island Rentals** (*©* **310/510-1456**), across from the boat terminal. Both companies offer a map of town for a self-guided tour. Rates are about $45 per hour plus a deposit. You must be 25 or older to drive.

EXPLORING THE ISLAND

ORGANIZED TOURS   The Santa Catalina Island Company's **Discovery Tours** (*©* **800/626-1496** or 310/510-TOUR; www.visitcatalinaisland.com) has a ticket and information office on Crescent Avenue across from the Green Pier. It offers the greatest variety of excursions from Avalon; many last just a couple of hours and don't monopolize your whole day. Tours are available in money-saving combo packs; inquire when you call.

Noteworthy excursions include the new **Cape Canyon** that takes you into the heart of Catalina's "outback" in an open-air 4WD Mercedes Benz Unimog Vehicle. The tour's rugged route includes the American Bald Eagle and Catalina Island Fox habitats at Middle Ranch, lunch at Airport-in-the-Sky, and plenty of photo stops ($99 per adults, $89 for children over the age of 6 years, $89 for seniors, includes lunch); the **Undersea Tour,** a leisurely 45-minute cruise of Lover's Cove Marine Preserve in a semi-submersible vessel that allows you to sit 5 feet under the water in a climate-controlled cabin where you comfortably observe Catalina's kelp forests by day or night ($36 adults, $18 kids, $32 seniors); the **Casino Tour,** a fascinating 1-hour look at the style and inventive engineering of this elegant ballroom (see "Catalina's Grand Casino" box, below; $16 adults, $8 kids, $15 seniors); nighttime **Flying Fish Boat Trips** (seasonal), a 50-minute Catalina tradition in searchlight-equipped open boats ($20 adults, $10 kids, $18 seniors); and the new **Classic Inland Motor Tour,** a 31-mile, 4-hour jaunt through the island's rugged

> **Tips** **Instant Massaging**
>
> After a full day of island activity, why not pamper yourself with a relaxing profes-
> sional massage in the privacy and comfort of your hotel room? Make a reserva-
> tion with **Massage by Michelle** (© 310/510-8920; www.catalinamassageby
> michelle.com) and she'll tote her table and oils to you. Michelle specializes in
> sports, deep tissue, Swedish, Thai, Swede-Thai combo, and pregnancy massage.
> Other treatments include heavenly aromatherapy wraps, sugar glow, body pol-
> ishing, foot scrubs, peppermint scalp massage, couples massages, and lavender
> or honey facial massages. Michelle works in 50- to 80-minute increments, offers
> packages, and caters to groups. If you're just visiting for the day, Michelle offers
> her own pampering facility for you to visit. Prices range from $75 to $125.

interior. The journey follows the 1800's stagecoach trail though Middle Ranch, where
you will enjoy the Native Plant Nursery and the Catalina Island Fox habitat. Continue
on to the beautiful windward shoreline and up to **El Rancho Escondido,** a working
ranch where some of America's finest Arabian horses are raised and trained. Returning to
Avalon, you'll visit the famous Airport-in-the-Sky ($69 adults, $62 seniors, $35 kids).

VISITING TWO HARBORS If you want to get a better look at the rugged natural
beauty of Catalina and escape the throngs of beachgoers, head over to Two Harbors, the
quarter-mile "neck" at the island's northwest end that gets its name from the "twin harbors" on each side, known as the Isthmus and Catalina Harbor. An excellent starting
point for campers and hikers, Two Harbors also offers just enough civilization for the
less-intrepid traveler.

The **Banning House Lodge** (© 800/626-1496; www.VisitTwoHarbors.com) is an
11-room bed-and-breakfast overlooking the Isthmus. The clapboard house was built in
1910 for Catalina's pre-Wrigley owners and has seen duty as on-location lodging for
movie stars such as Errol Flynn and Dorothy Lamour. Peaceful and isolated, the simply
furnished but comfortable lodge has spectacular views of both harbors. Rates range from
$199 to $299 including deluxe continental breakfast (June–Sept), and they'll even give
you a lift from the pier.

Everyone eats at the **Harbor Reef Restaurant** (© 310/510-4215) on the beach. This
nautical, tropical-themed saloon/restaurant serves breakfast, lunch, and dinner, the latter
consisting of hearty steaks, ribs, swordfish, chicken teriyaki, and buffalo burgers in summer. The house drink is sweet "buffalo milk," a potent concoction of vodka, crème de
cacao, banana liqueur, milk, whipped cream, and nutmeg.

WHAT TO SEE & DO IN AVALON Walk along horseshoe-shaped Crescent Avenue,
past private yachting and fishing clubs, toward the landmark **Casino** building. You can
see the Art Deco **theater** for the price of a movie ticket any night. Also on the ground
floor is the **Catalina Island Museum** (© 310/510-2414; www.catalinamuseum.org),
which explores 7,000 years of island history including fascinating exhibits of archaeology,
steamships, big bands, and natural history. The museum has a contour relief map of the
island that's helpful to hikers. Open daily. Admission is $5 for adults, $2 for kids, and $4
for seniors; it's included in the price of Discovery's Casino Tour (see above).

Around the point from the Casino lies **Descanso Beach Club** (© 310/510-7410), a
mini–Club Med in a private cove. While you can get on the beach year-round, the club's

facilities (including showers, restaurant/bar, sandy beach, volleyball lawns, dance area, and thatched beach umbrellas) are only open from Easter to September 30. Admission is $1.50.

About 1¹/₂ miles from downtown Avalon is **Wrigley Memorial and Botanical Garden** (© 310/510-2595). The specialized gardens, a project of Ada Wrigley, showcase plants endemic to California's coastal islands. It's open daily from 8am to 5pm; admission is $5 for adults, free for children under 12.

OUTDOOR ACTIVITIES

BEACHES   Unfortunately, Avalon's beaches leave much to be desired. The town's central beach, located off Crescent Avenue, is small and completely congested in the busy season. Be sure to claim your spot early in the morning before it's full. **Descanso Beach Club** offers the best beach in town but also gets crowded very quickly. Your best bet is to kayak out to a secluded cove where you have the beach virtually to yourself.

DIVING, SNORKELING & SEA KAYAKING ★   Snorkeling, scuba diving, and sea kayaking are among the main reasons mainlanders head to Catalina. Catalina Island's naturally clean water and giant kelp forests teeming with marine life have made it a renowned diving destination that attracts experts and beginning divers alike. **Casino Point Marine Park,** Southern California's first city-designated underwater park, was established in 1965 and is located behind the Casino. Due to its convenient location, it can get outrageously crowded in the summer (just like everything else at that time of year).

Catalina Divers Supply (© 800/353-0330 or 310/510-0330; www.catalinadivers supply.com) runs two full-service dive shops: one from a large trailer behind the Casino at the edge of Avalon's underwater park, where they offer guided snorkeling tours and introductory scuba dives; and another at the Green Pier, where they launch boat dives aboard the *Scuba Cat.* The three best locations for snorkeling are **Lover's Cove Marine Preserve, Casino Point Marine Park,** and **Descanso Beach Club. Catalina Snorkeling Adventures,** at Lover's Cove (© 877/SNORKEL), offers snorkel-gear rental. Snorkeling trips that take you outside of Avalon depart from **Joe's Rent-a-Boat** (© 310/510-0455), on the Green Pier.

At Two Harbors, stop by **West End Dive Center** (© 310/510-4272). Excursions range from half-day introductory dives to complete certification courses and multiday dive packages. It also rents snorkel gear and offers kayak rental, instruction, and tours.

HIKING & BIKING   When the summer crowds become overwhelming, it's time to head on foot for the peacefulness of the interior, where secluded coves and barren, rolling hills soothe frayed nerves. Visitors can obtain a free **hiking permit** at the Conservancy Office (125 Claressa Ave.; © 310/510-2595; www.catalinaconservancy.org), where you'll find maps, wildlife information, and friendly assistance from Conservancy staffers who love to share their knowledge of the interior. It's open daily from 9am to 5pm, and closed for lunch on weekends. Among the sights you may see are the many giant buffalo roaming the hills, scions of movie extras that were left behind in 1929 and have since flourished.

Mountain biking is allowed on the island's designated dirt roads, but requires a $20 permit (valid for 2 consecutive days) or a $60-per-person annual permit ($85 per family) that must be purchased in person at the Conservancy Office.

WHERE TO STAY

If you plan to stay overnight, be sure to reserve a room in advance because most places fill up quickly during the summer and holiday seasons. There are only a handful of hotels whose accommodations and amenities actually justify the rates that they charge. Some are downright scary, so book as far in advance as possible to get a room that makes the trip worthwhile. Don't stress too much over your accommodations, as you'll probably spend most of your time outdoors. Keep in mind that the best time to visit is in September or October when the water is warm, the crowds have somewhat subsided, and hotel occupancy is easier to come by. If you're having trouble finding a vacancy, try calling the Catalina Chamber of Commerce & Visitors Bureau ($ 310/510-1520); they keep daily tabs on last-minute cancellations.

Very Expensive

The Inn on Mt. Ada ★★   When William Wrigley, Jr., purchased Catalina Island in 1921, he built this ornate hilltop Georgian Colonial mansion as his summer vacation home; it's now one of the finest small hotels in California. The opulent inn—considered to be the best in town for its luxury accommodations and views—has several ground-floor salons, a club room with a fireplace, a deep-seated formal library, and a wickered sunroom where tea, cookies, and fruit are always available. The best guest room is the Grand Suite, fitted with a fireplace and a large private patio. Amenities include bathrobes and the use of a golf cart during your stay. TVs are in the rooms, but there are no phones. A hearty full breakfast, a light deli-style lunch, appetizers, fresh fruit, freshly baked cookies, soft drinks, beers, wines, and champagne are included in the rate. *Tip:* Even if you find that they're sold out or too pricey to fit your budget, make a lunch reservation and enjoy amazing views from the Inn's spectacular balcony.

398 Wrigley Rd. (P.O. Box 2560), Avalon, CA 90704. $ **800/608-7669** or 310/510-2030. Fax 310/510-2237. www.innonmtada.com. 6 units. Nov–April Mon–Thurs $350–$520 double, $605 suite; May–Oct and Fri–Sun year-round $390–$605 double, $730 suite. Rates include 2 meals daily. AE, MC, V. **Amenities:** Courtesy car; complimentary golf cart. *In room:* TV, hair dryer, iron, no phone.

Expensive

The Avalon Hotel   Catalina's newest boutique hotel is all about the details. The lot was originally developed at the turn of the last century as the Pilgrim Club, a gentleman's club that vanished in the great fire of 1915. After many incarnations, the dilapidated property was acquired in 2003 by locals Rock and Kathleen Gosselin and partner Carl Lambert, who have transformed it into one of the island's most luxurious hideaways. The cozy Craftsman-style hotel is decked out in rich, hand-carved mahogany and imported slate tastefully accented with handmade tile and local artwork. Catalina's silhouette is artfully etched into the slate, stained glass, and light fixtures, while shadowboxes showcase island memorabilia throughout the hotel's homey public space. Guest rooms, which come in a variety of sizes, feature local artwork, garden or ocean views (some with balconies), gleaming white bathrooms with natural skin-care products, fresh flowers, and an incredibly comfy queen- or king-size Supple-Pedic memory foam bed.

124 Whittley Ave. (P.O. Box 706), Avalon, CA 90704. $ **310/510-7070.** www.theavalonhotel.com. 15 units. Mid-Nov to mid-Mar and Mon–Thurs year-round $195–$395 double; mid-June to mid-Sept and Fri–Sun year-round $295–$495 double. Rates include continental breakfast, complimentary taxi pickup from the boat or helicopter, nightly turndown, wine and cheese service. AE, MC, V. **Amenities:** Rooftop deck w/360-degree views; garden patio w/fountain; laptops and DVDs to borrow at front desk. *In room:* Flatscreen TV/DVD, high-speed Internet, fridge w/refreshments, coffeemaker, hair dryer, microwave.

Moderate

Hotel Villa Portofino ★   Enjoy European elegance on the ocean front from your courtyard room or deluxe suite after a warm welcome from the hotel's efficient and friendly staff. The hotel boasts recently renovated rooms and a spacious rooftop deck

> **Tips** **For Travelers Who Use Wheelchairs**
>
> Visitors who use wheelchairs should request a room at **Hotel Metropole**
> (© **800/300-8528** or 310/510-1884). One of the most modern properties in
> Avalon, it has an elevator, a large sun deck that overlooks Avalon Bay, a shopping
> complex, and a very convenient location in the heart of Avalon.

overlooking the bay that is perfect for people-watching, sunbathing, cocktail sipping, or just enjoying the fantastic view. Some rooms have luxurious touches such as fireplaces, balconies, deep soaking tubs, and separate showers. The hotel is just steps away from the beach, shops, and sights.

111 Crescent Ave. (P.O. Box 127), Avalon, CA 90704. © **888/510-0555** or 310/510-0555. Fax 310/510-0839. www.hotelvillaportofino.com. 35 units. May–Oct $187–$249 double, from $335 suite; winter $95–$160 double, from $235 suite. Rates include continental breakfast, beach towels, and chairs. AE, DC, MC, V. **Amenities:** Award-winning restaurant; adjacent art gallery. *In room:* A/C, TV, fridge, coffeemaker, hair dryer, iron.

Hotel Vista Del Mar   The hotel's location smack-dab in the middle of town; lush, open-aired atrium garden courtyard; gigantic fish tank; freshly baked cookies and milk each evening; and friendly staff make it an island favorite for families and couples alike. The oceanview suites with double-Jacuzzi tubs are fantastic but hard to secure, as the only two are booked by regulars almost year-round.

417 Crescent Ave. (P.O. Box 1979), Avalon, CA 90704. © **310/510-1452.** www.hotel-vistadelmar.com. 15 units. May–Oct $125–$350 double; Nov–Apr $105–$300 double. Winter discounts and midweek rates available. Rates include continental breakfast and freshly baked cookies and milk in the evening. AE, DISC, MC, V. **Amenities:** Atrium courtyard w/sitting area; balcony w/harbor views; Free Wi-Fi; baggage storage facility. *In room:* A/C, TV/VCR, wet bar w/fridge, coffeemaker, Jacuzzi, fireplace.

Inexpensive

Our recommended choices for inexpensive lodgings are **Pavilion Lodge** (© **800/414-2754** or 310/510-2500; www.visitcatalinaisland.com), which recently completed an extensive renovation on all guest rooms, which are basic but affordable and clean (a great alternative when budgets and availability are tight); **Hotel Catalina** (© **800/540-0184** or 310/510-0027; www.hotelcatalina.com), a well-maintained Victorian-style hotel just a half-block from the beach, with tons of charm, family cottages, a courtyard with beautiful stained glass, and large verandas with bay views; **Zane Grey** (© **310/510-0966;** www.zanegreypueblohotel.com), a Hopi-style pueblo built in 1926 and former home of American author Zane Grey, situated above town and equipped with a cozy living room with fireplace and piano, free shuttle service, and a swimming pool; and **Hermit Gulch Campground** (© **310/510-8368;** www.visitcatalinaisland.com), Avalon's only campground, which can be crowded and noisy in peak season. Campsites can be tough to secure, especially when hotels are booked, so it's a good idea to make reservations in advance. The walk to town and back can be draining, so hop on the red trolley that runs you back and forth to town for a couple dollars each way.

WHERE TO DINE

Along with the choices below, recommended Avalon options include the **Busy Bee** on Crescent Avenue (© **310/510-1983**), an always-crowded waterfront diner with a heated and wind-protected patio. On the Two Harbors side of the island, the **Harbor Reef Restaurant** is the place to eat; see "Exploring the Island," above.

Expensive

Catalina Country Club ★ CALIFORNIA   You'll find some of Avalon's most elegant meals at this landmark Catalina Country Club, whose stylish Spanish-Mediterranean clubhouse was built by William Wrigley, Jr., during the 1920s. Recently restored, it exudes a chic and historical atmosphere; the menu is peppered with archival photos and vintage celebrity anecdotes. Sit outdoors in an elegant tiled Fountain Terrace courtyard, or inside the intimate, exquisite dining room. The executive chef infuses new American cuisine with creative influences from around the world, using only the finest free-range, organic meats, fresh produce, and seafood from environmentally sensitive fisheries. The Club is only a few minutes from the waterfront, but it's uphill, so shuttle service is available from Island Plaza (on Sumner Ave.) on weekends.

1 Country Club Dr. (above Sumner Ave.). ℂ **310/510-7404.** Reservations recommended. Main courses $9–$18 lunch, $26–$35 dinner. AE, DISC, MC, V. Daily 11:30am–2:30pm and 5–9pm (closing hour will vary seasonally).

Moderate

The Landing Bar and Grill AMERICAN   With a secluded and heated deck overlooking the harbor, the Landing is one of the most romantic dining spots in Avalon. It boasts beautiful Spanish-style architecture located in the historic El Encanto Center that manages to attract as many jeans-clad vacationers as dressed-up islanders. The menu is enticing, with local seafood offerings, pasta, Mexican cuisine, and gourmet pizzas that can be delivered to your hotel room if you wish.

Intersection of Crescent and Marilla. ℂ **310/510-1474.** Reservations recommended. Main courses $11–$22. AE, DISC, MC, V. Daily 11am–3pm and 4–10pm (subject to changes in winter).

Steve's Steakhouse AMERICAN   Step up above the busy bayside promenade into a fantastic collage of museum-quality photos capturing the Avalon of old. This setting overlooking Avalon Bay feels just right for the hearty menu of steaks, seafood, and pasta—all of which can be ordered from the full bar as well as the dining room. Catalina swordfish is their specialty, along with excellent cuts of meat. You can also make a respectable repast from the many appetizer selections, especially the fresh oysters and sashimi.

417 Crescent Ave. (directly across from the Green Pier, upstairs). ℂ **310/510-0333.** Reservations recommended on weekends. Main courses $7–$15 lunch, $15–$32 dinner. AE, DISC, MC, V. Daily 11am–3pm and 5–10pm.

Inexpensive

Note: Street addresses are useless in a town as small as Avalon, but all these restaurants are near each other on the main strip. Our three favorites for a low-bucks meal are **Rosie's Fish and Chips** (ℂ **310/510-0197**), on the Green Pier, which serves fresh seafood favorites such as fish and chips and seafood cocktails; **Casino Dock Café** (ℂ **310/510-2755**), with live summertime entertainment, marina views from the sun-drenched deck, breakfast burritos loaded with homemade salsa, and kicking Bloody Marys; and **Lori's Good Stuff** (ℂ **310/510-2489**), a tiny spot with fresh, healthy sandwiches, smoothies, and milkshakes—the best around.

Avalon doesn't have listed street addresses, but all these bars are within stumbling distance of each other on the main drag. The **Chi Chi Club** (✆ **310/510-2828**), the "noisy bar in Avalon" referred to in Crosby, Stills, and Nash's song "Southern Cross," is the island's only dance club and quite a scene on summer weekend evenings—the DJ spins an eclectic mixture of dance tunes. **Luau Larry's** (✆ **310/510-1919**) is Avalon's signature bar that everyone must visit; its tacky Tiki theme and signature Wicky Wack drink kicks you into island mode as soon as you step inside—sure to stumble out. Or go where the locals go and swill beers at the **Marlin Club** (✆ **310/510-0044**), Avalon's oldest drinking hole; catch the Dodgers game at **J. L.'s Locker Room** (✆ **310/510-0258**); and recover from your hangover with a spicy Bloody Mary at the rustic bar inside the **Busy Bee** (✆ **310/510-1983**).

SHOPPING

Don't worry—you won't have any trouble finding that must-have Catalina key chain or refrigerator magnet, as Crescent Avenue is lined with a myriad of schlocky souvenir shops. There are, however, a few stores that do offer unique and tasteful items. **C. C. Gallagher** (✆ **310/510-1278**) carries high-end gifts and also is a flower and coffee shop; they're best for finding beautiful art, music, and jewelry created by local artists. For colorful handmade pottery, stop by **Chet's Hardware** (✆ **310/510-0990**), in the Arcade—an arched shopping annex that connects Sumner and Metropole avenues. **Latitude 33** (✆ **310/510-0802**) is the place to get your vintage aloha shirts, shorts, hats, and sandals. **Buoys and Gulls** (✆ **310/510-0416**) offers men's and women's wear such as Nautica, Reyn Spooner islander shirts, Hurley, and Billabong. **The Steamer Trunk** (✆ **310/510-2600**) is loaded with unique gifts to take home to the dog-sitter or neighbor who collected your mail. **Leo's Drugstore** (✆ **310/510-0189**) is the obvious spot to pick up the sunscreen that you forgot to pack. **Von's,** located on Metropole Avenue in the center of town, and Von's Express on Catalina Avenue, are Avalon's main grocery stores where you'll find all your food staples.

3 BIG BEAR LAKE & LAKE ARROWHEAD

100 miles NE of downtown L.A.

These two deep-blue lakes, close to one another in the San Bernardino mountains, have long been favorite year-round alpine playgrounds for city-weary Angelenos.

Big Bear Lake is popular with skiers as well as boaters (it's much larger than Arrowhead, and equipment rentals abound), and in the past decade the area has received a much-needed face-lift. Big Bear Boulevard was widened to handle high-season traffic, and downtown Big Bear Lake (the "Village") was spiffed up but retains its woodsy charm. In addition to two excellent ski slopes less than 5 minutes from town, you can enjoy the comforts of a real supermarket and several video-rental shops, all especially convenient if you're staying in a cabin. Most people choose Big Bear over Arrowhead because there's so much more to do, from boating, fishing, and hiking to snow sports, mountain biking, and horseback riding. The weather is nearly always perfect at this 7,000-foot-plus elevation: If you want proof, ask CalTech, which operates a solar observatory here to take advantage of nearly 300 days of sunshine per year.

Lake Arrowhead has always been privately owned, as is apparent from the affluence of the surrounding homes, many of which are gated estates rather than rustic mountain

612 cabins. The lake and the private docks lining its shores are reserved for the exclusive use of homeowners, but visitors can enjoy Lake Arrowhead by boat tour or use of the summer-season beach clubs, a privilege included in nearly all private-home rentals. Reasons to choose a vacation at Lake Arrowhead? The roads up are less grueling than the winding ascent to Big Bear Lake and, being at a lower elevation, Arrowhead gets little snow (you can forget those pesky tire chains). It's very easy and cost effective to rent a luxurious house from which to enjoy the spectacular scenery, crisp mountain air, and relaxed resort atmosphere—and if you do ski, the slopes are only a half-hour away.

ESSENTIALS

GETTING THERE   Lake Arrowhead is reached by taking Highway 18 from San Bernardino. The last segment of this route takes you along the aptly named **Rim of the World Highway,** with its breathtaking view over the valley on clear days. Highway 18 then continues east to Big Bear Lake, but to get to Big Bear Lake, it's quicker to bypass Arrowhead by taking Highway 330 from Redlands, which meets Highway 18 in Running Springs. During heavy-traffic periods, it can be worthwhile to take scenic Highway 38, which winds up from Redlands through mountain passes and valleys to approach Big Bear from the other side.

Note: Nostalgia lovers can revisit legendary **Route 66** on the way from Los Angeles to the mountain resorts, substituting scenic motor courts and other relics of the "Mother Road" in place of impersonal I-10. For a complete driving tour, see "Get Your Kicks on Historic Route 66" in chapter 16.

VISITOR INFORMATION   National ski tours, mountain-bike races, and one of Southern California's largest Oktoberfest gatherings are just some of the events held year-round. Contact the **Big Bear Lake Resort Association,** 630 Bartlett Rd., Big Bear Lake Village (© **800/4-BIG-BEAR** or 909/866-7000; www.bigbearinfo.com), for schedules and information. They also provide information on sightseeing and lodging and will send you a free visitors guide.

In Lake Arrowhead, contact the **Lake Arrowhead Communities Chamber of Commerce** (© **800/337-3716** for the Lodging Information Line, or 909/337-3715; www.lakearrowhead.net). The visitor center is in the Lake Arrowhead Village lower shopping center.

ORIENTATION   The south shore of Big Bear Lake was the first resort area to be developed here and remains the most densely populated. Highway 18 passes first through the city of Big Bear Lake and its downtown village; then, as Big Bear Boulevard, it continues east to Big Bear City, which is more residential and suburban. Highway 38 traverses the north shore, home to pristine national forest and great hiking trails, as well as a couple of small marinas and a lakefront bed-and-breakfast inn (see the Windy Point Inn on p. 617).

Arrowhead's main town is Lake Arrowhead Village, on the south shore at the end of Highway 173. The village's commercial center is home to factory-outlet stores, about 40 chain and specialty shops, and the Lake Arrowhead Resort (p. 618). Minutes away is the town of Blue Jay (along Hwy. 189), where the Blue Jay Ice Castle skating rink is located (see "Winter Fun," below).

ENJOYING THE OUTDOORS

For up-to-date info on what outdoor activities are available in the region, call the **Big Bear Mountain Resorts Activities** hot line at © **909/866-5766,** or log on to their website at www.bigbearmountainresorts.com.

CALIFORNIA
Map Area □
Sacramento
San Francisco
Los Angeles

N

Ski Area

5 mi
5 km

18

Moonridge
Bear Mountain Ski Resort
Big Bear Lake
Snow Summit Ski Area
Fawnskin
Snow Valley Ski Area
38
Big Air Snowboard Park
Running Springs
18
Green Valley Lake
North Shore
Lake Arrowhead
Twin Peaks
Blue Jay
Lake Gregory
Dogwood
Crestline
Cedarpines Park
Rim of the World
330
San Manuel Indian Reservation
Waterman Canyon
206
18
215
SAN BERNARDINO MTNS.
NATIONAL
FOREST
Forest Falls
38
38
Redlands
10
Highland
30
Loma Linda

SAN BERNARDINO

Miller Canyon
Silverwood Lake
SILVERWOOD LAKE STATE REC. AREA
138
Barstow Fwy.
Glen Helen Regional Park
15
30
Colton
Rialto
Bloomington
Fontana
66
10
138

Santa Fe Trail 1849 Monument
15

SAN GABRIEL MTNS.
Day Canyon
CUCAMONGA WILDERNESS
138
Mt. Baldy Ski Area

SAN
BERNARDINO

LOS ANGELES CO.
SAN BERNARDINO CO.
Mt. Baldy Rd
Holiday Hill Ski Area

Rancho Cucamonga
Ontario Int'l Airport
Upland
Ontario
Mission Blvd.
Ontario Blvd.
Central Ave.
10

In addition to the activities described below, there's a great recreation spot for families near the heart of Big Bear Lake: **Alpine Slide at Magic Mountain,** 800 Wildrose Lane (© 909/866-4626; www.alpineslidebigbear.com), has a year-round bobsled-style Alpine Slide, a splashy double water slide open from mid-June to mid-September, and bunny slopes for snow tubing from November to Easter. The dry Alpine Slide is $4 a ride, the water slide is $1 (or $12 for a day pass), and snow play costs $22 per day including tube and rope tow.

Watersports

BOATING   You can rent all kinds of boats—including speedboats, rowboats, paddleboats, pontoons, sailboats, and canoes—at a number of Big Bear Lake marinas. Rates vary only slightly from place to place: A 14-foot dinghy with an outboard runs around $20 to $25 per hour; pontoon (patio) boats that can hold large groups range in size and price from $75 to $90 per hour or $170 to $225 for a half-day. **Pine Knot Landing** (© 909/866-2628) is the most centrally located marina, behind the post office at the foot of Pine Knot Boulevard in Big Bear Lake. **Big Bear Marina,** 500 Paine Rd. at Lakeview (© 909/866-3218; www.bigbearmarina.com), is close to Big Bear Lake Village and also rents a variety of watercraft. **Gray's Landing,** 38515 North Shore Dr. (© 909/866-2443), is on the western side of the lake.

FISHING   Big Bear Lake brims with rainbow trout, bass, and catfish in spring and summer, the best fishing seasons. Pine Knot Landing, Gray's Landing, and Big Bear Marina (see "Boating," above) all rent fishing boats and have bait-and-tackle shops that sell licenses.

JET-SKIING, WATER-SKIING & WAKE BOARDING   Personal water craft (PWCs) are available for rent at **Big Bear Marina** (see "Boating," above) and **North Shore Landing,** on Highway 38, 2 miles west of Fawnskin (© 909/878-4-FUN; www.800bigbear. com), rents jet skis and two- and three-person WaveRunners at rates ranging from $90 to $115 per hour plus gas. Call ahead to reserve your craft and check age and deposit requirements.

Other Warm-Weather Activities

GOLF   The **Bear Mountain Golf Course,** Goldmine Drive, Big Bear Lake (© 909/585-8002; www.bigbearmountainresorts.com), is a 9-hole, par-35, links-style course that winds through a gently sloping meadow at the base of the Bear Mountain Ski Resort. The course is open daily April through November. Weekend greens fees are $30 and $45 for 9 and 18 holes, respectively. Both riding carts and pull carts are available. Call ahead for tee times.

HIKING   Hikers love the **San Bernardino National Forest.** The gray squirrel is a popular native so you may see them scurrying around gathering acorns or material for their nests. You can sometimes spot deer, coyotes, and American bald eagles, which come here with their young in winter. The black-crowned Steller's jay and the talkative red, white, and black acorn woodpecker are the most common of the great variety of birds in this pine forest.

The best choice for a short mountain hike is the **Woodland Trail,** which begins near the ranger station. The best long hike is a section of the **Pacific Crest Trail,** which travels 39 miles through the mountains above Big Bear and Arrowhead lakes. The most convenient trail head is located at Cougar Crest, half a mile west of the Big Bear Ranger Station.

The best place to begin a hike in Lake Arrowhead is at the **Arrowhead Ranger Station** (© **909/337-2444**), in the town of Skyforest on Highway 18, a quarter mile east of the Lake Arrowhead turnoff (Hwy. 173). The staff will provide you with maps and information on the best area trails, which range from easy to difficult. The **Enchanted Loop Trail,** near the town of Blue Jay, is an easy half-hour hike. The **Heaps Peak Arboretum Trail** winds through a grove of redwoods; the trail head is on the north side of Highway 18, at an auxiliary ranger kiosk west of Running Springs.

The area is home to a **National Children's Forest,** a 20-acre area developed so that children, people in wheelchairs, and the visually impaired can enjoy nature. To get to the Children's Forest from Lake Arrowhead, take Highway 330 to Highway 18 east, past Deer Lick Station; when you reach a road marked IN96 (open only in summer), turn right and go 3 miles.

HORSEBACK RIDING   **Baldwin Lake Stables,** southeast of Big Bear City (© **909/585-6482;** www.baldwinlakestables.com), conducts hourly, lunch break, and sunset rides along a wide variety of terrains and trails—all with spectacular vistas—including the Pacific Crest Trail, which includes expansive views of the Mojave Desert. It's open year-round.

MOUNTAIN BIKING   Big Bear Lake has become a mountain-biking center, with most of the action around the Snow Summit ski area (see "Winter Fun," below), where a $15 lift ticket will take you and your bike to a web of trails, fire roads, and meadows at about 8,000 feet. The lake's north shore is also a popular destination; the forest-service ranger stations (see "Hiking," above) have maps to the historic Gold Rush–era Holcomb Valley and the 2-mile Alpine Pedal Path (an easy lakeside ride).

Bear Valley Bikes, 40298 Big Bear Blvd. (© **909/866-8000**), rents quality mountain bikes for about $15 an hour or $65 a day. At Lake Arrowhead, bikes are permitted on all hiking trails and back roads except the Pacific Crest Trail. See the local ranger station for an area map. Visitors can rent gear from the **Lake Arrowhead Resort** (© **909/336-1511**) or **Above & Beyond Sports,** 32877 Hwy. 18, Running Springs (© **909/867-5517**).

Winter Fun

ICE-SKATING   The **Blue Jay Ice Castle,** at North Bay Road and Highway 189 (© **909/337-0802;** www.icecastle.us), near Lake Arrowhead Village, was a training site for world champion Michelle Kwan, and boasts Olympic gold medalist Robin Cousins on its staff. Several public sessions each day—as well as hockey, broomball, group lessons, and private parties—give nonpros a chance to enjoy this impeccably groomed "outdoor" rink, open on three sides to the scenery and fresh air.

SKIING & SNOWBOARDING   When the L.A. basin gets wintertime rain, skiers rejoice, for they know snow is falling up in the mountains. The last few seasons have seen abundant natural snowfall at Big Bear, augmented by snowmaking equipment. While the slopes can't compare with those in Utah or Colorado, they do offer diversity, difficulty, and convenience.

Snow Summit at Big Bear Lake (© **909/866-5766;** www.bigbearmountainresorts. com) is the skiers' choice, especially because it installed its second high-speed quad express from the 7,000-foot base to the 8,200-foot summit. There are also green (easy) runs, even from the summit, so beginners can also enjoy the Summit Haus lodge and breathtaking lake views from the top. Advanced risk-takers will appreciate three double black-diamond runs. The resort offers midweek, beginner, half-day, night, and family specials, as well as ski and snowboard instruction. Other helpful Snow Summit phone numbers include advance lift-ticket sales (© **909/866-5841**), and a snow report (© **800/BEAR-MTN**).

The **Bear Mountain Resort** at Big Bear Lake (℗ **909/866-5766;** www.bigbearmountain resorts.com) has the largest beginner area, but experts flock to the double-black-diamond Geronimo run from the 8,805-foot Bear Peak. Natural-terrain skiers and snowboarders will enjoy legal access to off-trail canyons, but the limited beginner slopes and kids' areas get pretty crowded in season. One of two high-speed quad expresses rises from the 7,140-foot base to 8,440-foot Goldmine Mountain; most runs from here are intermediate. Bear Mountain has a ski-and-snowboard school, abundant dining facilities, and a well-stocked ski shop.

The **Snow Valley Ski Resort** in Arrowbear, midway between Arrowhead and Big Bear (℗ **909/867-2751;** www.snow-valley.com), has improved its snowmaking and facilities to compete with the other two major ski areas, and it's the primary choice of skiers staying at Arrowhead. From a base elevation of 6,800 feet, Snow Valley's 13 chairlifts (including five triples) can take you from the beginner runs all the way up to black-diamond challenges at the 7,898-foot peak. Children's programs, night skiing, and lesson packages are also available.

Organized Tours

LAKE TOURS The *Big Bear Queen* (℗ **909/866-3218;** www.bigbearmarina.com), a small version of a Mississippi-style paddle-wheeler, cruises Big Bear Lake on 90-minute tours daily from late April to the end of November. The boat departs from Big Bear Marina (at the end of Paine Ave.). Tours are $15 for adults, $14 for seniors 65 and older, $9 for children ages 3 to 12, and free for kids under 3. Call for reservations and information on the special Sunday brunch, champagne sunset, and dinner cruises.

Fifty-minute tours of Lake Arrowhead are available year-round on the *Arrowhead Queen* (℗ **909/336-6992**), a sister ship that departs hourly each day between 10am and 6pm from Lake Arrowhead Village. Tours are $15 for adults, $13 for seniors, $10 for children 3 to 12, and free for kids under 3. It's about the only way to really see this alpine jewel, unless you know a resident with a boat.

WHERE TO STAY
Big Bear Lake

Vacation rentals are plentiful in the area, from cabins to condos to private homes. Some can accommodate up to 20 people and can be rented on a weekly or monthly basis. For a wide range of rental properties, all pictured in detail online, contact the **Village Reservation Service** (℗ **800/693-0018** or 909/866-9689; www.villagereservations.net), which can arrange for everything from condos to lakefront homes, or call the **Big Bear Lake Resort Association** (℗ **800/4-BIG-BEAR;** www.bigbear.com) for referrals on all types of lodgings.

Besides the places below, I also recommend **Apples Bed & Breakfast Inn,** 42430 Moonridge Rd. (℗ **909/866-0903;** www.applesbedandbreakfast.com), a crabapple-red New England–style clapboard that blends hotel-like professionalism with B&B amenities (and lots of frilly touches); and **Gold Mountain Manor,** 1117 Anita Ave. (℗ **800/509-2604** or 909/585-6997; www.goldmountainmanor.com), a woodsy 1920s lodge that's now an ultracozy, affordable B&B.

Best Western Big Bear Chateau (Kids) This European-flavored property is one of only two traditional full-service hotels in Big Bear. Its location—just off Big Bear Boulevard at the base of the road to Bear Mountain—makes the Chateau a popular choice for skiers and families (kids 17 and under stay free in their parent's room, and there are also children's activities). The rooms are modern but more charming than your average Best

Western, with tapestries, brass beds, antique furniture, gas fireplaces, and marble bath- **617** rooms with heated towel racks and many with whirlpool tubs. The compound is surrounded by tall forest. Le Bistro restaurant (which provides room service) is advertised as "casually elegant," meaning you can dine on upscale California cuisine in après-ski duds.

42200 Moonridge Rd. (P.O. Box 1814), Big Bear Lake, CA 92315. **℃ 800/780-7234** or 909/866-6666. Fax 909/866-8988. www.bestwestern.com. 80 units. Winter $109–$190 double; summer $99–$170 double. Children 17 and under stay free in parent's room. Extra person $10. Winter-ski and summer-fun packages available. AE, DISC, MC, V. **Amenities:** Restaurant; lounge; heated outdoor pool; Jacuzzi; children's activities; limited room service. *In room:* A/C, TV, coffeemaker, hair dryer, iron.

Grey Squirrel Resort (Kids)
This is the most attractive of the many cabin-cluster-type motels near the city of Big Bear Lake, offering a wide range of rustic cabins, most with fireplace and kitchen. They're adequately, if not attractively, furnished—the appeal is the flexibility and privacy afforded large or long-term parties. Facilities include a heated pool that's enclosed in winter, a fire pit and barbecues, volleyball and basketball courts, and completely equipped kitchens.

39372 Big Bear Blvd., Big Bear Lake, CA 92315. **℃ 800/381-5569** or 909/866-4335. Fax 909/866-6271. www.greysquirrel.com. 18 cabins. $94–$151 1-bedroom cabin; $138–$160 2-bedroom cabin; $187–$239 3-bedroom cabin. Value rates available; higher rates on holidays. AE, DISC, MC, V. Pets accepted with $10-per-day fee. **Amenities:** Heated indoor/outdoor pool; Jacuzzi; coin-op laundry. *In room:* TV/DVD, free Wi-Fi, kitchen (some units), fireplace, microwave.

Knickerbocker Mansion Country Inn ★
Innkeepers Thomas Bicanic and Stan Miller faced quite a task reviving this landmark log house; when they moved in, it was empty of all furnishings and suffered from years of neglect. But Knickerbocker Mansion has risen to become the most charming and sophisticated inn on the lake's south side; chef Bicanic, who honed his craft in L.A.'s culinary temple Patina restaurant, even has plans to begin serving intimate gourmet dinners. The pair scoured antiques stores in Big Bear and Los Angeles for vintage furnishings, creating a warm and relaxing ambience in the grand-yet-quirky, house of legendary local character Bill Knickerbocker, who assembled it by hand almost 90 years ago. Today's guest rooms are a cedar-paneled dream, with luxury bed linens, cozy bathrobes, modern marble bathrooms with deluxe Australian showerheads, and refreshing mountain views. After Bicanic's memorable breakfast, you can spend the day relaxing on veranda rockers or garden hammocks; Big Bear's village is also an easy walk away.

869 Knickerbocker Rd. (P.O. Box 1907), Big Bear Lake, CA 92315. **℃ 877/423-1180** or 909/878-9190. Fax 909/878-4248. www.knickerbockermansion.com. 8 units. $140–$170 double; $240 suite. Rates include full breakfast, refreshments, and snacks. AE, DISC, MC, V. *In room:* TV/VCR/DVD, hair dryer, iron.

Windy Point Inn ★
A contemporary architectural showpiece on the scenic north shore, the Windy Point is the only shorefront B&B in Big Bear; ergo, all guest rooms have a view of the lake. Hosts Val and Kent Kessler's attention to detail is impeccable: If you're tired of knotty pine and Victorian frills, here's a grown-up place for you, with plenty of romance and all the pampering you can stand. Every room has a wood-burning fireplace, feather bed, private deck, and DVD player (guests may borrow DVDs from the inn's plentiful collection); some also feature whirlpool tubs and luxurious state-of-the-art bathrooms. The welcoming great room features a casual sunken fireplace nook with floor-to-ceiling windows overlooking the lake, a telescope for stargazing, a baby grand, and up-to-date menus for every local restaurant. You might not want to leave the cocoon of your room after Kent's custom gourmet breakfast, but if you do, you'll find a wintertime bald eagle

habitat just up the road, and the city of Big Bear Lake is only a 10-minute drive around the lake.

39015 N. Shore Dr., Fawnskin, CA 92333. © **909/866-2746.** Fax 909/866-1593. www.windypointinn.com. 5 units. $145–$265 double. Rates include welcome cookies, full breakfast, and afternoon hors d'oeuvres. Midweek discounts available. AE, DISC, MC, V. *In room:* TV/DVD, fridge, coffeemaker, hair dryer, CD player (some units), no phone.

Lake Arrowhead

Arrowhead has far more private homes than tourist accommodations, but rental properties abound, from cozy cottages to mansions; many can be economical for families or other groups. Two of the largest agencies are **Arrowhead Cabin Rentals** (© **800/244-5138** or 909/337-2403; www.arrowheadrent.com) and **Arrowhead Mountain Resorts Rentals** (© **800/743-0865** or 909/337-4413; www.lakearrowheadrentals.com). Overnight guests in rentals enjoy some resident lake privileges—ask when you reserve.

Two other options are **Chateau du Lac,** 911 Hospital Rd. (© **909/337-6488;** www.chateau-du-lac.com), an elegant and contemporary five-room B&B with stunning views of the lake; and the **Saddleback Inn,** 300 S. Hwy. 173 (© **800/858-3334** or 909/336-3571; www.saddlebackinn.com), an inn and restaurant that still boasts historic charm while offering up-to-date amenities, all at a prime location in the center of the village.

Bracken Fern Manor ★ (Finds) A half mile north of Highway 18, this "House of Now Fine Repute" is equally proud of its registered historical marker *and* its checkered past. The present owners work hard at evoking the inn's 1930s heyday: They've preserved the downstairs public rooms, along with many well-maintained antiques, and named each guest room for one of the "girls." There are many quiet corners for relaxing, including a game room, hidden library, whirlpool gazebo, and wood-lined sauna. Rooms are decorated in a fresh country style with private bathrooms. A detached cottage sleeps four and rents for $450 for 2 nights.

815 Arrowhead Villas Rd. (P.O. Box 1006), Lake Arrowhead, CA 92352. © **888/244-5612** or 909/337-8557. Fax 909/337-3323. www.brackenfernmanor.com. 10 units. $90–$225 double. Rates include full breakfast. MC, V. **Amenities:** Jacuzzi; sauna. *In room:* No phone.

Lake Arrowhead Resort & Spa ★★ (Kids) A $17-million resort-wide transformation greatly improved every part of this sprawling resort—including a new full-service **Spa of the Pines** and **Bin 189** restaurant—but its location is still its most outstanding feature. On the lakeshore adjacent to Lake Arrowhead Village, the hotel has its own beach, plus docks that are ideal for fishing. The newly renovated rooms are decked out with 32-inch swiveling flat-panel TVs, Essentiel Elements body and hair care products, and Anichini linens; most have balconies, king-size beds, and fireplaces as well. The suites, some in private cottages, are equipped with full kitchens and whirlpool tubs. The hotel caters primarily to groups and sports a businesslike ambience during the week, but you'll spend most of your time on the beach anyway. A full program of supervised children's activities, ranging from nature hikes to T-shirt painting, is offered on weekends year-round.

27984 Hwy. 189, Lake Arrowhead, CA 92352. © **800/800-6792** or 909/336-1511. Fax 909/744-3088. www.laresort.com. 173 units. $179–$349 double; $309–$785 suite. AE, DC, DISC, MC, V. **Amenities:** 2 restaurants; outdoor pool (summer only); 2 lit rooftop tennis courts; health club; Jacuzzi; children's programs; video arcade; business center; high-speed Internet access; salon; babysitting; laundry service; dry cleaning. *In room:* A/C, flat-panel TV w/pay movies, minibar, coffeemaker, hair dryer.

Pine Rose Cabins ★ (Kids) Pine Rose Cabins is a good choice for families. On 5 forested acres about 3 miles from the lake, the wonderful free-standing cabins offer lots of privacy. Innkeeper Tricia DuFour has 15 cabins, from romantic studios to a five-bedroom lodge, each decorated in a different theme: The Indian cabin has a tepeelike bed; the bed in Wild Bill's cabin is covered like a wagon. Multibedroom units have stocked kitchens and separate living areas; for all cottages, daily maid service is available at an extra charge. There are lots of diversions on hand, including swing sets, croquet, tetherball, and Ping-Pong.

25994 Hwy. 189 (P.O. Box 31), Twin Peaks, CA 92391. © 800/429-PINE or 909/337-2341. Fax 909/337-0258. www.lakearrowheadcabins.com. 17 units. $109–$189 studio for 2; $129–$219 1-, 2-, and 3-bedroom cabins for up to 10 people; $335–$460 large-group lodges. Ski packages available. AE, DISC, MC, V. Pets accepted with $10 fee per night and $100 refundable deposit. **Amenities:** Outdoor heated pool; Jacuzzi. *In room:* TV/VCR, kitchen, coffeemaker.

WHERE TO DINE
Big Bear Lake

A reliable option for all-day dining is **Stillwell's,** 40650 Village Dr. (© **909/866-3121,** ext. 3). You might otherwise bypass it, because Stillwell's is the dining room for convention-friendly Northwoods Resort at the edge of the village. Despite the unmistakable hotel feel, its American/Continental menu is surprisingly good with something for everyone, noted attention to detail, and fair prices (rare in this mountain resort town). Another dining option is the restaurant **Bin 189** at the Lake Arrowhead Resort & Spa (see above).

Note: Hours of operation often change depending on the season and weather conditions, so be sure to call ahead to see if these restaurants are open.

The Captain's Anchorage STEAK/SEAFOOD Historic and rustic, this knotty-pine restaurant has been serving fine steaks, prime rib, seafood, and lobster since 1947. Inside, the dark, nautical decor and fire-warmed bar are just right on blustery winter nights. It's got one of those mile-long soup-and-salad bars, plus some great early bird and weeknight specials.

Moonridge Way at Big Bear Blvd., Big Bear Lake. © **909/866-3997.** Reservations recommended. Full dinners $15–$35. AE, MC, V. Sun–Thurs 4:30–9pm; Fri–Sat 4:30–10pm.

Old Country Inn DINER/GERMAN The Old Country Inn has long been a favorite for hearty pre-ski breakfasts and stick-to-your-ribs dinners. The restaurant is casual and welcoming, and the adjacent cocktail lounge is raucous on weekends. At breakfast, enjoy German apple pancakes or colossal omelets. Lunch includes salads, sandwiches, and burgers. At lunch or dinner, feast on Wiener schnitzel, sauerbraten, and other gravy-topped German standards, as well as grilled steaks and chicken.

41126 Big Bear Blvd., Big Bear Lake. © **909/866-4521.** www.oldcountryinn.net. Main courses $6–$28. AE, DC, DISC, MC, V. Sun–Thurs 8am–9pm; Fri–Sat 8am–10pm.

Lake Arrowhead

For an affluent residential community, Lake Arrowhead has surprisingly few dining options. Not surprisingly, what's there tends to run toward pricey elegance—relative to a rustic mountain resort, that is. Although the town has both a California/Continental restaurant and a casual family place in the Lake Arrowhead Resort (p. 618), you might want to venture out to some of the local haunts. These include the **Chef's Inn & Tavern,** 29020 Oak Terrace, Cedar Glen (© 909/336-4488), a moderate to expensive Continental restaurant in a former bordello; the **Royal Oak,** 27187 Hwy. 189, Blue Jay Village

(© 909/337-6018), an expensive American/Continental steakhouse with a pub; and **Belgian Waffle Works,** dockside at Lake Arrowhead Village (© 909/337-5222), a bargain coffee shop with Victorian decor, known for crispy waffles with tasty toppings.

4 THE DISNEYLAND RESORT ★★★

30 miles SE of downtown L.A.

There are newer and larger Disney parks in Florida, Tokyo, France, and Hong Kong, but the original and the inspiration for all of them still opens its gates in Anaheim every day, proudly proclaiming itself "The Happiest Place on Earth." Smaller than Walt Disney World, Disneyland—which opened in 1955 on a 107-acre tract surrounded almost exclusively by orange groves—has always capitalized on being the world's first family-oriented mega–theme park. Nostalgia is a big part of the original park's appeal, and despite many advancements, changes, and expansions over the years, Disneyland remains true to the vision of founder Walt Disney.

In 2001, Disney unveiled a new theme park (Disney's California Adventure), a shopping/dining/entertainment district (Downtown Disney), and a third on-site hotel (Disney's Grand Californian Hotel). I'll give you the lowdown on the best of what's new, as well as on the classic Disneyland experience.

While the Disneyland Resort is the undisputed front-runner in family-friendly vacation destinations in Southern California, another amusement park that's a short drive away from Disneyland—Knott's Berry Farm (covered later)—has a far better selection of high-speed roller coasters and is a better choice for people who crave thrill rides.

ESSENTIALS

GETTING THERE To reach the Disneyland Resort by car from LAX, take I-105 east to I-605 north and then I-5 south. From Los Angeles, take I-5 south until you see signs for Disneyland. Dedicated off-ramps from I-5 lead to the attraction's parking lots and surrounding streets (follow signs leading to THEME PARKS). The drive from LAX takes approximately 40 minutes with no traffic (right!).

If Anaheim is your first—or only—destination and you want to avoid L.A. altogether, consider flying directly into **John Wayne Airport** in Santa Ana (© 949/252-5200; www.ocair.com), Orange County's largest airport. It's about 15 miles from Disneyland at the intersection of I-405 and California 55. Check to see if your hotel has a free shuttle to and from either airport (some will pick you up at LAX), or call one of the following commercial shuttle services: **Disneyland Resort Express** (© 714/978-8855; http://anaheim.coachusa.us) fares are adults $15 one-way, $25 round-trip, and children $13 one-way, $17 round-trip; **Xpress** (© 800/427-7483; www.xpressshuttle.com); **Prime Time** (© 800/733-8267; primetimeshuttle.com); or **SuperShuttle** (© 800/258-3826; www.supershuttle.com). Car-rental agencies located at the John Wayne Airport include **Budget** (© 800/527-0700; www.budget.com) and **Hertz** (© 800/654-3131; www.hertz.com). To reach Anaheim from the airport, take California 55 north to I-5 north, and then take the Harbor Boulevard exit and follow signs to theme parks. You can also catch a ride with **American Taxi** (© 888/482-9466), whose cabs queue up at the Ground Transportation Center on the lower level; reservations are not necessary. Expect the fare to Disneyland to cost about $30.

> ⓘ **Tips** **CityPass Savings**
>
> If your vacation includes a visit to San Diego, look into purchasing a Southern
> California CityPass (www.citypass.com). It includes a 3-Day Park Hopper ticket to
> Disneyland and Disney's California Adventure, plus a 1-day admission to Univer-
> sal Studios Hollywood, SeaWorld Adventure Park, and the San Diego Zoo or Wild
> Animal Park. It costs $247 for adults and $199 for children, and if you visit all
> these attractions you'll save more than $90.

VISITOR INFORMATION   For information on the **Disneyland Resort,** including
show schedules and ride closures that apply to the specific day(s) of your visit, call
ⓒ **714/781-4565** for automated information or ⓒ **714/781-7290** to speak to Guest
Relations (but expect a long wait). Better yet, log on to the Disneyland Resort's official
website at **www.disneyland.com.**

For general information on the entire Anaheim region, contact the **Anaheim/Orange
County Visitor and Convention Bureau,** 800 W. Katella Ave., inside the Anaheim
Convention Center (ⓒ **714/765-8888;** www.anaheimoc.org). It's open Monday to Friday from 8:30am to 5:30pm. Staffers can fill you in on area activities and shopping, as
well as send you their *Official Visitors Guide* and the AdventureCard, which offers discounts at dozens of local attractions, hotels, restaurants, and shops.

You can find out everything you need to know about the Disneyland Resort online,
beginning with the official site, **www.disneyland.com,** which contains the latest information on park improvements and additions, plus special offers (sometimes on airfare or
reduced admission) and an interactive trip planner that lets you build a custom Disney
vacation package. If you prefer human interaction, contact a Walt Disney Travel Company
specialist at ⓒ **866/60-DISNEY** (603-4763) and ask about money-saving package deals.

There are numerous unofficial Disney websites as well, which provide very detailed—
and often judgmental—information about the Disneyland Resort. The best we've found
are: **Disneyland: Inside & Out** (www.intercotwest.com), an active and friendly website
filled with detailed information on every corner of the Disneyland Resort; **Laughing
Place.com** and **MouseInfo.com,** which both feature daily updated headlines and columns on all things Disney; **Mouseplanet.com,** a comprehensive Disneyland information
resource that offers features and reviews by guest writers; and **MouseSavers.com,** which
offers in-depth information on Disney theme parks and helps users save money on lodging and admissions.

ADMISSION, HOURS & INFORMATION   As of press time, admission to *either* Disneyland or Disney's California Adventure, including unlimited rides and all festivities and
entertainment, is $66 for adults and children over 10, $56 for children 3 to 9, and free for
children under 3. Parking is $11. A 1-Day Park Hopper ticket is $91 for adults and $81
for children. A 2-day Park Hopper ticket, which allows you to go back and forth as much
as you'd like each day, is $132 for adults and children over 9, and $112 for children 3 to 9.
Other multiday, multipark combination passes are available as well. In addition, many area
accommodations offer lodging packages that include admission for 1 or more days. Be sure
to check the Disney website, **www.disneyland.com,** for seasonal ticket specials.

If you plan on arriving during a busy time (when the gates open in the morning, or
btw. 11am–2pm), purchase your tickets in advance and get a jump on the crowds at the

(Value) The Art of the (Package) Deal

If you intend to spend 2 or more nights in Disney territory, it pays to investigate the bevy of packaged vacation options. Start by logging onto **www. disneyland.com** to peruse their standard package offers, take a virtual tour of Disney hotel properties, and get online price quotes for customized, date-specific packages—including airline tickets. The packages are value-packed time-savers with abundant flexibility. Rates are highly competitive, considering each package includes multiday and multipark admission, plus keepsake souvenirs, preferred seating at Disney shows, Disney pocket guides, and coupon books. If you're staying in a non-Disney hotel (even those in Los Angeles or San Diego), ask whether they sell Disneyland admission packages; many hotels offer inclusive vacation packages that include Disneyland and Disney's California Adventure (and other attractions). To make sure you're getting the absolute best deal, call the official Disney travel planners at **Walt Disney Travel Co.** (© **866/60-DISNEY** or 714/520-5050) and compare their package deals with the ones you've already been quoted.

ticket counters. Advance tickets may be purchased through Disneyland's website (www. disneyland.com), at Disney stores in the United States, by calling the ticket mail-order line (© **714/781-4043**), at any nearby Disneyland Resort Good Neighbor Hotel, or as part of your travel package.

Disneyland and Disney's California Adventure are open every day of the year, but operating hours vary, so be sure to call for information that applies to the specific day(s) of your visit (© **714/781-7290**). The same information, including ride closures and show schedules, can also be found online at **www.disneyland.com**. Generally speaking, the parks are open from 9 or 10am to 6 or 7pm on weekdays, fall to spring; and from 8 or 9am to midnight or 1am on weekends, holidays, and during winter, spring, or summer vacation periods. *Tip:* The park's operating hours can give you some idea of what kinds of crowds Disney planners are expecting: The later the parks close, the more people will be there.

WHEN TO GO The Disneyland Resort is busiest in summer (btw. Memorial Day and Labor Day), on holidays (Thanksgiving week, Christmas week, Presidents' Day weekend, and Easter week), plus weekends year-round. All other periods are considered off season. Peak hours are from noon to 5pm; visit the most popular rides before and after these hours, and you'll cut your waiting times substantially. If you plan to arrive during a busy time, buy your tickets in advance and get a jump on the crowds at the ticket booths. Advance tickets may be purchased through Disneyland's website (www.disneyland.com), at Disney stores in the United States, or by calling the ticket mail-order line (© **714/781-4043**).

Attendance falls dramatically during the winter, so the park offers discounted or two-for-one admission to Southern California residents, who may buy up to five tickets per zip code verification. If you'll be visiting the park with someone who lives here, be sure to take advantage of this promotion.

Another secret time-saving tip is to enter Disneyland from the turnstile at the Monorail Station in Downtown Disney. The line is usually shorter and the Monorail will take you straight into Tomorrowland (but it doesn't stop in Disney's California Adventure).

Another time-saver is booking your vacation through the Walt Disney Travel Company—those package guests can enter Mickey's Toontown and Fantasyland 1 hour before the general public.

Once in the park, many visitors tackle Disneyland (or Disney's California Adventure) systematically, beginning at the entrance and working their way clockwise around the park. My advice: Arrive early and run to the most popular rides—the Indiana Jones Adventure, Star Tours, Big Thunder Mountain Railroad, Splash Mountain, the Haunted Mansion, and Pirates of the Caribbean, all in Disneyland; and Twilight Zone Tower of Terror, Soarin' Over California, California Screamin', Grizzly River Run, and It's Tough to Be a Bug rides in Disney's California Adventure. Waits for these rides can last an hour or more in the middle of the day.

This time-honored plan of attack may eventually become obsolete, thanks to Disney's complimentary **FASTPASS** system. Here's how it works: Say you want to ride Space Mountain, but the line is long—*so* long the current wait sign indicates a 75-minute standby. Instead, you can head to the automated FASTPASS ticket dispenser, where you pop in your park ticket to receive a free voucher listing a computer-assigned boarding time later that day. When you return at the assigned time, you enter through the FASTPASS gate and only have to wait about 10 minutes (to the envy of everyone in the slowpoke line). The hottest features at Disney's California Adventure had FASTPASS built in from the start; for a complete list for each park, check your official map/guide when you enter and look for the red FP symbol. *Note:* You can obtain a FASTPASS for only one attraction at a time. Also, the FASTPASS system doesn't eliminate the need to arrive at the theme park early because there's only a limited supply of FASTPASSes available for each attraction on a given day. So, if you don't show up until the middle of the afternoon, you might find that all the FASTPASSes have been distributed to other guests.

Disneyland ★★★

Disneyland is divided into eight sub-areas or "lands" arranged around a central hub, each of which has a number of rides and attractions that are, more or less, related to that land's theme. Be sure to pick up a free park map on the way in, or you'll probably get lost almost immediately.

MAIN STREET U.S.A. Located at the park's entrance, Main Street U.S.A. is an idealized version of a turn-of-the-20th-century American small-town street inspired by Marceline, Missouri (Walt Disney's childhood home), and built on a $^7/_8$ scale. Many visitors are surprised to discover that all the buildings are real, not elaborate props. Attention to detail here is exceptional—interiors, furnishings, and fixtures conform to the period. As with any real Main Street, the Disney version is essentially a collection of shops and eating places, with a city hall, a fire station, and an old-time silent cinema. Live performances include piano playing at the Carnation ice-cream parlor and Dapper Dan's barbershop quartet along the street. A mixed-media attraction combines a presentation on the life of Walt Disney (The Walt Disney Story) with a patriotic remembrance of Abraham Lincoln. Horse-drawn trolleys, fire engines, and horseless carriages give rides along Main Street and transport visitors to the central hub (properly known as the Central Plaza).

Because there are no major rides, it's best to tour Main Street during the middle of the afternoon, when lines for rides are longest, and in the evening, when walkways can be packed with visitors viewing Disneyland's parades and shows. There's always something happening on Main Street; stop in at the information booth to the left of the Main Entrance for a schedule of the day's events.

ADVENTURELAND Inspired by the most exotic regions of Asia, Africa, India, and the South Pacific, Adventureland is home to several popular rides. Here's where you can cavort inside **Tarzan's Treehouse,** a climb-around attraction based on the animated film. Its African-themed neighbor is the **Jungle Cruise,** where passengers board a large, authentic-looking Mississippi River paddleboat and float along an Amazon-like river; a spear's throw away is the **Enchanted Tiki Room,** one of the most sedate attractions in Adventureland. Inside, you can sit down and watch a 20-minute musical comedy featuring electronically animated tropical birds, flowers, and "Tiki gods."

The **Indiana Jones Adventure** is Adventureland's star ride. Based on the Steven Spielberg films, this ride takes adventurers into the Temple of the Forbidden Eye, in joltingly realistic all-terrain vehicles. Riders follow Indy and experience the perils of bubbling lava pits, whizzing arrows, fire-breathing serpents, collapsing bridges, and the familiar cinematic tumbling boulder (an effect that's very realistic to riders in the front seats).

NEW ORLEANS SQUARE A large, grassy green dotted with gas lamps, New Orleans Square is home to the **Haunted Mansion,** where the dated effects are more funny than scary. One of Disneyland's most popular rides, **Pirates of the Caribbean,** has a whole new look. Visitors still float on boats through mock underground caves, but now the plot is Captain Jack Sparrow and his cohorts from the hit film franchise doing battle with Davy Jones. Even in the middle of the afternoon you can dine by the cool moonlight and to the sound of crickets in the **Blue Bayou** restaurant, situated in the middle of the ride itself.

CRITTER COUNTRY An ode to the backwoods, Critter Country is a sort of Frontierland without those pesky settlers. Older kids and grown-ups head straight for **Splash Mountain,** one of the largest water flume rides in the world. Loosely based on the Disney movie *Song of the South,* the ride is lined with about 100 characters that won't stop singing "Zip-A-Dee-Doo-Dah." Be prepared to get wet, especially if someone sizable is in the front seat of your log-shaped boat. **The Many Adventures of Winnie the Pooh** is a children's attraction based on Winnie the Pooh and his friends from the Hundred-Acre Wood—Tigger, Eeyore, Piglet, and the gang. The attraction is of the kindler, gentler sort, where you board "hunny bee-hives" and take a slow-moving journey through the Hundred-Acre Wood in endless pursuit of "hunny." The high-tech gadgetry and illusions are spellbinding for kids and mildly entertaining for adults. (*Tip:* It's a very popular attraction, so be sure to arrive early or make use of FASTPASS.) While it may not be the fastest ride in the park, **Davy Crockett's Explorer Canoes** allow folks to row around Tom Sawyer Island. It's the only ride where you actively control your boat (no underwater rails!). Hop into replica canoes, grab a paddle, and away you go.

FRONTIERLAND Inspired by 19th-century America, Frontierland features a raft to **Pirate's Lair at Tom Sawyer's Island,** a do-it-yourself play area with live pirates, island caverns, and rope bridges leading to buried treasure. You'll also find the **Big Thunder Mountain Railroad,** a runaway roller coaster that races through a deserted 1870s gold mine. Children will dig the petting zoo, and there's an Abe Lincoln–style log cabin; both are great for exploring with the little ones. This is also where you board one of two large-capacity riverboats—*Mark Twain* and the *Sailing Ship Columbia*—that navigate the waters around Tom Sawyer Island and Fort Wilderness. Beautiful crafts, the riverboats provide lofty perches from which to see Frontierland and New Orleans Square. The *Sailing Ship Columbia,* however, has far more historic and aesthetic appeal. As with the other river craft, the riverboats suspend operations at dusk.

When it's showing (it's a seasonal presentation), head to Frontierland's **Rivers of**
America after dark to see the *FANTASMIC!* show. It mixes magic, music, 50 live performers, floats, and sensational special effects. Just as he did in *The Sorcerer's Apprentice,*
Mickey Mouse battles evil and conjures good, using his magical powers to create giant
water fountains, enormous flowers, and fantasy creatures. There's plenty of pyrotechnics,
lasers, and fog, as well as a 45-foot-tall dragon that breathes fire and sets the water of the
Rivers of America aflame.

MICKEY'S TOONTOWN   This is a colorful, whimsical world inspired by the Roger
Rabbit films—a wacky, gag-filled land populated by 'toons. It even looks like a cartoon
come to life, a trippy, smile-inducing world without a straight line or right angle in sight.
In addition to serving as a place where guests can be certain of finding Disney characters
at any time during the day, Mickey's Toontown also serves as an elaborate interactive
playground where it's okay for the kids to run, climb, and let off steam. There are several
rides and play areas, including **Roger Rabbit's CarToonSpin, Donald's Boat, Chip 'n'
Dale's Treehouse, Gadget's Go Coaster,** and **Mickey's House & Minnie's House.** *Tip:*
Because of its popularity with families, Toontown is most crowded during the day but
often deserted after dinnertime.

FANTASYLAND   With a storybook theme, this is the catchall "land" for stuff that
doesn't quite fit anywhere else. Most of the rides are geared to the under-6 set, including
the **King Arthur Carousel, Mad Tea Party, Dumbo the Flying Elephant ride,** and
Casey Jr. Circus Train. Some, such as **Mr. Toad's Wild Ride** and **Peter Pan's Flight,**
appeal to grown-ups as well, and are original attractions from opening day in 1955. You'll
also find **Alice in Wonderland, Snow White's Scary Adventures, Pinocchio's Daring
Journey,** and more.

The most lauded attraction is **It's a Small World,** a slow-moving indoor river ride
through a saccharine scenario of all the world's children singing the song everybody loves
to hate. (Perhaps the ride would be more entertaining if each person got four softballs on
the way in?) For a different kind of thrill, try the **Matterhorn Bobsleds,** a zippy roller
coaster through chilled caverns and drifting fog banks. It's one of the park's most popular
rides and the world's first steel tubular track roller coaster.

TOMORROWLAND   Conceived as an optimistic look at the future, Tomorrowland
employs an angular, metallic look popularized by futurists such as Jules Verne. Longtime
Tomorrowland favorites include the newly revamped **Space Mountain** (a pitch-black
indoor roller coaster that assaults your equilibrium and ears), and **Star Tours,** the original
Disney–George Lucas joint venture. It's a 40-passenger StarSpeeder that encounters a
space-load of misadventures on the way to the Moon of Endor, achieved with wired seats
and video effects—not for the queasy.

Other Tomorrowland attractions include: **Buzz Lightyear Astro Blasters,** where
guests pilot their own Star Cruiser through a comical interactive space mission to con-
quer the Evil Emperor Zurg; *Honey, I Shrunk the Audience,* an interactive 3-D movie
based on the popular movie series featuring Rick Moranis in the role of Wayne Szalinski;
the **Disneyland Monorail,** a "futuristic" elevated monorail that takes you to Downtown
Disney and back again (and offers the only practical opportunity for escaping the park
during the crowded lunch period and early afternoon); and **Innoventions,** a huge, busy
collection of industry-sponsored hands-on exhibits such as the **Dream Home**—a
5,000-plus-square-foot home belonging to the fictional Elias family—which provides a
glimpse of emerging technology for high-tech homes. Exhibits, many of which change

each year, demonstrate such products as virtual-reality games, voice-activated appliances, and various digital applications, among others.

Disney's California Adventure ★★

With a grand entrance designed to resemble one of those "Wish you were here" scenic postcards, the 55-acre Disney's California Adventure starts out with a bang. You walk beneath the scale model of the Golden Gate Bridge (keep watching—the monorail will pass overhead) into **Sunshine Plaza,** which is anchored by a perpetual wave fountain and an enormous gold titanium "sun" that shines all day (it's illuminated by six computerized heliostats that follow the real sun's path). From this point, visitors can head into four themed "districts," each containing rides, interactive attractions, live-action shows, and plenty of dining, snacking, and shopping opportunities.

THE GOLDEN STATE This multidimensional area represents California's history, heritage, and physical attributes. Sound boring? Actually, the park's splashiest attractions are here. **Condor Flats** is a tribute to daring aviators; inside a weathered corrugated test-pilots' hangar is **Soarin' Over California,** the simulated hang-glider ride that immediately rose to the top on everyone's "ride first" list (it's equipped with FASTPASS, and I highly recommend using it). It uses cutting-edge technology to combine elevated seats with a spectacular IMAX-style surround-movie—riders literally "soar" over California's scenic lands, feeling the Malibu ocean breeze and smelling the Central Valley orange groves and Yosemite pines.

Nearby, California Adventure's iconic Grizzly Peak towers over the **Grizzly River Run,** a splashy gold-country ride through caverns, mine shafts, and water slides; it culminates with a wet plunge into a spouting geyser. Kids can cavort nearby on the **Redwood Creek Challenge Trail,** a forest playground with smoke-jumper cable slides, net climbing, and swaying bridges.

Pacific Wharf was inspired by Monterey's Cannery Row and features mouthwatering demonstration attractions by **Boudin Sourdough Bakery** and **Mission Tortillas.** If you get hungry, each has a food counter where you can enjoy soup in a sourdough bowl; tacos, burritos, and enchiladas; and teriyaki bowls, egg rolls, and wonton soup.

PARADISE PIER Journey back to the glory days of California's beachfront amusement piers—remember Santa Monica, Santa Cruz, and Belmont Park?—on this fantasy board-walk. Highlights include **California Screamin',** a classic roller coaster that replicates the whitewashed wooden white-knucklers of the past—but with state-of-the-art steel construction and a smooth, computerized ride that catapults you from zero to 55 mph in less than 5 seconds, and then takes a loop-de-loop through a silhouette of Mickey Mouse's ears. There's also the **Maliboomer,** a trio of towers (giant strongman sledgehammer tests) that catapult riders to the tiptop bell and then lets them down bungee-style with dangling feet; the **Orange Stinger,** a whooshing swing ride inside an enormous orange, complete with orange scent piped in; **Mulholland Madness,** a wacky, wild trip along L.A.'s precarious hilltop street that is way scarier than it looks; and the **Sun Wheel Carousel,** featuring unique zigzagging cars that bring a new twist to the familiar ride. In 2008 the **Toy Story Mania** ride debuted. Guests donning 3-D glasses are "shrunk" to the size of a toy for a fanciful ride that twists along a midway-themed route. At each game booth, players aim for animated targets using their on-board "toy cannon."

Paradise Pier also has all the familiar boardwalk games (complete with stuffed prizes); guilty-pleasure fast foods such as pizza, corn dogs, and burritos; plus a full-service over-water restaurant called **Ariel's Grotto.**

HOLLYWOOD PICTURES BACKLOT   If you've visited Disney in Florida, you might recognize many elements of this *trompe l'oeil* re-creation of a Hollywood movie studio lot. Pass through a classic studio archway flanked by gigantic golden elephants and you'll find yourself on a surprisingly realistic Hollywood Boulevard. The resort's hottest attraction is the **Twilight Zone Tower of Terror.** This truly scary ride has been a huge hit since its debut at Walt Disney World. Legend has it that during a violent storm on Halloween night 1939, lightning struck the Hollywood Tower Hotel, causing an entire wing and an elevator full of people to disappear, and you're about to retrace their steps from that fateful night as you become the star in a special Disney episode of . . . *The Twilight Zone.* In this once glamorous but now eerily vacant hotel, you tour the lobby, library, and boiler room, and ultimately board the elevator to plunge 13 stories to the fifth dimension and beyond.

The Backlot's other main attraction is **Playhouse Disney—Live on Stage!,** starring the characters from the popular *Playhouse Disney* kid's program on the Disney Channel. It's a hugely popular high-energy show where Bear in the Big Blue House, Jo Jo, Stanley, and other television characters entertain kids with songs, music, and stories of friendship. Other popular shows include **Monsters, Inc. Mike & Sully to the Rescue!,** where guests ride taxis through Monstropolis on a mission to safely return "Boo" to her bedroom; and *Jim Henson's MuppetVision 3D,* an onscreen comedy romp featuring Kermit, Miss Piggy, Gonzo, Fozzie Bear—and even hecklers Waldorf and Statler. Although it's not nearly as entertaining as *It's Tough to Be a Bug,* it has its moments and won't scare the bejesus out of little kids.

At the end of the street, the replica movie palace **Hyperion Theater** presents Broadway-caliber live-action shows of classic Disney films such as *Aladdin—A Musical Spectacular.* In the **Disney Animation** building, visitors can participate in different interactive galleries and learn how stories become animated features as told by Disney artists in the Drawn to Animation studio.

A BUG'S LAND   This bug-themed land encompasses *It's Tough to Be a Bug,* **Flik's Fun Fair,** and **Bountiful Valley Farm.** Inspired by the movie *A Bug's Life, It's Tough to Be a Bug* uses 3-D technology to lead the audience on an underground romp in the insect kingdom with bees, termites, grasshoppers, stink bugs, spiders, and a few surprises that keep everyone hopping, ducking, and laughing along. (I could see how little kids might find the show rather terrifying, however.) The **Flik's Fun Fair** area features bug-themed rides and a water playground designed especially for little ones ages 4 to 7—but sized so their parents can ride along, too. **Bountiful Farm** pays tribute to California's agriculture (a real ho-hum if you're a Californian). Exhibits include a demonstration vineyard, Mission-style "aging room" (with *Seasons of the Vine,* a film presented by the late Robert Mondavi on the art of winemaking), wine bars, and the park's most upscale eatery, the **Vineyard Room,** a great place to sip champagne and watch Disney's Electrical Parade.

Downtown Disney District ★

Borrowing a page from central Florida's successful Disney compound, the **Downtown Disney District** is a colorful (and very sanitized) "street scene" filled with restaurants, shops, and entertainment for all ages. Options abound: Window-shop with kids in tow, have an upscale dinner for two, or party into the night. The promenade begins at the amusement park gates and stretches toward the Disneyland Hotel; there are nearly 20 shops and boutiques, and a dozen-plus restaurants, live music venues, and entertainment options.

Highlights include **House of Blues,** the blues-jazz restaurant/club that features Delta-inspired cuisine, big-name musicians, and the hand-clapping Sunday Gospel Brunch; **Ralph Brennan's Jazz Kitchen,** a spicy mix of New Orleans traditional foods and live jazz; **ESPN Zone,** the ultimate sports, dining, and entertainment experience, including an interactive game room with a rock climbing wall; and **World of Disney,** one of the biggest Disney shopping experiences anywhere, with a vast and diverse range of toys, souvenirs, and collectibles. There is also an AMC Theatres 12-screen multiplex, the LEGO Imagination Center, a Sephora cosmetics store, and much more.

WHERE TO STAY
Very Expensive

Disney's Grand Californian Hotel ★★★ (Kids)   Disney didn't miss the details when constructing this enormous version of an Arts and Crafts–era lodge (think Yosemite's Ahwahnee and Pasadena's Gamble House), hiring craftspeople throughout the state to contribute one-of-a-kind tiles, furniture, sculptures, and artwork. Taking inspiration from California's redwood forests, mission pioneers, and plein-air painters, designers created a nostalgic yet state-of-the-art high-rise hotel that has its own private entrance into Disney's California Adventure park and Downtown Disney District.

Enter through subtle (where's the door?) stained-glass sliding panels to the hotel's centerpiece, a six-story "living room" with a William Morris–designed marble "carpet," an angled skylight seen through exposed support beams, display cases of Craftsman treasures, and a three-story walk-in "hearth" whose fire warms Stickley-style rockers and plush leather armchairs.

Guest rooms are spacious and smartly designed, carrying through the Arts and Crafts theme surprisingly well considering the hotel's grand scale. The best ones overlook the park, but you'll pay for that view. Despite the sophisticated air of the Grand Californian, this is a hotel that truly caters to families, with a bevy of room configurations including one with a double bed plus bunk beds with a trundle. Since the hotel provides sleeping bags (rather than rollaways) for kids, this standard-size room will sleep a family of six—but you have to share the bathroom. *Tip:* Ask for a free upgrade to a room with a view of the park when you check in—they're pretty generous about this.

The hotel's two main restaurants are the upscale **Napa Rose** and the **Storytellers Cafe,** a "character dining" restaurant that's always bustling with excited kids who pay more attention to Chip and Dale than their eggs and bacon (be sure to make a breakfast reservation). Also on the property is **Mandara Spa,** offering a complete array of spa services for men and women.

1600 S. Disneyland Dr., Anaheim, CA 92802. (C) **714/956-MICKEY** (central reservations), or 714/635-2300. For vacation packages, call the Walt Disney Travel Company at 866/60-DISNEY. Fax 714/956-6099. www.disneyland.com. 745 units. $215–$345 double; from $355 suite. AE, DC, DISC, MC, V. Free self-parking; valet parking $6. **Amenities:** 3 restaurants; lounge; 2 outdoor pools; whirlpool; full service spa; children's center; game room/arcade; concierge; business center; 24-hr. room service; laundry service; dry cleaning; concierge-level rooms. *In room:* A/C, TV, minibar, coffeemaker, hair dryer, iron, safe, robes, portable crib.

Expensive

The Disneyland Hotel ★★ (Kids)   The Holy Grail of Disney-goers has always been this, the "Official Hotel of the Magic Kingdom." A monorail connection via Downtown Disney means you'll be able to return to your room anytime, whether to take a much-needed nap or to change your soaked shorts after riding Splash Mountain. The theme hotel is an attraction unto itself and is the best choice for families with small children. The rooms aren't fancy, but they're comfortably furnished and all have balconies. In-room amenities include movie channels (with free Disney Channel, naturally) and even Disneyland-themed toiletries and accessories such as Sneezy on the tissue box. When you turn out the lights in the guest room, the wallpaper glows with Tinker Bell's pixie dust. This all-inclusive resort offers several restaurants (a full review of **Goofy's Kitchen** is covered later), snack bars, and cocktail lounges; every kind of service desk imaginable; a video game center; and the Never Land Pool Complex with a white-sand beach and separate adult pool nearby.

1150 W. Magic Way, Anaheim, CA 92802. ℂ **714/956-MICKEY.** For vacation packages, call the Walt Disney Travel Company at 866/60-DISNEY. Reservations fax 714/956-6582. www.disneyland.com. 990 units. $80–$320 double; from $275 suite. AE, MC, V. Parking $10. **Amenities:** 4 restaurants; 3 lounges; 3 outdoor pools; health club; whirlpool; children's programs; game room; concierge; shopping arcade; room service; babysitting; laundry service; dry cleaning. *In room:* A/C, TV, minibar, hair dryer, safe.

Paradise Pier Hotel ★ Kids The whimsical beach boardwalk theme of this 15-story hotel ties in with the Paradise Pier section of Disney's California Adventure park across the street. The surfer theme salutes the heyday of seaside amusement parks with nautical and beach decor in the guest rooms, nostalgic California artwork, and a water slide modeled after the wooden roller coasters of yesteryear. Book a room at this smallest Disney property only if the other two are full—it's not as "magical" as the original Disneyland Hotel and is soundly trounced by the superlative Grand Californian. It's also not as centrally located as the other two hotels, which could be a problem if you're not fond of walking. It does, however, offer "family suites" that comfortably accommodate families of six or more, as well as Lilo & Stich's Aloha Breakfast featuring island songs and tableside visits at the hotel's **PCH Grill.** Kids even get to make their own pizzas (pseudo breakfast pizzas with peanut butter and gummy bears and such, or, for lunch/dinner, traditional pizzas baked in the kitchen oven). *Tip:* Request a room that either overlooks the Paradise Pier section of California Adventure or has direct access to the poolside cabanas.

1717 S. Disneyland Dr., Anaheim, CA 92802. ℂ **714/956-MICKEY.** For vacation packages, call the Walt Disney Travel Company at 866/60-DISNEY. Reservations fax 714/956-6582. www.disneyland.com. 489 units. $180–$320 double; from $275 suite. AE, MC, V. Parking $10. **Amenities:** 2 restaurants; lounge; outdoor pool; fitness center; whirlpool; children's programs; game room; concierge; shopping arcade; room service; babysitting; laundry service; dry cleaning. *In room:* A/C, TV w/pay movies, minibar, coffeemaker, hair dryer, safe.

Sheraton Anaheim Hotel ★ This hotel rises to the festive theme-park occasion with its fanciful English Tudor architecture; it's a castle that lures business conventions, Disney-bound families, and local high school proms. The public areas are quiet and elegant—intimate gardens with fountains and koi ponds, and a plush lobby and lounges—which can be a pleasing touch after a frantic day at the amusement park. The rooms are modern and unusually spacious, but otherwise not distinctive. A large swimming pool sits in the center of the complex, surrounded by attractive landscaping. Don't be put off by the high rack rates; rooms commonly go for $100 to $130, even on busy summer weekends.

900 S. Disneyland Dr. (at I-5), Anaheim, CA 92802. ℂ **800/325-3535** or 714/778-1700 in the U.S. Fax 714/535-3889. www.sheraton.com. 489 units. $210–$245 double; $300–$370 suite. AE, DC, MC, V. Parking $10; free Disneyland shuttle. **Amenities:** 2 restaurants; lounge; outdoor pool; fitness center; whirlpool; concierge; 24-hr. room service; coin-op laundry; laundry service; dry cleaning. *In room:* A/C, TV w/pay movies, minibar, coffeemaker, hair dryer, iron.

The Anabella Hotel ★   Uniting several formerly independent low-rise hotels across the street from Disney's California Adventure, the Anabella started from scratch, gutting each building to create carefully planned rooms for park-bound families and business travelers alike. The complex features a vaguely Mission-style facade of whitewashed walls and red-tiled roofs, though guest room interiors are strictly contemporary in style and modern in appointments. Bathrooms are generously sized and outfitted in honey-toned granite; most have a tub/shower combo—just a few are shower only. Though parking areas dot the grounds, you'll also find a pleasant garden around the central swimming pool and whirlpool; a separate adult pool hides out next to the street-side fitness room. Business travelers will appreciate the in-room executive desks with high-speed Internet access, while families can take advantage of "kids' suites" complete with bunk beds and separate bedrooms. There's a pleasant indoor-outdoor all-day restaurant, and the hotel is a stop on both the Disney and Convention Center shuttle routes. *Note:* Rooms and rates vary wildly in terms of room size, layout, and occupancy limits; extra time spent at the hotel's website and with the reservationist will pay off in the most comfortable room for your needs.

1030 W. Katella Ave., Anaheim, CA 92802. ✆ **800/863-4888** or 714/905-1050. Fax 714/905-1054. www. anabellahotel.com. 360 units. $99–$319 double. AE, DC, DISC, MC, V. Free parking. **Amenities:** Restaurant; lounge; 2 outdoor heated pools; exercise room; whirlpool; concierge; activities desk; business center; room service; self-service laundromat; laundry service; dry cleaning; nail salon. *In room:* A/C, TV w/ pay movies, Web TV, high-speed Internet, fridge, coffeemaker, hair dryer, iron, safe, PlayStation.

Anaheim Plaza Hotel & Suites ★ ⓥalue   Although it's located across the street from the Disneyland Resort's main gate, you'll appreciate the way this hotel's clever design shuts out the noisy world. In fact, the seven two-story garden buildings remind me more of 1960s Waikiki than busy Anaheim (maybe it's the palm trees). A key feature is the Olympic-size heated outdoor pool and whirlpool. The furnishings are motel-bland but you won't spend much time here anyway. On the plus side, little has changed about the friendly rates, which often drop as low as $59.

1700 S. Harbor Blvd., Anaheim, CA 92802. ✆ **800/631-4144** or 714/772-5900. Fax 714/772-8386. www. anaheimplazahotel.com. 300 units. $99–$170 double; from $205 suite. Rates include continental breakfast. AE, DC, DISC, MC, V. Free parking and Disneyland shuttle. **Amenities:** Restaurant; lounge; outdoor pool; whirlpool; room service; coin-op laundry; laundry service; dry cleaning. *In room:* A/C, TV, coffeemaker, hair dryer.

Portofino Inn & Suites ★ ⓚids   Emerging from the rubble of the former Jolly Roger Hotel renovation, this complex of low- and high-rise all-suite buildings sports a cheery yellow exterior and family-friendly interior. The location couldn't be better—directly across the street from California Adventure's backside. You can either walk or take the ART (Anaheim Resort Transit) to the front gate. Designed to work as well for business travelers from the nearby Convention Center as for Disney-bound families, the Portofino offers contemporary, stylish furnishings as well as vacation-friendly rates and suites for any family configuration. Families will want a Kids' Suite, which features bunk beds and a sleeper sofa, plus a TV, fridge, and microwave—and that's just in the kids' room; Mom and Dad have a separate bedroom with grown-up comforts such as a double vanity, shower massage, and their own TV. There's even a Kids Eat Free program at the inn's cafe.

1831 S. Harbor Blvd. (at Katella), Anaheim, CA 92802. ✆ **800/398-3963** or 714/782-7600. Fax 714/782-7619. www.portofinoinnanaheim.com. 190 units. $104–$169 double; $119–$229 suite. Midweek, off season, and other discounts available. AE, DC, DISC, MC, V. Free parking and Disneyland shuttle. **Amenities:**

Restaurant; outdoor pool; fitness center; whirlpool; game room; tour desk; Wi-Fi; coin-op laundry; laundry service; dry cleaning. *In room:* A/C, TV, coffeemaker, hair dryer, iron.

Inexpensive

Candy Cane Inn ★ (**Value**) Take your standard U-shaped motel court with outdoor corridors, spruce it up with cobblestone drives and walkways along with old-time street lamps, add flowering vines engulfing room balconies, and you have the Candy Cane. The face-lift worked, making this gem near Disneyland's main gate a treat for the stylish bargain hunter. The rooms are decorated in bright floral motifs with comfortable furnishings, including queen-size beds and a separate dressing and vanity area. Breakfast is served in the courtyard, where you can also splash around in a heated pool, spa, or kids' wading pool. If you feel like splurging, request one of the Premium Rooms with extended checkout and nightly turndown service.

1747 S. Harbor Blvd., Anaheim, CA 92802. (*C*) **800/345-7057** or 714/774-5284. Fax 714/772-1305. www. candycaneinn.net. 172 units. $82–$159 double. Rates include expanded continental breakfast. AAA discount available. AE, DC, DISC, MC, V. Free parking and Disneyland shuttle. **Amenities:** Outdoor pool; whirlpool; coin-op laundry; laundry service; dry cleaning. *In room:* A/C, TV, fridge, coffeemaker, hair dryer.

Travelodge Anaheim Located on the back side of Disneyland, this modest hotel appeals to the budget-conscious traveler who's looking for plenty of free perks such as wireless Internet and continental breakfast. All rooms have a refrigerator and microwave, and you can relax by the large outdoor heated pool and spa while using the laundry room. The extra-large family rooms accommodate virtually any brood, and shuttles run regularly to the park.

1057 W. Ball Rd., Anaheim, CA 92802. (*C*) **800/578-7878** or 714/774-7600. Fax 714/535-6953. www. travelodge.com. 95 units. $90–$110 double; $115 family room. Rates include full breakfast. AE, DC, DISC, MC, V. Free parking and Disneyland shuttle. **Amenities:** Restaurant; outdoor pool; whirlpool; Wi-Fi; self-service laundry. *In room:* A/C, TV, fridge, coffeemaker, hair dryer, iron, microwave.

WHERE TO DINE

There's nothing quite like an energetic family vacation to build an appetite, and sooner or later you'll have to make the inevitable Disney dining decisions: Where, when, and for how much? The expanded Disneyland Resort has something for everyone, a respectable lineup that can easily meet your needs for the duration of the typical visit. Until recently, dining options were pretty sparse, limited to those inside Disneyland and some old standbys at the Disneyland Hotel. But Disney's big expansion upped the ante with national theme/concept restaurants along Downtown Disney and competitive dining options at the resort hotels. The best of the bunch are reviewed below. For dining reservations at any place throughout the Disneyland Resort, call (*C*) **714/781-DINE.**

Expensive

Napa Rose ★★★ CALIFORNIA Situated inside the upscale Grand Californian Hotel, Napa Rose is the first really serious (read: on "foodie" radar) restaurant at the Disneyland Resort. Executive chef Andrew Sutton was lured away from the Napa Valley's chic Auberge du Soleil, bringing with him a wine-country sensibility and passion for fresh California ingredients and inventive preparations. You can see him keeping busy in the impressive exhibition kitchen, which showcases specialty items such as Sierra golden trout, artisan cheeses from Humboldt County and the Gold Country, and the Sonoma rabbit in Sutton's signature braised mushroom-rabbit tart. The tantalizing Seven Sparkling Sins starter platter (for two) features jewel-like portions of foie gras, caviar, oysters,

Tips **Standard Fruit**

As a welcome relief to those ubiquitous salty, sugary junk-food stands, both the Disneyland and California Adventure parks offer several bastions of healthful snacking: rustic wooden **fruit stands** teeming with a variety of quality seasonal fresh fruit and juices that sell for a fraction of the price you'd pay for a hot dog, fries, and a Coke. Ask a Disney "Cast Member" (any employee) for the nearest stand.

lobster, and other exotic delicacies; the same attention to detail is evident in seasonally composed main-course standouts such as grilled yellowtail with tangerine-basil fruit salsa atop savory couscous, or free-range veal *osso buco* in rich bacon–forest mushroom ragout. Leave room for dessert, to at least share one of pastry chef Jorge Sotelo's creative treats; our favorites are Sonoma goat cheese flan with Riesling-soaked tropical fruit, and chocolate crepes with house-made caramelized banana ice cream. Napa Rose boasts an impressive and balanced wine list, with 60 by-the-glass choices (and 40-plus sommeliers, the most of any restaurant in the world); and outdoor seating is arranged around a rustic fire pit, facing a landscaped arroyo toward California Adventure's distinctive Grizzly Peak. *Tip:* My favorite place to sit is at the counter facing the exhibition kitchen. Or skip all the pomp and circumstance of a full sit-down meal by dining at the restaurant's lounge.

1600 S. Disneyland Dr. (in Disney's Grand Californian Hotel). © **714/300-7170.** www.disneyland.com. Reservations strongly recommended. Main courses $19–$30. AE, DC, DISC, MC, V. Daily 11:30am–2pm and 5:30–10pm.

Yamabuki ★ JAPANESE Often ignored by all but their thriving clientele of Asian tourists and business folk, the low-profile Yamabuki restaurant has been tucked away in Paradise Pier Hotel for years. With a casual yet quietly traditional Japanese aesthetic, Yamabuki—the name of a Japanese rose—imparts a very un-Disney ambience. Lunch fare includes casual bento boxes, lunch specials, and sushi/sashimi selections (try the Crunchy Roll). At dinner, tradition demands a languorous procession of courses, from refreshing seafood starters and steaming noodle bowls to grilled teriyaki meats or table-cooked specialties such as sukiyaki or *shabu-shabu*.

1717 S. Disneyland Dr. (in Disney's Paradise Pier Hotel). © **714/239-5683,** or 714/956-6755 for reservations. www.disneyland.com. Reservations recommended at dinner. Main courses $7.50–$11 lunch, $20–$30 dinner. AE, DC, DISC, MC, V. Mon–Fri 11:30am–2pm; daily 5:30–10pm.

Moderate

Catal Restaurant/Uva Bar ★ MEDITERRANEAN/TAPAS Branching out from the acclaimed Patina restaurant in Los Angeles, high-priest-of-cuisine Joachim Splichal brings us this Spanish-inspired Mediterranean concept duo at the heart of Downtown Disney. The main restaurant, Catal, features a series of intimate second-floor rooms that combine rustic Mediterranean charm with fine dining. Complemented by an international wine list, the menu is a collage of flavors that borrow from France, Spain, Italy, Greece, Morocco, and the Middle East—all united in selections that manage to be intriguing but not overwhelming. Though the menu will vary seasonally, expect to find selections that range from seared sea scallops over saffron risotto or chorizo-spiked Spanish paella to herb-marinated rotisserie chicken or Sicilian rigatoni with ricotta cheese.

The Uva Bar (*uva* means "grape" in Spanish) is a casual tapas bar located at an outdoor courtyard right in the middle of the Downtown Disney walkway. Martinis are a standout here; there are also 40 different wines by the glass. The affordable menu features the same pan-Mediterranean influence, even offering many items from the Catal menu; standouts include cabernet-braised short ribs atop horseradish mashed potatoes, marinated olives, and cured Spanish ham; and Andalusian gazpacho with rock shrimp.

1580 Disneyland Dr. (at Downtown Disney). ℂ 714/774-4442. Reservations recommended Sun–Thurs, not accepted Fri–Sat for Catal; not accepted for Uva Bar. Main courses $14–$24; tapas $5–$8. AE, DC, DISC, MC, V. Mon–Thurs 11am–11pm; Fri–Sun 11am–midnight.

Goofy's Kitchen Kids AMERICAN   Your younger kids will never forgive you if they miss an opportunity to dine with their favorite Disney characters at this colorful, lively restaurant inside the Disneyland Hotel. Known for its entertainment and wacky and off-center Toontown-esque decor, Goofy's Kitchen features tableside visits by Disney characters (Goofy, Alice, Geppetto, Pocahontas, Aladdin, the Beast) who thrill the youngsters with dancing, autograph signing, and up-close-and-personal encounters. Meals are buffet-style and offer an adequate selection of crowd pleasers and reliable standbys, from bacon and eggs at breakfast to fried chicken, Caesar salad, deli sand-wiches, and Italian pastas at lunch and dinner. The most popular kid food is the peanut butter and jelly pizza (even for breakfast), the buffet of gummy worms, Mickey Mouse–shaped waffles, and Mickey ear–shaped chicken nuggets. This place isn't really about the food, though, and is definitely *not* for kidless grown-ups. Bring a camera and Disney autograph book for capturing the family's "candid" encounters. *Tip:* Make reservations for an early or late breakfast or dinner to avoid the mayhem.

1150 Magic Way (inside the Disneyland Hotel). ℂ 714/956-6755 or 714/781-DINE. www.disneyland. com. Reservations recommended. Buffet prices (child/adult): $10–$17 breakfast, $10–$18 lunch, $10–$27 dinner. AE, DC, DISC, MC, V. Daily 7am–9pm.

House of Blues AMERICAN/SOUTHERN   For years, fans have been comparing the House of Blues to Disneyland, so this celeb-backed restaurant/nightclub fits right into the Disney compound. Locations in Las Vegas, L.A., Orlando, and so forth all sport a calculated backwoods-bayou-meets-Country-Bear-Jamboree appearance that fits right into the Disneyfied world. The Anaheim HOB follows the formula, filled with made-to-look-old found objects, amateur paintings, uneven wood floors, seemingly decayed chandeliers, and a country-casual attitude. The restaurant features Delta-inspired stick-to-your-ribs cuisine such as Louisiana crawfish cakes, Creole seafood jambalaya, corn-meal-crusted catfish, baby back ribs glazed with Jack Daniel's sauce, and spicy Cajun meatloaf—plus some out-of-place Cal-lite stragglers such as seared ahi and pesto pasta. Sunday's Gospel Brunch is an advance-ticket event of hand-clapping, foot-stomping proportions. The adjacent Company Store offers logo ware interspersed with selected pieces of folk art. HOB's state-of-the-art Music Hall is a welcome addition to the local music scene (advance tickets are highly recommended for big-name bookings).

1530 S. Disneyland Dr. (at Downtown Disney). ℂ 714/778-2583. www.hob.com. Reservations not accepted for restaurant (tickets required for performances). Main courses $8–$17. AE, DC, DISC, MC, V. Mon–Sat 11am–midnight; Sun 10am–midnight.

Rainforest Cafe Kids INTERNATIONAL   Designed to suggest ancient temple ruins in an overgrown Central American jungle, this national chain favorite successfully com-bines entertainment, retail, and family-friendly dining in one fantasy setting. There are cascading waterfalls inside and out, a canopy of lush vegetation, simulated tropical mists,

(Tips) **For Sports Lovers**

Sports fans may prefer to dine at the **ESPN Zone** in Downtown Disney, 1545 Disneyland Dr. (✆ **714/300-ESPN** [300-3776]; www.espnzone.com). More than 175 TV monitors allow you to watch just about every current sporting event in the U.S. while dining on American grill food and pub fare.

and even a troupe of colorful parrots beckoning shoppers into the Retail Village. Once seated, diners choose from an amalgam of wildly flavored dishes inspired by Caribbean, Polynesian, Latin, Asian, and Mediterranean cuisines. Masquerading under such exotic-sounding names as Jungle Safari Soup (a meaty version of minestrone) and Mojo Bones (barbecued pork ribs), the food is really fairly familiar: A translated sampling includes Cobb salad, pita sandwiches, potstickers, shrimp-studded pasta, and charbroiled chicken. Fresh-fruit smoothies and tropical specialty cocktails are offered, as is a best-shared dessert called the Giant Chocolate Volcano. After your meal, you can browse through logo items, environmentally educational toys and games, stuffed jungle animals and puppets, straw safari hats, and other themed souvenirs in the lobby store. There's a children's menu, and the Rainforest Cafe is one of the few Downtown Disney eateries to have full breakfast service.

1515 S. Disneyland Dr. (at Downtown Disney). ✆ 714/772-0413. www.rainforestcafe.com. Reservations recommended for peak mealtimes. Main courses $9–$21. AE, DC, DISC, MC, V. Sun–Thurs 7am–11pm; Fri–Sat 7am–midnight.

Ralph Brennan's Jazz Kitchen ★ CAJUN-CREOLE   If you always thought Disneyland's New Orleans Square was just like the real thing, wait until you see this authentically Southern concept restaurant at Downtown Disney. Ralph Brennan, of the New Orleans food dynasty responsible for NOLA landmarks such as Commander's Palace and a trio of Big Easy hot spots, commissioned a handful of New Orleans artists to create the handcrafted furnishings that give the Jazz Kitchen its believable French Quarter ambience. Lacy wrought-iron grillwork, cascading ferns, and trickling stone fountains enhance three separate dining choices: The upstairs Carnival Club is an elegant dining salon with silk-draped chandeliers and terrace dining that overlooks the "street scene" below; casual Flambeaux is downstairs, where a bead-encrusted grand piano hints at the nightly live jazz that sizzles in this room; and the Creole Cafe is a quick stop for necessities such as muffulettas or beignets. Expect traditional Cajun-Creole fare with heavy-handed seasonings and rich, heart-stopping sauces—now *that's* authentically New Orleans.

1590 S. Disneyland Dr. (at Downtown Disney). ✆ 714/776-5200. www.rbjazzkitchen.com. Reservations strongly recommended. Main courses $16–$25 (cafe items $4–$8). AE, DC, DISC, MC, V. Daily 11am–3pm and 5–11pm.

Inexpensive

La Brea Bakery Express & Cafe BAKERY/MEDITERRANEAN   Fresh from the ovens of L.A.'s now nationally known artisan bakery, this La Brea Bakery duo occupies a coveted position at the beginning of Downtown Disney, right across from the theme parks' ticket kiosks. Each morning, still-groggy early bird parkgoers stumble from the parking-lot tram and head straight to La Brea's cafeteria-style Express for a caffeinated pick-me-up or a meal to start the day. Light breakfast items are served in addition to creator Nancy Silverton's irresistible breads and pastries. The outdoor patio is comfortably outfitted with woven bistro chairs (plus heat lamps for brisk mornings) and provides a relaxing setting before you brave the Disney throngs. Throughout the day, folks stop in for a lunch of sandwiches, filled brioche, or herb-laden focaccia. The kids' menu offers typical choices such as grilled cheese and PB&J.

1556 Disneyland Dr. (at Downtown Disney). © **714/490-0233.** www.labreabakery.com. Reservations recommended for Cafe. Light fare under $5 (Express); main courses $10–$20 (Cafe). AE, DISC, MC, V. Express daily 8am–11pm. Cafe daily 11am–11pm.

5 KNOTT'S BERRY FARM

30 miles SE of downtown L.A.

Although destined to always be in the shadow of Mickey's megaresort, the reality is that Knott's doesn't even attempt to compete with the Disney empire: Instead, it targets Southern California thrill-seekers (droves of them) by offering a far better selection of scream-inducing thrill rides.

Like Disneyland, Knott's Berry Farm is not without historical background. In 1920, Walter Knott began farming 20 acres of leased land on Highway 39 (now Beach Blvd.). When things got tough during the Depression, Mrs. Knott began selling pies, preserves, and home-cooked chicken dinners. Within a year, she was selling 90 meals a day. Lines became so long that Walter decided to create an Old West Ghost Town—America's first theme park—in 1940 as a diversion for waiting customers.

Today Knott's amusement park offers a whopping 165 shows, attractions, and state-of-the-art rides that are far more intense than most of the rides at the Disneyland Resort. Granted, it's less than half the size of the Disney Resort and doesn't have quite the same magical appeal, but if you're more into fast-paced amusement rides than swirling tea cups, spend your money here.

ESSENTIALS
Getting There
Knott's Berry Farm is at 8039 Beach Blvd. in Buena Park. It's about a 10-minute ride north on I-5 from Disneyland. From I-5 or California 91, exit south onto Beach Boulevard. The park is about half a mile south of California 91.

Visitor Information
The **Buena Park Convention and Visitors Office,** 6601 Beach Blvd., Suite 200, Buena Park (© **714/562-3560;** www.buenapark.com), provides specialized information on the area, including Knott's Berry Farm. To learn more about the amusement park before you arrive, call © **714/220-5200** or log on to **www.knotts.com.**

Admission Prices & Operating Hours
Admission to the park, including unlimited access to all rides, shows, and attractions, is $49 for adults and children 12 and over; $20 for kids 3 to 11 and seniors 62 and older; and free for children under 3. Admission after 4pm (on any day the park is open past 6pm) is $25 for adults and $18 for kids 3 to 11. Parking is $10. Tickets can also be purchased at many Southern California hotels, where discount coupons are sometimes available.

Like Disneyland, Knott's offers discounted admission—$36 for adults—for Southern California residents with zip codes 90000 through 93599, so if you're bringing local friends or family members along, try to take advantage of the bargain. Also like Disneyland,

Knott's Berry Farm's hours vary from week to week, so call ahead. The park generally opens daily at 10am and closes at 6 or 7pm, except Saturdays, when it stays open until 10pm. Operating hours and prices often change with seasonal promotions, so it's always a good idea to call Knott's Info at © **714/220-5200** for specific hours on the day you plan to visit. Stage shows and special activities are scheduled throughout the day; pick up a schedule at the ticket booth.

TOURING THE PARK

Despite all the high-tech multimillion-dollar rides, Knott's Berry Farm maintains much of its original Old West motif and also features the Peanuts gang: Snoopy, Charlie Brown, Woodstock, and pals are the official costumed characters of Knott's. The park is divided into six themed areas, each one of which features at least one of the thrill roller coasters that are the Knott's claim to fame. The California MarketPlace is located adjacent to, but outside of, the theme park, featuring 14 unique shops and restaurants, including the original favorite, Mrs. Knott's Chicken Dinner Restaurant and the TGI Friday's franchise.

Ghost Town

The park's original attraction is a collection of authentic 19th-century buildings relocated from deserted Old West towns in Arizona and California. You can pan for gold, ride an authentic stagecoach, take rickety train cars through the Calico Mine, and get held up aboard the Calico Railroad. If you love wooden roller coasters, don't miss the clackity GhostRider.

Calico Railroad Board this 1881 narrow-gauge steam-engine train—once part of the Denver and Rio Grande Southern Line—for a round-trip tour of half the theme park, interrupted by "bandit" holdups.

GhostRider ★★★ Looming 118 feet high, this coaster is the park's single largest attraction and one of the longest and tallest wooden roller coasters in the world. Riders enter through a replica mine and are strapped into gold, silver, or copper mining cars for an adventure that twists and careens through sudden dips, banked turns, and cheek-flattening G-forces. The ride isn't nearly as smooth and quiet as the steel roller coasters, and that's part of the thrill. Worldwide coaster enthusiasts worship this classic.

Ghost Town Artisans ★ (Finds) An entertaining holdover from the earliest days of the park, these living history booths present old-time crafts and tall tales presented by costumed blacksmiths, woodcarvers, a spinner, and storytellers who help bring Ghost Town to life for curious kids and history buffs.

Silver Bullet ★★ This inverted coaster dangles riders from the steel track that weaves its way through the center of the park. Flying over Reflection Lake from the edge of the stagecoach stop to the top of the Log Ride mountain at a height of 146 feet, this high-speed thriller sends riders head over heels six times with cobra rolls, spirals, cork-screws, and other whacked-out whirls.

Timber Mountain Log Ride ★ Riders emerge from a dark and twisting "sawmill" waterway and plummet down a 42-foot flume for the grand splash. Compared to the other water rides in the park, this one leaves you only slightly sprinkled.

Wild West Stunt Show This wild and woolly stunt spectacular is a raucous salute to the Old West presented throughout the day in the open-air Wagon Camp Theater.

Here you'll find a south-of-the-border theme—festive markets and an ambience that suggests old Spanish California. A cluster of carnival-style rides (in addition to the roller coasters listed below) includes a 100-year-old merry-go-round, plus Knott's version of Disneyland's Tea Cups, where you can sit-and-spin in your own sombrero. You can stroll the paths of Fiesta Village, which are lined with old-time carnival games and state-of-the-art electric arcades.

Jaguar! ★★   Loosely themed around a tropical jungle setting, this wild roller coaster includes two heart-in-the-mouth drops and a view of Fiesta Village from high above. It's a good family roller coaster for first-timers or the easily frightened.

La Revolución ★   A real stomach-churner, this ride both spins you in circles while swinging back and forth more than 65 feet in the air. It's like being in the rinse cycle of a washing machine that's swinging from a rope.

Montezooma's Revenge ★   Blasting from 0 to 60 mph in 5 seconds, this not-for-the-fainthearted thriller then propels riders through a giant 360-degree loop both forward and backward.

The Boardwalk

The park's Boardwalk area is a salute to Southern California's beach culture, where colorful architecture and palm trees are the backdrop for a trio of thrill rides. Other amusements include arcade and boardwalk games, and the **Charles M. Schulz Theatre,** where seasonal productions include a *Snoopy* ice show or holiday pageant (check the marquee or park entertainment schedule for showtimes).

Boomerang ★   This corkscrew scream machine sends you twisting through three head-over-heels loops in less than a minute—but it doesn't end there, since you're sent through the track again . . . backward.

Lazer Invaders (Kids)   In this adaptation of the classic Lazer Runner, participants equipped with phasers and fiber-optic vests battle for supremacy in a richly evocative atmosphere. Each combatant must make use of protective walls and laser power to vanquish opponents.

Perilous Plunge ★★   Just 34 feet shorter than Niagara Falls, this wet adventure sends riders to a height of 127 feet and then drops them down a 115-foot water chute at a 75-degree angle—15 degrees from a sheer vertical. Prepare for a thorough soaking (a boon on hot days, but best experienced before nightfall).

Sky Cabin ★   Just when you were thinking all the rides were for hard-core adrenaline-seekers (most are, actually), this quiet ride offers the same spectacular views at a calmer pace. The slowly rotating "cabin" ascends Knott's vertical tower, providing panoramic views of the park and surrounding area.

Supreme Scream ★★   They could've called this one the Evil Elevator: Seated and fully exposed riders are hoisted straight up a 30-story tower with their feet dangling in the air and then held at the top just long enough to rattle the nerves before plunging downward faster than gravity at more than 60 mph. The whole descent takes only a bowel-shaking 3 seconds. It's one of the tallest (and most unnerving) thrill rides in the world.

Xcelerator ★★★   It's scary just looking at this super-high-tech 1950s–themed roller coaster, which launches you from 0 to 82 mph in $2^1/_3$ seconds, then whips you straight

> **(Tips) Getting Soaked at Knott's**
>
> Surf's up at **Knott's Soak City Water Park,** a 13-acre water park next door to
> Knott's Berry Farm, with a theme of surf woodies and longboards of the 1950s
> Southern California coast. The fun includes the **Pacific Spin,** a multiperson raft
> ride that drops riders 75 feet into a six-story funnel tube, as well as body slides,
> speed slides, an artificial wave lagoon, and an area for youngsters with their own
> pool and beach shack fun house. The park is located at 8039 Buena Park (© **714/
> 220-5200;** www.soakcityusa.com). Admission prices are $29 for adults, $18 for
> kids 3 to 11, and free to children under 3; parking is $9. After 3pm, tickets for all
> ages are $18. Ask about special promotions and discount coupons (or check the
> website). The park is open daily May 24 to September 3 and weekends Septem-
> ber 8 to 30. Soak City Water Park opens at 10am and closes between 5 and 7pm,
> based on the season.

up 20 stories (with a half-twist thrown in for added addling), and takes you almost
straight back down again. It's like riding on the outer edge of a gigantic paper clip.

Camp Snoopy

This will probably be the youngsters' favorite area. The first-ever theme park area dedicated
solely to kids, it's meant to re-create a wilderness camp in the High Sierras. Six rustic acres
are the playgrounds of Charles Schulz's beagle and his pals, Charlie Brown and Lucy, who
greet guests and pose for pictures. There are over a dozen rides in the camp; several kid-size
rides are made especially for the younger set, while the entire family can enjoy others.
Scaled-down stock cars, locomotives, steamboats, 18-wheeler semis, hot-air balloons, and
even the Peanuts gang's school bus give kids a playland of their own. There's also a child-size
version of Supreme Scream, called Woodstock's Airmail, and Joe Cool's GR8 SK8, a mini–
thrill ride for the whole family. Interactive attractions include the **Camp Snoopy Theatre**
starring the Peanuts gang (little kids are transfixed by this show).

Wild Water Wilderness

This $10-million, 3^1/$_2$-acre area is styled like a turn-of-the-20th-century California wil-
derness park with a raging white-water river, cascading waterfalls, soaring geysers, and
old-style ranger stations.

Bigfoot Rapids ★★   The centerpiece of Wild Water Wilderness is this outdoor
white-water river raft ride, the longest of its kind in the world. Climb aboard a six-seat
circular raft, and prepare to be bounced, buffeted, tossed, spun, and splashed along fast-
moving currents, under cascading waterfalls, and around soaring geysers. Let there be no
doubt: You will get *extremely* wet on this one.

Mystery Lodge ★★   This amazing high-tech, trick-of-the-eye tribute to the magic
of Native American storytelling is a theater attraction for the whole family. The Old
Storyteller takes the audience on a mystical, multisensory journey into the culture of local
tribes by employing centuries-old legends passed down through oral history.

Indian Trails

Explore the ride-free Indian Trails cultural area, which offers demonstrations of native dance and music by authentically costumed Native American and Aztec dancers, singers, and musicians performed in the round on the Indian Trails stage. In addition, the compound showcases a variety of traditional Native American structures from the Pacific Northwest, Great Plains, and Southwest. The area includes four towering totem poles, standing from 15 to 27 feet high; three authentic tepees, representing the Arapaho, Blackfoot, and Nez Perce tribes; and more. The arts and crafts of Native American tribes from the western part of North America are also demonstrated and displayed. While exploring Indian Trails, visitors can enjoy a sampling of Native American foods, including Navajo tacos, Indian fry bread, and fresh-roasted ears of corn.

WHERE TO STAY

Knott's Berry Farm Resort Hotel ★ Kids Within easy walking distance of Knott's Berry Farm, this nine-story hotel is the only lodging located near the amusement park. Despite the hotel's lengthy moniker, the exterior and lobby have the look of a business hotel. There are two things I like best about this hotel: the Peanuts-themed rooms complete with Snoopy tuck-in service and Camp Kids bedtime stories (told via the in-room phone by the bed), and free shuttle service to Disneyland, 7 miles away. There's also a large family pool with a children's water play structure, and an arcade. Be sure to inquire about special rates and Knott's multiday vacation packages.

7675 Crescent Ave. (at Grand), Buena Park, CA 90620. © 866/752-2444 or 714/995-1111. Fax 714/828-8590. www.knottshotel.com. 320 units. $179 standard room; $224 Snoopy room. Prices vary depending on date of visit and room availability. Discount packages available. AE, DC, DISC, MC, V. Parking $10 per night. **Amenities:** Restaurant; lounge; outdoor pool; 2 outdoor tennis and basketball courts (lit for night play); fitness center; whirlpool; video arcade; concierge; free Disneyland shuttle; Wi-Fi (fee); room service; self-service laundry; laundry service; dry cleaning. *In room:* A/C, TV w/pay movies, fax, high-speed Internet (fee), coffeemaker, hair dryer, iron, safe, video games.

WHERE TO DINE

Mrs. Knott's Chicken Dinner Restaurant Kids AMERICAN Knott's Berry Farm got its start as a roadside diner in 1934, and you can still get a filling—albeit unhealthful—all-American meal without even entering the theme park. Cordelia Knott's down-home cooking was so popular that her husband created a few humble attractions to amuse patrons. Today more than 1.5 million annual visitors line up around the building to experience Cordelia's original recipe (very similar to the Colonel's, I must admit), served by sweet waitresses built more for comfort than speed. Looking just as you'd expect—country cute, with window shutters, old black-and-white photos of the original diner, and calico prints aplenty—the restaurant serves up its featured attraction of the original fried chicken dinner, complete with soup, salad, warm buttermilk biscuits, mashed potatoes and chicken gravy, and a slice of famous pie (the boysenberry pie is fantastic). Country-fried steak, pot roast, roast turkey, and pork ribs are options, as are sandwiches, salads, and a terrific chicken potpie. Boysenberries abound, from breakfast jam to traditional double-crust pies. The adjacent takeout shop is always crowded. *Tip:* If you're not visiting the amusement park, park in the lot that offers 3 free hours.

8039 Beach Blvd. (near La Palma), Buena Park. © 714/220-5080. Reservations not accepted. Main courses $7–$10; complete dinners $14. DC, DISC, MC, V. Open daily at 7am; closing times vary.

Seal Beach is 36 miles S of downtown L.A.; Newport Beach, 49 miles; Dana Point, 65 miles

Whatever you do, don't say "Orange County" here. The mere name evokes images of smoggy industrial parks, cookie-cutter housing developments, and the staunch Republicanism that prevails behind the so-called "orange curtain." We're talking instead about the Orange Coast, one of Southern California's best-kept secrets—a string of seaside jewels that have been compared with the French Riviera or the Costa del Sol. Forty-two miles of beaches offer pristine stretches of sand, tide pools teeming with marine life, ecological preserves, secluded coves, picturesque pleasure-boat harbors, and legendary surf breaks. My advice? Make it a day trip from L.A.—hit the road early for a scenic cruise down Pacific Coast Highway starting at Seal Beach, stop for lunch at Laguna Beach (the prettiest of all the So Cal beach towns), continue south to Dana Point where the *really* expensive resorts reside, and then take the freeway back to L.A. (I-5 to the I-405).

ESSENTIALS

GETTING THERE   See "Getting There" in chapter 3 for airport and airline information. By car from Los Angeles, take I-5 or I-405 south. The scenic, shore-hugging Pacific Coast Highway (Calif. 1, or just PCH to the locals) links the Orange Coast communities from Seal Beach in the north to Capistrano Beach just south of Dana Point, where it merges with I-5. To reach the beach communities directly, take the following freeway exits: **Seal Beach,** Seal Beach Boulevard from I-405; **Huntington Beach,** Beach Boulevard/California 39 from either I-405 or I-5; **Newport Beach,** California 55 from either I-405 or I-5; **Laguna Beach,** California 133 from I-5; **San Juan Capistrano,** Ortega Highway/California 74 from I-5; and **Dana Point,** Pacific Coast Highway/California 1 from I-5.

VISITOR INFORMATION   The **Seal Beach Chamber of Commerce,** 201 Eighth St., Suite 120, next to City Hall (© **562/799-0179;** www.sealbeachchamber.com), is open Monday through Friday from 10am to 4pm.

The **Huntington Beach Conference & Visitors Bureau,** 301 Main St., Suite 208 (© **800/729-6232** or 714/969-3492; www.surfcityusa.com), enthusiastically offers tons of information and personal anecdotes. Open Monday through Friday from 9am to 5pm.

The **Newport Beach Conference & Visitors Bureau,** 110 Newport Center Dr., Suite 120 (© **800/94-COAST** or 949/719-6100; www.newportbeach-cvb.com), distributes brochures, sample menus, a calendar of events, and the free *Visitor's Guide.* Call or stop in Monday through Friday from 8am to 5pm (plus weekends in summer).

The **Laguna Beach Visitors Bureau,** 252 Broadway (© **800/877-1115** or 949/497-9229; www.lagunabeachinfo.org), is in the heart of town and distributes lodging, dining, and art gallery guides. It's open Monday through Friday from 9am to 5pm, and Saturday from 10am to 4pm (plus Sun in summer).

The **San Juan Capistrano Chamber of Commerce,** Franciscan Plaza, 31781 Camino Capistrano, Suite 306 (© **949/493-4700;** www.sanjuancapistrano.com), is within walking distance of the mission and offers a walking tour guide to historic sites. Open Monday through Friday from 9am to 5pm.

The **Dana Point Chamber of Commerce Visitor Center,** located in the Clocktower Building at LaPlaza Center (© **800/290-DANA** or 949/496-1555; www.danapoint-chamber.com), is open Monday through Friday from 9am to 5pm (closed noon–1pm for

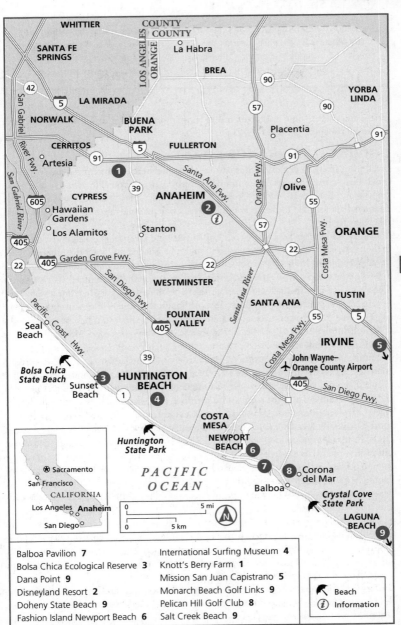

Balboa Pavilion **7**

Bolsa Chica Ecological Reserve **3**

Dana Point **9**

Disneyland Resort **2**

Doheny State Beach **9**

Fashion Island Newport Beach **6**

International Surfing Museum **4**

Knott's Berry Farm **1**

Mission San Juan Capistrano **5**

Monarch Beach Golf Links **9**

Pelican Hill Golf Club **8**

Salt Creek Beach **9**

🏖 Beach

ⓘ Information

Tips **A Special Arts Festival**

> A tradition for 60-plus years in arts-friendly Laguna, the **Festival of Arts & Pageant of the Masters** is held each summer throughout July and August. It's pretty large now, and it includes the formerly "alternative" Sawdust Festival across the street. See the "Calendar of Events" in chapter 3 for details, or log on to **www.foapom.com**.

lunch) and carries some restaurant and lodging information, as well as a comprehensive recreation brochure.

DRIVING THE ORANGE COAST

You'll most likely be exploring the coast by car, so the beach communities are covered in order, from north to south. Keep in mind, however, that if you're traveling between Los Angeles and San Diego, Pacific Coast Highway (Calif. 1) is a breezy, scenic detour that adds less than an hour to the commute—so pick out a couple of seaside destinations and take your time.

Seal Beach, on the border between Los Angeles and Orange counties, and a neighbor to Long Beach's Naples Harbor, is geographically isolated by both the adjacent U.S. Naval Weapons Station and the self-contained Leisure World retirement community. As a result, the beach town appears untouched by modern development—it's Orange County's version of small-town America. Take a stroll down Main Street for a walk back in time, culminating in the Seal Beach Pier. Although the clusters of sunbathing, squawking seals that gave the town its name aren't around any more, old-timers still fish, lovers still stroll, and families still cavort by the seaside, enjoying great food and retail shops or having a cold drink at Hennessey's tavern.

Huntington Beach—or Surf City, as it's known—is the largest Orange Coast city; it stretches quite a way inland and has seen the most urbanization. To some extent, this has changed the old boardwalk and pier to a modern outdoor mall where cliques of teens coexist with families and the surfers who continue to flock here, drawn by Huntington's legendary place in surf lore. Hawaiian-born George Freeth is credited with bringing the sport here in 1907, and some say the breaks around the pier and Bolsa Chica are the best in California. The world's top wave riders flock to Huntington each August for the rowdy but professional **U.S. Open of Surfing.** If you're around at Christmas time, try to see the gaily decorated marina homes and boats in Huntington Harbor by taking the **Cruise of Lights,** a 45-minute narrated sail through and around the harbor islands. The festivities generally last from mid-December until Christmas; call © **714/840-7542** for schedules and ticket information.

The name **Newport Beach** conjures comparisons to Rhode Island's Newport, where the well-to-do enjoy seaside living with all the creature comforts. That's the way it is here, too, but on a less grandiose scale. From the million-dollar Cape Cod–style cottages on sunny Balboa Island to elegant shopping complexes such as Fashion Island and South Coast Plaza (an über-mall with valet parking, car detailing, limo service, and concierge), this is where fashionable socialites, right-wing celebrities, and business mavens can all be found. Alternatively, you could explore **Balboa Peninsula's** historic Pavilion and old-fashioned pier, or board a passenger ferry to Catalina Island.

Laguna Beach, whose breathtaking geography is marked by bold elevated headlands, coastal bluffs, pocket coves, and a very inviting beach, is known as an artists' enclave, but the truth is that Laguna has became so "in" (read: expensive) that it's driven most of the true bohemians out. Their legacy remains, with the annual **Festival of Arts & Pageant of the Masters** (see "A Special Arts Festival," above), as well as a proliferation of art galleries mingling with high-priced boutiques along the town's cozy streets. In warm weather, Laguna Beach has an overwhelming Mediterranean-island ambience, which makes *everyone* feel beautifully, idly rich.

San Juan Capistrano, in the verdant headlands inland from Dana Point, is defined by Spanish missions and its loyal swallows. The mission architecture is authentic, and history abounds. Think of San Juan Capistrano as a compact, life-size diorama illustrating the evolution of a small Western town—from Spanish-mission era to secular rancho period, statehood, and into the 21st century. Surprisingly, Mission San Juan Capistrano (see "Seeing the Sights," below) is once again the center of the community, just as the founding friars intended 200 years ago.

Dana Point, the last town south, has been called a "marina development in search of a soul." Overlooking the harbor stands a monument to 19th-century author Richard Henry Dana, who gave his name to the area and described it in *Two Years Before the Mast.* Activities generally center on yachting and Dana Point's beautiful harbor. Nautical themes are everywhere, particularly the streets named for old-fashioned shipboard lights—a hodgepodge that includes Street of the Amber Lantern, Street of the Violet Lantern, Street of the Golden Lantern, and so on. Bordering the harbor is Doheny State Beach (see "Beaches & Nature Preserves," below), one of the very best for its seaside park and camping facilities.

ENJOYING THE OUTDOORS

BEACHES & NATURE PRESERVES   The **Bolsa Chica Ecological Reserve,** in Huntington Beach (© **714/846-1114;** www.bolsachica.org), is a 900-acre restored urban salt marsh that's a haven to more than 200 bird species, as well as a wide variety of protected plants and animals. Naturalists come to spot herons and egrets as well as California horn snails, jackknife clams, sea sponges, common jellyfish, and shore crabs. An easy 1.5-mile loop trail begins from a parking lot on Pacific Coast Highway (Calif. 1) a mile south of Warner Boulevard; docents lead a narrated walk the first Saturday of every month. The trail heads inland, over Inner Bolsa Bay and up Bolsa Chica bluffs. It then loops back toward the ocean over a dike that separates the Inner and Outer Bolsa bays and traverses a coastal sand-dune system. This beautiful hike is a terrific afternoon adventure. The Bolsa Chica Conservancy has been working since 1978 on reclaiming the wetlands from oil companies that began drilling here more than 70 years ago. It's an ongoing process, and you can still see those "seesaw" drills dotting the outer areas of the reserve.

Huntington City Beach, adjacent to Huntington Pier, is a haven for volleyball players and surfers; dense crowds abound, but so do amenities such as outdoor showers, beach rentals, and restrooms. Just south of the city beach is 3-mile-long **Huntington State Beach.** Both popular beaches have lifeguards and concession stands seasonally. The state beach also has restrooms, showers, barbecue pits, and a waterfront bike path. The main entrance is on Beach Boulevard, and there are access points all along Pacific Coast Highway (Calif. 1).

Newport Beach runs for about 5 miles and includes both Newport and Balboa piers. It has outdoor showers, restrooms, volleyball nets, and a vintage boardwalk that just may make you feel as though you've stepped 50 years back in time. **Balboa Bike and Beach**

Stuff (© 949/723-1516), at the corner of Balboa and Palm near the pier, rents a variety of items, from pier fishing poles to bikes, beach umbrellas, and body boards. The **Southwind Kayak Center,** 17855 Sky Park Circle, Irvine (© **800/768-8494** or 949/261-0200; www.southwindkayaks.com), rents sea kayaks for use in the bay or open ocean at rates starting at $70 per day; instructional classes are available on weekends, with some midweek classes in summer. The center also conducts several easygoing guided outings, including a $55 Back to Nature trip that highlights the marine life around Dana Point.

Crystal Cove State Park, which covers 3 miles of coastline between Corona del Mar and Laguna Beach and extends into the hills around El Moro Canyon, is a good alternative to the more popular beaches for seekers of solitude. (There are, however, lifeguards and restrooms.) The beach is a winding, sandy strip, backed with grassy terraces; high tide sometimes sections it into coves. The entire area offshore is an underwater nature preserve. There are four entrances, including Pelican Point and El Moro Canyon. For information, call © 949/494-3539 or log on to **www.crystalcovestatepark.com**.

Salt Creek Beach Park lies below the palatial Ritz-Carlton Laguna Niguel; guests who tire of the pristine swimming pool can venture down the staircase on Ritz-Carlton Drive to wiggle their toes in the sand. The setting is spectacular, with wide white-sand beaches looking out toward Catalina Island (which explains why the Ritz-Carlton was built here). The park has lifeguards, restrooms, a snack bar, and convenient parking near the hotel.

Doheny State Beach in Dana Point, just south of Dana Point Marina (enter off Del Abispo St.), has long been known as a premier surfing spot and camping site. Doheny has the friendly vibe of beach parties in days gone by: Tree-shaded lawns give way to wide beaches, and picnicking and beach camping are encouraged. There are 121 sites that can be used for either tents or RVs, plus a state-run visitor center featuring several small aquariums of sea and tide pool life. For more information and camping availability, call © 949/492-0802.

BICYCLING Biking is the most popular beach activity up and down the coast. A slower-paced alternative to driving, it allows you to enjoy the clean, fresh air and notice smaller details of these laid-back beach towns and harbors. The Newport Beach visitor center (see "Visitor Information," above) offers a free *Bike Ways* map of trails throughout the city and harbor. Bikes and equipment can be rented at **Balboa Bike & Beach Stuff,** 601 Balboa Blvd., Newport Beach (© 949/723-1516), and at **Laguna Beach Cyclery,** 240 Thalia St. (© **949/494-1522;** www.lagunacyclery.net).

GOLF Many golf-course architects have used the geography of the Orange Coast to its full advantage, molding challenging and scenic courses from the rolling bluffs. Most courses are private, but a few outstanding ones are open to the public. **The Links at Monarch Beach,** 50 Monarch Beach Resort North, Dana Point (© **877/635-8792** or 949/240-8247; www.monarchbeachgolf.com), is particularly impressive. This hilly, challenging course, designed by Robert Trent Jones, Jr., offers great ocean views. Afternoon winds can sneak up, so accuracy is essential. Weekend greens fees are $210 ($170 weekdays). The rates after 1pm drop to $135 weekends and $110 weekdays.

SEEING THE SIGHTS

Beyond the sights listed below, one of the most popular Orange Coast attractions is **Balboa Island** (www.balboaisland.com). The charm of this pretty little neighborhood isn't diminished by knowing that the island was man-made—and it certainly hasn't affected the price of real estate (it's hard to believe that the original property lots sold for $250). Tiny clapboard cottages in the island's center and modern houses with two-story

Biplane, Air Combat & Warbird Adventures: The Thrill of a Lifetime

For anyone with a thirst for adrenaline-pumping excitement, boy have I got a recommendation for you. At a small airport in the coastal town of Carlsbad, about 30 miles north of San Diego, is a company called Biplane, Air Combat & Warbird Adventures, run by husband-and-wife team Kate and Tom. Turning a passion for old planes into a thriving business, this cheerful duo offers a knock-out package of nostalgia, romance, fun, and—for the truly adventurous—a mind-blowing chance to fly a World War II fighter plane, an open-cockpit biplane, or a modern combat aircraft (or all three!).

For the mild-mannered, the 1920s-era biplane ride is pure romance: Couples wearing soft leather headgear and goggles (think Snoopy vs. the Red Baron) sit side-by-side at the front of the open cockpit while the pilot—seated in the back—flies a leisurely route along the sunny coast. At your request, the pilot will perform a few dips and lazy eights to add a touch of excitement, but nothing compares to the loops and rolls you'll perform (yes, you who's never flown a plane in your life) in their big blue AT-6 Texan, a 600-horsepower fighter aircraft equipped with machine-gun barrels that looks like a killer and flies like a pussycat. "Okay, it's your plane," are four words you'll remember forever as the pilot, seated in front, calmly talks you through the aerobatic procedures, which are surprisingly easy to perform (it's one of the most incredible things I've ever done).

Other toys on the tarmac include a pair of modern prop-driven dogfighters. Real fighter pilots from the nearby marine base will give you a preflight lesson on aerial combat maneuvers, then get you airborne, and let you fly the plane as you try to blast your partner—flying the "enemy" plane—out of the sky (figuratively, of course). For more information about Biplane, Air Combat & Warbird Adventures, call ⓒ **800/SKY-LOOP** or 760/930-0903. Be sure to visit their website, **www.barnstorming.com**, for special Internet rates and package deals.

windows and private docks along the perimeter make a colorful and romantic picture. You can drive onto the island on Jamboree Road to the north or take the three-car ferry from Balboa Peninsula (www.balboaislandferry.com). It's generally more fun to park and take the 30-minute ferry ride as a pedestrian, since the island is crowded and lacks parking, and the tiny alleys they call streets are more suitable for strolling. **Marine Avenue,** the main commercial street, is lined with small shops and cafes that evoke a New England fishing village. Shaved ices sold by sidewalk vendors will relieve the heat of summer.

Balboa Pavilion & Fun Zone ★ (Kids) This historic cupola-topped structure, a California Historical Landmark, was built in 1906 as a bathhouse for swimmers in their ankle-length bathing costumes. Later, during the Big Band era, dancers rocked the Pavilion doing the Balboa Hop. Now it serves as the terminal for Catalina Island passenger service, harbor and whale-watching cruises, and fishing charters. The surrounding boardwalk is the Balboa

Fun Zone (☏ **949/673-0408;** www.thebalboafunzone.com), a collection of carnival rides, game arcades, and vendors of hot dogs and cotton candy. For Newport Harbor or Catalina cruise information, call ☏ **949/673-5245;** for sportfishing and whale-watching, call ☏ **949/673-1434.**

600 E. Bay Ave., Balboa, Newport Beach. ☏ **949/675-1905.** www.balboapavilion.com. From Calif. 1, turn south onto Newport Blvd. (which becomes Balboa Blvd. on the peninsula); turn left at Main St.

International Surfing Museum   Nostalgic Gidgets and Moondoggies shouldn't miss this monument to the laid-back sport that has become synonymous with California beaches. You'll find gargantuan long boards from the sport's early days, memorabilia of Duke Kahanamoku and the other surfing greats represented on the Walk of Fame near Huntington Pier, and a gift shop where a copy of the *Surfin'ary* can help you bone up on your surfer slang even if you don't know which foot is goofy.

411 Olive Ave., Huntington Beach. ☏ **714/960-3483.** www.surfingmuseum.org. Admission $2 adults, $1 students, free for kids ages 6 and under. Mid-June to late Sept daily noon–5pm; rest of the year Wed–Sun noon–5pm (hours tend to vary, so call ahead).

Laguna Art Museum   This beloved local institution is working hard to position itself as the artistic cornerstone of the community. In addition to a small but interesting permanent collection, the museum presents installations of regional works definitely worth a detour. Past examples include a display of surf photography from the coast's 1930s and 1940s golden era, and dozens of plein-air Impressionist paintings (ca. 1900–30) by the founding artists of the original colony. The museum is also open during Laguna Beach Artwalk, the first Thursday each month, when all are admitted free.

307 Cliff Dr., Laguna Beach. ☏ **949/494-8971.** www.lagunaartmuseum.org. Admission $10 adults, $8 students and seniors, free for kids under age 12. Daily 11am–5pm.

Mission San Juan Capistrano   The seventh of the 21 California coastal missions, Mission San Juan Capistrano is continually being restored. The mix of old ruins and working buildings is home to small museum collections and various adobe rooms that are as quaint as they are interesting. The intimate mission chapel with its ornate baroque altar is still used for religious services, and the mission complex is the center of the community, hosting performing arts, children's programs, and other cultural events year-round.

This mission is best known for its **swallows,** which are said to return to nest each year at their favorite sanctuary. According to legend, the birds wing their way back to the mission annually on March 19, St. Joseph's Day, arriving at dawn; they are said to take flight again on October 23, after bidding the mission farewell. In reality, you'll probably see the well-fed birds here any day of the week, winter or summer.

Ortega Hwy. (Calif. 74), San Juan Capistrano. ☏ **949/234-1300.** www.missionsjc.com. Admission $9 adults, $8 seniors, $5 children. Daily 8:30am–5pm.

WHERE TO STAY
Very Expensive

Montage Resort & Spa ★★★   The rich have it good when it comes to vacationing. Spend a few minutes walking around the new 30-acre Montage resort in Laguna Beach and you'll see why. Unfazed by the two luxury resorts—the St. Regis and the Ritz-Carlton Laguna Niguel—just down the road, the investors behind this Arts and Crafts beauty have created yet another reason for big spenders to unwind along the Orange Coast. You can barely see it from the PCH, and the front entrance is rather understated, but as you

walk through the lobby and onto the balcony overlooking the . . . oh my. The change of
scenery is so breathtakingly abrupt that it takes composure not to sprint down to the
gorgeous mosaic-tiled pool or run barefoot along the sun-kissed beach. It's the same view
from the balcony of every room, and you never tire of it.

The Montage Resort is all about style. You don't even check in at the front desk: As
soon as you arrive you're warmly greeted and given a well-rehearsed tour of the resort by
attractive khaki-clad employees wearing tailored jackets. The tour ends at the neo-
Craftsman-style guest rooms, which are spacious, immaculate, and tastefully decorated
with muted color schemes, museum-quality plein-air artwork, huge marble bathrooms
with oversize tubs and plush robes, 27-inch flatscreen TVs with DVD players, quality
dark-wood furnishings, feather-top beds with goose-down pillows, and very inviting
balconies. But don't get too attached: You'll be spending very little time here as you
lounge by the infinity-edged pool sipping a lemonade, spend hours exploring the tide
pools, stroll through the hotel's impeccably manicured park and pristine beaches, spoil
yourself rotten with skin treatments and massages at the oceanfront Spa Montage, and
then feast on chef James Boyce's superb Mediterranean-style cuisine at the resort's signature restaurant, **Studio.** There's plenty for kids to do as well: They have their own pool
and several fun-filled programs to keep them entertained (and, of course, there's the
beach).

30801 S. Coast Hwy., Laguna Beach, CA 92651. © **866/271-6953** or 949/715-6000. Fax 949/715-6100.
www.montagelagunabeach.com. 262 units. $475–$735 double; from $1,100 suite. AE, DISC, MC, V. Valet
parking $25. **Amenities:** 3 restaurants and lobby lounge w/live entertainment; oceanfront fitness facili-
ties and spa; concierge and business services; 24-hr. in-room dining; daily laundry/valet service; newspaper delivery. *In room:* A/C, flatscreen TV and DVD/CD player, high-speed Internet access, minibar, hair
dryer, iron, safe, 3 multiline phones w/voice mail.

Ritz-Carlton Laguna Niguel ★★★   After a sorely needed $40-million renovation
to keep up with neighboring resorts such as the Montage and St. Regis, this Dana Point
grande dame has recaptured its status as one of the top resorts on the Orange Coast. From
its perch on the edge of a 150-foot-high bluff overlooking an idyllic 2-mile-long beach,
the view from most every window is spectacular (you can spend hours on your balcony
admiring the ocean view). The most welcome change is that every guest room and public
space has been completely remodeled with a much more chic and contemporary look
(gone are those frumpy prints of English fox hunts). The spacious rooms are now outfitted
with 42-inch plasma TVs with DVD players, sumptuous furnishings and fabrics, an
Italian-marble bathroom equipped with a double vanity, and the most comfortable feather
beds I've ever slept in. The resort's new **Restaurant 162'** is a dramatic improvement as
well, with gorgeous ocean views and superb cuisine (the Ocean Curry is fantastic). Other
improvements include a new luxury spa and oceanfront fitness center. As always, lush
terraces and colorful flower gardens abound throughout the well-tended property, and
service—in typical Ritz-Carlton style—is unassuming and impeccable. Garden tours,
beach shuttles, surf lessons, and excellent kids' programs are available as well.

1 Ritz-Carlton Dr., Dana Point, CA 92629. © **800/241-3333** or 949/240-2000. Fax 949/240-0829. www.
ritzcarlton.com. 393 units. From $475 garden-view/pool-view double; $775 oceanview double; from
$875 suite. Children age 17 and under stay free in parent's room. Midweek and special packages avail-
able. AE, DC, DISC, MC, V. Parking $35. **Amenities:** 2 restaurants; 1 lounge; 4 outdoor tennis courts; health
club; spa; children's programs; concierge; regular shuttle to/from the beach and the golf course; business
center; free Wi-Fi; 24-hr. room service; in-room massage; babysitting; laundry service; dry cleaning;
executive-level rooms. *In room:* A/C, TV w/pay movies, minibar, hair dryer, iron, safe, robes.

St. Regis Monarch Beach Resort & Spa ★★★ Let's cut to the chase: The St. Regis Monarch Beach Resort is one of the finest luxury hotels I have ever had the pleasure of reviewing—and I've reviewed a *lot* of luxury hotels. They nailed it with this one, setting a standard for all other resort hotels to follow. Everything oozes with indulgence, from the stellar service to the striking artwork, high-tech electronics, absurdly comfortable beds, stellar restaurants, and a 30,000-square-foot spa that will blow your mind. The $240-million, 172-acre resort opened on July 30, 2001, with a massive star-studded gala, and has since been wooing the wealthy with its gorgeous Tuscan-inspired architecture and soothing ocean views.

Perfection is all in the details, and the St. Regis is full of them: a three-lane lap pool with an underwater sound system; a yoga, spinning, and "movement" studio; a full-service Vogue salon; private poolside cabanas; fantastic cuisine at Michael Mina's popular **Stonehill Tavern** restaurant ★★★; couples' spa treatment rooms with whirlpool baths and fireplaces; an 18-hole Robert Trent Jones, Jr., golf course; and even a private beach club. The guest rooms are loaded with beautiful custom-designed furniture, 32-inch Sony Vega flatscreen TVs with CD/DVD audio systems and a 300-DVD library, huge marble-laden bathrooms with glass shower doors that must weigh 100 pounds, and the most comfortable bathrobe I've ever worn.

The resort's only caveat is that it's near the beach, but unlike the Ritz-Carlton Laguna Niguel and Montage (see reviews above), it's not on it. The view of the terraced pool area, golf course, and shimmering ocean beyond is fantastic, however, and the hotel offers complimentary shuttle service to the 2-mile-long beach, as well as exclusive access to the **St. Regis Beach Club,** where attendants set up chairs, towels, and umbrellas, and also take food and beverage (including alcohol) orders. You can even hire a "Surf Butler," who will take your measurements for a wet suit, bring out a long board, and give you surfing lessons.

1 Monarch Beach Rd., Dana Point, CA 92629. ✆ **800/722-1543** or 949/234-3200. Fax 949/234-3201. www.stregismb.com. 400 units. From $475 resort-view double; from $585 oceanview double; from $895 suite. Golf and spa packages available. AE, DC, DISC, MC, V. Valet parking $28. **Amenities:** 6 restaurants; lounge; wine cellar tasting room; 3 pools; 18-hole golf course; 3 tennis courts (lit for night play); Spa Gaucin and a fitness center; 2 hot tubs; kid's club; concierge; complimentary local shuttle; 24-hr. business center; retail shops; 24-hr. room service; in-room massage; babysitting; laundry service; dry cleaning; executive-level rooms; morning paper; 24-hr. butler service. *In room:* A/C, TV, CD/DVD player, DVD library, 3 phones, high-speed Internet access, minibar, hair dryer, safe, robes.

Surf and Sand Resort ★★ Perhaps the most beloved hotel on the Orange Coast, the nine-story Surf and Sand Resort has come a long way since it started in 1948 as a beachside motor lodge with 13 units. Still occupying the same fantastic oceanside location, it now features 152 guest rooms that, despite their simplicity and standard size, feel enormously decadent. They're all very bright and beachy; each has a private balcony with a dreamy ocean view, a marble bathroom accented handsomely with granite, and plush cotton terry robes. *Tip:* Try getting one of the deluxe corner rooms, with an expanded 90-degree view of the California coastline—it's well worth the additional dollars. Also, be sure to check their website for special package deals. Opened in early 2002, the hotel's Mediterranean-style **Aquaterra Spa** offers a tantalizing array of personalized massage, skincare, and body treatments. You'll find the requisite ocean-inspired treatments, but the menu also features eight different specialty massages, each with your choice of four aromatherapy oils. The spa's four Couples Rituals offer themed body treatments followed by a bubble bath for two (the tub has an ocean view) and a massage to finish. **Splashes**

restaurant serves breakfast, lunch, and dinner daily in a beautiful oceanfront setting; the
rich Mediterranean cuisine is perfect against a backdrop of sunlight and crashing waves.

1555 S. Coast Hwy. (south of Laguna Canyon Rd.), Laguna Beach, CA 92651. (C) **888/869-7569** or 949/
497-4477. Fax 949/494-2897. www.surfandsandresort.com. 152 rooms, 13 suites. Jan 3–Mar 28 $290–
$485 double, $475–$780 suite; Mar 29–June 27 $295–$375 double, $395–$1,085 suite; June 28–Oct 5
$385–$485 double, $475–$1,125 suite; Oct 6–Jan 2 $285–$465 double, $425–$725 suite. AE, DC, DISC,
MC, V. **Amenities:** Restaurant; bar; outdoor heated pool; fitness room; full-service spa; whirlpool; summer
children's programs; concierge; business center; room service (6:30am–10pm); in-room massage;
babysitting; laundry service; dry cleaning; concierge-level rooms. *In room:* TV w/pay movies, minibar, hair
dryer, iron, safe, robes, video games, CD player.

Moderate

Blue Lantern Inn ★★   A three-story New England–style gray clapboard inn, the Blue
Lantern is a pleasant cross between romantic B&B and modern, sophisticated small hotel.
Almost all the rooms, which are decorated with reproduction traditional furniture and
plush bedding, have a balcony or deck overlooking the harbor. All have a fireplace and
whirlpool tub. You can have your breakfast here in private (clad in the fluffy robe provided), or go downstairs to the sunny dining room that also serves complimentary afternoon tea. There's also an exercise room and a cozy lounge with menus for many area
restaurants. The friendly staff welcomes you with home-baked cookies at the front desk.

34343 St. of the Blue Lantern, Dana Point, CA 92629. (C) **800/950-1236** or 949/661-1304. Fax 949/496-
1483. www.bluelanterninn.com. 29 units. $175–$500 double. Rates include full breakfast and afternoon
wine and hors d'oeuvres. AE, DC, MC, V. **Amenities:** Exercise room; whirlpool; complimentary bikes;
laundry service; dry cleaning. *In room:* A/C, TV/VCR, minibar, coffeemaker, hair dryer.

Casa Laguna Inn & Spa ★   Once you see this romantic terraced complex of Spanish-style cottages amid lush gardens and secluded patios—which offers all the amenities
of a B&B *and* affordable prices—you might wonder, what's the catch? Well, the noise of
busy PCH wafts easily into Casa Laguna, so light sleepers may be disturbed. Still, the
Casa has been a favorite hideaway since Laguna's early days and now glows under the
watchful eye of a terrific owner, who has upped the ante by adding a spa. Some rooms—
especially the suites—are downright luxurious, with fireplace, kitchen, bathrobes, CD
player, VCR, and other in-room goodies. Throughout the property, Catalina tile adorns
fountains, and bougainvillea spills into paths; each room has an individual charm. Breakfast is served in the sunny morning room of the Craftsman-style Mission House, where
a cozy living room invites relaxation and conversation.

2510 S. Coast Hwy., Laguna Beach, CA 92651. (C) **800/233-0449** or 949/494-2996. Fax 949/494-5009.
www.casalaguna.com. 21 units. $150–$330 double; from $260 suite. Rates include breakfast, afternoon
wine, and hors d'oeuvres. Off-season and midweek discounts available. AE, DISC, MC, V. **Amenities:**
Heated outdoor pool; spa; whirlpool. *In room:* TV.

WHERE TO DINE

Options in Seal Beach are limited, but a good choice for seafood is **Walt's Wharf,** 201
Main St. ((C) **562/598-4433**), a bustling, polished restaurant featuring market-fresh
selections either plain or with Pacific Rim accents.

Expensive

Five Feet ★★ CALIFORNIA/ASIAN   While Five Feet may no longer break culinary
ground, the kitchen still combines the best in California cuisine with Asian technique and
ingredients. The restaurant has a minimalist, almost-industrial decor that's brightened by a

> ## (Tips) The Ramos House Café
>
> If you're anywhere near San Juan Capistrano, you *have* to stop for breakfast or lunch at the Ramos House Café, a petite restaurant within an adorable little old house in the historic Los Rios district of San Juan Capistrano. Chef John Humphreys's swoon-inducing menu changes daily and everything—from his roast turkey hash scramble with apple cider gravy to his corn and buttermilk crab cakes and southern fried chicken salad—is made from scratch (even the ice cream is turned by hand). And if that's not the best Soju Bloody Mary you'll ever have, send me a better recipe. The cafe is located at 31752 Los Rios St.—the oldest remaining residential street in California—near the train depot and is open for breakfast and lunch Tuesday through Sunday from 8:30am to 3pm (© **949/443-1342;** www.ramoshouse.com).

friendly staff and splendid cuisine. Menu selections run the gamut from tea-smoked filet mignon topped with Roquefort cheese and candied walnuts to a hot Thai-style mixed grill of veal, beef, lamb, and chicken stir-fried with sweet peppers, onions, and mushrooms in curry-mint sauce. The menu changes daily, but you can always find the house specialty, whole braised catfish.

328 Glenneyre, Laguna Beach. © **949/497-4955.** www.fivefeetrestaurants.com. Reservations recommended. Main courses $18–$49. AE, DC, DISC, MC, V. Sun–Thurs 5–10pm; Fri–Sat 5–11pm.

Roy's of Newport Beach ★★ HAWAIIAN REGIONAL/PACIFIC RIM Any foodie who's been to Hawaii in the past decade knows the name Roy Yamaguchi, father of Hawaiian Regional Cuisine (HRC) and the islands' answer to Wolfgang Puck. Roy's empire expanded to Southern California in 1999 with the opening of this dinner-only restaurant on the fringe of Fashion Island shopping center. Yamaguchi developed a menu that represents his groundbreaking East/West/Polynesian cuisine but can be reliably executed by chefs in far-flung kitchens. Most of each night's specials are fresh Pacific fish, given the patented HRC touch with Japanese, Thai, and even Latin accents. Signature dishes include island-style *ahi poke,* spicy Mongolian-glazed rack of lamb, and blackened yellowfin tuna in soy-mustard-butter sauce. The bar whips up "vacation" cocktails in tropical colors, and the chocolate soufflé is to-die-for.

453 Newport Center Dr., Fashion Island. © **949/640-7697.** www.roysrestaurant.com. Reservations suggested. Main courses $18–$32. AE, DC, DISC, MC, V. Sun–Thurs 5–10pm; Fri–Sat 5–11pm.

Moderate

Crab Cooker SEAFOOD Since 1951, folks in search of fresh, well-prepared seafood have headed to this bright-red former bank building. Also a fish market, the Crab Cooker has a casual atmosphere of humble wooden tables, uncomplicated smoked and grilled preparations, and meticulously selected fresh fare. The place is especially proud of its Maryland crab cakes; clams and oysters are also part of the repertoire.

2200 Newport Blvd., Newport Beach. © **949/673-0100.** www.crabcooker.com. Main courses dinner $10–$25, lunch $8–$19. AE, MC, V. Sun–Thurs 11am–9pm; Fri–Sat 11am–10pm.

Harbor Grill SEAFOOD/STEAK Located in a business/commercial mall right in the center of the Dana Point Marina, the Harbor Grill is enthusiastically recommended by locals for mesquite-broiled ocean-fresh seafood. Hawaiian mahimahi, with a mango- chutney baste, is on the menu, along with Pacific swordfish, crab cakes, and beef steaks.

34499 St. of the Golden Lantern, Dana Point. © **949/240-1416.** www.harborgrill.com. Reservations recommended. Main courses $10–$27. AE, DC, DISC, MC, V. Daily 11:30am–10pm; Sun brunch 9am–2pm.

Las Brisas (**Moments** MEXICAN SEAFOOD   Las Brisas's breathtaking view of the Pacific (particularly at sunset) and potent margaritas are a surefire combination for a *muy romantico* evening. In fact, it's so popular that it can get pretty crowded during the summer months, so be sure to make a reservation. Affordable during lunch but pricey at dinner, the menu consists mostly of seafood recipes from the Mexican Riviera. Even the standard enchiladas and tacos get a zesty update with crab or lobster meat and fresh herbs. Calamari steak is sautéed with bell peppers, capers, and herbs in a garlic-butter sauce, and king salmon is mesquite-broiled and served with a creamy lime sauce. Although a bit on the touristy side, Las Brisas can be a fun part of the Laguna Beach experience.

361 Cliff Dr. (off the PCH north of Laguna Canyon), Laguna Beach. © **949/497-5434.** www.lasbrisas lagunabeach.com. Reservations recommended. Main courses $10–$27. AE, DC, DISC, MC, V. Mon–Thurs 8am–10pm; Fri–Sat 8am–11pm; Sun 9am–10pm. Valet parking $4 lunch, $5 dinner.

The Southern California Desert

by Harry Basch

To the casual observer, the Southern California desert might seem like a desolate expanse under an unrelenting sun. Its splendor is subtle, though; its beauty unfolds over time.

If it looks as though nothing but insects could survive here, look again: You're bound to see a roadrunner or a tiny gecko dart across your path. Close your eyes and listen for the cry of a hawk or an owl. Check the ground for coyote or bobcat tracks. Notice the sparkle of fish in the streams running through palm oases. Check the road signs, which warn of desert tortoise crossings (the tortoise being one of many endangered species found only here, where it's protected by the federal government in a wildlife sanctuary). Visit in spring, when the ground throughout the Lancaster area is carpeted with the brilliant golds and oranges of the poppy,

California's state flower (which, like the autumn leaves in New England, draw seasonal tourists in droves).

Let your eyes adjust to take in the lushness of trees, flowering cacti, fragrant shrubs, and other singular plants that have adapted to this harsh climate—such as the gnarly Joshua tree, ugly to some but noble and eerily beautiful to many veteran explorers of the Mojave Desert.

If the beauty you seek is that of personal renewal, you're likely to find that too—if not in the shadow of purple-tinged mountains and otherworldly rock formations, then in a chaise longue beside a sparkling, impossibly blue swimming pool. Destinations here range from gloriously untouched national parks to luxurious resorts—united by the fact that it's a rare day when the sun doesn't shine.

1 EN ROUTE TO THE PALM SPRINGS RESORTS

If you're making the drive from Los Angeles via I-10, you'll spend your first hour or so extricating yourself from the L.A. metropolitan sprawl. But soon enough, you'll leave the Inland Empire auto plazas behind, sail past the last of the bedroom-community shopping malls, and edge ever closer to the snowcapped (if you're lucky) San Bernardino and San Jacinto mountain ranges (coming from San Diego via I-15 North, to I-215 North to I-60 East to I-10; the Palm Springs resorts are east of the junction with I-10).

Frequent travelers on this stretch of highway gauge their progress and orient themselves with certain landmarks. Here are two of our favorite roadside attractions.

Hadley's Fruit Orchards Since 1931, this friendly emporium has been a fixture here, packed with people shopping for dates, dried fruits, nuts, honey, preserves, and other regional products. A snack bar serves the beloved date shake; there are also plenty of gift-packed treats to carry home. (For more about the date mystique, see "Sweet Desert Treat: The Coachella Valley Date Gardens," on p. 666.)

48980 Seminole Dr. (off I-10), Cabazon. ℂ **800/854-5655** or 951/849-5255. www.hadleyfruitorchards. com. Mon–Thurs 9am–7pm; Fri–Sun 8am–8pm (call to verify).

Windmill Tours (Finds) For years, travelers through the San Gorgonio Pass have been struck by an awesome, otherworldly sight: never-ending, ever-expanding fields of windmills that harness the force of the breezes gusting through this passage and convert them to electricity, to power air-conditioners throughout the Coachella Valley. If you get a charge out of them, consider a guided tour, to understand more about this effective alternative energy source. Learn how designers have improved the efficiency of wind turbines (technically they're not windmills), and measure those long rotors against the average human height (about 10 people could lie along one span).

Interstate 10 (Indian Ave. exit), Palm Springs. ℂ **760/320-1365.** www.windmilltours.com. Admission $25 adults, $23 seniors, $10 kids 11 and under. Tours Wed–Sat at 9am, 11am, and 2pm (varies seasonally).

---

2 GET YOUR KICKS ON HISTORIC ROUTE 66

Until the final triumph of the multilane interstate system in the early 1960s, 2,300-mile-long Route 66 was the only automobile route between the Chicago shores of Lake Michigan and L.A.'s golden Pacific beaches. "America's Main Street" rambled through eight states, and today, in each one, organizations exist, such as Route 66 Tourism, just to preserve its remnants. California has a lengthy stretch of the original highway, many miles of which still proudly wear the designation "California State Highway 66." It's not just weed-split abandoned blacktop, either. These are active streets, often the main commercial drag of the communities they transect. Many stretches have become home to clusters of new developments, shopping centers, and fast-food chains. Pretty mundane—until you round a curve and unexpectedly see a vintage wood-frame house, from a ranch that predates the Great Depression. There's poignancy here: That house was probably set way back from the road, amid a shady grove, before highway workers buried the front yard under asphalt.

Other picturesque relics of that era—single-story motels, two-pump gas stations—exist beside their modern neighbors, inviting nostalgia for a time when the vacation began the moment you backed out of the driveway.

ESSENTIALS

THE ROUTE Our drive begins in Pasadena and ends in downtown San Bernardino, 56 miles west of Palm Springs. In San Bernardino, I-215 intersects Route 66; take it 4 miles south to rejoin I-10 and continue east.

Note: This detour works equally well if your destination is Lake Arrowhead or Big Bear Lake; take I-215 north 3 miles to Highway 30 and continue into the mountains. For more information, see chapter 15, "Side Trips from Los Angeles." The drive can take from 2 hours to 3 hours, depending on how many relics and photo opportunities you investigate. I've included some suitably retro meal suggestions, in case you want a lunch break.

VISITOR INFORMATION For more information, contact the **National Historic Route 66 Federation,** Box 1848 Dept WS, Lake Arrowhead, CA 92352-1848 (ℂ **909/336-6131;** www.national66.org). Or check out the quarterly *Route 66 Magazine* (four issues, $20; PO Box 66, Laughlin, NV 89025; ℂ **702/299-0856;** www.route66magazine.com).

LET'S HIT THE ROAD!

Route 66 terminated at the picturesque Pacific, but the heart of Los Angeles has very few remnants of the old road. In light of this fact, Pasadena is the best point to enter the time warp that exists along this highway.

One of my favorite establishments in Pasadena is the **Fair Oaks Pharmacy,** on the Southwest corner of Fair Oaks Avenue at 1526 Mission Street, 1½ miles south of Colorado Boulevard (© **626/799-1414;** www.fairoakspharmacy.net), a fixture since 1915. Try an authentic ice-cream soda, a sparkling phosphate, a "Route 66" sundae, or an old-fashioned malt (complete with the frosty mixing can), all served by fresh-faced soda jerks from behind the marble counter. They also serve soup, sandwiches, and snacks. The Fair Oaks is still a pharmacy and offers a variety of gifts, including an abundance of Route 66–themed items. It's open Monday through Friday from 9am to 7pm, Saturday 9am to 8pm, and Sunday from 9am to 5pm. The pharmacy is closed on Sunday.

For some driving music, reverse and go north on Fair Oaks to Colorado and turn right. **Canterbury Records,** 805 E. Colorado Blvd., a block west of Lake Avenue (© **626/792-7184**), has L.A.'s finest selection of big bands and pop vocalists on CDs; perhaps you'll choose one of the many renditions of the late Bobby Troup's "(Get Your Kicks on)

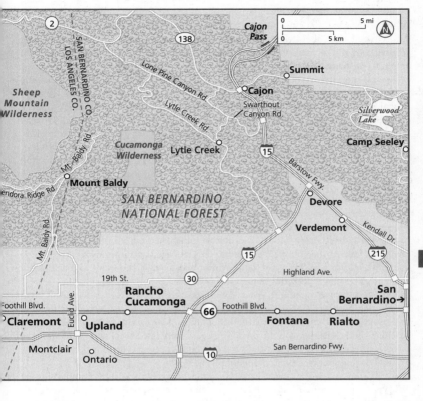

Route 66." The store is open Monday through Saturday from 9am to 9pm and Sunday from 10am to 7pm.

As you continue east on Colorado Boulevard, keep your eyes peeled for **motels** such as the Saga Motor Hotel, Vagabond, Astro (fabulous *Jetsons*-style architecture), and Hi-Way Host. Lodgings have proven the hardiest post-66 survivors, and you'll be seeing many motor courts frozen in time on the way.

Turn left on Rosemead Boulevard, passing under the freeway (boo, hiss) to Foothill Boulevard. Turning right, you'll soon be among the tree-lined streets of **Arcadia,** home to the Santa Anita Racetrack and the Los Angeles Arboretum, the picturesque former estate of "Lucky" Baldwin, whose Queen Anne cottage has been the setting for many movies and TV shows. Passing into Monrovia, look for the life-size plastic cow on the southeast corner of Mayflower. It marks the drive-through called **Mike's Dairy**—a splendid example of this auto-age phenomenon. If you're observant, you'll see other drive-through dairies along my route (mostly Alta-Dena brand). Mike's has all the typical features, including the refrigerated island display case still bearing a vintage DRIFTWOOD DAIRY PRODUCTS price sign.

Next, look for Magnolia Avenue and the **Aztec Hotel** on the northwest corner. Opened in 1925, the Aztec was a local showplace, awing guests with its overscale, dark, Native American–themed lobby, Maya murals, and exotic Brass Elephant bar. The arcade of shops once held the city's most prominent barbershop, beauty salon, and pharmacy. Little has changed about the interior, and a glance behind the front desk reveals the original cord-and-plug telephone switchboard still in use. If you care to wet your whistle, stop into the bar before continuing on.

Leaving the Aztec, you'll pass splendid Craftsman bungalows and other historic homes. Turn right on Shamrock Avenue and ogle the old gas station with its classic (if ornamental) gas pumps on the northwest corner of Almond Avenue; continue onward 2 more blocks, and then make a left turn on Huntington Drive. Now you're in **Duarte,** where Huntington is lit by graceful and ornate double street lamps on the center median. This stretch also has many fabulous old motor courts; see if you can spot the Ranch Inn, Evergreen, Oak Park, Duarte Inn, and Capri. Check out the **Justice Brothers Racing Museum,** 2734 E. Huntington Dr., in an officelike building at the east edge of town just before the river (open Mon–Fri 8am–5pm).

As you cross over the wide but nearly dry San Gabriel River, glance right from the bridge to see cars streaming along the interstate that supplanted Route 66. In Irwindale—which smells just like the industrial area it is, with plants ranging from a Miller brewery to Health Valley Foods—the street resumes the Foothill Boulevard name. At Irwindale Avenue, the 30-mile "neon cruise" begins. You'll pass into **Azusa,** with its elegant 1932 **Azusa City Hall and Auditorium,** with vintage lampposts and a Moorish fountain enhancing a charming courtyard.

Our route swerves right onto Alosta Avenue at the site of the former **Foothill Drive-In Theater,** Southern California's last single-screen drive-in. As you cruise by, think of the days when our cars were an extension of our living rooms (with the great snacks Mom wouldn't allow at home), and the outdoor theaters were filled every summer evening by dusk. Alas, the drive-in sign awaits demolition, but the new owners may donate it to the city of Los Angeles, relocate it, and refurbish the marquee.

Continuing on Alosta, you'll enter Glendora, named in 1887 by founder George Whitcomb for his wife, Ledora. Look for the **Palm Tropics,** one of the best-maintained old motels along the route. Farther along on the left-hand side is the **Golden Spur,** which began 70 years ago as a ride-up hamburger stand for the equestrian crowd. Unfortunately, the restaurant was remodeled in stucco, leaving only the original sign with its neon cowboy boot, as a reminder of its colorful past. At the corner of Cataract Avenue, a covered wagon announces the **Pinnacle Peak** restaurant, guarded by a giant steer atop the roof. In a mile or two, you'll pass through San Dimas, a ranchlike community where you must heed the HORSE CROSSING street signs.

Foothill Boulevard enters **La Verne** as you pass underneath the ramps to the I-30 freeway. **La Paloma** Mexican cafe, a fixture on the route for years, is on your left as you leave town. Continue on to Claremont, known for its highly respected group of **Claremont Colleges.** You'll pass several of them along this eucalyptus-lined boulevard. In days gone by, drivers would cruise along this route for mile upon mile, through orchards and open fields, the scenery punctuated only by ambling livestock or a rustic wood fence.

At Benson Avenue in Upland, a classic **1950s-style McDonald's** stands on the southeast corner, its golden arches flanking a low, white, walk-up counter with outdoor stools. The fast-food chain has its roots in this region: Richard and Maurice McDonald opened their first burger joint in San Bernardino in 1939. The brothers expanded their business,

(Tips) A Retro Pit Stop

If all this driving has made you hungry, consider the **Magic Lamp Inn,** 8189 Foothill Blvd. (© **909/981-8659**). It's open for lunch Tuesday through Friday from 11:30am to 2pm, and for dinner Tuesday through Sunday from 5pm until closing time, which varies (call first). Closed Mondays. Built in 1957, the Magic Lamp serves excellent Continental cuisine (nothing nouvelle about Rte. 66!) in a setting that's part manor house and part *Aladdin* theme park. Dark, stately dining rooms lurk behind a funky banquette cocktail lounge punctuated by a psychedelic fountain/fire pit and a panoramic view. The genie-bottle theme is everywhere, from the restaurant's dinnerware to the plush carpeting, which would be right at home in a Las Vegas casino. Lovers of kitsch and hearty retro fare shouldn't pass up this one.

opening locations throughout Southern California, until entrepreneur Ray Kroc purchased the chain in 1955 and franchised McDonald's nationwide. Farther along, look north at the intersection of Euclid Avenue for the regal **monument to pioneer women.**

Pretty soon you'll be cruising through Rancho Cucamonga, whose fertile soil still yields a reliable harvest. You might see **produce stands** springing up by the side of the road; stop and pick up a fresh snack. If you're blessed with clear weather, gaze north at the gentle slope of the **San Gabriel Mountains** and you'll understand how Foothill Boulevard got its name. The construction codes in this community are among the most stringent in California, designed to respect the region's heritage and restrict runaway development. All new buildings are Spanish-Mediterranean in style and amply landscaped. At the corner of San Bernardino Road, the architectural bones of a wonderful old service station now stand forsaken. Across the street is the **Sycamore Inn,** in a grove of trees, looking like an old-style stagecoach stop. This reddish-brown wooden house, dating from 1848, has been a private home and gracious inn; today, it serves the community of Cucamonga as a restaurant and civic hall.

Rancho Cucamonga has preserved two historic wineries. First you'll see the **Thomas Vineyards,** at the northeast corner of Vineyard Avenue, established in 1839. Legend holds that the first owner mysteriously disappeared, leaving hidden treasure still undiscovered on the property. The winery's preserved structures now house a restaurant, coffeehouse, country crafts store, and a garden-supply boutique in the former brandy still tower.

Continuing on to Hellman Avenue, look for the **New Kansan Motel** (on the northeast corner). With that name, it must have seemed welcoming to Dust Bowl refugees. Near the northwest corner of Archibald Avenue, you'll find remnants of a **1920s-era gas station.** Empty now, those service bays have seen many a Ford, Studebaker, and Packard in need of a helping hand. Nearby, on the left, is **Route 66 Memories,** 10150 Foothill Blvd. (© **909/476-3843**), in a three-story classic house with a collection of metallic dinosaurs in the front yard, and a gift shop for antiques and rustic furniture. Next you'll pass the **Virginia Dare Winery,** at the northwest corner of Haven Avenue, whose structures now house part of a business park/mall, but retain the flourish of the original (1830s) winery logo.

Soon you'll pass the I-15 junction and drive through Fontana, whose name in Italian means "fountain city." Slow down to have a look at the **motor-court hotels** lining both sides of the road. They're of various vintages, all built to cater to the once-vigorous stream of travelers passing through. Today they're dingy, but the melody of their names conjures up those glory days: Oasis, Rose Motel, Moana, El Rey, Rex, Fiesta, Dragon, Sand & Sage, and Sunset.

As you enter **San Bernardino,** be on the lookout for Meriden Avenue, site of the **Wigwam Motel.** Built in the 1950s (along with an identical twin motor court in Holbrook, Arizona), the whimsy of these stucco tepees lured in many a road-weary traveler for the night. Its catchy slogan, "Sleep in a wigwam, get more for your wampum," has been supplanted today by the more to-the-point "Do it in a tepee." But, as with many of the motor courts we'll pass, you need only picture a few large, shiny Buicks, T-bird convertibles, and "woodie" station wagons pulling in for the night, and your imagination will drift back to days gone by.

Soon Foothill Boulevard will become Fifth Street, where the San Bernardino sign must have been a welcome sight for hot and weary westbound travelers emerging from the Mojave Desert. Route 66 wriggled through the steep Cajon Pass into a land fragrant with orange groves, where agricultural prosperity earned this region a lasting sobriquet: "the Inland Empire."

The year 1928 saw the grand opening of an elegant movie palace, the **California Theatre,** 562 W. Fourth St., only a block from Route 66. From Fifth Street east, turn right at E Street, and then make a right on Fourth Street, where you can pull over to view the theater. Lovingly restored and still popular for nostalgic live entertainment and the rich tones of its original Wurlitzer pipe organ, the California was a frequent site of Hollywood "sneak previews." Humorist Will Rogers made his last public appearance here, in 1935. (Following his death, the highway was officially renamed the Will Rogers Memorial Hwy.) Notice the intricate relief of the theater's stone facade, and peek into the lobby to see the red velvet draperies, rich carpeting, and gold-banistered double staircase leading up to the balcony.

The theater is the last stop on your time-warp driving tour. Continue west on Fourth Street to the superslab highway only 2½ blocks away—that's I-215, your entry back to the present (see "Essentials" above).

3 THE PALM SPRINGS DESERT RESORTS

120 miles E of downtown L.A.; 135 miles NE of San Diego

Palm Springs had been known for years as a golf course–studded retirement mecca, invaded annually by hordes of libidinous college kids on spring break. Well, the city of Palm Springs has been quietly changing its image and attracting a whole new crowd. The late former mayor Sonny Bono's revolutionary "anti-thong" ordinance in 1991 halted the spring-break migration by eliminating public display of the bare derrière, and the upscale fairway-condo crowd now congregates in the outlying resort cities of Rancho Mirage, Palm Desert, Indian Wells, and La Quinta.

These days, no billboards are allowed in Palm Springs; all the palm trees in the center of town are backlit at night, and you won't see the word *motel* on any establishment. Seniors are everywhere, dressed to the nines in leisure suits, sustaining the retro-kitsch establishments from the days when Elvis, Liberace, and Sinatra made the desert a swingin' place. But they're not alone: Baby boomers and yuppies nostalgic for the kidney-shaped swimming pools and backyard luaus of the Eisenhower/Kennedy glory years are

ACCOMMODATIONS ■

Casa Cody **6**
The Colony Palms Hotel **6**
East Canyon Hotel & Spa **3**
Estrella Inn **6**
Holiday Inn
Palm Mountain Resort **6**
Korakia Pensione **6**
La Quinta Resort & Club **19**
Le Parker **9**
Marriott's Desert Springs
Spa & Resort **16**
Marriott's Rancho Las Palmas
Resort & Spa **15**
Miramonte Resort & Spa **21**
Orbit In **6**
Spa Resort Casino **4**
Villa Royale **8**
Westin Mission Hills Resort **13**

ATTRACTIONS ●

Coachella Valley Preserve **14**
El Paseo **17**
Indian Canyons **12**
Knott's Soak City **10**
The Living Desert
Wildlife & Botanical Park **18**
Palm Springs Aerial Tramway **2**
Palm Springs Desert Museum **5**
Palm Springs Oasis Waterpark **10**
Shields Date Gardens **20**
Smoke Tree Stables **11**
Tahquitz Canyon **7**
Windmill Tours **1**

buying ranch-style vacation homes and restoring them to their 1950s splendor. Holly-wood's young glitterati, along with upscale gays, are returning, too. Today, the city fancies itself a European-style resort with a dash of small-town Americana—think *Jetsons* archi-tecture and the crushed-velvet vibe of piano bars with the colors and attitude of a laid-back Aegean village. One thing hasn't changed: Swimming, sunbathing, golfing, and tennis are still the primary pastimes.

Another important presence in Palm Springs has little to do with socialites and Americana. The Agua Caliente Band of Cahuilla Indians settled in this area 1,000 years before the first golf ball was ever teed up. Recognizing the beauty and spirituality of this wide-open space, they lived a simple life around the mineral springs on the desert floor, migrating into the cool canyons during the summer months. Under a treaty with the railroad companies and the U.S. government, the tribe owns half the land on which Palm Springs is built and works to preserve Native American heritage. It's easy to learn about the American Indians during your visit, and it will definitely add to your appreciation of this part of California.

ESSENTIALS

GETTING THERE   Airlines that service the **Palm Springs International Airport,** 3400 E. Tahquitz Canyon Way (② 760/323-8161), include **Air Canada** (② 888/247-2262; www.aircanada.com) seasonal, **Alaska Airlines** (② 800/426-0333; www.alaskaair.com), **Allegiant Air** (② 702/505-8888; www.allegiantair.com) seasonal, **American** (② 800/433-7300; www.aa.com), **Continental** (② 800/525-0280; www.continental.com) sea-sonal, **Delta** and **Delta Connection** (② 800/221-1212; www.delta.com), **Horizon Air** (② 800/547-9308; www.horizonair.com), **Northwest** (② 800/225-2525; www.nwa.com) seasonal, **Sun Country Airlines** (② 800/359-6786; www.suncountry.com) sea-sonal, **United Airlines** and **United Express** (② 800/241-6522; www.united.com), **US Airways** (② 800/428-4322; www.usairways.com), and **WestJet** (② 800/538-5696; www.westjet.com) seasonal. Flights from Los Angeles take about 40 minutes.

If you're driving from Los Angeles, take I-10 east to the Highway 111 turnoff to Palm Springs. You'll breeze into town on North Palm Canyon Drive, the main thoroughfare. The trip from downtown L.A. takes 2 hours if traffic is light. If you're driving from San Diego, take I-15 north to I-215 and pick up I-10 east; it takes a bit more than 2 hours.

VISITOR INFORMATION   Be sure to pick up *Palm Springs Life* magazine's free monthly, *Desert Guide.* It contains copious visitor information, including a comprehensive calendar of events. Copies are distributed in hotels and newsstands and by the **Palm Springs Desert Resorts Convention & Visitors Authority,** 70–100 Hwy. 111, Rancho Mirage, CA 92270 (② **800/967-3767** or 760/770-9000). The bureau's office staff can help with maps, brochures, and advice Monday through Friday from 8:30am to 5pm. They also operate a website (www.palmspringsusa.com).

The **Palm Springs Visitors Information Center,** 2901 N. Palm Canyon Dr., Palm Springs, CA 92262 (② **800/34-SPRINGS [347-7746];** www.palm-springs.org), offers maps, brochures, advice, souvenirs, and a free hotel reservation service. The office is open Monday through Saturday from 9am to 5pm, and Sunday from 8am to 4pm.

Another site worth browsing is **www.thedesertsun.com**, an offshoot of the local newspaper the *Desert Sun,* with information for locals and visitors.

ORIENTATION   The commercial downtown area of Palm Springs stretches about half a mile along North Palm Canyon Drive between Alejo and Ramon streets. The street is one-way southbound through the heart of town, but its northbound counterpart is

Indian Canyon Drive, 1 block east. The mountains lie west and south, while the rest of Palm Springs is laid out in a grid to the southeast. Palm Canyon forks into South Palm Canyon (leading to the Indian Canyons) and East Palm Canyon (the continuation of Hwy. 111) traversing the towns of Cathedral City, Rancho Mirage, Palm Desert, Indian Wells, and La Quinta, before looping up to rejoin I-10 at Indio. Desert Hot Springs is north of Palm Springs, straight up Gene Autry Trail. Tahquitz Canyon Way creates North Palm Canyon's primary intersection, tracking a straight line between the airport and the heart of town.

WHAT TO SEE & DO
Great Golf Courses

The Palm Springs Desert Resorts are a mecca for golfers (see "Fairways & Five-Irons, Desert-Style," below), with 115 public, semiprivate, and private courses in the area. If you're the type who starts polishing your irons the moment you begin planning your vacation, you're best off staying at one of the valley's many golf resorts; many offer smart package deals. If, on the other hand, you like to squeeze a round of golf into an otherwise varied trip, you don't need to stay at a hotel with its own links; many courses, of all levels, are open to the public, many in Palm Springs, with others down the valley in Cathedral City, Palm Desert, Indian Wells, La Quinta, and Indio. Call ahead to see which will rent gear on short notice.

Beginners will enjoy **Tommy Jacobs' Bel-Air Greens,** 1001 El Cielo, Palm Springs (© 760/322-6062), a 9-hole, par-32 executive course that challenges golfers with water and sand traps but fosters a few confidence-boosting successes as well. Generally flat fairways and trees characterize the relatively short (3,350-yard) course. Greens fees are $20, less for a replay.

Slightly more intermediate amateurs will want to check out the **Tahquitz Creek Golf Resort,** 1885 Golf Club Dr., Palm Springs (© 760/328-1005; www.tahquitzcreek. com), whose two diverse courses both appeal to midhandicappers. The Legend's wide, water-free holes will appeal to anyone frustrated by the "target" courses popular with many architects, while the Ted Robinson–designed Resort course offers all those accuracy-testing bells and whistles more common to lavish private clubs. Greens fees, including cart, range from $59 to $109, depending on the day of the week.

The Classic Club (75–200 Northstar Resort Pkwy., north of I-10 at Cook St. exit, Palm Desert; © 760/601-3601; www.classicclubgolf.com) is a new 7,305-yard Arnold Palmer–designed course that won critical praise from the pros at the Bob Hope Classic. Greens fees in winter are $175 to $195, which includes a cart and a driving range; summer fees are half that.

One of our favorite desert courses is the **PGA West TPC Stadium Course,** La Quinta Resort & Club, 49499 Eisenhower Dr., La Quinta (© 800/598-3828 or 760/777-4827; www.laquintaresort.com), which once received *Golf* magazine's Gold Medal Award for the total golf-resort experience. The par-3 17th has a picturesque island green where Lee Trevino made Skins Game history with a spectacular hole in one. The rest of Pete Dye's 7,261-yard design is flat, with huge bunkers, lots of water, and severe mounding throughout. It's one of the most difficult courses in the U.S. Also open for semiprivate play is the **Mountain Course at La Quinta,** another Dye design that regularly appears on U.S. top-100 lists. It's set dramatically against the rocky mountains, which thrust into fairways to create tricky doglegs, and its small Bermuda greens are well guarded by boulders and deep bunkers. Greens fees for nonguests vary seasonally, from $190 to $209 on

THE SOUTHERN CALIFORNIA DESERT

THE PALM SPRINGS DESERT RESORTS

Fairways & Five-Irons, Desert-Style

Two hours outside of Los Angeles in the Coachella Valley, strung like ripe dates from I-10, lie the resort cities of Palm Springs, Rancho Mirage, Palm Desert, Indian Wells, and La Quinta. This all-season golfer's paradise boasts more than 100 courses, their lush fairways and velvety greens carved from the arid desert scruff. Both public and resort/semiprivate courses range in difficulty to accommodate low-handicappers and weekend duffers alike, and every imaginable service is available nearby.

In case you'd like to sharpen your game, all the principal clubs have resident pros, and there are several schools and clinics, including the **Indian Wells Golf School** at Indian Wells Resort (© **760/346-4653**), or the **1st Tee in Palm Desert** (© **760/779-1877**). If you're looking to pick up new equipment or golf attire, try **Lumpy's Discount Golf,** 67–625 Hwy. 111 in Cathedral City (© **800/553-2117**) and 78–267 Hwy. 111 in La Quinta (© **760/904-4911**); and **Lady Golf** at 42–412 Bob Hope Dr., Rancho Mirage (© **760/773-4949**).

Many fine resorts offer generous golf packages, among them **Marriott's Desert Springs Spa & Resort** in Palm Desert (© **760/341-2211**), **Marriott's Rancho Las Palmas Resort & Spa** in Rancho Mirage (© **760/568-2727**), the **Hyatt Grand Champions** in Indian Wells (© **760/341-1000**), and **La Quinta Resort & Club** in La Quinta (© **760/564-4111**).

Tee times at many courses cannot be booked more than a few days in advance for nonguests, but **Golf à la Carte** (© **877/887-6900** or 760/772-7663; www.palmspringsgolf.com) will make arrangements several months earlier or construct a package with accommodations, golf, meals, and other extras. A valuable service for the budget traveler, **Stand-By Golf** (© **760/321-2665;** www.stand-bygolf.com) helps more than 35 area courses—including semiprivate and resort courses—fill their bookings by offering players a last-minute discount of 40% to 60%. You can book some courses in advance, but many tee times are for the same or next day; call between 7am and 10pm daily.

weekends including the required cart. Also at La Quinta Resort is the Pete Dye–designed **Dunes Course,** the (Jack) **Nicklaus Tournament Course,** and the (Greg) **Norman Resort Course.**

A complete **golfer's guide** is available from the Palm Springs Desert Resorts Convention & Visitors Authority (see "Visitor Information," above).

More Outdoor Fun

The Coachella Valley Desert is a sunny playground, and what follows is but a sampling of outdoor pastimes for visitors. *Tip:* The abundant sunshine and dry air that are so appealing can also sneak up on you, in the form of sunburn and heat exhaustion. Especially during the summer, but even in milder times, always carry and drink plenty of water, and slather on the sunscreen.

BALLOONING This may be the most memorable way to see the desert: floating above the landscape in a hot-air balloon. Choose from such specialty themes as sunrise, sunset,

or romantic champagne flights, from $165 per person. Rides are offered by **Dream**
Flights (© 800/933-5628 or 760/321-5454; www.dreamflights.com) and **Fantasy Balloon Flights,** both at 74181 Parosella St., Palm Desert (© **800/GO-ABOVE [462-2683]** or 760/568-0997; www.fantasyballoonflights.com). Rates range from $170 to $185 per person for a 60- to 90-minute flight (two per day), including champagne and hors d'oeuvres.

BICYCLING The clean, dry desert air makes for the ideal conditions for pedaling your way around town or into the desert. Seek out **Adventure Bike Tours** (© 760/328-0282) for tour information; **Tri a Bike Rental,** 44841 San Pablo Ave., Palm Desert (© **760/ 340-2840**), rents road and mountain bikes for the hour ($12), the day ($30), or the week ($99), and offers children's and tandem models and helmets as well.

A FAMILY WATER PARK **Knott's Soak City,** off I-10 south on Gene Autry Trail between Ramon Road and East Palm Canyon Drive (© **760/327-0499;** www.knotts. com/soakcity/ps/index.shtml), is a 16-acre water playground with 12 water slides, body-and board surfing, a wave pool, and more. Dressing rooms, lockers, and private beach cabanas (with food service) are available. Admission is $28 for adults, $18 for seniors and kids 3 to 11, and free for kids under 3; rates are discounted after 3pm. The park is open Wednesday through Sunday mid-March through August, and weekends through October, from 11am to 5pm. Parking for a car is $8, for an RV, $16. Closed Mondays and Tuesdays.

GUIDED ALL-TERRAIN EXCURSIONS **Desert Adventures** (© **888/440-JEEP** or 760/340-2345; www.red-jeep.com), 74794 Lennon Place, Palm Desert, offers four-wheel-drive ecotours led by naturalist guides. Your off-road adventure may take you to a replica of an ancient Cahuilla village, the Santa Rosa Mountain roads overlooking the Coachella Valley, or picturesque ravines on the way to the San Andreas Fault. Tours run from 3 to 5 hours and cost from $129 to $150. Advance reservations are required. The company's red Jeeps depart from Coco's Restaurant at the Washington Street exit of I-10.

Elite Land Tours ★ (© **800/514-4866** or 760/318-1200; www.elitelandtours.com) offers a new way to visit the desert region: eco-exploration of the greater Palm Springs backcountry from the air-conditioned comfort of an all-terrain Hummer H2. Tours can include desert and mountain regions, exploration of ancient cultures, wildlife, and geological wonders. A Safari Trax Tour offers an up-close experience with two Siberian tigers, Asian leopards, and a caracal plus a safari lunch ($249 per person in a four-person group). The Night Discovery Tour lets you view the desert wildlife after dark with special night-vision equipment. Tours run from $109 per person for a four-person group.

HIKING The most popular spot for hiking is the nearby **Indian Canyons,** at the end of South Palm Canyon Drive (© **800/790-3398** or 760/699-6800). The Agua Caliente tribe dwelled here centuries ago, and remnants of its culture can be seen among the streams, waterfalls, and palm groves in Andreas, Murray, and Palm canyons. The striking rock formations and herds of bighorn sheep and wild ponies are more appealing than the Trading Post in Palm Canyon, but the shop sells detailed trail maps. The Tribal Council charges admission of $8 per adult; $6 for students, seniors, and military; and $4 for kids ages 6 to 12. The canyons are closed to visitors from late June to early September. The canyons are open 8am to 5pm, and guided hiking tours and ranger lectures are also available.

Don't miss the opportunity to explore **Tahquitz Canyon,** 500 W. Mesquite, west of Palm Canyon Drive, also in Agua Caliente territory. This scenic canyon, home of the waterfall in *Lost Horizon,* was closed to the public for nearly 30 years after careless squatters suffered injuries in the canyon, and hippies made it an all-night party zone, vandalizing land considered sacred. The tribe cleaned up decades' worth of dumping, and now that vegetation has regrown, they have begun offering 2¹/₂-hour ranger-led hikes into their most spiritual and beautiful place. The 2-mile round-trip hike is of moderate difficulty; hikes depart daily at 8am, 10am, noon, and 2pm. The fee is $13 for adults, $6 for children ages 6 to 12; call ☎ **760/416-7044** for reservations (recommended).

Ten miles east of Palm Springs is the 13,000-acre **Coachella Valley Preserve** (☎ **760/343-1234**), open daily from sunrise to sunset. It has springs, mesas, both hiking and riding trails, the Thousand Palms Oasis, a visitor center, and picnic areas.

If you're heading up to Joshua Tree National Park (see later in this chapter), consider stopping at the **Big Morongo Canyon Preserve** (☎ **760/363-7190**), which was once an Indian village and later a cattle ranch. It's open daily from 7:30am to sundown. The park's high water table makes it a magnet for birds and other wildlife; the lush springs and streams are an unexpected desert treat.

HORSEBACK RIDING   Novice and advanced equestrians alike can experience the desert's solitude and quiet on horseback, at **Smoke Tree Stables** (☎ **760/327-1372**). South of downtown, at 2500 Toledo Ave., and ideal for exploring the nearby Indian Canyon trails, Smoke Tree offers guided rides for $40 per hour, $80 for 2 hours; the 2-hour tour includes admission to an Agua Caliente Indian reservation. But don't expect your posse leader to spew facts about the natural features you'll encounter; this is strictly a do-it-yourself experience.

TENNIS   Virtually all the larger hotels and resorts have tennis courts. If you're staying at a B&B, you might want to play at the **Plaza Racquet Club,** 1300 Baristo Rd. (☎ **760/323-8997**). It has nine courts and runs day and evening clinics for adults, juniors, and seniors, and ball machines for solo practice. USPTA pros are on hand. Rates are $15 per hour for court rental, $15 for a 1¹/₂-hour group clinic. The night-lit courts at **Palm Springs High School,** 2248 E. Ramon Rd., are free, open to the public on weekends, holidays, and in summer. Beautiful **Ruth Hardy Park,** at Tamarisk and Caballero streets, also has eight free night-lit courts.

Exploring the Area

The Living Desert Zoo & Gardens ★ (Kids)

This 1,200-acre desert reserve, museum, zoo, and educational center is designed to acquaint visitors with the Southern California desert's unique habitats. You can walk or take a tram tour through sectors that re-create life in several distinctive desert zones. See and learn about a dizzying variety of plants, insects, and wildlife, including bighorn sheep, mountain lions, rattlesnakes, lizards, owls, golden eagles, and the ubiquitous roadrunner, plus new exhibits featuring frogs and butterflies. It's a nonstuffy learning experience for kids and grown-ups alike.

47–900 Portola Ave., Palm Desert. ☎ **760/346-5694.** www.livingdesert.org. Admission $12 adults, $11 seniors/military, $7.50 children 3–12, free for kids 2 and under. Reduced summer rates. Daily 9am–5pm (last entrance 4pm); summer (mid-June to Aug) 8am–1:30pm.

Palm Springs Aerial Tramway ★★

To gain a bird's-eye perspective on the Coachella Valley, take this 14-minute ascent up nearly 5,900 feet to the upper slopes of Mount San Jacinto. While the Albert Frey–designed boarding stations retain their 1960s ski-lodge feel, newly installed Swiss funicular cars are sleekly modern and rotate during the trip to allow each passenger a panoramic view. There's a whole other world once you arrive: alpine scenery, a ski-lodge-flavored restaurant and gift shop, and temperatures

Here's the Rub: Two Bunch Palms Desert Spa

Since the Native American Cahuilla learned how great it felt to soak in the Coachella Valley's natural hot springs, this desert has drawn stressed-out masses seeking relaxation. My number-one choice is heavenly **Two Bunch Palms.** Posh yet intimate, this spiritual sanctuary in Desert Hot Springs (about 20 min. north of Palm Springs) has been drawing weary city dwellers since Chicago mobster Al Capone hid out here in the 1930s. Two Bunch Palms later became a playground for the movie community, but today it's a friendly and informal haven, with 56 acres of renowned spa services, well appointed bungalows on lush grounds, and lagoons of steaming mineral water. Float in serenity at the Grotto, which consists of small mineral pools surrounded by tall tranquil greenery. Service is famously discreet; and legions of return guests will attest that the outstanding spa treatments (including 12 varieties of massage, mud baths, body wraps, facials, salt rubs, water therapy) and therapeutic waters are what make the luxury of Two Bunch Palms irresistible. To maintain the relaxed atmosphere, guests are requested to speak softly, just above a whisper. Loud argumentative guests will be asked to leave and denied access in the future. Room rates run from $225 to $425 (including breakfast) in high season, with substantial discounts midweek and off-season. Spa treatments cost between $75 and $125 per hour, and multiday money-saving room/spa packages run from $999 to $1,149 for two, with double occupancy. Other packages may be available. The quiet dining room serves delicious lunches and dinners, with a full bar and wine available. No one under 18 is allowed. The resort is off Palm Drive (Gene Autry Trail) at 67-425 Two Bunch Palms Trail in Desert Hot Springs (© **800/472-4334** or 760/329-8791; www.twobunchpalms.com).

typically 40° Fahrenheit cooler than the desert floor. The most dramatic contrast is during the winter, when the mountaintop is a snowy wonderland, irresistible to hikers and bundled-up kids with saucers. The excursion might not be worth the expense during the rest of the year. Guided mule rides and cross-country ski equipment are available at the top. An upscale restaurant, **Peaks,** serves California-modern cuisine. Appetizers begin at $10, entrees $21. Wait and take the tram to the top after 3pm for a lower rate and "Ride and Dine" at the **Pines Restaurant,** $36 adults, $23 children. Peaks is open 11am to 7:30pm daily and reservations are recommended (© **760/325-4537**).

Tramway Rd. off Hwy. 111, Palm Springs. © **888/515-TRAM** or 760/322-4800. www.pstramway.com. Tickets $22 adults, $20 seniors, $15 children 3–12, free for kids 2 and under. Mon–Fri 10am–8pm; Sat–Sun 8am–8pm. Tram runs every 30 min., last tram down at 9:45pm. Tram cars and stations are accessible to travelers w/disabilities.

Palm Springs Desert Museum ★ Unlikely though it may sound, this museum is well endowed and worth a look. Exhibits include world-class Western and Native American art collections, the natural history of the desert, and an outstanding anthropology department, primarily representing the local Cahuilla tribe. Tools, baskets, and other relics illustrate traditional Indian life, as it was lived for centuries. Check local schedules

Sweet Desert Treat: The Coachella Valley Date Gardens

In a splendid display of wishful thinking and clever engineering, the Coachella Valley has grown into a rich agricultural region, known internationally for grapefruit, figs, and grapes—and dates. Entrepreneurs, fascinated with Arabian lore and fueled by the Sahara-like conditions of the desert around Indio, planted these date palm groves in the 1920s. Launched with a few parent trees imported from the Middle East, the groves now produce 95% of the world's date crop.

Farmers hand-pollinate the trees, and the resulting fruit is bundled in wind-protective paper while still on the tree, which makes an odd sight indeed. You'll see them along Highway 111 through Indio, locally known as the "Date Highway."

The most picturesque place in the valley to sample dates is **Oasis Date Gardens,** 59111 Hwy. 111 (© **800/827-8017** or 760/399-5665), started in 1912 with nine Moroccan trees and now one of the nation's largest commercial date groves. It's a 40-minute drive from downtown Palm Springs—but there's a lot to do here. Picnic tables dot an inviting lawn, videos illustrate the history and art of date cultivation, and there's a cool palm arboretum and cactus exhibit. Many varieties of dates are laid out for free tasting. Oasis also sells date shakes, ice cream, date pie by the slice, homemade chili and sandwiches, and gourmet food gifts from all over the Southwest. Open daily (except Dec 25) from 8am to 5pm.

to find out about visiting exhibits (which are usually excellent). Plays, lectures, and other events are presented in the museum's **Annenberg Theater** (© 760/325-4490).

101 Museum Dr. (just west of the Palm Canyon/Tahquitz intersection), Palm Springs. © **760/325-7186.** www.psmuseum.org. Admission $13 adults, $11 seniors 62 and over, $5 military and children 6–17, free for children 5 and under. Free for all each Thurs after 4pm. Tues–Wed and Fri–Sun 10am–5pm; Thurs noon–8pm.

SHOPPING

Downtown Palm Springs revolves around **North Palm Canyon Drive;** many art galleries, souvenir shops, and restaurants are here, along with a couple of large-scale hotels and shopping centers. This wide one-way boulevard is designed for pedestrians, with many businesses set back from the street (don't be shy about poking around the little courtyards you'll encounter). On Thursday nights from 6 to 10pm, the blocks between Amado and Baristo roads are transformed into **VillageFest,** a town street fair. Handicrafts vendors and aromatic food booths vie for attention with wacky street performers and even wackier locals shopping at the fresh-produce stalls.

The northern section of Palm Canyon, known for collectibles, is touted as the **Antique and Heritage Gallery District.** Check out **Antiques Collector,** 798 N. Palm Canyon Dr. (© 760/323-4443), a discriminating mall-style store with 35 dealers displaying wares that range from vintage linens to handmade African crafts to prized Bakelite jewelry. The **111 Antique Mall** with vintage furnishings, art, and lighting, is at 2500 N. Palm Canyon Dr. in Palm Springs (© 760/864-9390).

Serious shoppers head south to Palm Desert with the delicious excesses of **El Paseo,** a **667**
cornucopia of high-rent boutiques, salons, and upscale restaurants reminiscent of Rodeo
Drive in Beverly Hills, along with more than a dozen major shopping malls.

Factory-outlet shopping is 20 minutes away in Cabazon (see "En Route to the Palm
Springs Resorts," earlier in this chapter).

GAY & LESBIAN LIFE IN PALM SPRINGS

The Palm Springs area is among America's top destinations for gay and lesbian travelers.
Real-estate agents cater to gay shoppers for vacation properties, and year-round condo
communities are also marketed toward gay residents. Advertisements for these and scores
of other gay-owned businesses can be found in the **Bottom Line** (www.psbottomline.
com), the desert's free biweekly magazine of articles, events, and community guides for
the gay reader, which is available at hotels, at newsstands, and from select merchants. The
Palm Springs Visitor and Hotel Information Center publishes an **Official Gay Visitors Guide.** Obtain it and additional information at their office at 2901 N. Palm Canyon Dr. (© 800/347-7746; www.palm-springs.org).

In March, the **Desert AIDS Walk** benefits the Desert AIDS Project, while one of the
world's largest organized gathering of lesbians—the **Dinah Shore Weekend** (www.club
skirts.com)—coincides with the LPGA's **Kraft Nabisco Championship** in March. The
predominantly male **White Party** (www.jeffreysanker.com), the area's largest circuit party
event, takes place Easter weekend. **Greater Palm Spring Pride** occurs the first weekend in
November, with a parade and 2-day cultural fair (© 760/416-8711; www.pspride.org).

Palm Springs has more than two dozen gay hotels, many concentrated on Warm Sands
Drive south of Ramon. Known simply as "Warm Sands," this area is home to many of
the private resorts—mostly discreet, gated inns, many of them clothing-optional. Try the
East Canyon Hotel & Spa, 288 E. Camino Monte Vista, a 15-unit luxurious hotel with
a pool and in-house spa that caters to the male guest. Clothing is not optional. Rates are
$119 to $369 including breakfast buffet (© 877/324-6835 or 760/320-1928; www.east
canyonps.com). **Casitas Laquita,** 450 E. Palm Canyon Dr. (© 760/416-9999; www.
casitaslaquita.com), is one of two all-women resorts in town. Rates are $135 to $350.

WHERE TO STAY

The city of Palm Springs has a wide range of accommodations, but we particularly like
the inns that have opened as a result of new owners renovating the many fabulous 40- to
60-year-old cottage complexes in the wind-shielded Tennis Club area west of Palm Canyon Drive. The other desert resort cities offer mostly sprawling complexes, many boasting world-class golf, tennis, or spa facilities and multiple on-site restaurants. Most are
destinations in and of themselves, with activities for the whole family (including a whole
lot of relaxing and pampering). If you're looking for a good base from which to shop or
sightsee, Palm Springs is your best bet.

Regardless of your choice, remember that the rates below are for high season (winter,
generally Nov–May). During the hotter summer months, it's common to find $300
rooms going for $99 or less, as part of off-season packages. Even in high season, discounts
for midweek stays are common.

Palm Springs
Expensive
The Colony Palms Hotel Palm Springs ★★★   Originally built in 1936 by a head
of the "Purple Gang" and later frequented by a number of Hollywood stars, this hotel

within walking distance of downtown has undergone a $15-million renovation. A two-story Spanish Hacienda–style building surrounds a lush patio area with a full-size swimming pool, large Jacuzzi, poolside cabanas, and a bevy of comfortable lounges for sunning. Along one side is the **Purple Palm** (p. 674), an inviting restaurant with indoor seating and outdoor patio tables by the pool. The 56 guest rooms are large and tastefully done in a '40s Hollywood decor with fireplaces; all are nonsmoking. Casitas set quietly behind the main building have private patios and outdoor hot tubs. The atmosphere is elegant-casual with friendly and efficient service.

572 North Palm Canyon Dr., Palm Springs, CA 92262. ℰ **800/557-2187** or 760/969-1800. www.colony palmshotel.com. 56 units. $209–$299 double; $359–$1,099 casitas and suites. Discounts available in summer. AE, DISC, MC, V. **Amenities:** Poolside full-service restaurant; pool bar; large heated pool; Jacuzzi; room service; nonsmoking; poolside cabanas. In room: A/C, flatscreen plasma TV, DVD/CD player, Wi-Fi, minibar, fridge.

Le Parker Meridien Palm Springs ★★★   Well ensconced on the superluxury Palm Springs hotel scene, is a $27-million renovation of the former Gene Autry Melody Ranch and then the Merv Griffin Givenchy Resort and Spa known simply as the Parker. If you have been to either of these, you won't recognize the makeover. The 13-acre property has 131 rooms, 12 one-bedroom villas, and the original Gene Autry house. In keeping with the desert decor, the rooms are basically a relaxed white with light wood overtones. And bathrooms include both tub and shower. Two restaurants serve your every desire: **Norma's** has all-day breakfast for late sleepers, including the renowned $1,000 sevruga caviar and lobster omelet, served indoors or on an outdoor terrace; **Mister Parker's** presents a daily changing dinner menu in an intimate atmosphere (closed Mon–Tues). A chic boutique, Veri Peri, features up-scale designs. Activities center around four red clay tennis courts, four pools (two of them heated), and the Palm Springs Yacht Club spa, to revive the jet-lagged body, and a 24-hour gym to get it back in shape. Golfers will be able to use the next door Seven Lakes Country Club's 18-hole golf course, where President Dwight D. Eisenhower reportedly scored his only hole in one.

4200 E. Palm Canyon Dr., Palm Springs, CA 92264. ℰ **760/770-5000.** www.theparkerpalmsprings.com. 144 units. Oct–May $255–$595 double; June–Sept $129–$369 double, $895–$2,000 12 private villas; $595–$1,200 private villas. There is a $30 resort fee. Guests under 30 can stay in the staff quarters for much less; call for details. AE, DC, DISC, MC, V. **Amenities:** 2 restaurants; lobby bar; 4 pools (2 heated); 4 red-clay tennis courts; gym; spa; Jacuzzi; steam and sauna rooms; room service and free morning coffee delivery upon request; twice-daily maid service; DVD library; helipad. In room: A/C, TV, CD/DVD/MP3 player, Wi-Fi, minibar, fridge.

Moderate

Korakia Pensione ★★   If you can handle the Korakia's rigid deposit-cancellation policy, you're in for a special stay at this Greek-Moroccan oasis, a few blocks from Palm Canyon Drive. This former artist's villa from the 1920s draws a hip international crowd of artists, writers, and musicians. The simply furnished rooms and spacious suites are peaceful and private, surrounded by flagstone courtyards and flowering gardens. Rooms are divided between the main house, a second restored villa across the street, and guest bungalows. Most have kitchens; many have fireplaces. All beds are blessed with thick duvets, and the windows are shaded by flowing white-canvas Mediterranean-style draperies. You also get a sumptuous breakfast served in your room or poolside. *Korakia* is Greek for "crow," and a tile mosaic example graces the pool bottom. *Note:* You must pay a deposit to book a room, there's a 2-night minimum on weekends, and you have to give at least 2 weeks' cancellation notice (*45 days*' advance notice for holidays) or you'll lose your deposit.

The Old Is New Again

Bring back the romance of the '50s with a vacation stay at the Twin Palms Sinatra Estate. Built in 1947 by Stewart Williams for Frank and his then wife, Nancy, it became the center of desert social life when Frank brought home a new bride, Ava Gardner. The 4,500-square-foot home has three bedrooms, seven bathrooms, a living room with massive glass doors that open to the patio, and the piano-shaped swimming pool. Period furniture sustains the atmosphere, with artwork, pottery, and textiles. It wasn't all peaches and cream in the Sinatra household—note the chip in the sink, from a champagne bottle tossed during one of Frank's loving tiffs with Ava. But if you still dote on Ol' Blue Eyes, nostalgia is your bag, and you can afford $7,800 for 3 nights ($2,600 for each additional night), see **www.timeandplace.com** for availability, rates, and other information.

257 S. Patencio Rd., Palm Springs, CA 92262. ✆ **760/864-6411.** Fax 760/864-4147. www.korakia.com. 29 units. $169–$229 double; $279–$369 suite; $499–$789 house. Rates include breakfast. MC, V. Free parking. **Amenities:** 2 outdoor heated pools; in-room massage. *In room:* A/C, fridge, coffeemaker, hair dryer and iron on request, safe.

Orbit In ★★ This much-hyped renovation of a classic 1950s motel gets our vote as the grooviest digs in town. With its cocktails-by-the-pool Rat Pack aesthetic, it has exceeded everyone's expectations, with an almost scholarly appreciation of the architects and designers responsible for Palm Springs's reign as a mecca of vintage modernism. Serious connoisseurs of interior design will find a museum's worth of furnishings in these rooms, each of which adheres to a theme (Martini Room, Atomic Paradise, and so on) down to customized lounge-music CDs. Contemporary comforts abound, from cushy double pillow-top mattresses to poolside misters that create an oasis of cool even during midsummer scorchers. Kitchenettes all boast charming restored fixtures, as do the candy-pink-tiled original bathrooms, which have only stall showers but make up for the lack of tubs by being surprisingly spacious—and naturally sunlit. Guests gather at the poolside "boomerang" bar, or in the **Albert Frey Lounge** (homage to the late, great architect whose unique home sits midway up the mountain backdrop); a central "movies, books, and games" closet encourages old-fashioned camaraderie. Nearby, the eight-unit **Hideaway** is a quieter, more secluded lodging with a large saltwater pool; no Jacuzzi but access to the Orbit amenities is available.

562 W. Arenas Rd., Palm Springs, CA 92262. ✆ **877/99-ORBIT (996-7248)** or 760/323-3585. Fax 760/323-3599. www.orbitin.com. 10 units. $179–$259 double. Rates include deluxe continental breakfast. AE, DISC, MC, V. Free parking. **Amenities:** Poolside bar; outdoor heated saltwater pool; Jacuzzi; spa facilities; bikes available for rental; private patios. *In room:* A/C, TV/VCR, kitchenette, fridge, coffeemaker, hair dryer, iron, safe, CD player.

Spa Resort Casino This is one of the more unusual choices in town. It's on the Indian-owned parcel of land containing the mineral springs for which Palm Springs was named. The Cahuilla claimed the springs had magical powers to cure illness. Today's travelers still come here to pamper body and soul by "taking the waters," though now the facility is sleekly modern. There are three pools on the premises: One is a conventional outdoor swimming pool; the other two are filled from the underground natural springs brimming with revitalizing minerals. Inside the hotel's extensive spa are private sunken marble swirl-pools fed by the springs. After your bath, you can pamper yourself with one of many treatments. Despite the addition of the Vegas-style casino (a separate unit across the street), the Cahuilla have integrated modern hotel comforts with this land's ancient healing tradition and Indian spirit.

100 N. Indian Canyon Dr., Palm Springs, CA 92263. ℂ 888/999-1995 or 760/325-1461. Fax 760/325-3344. www.sparesortcasino.com. 228 units. $189–$259 double; $369–$1,500 suite. AE, DC, MC, V. Free parking. **Amenities:** 3 restaurants; 2 bars; Olympic-size outdoor heated pool; fitness center; full-service spa; concierge; car-rental desk; room service. *In room:* A/C, TV, fridge, hair dryer, iron.

Viceroy Palm Springs ★★   Once the choice of Hollywood celebrities, this outstanding historic hotel, formerly the Estrella, is quiet and secluded yet close to the action. It's composed of three distinct properties from three different eras, which benefited from a chic transformation in 2002—sort of a Grecian-meets-modern Regency style popular during Palm Springs's golden era. Guest rooms vary in terms of size and amenities—some have fireplaces and/or full kitchens, others have wet bars or private balconies. The color scheme is black-and-white with lemon-yellow accents. The real deals are the studio bungalows, even though they have tiny 1930s bathrooms. Lavish landscaping is an elegant finishing touch. The restaurant, **Citron,** serves lunch, dinner, and Sunday brunch (entrees $24–$34; three-course brunch $35) and has a full bar. There is also pool food service.

415 S. Belardo Rd. (south of Tahquitz Way), Palm Springs, CA 92262. ℂ 800/670-6184 or 760/320-4117. Fax 760/323-3303. www.viceroypalmsprings.com. 68 units. $189–$229 double; $425 suite; $569–$719 villa. AE, DC, MC, V. Free parking. **Amenities:** Restaurant; bar; 3 outdoor heated pools (including children's pool); fitness room; full-service spa; 2 Jacuzzis. *In room:* A/C, flatscreen TV/DVD, fridge, hair dryer.

Villa Royale ★★   This charming inn, 5 minutes from the hustle and bustle of downtown, evokes a European cluster of villas, complete with climbing bougainvillea and rooms filled with international antiques and artwork. Uniform luxuries (down comforters and other pampering touches) appear throughout. Rooms vary widely in size and ambience; larger isn't always better, as some of the inn's most appealing rooms are in the smaller, more affordable range. Many rooms have fireplaces, private patios, full kitchens, and a variety of other amenities. A full breakfast is served in an intimate garden setting surrounding the main pool. This is a genuine desert oasis. The hotel's romantic restaurant, **Europa** (p. 674), is a sleeper, offering some of Palm Springs's very best meals.

1620 Indian Trail (off E. Palm Canyon), Palm Springs, CA 92264. ℂ 800/245-2314 or 760/327-2314. Fax 760/322-3794. www.villaroyale.com. 30 units. $200–$275 suite; $350–$450 villa. Rates include full breakfast. AE, DC, DISC, MC, V. Free parking. **Amenities:** Restaurant; 2 outdoor heated pools; Jacuzzi; in-room massage. *In room:* A/C, TV, hair dryer, iron.

Inexpensive

Calla Lily Inn   With a recent, extensive renovation, this nine-unit inn offers deluxe rooms with kitchens and poolside suites, all with tile floors and luxurious beds. Instead of wine at cocktail time, the Calla Lily offers a nighttime cordial or brandy. The tropical decor is enhanced by the lush landscaping with, what else, calla lilies. A 2-day minimum is required on weekends and holidays, and pets and smoking are prohibited.

350 S. Belardo Rd., Palm Springs, CA 92262. ℂ 888/888-5787 or 760/323-3654. Fax 760/323-4964. www. callalilypalmsprings.com. 9 units. $129–$179 double; $159–$398 suite. AE, DC, DISC, MC, V. **Amenities:** Heated pool; Jacuzzi; on-site massage. *In room:* A/C, TV/VCR/DVD, Wi-Fi, coffeemaker, iron, robes.

Casa Cody ★ Once owned by "Wild" Bill Cody's niece, this 1920s house with a double courtyard (each with swimming pool) has been restored to fine condition. It now sports a southwestern decor and peaceful grounds marked by large lawns and mature, blossoming fruit trees. You'll feel more like a houseguest than a hotel client at the Casa Cody. It's in the residential, tennis clubby part of town, a couple of easy blocks from Palm Canyon Drive. Most of the 27 units here have fireplaces and full-size kitchens. Breakfast is served poolside, as are complimentary wine and cheese on Saturday afternoons. Kids are welcome.

175 S. Cahuilla Rd. (btw. Tahquitz Way and Arenas Rd.), Palm Springs, CA 92262. (C) **800/231-2639** or 760/320-9346. Fax 760/325-8610. www.casacody.com. 27 units. $69–$189 double; $209–$279 suite; $429 2-bedroom house; $639 4-bedroom house. Rates include expanded continental breakfast. AE, DC, DISC, MC, V. Pets accepted for $15 extra per night. **Amenities:** 2 outdoor heated pools; Jacuzzi; in-room massage. *In room:* A/C, TV, fridge.

Palm Mountain Resort and Spa (Kids) Within easy walking distance of Palm Springs's main drag, this former Holiday Inn welcomes kids under 18 free in their parent's room, making it a good choice for families. Rooms are in the two- or the three-story wing, and many have a patio or balcony, with a view of the mountains or the large Astroturf courtyard. Midweek and summer rates are as low as $99. For the best rates, book online or ask for "Great Rates."

155 S. Belardo Rd., Palm Springs, CA 92262. (C) **800/622-9451** or 760/325-1301. Fax 760/323-8937. www.palmmountainresort.com. 119 units. Jan–Apr $109–$209 double; May–Sept $69–$139 double; Oct–Dec $99–$169 double. Rates include continental breakfast. Children 17 and under stay free in parent's room. AE, DC, DISC, MC, V. Free parking. **Amenities:** Restaurant; lounge; heated pool; day spa. *In room:* A/C, TV, fridge, coffeemaker, hair dryer, iron.

Rancho Mirage

Marriott's Rancho Las Palmas Resort & Spa ★★ The early California charm of this relaxing Spanish hacienda makes Rancho Las Palmas one of the least pretentious luxury resorts in the desert. Dedicated golfers play on the adjoining country club's 27 holes; tennis buffs flock to the 25 hotel courts (three of them red clay); everybody enjoys the world-class health spa, plus a new aquatic adventure called Splastopia. Guest rooms are in a complex of low-rise, tile-roofed structures, and the public areas have an easygoing elegance, filled with flower-laden stone fountains, smooth terra-cotta tile floors, and rough-hewn wood trim. Each room has a balcony or patio.

41000 Bob Hope Dr., Rancho Mirage, CA 92270. (C) **866/4233-1195** or 760/568-2727. Fax 760/568-5845. www.rancholaspalmas.com. 450 units. $119–$459 double. Children 17 and under stay free in parent's room. AE, DISC, MC, V. Self-parking. **Amenities:** 2 restaurants; cocktail lounge; 2 outdoor heated pools; night-lit outdoor tennis courts; health club; full-service spa; 2 Jacuzzis; children's programs; concierge; business center; room service; babysitting; laundry/dry-cleaning service. *In room:* A/C, TV w/pay movies, minibar, coffeemaker, hair dryer, iron, safe.

Westin Mission Hills Resort ★★ Designed to resemble a Moroccan palace surrounded by pools, waterfalls, and lush gardens, this self-contained resort stands on 360 acres. It's an excellent choice for families and travelers who take their golf game seriously. (Regular desert visitors will note the Westin is situated so Palm Springs and Palm Desert are equally accessible without driving on congested Hwy. 111.) Rooms are arranged around the grounds in a series of two-story buildings, and accommodations range from basic to palatial. All have terraces and come with an array of creature comforts befitting this price range—including the Westin trademark Heavenly Bed, an ultracomfy white confection that many guests order for their homes.

The Westin has the business demeanor of a practiced group-and-meeting hotel, but it offers a multitude of recreation options for leisure travelers, gamblers attracted to the nearby Agua Caliente Casino, or professionals after the day's business is concluded. In addition to their championship golf course, you'll find a running track, bike trails, lawn games, and the freshly expanded Spa at Mission Hills, a boutiquelike oasis whose treatments range from sports massage to pampering Hawaiian body treatments.

71–333 Dinah Shore Dr. (at Bob Hope Dr.), Rancho Mirage, CA 92270. ℂ **800/WESTIN-1** (937-8461) or 760/770-8250. Fax 760/324-6343. www.starwood.com. 512 units. $279–$449 double. Extra person $35. Children 17 and under stay free in parent's room. Golf, spa, and family packages available. AE, DC, DISC, MC, V. Free valet and self-parking. **Amenities:** 3 restaurants; 2 lounges; 3 poolside cabana bars; multiple outdoor heated pools and Jacuzzis; night-lit outdoor tennis courts; health club; full-service spa; bike rental; children's activity center; concierge; business center; room service; in-room massage; babysitting; dry-cleaning/laundry service; water slide. *In room:* A/C, TV w/pay movies, minibar, coffeemaker, hair dryer, iron, safe.

Palm Desert

Desert Springs—A JW Marriott Resort & Spa ★★ (Kids)

A tourist attraction in its own right, Marriott's Desert Springs resort is worth a peek even if you're not lucky enough to stay here. Most guests come for the golf and tennis facilities, and the luxurious, full-service spa is an added perk. Visitors enter this artificial desert oasis via a sweeping palm-tree-lined road wending its way past a small pond that's home to a gaggle of pink flamingos. Once inside, guests are greeted by a shaded marble lobby featuring a 60-foot bar backed by waterfalls spilling into reflecting pools. The "dock" at the end of the lobby has been enlarged to enable two gondolas to transport guests through a network of Venetian inspired waterways to view the fairways and lush gardens of the property.

Rooms here are not as fancy as the lobby would lead you to believe, but they're exceedingly comfortable, decorated with muted pastels and contemporary furnishings. All have terraces with views of the golf course and the San Jacinto Mountains. Recreational options include a jogging trail, 36 holes of golf, driving range, a unique 18-hole putting range, basketball courts, lawn croquet, and a sunbathing "beach" with volleyball court. An enlarged spa now has 47 treatment rooms and suites with private showers, fireplaces, and outdoor whirlpools. You need not ever leave the premises if you don't want to.

74855 Country Club Dr., Palm Desert, CA 92260. ℂ **800/331-3112** or 760/341-2211. Fax 760/341-1872. www.desertspringsresort.com. 884 units. $229–$459 double; from $600 suite. Children 17 and under stay free in parent's room; senior discount available. AE, DC, DISC, MC, V. **Amenities:** 5 restaurants; 4 snack bars; 3 lounges; 5 heated outdoor pools; 20 tennis courts (hard, clay, and grass; 7 lit); full-service spa and health club; 5 outdoor Jacuzzis; bike rental; children's programs; game room; concierge; tour desk; car-rental desk; business center; shopping arcade; salon; room service; in-room massage; babysitting; dry-cleaning/laundry service. *In room:* A/C, TV w/pay movies, minibar, coffeemaker, hair dryer, iron, safe.

The Mod Resort ★

This 14-unit hideaway is a remembrance of the '70s as a vision in white. In fact, in the rooms, it's white on white, with accents of chrome and mirrors. The bathroom has a glass bowl sink and a glass tile showers with rain shower head. The suites have private patios, some with kitchenettes, some with full kitchens. The units flank a full-size pool set among palm trees and augments with white and chrome loungers and tables. Truly, a place to relax and still be a short walk to El Paseo's shopping and restaurants.

73758 Shadow Mountain Dr., Palm Desert, CA 92260. ℂ **888/MOD-1970** or 760/674-1966. www. modresort.com. 14 units. $159–$349 double. Rates include continental breakfast. AE, MC, V. **Amenities:**

> ## Tips A La Quinta Bed & Breakfast Hideaway
>
> Devotees of bed-and-breakfasts or boutique inns might be daunted by the La Quinta Resort's 800 rooms, but there's a way to enjoy this quiet, affluent end of the valley with a little more intimacy. Check out the hidden-secret **Lake La Quinta Inn,** 78–120 Caleo Bay ((© **888/226-4546** or 760/564-7332; www.lake laquintainn.com), a 13-room Norman-style B&B on the shores of a man-made lake, blocks from the famous resort. Exquisitely outfitted rooms, delightful hosts, on-site facials and massage, and a 24-hour pool and Jacuzzi complete the fantasy. Rates are $219 to $319 (double); suites are $267 to $449, including breakfast and wine in the afternoon.

Pool; Jacuzzi. *In room:* Flatscreen LCD TV/DVD, high-speed Internet, Wi-Fi, some with kitchenettes or full kitchens, CD player, private patios for suites.

La Quinta

La Quinta Resort & Club ★★★   A luxury resort amid citrus trees, towering palms, cacti, and desert flowers at the base of the Santa Rosa Mountains, La Quinta is *the* place to be if you're serious about golf or tennis. The resort is renowned for its five championship golf courses—including one of California's best, Pete Dye's PGA West TPC Stadium Course. All guest rooms are in single-story, Spanish-style buildings throughout the grounds. Each has its own patio and access to one of several dozen small pools, enhancing the feeling of privacy at this retreat. Some units have a fireplace or Jacuzzi. The tranquil lounge and library in the original hacienda hearken back to the early days of the resort, when Clark Gable, Greta Garbo, Frank Capra, and other luminaries chose La Quinta as their hideaway. The resort includes Spa La Quinta, a Mission-style complex with more than 35 treatment rooms for every pampering luxury.

16

49499 Eisenhower Dr., La Quinta, CA 92253. (© **800/598-3828** or 760/564-4111. Fax 760/564-7656. www.laquintaresort.com. 796 units. $329–$629 double; from $1,000 suite. $27 resort fee per night. Extra person $25. Children 17 and under stay free in parent's room. Packages available. AE, MC, V. Free self-parking; valet parking. Pets welcome for a fee. **Amenities:** 5 restaurants; 3 bars (2 featuring entertainment); 41 outdoor pools; 23 outdoor tennis courts (10 lit); full-service spa; 53 Jacuzzis; bike rental; children's programs; concierge; business center; room service; laundry service. *In room:* A/C, flatscreen TV/VCR w/pay movies, Wi-Fi, minibar, coffeemaker, hair dryer, iron, safe.

Indian Wells

Miramonte Resort & Spa ★★   This collection of 215 rooms in 12 Mediterranean villas covers 11 acres of bougainvillea-filled gardens and Italian fountains. Standard rooms are enlarged to become luxurious minisuites adding a living room area with a second TV. Suites add one or two bedrooms. An extra-large pool has cabanas that can be rented by the day, plus whirlpools, and is the center of activity in the main area. Another pool is designated as adults only, making it a quiet respite for relaxing. An $18 resort fee includes local phone calls, 24-hour fitness center, valet and self-parking, daily newspaper, and Wi-Fi. Dining is especially fine in the Restaurante Brissago, which features a Mediterranean-inspired menu. The Vineyard Lounge offers tapas and local jazz on the weekends. The WELL SPA is a 14,000-square-foot expanse with relaxation suites, mud bars, river benches, and a Watsu pool.

45–000 Indian Wells Lane (on Hwy. 111), Indian Wells, CA 82210. ✆ **800/237-2926** or 760/341-2200. Fax 760/568-0541. www.miramonteresort.com. 215 units. $119–$359 double; $379–$480 suite; $899 1-bedroom villa. $20 resort fee per night. Free self- and valet parking. **Amenities:** Restaurant; bar; lounge; 2 pools; full spa w/fitness room and pool; 2 Jacuzzis; concierge; golf desk; business center; room service. *In room:* AC, TV, Wi-Fi, minibar, coffeemaker, hair dryer, iron, safe, patio.

WHERE TO DINE
Palm Springs
Expensive

Europa Restaurant ★★ CALIFORNIA/CONTINENTAL　Long advertised as the "most romantic dining in the desert," Europa is a sentimental favorite of many regulars, equal parts gay and straight. This European-style hideaway exudes charm and ambience. Whether you sit under the stars on Europa's garden patio or in subdued candlelight indoors, you'll savor dinner prepared by one of Palm Springs's most dedicated kitchens and served by a discreetly attentive staff. Standout dishes include a tender *osso buco* that falls off the bone, filet mignon on a bed of crispy onions with garlic butter, and a show-stopping salmon baked in parchment with crème fraîche and dill. And don't miss the signature chocolate mousse—smooth and addictive.

1620 Indian Trail (at the Villa Royale). ✆ **760/327-2314.** Reservations recommended. Main courses $26–$42. AE, DC, DISC, MC, V. Tues–Sun 5–10pm.

The Purple Palm ★★ FRENCH/MEDITERRANEAN　Set poolside at the Colony Palms Hotel, this fresh, innovative addition to Palm Springs dining has quickly become *the* place to dine. Relax in the comfortable dining room or dine by candlelight alongside of the pool. Specialties include grilled divers sea scallops, charred ahi tuna steak, and roasted saddle of spring Colorado lamb, with starters such as cream of artichoke soup, or Kumomoto oysters. Don't leave without tasting the tiramisu with a raspberry soda shooter.

572 North Indian Canyon Dr. (at the Colony Palms Hotel). ✆ **800/557-2187.** www.colonypalmshotel. com. Reservations recommended. Main courses $24–$42. AE, DISC, MC, V. Open daily 9am–10pm summer; 7:30–10pm winter.

Inexpensive

Davey's Hideaway American　For a relaxed, casual, inexpensive evening, you must try Davey's Hideaway at the beginning of East Palm Canyon. Featuring patio dining and piano entertainment, this small cookshop serves salads, pasta, beef, rack of lamb, and their special fresh Atlantic salmon charbroiled or Cajun style. Nightly specials sell for $20 from 5 to 6pm, and wines are $26 to $60 per bottle.

292 E. Palm Canyon, Palm Springs (across the street from Lyon's). ✆ **760/320-4480.** Reservations suggested. Main courses $18–$32. MC, V. Sun–Thurs 5–9pm; Fri–Sat 5–10pm.

Murph's Gaslight ★ PAN-FRIED CHICKEN　Join those in the know at this budget-saving lunch-and-dinner meeting place, where the chicken just keeps coming, with all the trimmings: black-eyed peas, mashed potatoes, corn bread, hot biscuits, country gravy, and fruit cobbler. Call ahead for takeout or join the family-style crowd, on a first-come, first-served basis. An early bird special starts at 5pm for $10. If there's a wait, relax in Murph's Irish Pub.

79–860 Ave. 42, next to the airport in Bermuda Dunes near Jefferson. ✆ **760/345-6242.** $16 for full dinner. MC, V. Mon–Sat 11am–3pm and 5–9pm; Sun 3–9pm.

Sherman's Deli and Bakery ★ KOSHER DELI　Join the locals at this indoor and outdoor-patio restaurant with 2-inch-thick deli sandwiches, lox and bagels, and a bakery with rich, delicious cakes and pastries that would put any calorie-conscious dieter into trauma if it weren't for the Lite Lunch Special: mushroom barley or matzo ball soup with half of any regular deli-variety sandwich. Iced tea is the official drink, but wine and beer are also available. Sherman's has another branch in Palm Desert (73–161 Country Club Dr.; ✆ **760/568-1350**).

401 Tahquitz, Palm Springs. ✆ **760/325-1199.** Breakfast omelets $6.75–$9.45; deli sandwich board $8.45–$13 (includes potato salad); dinner $15–$21, early bird dinner 4–7pm $12. AE, DC, DISC, MC, V. Daily 7am–9pm.

Rancho Mirage
Expensive
Villa Abbate ITALIAN   Southern Italian cooking has come to the desert in high style at the Villa Abbate. Try the three-tier selection of antipasto for a starter at $30 for two. From there, choose from pasta, fish, or veal prepared to perfection.

69820 Hwy. 111 (at Frank Sinatra Dr.). ✆ **760/321-6835.** Entrees $26–$40. AE, MC, V. Tues–Sun 5:30–10pm.

Palm Desert
Louise's Pantry ★ COFFEE SHOP/DINER   A real old-fashioned luncheonette, Louise's was a fixture in Palm Springs since opening as a drugstore lunch counter in 1945. The original location on Palm Canyon Drive fell victim to skyrocketing property values, but devoted patrons—young and old—flocked to the new location in La Quinta, for premium-quality comfort foods such as Cobb salad, Reuben and French dip sandwiches, burgers, pantry sandwiches, chicken and dumplings, hearty breakfasts with biscuits and gravy, and tasty fresh-baked pies. Beer and wine are available. The new branch is on Washington Street in La Quinta, serving the same menu through dinner.

47–150 Washington (south of Hwy. 111). ✆ **760/771-3330.** Reservations not accepted. Most menu items under $10. MC, V. Daily 7am–3pm.

Palmie ★ CLASSIC FRENCH   Martine and Alain Clerc's cozy bistro is filled with Art Deco posters of French seaside resorts. Chef Alain sends out masterful traditional French dishes such as braised lamb shank, *cassoulet des confit de canard*, and ravioli stuffed with lobster. In fact, every carefully garnished plate is a work of art. To the charming background strains of French chanteuses that can sometimes be heard over the noise of happy diners, hostess and manager Martine circulates between tables, determined that visitors enjoy their meals as do the loyal regulars she greets by name. Don't leave without sampling dessert: Our favorite is the trio of petite crème brûlées, flavored with ginger, vanilla, and Kahlúa.

44–491 Town Center Way, Suite G, Palm Desert. Go north on Town Center Way, then take the 1st left into the mall, and a direct left to the restaurant. ✆ **760/341-3200.** Reservations recommended. Main courses $17–$32. AE, DC, MC, V. Mon–Sat 5:30–9pm.

Sammy's Woodfired Pizza PIZZA   In the same mall complex as Tommy Bahama's is a great inexpensive restaurant for families. The large room with booths and tables is fronted by a misted outdoor patio. Choose from 21 wood-fired pizza drizzled with chili oil, such as the N.Y. pizza: homemade tomato sauce, sautéed mushrooms, pepperoni, salami, and Italian sausage for $13. The menu also has a variety of salads and pasta. Beer and wine are available.

73595 El Paseo (at Larkspur Ave.). ✆ **760/836-0500.** Pizzas $9.75–$13, salads $9.50–$17, pastas $13–$17. AE, MC, V. Daily 11am–9pm.

Tommy Bahama's Tropical Cafe CARIBBEAN   If all this desert terrain makes you long for *de islands, mon,* step upstairs from fashionable Tommy Bahama's boutique for a dose of Caribbean relaxation, without the humidity. The decor alone is worth a visit: a fantasy port of call, around 1940, with ceiling fans, plenty of rattan and palms, and upholstery in TB's signature tropical prints. Enormous umbrellas shade patio seating with valley views, and spacious indoor booths make for easy relaxing over a series of sweet umbrella drinks. The food is a delicious change of pace, its Caribbean zing not overly spiced; check out coconut shrimp with mango dip, conch fritters, mango shrimp salad, Boca Chica chicken, Jamaican jerk pork, and Key lime pie for dessert. Diners are an entertaining mix of socialites fresh from the tennis courts, perennially vacationing retirees, and well-heeled shoppers.

73595 El Paseo (at Larkspur Ave.). (C) **760/836-0188.** Reservations recommended in season. Main courses $8–$18 lunch, $18–$37 dinner. AE, MC, V. Daily 11am–10pm.

THE DESERT RESORTS AFTER DARK

Every month a different club or disco is the hot spot in the Springs, and the best way to tap into the trend is by consulting the *Desert Guide,* the *Bottom Line* (see "Gay & Lesbian Life in Palm Springs," earlier in this chapter), or one of the many other free newsletters available from area hotels and merchants. **VillageFest** (see "Shopping," earlier in this chapter) turns Palm Canyon Drive into an outdoor party every Thursday night. For a trip back into Rat Pack days, drop in at Buddy Greco's Dinner Restaurant. There is a show at 8pm with a cover charge of $40 per person if you are dining, $60 if just in for drinks. Below, I've described a couple of the enduring arts and entertainment attractions around the desert resorts.

The **Fabulous Palm Springs Follies,** at the Plaza Theatre, 128 S. Palm Canyon Dr., Palm Springs ((C) **760/327-0225;** www.psfollies.com), a vaudeville-style show filled with highly polished and lavishly costumed production numbers reminiscent of the Ziegfeld days, is a long-running hit in the historic Plaza Theatre in the heart of town. With a cast of retired showgirls, singers, dancers, and comedians, the revue is hugely popular. In addition, there are guest stars such as Mimi Hines, Kaye Ballard, Anna Maria Alberghetti, and the Four Aces. The season runs November through May; call for exact schedule. Tickets range from $42 to $95. Matinees are at 1:30pm, evening shows at 7pm.

The **McCallum Theatre for the Performing Arts,** 73000 Fred Waring Dr., Palm Desert ((C) **866/889-2787**), offers the only cultural high road around. Frequent symphony performances feature visiting virtuosos such as conductor Seiji Ozawa or violinist Itzhak Perlman; musicals such as *Hairspray,* and *Gypsy;* and pop performers such as Steve and Edie (Lawrence and Gorme) or Patti Lu Pone, were among recent offerings. Call for upcoming events.

CASINOS

Native American gaming has been part of desert life for years now, but recently the industry seems to have joined the major leagues, with a professionalism and polish that have given rise to a "virtual Vegas."

The best-known and most centrally located casino is the **Spa Resort Casino** in the heart of Palm Springs (p. 669). Gaming rooms that were once an afterthought now share the spotlight with the hot springs. Attendees at the hotel's conference center on business can often be found playing hooky at one or both.

You can't help but be impressed by the brilliant neon fireballs of the **Agua Caliente Casino,** northeast of Palm Springs at 32–250 Bob Hope Dr., Rancho Mirage ((C) **888/999-1995** or

The new hotel has 340 rooms, a 10,000-square-foot spa, three restaurants, and a 2,000-seat showroom; call © **866/923-7244** for reservations.

The former Trump 29, now run by the owning Indian tribe, is called **Spotlight 29,** 46–200 Harrison Place, Coachella (© **866/878-6729**), about a half-hour from Palm Springs. Although the land is tribal-owned, this sophisticated complex is Vegas all the way, with its big-name shows and high-roller players club to its 24-hour fine dining and all-you-can-eat prime-rib buffets.

Other tribal casino/resorts flank the valley, with the **Morongo Casino, Resort and Spa** to the northwest, at 49500 Seminole Dr., Cabazon, CA 92230 (© **888-MORONGO** [667-6646]), with 310 rooms, 32 suites, and six casitas by the pool. Four restaurants, food court, and full-service salon and spa augment the three nightclubs, not to mention the tables.

4 JOSHUA TREE NATIONAL PARK ★

40 miles NE of Palm Springs; 128 miles E of downtown L.A.

The Joshua trees in this national park are merely a jumping-off point for exploring this seemingly barren desert. Viewed from the roadside, the dry land only hints at hidden vitality, but closer examination reveals a giant mosaic of intense beauty and complexity. From lush oases teeming with life to rusted-out relics of human attempts to tame the wilderness, from low plains of tufted cacti to mountains of exposed, twisted rock, the park is much more than a tableau of the curious tree for which it is named.

The Joshua tree is said to have received its name from early Mormon settlers traveling west, for its upraised limbs and bearded appearance reminded them of the prophet Joshua leading them to the promised land. Other observers were not so kind. Explorer John C. Frémont called it "the most repulsive tree in the vegetable kingdom."

That's harsh criticism for this hardy desert dweller—really not a tree but a variety of yucca and member of the lily family. The relationship is apparent when pale-yellow, lily-like flowers festoon the limbs of the Joshuas when they bloom in March, April, or May (depending on rainfall). When Mother Nature cooperates, the park also puts on quite a wildflower display. Call the park ranger (see "Essentials," below) for an updated report on prime viewing sites.

The park, which reaches the southernmost boundary of this special tree's range, straddles two desert environments. There's the mountainous, Joshua tree–studded Mojave Desert, forming the northwestern part of the park, while the Colorado Desert—hotter, drier, lower, and characterized by a wide variety of desert flora, including cacti,

---

Tips Load Up on Everything

Joshua Tree National Park has no restaurants, lodging, gas stations, or stores. Water is available only at five park locations: Cottonwood Springs, the Black Rock Canyon Campground, the Indian Cove Ranger Station, the West Entrance (the hamlet of Joshua Tree), and the Oasis Visitor Center. Joshua Tree, Twentynine Palms, and Yucca Valley have lots of restaurants, markets, motels, and B&Bs.

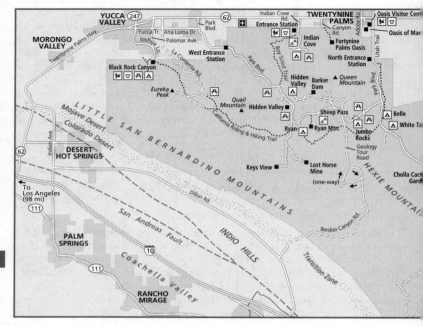

cottonwood, and native California fan palms—comprises the southern and eastern sections of the park. Between them runs the "transition zone," displaying characteristics of each.

The area's geological timeline is fascinating, stretching back 8 million years to a time when the Mojave landscape was one of rolling hills and grasslands; horses, camels, and mastodons abounded, preyed upon by saber-toothed tigers and wild dogs. Displays at the Oasis Visitor Center show how resulting climatic, volcanic, and tectonic activity created the park's signature cliffs and boulders and turned Joshua Tree into the arid desert it is today.

Human presence has been traced back nearly 10,000 years, with the discovery of Pinto Man, and evidence of more recent habitation can be seen in the form of Native American pictographs carved into rock faces throughout the park. Miners and ranchers began coming in the 1860s, but the boom went bust by the turn of the 20th century. Then a Pasadena doctor, treating World War I veterans suffering from respiratory and heart ailments caused by mustard gas, prescribed the desert's clean, dry air—and the town of Twentynine Palms was (re)born.

In the 1920s, cactus gardens were very much in vogue. Entrepreneurs hauled truckloads of desert plants into Los Angeles for quick sale or export, and souvenir hunters removed archaeological treasures. Incensed that the beautiful Mojave was in danger of being picked clean, Los Angeles socialite Minerva Hoyt organized a conservation movement and successfully lobbied for the establishment of Joshua Tree National Monument in 1936. The park got an unexpected boost when the first rock-climbing route was put up in 1956, near Jumbo Rock. The sport didn't take off until the late 1960s, but today the park is considered Southern California's best rock-climbing area, and in winter (when places such as Yosemite are embraced by cold weather), Joshua Tree is crawling with climbers.

In 1994, under provisions of the federal California Desert Protection Act, Joshua Tree rose to national park status and expanded to nearly 800,000 acres. The park is popular with everyone from campers to wildflower lovers and even RVers just cruising through. It's a must-see for nature and geology lovers visiting during temperate weather, and it's more "user-friendly" than the other two hard-core desert parks.

ESSENTIALS

GETTING THERE From metropolitan Los Angeles, the usual route to the **Oasis Visitor Center** in Joshua Tree National Park is via I-10 to its intersection with Highway 62 (some 92 miles east of downtown). Highway 62 (the Twentynine Palms Hwy.) leads northeast for about 43 miles to the town of **Twentynine Palms.** Total driving time is around 2¹/₂ hours. In town, follow the signs at National Park Drive or Utah Trail to the visitor center and ranger station. Admission to the park is $15 per car (good for 7 days). Camping fees are $10 with no water, $15 with water.

WHEN TO GO The park is busiest—relatively speaking, since it rarely feels crowded—in winter (Nov–Mar). Rock climbers flock to Joshua Tree in winter and spring, along with day-trippers drawn by brilliant wildflower displays (if winter rainfall was sufficient) in March, April, and May. The sizzling summer months are popular with international visitors curious about the legendary extremes of temperature, and hardy campers looking for the solitude of balmy evenings.

VISITOR CENTERS & INFORMATION   In addition to the **Oasis Visitor Center** (© 760/367-5500) at the Twentynine Palms entrance, **Cottonwood Visitor Center** is at the south entrance, and the privately operated **Park Center** is in the town of Joshua Tree, close to the West Entrance, the unofficial portal for rock climbers.

The Oasis Visitor Center is open daily (except Dec 25) from 8am to 5pm. Check here for a detailed map of park roads, plus schedules of ranger-guided walks and interpretive programs. Ask about weekend tours of the Desert Queen Ranch, once a working homestead and now part of the park.

For information before you go, contact the **Park Superintendent's Office,** 74485 National Park Dr., Twentynine Palms, CA 92277 (© **760/367-5525;** www.nps.gov/jotr). The **Joshua Tree National Park Association** is another good resource; reach them at © **760/367-5525** (www.joshuatree.org). Another outfit focused on the surrounding communities is **www.desertgold.com**.

EXPLORING THE PARK

An excellent first stop, outside the park's north entrance, is the main **Oasis Visitor Center,** alongside the Oasis of Mara, also known as the Twentynine Palms Oasis. For many generations, the native Serrano tribe lived at this "place of little springs and much grass." Get maps, books, and the latest in road, trail, and weather conditions before beginning your tour.

From the Oasis Center, drive south to **Jumbo Rocks,** which captures the essence of the park: a vast array of rock formations, a Joshua tree forest, and the yucca-dotted desert, open and wide. Check out Skull Rock (one of the many rocks in the area that appear to resemble humans, dinosaurs, monsters, cathedrals, or castles) via a 1.5-mile nature trail that provides an introduction to the park's flora, wildlife, and geology.

At Cap Rock Junction, the main park road swings north toward the **Wonderland of Rocks,** 12 square miles of massive jumbled granite. This curious maze of stone hides groves of Joshua trees, trackless washes, and several small pools of water. To the south is Keys View Road, which dead-ends at mile-high **Keys View.** From the crest of the Little San Bernardino mountains, enjoy grand desert views that encompass both the highest (Mt. San Gorgonio) and lowest (Salton Sea) points in Southern California.

Don't miss the contrasting Colorado Desert terrain found along Pinto Basin Road. To conserve time, you might plan to exit the park via this route, which ends up at I-10. You'll pass both the **Cholla Cactus Garden** and spindly **Ocotillo Patch** on your way to vast, flat **Pinto Basin,** a barren lowland surrounded by austere mountains and punctuated by trackless sand dunes. The dunes are an easy 2-mile round-trip hike from the backcountry camping board (one of the few man-made markers along this road and one of the only designated parking areas), or simply continue to **Cottonwood Springs,** near the southern park entrance. Besides a small ranger station and well-developed campground, Cottonwood has a cool, palm-shaded oasis that is the trail head for a tough hike to Lost Palms Oasis.

HIKING, BIKING & CLIMBING

HIKING & NATURE WALKS   The national park has a variety of nature trails, from strenuous challenges to kid-friendly interpretive walks; two of these (**Oasis of Mara** and interpretive trails, is **Cholla Cactus Garden,** in the park's center, where you stroll through dense clusters of the deceptively fluffy-looking "teddy bear cactus."

For the more adventurous, **Barker Dam** is an easy 1-mile loop accessible by a graded dirt road east of Hidden Valley. A small, man-made lake is framed by the majestic Wonderland of Rocks. It's fun to scramble atop the old dam or search out Native American petroglyphs carved into the cliffs lining your return to the trail head.

The challenging **Lost Horse Mine Trail** near Keys View leads through rolling hills to the ruins of a successful gold-mining operation; from here, a short, steep hike leads uphill behind the ruins for a fine view into the heart of the park.

When you're ready for a strenuous hike, try the **Fortynine Palms Oasis Trail,** accessible from Canyon Road in Twentynine Palms. After a steep, harsh ascent to a cactus-fringed ridge, the rocky canyon trail leads to a spectacular oasis, complete with palm-shaded pools of green water and abundant birds and other wildlife. Allow 2 to 3 hours for the 3-mile round-trip hike.

Another lush oasis lies at the end of **Lost Palms Oasis Trail** at Cottonwood Springs. The first section of the 7.5-mile trail is moderately difficult, climbing slowly to the oasis overlook; from here, a treacherous path continues to the canyon bottom, a remote spot that the elusive bighorn sheep find attractive.

Joshua Tree Hiking Adventures (© 760/366-7985; www.joshuatreehike.com) offers half- and full-day guided hikes in the nearby mountains and washes. Half-day costs run from $50 per person for groups of five or more to $150 for one person, full-day $70 to $240.

Desert Adventures Jeep Eco-Tours (© 888/440-5337 or 760/340-2345; www.redjeep.com) offers four-wheel-drive ecotours led by naturalist guides. Desert Adventures is the only outdoor adventure company that can take you to a private 1,000-acre preserve located on the San Andreas Fault. They offer miles of pristine desert, a private natural palm oasis, and amazing steep-walled canyons to explore. Their award-winning tours feature interactive displays to bring your tour to life. Your off-road adventure may take you to a replica of an ancient Cahuilla village filled with Indian interpretive displays, a replica Old Mining Camp where you can pan for gold, an EPICENTER Earthquake Education Center where you can learn about geology and earthquakes, or visit a homestead and discover how early Coachella Valley pioneers survived in the harsh desert. Desert Adventures also offers jeep adventures to Joshua Tree National Park

MOUNTAIN BIKING Much of the park is designated wilderness, meaning that bicycles are limited to roads (they'll damage the fragile ecosystem if you venture off the beaten track). None of the paved roads have bike lanes, but rugged mountain bikes are a great way to explore the park via unpaved roads, where there aren't many cars.

Try the 18-mile **Geology Tour Road,** which begins west of Jumbo Rocks. Dry lake beds contrast with towering boulders along this sandy downhill road, and you'll also encounter abandoned mines.

A shorter but still rewarding ride begins at the **Covington Flats** picnic area. A steep 4-mile road climbs through Joshua trees, junipers, and pinyon pines to Eureka Peak, where you'll be rewarded with a panoramic view. For other bike-friendly unpaved and four-wheel-drive roads, view the official park map.

ROCK CLIMBING From Hidden Valley to the Wonderland of Rocks, the park has emerged as one of the state's premier rock-climbing destinations. The park offers some 4,000 climbing routes, from the easiest bouldering to some of the sport's most difficult climbs. November through May is the prime season to watch lizardlike humans scale sheer rock faces with impossible grace. Beginners can get into the act with the **Joshua Tree Rock Climbing School** (𝄪 800/890-4745 or 760/366-4745; www.joshuatree rockclimbing.com). In business since 1988, it offers weekend and 4-day group lessons ($110 for 1 day, $215–$315 for 2 days, and $530 for 4 days, including equipment), plus private guiding ($295 for one person per day; less if more in the group, such as $125 per person if five in the group). **Nomad Adventures** in Joshua Tree (𝄪 760/366-4684) is the local climbing store for gear sales and shoe rentals ($7.50 a day). Open weekdays from 8am to 6pm, weekends 8am to 8pm.

WHERE TO STAY

If you're staying in the Palm Springs area, it's possible to visit the national park as a day trip. But if you'd like to stay close by or spend more time here, consider Twentynine Palms, just outside the north boundary of the national park on Highway 62, which offers budget-to-moderate lodging. There are also accommodations in Blackrock and Joshua Tree (West Entrance). For a complete listing of Twentynine Palms lodging, contact the **29 Palms Chamber of Commerce,** 73660 Civic Center Drive, Twentynine Palms, CA 92277 (𝄪 760/367-3445; www.29chamber.com). Blackrock information is available through the **Yucca Valley Chamber of Commerce,** 56711 Twentynine Palms Hwy., Yucca Valley, CA 92284 (𝄪 760/365-6323; www.yuccavalley.org). For Joshua Tree (West Entrance), contact the **Joshua Tree Chamber of Commerce,** 61325 Twentynine Palms Hwy. #F, Joshua Tree, CA 92252 (𝄪 760/366-3723; www.joshuatreechamber. org).

Near the visitor center in the Oasis of Mara is the rustic **29 Palms Inn,** 73950 Inn Ave. (𝄪 760/367-3505; www.29palmsinn.com), a cluster of adobe cottages and old cabins from the 1920s; its garden-fresh restaurant is the best in town. The 100-room **Best Western Garden Inn,** 71487 Palm Hwy. (𝄪 760/367-9141; www.bestwestern. com), is also a comfortable base from which to maximize your outdoor time. Also recommended in Twentynine Palms is the 53-room **Holiday Inn Express Hotel and Suites,** 71809 Twentynine Palms Hwy. (𝄪 760/361-4009).

Nine **campgrounds** scattered throughout the park offer pleasant though often spartan accommodations, with just picnic tables and pit toilets for the most part. Only two— **Black Rock Canyon** and **Cottonwood Springs**—have potable water and flush toilets, for a $15 overnight fee. Indian Cove and West Entrance have water at the ranger station, less than 2 miles from their closest campgrounds. You can make reservations online at **http://reservations.nps.gov** or by calling 𝄪 800/365-2267. Hot showers are available at **Coyote Corner,** 6535 Park Blvd. in Joshua Tree (𝄪 760/366-9683); they also rent climbing and camping gear.

---

5 ANZA-BORREGO DESERT STATE PARK ★

90 miles NE of San Diego; 31 miles E of Julian

The 600,000-acre Anza-Borrego Desert State Park, the nation's largest contiguous state park, lies mostly within San Diego County, and getting to it is almost as much fun as being there. From Julian, the first 20 minutes of the winding hour-long drive feel as if you're going straight downhill; in fact, it's a 7-mile drop called Banner Grade. A famous scene from the 1954 movie *The Long, Long Trailer,* with Lucille Ball and Desi Arnaz, was

Desert. An easier access is from Indio: Go south on Highway 86 to Salton City and west on County Road S22 into Borrego Springs.

The desert is home to fossils and rocks dating from 540 million years ago (humans arrived only 10,000 years ago). The terrain ranges in elevation from 15 feet to 6,100 feet above sea level. It incorporates dry lakebeds, sandstone canyons, granite mountains, palm groves fed by year-round springs, and more than 600 kinds of desert plants. After the spring rains, thousands of wildflowers burst into bloom, transforming the desert into a brilliant palette of pink, lavender, red, orange, and yellow. The rare bighorn sheep can sometimes be spotted navigating rocky hillsides, and an occasional migratory bird stops off on the way to the Salton Sea. A sense of timelessness pervades this landscape; it's worth slowing down to take a long look around.

When planning a trip here, keep in mind that temperatures rise to as high as 115°F (46°C) in summer. Winters days are comfortable with temperatures in the low to mid 70s Fahrenheit (mid-20s Celsius), but nighttime temps can drop to freezing. *Note:* Hypothermia is as big a killer out here as the heat.

ESSENTIALS

GETTING AROUND You don't need four-wheel-drive to tour the desert, but you'll probably want to get off the highways and onto the jeep trails. The Anza-Borrego Desert State Park Visitor Center staff can tell you which jeep trails are in condition for two-wheel-drive vehicles. A free Back Country Permit is required to camp or use the jeep trails in the park. The Ocotillo Wells area has been set aside for off-road vehicles such as dune buggies and dirt bikes. A vehicle must be licensed for highway use to ride the jeep trails.

ORIENTATION & VISITOR INFORMATION In Borrego Springs, the shopping center known as "the Mall" is on Palm Canyon Drive, the main drag. Christmas Circle surrounds a grassy park at the entry to town. The **Anza-Borrego Desert State Park Visitor Center** (© 760/767-4205; www.parks.ca.gov) is just west of the town of Borrego Springs. It supplies information, maps, and two 15-minute audiovisual presentations, one on the desert's changing faces and the other on wildflowers. The visitor center is open October through May daily from 9am to 5pm, June through September weekends from 9am to 5pm. The **Desert Natural History Association,** 652 Palm Canyon Dr. (© 760/767-3098; www.abdnha.org), runs the sleek Borrego Desert Nature Center and Bookstore with an impressive selection of guidebooks, historical resources, educational materials for kids, native plants and regional crafts, and a small museum display that includes a frighteningly real stuffed bobcat. This is also your best source for information on the nearby Salton Sea. It's open daily 9am to 5pm.

Moments   The Desert in Bloom

From mid-March to the beginning of April, the desert wildflowers and cacti are usually in bloom—a hands-down, all-out natural special event that's not to be missed. It's so extraordinary, there's a hot line to let you know when the blossoms are expected to burst forth: © **760/767-4684.**

For information on lodging, dining, and activities, contact the **Borrego Springs Chamber of Commerce,** 786 Palm Canyon Dr., Borrego Springs, CA 92004 (© **800/ 559-5524** or 760/767-5555; www.borregosprings.org).

EXPLORING THE DESERT

Remember that when you're touring in this area, hydration is of paramount importance. Whether you're walking, cycling, or driving, always have a bottle of water at your side. If you will be out after dusk, or anytime during January and February, warm clothing is also essential.

You can explore the desert terrain on a trail or self-guided driving tour; the visitor center can supply maps. For starters, the **Borrego Palm Canyon self-guided hike** (1.5 miles each way) starts at the campgrounds near the visitor center. It is beautiful and easy, leading to a waterfall and massive fan palms in about 30 minutes. There is a $4 to $6 per vehicle day-use fee.

Note: Don't miss the sunset from Font's Point (accessible via four-wheel-drive; check at the visitor center). Plan ahead and bring champagne and beach chairs for the nightly ritual.

WHERE TO STAY

Borrego Springs is small but has enough lodgings to suit all travel styles and budgets. Peak season corresponds with the most temperate weather and wildflower viewing—mid-January through mid-May. Other decent options include **Palm Canyon Resort,** 221 Palm Canyon Dr. (© **800/242-0044** or 760/767-5341; www.pcresort.com), a large complex that includes a moderately priced hotel ($70–$195), RV park ($36 for full hookup), restaurant, and recreational facilities; and **Borrego Valley Inn,** 405 Palm Canyon Dr. (© **800/333-5810** or 760/767-0311; www.borregovalleyinn.com), a luxury southwestern complex featuring sand-colored pueblo-style rooms and upscale bed-and-breakfast amenities. High-season rates are $175 to $295.

La Casa del Zorro Desert Resort ★★   This pocket of heaven on earth was built in 1937, and the tamarisk trees planted then have grown up around it. So have the many charming tile-roofed casitas, originally neighboring homes bought by the resort's longtime owners, San Diego's Copley newspaper family. Over time the property has grown into a cohesive blend of discreet private cottages and luxurious two-story hotel buildings—each blessed with personalized service and unwavering standards—that make La Casa del Zorro unequaled in Borrego Springs. Courtesy carts ferry you around the lushly planted grounds, and to the resort's stunning pool area by the resurfaced tennis courts. It's easy to understand why repeat guests book their favorite casita year after year; some have a fireplace or pool, every bedroom has a separate bathroom, and they all have minifridges and microwaves (though the absence of dishes and utensils is calculated, to get you into the Spanish-style main lodge's fine dining room). Outdoor diversions include horseshoes, Ping-Pong, volleyball, jogging trails, basketball, shuffleboard, and a life-size chess set. By the way, *zorro* means fox, and you'll find subtle fox motifs throughout the property.

3845 Yaqui Pass Rd., Borrego Springs, CA 92004. © **800/824-1884** or 760/767-5323. Fax 760/767-5963. www.lacasadelzorro.com. 63 units. $365–$450 double; from $395–$555 1-bedroom casita, 3- and 4-bedroom casitas available. Rates include breakfast. AE, DC, DISC, MC, V. **Amenities:** Restaurant; lounge; 5 outdoor pools; 9-hole putting green; 6 tennis courts; health club and spa; 4 whirlpools; bike rental; activities desk; courtesy car to golf; business center; salon; room service; in-room massage; babysitting. *In room:* A/C, TV w/pay movies, VCR/DVD player, minibar, coffeemaker, hair dryer, iron.

The Palms at Indian Head ★★ (Finds)   It takes a sense of nostalgia and an active imagination for most visitors to appreciate Borrego Springs's only bed-and-breakfast. Its fervent owners, David and Cynthia Leibert, have renovated the once-chic resort. Originally opened in 1947, then rebuilt after a fire in 1958, the Art Deco–style hilltop lodge was a favorite hideaway for San Diego's and Hollywood's elite. It hosted stars such as Bing Crosby, Clark Gable, and Marilyn Monroe. The Leiberts rescued it from disrepair in 1993, uncovering original wallpaper, light fixtures, and priceless memorabilia. As soon as they'd restored several rooms in luxurious southwestern style, they began taking in guests.

The inn has 12 rooms and a popular restaurant, the **Krazy Coyote** (see "Where to Dine," below). Also restored is the 42-by-109-foot pool, soon to be joined by the original subterranean grotto bar behind viewing windows at the deep end and solar heating. The inn occupies the most envied site in the valley—shaded by palms, next to the state park, with a view across the entire Anza-Borrego region. A hiking trail begins steps from the hotel. The Palms at Indian Head rewards you with charm, comfort, and convenience.

2220 Hoberg Rd., Borrego Springs, CA 92004. (℃) **800/519-2624** or 760/767-7788. Fax 760/767-9717. www.thepalmsatindianhead.com. 12 units. $129–$229 double. Extra person $20. Rates include continental breakfast. DC, DISC, MC, V. Take S22 into Borrego Springs; at Palm Canyon Dr., S22 becomes Hoberg Rd. Continue north ¹/₂ mile. **Amenities:** Restaurant; bar; outdoor pool; room service; in-room massage; laundry service. In room: A/C, TV, fridge, coffeemaker.

Camping

The park has two developed campgrounds. **Borrego Palm Canyon,** with 117 sites, is 2¹/₂ miles west of Borrego Springs, near the visitor center. Full hookups are available, and there's an easy hiking trail. **Tamarisk Grove,** at Highway 78 and County Road S3, has 27 sites. The overnight rate at both ranges from $20 to $29. Both have restrooms with pay showers (bring quarters!) and a campfire program; reservations are a good idea. The park allows open camping along all trail routes. For more information, check with the visitor center (℃ **760/767-4205;** www.anzaborrego.statepark.org).

WHERE TO DINE

Pickings are slim, but your best bet—if you're not willing to break the bank at La Casa del Zorro's classy dining room (dinner $25–$60)—is the surprisingly good **Krazy Coyote** (see below), which presents a new menu of steaks and seafood. Follow legions of locals into downtown mainstay **Carlee's Place,** 660 Palm Canyon Dr. (℃ **760/767-3262**), a casual bar and grill with plenty of neon beer signs, a pool table, and fuzzy-sounding jukebox. It's easy to understand why Carlee's is the watering hole of choice for motorcycle brigades that pass through town on recreational rides—and the food is tasty, hearty, and priced just right. Open daily from 11am "till whenever," and food service stops at 9pm. If you have a sweet tooth, check out the **Fudge Factory,** 202 Palm Canyon (℃ **760/767-7782**), for a wide variety of fudge, ice creams, pastries, and espresso. It's open Tuesday through Sunday 8am to 4pm. Closed Monday.

Assaggio ITALIAN   This new addition to the Borrego Springs dining scene has daily specials to augment the inexpensive menu of seafood, pasta, veal, beef, and chicken. The decor is uninspired, but the traditional trattoria dining hits the mark. The restaurant is open for breakfast, lunch, and dinner; and beer and house wine is available.

1816 Palm Canyon Dr. (℃ **760/767-3388.** Main courses mostly under $16. Daily 7am–9:30pm.

Kendall's Cafe ★ COFFEE SHOP   Here's an economical spot to grab a bite. Buffalo burgers and Mexican dishes are popular. The best bet here is breakfast or anything that can be packed to go so you can dine overlooking the desert.

In the Mall. ℂ **760/767-3491.** Lunch $6–$10; dinner $7–$14. MC, V. Daily 6am–8pm.

Krazy Coyote Saloon & Grille ★ MEAT AND SEAFOOD   The same style and perfectionism that pervades David and Cynthia Leibert's bed-and-breakfast is evident in this restaurant, overlooking the inn's swimming pool and the desert beyond. The menu includes prime steaks, New Zealand rack of lamb or lobster, scampi, salmon, and chicken. The evening ambience is welcoming and romantic, as the sparse lights of tiny Borrego Springs twinkle on the desert floor below.

In the Palms at Indian Head, 2220 Hoberg Rd. ℂ **760/767-7788.** Main courses $10–$50. AE, MC, V. Open daily; call for seasonal hours.

The Red Ocotillo OLD-FASHIONED DINER   For hearty breakfast (served all day) or a casual lunch, join the crowd at the Red Ocotillo. Dining is casual indoors or in the patio. Eggs Benedict and omelets go for $9.95, and sandwiches are $8.95. Beer and wine are available.

818 Palm Canyon (as you enter town). ℂ **760/767-7400.** Daily 7am–9pm.

THE SOUTHERN CALIFORNIA DESERT

16

MOJAVE NATIONAL PRESERVE

6 MOJAVE NATIONAL PRESERVE

235 miles E of downtown L.A.; 125 miles SW of Las Vegas

Two decades of park politicking ended in 1994 when President Bill Clinton signed into law the California Desert Protection Act, which created the Mojave National Preserve. Thus far, the Mojave's elevated status has not attracted hordes of sightseers, and devoted visitors are happy to keep it that way. Unlike a fully protected national park, the "national preserve" designation allows hunting and certain commercial land uses, and the continued grazing and mining within the preserve's boundaries goad ardent environmentalists.

To most Los Angelenos, the East Mojave is that vast, bleak, interminable stretch of desert to be crossed as quickly as possible while leaving California via I-15 or I-40. Few realize that these highways are the boundaries of what some have long considered the crown jewel of the California desert.

This land is hard to get to know; unlike more developed desert parks, it has no lodgings or concessions, few campgrounds, and a handful of roads suitable for the average passenger vehicle. It takes a love of the desert to appreciate the stark, barren terrain. But gems are hidden within this natural fortress: The preserve's 1.6 million acres include the world's largest Joshua tree forest; abundant wildlife; spectacular canyons, caverns, and volcanic formations; nationally honored scenic back roads and footpaths to historic mining sites; tabletop mesas; and a dozen mountain ranges.

ESSENTIALS
GETTING THERE   I-15, the major route between the Southern California metropolis and the state line for Las Vegas–bound travelers, extends along the northern boundary of Mojave National Preserve. I-40 is the southern access route to the East Mojave. It's a 3¹/₂-hour drive from L.A. to Kelso Depot, in the center of the preserve. The closest major airport is in Las Vegas.

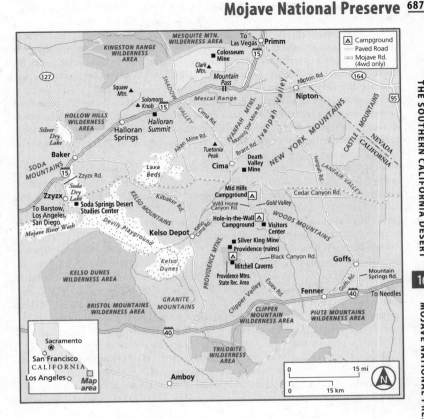

WHEN TO GO   Spring and autumn are splendid times to visit this desert. From March to May temperatures are mild, the Joshua trees are in bloom, and the lower Kelso Dunes are bedecked with yellow and white desert primrose and pink sand verbena.

VISITOR CENTERS & INFORMATION   The best source for up-to-date weather conditions and a free topographical map is the new **Kelso Visitor Center** in the Kelso Depot (℃ **760/252-6108**), open daily 9am to 5pm. Additional information and maps are available inside the preserve at the **Hole-in-the-Wall Visitor Center** (℃ **760/928-2572**), which is open 9am to 4pm Wednesday to Sunday for most of the year, Friday to Sunday in summer. You can visit the preserve online at **www.nps.gov/moja**.

EXPLORING THE PARK

One of the preserve's spectacular sights is the **Kelso Dunes,** the West's most extensive dune field. The 45-square-mile formation of magnificently sculpted sand is famous for "booming": Visitors' footsteps cause mini-avalanches that go "sha-boom-sha-boom-sha-boom." Geologists speculate that the extreme dryness of the East Mojave Desert, combined with the wind-polished, rounded nature of the individual sand grains, has something to do with their musicality. Sometimes the low rumbling sound resembles a Tibetan gong; other times it sounds like a 1950s doo-wop musical group.

A 10-mile drive from the Kelso Dunes, **Kelso Depot,** built by the Union Pacific in 1924, now houses the visitor center. The Spanish Revival–style structure was designed with a red-tile roof, graceful arches, and a brick platform. The depot remained open for freight-train crew use through the mid-1980s, although it ceased to be a passenger railroad stop after World War II.

On and around **Cima Dome,** a rare geological anomaly, grows the world's largest and densest Joshua tree forest. Botanists say Cima's Joshuas are more symmetrical than their cousins elsewhere in the Mojave. The dramatic colors of the sky at sunset provide a breathtaking backdrop for Cima's Joshua trees, some more than 25 feet tall and several hundred years old.

Tucked into the Providence Mountains, in the southern portion of the preserve, is a treat everyone should try to see. The **Mitchell Caverns ★**, contained in a state recreation area within the national preserve, is a geological oddity exploited for tourism but still quite fascinating. Regular tours are conducted of these cool rock "rooms"; in addition to showcasing stalactites, stalagmites, and other limestone formations, the caves have proven to be rich in Native American archaeological finds.

Hole-in-the-Wall and **Mid Hills** are the centerpieces of Mojave National Preserve. Both offer diverse desert scenery, fine campgrounds, and the feeling of being in the middle of nowhere. The preserve's best drive links the two sites. In 1989, **Wildhorse Canyon Road,** which loops from Mid Hills Campground to Hole-in-the-Wall Campground, was declared the nation's first official "Back Country Byway," an honor federal agencies bestow upon America's most scenic back roads. The 11-mile, horseshoe-shaped road crosses open country dotted with *cholla* and, in season, purple, yellow, and red wildflowers. Volcanic slopes and flattop mesas tower over the low desert.

Mile-high Mid Hills, named for its location between the Providence and New York mountains, recalls the Great Basin Desert topography of Nevada and Utah. Mid Hills Campground offers a grand observation point from which to gaze out at the creamy, coffee-colored Pinto Mountains to the north and the rolling Kelso Dunes shining on the western horizon.

Hole-in-the-Wall is the kind of place Butch Cassidy and the Sundance Kid would have chosen as a hideout. This twisted maze of rhyolite rocks is a form of crystallized red-lava rock. A series of iron rings aids descent into Hole-in-the-Wall; they're not particularly difficult for those who are reasonably agile.

Kelso Dunes, Mitchell Caverns, Cima Dome, and Hole-in-the-Wall are highlights of the preserve that can be viewed in a weekend. But you'll need a week to see all the major sights, and maybe a lifetime to get to know the East Mojave. And right now, without much in the way of services, the traveler to this desert must be well prepared and self-reliant. For many, this is what makes a trip to the East Mojave an adventure.

If Mojave National Preserve attracts you, you'll want to return again and again to see its wonders, including **Caruthers Canyon,** a "botanical island" of pinyon pine and juniper woodland, and **Ivanpah Valley,** which supports the largest desert-tortoise population in the California desert.

HIKING & BIKING

HIKING The free-form ambling climb to the top of the **Kelso Dunes** is 3 miles round-trip. The **Caruthers Canyon Trail,** 3 miles round-trip, wends through a cool, inviting pinyon pine/juniper woodland. The longest path, **Mid Hills to Hole-in-the-Wall Trail,**

is a grand tour of basin and range tabletop mesas, large pinyon trees, and colorful cacti; it's 8 miles one-way. The 1-mile trip from **Hole-in-the-Wall Campground** to **Banshee Canyon** and the 5-mile jaunt to **Wildhorse Canyon** are easier options. Pick up trail maps at one of the visitor centers.

MOUNTAIN BIKING   Opportunities are as extensive as the preserve's hundreds of miles of lonesome dirt roads. The 140-mile historic **Mojave Road,** a rough four-wheel-drive route, visits many of the most scenic areas in the East Mojave; sections of this road make excellent bike tours. Prepare well: These are rugged routes through desert wilderness.

CAMPING

The **Mid Hills Campground** is in a pinyon-pine/juniper woodland and offers outstanding views. This mile-high camp is the coolest in the East Mojave. Nearby **Hole-in-the-Wall Campground** sits above two canyons. Both campgrounds have pit toilets and potable water but no utility hookups. There is a graded dirt road between the two, but it's suitable for two-wheel-drive passenger cars.

There are also some sites at **Providence Mountain State Recreation Area** (Mitchell Caverns; see "Exploring the Park," above).

One of the highlights of the East Mojave Desert is camping in the open desert all by your lonesome, but certain rules apply. Call the **Kelso Visitors Center** at ✆ 760/252-6108 for suggestions.

NEARBY TOWNS WITH TOURIST SERVICES

BARSTOW   This sizable town has many restaurants and motels, about a 1-hour drive from the center of the preserve. On the east end of Main Street is Barstow Station, looking like a collection of railway cars, but inside is a rambling shop with an amazing collection of tacky souvenirs: everything from life-size plaster of Paris howling wolves to Marilyn Monroe cookie jars. The **Route 66 museum** (681 N. First St.; ✆ 760/255-1890; www.route66museum.org), on the other end of Main Street, at the Harvey House Casa del Desierto is free but open only Friday through Sunday from 11am to 4pm. Of the town's dozen motels, the most reliable are **Best Western Desert Villa** (1984 E. Main St.; ✆ 760/256-1781), and the **Ramada Inn** (1511 E. Main St.; ✆ 760/256-5673).

BAKER   Lodgings and food are available in this small desert town, which is a good place to fill your gas tank and purchase supplies before entering Mojave National Preserve. Inexpensive lodging can be secured at the **Bun Boy Motel and Country Store** (✆ 760/733-4252). The Bun Boy Coffee Shop is open 24 hours. For a tasty surprise, hop across the street to the **Mad Greek** (✆ 760/733-4354), open daily 24 hours. Order a gyro, Greek salad, souvlakia, or baklava, and marvel at your good fortune for finding such tasty food and pleasant surroundings in the middle of nowhere.

NEWBERRY SPRINGS   The only reason for venturing 18 miles southeast of Barstow on Route 66 is to visit the **Bagdad Café** (✆ 760/257-3101). It's noted for the location of a movie of the same name, which went unnoticed in the States but became a cult favorite among Europeans. They come in busloads to see the site, munch on Jack Palance burgers (with bacon), and mix with some of the colorful locals.

NIPTON   This tiny (pop. 30), charming town boasts a "trading post" with snacks, maps, ice, and native jewelry; and the **Hotel Nipton** (✆ 760/856-2335; www.nipton.com), a B&B with a sitting room, two bathrooms down the hall, and five guest rooms, each for $75 a night. There are also four eco-tents on platforms that sleep four for $58 per night. Owners Jerry and Roxanne Freeman, a former hard-rock miner who purchased the entire town in 1984, moved from Malibu to the abandoned ghost town, and brought it back to life. Nipton is on Nipton Road, a few miles from I-15 near the Nevada state line.

PRIMM (FORMERLY STATELINE)   This town on the California-Nevada border has three hotel/casinos—Whiskey Pete's, Buffalo Bill's, and Primadonna—each as large and garish as an amusement park, all managed by the same company. Rooms are pretty nice, cheap, and (if you have a twisted sense of humor) an ironic counterpoint to the wilderness. With a dozen restaurants, including low-cost Vegas-style buffets, Primm might also be your best dining bet. For reservations, call ✆ **800/FUN-STOP** (386-7867).

---

7 DEATH VALLEY NATIONAL PARK ★

290 miles NE of downtown L.A.; 120 miles NW of Las Vegas

Park? Death Valley National Park? The forty-niners, whose suffering gave the valley its name, would have howled at the notion. To them, other four-letter words would have been more appropriate: gold, mine, heat, lost, dead. And when you trace the whole history, you can imagine a host of other four-letter words shouted by teamsters who drove the 20-mule-team borax wagons.

Americans looking for gold in California's mountains in 1849 were forced to cross the burning sands to avoid severe snowstorms in the nearby Sierra Nevada. Some perished en route, and the land became known as Death Valley.

Mountains stand naked, unadorned. The bitter waters of saline lakes evaporate into bizarre, razor-sharp crystal formations. Jagged canyons jab deep into the earth. Ovenlike heat, frigid cold, and the driest air imaginable combine to make this one of the most inhospitable locations in the world.

But, human nature being what it is, it's not surprising that people have long been drawn to challenge the power of Mother Nature, even in this, her home court. Tourism here began in 1925, a scant 76 years after the forty-niners' harrowing experiences. It probably would have begun sooner, but the valley had been consumed with lucrative borax mining since the late 1880s.

Death Valley is raw, bare earth, the way it must have looked before life began. Here, forces of the earth are exposed to view with dramatic clarity; just looking out on the landscape, it's impossible to know what year—or what century—it is. It's no coincidence that many of Death Valley's topographical features are associated with hellish images—the Funeral Mountains, Furnace Creek, Dante's View, Coffin Peak, and the Devil's Golf Course. But it can be a place of serenity.

President Herbert Hoover signed a proclamation designating Death Valley a national monument on February 11, 1933. With the stroke of a pen, he not only authorized the protection of a vast and wondrous land but also helped transform one of the earth's least hospitable spots into a tourist destination.

The naming of Death Valley National Monument came at a time when Americans began to discover the romance of the desert. Land that had been considered devoid of life was now celebrated for its spare beauty; places that had been feared for their harshness were now admired for their uniqueness. In 1994, when President Clinton signed the California Desert Protection Act, Death Valley became the largest national park outside Alaska, with more than 3.3 million acres. It's remote but one of the most popular, and you're likely to hear less English than German, French, and Japanese.

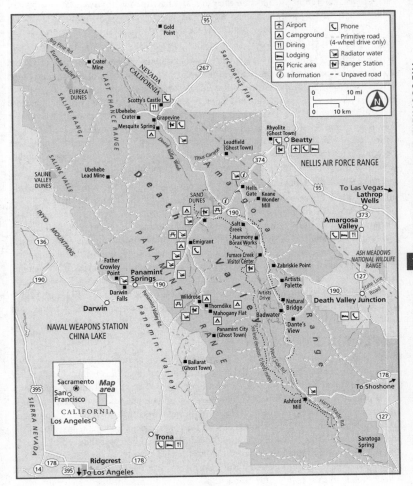

Today's visitor to Death Valley drives in air-conditioned comfort, stays in comfortable hotels or well-maintained campgrounds, orders meals and provisions at park concessions, even quaffs a beer at the local saloon. You can swim in the Olympic-size pool, tour a Moorish castle, shop for souvenirs, and enjoy the landscape while hiking along a nature trail with a park ranger.

ESSENTIALS

GETTING THERE Several routes lead into the park, all of which involve crossing one of the steep mountain ranges that isolate Death Valley from, well, everything. Perhaps the most scenic entry is via Calif. 190, east of Calif. 178 from Ridgecrest. Another scenic drive is by way of Calif. 127 and Calif. 190 from Baker. For a first-time visitor, I recommend the road 1 mile north of Tecopa, marked to Badwater and Death Valley. It's longer and rougher, but you dip down from the hills into the valley and have the full approach into the region. Otherwise, for the shorter route, continue to 190, which will bring you into Death Valley Center. The $15-per-car entrance fee is valid for 7 days. The closest major airport is in Las Vegas. *Note:* Top off your gas tank in Tecopa—it's pricey but not as bad as in the valley.

WHEN TO GO   Death Valley is popular year-round, with the greatest number of visitors during the temperate winter and spring (Nov–Mar). The heavy rains of 2005 caused road washouts and brought forth a carpet of multicolor wildflowers, and the floor of the desert became a lake, 2 feet deep, offering rare kayak adventures. All disappeared when the summer temperatures returned. But the park is never deserted, not even in the scorching months of July, August, and September, as international visitors and extreme-heat seekers come to experience record-breaking temperatures. Even during the "cool" months (when evenings can become chilly), it's essential to wear sunscreen by day to protect against unfiltered rays, and to drink plenty of water to avoid becoming dehydrated in the ultra-arid climate.

VISITOR CENTER & INFORMATION   For camping and road information before you go, contact the Superintendent, Death Valley National Park, Death Valley, CA 92328 (© **760/786-3200** for road, camping, and weather information; www.nps.gov/deva). The **Furnace Creek Visitor Center & Museum,** 15 miles inside the eastern park boundary on Calif. 190 (© **760/786-3200**), offers interpretive exhibits and an hourly slide program. Ask at the information desk for ranger-led nature walks and evening naturalist programs. The center is open daily from 8am to 6pm in summer (to 5pm in winter). In November, a group called Death Valley 49ers (www.deathvalley49ers.org) gathers for 5 days to celebrate the pioneers who first traveled through this harsh environment. A $20 fee per family gives access to hootenannies, hoedowns, covered-wagon parades, gold panning, hiking, and four-wheel-drives in the area. *Tip:* Make your reservations months in advance.

EXPLORING THE PARK

A good first stop, after checking in at the main park visitor center in Furnace Creek, is the **Harmony Borax Works**—a rock-salt landscape as tortured as you'll ever find. Death Valley prospectors called borax "white gold," and though it wasn't exactly a glamorous substance, it was profitable. From 1883 to 1888, more than 20 million pounds (used to make laundry detergent) were transported from the Harmony Borax Works, and borax mining continued in Death Valley until 1928. A short trail with interpretive signs leads past the ruins of the old refinery and some outlying buildings. Transport of the borax was the stuff of legends, too. The famous 20-mule teams hauled the huge loaded wagons 165 miles to the rail station at Mojave. To learn more about this colorful era, visit the Borax Museum at Furnace Creek Ranch and the park visitor center, also located in Furnace Creek.

Badwater—at 282 feet below sea level, the lowest point in the Western Hemisphere— is possibly the hottest place in the world, with regularly recorded summer temperatures of 120°F (49°C). Badwater is mostly a curiosity, and not that much hotter or more brutal than the rest of Death Valley; most folks like to make a brief detour to see the otherworldly landscape and say they were there.

Salt Creek is home to the **Salt Creek pupfish,** found nowhere else on earth. The little fish, which has made amazing adaptations to survive in this land, can be glimpsed from a boardwalk nature trail. In spring a million pupfish wriggle in the creek, but by summer's end only a few thousand remain.

Before sunrise, photographers set up tripods at **Zabriskie Point** and aim their cameras down at the magnificent panoramic view of Golden Canyon's pale mudstone hills and

foot viewpoint overlooking the shimmering Death Valley floor, backed by the high
Panamint Mountains.

South of Furnace Creek is the 9-mile loop of **Artists Drive,** an easy must-see for visitors (except those in RVs, which can't negotiate the sharp, rock-bordered curves in the road). From the highway, you can't see the splendid palette of colors splashed on the rocks behind the foothills; once inside, though, stop and climb a hill that offers an overhead view, and then continue through to aptly named **Artists Palette,** where an interpretive sign explains the source of nature's rainbow.

Scotty's Castle & the Gas House Museum (© 760/786-2392), the Mediterranean hacienda in the northern part of the park, is Death Valley's premier tourist attraction. Visitors are wowed by the elaborate Spanish tiles, well-crafted furnishings, and construction that included solar water heating. Even more compelling is the colorful history of this villa in Grapevine Canyon, brought to life by park rangers dressed in 1930s period clothing. Don't be surprised if the castle cook or a friend of Scotty's gives you a special insight into castle life.

Construction of the "castle"—more officially, Death Valley Ranch—began in 1924. It was to be a winter retreat for eccentric Chicago millionaire Albert Johnson. The insurance tycoon's unlikely friendship with prospector, cowboy, and spinner-of-tall-tales Walter Scott put the $2.3-million structure on the map and captured the public's imagination. Scotty greeted visitors and told them fanciful stories from Death Valley's early hard-rock mining days.

The 1-hour walking tour of Scotty's Castle is excellent, for its inside look at the mansion and its exploration of Johnson and Scotty's eccentricities. Tours (9am–5pm daily) fill up quickly; arrive early for the first available spots ($11 adult, $9 senior, and $6 child fee). Its open daily from 8am to 5pm.

Near Scotty's Castle is **Ubehebe Crater.** It's known as an explosion crater—one look and you'll know why. When hot magma rose from the depths of the earth to meet the groundwater, the resultant steam blasted out a crater.

BIKING & HIKING

BIKING   Because most of the park is federally designated wilderness, cycling is allowed only on roads used by cars. Bikes are not allowed on hiking trails. Check © 760/786-3200 for road and trail conditions.

Good routes for bikers include Racetrack (28 miles, mainly level), Greenwater Valley (30 miles, mostly level), Cottonwood Canyon (20 miles), and West Side Road (40 miles, fairly level with some washboard sections). Artists Drive is 8 miles long and paved, with some steep uphills. A favorite is Titus Canyon, a 28-mile one-way route that starts 2³/₄ miles east of the park boundary on Nevada Highway 374.

HIKING   The trails in Death Valley range from the .5-mile **Salt Creek Nature Trail,** an easy boardwalk suitable for everyone in the family, to the grueling **Telescope Peak Trail** (14 miles round-trip). Telescope Peak is a day-long, 3,000-foot climb to the 11,049-foot summit. Snow-covered in winter, the peak is best climbed between May and November.

For moderate hikes, try the trail into **Mosaic Canyon,** near Stovepipe Wells, where water has polished the marble rock into mosaics. It's an easy, 2.5-mile scramble through long, narrow walls that provide shade at every turn.

Romping among the **Sand Dunes** on the way to Stovepipe Wells is also fun, particularly for kids. It's a free-form adventure, and the dunes aren't particularly high—but the sun can be merciless. The sand in the dunes is actually tiny pieces of rock, most of them quartz fragments. As with all desert activities, having an adequate water supply is crucial.

694 Near the park's eastern border, two trails lead from the **Keane Wonder Mill,** site of a successful gold mine. The first is a steep and strenuous 2-mile challenge leading to the mine itself, passing along the way the solid, efficient wooden tramway that carried ore out of the mountain. The 2-mile **Keane Wonder Spring Trail** is much easier. The spring announces itself with a sulfur smell and piping birdcalls.

If you're visiting **Ubehebe Crater,** check out the steep but plain trail leading from the parking area up to the crater's lip and around some of the contours. Fierce winds can hamper your progress, but you'll feel like you're on another planet.

Park rangers can provide topographical maps and detailed directions to these and a dozen other hiking trails within the national park.

WHERE TO STAY

The park's nine campgrounds are at elevations ranging from below sea level to 8,000 feet. In Furnace Creek, **Sunset** has 1,000 spaces with water and flush toilets. **Furnace Creek Campground** has 200 similarly appointed spaces. **Stovepipe Wells** has 200 spaces with water and flush toilets. Make reservations online at **http://reservations.nps.gov** or call C 877/444-6777.

The **Furnace Creek Ranch** (C 760/786-2345; www.furnacecreekresort.com), a private in-holding within the park, has 224 no-frills cottage units with air-conditioning and showers ($141–$191). The swimming pool is a popular hangout. Nearby are a coffee shop, saloon, steakhouse, and general store. **Stovepipe Wells Village** (C 760/786-2387) has 74 modest rooms with air-conditioning and showers, plus a casual dining room that closes between meals ($75–$115).

The only lodging in the park not run by the official concessionaire is the **Panamint Springs Resort** (C 775/482-7680; www.deathvalley.com), a rustic motel, cafe, and snack shop an hour east of Furnace Creek ($89–$167). Because accommodations in Death Valley are limited and expensive, you might consider the money-saving (but inconvenient) option of spending a night at one of the two gateway towns: **Lone Pine,** on the west side of the park, or **Baker,** on the south. **Beatty, Nevada,** which has inexpensive lodging, is an hour's drive from the park's center. The restored **Amargosa Hotel** (C 760/852-4441) in Death Valley Junction offers 14 rooms in a historic, out-of-the-way place, 40 minutes from Furnace Creek ($67–$84).

Tip: Meals and groceries are very costly due to the park's remoteness. If possible, bring a cooler with some snacks, sandwiches, and beverages to last the duration of your visit. Ice is easily obtainable, and you'll also be able to keep water chilled.

Furnace Creek Inn ★★ Like an oasis in the middle of Death Valley, the inn's red-tiled roofs and sparkling blue mineral-spring-fed swimming pool hint at the elegance within. The hotel has equipped its 66 deluxe rooms and suites with every modern amenity while successfully preserving the charm of this 1930s resort. Stroll the palm-shaded gardens before sitting down to a meal in the elegant dining room, where the food is excellent but the formality a bit out of place. Don tennis whites for a match in the midwinter sunshine, enjoy 18 holes of golf nearby, take an excursion on horseback—there's even a shuttle from the Furnace Creek airstrip for well-heeled clientele. Reserve early: The inn is booked solid in winter with guests who appreciate a little pampering after a day in the park.

Hwy. 190 (P.O. Box 1), Death Valley, CA 92328. C **800/236-7916** or 760/786-2345. Fax 760/786-2514. www.furnacecreekresort.com. 66 units. $275–$395 double; $410–$425 suite. Extra person $20. AE, DISC, MC, V. **Amenities:** Restaurant; lounge; naturally heated outdoor pool; nearby golf course (greens fees $35–$55, cart $25); 4 night-lit tennis courts; room service; in-room massage. *In room:* A/C, TV w/pay movies, fridge, hair dryer, iron.

San Diego & Environs

by Mark Hiss

High-end nightclubs. Adventurous dining. Hypermodern architecture. What's going on here? What happened to that sleepy Navy town—that *nice* little city of San Diego?

Well, that sleepy burg has woken up and it wants to party. Growth has been fast and furious over the last decade, and although it has been awkward at times, as growth can be, San Diego now finds itself with a new skyline and a new attitude. With 70 miles of coastline, an array of theme parks and attractions, and, yes, those killer whales, it's still a family-friendly destination, but the nearly nightly bacchanalia in the Gaslamp Quarter is evidence of something new—something young and exciting.

San Diego is the "Plymouth Rock of the Pacific Coast," the site of the first European settlement along the western shores of what would become the United States. The city is now the nation's eighth largest, and the border it shares with Tijuana, Mexico, is believed to be the world's busiest international crossing. These historical and geographical facts only begin to tell the local story, though. In fact, there really is no easy way to sum up San Diego. Whatever you're interested

in, from astronomy to zebras, it's here. It's an embarrassment of riches, really, including the country's best weather.

Despite a wobbly economy, the city is still riding the crest of a wave unlike anything seen since its rootin'-tootin' boomtown days in the 1880s, when real-estate speculation doubled and tripled the price of land, and the population swelled. San Diego's most recent boom, though, goes beyond sky-high property values and the opening of new hotels, bars, and restaurants. Swords are being sculpted—not beaten—into ploughshares at NTC Promenade, a former Navy base that's on track to become one of the country's most exciting performing arts facilities. Additionally, the Museum of Contemporary Art San Diego opened its third space, a sleek downtown annex at the historic Santa Fe Depot Baggage Building, while the new, architecturally striking Children's Museum is poised to take child's play to a whole new level.

Of course, that boom in the 1880s was followed by an inevitable bust that cast a pall over downtown San Diego for nearly 100 years. So my advice to you? Come now while the party is still rolling. This is not your father's San Diego. It's more like your great-great-grandfather's San Diego.

---

1 ORIENTATION

GETTING THERE
By Plane

San Diego International Airport, 3707 N. Harbor Dr. (© **619/231-2100;** www.san. org; airport code **SAN**), locally known as Lindbergh Field, is just 2 miles from downtown. All the major domestic carriers fly here, plus **AeroMéxico** from Los Cabos and Mexico City, and **Air Canada** from Toronto and Vancouver. The airport has three passenger buildings, with short local flights departing from the Commuter Terminal, a half mile away.

TRANSPORTATION FROM THE AIRPORT   All the major car-rental agencies have offices at the airport, including **Avis** (© 800/331-1212; www.avis.com), **Budget** (© 800/527-0700; www.budget.com), **Dollar** (© 800/800-4000; www.dollar.com), and **Hertz** (© 800/654-3131; www.hertz.com). If you're driving to downtown from the airport, take Harbor Drive south to Broadway, the main east-west thoroughfare, and turn left. To reach Hillcrest or Balboa Park, exit the airport toward I-5, and follow the signs for Laurel Street. To reach Mission Bay and the beaches, take I-5 north to I-8 west. To reach La Jolla, take I-5 north to the La Jolla Parkway exit, which turns into Torrey Pines Road.

   Metropolitan Transit System (MTS; © 619/233-3004; www.transit.511sd.com) bus route no. 992 provides service between the airport and downtown San Diego, running along Broadway. Bus stops are located at each of the three terminals, and the one-way fare is $2.25. If you're connecting to another bus or the San Diego Trolley, you'll need to purchase a Day Pass; free transfers are no longer given. A 1-day pass starts at $5 and is available from the driver or online. The ride downtown takes 15 minutes, with buses coming at 10- to 15-minute intervals. At Broadway and First Avenue is the **Transit Store** (© 619/234-1060), where you can get information about San Diego's mass transit system (bus, rail, and ferry) and pick up passes, free brochures, route maps, and timetables. The shop is open Monday to Friday, 9am to 5pm.

   Shuttle services run regularly from the airport to points around the city; you'll see designated pickup areas outside each terminal. The fare is about $8 per person to downtown hotels; Mission Valley and Mission Beach are $12; La Jolla $19; and Coronado $15. Rates to a residence in these areas are about $8 more than the above rates, for the first person. One company that serves all of San Diego County is **Super Shuttle** (© 800/974-8885; www.supershuttle.com). Reservations can be made online, but advance notification is not needed for service from the airport or from a hotel. **Taxis** line up outside all terminals, and the trip downtown, usually a 10-minute ride, is about $10 (plus tip); budget $20 to $25 for Coronado or Mission Beach, and about $30 to $35 for La Jolla.

By Car

From Los Angeles, you'll enter San Diego via coastal route **I-5.** From points northeast of the city, you'll come down on **I-15** and **Highway 163** south to drive into downtown (where 163 turns into 10th Ave.), or hook up with **I-8** west for the beaches. From the east, you'll come in on I-8, connecting with Highway 163 south. The freeways are well marked, pointing the way to downtown streets.

By Train

Amtrak (© 800/872-7245; www.amtrak.com) connects San Diego to the rest of the country via Los Angeles. Trains pull into San Diego's Mission-style **Santa Fe Train Depot,** 1050 Kettner Blvd. (at Broadway), within walking distance of some downtown hotels and the Embarcadero. It's $29 one-way from L.A.

By Bus

Greyhound (© 800/231-2222; www.greyhound.com) buses from Los Angeles, Phoenix, Las Vegas, and other points in the southwest U.S. arrive at the station in downtown San Diego at 120 W. Broadway. The one-way fare from Los Angeles is $32, but half-price discounts are available for travel Monday through Thursday. Local buses stop in front of the station, and the San Diego Trolley is nearby.

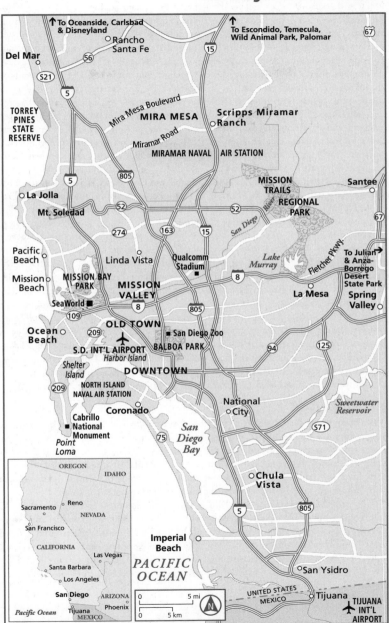

You'll find staffed information booths at the airport, train station, and the cruise-ship terminal. Downtown, the Convention & Visitors Bureau's **International Visitor Information Center** (✆ 619/236-1212; www.sandiego.org) is at 1040¹/₃ W. Broadway at Harbor Drive (across from the cruise ship terminal). Daily summer hours are from 9am to 5pm; it's open 9am to 4pm daily the rest of the year and is closed on major holidays. The bureau offers great info and deals on its website, but you can also get your hands on the glossy *Official Visitors Planning Guide* from the information center. The guide includes information on dining, activities, attractions, tours, and transportation. ConVis also publishes *San Diego Travel Values,* which is full of discount coupons for hotels, restaurants, and attractions (it's available online, too). A walk-up-only facility (sans phone) at the **La Jolla Visitor Center,** 7966 Herschel Ave., near the corner of Prospect Street, is open daily, in summer from 10am to 7pm (until 6pm Sun), with a more limited schedule from September to May.

Specialized visitor information outlets include the **Coronado Visitors Center,** 1100 Orange Ave., Coronado (✆ 619/437-8788; www.coronadovisitorcenter.com); and **Promote La Jolla,** 1150 Silverado St. (✆ 858/454-5718; www.lajollabythesea.com). The **Mission Bay Visitor Information Center,** 2688 E. Mission Bay Dr., San Diego (✆ 866/746-8440 or 619/276-8200; www.infosandiego.com), is conveniently located on Mission Bay next to I-5 (exit Clairemont Dr./Mission Bay Dr. and head toward the water). The **San Diego North Convention & Visitors Bureau,** 360 N. Escondido Blvd., Escondido (✆ 800/848-3336 or 760/745-4741; www.sandiegonorth.com), can provide information on North County excursion areas, including Del Mar, Carlsbad, Escondido, Julian, and Anza-Borrego Desert State Park.

To find out what's playing in clubs and theaters, pick up a copy of the *San Diego Weekly Reader* (www.sdreader.com), a free newspaper available all over the city every Thursday; in tourist areas it is distributed in a condensed version, called the *Weekly.* "Night & Day," the entertainment supplement in the *San Diego Union-Tribune* (www. signonsandiego.com), the city's main daily newspaper, appears on Thursday; the free alternative weekly *San Diego CityBeat* comes out on Wednesday.

CITY LAYOUT

San Diego has a clearly defined downtown, surrounded by about a dozen separate neighborhoods—each with its own personality, but all incorporated into the city. The street system is straightforward, so getting around is fairly easy: Broadway is the main street downtown, intersected by Fourth and Fifth avenues (running south and north, respectively). Harbor Drive hugs the waterfront (Embarcadero), connecting downtown with the airport to the northwest and the Convention Center to the south.

The San Diego–Coronado Bay Bridge leading to Coronado is accessible from I-5 south of downtown, and I-5 north leads to Old Town, Mission Bay, La Jolla, and North County coastal areas. Balboa Park (home of the San Diego Zoo), Hillcrest, and uptown areas lie north of downtown San Diego. The park and zoo are easily reached via Park Boulevard (which would otherwise be 12th Ave.), which leads to parking lots. Fifth Avenue leads to the Hillcrest and uptown neighborhoods. Highway 163, which heads north from 11th Avenue, leads into Mission Valley.

NEIGHBORHOODS IN BRIEF

Downtown The business, shopping, dining, and entertainment heart of the city encompasses Horton Plaza, the Embarcadero (waterfront), and the Convention Center, sprawling over eight "neighborhoods." This is the most convenient place to stay for those with downtown appointments or meetings at the Convention Center. The **Gaslamp Quarter** is jam-packed with boutiques, restaurants, and nightspots; immediately southeast of the Gaslamp is the **East Village** and **PETCO Park,** home of the San Diego Padres. Northwest, **Little Italy** is another rejuvenated neighborhood, along India and Kettner streets between Cedar and Laurel. It's a great place to find Italian food and upscale shopping. Downtown is the easiest place to stay if you don't have a car.

Hillcrest & Uptown First established about 1907, Hillcrest was the city's first self-contained suburb. Despite the cachet of being close to **Balboa Park** (home of the San Diego Zoo and numerous museums), the area fell into neglect in the 1960s. However, in the late 1970s, legions of preservation-minded residents—particularly its lively gay community—began to restore Hillcrest's charms, making it the local equivalent of a West Hollywood or SoHo. Centrally located and brimming with popular restaurants and shops, Hillcrest also offers less expensive, more personalized accommodations. Other uptown neighborhoods of interest are **Mission Hills** west of Hillcrest, **University Heights, Normal Heights, North Park,** and **Kensington,** to the east.

Old Town & Mission Valley These two busy areas wrap around the neighborhood of Mission Hills. On one end are Old Town State Historic Park (where California "began"), Presidio Park, Heritage Park, and several museums that focus on local history. Shopping and dining here largely target visitors. Not far from Old Town lies the congested, suburban sprawl of Mission Valley, home to gigantic shopping centers, Qualcomm Stadium, and numerous condo developments. Hotel Circle is an elongated loop road paralleling I-8, featuring a string of budget and moderately priced hotels.

Mission Bay & the Beaches Here's where they took the picture on the postcard you'll send home. Mission Bay is a watery playground perfect for waterskiing, sailing, and windsurfing. The adjacent communities of **Ocean Beach, Mission Beach,** and **Pacific Beach** are known for their wide stretches of sand, nightlife, and casual dining. The boardwalk, which runs from South Mission Beach to Pacific Beach, is a popular place for skating, biking, people-watching, and sunsets. It's the best place to stay if you are traveling with beach-loving kids.

La Jolla Mediterranean in design and ambience, La Jolla is the Southern Californian Riviera. This seaside community of about 25,000 is home to an inordinate number of wealthy folks who could afford to live anywhere. They choose La Jolla for good reason—it has one of the state's most stunning coastlines and offers an outstanding array of restaurants, shops, and galleries, as well as a host of cultural and recreational attractions. There are really two La Jollas: the original seaside community—the so-called "village"—and the residential and business areas that have sprouted along La Jolla Village Drive east of I-5, which are of less interest. Public transportation is limited, so La Jolla is not an ideal base if you don't have a car.

Coronado You might be tempted to think of Coronado as an island—it does have a self-contained, resort ambience and it's most easily accessed by the sweeping Coronado Bridge or by ferry. The city is actually on a peninsula, though, connected to the mainland by a long, sandy isthmus known as the **Silver Strand.** Coronado is home to a U.S. Naval Air Station, in use since World War I, and also has a history as

an elite playground for snowbirds. This charming, wealthy community is home to the iconic Hotel Del Coronado as well. Built in 1888, the "Hotel Del," as it's known, sits on one of the area's finest beaches and is a major attraction for both guests and nonguests.

2 GETTING AROUND

BY CAR

San Diego traffic can be problematic. It's not L.A., by any means, but the construction of dense, outlying suburbia over the last 20 years has made morning and evening rush-hour traffic a headache. Aside from that, it's car friendly and easy to navigate. For up-to-the-minute traffic info, dial © **511.**

Downtown, many streets run one-way, and finding a parking space can be tricky. There are several centrally located parking lots, where prices fluctuate wildly according to the day and time.

RENTALS All the large, national car-rental firms have outlets at the airport (see "Getting There," above), in the major hotels, and at other locations around the city. Some car-rental companies allow their cars into Mexico as far as Ensenada, provided that you stop before crossing the border to buy Mexican auto insurance. Mexican insurance is also highly advised if you drive your own car over the border.

PARKING Parking meters are common in most San Diego areas, including downtown, Hillcrest, the beaches, and La Jolla. Signs post operating hours—generally between 9am and 6pm, daily except Sunday; meters devour one quarter every 12 minutes. The Gaslamp Quarter has two large parking structures (on Sixth Ave. at Market and K sts.). Parking is free in Balboa Park and Old Town.

BY PUBLIC TRANSPORTATION

The **San Diego Metropolitan Transit System (MTS;** © **619/233-3004;** www.transit.511sd.com) runs both city buses and the San Diego Trolley. The website displays timetables, maps, and fares online, and provides information for travelers with disabilities. The system's **Transit Store,** 102 Broadway at First Avenue (© **619/234-1060**), is an information center, supplying travelers with passes, tokens, timetables, maps, and brochures. Get a copy of the useful pamphlet *San Diego's Fun Places,* which details routes to the city's most popular tourist attractions. The store is open Monday through Friday from 9am to 5pm. If you know your route and just need schedule information—or automated answers to FAQs—call **Info Express** (© **619/685-4900**) from any touch-tone phone, 24 hours a day. A $5 **Day-Tripper pass** allows for 1 day of unlimited rides (you can buy a 2-day pass for $9, a 3-day pass for $12, or a 4-day pass for $15); it's available from the Transit Store, at all trolley ticket vending machines, or online (Web orders require 7 working days to process). Monthly passes start at $64 ($32 for ages 6–18).

BY BUS San Diego's bus system is adequate and will get you where you want to go—eventually. Bus stops are marked by rectangular red, white, and black signs every other

block or so on local routes, farther apart on express routes. Most fares are $2.25. Buses
accept dollar bills, but the driver can't give change. Transfers are no longer issued, so if
you need to make a connection with another bus or trolley, purchase a $5 day pass from
the driver, at the Transit Store, trolley station ticket vending machine, or online. It gives
you unlimited use of most bus and trolley routes for the rest of the service day. Some
routes stop at 6pm, while other lines continue until 9pm, midnight, and 2am. Ask your
bus driver for more specific information.

BY TROLLEY   The San Diego Trolley is great for visitors, particularly if you're staying
downtown and plan to visit Tijuana, Old Town, or Mission Valley. The Blue Line travels
from the Mexican border north through downtown, Old Town, and then east through
Mission Valley. The trip to the border takes 40 minutes from downtown. The Orange
Line runs from downtown east through Lemon Grove and El Cajon to the city of Santee;
while the Green Line heads from Old Town to San Diego State University and on to El
Cajon.

Riders buy trolley tickets from machines in stations before boarding. The machines
list fares for each destination ($1.25–$3) and dispense change. Tickets are valid for 2
hours from the time of purchase, in any direction. Fare inspectors board trains at random
to check tickets. A round-trip ticket is double the price, but it's valid all day between the
origination and destination points.

Trolleys run every 15 minutes during the day and every 30 minutes at night; during
peak weekday rush hours the Blue Line runs every 10 minutes. There is also expanded
service to accommodate events at PETCO Park and Qualcomm Stadium. The trolleys
generally operate daily from 5am to about midnight; the Blue Line provides late-night
service between the border and Old Town on Saturday night/Sunday morning.

BY TRAIN   San Diego's express rail commuter service, the **Coaster,** travels between the
downtown Santa Fe Depot station and the Oceanside Transit Center, with stops at Old
Town, Sorrento Valley, Solana Beach, Encinitas, and Carlsbad. Fares range from $4 to
$5.50 each way and can be paid by credit card at machines at each station. Eligible
seniors and riders with disabilities pay $2 to $2.75. The trip from downtown to Oceanside takes an hour. Trains run Monday through Friday, from about 6:30am–5:30am
heading south from Oceanside) to 7pm, with four trains each direction on Saturday (no
service Sun); call © **800/262-7837** or 511, or visit www.transit.511sd.com, for the current schedule. The new **Sprinter** rail service runs west to east alongside Highway 78,
from Oceanside to Escondido. The Sprinter operates from about 4am to 8pm daily, with
trains every half-hour during the week and hourly on the weekends. Basic one-way fare
is $2 ($1 for seniors and those with disabilities).

Amtrak (© **800/872-7245;** www.amtrak.com) trains run between San Diego and
downtown L.A. about 11 times daily each way. Trains depart from the Santa Fe Depot
and stop in Solana Beach, Oceanside, San Juan Capistrano, Santa Ana, and Anaheim
(Disneyland). Two trains per day also stop in San Clemente. One-way to Los Angeles is
$29, $43 in business class. One-way to Solana Beach is $9, to Oceanside $13, to San
Clemente or San Juan Capistrano $15, and to Anaheim $20.

BY FERRY & WATER TAXI   Ferries between San Diego and Coronado (© **800/442-
7847** or 619/234-4111; www.sdhe.com) leave from the Broadway Pier (1050 N. Harbor
Dr., at the intersection of Broadway) on the hour from 9am to 9pm Sunday through
Thursday, and until 10pm Friday and Saturday. They return from the Ferry Landing in
Coronado to the Broadway Pier every hour on the half-hour from 9:30am to 9:30pm

Sunday through Thursday and until 10:30pm Friday and Saturday. The ride takes 15 minutes. The fare is $3 each way (50¢ extra if you bring your bike).

Water taxis (© **619/235-8294**; www.sdhe.com) will pick you up from any dock around San Diego Bay, daily from 3 to 10pm, with extended hours on weekends and in summer. If you're staying in a downtown hotel, this is a great way to reach Coronado. Boats are sometimes available on the spur of the moment, but reservations are advised. Fares are $7 per person to most locations.

BY TAXI

Half a dozen taxi companies serve the area. Rates are based on mileage and can add up quickly in sprawling San Diego; a trip from downtown to La Jolla, for example, will cost $30 to $35. Other than in the Gaslamp Quarter after dark, taxis don't cruise the streets as they do in other cities, so you have to call ahead for quick pickup. If you are waiting at a hotel or restaurant, the front-desk attendant or host will call one for you. Local companies include **Orange Cab** (© **619/291-3333**), **San Diego Cab** (© **619/226-8294**), **Yellow Cab** (© **619/234-6161**), and **Coronado Cab Company** (© **619/435-6211**).

BY BICYCLE

San Diego is ideal for exploration by bike and was named "one of the top 10 cities in the U.S. to bicycle" by *Bicycling* magazine.

Many major thoroughfares offer bike lanes; bikes are also allowed on the San Diego–Coronado ferry (50¢ extra), as well as on the San Diego Trolley and most city buses (no additional charge). To request a detailed map of San Diego County's bike lanes and routes, call **RideLink Bicycle Information** (© **511** or 619/699-1900), or go to www.511sd.com for a downloadable version. You might also want to talk to the **San Diego County Bicycle Coalition** (© **858/487-6063**; www.sdcbc.org). *Cycling San Diego*, by Nelson Copp and Jerry Schad (Sunbelt Publications), is a good resource for bicyclists; the book is sold at most local bike shops. For information on rentals, see "Outdoor Pursuits," later in this chapter.

⒡*Fast Facts*　San Diego

Area Codes San Diego's main area code is **619,** used primarily by downtown, uptown, Mission Valley, Point Loma, Coronado, La Mesa, Chula Vista, and El Cajon. The area code **858** is used for northern and coastal areas, including Mission Beach, Pacific Beach, La Jolla, Del Mar, and Rancho Santa Fe. Use **760** to reach the remainder of San Diego County, including Encinitas, Carlsbad, Oceanside, Escondido, Julian, and Anza-Borrego.

Babysitters Marion's Childcare (© **888/891-5029**; www.hotelchildcare.com) will send bonded babysitters to your hotel. **Panda's Domestic Service Agency** (© **858/292-5503;** www.sandiegobabysitters.com) is also available.

Dentists/Doctors For dental referrals, contact the **San Diego County Dental Society** at © **800/201-0244,** or call © **800/DENTIST** (336-8478). Miami-based **Hotel Docs** (© **800/468-3537**) is a 24-hour network of physicians, dentists, and chiropractors. They accept credit cards, and their services are covered by most insurance. In a life-threatening situation, dial © **911.**

Emergencies Call 🕾 **911** for fire, police, and ambulance.

Hospitals In Hillcrest, near downtown San Diego, **UCSD Medical Center–Hillcrest,** 200 W. Arbor Dr. (🕾 **619/543-6222**), has the most convenient emergency room. In La Jolla, **UCSD Thornton Hospital,** 9300 Campus Point Dr. (🕾 **858/657-7000**), has a good emergency room, and you'll find another in Coronado, at **Sharp Coronado Hospital,** 250 Prospect Place, opposite the Marriott Resort (🕾 **619/522-3600**). Twenty-four-hour pharmacies include **CVS,** 313 E. Washington St., Hillcrest (🕾 **619/291-7170**), and 8831 Villa La Jolla Dr., La Jolla (🕾 **858/457-4390**). For 24-hour **Rite Aid** pharmacies, call 🕾 **800/748-3243.**

Police The downtown police station is at 1401 Broadway (🕾 **619/531-2000,** or 619/233-3323 for the hearing impaired).

Post Office San Diego's main post office is in the boondocks, but the former main office, located at 2535 Midway Dr., just west of Old Town, is a good alternative. It's open Monday through Friday from 8am to 5pm, and Saturdays from 8am to 4pm. For branch locations, call 🕾 **800/275-8777** or log on to www.usps.com.

Safety Of the 10 largest cities in the United States, San Diego historically has had the lowest incidence of violent crime per capita. Virtually all areas of the city are safe during the day, but caution is advised in parts of Balboa Park not frequented by regular foot traffic. Transients are common—especially downtown, in Hillcrest, and in beach areas. Downtown areas to the east of PETCO Park are sparsely populated and poorly lighted after dusk.

Taxes Sales tax in restaurants and shops is 7.75%. Hotel tax is 10.5%, or 12.5% for lodgings with more than 70 rooms.

Useful Telephone Numbers For the latest San Diego arts and entertainment info, call 🕾 **619/238-0700;** for half-price day-of-performance tickets, call 🕾 **619/497-5000;** for a beach and surf report, call 🕾 **619/221-8824.** For the time, call 🕾 **853-1212** (works in all area codes). For **weather,** call 🕾 **619/289-1212.**

3 WHERE TO STAY

Rates tend to be highest in summer at beach hotels, and midweek downtown when a big convention is in town. Remember to factor in the city's hotel tax—it's 10.5% or 12.5% for lodgings with more than 70 rooms. The **San Diego Convention & Visitors Bureau** is a good place to start looking for hotel deals (🕾 **619/232-3101;** www.sandiego.org); while the **San Diego Bed & Breakfast Guild** (🕾 **800/619-7666;** www.bandbguildsandiego.org) is a helpful resource if you are interested in staying someplace cozy.

DOWNTOWN

San Diego's downtown is an excellent place for leisure travelers to stay. The nightlife and dining in the Gaslamp Quarter and Horton Plaza shopping are close at hand; Balboa Park, Hillcrest, Old Town, and Coronado are less than 10 minutes away by car; and beaches aren't much farther. It's also the city's public-transportation hub and thus very convenient for car-free visitors.

ACCOMMODATIONS ■

Balboa Park Inn **65**
The Beach Cottages **31**
Best Western Seven Seas **57**
Bristol Hotel **9**
Britt Scripps Inn **61**
Catamaran Resort Hotel **32**
The Cottage **55**
Crone's Cobblestone Cottage **51**
Crowne Plaza Hotel **48**
Crystal Pier Hotel **29**
The Dana on Mission Bay **38**
El Cordova Hotel **72**
500 West **8**
Gaslamp Plaza Suites **11**
Glorietta Bay Inn **73**
Hard Rock Hotel **24**
Heritage Park Bed & Breakfast **49**
HI Downtown Hostel **17**

Hilton San Diego Gaslamp
    Quarter **22**
Holiday Inn Express–Old Town **49**
Holiday Inn on the Bay **6**
Horton Grand **20**
Hostelling International Point
    Loma **42**
Hotel del Coronado **74**
Hotel Occidental **1**
Ivy Hotel **12**
Keating Hotel **13**
Keating House **63**
La Pensione Hotel **3**
Loews Coronado Bay Resort **75**
Mission Valley Travelodge **57**
Motel 6 Hotel Circle **46**
Ocean Beach International
    Hostel **40**
Ocean Park Inn **31**

Pacific Terrace Hotel **27**
Paradise Point Resort & Spa **37**
Park Manor Suites **60**
The Pearl Hotel **43**
Ramada Plaza **57**
Tower 23 **29**
USA Hostels **15**
U.S. Grant Hotel **10**
Vagabond Inn–Hotel Circle **57**
Village Inn **69**
W San Diego **7**

DINING ◆

Anthology **5**
Baleen **37**
Bay Park Fish Co. **36**
Berta's Latin American
    Restaurant **50**
Bertrand at Mister A's **62**

Bite **66**
Blue Water Seafood Market
    and Grill **52**
Bread & Cie. **58**
The Brigantine **45, 71**
Bronx Pizza **56**
Cafe Chloe **16**
Café Lulu **14**
Cafe Pacifica **50**
Caffè Bella Italia **34**
Candelas **19**
Chez Loma **70**
Chive **18**
El Agave Tequileria **50**
Extraordinary Desserts **4, 59**
1500 Ocean **74**
Filippi's Pizza Grotto **2, 28**
The Fishery **26**
Gringos **30**

The Guild **25**
Island Prime **53**
Laurel **62**
Living Room
    Coffeehouse **44, 47**
Mamá Testa **66**
The Mission **23, 33, 68**
Modus **64**
Oceanaire Seafood Room **21**
Parallel 33 **54**
Point Loma Seafoods **44**
Red Pearl Kitchen **21**
Rhinoceros Cafe & Grill **70**
Rubio's Baja Grill **35**
South Beach Bar & Grill **41**
Sushi Ota **35**
Thee Bungalow **39**
Villa Nueva Bakery Cafe **70**
Whahoo's Fish Taco **67**

Many downtown hotels seem designed for the expense-account or trust-fund crowd, but some accommodations have more moderate rates. There's the colorful, modern **Bristol Hotel,** 1055 First Ave. (© 800/662-4477 or 619/232-6141; www.thebristolsandiego. com), adjacent to the Gaslamp Quarter; and in the budget category, you can't beat the 258-room **500 West,** 500 W. Broadway (© **866/315-4251;** www.500westhotel.com). It offers small but comfortable rooms for $79 to $99 a night in a seven-story building dating from 1924. It has contemporary style, history, and a good location, but bathrooms are down the hall. Cheaper still are downtown's two hostels, where private rooms start at about $45 and dorm rooms are around $20: **USA Hostels** (© 800/438-8622 or 619/232-3100; www.usahostels.com) is in the Gaslamp, at 726 Fifth Ave.; **HI Downtown Hostel** (© **888/464-4872,** ext. 156, or 619/525-1531; www.sandiegohostels.org) is nearby, at 521 Market St.

Very Expensive

Hilton San Diego Gaslamp Quarter ★★★
At the foot of the Gaslamp Quarter, across from the Convention Center, this hotel is ideally situated for business travelers. Yet unlike some of its competitors, the Hilton doesn't overwhelm with size, making it a great place for guests who want to stay near the action but out of the fray. The hotel opened in 2001 on the site of the old Bridgeworks building, part of San Diego's original wharf a century ago; much of the brick facade was incorporated into the hotel's polished design. Standard rooms boast upmarket furniture, down comforters, and pillow-top mattresses. There are suites and an executive floor, but the really snazzy picks are rooms in the Lofts at Fifth Avenue, a hotel within the hotel that features 30 oversize guest rooms with towering ceilings, custom furnishings, and lavish tubs. These are some of the handsomest hotel rooms available downtown.

401 K St. (at Fourth Ave.), San Diego, CA 92101. © **800/445-8667** or 619/231-4040. Fax 619/231-6439. 282 units. $329 double; from $399 suite. Children under 12 stay free in parent's room. AE, DC, DISC, MC, V. Valet parking $30. Trolley: Gaslamp Quarter or Convention Center. **Amenities:** 2 restaurants; 2 bars; outdoor pool; health club and full-service spa; Jacuzzi; concierge; business center; salon; room service; laundry service; dry cleaning. *In room:* A/C, TV w/pay movies, minibar, coffeemaker, hair dryer, iron.

Ivy Hotel ★★★
The Maryland Hotel, a dowdy property built in 1914, has been magically transformed into a world-class, high-style luxury destination called the Ivy Hotel. Its unbeatable Gaslamp Quarter address assures a steady stream of beautiful people making their way into **Envy,** the hotel's four-level nightclub. The Ivy also boasts downtown's largest rooftop pool and entertainment area: a 17,000-square-foot playground dubbed **Eden;** and modern, regional cuisine is dished out at the street-level **Quarter Kitchen.** The $75-million renovation was overseen by a design team that has not only worked on various W Hotels, but also made a name for itself in Hollywood, art-directing projects for such directors as Jim Jarmusch and Ridley Scott. The fashionable rooms are modern but warm; be sure to take advantage of a blissful soak prepared in-room by your personal Bath Butler.

650 F St. (btw. Sixth and Seventh aves.), San Diego, CA 92101. © **877/489-4489** or 619/814-1000. Fax 619/531-7955. www.ivyhotel.com. 159 units. $349–$449 double; from $549 suite. Children 12 and under stay free in parent's room. Packages available. AE, DC, DISC, MC, V. Valet parking $30. Bus: 3 or 120. Pets less than 35 lb. accepted with $150 fee. Nonsmoking. **Amenities:** Restaurant; bar; nightclub; pool; fitness center; spa services; concierge; free local transportation; business services via personal butler; boutique; room service; butler service; laundry/dry cleaning/pressing service. *In room:* A/C, TV w/DVD/CD/MP3 docking station, Wi-Fi, full bar with retail items, coffeemaker, hair dryer, safe, 2-line phone.

Keating Hotel ★★   Pininfarina, the Italian design group that is the driving force behind Ferrari and Maserati, has made its first foray into hotel design right here in San Diego. The Keating is located in the heart of the Gaslamp Quarter in a gorgeous Romanesque-style structure built in 1890. Boutique in size, with 35 rooms, it features sleek, ultra-modern interiors and luxury amenities, such as goose-down beds, Frette linens, Bang & Olufsen electronics, and even in-room espresso machines (gotta love those Italians). The rooms (or *"stanzas"* as they say in Italy and at the Keating) are highly contemporary—some may find them cold—and feature an interior design that does away with walls between the bed and bath areas. The guests-only lounge and wine bar (nestled in what was once a basement vault) keeps the high-tech theme going with its accents of aluminum, steel, and brick swathed in a deep red palette. Packages are available that include the use of a Ferrari. The hotel is nonsmoking.

432 F St. (btw. Fourth and Fifth aves.), San Diego, CA 92101. **(C)** **877/753-2846** or 619/814-5700. Fax 619/814-5750. www.keatinghotel.com. 35 units. $499 double; $2,400 suite. 1 child under 12 stays free in parent's room. Packages available. AE, DC, DISC, MC, V. Valet parking $30. Bus: 3 or 120. Pets less than 20 lb. accepted with $150 fee. **Amenities:** Bar w/limited food menu; spa services; concierge; in-room dining; babysitting service; laundry/dry cleaning service. *In room:* A/C, TV/DVD, Wi-Fi, minibar, espresso machine, hair dryer, iron, CD/MP3 docking station, 2-line phone.

The US Grant ★★★   Following a 20-month, $56-million renovation, one of San Diego's most historic properties reopened in the fall of 2006. Originally built in 1910 by the son of Ulysses S. Grant, this grandiose 11-story property sits at the northern edge of the Gaslamp Quarter. An impressive Beaux Arts beauty, the Grant is part of the Starwood Hotel & Resorts' Luxury Collection and is owned by the Sycuan Band of the Kumeyaay Nation (in a nice touch of irony, the Kumeyaay were given their sovereignty in 1875 by President Grant). Guest rooms all have 9-foot ceilings, plush wool carpets, ornate moldings, custom furniture, Italian linens, and Native American artwork in the foyer. In-room spa services incorporating Native American traditions and local herbs and plants are also available. The **Grant Grill,** long a clubby spot for power lunches and dinners, has been given an Art Deco, modern makeover, with plenty of curves, creamy white leather booths, rich mahogany, and iron filigrees.

326 Broadway (btw. Third and Fourth aves., main entrance now on Fourth Ave.), San Diego, CA 92101. **(C)** **800/237-5029** or 866/837-4270. Fax 619/239-9517. www.usgrant.net. 270 units (47 suites). $339–$619 double; $699–$3,500 suite. Children under 18 stay free in parent's room. Packages available. AE, DC, DISC, MC, V. Valet parking $28. Bus: Numerous downtown routes, including 2, 3, 7, 20, 120, 923, 929, and 992. Trolley: Civic Center. Most dogs less than 35 lb. accepted with $150 fee. **Amenities:** Restaurant; 2 bars; fitness facility; concierge; business center; boutique; room service; babysitting service; laundry/valet service; shoeshine service; luggage storage; afternoon tea daily (1–4pm). *In room:* A/C, TV w/pay movies, Wi-Fi, minibar, coffeemaker, hair dryer, iron, safe, CD player, 2-line phone.

W San Diego ★★   The W took the city by storm when it opened in 2003, delivering swanky nightlife beyond the Gaslamp Quarter. Rooms are bright, cheery—like mod beach cabanas beamed into downtown—and replete with a sexy shower. *Nouveau nautique* is the theme, with elegant aqua and sand tones accenting the whites, a window seat (great idea), and a beach-ball-shaped pillow. The WoW suite on the 19th floor is a 1,250-square-foot luxury accommodation with a host of state-of-the-art features and killer skyline views. The restaurant, **Rice,** has an adventurous and playful menu featuring contemporary global cuisine. The adjoining lounge, **Karma,** offers small-plates and a champagne menu, while the airy lobby bar, **Living Room,** has turntables and board games (good luck concentrating on your chess match). **Beach,** on the third floor, is where the designers let it rip: The open-air bar has a sand floor (heated at night), a fire pit, and cabanas.

421 W. B St. (at State St.), San Diego, CA 92101. (✆ **888/625-5144** or 619/231-8220. Fax 619/231-5779. www.whotels.com/sandiego. 259 units. $279–$429 double; $599–$3,000 suite. AE, DC, DISC, MC, V. Valet parking $26. Bus: 810 or 820. Trolley: American Plaza. **Amenities:** Restaurant; 3 lounges; concierge; room service; laundry service; dry cleaning. *In room:* A/C, TV/VCR/DVD, minibar, coffeemaker, hair dryer, iron, safe, CD player.

Expensive

Hard Rock Hotel San Diego ★★ A far cry from the tired burger-and-memorabilia joint over on Fourth Avenue, this new 12-story condo-hotel has a sweet location—right at the gateway to the Gaslamp Quarter—and plenty of star power in the personages of master chef Nobuyuki Matsuhisa and nightlife tastemaker Rande Gerber. Matsuhisa, who has partnered with Robert De Niro on restaurants in New York, Milan, Tokyo, and London, adds San Diego to the list with **Nobu,** the hotel's signature eatery. Lounge impresario Gerber works his magic with two bars, one on the ground floor, **Sweetwater Saloon,** and one on the fourth-floor pool deck, **Moonstone Lounge.** The Black Eyed Peas weigh in, too, with a million-dollar "doped-out" suite specially designed by the group. It's one of 17 "Rock Star" suites, some of which include private decks, fire pits, outdoor hot tubs, and 270-degree city views. Standard rooms are hip and modern; all rooms are well soundproofed from the Gaslamp hubbub.

207 Fifth Ave. (btw. K and L sts.), San Diego, CA 92101. (✆ **866/751-7625** or 619/702-3000. Fax 619/702-3007. www.hardrockhotelsd.com. 420 units. $250–$500 double; from $600 suite. AE, DC, DISC, MC, V. Valet parking $30. Trolley: Gaslamp Quarter. **Amenities:** 2 restaurants; 2 bars; 2 music venues; pool; fitness center; spa; concierge; business center; gift shop; room service. *In room:* A/C, HDTV w/on-demand video and video games, Wi-Fi, minibar, hair dryer, iron, safe, personal electronics docking station.

Holiday Inn on the Bay ★★ (Kids) This better-than-average Holiday Inn is reliable and nearly always offers great deals. The three-building high-rise complex is on the Embarcadero across from the harbor and the Maritime Museum. This scenic spot is only 1 1/2 miles from the airport (you can watch planes landing and taking off) and 2 blocks from the train station and trolley. Rooms, while basic, always seem to sport clean new furnishings and plenty of thoughtful comforts. They are identical inside, so the only choice is whether you want marvelous bay views or a look at San Diego's still-evolving skyline. In either case, request the highest floor possible.

1355 N. Harbor Dr. (at Ash St.), San Diego, CA 92101-3385. (✆ **800/465-4329** or 619/232-3861. Fax 619/232-4924. www.holiday-inn.com/san-onthebay. 600 units. $224 double; from $339 suite. Children under 18 stay free in parent's room. AE, DC, MC, V. Valet parking $26; self-parking $20. Bus: 2, 210, 810, 820, 850, 860, 923, or 992. Trolley: American Plaza. Pets accepted w/$25 nonrefundable fee and $100 deposit. **Amenities:** 4 restaurants; lounge; outdoor heated pool; exercise room; concierge; business center; room service; babysitting; coin-op laundry and laundry service. *In room:* A/C, TV w/pay movies, Wi-Fi, coffeemaker, hair dryer, iron.

Moderate

Gaslamp Plaza Suites ★★ (Value) You can't get closer to the center of the vibrant Gaslamp Quarter than this restored, 11-story Edwardian beauty. Built in 1913, it was San Diego's first skyscraper. Crafted (at great expense) of Australian gumwood, marble, brass, and exquisite etched glass, the splendid building originally housed the San Diego Trust & Savings. Various other businesses set up shop here until 1988, when the elegant structure was placed on the National Register of Historic Places and reopened as a boutique hotel. Most rooms are spacious and offer luxuries rare in this price range, such as pillow-top mattresses and premium toiletries; microwaves and dinnerware; and impressive luxury bathrooms. The cheapest rooms on the back side have no view and are uncomfortably small. The higher floors boast splendid city and bay views, as do the rooftop patio and breakfast room. Don't be surprised to hear a hum from the street below when things gets rockin' on weekends.

520 E St. (corner of Fifth Ave.), San Diego, CA 92101. ✆ **800/874-8770** or 619/232-9500. Fax 619/238-9945. www.gaslampplaza.com. 64 units. $139–$179 double; from $249 suite. Extra person $15. Rates include continental breakfast. AE, DC, DISC, MC, V. Valet parking $24. Bus: 3 or 120, plus numerous downtown routes. Trolley: Fifth Ave. **Amenities:** Room service (lunch and dinner). *In room:* A/C, TV/VCR, fridge, coffeemaker, hair dryer, iron, safe, microwave.

Horton Grand ★ ⒻInds   A cross between an elegant hotel and a charming inn, the Horton Grand combines two hotels that date from 1886—one of which was the residence of lawman Wyatt Earp during his San Diego days. Both properties were saved from demolition, moved to this spot, and connected by an airy atrium lobby filled with white wicker. The facade, with its graceful bay windows, is original. Each room is unique, with vintage furnishings and gas fireplaces; bathrooms are lush with reproduction floor tiles, fine brass fixtures, and genteel appointments. Rooms overlook either the city or the fig tree–filled courtyard; the suites (really just large studio-style rooms) are in a newer wing—choosing one means sacrificing historic character for a sitting area/sofa bed and minibar with microwave. If you're lonely, request room no. 309, where Roger the ghost hangs out.

311 Island Ave. (at Fourth Ave.), San Diego, CA 92101. ✆ **800/542-1886** or 619/544-1886. Fax 619/239-3823. www.hortongrand.com. 132 units. $169–$199 double; from $269 suite. Extra person $20. Children under 18 stay free in parent's room. AE, DC, MC, V. Valet parking $24. Bus: 3, 11, or 120. Trolley: Convention Center. **Amenities:** Restaurant (breakfast only); bar; business center. *In room:* A/C, TV, hair dryer.

Inexpensive

Hotel Occidental ★ ⒻInds   While almost every new hotel in San Diego caters to those with fat wallets, exceptions include the Hotel Occidental, which opened in late 2005. Located in Bankers Hill between Hillcrest and downtown, the Hotel Occidental is also just a block from Balboa Park. Built as a Knights of Columbus meeting place in 1923, the attractive Mission-style architecture has been restored to its original glory, and the hotel features kitchenettes in all rooms, free Wi-Fi, free bicycle rental, and a daily continental breakfast. Rooms are available with both shared and private bathrooms. Other nice touches include a business center, laundry service, and a garden patio. The hotel is entirely nonsmoking.

410 Elm St. (btw. Fourth and Fifth aves.), San Diego, CA 92101. ✆ **800/205-9897** or 619/232-1336. Fax 619/232-1331. www.hoteloccidental-sandiego.com. 54 units. $79–$129 double; $139 suite. Rates include continental breakfast. AE, MC, V. Limited self-parking $10; street parking. Bus: 3 or 120. **Amenities:** Free bike rental; business center; free Wi-Fi; coin-op laundry; valet dry cleaning; garden patio. *In room:* A/C, TV/DVD, kitchenette, fridge, hair dryer, iron, safe, microwave, minirange (suites only).

La Pensione Hotel ★ Ⓥalue   This place has a lot going for it: modern amenities, remarkable value, a location in Little Italy within walking distance of the central business district, a friendly staff, and free parking (a premium for small hotels in San Diego). The four-story hotel is built around a courtyard and feels like a small European hotel. The decor is modern and streamlined, with plenty of sleek black and metallic surfaces, crisp white walls, and modern wood furnishings. Guest accommodations, while not overly large, make the most of their confines and allow you space to move around. Each room offers a ceiling fan (but no air-conditioning) and minifridge; some have a small balcony. La Pensione is within walking distance of eateries (two restaurants are directly downstairs), nightspots, and a trolley station. If you're sensitive to noise, request a room away from the street, though this means no bay or city view.

606 W. Date St. (at India St.), San Diego, CA 92101. ☎ **800/232-4683** or 619/236-8000. Fax 619/236-8088. www.lapensionehotel.com. 75 units. $90 double. AE, DC, DISC, MC, V. Limited free underground parking. Bus: 83. Trolley: Little Italy. **Amenities:** Self-service laundry. *In room:* TV, fridge.

HILLCREST/UPTOWN

The gentrified historic neighborhoods north of downtown are still something of a bargain. They're convenient to Balboa Park, with easy access to the rest of town. Filled with casual and upscale restaurants, eclectic shops, and upbeat nightlife, the area is also easy to navigate. All the following accommodations cater to the mainstream market but attract a gay/lesbian clientele as well.

Several bed-and-breakfasts in elegant, older neighborhoods invite consideration. **Keating House** ★★, 2331 Second Ave. (☎ **800/995-8644** or 619/239-8585; www.keating house.com), is an 1880s Victorian mansion with period decor, between Hillcrest and downtown; **Crone's Cobblestone Cottage** ★, 1302 Washington Place (☎ **619/295-4765;** www.cobblestonebandb.com), is a beautifully restored Craftsman bungalow in Mission Hills; and the **Cottage,** 3829 Albatross St. (☎ **619/299-1564**), is a 1913 Mission Hills home tucked into a quiet cul-de-sac.

Very Expensive

Britt Scripps Inn ★★★   Built around 1887, this property was home to one of San Diego's most prominent families, the Scripps. Today, the house and its grounds function as a nine-room "estate hotel"—part B&B, part luxury hotel. With first-class amenities, such as 1,000-thread-count sheets, flatscreen TVs (most hidden in antique armoires), free Wi-Fi, and heated towel racks, this gracious lady lays on the personal charm as well, with gourmet breakfasts including homemade pastries and breads, late-afternoon wine and cheese, and a vintage Steinway piano in the music alcove. Staff is always on-site, but usually out of sight. Striking architectural elements include seven gables, a dramatic turret, wraparound porch, twisting oak staircase, and a two-story, three-paneled stained-glass window. And it's all just a block away from Balboa Park.

406 Maple St. (at Fourth Ave.), San Diego, CA 92103. ☎ **888/881-1991** or 619/230-1991. Fax 619/230-1188. www.brittscripps.com. 9 units. $435–$525 double. Rates include full breakfast and afternoon wine and hors d'oeuvres. AE, DC, MC, V. Bus: 3 or 120. Take the Laurel St. exit off I-5, make a left on Laurel, a left on Fifth Ave., and a left on Maple St. *In room:* A/C, TV/DVD, Wi-Fi, coffeemaker, hair dryer, iron, safe, CD/MP3 player, 2-line phone.

Moderate

Park Manor Suites ★ Ⓥⓐⓛⓤⓔ   On a prime corner overlooking Balboa Park, this hotel became a popular stopping-off point for celebrities headed for Mexican vacations in the 1920s and 1930s. Although dated, guest rooms are huge and very comfortable, featuring full kitchens, dining rooms, living rooms, and bedrooms with a separate dressing area. A few have glassed-in terraces; request one when you book. The overall feeling is that of a prewar East Coast apartment building, complete with steam heat and lavish moldings. Park Manor Suites does have its weaknesses, particularly bathrooms that have mostly original fixtures and could use some renovation. The old-world restaurant on the ground floor also has a piano bar; and lunch is served weekdays in the penthouse banquet room (the view is spectacular). On Friday evenings, the penthouse bar becomes the launching pad for the gay party scene, drawing big crowds.

525 Spruce St. (btw. Fifth and Sixth aves.), San Diego, CA 92103. ☎ **800/874-2649** or 619/291-0999. Fax 619/291-8844. www.parkmanorsuites.com. 74 units. $159–$199 studio; $189–$229 1-bedroom suite; $249–$269 2-bedroom suite. Extra person $15. Children under 12 stay free in parent's room. Rates

include continental breakfast. AE, DC, DISC, MC, V. Free parking. Bus: 3 or 120. Take Washington St. exit **711**
off I-5, right on Fourth Ave., left on Spruce. **Amenities:** Restaurant; bar; access to nearby health club ($5);
coin-op laundry and laundry service; dry cleaning. *In room:* TV, Wi-Fi, kitchen, coffeemaker, hair dryer,
iron, safe, microwave.

Inexpensive

Balboa Park Inn ★   Insiders looking for unusual accommodations head straight for
this small pink inn at the northern edge of Balboa Park. It's a cluster of four Spanish
Colonial–style former apartment buildings in a mostly residential neighborhood a half
mile east of Hillcrest's heart. The hotel is popular with gay travelers drawn to Hillcrest's
restaurants and clubs, which crop up within several blocks of the property. The rooms
and standard suites are tastefully decorated, but the specialty suites are over-the-top:
Choose the "Tara Suite," as in *Gone With the Wind;* or the "Greystoke" suite, a jumble of
jungle, safari, and tropical themes with a completely mirrored bathroom and Jacuzzi tub.
Seven rooms have Jacuzzi tubs, and most have kitchens—all have private entrances,
though the front desk operates 24 hours. *Tip:* You'll be close enough to walk to the San
Diego Zoo and Balboa Park.

3402 Park Blvd. (at Upas St.), San Diego, CA 92103. ✆ **800/938-8181** or 619/298-0823. Fax 619/294-
8070. www.balboaparkinn.com. 26 units. $99 double; $149–$239 suite. Extra person $10. Children under
12 stay free in parent's room. Rates include continental breakfast. AE, DC, DISC, MC, V. Parking available
on street. Bus: 7. From I-5, take Washington St. east, follow signs to University Ave. E., and turn right at
Park Blvd. *In room:* TV, fridge, coffeemaker, microwave.

OLD TOWN & MISSION VALLEY

Old Town is popular with families because of its proximity to Old Town State Historic
Park and other attractions within walking distance, and SeaWorld and the San Diego
Zoo are within a 10-minute drive. Around the corner, in Mission Valley, you'll find the
city's largest collection of hotels with rooms under $100 a night. Mission Valley lacks
homegrown personality—this is the spot for chain restaurants and huge shopping malls,
not gardens or water views. But it caters to convention groups and leisure travelers drawn
by the lower prices and competitive facilities.

Room rates at properties on Hotel Circle are significantly cheaper than those in many
other parts of the city. You'll find a cluster of inexpensive chain hotels and motels, including **Best Western Seven Seas** (✆ **800/421-6662** or 619/291-1300), **Mission Valley
Travelodge** (✆ **800/255-3050** or 619/297-2271), **Motel 6 Hotel Circle** (✆ **800/466-
8356** or 619/296-1612), **Ramada Plaza** (✆ **800/532-4241** or 619/291-6500), and
Vagabond Inn–Hotel Circle (✆ **800/522-1555** or 619/297-1691). Summer and weekend rates tend to be higher.

Moderate

Crowne Plaza San Diego ★   Formerly known as the Red Lion Hanalei, this Mission Valley hotel has a Polynesian theme and a comfort-conscious sophistication that sets
it apart from the rest of the pack. Most rooms are split between two eight-story towers
and cleverly positioned so that the balconies open onto the tropically landscaped pool
courtyard or the attractive links of an adjacent golf club. A few more rooms are found in
a third structure, which is a little too close to the freeway. The heated outdoor pool is
large enough for any luau, as is the oversize Jacuzzi beside it. Guest rooms are outfitted
with contemporary furnishings and conveniences; those on the sixth through eighth
floors have a microwave and fridge. Services include a free shuttle to Old Town and the
Fashion Valley Shopping Center.

2270 Hotel Circle N., San Diego, CA 92108. ✆ **800/227-6963** or 619/297-1101. Fax 619/297-6049. www.
cp-sandiego.com. 417 units. $147–$189 double; $300–$550 suite. AE, DISC, MC, V. Parking $10. Bus: 14.
From I-8, take Hotel Circle exit, follow signs for Hotel Circle N. **Amenities:** 2 restaurants; bar; outdoor
pool; nearby golf course (packages available); fitness center; spa/massage facility; Jacuzzi; game room;
activities desk; business center; salon; gift shop; room service; coin-op laundry and laundry service; dry
cleaning. *In room:* A/C, TV w/pay movies, coffeemaker, hair dryer, iron, safe.

Heritage Park Bed & Breakfast Inn ★★   This exquisite 1889 Queen Anne mansion is set in a Victorian park that is an artfully arranged cobblestone cul-de-sac lined
with historic buildings saved from the wrecking ball. Most of the Inn's rooms are in the
main house, with a handful of equally appealing choices in an adjacent 1887 Italianate
companion. A stay here is about surrendering to the pampering of breakfast by candlelight, afternoon tea, or watching the sunset from a veranda rocking chair. Like the gracious parlors and porches, each guest room is meticulously outfitted with period antiques
and luxurious fabrics; although the fireplaces are all ornamental, some rooms have whirlpool baths. In the evenings, classic films are shown in the Victorian parlor, where screenings are complete with popcorn.

2470 Heritage Park Row, San Diego, CA 92110. ✆ **800/995-2470** or 619/299-6832. Fax 619/299-9465.
www.heritageparkinn.com. 12 units. $125–$295 double. Extra person $20. Rates include full breakfast
and afternoon tea. AE, DC, DISC, MC, V. Free parking. Bus: Numerous Old Town routes including 10, 14,
and 30. Trolley: Old Town. Take I-5 to Old Town Ave., turn left onto San Diego Ave., and then turn right
onto Harney St. *In room:* A/C, hair dryer, iron.

Holiday Inn Express–Old Town ★   A couple blocks from the heart of Old Town,
this Holiday Inn's Spanish Colonial exterior suits the neighborhood. Inside, above-par
contemporary furnishings and small touches make this hotel an affordable favorite of
business travelers and families alike. Adjacent streets are unspectacular, so the hotel is
smartly oriented toward the interior; request a room with a patio or balcony that opens
onto the pleasant courtyard. Rooms are thoughtfully, practically appointed, with extras
such as microwave ovens and writing tables. The lobby, surrounded by French doors, has
a large fireplace, several sitting areas, and a TV.

3900 Old Town Ave., San Diego, CA 92110. ✆ **800/972-2802** or 619/299-7400. Fax 619/299-1619. www.
hiexpress.com/ex-oldtown. 125 units. $161–$169 double; from $199 suite. Extra person $10. Children
under 18 stay free in parent's room. Rates include continental breakfast. AE, DC, DISC, MC, V. Parking $12.
Bus: 10, 30. Trolley: Old Town. Take I-5 to Old Town Ave. exit. **Amenities:** Outdoor pool; whirlpool; Wi-Fi;
laundry/dry-cleaning service. *In room:* A/C, TV, fridge, coffeemaker, iron, microwave.

MISSION BAY & THE BEACHES

If the beach and aquatic activities are the focus of your San Diego agenda, this part of
town may be for you. Even though the beach communities feel removed from the city,
downtown and Balboa Park are only a 15-minute drive away. Some hotels are right on
Mission Bay, San Diego's water playground; they're usually good choices for families.
Ocean Beach, Mission Beach, and Pacific Beach provide a taste of the beach-bum lifestyle. They can be raucous at times, especially on summer weekends, and dining options
are largely limited to chains and casual restaurants. If you're looking for a more refined
landing, head to La Jolla or Coronado (covered later in this chapter).

   Hostelling International has a 53-bed location in **Point Loma** (✆ **888/464-4872**, ext.
157, or 619/223-4778; www.sandiegohostels.org), 3790 Udall St., about 2 miles inland
from Ocean Beach; rates start at $17 per person, and private rooms that sleep two or
three are $42 and $48. The **Ocean Beach International Hostel,** 4961 Newport Ave.

and is just 2 blocks from the beach; bunk rates are $16 per person. Free pickup from the airport, train, or bus station is offered. U.S residents must show proof of international travel within the last 6 months or be a member of Hostelling International in order to stay.

Very Expensive

Crystal Pier Hotel ★★ (Finds) (Kids)   If historic charm is higher on your wish list than hotel-style service, head to this utterly unique cluster of cottages sitting literally over the surf on the vintage Crystal Pier in Pacific Beach. It's a self-contained hideaway—you'll get a separate living room and bedroom, a fully equipped kitchen, and a private patio with breathtaking ocean views—all within the whitewashed walls of sweet, blue-shuttered cottages that date from 1936 but have been carefully renovated. Each of the Cape Cod–style cottages has a deck, and the more expensive units farthest out have more privacy. Six cheaper units are not actually on the pier, but still offer sunset-facing sea views. Guests drive right out and park beside their cottages, a real boon on crowded weekends. These accommodations book up fast; reserve for summer and holiday weekends 8 to 11 months in advance, 4 to 6 months in advance for winter. Or, with luck, you might be able to nab someone's cancelled reservation.

4500 Ocean Blvd. (at Garnet Ave.), San Diego, CA 92109. (© 800/748-5894 or 858/483-6983. Fax 858/483-6811. www.crystalpier.com. 29 units. $300–$375 double; $500 for larger units sleeping 4 or 6. 3-night minimum in summer, 2-night minimum in winter. DISC, MC, V. Free parking. Bus: 8, 9, 27, or 30. Take I-5 to Grand/Garnet exit; follow Garnet to the pier. **Amenities:** Beach equipment rental. *In room:* TV, kitchen.

Pacific Terrace Hotel ★   This modern hotel on the boardwalk swaggers with a heavy-handed South Seas–meets–Spanish Colonial ambience. More upscale than most places nearby, it's at the north end of the Pacific Beach boardwalk; the surfer contingent tends to stay a few blocks south. Large, comfortable guest rooms each come with a balcony or terrace; bathrooms, designed with warm-toned marble and natural woods, have a separate sink/vanity area. About half the rooms have kitchenettes, and top-floor rooms in this three-story hotel enjoy particularly nice views. Management keeps cookies, coffee, and iced tea at the ready throughout the day; the lushly landscaped pool and hot tub overlook a relatively quiet stretch of beach. Five nearby restaurants allow meals to be billed to the hotel, but no restaurant is on the premises.

610 Diamond St., San Diego, CA 92109. (© 800/344-3370 or 858/581-3500. Fax 858/274-3341. www. pacificterrace.com. 73 units. $359–$500 double; from $490 suite. Children 12 and under stay free in parent's room. 2- to 4-night minimums apply in summer. Rates include continental breakfast and afternoon wine reception. AE, DC, DISC, MC, V. Parking $20; limited free parking in off-street lot. Bus: 30. Take I-5 to Grand/Garnet exit and follow Grand or Garnet west to Mission Blvd., turn right (north), and then left (west) onto Diamond. **Amenities:** Pool; fitness room; Jacuzzi; bike rental nearby; activities desk; room service; in-room massage; coin-op laundry and laundry service; dry cleaning. *In room:* A/C, TV w/pay movies, minibar, coffeemaker, hair dryer, iron, safe.

Paradise Point Resort & Spa ★★ (Kids)   Smack dab in the middle of Mission Bay, this hotel complex is almost as much a theme park as its closest neighbor, SeaWorld (a 3-min. drive away). Single-story accommodations are spread across 44 tropically landscaped acres of duck-filled lagoons, lush gardens, and swim-friendly beaches; all have private lanais and plenty of thoughtful conveniences. Standard "lanai" rooms range considerably in price, based solely on view. The resort was updated to keep its low-tech 1960s charm but rooms now have a refreshingly colorful beach cottage decor. The upscale waterfront restaurant, **Baleen,** features fine dining in a contemporary, fun space, and a stunning Indonesian-inspired spa—this facility is a vacation in itself—offers cool serenity and aroma-tinged Asian treatments.

1404 Vacation Rd. (off Ingraham St.), San Diego, CA 92109. ✆ **800/344-2626** or 858/274-4630. Fax 858/581-5924. www.paradisepoint.com. 462 units. $356–$421 double; from $421 suite. Extra person $20. Children 17 and under stay free in parent's room. AE, DC, DISC, MC, V. Parking $20. Bus: 8 or 9. Follow I-8 west to Mission Bay Dr. exit; take Ingraham St. north to Vacation Rd. **Amenities:** 2 restaurants; bar; pool bar; 5 outdoor pools; 18-hole putting course; tennis courts; basketball court; fitness center; full-service spa; Jacuzzi; bike rental; concierge; business center; gift shop/market; room service; laundry service; dry cleaning. *In room:* A/C, TV w/pay movies, fridge, coffeemaker, hair dryer, iron.

Tower 23 ★★   Named for a nearby lifeguard station, Tower 23 is a modernist beach resort that opened in 2005. On the Pacific Beach (aka P.B.) boardwalk, the hotel enjoys a people-watching quotient matched only by its first-class contemporary amenities, including Wi-Fi right on the beach. Featuring clean lines and glass-box architecture, the three-story Tower 23 has 44 rooms, all with private balconies (though not all with ocean views). A guest-only second-story deck with fire pit overlooks the beach. The hotel's **Tower Bar** and **Jordan** restaurant, which serves contemporary steak and seafood and has an eight-seat sushi bar, have become the sophisticated heart of the P.B. scene. Jordan sometimes takes a rap for poor service (a common San Diego complaint), but you can always wile away long waits by sipping a cocktail and gazing at the hypnotic, 75-foot-long "wave wall" and its morphing color scheme.

723 Felspar St., San Diego, CA 92109. ✆ **866/869-3723.** Fax 858/274-2333. www.t23hotel.com. 44 units. $409–$489 double; from $789 suite. Children 17 and under stay free in parent's room. AE, DC, DISC, MC, V. Valet parking $15. Bus: 8, 9, 27, or 30. Take I-5 to Grand/Garnet exit, left on Grand Ave., right on Mission Blvd., left on Felspar St. Pets 25 lb. and under accepted with a $250 cleaning charge. **Amenities:** Restaurant; bar; Wi-Fi; room service; in-room massage and spa services; laundry; valet; private deck. *In room:* A/C, TV w/on-demand video, DVD player, hair dryer, iron, safe, Jacuzzi tubs (suites only), 2-line phone, CD player, Xbox, hypoallergenic bedding (on request).

Expensive

Catamaran Resort Hotel ★★ (Kids)   Right on Mission Bay, the Catamaran has its own beach, complete with watersports facilities. Built in the 1950s, the hotel has been fully renovated to modern standards without losing its trademark Polynesian theme. Guest rooms—in either a 13-story building or one of the six two-story buildings—have subdued South Pacific decor, and each has a balcony or patio. Tower rooms on higher floors have commanding views, and studios and suites have kitchenettes. A 9,300-square-foot spa, featuring a menu of South Pacific and Asian-inspired treatments, was added in 2005. The Catamaran is within a few blocks of Pacific Beach's restaurant-and-nightlife scene, and the resort's **Moray's Lounge** features live music nightly. During the summer, kids can take advantage of the daily Mad Science Kid's Camp.

3999 Mission Blvd. (4 blocks south of Grand Ave.), San Diego, CA 92109. ✆ **800/422-8386** or 858/488-1081. Fax 858/488-1387. www.catamaranresort.com. 315 units. $319–$409 double; from $539 suite. Children under 12 stay free in parent's room. AE, DC, DISC, MC, V. Valet parking $16; self-parking $12. Bus: 8 or 9. Take Grand/Garnet exit off I-5 and go west on Grand Ave., and then south on Mission Blvd. **Amenities:** Restaurant; 2 bars; outdoor pool; fitness room; full-service spa; Jacuzzi; watersports equipment rental; bike rental; children's programs; game room; business center; concierge; room service; in-room massage; laundry service; dry cleaning. *In room:* A/C, TV w/pay movies, fridge in most units, coffeemaker, hair dryer, iron.

The Dana on Mission Bay ★   The Dana completed a $20-million renovation and expansion in 2004, adding 74 contemporary rooms in a three-story arc wrapping around

an infinity pool. Some rooms overlook bobbing sailboats in the recreational marina; others
face onto the original kidney-shaped pool whose surrounding tiki-torch-lit gardens offer
shuffleboard and Ping-Pong. You'll pay a little extra for bay and marina views; if the view
doesn't matter, save your money—every one of the old rooms is plain but well-maintained.
The new rooms are bigger and feature water views and reclaimed redwood beam ceilings.
Beaches and SeaWorld are a 15-minute walk away (or take the complimentary shuttle that
also goes to the airport, zoo, and Gaslamp Quarter, among other destinations).

1710 W. Mission Bay Dr., San Diego, CA 92109. (*C*) **800/345-9995** or 619/222-6440. Fax 619/222-5916.
www.thedana.com. 270 units. $259–$329 double (sleeps up to 4); from $349 suite. AE, DC, DISC, MC, V.
Parking $12. Bus: 8 or 9. Follow I-8 west to Mission Bay Dr. exit; take W. Mission Bay Dr. **Amenities:** 2
restaurants; 2 outdoor heated pools; fitness room; spa services; 2 Jacuzzis; watersports equipment/rent-
als; bike rentals; concierge; gift shop; room service; coin-op laundry and laundry service; dry cleaning. *In
room:* A/C, TV, fridge, coffeemaker, hair dryer, iron.

Ocean Park Inn ★   This oceanfront motor hotel offers simple, attractive, spacious
rooms with contemporary furnishings. Although the inn has a smidgen of sophistication
uncommon in this casual, surfer-populated area, you won't find much solitude with the
boisterous scene outside; but you can't beat the direct beach access. Most rooms have at
least a partial ocean view; all have a private balcony or patio. Units in front are most
desirable, but it can get noisy directly above the boardwalk; try for the second or third
floor, or pick one of the three junior suites, which have huge bathrooms and pool views.
The entire hotel is nonsmoking.

710 Grand Ave., San Diego, CA 92109. (*C*) **800/231-7735** or 858/483-5858. Fax 858/274-0823. www.
oceanparkinn.com. 73 units. $219–$329 double; from $369 suite. Rates include continental breakfast. AE,
DC, DISC, MC, V. Parking $10. Bus: 8, 9, or 30. Take Grand/Garnet exit off I-5; follow Grand Ave. to ocean.
Amenities: Outdoor pool; Jacuzzi; laundry service; dry cleaning. *In room:* A/C, TV, fridge, coffeemaker,
hair dryer, iron, safe.

Moderate
The Beach Cottages   This family-owned operation has been around since 1948 and
offers a variety of guest quarters, most of them geared to the long-term visitor. It's the 17
cute detached cottages just steps from the sand that give it real appeal: Some of them lack
a view (of anything), but each has a patio with tables and chairs. The cottages themselves
aren't pristine, but they have a rustic charm—reserve one well in advance. Adjoining
apartments are perfectly adequate, especially for budget-minded families who want to log
major hours on the beach—all cottages and apartments sleep four or more and have full
kitchens. The standard motel rooms are worn but cheap (most of these sleep two). The
property features shared barbecue grills, shuffleboard courts, and table tennis, and is also
within walking distance of shops and restaurants.

4255 Ocean Blvd. (1 block south of Grand Ave.), San Diego, CA 92109-3995. (*C*) **858/483-7440.** Fax
858/273-9365. www.beachcottages.com. 61 units, 17 cottages. $135–$155 double; from $285 cottage
and apt. for 4 to 6. Monthly rates available mid-Sept to Mar. AE, DC, DISC, MC, V. Free parking. Bus: 8 or 9.
Take I-5 to Grand/Garnet exit, go west on Grand Ave. and left on Mission Blvd. **Amenities:** Coin-op laundry. *In room:* TV, fridge, coffeemaker.

The Pearl Hotel ★ (Finds)   The designers of this midcentury modernist gem took a
run-down motel property dating from 1959 and let fly with the vintage cool. Accommodations are modest in size but have been refreshed with amenities such as Internet
radios and contemporary chrome bathroom fixtures; thoughtful design touches include
custom mosaic artwork and a pet fish. The Pearl's restaurant and lounge area is cozy and
features outdoor dining spaces alongside the saltwater pool (where "dive-in" movies are

screened weekly). Although the closest beach is over the hill in Ocean Beach, Point Loma is a nautical neighborhood, with the marinas, bars, and restaurants of Shelter Island nearby; the airport and Cabrillo National Monument are also just minutes away. The hotel is entirely nonsmoking.

1410 Rosecrans St. (at Fenelon St.), San Diego, CA 92106. ℂ **877/732-7573** or 619/226-6100. Fax 619/226-6161. www.thepearlsd.com. 23 units. $159–$229 double; "Play & Stay" rate $89 after midnight (subject to availability). AE, DISC, MC, V. Parking $10. Bus: 28. Take I-5 south to Rosecrans St. exit. **Amenities:** Restaurant; bar; outdoor saltwater pool; spa services; bike rental; computer rental; laundry service. *In room:* A/C, TV, Wi-Fi, hair dryer, iron.

LA JOLLA

No one is quite sure, but the name "La Jolla" may be misspelled Spanish for "the jewel"— a fitting comparison for this section of the city with its beautiful coastline and compact downtown village. You'll have a hard time finding bargain accommodations in this upscale, conservative community. But remember, most hotels—even those in our "Very Expensive" category—have occupancy-driven rates, meaning you can score surprising discounts during the off season (winter).

Very Expensive

Estancia La Jolla Hotel and Spa ★★★ This 9¹/₂-acre California rancho-style property has some pretty cool neighbors: the Louis I. Kahn–designed Salk Institute, UC San Diego, the Torrey Pines Gliderport, and Black's Beach. You won't see any of those things from this self-contained retreat, but the romance created by the hacienda flavor and the meticulously maintained gardens with their native flora and bubbling fountains is diversion enough. Guest rooms face a central courtyard, so many rooms have balconies or patios; and all are tastefully appointed with comfy furnishings that would be at home in an upscale residence. With its old *Californio* exterior, outdoor fireplace, and live Spanish guitar music, the Mustangs & Burros lounge and bar is a great place to chill out; there is also an award-winning restaurant on-site. The full-service spa offers organic-based treatments such as the garden vegetable wrap.

9700 N. Torrey Pines Rd., La Jolla, CA 92037. ℂ **877/437-8262** or 858/550-1000. Fax 858/550-1001 www. estanciajolla.com. 210 units. $349–$399 double; from $499 suite. B&B packages available for an additional $20. AE, DC, DISC, MC, V. Valet parking $21; self-parking $17. Bus: 101. From I-5 take the Genesee Ave. exit westbound, go left on N. Torrey Pines Rd. **Amenities:** Restaurant; 2 bars; pool; fitness center; yoga and personal training; full-service spa; Jacuzzi; concierge; free area transportation (5-mile radius); car rental; business center; gift shop; room service; babysitting service; laundry service; dry cleaning. *In room:* A/C, TV w/pay movies and video games, Wi-Fi, minibar, coffeemaker, hair dryer, iron, safe.

Hotel Parisi ★★★ (Finds) This intimate hotel overlooking one of La Jolla village's main intersections offers a nurturing, wellness-inspired vibe. The Italy-meets-Zen composition includes custom guest-room furnishings that are modern yet comfy; Parisi calls the spacious accommodations "suites" (some are more like junior suites), and each has an ergonomic desk, dimmable lighting, and superluxe goose-down bedding. Each darkly cool marble bathroom boasts a shower (some with dual shower heads), a separate tub with contoured backrest, and smoothly sculpted fixtures. Less expensive rooms are smaller with little or no view; across the street from the hotel is Parisi Apart—four luxury units (one- and two-bedrooms) available for extended stays. Though primped and elegant, Parisi is not stuffy, and the personal service stops at nothing—there's even a menu of 24-hour in-room holistic health services, ranging from yoga to psychotherapy. The Parisi does not allow smoking.

ACCOMMODATIONS ■

Bed & Breakfast Inn
at La Jolla **20**

Estancia La Jolla **11**

The Grande Colonial **1**

Hotel Parisi **5**

La Jolla Village Lodge **17**

La Valencia Hotel **4**

The Lodge at
Torrey Pines **10**

Scripps Inn **21**

DINING ◆

Brockton Villa **8**

The Cottage **22**

Georges California Modern **7**

Jack's La Jolla **18**

Living Room Coffeehouse **3**

The Marine Room **15**

Nine-Ten **1**

Piatti **14**

Whahoo's Fish Taco **24**

Zenbu **23**

ATTRACTIONS ●

Birch Aquarium at Scripps **13**

Children's Pool **2**

Ellen Browning Scripps Park **6**

La Jolla Playhouse **12**

Mount Soledad **16**

Museum of Contemporary
Art San Diego **19**

Torrey Pines State Reserve **9**

1111 Prospect St. (at Herschel Ave.), La Jolla, CA 92037. © **877/472-7474** or 858/454-1511. Fax 858/454-1531. www.hotelparisi.com. 27 units. $295–$495 double; from $525 suite. Rates include continental breakfast. AE, DC, DISC, MC, V. Parking $15. Bus: 30. Take Torrey Pines Rd. to Prospect Place and turn right; Prospect Place becomes Prospect St., turn left on Herschel Ave. **Amenities:** Restaurant; in-room spa treatments; room service; laundry service; dry cleaning. *In room:* A/C, TV, DVD, Wi-Fi, minibar w/complimentary beverages, coffeemaker, hair dryer, iron, safe, CD.

La Valencia Hotel ★★★   Looking much like a Mediterranean villa, "La V" has been the centerpiece of La Jolla since it opened in 1926. Brides still pose in front of the lobby's picture window, well-coiffed ladies lunch in the dappled shade of the garden patio, and neighborhood cronies quaff libations in the clubby **Whaling Bar.** All rooms are comfortably and traditionally furnished, with lavish appointments and all-marble bathrooms with signature toiletries. Because rates vary wildly according to the view (from sweeping to *nada*), get a cheaper room and enjoy the scene from one of the many lounges, serene garden terraces, or the amazing pool, which fronts the Pacific and nearby Scripps Park. Room decor, layouts, and size are all over the map, too; a few extra minutes with the reservationist will ensure a custom match for you. If you've got the bucks, spring for one of the newer villas (with fireplaces and butler service) and a meal at the hotel's 12-table **Sky Room,** one of the city's most celebrated dining rooms.

1132 Prospect St. (at Herschel Ave.), La Jolla, CA 92037. © **800/451-0772** or 858/454-0771. Fax 858/456-3921. www.lavalencia.com. 117 units. $285–$575 double; from $600 suites and villas; B&B packages from $358. 2-night minimum summer weekends. AE, DC, DISC, MC, V. Valet parking $17. Bus: 30. Take Torrey Pines Rd. to Prospect Place and turn right. Prospect Place becomes Prospect St. **Amenities:** 3 restaurants; bar; outdoor pool; exercise room with spa treatments; Jacuzzi; sauna; concierge; secretarial services; Wi-Fi; room service; babysitting; laundry service; dry cleaning. *In room:* A/C, TV/VCR/DVD, minibar, coffeemaker, hair dryer, iron, safe.

The Lodge at Torrey Pines ★★★   Patterned largely after the 1908 Greene & Greene–designed Gamble House (see chapter 14), the Lodge brims with perfectly assembled odes to Arts and Crafts style: clinker-brick masonry, art glass windows and doors, Stickley furniture, and exquisite pottery. The least expensive rooms are an unstinting 520 square feet, lavished with Tiffany-style lamps, period wallpaper, and framed Hiroshige prints, with lots of wood accents. Views face a courtyard carefully landscaped to mimic the rare coastal environment that exists just beyond the hotel grounds. More expensive rooms overlook the Torrey Pines Golf Course and the sea in the distance; most of these have balconies, fireplaces, and giant bathrooms with separate tub and shower. Sumptuous suites are also available. The 9,500-square-foot spa specializes in treatments utilizing coastal sage and other local plants; **A. R. Valentien,** the resort's excellent restaurant, also makes use of the region's top-quality seasonal products.

11480 N. Torrey Pines Rd., La Jolla, CA 92037. © **800/656-0087** or 858/453-4420. Fax 858/453-7464. www.lodgetorreypines.com. 175 units. From $575 double; from $900 suite. Children under 18 stay free in parent's room. AE, DC, DISC, MC, V. $27 valet parking; $22 self-parking. Bus: 101. From I-5 take La Jolla Village Dr. west, bear right (north) onto N. Torrey Pines Rd. **Amenities:** 2 restaurants; outdoor pool; preferential tee times at the golf course; fitness center; spa; whirlpool; concierge; pool table; gift shop; room service; laundry service; dry cleaning. *In room:* A/C, TV, Wi-Fi, minibar, coffeemaker, hair dryer, safe, fireplace and balcony in many units.

Expensive

The Bed & Breakfast Inn at La Jolla ★★ (Finds)   A house designed in 1913 by San Diego's first important architect, Irving Gill—and occupied in the 1920s by John Philip Sousa and his family—is the setting for this cultured and elegant B&B. Reconfigured as

lodging, the house has lost none of its charm, and its appropriately unfrilly period furnishings add to the sense of history. The inn also features lovely enclosed gardens and a
cozy library and sitting room. Sherry and fresh-cut flowers await in every room, some of
which feature a fireplace or ocean view. Each room has a private bathroom, most of
which are on the compact side. The furnishings are tasteful and cottage-style, with plenty
of historic photos of La Jolla. Gourmet breakfast is served wherever you desire—dining
room, patio, sun deck, or in your room.

7753 Draper Ave. (near Prospect), La Jolla, CA 92037. ✆ 800/582-2466 or 858/456-2066. Fax 858/456-
1510. www.innlajolla.com. 15 units. $210–$329 double; from $359 suite. 2-night minimum on weekends.
Rates include full breakfast and afternoon wine and cheese. AE, DISC, MC, V. Limited free parking. Bus: 30.
Take Torrey Pines Rd. to Prospect Place and turn right. Prospect Place becomes Prospect St.; proceed to
Draper Ave. and turn left. *In room:* A/C, hair dryer, iron.

The Grande Colonial ★★ (Finds)
Possessed of an old-world European flair that's
more London or Georgetown than seaside La Jolla, the Grande Colonial has earned
accolades for its meticulous restorations over the past decade. The most recent involves
the renovation of two adjacent properties, dating from 1925 and 1926, that add 18 more
suites to the Grande Colonial; some of the new suites feature ocean views, fireplaces, and
full kitchens. A large spray of fresh flowers is the focal point in the hotel lounge, where
guests gather in front of the fireplace for drinks—often before enjoying dinner at the
hotel's excellent **Nine-Ten** restaurant. Guest rooms are quiet and elegantly appointed,
with beautiful draperies and traditional furnishings. Many rooms in the original building
have sea views.

910 Prospect St. (btw. Fay and Girard), La Jolla, CA 92037. ✆ 888/530-5766 or 858/454-2181. Fax
858/454-5679. www.thegrandecolonial.com. 93 units. $305–$489 double; from $450 suite. Children
under 12 stay free in parent's room. AE, DC, DISC, MC, V. Valet parking $18. Bus: 30. Take Torrey Pines Rd.
to Prospect Place and turn right. Prospect Place becomes Prospect St. **Amenities:** Restaurant; outdoor
pool; access to nearby health club; concierge; room service; laundry service; dry cleaning. *In room:* A/C,
TV w/pay movies, Wi-Fi, hair dryer, iron, safe.

Moderate
Scripps Inn ★★ (Finds)
This secluded and meticulously maintained inn is hidden
away behind the Museum of Contemporary Art, with the attractions of La Jolla just a
short walk away. Only a small, grassy park comes between the inn and the beach, cliffs,
and tide pools; the view from the second-story deck can mesmerize guests, who gaze out
to sea indefinitely. Rates vary depending on ocean view (all have one, but some are better
than others). Rooms have a pleasantly pale palette and are furnished in "early American
comfortable," with new bathroom fixtures and appointments. All rooms have sofa beds;
two have wood-burning fireplaces, and four have kitchenettes. The inn supplies beach
towels, firewood, and French pastries each morning. Book a room here well in advance.

555 Coast Blvd. S. (at Cuvier), La Jolla, CA 92037. ✆ 858/454-3391. Fax 858/456-0389. www.scrippsinn.
com. 14 units. $175 double; from $265 suite. Extra person $10. Children under 5 stay free in parent's
room. Rates include continental breakfast. AE, DC, DISC, MC, V. Free parking. Bus: 30. Take Torrey Pines
Rd., turn right on Prospect Place; past the museum, turn right onto Cuvier. *In room:* Ceiling fans, TV, Wi-Fi,
fridge, coffeemaker, hair dryer, iron, safe.

Inexpensive
Wealthy, image-conscious La Jolla is not the best place for deep bargains, but if you're
determined to stay here on a budget, try the 30-room **La Jolla Village Lodge,** 1141
Silverado St. (✆ 877/551-2001 or 858/551-2001; www.lajollavillagelodge.com). This

motel with small, basic rooms has rates that vary wildly by season and day of the week—a room going for $90 midweek in winter doubles in price for a summer weekend.

CORONADO

Coronado is a great escape—with quiet, architecturally rich streets, a small-town, Navy-oriented atmosphere, and one of the state's most beautiful, welcoming beaches. Coronado's resorts are especially popular with Southern California and Arizona families for weekend escapes. Although downtown San Diego is just a 10-minute drive or 15-minute ferry ride away, you may feel pleasantly isolated on this peninsula, but it isn't the best choice if you plan to spend time in central parts of the city.

Very Expensive

Hotel del Coronado ★★★ Opened in 1888 and designated a National Historic Landmark in 1977, the "Hotel Del" is the last of California's stately old seaside hotels. This monument to Victorian grandeur boasts tall cupolas, red turrets, and gingerbread trim, all spread out over 31 acres. Even if you don't stay here, take a stroll through the sumptuous, wood-paneled lobby and along the wide, pristine beach, or enjoy Sunday brunch in the amazing **Crown Room.** Guest rooms—almost no two alike—run the gamut from compact to extravagant, and all are packed with antique charm. The least expensive rooms are snug and have views of a roof or parking lot; the best are junior suites with large windows and balconies fronting one of the state's finest white-sand beaches. Almost half the hotel's rooms are in the renovated, seven-story contemporary tower—it has more living space, but none of the historical ambience. Since 2001, the Del has done nonstop restoration and upgrading, most recently adding a state-of-the-art spa and creating Beach Village, a collection of 78 "coastal cottages." These privately owned two- and three-bedroom rental condos ($875–$2,275) feature fireplaces and oceanview balconies or terraces.

1500 Orange Ave., Coronado, CA 92118. ℂ **800/468-3533** or 619/435-6611. Fax 619/522-8238. www.hoteldel.com. 757 rooms. $300–$545 double; from $780 suite. Extra person $25. Children under 18 stay free in parent's room. Minimum stay requirements apply most weekends. $25/day resort fee. AE, DC, DISC, MC, V. Valet parking $30; self-parking $23. Bus: 901 or 904. From Coronado Bridge, turn left onto Orange Ave. **Amenities:** 5 restaurants; 4 bars; 2 outdoor pools; health club; full-service spa; 2 Jacuzzis; bike rental; children's activities; concierge; car-rental desk; airport shuttle; business center; shopping arcade; room service; babysitting; laundry service; dry cleaning. *In room:* A/C, TV w/pay movies, minibar, hair dryer, iron, safe.

Loews Coronado Bay Resort ★★ (Kids) The area's most removed hotel, this is the perfect place to really get away from it all. Located on its own private peninsula 4 miles south of downtown Coronado, across the highway from the Silver Strand State Beach, the Loews is an all-inclusive resort destination. There is a plethora of water-related activities such as sailing and jet-skiing from the private 80-slip marina; the Loews also has direct, private access to the beach. This is a family-friendly place with special (healthy) kids' menus, supervised children's activities, and teen-themed DVDs and Gameboys to borrow; pets are always welcome at Loews, too. Adult pleasures are plentiful as well, including romantic gondola rides through the canals of the adjacent Coronado Cays, an exclusive, waterside community; fine dining at the wonderful **Mistral** restaurant (ask for table 61 or 64 for best vistas); and a full-service spa.

4000 Coronado Bay Rd., Coronado, CA 92118. ℂ **866/563-9792** or 619/424-4000. Fax 619/424-4400. www.loewshotels.com. 440 units. $329–$379 double; from $575 suite. Children under 18 stay free in parent's room. AE, DC, DISC, MC, V. Valet parking $25; self-parking $19. Bus: 901. From Coronado Bridge, turn left on Orange Ave., left on Coronado Bay Rd. Packages available. Pets accepted w/$25 fee. **Amenities:**

2 restaurants; 1 bar; 3 outdoor pools; 3 tennis courts and lessons; fitness center and classes; spa; 2 Jacuzzis; watersports; gondola rides; surf lessons; kids and teens programs and services; concierge; business center; boutique; room service; babysitting; pet-sitting service; laundry/dry cleaning service; shoeshine service; private beach access. *In room:* A/C, TV w/pay movies, DVD player upon request, minibar, coffeemaker, hair dryer, iron, safe, CD player, 2-line phone.

Moderate

El Cordova Hotel ★ This Spanish hacienda across the street from the Hotel del Coronado began life as a private mansion in 1902. By the 1930s, it had become a hotel, the original building augmented by a series of attachments housing retail shops along the ground-floor arcade. Shaped like a baseball diamond and surrounding a courtyard with meandering tiled pathways, flowering shrubs, a swimming pool, and patio seating for **Miguel's Cocina** Mexican restaurant, El Cordova hums pleasantly with activity. Each room differs from the next—some have a Mexican Colonial feel, while others evoke comfy beach cottages. Most rooms have kitchenettes with gas stoves; all are no-frills, with ceiling fans and brightly tiled bathrooms. El Cordova's prime location makes it a popular option; make reservations well in advance of a summer stay.

1351 Orange Ave. (at Adella Ave.), Coronado, CA 92118. © **800/229-2032** or 619/435-4131. Fax 619/435-0632. www.elcordovahotel.com. 40 units. $185–$269 double; from $255 suite. Children under 12 stay free in parent's room. Weekly/monthly rates available in winter. AE, DC, DISC, MC, V. Parking nearby $6. Bus: 901 or 904. From Coronado Bridge, turn left onto Orange Ave. **Amenities:** 3 restaurants; outdoor pool; Jacuzzi; shopping arcade; coin-op laundry. *In room:* A/C, TV.

Glorietta Bay Inn ★★ Across the street from the Hotel Del, this pretty property consists of the historic John D. Spreckels mansion (1908) and several younger, motel-style buildings. The mansion has 11 rooms with original fixtures, a grand staircase, and old-fashioned wicker furniture; the guest rooms are also decked out in antiques. Rooms and suites in the 1950s annexes are much less expensive but only somewhat better than motel-plain; some have kitchenettes and marina views. The least expensive units are small with views of the parking lot. The hotel offers bikes as well as boat rentals on Glorietta Bay across the street, and it's within easy walking distance of the beach, golfing, tennis, watersports, shopping, and dining. Rooms in the mansion fill up early, but they're worth the extra effort and expense.

1630 Glorietta Blvd. (near Orange Ave.), Coronado, CA 92118. © **800/283-9383** or 619/435-3101. Fax 619/435-6182. www.gloriettabayinn.com. 100 units. Double $185–$650; from $425 suite. Extra person $10. Children under 18 stay free in parent's room. Minimum stays in summer. Rates include continental breakfast and afternoon refreshment. AE, DC, DISC, MC, V. Self-parking $10. Bus: 901 or 904. From Coronado Bridge, turn left on Orange Ave. After 2 miles, turn left onto Glorietta Blvd.; the inn is across the street from the Hotel del Coronado. **Amenities:** Outdoor pool; Jacuzzi; concierge; business center; babysitting; in-room massage; coin-op laundry and laundry service; dry cleaning. *In room:* A/C, TV w/pay movies, DVD player, fridge, coffeemaker, hair dryer, safe, CD player.

Inexpensive

The Village Inn (Value) Its location a block or two from Coronado's main sights—the Hotel Del, the beach, shopping, and cafes—is this inn's most appealing feature. Historic charm runs a close second; a plaque outside identifies the three-story brick-and-stucco hotel as the once-chic Blue Lantern Inn, built in 1928. The charming vintage lobby sets the mood in this European-style hostelry; each simple but well-maintained room holds a four-poster bed and antique dressers and armoires, plus lovely Battenberg lace bedcovers and shams. Front rooms enjoy the best view, and the communal full kitchen is available day and night for guest use. This appealing inn's only Achilles' heel is its tiny bathrooms, though some have been updated with Jacuzzi tubs to compensate.

1017 Park Place (at Orange Ave.), Coronado, CA 92118. ✆ **619/435-9318.** www.coronadovillageinn.com. 15 units. $85–$95 double. Rates include continental breakfast. AE, MC, V. Parking available on street. Bus: 901 or 904. From Coronado Bridge, turn left onto Orange Ave., and then right on Park Place. **Amenities:** Kitchen; library. *In room:* TV, whirlpool tubs (in some).

4 WHERE TO DINE

While San Diego hasn't achieved top-tier foodie status, its culinary profile is at an all-time high. Exciting, sophisticated restaurants seem to open monthly; Young Turk chefs mentored by major players are setting up shop here; and the region's longtime ace in the hole—year-round fresh produce and seafood—is finally receiving its full due at many establishments. The city still clings to conservative tastes and lacks a professional server class, but the pieces are in place and San Diego's dining renaissance is well underway.

What follows is an abbreviated sampling of highlights from the local dining scene, with an emphasis on the best of the best in all price categories, locations, and cuisines. For a greater selection of reviews, see *Frommer's San Diego 2009* (Wiley Publishing, Inc.). To locate these restaurants, see the "San Diego Accommodations & Dining" map, on p. 704, and the "La Jolla" map, on p. 717.

DOWNTOWN
Very Expensive

Candelas ★★ MEXICAN   This Gaslamp Quarter restaurant will forever alter your notion of Mexican food. If you're looking for tacos and burritos, go somewhere else. But for a sophisticated, romantic fine dining experience, look no further than Candelas. Owner Alberto Mestre and executive chef Eduardo Baeza are both natives of Mexico City and brought with them that city's culinary influences, which often blend Mexican and European elements. (After all, it was not so long ago Spanish and French flags flew over Mexico.) The chef's signature creation is *langosta Baeza:* fresh lobster in its shell, stuffed with mushrooms, chiles, onions, bacon, and tequila. Candelas also has a sexy lounge next door.

416 Third Ave. (at J St.), Gaslamp Quarter. ✆ **619/702-4455.** www.candelas-sd.com. Reservations recommended. Main courses $22–$53 dinner. AE, DC, DISC, MC, V. Mon–Sun 5–11pm. Valet parking Fri–Sat $15. Bus: 11 or 120. Trolley: Convention Center.

The Oceanaire Seafood Room ★★ SEAFOOD   As you sweep up the dramatic staircase of the Oceanaire, the retro-nautical decor may evoke the grand elegance of a *Titanic*-style luxury liner. The only iceberg ahead is of the lettuce variety, though, and this seafood eatery made it through its maiden voyage with flying colors to become a popular Gaslamp Quarter addition. A Minneapolis-based chain that opened here in 2004, Oceanaire features top local products as well as fish brought in daily from around the globe. Executive chef Brian Malarkey's preparations incorporate elements of Pacific Rim, Italian, classic French, and Asian cuisine; or you can have your catch-of-the-day simply grilled or broiled. Non–fish eaters can enjoy top-quality prime beef, chicken, and pork.

400 J St. (at Fourth Ave.), Gaslamp Quarter. ✆ **619/858-2277.** www.theoceanaire.com. Reservations recommended. Main courses $15–$50. AE, DISC, MC, V. Sun–Thurs 5–10pm; Fri–Sat 5–11pm. Valet parking from 6pm $10–$20. Bus: 3, 11, or 120. Trolley: Convention Center.

Expensive
Anthology ★★★ AMERICAN   It's difficult to categorize Anthology: Is it a fine-dining establishment or a world-class live music venue? The answer to both is a resounding yes.

Featuring a modern American menu created by James Beard–award winner Bradley Ogden (mastermind behind Northern California's acclaimed Lark Creek Inn and his own eponymous eatery at Caesar's Palace in Las Vegas, among others), Anthology is also a sophisticated, acoustically excellent concert hall. The music is eclectic, with an emphasis on jazz (think heavy hitters like Stanley Clarke, Poncho Sanchez, and Chick Corea), world music, and blues. The music won't drown out the food, though—in fact, you'll know the band onstage is really jamming when you're able to tear your attention away from your meal.

1337 India St. (btw. A and Ash sts.), downtown. ✆ **619/595-0300.** www.anthologysd.com. Reservations recommended. Main courses $19–$28. AE, DISC, MC, V. Tues–Thurs and Sun 5–11:30pm; Fri–Sat 5pm–1:30am. Valet parking $7. Bus: 83.

Chive ★★★ CALIFORNIAN   When it opened in 1999, this sleek and chic restaurant took the city by storm and put to rest any lingering doubts that local dining had come of age. The minimalist design and urban ethos were new to San Diego, and Chive struck an immediate chord. In 2006, the restaurant took a new tack, moving away from traditional three-course meals. Chive—still stylish as ever—now concentrates on small, shared plates (with some available as entree-size portions). The cuisine is as modern as the decor, taking a global approach with dishes such as a Moroccan-spiced chicken kabob and Kung Pao–style sweetbreads, while still making room for such unique comfort food as the crab mac 'n' cheese. The always-evolving wine list offers many intriguing selections by "cork" or "stem" from around the world. One lament: the cement floors and other hard surfaces amplify the noise level.

558 Fourth Ave. (at Market St.), Gaslamp Quarter. ✆ **619/232-4483.** www.chiverestaurant.com. Reservations recommended. Main courses $10–$36. AE, DISC, MC, V. Sun–Thurs 5–10pm; Fri–Sat 5–11pm. Valet parking Thurs–Sat $12–$17. Bus: 3, 11, or 120. Trolley: Convention Center.

Island Prime ★★ SEAFOOD   With its over-the-water dining, patio with fireplace, plentiful free parking, and spectacular bay and skyline views, it would be easy to understand if Island Prime didn't even bother to make its food interesting. Executive chef/partner Deborah Scott isn't just going through the motions here, though. With such dishes as shaved corn with black truffle and fresh herbs, hazelnut-crusted diver scallops, and porcini-dusted rack of Colorado lamb with Moroccan-spiced tomato jam, the views actually have some competition. The restaurant's C-Level Lounge serves lunch and has a bar menu of both food and specialty cocktails. Scott is also the mastermind behind the successful eateries **Kemo Sabe** and **Indigo Grill.** Both do mash-ups of Pacific Coast and Mexican/southwestern cuisine to good effect and are worth a visit. Kemo Sabe is at 3958 Fifth Ave., Hillcrest (✆ **619/220-6802**); Indigo Grill is at 1536 India St., Little Italy (✆ **619/234-6802**).

880 Harbor Island Dr., Embarcadero. ✆ **619/298-6802.** www.cohnrestaurants.com. Reservations recommended. Main courses $11–$29 lunch; $30–$49 dinner. AE, DC, DISC, MC, V. Sun–Thurs 11:30am–10pm; Fri–Sat 11:30am–11pm. Free parking. Bus: 923 or 992.

Moderate

Cafe Chloe ★★ FRENCH   This East Village restaurant created an immediate buzz when it opened in 2004. Had the owners struck upon some cutting-edge trend? No, it was a simple idea, really; something you'll find everywhere from Amsterdam to Zanzibar. It's a bistro. Whimsical touches abound, for sure—such as the children's area, a retail space, and a patio built for two—but this is a pretty straightforward enterprise, infused with its proprietors' refined tastes and *joie de vivre.* Yes, Cafe Chloe is small, it's loud when at capacity, and its tiny kitchen can get backed up. So what's the fuss about? The neighborly conviviality, combined with a short-but-sweet French-inspired menu covering breakfast, lunch, and dinner, makes for a winning experience—and one unique enough to create a stir in ever-morphing San Diego.

721 Ninth Ave. (at G St.), East Village. ✆ **619/232-3242.** www.cafechloe.com. Reservations for parties of 5 or more only. Main courses $8–$13 breakfast, $9–$13 lunch, $15–$28 dinner. AE, MC, V. Mon 11am–10pm; Tues–Fri 7am–10pm; Sat 8am–10pm; Sun 9am–9pm. Bus: 3, 5, 11, 901, or 929.

The Guild ★★ CALIFORNIAN   Just southeast of downtown in the decidedly non-touristy, rough-around-the-edges neighborhood of Barrio Logan, the Guild is flat-out one of the coolest places in town. Fans of contemporary food and design shouldn't miss it. Serving a small-plates menu that derives inspiration from Asian, Latin American, and Mediterranean cuisine, the Guild is also the base of operations for owner Paul Basile's design studio. Known throughout the city for his architectural metalwork, you can literally see the sparks fly in the large workshop attached to the rear of the restaurant. The restaurant itself features lots of glass, steel, and concrete elements, exposed raw materials, and linear forms. The Guild serves lunch, dinner, and Saturday brunch, with weekday happy hours from 3 to 6pm and 10 to 11pm.

1805 Newton Ave. (at Beardsley St.), Barrio Logan. ✆ **619/564-7584.** www.theguildrestaurant.com. Dinner reservations recommended. Main courses $7–$18 lunch, $12–$25 dinner. AE, MC, V. Tues–Fri 11am–11pm; Sat 9:30am–11pm (brunch served till 2pm). Free parking in lot. Bus: 929.

Red Pearl Kitchen ★★ CHINESE/ASIAN FUSION   Specializing in dim sum dishes with a contemporary, Pan Asian flair, this sexy Gaslamp Quarter restaurant is decorated in hues of deep red and features stone and tile accents, a cool pebbled floor, some nice deep booths, and two private dining areas. At Red Pearl, you may see a kung fu flick on one of the flatscreens over the bar or hear some chill tunes to go along with your strawberry-cinnamon short ribs, duck lettuce wraps, or wok-fired Kobe beef with papaya and mint; for dessert, don't miss the airy *andagi,* the Japanese version of a doughnut hole. Red Pearl also has an in-kitchen chef's table seating 4 to 12 people; bottles of wine are half-price on Sunday; and if you dine Tuesday through Sunday, bring your bill back on Monday and eat for half-off. Like any Chinese restaurant worth its noodles, Red Pearl also has takeout.

440 J St. (btw. Fourth and Fifth aves.), Gaslamp Quarter. ✆ **619/231-1100.** www.redpearlkitchen.com/sandiego. Reservations recommended. Main courses $7–$20. AE, MC, V. Sun–Wed 5pm–2am (dinner served until 10pm); Thurs–Sat 5pm–2am (dinner served until 11pm). Valet parking $15. Bus: 3, 11, or 120. Trolley: Convention Center or Gaslamp Quarter.

Inexpensive

Café Lulu COFFEE & TEA/LIGHT FARE   Smack-dab in the heart of the Gaslamp Quarter, Café Lulu aims for a hip, bohemian vibe, but if you're straight-arrow conservative, don't be put off—it's an inclusive place. Ostensibly a coffee bar, the cafe also makes a good choice for casual dining; you can keep an eye on the action from a sidewalk table or repair to the stylishly dark interior. The food is health conscious, largely prepared with organic ingredients. Soups, salads, cheese melts, and veggie lasagna are on the list; breads come from **Bread & Cie.** uptown (p. 726). Try one of the inventive coffee drinks, such as cafe Bohème (mocha with almond syrup); beer and wine are served, too. Café Lulu also stays open later than just about any other place downtown.

419 F St. (near Fourth Ave.), Gaslamp Quarter. ✆ **619/238-0114.** Main courses $6–$9. No credit cards. Sun–Thurs 11am–1am; Fri–Sat 11am–3am. Bus: 3 or 120. Trolley: Convention Center.

Filippi's Pizza Grotto (Value) ITALIAN   When longtime locals think "Little Italy,"
Filippi's often comes to mind. To get to the dining area, decorated with chianti bottles
and red-checked tablecloths, you walk through a "cash and carry" Italian grocery store
and deli stocked with cheeses, pastas, wines, bottles of olive oil, and salamis. You might
even end up eating behind shelves of canned olives, but don't feel bad—this has been a
tradition since 1950. Filippi's has more than 15 pizza varieties (including vegetarian),
plus huge portions of spaghetti, lasagna, and other pasta; children's portions are available,
too. The line to get in on Friday and Saturday can look intimidating, but it moves
quickly. This was the first of a dozen branches throughout the county, including one in
Pacific Beach at 962 Garnet Ave. (© **858/483-6222**).

1747 India St. (btw. Date and Fir sts.), Little Italy. © **619/232-5094.** www.realcheesepizza.com. Reservations Mon–Thurs for groups of 8 or more. Main courses $6–$13. AE, DC, DISC, MC, V. Sun–Mon 11am–10pm; Tues–Thurs 11am–10:30pm; Fri–Sat 11am–11:30pm. Deli opens daily at 8am. Free parking. Bus: 83. Trolley: Little Italy.

HILLCREST/UPTOWN
Very Expensive
Bertrand at Mister A's ★★★ AMERICAN/MEDITERRANEAN   Since 1965,
San Diegans have come to high-rise Mister A's for proms, anniversaries, power meals, and
other special occasions. Mister A's star began to wane in the '80s, though, despite its
unsurpassed views of Point Loma, downtown, and Balboa Park. In 2000, it finally
closed—only to reopen 4 months later, after a reported $1-million makeover under the
stewardship of one of San Diego's most successful restaurateurs, Bertrand Hug. The
original Mister A's, with its dark, red-velvet interiors and cocktail waitresses in campy
one-shouldered gowns, was reborn into Bertrand at Mister A's—an elegant, bright,
sophisticated space, with an array of modern art. The seasonal menu is modern American
with a French/Mediterranean twist; a bar/patio menu gives diners on a budget access to
the unsurpassed vistas.

2550 Fifth Ave. (at Laurel St.), Hillcrest. © **619/239-1377.** www.bertrandatmisteras.com. Reservations recommended. Main courses $13–$27 lunch, $28–$45 dinner. AE, DC, MC, V. Mon–Fri 11:30am–2:30pm and 5:30–9:30pm; Sat–Sun 5–9:30pm. Valet parking $7.50 (after 6pm). Bus: 3 or 120.

Expensive
Laurel Restaurant & Bar ★★ FRENCH/MEDITERRANEAN   Restaurateur
Tracy Borkum brought upscale, minimalist chic to the Gaslamp Quarter when she
opened **Chive** in 1999 (p. 723). Five years later she took ownership of, and completely
reinvented, Laurel, one of the city's premier dining destinations. Laurel offers a wonderful cassoulet; a main-course vegetable sampler; a seven-course chef's tasting meal; and a
daily three-course, prix-fixe meal from 5 to 6:30pm for $35. Many bottles of wine are
half-price on Sundays. Laurel's quirky interior design features bold black and white patterns, punctuated by highlights of chartreuse, Kelly green, and lipstick red. Mirrored
walls with arabesque and Joan Miró–inspired patterns reflect Swarovski crystal chandeliers, and bouquets of roses are suspended in large cylindrical vases like lab experiments.

505 Laurel St. (at Fifth Ave.), Balboa Park. © **619/239-2222.** www.sdurbankitchen.com. Reservations recommended. Main courses $22–$44. AE, DC, DISC, MC, V. Sun–Thurs 5–9:30pm; Fri–Sat 5–10:30pm. Valet parking $7. Bus: 3 or 120.

Parallel 33 ★★ (Finds) INTERNATIONAL   What do Morocco, Lebanon, India,
China, Iran, Iraq, and San Diego all have in common? They are all intersected by the

SAN DIEGO & ENVIRONS

same latitude—the 33rd parallel. In the upscale neighborhood of Mission Hills, Parallel 33 unites the unique flavors of those far-flung locales. Sit back and savor the creativity displayed in a menu that leaps enthusiastically from fragrant Moroccan lamb tagine to Goan shrimp curry. The ahi poke (raw tuna) appetizer fuses a Hawaiian mainstay with Asian pear, mango, and Japanese wasabi, and it's a winner. Next door is the restaurant's intimate, very chill lounge, **Blue Lotus,** which serves food from the same menu and warrants a visit on its own.

741 W. Washington St. (at Falcon), Mission Hills. ℂ **619/260-0033.** www.parallel33sd.com. Reservations suggested. Entrees $20–$34. AE, DISC, MC, V. Mon–Thurs 5:30–10pm; Fri–Sat 5:30–11pm. Bus: 10 or 83.

Moderate

Bite ★★ (Finds) CALIFORNIAN   San Diego gourmands are devoted to chef Chris Walsh, following him along the creative path he has cut through various local establishments. After his most recent tenure at the glitzy downtown supper club, fans are relieved to find him in the friendly confines of his own neighborhood restaurant. Stylishly modern with a hint of industrial lounge, Bite features a tapas-style roster of small plates that encourage grazing and sharing. The menu is seasonally driven and influenced by Northern Italian and French bistro fare; the wine list has nearly 30 interesting, reasonably priced wines by the glass. Bite allows you to invent your own cocktail, too: You can select mixers from a lineup of specialty sodas (pomegranate, pear, and so on), fresh juices, and house-infused sakes. Champagne fans can indulge in a bubbly happy hour from 5 to 7pm on weekdays.

1417 University Ave. (at Richmond St.), Hillcrest. ℂ **619/299-2483.** www.bitesd.com. No reservations, but call ahead to be placed on a priority-seating list. Small plates $6–$14. AE, DISC, MC, V. Mon and Wed–Thurs 5–10:30pm; Fri–Sat 5–11pm; Sun 5–10pm. Bus: 1, 10, or 11.

Modus ★ (Finds) CALIFORNIAN   Livening up sedate Bankers Hill, this cool little "gastro-lounge" has been a hit since opening in 2006. It features mood lighting, a zigzagging bar, a mod fireplace, DJs, and a patio with a water-wall feature. The modern European bistro cuisine has a California flair, incorporating fresh, local, organic products. Look for classics such as onion soup and confit of duck, as well as vegetarian items, cheese and charcuterie plates, and a killer hamburger. A bar menu is served until 1am. Modus also takes its wine and cocktail program seriously, and has a roster of creative drinks and boutique wines.

2202 Fourth Ave. (at Ivy St.), Bankers Hill. ℂ **619/236-8516.** www.modusbar.com. Reservations recommended Fri–Sat. Main courses $14–$24. AE, DISC, MC, V. Tues–Sun 5pm–1:30am. Free parking after 6pm. Bus: 3 or 120.

Inexpensive

Bread & Cie. ★★ LIGHT FARE/MEDITERRANEAN   The traditions of European artisan bread-making and attention to the fine points of texture and crust quickly catapulted Bread & Cie. to local stardom—they now supply bread to more than 75 local restaurants. Some favorites are available daily, such as anise and fig, black olive, and jalapeño and cheese; others are available just 1 or 2 days a week: say, the garlic and goat cheese (Sun and Thurs), or the hunky walnut and scallion (Wed and Sat). Ask for a free sample or order one of the many Mediterranean-inspired sandwiches. A specialty coffee drink, delivered in a bowl-like mug, perfectly accompanies a light breakfast of fresh scones, muffins, or homemade granola with yogurt.

350 University Ave. (at Fourth St.), Hillcrest. ℂ **619/683-9322.** www.breadandcie.com. Reservations not accepted. Sandwiches and light meals $4–$9. DISC, MC, V. Mon–Fri 7am–7pm; Sat 7am–6pm; Sun 8am–6pm. Bus: 1, 3, 10, 11, or 120.

Bronx Pizza ★ (Finds) ITALIAN   No one is going to confuse San Diego with New
York—unless you walk into Bronx Pizza in Hillcrest. This pizzeria, serving up what are arguably San Diego's best pies, has two small dining areas separated by a covered patio. With its red vinyl booths, checkered curtains, and pictures of boxers on the walls, the interior dining room looks as if it were airlifted straight out of the boroughs. Bronx Pizza makes only pizzas and calzones—no salads, no chicken wings. And if there's a line out the door (which is a pretty frequent occurrence), don't hesitate to order when you get to the counter: These guys will definitely drop a little New York attitude on you, and you may find yourself living out the *Seinfeld* Soup Nazi episode. Choices are simple, though. It's all thin-crust, 18-inch pies, or by the slice, with straightforward toppings—although Bronx Pizza has made concessions to the locals by including such ingredients as marinated artichokes and pesto.

111 Washington St. (at First Ave.), Hillcrest. (C) 619/291-3341. www.bronxpizza.com. Phone orders accepted for full pies. Pies $13–$19; $2.50 by the slice. No credit cards. Sun–Thurs 11am–10pm; Fri–Sat 11am–11pm. Street parking. Bus: 3, 10, or 83.

Extraordinary Desserts ★★★ DESSERTS   Dozens of divine creations are available daily, and many are garnished with edible gold or flowers. Among them: a passion fruit–ricotta torte bursting with kiwis, strawberries, and bananas; a *gianduia* of chocolate cake lathered with hazelnut butter cream, chocolate mousse, and boysenberry preserves, and sprinkled with shards of praline; or the *bête noir*, which is a dark-chocolate cake layered with vanilla crème brûlée, chocolate mousse, and chocolate truffle cream. An exclusive line of jams, chutneys, syrups, spices, and confections is carried at both the original location and the architecturally striking second space in Little Italy, 1430 Union St. ((C) 619/294-7001). The Little Italy location also serves panini, salads, and artisan cheeses, as well as wine and beer.

2929 Fifth Ave. (btw. Palm and Quince sts.). (C) 619/294-2132. www.extraordinarydesserts.com. Desserts $2–$9. MC, V. Mon–Thurs 8:30am–11pm; Fri 8:30am–midnight; Sat 10am–midnight; Sun 10am–11pm. Street parking usually available. Bus: 3 or 120.

OLD TOWN & MISSION VALLEY
Expensive
Cafe Pacifica ★★ CALIFORNIA/SEAFOOD   Inside this cozy Old Town casita, the decor is cleanly contemporary (but still romantic), and the food is anything but Mexican. Established in 1980, Cafe Pacifica serves upscale, imaginative seafood at decent prices; among the temptations are crab-stuffed portobello mushrooms topped with grilled asparagus, anise-scented bouillabaisse, and daily fresh-fish selections grilled with your choice of six sauces. Signature items include Hawaiian ahi with shiitake mushrooms and ginger butter, griddled mustard catfish, and the "Pomerita," a pomegranate margarita. Arrive before 6:30pm and you can take advantage of the early bird special: entree with soup or salad and dessert for $21.

2414 San Diego Ave., Old Town. (C) 619/291-6666. www.cafepacifica.com. Reservations recommended. Main courses lunch $12–$30, dinner $13–$30. AE, DC, DISC, MC, V. Wed–Fri 11:30am–2pm; Mon–Sat 5–10pm; Sun 4:30–9:30pm. Valet parking $5. Bus: Numerous Old Town routes including 8, 9, 10, 14, 28, and 30. Trolley: Old Town.

El Agave Tequileria ★★ MEXICAN   Don't be misled by this restaurant's less-than-impressive location above a liquor store. The regional Mexican cuisine here leaves Old Town's touristy fajitas and *cerveza* joints far behind. El Agave is named for the plant from which tequila and its smoky cousin mescal are derived, and the restaurant boasts more than 850 different brands—bottles of every size, shape, and jewel-like hue fill shelves and cases throughout the dining room. Needless to say, El Agave serves some of the best margaritas in town. Even teetotalers, though, will enjoy the restaurant's authentically flavored mole sauces—from Taxco, rich with walnuts; tangy tomatillo from Oaxaca; and the more familiar dark mole flavored with chocolate and sesame. Lunches are inexpensive and simple, without the exotic sauces.

2304 San Diego Ave., Old Town. ✆ 619/220-0692. www.elagave.com. Reservations recommended. Main courses $8–$11 lunch, $16–$32 dinner. AE, MC, V. Daily 11am–10pm. Street parking. Bus: Numerous Old Town routes including 8, 9, 10, 14, 28, and 30. Trolley: Old Town.

Moderate

Berta's Latin American Restaurant ★ (Finds) LATIN AMERICAN Berta's is a welcome change from the nacho-and-taco joints that dominate Old Town. Housed in a cottage tucked on a side street, Berta's faithfully re-creates the sunny flavors of Central and South America, where slow cooking mellows the heat of chiles and other spices. Everyone starts with a basket of fresh flour tortillas and mild salsa verde, which usually vanishes before you're through contemplating such mouthwatering dishes as Guatemalan *chilemal,* a rich pork-and-vegetable casserole with chilies, tomatoes, cornmeal *masa,* cilantro, and cloves. For lunch, try the Salvadoran *pupusas*—dense corn-mash turnovers with melted cheese and black beans. Or graze on a table full of Spanish-style tapas—crispy empanadas, strong Spanish olives, or *pincho moruno,* skewered lamb and onion redolent of spices and red saffron.

3928 Twiggs St. (at Congress St.), Old Town. ✆ 619/295-2343. www.bertasinoldtown.com. Main courses $7–$12 lunch, $13–$17 dinner. AE, DISC, MC, V. Tues–Sun 11am–10pm (lunch menu till 3pm). Free parking. Bus: Numerous Old Town routes including 8, 9, 10, 14, 28, and 30. Trolley: Old Town.

Inexpensive

The Living Room COFFEE/TEA/LIGHT FARE Grab a patio table in the courtyard of this lovely old house and enjoy splendid people-watching. The pastries are fine, but it's the light meals—breakfast, lunch, and dinner—that make this a good choice. Breakfast includes omelets and waffles; later in the day, try the turkey lasagna, tuna melt, or one of several hearty entree salads. You'll also find exotic iced or hot coffees and Italian sodas. Additional locations are in **La Jolla** at 1010 Prospect St. (✆ 858/459-1187), **Point Loma** at 1018 Rosecrans (✆ 619/222-6852), and near **San Diego State University,** at 5900 El Cajon Blvd. (✆ 619/286-8434).

2541 San Diego Ave., Old Town. ✆ 619/325-4445. www.livingroomcafe.com. Most menu items $6–$9. AE, DISC, MC, V. Sun–Thurs 7am–10pm; Fri–Sat 7am–midnight. Bus: Numerous Old Town routes including 8, 9, 10, 14, 28, and 30. Trolley: Old Town.

MISSION BAY & THE BEACHES
Very Expensive

Baleen ★★ SEAFOOD/CALIFORNIAN This attractive waterfront eatery is right in the middle of Mission Bay at the Paradise Point Resort. With its lush bayfront view (and a dining deck that's sublime on warm evenings), it's easy to miss the design details indoors—from a monkey motif that includes simians hanging off chandeliers to specialized serving platters for many of Baleen's artistically arranged dishes. Ocean fare takes precedence, and local fish and shellfish are featured in a chef's tasting menu; also on offer is the classic surf and turf or a selection of wood-roasted meats and seafood. ***Note:*** This is a family-oriented

Tips   **Eating on the Go: Baja Fish Tacos**

A native of Baja California, fish tacos were popularized in San Diego by **Rubio's Baja Grill** in the early 1980s. Rubio's has since grown into a sizable chain, and it's a good option if you're on the go—the original stand is still operating at the east end of Pacific Beach, 4504 E. Mission Bay Dr. (℃ 858/272-2801). Better yet are such retail fish market/eateries as **Bay Park Fish Co.** ★, 4121 Ashton St., Bay Park (℃ 619/276-3474); **Blue Water Seafood Market and Grill** ★, 3667 India St., Mission Hills (℃ 619/497-0914); and **Point Loma Seafoods** ★, 2805 Emerson St., Point Loma (℃ 619/223-1109).

Other top choices include the **Brigantine,** 2725 Shelter Island Dr., Shelter Island (℃ 619/224-2871), 1333 Orange Ave., Coronado (℃ 619/435-4166), and 3263 Camino del Mar, Del Mar (℃ 858/481-1166); **Mamá Testa** ★, 1417A University Ave., Hillcrest (℃ 619/298-8226); **South Beach Bar & Grill,** 5059 Newport Ave., Ocean Beach (℃ 619/226-4577); and **Wahoo's Fish Taco,** 639 Pearl St., La Jolla (℃ 858/459-0027) and 2195 Station Village Way, Mission Valley (℃ 619/299-4550).

resort, so knee-high types may be sharing the space; a children's menu goes beyond the usual burgers-and-fries option to include items such as shrimp scampi and petit filet.

1404 Vacation Rd. (Paradise Point Resort), Mission Bay. ℃ **858/490-6363.** www.paradisepoint.com. Reservations recommended. Main courses $22–$75. AE, DC, DISC, MC, V. Sun–Thurs 5–9pm; Fri–Sat 5–10pm. Free parking. Bus: 8 or 9.

Expensive

Thee Bungalow ★★ FRENCH   For some 35 years, this small cottage, standing alone at the edge of Robb Field near the Ocean Beach channel, has been a romantic hideaway beckoning diners for consistently rewarding Continental cuisine. By far the fanciest restaurant in laid-back Ocean Beach, Thee Bungalow has endeared itself with its excellent wine list and house specialties such as crispy roast duck served with a choice of sauces (such as black cherry), *osso-buco*-style lamb shank with shallot–red wine purée, and decadent made-to-order dessert soufflés for two (chocolate or orange liqueur). Thee Bungalow also offers early bird specials (Mon–Thurs 5:30–6:15pm, Sun 5–5:45pm), along with a selection of bottled wines for $20 each.

4996 W. Point Loma Blvd. (at Bacon St.), Ocean Beach. ℃ **619/224-2884.** www.cohnrestaurants.com. Reservations recommended. Main courses $19–$34, early bird specials $16–$19. AE, DC, DISC, MC, V. Mon–Thurs 5:30–9:30pm; Fri–Sat 5–10pm; Sun 5–9pm. Free parking. Bus: 35 or 923.

Moderate

Caffé Bella Italia ★★ ITALIAN   Caffé Bella's odd-looking stucco exterior, in a less-than-promising section of P.B., looks like a dry cleaner adorned with umbrellas because it once *was* a spot for 1-hour Martinizing. It's lovely inside, however, with romantic lighting, sheer draperies, and earthy walls. Staff members, many with lilting Milanese accents, welcome guests like family. And the food can knock your socks off—every item on the menu bears the unmistakable flavor of freshness and homemade care. It's the best spot in the area for shellfish-laden pasta and wood-fired pizzas; even the simplest curled-edge ravioli stuffed with ricotta, spinach, and pine nuts is elevated to culinary perfection. Lunch is served on Saturday only.

1525 Garnet Ave. (btw. Ingraham and Haines), Pacific Beach. ✆ **858/273-1224.** www.caffebellaitalia. com. Reservations suggested for dinner. Main courses $9–$17 lunch, $13–$27 dinner. AE, DC, DISC, MC, V. Daily 4:30–10pm; Sat noon–10pm. Free (small) parking lot. Bus: 8, 9, or 27.

The Fishery ★ (Finds) SEAFOOD You're guaranteed fresh-off-the-boat seafood at this off-the-beaten-track establishment, which is really a wholesale warehouse and retail fish market with a casual restaurant attached. Regular menu favorites include spicy mahi-mahi, chargrilled and topped with jalapeño butter; king salmon Oscar, layered with garlic mashed potatoes and grilled asparagus, Dungeness crab, and hollandaise; or—the favorite—sea bass, charbroiled with a soy-ginger marinade. You can keep it simple at lunch or dinner with bacon-wrapped scallops over a delectable salad, or the very reliable fish and chips; a couple of vegetarian stir-fry entrees are always available, too. *Note:* As of this writing, the Fishery was undergoing major renovations that will add two-dozen more seats and a small wine bar.

5040 Cass St. (at Opal, ¾ mile north of Garnet), Pacific Beach. ✆ **858/272-9985.** www.pacshell.com. Reservations recommended for dinner. Main courses $8–$21 lunch, $9–$28 dinner. AE, DC, DISC, MC, V. Daily 11am–10pm. Street parking usually available. Bus: 30.

Gringo's ★ MEXICAN This upscale space features warm woods, cool flagstone, and trendy lighting; a large patio is primed with heaters and fire pits most evenings. The menu offers dishes the average gringo will recognize (quesadillas, fajitas, burritos), but flip it over and you'll find regional specialties from all over Mexico—Oaxaca, the Yucatán, and Mexico's Pacific coast. Look for chicken breast stuffed with goat cheese and corn, and then lathered in a sauce of *huitlacoche;* or a poblano chile stuffed with *picadillo* and draped in walnut-cream sauce with a drizzle of pomegranate reduction. The margarita options, with more than 100 tequilas available, are worth inspecting, as are the Mexican wines. Sunday brunch is available from 9am to 2pm.

4474 Mission Blvd. (at Garnet Ave.), Pacific Beach. ✆ **858/490-2877.** www.gringoscantina.com. Reservations suggested for weekends. Main courses $6–$14 lunch, $8–$31 dinner, $20 brunch. AE, DC, DISC, MC, V. Mon–Sat 11am–11pm; Sun 9am–11pm. Bus: 8, 9, 27, or 30.

Sushi Ota ★★★ (Finds) SUSHI Masterful chef/owner Yukito Ota creates San Diego's finest sushi. This sophisticated, traditional restaurant (no Asian fusion here) is a minimalist bento box with stark white walls and black furniture, softened by indirect lighting. The sushi menu is short—discerning regulars look first to the daily specials posted behind the counter. The city's most experienced chefs, with nimble fingers and seriously sharp knives, turn the day's fresh catch into artful bundles. The rest of the varied menu features seafood, teriyaki-glazed meats, tempura, and appetizers perfect for accompanying sushi. The restaurant is in a nondescript part of Pacific Beach, behind a laundromat and convenience store in a mini-mall, though none of that should discourage you from seeking it out.

4529 Mission Bay Dr. (at Bunker Hill), Pacific Beach. ✆ **858/270-5670.** Reservations strongly recommended on weekends. Main courses $6–$14 lunch, $9–$22 dinner, sushi $4–$13. AE, MC, V. Tues–Fri 11:30am–2pm; Tues–Thurs 5:30–10:30pm; Fri–Sun 5–10:30pm. Free parking (additional lot behind the mall). Bus: 30.

Inexpensive

The Mission ★ (Value) BREAKFAST/LIGHT FARE Set alongside the funky surf shops and bikini boutiques of bohemian Mission Beach, this is the neighborhood's central meeting place. It attracts more than just locals, however, and it has siblings near the ballpark and east of Hillcrest. The menu features all-day breakfasts, from traditional pancakes to nouvelle egg dishes to burritos and quesadillas; standouts include tamales and eggs with tomatillo sauce, chicken-apple sausage with eggs and a mound of rosemary potatoes, and cinnamon French toast with blackberry purée. At lunch, the menu expands for sandwiches, salads, and a few Chino-Latino items such as ginger-sesame chicken tacos. The other locations are at 2801 University Ave., in North Park (© **619/220-8992**), and in a historic building at 1250 J St., downtown (© **619/232-7662**). Expect waits of half an hour or more on weekends.

3795 Mission Blvd. (at San Jose), Mission Beach. © **858/488-9060.** www.themission1.signonsandiego. com. All items $6–$10. AE, MC, V. Daily 7am–3pm. Bus: 8 or 9.

LA JOLLA
Very Expensive

Georges California Modern ★★★ CALIFORNIAN   This is perhaps La Jolla's signature restaurant. It has it all: stunning ocean views, style, impeccable service, and above all, a world-class chef. Not resting on its considerable laurels, though, Georges closed briefly in early 2007, undergoing a $2.5-million renovation. It reemerged with a slightly new name (it had been known as George's at the Cove since opening in 1984), and a new design-forward environment. Most importantly, though, Trey Foshee can still be found in the kitchen. Foshee, named one of America's top-10 chefs by *Food & Wine*, has been set loose stylistically—the menu is larger and more adventurous than before (still driven by the freshest local ingredients available), incorporating more cross-cultural influences. Those seeking fine food and incomparable views at more modest prices can head upstairs to the **Ocean Terrace** and **George's Bar.** These two spaces offer indoor and outdoor seating, as well as food from the same kitchen as the pricey main dining room. Lunch is served here daily.

1250 Prospect St., La Jolla. © **858/454-4244.** www.georgesatthecove.com. Reservations strongly recommended. Main courses $26–$90. AE, DC, DISC, MC, V. Sun–Thurs 5:30–10pm; Fri–Sat 5–10:30pm. Ocean Terrace Bistro main courses $10–$15 lunch, $16–$29 dinner. Daily 11am–10pm (Fri–Sat till 10:30pm). Valet parking $7. Bus: 30.

Jack's La Jolla ★★★ AMERICAN   Centering on an open-air courtyard that takes full advantage of sunny days and mild nights, this multistory epicurean funhouse ranges from sidewalk coffee stop to third-floor sushi bar, plus has a fine-dining component and a couple of bars and lounges (with live music and DJs) thrown in for good measure. Jack's is built around the talents and modern American fare of chef/owner Tony DiSalvo, formerly chef de cuisine at Jean-Georges in New York City. Jack's middle level features the chic **Wall Street Bar,** the most sedate of Jack's lounge areas, and the **Dining Room at Jack's.** This formal dining space is modern but warm (one caveat: the closer you get to the atrium, the more sound you'll hear welling up from the lower depths). **Jack's Grille** provides more casual dining; the **Ocean Room** offers lunch and dinner (and has private cabanas with ocean views); while the **Sidewalk Cafe** serves baked goods, pizzas, panini, smoothies, and salads.

7863 Girard Ave., La Jolla. © **858/456-8111.** www.jackslajolla.com. Reservations recommended. The Dining Room main courses $22–$44. AE, DC, DISC, MC, V. Sun 5:30–8:30pm; Tues 5:30–9pm; Wed–Sat 5:30–10pm. Jack's Grille main courses $10–$44. Sun–Wed 5–9:30pm; Thurs–Sat 5–11pm. Ocean Room main courses $11–$14 lunch, $22–$40 dinner. Daily 11:30am–2:30pm; Sun–Wed 5:30–9:30pm; Thurs–Sat 5:30–11pm. Sidewalk Cafe Sun–Tues 8am–8pm; Wed–Thurs 8am–10pm; Fri–Sat 8am–11pm. Bars and lounges till 2am Thurs–Sat (Wall St. Bar and sushi bar closed Mon). Valet parking Tues–Sun 11:30am–close $5. Bus: 30.

The Marine Room ★★★ ⓜ(Moments FRENCH/CALIFORNIAN   Since 1941, San Diego's most celebrated dining room has been this shorefront institution. It wasn't until the 1994 arrival of Executive Chef Bernard Guillas of Brittany, though, that the food finally lived up to its glass-fronted room with a view. Guillas and Chef de Cuisine Ron Oliver work with local produce, but never hesitate to pursue unusual flavors from other corners of the globe—such as pomegranate-macadamia-coated organic salmon with red quinoa, bok choy, Serrano ham, and Kaffir lime-leaf infusion. The Marine Room ranks as one of San Diego's most expensive venues, but it's usually filled to the gills on weekends; weekdays it's much easier to score a table. Ideally, schedule your reservation a half-hour or so before sunset; or experience sundown by the bar, where a lounge menu is available.

2000 Spindrift Dr., La Jolla. ⓒ **866/644-2351.** www.marineroom.com. Reservations recommended, especially weekends. Main courses $27–$44. AE, DC, DISC, MC, V. Sun–Thurs 5:30–9:30pm; Fri–Sat 5:30–10pm. Valet parking $6. Bus: 30.

Expensive

Nine-Ten ★★ CALIFORNIA   This warmly stylish space is the place for market-fresh cuisine, prepared by Jason Knibb, another member of San Diego's cadre of skilled young chefs. Knibb, who was mentored by such culinary figures as Wolfgang Puck, Roy Yamaguchi, and Hans Rockenwagner, presides over a shape-shifting, seasonal menu that's best enjoyed via small-plate grazings—past offerings have included espresso-and-chocolate-braised boneless short ribs, Maine scallops with apple risotto, and harissa-marinated shrimp. Or better yet, you can turn yourself over to the "Mercy of the Chef," a five-course tasting menu for $80, or $120 with wine pairings (your whole table has to play along, though). When you're looking for a classy fine-dining experience—without the old-guard attitude—this hotel eatery fits the bill.

910 Prospect St. (btw. Fay and Girard), La Jolla. ⓒ **858/964-5400.** www.nine-ten.com. Reservations recommended. Main courses $6–$18 breakfast, $11–$18 lunch, $13–$40 dinner. AE, DC, DISC, MC, V. Daily 6:30–11am (Sun 12:30pm), 11:30am–2:30pm, and 6–10pm. Valet parking $2. Bus: 30.

Zenbu ★★ SUSHI/SEAFOOD   La Jolla native Matt Rimel loved fishing so much, he bought a commercial fishing boat. "Nobody buys local fish, so in order to keep doing it, I had to open a restaurant," he says. He still owns that local boat, as well as two additional restaurants; he also launched Ocean Giant, an international fleet that fishes exclusively for himself and other clients. There are so many fresh, tempting things on the menu that decision-making at Zenbu is no easy task. You can order something from the sushi bar such as exquisite toro, creamy *uni* (sea urchin), or one of the specialty rolls. Or maybe an entree such as steak of locally harpooned swordfish, or grilled local fish of the day. There's also the fabulous lobster dynamite, a half lobster (local, naturally) and crab baked in a special sauce and given a dramatic, flaming presentation. Next door, intimate **Zenbu Lounge** (Thurs–Sat) has a sushi bar and DJs.

7660 Fay Ave. (at Kline St.), La Jolla. ⓒ **858/454-4540.** www.zenbusushi.com. Reservations not accepted. Main courses $22–$30. AE, DC, DISC, MC, V. Sun–Wed 5–9:30pm; Thurs–Sat 5–10:30pm. Happy hour all night Sun–Tues; Wed–Thurs till 6:30pm. Lounge Thurs–Sat 8pm–1am. Free parking. Bus: 30.

Moderate

Brockton Villa ★ BREAKFAST/CALIFORNIA   A restored 1894 beach bungalow, this charming cafe occupies a breathtaking perch overlooking La Jolla Cove. The biggest buzz is at breakfast, when you can enjoy inventive dishes such as soufflélike "Coast Toast" (the house take on French toast) and Greek "steamers" (eggs scrambled with an espresso steamer, and then mixed with feta cheese, tomato, and basil). Breakfasts are served till noon weekdays; till 3pm weekends. Lunch highlights include homemade soups and salads, plus such sandwiches as the grilled organic salmon BLT. The somewhat less successful supper menu includes seafood and steak dishes, plus paella, pastas, and grilled meats. *Note:* Steep stairs from the street limit wheelchair access.

1235 Coast Blvd. (across from La Jolla Cove), La Jolla. © **858/454-7393**. www.brocktonvilla.com. Reservations recommended. Main courses $7–$12 breakfast, $10–$15 lunch, $16–$30 dinner. AE, DISC, MC, V. Mon 8am–3pm; Tues–Sun 8am–9pm. Bus: 30.

Piatti ★ ITALIAN/MEDITERRANEAN La Jolla's version of the neighborhood hangout is this pasta-centric trattoria a couple of blocks inland from La Jolla Shores. Come here on Friday or Saturday evening and you're likely to be surrounded by a crew of regulars who pop in once or twice a week and know all the staff by name. You won't feel left out, however, and the food is well priced. The lemon herb-roasted chicken and *bistecca* (rib-eye) are fantastic, but it's the pastas that parade out to most tables. Try *orecchiette* bathed in Gorgonzola or *pappardelle* "fantasia"—shrimp-crowned ribbons of saffron pasta, primed with garlic, tomato, and white wine. The outdoor patio, beneath the sprawl of an enormous ficus tree, is ideal for dining any night.

2182 Avenida de la Playa. © **858/454-1589**. www.piatti.com. Reservations recommended. Main courses $11–$27; Sat–Sun brunch $9–$18. AE, DC, DISC, MC, V. Mon–Thurs 11:30am–10pm; Fri 11:30am–11pm; Sat 11am–11pm; Sun 11am–10pm. Street parking usually available. Bus: 30.

Inexpensive
The Cottage ★ BREAKFAST/LIGHT FARE La Jolla's best breakfast is served at this turn-of-the-20th-century bungalow on a sunny village corner. The cottage is light and airy, but most diners opt for tables outside, where a charming white picket fence encloses the trellis-shaded brick patio. Omelets and egg dishes feature Mediterranean, Cal-Latino, and classic American touches. Homemade granola is a favorite as well (it's even packaged and sold to go). The Cottage also bakes its own muffins, rolls, and coffee cakes. Breakfast dishes are served all day, but toward lunchtime the kitchen begins turning out freshly made, healthful soups, light meals, and sandwiches. Dinners, served during summer only, are a delight, particularly when you're seated before dark on a balmy night.

7702 Fay Ave. (at Kline St.), La Jolla. © **858/454-8409**. www.cottagelajolla.com. Reservations accepted for dinner only. Main courses $8–$11 breakfast, $9–$14 lunch, $9–$30 dinner. AE, DISC, MC, V. Daily 7:30am–3pm; dinner (June–Aug only) Tues–Sat 5–9:30pm. Bus: 30.

CORONADO
Very Expensive
1500 Ocean ★★ CALIFORNIA The Hotel del Coronado's longtime fine dining option, the **Prince of Wales,** was dethroned by 1500 Ocean, which opened to enthusiastic reviews in 2006. This smart, contemporary space eschews the Del's ever-present Victoriana for a stylish California Craftsman look. The menu is California oriented as well, featuring a Southland coastal cuisine that draws inspiration—and top-quality product—from throughout the region, from Baja to Santa Barbara. A three-course tasting menu is offered, as well as such entrees as lamb porterhouse with stewed fennel and pan-seared scallops in a black truffle vinaigrette. For dessert, don't miss the spicy chipotle chocolate cake. There's also fabulous patio dining, with views of the ocean and Point Loma.

1500 Orange Ave., Coronado. ✆ **619/522-8490.** www.dine1500ocean.com. Reservations recommended. Main courses $27–$42. AE, DC, DISC, MC, V. Daily 5:30–10:30pm. Bar until midnight. Bus: 901 or 904.

Expensive

Chez Loma ★ FRENCH   This intimate Victorian cottage filled with antiques and subdued candlelight makes for romantic dining. The structure dates from 1889, the French-Continental restaurant from 1975. Tables are scattered throughout the house and on the enclosed garden terrace; an upstairs wine salon, reminiscent of a Victorian parlor, is a cozy spot for coffee or conversation. Among the entrees are salmon with smoked-tomato vinaigrette; and roast duckling with lingonberry, port, and burnt-orange sauce. Follow dinner with a silky crème caramel or a desert sampler. California wines and American microbrews are available, in addition to a full bar; early birds enjoy special prices—$25 for a three-course meal before 6pm and all night on Tuesday.

1132 Loma (off Orange Ave.), Coronado. ✆ **619/435-0661.** www.chezloma.com. Reservations recommended. Main courses $23–$36. AE, DC, DISC, MC, V. Tues–Sun 5–10pm. Bus: 901 or 904.

Moderate

Rhinoceros Cafe & Grill AMERICAN   This bright bistro is more casual than it looks from the street and offers large portions, although the kitchen can be a little heavy handed with sauces and spices. At lunch, every other patron seems to be enjoying the *penne à la vodka* in creamy tomato sauce; favorite dinner specials are Italian cioppino and southwestern-style meatloaf. Plenty of crispy fresh salads balance out the main courses. The wine list is fair.

1166 Orange Ave., Coronado. ✆ **619/435-2121.** www.rhinocafe.com. Main courses $6–$12 lunch, $12–$27 dinner. AE, DC, DISC, MC, V. Daily 11am–2:30pm; Sun–Thurs 5–9pm; Fri–Sat 5–10pm. Street parking available. Bus: 901 or 904.

Inexpensive

Villa Nueva Bakery Café (Value) BREAKFAST/LIGHT FARE   In addition to fresh-roasted coffee and espresso drinks, this sometimes-too-casual cafe serves omelets, bagels and lox, and other breakfast treats (until 2pm), deli sandwiches on delicious house bread, and a daily fresh soup. It's the kind of spot where half the customers are greeted by name. Regulars rave about the "Yacht Club" sandwich, a croissant filled with yellowfin tuna, and the breakfast croissant, topped with scrambled eggs, ham, and cheddar cheese. Those fat, gooey cinnamon buns are every bit as good as they look.

956 Orange Ave., Coronado. ✆ **619/435-4191.** Main courses $5–$9. AE, DC, DISC, MC, V. Daily 6:30am–6pm. Bus: 901 or 904.

5 THE THREE MAJOR ANIMAL PARKS

San Diego Wild Animal Park ★★★ (Kids)   Thirty-four miles north of San Diego, outside Escondido, this terrific "zoo of the future" will transport you to the African plains and other faraway landscapes. Originally a breeding facility for the San Diego Zoo, the 1,800-acre Wild Animal Park now holds 3,500 animals representing some 430 species. Many of the animals roam freely in vast enclosures, allowing giraffes to interact with antelopes, much as they would in Africa. You'll find the largest crash of rhinos at any zoological facility in the world, an exhibit for the endangered California condor, and a mature landscape of exotic vegetation. The San Diego Zoo is world famous, but many visitors end up preferring the Wild Animal Park.

The easiest way to see critters is on the "Journey into Africa" tour aboard the **African** **Express,** an open-air, soft-wheeled tram that runs on biodiesel. Although it visits less park space than the now-retired monorail, the 2.5-mile circuit (which takes about 30 min.) brings guests much nearer to the animals, in some locations up to 300 feet closer. Depending on the crowd size, trams leave every 10 minutes or so. Lines build up by late morning, so make this your first or last attraction of the day (the animals are more active then, anyway). The **Savanna Safari** is a deluxe, 50-minute tour for up to 10 people. It visits the same places as the "Journey into Africa," but also includes places not on the regular tour; tickets are $35 (not including admission), and no reservations are necessary.

There are also three self-guided **walking tours,** which visit various habitats, including the most recent, **Lion Camp.** The commercial hub of the park is **Nairobi Village,** but even here animal exhibits are interesting, including the **nursery area,** a **petting station,** the **lowland gorillas,** and the **African Aviary.** There are amphitheaters for a bird show and another featuring elephants, scheduled two or three times daily. Nairobi Village has souvenir stores and several spots for mediocre dining. Visitors should be prepared for sunny, often downright hot weather; it's not unusual for temperatures to be 5° to 10° Fahrenheit warmer here than in San Diego.

If you want to get really close to the animals, take one of the park's **Photo Caravans,** which shuttle groups in flatbed trucks into the open areas that are inaccessible to the general public. There are a variety of itineraries (some are seasonal with varying age requirements), and each is a minimum of 2 hours. Prices start at $90, and you'll want to make reservations ahead of your visit (© 619/718-3000). The park also schedules a variety of 1- and 2-night **sleepovers** year-round. Programs for families, kids, teens, and adults let you camp out next to the animal compound in spacious canvas tents. Reservations required; © 619/718-3000. The **Cheetah Run Safari** allows a limited number of guests (reservations required; © 619/718-3000) to watch the world's fastest land mammal sprint after a mechanical lure. Cost is $69 per person, excluding park admission.

15500 San Pasqual Valley Rd., Escondido. © 760/747-8702. www.wildanimalpark.org. Admission $29 adults, $18 children 3–11, free for children 2 and under and military in uniform. AE, DISC, MC, V. Daily 9am–4pm (grounds close at 5pm); extended hours during summer and Festival of Lights (2 weekends in Dec). Parking $9, $14 RVs. Bus: 386 (Mon–Sat). Take I-15 to Via Rancho Pkwy.; follow signs for about 3 miles.

San Diego Zoo ★★★ Kids   More than 4,000 creatures reside at this influential zoo, started in 1916 and run by the Zoological Society of San Diego. The zoo's founder, Dr. Harry Wegeforth, traveled the world and bartered native southwestern animals such as rattlesnakes and sea lions for more exotic species. "Dr. Harry" also brought home plants, which flourish in the zoo's botanical garden, with more than 700,000 plants.

The zoo is one of only four in the U.S. with giant pandas, and many other rare species are here, including Buerger's tree kangaroos of New Guinea, long-billed kiwis from New Zealand, wild Przewalski's horses from Mongolia, lowland gorillas from Africa, and giant tortoises from the Galapagos. The Zoological Society is involved with animal preservation efforts around the world and has engineered many "firsts" in breeding. The zoo was also a forerunner in creating barless, moated enclosures that allow animals to roam in sophisticated environments resembling their natural ones.

Monkey Trails and Forest Tales is the largest, most elaborate habitat in the zoo's history, re-creating a wooded forest full of endangered species such as the mandrill monkey, clouded leopard, and pygmy hippopotamus. An elevated trail through the treetops allows for close observation of the primate, bird, and plant life that thrives in the forest canopy. **Absolutely Apes** showcases orangutans and siamangs of Indonesia; while next door is **Gorilla Tropics,**

SAN DIEGO & ENVIRONS

THE THREE MAJOR ANIMAL PARKS

17

The Art and Design District **1**
Balboa Theatre **8**
Belmont Park **18**
Cabrillo National Monument **33**
Fashion Valley
Shopping Center **24**
Ferry Landing Marketplace **30**
Greyhound Bus Station **7**
Horton Plaza Shopping Center **9**
Hotel Del Coronado **32**
International Visitor
Information Center **4**
Junípero Serra Museum **23**
Lamb's Players Theatre **31**
Maritime Museum **2**
Mission Basílica San Diego
de Alcalá **17**
Mission Valley
Shopping Center **25**
Museum of Contemporary Art
San Diego **3, 6**
The New Children's Museum **12**
North Park Theatre **27**
NTC Promenade **21**
Ocean Beach Antique District **19**
Old Globe Theatre **29**
Old Town State Historic Park **22**
PETCO Park **15**
San Diego Aircraft Carrier
Museum **10**
San Diego Convention Center **14**
San Diego Wild Animal Park **16**
San Diego Zoo **28**
Santa Fe Train Depot (Amtrak) **5**
Seaport Village **11**
SeaWorld San Diego **20**
William Heath Davis House
Museum **13**

where two troops of Western lowland gorillas roam an 8,000-square-foot habitat. Despite the hype, I find the **Giant Panda Research Center** *not* worth the hassle when a long line is in place (lines are shortest first thing in the morning or toward the end of the day). More noteworthy is **Ituri Forest,** which simulates a central African rainforest with forest buffalos, otters, okapis, and hippos, which are viewed underwater from a glassed-in enclosure; and the **Polar Bear Plunge,** where you'll find a 4¹/₂-acre summer tundra habitat populated by Siberian reindeer, yellow-throated martens, and diving ducks, as well as polar bears. The **Children's Zoo** features a nursery with baby animals and a petting area where kids can cuddle up to sheep, goats, and the like. There's also a **sea lion show** at the 3,000-seat amphitheater (easy to skip if you're headed to SeaWorld).

A 35-minute **Guided Bus Tour** provides a narrated overview and covers about 75% of the facility. It costs $10 for adults, $7 for children 3 to 11; it's included in the "Best Value" admission package. Since you get only brief glimpses of the enclosures, and animals won't always be visible, you'll want to revisit some areas. Included in the bus ticket is access to the unnarrated **Express Bus,** which allows you to get on and off at one of five different stops along the same route. You can also get an aerial perspective from the **Skyfari,** which is $3 per person each way, though you won't see many creatures. Ideally, take the complete bus tour early in the morning, when the animals are more active (waits for the bus tour can be long on a busy day). After the bus tour, take the Skyfari to the far side of the park and wend your way back on foot or by Express Bus to revisit animals you missed.

In addition to several fast-food options, **Albert's** restaurant is a beautiful oasis at the lip of a canyon and a lovely place to take a break.

2920 Zoo Dr., Balboa Park. © **619/234-3153** (recorded info), or 619/231-1515. www.sandiegozoo.org. Admission $25 adults, $17 children 3–11, free for military in uniform; "Best Value" package (admission, guided bus tour, round-trip Skyfari aerial tram) $34 adults, $31 seniors, $24 children. AE, DISC, MC, V. Sept to mid-June daily 9am–4pm (grounds close at 5 or 6pm); mid-June to Aug daily 9am–8pm (grounds close at 9pm). Bus: 7. I-5 south to Pershing Dr., follow signs.

(Value) Now That's a Deal!

If you plan to visit both the zoo and the Wild Animal Park, a two-park ticket (the "Best Value" zoo package, plus Wild Animal Park admission) is $60 for adults, $43 for children 3 to 11. You get unlimited visits to each attraction, to be used within 5 days of purchase. Or throw in SeaWorld within the same 5 days, and the combo works out to $109 for adults, $89 children ages 3 to 9.

Other value options include the **Southern California CityPass** (© **707/256-0490;** www.citypass.com), which covers the zoo or Wild Animal Park, plus Sea-World, Disneyland Resorts, and Universal Studios in Los Angeles; passes are $247 for adults, or $199 for kids age 3 to 9 (a savings of about 25%), and are valid for 14 days. The **Go San Diego Card** (© **800/887-9103;** www.gosandiegocard.com) offers unlimited general admission to more than 35 attractions, including the zoo and LEGOLAND, as well as deals on shopping, dining, and day trips to Mexico and the local wine country. One-day packages start at $55 for adults and $45 for children (ages 3–12). The **San Diego Passport** ($89 for adults, $45 for children 3–11) includes zoo admission, an Old Town Trolley city tour, Hornblower bay cruises, and more; passports are sold at the attractions themselves.

SeaWorld San Diego ★★ (Kids)   Opened in 1964, this aquatic theme park—owned by the Anheuser-Busch corporation—is perhaps the country's premiere showplace for marine life, in a nominally informative atmosphere. At its heart, SeaWorld is a shore-side family entertainment center where the performers are whales, dolphins, otters, sea lions, walruses, and seals. The 20-minute shows run several times each during the day, with visitors cycling through the various open-air amphitheaters.

Several successive 4-ton, black-and-white killer whales have taken turns as the park's mascot, and *Believe,* starring Shamu, is SeaWorld's most popular show. Performed in a 5,500-seat stadium, the stage is a 7-million-gallon pool lined with plexiglass walls with magnified views of the huge performers. But think twice before you sit in the seats down front—a highlight of the act is multiple drenchings in the first 12 or so rows of spectators. A nighttime show, *Shamu Rocks,* features concert lighting, animation, and a rock soundtrack. The slapstick *Clyde and Seamore's Risky Rescue* (sea lions and otters), the fast-paced *Dolphin Discovery,* and *Pets Rule!* are other performing animal routines, all in venues seating more than 2,000; during the summer, human acrobats are added to the mix with *Cirque de la Mer.* A small collection of rides is led by **Journey to Atlantis,** a roller coaster and log flume; **Shipwreck Rapids** is a splashy adventure on raftlike inner tubes, and **Wild Arctic** is a simulated helicopter trip to the frozen North. Enjoy a passel of new *Sesame Street*–related attractions, including rides, a musical production *(Big Bird's Beach Party),* and a "4-D" interactive movie experience.

SeaWorld's real specialties are simulated marine environments, such as the **arctic research station,** surrounded by beluga whales and polar bears. Other animal environments worth seeing are **Manatee Rescue, Shark Encounter,** and **Penguin Encounter.**

The **Dolphin** and **Wild Arctic Interaction Programs** are a chance for people to wade waist-deep with dolphins and beluga whales. This program includes some classroom time before participants wriggle into a wet suit and climb into the water for 20 minutes. It costs $160 to $170 per person (not including park admission); participants must be age 6 or older for the dolphin program, 10 for the arctic. Advance reservations required (© **800/257-4268**).

500 SeaWorld Dr., Mission Bay. © **800/257-4268** or 619/226-3901. www.seaworld.com. Admission $59 adults, $49 children 3–9, free for children 2 and under. AE, DISC, MC, V. Hours vary seasonally, but always at least daily 10am–5pm; most weekends and during summer 9am–11pm. Parking $10, $15 RVs. Bus: 8 or 9. From I-5, take SeaWorld Dr. exit; from I-8, take W. Mission Bay Dr. exit to SeaWorld Dr.

6   BEACHES

San Diego County is blessed with 70 miles of sandy coastline and more than 30 individual beaches, probably the state's best collection. The beaches cater equally to surfers, snorkelers, swimmers, sailors, divers, walkers, volleyballers, sunbathers—you get the drift. Even in winter and spring, when water temps drop to the high 50s (teens Celsius), they are great places to walk and jog, and surfers happily don wet suits to pursue their passion. In summer, the beaches teem with locals and visitors alike—the bikinis come out, the pecs are bared, and a party-hearty atmosphere prevails. From mid-May through mid-July, however, prepare for **May Gray** and **June Gloom,** a local phenomenon caused as inland deserts heat up at the end of spring and suck the marine layer—a thick bank of fog—inland for a few miles. Expect moist mornings and evenings.

Warning: A **1-year trial ban of alcohol** has been put in place at all city beaches, bay shores, and coastal parks; it will expire in January '09. It's unknown if the ban will be made permanent or not, so check signage—first offense is a maximum fine of $250.

Here's a list of San Diego's best stretches of sand, each with its own personality and devotees. They are listed geographically from south to north.

CORONADO Lovely, wide, and sparkling, this beach is conducive to strolling and lingering, especially in the late afternoon. At the north end, you can watch fighter jets in formation flying from the Naval Air Station, while just south is the pretty section fronting Ocean Boulevard and the Hotel del Coronado. Waves are gentle here, so the beach draws many Coronado families—and their dogs, which are allowed off-leash at the northwestern end. South of the Hotel Del, the beach becomes the beautiful, often deserted, **Silver Strand.**

OCEAN BEACH The northern end of Ocean Beach Park is officially known as **Dog Beach,** and it's one of a few in the county where your pooch can roam freely. Surfers congregate around the O.B. Pier, mostly in the water but often at the snack shack on the end. Rip currents can be strong—check with the lifeguard stations. Facilities at the beach include restrooms, showers, picnic tables, volleyball courts, and metered parking lots. To reach the beach, take West Point Loma Boulevard to the end.

MISSION BEACH Anchored by the **Giant Dipper** roller coaster, built in 1925, the sands and wide cement "boardwalk" sizzle with activity for most of the year. At the southern end, volleyball and basketball games are always underway. Parking can be tough, with your best bet being the public lots around the Giant Dipper or at the south end of Mission Boulevard. This street is the centerline of a 2-block-wide isthmus that leads a mile north to Pacific Beach.

PACIFIC BEACH There's always action here, particularly along **Ocean Front Walk**—a paved promenade showcasing a human parade akin to the one at L.A.'s Venice Beach boardwalk. It runs along Ocean Boulevard (just west of Mission Blvd.) to the pier. Surfing is popular year-round, in marked sections, and the beach is well-staffed with lifeguards. You're on your own to find street parking. A half mile north of the pier is **Tourmaline Surfing Park,** where the sport's old guard gathers to surf waters where swimmers are prohibited.

MISSION BAY PARK This man-made, 4,600-acre aquatic playground features 27 miles of bay front, picnic areas, playgrounds, and paths for biking, in-line skating, and jogging. The bay lends itself to windsurfing, sailing, water-skiing, and fishing. There are dozens of access points; at the southwest corner is **Bonita Cove,** a protected inlet with calm waters, grassy picnic areas, and playground equipment. Parts of the bay have been subject to closure over the years due to high levels of bacteria—check for posted warnings. Get there from Mission Boulevard in south Mission Beach.

LA JOLLA COVE These protected, calm waters—celebrated as the clearest along the coast—attract kayakers, snorkelers and scuba divers, and families. The stunning setting offers a small sandy beach and a lovely park, as well as the nearby cove known as the **Children's Pool,** inhabited by a colony of harbor seals. Smaller fish huddle in the tide pools between the two beaches. La Jolla Cove is terrific for swimming, cramped for sunbathing, and accessible from Coast Boulevard; street parking is free, if sparse.

LA JOLLA SHORES The wide, flat mile of sand at La Jolla Shores is popular with joggers, swimmers, and beginning body- and board surfers, as well as with families. Weekend crowds can be enormous, quickly claiming fire rings and occupying both the areas here, as well the grassy, palm-lined Kellogg Park across the street.

BLACK'S BEACH   The area's unofficial nude beach (technically, it's illegal), 2-mile-long Black's lies north of La Jolla Shores, at the base of steep, 300-foot-high cliffs. It's tricky to reach, but it draws scores with its secluded beauty and good swimming and surfing conditions. The spectacle of hang gliders launching from the cliffs above adds to the show. To get here, take North Torrey Pines Road, park at the Gliderport, and clamber down the makeshift path. To bypass the cliff descent, you can walk to Black's from beaches north (Torrey Pines) or south (La Jolla Shores). *Note:* Lifeguards are usually present from spring break through October; citations for nude sunbathing are rarely issued. There are no restroom facilities.

TORREY PINES   At the north end of Black's Beach, at the foot of Torrey Pines State Park, this fabulous strand is accessed by a pay parking lot at the park entrance. A visit to the park combined with a day at the beach is the quintessential outdoor San Diego experience. It's rarely crowded, though you need to be aware that at high tide, most of the sand gets a bath. In almost any weather, it's a great beach for walking. *Note:* At Torrey Pines and other bluff-side beaches, never sit at the bottom of the cliffs. The hillsides are unstable and could collapse.

7 EXPLORING THE AREA

BALBOA PARK

Established in 1868, 1,174-acre Balboa Park is not only the nation's second oldest city park (after New York's Central Park), it's also the largest urban cultural park in the United States. Tree plantings began in the late 19th century and the initial buildings were created to host the 1915–16 Panama-California Exposition; another expo in 1935–36 brought additional developments. Today, Balboa Park's most distinctive features include mature landscaping, the architectural beauty of the Spanish Colonial Revival buildings lining the pedestrian thoroughfare, and a diverse collection of museums. You'll also find the **Old Globe Theatre** complex (p. 756) and the **San Diego Zoo** (p. 735) here.

Entry to Balboa Park is free, as is parking, but most of the museums have admission charges and varying hours (some are closed on Mon); a free tram can transport you around the park. Get details from the **Balboa Park Visitor Center,** in the House of Hospitality (✆ 619/239-0512; www.balboapark.org). The visitor center is also the starting point for several free tours of the park that focus on architecture, horticulture, and so on. Top museums include:

Mingei International Museum ★★   This captivating museum (pronounced *Min-gay,* meaning "art of the people" in Japanese) offers exhibitions one could generally describe as folk art. The exhibits—usually four at a time—feature artists from countries across the globe; displays include textiles, costumes, jewelry, toys, pottery, paintings, and sculpture. The permanent collection includes whimsical contemporary sculptures by the late French artist Niki de Saint Phalle, who made San Diego her home in 1993. As one of the only major museums in the United States devoted to folk crafts on a worldwide scale, it's well worth a look. It has a wonderful gift store as well.

1439 El Prado, in the House of Charm. ✆ **619/239-0003.** www.mingei.org. Admission $7 adults; $5 seniors; $4 children 6–17, students, and military with ID; free for children 5 and under. Free the 3rd Tues of each month. Tues–Sun 10am–4pm. Bus: 7.

(Tips) **Balboa Park Money-Savers**

Most Balboa Park attractions are free one Tuesday each month; the schedule rotates so two or three venues participate each Tuesday (the visitor center has a schedule). If you plan to visit more than three of the park's museums, buy the **Passport to Balboa Park**—it allows entrance to 13 major museums; it's valid for 1 week and costs $39 for adults, $21 for children 3 to 12. If you plan to spend a day at the zoo and return for the museums, buy the **Deluxe Passport** which provides one ticket to the zoo and 7 days' admission to the museums for $65 adults, $36 children. Passports are available at any museum (but not the zoo), the visitor center, or online at www.balboapark.org.

Museum of Photographic Arts ★★ Fans of Ansel Adams and Edward Weston shouldn't miss a sampling of the 7,000-plus images housed by this museum—one of few in the United States devoted exclusively to the photographic arts (encompassing cinema, video, and digital photography as well). Provocative traveling exhibits change every few months, and the permanent collection includes photos by Alfred Stieglitz, Margaret Bourke-White, Imogen Cunningham, and Manuel Alvarez Bravo. The plush cinema hosts special screenings on an ongoing basis.

1649 El Prado. (C) **619/238-7559.** www.mopa.org. Admission $6 adults; $4 seniors, students, and military; free for children 11 and under with adult. Free 2nd Tues of each month. Tues–Sun 10am–5pm. Bus: 7.

Reuben H. Fleet Science Center ★ (Kids) A park highlight for kids, this tantalizing collection of interactive exhibits and attractions is designed to provoke the imagination and teach scientific principles. The Virtual Zone features a 23-passenger motion simulator that offers virtual-reality rides with a scientific bent. The Fleet also has a 76-foot-high IMAX Dome Theater for large-format movies, as well as planetarium shows (held the first Wed of each month).

1875 El Prado. (C) **619/238-1233.** www.rhfleet.org. Fleet Experience admission includes 1 IMAX film and exhibit galleries: $13 adults, $10 seniors 65 and over and children 3–12 (exhibit gallery can be purchased individually). Free 1st Tues of each month (exhibit galleries only). AE, DISC, MC, V. Daily 9:30am; closing times vary but always until at least 5pm. Bus: 7.

San Diego Air & Space Museum ★★ (Kids) The other big kid pleaser, this facility provides an overview of air-and-space history, from the days of hot-air balloons to the space age, with plenty of biplanes and military fighters in between. It emphasizes local aviation history, particularly the construction here of the *Spirit of St. Louis*. The museum is housed in a cylindrical hall built by the Ford Motor Company in 1935 for the park's second international expo.

2001 Pan American Plaza. (C) **619/234-8291.** www.sandiegoairandspace.org. Admission $15 adults, $12 seniors and students with ID, $9 juniors 12–17, $6 children 6–11, free for active military with ID and children 5 and under. Free 4th Tues of each month. Sept–May daily 10am–4pm; June–Aug daily 10am–5pm. Bus: 7.

San Diego Museum of Art (SDMA) ★ This museum is known in the art world for its collection of Spanish baroque painting and possibly the largest horde of South Asian paintings outside India. The American collection includes works by Georgia O'Keeffe and Thomas Eakins. Only a small percentage of the 12,000-piece permanent collection is on

Balboa Park Municipal Golf Course **31**
Botanical Building and Lily Pond **8**
Carousel **4**
Casa de Balboa **15**
   Model Railroad Museum
   Museum of Photographic Arts
   Museum of San Diego History
Casa del Prado **7**
Centro Cultural de la Raza **30**
Hall of Nations **20**
House of Charm **13**
   Mingei International Museum
   SDAI Museum of the Living Artist
House of Hospitality **14**
   Balboa Park Visitors Center
   Prado Restaurant
House of Pacific Relations
International Cottages **22**
Japanese Friendship Garden **18**
Marie Hitchcock Puppet Theatre **23**

Marston House **1**
Old Globe Theatre **11**
Reuben H. Fleet Science Center **16**
Rose and Desert Gardens **17**
San Diego Air & Space Museum **25**
San Diego Automotive Museum **24**
San Diego Hall of Champions
   Sports Museum **27**
San Diego Miniature Railroad **3**
San Diego Museum of Art **10**
San Diego Museum of Man **12**
San Diego Natural History Museum **6**
San Diego Zoo entrance **2**
Spanish Village Art Center **5**
Spreckels Organ Pavilion **19**
Starlight Bowl **26**
Timken Museum of Art **9**
United Nations Building **21**
Veterans Museum & Memorial Center **29**
WorldBeat Center **28**

display at any given time, in favor of prestigious touring shows. SDMA also has an ongoing schedule of concerts, films, and lectures, usually themed with a current exhibition.

1450 El Prado. ℭ **619/232-7931.** www.sdmart.org. Admission $10 adults, $8 seniors and military, $7 college students, $4 children 6–17, free for children 5 and under. Admission to traveling exhibits varies. Free 3rd Tues of each month. Tues–Sun 10am–6pm (Thurs until 9pm). Bus: 7.

San Diego Natural History Museum (SDNHM) (Kids) The main focus of this museum is the flora, fauna, and mineralogy of Southern and Baja California. There's a 300-seat large-format movie theater, and two films are included in the price of admission. The interactive installation *Fossil Mysteries* includes life-size models of prehistoric animals, including the megalodon shark, the largest predator the world has ever known. SDNHM also leads free nature hikes and has a schedule of events and overnight expeditions for both children and adults.

1788 El Prado. ℭ **619/232-3821.** www.sdnhm.org. Admission $9 adults; $7 seniors; $6 students, youth age 13–17, and active-duty military; $4 children 3–12; free for children 2 and under. Free 1st Tues of each month. Daily 10am–5pm. Bus: 7.

MORE ATTRACTIONS IN & AROUND SAN DIEGO
Downtown & Beyond

Downtown, you can wander through the turn-of-the-20th-century **Gaslamp Quarter** ★★, with 17 blocks of restored historic buildings. You'll find dozens of restaurants and a vigorous nightlife scene here. More information about the Gaslamp Quarter—as well as walking tours on Saturdays at 11am—are available at the **William Heath Davis House,** a museum in downtown's oldest structure and home to the quarter's historical foundation; it's at 410 Island Ave., at Fourth Avenue (ℭ 619/233-4692; www.gaslampquarter.org). At **Horton Plaza** ★, notable for its colorful, jumbled architecture, you can shop, dine, see a movie or play, and people-watch (p. 754).

The long-awaited, oft-delayed **New Children's Museum,** 200 W. Island Ave. (ℭ **619/ 233-8792;** www.childrensmuseumsd.org), opened in May 2008. Designed by the city's most acclaimed architect, this $25-million, state-of-the-art facility will feature cultural and educational programs, including hands-on art projects, storytelling, music, and visual and performing arts. The museum is intended to engage all ages, from toddlers to parents.

In 2004, the city completed $474-million **PETCO Park,** home to San Diego's Major League Baseball team, the **Padres.** The 42,000-seat ballpark incorporates seven historic structures into the stadium, including the Western Metal Supply building, a four-story brick edifice dating from 1909 that now sprouts left-field bleachers from one side. The San Diego Padres play April through September; for information or tickets, call ℭ **877/374-2784** or 619/795-5000, or visit www.padres.com. PETCO parking is limited and costly—for a space within a couple blocks, expect to pay at least $17. Better yet, take the San Diego Trolley.

Cabrillo National Monument ★★★ Breathtaking views mingle with the history of San Diego, starting with the arrival of Juan Rodríguez Cabrillo in 1542. This tip of Point Loma is also a vantage point for viewing migrating Pacific gray whales en route from Alaska to Baja California (and back again), December through March. A tour of the restored lighthouse, built in 1855, illuminates what life was like here more than a century ago. National Park Service rangers lead walks at the monument, and tide pools at the base of the peninsula beg for exploration. Free 25-minute films on Cabrillo, tide pools, and the whales screen daily on the hour from 10am to 4pm. The drive from downtown takes 20 minutes.

1800 Cabrillo Memorial Dr., Point Loma. ℂ **619/557-5450.** www.nps.gov/cabr. Admission $5 per vehicle, $3 for walk-ins (valid for 7 days from purchase). Daily 9am–5pm. Bus: 84. By car, take I-8 west to Rosecrans St., turn right on Canon St., left on Catalina, and follow signs.

Maritime Museum ★★ (Kids)   This flotilla of classic ships is led by the full-rigged merchant vessel *Star of India* (1863), a National Historic Landmark and the world's oldest ship that still goes to sea. The gleaming white San Francisco–Oakland steam-powered ferry *Berkeley* (1898) worked round-the-clock to ferry people to safety after the 1906 San Francisco earthquake; it now pulls duty as a museum. The elegant *Medea* (1904) is one of the world's few remaining large steam yachts, and *Pilot* (1914) was San Diego Bay's official pilot boat for 82 years. There's also the HMS *Surprise,* a reproduction of an 18th-century Royal Navy Frigate which played a supporting role to Russell Crowe in the film *Master and Commander,* and a 300-foot-long Cold War–era B-39 Soviet attack submarine. You can board and tour each vessel.

1492 N. Harbor Dr. ℂ **619/234-9153.** www.sdmaritime.org. Admission $12 adults, $9 seniors 63 and over and active military with ID, $8 children 6–17, free for children 5 and under. Daily 9am–8pm (till 9pm in summer). Bus: 2, 210, 810, 820, 850, 860, 923, or 992. Trolley: County Center/Little Italy.

Museum of Contemporary Art San Diego Downtown ★★★   In 2007, the Museum of Contemporary Art opened a new downtown space known as the Jacobs Building. The annex is boldly grafted onto the end of historic Santa Fe Depot, built in 1915, and transforms what had been the train station's baggage building into a state-of-the-art museum and educational facility. Across the street at America Plaza are MCASD's original downtown galleries and gift store (MCASD's flagship museum is in La Jolla, p. 747). Lectures and special events for adults and children are also offered, and the first Thursday evening of every month is "TNT" (Thursday Night Thing), an engaging music and arts program that's part cocktail party, part concert, part gallery opening. Free tours are given on Thursdays at 6pm and weekends at 2pm.

1100 and 1001 Kettner Blvd. (btw. B St. and Broadway). ℂ **858/454-3541** or 619/234-1001. www.mcasd. org. Admission $10 adults, $5 seniors and military, free for anyone 25 and under, free admission Thurs 5–7pm, paid ticket good for admission to MCASD La Jolla within 7 days. Fri–Mon 11am–5pm; Wed 11am–5pm; Thurs 11am–7pm. Discounted parking with validation at 5 Star Garage (501 W. C St. at Columbia). Bus: 83. Trolley: America Plaza.

San Diego Aircraft Carrier Museum   The USS *Midway's* 47-year military history began 1 week after the Japanese surrender of World War II in 1945. By the time *Midway* was decommissioned in 1991, the aircraft carrier had patrolled the Taiwan Straits in 1955, operated in the Tonkin Gulf, and served as the flagship from which Desert Storm was conducted. In all, more than 225,000 men served aboard the warship. The carrier is now moored at the Embarcadero and in 2004 became San Diego's first naval-aviation museum. A self-guided audio tour takes visitors to several levels of the ship, telling the story of life onboard. The highlight is climbing up the superstructure to the bridge and gazing down on the 1,001-foot-long flight deck, with various aircraft poised for duty.

910 Harbor Dr. (at Navy Pier). ℂ **619/544-9600.** www.midway.org. Admission $15 adults; $10 seniors, students, and military; $8 children 6–17; free for children 5 and under and military in uniform. Daily 10am–5pm. Limited parking on Navy Pier, $7 for 4 hr.; metered parking available nearby. Bus: 2, 210, or 992.

Old Town & Beyond: California's Beginnings

The birthplace of San Diego—indeed, of California—Old Town takes you back to the Mexican California of the mid-1800s. Today the spot suffers a daily invasion of tourists, many of them headed to **Plaza del Pasado,** a one-time 1930s-era motel that is now a collection of restaurants and shops (see "Shopping," later in this chapter).

Mission Valley, which starts at Presidio Park and heads straight east, is anything but old; until Highway 8 was built in the 1950s, it was little more than cow pastures with a couple of dirt roads. Shopping malls, motels, a golf course, condos, and car dealerships fill it today. It's also the site of **Qualcomm Stadium,** 9449 Friars Rd., where San Diego's National Football League team, the **Chargers,** play. The season runs from August to December; for information, call ✆ 877/242-7437 or go to www.chargers.com.

Old Town and Mission Valley are easily accessed via the San Diego Trolley.

Junípero Serra Museum ★   On the hill above Old Town, this iconic Spanish Mission–style building built in 1929 overlooks the slopes where, in 1769, the first mission, first presidio (fort), and first nonnative settlement on the west coast of the United States and Canada were founded. The museum's exhibits introduce visitors to the Native American, Spanish, and Mexican people who first called this place home. On display are their belongings, from cannons to cookware. From the 70-foot tower, visitors can compare the spectacular view with historic photos to see how this land has changed over time. Designed by William Templeton Johnson, the structure can be seen for miles around.

2727 Presidio Dr., Presidio Park. ✆ 619/297-3258. www.sandiegohistory.org. Admission $5 adults; $4 seniors, students, and military; $2 children 6–17; free for children 5 and under. Mon–Fri 11am–3pm; Sat–Sun 10am–4:30pm; daily 10am–4:30pm in summer. Bus: 8, 9, 10, 14, 28, 30, 35, 44, 83, 105, or 150. Trolley: Old Town. Take I-8 to the Taylor St. exit. Turn right on Taylor, and then left on Presidio Dr.

Mission Basilica San Diego de Alcalá   This was the first link in a chain of 21 California missions founded by Spanish missionary Junípero Serra (the mission was moved from Old Town to this site in 1774 for agricultural reasons, and to separate Native American converts from the fortress that included the original building). The mission was sacked by Indians a year after it was built—Father Serra rebuilt the structure using 5- to 7-foot-thick adobe (mud) walls and clay tile roofs, rendering it harder to burn. In the process he inspired a bevy of 20th-century California architects. Mass is said daily in this active Catholic parish.

10818 San Diego Mission Rd., Mission Valley. ✆ 619/281-8449. www.missionsandiego.com. Admission $3 adults, $2 seniors and students, $1 children 11 and under. Free Sun and for daily Masses. Museum and gift shop daily 9am–4:45pm; Mass daily 7am and 5:30pm, with additional Sun Mass at 8am, 10am, 11am, and noon. Bus: 14. Trolley: Mission San Diego. Take I-8 to Mission Gorge Rd. to Twain Ave., which turns into San Diego Mission Rd.

Old Town State Historic Park ★   The Stars and Stripes weren't raised over Old Town until 1846, and this historic park is dedicated to re-creating the city as it was during this era of Mexican influence, from around 1821 to 1872. Seven of the park's 20 structures are original, including the adobe homes. La Casa de Estudillo represents the living conditions of a wealthy family in 1872; Seeley Stables is named after A. L. Seeley, who ran the stagecoach and mail service in these parts from 1867 to 1871. Pick up a map at Park Headquarters, and peruse the model of Old Town as it looked in 1872. On Wednesdays, from 10am to 2pm, costumed park volunteers reenact 19th-century life with cooking and crafts demonstrations, a working blacksmith, and parlor singing. Free 1-hour walking tours leave daily at 11am and 2pm from the Robinson-Rose House.

4002 Wallace St., Old Town. ✆ 619/220-5422. www.parks.ca.gov. Free admission (donations welcome). Museums daily 10am–5pm; most restaurants till 9pm. Bus: 8, 9, 10, 14, 28, 30, 35, 44, 105, or 150. Trolley: Old Town. Take I-5 to the Old Town exit and follow signs.

Opened to the public in 1949, **Mission Bay** is a 4,600-acre aquatic playground created by dredging tidal mud flats and opening them to sea water. Today it's a great area for walking, jogging, in-line skating, biking, and boating. The boardwalk connecting **Mission Beach** and **Pacific Beach** is almost always bustling and colorful. For Mission Bay recreational activities, see "Outdoor Pursuits" p. 749.

A 1925 wooden roller coaster, the **Giant Dipper,** is just one of the attractions at **Belmont Park,** 3146 Mission Blvd. (© **858/228-9283;** www.belmontpark.com), a shore-side amusement park. It's open daily (weekends only in Jan and Feb) with extended summer hours. The surf's always up at the adjacent **Wavehouse,** where a unique wave machine provides stand-up board rides. The Wavehouse is also the location of the **Plunge,** a 175-foot-long indoor pool that dates from the 1920s.

For information on **SeaWorld San Diego,** see p. 739.

La Jolla

One of San Diego's most photogenic spots is **La Jolla Cove** and the **Ellen Browning Scripps Park** on the bluff above it. Take a stroll along Coast Walk, which offers some of California's most resplendent coastal scenery. Just south is the **Children's Pool,** a beach where dozens of harbor seals laze in the sun. For a fine scenic drive, follow La Jolla Boulevard to Nautilus Street and turn east to get to 800-foot-high **Mount Soledad** ★, with a 360-degree view of the area.

Birch Aquarium at Scripps ★★ This beautiful aquarium and museum is run as the interpretive arm of the world-famous Scripps Institution of Oceanography. The aquarium affords close-up views of the Pacific Northwest, the California coast, Mexico's Sea of Cortés, and the tropical seas, presented in more than 60 marine-life tanks. The giant kelp forest is particularly impressive, with sharks and eels; and don't miss the fanciful white anemones and ethereal moon jellyfish. A re-created tide pool demonstrates marine coastal life and affords an amazing view of Scripps Pier and La Jolla. Off-site adventures are conducted year-round.

2300 Expedition Way. © **858/534-3474.** www.aquarium.ucsd.edu. Admission $11 adults, $9 seniors, $8 college students with ID, $7.50 children 3–17, free for kids 2 and under. Free 3-hr. parking. AE, MC, V. Daily 9am–5pm. Bus: 30. Take I-5 to La Jolla Village Dr. exit, go west 1 mile, and turn left at Expedition Way.

Museum of Contemporary Art San Diego (MCASD) ★★★ Focusing on works produced since 1950, this museum is known internationally for its permanent collection and thought-provoking exhibitions. The 4,000-plus holdings represent every major art movement of the past half-century, with a strong showing by California artists. You'll see particularly noteworthy examples of minimalism, light and space work, conceptualism, installation, and site-specific sculptures. The museum is on a bluff overlooking the ocean, and the views from the galleries are gorgeous. The original building was the residence of the legendary Ellen Browning Scripps, designed by Irving Gill in 1916. Free docent tours are available Thursdays at 6pm and weekends at 2pm. The bookstore is a great place for contemporary gifts, and the cafe is a pleasant stop before or after your visit. Admission is free for those 25 and under; a paid ticket to the La Jolla museum will get you into the downtown galleries for free.

700 Prospect St. © **858/454-3541.** www.mcasd.org. Admission $10 adults, $5 seniors and military, free for anyone 25 and under; free admission Thurs 5–7pm; paid ticket good for admission to MCASD Downtown within 7 days. Fri–Tues 11am–5pm; Thurs 11am–7pm. Bus: 30. Take I-5 north to La Jolla Pkwy. or

SAN DIEGO & ENVIRONS

17

EXPLORING THE AREA

take I-5 south to La Jolla Village Dr. west. Take Torrey Pines Rd. to Prospect Place and turn right; Prospect Place becomes Prospect St.

Torrey Pines State Reserve ★★★ (Moments) The rare Torrey pine grows only two places in the world: Santa Rosa Island, 175 miles northwest of San Diego, and here, at the north end of La Jolla. If the gnarled beauty of these trees doesn't move you, the equally rare, undeveloped coastal scenery should. This 1,750-acre reserve encompasses the 300-foot-high, water-carved sandstone bluffs, which provide a precarious footing for the trees. Six trails, less than 1.5 miles in length, travel from the road to the cliff edge or to the beach. A small visitor center, built in the adobe style of the Hopi Indians, features a lovely, 12-minute video about the park. This delicate spot is one of San Diego's unique treasures. *Note:* The park has no food or drink facilities.

Hwy. 101, La Jolla. ✆ **858/755-2063.** www.torreypine.org. Admission $8 per car, seniors $7. Daily 8am–sunset. Bus: 101. From I-5, take Carmel Valley Rd. west; turn left at Hwy. 101.

Coronado

It's hard to miss San Diego Bay's most iconic landmark: the **San Diego–Coronado Bay Bridge ★**. Completed in 1969, this graceful five-lane bridge spans 2^1/$_4$ miles and links the city and the "island" of Coronado. At 246 feet in height, the bridge is tall enough to allow Navy aircraft carriers to pass under it. It still looks more elegant than utilitarian, with a sweeping curve that maximizes the view, encompassing Mexico and the shipyards of National City to the south, the city skyline to the north, and Coronado, the naval station, and Point Loma before you—designated drivers are hard pressed to keep their eyes on the road. Bus no. 901 from downtown will also take you across the bridge. The **Hotel del Coronado ★★★** is also worth checking out, even if you're not checking in. This turreted Victorian seaside resort is a national treasure (p. 720).

SIGHTSEEING TOURS

City Sightseeing Narrated tours are conducted aboard double-decker buses along two routes, the Harbor Loop (which includes downtown) and the Park & Zoo Loop (which includes Old Town). There are on-and-off privileges, and each tour is about an hour; your ticket is good for 48 hours. Tours commence in Old Town, and both day and evening (May–Oct) tours are offered. Coronado is not part of these tours, but passes for the Coronado ferry are included in some ticket prices.

2415 San Diego Ave. ✆ **619/296-2400.** www.citysightseeing-sd.com. Day tours $25–$30 adults; $15–$20 children; night tours $20 adults, $12 children. Daily 8:30am–5pm. Bus: 8, 9, 10, 14, 28, 30, 35, 44, 105, or 150. Trolley: Old Town.

Hornblower Cruises These 1- or 2-hour narrated tours lead passengers through San Diego harbor on one of eight different vessels, ranging from a 61-passenger antique yacht to a three-deck, 800-passenger behemoth. You'll see the *Star of India,* cruise under the San Diego–Coronado Bridge, and swing by a submarine base and an aircraft carrier or two. Guests can visit the captain's wheelhouse for a photo op, and harbor seals and sea lions on buoys are a regular sighting. Whale-watching trips (mid-Dec to late Mar) are a blast; a 2-hour weekend champagne brunch cruise departs at 11am, and dinner/dance cruises run nightly.

1066 N. Harbor Dr. ✆ **888/467-6256** or 619/686-8715. www.hornblower.com. Harbor tours $18–$23 adults; $2 off for seniors and military; half price children 4–12. Dinner cruises start at $65; brunch cruise $47; whale-watching trips $30–$35 ($5 off for seniors and military), $15 children. Bus: 2, 210, or 992. Trolley: America Plaza.

Old Town Trolley Tours   Not to be confused with the public transit trolley, these narrated excursions are an easy way to get an overview of the city. The trackless trolleys do a 30-mile circular route, and you can hop off at any one of 10 stops, explore at leisure, and reboard when you please (trolleys run every half-hour). Stops include Old Town, the Gaslamp Quarter, Coronado, the San Diego Zoo, and Balboa Park. You can begin wherever you want, but you must purchase tickets before boarding (most stops have ticket kiosks). Old Town Trolley also operates **Sea and Land Adventures,** a 90-minute tour in amphibious vehicles that hold 46 passengers. After cruising along the Embarcadero, you'll dip into the bay to experience the maritime and military history of San Diego. The trip is $30 for adults and $15 for kids 4 to 12.

4040 Twiggs St., Old Town. ℂ 619/298-8687. www.historictours.com. $30 adults, $15 for kids 4–12, free for children 3 and under. The route takes 2 hr. Trolleys run daily 9am–4pm in winter, 9am–5pm in summer.

San Diego Harbor Excursion   This company also offers daily 1- and 2-hour narrated tours of the bay, using its fleet of eight boats ranging from a 1940s passenger launch to plush, modern vessels. Two 1-hour itineraries each cover about 12 miles—the south bay tour includes the San Diego–Coronado Bridge and Navy shipyards, the north bay route motors past Naval Air Station North Island and Cabrillo National Monument. The 25-mile, 2-hour tour encompasses the entire bay. Two-hour Sunday brunch and nightly dinner cruises are also available. In winter, whale-watching excursions feature naturalists from the Birch Aquarium; a 5¹/₂-hour nature cruise plies international waters to view the Coronado Islands (Jan–May).

1050 N. Harbor Dr. (foot of Broadway). ℂ 800/442-7847 or 619/234-4111. www.sdhe.com. Harbor tours $18–$23, $2 off for seniors and military, half price for children 4–12. Dinner cruises start at $63 adults, $38 children; brunch cruise $53 adults, $38 children; whale-watching trips $30–$35 adults, $25–$30 seniors and military, $15 children; nature cruise $50 adults, $45 seniors and military, $40 children. Bus: 2, 210, or 992. Trolley: America Plaza.

Xplore Offshore ★★ Ⓕⁱⁿᵈˢ   This fleet has only two small boats, and the one to ride is the tricked-out, 24-foot RIB (rigid-inflatable boat), similar to the crafts used by Navy SEALs. Capable of cruising at up to 45 mph, the RIB is built for speed and comfort—there's lots of padding and straddle-seating up front, and a roomy head (not bad for a 24-ft. boat). Other special features include hot water for showering after a swim and an underwater camera, for those who don't want to get wet. Trips are unscripted; you go where you want and do what you'd like: rip-roaring wave riding or serene pleasure boating; whale-watching or a booze cruise to a bayside restaurant—it's your call.

Pickup points are flexible, but usually Dana Landing in Mission Bay. ℂ 858/456-1636. www.xplore offshore.com. 3-hr. rates start at $49 per person. Bus: 8 or 9 (for Dana Landing).

8 OUTDOOR PURSUITS

BALLOONING & SCENIC FLIGHTS   A peaceful balloon ride reveals sweeping vistas of the Southern California coast, the wine country surrounding Temecula (70 min. north of downtown), or rambling estates and golf courses around Rancho Santa Fe (25 min. north of downtown). For a champagne-fueled flight at sunrise or sunset, followed by hors d'oeuvres, contact **Skysurfer Balloon Company** (ℂ 800/660-6809 or 858/481-6800; www.sandiegohotairballoons.com) or **California Dreamin'** (ℂ 800/373-3359 or 951/699-0601; www.californiadreamin.com). Rates range from $158 to $248. California Dreamin' also offers a **biplane excursion** over Temecula's wine country starting at $248 for two people.

Biplane, Air Combat & Warbird Adventures (© **800/759-5667** or 760/438-7680; www.barnstorming.com) offers just about everything but wing-walking. Vintage biplane flights leave from McClellan-Palomar Airport in Carlsbad, taking up to two passengers per plane on scenic flights down the coast; rates start at $199 for two-person, 20-minute rides. Air Combat flights, most piloted by active-duty fighter pilots, offer simulated dogfights (if you're bringing your own adversary, you need to reserve space 1 to 2 weeks in advance; if you need your target assigned, call 3 weeks in advance); rates start at $298. You can also opt for a flight—with or without aerial acrobatics—in a 1941 SNJ-4 warbird, and you might even get a chance at the controls; no pilot's license is necessary ($445 and up). A 60-minute fly/dine package features a sunset flight for two aboard a 1920s biplane followed by dinner at the Four Seasons Resort Aviara ($569).

BIKING The paths around **Mission Bay** are great for leisurely rides, but the oceanfront **boardwalk** between Pacific Beach and Mission Beach can get very crowded, especially on weekends (and that's half the fun). The road out to **Point Loma** (Catalina Dr.) is hilly with wonderful scenery. Traveling old **State Route 101** (aka the Pacific Coast Hwy.) from La Jolla north to Oceanside yields terrific coastal views, with plenty of places to refuel with coffee, a snack, or a swim.

For rentals, call **Bike Tours San Diego,** 509 Fifth Ave. (© **619/238-2444;** www.biketours.com), which offers delivery ($5) as far north as Del Mar. Rates for a city/hybrid bike start at $22 for a day and include helmets, locks, maps, and roadside assistance. Other rental outlets include **Mission Beach Surf & Skate,** 704 Ventura Place, off Mission Boulevard at Ocean Front Walk (© **858/488-5050**), for one-speed beach cruisers, and **Cheap Rentals,** 3685 Mission Blvd. (© **858/488-9070**), for mountain bikes and more. In La Jolla, try **California Bicycle,** 7462 La Jolla Blvd. (© **858/454-0316;** www.calbike.com), for front-suspension mountain bikes. In Coronado, check out **Bikes and Beyond,** 1201 First St., at the Ferry Landing Marketplace (© **619/435-7180;** www.hollandsbicycles.com), for beach cruisers and mountain bikes. Expect to pay $7 and up per hour for bicycles, $30 for 24 hours.

Hike Bike Kayak San Diego (© **866/425-2925** or 858/551-9510; www.hikebikekayak.com) has a variety of bike tours, including a plunge down La Jolla's Mount Soledad.

BIRD-WATCHING More than 480 bird species have been observed in San Diego county—more than anywhere else in the United States. The area is a haven along the Pacific Flyway—the migratory route along the Pacific Coast—and the diverse range of ecosystems helps to lure a wide range of winged creatures. From the tidal marshes to the desert, it's possible for birders to enjoy four distinct bird habitats in a single day.

Among the best places for bird-watching is the **Chula Vista Nature Center** at **Sweetwater Marsh National Wildlife Refuge** (© **619/409-5900;** www.chulavistanaturecenter.org), where you may spot rare residents such as the light-footed clapper rail and the western snowy plover, as well as predatory species such as the American peregrine falcon and northern harrier. **Torrey Pines State Reserve** (p. 748) is a protected habitat for swifts, thrashers, woodpeckers, and wren-tits. Inland, the **Anza-Borrego Desert State Park** (see chapter 16) makes an excellent day trip from San Diego—with some 268 species of birds.

Get the free brochure *Birding Hot Spots of San Diego* from the Port Administration Building (3165 Pacific Hwy.), the San Diego Zoo, Wild Animal Park, San Diego Natural History Museum, or Birch Aquarium. It's also posted online at www.portofsandiego.org/

FISHING   Summer and fall are ideal for boat fishing, when the waters around **Point Loma** are brimming with bass, bonito, and barracuda; the nearby **Islas los Coronados,** which belong to Mexico, are popular for abalone, yellowtail, yellowfin, and big-eyed tuna. Some outfitters will take you deeper into Baja California waters on multiday trips. Fishing charters depart from Harbor and Shelter islands, Point Loma, Imperial Beach, and Quivira Basin in Mission Bay. Participants over age 16 need a California fishing license, but anglers of any age can fish free without a license off any **municipal pier** in the state, including those of Shelter Island, Ocean Beach, and Imperial Beach.

San Diego's sportfishing fleet consists of more than 75 large commercial vessels and several dozen private charter yachts. A variety of half-, full-, and multiday trips are available. Rates for trips on a large boat average $42 for half a day or $90 for three-quarters of a day. Or spring $120 to $225 for a 20-hour overnight trip to the Coronados (call around and compare prices). Rates are lower for kids, and discounts are available for twilight sailings; charters or "limited load" rates are also to be had. The following outfitters offer short or extended outings with daily departures: **H&M Landing,** 2803 Emerson St. (C **619/222-1144;** www.hmlanding.com); **Lee Palm Sportfishers,** 2801 Emerson St. (C **619/224-3857;** www.redrooster3.com); **Point Loma Sportfishing,** 1403 Scott St. (C **619/223-1627;** www.pointlomasportfishing.com); and **Seaforth Sportfishing,** 1717 Quivira Rd. (C **619/224-3383;** www.seaforthlanding.com).

GOLF   San Diego County has 90-plus courses, and more than 50 of them are open to the public. For a full listing of area courses, visit www.golfsd.com, or request the *Golf Guide* from the San Diego Convention and Visitors Bureau (C **619/236-1212;** www. sandiego.org). **San Diego Golf Reservations** (C **866/701-4653** or 858/964-5980; www.sandiegogolf.com) can arrange tee times for you.

The city's most famous links are at the **Torrey Pines Golf Course** ★★★, a pair of 18-hole championship courses on the cliffs between La Jolla and Del Mar. Home of the Buick Invitational Tournament and the setting for the 2008 U.S. Open, Torrey Pines tee times are taken 8 to 90 days in advance by automated telephone system ($37 booking fee); first-come, first-served tee times are offered from sunup to 7:30am. Weekday greens fees on the south course are $145, $181 weekends; the north course is $85 weekdays, $106 weekends. Cart rentals are $30, and twilight rates are available. You can also arrange for lessons, which assure you a spot on the course. For automated reservations, call C **877/ 581-7171** option 6; for information, call C **800/985-4653** or go to www.torreypines golfcourse.com.

Other acclaimed links include the **Four Seasons Resort Aviara Golf Club** in Carlsbad (C 760/603-6900; www.fourseasons.com); Ramona's **Mt. Woodson Golf Club** (C 760/ 788-3555; www.mtwoodson.com); the **Grand Del Mar Golf Club** (C 858/792-6200; www.thegrandgolfclub.com); **Maderas Golf Club** in Poway (C 858/451-8100; www. maderasgolf.com); **Barona Creek Golf Club** in Lakeside (C 619/387-7018; www. barona.com); **Salt Creek Golf Club** in Chula Vista (C 619/482-4666; www.saltcreekgc. com); and **Sycuan Resort & Casino** in El Cajon (C 800/457-5568; www.sycuanresort. com). More convenient for most visitors is the **Riverwalk Golf Club** (C 619/296-4653; www.riverwalkgc.com), which wanders along the Mission Valley floor; humble **Balboa Park Municipal Golf Course** (C 619/239-1660; www.sandiego.gov/golf); or **Coronado Municipal Golf Course** (C 619/435-3121; www.golfcoronado.com). The latter two feature distractingly nice views of the city skyline.

SAN DIEGO & ENVIRONS

17

OUTDOOR PURSUITS

HANG GLIDING & PARAGLIDING The windy cliffs at the **Torrey Pines Gliderport,** 2800 Torrey Pines Scenic Dr., La Jolla (© 877/359-8326 or 858/452-9858; www.fly torrey.com), are one of the country's top spots for hang gliding and paragliding. A 20- to 30-minute tandem flight with a qualified instructor costs $150 for paragliding and $175 for hang gliding. Even if you don't muster the courage to try a tandem flight, sitting at the cafe here and watching the graceful aerobatics is stirring.

HIKING & WALKING The best **beaches** for walking are Coronado, Pacific Beach, La Jolla Shores, and Torrey Pines, but pretty much any shore is a good choice. You can also walk around most of Mission Bay on a series of connected footpaths. If a four-legged friend is walking with you, head for Dog Beach in Ocean Beach or Fiesta Island in Mission Bay—two of the few areas where dogs can legally go unleashed. The **Coast Walk** offers supreme surf-line views above the bluffs of La Jolla. Other places for hikes listed elsewhere in this chapter include **Torrey Pines State Reserve** (p. 748) and **Cabrillo National Monument** (p. 744).

The **Sierra Club** sponsors many hikes in the San Diego area, and nonmembers are welcome to participate. Most are free. Contact the office at © 619/299-1743, or check the website www.sandiego.sierraclub.org. Volunteers from the **Natural History Museum** (© 619/232-3821; www.sdnhm.org) also lead free nature walks throughout San Diego County.

Walkabout International, 2825 Dewey Rd., Suite 202, Point Loma (© 619/231-7463; www.walkabout-int.org), sponsors more than 100 free walking tours every month. Led by local volunteers, they're listed on the website and hit all parts of the county, including the Gaslamp Quarter, La Jolla, and the beaches. Mountain hikes take place most Wednesdays and Saturdays.

SAILING & MOTOR YACHTS Sailors can choose from among the calm waters of 4,600-acre **Mission Bay,** with its 26 miles of shoreline; **San Diego Bay,** one of the most beautiful natural harbors in the world; or the open **Pacific Ocean,** where you can sail south to the Islas los Coronados (the trio of uninhabited islets on the Mexico side of the border).

Next Level Sailing (© 800/644-3454; www.nextlevelsailing.com) offers bay sails aboard one of two 80-foot America's Cup Class racing yachts. The 2-hour excursions, either on *Stars and Stripes* or *Abracadabra,* are $99. **Classic Sailing Adventures** (© 800/659-0141 or 619/224-0800; www.classicsailingadventures.com) offers two 4-hour sailing trips daily aboard the *Soul Diversion,* a 38-foot Ericson. The afternoon cruise leaves at 1pm and a champagne sunset sail departs at 5pm, with a maximum of six passengers ($75 per person, minimum two people).

If you have sailing or boating experience, consider a nonchartered rental. **Seaforth Boat Rental,** 1641 Quivira Rd., Mission Bay (© 888/834-2628 or 619/223-1681; www.seaforth boatrental.com), has a variety of boats for the bay or the ocean. Powerboats range from mini-runabouts ($48 an hour) to 240-horsepower cabin cruisers ($395, 2-hr. minimum); 16.5- to 36-foot sailboats start at $35 an hour; and jet skis begin at $90 an hour. Half- and full-day rates are available. Canoes, kayaks, and pedal boats are also for rent, as are fishing boats and equipment. Seaforth has a location downtown at the Marriott San Diego Hotel & Marina, 333 W. Harbor Dr. (© 619/239-2628), and in Coronado at 1715 Strand Way (© 619/437-1514). **Mission Bay Sportcenter,** 1010 Santa Clara Place (© 858/488-1004; www.missionbaysportcenter.com), rents sailboats (from $18 per hour), catamarans (from $30 per hour), sailboards ($18 per hour), kayaks (from $13 per hour), jet skis ($90 per hour), pedal boats ($17 per hour), and motorboats (from $85 per hour). Discounts are given for 4-hour and full-day rentals; private instruction and group lessons are offered.

SAN DIEGO & ENVIRONS

17

OUTDOOR PURSUITS

San Diego's underwater scene ranges from the magnificent giant kelp forests of Point Loma to a nautical graveyard off Mission Beach called Wreck Alley, where a 366-foot Canadian destroyer and other ships (and the remains of a toppled research platform) sit on the sea floor. Fishing and boating activity are banned in the 533-acre Ecological Reserve off the La Jolla Cove, but diving and snorkeling are welcome. It's a reliable place to spot garibaldi, California's state fish, as well as giant black sea bass. Shore diving here, or at nearby La Jolla Shores, is common, and a number of dive shops will help set you up. Boat dives are the rule, however, particularly to the Islas los Coronados, a trio of uninhabited islets off Tijuana, where seals, sea lions, and eels cavort against a landscape of boulders.

The **San Diego Oceans Foundation** (✆ 619/523-1903; www.sdoceans.org) is devoted to the stewardship of local marine waters. The website contains good information about local diving opportunities. Notable dive outfits include **Ocean Enterprises** (✆ 858/565-6054; www.oceanenterprises.com), **Lois Ann Dive Charters** (✆ 800/201-4381; www.loisann.com), **Scuba San Diego** (✆ 800/586-3483 or 619/260-1880; www.scubasandiego.com), and **OEX Dive & Kayak Centers** (www.oexcalifornia.com), which has four locations in the county—La Jolla (✆ 858/454-6195), Mission Bay (✆ 619/224-6195), Point Loma (✆ 619/758-9531), and Oceanside (✆ 760/721-6195).

SKATING Gliding around on in-line skates, especially in the Mission Bay area, is a quintessential Southern California experience. In Pacific Beach, rent a pair of regular or in-line skates from **Resort Watersports** (✆ 858/539-8696), based at the Catamaran Resort, 3999 Mission Blvd.; or **Play It Again Sports,** 1401 Garnet Ave. (✆ 858/490-0222). In Coronado, go to **Bikes and Beyond,** 1201 First St., at the Ferry Landing (✆ 619/435-7180).

SURFING San Diego is a popular year-round surf destination. Some of the best spots include Black's Beach, La Jolla Shores, Windansea, Pacific Beach, Mission Beach, Ocean Beach, and Imperial Beach. In North County, there's Swami's in Encinitas, Carlsbad State Beach, and Oceanside. If you didn't bring a board, you can rent one from stands at many popular beaches. Local surf shops also rent equipment; they include **La Jolla Surf Systems,** 2132 Avenida de la Playa, La Jolla Shores (✆ 858/456-2777; www.lajollasurf systems.com), and **Emerald City–The Boarding Source,** 1118 Orange Ave., Coronado (✆ 619/435-6677).

For surfing lessons, check with **San Diego Surfing Academy** (✆ 800/447-7873 or 760/230-1474; www.surfsdsa.com), which offers lessons at South Carlsbad State Beach; and La Jolla–based **Surf Diva** (✆ 858/454-8273; www.surfdiva.com), billed as the world's first surfing school for women and girls. The company has become so popular it now offers private lessons for guys too.

9 SHOPPING

San Diegans have embraced the suburban shopping mall with vigor, and many residents do the bulk of their shopping at two massive complexes in Mission Valley. Downtown has even adopted the mall concept at Horton Plaza. Sales tax in San Diego is 7.75%, but savvy out-of-state shoppers avoid the tax by shipping larger items home at the point of purchase.

The Disneyland of shopping malls, **Horton Plaza** ★, 324 Horton Plaza (© **619/239-8180;** www.westfield.com/hortonplaza), is in the heart of the revitalized city center. The multilevel facility has more than 180 specialty shops and kiosks. There's a 14-screen cinema, a performing arts theater, two major department stores, several restaurants, and a roster of short-order dining spots. It transcends its genre with a conglomeration of rambling paths, bridges, towers, piazzas, sculptures, fountains, and greenery. Horton Plaza opened in 1985 to rave reviews and was a catalyst for the Gaslamp's redevelopment. Three hours of free parking are available from 7am to 9pm; you can self-validate your ticket at machines scattered throughout the mall (validation in food court offered until 11pm). It's $2 per 20 minutes without validation. The garage is confusing (losing your car is part of the Horton Plaza experience) and is open 24 hours.

Fourteen-acre **Seaport Village,** 849 W. Harbor Dr. (© **619/235-4014;** www.seaport village.com), alongside San Diego Bay, was built to resemble a Cape Cod community, but the more than 50 shops are Southern California cutesy. The waterfront atmosphere is still pleasant, and 2 hours of parking are free with a purchase.

Seekers of serious art, design, and home furnishings should head to Little Italy. The conglomeration of hip stores and galleries along Kettner Boulevard and India Street, from Laurel to Date streets, has become known as the **Art and Design District** (© **619/702-7777;** www.taddsd.com). Highlights include **DNA European Design Studio** (© **619/235-6882;** www.dnaeuropeandesign.com), featuring Euro-style furniture; **Mixture** (© **619/239-4788;** www.mixturedesigns.com) for modern furniture and accessories; and **David Zapf Gallery** (© **619/232-5004**) and **Scott White Contemporary Art** (© **619/501-5689;** www.scottwhiteart.com), two of the city's most prominent galleries.

HILLCREST/UPTOWN

Compact Hillcrest is an ideal shopping destination for vintage-clothing, books, and home furnishings; there are plenty of cafes and wine bars as well. Start at the intersection of University and Fifth avenues. Street parking is available.

To the north and east of Hillcrest are the Uptown neighborhoods of University Heights and North Park, which are brimming with boutiques. You'll find independent-minded clothing stores and unusual gift shops along Park Boulevard and University Avenue. Running east from where Park Boulevard T-bones Adams Avenue is **Adams Avenue Antique Row.** It doesn't have the number of antiques stores it once had, but plenty of shops, restaurants, and bars still enliven the excursion. The district is best tackled by car; for more information and an area brochure with a map, contact the **Adams Avenue Business Association** (© **619/282-7329;** www.adamsaveonline.com).

OLD TOWN & MISSION VALLEY

Old Town State Historic Park features restored historic sites and adobe structures, a number of which now house shops that cater to tourists. Many have a "general-store" theme and carry gourmet treats and inexpensive Mexican crafts alongside standard issue souvenirs. **Plaza del Pasado,** 2754 Calhoun St. (© **619/297-3100;** www.plazadelpasado.com), maintains the park's old *Californio* theme and has nearly a dozen specialty shops and three restaurants. Costumed employees, special events and activities, and strolling musicians heighten the festive atmosphere. You'll have plenty of shopping opportunities outside the park perimeter as well.

Mission Valley is home to two giant malls (**Fashion Valley** and **Mission Valley**), with more than enough stores to satisfy any shopper, and free parking. Both are accessible via San Diego Trolley from downtown.

The beach communities offer laid-back shopping options: surf shops, recreational gear, and casual clothing stores. The best selection of bikinis is at **Pilar's,** 3745 Mission Blvd., Pacific Beach (© **858/488-3056;** www.pilarsbeachwear.com). Across the street is **Liquid Foundation Surf Shop,** 3731 Mission Blvd. (© **858/488-3260;** www.liquidfoundation surf.com), which specializes in board shorts for guys.

In Pacific Beach, **Pangaea Outpost,** 909 Garnet Ave. (© **858/581-0555;** www.pangaea outpost.com), gathers more than 60 diverse shops under one roof; while San Diego's greatest concentration of antiques stores is found in the **Ocean Beach Antique District** (www. obantiquedistrict.com), along the 4800 block of Newport Avenue. Several stores are mall-style, with multiple dealers. Most of the O.B. antiques stores are open daily from 10am to 6pm, with reduced hours Sunday.

LA JOLLA

Shopping is a major pastime in this upscale community of moneyed professionals and retirees. Women's-clothing boutiques tend toward conservative and costly, such as those lining Girard and Prospect streets (**Ann Taylor, Armani Exchange, Polo/Ralph Lauren, Nicole Miller,** and **Sigi's Boutique**), but you'll also find less pricey, mainstream stores such as **Banana Republic** and **American Apparel.** Even if you're not in the market to buy, the many home-decor boutiques make for great window-shopping, as do La Jolla's ubiquitous jewelers. La Jolla also has more than 20 art galleries—although most won't appeal to serious collectors.

CORONADO

This insular, conservative Navy community doesn't have many shopping opportunities beyond the stores on Orange Avenue at the western end of the island. In addition to some scattered housewares and home-furnishing stores and women's boutiques, there are gift shops at Coronado's major resorts. The **Ferry Landing Marketplace,** 1201 First St., at B Avenue (© **619/435-8895**), is a touristy faux-seaport with shops and restaurants and a sweeping view of the bay and downtown skyline.

10 SAN DIEGO AFTER DARK

Historically, San Diego's cultural scene has lounged in the shadows of Los Angeles and San Francisco, but the go-go '90s brought new blood and money into the city, and arts organizations reaped the benefits. The San Diego Symphony, Old Globe Theatre, and Museum of Contemporary Art San Diego each received mega-millions from individual donors, but don't think "after-dark" activity in this city is limited to highfalutin affairs for the Lexus crowd. Rock and pop concerts, swank martini bars, and nightclubs crank up the volume on a nightly basis.

THE PERFORMING ARTS

The San Diego Convention and Visitors Bureau's **Art + Sol** campaign publishes a calendar of performing and visual arts events; check it out at www.sandiegoartandsol.com. The San Diego Performing Arts League produces the **What's Playing?** guide every 2 months. You can pick one up at the ARTS TIX booth (see below) or view it online (© **619/238-0700;** www.sandiegoperforms.com).

Half-price tickets to theater, music, and dance events are available at the **ARTS TIX** booth, in Horton Plaza Park at Broadway and Third Avenue. For a daily roster of offerings, call © **619/497-5000** or visit www.sandiegoperforms.com.

Thankfully, San Diego's orgy of development has included more than high-rise condos. **NTC Promenade** (© **619/573-9260**; www.ntcpromenade.org) consists of 26 historic buildings on 28 acres in Point Loma, the remnants of a huge Navy base. It is being transformed into a flagship hub of creative activity and includes office, studio, and performance space for nearly two dozen arts and educational groups. The **North Park Theatre**, 2891 University Ave. (© **619/239-8836**; www.birchnorthparktheatre.net), is a resurrected 1928 vaudeville and movie house. It's now the home base for Lyric Opera San Diego and hosts numerous other groups throughout the year. Most recently unveiled is the **Balboa Theatre**, 868 Fourth Ave. (© **619//570-1100**; www.sdbalboa.org), which opened in early 2008 following a 5-year, $27-million restoration. Originally built in 1924, the Balboa sat empty and decaying for years, barely avoiding several brushes with the wrecking ball. This Gaslamp Quarter icon is once again presenting music, dance, theater, and films.

Theater

A complex of three performance venues in Balboa Park, the **Old Globe Theatre** ★★★ includes the 581-seat Old Globe Theatre (fashioned after Shakespeare's wooden-O theater), the 225-seat Cassius Carter Centre Stage, and the 612-seat open-air Lowell Davies Festival Theatre. This Tony Award–winning company stages more than a dozen productions year-round, from world premieres of subsequent Broadway hits such as *Dirty Rotten Scoundrels* and *The Full Monty*, to an excellent outdoor summer Shakespeare festival. High-profile actors, writers, and directors are often involved with productions here. Backstage tours are offered most weekends at 10:30am ($5 adults; $3 students, seniors, and military). Tickets range from $19 to $79. For more information, call © **619/234-5623** or see www.theoldglobe.org.

Founded in 1947 by Gregory Peck, Dorothy McGuire, and Mel Ferrer, **La Jolla Playhouse** ★★★ won a 1993 Tony Award for outstanding regional theater. The Playhouse is a three-theater complex located on the campus of UC San Diego and is known for its contemporary takes on classics and commitment to commedia dell'arte style—as well as producing Broadway-bound blockbusters. Past hits include the world premieres of *Jersey Boys*, *Thoroughly Modern Millie*, *The Who's Tommy*, and *Big River*. Tickets are $28 to $72, but discounted tickets ($15–$20) for seniors and students, subject to availability, are offered 10 minutes prior to curtain on Wednesday, Thursday, and Sunday evenings, and Saturday matinees. For details, call © **858/550-1010** (www.lajollaplayhouse.org).

Also noteworthy are **San Diego Repertory Theatre** ★, which mounts plays and musicals at the Lyceum Theatre in Horton Plaza (© **619/544-1000**; www.sandiegorep.com); **Lamb's Players Theatre** ★ (© **619/437-0600**; www.lambsplayers.org), a resident-professional company based in Coronado; iconoclastic **Sledgehammer Theatre** ★ (© **619/544-1484**; www.sledgehammer.org); and **Cygnet Theatre** ★ (© **619/337-1525**; www.cygnettheatre.com), which produces work at the **Old Town Theatre**, 4040 Twiggs St., as well as at it's original space, the **Rolando Theatre**, 6663 El Cajon Blvd., near San Diego State University.

Classical Music, Opera & Dance

The **San Diego Symphony** ★ lures top talent for its year-round programs. Under the leadership of music director Jahja Ling, the symphony presents a traditional season October through May at Copley Symphony Hall, a 1929 French rococo-style downtown landmark (well hidden within a modern office tower). The Summer Pops series, devoted to a mix of big band, Broadway, Tchaikovsky, and sundry "pops," runs weekends from July through early September at the Embarcadero. Tickets are $20 to $90; select performances offer $10 student tickets 1 hour prior to curtain. For additional information, call ℂ **619/235-0804** (www.sandiegosymphony.com).

The well-respected **La Jolla Music Society ★★** has been bringing marquee names to San Diego since 1968, including Pinchas Zukerman, Emanuel Ax, and Joshua Bell. Many of the 40-plus annual shows are held October through May in La Jolla's Sherwood Auditorium at the Museum of Contemporary Art. The annual highlight is SummerFest, a 3-week series of eclectic concerts, forums, open rehearsals, talks, and artist encounters, held in August. Tickets range from $20 to $95; for more information, call ℂ **858/459-3728** (www.ljms.org).

The **San Diego Opera ★★★** is perhaps the community's most successful arts organization. The annual season runs from late January through mid-May, with five offerings at downtown's 3,000-seat Civic Theatre, and occasional recitals at smaller venues. Productions range from well-trod warhorses such as *Carmen* to edgier works such as Alban Berg's *Wozzeck*, performed by local singers and international name talent. Tickets run $28 to $192; rush tickets ($20–$50) become available 90 minutes before curtain. For details, call ℂ **619/533-7000** (box office), or 619/232-7636 (www.sdopera.com).

Dance Place at NTC Promenade (p. 756) has become the heart of the city's dance scene, providing studio, performance, and educational space for several of San Diego's leading companies, including **San Diego Ballet** (ℂ **619/294-7378**; www.sandiegoballet. org), **Malashock Dance** (ℂ **619/260-1622**; www.malashockdance.org), and **Jean Isaacs San Diego Dance Theater** (ℂ **619/225-1803**; www.sandiegodancetheater.org).

THE CLUB & MUSIC SCENE

Comprehensive listings are found in the free *San Diego Weekly Reader* (www.sdreader. com), published Thursdays and distributed all over town (in tourist areas, it's a condensed version called the *Weekly*).

Live Rock, Pop, Folk, Jazz & Blues

San Diego's downtown **House of Blues,** 1055 Fifth Ave. (ℂ **619/299-2583;** www.hob.com/sandiego), features an eclectic lineup of rock, blues, reggae, and world music. **Anthology** (p. 722) is a fine-dining establishment masquerading as a top-notch music venue, presenting jazz, blues, world, and rock music. You'll find live music nightly at **Croce's Restaurant & Jazz Bar,** 802 Fifth Ave. at F Street (ℂ **619/233-4355;** www.croces.com), a mainstream gathering place for jazz and rhythm and blues in the Gaslamp. **The Casbah,** 2501 Kettner Blvd. at Laurel (ℂ **619/232-4355;** www.casbahmusic.com), is a Little Italy dive with a well-earned rep for presenting alternative bands that are, were, or will be famous. May through October, San Diegans flock to **Humphrey's,** 2241 Shelter Island Dr. (ℂ **619/523-1010;** www.humphreysconcerts.com), a 1,300-seat outdoor venue overlooking a marina. The lineup spans the musical spectrum. Jazz fans should look into **Dizzy's,** 200 Harbor Dr. (ℂ **858/270-7467;** www.dizzyssandiego.com). It's conveniently located at the San Diego Wine & Culinary Center in the Gaslamp. Tickets are cash only, available at the door.

The Gaslamp Quarter is the hub of nightlife in San Diego, and high-end dance clubs where you can also enjoy a fancy sit-down meal have become popular. Options include: **Stingaree**, 454 Sixth Ave. at Island Street (© **619/544-9500;** www.stingsandiego.com), a three-level, 22,000-square-foot megaclub with a cool rooftop lounge; **Confidential,** 901 Fourth Ave. (© **619/696-8888;** www.confidentialsd.com), a sexy spot with a tapas menu created by one of San Diego's favorite chefs; **On Broadway,** 615 Broadway at Sixth Avenue (© **619/231-0011;** www.obec.tv), a converted 1925 bank building with a sushi bar and billiards parlor (Fri and Sat only); and **belo,** located on E Street, between Fourth and Fifth avenues (© **619/231-9200;** www.belosandiego.com), a huge, three-room space with a retro design. At **Sevilla,** 555 Fourth Ave. (© **619/233-5979;** www.cafe sevilla.com), you can salsa (lessons Tues–Thurs, samba lessons Sun, at 8:30pm, followed by live bands) or nibble on tapas. **Envy** and **Eden** (© **619/814-2055;** www.envysan diego.com) are the hip and very happening clubs located in the ultrastylish Ivy Hotel (p. 706). Multilevel Envy is chic and sexy, with a definite A-lister vibe; Eden is the open-air rooftop bar. Just opening at press time is the city's latest über-club, **Universal,** 1202 University Ave., in Hillcrest (© **619/544-9704;** www.universalhillcrest.com). It will feature alfresco spaces and a restaurant.

Bars & Cocktail Lounges

Beach, the rooftop bar of the W Hotel at 421 B St. downtown (© **619/398-3100;** www. wbeachbar.com), features a heated sand floor, cabanas, and fire pit. **Altitude Skybar,** 660 K St. (© **619/696-0234;** www.altitudeskybar.com), 22 stories up, and **J6Bar,** 616 J St. (© **619/531-8744;** www.jsixsandiego.com), join the open-air lounge derby. San Diego's ultimate bar with a view is **Top of the Hyatt,** 1 Market Place, at Harbor Drive (© **619/232-1234**)—on the 40th floor of the West Coast's tallest waterfront building. **Sidebar,** 536 Market St. at Sixth Avenue (© **619/696-0946;** www.sidebarsd.com), is too cool for signage, while hypermodern **Thin** (© **619/231-7529**) and its downstairs sister club, the **Onyx Room,** 852 Fifth Ave., Gaslamp Quarter (© **619/235-6699;** www. onyxroom.com), let you move from a contemporary vibe to classic lounge. The Onyx Room also has a live jazz jam on Tuesday. Sleek, retro-cool **Airport,** 2400 India St. (© **619/ 685-3881;** www.airportsd.com), has a back patio where you can practically touch the planes landing at nearby Lindbergh Field. Off the main tourist grid are **Starlite,** 3175 India St. (at Spruce St.), in Mission Hills (© **619/358-9766;** www.starlitesandiego. com), a nifty drinking and dining spot with a great patio; and **Beauty Bar,** 4746 El Cajon Blvd. (at Euclid Ave.), in City Heights (© **619/516-4746;** www.beautybar.com). Located in a rather sketchy part of town, Beauty Bar is favored by the indie set that avoids the glitz of the Gaslamp.

Gay & Lesbian Clubs & Bars

The **Brass Rail,** 3796 Fifth Ave., Hillcrest (© **619/298-2233;** www.thebrassrailsd.com), is San Diego's oldest gay bar but courts a mixed crowd. Across the street from one another, **Numbers,** 3811 Park Blvd. (near University Ave.), Hillcrest (© **619/294-9005**), and the **Flame,** 3780 Park Blvd. (© **619/295-4163;** www.flamesd.com), are popular dance emporiums with theme nights. Numbers has ladies' night on Fridays, while the girls take over the Flame on Saturdays (with a Goth night scheduled every second Sat). **Bourbon Street,** 4612 Park Blvd., University Heights (© **619/291-4043;** www.bourbonstreetsd.com), is a gay bar featuring karaoke, drag shows, and DJs; Sunday is ladies' night. **Rich's,** 1051 University Ave., between 10th and 11th avenues (© **619/295-2195;** www.richssandiego.com), is a high-energy dance club, with house music and a video bar; Thursday is ladies' night. **Club Montage,** 2028 Hancock St., Middletown (© **619/294-9590;** www.clubmontage. com), is a three-level dance club with an industrial, funhouse interior; the rooftop lounge has bay views. The club is usually open Wednesday through Sunday, and the party often keeps rolling here until 3 or 4am.

11 NORTH COUNTY BEACH TOWNS

The string of picturesque beach towns that dot the coast of San Diego County from Del Mar to Oceanside make great day trips. Be forewarned: You'll be tempted to spend the night.

ESSENTIALS

Del Mar is only 18 miles north of downtown San Diego; **Carlsbad** is about 33 miles. If you're driving, follow I-5 north; Del Mar, Solana Beach, Encinitas, Carlsbad, and Oceanside all have freeway exits. The farthest point, Oceanside, will take about 45 minutes. The other choice by car is the coast road, known as Camino del Mar, "PCH" (Pacific Coast Hwy.), Old Highway 101, and County Highway S21.

From downtown San Diego, the **Coaster** commuter train provides service to Solana Beach, Encinitas, Carlsbad, and Oceanside, and **Amtrak** stops in Solana Beach—just a few minutes north of Del Mar—and Oceanside. The Coaster makes the trip a number of times (6:30am–7pm) weekdays, four times on Saturday; Amtrak passes through about 11 times daily each way. Call © **800/262-7837** or 511, or visit www.transit.511sd.com for transit information; for Amtrak call © **800/872-7245** (www.amtrak.com).

DEL MAR ★★

Del Mar is a small community with some 4,500 inhabitants in 2 square miles. The town has adamantly maintained its independence, eschewing incorporation into the city of San Diego. It's one of the most upscale communities in the metropolitan area, yet Del Mar maintains a casual, small-town personality and charm. The town swells in summer, as visitors flock to thoroughbred horse races and the county's San Diego Fair.

The history and popularity of Del Mar are inextricably linked to the **Del Mar Racetrack & Fairgrounds,** 2260 Jimmy Durante Blvd. (© **858/793-5555;** www.delmarfair. com). In 1933, actor/crooner Bing Crosby developed the Del Mar Turf Club, enlisting the help of celebrity friends. Soon, Hollywood stars were seen around Del Mar, and the town became famous as the place where "the turf meets the surf." Racing season is mid-July through early September.

Two excellent beaches flank Del Mar: **Torrey Pines State Beach** to the south and **Del Mar State Beach.** Both are wide, well-patrolled strands popular for sunbathing, swimming, and surfing (in marked areas). The sand stretches north to the mouth of the San Dieguito Lagoon, where people bring their dogs for a romp in the sea. The hub of activities for most residents and visitors, **Del Mar Plaza,** 1555 Camino del Mar, is an open-air shopping center with fountains, sculptures, palazzo-style terraces, good restaurants and shops, and wonderful views of the sea.

For more information about Del Mar, contact or visit the **Del Mar Regional Chamber of Commerce Visitor Information Center,** 1104 Camino del Mar, Del Mar, CA 92014 (© **858/755-4844;** www.delmarchamber.org), which distributes a detailed folding map.

Hours vary according to volunteer staffing but approximate weekday business hours. The city-run website is www.delmar.ca.us.

Where to Stay

Del Mar Motel on the Beach (Finds)   The only property in Del Mar on the beach, this simply furnished, white-stucco motel has been here since 1946. The rooms are large and well kept; upstairs units have one king-size bed, downstairs rooms have two double beds. Most of them have scant views, but two oceanfront rooms, dressed up with faux plants and larger bathrooms, sit right over the sand. You can walk the shore for miles, and the popular seaside restaurants **Poseidon** and **Jake's** are right next door.

1702 Coast Blvd. (at 17th St.), Del Mar, CA 92014. (C) **800/223-8449** for reservations, or 858/755-1534. www.delmarmotelonthebeach.com. 44 units, upper units with shower only. $259–$299 double (reduced rates Oct–May). AE, DC, DISC, MC, V. Free parking. Take I-5 to Via de la Valle exit. Go west, and then south on Hwy. 101 (Pacific Coast Hwy.); veer west onto Coast Blvd. **Amenities:** Picnic and barbecue area. *In room:* A/C, TV, fridge, coffeemaker, hair dryer, iron.

The Grand Del Mar ★★★   A faux Tuscan villa nestled in the foothills of Del Mar, this new resort features ornate, Vegas-style luxury and high-end comforts. Liberally accented with fountains, courtyards, terraces, sweeping staircases, and outdoor fireplaces, the hotel is so grandly European you'll feel as if you are visiting the doge at his country estate. It even has a canyon-side walking path overlooking the golf course (dramatically lit at night), tennis courts, four swimming pools, a tricked-out kids' activity center, and a 21,000-square-foot spa. The signature restaurant, **Addison,** is one of San Diego's most sumptuous dining rooms: plush, elegant, and refined, it serves cuisine to match—and the wine list is more fairly described as a wine novel. This is simply San Diego's most opulent resort.

5300 Grand Del Mar Court, San Diego, CA 92130. (C) **888/314-2030** or 858/314-2000. Fax 858/314-2001. www.thegranddelmar.com. 249 units. From $575 doubles; from $1,100 suites. Children under 18 stay free in parent's room. Packages available. AE, DC, DISC, MC, V. Valet parking. From I-5 merge onto Ted Williams Pkwy. east, exit Carmel Country Road and turn right, left at Meadows Del Mar. **Amenities:** 4 restaurants; 5 bars; live entertainment; 4 swimming pools; 18-hole championship golf course; 2 tennis courts; fitness center; spa; activity center with games, computers, kids and teens programs; concierge; complimentary town car transportation within a 10-mile radius; business center; retail shops; room service; laundry/dry cleaning service; shoeshine service; croquet lawn; hiking and jogging trails. *In room:* A/C, TV/DVD player, Wi-Fi, minibar, hair dryer, iron, laptop safe, cordless phone.

L'Auberge Del Mar Resort and Spa ★★★   Reopened in June 2008 after a 7-month closure, this longtime luxury favorite has undergone a top-to-bottom, $25-million renovation bent on taking it to another, more modern level. All guest rooms have been upgraded, a new lobby features a wine and cheese bar, lush landscaping abounds, and the pool areas sport private cabanas and a bar. By December, a new 4,100-square-foot spa will have added amenities such as a juice bar, bakery, and a boutique; Waterfall Terrace (the signature restaurant opened in Sept) offers indoor and outdoor dining alongside water features and fire pits. Unchanged, of course, is the hotel's prime location across the street from Del Mar's main shopping and dining scene, and a short jog from the sand.

1540 Camino del Mar (at 15th St.), Del Mar, CA 92014. (C) **800/245-9757** or 858/259-1515. Fax 858/755-4940. www.laubergedelmar.com. 120 units. $395–$465 double; from $600 suite. AE, DC, MC, V. Valet parking $20. Take I-5 to Del Mar Heights Rd. west, and then turn right onto Camino del Mar Rd. **Amenities:** Restaurant; bars; 2 outdoor pools; full-service spa; Jacuzzi; concierge; courtesy van; room service; laundry service; dry cleaning. *In room:* A/C, TV w/pay movies, Wi-Fi, minibar, coffeemaker, hair dryer, iron, safe, CD player.

Les Artistes (Finds)   What do you get when you take a 1940s motel and put it in the hands of an owner with a penchant for prominent painters? An intriguingly funky, disarmingly informal hotel, a few blocks from downtown Del Mar. None of the rooms **761** have ocean views, but charming touches abound, such as a lily-and-koi pond, Asian chimes, and bougainvillea. Ten rooms are tributes to artists: The Diego Rivera room feels like a warm Mexican painting come to life; the Monet room has a distractingly abstract swirl of color. The Japanese Furo room features a soaking tub carved into the bathroom floor; downstairs rooms have tiny private garden decks.

944 Camino del Mar, Del Mar, CA 92014. (℃) **858/755-4646**. www.lesartistesinn.com. 12 units. $115–$195 double. Rates include continental breakfast. AE, DISC, MC, V. Free parking. From I-5 go west on Del Mar Heights Rd., and then left onto Camino Del Mar Rd. Pets accepted for $30, with $50 cash deposit. *In room:* TV.

Where to Dine

Head to the upper level of the centrally located Del Mar Plaza, at Camino del Mar and 15th Street. Here you'll find **Il Fornaio Cucina Italiana** ★ ((℃) **858/755-8876**; www. ilfornaio.com) for pleasing Italian cuisine and an *enoteca* (wine bar) with great ocean views; **Pacifica Del Mar** ★★ ((℃) **858/792-0476**; www.pacificadelmar.com), which serves outstanding seafood; and **Epazote Oceanview Steakhouse** ★ ((℃) **858/259-9966**; www.epazotedelmar.com), where they whip up a wicked margarita. West from the plaza on 15th Street is neighborhood favorite **Sbicca** ★★, 215 15th St. ((℃) **858/481-1001**; www.sbiccabistro.com), serving modern American cuisine sweetened with great wine deals. Fabulous vistas come with your meal at **Poseidon,** 1670 Coast Blvd. ((℃) **858/755-9345**; www.poseidonrestaurant.com), set right on the beach. While there's no view at **Arterra** ★★★, 11966 El Camino Real ((℃) **858/369-6032**; www.arterrarestaurant. com), the seasonally driven menu is attractive enough—not to mention the fairly swanky outdoor lounge. Ensconced in an uninspiring Marriott hotel, the restaurant is under the stewardship of high-profile chef Bradley Ogden.

Jake's Del Mar ★ SEAFOOD/CALIFORNIA This Hawaiian-owned seafood restaurant with a killer view occupies a building originally constructed in 1910. Jake's has a perfect seat beside the sand, and diners get straight-on views of the beach scene. The predictable menu can't live up to the panorama, but it's prepared competently and service is swift (too swift, actually—don't let them rush you). At lunch, you'll find sandwiches and salads. Dinner brings in the big boys: Maine lobster tails, giant scampi, rack of lamb, and so on. Happy hour features a shorter bar/bistro menu at half price.

1660 Coast Blvd. (at 15th St.), Del Mar. (℃) **858/755-2002**. www.jakesdelmar.com. Reservations recommended. Main courses $10–$16 lunch, $10–$53 dinner, $11–$17 brunch. AE, DISC, MC, V. Tues–Sat 11:30am–2:30pm; Sun brunch 10am–2pm; daily 5–9pm (Fri–Sat until 9:30pm). Valet parking $3. Bus: 101.

Market Restaurant + Bar ★★★ CALIFORNIA Comfortably elegant Market specializes in a regional San Diego cuisine, showcasing the best ingredients from the area's top farms, ranches, and seafood providers. The menu is printed daily, depending on what is available at the produce stands; the wine list, which is reprinted about every week, is no less quality obsessed, focusing on small and nontraditional wineries. Past Market menu items have included blue cheese soufflé with roasted pears, candied pecans, and fig-port reduction; tempura black sea bass; and a tasting of game hen served three ways. Truly fine dining in a relaxed atmosphere.

3702 Via de la Valle (at El Camino Real), Del Mar. (℃) **858/523-0007**. www.marketdelmar.com. Reservations recommended. Main courses $23–$70. AE, MC, V. Daily 5–10pm. Free valet parking. Bus: 308.

Pamplemousse Grille ★★★ CONTEMPORARY FRENCH The whimsical interior murals of pigs on parade and a slouched chef with a cigarette dangling from his lips might lead one to believe this isn't a serious restaurant. Even the name, which is French for grapefruit, is a bit silly. But make no mistake—this is one of the county's upper-echelon dining destinations. The internationally inspired menu also has room for personal input: You can create your own entree of grilled meats (prime rib-eye, rack of lamb, and so on) with a choice of sauce (wild mushroom, peppercorn, grain mustard, au jus, or béarnaise), along with a selection of veggies and potatoes (truffled and mashed, gratin, *pommes frites*, and so on).

514 Via de la Valle (across from the Del Mar Fairgrounds), Solana Beach. © **858/792-9090.** www.pgrille. com. Dinner reservations recommended (and a necessity during race season). Main courses $20–$25 lunch (served Fri only), $23–$43 dinner. AE, MC, V. Daily 5–9pm; Fri 11:30am–2pm. Bus: 308.

SOLANA BEACH, ENCINITAS & CARLSBAD ★

North of Del Mar and a 45-minute drive from downtown San Diego, the pretty communities of Solana Beach, Encinitas, and Carlsbad provide many reasons to linger on the California coast: good swimming and surfing beaches, small-town atmosphere, antiques and boutiques, and the region's most beautiful flowers.

Carlsbad was named for Karlsbad, Czech Republic, because of the similar mineral waters (some say they're curative) each produced. Carlsbad's once-famous artesian well was capped in the 1930s, but was redrilled in 1994, and the healthful water is flowing once more. Carlsbad is also a noted commercial flower-growing region, along with its neighbor Encinitas. Each spring at **Carlsbad Ranch** (© **760/431-0352;** www.theflower fields.com), 45 acres of solid ranunculus fields bloom into a rainbow visible even from the freeway. In December, the nurseries are alive with holiday poinsettias.

The **Solana Beach Visitor Center** is near the train station at 103 N. Cedros (© **858/ 350-6006;** www.solanabeachchamber.com). The **Encinitas Visitors Center** is at 859 Second St. (corner of H St.) in downtown Encinitas (© **800/953-6041** or 760/753-6041; www.encinitaschamber.com). The **Carlsbad Visitor Information Center,** 400 Carlsbad Village Dr. (in the old Santa Fe Depot; © **800/227-5722** or 760/434-6093; www. carlsbadca.org), has information on flower fields and nursery touring.

Fun Things to See & Do

Going from south to north, the main area of activity for **Solana Beach** is South Cedros Avenue, parallel to Pacific Coast Highway, 1 block east. A 2-block stretch is lined with many of San Diego County's best furniture and home-design shops, antiques stores, art dealers, and boutiques selling imported goods. The **Belly Up Tavern,** 143 S. Cedros Ave. (© **858/481-9022;** www.bellyup.com), is one of San Diego's most appealing concert venues.

If you've ever wanted to get a glimpse into the artistic process, get yourself to the **Lux Art Institute** in Encinitas, 1550 S. El Camino Real (© **760/436-6611;** www.luxartinstitute. com). This unique facility—a work of art in itself—allows visitors to watch as an artist-in-residence paints, sculpts, or draws in a studio environment. It's open to the public Thursday and Friday, 1 to 5pm, and Saturday from 11am to 5pm ($10). Every third Wednesday of the month is Lux@night, a free wine and cheese reception from 7 to 9pm.

Another popular spot is **Moonlight Beach,** where you'll find plenty of facilities, including free parking, a playground, restrooms, showers, picnic tables, and fire grates. The beach entrance is at the end of B Street (at Encinitas Blvd.). A mile south is the appropriately serene **Swami's Beach,** named for the adjacent spiritual retreat (see below). To the north, it adjoins little-known **Boneyard Beach,** where low-tide coves shelter romantics and nudists; this isolated stretch is accessible only from Swami's Beach. Swami's has a free parking lot, restrooms, and a picnic area.

The **Self-Realization Fellowship** was founded in 1920 by guru Paramahansa Yogananda, and these exotic-looking domes are what remain of the retreat originally built in 1937. Today the site is a sanctuary for holistic healers and their followers, featuring serene, cliffside gardens with koi ponds and beautiful flower displays. Enter the garden at 215 K St., at the south end of Encinitas; it's open Tuesday through Sunday, admission is free, and you won't be pitched any philosophy. Also on-site, the **Hermitage,** where Yogananda lived and worked for many years, is usually open Sundays from 2 to 5pm. The gift shop is at 1105 Second St., between J and K streets (© **760/753-2888;** www.yogananda-srf.org).

Carlsbad is a great place for antiquing. Whether you're a serious shopper or seriously window-shopping, park the car and stroll the 3 blocks of **State Street** between Oak and Beech streets. There are about two dozen shops in this part of town, which has a village atmosphere.

Carlsbad State Beach runs alongside downtown. It's a great place to stroll along a wide concrete walkway. Enter on Ocean Boulevard at Tamarack Avenue; there's a $4 fee per vehicle. South of town is **South Carlsbad State Beach,** with its nearly 3 miles of cobblestone-strewn sand. A state-run campground at the north end is popular year-round, and the southern portion is favored by surfers. There's a $4 fee at the beach's entrance, along Carlsbad Boulevard at Poinsettia Lane.

Dedicated shoppers won't want to miss the **Carlsbad Premium Outlets,** Paseo del Norte, via Palomar Airport Road (© **888/790-7467** or 760/804-9000; www.premium outlets.com), a smart, upscale outlet mall featuring some 90 stores. Also of note is the **Museum of Making Music,** 5790 Armada Dr. (© **877/551-9976** or 760/438-5996; www.museumofmakingmusic.org), which chronicles the American music industry from Tin Pan Alley to MTV, pausing along the way for anecdotes. It's open Tuesday through Sunday from 10am to 5pm; admission is $5 for adults; $3 for children ages 4 to 18, seniors, students, and military. For a real thrill—or serene sunset flight—check out **Biplane, Air Combat & Warbird Adventures** (p. 750).

LEGOLAND California ★ (Kids) One of four such theme parks in the world (including Denmark, Britain, and Germany), the Carlsbad park features more than 50 rides, shows, and attractions, as well as 5,000 LEGO models. There are hands-on interactive displays; a life-size menagerie; scale models of international landmarks (such as the Eiffel Tower or Sydney Opera House)—all constructed of LEGO bricks. Three relatively gentle roller coasters give the park a little more weight for older kids, but the park caters to children ages 2 to 12. Four new rides make up the park's latest draw, the Egyptian-themed **Land of Adventure.** The signature ride, **Lost Kingdom Adventure,** takes you on a search for stolen treasure and tests your laser shooting skills. An even bigger expansion—in fact, an entirely new sister park—**Sea Life LEGOLAND California Resort** is an interactive, educational aquarium experience, focusing on the creatures (the real things—not models) found in regional waters from the Sierra Mountains to the depths of the Pacific. Separate admission is required ($19 adults, $16 seniors, $12 kids).

1 Legoland Dr. © **877/534-6526** or 760/918-5346. www.legoland.com. $59 adults, $47 seniors and kids 3–12, free for children 2 and under. AE, DISC, MC, V. Summer (late June–Aug) daily 10am–8pm; off season Thurs–Mon 10am–5 or 6pm. Closed Tues–Wed Sept–May, but open daily during winter and spring vacation periods. Parking $10. From I-5 take Cannon Rd. exit east, following signs for Legoland Dr.

Quail Botanical Gardens ★ You don't need a green thumb to appreciate this wonderful botanical facility. It has the country's largest bamboo collection, plus more than 35 acres of California natives, exotic tropicals, palms, cacti, Mediterranean, Australian, and other unusual collections. Scenic walkways and trails crisscross the compound. Guided tours take place Saturdays at 10am, and you can shop afterward at the on-site gift shop and nursery. The gardens are free on the first Tuesday of the month.

230 Quail Gardens Dr., Encinitas. ⓒ 760/436-3036. www.qbgardens.com. Admission $10 adults; $7 students, seniors, and military; $5 children 3–12; free for children 2 and under. Daily 9am–5pm. Parking $1. From San Diego take I-5 north to Encinitas Blvd.; go 1/2 mile east, left on Quail Gardens Dr.

Where to Stay

Beach Terrace Inn   At Carlsbad's only beachside hostelry (others are across the road or a little farther away), almost all the rooms—as well as the swimming pool/whirlpool—have ocean views. This downtown property's scenic location, between rows of high-rent beach cottages, is its best quality. The rooms are extra-large, and although they suffer from generic "furnished bachelor pad"–style interiors, some have balconies, fireplaces, and kitchenettes. Suites are affordable and have separate living rooms and bedrooms, making this a good choice for families. You can walk everywhere from here—except LEGOLAND, which is a 5-minute drive away.

2775 Ocean St., Carlsbad, CA 92008. ⓒ **800/433-5415** or 760/729-5951. Fax 760/729-1078. www.beach terraceinn.com. 49 units. $185–$265 double; from $255 suite. Children 12 and under stay free in parent's room. Extra person $20. Rates include continental breakfast. AE, DC, DISC, MC, V. Free parking. **Amenities:** Outdoor pool; whirlpool; self-service laundry; dry-cleaning service. *In room:* A/C, TV w/pay movies, fridge, coffeemaker, hair dryer, iron, safe.

Four Seasons Resort Aviara ★★★   This resort offers every over-the-top comfort with the ease that sets Four Seasons apart. When not wielding club or racquet, guests can lie by the dramatically perched pool, relax in a series of carefully landscaped gardens, or luxuriate in the spa where treatments incorporate regional flowers and herbs; the signature restaurant, **Vivace,** is also one of the region's premier dining destinations. A recreation center offers everything from basketball and sand volleyball to croquet and bocce ball; there's even a surf concierge who can give lessons and a beach butler who will arrange a perfect day at the shore for you. Rooms are decorated with soothing neutrals and nature prints that evoke the 130 bird species that nest in the surrounding Batiquitos Lagoon. The hotel's Arnold Palmer–designed golf course was designed to keep the wetlands intact.

7100 Four Seasons Point, Carlsbad, CA 92009. ⓒ **800/332-3442** or 760/603-6800. Fax 760/603-6801. www.fourseasons.com/aviara. 329 units. $405–$585 double; from $725 suite. Children 17 and under stay free in parent's room. AE, DC, DISC, MC, V. Valet parking $29. From I-5, take Poinsettia Lane east to Aviara Pkwy. S. **Amenities:** 4 restaurants; 2 bars; 2 outdoor pools; golf course; tennis courts; health club; spa; Jacuzzi; bike rental; concierge; business center; salon; room service; in-room massage; babysitting; laundry service; dry cleaning; recreation center; surf lessons. *In room:* A/C, TV w/pay movies, DVD player, VCR, Wi-Fi, minibar, coffeemaker, hair dryer, iron, safe, CD player, PlayStation.

La Costa Resort and Spa ★★   With a 45-foot bell tower, white stucco walls, and red tile roofs, this California rancho-style resort has a campuslike setting. Rooms feature leather headboards and beds trimmed in Egyptian cotton linens, dark walnut desks, metal accents, and bathrooms with pedestal sinks. The resort has also added 149 privately owned luxury villas. The huge spa has 42 treatment rooms and outdoor sunning areas, a sprawling gym, and the (Dr. Deepak) **Chopra Center,** which offers services and products relating to mind/body healing and transformation. **BlueFire Grill,** the stylish bar and restaurant, faces onto a lovely plaza and features three chic spaces. The 400-acre property boasts two championship 18-hole golf courses and a 17-court racquet club. A dedicated areas for kids features high- and low-tech entertainments, and several new pools have theme park–style water slides.

Costa del Mar Rd., Carlsbad, CA 92009. © **800/854-5000** or 760/438-9111. Fax 760/931-7585. www.
lacosta.com. 511 units. $300–$500 double; from $500 suite; from $760 villa. Children under 18 stay free
in parent's room. $22 per day resort fee. Golf, spa, and tennis packages available. AE, DC, DISC, MC, V.
Valet parking $25 overnight; self-parking $15. From I-5 take La Costa Ave. east; left on El Camino Real.
Amenities: 6 restaurants; bar; 7 outdoor pools; 2 golf courses; tennis courts; spa; 6 Jacuzzis; bike rentals;
concierge; business center; salon; room service; babysitting; laundry service; dry cleaning. *In room:* A/C,
TV w/pay movies, minibar, coffeemaker, hair dryer, iron.

Pelican Cove Inn ★ Two blocks from the beach, this Cape Cod–style bed-and-
breakfast combines romance with luxury. Hosts Kris and Nancy Nayudu furnish guest
rooms with soft feather beds and down comforters, provide beach chairs and towels, and
prepare picnic baskets (with 24-hr. notice). Each room has a fireplace and private
entrance; some have private spa tubs. The Pacific room is most spacious, while the airy
La Jolla room has bay windows and a cupola ceiling. Courtesy transportation from the
Carlsbad or Oceanside train stations is available.

320 Walnut Ave., Carlsbad, CA 92008. © **888/735-2683** or 760/434-5995. www.pelican-cove.com. 10
units. $95–$215 double. Rates include full breakfast. Extra person $15. AE, MC, V. Free parking. From
downtown Carlsbad, follow Carlsbad Blvd. south to Walnut Ave.; turn left and drive 2¹⁄₂ blocks. *In room:*
TV, no phone.

Where to Dine

Sleek and sophisticated **Blanca** ★★★, 437 S. Coast Hwy. 101, Solana Beach (© **858/
792-0072;** www.dineblanca.com), caters to a discerning crowd that enjoys the finer
things in life and doesn't mind paying for them—It's foodie nirvana. Always crowded,
Fidel's Little Mexico is reliable for tasty Mexican food and kickin' margaritas; it's in
Solana Beach at 607 Valley Ave. (© **858/755-5292**). Perfect for breakfast, lunch, or
dinner, **Beach Grass Café** ★★ has two locations: 159 S. Coast Hwy. 101, Solana Beach
(© **858/509-0632;** www.beachgrasscafe.com), and 1476 Encinitas Blvd., Encinitas.

Also in Encinitas, look for **Vigilucci's Trattoria Italiana** ★, 505 S. Coast Hwy. 101,
at D Street (© **760/942-7332;** www.vigiluccis.com). It's part of a mini-empire of North
County bistros, pizzerias, and steakhouses, but this is where it all started. Other local
hangouts include the **Potato Shack** ★, in Encinitas, 120 W. I St. (© **760/436-1282**),
good for breakfast carbo-loading; and casual **Swami's Cafe** ★, 1163 S. Coast Hwy. 101
(© **760/944-0612;** www.swamis.signonsandiego.com). At **Siamese Basil** ★, 527 S.
Coast Hwy. 101 (© **760/753-3940**), the bland surroundings belie the restaurant's well-
deserved reputation for zesty Thai food. Chocoholics should not miss **Chuao Chocolatier** ★★, which has several North County locations, including the Lumberyard mall,
937 S. Coast Hwy. (© **760/635-1444;** www.chuaochocolatier.com).

One of the county's finest dining destinations is in Carlsbad—the Aviara resort's
Vivace ★★★, 7100 Four Seasons Point (© **760/603-6999;** www.fourseasons.com/
aviara). The architectural centerpiece of Carlsbad is **Ocean House,** 300 Carlsbad Village
Dr. (© **760/729-4131;** www.oceanhousecarlsbad.com), a restored Victorian mansion.
Inside, there's a casual cafe and bar; most evenings feature live music or a DJ. In the
Carlsbad Premium Outlets shopping center, **Bellefleur** ★, 5610 Paseo del Norte (© **760/
603-1919;** www.bellefleur.com), re-creates a wine country experience with wood-fired
grills, a tasting bar, and glassed-in aging room. Lunch, dinner, and Sunday brunch fare
surpasses shopping-mall standards.

12 JULIAN: GOLD, APPLE PIES & A SLICE OF SMALL-TOWN CALIFORNIA

60 miles NE of San Diego; 31 miles W of Anza-Borrego Desert State Park

A trip to Julian (pop. 3,000) is a trip back in time. The old gold-mining town, now best known for its apples, has a handful of cute B&Bs, but its popularity is based on the fact it provides a chance for city-weary folks to get away from it all. It's at its best on weekdays, when things are a little quieter.

Prospectors first ventured into these fertile hills (elevation 4,225 ft.) in search of gold in the late 1860s. They discovered it in 1870 near where the Julian Hotel stands today, and 18 mines sprang up like mushrooms. Four cousins—all former Confederate soldiers from Georgia, two with the last name Julian—founded the town. The mines produced an estimated $13 million worth of gold in their day.

In October 2003, Julian was virtually engulfed by the devastating Cedar Fire, and firefighters made a valiant stand to protect the town against what seemed insurmountable odds. The central historic part of Julian was saved, though, along with the town's famed apple orchards. You can stand on Main Street again without knowing catastrophe visited just a few hundred yards away.

ESSENTIALS

GETTING THERE   The drive can be made in 90 minutes via Highway 78 or I-8 to Highway 79. Highway 78 traverses countryside and farmland severely burned by the Witch Fire, one of Southern California's epic wildfires in 2007, while Highway 79 winds through scenic Cuyamaca Rancho State Park, where you'll still see residual damage from the 2003 fire.

VISITOR INFORMATION   For a brochure on what to see and do, contact the **Julian Chamber of Commerce,** corner of Main and Washington streets, P.O. Box 1866, Julian, CA 92036 (© **760/765-1857;** www.julianca.com), where staffers offer enthusiastic suggestions. The office is open daily 10am to 4pm.

EXPLORING THE TOWN

This 1880s gold-mining town offers an abundance of early California history, Old West streets with apple-pie shops and antiques stores, fresh air, and friendly people. *Note:* Julian's downtown can be crowded during the fall harvest season, so consider making your trip at another time. At an elevation of 4,225 feet, the autumn air is crisp and Julian often sees a dusting of snow during the winter months. Don't worry, though: They bake their famous apple pies year-round.

The best way to experience tiny Julian is on foot. The **Julian Drug Store & Miner's Diner,** 2130 Main St. (© **760/765-3753**), is an old-style soda fountain serving sparkling sarsaparilla; the **Eagle and High Peak Mines** (ca. 1870) at the end of C Street (© **760/765-0036**), although seemingly a tourist trap, offers an educational look at the town's one-time economic mainstay. The town's **Pioneer Cemetery** is a hilltop graveyard straight out of *Our Town;* and there's more local history on view at the **Julian Pioneer Museum,** 2811 Washington St. (© **760/765-0227**); it's open April through November, Wednesday through Sunday, 10am to 4pm, weekends 10am to 4pm the rest of the year. African-American roots are deep in Julian (it was a black settler who originally found gold here in 1869), and the "soul of Julian" is presented by the **Julian Black Historical**

Society at its museum and gift shop, 2030 Third St. (© **760/765-1120;** www.julian blackhistoricalsociety.org).

The **California Wolf Center** ★, 18457 Hwy. 79 (© **760/765-0030** or 619/234-9653; www.californiawolfcenter.org), is a conservation facility with public programs on Saturdays at 1:30pm (reservations required; $10 adults, $7 seniors, $6 kids); programs include a visit with the resident wolf pack. Private tours can be arranged during the week for $25 per person.

The Julian hills are rife with **roadside fruit stands** and **orchards;** in autumn they're open all day, every day, but in the off season, many are open only on weekends. Many line Highway 78 between Julian and Wynola; Farmers Road, a country lane leading north from downtown, also has stands. Wineries have a presence in the area, too, including rustic **Menghini Winery,** 1150 Julian Orchards Dr. (© **760/765-2072**), and **Witch Creek Winery,** 2100 Main St. (© **760/765-2023;** www.witchcreekwinery.com).

Apple pie is the town's mainstay, though, and you'll need to sample them all to judge whether the best pies come from **Mom's Pies** ★, 2119 Main St. (© **760/765-2472;** www.momspiesjulian.com), **Julian Pie Company** ★, 2225 Main St. (© **760/765-2449;** www.julianpie.com), **Apple Alley Bakery** ★, a nook on Main Street between Washington and B streets (© **760/765-2532**), or the **Julian Café & Bakery** ★, 2112 Main St. (© **760/765-2712**). At the **Julian Cider Mill,** 2103 Main St. (© **760/765-1430**), you can see cider presses at work October through March; it offers free fresh tastes and sells jugs to take home.

OUTDOOR PURSUITS

Within 10 miles of Julian, numerous hiking trails traverse rolling meadows, high chaparral, and oak and pine forests; damage from the 2003 fire is visible—oaks have recovered, pine trees have not, though seedlings have sprung up. The most spectacular hike is at **Volcan Mountain Preserve** (© **760/765-2300;** www.volcanmt.org), north of town along Farmers Road; the trail to the top is a moderately challenging hike of about 5 miles round-trip, with a 1,400-foot elevation gain. From the top, hikers have a panoramic view of the desert, mountains, and sea.

The 26,000-acre **Cuyamaca Rancho State Park,** on Highway 79 between Julian and the I-8, was badly burned during the October 2003 forest fires but is regenerating nicely. For a map or information, stop at **park headquarters,** 12551 Highway 79, Descanso, or check in with the **Cuyamaca Rancho State Park Interpretive Association** (© **760/765-3020;** www.cuyamaca.us).

Eight miles south of Julian, **Lake Cuyamaca** is a tiny community that is centered on lake activities, primarily boating and fishing for trout (stocked year-round), plus bass, catfish, bluegill, and sturgeon. The fishing fee is $6 per day, $3.50 per day for kids 8 to 15, free for children under 8. A California state fishing license is required and sold here; it's $12 for the day. Rowboats are $15 per day, and motorboat rentals run $40 for the day ($30 after 1pm). In summer, you can rent canoes and paddleboats by the hour for $10. For boat rental, fishing information, and RV or tent sites, call © **877/581-9904** or 760/765-0515 or see www.lakecuyamaca.org.

WHERE TO STAY

Julian is B&B country, and they fill up months in advance for the fall harvest season. The **Julian Bed & Breakfast Guild** (© **760/765-1555;** www.julianbnbguild.com) has more than 10 members and is a terrific resource for locating accommodations.

Julian Gold Rush Hotel ★   Built in 1897 by freed slave Albert Robinson, this frontier-style hotel is a living monument to the area's gold boom days and one of Southern California's oldest continually operating hotels. Downtown, it isn't as secluded or plush as some of the area's B&Bs, but if you seek historically accurate Queen Anne–style lodgings, it's ideal. The 14 rooms and two cottages were authentically restored with antiques, with nicely designed private bathrooms added where necessary. Some rooms are tiny, so claustrophobics should ask about room size before booking. An inviting private lobby is stocked with books, games, literature on local activities, and a wood-burning stove.

2032 Main St. (at B St.), Julian, CA 92036. © **800/734-5854** or 760/765-0201. Fax 760/765-0327. www. julianhotel.com. 14 units, 2 cottages. $120–$165 double; $160–$210 cottage. Rates include full breakfast and afternoon tea. AE, MC, V. *In room:* No phone.

Orchard Hill Country Inn ★★ ⟨**Value**⟩   Hosts Darrell and Pat Straube offer the most upscale lodgings in Julian—a posh, two-story Craftsman lodge and 12 cottages on a hill overlooking town. The lodge has 10 guest rooms, a guests-only dining room (open 4 nights a week), and a great room with a massive stone fireplace. The 12 cottages are romantic hideaways, spread over 3 acres. All units have contemporary country furnishings and snacks. Rooms in the main lodge feel hotel-ish, but the cottage suites are secluded and luxurious, with private porches, fireplaces, wet bars, and whirlpool tubs in most. Hiking trails lead from the lodge into the adjacent woods. Check the website for midweek specials.

2502 Washington St., at Second St. (P.O. Box 2410), Julian, CA 92036. © **800/716-7242** or 760/765-1700. Fax 760/765-0290. www.orchardhill.com. 10 units, 12 cottages. $195–$250 double; from $295 cottage. Extra person $25. 2-night minimum for Sat stays. Rates include breakfast and hors d'oeuvres. AE, MC, V. From Hwy. 79, turn left on Main St., right on Washington St. **Amenities:** Restaurant; bar; mountain bikes; gift shop; library; hiking trails. *In room:* A/C, TV/VCR (extensive video library), hair dryer, iron, CD player.

WHERE TO DINE

In a cozy cottage with lacy draperies, flickering candles, and a warm hearth, the **Julian Grille** ★, 2224 Main St. (© 760/765-0173), is the nicest restaurant in Julian. It serves soups, sandwiches, large salads, charbroiled burgers, and hearty omelets for lunch; dinner (served nightly except for Mon) features grilled and broiled meats, seafood, and prime rib. In a historic home off Main Street, **Romano's Dodge House** ★, 2718 B St. (© 760/765-1003; www.romanosjulian.com), serves home-style Italian, with red-checkered tablecloths and straw-clad chianti bottles. The small lounge features live music on Saturday nights.

Appendix: Fast Facts

FAST FACTS: CALIFORNIA

AMERICAN EXPRESS Call ℂ **800/221-7282** for locations near you.

ATM NETWORKS See "Money & Costs," p. 48.

BUSINESS HOURS Offices are usually open weekdays from 9am to 5pm. Banks are open weekdays from 9am to 3pm or later and sometimes Saturday mornings. Stores typically open between 9 and 10am and close between 5 and 6pm from Monday through Saturday. Stores in shopping complexes or malls tend to stay open late: until about 9pm on weekdays and weekends; many malls and department stores are open on Sundays.

CAR RENTALS See "Getting Around," p. 46.

CASHPOINTS See "Money & Costs," p. 48.

CURRENCY The most common bills are the $1 (a "buck"), $5, $10, and $20 denominations.

Coins come in seven denominations: 1¢ (1 cent, or a penny); 5¢ (5 cents, or a nickel); 10¢ (10 cents, or a dime); 25¢ (25 cents, or a quarter); 50¢ (50 cents, or a half dollar); and the gold-colored Sacagawea coin, worth $1. For additional information, see "Money & Costs," p. 48.

DRINKING LAWS The legal age for purchase and consumption of alcoholic beverages is 21; proof of age is required and often requested at bars, nightclubs, and restaurants, so it's always a good idea to bring ID when you go out. Supermarkets and convenience stores in California sell beer, wine, and liquor.

Most restaurants serve alcohol, but some only serve beer and wine. By law, all bars, clubs, restaurants, and stores cannot sell or serve alcohol after 2am, and "last call" tends to start at 1:30am. Do not carry open containers of alcohol in your car or any public area that isn't zoned for alcohol consumption. The police can fine you on the spot. And nothing will ruin your trip faster than getting a citation for DUI ("driving under the influence").

DRIVING RULES See "Getting Around," p. 46.

EARTHQUAKES In the rare event of an earthquake, *don't panic.* If you're in a tall building, don't run outside; instead, move away from windows and toward the building's center. Crouch under a desk or table, or stand against a wall or under a doorway. If you're in bed, get under the bed, stand in a doorway, or crouch under a sturdy piece of furniture. When exiting the building, use stairwells, *not* elevators. If you're in your car, pull over to the side of the road and stop, but wait until you're away from bridges or overpasses, as well as telephone or power poles and lines. Stay in your car. If you're outside, stay away from trees, power lines, and the sides of buildings.

ELECTRICITY Like Canada, the United States uses 110 to 120 volts AC (60 cycles), compared to 220 to 240 volts AC (50 cycles) in most of Europe, Australia, and New Zealand. Downward converters that change 220 to 240 volts to 110 to 120 volts are difficult to find in the United States, so bring one with you.

EMBASSIES & CONSULATES All embassies are located in the nation's capital, Washington, D.C. Some consulates are located in major U.S. cities, and most nations have a mission to the United Nations in New York City. If your country isn't listed below, call for directory information in Washington, D.C. (© 202/555-1212) or log on to **www.embassy.org/embassies.**

The embassy of **Australia** is at 1601 Massachusetts Ave. NW, Washington, DC 20036 (© **202/797-3000;** www.austemb.org). There are consulates in New York, Honolulu, Houston, Los Angeles, and San Francisco.

The embassy of **Canada** is at 501 Pennsylvania Ave. NW, Washington, DC 20001 (© **202/682-1740;** www.canadianembassy.org). Other Canadian consulates are in Buffalo (New York), Detroit, Los Angeles, New York, and Seattle.

The embassy of **Ireland** is at 2234 Massachusetts Ave. NW, Washington, DC 20008 (© **202/462-3939;** www.irelandemb.org). Irish consulates are in Boston, Chicago, New York, San Francisco, and other cities. See website for complete listing.

The embassy of **New Zealand** is at 37 Observatory Circle NW, Washington, DC 20008 (© **202/328-4800;** www.nzemb.org). New Zealand consulates are in Los Angeles, Salt Lake City, San Francisco, and Seattle.

The embassy of the **United Kingdom** is at 3100 Massachusetts Ave. NW, Washington, DC 20008 (© **202/588-7800;** www.britainusa.com). Other British consulates are in Atlanta, Boston, Chicago, Cleveland, Houston, Los Angeles, New York, San Francisco, and Seattle.

EMERGENCIES Call © **911** to report a fire, call the police, or get an ambulance anywhere in the United States. This is a toll-free call. (No coins are required at public telephones.)

If you encounter traveler's problems, call the Los Angeles chapter of the **Traveler's Aid Society** (© 310/646-2270; www.travelersaid.org), a nationwide, nonprofit, social service organization.

GASOLINE (PETROL) At press time, in the U.S., the cost of gasoline (also known as gas, but never petrol), is abnormally high—about $4.20 per gallon at press time—and in California it's typically more expensive than most other states. Taxes are included in the printed price. One U.S. gallon equals 3.8 liters or .85 imperial gallons. Fill-up locations are known as gas or service stations.

HOLIDAYS Banks, government offices, post offices, and many stores, restaurants, and museums are closed on the following legal national holidays: January 1 (New Year's Day), the third Monday in January (Martin Luther King, Jr., Day), the third Monday in February (Presidents' Day), the last Monday in May (Memorial Day), July 4 (Independence Day), the first Monday in September (Labor Day), the second Monday in October (Columbus Day), November 11 (Veterans' Day/Armistice Day), the fourth Thursday in November (Thanksgiving Day), and December 25 (Christmas). The Tuesday after the first Monday in November is Election Day, a federal government holiday in presidential-election years (held every 4 years, and next in 2012).

For more information on holidays, see "Calendar of Events," p. 39.

INTERNET ACCESS See "Staying Connected," p. 54.

LEGAL AID If you are "pulled over" for a minor infraction (such as speeding), never attempt to pay the fine directly to a police officer; this could be construed as attempted bribery. Pay fines by mail or directly into the hands of the clerk of the court. If accused of a more serious offense, say and do nothing before consulting a lawyer. Here the burden is on the state to prove a person's guilt beyond a reasonable doubt, and everyone has the right to remain silent, whether he or she is suspected of a crime or actually arrested. Once arrested, a person can make one telephone call to a party of his or her choice. International visitors should call your embassy or consulate.

MAIL At press time, domestic postage rates were 27¢ for a postcard and 42¢ for a letter. For international mail, a first-class letter of up to 1 ounce costs 90¢ (69¢ to Canada and Mexico); a first-class postcard costs the same as a letter. For more information, go to **www.usps.com** and click on "Calculate Postage."

Always include zip codes when mailing items in the U.S. If you don't know your zip code, visit **www.usps.com/zip4.**

MEASUREMENTS See the chart on the inside front cover of this book for details on converting metric measurements to U.S. equivalents.

PASSPORTS For Residents of Australia: You can pick up an application from your local post office or any branch of Passports Australia, but you must schedule an interview at the passport office to present your application materials. Call the **Australian Passport Information Service** at ✆ **131-232,** or visit the government website at **www.passports.gov.au.**

For Residents of Canada: Passport applications are available at travel agencies throughout Canada or from the central **Passport Office,** Department of Foreign Affairs and International Trade, Ottawa, ON K1A 0G3 (✆ **800/567-6868;** www. ppt.gc.ca). *Note:* Canadian children who travel must have their own passport. However, if you hold a valid Canadian passport issued before December 11, 2001, that bears the name of your child, the passport remains valid for you and your child until it expires.

For Residents of Ireland: You can apply for a 10-year passport at the **Passport Office,** Setanta Centre, Molesworth Street, Dublin 2 (✆ **01/671-1633;** www.irlgov.ie/ iveagh). Those under age 18 and over 65 must apply for a 3-year passport. You can also apply at 1A South Mall, Cork (✆ **021/ 272-525**), or at main post offices.

For Residents of New Zealand: You can pick up a passport application at any New Zealand Passports Office or download it from their website. Contact the **Passports Office** at ✆ **0800/225-050** in New Zealand, or 04/474-8100, or log on to www.passports.govt.nz.

For Residents of the United Kingdom: To pick up an application for a standard 10-year passport (5-year passport for children under 16), visit your nearest passport office, major post office, or travel agency or contact the **United Kingdom Passport Service** at ✆ **0870/521-0410** or search its website at www.ukpa.gov.uk.

POLICE For any emergency, dial ✆ **911** from any phone, including cellphones and pay phones.

SAFETY See "Health & Safety," p. 49.

SMOKING Heavy smokers are in for a tough time in California. Smoking is illegal in public buildings, sports arenas, elevators, theaters, banks, lobbies, restaurants, offices, stores, bed-and-breakfasts, most small hotels, and bars. That's right: As of January 1, 1998, you can't even smoke in California bars unless drinks are served solely by the owner (though you will find that many neighborhood bars turn a blind eye and pass you an ashtray).

TAXES The United States has no value-added tax (VAT) or other indirect tax at the national level. Every state, county, and city may levy its own local tax on all purchases, including hotel and restaurant checks and airline tickets. These taxes will not appear on price tags. Sales tax in California is generally around 8%. Hotel tax is charged on the room tariff only (which is not subject to sales tax) and is set by the city, ranging from 12% to 17% throughout California.

TIME   California is on Pacific Standard Time (PST). The continental United States is divided into **four time zones:** Eastern Standard Time (EST), Central Standard Time (CST), Mountain Standard Time (MST), and Pacific Standard Time (PST). Alaska and Hawaii have their own zones. For example, when it's 9am in Los Angeles (PST), it's 7am in Honolulu (HST), 10am in Denver (MST), 11am in Chicago (CST), noon in New York City (EST), 5pm in London (GMT), and 2am the next day in Sydney.

Daylight saving time takes effect at 2am the second Sunday in March until 2am the first Sunday in November, except in Arizona, Hawaii, the U.S. Virgin Islands, and Puerto Rico. Daylight saving moves the clock 1 hour ahead of standard time.

TIPPING   Tips are a very important part of many workers' incomes, and gratuities are the standard way of showing appreciation for good service. In hotels, tip **bellhops** at least $1 per bag ($2–$3 if you have a lot of luggage) and tip the **chamber staff** $1 to $2 per day (more if you've left a disaster area for him or her to clean up). Tip the **doorman** or **concierge** only if he or she has provided you with some specific service (for example, calling a cab for you or obtaining difficult-to-get theater tickets). Tip the **valet-parking attendant** $1 every time you get your car.

In restaurants, bars, and nightclubs, tip **service staff** 15% to 20% of the check, tip **bartenders** 10% to 15%, tip **checkroom attendants** $1 per garment, and tip **valet-parking attendants** $1 per vehicle.

As for other service personnel, tip **cab drivers** 15% of the fare; and tip **skycaps** at airports at least $1 per bag ($2–$3 if you have a lot of luggage).

TOILETS   You won't find public toilets or "restrooms" on the streets in most California cities (except San Francisco), but they can be found in hotel lobbies, bars, restaurants, museums, department stores, railway and bus stations, and service stations. Large hotels and fast-food restaurants are often the best bet for clean facilities. If possible, avoid the toilets at parks and beaches, which tend to be dirty; some may even be unsafe. Restaurants and bars in heavily visited areas may reserve their restrooms for paying customers.

VISAS   For information about U.S. Visas go to **http://travel.state.gov** and click on "Visas." Or go to one of the following websites:

Australian citizens can obtain up-to-date visa information from the **U.S. Embassy Canberra,** Moonah Place, Yarralumla, ACT 2600 (© **02/6214-5600),** or by checking the U.S. Diplomatic Mission's website at **http://usembassy-australia.state.gov/consular.**

British subjects can obtain up-to-date visa information by calling the **U.S. Embassy Visa Information Line** (© **0891/200-290),** or by visiting the "Visas to the U.S." section of the American Embassy London's website at **www.usembassy.org.uk.**

Irish citizens can obtain up-to-date visa information through the **Embassy of the USA Dublin,** 42 Elgin Rd., Dublin 4, Ireland (© **353/1-668-8777);** or by checking the "Consular Services" section of the website at **http://dublin.usembassy.gov.**

Citizens of **New Zealand** can obtain up-to-date visa information by contacting the **U.S. Embassy New Zealand,** 29 Fitzherbert Terrace, Thorndon, Wellington (© **644/472-2068),** or get the information directly from the website at **http://wellington.usembassy.gov.**

INDEX